COBOL

From Micro to Mainframe

Preparing for the New Millennium

Fujitsu Version

THIRD EDITION

ROBERT T. GRAUER

University of Miami

CAROL VAZQUEZ VILLAR

Andersen Consulting

ARTHUR R. BUSS

William Jewell College

Prentice Hall

PRENTICE HALL
Upper Saddle River, NJ 07458

Library of Congress Cataloging-in-Publication Data

Grauer, Robert T.
    COBOL: from micro to mainframe: preparing for the
new millennium: Fujitsu version/Robert T. Grauer, Carol Vazquez Villar,
Arthur R. Buss.—3rd ed.
      p. cm.
    ISBN: 0-13-085849-8
    1. COBOL (Computer program language) I. Vazquez Villar, Carol
II. Buss, Arthur R. III. Title.
QA76.73.C25 G734 2000
005.13'3—dc21
                  99-053322

To Marion, Benjy, and Jessica
To Mario, Mom & Dad, and Fefa
To Pat, Betsy, and Carolyn

Acquisitions editor: **PETRA RECTER**
Publisher: **ALAN APT**
Editor-in-chief: **MARCIA HORTON**
Production editor: **IRWIN ZUCKER**
Managing editor: **DAVID A. GEORGE**
Executive managing editor: **VINCE O'BRIEN**
Assistant vice president, production and manufacturing: **DAVID W. RICCARDI**
Copy editor: **BOB LENTZ**
Art director: **HEATHER SCOTT**
Cover designer: **JOHN CHRISTIANA**
Cover illustration: **PATRICE VAN ACKER**
Manufacturing buyer: **PAT BROWN**
Editorial assistant: **SARAH BURROWS**

©2000, 1998, 1994, 1991 by Prentice-Hall, Inc.
Prentice Hall, Inc.
Upper Saddle River, New Jersey 07458

The author and publisher of this book have used their best efforts in preparing this book. These efforts include the
development, research, and testing of the theories and programs to determine their effectiveness. The author and
publisher make no warranty of any kind, expressed or implied, with regard to these programs or the documentation
contained in this book. The author and publisher shall not be liable in any event for incidental or consequential damages
in connection with, or arising out of, the furnishing, performance, or use of these programs.

TRADEMARK INFORMATION: Fujitsu COBOL is a registered trademark of Fujitsu Software Corporation. Micro Focus® Personal COBOL™ for
Windows™ is a registered trademark of Micro Focus Ltd. Windows® and Windows 95® are registered trademarks of Microsoft Corporation.
Windows NT™ is a trademark of Microsoft Corporation.

Printed in the United States of America

10 9 8 7 6 5 4 3

ISBN 0-13-085849-8

Prentice-Hall International (UK) Limited, London
Prentice-Hall of Australia Pty. Limited, Sydney
Prentice-Hall Canada Inc., Toronto
Prentice-Hall Hispanoamericana, S.A., Mexico
Prentice-Hall of India Private Limited, New Delhi
Prentice-Hall of Japan, Inc., Tokyo
Pearson Education Asia Pte. Ltd., Singapore
Editora Prentice-Hall do Brasil, Ltda., Rio de Janeiro

Contents

Preface xi

Chapter 1: Introduction   1

Overview 2
The First Problem 2
   Programming Specifications 3
Required Logic 5
   Flowcharts 6
   Pseudocode 8
A First Look at COBOL 9
   Identification Division 11
   Environment Division 11
   Data Division 11
   Procedure Division 12

Test Data 13
Elements of COBOL 13
   Reserved Words 13
   Programmer-Supplied Names 14
   Literals 15
   Symbols 16
   Level Numbers 16
   Picture Clauses 17
An Alternate Look at COBOL 17
Summary 19
Fill-in 20   True/False 20   Problems 21

Chapter 2: From Coding Form to Computer   25

Overview 26
From Coding Form to Computer 26
   The COBOL Coding Form 28
   Use of an Editor 28
   The Compile, Link, and Execute Sequence 30
Learning by Doing 32
   Errors in Entering the Program 33
   Errors in Operating System Commands 33

   Errors in Compilation 33
   Errors in Execution 35
   Errors in Data Input 37
Evolution of COBOL 38
There's Always a Reason 40
Summary 41
Fill-in 41   True/False 42   Problems 43

Chapter 3: A Methodology for Program Development   47

Overview 48
The Tuition Billing Problem 48
Structured Design 50
Evaluating the Hierarchy Chart 52
   Completeness 53
   Functionality 54
   Span of Control 54
Structured Programming 54

   Sufficiency of the Basic Structures 56
Expressing Logic 57
   The Traditional Flowchart 57
   Pseudocode 57
   Warnier-Orr Diagrams 59
Top-Down Testing 61
Summary 66
Fill-in 67   True/False 68   Problems 68

Chapter 4: The Identification, Environment, and Data Divisions 73

Overview 74
COBOL Notation 74
IDENTIFICATION DIVISION 75
ENVIRONMENT DIVISION 76
   CONFIGURATION SECTION 76
   INPUT-OUTPUT SECTION 76
DATA DIVISION 77
   FILE SECTION 77

WORKING-STORAGE SECTION 82
The Tuition Billing Program 84
   Programming Specifications 84
   COBOL Entries 87
Limitations of COBOL-74 90
Summary 90
Fill-in 92   True/False 92   Problems 93

Chapter 5: The Procedure Division 97

Overview 98
OPEN 98
CLOSE 99
READ 99
   Placement of the READ Statement 100
WRITE 100
STOP RUN 102
MOVE 102
   Restrictions on the Move Statement 103
   Alphanumeric Field to Alphanumeric Field 103
   Numeric Field to Numeric Field 104
   Group Moves 105
PERFORM 105
IF 106
   The ELSE Clause 106
   Indentation 106
EVALUATE 109
Arithmetic Statements 109

The ROUNDED Clause 109
The SIZE ERROR Clause 110
COMPUTE 110
ADD 112
SUBTRACT 112
MULTIPLY 114
DIVIDE 115
   Programming Tip: Use the COMPUTE Statement for Multiple Arithmetic Operations 116
   Assumed Decimal Point 117
The Tuition Billing Program 118
   Test Data 127
   Hierarchy Chart 127
COBOL Program Skeleton 128
Limitations of COBOL-74 128
Summary 130
Fill-in 131   True/False 132   Problems 133

Chapter 6: Debugging 139

Overview 140
Errors in Compilation 140
   Common Compilation Errors 149
Errors in Execution 151
   Run Time Error 156
   Logic Errors 158

Tips for Debugging 159
   DISPLAY Statement 161
The Structured Walkthrough 162
Summary 163
Fill-in 164   True/False 165   Problems 165

Chapter 7: Editing and Coding Standards 169

Overview 170
Editing 170
  The Decimal Point 172
  Zero Suppression 172
  Dollar Signs 174
  Comma 174
  Asterisks for Check Protection 175
  Insertion Characters 175
  Synopsis 175
Signed Numbers 176
  CR and DB 176
  Plus and Minus Signs 177

BLANK WHEN ZERO Clause 177
The Tuition Billing Program Revisited 178
Coding Standards 179
  Data Division 179
  Programming Tip: Avoid Literals 180
  Procedure Division 181
  Programming Tip: Use Scope Terminators 182
  Both Divisions 183
A Well-Written Program 184
Summary 189
Fill-in 190   True/False 191   Problems 191

Chapter 8: Data Validation 195

Overview 196
System Concepts: Data Validation 196
The IF Statement 197
  Relational Condition 198
  Class Test 199
  Sign Test 200
  Condition-Name Test 200
  Compound Test 200
  Hierarchy of Operations 201
  Implied Conditions 203
  Nested IFs 203
  NEXT SENTENCE 205

ACCEPT Statement 206
  Calculations Involving Dates 206
The Stand-Alone Edit Program 207
  Programming Specifications 208
  Error Messages 211
  Pseudocode 211
  Hierarchy Chart 212
  The Completed Program 220
Limitations of COBOL-74 221
Summary 223
Fill-in 224   True/False 224   Problems 225

Chapter 9 : More About the Procedure Division 229

Overview 230
PERFORM 231
  TEST BEFORE/TEST AFTER 231
  In-line Perform 232
  Performing Sections 232
  PERFORM THRU 233
  Programming Tip: Perform Paragraphs, Not
    Sections 233
READ 234
  False-Condition Branch 235
  READ INTO 235
WRITE FROM 236
INITIALIZE 236
String Processing 237
  INSPECT 237

STRING 238
UNSTRING 240
Reference Modification 240
ACCEPT 242
Duplicate Data Names 243
  Qualification 244
  MOVE CORRESPONDING 245
The Car Billing Program 246
  Programming Specifications 246
  Program Design 248
  The Completed Program 249
Limitations of COBOL-74 258
Summary 258
Fill-in 259   True/False 260   Problems 260

Chapter 10: Screen I-O   265

Overview   266
ACCEPT   266
   Programming Tip: Special Names Section and
      Symbolic Constants to Specify Color
      Names   267
DISPLAY   269
The Tuition Billing Program Revisited   270
   Programming Specifications   270
   Hierarchy Chart   271
   Pseudocode   271
   The Completed Program   273
   Programming Tip: Advanced Use of Evaluate   274

Car Validation and Billing Program   278
   Programming Specifications   279
   The Screen Section   280
   Hierarchy Chart   284
   Pseudocode   284
   The Completed Program   287
Limitations of COBOL-74   297
Summary   297
Fill-in   298   True/False   299   Problems   299

Chapter 11: Introduction to Tables   301

Overview   302
Introduction to Tables   302
   OCCURS Clause   303
   Processing a Table   304
   PERFORM VARYING   304
A Second Example   306
   Problems with the OCCURS Clause   308
   Rules for Subscripts   308
   Relative Subscripting   308
   USAGE Clause   309

OCCURS DEPENDING ON   310
The Student Transcript Program   311
   Programming Specifications   311
   Program Design   313
   The Completed Program   314
Indexes versus Subscripts   321
   The SET Statement   322
Limitations of COBOL-74   322
Summary   325
Fill-in   326   True/False   326   Problems   327

Chapter 12: Table Lookups   331

Overview   332
System Concepts   332
   Types of Codes   333
   Characteristics of Codes   333
   Sequential Table Lookup   334
   Binary Table Lookup   335
   Positional Organization and Direct Lookups   336
Initializing a Table   336
   Hard Coding   336
   Input-Loaded Tables   338
Table Lookups   339
   PERFORM VARYING Statement   340
   SEARCH Statement   340

Programming Tip—Restrict Subscripts
   and Switches to a Single Use   342
   SEARCH ALL Statement   344
   Direct Lookup   344
   Range-Step Tables   345
A Complete Example   347
   Programming Specifications   347
   Program Design   349
   The Completed Program   350
Limitations of COBOL-74   357
Summary   357
Fill-in   358   True/False   359   Problems   360

Chapter 13: Multilevel Tables   363

Overview   364
System Concepts   364
COBOL Implementation   366
One-Level Tables   366
    PERFORM VARYING   366
Two-Level Tables   368
    Errors in Compilation   369
    PERFORM VARYING   370
A Sample Program   373
    Programming Specifications   373
    Program Design   375
    The Completed Program   375
Three-Level Tables   380

    PERFORM VARYING   382
A Sample Program   384
    Programming Specifications   384
    The Completed Program   386
Table Lookups   390
A Calorie Counter's Delight   392
    Programming Specifications   392
    Range-Step Tables   392
    The Completed Program   394
Limitations of COBOL-74   398
Summary   398
Fill-in   399   True/False   399   Problems   400

Chapter 14: Sorting   403

Overview   404
System Concepts   405
Collating Sequence   405
    Embedded Sign   406
COBOL Implementation   408
    SORT Statement   409
    SD (Sort Description)   410
    RELEASE and RETURN   410
    Programming Specifications   411

USING/GIVING Option   414
INPUT PROCEDURE/OUTPUT PROCEDURE
    Option   419
Comparing Options   426
MERGE Statement   426
Limitations of COBOL-74   428
Summary   428
Fill-in   429   True/False   430   Problems   431

Chapter 15: Control Breaks   435

Overview   436
System Concepts   436
    Running versus Rolling Totals   440
One-Level Control Breaks   443
    Programming Specifications   443
    Hierarchy Chart   444
    Pseudocode   446
    The Completed Program   446
Two-Level Control Breaks   451
    Hierarchy Chart   451
    Pseudocode   452

    The Completed Program   454
Three-Level Control Breaks   460
    Hierarchy Chart   460
    Pseudocode   462
    The Completed Program   463
    Programming Tip: How to Write a Control Break
      Program   471
Limitations of COBOL-74   471
Summary   472
Fill-in   472   True/False   473   Problems   473

Chapter 16: Subprograms

475

Overview 476
Subprograms 477
   Called and Calling Programs 477
   COPY Statement 479
   Calling BY CONTENT and BY REFERENCE 480
   Programming Tip: Use COPY to Pass
      Parameters 481
INITIAL Clause 482
A System for Physical Fitness 482
   Programming Specifications 482
   Hierarchy Chart 485
   Pseudocode 485

The Completed Programs 486
   Main Program (FITNESS) 486
   Input Program (INPUTSUB) 490
   Weight-Range Program (WGTSUB) 494
   Training Program (TRAINSUB) 498
   Display Program (DSPLYSUB) 498
   Time Program (TIMESUB) 503
The Linkage Editor 504
   Problems with the Linkage Editor 505
Limitations of COBOL-74 506
Summary 508
Fill-in 509   True/False 509   Problems 510

Chapter 17: Sequential File Maintenance

515

Overview 516
System Concepts 516
   Sequential versus Nonsequential Processing 518
   Periodic Maintenance 518
Data Validation 519
   Programming Specifications 520
   Designing the Program 523
   The Completed Program 524
Sequential File Maintenance 528

   Programming Specifications 528
   The Balance Line Algorithm 529
   Designing the Hierarchy Chart 531
Top-Down Testing 535
   The Stubs Program 535
   The Completed Program 540
Summary 545
Fill-in 546   True/False 546   Problems 547

Chapter 18: Indexed Files

549

Overview 550
System Concepts 550
COBOL Implementation 554
Creating an Indexed File 556
   Programming Specifications 556
   Pseudocode 557
   The Completed Program 557
Additional COBOL Elements 559
   OPEN 559
   READ 561
   WRITE 562
   REWRITE 562
   DELETE 562

Maintaining an Indexed File 563
   Programming Specifications 563
   Hierarchy Chart 565
   Pseudocode 566
   The Completed Program 566
Alternate Record Key 570
   Programming Specifications 570
Concatenated Key 573
   The START Statement 574
Limitations of COBOL-74 574
Summary 576
Fill-in 577   True/False 578   Problems 578

Chapter 19: The Year 2000 Problem   583

Overview   584
The Year 2000 Problem   584
Date Arithmetic   590
    COBOL Intrinsic Calendar Functions   591

Leap-Year Problem   594
Retirement Program Revisited   594
Summary   599
Fill-in   600   True/False   600   Problems   601

Chapter 20: Object-Oriented COBOL Programming   603

Overview   604
The Next Generation of COBOL   605
    The Development of Structured Programming   606
    Terminology   607
    The Object-Oriented versus Structured Paradigm   608
The Student-Look-Up System   610
    Programming Specifications   610
    Student-Look-UP Program   612
    Programming Specifications   613
Programming Tip: Object-Oriented Coding
    Conventions   614
The Registrar Class   616
    Programming Specifications   616
    Classes and Inheritance   619
    ProcessRequests Method   619

Programming Tip: Memory Leakage   621
The StudentDM Class   621
    Programming Specifications   622
    The StudentDM Instance Definition   625
The Student Class   627
    Programming Specifications   627
The Person Class   630
    Programming Specifications   630
The Student UI Class   633
    Programming Specifications   633
The Student PRT Class   635
Conclusion   639
Summary   640
Fill-in   641   True/False   641   Problems   642

Appendix A: Getting Started   643

Appendix B: Connecting COBOL97 and Visual Basic   693

Appendix C: Reserved Words   711

Appendix D: COBOL-85 Reference Summary   713

Appendix E: COBOL in the New Millennium   739

Appendix F: Answers to Odd-Numbered Exercises   747

Appendix G: Projects   755

Index   897

Preface

The *Fujitsu Version* of *COBOL: From Micro to Mainframe, Third Edition* parallels our earlier work, but has been updated to support *Fujitsu COBOL Version 4.0*. All listings in the text have been modified for the new compiler, especially those listings pertaining to screen I/O. We have added an extensive appendix with supporting documentation and hands-on exercises that describe how to use the new software to full advantage. The set of student programming projects has also been thoroughly revised. As in the previous edition, the Fujitsu software is provided with the text at no additional cost. (The text may also be ordered with one of two compilers from Micro Focus, Net Express COBOL or Personal COBOL, but at an additional cost.)

The Fujitsu version is supported by our Web site at www.prenhall.com/grauer. Students can download the practice files and PowerPoint lectures as before, but now have access to an online study guide that provides an interactive review on a chapter-by-chapter basis. Each chapter contains a variety of short answer questions that can be taken for self-evaluation or e-mailed to instructors.

The *Fujitsu Version* of *COBOL: From Micro to Mainframe* includes all subjects normally covered in the one-year COBOL sequence. The scope is extensive, ranging from an introduction to COBOL, to maintaining sequential files and non-sequential files, to object-oriented COBOL, to linking COBOL programs and Visual Basic.

Benefits and Features

Both the new Fujitsu version, and the earlier Micro Focus version, on which it is based, respond to the requests of students and instructors to provide access to Windows-based tools, while maintaining the proven approach to teaching COBOL. Its many features include:

- Appendix A provides extensive coverage of the Fujitsu compiler through a series of hands-on exercises. Students are shown how to create and edit COBOL programs, how to compile, link, and edit a program, and how to use the debugging facility.

- A new chapter (Chapter 19) on the Y2K problem discusses the sources of the problem, and techniques to correct it. The chapter also provides a list of Web sites to obtain further information.

- Another new chapter (Chapter 20) demonstrates the concepts of object-oriented COBOL. This new approach to COBOL promises to be a way for companies to maintain the value of their legacy COBOL programs, while still being able to use the benefits of object-oriented programming.

- Appendix B shows how Visual Basic can be used to create Windows-based user interfaces for COBOL programs.

- Coverage of COBOL 2002 and intrinsic functions has been added in Appendix E. The 1989 extensions to COBOL 85 allow the use of predefined functions that had been missing in COBOL. This appendix also discusses the changes anticipated in COBOL 2002.

- Appendix G, on student programming projects has been thoroughly revised. Many of the projects are continued from one chapter to the next, enabling students to experience system development and programming maintenance.

- Immediate entry into COBOL programming, beginning in Chapter 1. Programming is learned by doing, and the book has students writing a complete program from the very beginning.

- Over 30 illustrative COBOL programs reinforce the discussion in the text and serve as both pedagogical aids and subsequent reference material. Every program is presented in a uniform and detailed format, including program narrative, record layouts, report layouts, test data, and processing specifications.

- A thorough discussion of structured methodology, hierarchy charts, pseudocode, and top-down testing is presented in Chapter 3 and followed throughout the text. Students learn the proper way to develop programs early on and follow the procedure throughout the text.

- An enhanced Web site (www.prenhall.com/grauer) from where students can download the COBOL listings in the text, data files for student projects, and PowerPoint lectures. The availability of the sample listings enables students to reproduce and/or modify any of the programs without the tedium of data entry and further enhances the learning experience. The Web site also provides access to an online study guide containing review questions for every chapter.

- An abundance of short-answer (true-false, multiple choice and fill-in-the blank) questions, COBOL problems, and programming projects for every chapter, with answers to the odd-numbered questions provided in Appendix F.

- Programming tips, dispersed throughout the text, which go beyond the syntactical rules of COBOL, and suggest stylistic considerations to make programs easier to read and maintain.

- Extensive use of graphic aids, featuring a two-color presentation, with annotated figures to further clarify the presentation.

- System concept presentation at the beginning of most chapters, as COBOL instruction has come to require additional material beyond the language itself. There are detailed discussions of control breaks, data validation, techniques for table lookups and initialization, storing, the balance line algorithm for file maintenance and the organization of indexed files.

Software and Supplements

The *Fujitsu Version* of *COBOL: From Micro to Mainframe,* Third Edition is bundled with a free copy of Version 4.0 of the Fujitsu COBOL compiler and includes the associated documentation in the text. The Fujitsu version may also be ordered with one of two Micro Focus compilers. For more information please see our Web site (www.prenhall.com/grauer).

Instructors may also obtain the **Instructor's Resource CD** (ISBN# 0-13-088457-X) from their local Prentice Hall representative. The CD contains the Instructor Manual in Word format, solutions to programming projects, and Prentice Hall Testing software. The latter is based on technology developed by Engineering Software Associates, Inc. (EAS), Prentice Hall Custom Test allows the educator to create and tailor the exam to their own needs.

Acknowledgments

We are especially grateful to our editors at Prentice Hall, Petra Recter, Alan Apt, and Marcia Horton, without whom this project would not have been possible. We also want to thank the many other individuals who helped produce the text. Erik Unhjem developed our innovative Web site. John Innanen provided the solutions to the COBOL projects. Paul Ross created the Instructor Manual. Irwin Zucker supervised the production. We also want to acknowledge our reviewers, who through their comments and constructive criticism, made this a far better book:

Robert V. Binder, Robert Binder Systems Consulting, Inc.
Harvey Blessing, Essex Community College
Dinon Boyer, University of Akron
Georgia Brown, Northern Illinois University
Jan De Lassen, Brigham Young University
Ida M. Flynn, University of Pittsburgh
Frank T. Gergelyi, NJIT
Ken Goldsmith, University of Miami
Tom Gorecki, St. Charles Community College
Carol C. Grimm, Palm Beach Community College
Monica Holmes, Central Michigan University
Ann W. Houck, Pima Community College
David Lee
James W. Payne, Kellogg Community College
Nicholas Ross, University of Illinois at Chicago
Wendell I. Pope, Utah State University
Daniel H. Rindfleisch, Computer Specialist with Federal Government
Daniel R. Rota, Robert Morris College
Richard H. Saracusa, Northeastern University
Ron Teemley, DeVry Institute of Technology
Donat Valcourt, Northeastern University
Ron Williams, McLennon Community College
Jackie Zucker, University of Miami

A final word of thanks to you, our readers, for choosing this book. Please feel free to contact us with any comments or suggestions via email.

Robert Grauer
rgrauer@sba.miami.edu

Carol Vazquez Villar

Arthur R. Buss
bussa@william.jewell.edu

Introduction

CHAPTER OUTLINE

Overview

The First Problem

Programming Specifications

Required Logic

Flowcharts

Pseudocode

A First Look at COBOL

Identification Division

Environment Division

Data Division

Procedure Division

Test Data

Elements of COBOL

Reserved Words

Programmer-Supplied Names

Literals

Symbols

Level Numbers

PICTURE Clauses

An Alternate Look at COBOL

Summary

Fill-in

True/False

Problems

OBJECTIVES

After reading this chapter you will be able to:

- Define the terms: field, record, and file.

- Name two techniques used to express program logic.

- Identify the four divisions of a COBOL program.

- State the six COBOL language elements.

- State the rules for creating a programmer-supplied name; distinguish between examples of valid and invalid names.

- State the difference between numeric and nonnumeric literals; recognize valid and invalid examples of each.

- Follow the logic of a simple program as expressed in a flowchart or pseudocode.

OVERVIEW

This book is about computer programming. In particular, it is about COBOL, a widely used commercial programming language. Programming involves the translation of an algorithm (a precise means of solving a problem) into a form the computer can understand. Programming is necessary because, despite reports to the contrary, computers cannot think for themselves. Instead, they do exactly what they have been instructed to do, and these instructions take the form of a computer program. The advantage of the computer stems from its speed and accuracy. It does not do anything that a human being could not do, given sufficient time and memory capacity.

We begin our study of computer programming by describing a simple problem and then developing the logic and COBOL program to solve it. This rapid entrance into COBOL is somewhat different from the approach followed by most textbooks, but we believe in learning by doing. There is nothing very mysterious about COBOL programming, so let's get started.

The First Problem

Our first problem is set in the context of a university, and involves a set of student records, one record per student. Each record contains the student's name, number of completed credits, and major. Implicit in this statement are the definitions of three fundamental terms: field, record, and file. A *field* is a basic fact, such as the name, address, major, grade point average, or number of completed credits. A *record* is a set of fields, and a *file* is a set of records. Thus, if there were 1,000 students, there would be 1,000 records (one for each student), each consisting of five fields, and comprising a single student file.

To clarify this relationship, we create four hypothetical students for our problem: John Adams, Amelia Earhart, Orville Wright, and Georgia O'Keeffe. There are many facts about each of our students, but our problem utilizes only three:

Figure 1.1   Fields, Records, and Files

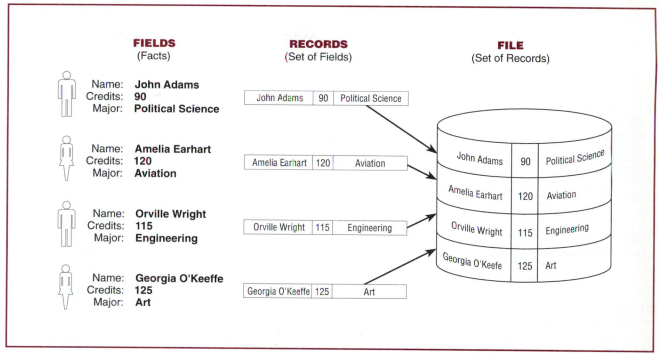

name, major, and credits completed. Figure 1.1 represents these concepts in pictorial fashion. Each fact about each student comprises a single field. The three fields collectively make up that student's record. The four records (one for each of our students) compose the student file.

The problem is to process the file of student records and produce a list of engineering students who have completed more than 110 credits. It is a typical problem, in that its solution will address the three elements common to all computer applications: input, processing, and output. As shown in Figure 1.2, the student file, just defined, is the *input*; this file is *processed* by determining which students are engineering majors with more than 110 credits; and consequently, a report is created as *output*, reflecting these students.

The input to a computer program; that is, the precise arrangement of the various fields in each incoming record, has to be specified exactly. Figure 1.3a is a common way to communicate this information, and shows that the student's name is contained in positions 1–25, the number of credits in positions 26–28, and the student's major in positions 29–43. Note too, that every record in a given file must have the identical record layout.

In similar fashion, the report produced as output is also precisely designed. Figure 1.3c shows a print layout chart, in which descriptive information appears on line one, with the names of selected students in columns 9–33 of subsequent lines. Observe also that the location of the name field is different in the input and output records (positions 1–25 and 9–33, respectively), and that each input record contains three fields, but that each line of output has been designed to contain only one field.

Programming Specifications

It is important that programming specification—that is, the input, processing, and output requirements—be presented in a clear and unambiguous fashion.

Figure 1.2 Input, Processing, and Output

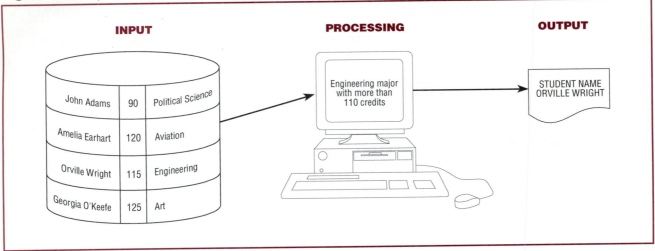

Figure 1.3 Engineering Senior (Input and Output)

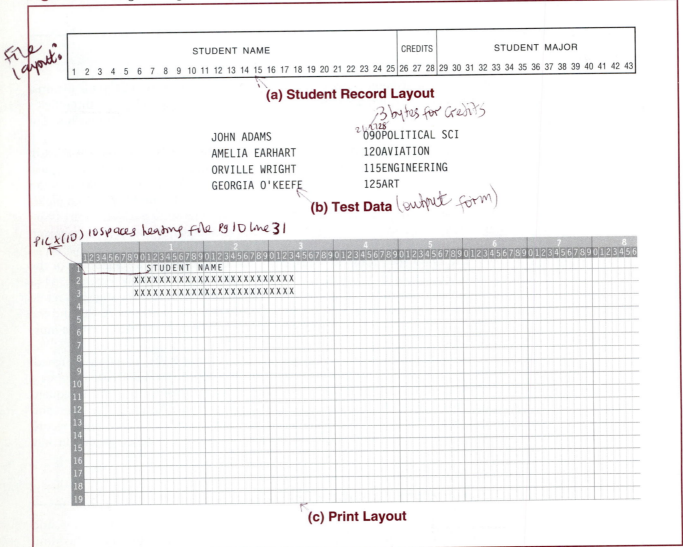

Accordingly, the authors have adopted the format shown below, and use it throughout the text for both illustrative programs and student assignments. The programming specifications begin with the program name and a brief narrative, followed by a detailed description of the various requirements. Note, too, that the specification document is entirely self-contained, and that if the person preparing the specifications has done a complete job, there will be little need for the programmer to seek additional information.

Programming Specifications

Program Name: Engineering Senior Program

Narrative: This program processes a file of student records and prints the name of every student who is an engineering major with more than 110 credits.

Input File(s): STUDENT-FILE

Input Record Layout: See Figure 1.3a

Test Data: See Figure 1.3b

Report Layout: See Figure 1.3c

Processing Requirements:
1. Print a heading line.

2. Read a file of student records.

3. For every record, determine whether that student has a major of engineering and has completed more than 110 credits.

4. Print the name of every student who satisfies the requirements in item 3 above. Single-space the output.

Required Logic

Let us imagine momentarily that the student records are physically in the form of manila folders, stored in a filing cabinet, and further that a clerk is available to do our work. Our problem is to instruct the clerk on how to go through the folders. We would say something to the following effect:

Repeat steps 1 through 4 until there are no more folders:

1. Select a folder.

2. Examine the folder to see if that student is an engineering major *and* has more than 110 credits.

3. If the student meets both qualifications, write the student's name on a running list.

4. Return the folder to the file cabinet.

Stop

In essence, we have prepared a series of instructions for the clerk to follow. If our instructions are correct and if they are followed exactly, then the clerk will produce the desired results.

A *computer program* is a set of instructions, written according to a precise set of rules, which the computer interprets and subsequently executes. Unlike the clerk, however, the computer always follows our instructions exactly. In other words, *the computer does what we tell it to do, which is not necessarily what we want it to do*. A human clerk, on the other hand, has a mind of his or her own and can question or alter erroneous instructions. Since the computer does precisely what it is told, it is imperative that you strive to write logically correct programs. Accordingly, you must expend significant effort *prior to actual coding* to develop a program's logic correctly. Two common techniques for expressing that logic are *flowcharts* and *pseudocode*.

Flowcharts

A flowchart is a pictorial representation of the logic inherent in a program. It is the translation of a problem statement into a logical blueprint that is subsequently incorporated into the COBOL program. A flowchart to list the engineering students with more than 110 credits is shown in Figure 1.4.

A flowchart uses blocks with specific shapes to indicate the nature of an operation. Using Figure 1.4 as a guide, we see that a diamond-shaped block indicates a decision, a parallelogram depicts input or output, an ellipse shows the beginning or end, and a rectangle implies straightforward processing. A rectangle with vertical lines implies that the processing within the rectangle will be expanded into a flowchart of its own.

To understand the flowchart in Figure 1.4, consider the nature of a READ statement. The function of a READ instruction is to obtain a record, but there will always be a point when a READ is attempted and no record is found, that is, when all the records in the file have already been read. Since one does not know in advance how many records a file contains, the READ instruction must also test for the *end-of-file* condition. Thus, if a file contains two records, it is actually read three times (once for each record, and once to sense the end-of-file condition).

The flowchart in Figure 1.4 begins with a start block (block 1), and continues with various housekeeping blocks. Housekeeping consists of statements that are done once at the start of processing, for example, opening files (block 2), reading the first record (block 3), and writing a heading at the start of a report (block 4). Control then passes through a connector block (block 5) to a decision statement (block 6).

If the end-of-file has not been reached, control goes to the PROCESS-RECORDS block, which is expanded in the right side of the figure. Each incoming record is checked in block 9 to determine if it meets both qualifications. If so, that student's name is written to the output report in block 10; if not, control goes directly to the connector in block 11. (Note that both the true and false branches for the condition in block 9 meet at a single connector in block 11.) The next record is read in block 12, and the PROCESS-RECORDS block is finished. Control then moves to the left side of the figure, to the connector in block 5 to the end-of-file test in block 6. Eventually, when the end-of-file has been reached, control will pass to close files (block 7), then to the stop statement in block 8.

To better understand how the flowchart works, we can use the test data of Figure 1.1 and play computer, by running the data through the flowchart. Execution begins by opening the files, reading the first record (John Adams), and writing the heading line. The end-of-file has not been reached, so block 6 directs flow to block 9, the test for engineering majors with more than 110 credits. John Adams fails the test, so control passes to the connector in block 11, to the READ in block 12, whereupon the data for Amelia Earhart are read into memory. Control flows through

Figure 1.4   Flowchart to Select Engineering Seniors

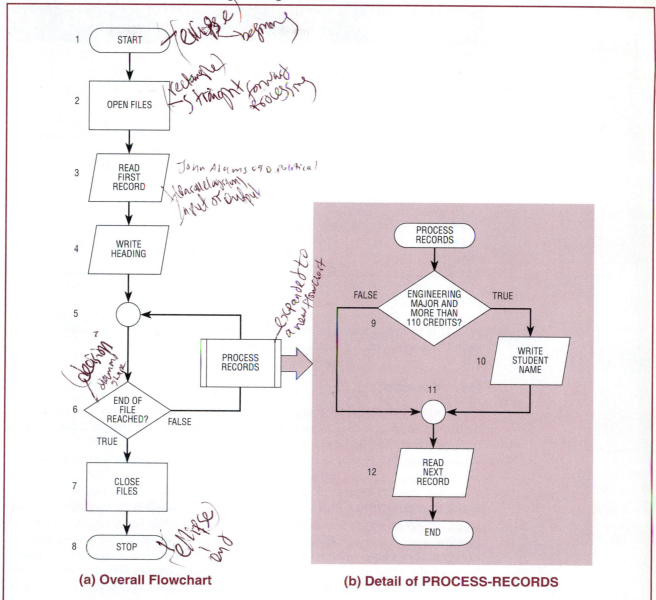

(a) Overall Flowchart   **(b) Detail of PROCESS-RECORDS**

the connector of block 5, to the end-of-file test in block 6, and then to the qualification test in block 9. Amelia Earhart fails the test, again passing control to the connector in block 11, to the READ in block 12, at which point Orville Wright is read into memory. However, Wright is an engineering major with more than 110 credits, so he passes the test and his name is written in block 10.

The data for Georgia O'Keeffe are read in block 12, and control flows once more to the connector in block 5, to the end-of-file test in block 6. Realize, however, that even though O'Keeffe is the last record, the end-of-file condition has *not* yet been detected. O'Keeffe fails the qualification test, whereupon control flows to the READ in block 12. This time the end-of-file is detected so that, when control again reaches the end-of-file test in block 6, processing will be directed to the CLOSE FILES and STOP statements in blocks 7 and 8.

TABLE 1.1   The Flow chart and Test Data

BLOCK & DESCRIPTION	TIMES EXECUTED	EXPLANATION
1 Start	1	At beginning of program
2 Open files	1	At beginning of program
3 Initial read	1	Reads the first record (Adams)
4 Write heading	1	At beginning of program
5 Connector	5	Entered five times
6 End-of-file test	5	Once for each of four records; once to sense end-of-file condition
7 Close files	1	Once, before execution stops
8 Stop	1	Executed once, at program's end
9 Qualifying test	4	Once for each student
10 Write	1	Executed for Wright only
11 Connector	4	Entered four times
12 Read	4	Reads every record but the first, and detects the end-of-file condition

It is useful to summarize this discussion by tabulating the number of times each block in Figure 1.4 is executed. This is shown in Table 1.1.

Pseudocode

Pseudocode expresses a program's logic more concisely than a flowchart. One definition of pseudocode is *neat notes to oneself,* and since programmers do this naturally, pseudocode has replaced the traditional flowchart in many installations. Consider Figure 1.5, which contains identical logic to the flowchart in Figure 1.4, albeit in a more concise fashion.

As shown in Figure 1.5, the logic of most programs can be divided into three major portions: *initialization, processing,* and *termination.* Initialization is done once at the start of processing—for example, opening files, reading the first record in a file, and writing a heading. This is followed by a series of instructions that are executed repeatedly, once for each incoming record; e.g., each record is evaluated for an engineering major with the requisite number of credits. If both conditions are met, the name will be written on the registrar's list; if the conditions are not met,

Figure 1.5 Pseudocode

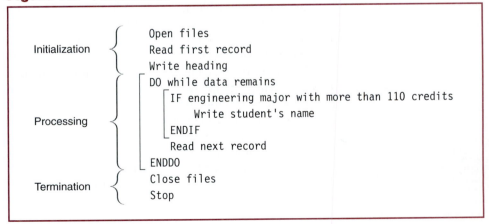

```
                      Open files
      Initialization  Read first record
                      Write heading
                      DO while data remains
                          IF engineering major with more than 110 credits
                              Write student's name
      Processing      ENDIF
                          Read next record
                      ENDDO
      Termination     Close files
                      Stop
```

nothing further is done with the particular record. When *all* of the records in the file have been read, the loop is finished, and a termination routine is entered to print a total or simply stop processing.

Figure 1.5 also contains vertical lines connecting the words IF and ENDIF, and DO and ENDDO. This notation indicates two of the basic building blocks (**selection** and **iteration**) of a discipline known as **structured programming** which is fully explained in Chapter 3.

Pseudocode uses instructions similar to those of a computer language to describe program logic, but is *not* bound by precise syntactical rules found in formal programming languages. For example, the vertical lines referred to previously are the authors' convention and do not necessarily appear in the pseudocode of others. Nor is pseudocode bound by any rules for indentation, which is done strictly at the discretion of the person using it. The purpose of pseudocode is simply to convey program logic in a straightforward and easily followed manner.

A First Look at Cobol

We proceed to the COBOL program in Figure 1.6, which corresponds to the flowchart in Figure 1.4 and the pseudocode in Figure 1.5. The syntactical rules for COBOL are extremely precise, and you are certainly *not* expected to remember them after a brief exposure to Figure 1.6. The authors believe, however, *that immediate exposure to a real program is extremely beneficial in stripping the mystical aura that too often*

Figure 1.6   The First COBOL Program

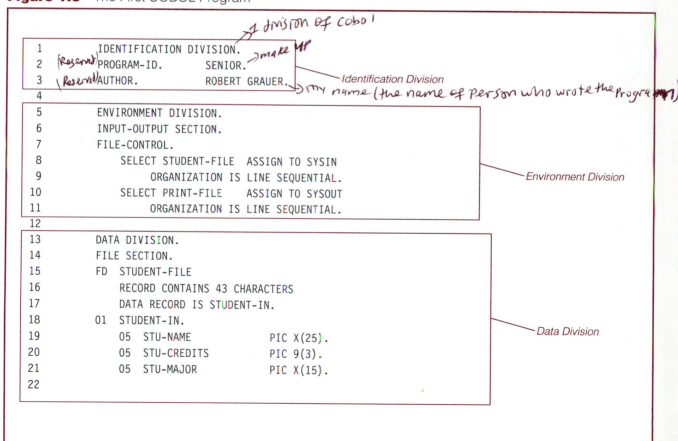

Figure 1.6 *(continued)*

```
23        FD   PRINT-FILE
24             RECORD CONTAINS 132 CHARACTERS
25             DATA RECORD IS PRINT-LINE.
26        01   PRINT-LINE             PIC X(132).
27
28        WORKING-STORAGE SECTION.
29        01   DATA-REMAINS-SWITCH    PIC X(2)      VALUE SPACES.
30
31        01   HEADING-LINE.
32             05   FILLER            PIC X(10)     VALUE SPACES.
33             05   FILLER            PIC X(12)     VALUE 'STUDENT NAME'.
34             05   FILLER            PIC X(110)    VALUE SPACES.
35
36        01   DETAIL-LINE.
37             05   FILLER            PIC X(8)      VALUE SPACES.
38             05   PRINT-NAME        PIC X(25).
39             05   FILLER            PIC X(99)     VALUE SPACES.
40
```

Data Division

```
41        PROCEDURE DIVISION.
42        PREPARE-SENIOR-REPORT.
43            OPEN INPUT  STUDENT-FILE
44                 OUTPUT PRINT-FILE.
45            READ STUDENT-FILE
46                AT END MOVE 'NO' TO DATA-REMAINS-SWITCH
47            END-READ.
48            PERFORM WRITE-HEADING-LINE.
49            PERFORM PROCESS-RECORDS
50                UNTIL DATA-REMAINS-SWITCH = 'NO'.
51            CLOSE STUDENT-FILE
52                  PRINT-FILE.
53            STOP RUN.
54
55        WRITE-HEADING-LINE.
56            MOVE HEADING-LINE TO PRINT-LINE.
57            WRITE PRINT-LINE.
58
59        PROCESS-RECORDS.
60            IF STU-CREDITS > 110 AND STU-MAJOR = 'ENGINEERING'
61                MOVE STU-NAME TO PRINT-NAME
62                MOVE DETAIL-LINE TO PRINT-LINE
63                WRITE PRINT-LINE
64            END-IF.
65            READ STUDENT-FILE
66                AT END MOVE 'NO' TO DATA-REMAINS-SWITCH
67            END-READ.
```

Procedure Division

surrounds programming. Further, Figure 1.6 will become easier to understand after some brief explanation.

Every COBOL program consists of four divisions, which must appear in the following order:

IDENTIFICATION DIVISION	The Identification Division contains the program name and author's name.
ENVIRONMENT DIVISION	The Environment Division associates the file names referenced in a program to the input and output (I/O) devices recognized by the operating system.
DATA DIVISION	The Data Division describes the record layout of the incoming record(s) and the location of data in the generated report.
PROCEDURE DIVISION	The Procedure Division contains the program logic, that is, the instructions the computer is to execute in solving the problem.

Since COBOL is intended to resemble English, you may be able to get an overall sense of what is happening, merely by reading the program. We provide an intuitive explanation and reiterate that, at this time, you should in no way be concerned with the precise syntax of the language; that is, our present intent is to teach COBOL by example, with the short-term objective of achieving a conceptual understanding of a COBOL program.

The Identification Division

The **IDENTIFICATION DIVISION** (Lines 1–3) appears at the beginning of every program. It serves to identify the program (SENIOR) and the author (Robert Grauer). There is nothing complicated about this division, and it has no effect on the results of the program.

The Environment Division

The **ENVIRONMENT DIVISION** (lines 5–11) contains the INPUT-OUTPUT SECTION, which describes the files used by the program. The engineering senior program uses two files, an input file containing the student records and an output file for the report. Both of these files are defined in SELECT statements.

The names chosen by the programmer for these files (that is, STUDENT-FILE and PRINT-FILE) are assigned to logical devices by the SELECT statement and associated ASSIGN clause. Line 8, for example, ties the incoming STUDENT-FILE to the logical device, SYSIN; this tells the operating system to read the file containing the incoming student records from the device SYSIN. (The name of the device, such as SYSIN, is installation dependent and varies from computer to computer.) The clause ORGANIZATION IS LINE SEQUENTIAL is required to properly process sequential files on personal computers. Mainframe sequential files have a different format and do not require this clause.

The Data Division

The **DATA DIVISION** (lines 13–39) describes all data elements used by the program. It is divided into two sections, the FILE SECTION (lines 14–26) and the WORKING-STORAGE SECTION (lines 28–39).

The **FILE SECTION** contains file description (FD) entries for files previously defined in SELECT statements. The FD for STUDENT-FILE extends from line 15 to line 17 and contains clauses that describe the physical characteristics of the file. The FD is followed by a *record description*, which defines the various fields within the record (lines 18–21).

The statements within the record description are preceded by *level numbers*, in this example, 01 and 05. The level number 01 is special and indicates the beginning of a *record description* entry. The fields within a record are defined through a series of PICTURE clauses (PIC is an acceptable abbreviation), which indicate the *type* and *size* of the field. A picture of 9's indicates a numeric field, whereas a picture of X's signifies an alphanumeric field. The number in parentheses indicates the size of the field; for example, PIC 9(3) indicates a three-position numeric field, and PIC X(25) is a 25-position alphanumeric field. The PICTURE clauses in lines 19–21 of Figure 1.6 are consistent with the record description in the original problem statement.

The **WORKING-STORAGE SECTION** (lines 28–39) is used to define any data names that do not appear in an input or output file. The programming specifications called for two distinct print lines (a heading line and a detail line), each of which contains a different format as per the print layout of Figure 1.3. Accordingly, two different 01 entries are defined, HEADING-LINE and DETAIL-LINE, each with a different layout. The function of DATA-REMAINS-SWITCH will be made clearer after an examination of the Procedure Division.

The Procedure Division

The **PROCEDURE DIVISION** (lines 41–67) contains the logic required to solve the problem. The Procedure Division is divided into *paragraphs*, with each paragraph consisting of one or more sentences.

The first paragraph, PREPARE-SENIOR-REPORT, extends from line 42 to line 53. It begins by opening the files, then reading the first student record. The PERFORM statement in line 48 transfers control to the paragraph WRITE-HEADING-LINE (lines 55–57), which prints the heading, then returns control back to line 49 in the PREPARE-SENIOR-REPORT paragraph. This too is a PERFORM statement, which transfers control to the paragraph PROCESS-RECORDS (lines 59–67), which processes incoming student records until the data file is exhausted.

The IF statement in line 60 determines whether an incoming record meets both qualifications, that is, whether the student is an engineering major and has more than 110 credits. If both conditions are met, that student's name is written to the output report. The IF statement extends to the END-IF *scope terminator* in line 64; that is, if the condition in line 60 is met, *every* statement between the condition and the END-IF in line 64 will be executed. Note, too, that three COBOL statements are required to produce a detail line; the incoming name is moved to the output name in line 61, the detail line is moved to the print line in line 62, and the line is written in line 63.

The action of the PERFORM statement is explained with the aid of Figure 1.7. The PERFORM statement in line 49 transfers control to the paragraph PROCESS-RECORDS, until DATA-REMAINS-SWITCH = 'NO', that is, until the data file is empty. Accordingly, the last statement of the performed routine is a READ statement to read the next record. When the end-of-file is reached, the AT END clause of the READ statement will move 'NO' to DATA-REMAINS-SWITCH to terminate the PERFORM; the READ statement itself is ended by the END-READ scope terminator. Control then returns to the statement under the PERFORM statement (to line 51), which closes the files, and finally to the STOP RUN statement, which terminates the program.

Figure 1.7 Procedure Division Logic

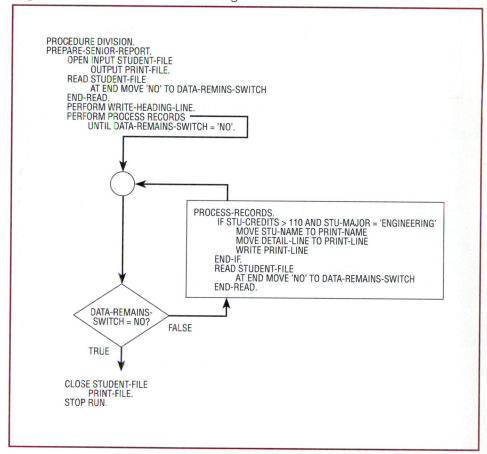

Test Data

Figure 1.8 contains test data and the associated output produced by the program in Figure 1.6. (Five more records have been added to provide additional examples.) You should be able to state the reasons why individual records were not selected for the output report; for example, Amelia Earhart and Alex Bell were rejected for the wrong major and an insufficient number of credits, respectively. (Can you identify all nine of our famous students?)

Elements of COBOL

Although you are not yet expected to write a COBOL program, you should be able to follow simple programs like the one in Figure 1.6 intuitively. This section begins a formal discussion of COBOL so that you will eventually be able to write an entire program.

COBOL consists of six language elements: reserved words, programmer-supplied names, literals, symbols, level numbers, and pictures.

Reserved Words

Reserved words have special significance to COBOL and are used in a rigidly prescribed manner. They must be spelled correctly, or the compiler will not be able

Figure 1.8 Test Data and Associated Output

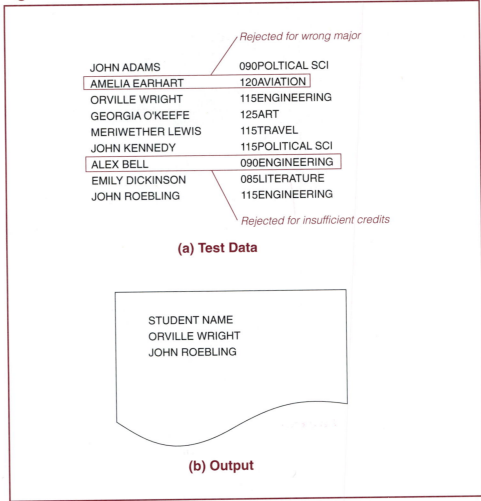

Rejected for wrong major

JOHN ADAMS	090POLTICAL SCI
AMELIA EARHART	120AVIATION
ORVILLE WRIGHT	115ENGINEERING
GEORGIA O'KEEFE	125ART
MERIWETHER LEWIS	115TRAVEL
JOHN KENNEDY	115POLITICAL SCI
ALEX BELL	090ENGINEERING
EMILY DICKINSON	085LITERATURE
JOHN ROEBLING	115ENGINEERING

Rejected for insufficient credits

(a) Test Data

STUDENT NAME
ORVILLE WRIGHT
JOHN ROEBLING

(b) Output

to recognize them. The list of reserved words varies from compiler to compiler. A comprehensive list of reserved words is given in Appendix C. The beginner is urged to refer frequently to this appendix for two reasons: (1) to ensure the proper spelling of reserved words used in his or her program; and (2) to avoid the inadvertent use of reserved words as programmer-supplied names.

Programmer-Supplied Names

You, the programmer, supply names for paragraphs, data elements, and files. A ***paragraph name*** is a tag to which the program refers, for example, PROCESS-RECORDS or PREPARE-SENIOR-REPORT in Figure 1.6. ***Data names*** are the elements on which instructions operate, for example, STU-NAME, STU-CREDITS, and STU-MAJOR in Figure 1.6. ***File names*** are specified in several places throughout a COBOL program, but their initial appearance is in the Environment Division, for example, STUDENT-FILE and PRINT-FILE in Figure 1.6. All programmer-supplied names are chosen according to the following rules:

1. A programmer-supplied name may contain the letters A to Z, the digits 0 to 9, and the hyphen; no other characters are permitted, not even blanks.

2. A programmer-supplied name may *not* begin or end with a hyphen.

3. A programmer-supplied name must be 30 characters or fewer in length.

4. A reserved word may *not* be used as a programmer-supplied name.

5. Data names must contain at least one letter.

6. Paragraph names may be all numeric.

Table 1.2 illustrates examples of the rules associated with programmer-supplied names.

TABLE 1.2   Programmer-Supplied Names

Programmer-Supplied Name	Explanation
SUM	**Invalid**—reserved word
SUM-OF-X	**Valid**
SUM OF X	**Invalid**—contains blanks
SUM-OF-X-	**Invalid**—ends with a hyphen
SUM-OF-ALL-THE-XS	**Valid**
SUM-OF-ALL-THE-XS-IN-ENTIRE-PROGRAM	**Invalid**—more than 30 characters
GROSS-PAY-IN-$	**Invalid**—contains a $
12345	**Valid** as a paragraph name but *invalid* as a data name

Literals

A *literal* is an exact value or constant. Literals are of two types, ***numeric*** (a number) or ***nonnumeric*** (a character string). Literals of both types appear throughout a program and are used to compare the value of a data name to a specified constant. Consider line 60 of Figure 1.6:

```
IF STU-CREDITS > 110 AND STU-MAJOR = 'ENGINEERING'
```

In the first portion of the statement, STU-CREDITS is compared to 110, a numeric literal. Numeric literals adhere to the following rules:

1. A numeric literal can be up to 18 digits long.

2. A numeric literal may begin with a leading (leftmost) plus or minus sign.

3. A numeric literal may contain a decimal point, but it may *not* end with a decimal point.

The second part of the IF statement contains a nonnumeric literal, 'ENGINEERING'. Nonnumeric literals adhere to the following rules:

1. A nonnumeric literal is enclosed in apostrophes (or quotation marks) as specified by the compiler.

2. A nonnumeric literal may be up to 160 characters in length.

3. A nonnumeric literal may contain anything, including blanks, numbers, and reserved words, but not another apostrophe (or quotation mark).

Examples of both numeric and nonnumeric literals are shown Table 1.3.

TABLE 1.3   Numeric and Nonnumeric Literals

Literal	Explanation
123.4	Valid numeric literal
'123.4'	Valid nonnumeric literal
+123	Valid numeric literal
'IDENTIFICATION DIVISION'	Valid nonnumeric literal
123.	Invalid numeric literal—may not end with a decimal point
123-	Invalid numeric literal—the minus sign must be in the leftmost position

Symbols

Symbols are of three types—punctuation, arithmetic, and relational, as listed in Table 1.4.

TABLE 1.4   Symbols

Category	Symbol	Meaning
Punctuation	.	Denotes end of COBOL entry
	,	Delineates clauses
	' or "	Sets off nonnumeric literals
	( )	Encloses subscripts or expressions
Arithmetic	+	Addition
	-	Subtraction
	*	Multiplication
	/	Division
	**	Exponentiation
Relational	=	Equal to
	>	Greater than
	<	Less than
	>=	Greater than or equal to
	<=	Less than or equal to

The use of relational and arithmetic symbols is described in detail later in the text, beginning in Chapter 4. A period terminates an entry, and its omission (in the absence of a scope terminator) can cause difficulty. A comma, on the other hand, is entirely optional, and its omission (or inclusion) has no effect whatsoever on the program. The use of commas is discouraged, however, as a comma can be mistaken for a period on older printers, which tend to blur the output.

Level Numbers

Level numbers describe the relationship of items in a record. For example, under STUDENT-FILE in Figure 1.6, there was a single 01-level entry and several 05-level entries. In general, the higher (numerically) the level number, the less significant the entry; thus 05 is less important than 01. Entries with higher numeric values are said to belong to the levels above them. Thus, in Figure 1.6 the several 05-level entries belong to their respective 01-level entries.

Picture Clauses

Pictures describe the nature of incoming or outgoing data. A picture of 9's means the entry is numeric; a picture of X's means the entry is alphanumeric, that is, it can contain letters, numbers, and special characters. (Alphabetic pictures, with a picture of A, are seldom used; even names can contain apostrophes or hyphens, which are alphanumeric rather than alphabetic in nature.) Level numbers and pictures are discussed more fully in Chapter 4.

An Alternate Look at COBOL

Many newcomers to COBOL, especially programmers familiar with other languages, are put off by the "priming read" that results in two distinct Read statements within a program. For example, see lines 45 and 65 in Figure 1.6. The requirement for the extra READ statement stems from a limitation of COBOL-74, an earlier version of the language. Believe it or not, COBOL-74 is still common in the workplace for older systems.

Figure 1.9   The Engineering Senior Program (An Alternate Look)

```
 1        IDENTIFICATION DIVISION.
 2        PROGRAM-ID.      SENIORAV.
 3        AUTHOR.          ROBERT GRAUER.
 4
 5        ENVIRONMENT DIVISION.
 6        INPUT-OUTPUT SECTION.
 7        FILE-CONTROL.
 8            SELECT STUDENT-FILE  ASSIGN TO SYSIN
 9                ORGANIZATION IS LINE SEQUENTIAL.
10            SELECT PRINT-FILE    ASSIGN TO SYSOUT
11                ORGANIZATION IS LINE SEQUENTIAL.
12
13        DATA DIVISION.
14        FILE SECTION.
15        FD  STUDENT-FILE
16            RECORD CONTAINS 43 CHARACTERS
17            DATA RECORD IS STUDENT-IN.
18        01  STUDENT-IN.
19            05  STU-NAME          PIC X(25).
20            05  STU-CREDITS       PIC 9(3).
21            05  STU-MAJOR         PIC X(15).
22
23        FD  PRINT-FILE
24            RECORD CONTAINS 132 CHARACTERS
25            DATA RECORD IS PRINT-LINE.
26        01  PRINT-LINE            PIC X(132).
27
28        WORKING-STORAGE SECTION.
29        01  DATA-REMAINS-SWITCH   PIC X(2)      VALUE SPACES.
30
31        01  HEADING-LINE.
32            05  FILLER            PIC X(10)     VALUE SPACES.
33            05  FILLER            PIC X(12)     VALUE 'STUDENT NAME'.
34            05  FILLER            PIC X(110)    VALUE SPACES.
```

Programmer-supplied file name appears in several places (see lines 43, 47, and 54)

Picture clauses describe incoming record and are consistent with the data in Figure 1.3

Reserved words

Figure 1.9 *(continued)*

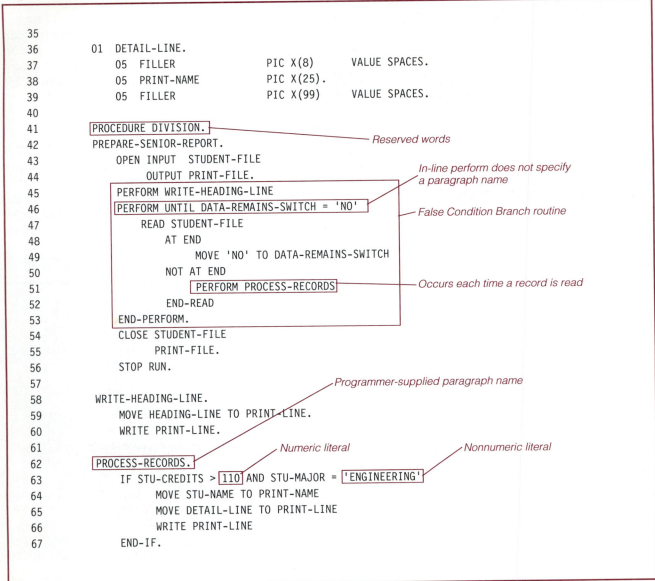

```
35
36    01  DETAIL-LINE.
37        05  FILLER              PIC X(8)      VALUE SPACES.
38        05  PRINT-NAME          PIC X(25).
39        05  FILLER              PIC X(99)     VALUE SPACES.
40
41    PROCEDURE DIVISION.                          ── Reserved words
42    PREPARE-SENIOR-REPORT.
43        OPEN INPUT  STUDENT-FILE
44             OUTPUT PRINT-FILE.                  ── In-line perform does not specify
45        PERFORM WRITE-HEADING-LINE                  a paragraph name
46        PERFORM UNTIL DATA-REMAINS-SWITCH = 'NO'  ── False Condition Branch routine
47            READ STUDENT-FILE
48                AT END
49                    MOVE 'NO' TO DATA-REMAINS-SWITCH
50                NOT AT END
51                    PERFORM PROCESS-RECORDS       ── Occurs each time a record is read
52            END-READ
53        END-PERFORM.
54        CLOSE STUDENT-FILE
55              PRINT-FILE.
56        STOP RUN.
57                                                  ── Programmer-supplied paragraph name
58    WRITE-HEADING-LINE.
59        MOVE HEADING-LINE TO PRINT-LINE.
60        WRITE PRINT-LINE.
61                             ── Numeric literal        ── Nonnumeric literal
62    PROCESS-RECORDS.
63        IF STU-CREDITS > 110 AND STU-MAJOR = 'ENGINEERING'
64            MOVE STU-NAME TO PRINT-NAME
65            MOVE DETAIL-LINE TO PRINT-LINE
66            WRITE PRINT-LINE
67        END-IF.
```

COBOL-85 provides a way to eliminate the priming read using an in-line PERFORM and the NOT AT END clause or False Condition Branch of the READ statement. This technique, incorporating the two new features, is shown in lines 46 to 53 of Figure 1.9. Line 46 controls a loop that runs to line 53. Inside the loop, the program reads the STUDENT-FILE until the last record has been read. When this occurs, the READ follows the AT END branch and moves "NO" to the DATA-REMAINS-SWITCH to stop the loop. In all other cases, the READ follows the NOT AT END or False Condition Branch and performs PROCESS-RECORDS. In Chapter 9 we discuss these two new techniques in more detail.

In the early chapters of the book we stay with the priming read technique, because this practice is still widespread in the industry. In addition, there are cases where priming reads are necessary—for example when several input files must be read. We switch to the alternate structure in Chapter 9. You, however, should use the form your professor prefers.

Summary

Points to Remember

■ A field is a basic fact, such as the name, address, major, grade point average, or number of completed credits. A record is a set of fields, and a file is a set of records.

■ Every computer application consists of input, processing, and output.

■ The computer cannot think for itself but must be told precisely what to do. This is done through a series of instructions known as a program.

■ The computer does not do anything that a human being could not do if given sufficient time. The advantages of a computer stem from its speed and accuracy.

■ A flowchart and/or pseudocode represent the logic embodied in a computer program.

■ Every COBOL program contains four divisions, which appear in the sequence: Identification, Environment, Data, and Procedure.

■ COBOL contains six language elements; reserved words, programmer-supplied names, literals, symbols, level numbers, and pictures.

Key Words and Concepts

Alphabetic data
Alphanumeric data
Arithmetic symbol
End-of-file
Field
File
Flowchart
Initialization
Level number
Nonnumeric literal
Numeric data
Numeric literal
Paragraph

Processing
Programmer-supplied name
Programming specifications
Pseudocode
Punctuation symbol
Record
Record description
Relational symbol
Reserved words
Scope terminator
Symbol
Termination
Test Data

COBOL Elements

```
DATA DIVISION
ENVIRONMENT DIVISION
FILE SECTION
IDENTIFICATION DIVISION
INPUT-OUTPUT SECTION
```

```
LINE SEQUENTIAL
PICTURE
PROCEDURE DIVISION
WORKING-STORAGE SECTION
```

F i l l - I n

1. All computer applications consist of _____, _____, and _____.

2. The divisions of a COBOL program appear in the order: _____, _____, _____, and _____.

3. A _____ is a pictorial representation of the logic in a program.

4. _____ may be described as neat notes to oneself.

5. A diamond-shaped block in a flowchart indicates a _____.

6. _____ _____ have special significance to COBOL and must be used in a rigidly prescribed manner and be spelled correctly.

7. A _____-_____ _____ may contain the letters A to Z, the digits 0 to 9, and the hyphen.

8. ** is the COBOL symbol for _____.

9. =, > , and < are examples of _____ symbols in COBOL.

10. A _____ is a set of records.

11. A record consists of one or more _____.

12. A _____ is a set of instructions to a computer.

T r u e / F a l s e

1. Nonnumeric literals may not contain numbers.

2. Numeric literals may not contain letters.

3. A data name may not contain any characters other than letters or numbers.

4. The rules for forming paragraph names and data names are exactly the same.

5. A data name may not consist of more than 30 characters.

6. A nonnumeric literal may not contain more than 30 characters.

7. A numeric literal may contain up to 18 digits.

8. There are four divisions in a COBOL program.

9. The divisions of a COBOL program may appear in any order.

10. Data description appears in the Identification Division.

11. A record contains one or more fields.

12. A file is a set of records.

13. Computers can think for themselves.

14. No statement in a computer program may be executed more than once.

15. A rectangle is the standard flowchart symbol for a decision block.

16. Reserved words may appear in a nonnumeric literal.

17. Reserved words may be used as data names.

18. Pseudocode serves the same function as a flowchart.

19. Pseudocode must be written according to precise syntactical rules.

20. The COBOL compiler needs to be installed every time a program is executed.

P r o b l e m s

1. Indicate whether the entries below are valid as data names. If any entry is invalid, state the reason.
   a. NUMBER-OF-TIMES
   b. CODE
   c. 12345
   d. ONE TWO THREE
   e. IDENTIFICATION-DIVISION
   f. IDENTIFICATION
   g. HOURS
   h. GROSS-PAY
   i. GROSS-PAY-IN-$

2. Classify the entries below as being valid or invalid literals. For each valid entry, indicate whether it is numeric or nonnumeric; for each invalid entry, state why it is invalid.
   a. 567
   b. 567.
   c. -567
   d. +567
   e. +567.
   f. '567.'
   g. 'FIVE SIX SEVEN'
   h. '-567'
   i. 567-
   j. 567+
   k. '567+'

3. a. Which division(s) contain paragraph names?
   b. Which division(s) contain the SELECT statement(s)?
   c. Which division(s) contain level numbers?
   d. Which division(s) contain data names?
   e. Which division(s) contain reserved words?
   f. Which division(s) contain PICTURE clauses?
   g. Which division(s) do not contain file names?

4. Given the COBOL program in Figure 1.6, indicate what changes would have to be made if
   a. We wanted music students rather than engineering students.
   b. We wanted students with 60 or fewer credits.
   c. The student major was contained in columns 60–74 of the incoming record.
   d. We wanted engineering students *or* students with 110 credits or more.
   Note: Treat parts (a), (b), (c), and (d) independently.

5. Which division in a COBOL program contains
   a. The File Section?
   b. Statements to open and close files?
   c. The description of incoming data?
   d. The description of outgoing data?
   e. The author's name?
   f. The program's name?
   g. Statements to read information?
   h. Statements to write information?

6. Your programming supervisor has drawn a flowchart for you to code. He left the flowchart on his dining room table at home, and unfortunately his three-year-old son, Benjy, cut it up into pieces with a pair of scissors. Your supervisor has collected the pieces (shown in Figure 1.10) and has asked you to rearrange them properly into a correct flowchart; do so. The flowchart is to read a file with each record containing three unequal numbers, A, B, and C. Write out the greater of the two sums (A + B) and (B + C) for each record only if A is less than 50. Develop the equivalent pseudocode.

7. World Wide Sales, Inc., wishes to promote one of its employees to head the South American Division. The selected employee must speak Spanish, be 40 or younger, and hold a college degree. The programming manager has prepared the necessary flowchart (see Figure 1.11), but unfortunately Benjy and his scissors got to it first (see Problem 6). Your job is to put the flowchart together. Note that there may be more than one employee who qualifies for the position. Accordingly, the flowchart includes the necessary logic to count and print the number of qualified employees and to print the name of every such employee. Develop the equivalent pseudocode.

8. Figure 1.12 contains a COBOL program to process a file of employee records and print the names of programmers under 30. Using Figure 1.6 as a guide, restore the missing information so that the program will run as intended.

Figure 1.10   Flowchart Blocks for Problem 6

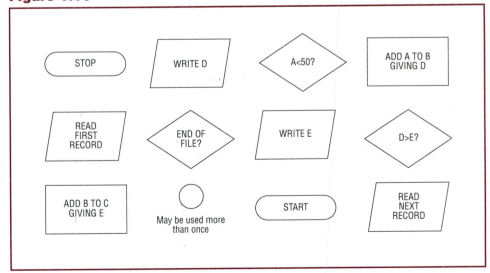

Figure 1.11 Flowchart Blocks for Problem 7

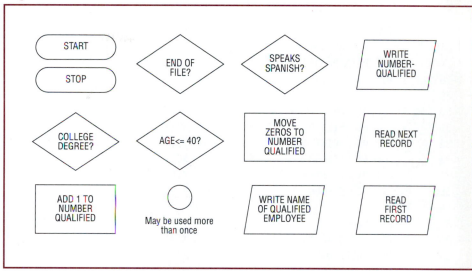

Figure 1.12 COBOL Listing for Problem 8

```
1          IDENTIFICATION DIVISION.
2          PROGRAM-ID.  FIRSTTRY.
3       1  ▭▭▭▭▭▭       GRAUER.
4
5          ENVIRONMENT DIVISION.
6          INPUT-OUTPUT SECTION.
7          FILE-CONTROL.
8             SELECT EMPLOYEE-FILE  ASSIGN TO SYSIN
9                 ORGANIZATION IS LINE SEQUENTIAL.
10        2 ▭▭▭▭  PRINT-FILE      ASSIGN TO SYSOUT
11                ORGANIZATION IS LINE SEQUENTIAL.
12
13      3 ▭▭▭▭▭▭▭▭▭
14         FILE SECTION.
15         FD  EMPLOYEE-FILE
16             RECORD CONTAINS 44 CHARACTERS
17             DATA RECORD IS EMPLOYEE-RECORD.
18         01  EMPLOYEE-RECORD.
19             05  EMP-NAME          PIC X(25).
20             05  EMP-TITLE         PIC X(10).
21             05  EMP-AGE           PIC 99.
22             05  FILLER            PIC XX.
23             05  EMP-SALARY        PIC 9(5).
24
```

Figure 1.12 COBOL Listing for Problem 8 *(continued)*

```
25      FD   �220000  4
26           RECORD CONTAINS 132 CHARACTERS
27           DATA RECORD IS PRINT-LINE.
28      01   PRINT-LINE.
29           05  FILLER              PIC X.
30           05  PRINT-NAME          �220000  5
31           05  FILLER              PIC X(2).
32           05  PRINT-AGE           PIC 99.
33           05  FILLER              PIC X(3).
34           05  PRINT-SALARY        PIC 9(5).
35           05  FILLER              PIC X(94).
36
37   6 �220000000000000
38      01  END-OF-DATA-FLAG         PIC X(3)      �220000  7
39      PROCEDURE DIVISION.
40      MAINLINE.
41        8 �220   INPUT EMPLOYEE-FILE
42               OUTPUT PRINT-FILE.
43           MOVE SPACES TO PRINT-LINE.
44           MOVE 'SALARY REPORT FOR PROGRAMMERS UNDER 30' TO PRINT-LINE.
45           WRITE PRINT-LINE
46               AFTER ADVANCING 2 LINES.
47           READ EMPLOYEE-FILE
48               AT END MOVE 'YES' TO END-OF-DATA-FLAG
49           END-READ.
50        9 �220000   PROCESS-EMPLOYEE-RECORDS
51               UNTIL END-OF-DATA-FLAG = 'YES'.
52           CLOSE EMPLOYEE-FILE
53                 PRINT-FILE.
54           STOP RUN.
55
56      PROCESS-EMPLOYEE-RECORDS.                    10
57           IF EMP-TITLE = 'PROGRAMMER' AND EMP-AGE < 30
58               MOVE SPACES TO PRINT-LINE
59               MOVE EMP-NAME TO PRINT-NAME
60               MOVE �220000 TO PRINT-AGE
61               MOVE EMP-SALARY TO PRINT-SALARY
62               WRITE PRINT-LINE
63           END-IF.                                 11
64           READ EMPLOYEE-FILE
65               AT END MOVE �220000 TO END-OF-DATA-FLAG
66           END-READ.
```

2

From Coding Form to Computer

CHAPTER OUTLINE

Overview
From Coding Form to Computer
    The COBOL Coding Form
    Use of an Editor
    The Compile, Link, and Execute Sequence
Learning by Doing
    Errors in Entering the Program
    Errors in Operating System Commands
    Errors in Compilation
    Errors in Execution
    Errors in Data Input
Evolution of COBOL
There's Always a Reason
Summary
Fill-in
True/False
Problems

OBJECTIVES

After reading this chapter you will be able to:

- State the rules associated with the COBOL coding sheet, and enter a program appropriately.

- Distinguish between compilation and execution; describe the function of a link program.

- Describe the environmental differences between a PC and a mainframe as they relate to execution of COBOL programs.

- Compile, link, and execute a COBOL program.

- Find and correct simple errors in compilation or execution.

OVERVIEW

This chapter continues with the engineering senior program of Chapter 1, describing how to actually run a COBOL program. We discuss the COBOL coding form and its associated rules, the use of an editor (or word processor) to create COBOL programs and/or data files, and the procedure for submission to the computer. We describe the compile, link, and execute sequence. We also prepare you for the errors you will inevitably make, discuss fundamentals of debugging, and alert you to the subtle differences between the two standards in use today, COBOL-74 and COBOL-85.

At the conclusion of the chapter we ask you to run the engineering senior program of Chapter 1. *Seeing is believing* may be a cliché, but it is only after you have seen output from your own program that the material truly begins to make sense. Suffice it to say then, that the sooner you are on the computer, the sooner you will appreciate the subtleties inherent in programming.

From Coding Form to Computer

Chapter 1 ended with presentation of a completed COBOL program, and a discussion of the elements that make up the COBOL language. The program, however, is not yet in a form suitable for execution on the computer, and much has to be done in order for this to be accomplished. That is the overriding objective of this chapter.

The flowchart in Figure 2.1 depicts the various steps in solving a problem through use of a computer. The first step is to obtain a clear statement of the problem, containing a complete description of the input and desired output. The problem statement should also contain detailed processing specifications. It is not enough, for example, to say calculate a student's grade point average; instead the method for calculating the average must be provided as well.

Once the input, output, and processing specifications have been enumerated, a hierarchy chart (see Chapter 3) is created, then a flowchart or pseudocode is developed. Careful attention to these steps will simplify the subsequent program and increase the likelihood it will be correct.

Coding is the translation of the hierarchy chart, flowchart, and/or pseudocode into COBOL. Coding must be done within the well-defined rules of COBOL regarding

Figure 2.1 The Programming Process

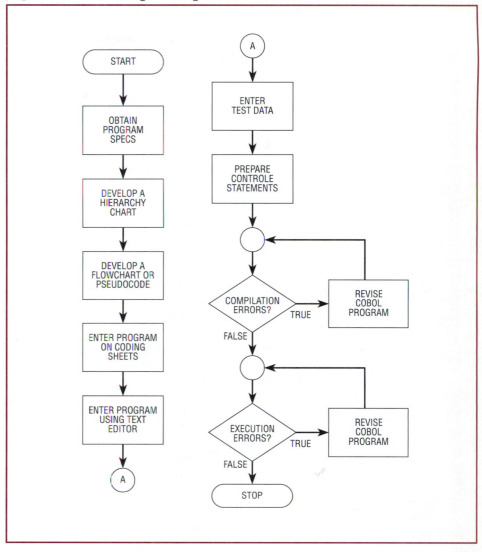

the placement of various statements in specific areas of the coding form. After coding, the program is entered into a file suitable for input to a computer through use of an editor.

The program is then submitted to the computer in conjunction with a set of control statements. The latter provide information to the operating system as to the location of the COBOL program and/or its associated data. The control statements vary greatly from installation to installation.

Next comes compilation in which the COBOL program is translated into machine language. Initial attempts at compilation are apt to identify several errors, due to misspellings, missing periods, misplaced parentheses, etc. Corrections are made, and the program is recompiled. Only after the compilation has been successfully completed can we proceed to execution.

During execution the computer does exactly what it was instructed to do, which may be different from what you want it to do. For example, if OR were substituted for AND in line 60 of the engineering senior program, the program would select *either* engineering majors *or* seniors. Either way, it would function differently from the original, logically correct version, although the program would still compile cleanly. Corrections are made, the program is recompiled, and testing continues.

The presence of the two decision blocks in Figure 2.1 indicates the iterative nature of the entire process. Few, if any, programs compile correctly on the first try—hence the need to recode specific statements. Similarly, programs may not execute properly on the first attempt, and thus the need to revise the program, recompile, reexecute, and so on.

The COBOL Coding Form

The COBOL compiler is very particular about the information it receives, and requires a program to be written within its well-defined syntax. For example, division and section headers are required to begin between columns 8 and 11, whereas most other statements begin in or past column 12. There are additional rules for continuation (what happens if a statement does not fit on one line), comments, optional sequencing of source statements in columns 1–6, and program identification in columns 73–80.

The rules of the coding sheet are summarized in Table 2.1, and illustrated in Figure 2.2. The latter shows completed forms for the engineering senior problem of Chapter 1. Several features in Figure 2.2 bear mention. Note in particular the wavy line under various PIC entries to indicate that identical information is to be entered on subsequent lines. Of greatest import, however, is the conformity between the entries in Figure 2.2 and the COBOL requirements of Table 2.1.

Coding sheets are not mandatory and you can use ordinary paper instead. You will find, however, that programming is much easier, if you are well organized. A good start is to have the program neatly entered in appropriate columns before sitting down at the computer.

Use of an Editor

Once a program has been written on coding sheets, it is entered through an editor (or word processor) into a file for subsequent input to the computer. In all likelihood you are already familiar with a word processor, and can use that to create and edit COBOL programs as well. Accordingly, be sure you can do all of the following:

1. Save the program as an unformatted (ASCII text) file, with a file name of your own choosing, consistent with the computer on which you will execute the program.

2. Retrieve the file, then resave it after making additional modifications.

3. Toggle between the insertion and replacement modes to change characters within a statement, and/or to insert and/or delete statements within a program.

4. Print a listing of the file.

   You will also find it useful to learn the commands to:

1. Set tabs to move to designated columns; for example, columns 8 and 12 for the A and B margins, respectively.

2. Search and/or replace character strings.

3. Move to specified places within the program; for example, the beginning or end, a particular line, the start of the Procedure Division, and so on.

The availability of an on-line editor facilitates programming to an extent that was unimaginable to tens of thousands of COBOL programmers of the 1960s and

TABLE 2.1   Rules for the COBOL Coding Form

COLUMN	EXPLANATION and USE
1–6	*Optional sequence numbers*; If this field is coded, the compiler performs a sequence check on incoming COBOL statements by flagging any statements out of order. Although some commercial installations encourage this option, we advise against it, especially since you are entering your own programs, and the more you type, the more chance for error.
7	An asterisk in column 7 indicates a **comment**, while a hyphen is used for the **continuation of nonnumeric literals** (described further on page 180). Comments may appear anywhere in a program; they are shown on the source listing but are otherwise ignored.
8–11	Known as the **A margin**; Division headers, section headers, paragraph names, FD's, and 01's all begin in the A margin.
12–72	Known as the **B margin**; All remaining entries begin in or past column 12. COBOL permits considerable flexibility here, but individual installations have their own requirements. We, for example, begin PICTURE clauses in the same column, for example, column 37, for better readability. (We shall discuss this further in Chapter 7.)
73–80	**Program identification**; a second optional field, which is ignored by the compiler. Different installations have different standards regarding use of this field.

[handwritten margin note: Not Coded just by programmers but by the computer]

Figure 2.2   The COBOL Coding Form

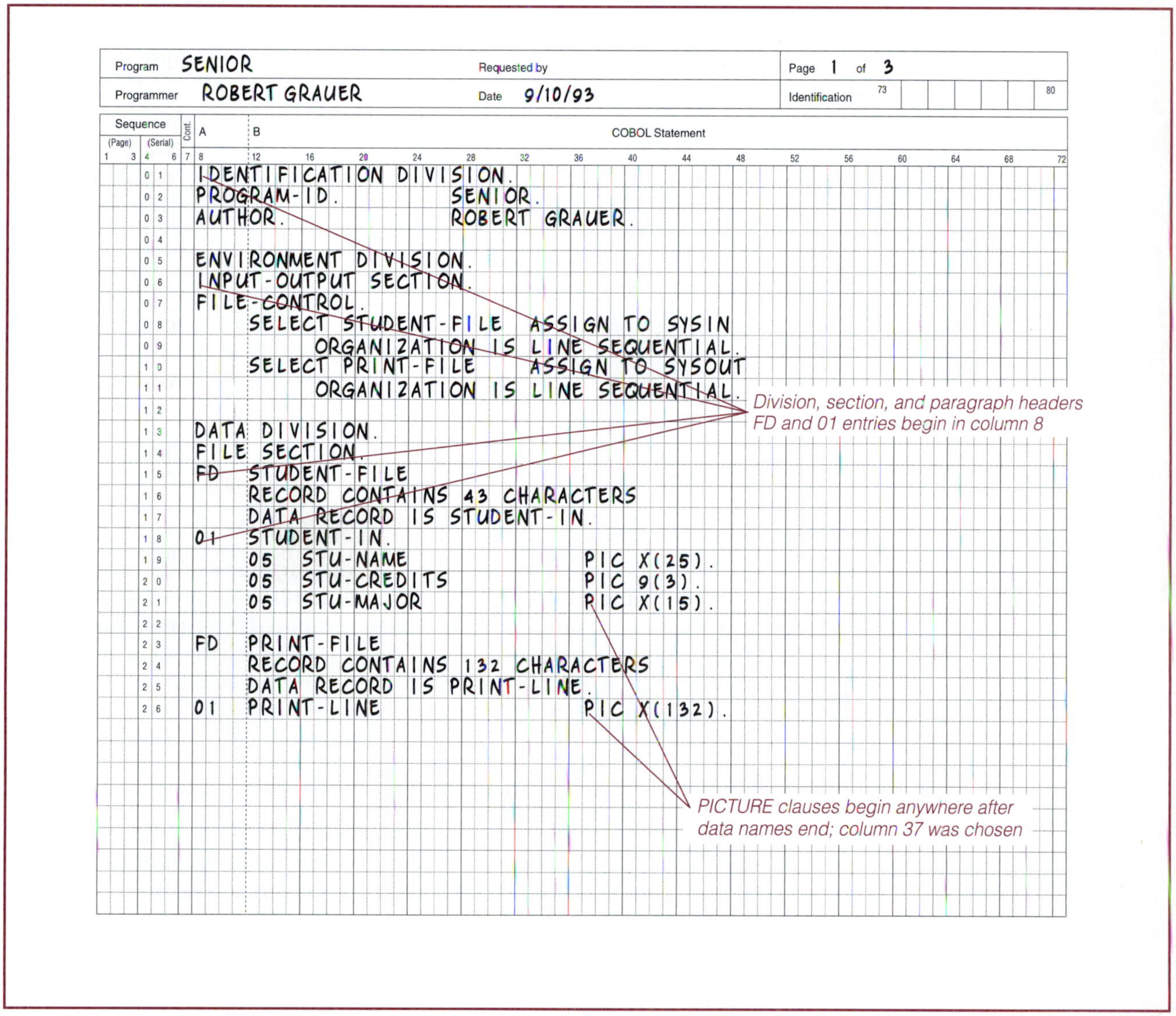

Program	SENIOR	Requested by		Page **1** of **3**
Programmer	ROBERT GRAUER	Date 9/10/93		Identification

```
IDENTIFICATION DIVISION.
PROGRAM-ID.          SENIOR.
AUTHOR.              ROBERT GRAUER.

ENVIRONMENT DIVISION.
INPUT-OUTPUT SECTION.
FILE-CONTROL.
     SELECT STUDENT-FILE    ASSIGN TO SYSIN
         ORGANIZATION IS LINE SEQUENTIAL.
     SELECT PRINT-FILE       ASSIGN TO SYSOUT
         ORGANIZATION IS LINE SEQUENTIAL.

DATA DIVISION.
FILE SECTION.
FD  STUDENT-FILE
     RECORD CONTAINS 43 CHARACTERS
     DATA RECORD IS STUDENT-IN.
01  STUDENT-IN.
     05  STU-NAME            PIC X(25).
     05  STU-CREDITS         PIC 9(3).
     05  STU-MAJOR           PIC X(15).

FD  PRINT-FILE
     RECORD CONTAINS 132 CHARACTERS
     DATA RECORD IS PRINT-LINE.
01  PRINT-LINE               PIC X(132).
```

Division, section, and paragraph headers FD and 01 entries begin in column 8

PICTURE clauses begin anywhere after data names end; column 37 was chosen

[handwritten notes at bottom:]
→ The logic of a COBOL Program is contained in the Procedure Division.
→ Pseudocode is used to develop the logic of a program.

Figure 2.2 *(continued)*

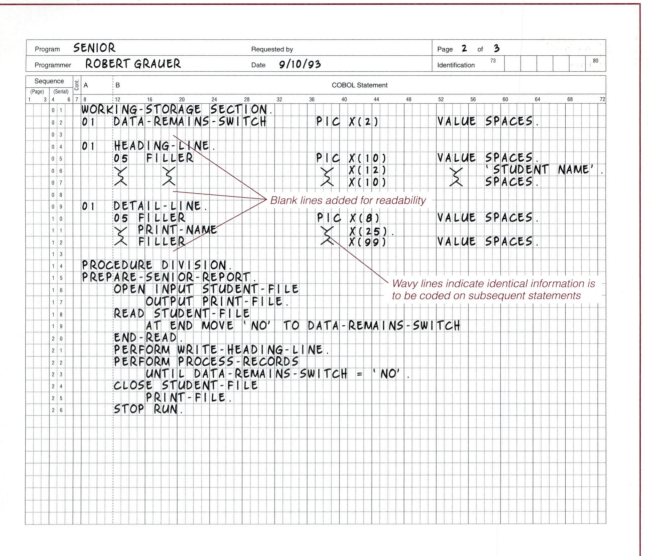

early 1970s. COBOL itself is over 30 years old, and for much of its existence the punched card and batch processing (often with turnaround times of several hours or more) was the way in which programs were submitted. Students today are far more fortunate in the available technology, taking for granted the ability to execute a program many times in a single session, instead of having to wait hours (or days) to retrieve a single run, wait hours more for the next run, etc.

The Compile, Link, and Execute Sequence

The material on the coding sheet and use of an editor is straightforward, and should pose little difficulty. The execution of a COBOL program, however, is more complex, and is explained in conjunction with Figure 2.3. The figure shows the execution of three distinct programs, a *compiler*, *linker* (or linkage-editor on IBM mainframes), and *load module*, each of which is necessary to produce the list of engineering seniors. Realize, too, that the process described in Figure 2.3 is required for any COBOL program, even one as simple as the engineering senior example.

Figure 2.2   *(continued)*

Program	SENIOR	Requested by	Page **3** of **3**
Programmer	ROBERT GRAUER	Date **9/10/93**	Identification 73 ... 80

```
WRITE-HEADING-LINE.
    MOVE HEADING-LINE TO PRINT-LINE.
    WRITE PRINT-LINE.

PROCESS-RECORDS.
    IF STU-CREDITS > 110 AND STU-MAJOR = 'ENGINEERING'
        MOVE STU-NAME TO PRINT-NAME
        MOVE DETAIL-LINE TO PRINT-LINE
        WRITE PRINT-LINE
    END-IF.
    READ STUDENT-FILE
        AT END MOVE 'NO' TO DATA-REMAINS-SWITCH
    END-READ.
```

Procedure Division statements begin in or past column 12

Optional indentation to indicate these statements "belong" to the IF

The procedure begins with the COBOL *compiler*, a program that accepts a COBOL (source) program as input, and produces a machine-language (object) program as output. The result of the compilation, the object program, is input into a second program called the *linker*, that combines the object program with subroutines and other object modules to produce a load module. Execution of the compiled COBOL program takes place in the third step as the *load module* accepts input data and produces an output report.

The execution of the various programs in Figure 2.3 does not happen through wishful thinking, but through specification of commands to the *operating system* to describe these programs and their associated data files. Every operating system has its own specific commands, but the underlying concept is the same, namely that three different programs (a compiler, linker, and load module) are required. It will be necessary, therefore, to learn the commands for your particular configuration in order to compile, link, and execute a COBOL program.[1]

---

1. Appendices A and B describe the Fujitsu COBOL97 compiler that accompanies this text.

Figure 2.3   Compile, Link, and Execute Sequence

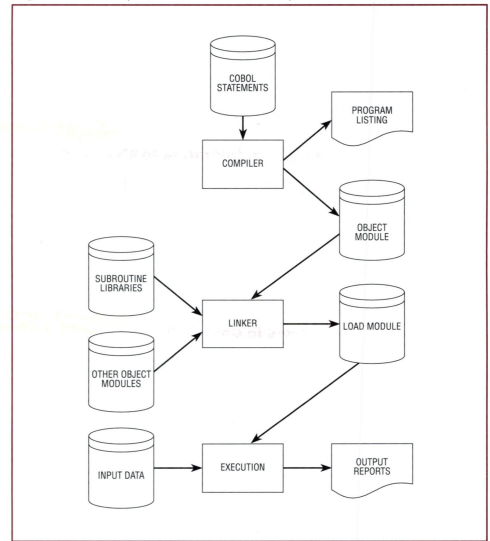

One learns by doing. This time-worn axiom is especially true for programming. We have covered a lot of material since you first began reading Chapter 1. Now it is time to put everything together and actually run your first program. Enter the program on the coding sheets in Figure 2.2, using the appropriate editor. Prepare the necessary control statements for the operating system. Create your own test data, or use Figure 1.8a. Submit the job and retrieve your output.

    We believe—in fact we are very sure—that after you receive your first computer printout, many things will fall into place. Nevertheless, the first program is in many ways the most difficult you will attempt, and you should be prepared for problems along the way. The difficulty is not in the program's complexity (the engineering senior program is logically trivial). Nor is it in the COBOL syntax, in that the program uses only a fraction of the COBOL features you will eventually employ. The problems arise in interacting with the computer, using the editor, entering the proper commands to the operating system, and so on. Murphy's Law is perhaps the most eloquent statement of what to expect, and thus you should be prepared for any or all of the ensuing errors.

Types of Errors [handwritten]

Errors in Entering the Program

The errors that occur as you enter the program are potentially the most damaging, especially if you spend hours entering the program and then forget to save it, save it incorrectly, or delete it unintentionally. A suggested course of action for your first attempt is to enter only the first two lines of the program, save these, log off the system, then log on and retrieve the file. In this way you are sure you know how to use the editor. Other frequent errors are to enter information in the wrong columns, to misuse a tab key, and so on.

Forgot to move the filing [handwritten]

Errors in Operating System Commands

The syntax of operating system commands has to be followed exactly, in order for the system to do your bidding. Simple mistakes result in baffling errors; for example, *Bad command or file name*, when you misspell an MS-DOS command, and/or fail to indicate the proper subdirectory where the command is located. In similar fashion the control statements submitted on a mainframe must be syntactically correct, or everything else will fail. Invalid job streams result in the system being unable to execute the job, leaving you with the most frustrating of all messages, *Job not run due to JCL error.*

→ Syntax errors e.g mispelled words, put in wrong columns etc misplacing periods [handwritten]

Errors in Compilation

A ***compilation error*** occurs whenever you violate a rule of COBOL, for example, misspelling a reserved word or misplacing a period. The result of the error is that the compiler is unable to translate a portion of the COBOL program to machine language, and any subsequent attempt at execution will (most likely) be incorrect.

Consider, for example, Figure 2.4a, which contains a slightly modified version of the Engineering Senior Program of Figure 1.6, in which lines 59–64 have been

Figure 2.4   Engineering Senior Program with Compilation Errors

```
 1        IDENTIFICATION DIVISION.
 2        PROGRAM-ID.       SENIORCE.
 3        AUTHOR.           ROBERT GRAUER.
 4
 5        ENVIRONMENT DIVISION.
 6        INPUT-OUTPUT SECTION.
 7        FILE-CONTROL.
 8           SELECT STUDENT-FILE   ASSIGN TO SYSIN
 9               ORGANIZATION IS LINE SEQUENTIAL.
10           SELECT PRINT-FILE     ASSIGN TO SYSOUT
11               ORGANIZATION IS LINE SEQUENTIAL.
12
13        DATA DIVISION.
14        FILE SECTION.
15        FD  STUDENT-FILE
16            RECORD CONTAINS 43 CHARACTERS
17            DATA RECORD IS STUDENT-IN.
18        01  STUDENT-IN.
19            05  STU-NAME          PIC X(25).
```

Figure 2.4 *(continued)*

```
20          05  STU-CREDITS        PIC 9(3).
21          05  STU-MAJOR          PIC X(15).
22
23      FD  PRINT-FILE
24          RECORD CONTAINS 132 CHARACTERS
25          DATA RECORD IS PRINT-LINE.
26      01  PRINT-LINE             PIC X(132).
27
28      WORKING-STORAGE SECTION.
29      01  DATA-REMAINS-SWITCH    PIC X(2)      VALUE SPACES.
30
31      01  HEADING-LINE.
32          05  FILLER             PIC X(10)     VALUE SPACES.
33          05  FILLER             PIC X(12)     VALUE 'STUDENT NAME'.
34          05  FILLER             PIC X(110)    VALUE SPACES.
35
36      01  DETAIL-LINE.
37          05  FILLER             PIC X(8)      VALUE SPACES.
38          05  PRINT-NAME         PIC X(25).
39          05  FILLER             PIC X(99)     VALUE SPACES.
40
41      PROCEDURE DIVISION.
42      PREPARE-SENIOR-REPORT.
43          OPEN INPUT  STUDENT-FILE
44               OUTPUT PRINT-FILE.
45          READ STUDENT-FILE
46              AT END MOVE 'NO' TO DATA-REMAINS-SWITCH
47          END-READ.
48          PERFORM WRITE-HEADING-LINE.
49          PERFORM PROCESS-RECORDS
50              UNTIL DATA-REMAINS-SWITCH = 'NO'.
51          CLOSE STUDENT-FILE
52                PRINT-FILE.
53          STOP RUN.
54
55      WRITE-HEADING-LINE.
56          MOVE HEADING-LINE TO PRINT-LINE.
57          WRITE PRINT-LINE.
58
59      PROCESS-RECORDS                          ← Period missing after paragraph header
60          IF STU-CREDITS > 110 AND STU-MAJOR = 'ENGINEERING'
61              MOVE STU-NAME TO PRINT-NAME
62              MOVE DETAIL-LINE TO PRINT-LINE
63              WRTE PRINT-LINE.                  ← WRITE is misspelled
64          END-IF.                                 Period does not belong before END-IF terminator
65          READ STUDENT-FILE
66              AT END MOVE 'NO' TO DATA-REMAINS-SWITCH
67          END-READ.
```

(a) COBOL Listing

Figure 2.4   *(continued)*

```
                                          ┌─ COBOL statement number where error occurred
                                          │
** DIAGNOSTIC MESSAGE ** (SENIORCE)
SENIORCE.CBL  59:  JMN1103I-W PERIOD IS MISSING. ASSUMED TO BE CODED.
SENIORCE.CBL  63:  JMN2503I-S USER WORD 'WRTE' IS UNDEFINED.
SENIORCE.CBL  64:  JMN2510I-S NO CORRESPONDING 'END-IF' IS SPECIFIED. 'END-IF' IS IGNORED.
STATISTICS: HIGHEST SEVERITY CODE=S. PROGRAM UNIT=1
```

(b) COBOL Diagnostics

changed to produce compilation errors. Figure 2.4b shows the resulting compiler diagnostics. The error message associated with line 59 is caused by the missing period at the end of the line. The diagnostic in line 63 resulted from misspelling a reserved word, and the diagnostic in line 64 is produced by the superfluous period in line 63.

Compiler diagnostics are discussed fully in Chapter 6. Corrections are made, and the program is recompiled. Only after the compilation has been successfully completed should we proceed to execution.

 ## Errors in Execution

Execution errors occur after compilation and are generally due to errors in logic. Figure 2.5a contains yet another version of the engineering senior program in which the credits test was *deliberately* omitted in line 60. The program is syntactically correct and will compile without error; it is, however, logically incorrect and hence the associated output in Figure 2.5b is wrong. (Review the original program specifications and test data; Alex Bell should not be selected because of an insufficient number of credits.)

Figure 2.5   Engineering Senior Program with Execution Errors

```
     1          IDENTIFICATION DIVISION.
     2          PROGRAM-ID.      SENIOREE.
     3          AUTHOR.          ROBERT GRAUER.
     4
     5          ENVIRONMENT DIVISION.
     6          INPUT-OUTPUT SECTION.
     7          FILE-CONTROL.
     8              SELECT STUDENT-FILE  ASSIGN TO SYSIN
     9                  ORGANIZATION IS LINE SEQUENTIAL.
    10              SELECT PRINT-FILE    ASSIGN TO SYSOUT
    11                  ORGANIZATION IS LINE SEQUENTIAL.
    12
    13          DATA DIVISION.
```

Figure 2.5   *(continued)*

```
14        FILE SECTION.
15        FD  STUDENT-FILE
16            RECORD CONTAINS 43 CHARACTERS
17            DATA RECORD IS STUDENT-IN.
18        01  STUDENT-IN.
19            05  STU-NAME          PIC X(25).
20            05  STU-CREDITS       PIC 9(3).
21            05  STU-MAJOR         PIC X(15).
22
23        FD  PRINT-FILE
24            RECORD CONTAINS 132 CHARACTERS
25            DATA RECORD IS PRINT-LINE.
26        01  PRINT-LINE            PIC X(132).
27
28        WORKING-STORAGE SECTION.
29        01  DATA-REMAINS-SWITCH   PIC X(2)      VALUE SPACES.
30
31        01  HEADING-LINE.
32            05  FILLER            PIC X(10)     VALUE SPACES.
33            05  FILLER            PIC X(12)     VALUE 'STUDENT NAME'.
34            05  FILLER            PIC X(110)    VALUE SPACES.
35
36        01  DETAIL-LINE.
37            05  FILLER            PIC X(8)      VALUE SPACES.
38            05  PRINT-NAME        PIC X(25).
39            05  FILLER            PIC X(99)     VALUE SPACES.
40
41        PROCEDURE DIVISION.
42        PREPARE-SENIOR-REPORT.
43            OPEN INPUT  STUDENT-FILE
44                 OUTPUT PRINT-FILE.
45            READ STUDENT-FILE
46                AT END MOVE 'NO' TO DATA-REMAINS-SWITCH
47            END-READ.
48            PERFORM WRITE-HEADING-LINE.
49            PERFORM PROCESS-RECORDS
50                UNTIL DATA-REMAINS-SWITCH = 'NO'.
51            CLOSE STUDENT-FILE
52                  PRINT-FILE.
53            STOP RUN.
54
55        WRITE-HEADING-LINE.
56            MOVE HEADING-LINE TO PRINT-LINE.
57            WRITE PRINT-LINE.
58
59        PROCESS-RECORDS.
60            IF STU-MAJOR = 'ENGINEERING'                    Credits test missing
61                MOVE STU-NAME TO PRINT-NAME
62                MOVE DETAIL-LINE TO PRINT-LINE
63                WRITE PRINT-LINE
```

Figure 2.5   *(continued)*

```
64          END-IF.
65          READ STUDENT-FILE
66              AT END MOVE 'NO' TO DATA-REMAINS-SWITCH
67          END-READ.
```

(a) COBOL Listing

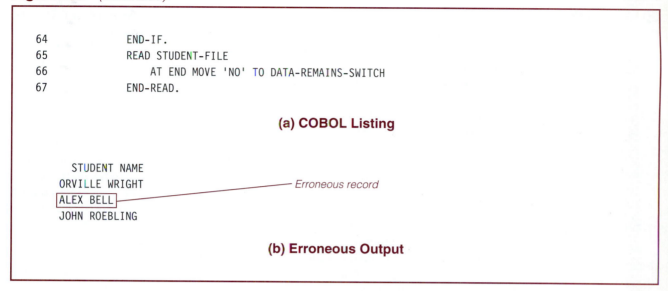

(b) Erroneous Output

It is important to remember, therefore, that *a computer does exactly what it is instructed to do, which may be different from what you want it to do.* In other words if you (incorrectly) tell the computer to ignore the credits test, then that is precisely what the program will do.

Errors in Data input

A program may also produce erroneous output, even if it is logically correct, when the data on which the program operates are invalid. If, for example, the *erroneous* data in Figure 2.6 are submitted to the *valid* program in Figure 2.2, neither Orville Wright nor John Roebling will be selected! Wright's major appears in the data as ENGINEER, whereas line 60 in the program is looking for ENGINEER*ING*. Roebling's credits are entered in the wrong column. In other words, a computer operates on data exactly as it is submitted, with no regard for its correctness. Stated another way, the output produced by a program is only as good as its input, or put even more simply, **garbage in, garbage out**, giving rise to the well known acronym, **GIGO**.

Figure 2.6   Erroneous Input Data

```
JOHN ADAMS            090POLITICAL SCI
AMELIA EARHART        120AVIATION
ORVILLE WRIGHT        115 ENGINEER          "Engineering" is spelled incorrectly
GEORGIA O'KEEFFE      125ART
MERIWETHER LEWIS      115TRAVEL
JOHN KENNEDY          115POLITICAL SCI
ALEX BELL             090ENGINEERING
EMILY DICKINSON       085LITERATURE
JOHN ROEBLING             115ENGINEERING    Data entered in wrong columns
```

Evolution of COBOL

COBOL was introduced in 1959 through the efforts of Captain Grace Murray Hopper of the United States Navy. It was designed to be an open ended language, capable of accepting change and amendment. It was also intended to be a highly portable language; i.e., a COBOL program written for an IBM mainframe computer should run equally well on any other computer with a COBOL compiler. Over the years the needs of an evolving language, and the desire for compatibility among vendors have given rise to several COBOL standards, two of which are in common use today, *COBOL-74* and *COBOL-85*.

All of the listings in this text, aside from Chapter 20, are written to take advantage of the newer standard. We think it important to emphasize COBOL-85 because it has been the current standard for about fifteen years. However, even today many COBOL programs still adhere to the COBOL-74 standard. You should be aware that an even newer standard is currently under development and should be released in 2002. We discuss aspects of this new standard, COBOL 2002, in Chapter 20 and Appendix E. Until the new standard is released and for several years beyond, it is important to understand that COBOL-85 will remain as the industry standard. Industry is slow to change and will continue to use COBOL-85. The reason for slow conversion is the subtle *incompatibilities* that exist between the two compilers. In theory, a program written to the earlier standard is supposed to run without modification under the later standard. In practice, however, this is not always the case.

Consider, for example, the incompatibility brought about by the introduction of new features and associated new reserved words, words such as CONTENT, EVALUATE, FALSE, OTHER, TEST, and so on. A programmer writing under COBOL-74 could logically have used any or all of these words as data names, which posed no problem under the older compiler, but which produces numerous compilation errors under COBOL-85. Thus, a blanket conversion by an installation of its hundreds (thousands, or tens of thousands) of COBOL programs, would prove disastrous, unless each program was manually checked for compatibility with the new standard.

When the new standard is issued, many installations may maintain support for two or even three compilers, using COBOL-85 and COBOL-74 to maintain existing programs and COBOL 2002 for development. It is important, therefore, that you become aware of the differences between standards. Accordingly, we end most chapters with a section describing differences between the two older standards as they relate to the program being discussed in that chapter. The changes in COBOL 2002 are addressed in Chapter 20 and Appendix E.

Figure 2.7 represents our final look at the engineering senior program as it would be implemented in COBOL-74. Note the following differences between this program and the COBOL-85 implementation of Figure 1.6:

Figure 2.7 Engineering Senior Program (COBOL-74 Implementation)

```
1        IDENTIFICATION DIVISION.
2        PROGRAM-ID.       SENIOR74.
3        AUTHOR.           ROBERT GRAUER.
4
5        ENVIRONMENT DIVISION.
6        CONFIGURATION SECTION.                     — Configuration section is required
7        SOURCE-COMPUTER.   IBM-PC.
8        OBJECT-COMPUTER.   IBM-PC.
9        INPUT-OUTPUT SECTION.
10       FILE-CONTROL.
                                                      Mainframe technique for
                                                      assigning I/O devices and files
11           SELECT STUDENT-FILE   ASSIGN TO UT-S-SYSIN.
13           SELECT PRINT-FILE
14               ASSIGN TO UT-S-SYSOUT.
15
```

Figure 2.7 *(continued)*

```
16        DATA DIVISION.
17        FILE SECTION.
18        FD  STUDENT-FILE
19            LABEL RECORDS ARE STANDARD
20            RECORD CONTAINS 43 CHARACTERS
21            DATA RECORD IS STUDENT-IN.
22        01  STUDENT-IN.
23            05  STU-NAME          PIC X(25).
24            05  STU-CREDITS       PIC 9(3).
25            05  STU-MAJOR         PIC X(15).
26
27        FD  PRINT-FILE
28            LABEL RECORDS ARE STANDARD
29            RECORD CONTAINS 132 CHARACTERS
30            DATA RECORD IS PRINT-LINE.
31        01  PRINT-LINE            PIC X(132).
32
33        WORKING-STORAGE SECTION.
34        01  DATA-REMAINS-SWITCH   PIC X(2)      VALUE SPACES.
35
36        01  HEADING-LINE.
37            05  FILLER            PIC X(10)     VALUE SPACES.
38            05  FILLER            PIC X(12)     VALUE 'STUDENT NAME'.
39            05  FILLER            PIC X(110)    VALUE SPACES.
40
41        01  DETAIL-LINE.
42            05  FILLER            PIC X(8)      VALUE SPACES.
43            05  PRINT-NAME        PIC X(25).
44            05  FILLER            PIC X(99)     VALUE SPACES.
45
46        PROCEDURE DIVISION.
47        PREPARE-SENIOR-REPORT.
48            OPEN INPUT  STUDENT-FILE
49                 OUTPUT PRINT-FILE.
50            READ STUDENT-FILE
51                AT END MOVE 'NO' TO DATA-REMAINS-SWITCH.
52            PERFORM WRITE-HEADING-LINE.
53            PERFORM PROCESS-RECORDS
54                UNTIL DATA-REMAINS-SWITCH = 'NO'.
55            CLOSE STUDENT-FILE
56                  PRINT-FILE.
57            STOP RUN.
58
59        WRITE-HEADING-LINE.
60            MOVE HEADING-LINE TO PRINT-LINE.
61            WRITE PRINT-LINE.
62
63        PROCESS-RECORDS.
64            IF STU-CREDITS > 110 AND STU-MAJOR = 'ENGINEERING'
65                MOVE STU-NAME TO PRINT-NAME
66                MOVE DETAIL-LINE TO PRINT-LINE
67                WRITE PRINT-LINE.
68            READ STUDENT-FILE
69                AT END MOVE 'NO' TO DATA-REMAINS-SWITCH.
```

Label records clause is required

END-IF scope terminator is not recognized in COBOL-74

1. COBOL-74 requires a CONFIGURATION SECTION with both a SOURCE-COMPUTER and an OBJECT-COMPUTER paragraph, to indicate the computer on which the program will compile and execute. The CONFIGURATION SECTION is optional in COBOL-85, and since these entries are treated as comments by the compiler, they are omitted in the COBOL-85 listing.

2. COBOL-74 requires the LABEL RECORDS clause in a file description to indicate whether standard, nonstandard, or no labels are in effect. (A label contains information about a file such as the date it was created and the intended expiration date.) The clause is optional in COBOL-85 where its omission defaults to LABEL RECORDS ARE STANDARD.

3. Scope terminators (END-IF and END-READ) are not permitted in COBOL-74 and hence do not appear in Figure 2.7. Scope terminators are optional in COBOL-85, but are used throughout the text because of advantages that will be clearly explained in Chapter 7.

Despite these differences the COBOL-74 implementation of the engineering senior program is upward compatible with COBOL-85; that is, the program in Figure 2.7 will run *without* modification under the new compiler. The converse is not true; the COBOL-85 listing in Figure 1.6 will not run under the earlier standard.

There's Always a Reason

We expect that you completed the chapter with little difficulty and that you were able to successfully run the engineering senior program. There will be times, however, when not everything will go as smoothly and so we relate a favorite anecdote ("Mystery of the Month," PC World Magazine, April 1983) that is as relevant today as when it was written. As you read our tale, remember that a computer does exactly what you tell it to do, which is not necessarily what you want it to do. It is a source of wonderful satisfaction when everything works, but also the cause of nearly unbelievable frustration when results are not what you expect.

Our story concerns a manager who purchased a PC and began to use it enthusiastically. Unfortunately, the feeling did not rub off on his assistant, who was apprehensive of computers in general, but who finally agreed to try the new technology.

As is frequently the case, the assistant's experience with the computer was as frustrating as the manager's was rewarding. Every time the assistant tried using the computer an error message appeared, yet when the manager tried the same procedure it worked fine. Finally, manager and assistant went through a systematic comparison of everything they did: turning the machine on and off, handling disks, using the keyboard, etc. They could find no difference in their procedures and could not account for the repeated disk errors which plagued the assistant but left the manager alone.

Just as they were about to give up the manager noticed that his assistant was wearing a charm bracelet. He looked closely, and sure enough one of the charms was a tiny magnet containing just enough force to interfere with reading the disk. The assistant stored the bracelet in a drawer and the machine has been fine ever since.

The point of our story is that there is always a logical reason for everything a computer does or does not do, although discovering that reason may be less than obvious. You are about to embark on a wonderful journey toward the productive use of a computer, with a virtually unlimited number of potential applications. Be patient, be inquisitive, and enjoy.

→) Errors in Entering a program's: misusing a tab key / Entering information in the wrong column.

→) Errors in Operating System: entering a wrong file name / bad command) mispelling a DOS command

→) Errors in Compilation: misplacing a period / mispelling a reserved word

→) Errors in execution: Errors after Compilation, due to errors in logic

→) Errors in Data Input: Data in which program operates is invalid

→) The logic of a program is in the Procedure Division & Pseudocode is used to develop the logic of a program.

Fill-In

41

SUMMARY

Points to Remember

■ The A margin consists of columns 8–11 whereas the B margin is defined as columns 12–72. Division and section headers, paragraph names, FD's, and 01-level entries must begin in the A margin; all other entries begin in the B margin (that is, in or past column 12).

■ The execution of a COBOL program is a three-part process, involving three distinct programs—a compiler, a linker, and the resultant load module. The means of communicating information about these programs (and their associated files) is dependent on the operating system.

■ A compiler is a computer program that translates a higher-level (problem-oriented) language such as COBOL into machine language; the input to a compiler is referred to as a source program, whereas the output is an object program.

■ The linker combines the output produced by the compiler, with additional object modules (such as subroutines and/or Input/Output modules) to produce a load module.

■ Execution of the COBOL program occurs when the load module processes the input file(s) to produce the required reports.

■ COBOL-74 is intended to be upward compatible with COBOL-85 although subtle incompatibilities do exist between the two standards. The converse is not true, as COBOL-85 programs will not run under the earlier standard.

Key Words and Concepts

A margin
ASCII file
B margin
COBOL-74
COBOL-85
COBOL 2002
Coding form
Comments
Compilation error
Compiler
Continuation

Debugging
Editor
Execution error
GIGO
Incompatibility
Load module
Object program
Operating system
Source program
Test data

Fill-in

1. A ___Compiler___ translates a ___higher-level___ language into an ___machine___ language.

2. ___Cobol-85___ is the most recently approved COBOL standard, but ___it___ is still widely used in industry.

3. The ___*A. Margin*___ is in columns 8 to 11 of the coding sheet.

4. A comment is indicated by an ___*asterik*___ in column ___*7*___.

5. Entries that are not required to begin in the A margin may begin anywhere in columns ___*12*___ to ___*72*___.

6. Division headers and paragraph names must begin in the ___*A Margin*___.

7. An ___*text editor*___ is used to enter programs into the computer.

8. The compile, link, and execute process requires the execution of ___*three*___ distinct programs.

9. ___*Compiling errors*___ is the process of finding and correcting errors in a program.

10. Picture clauses may begin anywhere within the ___*B*___ margin.

11. The output of compilation is input to a second program called the ___*linker*___.

12. A clean compile (does/~~does not~~) guarantee that the resulting program execution will be correct.

13. Different mainframe computers will most likely use (different/identical) COBOL compilers.

14. Misspelling a reserved word will result in a ___*Compilation*___ error.

15. Entering test data in the wrong columns will result in an ___*entering the program*___ error.

True / False

1. A compiler translates a machine-oriented language into a problem-oriented language.

2. A well-written program will always produce correct results, even with bad data.

3. A compiler is a computer program.

4. The COBOL compiler for an IBM mainframe is identical to the compiler for a PC.

5. A COBOL program can run on a variety of computers.

6. Division headers must begin in the A margin.

7. Division headers must begin in column 8.

8. Section headers must begin in column 12.

9. Paragraph names must begin in column 8.

10. PICTURE clauses may appear in column 12 or after.

11. If a program compiles correctly, then it must execute correctly.

12. Columns 1–6 are never used on the coding sheet.

13. The use of columns 73–80 is optional.

14. Column 8 is used as a continuation column.

15. All editors have identical commands.

16. All computers use the same operating system.

17. Successful execution of the COBOL compiler produces a load module.

P r o b l e m s

1. Figure 2.8a contains data for the COBOL program in Figure 2.8b, which will process a file of employee records and print the names of all programmers under 30.

Figure 2.8   COBOL Program and Associated Data for Problems 1 & 2

```
WALT BECHTEL           PROGRAMMER34  39700
NELSON KERBEL          PROGRAMMER23  30000
MARGOT HUMMER          PROGRAMMER30  45000
CATHY BENWAY           DATA BASE 23  50000
JUD MCDONALD           DATA BASE 29  55000
JACKIE CLARK           PROGRAMMER22  47500
LOUIS NORIEGA          PROGRAMER 24  42500
JEFF SHEESLEY          ANALYST   28  46400
```

(a) Data

```
 1         IDENTIFICATION DIVISION.
 2         PROGRAM-ID.  FIRSTTRY.
 3         AUTHOR.      GRAUER.
 4
 5         ENVIRONMENT DIVISION.
 6         INPUT-OUTPUT SECTION.
 7         FILE-CONTROL.
 8             SELECT EMPLOYEE-FILE  ASSIGN TO SYSIN
 9                 ORGANIZATION IS LINE SEQUENTIAL.
10             SELECT PRINT-FILE     ASSIGN TO SYSOUT
11                 ORGANIZATION IS LINE SEQUENTIAL.
12
13         DATA DIVISION.
14         FILE SECTION.
15         FD  EMPLOYEE-FILE
16             RECORD CONTAINS 44 CHARACTERS
17             DATA RECORD IS EMPLOYEE-RECORD.
18         01  EMPLOYEE-RECORD.
19             05  EMP-NAME           PIC X(25).
20             05  EMP-TITLE          PIC X(10).
21             05  EMP-AGE            PIC 99.
22             05  FILLER             PIC XX.
23             05  EMP-SALARY         PIC 9(5).
24
25         FD  PRINT-FILE
26             RECORD CONTAINS 132 CHARACTERS
27             DATA RECORD IS PRINT-LINE.
28         01  PRINT-LINE.
```

Figure 2.8 *(continued)*

```
29        05   FILLER              PIC X.
30        05   PRINT-NAME          PIC X(25).
31        05   FILLER              PIC X(2).
32        05   PRINT-AGE           PIC 99.
33        05   FILLER              PIC X(3).
34        05   PRINT-SALARY        PIC 9(5).
35        05   FILLER              PIC X(94).
36
37     WORKING-STORAGE SECTION.
38     01  END-OF-DATA-FLAG        PIC X(3)        VALUE SPACES.
39     PROCEDURE DIVISION.
40     PREPARE-PROGRAMMER-REPORT.
41         OPEN INPUT EMPLOYEE-FILE
42              OUTPUT PRINT-FILE.
43         MOVE SPACES TO PRINT-LINE.
44         MOVE 'SALARY REPORT FOR PROGRAMMERS UNDER 30' TO PRINT-LINE.
45         WRITE PRINT-LINE
46            AFTER ADVANCING 2 LINES.
47         READ EMPLOYEE-FILE
48              AT END MOVE 'YES' TO END-OF-DATA-FLAG
49         END-READ.
50         PERFORM PROCESS-EMPLOYEE-RECORDS
51              UNTIL END-OF-DATA-FLAG = 'YES'.
52         CLOSE EMPLOYEE-FILE
53              PRINT-FILE.
54         STOP RUN.
55
56     PROCESS-EMPLOYEE-RECORDS.
57         IF EMP-TITLE = 'PROGRAMMER' AND EMP-AGE < 30
58              MOVE SPACES TO PRINT-LINE
59              MOVE EMP-NAME TO PRINT-NAME
60              MOVE EMP-AGE TO PRINT-AGE
61              MOVE EMP-SALARY TO PRINT-SALARY
62              WRITE PRINT-LINE
63         END-IF.
64         READ EMPLOYEE-FILE
65              AT END MOVE 'YES' TO END-OF-DATA-FLAG
66         END-READ.
```

(b) COBOL Program

a. Compile, link, and execute the COBOL program, using the appropriate commands for your system. (The program is on the data file available on our web site.)

b. Are any potential problems introduced by checking age rather than date of birth?

c. Would processing be simplified if the employee records contained an abbreviated title code (for example, 010) rather than an expanded title (for example, programmer)? Are there any other advantages to storing codes rather than expanded values?

2. Modify the program in Figure 2.8b to accommodate all of the following.
   a. Employee age is stored in positions 38 and 39 of the incoming record.
   b. The report should list all employees under age 30 who earn at least $30,000, regardless of title.
   c. The report should include the title of all selected employees in positions 41–52.

3. Match each item with its proper description.

   ___ 1. A Margin
   ___ 2. B Margin
   ___ 3. Comment
   ___ 4. IDENTIFICATION DIVISION
   ___ 5. PROCEDURE DIVISION
   ___ 6. Hyphen
   ___ 7. Nonnumeric literal
   ___ 8. Reserved word
   ___ 9. Compiler
   ___ 10. Literal

   a. An asterisk in column 7
   b. First line of any COBOL program
   c. Often appears in data names
   d. Columns 12 through 72
   e. Contains the logic of a program
   f. Limited to 160 characters, and enclosed in quotes or apostrophes
   g. Where division, section, and paragraph headers begin
   h. Translates COBOL to machine language
   i. Preassigned meaning
   j. A constant; may be numeric or nonnumeric

4. Indicate the starting column (or columns) for each of the following.
   a. Division headers
   b. Comments
   c. Paragraph names
   d. Statements in the Procedure Division (except paragraph names)
   e. WORKING-STORAGE SECTION
   f. FD
   g. 01 entries
   h. 05 entries
   i. PICTURE clauses
   j. OPEN statement
   k. WRITE statement
   l. SELECT statement

5. Explain how it is possible for a program to compile perfectly, be logically correct, and still produce invalid results; provide specific examples in conjunction with the engineering senior program.

A Methodology for Program Development

CHAPTER OUTLINE

Overview

The Tuition Billing Problem

Structured Design

Evaluating the Hierarchy Chart

    Completeness

    Functionality

    Span of Control

Structured Programming

    Sufficiency of the Basic Structures

Expressing Logic

    The Traditional Flowchart

    Pseudocode

    Warnier-Orr Diagrams

Top-Down Testing

Summary

Fill-in

True/False

Problems

OBJECTIVES

After reading this chapter you will be able to:

- Describe how a hierarchy chart is developed; discuss three criteria for evaluating a completed hierarchy chart.

- Define structured programming; describe its three fundamental building blocks and an optional extension.

- Explain the one entry point/one exit point philosophy of structured programming.

- Differentiate between structured programming and structured design; distinguish between a functionally oriented technique and one that is procedurally oriented.

- Describe what is meant by top down design and implementation.

OVERVIEW

We stated at the outset that programming is best learned by doing, and so our objective in the first two chapters was to put you on the computer as quickly as possible. Thus, we jumped immediately into COBOL, without giving much thought to the underlying logic of the program you developed. While that approach works well initially, it is also important for you to learn how to properly design programs, so that they will work correctly, and further so that they can be easily read and maintained by someone other than yourself.

Accordingly, this chapter presents a methodology for program development, embracing the techniques of structured design, structured programming, and top down testing. We stress that structured design is functionally oriented and describes what is to be accomplished; structured programming, on the other hand, is procedurally oriented and focuses on how the objectives of the program will be realized. The discussion includes hierarchy charts, pseudocode, flowcharts, and Warnier-Orr diagrams.

The presentation is of a practical nature, and stresses application rather than theory. Accordingly, we introduce a new program at the beginning of the chapter, and develop the methodology in the context of that program. We begin with presentation of the program specifications.

The Tuition Billing Program

This section contains the specifications for a new problem, known simply as the tuition billing program. The requirements are straightforward and parallel those of many other COBOL programs, namely to print a heading line(s) at the start of processing, one or more detail lines for every record processed, and a total line(s) at the end of processing. As simple as these specifications may be, it is critical that you avoid the temptation to rush immediately into COBOL, and concentrate instead on designing the program you will eventually write.

The approach we follow begins with a determination of the most general function the program is to accomplish, then divides that task into smaller and smaller pieces, until the requirements of each piece are clearly recognized. Initially the design process may seem superfluous in that you are confident of your ability to begin coding immediately. Rest assured, however, that design is productive work, and does in fact pay dividends in the long run. A well-designed program is far more likely to be correct than one written off-the-cuff. Moreover, and this may be the argument that most appeals to you, a well-designed program will ultimately be completed in less time than one that is poorly designed or one that has no design at all.

Programming Specifications

Program Name: Tuition Billing Program

Narrative: This program processes a file of student records, computes and prints the tuition bill for each student, and prints the total amounts for all students.

Input File(s): STUDENT-FILE

Input Record Layout: See Figure 3.1a

Test Data:

```
SMITH           JB15Y0000230
JAMES           HR15 0500245
BAKER           SR09 0500350
PART-TIMER      JR03Y0000300
JONES           PL15Y0000280
HEAVYWORKER     HM18 0000200
LEE             BL18 0000335
CLARK           JC06 0000310
GROSSMAN        SE07 0000215
FRANKEL         LF10 0000350
BENWAY          CT03 0250395
KERBEL          NB04 0000100
```

Report Layout: See Figure 3.1b

Processing Requirements:

1. Print a suitable heading at the beginning of the report.

2. Read a file of student records.

3. Process each record read by:

   a. Computing an individual bill, equal to the sum of tuition, union fee, and activity fee, minus a scholarship (if any), by:

   i. Calculating the tuition due, at a rate of $200 per credit.

   ii. Billing the student $25 for the union fee, if there is a "Y" in the Union Member position.

   iii. Computing the activity fee based on the number of credits taken:

ACTIVITY FEE	CREDITS
$25	6 or fewer
$50	7 – 12
$75	more than 12

Figure 3.1   Record Layouts for Tuition Billing Program

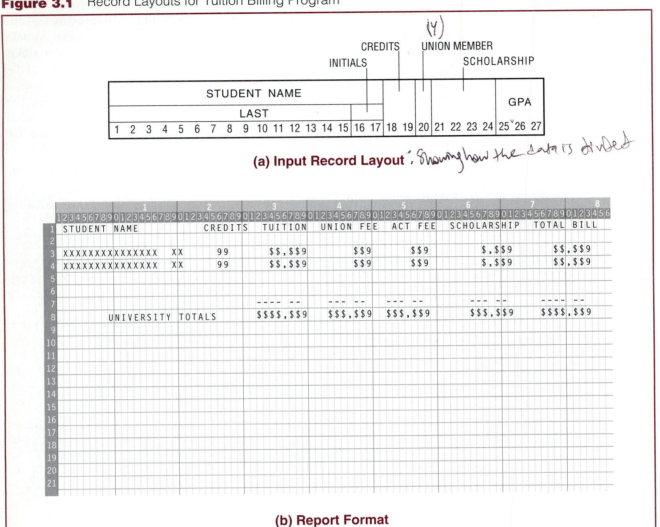

(a) Input Record Layout *Showing how the data is divided*

(b) Report Format

iv. Awarding a scholarship equal to the amount in the incoming record if, and only if, the GPA is greater than 2.5. (Observe that in the test data on the previous page James does *not* qualify for the $500 scholarship he would otherwise have been awarded.)

v. Incrementing the university totals for tuition, union fee, activity fee, scholarship, and overall total.

b. Printing a detail line for each record read.

4. Print a total line at the end of the report.

Structured Design

Structured design identifies the tasks a program is to accomplish, then relates those tasks to one another in a ***hierarchy chart***. Figure 3.2 contains a very basic example, applicable to any COBOL program. The hierarchy chart divides the program into its functional components, for example, initialization, processing, and termination, and indicates the manager/subordinate relationships between these components. In this example all three modules are subordinate to the module labeled any COBOL program.

To better appreciate the significance of a hierarchy chart and its role in program development, consider Figure 3.3, depicting the hierarchy chart for the tuition billing program. The development takes place in stages, beginning at the top and working down to the bottom. At every level, the major function(s) are subdivided into other functions that are placed on the next lower level in the hierarchy chart. Those functions are in turn further subdivided into still other functions, until finally the lowest-level functions cannot be further subdivided.

The specifications for the tuition billing problem suggest a suitable name for the highest-level module, PREPARE-TUITION-REPORT. This in turn is divided into its basic functions of initialization (consisting of WRITE-HEADING-LINE and READ-STUDENT-FILE), processing (PROCESS-STUDENT-RECORD), and termination (WRITE-UNIVERSITY-TOTALS). Levels 1 and 2 of the hierarchy chart are shown in Figure 3.3a.

Of these four modules, only one, PROCESS-STUDENT-RECORD, needs to be subdivided. In other words ask yourself which additional lower-level functions should be included under PROCESS-STUDENT-RECORD in order to process individual student records. The program specifications contain the requirement to compute the individual's bill, increment the university totals to include the amount just computed, and write a detail line for the particular student. Each of these tasks requires its own module as indicated in Figure 3.3b. In addition, PROCESS-STUDENT-RECORD must also read the next record so that the program can continue. (The module READ-STUDENT-FILE appears twice in the hierarchy chart; on level two to read the first record, and on level three to read all subsequent records. The necessity for the dual appearance stems from a limitation in COBOL-74 rather than a requirement of structured design).

The development of a hierarchy chart continues until its lowest-level modules cannot be further subdivided, that is, until the designer believes they can be easily translated into programming statements. The decision is *subjective* in that there is no single correct answer; you could, for example, stop at three levels or continue to a fourth level as in Figure 3.3c. We chose to divide COMPUTE-INDIVIDUAL-BILL into four additional modules: COMPUTE-TUITION, COMPUTE-UNION-FEE, COMPUTE-ACTIVITY-FEE, and COMPUTE-SCHOLARSHIP.

The hierarchy chart is now complete and consists of four levels, each of which will correspond to a PERFORM statement in the eventual COBOL program;

Figure 3.2 Overall COBOL Hierarchy Chart

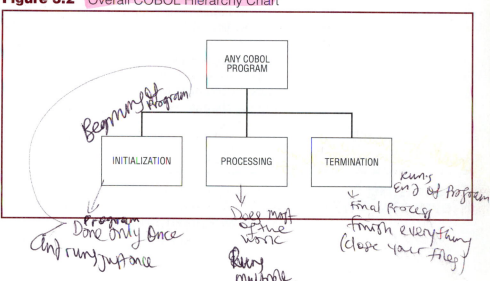

Figure 3.3 Hierarchy Chart for Tuition Billing Program

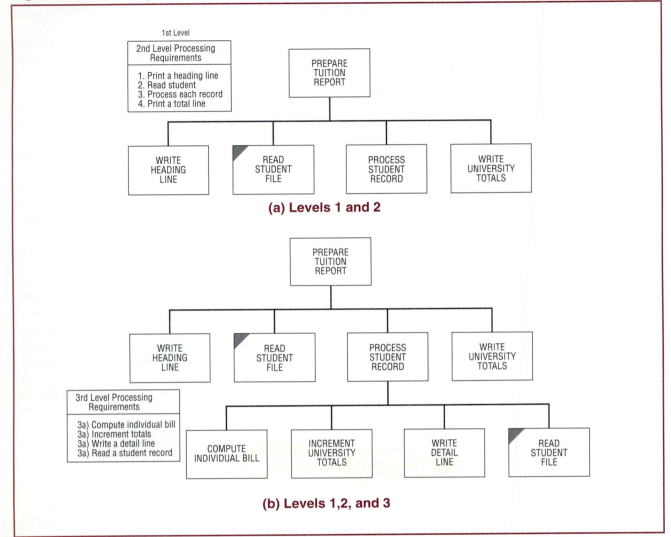

(a) Levels 1 and 2

(b) Levels 1,2, and 3

that is, the module (paragraph) on level one will perform the modules (paragraphs) on level two, those on level two will perform the modules on level three, and so on. The hierarchy chart does not specify how often these paragraphs will be called, nor does it indicate the conditions for calling one subordinate in lieu of another. In other words, the hierarchy chart indicates only what functions are necessary, but not when they are executed. It contains no decision-making logic, nor does it imply anything about the order or frequency in which various paragraphs within a program are executed. That, in turn, is specified within the logic of the program, developed according to the discipline of structured programming as discussed later in the chapter.

Evaluating the Hierarchy Chart

As we have already indicated, the decision of how many modules to include in a hierarchy chart and how they should be related to one another is necessarily subjective. Nevertheless, there are certain evaluation criteria that result in selecting one design over another. Among these are the following:

Figure 3.3 *(continued)*

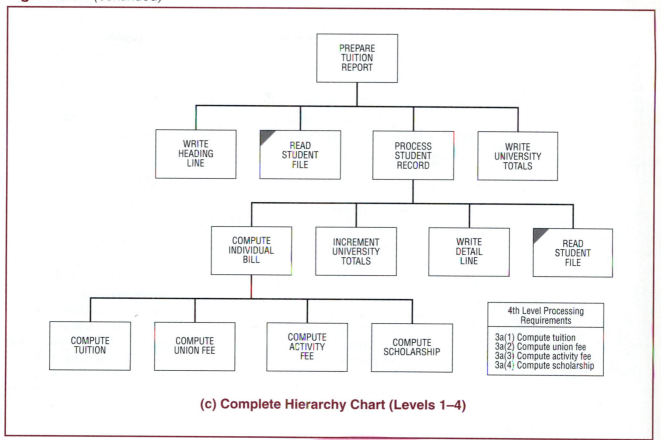

(c) Complete Hierarchy Chart (Levels 1–4)

Evaluating the Hierarchy Chart

1. Is the hierarchy chart complete?
2. Are the modules functional?
3. Is there effective span of control?

Completeness

A hierarchy chart must be complete; that is, it has to provide for every function required by the program as specified in the programming specifications. You test for completeness level by level, starting at the top of the hierarchy chart, and working your way down, one level at a time, by asking the question, "Do the subordinate modules at the next level completely develop their corresponding modules at this level?" If the answer is yes, move to the next module on the present level, or to the first module on the next level, and repeat the question. If the answer is no, add functions as necessary and continue to the next module.

For example, begin with the completed hierarchy chart of Figure 3.3c and ask yourself whether the modules on level two are adequate to expand the single module of level one; that is, do the four modules on level two completely expand the PREPARE-TUITION-REPORT module to which they are subordinate? The answer is yes, so you move to level three and see whether the modules on this level adequately expand the PROCESS-STUDENT-RECORD module from level two. Once again the answer is yes, and so you progress to level four. The process continues until you have checked every module on every level and are satisfied that all necessary functions are included.

Functionality

Every module in a hierarchy chart should be dedicated to a *single* function, the nature of which should be clear from examining the module's name. Each of the module names in Figure 3.3 consists of a verb, adjective (or two), and an object—for example, COMPUTE-INDIVIDUAL-BILL or WRITE-DETAIL-LINE. Indeed, if a module cannot be named in this way, its function is probably not well defined and thought should be given to revising the hierarchy chart.

Stated another way, you should reject (or redesign) any module that does not appear to be functional; that is, modules whose names contain:

1. More than one verb—for example, READ-AND-WRITE.

2. More than one object—for example, EDIT-NAME-AND-ACCOUNT-DATA.

3. Nondescriptive or time-related terms—for example, HOUSEKEEPING, TERMINATION-ROUTINE, INITIALIZATION, or MAINLINE.

Another way of expressing the need for functional modules is to strive for module independence; that is, the internal workings of one module should not affect those of another. Perhaps you have already been associated with a working program in which changes were implemented, only to have some other, apparently unrelated, portion of the program no longer work properly. The problem may be due to paragraphs in the program being unnecessarily dependent on one another.

What we are saying is that in an ideal situation, changes made to one paragraph should not affect the results of any other. In a more practical sense, the paragraphs have to be somewhat related, otherwise they would not be parts of the same program; however, the amount of interdependence between paragraphs should be minimized to the greatest extent possible. With respect to Figure 3.3, for example, a change in the procedure for computing the union fee should not affect how the activity fee is determined. That is because the modules COMPUTE-UNION-FEE and COMPUTE-ACTIVITY-FEE are functional in their own right, and consequently are independent of one another.

Span of Control

The **span of control** of a module is the number of subordinates it contains. In Figure 3.3, for example, the span of control of both PREPARE-TUITION-REPORT and COMPUTE-INDIVIDUAL-BILL is four. An effective span of control (for hierarchy charts associated with COBOL programs) is generally from two or three to seven, although that may vary depending on the situation. You should, however, avoid extremes in either direction. Programs with ineffective spans of control (too many subordinates or too few) are poorly designed and difficult to follow and/or maintain.

Structured Programming

Let us pause for a moment to see what has been accomplished. We have taken the original problem and divided it into a series of manageable pieces, each of which describes a particular job that needs to be accomplished. In other words, we have said what needs to be done to solve the problem, but have not as yet said how we will solve it. That in essence is the difference between structured design and structured programming.

A structured program is one consisting entirely of three types of logic structures: sequence, selection (a decision), and iteration (a loop). The fact that these structures (or basic building blocks) are sufficient to express any desired logic was first postulated in a now-classic paper by Bohm and Jacopini.[1]

The elementary building blocks of structured programming are shown in flowchart form in Figure 3.4. Flowcharts use special symbols to communicate information. A rectangle indicates a processing statement, a diamond indicates a decision, and a small circle connects portions of the flowchart. All of the flowcharts have one key feature in common, namely, a *single entry point* and a *single exit point*; that is, there is only one way to enter each structure and only one way to leave.

The ***sequence*** structure in Figure 3.4a specifies that the program statements are executed sequentially, in the order in which they appear. The two blocks, A and B, may denote anything from single statements to complete programs, and it is clear that there is a single entry point and a single exit point to the structure.

---

1 Bohm and Jacopini, "Flow Diagrams, Turing Machines and Languages with Only Two Formation Rules," *Communications of the ACM* (May 1966).

Figure 3.4 The Building Blocks of Structured Programming

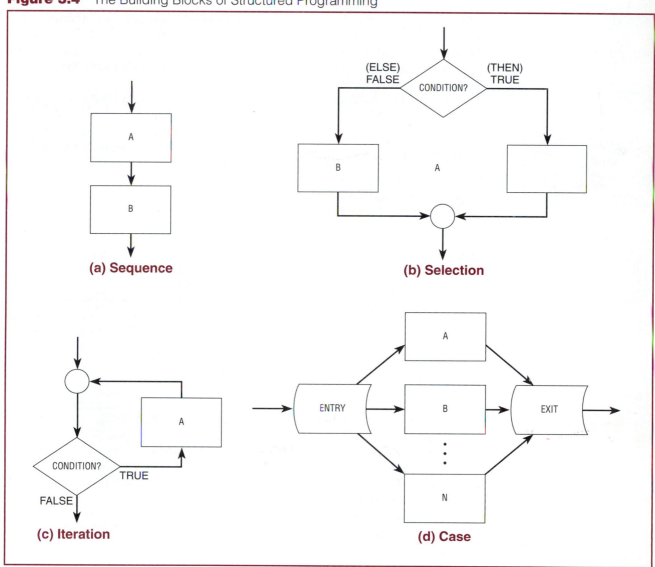

The *selection* (or IF . . . THEN . . . ELSE) structure in Figure 3.4b specifies a choice between two actions. A condition is tested with one of two outcomes; if the condition is true, block A is executed, while if it is false, block B is executed. The condition itself is the single entry point, and both paths meet to form a single exit point.

The *iteration* (or DO . . . WHILE) structure in Figure 3.4c specifies repeated execution of one or more statements while a condition is true. A condition is tested and, if it is true, block A is executed after which the condition is retested. If, however, the condition is false, control passes to the next sequential statement after the iteration structure. Again, there is a single entry point and a single exit point from the structure.

The *case structure* in Figure 3.4d expresses a multibranch situation. Although case is actually a special instance of selection, it is convenient to extend the definition of structured programming to include this fourth type of building block. The case structure evaluates a condition and branches to one of several paths, depending on the value of the condition. As with the other building blocks, there is one entry point and one exit point.

Sufficiency of the Basic Structures

The theory of structured programming says simply that an appropriate combination of the basic building blocks may be derived to solve any problem. This is possible because an entire structure (sequence, selection, iteration, or case) may be *substituted* anywhere block A or B appears. Figure 3.5 shows a combination of the basic structures to illustrate this concept.

Figure 3.5 is essentially a selection structure. However, instead of specifying a single statement for the true or false branches, as was done in Figure 3.4, a complete building block is used instead. Thus, if condition-1 is true, an iteration structure is entered, whereas, if it is false, a sequence structure is executed. Both the iteration and sequence structures meet at a single exit point which becomes the exit point for the initial selection structure.

Figure 3.5   Sufficiency of the Basic Structures

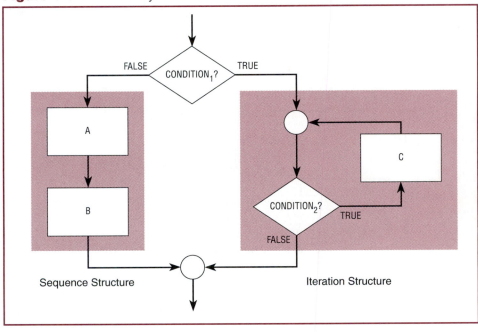

Expressing Logic

We now turn our attention to ways in which programmers express logic, to themselves and to others. We begin with the traditional flowchart, then move to newer techniques more closely associated with structured programming: pseudocode and Warnier-Orr diagrams.

The Traditional Flowchart

Every programmer is familiar with the traditional *flowchart* as described in Chapter 1. Although flowcharts have declined in popularity, they remain in widespread use, primarily for documentation. Our personal preference is to use pseudocode, but we include Figure 3.6 for completeness. The decision as to which technique to use is between you and your instructor.

Pseudocode

The fact that most programmers write simple notes to themselves prior to coding a program gave rise to *pseudocode*, a technique associated with structured programming. As we indicated in Chapter 1, pseudocode is defined simply as neat notes to yourself, and uses statements similar to computer instructions to describe logic. Figure 3.7 represents the building blocks of structured programming as they would be written in pseudocode and corresponds to the flowcharts shown in Figure 3.4.

Pseudocode comes into play after the design phase of a program has been completed, and prior to actual coding. Recall that a hierarchy chart is *functional* in nature and indicates *what* has to be done, but not necessarily *when* or *how*. Pseudocode, on the other hand, is *procedural* and contains sequence and decision-making logic. In other words, pseudocode connects the modules in a hierarchy chart through loops and decision making.

To better appreciate how pseudocode expresses programming logic, consider Figure 3.8, which contains pseudocode for the tuition billing program. Two versions of the pseudocode are presented—an initial attempt in Figure 3.8a, and an expanded (more detailed) version in Figure 3.8b. Both versions are equally appropriate, with the choice between them depending entirely on the individual, and the level of detail he or she desires.

The logic is straightforward and begins with the steps for initialization; to open files, write a heading line(s), and read the first record. Then, a loop (or iteration structure) is entered in which the program computes the student's bill (tuition plus union and activity fees minus scholarship), increments the university totals to include this amount, writes a detail line, and finally reads the next student record. The statements in the loop are executed continually until all the records have been read, at which point university totals are written, and the program terminates.

Pseudocode has a distinct block structure that is conducive to structured programming. It is not, however, bound by formal syntactical rules (although some organizations have implemented standards), nor does it have specific rules of indentation, which is done strictly at the programmer's discretion. Its only limitation is a restriction to the building blocks of structured programming (sequence, selection, iteration, and case).

With practice, pseudocode can be developed quickly and easily. Good pseudocode should be sufficiently precise to be a real aid in writing a program, while informal enough to be understood by nonprogrammers. The informality of

Figure 3.6   Flowchart for Tuition Billing Program

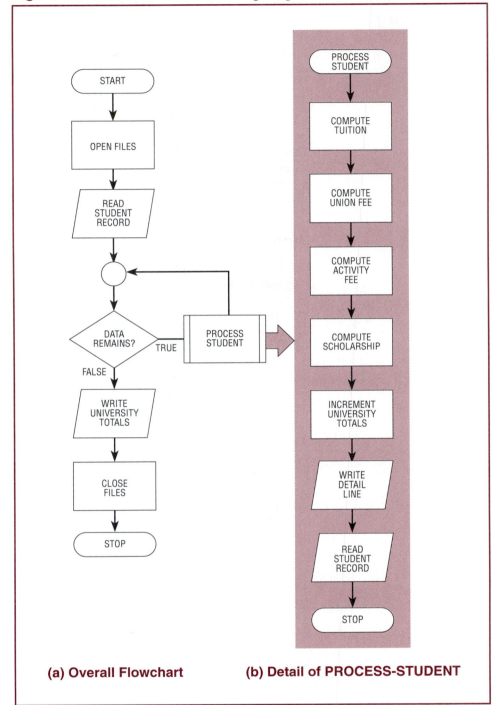

(a) Overall Flowchart   **(b) Detail of PROCESS-STUDENT**

the technique precludes exact rules, but we urge the use of consistent conventions to make it easier to read. Our suggestions:

1. Indent for readability.

2. Use ENDIF, ENDDO, and ENDCASE to indicate the end of a logic structure; use vertical lines to indicate the extent of a block.

Figure 3.7 Pseudocode for Building Blocks

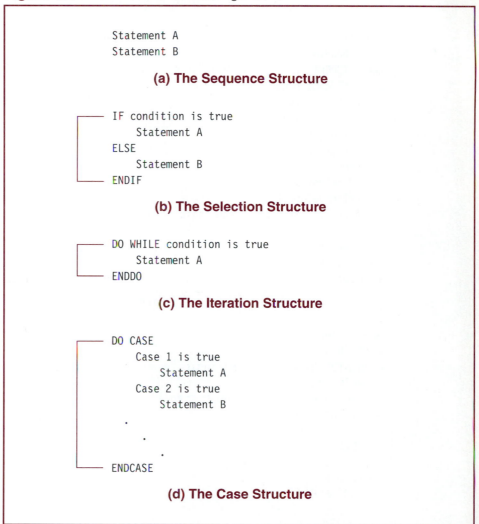

```
Statement A
Statement B
```

(a) The Sequence Structure

```
IF condition is true
    Statement A
ELSE
    Statement B
ENDIF
```

(b) The Selection Structure

```
DO WHILE condition is true
    Statement A
ENDDO
```

(c) The Iteration Structure

```
DO CASE
    Case 1 is true
        Statement A
    Case 2 is true
        Statement B
    .
      .
        .
ENDCASE
```

(d) The Case Structure

3. Use parenthetical expressions to clarify statements associated with the ELSE portion of an IF statement.

4. Minimize or avoid the use of adjectives and adverbs.

Warnier-Orr Diagrams

Warnier-Orr diagrams (named for their co-developers, Jean-Dominique Warnier and Kenneth Orr) combine elements of structured design and structured programming. The diagrams use specific symbols to represent the basic building blocks of structured programming, then combine these elements in hierarchical fashion.

Figure 3.9 shows how the basic building blocks of structured programming would be represented in a Warnier-Orr diagram. Sequential statements (Figure 3.9a) are listed vertically, one under the other, and are grouped in braces. A plus sign enclosed in a circle indicates selection, and is placed between the true and false conditions of the selection structure (a bar denotes the false condition). Parentheses indicate iteration (Figure 3.9c), with the number inside the parentheses indicating

Figure 3.8   Pseudocode for Tuition Billing Program

```
Open files
Write heading line(s)
Read STUDENT-FILE at end indicate no more data
DO WHILE data remains
      Compute tuition
      Compute union fee
      Compute activity fee
      Compute scholarship
      Compute bill
      Increment university totals
      Write detail line
      Read STUDENT-FILE at end indicate no more data
ENDDO
Write university totals
Close files
Stop run
```

(a) Initial attempt

```
Open files
Write heading line(s)
Read STUDENT-FILE at end indicate no more data
DO WHILE data remains
      Compute tuition = 200 * credits
      IF union member
          Union fee = $25
      ELSE
          Union fee = 0
      ENDIF
      DO CASE
          CASE credits <= 6
              Activity fee = 25
          CASE credits > 6 and <= 12
              Activity fee = 50
          CASE credits > 12
              Activity fee = 75
      END CASE
      IF gpa > 2.5
          Scholarship = Scholarship amount
      ELSE (no scholarship)
          Scholarship = 0
      ENDIF
      Compute Bill = Tuition + Union fee + Activity fee - Scholarship
      Increment university totals
      Write detail line
      Read STUDENT-FILE at end indicate no more data
ENDDO
Write university totals
Close files
Stop run
```

(b) Detailed pseudocode

Figure 3.9   Warnier-Orr Diagrams for Building Blocks

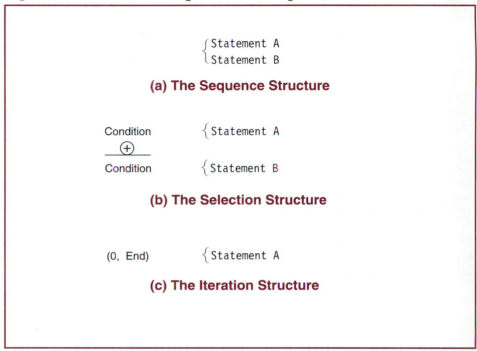

how often the loop is to be performed. A variable number of iterations is implied by enclosing two numbers, for example (0, End) to indicate execution until an end-of-file condition is reached. There is no specific notation for the case construct.

Figure 3.10 contains a Warnier-Orr diagram for the tuition billing program. The diagram depicts the same manager/subordinate relationships as the hierarchy chart of Figure 3.3c, but unlike the hierarchy chart, is read from left to right rather than from top to bottom. The diagram also contains additional information not found in the hierarchy chart, namely the logic to indicate how often, and in what sequence, subordinate modules are executed.

Top-Down Testing

All programs require extensive testing to ensure that they conform to the original specifications. However, the question of when coding ends and testing begins is not as straightforward as it may appear, and gives rise to the philosophy of ***top-down testing***.

Top-down testing suggests that coding and testing are parallel activities, and espouses the philosophy that testing begins even before a program is completely finished. This is accomplished by initially coding the intermediate- and/or lower-level paragraphs as ***stubs***, that is, partially coded paragraphs whose purpose is to indicate only that the paragraph has been executed. The stub paragraphs do no useful work per se, and are used only to test the overall flow of the program. The rationale is that the highest (and most difficult) modules should be tested earlier and more often than the lower-level routines; the latter contain detailed but often trivial logic, and are least important with respect to the overall program flow.

Figure 3.11 is an example of such a program. It is *complete* in the sense that it contains a paragraph for every module in the hierarchy chart of Figure 3.3, yet *incomplete* in that most of its paragraphs consist of a single DISPLAY statement.

Figure 3.10 Warnier-Orr Diagram for Tuition Billing Program

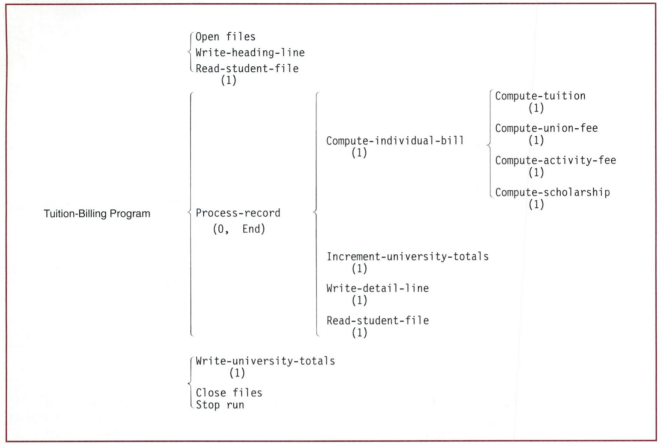

(DISPLAY is one of the most useful statements in COBOL as it allows the programmer to print a message on the screen—for example, DISPLAY "COMPUTE-INDIVIDUAL-BILL paragraph has been entered"—or to print the contents of a data name—for example, DISPLAY STUDENT-RECORD—without having to open a file. The DISPLAY statement is covered in Chapter 6.)

The program in Figure 3.11 was tested with the data of Figure 3.12a, and produced the output of Figure 3.12b. You may not think that much has been accomplished, but closer examination shows that all of the paragraphs in the program were executed, and further that they were executed in the correct sequence. The testing has demonstrated that the overall program flow is correct.

Execution began with the paragraph PREPARE-TUITION-REPORT followed by the the paragraph WRITE-HEADING-LINE. The record for the first student (JB Smith) was read, and the paragraph PROCESS-STUDENT-RECORD was entered. The paragraph COMPUTE-INDIVIDUAL-BILL was executed next, and called its four subordinates to compute the tuition, union fee, activity fee, and scholarship. The paragraphs to increment university totals and to write a detail line were also called. The data for the second student (HR James) was read, and PROCESS-STUDENT-RECORD (and all its subordinates) were re-executed. Eventually the end of file was reached, the paragraph WRITE-UNIVERSITY-TOTALS was executed, and the program ended.

Yes, the program requires additional development, but the hardest part is over. Any errors that may have existed in the highest-level modules have already

Figure 3.11   Tuition Billing Program with Stubs

```
 1          IDENTIFICATION DIVISION.
 2          PROGRAM-ID.    TUITION3.
 3          AUTHOR.         CAROL VAZQUEZ VILLAR.
 4
 5          ENVIRONMENT DIVISION.
 6          INPUT-OUTPUT SECTION.
 7          FILE-CONTROL.
 8              SELECT STUDENT-FILE   ASSIGN TO SYSIN
 9                  ORGANIZATION IS LINE SEQUENTIAL.
10
11          DATA DIVISION.
12          FILE SECTION.
13          FD  STUDENT-FILE
14              RECORD CONTAINS 27 CHARACTERS.
15          01  STUDENT-RECORD        PIC X(27).
16
17          WORKING-STORAGE SECTION.
18          01  DATA-REMAINS-SWITCH    PIC X(2)    VALUE SPACES.
19
20          PROCEDURE DIVISION.
21          PREPARE-TUITION-REPORT.
22              DISPLAY 'PREPARE-TUITION-REPORT paragraph entered'.
23              OPEN INPUT   STUDENT-FILE.
24              PERFORM WRITE-HEADING-LINE.
25              PERFORM READ-STUDENT-FILE.
26              PERFORM PROCESS-STUDENT-RECORD
27                  UNTIL DATA-REMAINS-SWITCH = 'NO'.
28              PERFORM WRITE-UNIVERSITY-TOTALS.
29              CLOSE STUDENT-FILE.
30              STOP RUN.
31
32          WRITE-HEADING-LINE.
33              DISPLAY 'WRITE-HEADING-LINE paragraph entered'.
34
35          READ-STUDENT-FILE.
36              READ STUDENT-FILE
37                  AT END MOVE 'NO' TO DATA-REMAINS-SWITCH
38              END-READ.
39
40          PROCESS-STUDENT-RECORD.
41              DISPLAY ' '.
42              DISPLAY 'PROCESS-STUDENT-RECORD paragraph entered'.
43              DISPLAY 'Student record being processed: ' STUDENT-RECORD.
44              PERFORM COMPUTE-INDIVIDUAL-BILL.
45              PERFORM INCREMENT-UNIVERSITY-TOTALS
46              PERFORM WRITE-DETAIL-LINE.
47              PERFORM READ-STUDENT-FILE.
48
```

Display statement shows current record

Figure 3.11   *(continued)*

```
49      COMPUTE-INDIVIDUAL-BILL.
50          DISPLAY '  COMPUTE-INDIVIDUAL-BILL paragraph entered'.
51          PERFORM COMPUTE-TUITION.
52          PERFORM COMPUTE-UNION-FEE.
53          PERFORM COMPUTE-ACTIVITY-FEE.
54          PERFORM COMPUTE-SCHOLARSHIP.
55
56      COMPUTE-TUITION.
57          DISPLAY '  COMPUTE-TUITION paragraph entered'.
58
59      COMPUTE-UNION-FEE.
60          DISPLAY '  COMPUTE-UNION-FEE paragraph entered'.
61
62      COMPUTE-ACTIVITY-FEE.
63          DISPLAY '  COMPUTE-ACTIVITY-FEE paragraph entered'.
64
65      COMPUTE-SCHOLARSHIP.
66          DISPLAY '  COMPUTE-SCHOLARSHIP paragraph entered'.
67
68      INCREMENT-UNIVERSITY-TOTALS.
69          DISPLAY '  INCREMENT-UNIVERSITY-TOTALS paragraph entered'.
70
71      WRITE-DETAIL-LINE.
72          DISPLAY '  WRITE-DETAIL-LINE paragraph entered'.
73
74      WRITE-UNIVERSITY-TOTALS.
75          DISPLAY ' '.
76          DISPLAY 'WRITE-UNIVERSITY-TOTALS paragraph entered'.
```

Program stub

been found, and were easier to correct than had testing been deferred. Of course, later versions of the program can still contain bugs, but these errors will occur in lower level modules where correction is generally easier. The more difficult problems will already have been resolved in the initial tests, and that is precisely the goal of top-down testing.

We urge you to implement the top-down approach to program testing, and offer Figure 3.13 as our last word on the subject. In the traditional mode of Figure 3.13a, no testing is done until the weekend before the program goes live (or your assignment is due). Inevitably last-minute panic sets in, giving rise to overtime and chaos, an environment unlikely to produce logically correct programs. By contrast, the top down approach of Figure 3.13b provides a more uniform testing pattern, beginning almost immediately with the project's inception and continuing throughout its duration. The results are vastly superior.

Figure 3.12 Testing the Tuition Billing Program

```
SMITH          JB15Y0000230
JAMES          HR15 0500245
BAKER          SR09 0500350
PART-TIMER     JR03Y0000300
JONES          PL15Y0000280
HEAVYWORKER    HM18 0000200
LEE            BL18 0000335
CLARK          JC06 0000310
GROSSMAN       SE07 0000215
FRANKEL        LF10 0000350
BENWAY         CT03 0250395
KERBEL         NB04 0000100
```

(a) Test Data

```
PREPARE-TUITION-REPORT paragraph entered
WRITE-HEADING-LINE paragraph entered

PROCESS-STUDENT-RECORD paragraph entered
Student record being processed: SMITH          JB15Y0000230
  COMPUTE-INDIVIDUAL-BILL paragraph entered
  COMPUTE-TUITION paragraph entered
  COMPUTE-UNION-FEE paragraph entered
  COMPUTE-ACTIVITY-FEE paragraph entered
  COMPUTE-SCHOLARSHIP paragraph entered
  INCREMENT-UNIVERSITY-TOTALS paragraph entered
  WRITE-DETAIL-LINE paragraph entered

PROCESS-STUDENT-RECORD paragraph entered
Student record being processed: JAMES          HR15 0500245
  COMPUTE-INDIVIDUAL-BILL paragraph entered
  COMPUTE-TUITION paragraph entered
  COMPUTE-UNION-FEE paragraph entered
  COMPUTE-ACTIVITY-FEE paragraph entered
  COMPUTE-SCHOLARSHIP paragraph entered
  INCREMENT-UNIVERSITY-TOTALS paragraph entered
  WRITE-DETAIL-LINE paragraph entered
        .
          .
            .
PROCESS-STUDENT-RECORD paragraph entered
Student record being processed: KERBEL          NB04 0000100
  COMPUTE-INDIVIDUAL-BILL paragraph entered
  COMPUTE-TUITION paragraph entered
  COMPUTE-UNION-FEE paragraph entered
  COMPUTE-ACTIVITY-FEE paragraph entered
  COMPUTE-SCHOLARSHIP paragraph entered
  INCREMENT-UNIVERSITY-TOTALS paragraph entered
  WRITE-DETAIL-LINE paragraph entered

WRITE-UNIVERSITY-TOTALS paragraph entered
```

(b) Output of Stubs Program

Figure 3.13 Advantages of Top-Down Testing

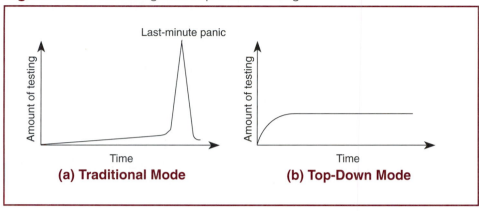

(a) Traditional Mode   **(b) Top-Down Mode**

SUMMARY

Points to Remember

■ Structured design is a functionally oriented technique that identifies the tasks a program is to accomplish, then relates those tasks to one another in a hierarchy chart.

■ The modules in a hierarchy chart correspond one to one with paragraphs in a COBOL program. A module (paragraph) can be entered only from the module immediately above it, and must return control to that module when execution is complete.

■ A hierarchy chart is evaluated for completeness, functionality, and span of control.

■ Structured programming is procedural in nature and contains decision-making logic depicting the sequence in which the program tasks will be executed.

■ A structured program consists entirely of the basic building blocks of sequence, selection, and iteration; a fourth construct, case, is commonly included in the definition of structured programming.

■ Each of the elementary building blocks in structured programming has one entry point and one exit point.

■ Flowcharts and/or pseudocode (defined as neat notes to yourself) describe the logic in a program. Warnier-Orr diagrams combine elements of structured design and structured programming.

■ Top down testing begins early in the development process, even before a program is completely coded; it is accomplished through the use of program stubs.

Pg 64. Difference between structured design & structured programming. Said what needs to be done to solve the problem but have not said how the problem would be solved.

Key Words and Concepts

Bohm and Jacopini	Pseudocode
Case structure	Selection structure
Flowchart	Sequence structure
Functional technique	Span of control
Hierarchy chart	Structured design
Iteration structure	Structured programming
One entry point/one exit point	Top-down development
Procedural technique	Warnier-Orr diagram
Program stub	

Fill-In

1. The fundamental building blocks of structured programming are: _____, _____, and _____.

2. The _____ construct is a fourth structure, which is convenient for expressing multibranch situations.

3. All of the basic building blocks of structured programming have _____ entry point and _____ exit point.

4. In the iteration, or DO WHILE construct, the condition is tested (<u>before/after</u>) the procedure is executed.

5. The primary tool of structured design is the _____ _____.

6. _____ diagrams combine elements of a hierarchy chart and pseudocode.

7. A hierarchy chart is evaluated according to the criteria of _____, _____, and _____.

8. Structured design is a _____ oriented technique, whereas structured programming is _____ in nature.

9. _____, rather than flowcharting, is the most common technique for expressing program logic.

10. Each module in a _____ _____ represents a _____ in a COBOL program.

11. _____ __ _____ is the management term for the number of subordinate modules.

12. A well-chosen paragraph name should indicate the function of that paragraph, and consist of a _____, _____, and _____.

13. _____ and _____ are the individuals credited with first postulating the structured theorem.

14. Structured (<u>programming/design</u>) is intended to produce a _____ solution with the same components and relationships as the problem it is intended to solve.

15. A program should be tested from the (<u>top down/bottom up</u>).

T r u e / F a l s e

1. A structured program is guaranteed not to contain logical errors.

2. Structured programming can be implemented in a variety of programming languages.

3. INITIALIZATION and TERMINATION are good module names.

4. The logic of any program can be expressed as a combination of only three types of logic structures.

5. The one entry/one exit philosophy is essential to structured programming.

6. Decision making should generally occur in higher-level, rather than lower-level, modules.

7. The case construct is one of the three basic logic structures.

8. A flowchart is the only way to communicate program logic.

9. Pseudocode has precise syntactical rules.

10. A program's hierarchy chart is developed from the bottom up.

11. A program must be completely coded before testing can begin.

12. A Warnier-Orr diagram combines elements of structured design and structured programming.

13. READ-WRITE-AND-COMPUTE is a good module name.

14. A single COBOL paragraph should accomplish many functions for optimal efficiency.

15. Program testing should be concentrated in the last 25% of the development phase.

16. A span of control from 15 to 25 COBOL paragraphs is desirable for the highest-level modules.

17. The optimal number of modules in a system is equal to the number of programmers available for coding.

18. A module in a hierarchy chart can be called from another module on its own level.

P r o b l e m s

1. Given the flowchart in Figure 3.14, respond "true" or "false" to the following on the basis of the flowchart.
   a. If X > Y and W > Z, then *always* add 1 to B.
   b. If X < Y, then *always* add 1 to D.
   c. If Q > T, then *always* add 1 to B.
   d. If X < Y and W < Z, then *always* add 1 to D.
   e. There are no conditions under which 1 will be added to both A and B simultaneously.
   f. If W > Z and Q < T, then *always* add 1 to C.

2. Assume that a robot is sitting on a chair, facing a wall a short distance away. Restricting yourself to the basic building blocks of structured programming, develop the necessary logic to have the robot walk to the wall and return to its initial position. Express your solution in pseudocode. The robot understands the following commands:

Figure 3.14 Flowchart for Problem 1

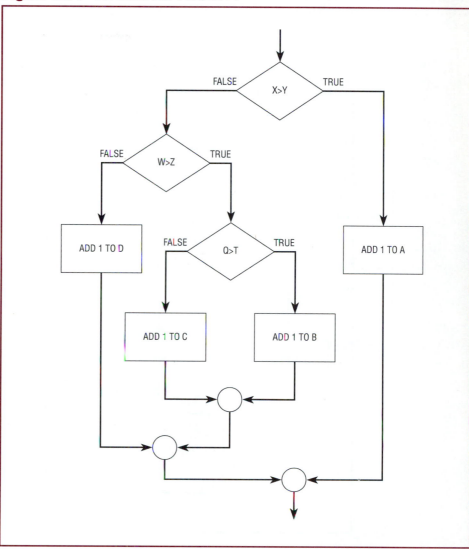

```
STAND
SIT
TURN (turns right 90 degrees)
STEP
```

In addition, the robot can raise its arms and sense the wall with its fingertips. (However, it cannot sense the chair on its return trip, since the chair is below arm level.) Accordingly the robot must count the number of steps to the wall or chair by using the following commands:

```
ADD (increments counter by 1)
SUBTRACT (decrements counter by 1)
ZERO COUNTER (sets counter to zero)
ARMS UP
ARMS DOWN
```

The wall is assumed to be an integer number of steps away. Select a volunteer to act as the robot, and see whether the submitted solutions actually accomplish the objective.

Figure 3.15 Flowchart for Problem 3

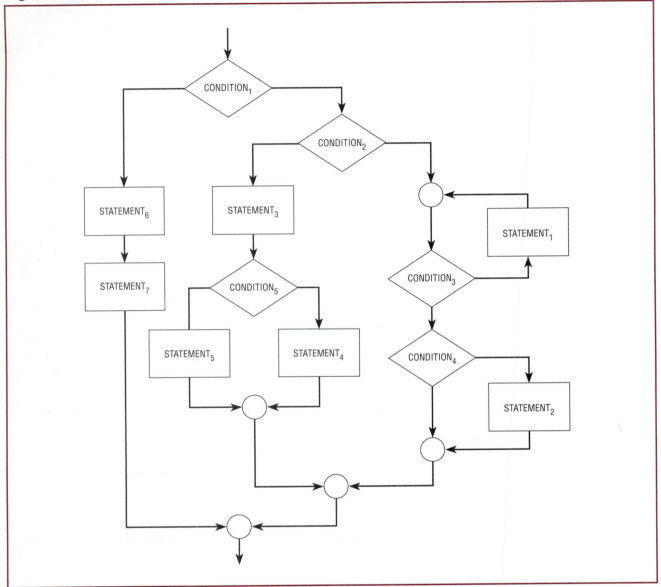

3. Identify the elementary building blocks in Figure 3.15. Be sure you get all of them (the authors can find eight).

4. Indicate the output that will be produced by each of the following DISPLAY statements.
    a. DISPLAY 'STUDENT RECORD'.
    b. DISPLAY STUDENT-RECORD.
    c. DISPLAY 'STUDENT RECORD IS ' STUDENT-RECORD.
    d. DISPLAY.
    e. DISPLAY STUDENT-NAME, SOC-SEC-NUM.

5. This non-data-processing problem specifically avoids a business context, and was chosen because you are unlikely to have a preexisting bias toward a solution.

Develop a hierarchy chart to allow a user to play a series of tic-tac-toe games interactively against a computer. The following modules were used in the author's solution: PLAY-SERIES, PLAY-GAME, CLEAR-BOARD, GET-USER-MOVE, VALIDATE-USER-MOVE, CHECK-FOR-WINNER, UPDATE-BOARD, GET-COMPUTER-MOVE, DISPLAY-BOARD, DISPLAY-MESSAGE. (The last module, DISPLAY-MESSAGE, may be called from several places.) The module names should in themselves be indicative of the module functions.

6. Again we have chosen a nonbusiness problem to give you further practice with structured design. This time you are asked to develop a hierarchy chart for the game of blackjack (also known as "21"). The game is played with a deck of 52 cards (or more commonly with multiple decks). The player places a bet, and the player and dealer are each dealt two cards. Both of the player's cards are face up (showing), but one of the dealer's cards is hidden. The player is asked whether he or she wishes to draw additional card(s), after which the dealer has the same option (provided the player has not gone over 21). The player closest to 21 (without going over) wins. The rules of the game require the dealer to draw with 16 or less, and stand (not draw) with 17 or more. Your hierarchy chart should contain the necessary modules to keep a running total of the player's winnings (or losses) as well as the following special situations:

   a. Doubling down—if the player's first two cards total 11, he or she may double the bet and receive one additional card.

   b. Purchasing insurance—if the dealer's "up" card is an ace, the player may place an additional side bet. If the dealer has "blackjack," the player receives a payout of 2 to 1 on the side bet, but loses the initial bet. If the dealer does not have blackjack, the side bet is lost and play continues.

   c. Splitting pairs—if the player has a pair, he or she may double the bet and play two hands.

The Identification, Environment, and Data Divisions

CHAPTER OUTLINE

Overview
COBOL Notation
Identification Division
Environment Division
    CONFIGURATION SECTION
    INPUT-OUTPUT SECTION
Data Division
    FILE SECTION
        File Description (FD)
        Record Description
        PICTURE Clause
        Level Numbers
        Assumed Decimal Point
    WORKING-STORAGE SECTION
        VALUE Clause
The Tuition Billing Program
    Programming Specifications
    COBOL Entries
Limitations of COBOL-74
Summary
Fill-in
True/False
Problems

OBJECTIVES

After reading this chapter you will be able to:

■ Describe the COBOL notation and determine the appropriate syntax for any statement.

■ Complete the Identification Division of a COBOL program.

■ Complete the Environment Division of a COBOL program.

■ Code a record description to show hierarchical relationships among fields containing numeric and alphanumeric entries.

■ Code a Working-Storage Section to define various print lines.

■ Explain the use of an assumed decimal point.

OVERVIEW

The overall approach of this book is to provide a rapid introduction to computer programming; thus we presented a complete COBOL program in Chapter 1. Our objective at that time was to put you on the computer immediately, without too much concern for the syntactical rules, which you must eventually master.

We move now to a formal study of COBOL, beginning with a notation that fully explains the variations permitted within any COBOL statement. The chapter focuses on the Identification, Environment, and Data Divisions, and concludes with a COBOL listing expanding on this material.

COBOL Notation

COBOL is an English-like language with inherent flexibility in the way a particular entry may be expressed. In other words, there are a number of different, but equally acceptable, ways to say the same thing. It is necessary, therefore, to develop a standard notation to provide a clear and unambiguous means of indicating precisely what is, and is not, permitted within any given statement. The notation is illustrated in Figure 4.1 and adheres to the following conventions:

1. Lowercase letters signify programmer-supplied information—for example, identifier-1 or literal-1.

2. Uppercase letters indicate reserved words—for example, IF, GREATER, or THAN.

3. Uppercase letters that are underlined are required; uppercase letters that are not underlined are optional reserved words.

4. Brackets [ ] symbolize an optional entry—for example, [NOT].

5. Braces { } imply that one of the enclosed items must be chosen—for example, a choice is required between identifier-1, literal-1, and arithmetic expression-1.

6. Three dots . . . mean that the last syntactical unit can be repeated an arbitrary number of times.

Figure 4.1 COBOL Notation

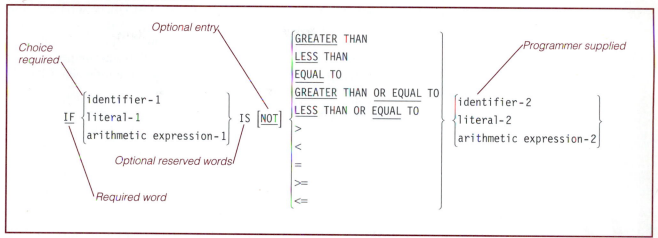

The example in Figure 4.1 is associated with the condition portion in the IF statement. IF is underlined and appears in capital letters, indicating it is a required reserved word. It is followed by a set of braces containing three options, one of which must be chosen. The reserved word IS appears in uppercase letters but is not underlined, meaning its use is optional. The brackets surrounding NOT imply that the clause is optional, but if the clause is chosen, NOT is required because it is underlined.

The next set of braces indicates a second mandatory choice among five relationships: GREATER THAN, GREATER THAN OR EQUAL TO, LESS THAN, LESS THAN OR EQUAL TO, or EQUAL TO. The reserved words THAN and TO are not underlined and are, therefore, optional. Alternatively, you can choose the appropriate symbol: >, >= <, <=, or = instead of spelling out the relationship. The third set of braces indicates yet another choice, this time from the entries identifier-2, literal-2, and arithmetic expression-2.

Returning to the engineering senior problem of Chapter 1, in which STU-MAJOR is compared to engineering, we see that all of the following are acceptable as the condition portion of the IF statement:

```
IF STU-MAJOR IS EQUAL TO 'ENGINEERING'
IF STU-MAJOR EQUAL 'ENGINEERING'
IF 'ENGINEERING' IS EQUAL TO STU-MAJOR
IF STU-MAJOR = 'ENGINEERING'
```

Identification Division

The **IDENTIFICATION DIVISION** is the first of the four divisions in a COBOL program. Its function is to provide identifying information about the program, such as author, date written, and security. The division consists of a division header and up to six paragraphs:

```
IDENTIFICATION DIVISION.
PROGRAM-ID.        program-name.(Required)
[AUTHOR.           [comment-entry] ... ]
[INSTALLATION.     [comment-entry] ... ]
[DATE-WRITTEN.     [comment-entry] ... ]
[DATE-COMPILED.    [comment-entry] ... ]
[SECURITY.         [comment-entry] ... ]
```

The division header and PROGRAM-ID paragraph are the only required entries. The five remaining paragraphs are optional (as indicated by the COBOL notation), and only the DATE-COMPILED paragraph merits special mention. If the paragraph is specified, the compiler will insert the current date during program compilation. (The paragraph is redundant, however, since most compilers automatically print the date of compilation on the top of each page.) A completed Identification Division is shown:

```
IDENTIFICATION DIVISION.
PROGRAM-ID.             FIRSTTRY.
AUTHOR.                 ROBERT  T.  GRAUER.
INSTALLATION.           UNIVERSITY OF MIAMI.
DATE-WRITTEN.           MARCH 16, 1999.
DATE-COMPILED.          The compiler supplies compilation date.
SECURITY.               TOP SECRET-INSTRUCTORS  ONLY.
```

Coding for the Identification Division follows the general rules described in Chapter 2. The division header and paragraph names begin in the A margin, with all corresponding entries beginning in or past column 12 (B margin).

Environment Division

The ENVIRONMENT DIVISION contains two sections:

1. The CONFIGURATION SECTION identifies the computers for compiling and executing the program, usually one and the same.

2. The INPUT-OUTPUT SECTION associates the files in the COBOL program with the files known to the operating system.

The nature of these functions makes the Environment Division dependent on the computer on which you are working; that is, the Environment Division for a program on a VAX is different from that for a program on an IBM mainframe.

Configuration Section

The **CONFIGURATION SECTION** is enclosed in brackets within the COBOL notation and is therefore optional. An abbreviated format is shown below:

```
[CONFIGURATION SECTION.
[SOURCE-COMPUTER.  computer-name.]
[OBJECT-COMPUTER.  computer-name.]]
```

The section header and paragraph names begin in the A margin whereas the computer-name entries begin in or past column 12. The CONFIGURATION SECTION does little to enhance (the documentation of) a COBOL program and is typically omitted.

Input-Output Section

The **INPUT-OUTPUT SECTION** associates the files in a COBOL program with files known to the operating system. It contains a FILE-CONTROL paragraph, which in turn contains a **SELECT** statement for every file in the program. Syntactically it has the format:

```
[INPUT-OUTPUT SECTION.
 FILE-CONTROL.
      SELECT file-name-1 ASSIGN TO implementor-name.]
```

A program may be written without any files and hence the INPUT-OUTPUT section is optional. (See Chapter 10 on screen I/O for an example of a program written without any files.)

The section header (INPUT-OUTPUT SECTION) and paragraph name (FILE-CONTROL) begin in the A margin (columns 8 through 11). The SELECT statements for the individual files begin in the B margin (column 12 and beyond).

The precise format of the ***implementor-name*** in the SELECT statement varies from compiler to compiler, with the example below taken from lines 8 through 11 in the engineering senior problem.

```
INPUT-OUTPUT SECTION.
FILE-CONTROL.
    SELECT STUDENT-FILE    ASSIGN TO SYSIN
        ORGANIZATION IS LINE SEQUENTIAL.
    SELECT PRINT-FILE      ASSIGN TO SYSOUT
        ORGANIZATION IS LINE SEQUENTIAL.
```

The dependence of the Environment Division on the individual computer installation bears repeating. You should consult either your instructor or your computer center for the proper statements to use in your program. For example, the use of ORGANIZATION IS LINE SEQUENTIAL is necessary for personal computers but not for mainframes.

Data Division

The Data Division describes the data items that appear in a program. It contains several sections, two of which, the FILE SECTION and the WORKING-STORAGE SECTION, will be discussed in this chapter. Two other sections, the SCREEN SECTION and the LINKAGE SECTION, are presented in later chapters.

File Section

The **FILE SECTION** is the first section in the Data Division and contains a file description (FD) for every file previously defined in a SELECT statement in the Environment Division. (If, however, a program is written without any files, then the FILE SECTION will not appear.) The file description is followed by the associated record description which is accomplished through PICTURE clauses and level numbers. Each of these elements is discussed in turn.

File Description (FD)   The ***file description*** (FD) provides information about the physical characteristics of a file. It contains four clauses, all of which are optional, and which may appear in any order. The final entry, however, must be terminated by a period. An abbreviated format for the file description is as follows:

```
FD  file-name
      [BLOCK CONTAINS integer-1 RECORDS ]
      [RECORD CONTAINS integer-1 CHARACTERS]
      [      {RECORDS ARE}  {OMITTED }  ]
      [LABEL {RECORD IS  }  {STANDARD}  ]

      [DATA RECORD IS data-name-1].
```

The **BLOCK CONTAINS** clause is used to speed up input/output operations for files on tape or disk, by reducing the number of physical records (blocks) in a file, and thus reducing the number of times the input/output device is accessed. In other words, it is more efficient to access a disk once and read a block containing 10 records, than it is to access the disk 10 times and read each record individually. The *blocking factor* is defined as the number of *logical records* in a *physical record*. The concept is illustrated in Figure 4.2 where the records of Figure 4.2a are unblocked, whereas those in Figures 4.2b and 4.2c have blocking factors of 2 and 3, respectively.

The higher the blocking factor, the fewer the number of physical records, and the more efficient the processing. Thus, the blocking factor should always be as high as possible, within the limitations of the physical device. The actual determination of the blocking factor need not concern us now; what is important is the implementation of blocking in a COBOL program.

Assume, for example, a blocking factor of 5, with the associated entry, BLOCK CONTAINS 5 RECORDS. The initial execution of the READ statement places a block of 5 logical records in memory, with only the first record available to the program. The second (third, fourth, and fifth) execution of the READ statement makes a new logical record available, without a corresponding physical operation taking place. In similar fashion the sixth execution of the READ statement will bring a new physical record into the I/O area, with new logical records made available on the seventh through tenth executions of the READ statement. All of this is automatically done for the programmer as long as the BLOCK CONTAINS statement is specified in the COBOL FD.

Figure 4.2   Blocked versus Unblocked Records

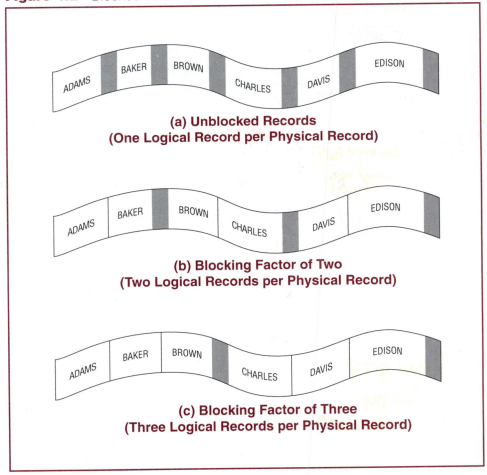

(a) Unblocked Records
(One Logical Record per Physical Record)

(b) Blocking Factor of Two
(Two Logical Records per Physical Record)

(c) Blocking Factor of Three
(Three Logical Records per Physical Record)

COBOL programs that are written to run on an IBM mainframe typically contain the entry, BLOCK CONTAINS 0 RECORDS. This entry does not mean what it says literally, but rather that the block size will be entered at execution time.

The **RECORD CONTAINS** clause indicates the number of characters in a record and is useful for documentation. The clause also causes the compiler to verify that the sizes of the individual data items sum to the stated value.

The **LABEL RECORDS** clause determines whether or not label processing is to take place. Label records appear at the beginning and end of files stored on tape or disk, and contain information about the file, such as the date created, the logical record size and the block size. Label records are created automatically whenever a file is opened as output and are checked automatically whenever a file is opened as input. Label processing is necessary to ensure that the proper file is being processed. The LABEL RECORDS clause is optional and its omission defaults to standard labels.

The DATA RECORD clause specifies the name of the 01 entry (or entries) associated with the particular file. It has limited value in documentation and has no other function. An example of a completed FD is shown below:

```
FD  STUDENT-FILE
        BLOCK CONTAINS 10 RECORDS
        RECORD CONTAINS 43 CHARACTERS
        LABEL RECORDS ARE STANDARD
        DATA RECORD IS STUDENT-IN.
```

Record Description   A file description is followed by an associated *record description* that conveys the following information:

1. The size and type of each field within a record

2. The order in which the fields appear

3. The relationship of the fields to one another

through a combination of PICTURE clauses and level numbers.

PICTURE Clause   A **PICTURE** clause describes the size and type of a field. The *size* of a field is equivalent to the number of characters (positions) in the field. The *type* of field is either numeric or alphanumeric, and is denoted by a 9 or an X, respectively, in the associated PICTURE clause. A *numeric item* can contain the numbers 0–9, whereas an *alphanumeric item* may contain A–Z (alphabetic), 0–9 (numeric), and/or special characters.

The size of a field is indicated by the number of times the 9 or X is repeated. A data item with a picture of XXXX or X(4) is a four-position alphanumeric field. In similar fashion 999 or 9(3) denotes a three-position numeric field. (Alphabetic data items, denoted by an A in the associated PICTURE clause, are seldom used because even a field as simple as a person's name can contain apostrophes or hyphens, which are alphanumeric rather than alphabetic in nature.)

Level Numbers   *Level numbers* describe the relationships that exist between fields within a record. Each field is classified as either a group item or an elementary item. A *group item* is a field that can be further divided—an *elementary item* can not.

Consider, for example, Figure 4.3, which depicts a student examination record. The field STUDENT-NAME is a group item because it is divided into three fields: LAST-NAME, FIRST-NAME, and INIT. LAST-NAME, FIRST-NAME, and INIT, however, are elementary items, since they are not further divided. In similar fashion, SS-NUM is an elementary item. EXAM-SCORES is a group item, as are MATH and ENGLISH. ALG, GEO, READ, etc., are elementary items.

Figure 4.3   Student Exam Record

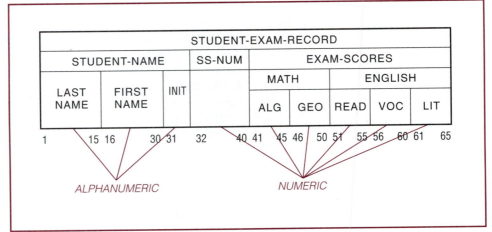

Level numbers and PICTURE clauses are used in Figure 4.4 to define a record corresponding to the STUDENT-EXAM-RECORD in Figure 4.3. Two equivalent sets of COBOL statements (Figures 4.4a and 4.4b) are presented and follow the rules below:

1. The level numbers within a record description can assume any value from 01 to 49 inclusive.

2. The level number 01 denotes the record as a whole.

3. Any level number from 02 to 49 can be used for field(s) within the record, so long as elementary items have a numerically higher number than the group item to which they belong.

4. An elementary item *must* have a PICTURE clause—a group item *cannot* have a PICTURE clause.

In Figure 4.4 STUDENT-EXAM-RECORD has a level number of 01 to indicate the record as a whole. STUDENT-NAME is a subfield of STUDENT-EXAM-RECORD; hence it has a higher level number (05). LAST-NAME, FIRST-NAME, and MID-INITIAL are subordinate to STUDENT-NAME and thus have a higher level number (10). SOC-SEC-NUM and EXAM-SCORES are also subfields of STUDENT-EXAM-RECORD and have the same level number as STUDENT-NAME. EXAM-SCORES is subdivided into two group items, MATH and ENGLISH, which in turn are further subdivided into elementary items.

Every elementary item must have a PICTURE clause, whereas a group item cannot have a PICTURE clause. Thus, LAST-NAME has the entry PICTURE IS X(15) to denote a 15-position alphanumeric field; STUDENT-NAME, however, is a group item and does not have a PICTURE clause. The parentheses in a PICTURE clause imply repetition; that is, the entry 9(5) for ALGEBRA depicts a 5-position numeric field.

There is considerable latitude within COBOL as to the specification of level numbers and PICTURE clauses. You can, for example, choose any level numbers from 02 to 49 to describe subordinate fields; for example, 04, 08, and 12 are used in Figure 4.4b as opposed to the levels 05, 10, and 15 in Figure 4.4a. The 01 level is used in both figures for the record as a whole.

Figure 4.4 Level Numbers and PICTURE Clauses

```
01  STUDENT-EXAM-RECORD.
    05   STUDENT-NAME.
         10   LAST-NAME        PICTURE IS X(15).
         10   FIRST-NAME       PICTURE IS X(15).
         10   MID-INITIAL      PICTURE IS X.
    05   SOC-SEC-NUM           PICTURE IS 9(9).
    05   EXAM-SCORES.
         10   MATH.
              15   ALGEBRA     PICTURE IS 9(5).
              15   GEOMETRY    PICTURE IS 9(5).
         10   ENGLISH.
              15   READING     PICTURE IS 9(5).
              15   VOCABULARY  PICTURE IS 9(5).
              15   LITERATURE  PICTURE IS 9(5).
```

(a) Initial Coding

```
01  STUDENT-EXAM-RECORD.
    04   STUDENT-NAME.
         08   LAST-NAME        PIC X(15).
         08   FIRST-NAME       PIC X(15).
         08   MID-INITIAL      PIC X.
    04   SOC-SEC-NUM           PIC 9(9).
    04   EXAM-SCORES.
         08   MATH.
              12   ALGEBRA     PIC 99999.
              12   GEOMETRY    PIC 99999.
         08   ENGLISH.
              12   READING     PIC 99999.
              12   VOCABULARY  PIC 99999.
              12   LITERATURE  PIC 99999.
```

(b) Alternative Specification

The PICTURE clause itself can assume any one of four forms: PICTURE IS, PICTURE, PIC IS, or PIC. Parentheses may be used to signal repetition of a picture type; that is, X(3) is equivalent to XXX. Figure 4.4b is the exact equivalent of Figure 4.4a with emphasis on the aforementioned flexibility.

Assumed Decimal Point Incoming numeric data may not contain *actual* decimal points. On first reading, that statement may be somewhat hard to accept. How, for example, does one read a field containing dollars and cents? The answer is an assumed (implied) decimal point as illustrated in the COBOL entry:

```
05  HOURLY-RATE   PICTURE IS 99V99.
```

Everything is familiar except the V embedded in the PICTURE clause. The V means an ***implied decimal point***; that is, HOURLY-RATE is a four-digit (there are

Figure 4.5   Assumed Decimal Point

INCOMING RECORD:	DATA DIVISION RECORD DESCRIPTION:	VALUES:
9˅87|65˅4|3|˅210	01 INCOMING-DATA-RECORD.	
	05 FIELD-A PIC 9V99. ⟶	9.87
	05 FIELD-B PIC 9V99. ⟶	65.4
	05 FIELD-C PIC 9. ⟶	3
	05 FIELD-D PIC V999. ⟶	.210

four 9's) numeric field, with two of the digits coming after the decimal point. Simply stated, the V indicates the position of the decimal point.

To check your understanding, assume that 9876543210 is found in positions 1–10 of an incoming record and that the following Data Division entries apply:

```
01   INCOMING-DATA-RECORD.
     05   FIELD-A         PIC 9V99.
     05   FIELD-B         PIC 99V9.
     05   FIELD-C         PIC 9.
     05   FIELD-D         PIC V999.
```

The values of FIELD-A, FIELD-B, FIELD-C, and FIELD-D are 9.87, 65.4, 3, and .210, respectively, as shown in Figure 4.5. FIELD-A is contained in the first three positions with two of the digits to the right of the decimal point. FIELD-B is contained in the next three positions (i.e., 6, 5, and 4) with one digit to the right of the decimal point. FIELD-C is contained in position 7 with no decimal places. Finally, FIELD-D is contained in positions 8, 9, and 10, with all three to the right of the decimal.

Working-Storage Section

Setting aside space for variable needed but are not part of the file

The **WORKING-STORAGE SECTION** defines any data name that was not previously referenced in the FILE SECTION, that is, any data name that does not appear in a file. The WORKING-STORAGE SECTION contains data names to store the results of calculations, switches to control the execution of performed paragraphs, and/or data names to hold constants needed by the program. The WORKING-STORAGE SECTION will also define various print lines (a heading, detail, and/or total line) required by a program.

Figure 4.6 contains a WORKING-STORAGE SECTION for an expanded version of the engineering senior program to count the number of qualified students. There are separate record descriptions for the counters and constants needed by the program, as well as a separate record description (01 entry) for each type of print line.

A **FILLER** entry defines a field that is not referenced elsewhere in the COBOL program. The layout of DETAIL-LINE, for example, begins with eight spaces, followed by the value of PRINT-NAME, an additional 10 spaces, the value of PRINT-MAJOR, and a final set of 74 spaces to complete the print line. The three fields containing spaces are not referenced anywhere else in the program yet need to be accounted for—hence the FILLER entry.

The word FILLER is optional, however, and could be omitted as shown in the definition of TOTAL-LINE. The entries under TOTAL-LINE look strange initially, but make perfect sense when your realize that the "missing" FILLER entries are not

Figure 4.6 The Working-Storage Section

```
WORKING-STORAGE SECTION.

01   COUNTERS-AND-SWITCHES.
     05   TOTAL-STUDENTS          PIC 9(3)      VALUE ZEROS.
     05   DATA-REMAINS-SWITCH     PIC X(2)      VALUE SPACES.

01   PROGRAM-CONSTANTS.
     05   REQUIRED-CREDITS        PIC 999       VALUE 110.
     05   REQUIRED-MAJOR          PIC X(10)     VALUE 'ENGINEERING'.
     05   REQUIRED-GPA            PIC 9V99      VALUE 3.00.

01   HEADING-LINE.
     05   FILLER                  PIC X(10)     VALUE SPACES.
     05   FILLER                  PIC X(12)     VALUE 'STUDENT NAME'.
     05   FILLER                  PIC X(110)    VALUE SPACES.

01   DETAIL-LINE.
     05   FILLER                  PIC X(8)      VALUE SPACES.
     05   PRINT-NAME              PIC X(25).
     05   FILLER                  PIC X(10)     VALUE SPACES.
     05   PRINT-MAJOR             PIC X(15).
     05   FILLER                  PIC X(74)     VALUE SPACES.
                                                                    FILLER IS OPTIONAL IN COBOL-85
01   TOTAL-LINE.
     05                           PIC X(4)      VALUE SPACES
     05                           PIC X(14)     VALUE 'TOTAL STUDENTS'.
     05                           PIC X(2)      VALUE SPACES.
     05   TOT-STUDENTS            PIC 9(3)      VALUE ZEROS.
     05                           PIC X(110)    VALUE SPACES.

01   DASHED-LINE
     05   FILLER                  PIC X(132)    VALUE ALL '-'.
```

referenced in the Procedure Division, and hence their omission has no effect on the remainder of the program.

VALUE Clause The **VALUE** clause initializes the contents of a data name within the WORKING-STORAGE SECTION and has the general form:

VALUE IS literal

Literals are of three types—numeric, nonnumeric, and figurative constants. Numeric literals—for example, 110 or 3.00—contain a number and are used in calculations. Nonnumeric literals, such as 'ENGINEERING', contain a character string and are enclosed in apostrophes or quotations marks. (Additional rules for numeric and nonnumeric literals were presented in Chapter 1.)

A *figurative constant* (ZERO or SPACE) is a COBOL reserved word with a pre-assigned value. The singular and plural forms of a figurative constant are interchangeable; that is, one can use SPACE or SPACES, or ZERO, ZEROS, or ZEROES.

Figurative constants are *not* enclosed in quotation marks. COBOL also permits the use of the **ALL** literal to repeat a character string.

The VALUE clause associated with a particular data name must be consistent with the corresponding PICTURE clause; that is, it is *incorrect* to use a nonnumeric literal with a numeric picture clause or a numeric literal with a nonnumeric picture. Consider:

```
REQUIRED-CREDITS    PIC 999     VALUE 110.              (valid)
REQUIRED-MAJOR      PIC X(10)   VALUE 'ENGINEERING'.    (valid)
REQUIRED-CREDITS    PIC 999     VALUE '110'.            (invalid)
REQUIRED-MAJOR      PIC X(10)   VALUE ENGINEERING.      (invalid)
```

REQUIRED-CREDITS is defined as a numeric item and must have a numeric value. In similar fashion, REQUIRED-MAJOR is defined as alphanumeric and requires an alphanumeric VALUE clause.

The Tuition Billing Program

The tuition billing program was introduced in Chapter 3 in conjunction with structured programming and design. The stubs program did not, however, show the detailed output as presented in the programming specifications, because the objective at that time was only to test the overall flow of the program. It is necessary, therefore, to return to the original specifications to develop the Identification, Environment, and Data Divisions. We will, however, amplify the development of the Data Division by presenting three figures that relate various portions of the programming specifications to their associated COBOL entries.

Programming Specifications

Figure 4.7a displays the input record layout from the programming specifications; Figure 4.7b shows the corresponding FD and record description. STUDENT-RECORD corresponds to the record as a whole and thus is assigned the level number 01. STUDENT-RECORD in turn is divided into the subordinate fields STU-NAME (which is further divided into STU-LAST-NAME and STU-INITIALS), STU-CREDITS, STU-UNION-MEMBER, and STU-SCHOLARSHIP. STUDENT-RECORD and STU-NAME are group items and do not have a PICTURE clause; all of the other data names are elementary items and have a PICTURE clause. An implied decimal point appears within the PICTURE clause for STU-GPA.

Figure 4.8a excerpts the processing specifications for the computation of a student's bill; Figure 4.8b shows the associated record description as it appears in WORKING-STORAGE. The entries in Figure 4.8b are not required by COBOL per se, and are included to facilitate documentation and maintenance. It would be possible, for example, to use the constants 200 and 25 in the Procedure Division rather than the corresponding data names PRICE-PER-CREDIT and UNION-FEE. The data names, however, facilitate program maintenance; that is, a change in the value of a constant is easier to implement in the Data Division than (in multiple statements) in the Procedure Division.

Figure 4.9a contains the programming specifications for the heading and detail lines; Figure 4.9b shows the associated COBOL entries. Note carefully the exact correspondence between the COBOL entries and report layout. The print layout calls for 10 spaces between the literals STUDENT NAME and CREDITS; thus there is a 10 position FILLER entry between these literals within the COBOL entries.

Figure 4.7 Development of a COBOL Program (File Section)

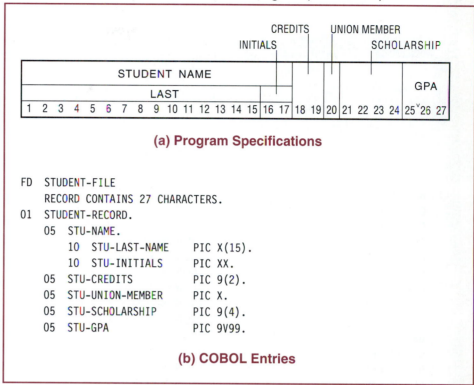

(a) Program Specifications

```
FD  STUDENT-FILE
    RECORD CONTAINS 27 CHARACTERS.
01  STUDENT-RECORD.
    05  STU-NAME.
        10  STU-LAST-NAME     PIC X(15).
        10  STU-INITIALS      PIC XX.
    05  STU-CREDITS           PIC 9(2).
    05  STU-UNION-MEMBER      PIC X.
    05  STU-SCHOLARSHIP       PIC 9(4).
    05  STU-GPA               PIC 9V99.
```

(b) COBOL Entries

Figure 4.8 Development of a COBOL Program (Constants and Rates)

1. Calculate tuition due at the rate of $200 per credit.
2. The union fee is $25.
3. Compute the activity fee based on the number of credits taken; $25 for 6 credits or less, $50 for 7 to 12 credits, and $75 for more than 12 credits.
4. Award a scholarship equal to the amount in the incoming record if, and only if, the GPA is greater than 2.5.

(a) Excerpt from the Program Specifications

```
WORKING-STORAGE SECTION.
01  CONSTANTS-AND-RATES.
    05  PRICE-PER-CREDIT      PIC 9(3)   VALUE 200.
    05  UNION-FEE             PIC 9(2)   VALUE 25.
    05  ACTIVITY-FEES.
        10  1ST-ACTIVITY-FEE  PIC 99     VALUE 25.
        10  1ST-CREDIT-LIMIT  PIC 99     VALUE 6.
        10  2ND-ACTIVITY-FEE  PIC 99     VALUE 50.
        10  2ND-CREDIT-LIMIT  PIC 99     VALUE 12.
        10  3RD-ACTIVITY-FEE  PIC 99     VALUE 75.
    05  MINIMUM-SCHOLAR-GPA   PIC 9V9    VALUE 2.5.
```

(b) COBOL Entries

Figure 4.9   Development of a COBOL Program (Print Lines)

		1	2	3	4	5	6	7	8
1	STUDENT NAME		CREDITS	TUITION	UNION FEE	ACT FEE	SCHOLARSHIP	TOTAL BILL	
2									
3	XXXXXXXXXXXXXX	99	99	999999	999	999	99999	999999	
4	XXXXXXXXXXXXXX	XX	99	999999	999	999	99999	999999	
5									
6									

(a) Report Layout

```
01  HEADING-LINE.
    05  FILLER              PIC X        VALUE SPACES.
    05  FILLER              PIC X(12)    VALUE 'STUDENT NAME'.
    05  FILLER              PIC X(10)    VALUE SPACES.
    05  FILLER              PIC X(7)     VALUE 'CREDITS'.
    05  FILLER              PIC X(2)     VALUE SPACES.
    05  FILLER              PIC X(7)     VALUE 'TUITION'.
    05  FILLER              PIC X(2)     VALUE SPACES.
    05  FILLER              PIC X(9)     VALUE 'UNION FEE'.
    05  FILLER              PIC X(2)     VALUE SPACES.
    05  FILLER              PIC X(7)     VALUE 'ACT FEE'.
    05  FILLER              PIC X(2)     VALUE SPACES.
    05  FILLER              PIC X(11)    VALUE 'SCHOLARSHIP'.
    05  FILLER              PIC X(2)     VALUE SPACES.
    05  FILLER              PIC X(10)    VALUE 'TOTAL BILL'.
    05  FILLER              PIC X(48)    VALUE SPACES.

01  DETAIL-LINE.
    05  FILLER              PIC X        VALUE SPACES.
    05  DET-LAST-NAME       PIC X(15).
    05  FILLER              PIC X(2)     VALUE SPACES.
    05  DET-INITIALS        PIC X(2).
    05  FILLER              PIC X(5)     VALUE SPACES.
    05  DET-CREDITS         PIC 9(2).
    05  FILLER              PIC X(6)     VALUE SPACES.
    05  DET-TUITION         PIC 9(6).
    05  FILLER              PIC X(7)     VALUE SPACES.
    05  DET-UNION-FEE       PIC 9(3).
    05  FILLER              PIC X(6)     VALUE SPACES.
    05  DET-ACTIVITY-FEE    PIC 9(3).
    05  FILLER              PIC X(8)     VALUE SPACES.
    05  DET-SCHOLARSHIP     PIC 9(5).
    05  FILLER              PIC X(6)     VALUE SPACES.
    05  DET-IND-BILL        PIC 9(6).
    05  FILLER              PIC X(49)    VALUE SPACES.
```

(b) COBOL Entries

COBOL Entries

Figure 4.10 contains the completed entries for the first three divisions. (The completed Procedure Division appears at the end of Chapter 5.) The Identification Division is unchanged from the stubs program in Chapter 3 and contains only the required PROGRAM-ID paragraph and an optional AUTHOR paragraph. The Environment Division has expanded slightly to include an additional SELECT statement for the print file (lines 10 and 11).

The Data Division, however, has grown significantly. The FILE SECTION contains the FD for the incoming student record (lines 15 and 16) followed by the associated record description in lines 17 through 24. A file description has also been added for PRINT-FILE. Note, too, the correspondence between the SELECT statements in the Environment Division and the associated FD entries in the Data Division.

The programming specifications call for multiple calculations for each student (tuition, union fee, activity fee, scholarship) as well as university totals for each item. Each of these calculations requires a separate data name in WORKING-STORAGE to store the result. Observe, therefore, the definition of the elementary items IND-TUITION, IND-ACTIVITY-FEE, and so on, which appear together (for convenience) under the group item INDIVIDUAL-CALCULATIONS (line 33). In similar fashion, the elementary items UNI-TUITION, UNI-ACTIVITY-FEE, and so on, appear under the group item UNIVERSITY-TOTALS (line 40). There is also a separate 01 entry to hold the constants and rates required by the program (lines 47–56).

The program requires several different types of print lines—a heading line, a detail line, and a total line, each with a different format. Thus, there are separate 01 entries for HEADING-LINE (lines 58–73), DETAIL-LINE (lines 75–92), and TOTAL-LINE in lines 107–121. Note, too, the separate entry for DASH-LINE (lines 94–105), which makes use of the ALL literal to establish a row of dashes. Look carefully at the use of the FILLER and associated VALUE clauses in each of these print lines, to create the necessary literal information, and the correspondence between these entries and the COBOL specifications.

Figure 4.10   Identification, Environment, and Data Divisions for Tuition Billing Program

```
1        IDENTIFICATION DIVISION.
2        PROGRAM-ID.     TUITION5.
3        AUTHOR.         CAROL VAZQUEZ VILLAR.
4
5        ENVIRONMENT DIVISION.
6        INPUT-OUTPUT SECTION.
7        FILE-CONTROL.
8           SELECT STUDENT-FILE  ASSIGN TO SYSIN
9              ORGANIZATION IS LINE SEQUENTIAL.
10          SELECT PRINT-FILE    ASSIGN TO SYSOUT
11             ORGANIZATION IS LINE SEQUENTIAL.
12
```

Figure 4.10   Identification, Environment, and Data Divisions for Tuition Billing Program *(continued)*

```
13      DATA DIVISION.
14      FILE SECTION.
15      FD  STUDENT-FILE
16          RECORD CONTAINS 27 CHARACTERS.
17      01  STUDENT-RECORD.
18          05  STU-NAME.                              ─── STU-NAME is a group item with two elementary items
19              10  STU-LAST-NAME    PIC X(15).
20              10  STU-INITIALS     PIC XX.
21          05  STU-CREDITS          PIC 9(2).
22          05  STU-UNION-MEMBER     PIC X.
23          05  STU-SCHOLARSHIP      PIC 9(4).         ─── Implied decimal point
24          05  STU-GPA              PIC 9V99.
25
26      FD  PRINT-FILE
27          RECORD CONTAINS 132 CHARACTERS.
28      01  PRINT-LINE               PIC X(132).
29
30      WORKING-STORAGE SECTION.
31      01  DATA-REMAINS-SWITCH      PIC X(2)   VALUE SPACES.
32
33      01  INDIVIDUAL-CALCULATIONS.
34          05  IND-TUITION          PIC 9(4)   VALUE ZEROS.   ─── VALUE clauses initialize data names
35          05  IND-ACTIVITY-FEE     PIC 9(2)   VALUE ZEROS.
36          05  IND-UNION-FEE        PIC 9(2)   VALUE ZEROS.
37          05  IND-SCHOLARSHIP      PIC 9(4)   VALUE ZEROS.
38          05  IND-BILL             PIC 9(6)   VALUE ZEROS.
39
40      01  UNIVERSITY-TOTALS.
41          05  UNI-TUITION          PIC 9(6)   VALUE ZEROS.
42          05  UNI-UNION-FEE        PIC 9(4)   VALUE ZEROS.
43          05  UNI-ACTIVITY-FEE     PIC 9(4)   VALUE ZEROS.
44          05  UNI-SCHOLARSHIP      PIC 9(6)   VALUE ZEROS.
45          05  UNI-IND-BILL         PIC 9(6)   VALUE ZEROS.
46
47      01  CONSTANTS-AND-RATES.
48          05  PRICE-PER-CREDIT     PIC 9(3)   VALUE 200.
49          05  UNION-FEE            PIC 9(2)   VALUE 25.
50          05  ACTIVITY-FEES.
51              10  1ST-ACTIVITY-FEE PIC 99     VALUE 25.
52              10  1ST-CREDIT-LIMIT PIC 99     VALUE 6.
53              10  2ND-ACTIVITY-FEE PIC 99     VALUE 50.
54              10  2ND-CREDIT-LIMIT PIC 99     VALUE 12.
55              10  3RD-ACTIVITY-FEE PIC 99     VALUE 75.
56          05  MINIMUM-SCHOLAR-GPA  PIC 9V9    VALUE 2.5.
57                                              ─── Separate areas for heading and detail lines
58      01  HEADING-LINE.
59          05  FILLER               PIC X      VALUE SPACES.
60          05  FILLER               PIC X(12) VALUE 'STUDENT NAME'.
61          05  FILLER               PIC X(10) VALUE SPACES.
62          05  FILLER               PIC X(7)  VALUE 'CREDITS'.
```

Figure 4.10 *(continued)*

```
63              05  FILLER              PIC X(2)   VALUE SPACES.
64              05  FILLER              PIC X(7)   VALUE 'TUITION'.
65              05  FILLER              PIC X(2)   VALUE SPACES.
66              05  FILLER              PIC X(9)   VALUE 'UNION FEE'.
67              05  FILLER              PIC X(2)   VALUE SPACES.
68              05  FILLER              PIC X(7)   VALUE 'ACT FEE'.
69              05  FILLER              PIC X(2)   VALUE SPACES.
70              05  FILLER              PIC X(11) VALUE 'SCHOLARSHIP'.
71              05  FILLER              PIC X(2)   VALUE SPACES.
72              05  FILLER              PIC X(10) VALUE 'TOTAL BILL'.
73              05  FILLER              PIC X(48) VALUE SPACES.
74
75          01  DETAIL-LINE.                                  ── Separate areas for heading and detail lines
76              05  FILLER              PIC X      VALUE SPACES.
77              05  DET-LAST-NAME       PIC X(15).
78              05  FILLER              PIC X(2)   VALUE SPACES.
79              05  DET-INITIALS        PIC X(2).
80              05  FILLER              PIC X(5)   VALUE SPACES.
81              05  DET-CREDITS         PIC 9(2).
82              05  FILLER              PIC X(6)   VALUE SPACES.
83              05  DET-TUITION         PIC 9(6).
84              05  FILLER              PIC X(7)   VALUE SPACES.
85              05  DET-UNION-FEE       PIC 9(3).
86              05  FILLER              PIC X(6)   VALUE SPACES.
87              05  DET-ACTIVITY-FEE    PIC 9(3).
88              05  FILLER              PIC X(8)   VALUE SPACES.
89              05  DET-SCHOLARSHIP     PIC 9(5).
90              05  FILLER              PIC X(6)   VALUE SPACES.
91              05  DET-IND-BILL        PIC 9(6).
92              05  FILLER              PIC X(49) VALUE SPACES.
93                                                            ── Separate areas for dash and total lines
94          01  DASH-LINE.
95              05  FILLER              PIC X(31) VALUE SPACES.
96              05  FILLER              PIC X(8)   VALUE ALL '-'.
97              05  FILLER              PIC X(2)   VALUE SPACES.
98              05  FILLER              PIC X(8)   VALUE ALL '-'.
99              05  FILLER              PIC X(2)   VALUE SPACES.
100             05  FILLER              PIC X(7)   VALUE ALL '-'.
101             05  FILLER              PIC X(6)   VALUE SPACES.
102             05  FILLER              PIC X(7)   VALUE ALL '-'.
103             05  FILLER              PIC X(5)   VALUE SPACES.
104             05  FILLER              PIC X(7)   VALUE ALL '-'.
105             05  FILLER              PIC X(49) VALUE SPACES.
106
107         01  TOTAL-LINE.
108             05  FILLER              PIC X(8)   VALUE SPACES.
109             05  FILLER              PIC X(17)
110                         VALUE 'UNIVERSITY TOTALS'.
111             05  FILLER              PIC X(8)   VALUE SPACES.
112             05  TOT-TUITION         PIC 9(6).
```

Figure 4.10 *(continued)*

```
113          05  FILLER          PIC X(6)  VALUE SPACES.
114          05  TOT-UNION-FEE    PIC 9(4).
115          05  FILLER          PIC X(5)  VALUE SPACES.
116          05  TOT-ACTIVITY-FEE PIC 9(4).
117          05  FILLER          PIC X(7)  VALUE SPACES.
118          05  TOT-SCHOLARSHIP  PIC 9(6).
119          05  FILLER          PIC X(6)  VALUE SPACES.
120          05  TOT-IND-BILL     PIC 9(6).
121          05  FILLER          PIC X(49) VALUE SPACES.
```

Limitations of COBOL-74

The CONFIGURATION SECTION, SOURCE-COMPUTER, and OBJECT-COMPUTER entries are optional in COBOL-85 but are required in COBOL-74. The LABEL RECORDS clause is optional in COBOL-85 but is required in COBOL-74.

The BLOCK CONTAINS clause is optional in both compilers, but its omission has different effects. Omitting the clause in COBOL-85 causes the system to take the blocking factor from the operating environment (and is equivalent to the IBM entry BLOCK CONTAINS 0 RECORDS). Omission of the clause in COBOL-74 defaults to the implementor-designated number, regardless of what was specified in the control statements to the operating system.

COBOL-85 allows two new relationships, GREATER THAN OR EQUAL TO and LESS THAN OR EQUAL TO, in the condition portion of an IF statement. These were not allowed in COBOL-74, which used NOT LESS THAN as the equivalent of GREATER THAN OR EQUAL TO.

The word FILLER is optional in COBOL-85, whereas it is required in COBOL-74.

SUMMARY

 **Points to Remember**

 COBOL notation is the standardized form used to express permissible COBOL formats. Uppercase letters indicate COBOL reserved words, whereas lowercase letters denote programmer-supplied information. Brackets [ ] imply an optional entry, whereas braces { } indicate a choice between required entries. Any underlined item is required.

 The PROGRAM-ID paragraph is the only required entry in the Identification Division; the AUTHOR paragraph is strongly recommended. The

Environment Division contains the FILE-CONTROL paragraph that defines the files used in a program through SELECT statements.

 The FILE SECTION contains a file description for every file previously defined in a SELECT statement in the Environment Division. The file description is followed by a record description to describe the fields within a file.

 The PICTURE clause indicates the size and type of a data name. An elementary item always has a PICTURE clause, whereas a group item does not. Level numbers assume values from 01 to 49 inclusive, with 01 assigned to the record as a whole. Level numbers need not be assigned consecutive values.

 The WORKING-STORAGE SECTION contains additional record descriptions for data names not found in the FILE SECTION. VALUE clauses assign an initial value to a data name of a numeric literal, a nonnumeric literal, or a figurative constant. (pg 83)

Key Words and Concepts

Alphanumeric item	Group item
Assumed (implied) decimal point	Heading line
Blocking factor	Level numbers
Braces	Logical record
Brackets	Numeric item
COBOL notation	Physical record
Detail line	Record description
Elementary item	Size
Figurative constant	Total line
File description	Type

COBOL Elements

ALL	INSTALLATION
ASSIGN	LABEL RECORDS
AUTHOR	PICTURE
BLOCK CONTAINS	PROGRAM-ID
DATA RECORD IS	RECORD CONTAINS
DATE-COMPILED	SECURITY
DATE-WRITTEN	SELECT
FD	SPACES
FILE SECTION	VALUE
FILE-CONTROL	WORKING-STORAGE SECTION
FILLER	ZEROS
INPUT-OUTPUT SECTION	

Fill-In

1. The _____ Division is the first division in a COBOL program.

2. The _____ paragraph is the only required entry in the Identification Division.

3. In the COBOL notation, _____ indicate that one of the enclosed elements must be included.

4. Required reserved words are written in _____ letters and are _____.

5. Lowercase letters indicate _____ _____ information.

6. The Environment Division contains _____ sections.

7. The _____ statement ties a programmer-chosen file name to a system name.

8. A _____ item is divided into one or more elementary items.

9. An elementary item always has a _____ clause.

10. Level numbers appearing under a 01 record may range from _____ to _____.

11. The Data Division contains the _____ and _____ sections.

12. The presence of a V in a numeric picture indicates an _____ decimal point.

13. Incoming numeric fields (<u>may/may not</u>) contain an actual decimal point.

14. _____ denotes a field that is not referenced by name.

15. The _____ _____ specifies the number of _____ records in one _____ record.

True/False

1. The Identification Division may contain up to six paragraphs.

2. The PROGRAM-ID paragraph is the only required paragraph in the Identification Division.

3. Square brackets indicate a required entry.

4. Braces imply that one of the enclosed entries must be chosen.

5. A COBOL program that runs successfully on a PC would also run successfully on a mainframe with no modification whatever.

6. A level number may assume any value from 01 to 49.

7. A 01-level entry cannot have a PICTURE clause.

8. All elementary items have a PICTURE clause.

9. A group item may have a PICTURE clause.

10. 01-level entries may appear in both the File and Working-Storage Sections of the Data Division.

11. A data name at the 10 level will always be an elementary item.

12. A data name at the 05 level may or may not have a PICTURE clause.

13. PICTURE, PICTURE IS, PIC, and PIC IS are all acceptable forms of the PICTURE clause.

14. PICTURE IS 9(3) and PICTURE IS 999 are equivalent entries.

15. The File Section is required in every COBOL program.

16. An incoming numeric field may contain an actual decimal point.

17. The RECORD CONTAINS clause is required in an FD.

P r o b l e m s

1. Consider the accompanying time card. Show an appropriate record description for this information in COBOL; use any PICTURE clauses you think appropriate.

Time-Record								
Name			Number	Date			Hours	
First	Middle	Last		MO	DA	YR		

2. In which division(s) do you find the
   - a. PROGRAM-ID paragraph?
   - b. FILE-CONTROL paragraph?
   - c. CONFIGURATION SECTION?
   - d. WORKING-STORAGE SECTION?
   - e. FILE SECTION?
   - f. FD's?
   - g. AUTHOR paragraph?
   - h. DATE-COMPILED paragraph?
   - i. INPUT-OUTPUT SECTION?
   - j. File names?
   - k. Level numbers?
   - l. SELECT statements?
   - m. VALUE clauses?
   - n. PICTURE clauses?

3. Given the following record layout:

```
01  EMPLOYEE-RECORD.
    05  SOC-SEC-NUMBER          PIC 9(9).
    05  EMPLOYEE-NAME.
        10  LAST-NAME           PIC X(12).
        10  FIRST-NAME          PIC X(10).
        10  MIDDLE-INIT         PIC X.
    05  FILLER                  PIC X.
    05  BIRTH-DATE.
        10  BIRTH-MONTH         PIC 99.
        10  BIRTH-DAY           PIC 99.
        10  BIRTH-YEAR          PIC 9(4).
    05  FILLER                  PIC X(3).
```

```
            05  EMPLOYEE-ADDRESS.
                10  NUMBER-AND-STREET.
                    15  HOUSE-NUMBER    PIC X(6).
                    15  STREET-NAME     PIC X(10).
                10  CITY-STATE-ZIP.
                    15  CITY            PIC X(10).
                    15  STATE           PIC X(4).
                    15  ZIP             PIC 9(5).
            05  FILLER                  PIC X(3).
```

a. List all group items.

b. List all elementary items.

c. State the record positions in which the following fields are found:

- SOC-SEC-NUMBER
- EMPLOYEE-NAME
- LAST-NAME
- FIRST-NAME
- MIDDLE-INIT
- BIRTH-DATE
- BIRTH-MONTH
- BIRTH-DAY
- BIRTH-YEAR
- EMPLOYEE-ADDRESS
- NUMBER-AND-STREET
- HOUSE-NUMBER
- STREET-NAME
- CITY-STATE-ZIP
- CITY
- STATE
- ZIP

4. Given the following record layout (assume that FIELD-I is the last entry under FIELD-A),

```
    01  FIELD-A
        05  FIELD-B
            10  FIELD-C
            10  FIELD-D
        05  FIELD-E
        05  FIELD-F
            10  FIELD-G
            10  FIELD-H
            10  FIELD-I
```

answer true or false.

a. FIELD-C is an elementary item.

b. FIELD-E is an elementary item.

c. FIELD-E should have a picture.

d. FIELD-F should have a picture.

e. FIELD-B must be larger than FIELD-C.

f. FIELD-C must be larger than FIELD-D.

g. FIELD-C must be larger than FIELD-H.

h. FIELD-B and FIELD-D end in the same column.

i. FIELD-A and FIELD-I end in the same column.

j. FIELD-E could be larger than FIELD-F.

k. FIELD-D could be larger than FIELD-E.

l. FIELD-F and FIELD-G start in the same column.

5. Use the COBOL notation introduced at the beginning of the chapter and the general format of the FD entry to determine whether the following are valid FD entries.

a. `FD EMPLOYEE-FILE.`

b. `FD EMPLOYEE-FILE`
   ```
        BLOCK CONTAINS 10 RECORDS
        RECORD CONTAINS 100 CHARACTERS
        LABEL RECORDS ARE STANDARD
        DATA RECORD IS EMPLOYEE-RECORD.
   ```

c. `FD EMPLOYEE-FILE`
   ```
        BLOCK 10 RECORDS
        RECORD 100 CHARACTERS
        LABEL RECORDS STANDARD
        DATA RECORD EMPLOYEE-RECORD.
   ```

6. Indicate whether each of the following entries is spelled correctly and whether it is syntactically valid.

a. ENVIRONMENT DIVISION

b. WORKING-STORAGE-SECTION

c. IDENTIFICATION-DIVISION

d. WRITTEN-BY

e. DATA-DIVISION

f. FILE SECTION

g. PROGRAM ID

h. DATE-WRITTEN

i. DATE-EXECUTED

j. INPUT-OUTPUT SECTION

k. FILE-CONTROL SECTION

l. DATE DIVISION

m. COMMENTS

The Procedure Division

CHAPTER OUTLINE

Overview
OPEN
CLOSE
READ
    Placement of the READ Statement
WRITE
STOP RUN
MOVE
    Restrictions on the MOVE Statement
    Alphanumeric Field to
        Alphanumeric Field
    Numeric Field to Numeric Field
    Group Moves
PERFORM
IF
    The ELSE Clause
    Indentation
EVALUATE
Arithmetic Statements

The ROUNDED Clause
The SIZE ERROR Clause
COMPUTE
ADD
SUBTRACT
MULTIPLY
DIVIDE
Programming Tip: Use the
    COMPUTE Statement
Assumed Decimal Point
The Tuition Billing Program
    Test Data
    Hierarchy Chart
COBOL Program Skeleton
Limitations of COBOL-74
Summary
Fill-in
True/False
Problems

OBJECTIVES

After reading this chapter you will be able to:

■ Write the OPEN, CLOSE, READ, and WRITE statements necessary for sequential file processing.

■ Describe the purpose of the priming (initial) READ statement, and place it correctly in the Procedure Division.

■ Discuss the rules of the MOVE statement as they apply to numeric and alphanumeric fields.

■ Describe the PERFORM statement; show how this statement is used to process a file until all of its records have been read.

■ Describe the IF statement and how it is used with and without an ELSE clause; explain the significance of the END-IF scope terminator.

■ Use the EVALUATE statement to implement a case (multibranch) construct.

■ State the hierarchy of operations for a COMPUTE statement; describe the individual arithmetic statements, ADD, SUBTRACT, MULTIPLY, and DIVIDE.

■ Describe the ROUNDED and SIZE ERROR options as they apply to any of the arithmetic statements.

■ Explain the relationship between a Procedure Division and its associated hierarchy chart.

OVERVIEW

This is a long chapter—the longest in the text. It focuses on the Procedure Division, which is the portion of a COBOL program that contains the logic. The chapter is long because it presents the many statements needed to write a basic program such as the tuition billing program introduced in Chapter 3.

We begin with the COBOL statements used for I/O (input/output) operations; OPEN, CLOSE, READ, and WRITE, and continue with the STOP RUN statement to terminate program execution. We learn about the PERFORM statement to implement a loop, the IF statement to implement the selection structure, and the EVALUATE statement to implement a case structure. We study the MOVE statement to copy data from one location to another and end with the arithmetic statements: COMPUTE, ADD, SUBTRACT, MULTIPLY, and DIVIDE.

The chapter concludes with the completed COBOL listing for the tuition billing program of Chapter 3.

Open

The **OPEN** statement initiates processing for a file. It indicates the nature of the file (input or output) and ensures that a specific device is available for the I/O operations. The OPEN statement also performs validation functions in conjunction with the LABEL

RECORDS clause of the FD; for example, if label records are specified for an input file, the OPEN statement checks the header label of that file to ensure that the proper file is available for processing. An abbreviated format of the OPEN statement is:

```
OPEN {[INPUT ]  file-name-1 . . .} . . .
     [OUTPUT]
```

The syntax of the OPEN statement indicates a mandatory selection for the type of file—INPUT is used for a file that is read, whereas OUTPUT is used for a file that is written to. The brackets and ellipsis associated with file-name-2 imply that multiple files can be opened in the same statement as was done in lines 43 and 44 of the engineering senior program in Figure 1.6:

```
OPEN INPUT STUDENT-FILE
     OUTPUT PRINT-FILE.
```

Each file referenced in an OPEN statement must have been previously defined in a SELECT statement in the Environment Division, and in a corresponding FD in the Data Division. All files must be opened before they can be accessed; the operating system will terminate execution of a COBOL program that attempts to read (or write) an unopened file.

Close

The **CLOSE** statement is executed when access to a file is no longer necessary, such as when all records have been read from an input file or when all records have been written to an output file. The CLOSE statement releases the I/O devices associated with the file; it also writes trailer labels at the end of files on disk or tape in conjunction with the LABEL RECORDS clause of the FD. All open files should be closed before processing terminates. The format of the CLOSE is simply:

```
CLOSE file-name-1 [, file-name-2 ...]
```

The brackets and ellipsis associated with file-name-2 indicate that multiple files can be closed in the same statement. The type of file, INPUT or OUTPUT, is not specified when the file is closed because the distinction between input and output is no longer important. Lines 51 and 52 in the engineering senior program provide an example:

```
CLOSE STUDENT-FILE
      PRINT-FILE.
```

A CLOSE statement can appear anywhere within a program but typically appears immediately before the program terminates, that is, immediately before the STOP RUN statement.

Read

The **READ** statement transfers data from an open file into memory, provided a record is available. If, however, no record is present—that is, the *end-of-file* condition has been reached—control passes to the statement(s) following the AT END clause. An abbreviated format of the READ statement is shown below:

```
READ file-name
    AT END statement
[END-READ]
```

(handwritten notes: "Read a file with a Record (sentence out)", "End-of-file is a Switch")

The END-READ scope terminator is optional but strongly recommended. The READ statement is illustrated in lines 45–47 of the engineering senior program.

```
READ STUDENT-FILE
    AT END MOVE 'NO' TO DATA-REMAINS-SWITCH
END-READ.
```

Placement of the READ Statement

The engineering senior program in Figure 1.6 contained two distinct READ statements. There was an initial, or priming, READ in lines 45–47 and a second READ statement as the *last* instruction of the performed paragraph (lines 65–67). The necessity for *both* statements is explained by considering Figure 5.1, which shows correct and incorrect ways to process a file of transactions.

Figure 5.1a, the *incorrect* implementation, causes the last record of INPUT-FILE to be processed twice. To see how this happens, consider a file with only two records, A and B, realizing that such a file is read three times—once for each record and once to sense the end of file. Realize, too, that the PERFORM statement evaluates the UNTIL condition *before* branching (a detailed description of the PERFORM statement is found in an upcoming section).

In Figure 5.1a, record A is read the first time PROCESS-RECORDS is performed, with execution continuing through the remainder of the PROCESS-RECORDS paragraph, at which point DATA-REMAINS-SWITCH is still set to 'YES'. Hence, PROCESS-RECORDS is executed a second time, during which time it reads and processes record B. Since DATA-REMAINS-SWITCH is still set to 'YES', PROCESS-RECORDS is executed a third time, during which the end-of-file condition is sensed immediately. Execution continues, however, to the end of the paragraph, causing the last record (record B) to be processed twice.

In the *correct* implementation of Figure 5.1b, an initial (priming) READ is executed *before* performing the paragraph PROCESS-RECORDS, which also contains a READ statement. The first time PROCESS-RECORDS is performed, it processes record A, and its *last* statement reads record B. Since DATA-REMAINS-SWITCH is still set to 'YES', PROCESS-RECORDS is executed a second time to process record B, with the ending READ statement sensing the end-of-file condition. DATA-REMAINS-SWITCH is set to 'NO', which in turn terminates the PERFORM statement.

In Chapter 1 we demonstrated another way to place the READ statement. This technique is further explained in Chapter 9.

Write

The **WRITE** statement transfers data from memory to the printer (or other open output device). Consider:

```
WRITE record-name

    [ {AFTER }  ADVANCING  {integer [LINE ]} ]
    [ {BEFORE}             {        [LINES]} ]
    [                      {PAGE            } ]
```

The ADVANCING option controls the line spacing on a printer; for example, specification of AFTER ADVANCING 3 LINES produces triple spacing (the printer skips two lines and writes on the third). Conversely, specification of the BEFORE option first writes the line, then skips the designated amount. Specification of

Figure 5.1   Placement of the READ Statement

```
PREPARE-TUITION-REPORT.
    .
        .
            .
        MOVE 'YES' TO DATA-REMAINS-SWITCH.
        PERFORM PROCESS-RECORDS
            UNTIL DATA-REMAINS-SWITCH = 'NO'.
        .
            .
                .
PROCESS-RECORDS.                             ─── First statement of performed paragraph is the READ
        READ INPUT-FILE
            AT END MOVE 'NO' TO DATA-REMAINS-SWITCH
        END-READ.
        .
            .
                .
```

(a) Incorrect Implementation

```
PREPARE-TUITION-REPORT.
    .
        .
            .
        MOVE 'YES' TO DATA-REMAINS-SWITCH.      ─── Initial READ is executed once and only once
        READ INPUT-FILE
            AT END MOVE 'NO' TO DATA-REMAINS-SWITCH
        END-READ.
        PERFORM PROCESS-RECORDS
            UNTIL DATA-REMAINS-SWITCH = 'NO'.
        .
            .
                .
PROCESS-RECORDS.
    .
        .
            .                                   ─── Last statement of performed paragraph is another READ
        READ INPUT-FILE
            AT END MOVE 'NO' TO DATA-REMAINS-SWITCH
        END-READ.
```

(b) Correct Implementation

PAGE, in lieu of LINES, will cause output to begin on top of a new page. Omission of the ADVANCING option defaults to single spacing. The examples below

```
WRITE PRINT-LINE.
WRITE PRINT-LINE
    AFTER ADVANCING 2 LINES.
WRITE PRINT-LINE
    AFTER ADVANCING PAGE.
```

will single space, double space, and advance to the top of a new page, respectively.

The WRITE statement contains a *record* name, whereas the READ statement contains a *file* name. The record name in the WRITE statement will appear as a 01 entry in the File Section of the Data Division. The file in which it is contained will appear in SELECT, FD, OPEN, and CLOSE statements.

Stop Run

The format of the **STOP RUN** statement is simply:

```
STOP RUN
```

The STOP RUN statement terminates execution of a COBOL program and returns control to the operating system. [STOP RUN need not be (and typically is not) the last physical statement in the program.] All files should be closed prior to executing the STOP RUN statement.

Move

The **MOVE** statement copies data from one location to another; for example, the statement MOVE A TO B copies the value in location A to location B. The value of A is in two places after the move has taken place, while the initial value of B is gone (having been replaced by the value of A). The syntax of the MOVE statement is:

$$\underline{MOVE} \begin{Bmatrix} \text{identifier-1} \\ \text{literal-1} \end{Bmatrix} \underline{TO} \text{ identifier-2} \begin{bmatrix} \text{identifier-3} \end{bmatrix} \ldots$$

Consider the following examples:

1. MOVE 200 TO PRICE-PER-CREDIT.

2. MOVE 'ABC UNIVERSITY' TO SCHOOL-NAME.

3. MOVE STU-NAME TO PRINT-NAME.

4. MOVE ZEROS TO TOTAL-NUMBER.

5. MOVE SPACES TO PRINT-LINE.

Example one moves a numeric literal, 200, to the data name PRICE-PER-CREDIT. Example two moves a nonnumeric literal, 'ABC UNIVERSITY', to SCHOOL-NAME. Example three copies data from an input area to an output area for subsequent printing. Examples four and five use the figurative constants, ZEROS and SPACES, to initialize a counter and print line, respectively.

The brackets and ellipsis associated with identifier-3 in the COBOL syntax indicate the same item can be moved to multiple data names. Thus the single statement:

```
MOVE 10 TO FIELD-A FIELD-B FIELD-C.
```

is equivalent to the three individual statements:

```
MOVE 10 TO FIELD-A.
MOVE 10 TO FIELD-B.
MOVE 10 TO FIELD-C.
```

Restrictions on the MOVE Statement

The results of a MOVE statement depend on the type of data in the sending and/or receiving field. We concentrate initially on MOVE statements involving only elementary items, since these statements are by far the most common. Recall (from Chapter 4) that elementary data items may be of four types:

Numeric PIC(9)	Numeric data items, numeric literals, and the figurative constants, ZERO, ZEROS, or ZEROES.
Alphabetic PIC(A)	Alphabetic data items and the figurative constants, SPACE and SPACES
Alphanumeric PIC(X)	Alphanumeric data items, nonnumeric literals and the figurative constants, SPACE and SPACES
Numeric Edited	Numeric edited data items (to be discussed in Chapter 7)

In theory a MOVE statement could involve any combination of these four types; in actuality, however, certain types of moves are not permitted as indicated by Table 5.1. (You do not have to commit the table to memory; simply be aware that certain restrictions exist, and know where to turn should questions arise later.)

TABLE 5.1   Rules of the MOVE Statement (Elementary Data Items)

SENDING FIELD	RECEIVING FIELD			
	Alphabetic	Alphanumeric	Numeric	Numeric Edited
Alphabetic	Valid	Valid	Invalid	Invalid
Alphanumeric	Invalid	Valid	Invalid	Invalid
Numeric	Invalid	Integers only	Valid	Valid
Numeric Edited	Invalid	Valid	Valid	Invalid

At first glance Table 5.1 seems overwhelming, but a second look shows it to make intuitive sense. You cannot, for example, move an alphanumeric field to an alphabetic field (because the alphanumeric field may contain numbers, which are invalid in an alphabetic field). You can, however, do the move in the opposite direction; that is, you can move an alphabetic field to an alphanumeric field.

Even Table 5.1 does not tell us everything we need to know about the MOVE statement. What happens, for example, when moves with like fields (an alphanumeric sending field to an alphanumeric receiving field) involve PICTURE clauses of different lengths? Additional explanation is required as explained in the next two sections.

Alphanumeric Field to Alphanumeric Field

Data moved from an alphanumeric field to an alphanumeric field are moved one character at a time from left to right. If the receiving field is larger than the sending field, it is padded on the right with blanks; if the receiving field is smaller than the sending field, the rightmost characters are truncated.

Alphanumeric moves are illustrated in Table 5.2. Example (a) is trivial, in that the sending and receiving fields have the same picture clause. In example (b) the sending field is one character longer than the receiving field; hence the rightmost character is truncated. Data are moved from left to right one character at a time; thus A, B, C, and D are moved in that order, and E is dropped. In example (c), however, the receiving field is one character longer than the sending field. A, B, C, D, and E are moved in that order, and a blank is added at the right.

TABLE 5.2   Illustration of the MOVE Statement: Alphanumeric Sending Field to Alphanumeric Receiving Field

	SENDING FIELD		RECEIVING FIELD	
	Picture	Contents	Picture	Contents
(a)	X(5)	A B C D E	X(5)	A B C D E
(b)	X(5)	A B C D E	X(4)	A B C D
(c)	X(5)	A B C D E	X(6)	A B C D E

Numeric Field to Numeric Field

All moves involving numeric fields maintain decimal alignment. If the integer portion of the receiving field is larger than that of the sending field, high-order (insignificant) zeros are added to the receiving field. If, however, the integer portion of the receiving field is smaller than that of the sending field, the high-order (significant) digits of the sending field are truncated.

In similar fashion if the decimal portion of the receiving field is larger than that of the sending field, low-order zeros are added. And finally, if the decimal portion of the receiving field is smaller than that of the sending field, the extra positions are truncated. These points are clarified in Table 5.3.

TABLE 5.3   Illustration of the MOVE Statement: Numeric Sending Field to Numeric Receiving Field

	SENDING FIELD		RECEIVING FIELD	
	Picture	Contents	Picture	Contents
(a)	9(5)	1 2 3 4 5	9(5)	1 2 3 4 5
(b)	9(5)	1 2 3 4 5	9(4)	2 3 4 5
(c)	9(5)	1 2 3 4 5	9(6)	0 1 2 3 4 5
(d)	9(3)V99	1 2 3 ⌄ 4 5	9(3)	1 2 3
(e)	9(3)V99	1 2 3 ⌄ 4 5	9V99	3 ⌄ 4 5
(f)	9(3)	1 2 3	9(3)V99	1 2 3 ⌄ 0 0

Example (a) is trivial. Example (b) attempts to move a five-position field to a four-position field. Since decimal alignment is always maintained, the leftmost digit (i.e., the *most significant* digit) is truncated. Example (c) moves a five-position sending field to a six-position receiving field, causing the addition of a leading (nonsignificant) zero. The sending field in example (d) has two digits after the decimal point, but the receiving field has none. Hence the 4 and 5 do not appear in the receiving field. Example (e) truncates the most significant digits. Example (f) adds two nonsignificant zeros to the receiving field.

Group Moves

The preceding discussion concerned MOVE statements in which the receiving field was an elementary item. The results are very different if a group item is involved, because *if the receiving field is a group item, the move takes place as though the receiving field were an alphanumeric item, with padding or truncation on the right as necessary.* MOVE statements involving group items often produce unexpected results and should be avoided.

Perform

The **PERFORM** statement transfers control to a procedure (paragraph) elsewhere in the program, allowing the program to be divided into functional modules. An abbreviated format of the PERFORM statement is:

```
PERFORM procedure-name
     [UNTIL condition]
```

Consider first the statement *without* an UNTIL clause as illustrated below:

```
            COMPUTE TUITION = CREDITS * CHARGE-PER-CREDIT.
            PERFORM WRITE DETAIL-LINE.
            ADD 1 TO NUMBER-OF-STUDENTS.
            .
            .
            .
        WRITE-DETAIL-LINE.
            MOVE STUDENT-NAME TO PRINT-NAME.
            MOVE TUITION TO PRINT-TUITION.
            WRITE PRINT-LINE AFTER ADVANCING 2 LINES.
        WRITE-TOTAL-LINE.
```

Transfer to   *Return to*

The statement PERFORM WRITE-DETAIL-LINE transfers control to the first statement in the paragraph WRITE-DETAIL-LINE. When every statement in WRITE-DETAIL-LINE has been executed (i.e., when the next paragraph name is encountered), control returns to the statement immediately after the original PERFORM, in this case, to the ADD statement.

A loop (iteration) is implemented through inclusion of an UNTIL clause. The condition in the UNTIL clause is tested *before* the paragraph is executed, and if the condition is not met, control is transferred to the designated paragraph. When the paragraph has completed execution, the condition is retested, and if it (the condition) is still not met, the paragraph is executed a second time. The process continues until the condition is finally satisfied. Consider:

```
        PERFORM PROCESS-RECORDS
             UNTIL DATA-REMAINS-SWITCH = 'NO'.
            .
            .
            .
        PROCESS-RECORDS.
            .
            .
            .
            READ STUDENT-FILE
                AT END MOVE 'NO' TO DATA-REMAINS-SWITCH
            END-READ.
```

The paragraph PROCESS-RECORDS is executed repeatedly until DATA-REMAINS-SWITCH equals 'NO', that is, until there are no more incoming records. The last statement of the performed paragraph is a READ statement, so that when the end of file is reached, DATA-REMAINS-SWITCH will be set to 'NO'. This causes the next test of the UNTIL condition to be successful and prevents further execution of the PROCESS-RECORDS paragraph.

IF

The **IF** statement is one of the most powerful statements in COBOL. Our present concern, however, is with only a few of the available options, with additional consideration deferred to Chapter 8. An abbreviated format of the IF statement is

```
IF condition THEN
      statement-1
[ELSE
      statement-2 ]
[END-IF]
```

The IF statement is terminated by the optional (but highly recommended) END-IF scope terminator and/or a period. Consider:

```
IF STU-CREDITS > 110 AND STU-MAJOR = 'ENGINEERING'
    MOVE STU-NAME TO PRINT-NAME
    MOVE STU-CREDITS TO PRINT-CREDITS
    MOVE STU-GPA TO PRINT-GPA
    WRITE PRINT-LINE
END-IF.
```

If the condition is true, then *every* statement between the IF (condition) and the END-IF (and/or period) will be executed. Hence, when an engineering senior is processed, three MOVE statements and one WRITE statement are executed. If, however, the condition is false, then all four statements—three MOVEs and a WRITE—are bypassed.

As indicated, the IF statement is terminated by the END-IF scope terminator and/or a period, and the inclusion of both appears redundant. (Many programmers do, however, use both entries.) END-IF, despite the fact that it is an optional entry, has distinct advantages (as will be explained in Chapter 7) and should be used in every instance.

The ELSE Clause

The **ELSE** clause is optional as implied by the square brackets in its syntax. Figure 5.2a contains an ELSE clause, whereas it is omitted in Figure 5.2b. If the condition in Figure 5.2a is true, statement-1 is executed; whereas if it is false, statement-2 is executed—in either case execution continues with statement-3. Figure 5.2b, however, omits the ELSE clause so that if the condition is false, the IF statement is terminated immediately.

Indentation

Indentation in an IF statement is extremely important to emphasize a programmer's understanding of a statement's intended effect. Consider Figure 5.3, which contains a flowchart and corresponding COBOL code.

Figure 5.2 The IF Statement

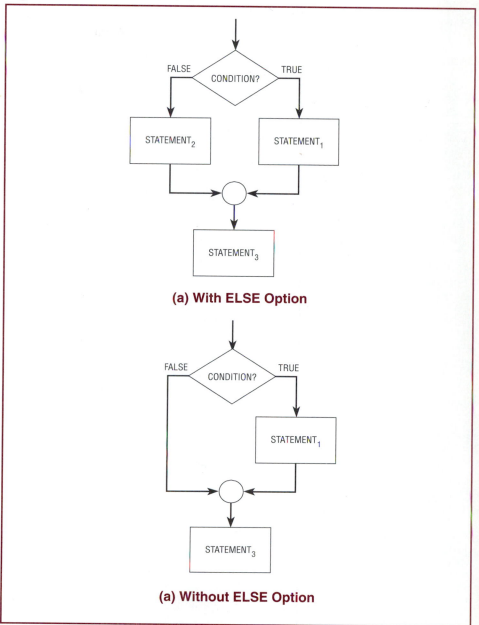

(a) With ELSE Option

(a) Without ELSE Option

The flowchart in Figure 5.3a indicates that if the condition A = B is true, the statements MOVE 1 TO C and MOVE 1 TO D are to be executed. If, however, the condition is false, then the statements MOVE ZERO TO C and MOVE ZERO TO D are to be executed instead. In either case—that is, whether the condition is true or false—we are to write a detail line. The latter is indicated by the IF and ELSE branches meeting in a common exit point, which leads to the final WRITE statement.

The COBOL code in Figure 5.3b is carefully aligned to reflect this interpretation. Recall that the rules of COBOL require only that an IF statement appear in the B margin, that is, in columns 12–72. Hence the indentation in Figure 5.3b is done solely for the purpose of making a program easier to read, rather than to satisfy a

Figure 5.3   The ELSE Clause/II

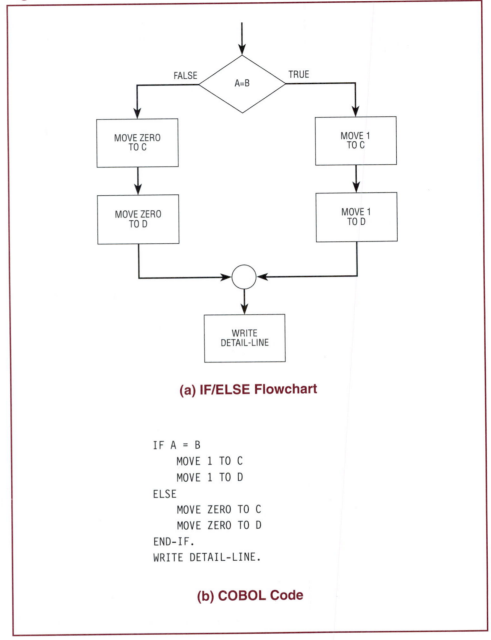

(a) IF/ELSE Flowchart

```
IF A = B
    MOVE 1 TO C
    MOVE 1 TO D
ELSE
    MOVE ZERO TO C
    MOVE ZERO TO D
END-IF.
WRITE DETAIL-LINE.
```

(b) COBOL Code

rule of COBOL. Nevertheless, proper indentation is essential and goes a long way to improve the quality of your work. Accordingly, we suggest the following guidelines:

1. Begin the IF statement in column 12.

2. Put the word ELSE on a line by itself and directly under the IF.

3. Indent detail lines associated with either the IF or ELSE four columns.

4. Put END-IF on a line by itself directly under the IF statement.

Evaluate

The **EVALUATE** statement implements the case (multibranch) construct of structured programming. It has what first appears to be a rather complicated syntax, but in actuality is quite easy to use. Consider:

$$
\underline{\text{EVALUATE}} \left\{ \begin{array}{l} \text{identifier-1} \\ \text{expression-1} \\ \underline{\text{TRUE}} \\ \underline{\text{FALSE}} \end{array} \right\}
$$

$$
\left\{ \underline{\text{WHEN}} \left\{ \begin{array}{l} \text{condition-1} \\ \underline{\text{TRUE}} \\ \underline{\text{FALSE}} \end{array} \right\} \text{imperative-statement-1} \ . \ . \ . \right\}
$$

$$
\left[\underline{\text{WHEN}} \ \underline{\text{OTHER}} \ \text{imperative-statement-2} \right]
$$

$$
\left[\underline{\text{END-EVALUATE}} \right]
$$

An example of the EVALUATE statement is shown below in conjunction with the tuition billing program presented in Chapter 3. The specifications for the program indicate that activity fee is dependent on the number of credits ($25 for 6 credits or fewer, $50 for 7 to 12 credits, and $75 for 13 credits or more). Consider:

```
EVALUATE TRUE
    WHEN STU-CREDITS <= 6
        MOVE 25 TO IND-ACTIVITY-FEE
    WHEN STU-CREDITS > 6 AND STU-CREDITS <= 12
        MOVE 50 TO IND-ACTIVITY-FEE
    WHEN STU-CREDITS > 12
        MOVE 75 TO IND-ACTIVITY-FEE
END-EVALUATE.
```

The different conditions (i.e., the ranges for the number of student credits) are presented in the various WHEN clauses. The END-EVALUATE scope terminator is a required entry.

Arithmetic Statements

COBOL does arithmetic in one of two ways. It has individual statements for the basic arithmetic operations (addition, subtraction, multiplication, and division), and a COMPUTE statement that combines multiple operations into one statement. As you shall see, the COMPUTE statement is generally easier to use, and so we begin with it. Note, too, that all of these statements have optional ROUNDED and SIZE ERROR clauses, which are discussed prior to the individual statements.

The ROUNDED Clause

The **ROUNDED** clause (in any arithmetic statement) causes COBOL to carry a calculation to one more decimal place than is specified in the result field. If the value of the extra decimal place is 5 or larger, the answer is rounded up; if it is 4 or less, the answer is unchanged. If the ROUNDED clause is omitted, COBOL truncates any extra decimal positions regardless of their value. Table 5.4 shows the effect of the ROUNDED option in which the values of A and B are added to produce a value for C.

TABLE 5.4   The ROUNDED Clause

Data Name	A	B	C
Picture	**9V99**	**9V99**	**9V9**
Value before execution	123	456	(immaterial)
Value after execution of			
ADD A B GIVING C	123	456	57
ADD A B GIVING C ROUNDED	123	456	58

Both of the examples in Table 5.4 add the same numbers (1.23 and 4.56) to produce a sum of 5.79. Both examples also specify the same PICTURE clause for the sum, which contains only a single decimal place. The first statement, however, does not contain the ROUNDED clause, and hence the .09 is truncated, leaving 5.7 as the final answer. The second example contains the ROUNDED clause, producing a more accurate 5.8.

The SIZE ERROR Clause

The **SIZE ERROR** clause is available for all arithmetic statements and produces a warning when the result of calculation is too large for the designated field. Consider:

```
05  HOURLY-RATE      PIC 99.
05  HOURS-WORKED     PIC 99.
05  GROSS-PAY        PIC 999.
   .
     .
       .
        COMPUTE GROSS-PAY = HOURLY-RATE * HOURS-WORKED.
```

Let us assume that HOURLY-RATE and HOURS-WORKED are 25 and 40, respectively. The result of the multiplication should be 1,000. GROSS-PAY, however, is defined as a three-position numeric field and is too small to hold the result. Hence its value is *truncated* and only the three rightmost digits are retained; in other words, GROSS-PAY becomes 000.

The situation is prevented by the inclusion of the SIZE ERROR clause:

```
COMPUTE GROSS-PAY = HOURLY-RATE * HOURS-WORKED
    ON SIZE ERROR PERFORM ERROR-ROUTINE
END-COMPUTE.
```

This time, if the results of the computation are too large and exceed the size allotted in the PICTURE clause, control passes to the statement(s) following the SIZE ERROR clause. The latter contains an error routine to display an error message or take other corrective action. When SIZE ERROR occurs, no fields are changed.

COMPUTE

The **COMPUTE** statement combines multiple arithmetic operations into a single statement of the form:

```
COMPUTE {identifier-1 [ROUNDED]}...= expression-1

   [ON SIZE ERROR imperative-statement-1]

[END-COMPUTE]
```

The COMPUTE statement first calculates the value of the expression on the right side of the equal sign, then stores that value in the data name on the left. The expression within the COMPUTE statement consists of data names, numeric literals, arithmetic symbols, and parentheses. Spaces should precede and follow arithmetic symbols. A space is also required before a left parenthesis and after a right parenthesis.

Parentheses are used to clarify, and in some cases, alter the sequence of, operations within an expression, but anything contained within parentheses must also be a valid expression. Expressions are evaluated according to the following rules:

1. Anything contained in parentheses is evaluated first as a separate expression.

2. The symbols +, –, *, /, and ** denote addition, subtraction, multiplication, division, and exponentiation, respectively. Exponentiation is done first, then multiplication or division, then addition or subtraction.

3. If rule 2 results in a tie (e.g., if both multiplication and division are present), then evaluation proceeds from left to right.

Table 5.5 contains examples to illustrate the formation and evaluation of expressions in a COMPUTE statement.

TABLE 5.5   The COMPUTE Instruction

Data Name	A	B	C	Comments
Value *before* execution	2	3	10	Initial Values
Value *after* execution of				
COMPUTE C = A + B.	2	3	5	Simple addition
COMPUTE C = A + B * 2.	2	3	8	Multiplication before addition
COMPUTE C = (A + B) * 2.	2	3	10	Parenthesis evaluated first
COMPUTE C = A ** B.	2	3	8	Algebraically, c = a^b
COMPUTE C = B ** A.	2	3	9	Algebraically, c = b^a

Table 5.6 should further clarify the use of this all-important statement. This table contains several algebraic expressions and the corresponding COMPUTE statements to accomplish the intended logic.

TABLE 5.6   The COMPUTE Instruction *(continued)*

Algebraic Expression	COBOL COMPUTE
$x = a + b$	`COMPUTE X = A + B.`
$x = \dfrac{a+b}{2}$	`COMPUTE X = (A + B) / 2.`
$x = \dfrac{(a+b)c}{2}$	`COMPUTE X = (A + B) * C / 2.`
$x = \dfrac{a+b}{2c}$	`COMPUTE X = (A + B) / (2 * C).`
$x = \sqrt{a}$	`COMPUTE X = A ** .5.`
$x = \dfrac{a^2 + b^2}{c^2}$	`COMPUTE X = (A ** 2 + B ** 2) / C ** 2.`

ADD

The **ADD** statement has two basic formats:

$$\text{\underline{ADD}} \begin{Bmatrix} \text{identifier-1} \\ \text{literal-1} \end{Bmatrix} \cdots \text{\underline{TO}} \left\{ \text{identifier-2} \left[\text{\underline{ROUNDED}} \right] \right\} \cdots$$

$$\left[\text{ON \underline{SIZE} \underline{ERROR} imperative-statement-1} \right]$$

$$\left[\text{\underline{END-ADD}} \right]$$

$$\text{\underline{ADD}} \begin{Bmatrix} \text{identifier-1} \\ \text{literal-1} \end{Bmatrix} \cdots \text{\underline{TO}} \begin{Bmatrix} \text{identifier-2} \\ \text{literal-2} \end{Bmatrix}$$

$$\text{\underline{GIVING}} \left\{ \text{identifier-3} \left[\text{\underline{ROUNDED}} \right] \right\} \cdots$$

$$\left[\text{ON \underline{SIZE} \underline{ERROR} imperative-statement-1} \right]$$

$$\left[\text{\underline{END-ADD}} \right]$$

In the first format the value of identifier-2 is *replaced* by the result of the addition; in the second format the value of identifier-2 is *unchanged*, because the result is stored in identifier-3 (and beyond). The word TO is *required* in the first format, but *optional* in the second. The three dots in either format indicate that identifier-1 or literal-1 can be repeated as many times as necessary (so that multiple items can be added together.)

Examples 5.1 and 5.2 illustrate the ADD statement. The first instruction adds the values of A and B (5 and 10) to the value of C (20), and puts the sum of 35 back into C. Example 5.2, however, does not include the initial value of C in the calculation; it adds the values of A and B (5 and 10), and places the sum of 15 in C.

Example 5.1   ADD A B TO C

	A	B	C
Before execution:	5	10	20
After execution:	5	10	35

Example 5.2   ADD A TO B GIVING C

	A	B	C
Before execution:	5	10	20
After execution:	5	10	15

Table 5.7 contains additional examples of the ADD statement, with all examples operating on the *initial* values of A, B, and C (5, 10, and 30, respectively). The last example changes the values of both B and C.

TABLE 5.7 The ADD Instruction

Data Name	A	B	C
Value before execution	5	10	30
Value after execution of			
ADD A TO C.	5	10	35
ADD A B TO C.	5	10	45
ADD A TO B GIVING C.	5	10	15
ADD A 18 B GIVING C.	5	10	33
ADD A 18 B TO C.	5	10	63
ADD 1 TO B C.	5	11	31

SUBTRACT

The **SUBTRACT** statement has two formats:

$$\underline{\text{SUBTRACT}} \begin{Bmatrix} \text{identifier-1} \\ \text{literal-1} \end{Bmatrix} \ldots \underline{\text{FROM}} \{ \text{identifier-2}\ [\underline{\text{ROUNDED}}] \} \ldots$$

$$[\text{ON } \underline{\text{SIZE}}\ \underline{\text{ERROR}}\ \text{imperative-statement-1}]$$

$$[\underline{\text{END-SUBTRACT}}]$$

$$\underline{\text{SUBTRACT}} \begin{Bmatrix} \text{identifier-1} \\ \text{literal-1} \end{Bmatrix} \ldots \underline{\text{FROM}} \begin{Bmatrix} \text{identifier-2} \\ \text{literal-2} \end{Bmatrix}$$

$$\underline{\text{GIVING}} \{ \text{identifier-3}\ [\underline{\text{ROUNDED}}] \} \ldots$$

$$[\text{ON } \underline{\text{SIZE}}\ \underline{\text{ERROR}}\ \text{imperative-statement-1}]$$

$$[\underline{\text{END-SUBTRACT}}]$$

In the first format the initial value of identifier-2 is replaced by the result of the subtraction. In the second format the initial value of either identifier-2 or literal-2 is unchanged, as the result is stored in identifier-3 (and beyond).

Examples 5.3 and 5.4 illustrate the SUBTRACT statement. In Example 5.3 the SUBTRACT statement causes the value of A (5) to be subtracted from the initial value of B (15) and the result (10) to be stored in B. Only the value of B was changed.

In the FROM . . . GIVING format of Example 5.4 the value of A (5) is subtracted from the value of B (15), and the result (10) is placed in C. The values of A and B are unchanged, and the initial value of C (100) is replaced by 10. Table 5.8 contains additional examples.

Example 5.3   SUBTRACT   A   FROM   B

	A	B
Before execution:	5	15
After execution:	5	10

Example 5.4   SUBTRACT   A   FROM   B   GIVING   C

		A	**B**	**C**
Before execution:		5	15	100
After execution:		5	15	10

TABLE 5.8   The SUBTRACT Instruction

Data Name	A	B	C	D
Value before execution	5	10	30	100
Value after execution of				
SUBTRACT A FROM C.	5	10	25	100
SUBTRACT A B FROM C.	5	10	15	100
SUBTRACT A B FROM C GIVING D.	5	10	30	15
SUBTRACT 10 FROM C D.	5	10	20	90

MULTIPLY

The **MULTIPLY** statement has two formats:

$$\underline{\text{MULTIPLY}} \begin{Bmatrix} \text{identifier-1} \\ \text{literal-1} \end{Bmatrix} \underline{\text{BY}} \left\{ \text{identifier-2} \; [\underline{\text{ROUNDED}}] \right\} \; \ldots$$

$$\left[\text{ON} \; \underline{\text{SIZE}} \; \underline{\text{ERROR}} \; \text{imperative-statement-1} \right]$$

$$\left[\underline{\text{END-MULTIPLY}} \right]$$

$$\underline{\text{MULTIPLY}} \begin{Bmatrix} \text{identifier-1} \\ \text{literal-1} \end{Bmatrix} \underline{\text{BY}} \begin{Bmatrix} \text{identifier-2} \\ \text{literal-2} \end{Bmatrix}$$

$$\underline{\text{GIVING}} \left\{ \text{identifier-3} \; [\underline{\text{ROUNDED}}] \right\} \; \ldots$$

$$\left[\text{ON} \; \underline{\text{SIZE}} \; \underline{\text{ERROR}} \; \text{imperative-statement-1} \right]$$

$$\left[\underline{\text{END-MULTIPLY}} \right]$$

If GIVING is used, then the result of the multiplication is stored in identifier-3 (and beyond). If GIVING is omitted, then the result is stored in identifier-2 (and beyond).

Example 5.5   MULTIPLY   A   BY   B

		A	**B**
Before execution:		10	20
After execution:		10	200

Example 5.6   MULTIPLY A BY B GIVING C

	A	B	C
Before execution:	10	20	345
After execution:	10	20	200

Table 5.9 contains additional examples of the MULTIPLY statement. As in the previous examples, the instructions operate on the initial values of A, B, and C.

TABLE 5.9   The MULTIPLY Instruction

Data Name	A	B	C
Value before execution	5	10	30
Value after execution of			
MULTIPLY B BY A GIVING C.	5	10	50
MULTIPLY A BY B GIVING C.	5	10	50
MULTIPLY A BY B.	5	50	30
MULTIPLY B BY A.	50	10	30
MULTIPLY A BY 3 GIVING B C.	5	15	15

DIVIDE

The **DIVIDE** statement has two formats. In the second format, the primary distinction is between the words BY and INTO, which determine whether identifier-2 is the divisor or the dividend. As with the other arithmetic statements, the GIVING option implies that the result is stored in identifier-3 so that the initial value of identifier-2 or literal-2 is unchanged. Only the second format makes explicit provision for storing the remainder.

DIVIDE $\begin{Bmatrix} \text{identifier-1} \\ \text{literal-1} \end{Bmatrix}$ INTO $\{\text{identifier-2} [\text{ROUNDED}]\}$ . . .

[ON SIZE ERROR imperative-statement-1]

[END-DIVIDE]

DIVIDE $\begin{Bmatrix} \text{identifier-1} \\ \text{literal-1} \end{Bmatrix}$ $\begin{Bmatrix} \text{INTO} \\ \text{BY} \end{Bmatrix}$ $\begin{Bmatrix} \text{identifier-2} \\ \text{literal-2} \end{Bmatrix}$ GIVING $\{\text{identifier-3} [\text{ROUNDED}]\}$ . . .

[REMAINDER identifier-4]

[ON SIZE ERROR imperative-statement-1]

[END-DIVIDE]

In Example 5.7 the value of B (50) is divided by the value of A (10), and the quotient (5) replaces the initial value of B. In Example 5.8, which uses the GIVING option, the quotient goes into C, the remainder into D, and the values of A and B are

The COMPUTE statement should always be used when multiple arithmetic operators are involved. Consider two sets of equivalent code:

Poor Code:

```
MULTIPLY B BY B GIVING B-SQUARED.
MULTIPLY 4 BY A GIVING FOUR-A.
MULTIPLY FOUR-A BY C GIVING FOUR-A-C.
SUBTRACT FOUR-A-C FROM B-SQUARED GIVING RESULT-1.
COMPUTE RESULT-2 = RESULT-1 ** .5.
SUBTRACT B FROM RESULT-2 GIVING NUMERATOR.
MULTIPLY 2 BY A GIVING DENOMINATOR.
DIVIDE NUMERATOR BY DENOMINATOR GIVING X.
```

Improved Code:

```
COMPUTE X = (-B + (B ** 2 - (4 * A * C)) ** .5) / (2 * A).
```

Both sets of code apply to the quadratic formula,

$$X = \frac{-B + \sqrt{B^2 - 4AC}}{2A}$$

It is fairly easy to determine what is happening from the single COMPUTE statement, but next to impossible to realize the cumulative effect of the eight arithmetic statements. Interpretation of the unacceptable code is further clouded by the mandatory definition of data names for intermediate results, RESULT-1, RESULT-2, etc.

Parentheses are often required in COMPUTE statements to alter the normal hierarchy of operations; for example, parentheses are required around 2 * A in the denominator. If they had been omitted, the numerator would have been divided by 2 and then the quotient would have been multiplied by A. Sometimes the parentheses are optional to the compiler but should be used to clarify things for the programmer. The parentheses around 4 * A * C do not alter the normal order of operations and hence are optional.

Individual arithmetic statements are preferable to the COMPUTE statement when only a *single* operation is required. Hence, ADD 1 TO COUNTER is easier to read than COMPUTE COUNTER = COUNTER + 1.

unaffected. Example 5.9 parallels 5.8 except that BY replaces INTO, resulting in a quotient of zero and a remainder of 10. Table 5.10 contains additional examples of the DIVIDE statement.

Example 5.7   `DIVIDE A INTO B.`

	A	**B**
Before execution:	10	50
After execution:	10	5

Example 5.8   `DIVIDE A INTO B GIVING C REMAINDER D.`

	A	**B**	**C**	**D**
Before execution:	10	51	13	17
After execution:	10	51	5	1

Example 5.9   `DIVIDE A BY B GIVING C REMAINDER D.`

	A	**B**	**C**	**D**
Before execution:	10	51	13	17
After execution:	10	51	0	10

TABLE 5.10   The DIVIDE Instruction

Data Name	**A**	**B**	**C**
Value before execution	5	10	30
Value after execution of			
DIVIDE 2 INTO B.	5	5	30
DIVIDE 2 INTO B GIVING C.	5	10	5
DIVIDE B BY 5 GIVING A.	2	10	30
DIVIDE A INTO B C.	5	2	6
DIVIDE A INTO B GIVING C.	5	10	2
DIVIDE 3 INTO A GIVING B REMAINDER C.	5	1	2

Assumed Decimal Point

Arithmetic is performed on decimal as well as integer fields. You must be aware of the decimal point, and in particular, *be sure to define the field holding the result with a sufficient number of decimal places.* Consider Example 5.10, in which A and B have pictures of 99 and 99V9, respectively.

Example 5.10   `ADD A TO B.`

	A	**B**
Before execution:	1 2	3 4 ⌄ 5
After execution:	1 2	4 6 ⌄ 5

In the example, field B is stored with an implied decimal point. The compiler generates instructions to add an integer number (12) to a number with one decimal place (34V5). It maintains decimal alignment, obtains 46V5 as an answer, and stores the result in field B.

Now consider what happens if the operation is reversed, that is, ADD B TO A. The result of the addition is still 46V5; however, the field that stores the sum, A, is defined without a decimal point; hence, the .5 will be truncated. *It is critical, therefore, to define the receiving field with a sufficient number of decimal places.* Table 5.11 contains additional examples. In each instance the instruction is assumed to operate on the initial values of A, B, and C.

TABLE 5.11   Arithmetic on Fields with Assumed Decimal Points

Data Name	A	B	C
Picture	**99**	**99V9**	**99V99**
Value before execution	12	345	4712
Value after execution of			
ADD B TO A.	46	345	4712
ADD A TO B.	12	465	4712
ADD B TO C.	12	345	8162
ADD C TO B.	12	816	4712
ADD C TO A.	59	345	4712
ADD A TO C.	12	345	5912

The Tuition Billing Program

The tuition billing program was first presented in Chapter 3, where we produced the hierarchy chart, pseudocode, and stubs program. We continued the development of the program in Chapter 4, with specifics of the Identification, Environment, and Data divisions. Now we are able to write the Procedure Division and complete the program.

We emphasize, however, that the Procedure Division is not written from scratch, but is developed from work already done in Chapters 3 and 4. Consider, therefore, Figure 5.4, which contains the hierarchy chart and detailed pseudocode, and most importantly the *already working* stubs program. The stubs program is complete in the sense that it contains all of the paragraphs needed for the eventual program; it is incomplete because many of its paragraphs exist as one sentence DISPLAY statements that need to be expanded to perform the indicated task. The most difficult work has already been done, however, because the testing in Chapter 3 demonstrated that the overall program flow is correct.

Thus, it is relatively simple to expand the various stub paragraphs in favor of more detailed Procedure Division statements presented in this chapter. The paragraphs can be implemented one (or several) at a time; for example, begin with the paragraph to write a heading line, expand it, then test it to be sure it executes correctly. Develop the paragraph to write a detailed line, then expand the paragraphs to compute the individual amounts (tuition, union fee, activity fee, and scholarship), testing each paragraph to be sure it works properly. Finally, add the paragraphs to increment the university totals and write the summary line at the end of the report.

The completed program is shown in Figure 5.5. The Identification, Environment, and Data divisions were developed at the end of Chapter 4 and are

Figure 5.4 Developing the Procedure Division

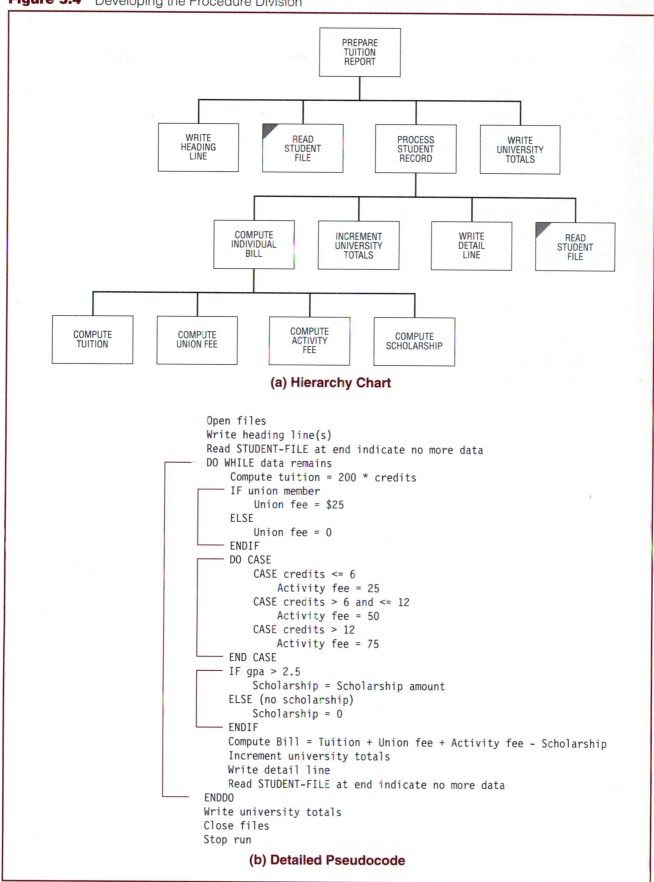

(a) Hierarchy Chart

```
Open files
Write heading line(s)
Read STUDENT-FILE at end indicate no more data
DO WHILE data remains
    Compute tuition = 200 * credits
    IF union member
        Union fee = $25
    ELSE
        Union fee = 0
    ENDIF
    DO CASE
        CASE credits <= 6
            Activity fee = 25
        CASE credits > 6 and <= 12
            Activity fee = 50
        CASE credits > 12
            Activity fee = 75
    END CASE
    IF gpa > 2.5
        Scholarship = Scholarship amount
    ELSE (no scholarship)
        Scholarship = 0
    ENDIF
    Compute Bill = Tuition + Union fee + Activity fee - Scholarship
    Increment university totals
    Write detail line
    Read STUDENT-FILE at end indicate no more data
ENDDO
Write university totals
Close files
Stop run
```

(b) Detailed Pseudocode

Figure 5.4 (continued)

```
PROCEDURE DIVISION.
PREPARE-TUITION-REPORT.
    DISPLAY 'PREPARE-TUITION-REPORT paragraph entered'.
    OPEN INPUT  STUDENT-FILE.
    PERFORM WRITE-HEADING-LINE.
    PERFORM READ-STUDENT-FILE.
    PERFORM PROCESS-STUDENT-RECORD
        UNTIL DATA-REMAINS-SWITCH = 'NO'.
    PERFORM WRITE-UNIVERSITY-TOTALS.
    CLOSE STUDENT-FILE.
    STOP RUN.
WRITE-HEADING-LINE.
    DISPLAY 'WRITE-HEADING-LINE paragraph entered'.

READ-STUDENT-FILE.
    READ STUDENT-FILE
        AT END MOVE 'NO' TO DATA-REMAINS-SWITCH
    END-READ.

PROCESS-STUDENT-RECORD.
    DISPLAY ' '.
    DISPLAY 'PROCESS-STUDENT-RECORD paragraph entered'.
    DISPLAY 'Student record being processed: ' STUDENT-RECORD.
    PERFORM COMPUTE-INDIVIDUAL-BILL.
    PERFORM INCREMENT-UNIVERSITY-TOTALS
    PERFORM WRITE-DETAIL-LINE.
    PERFORM READ-STUDENT-FILE.

COMPUTE-INDIVIDUAL-BILL.
    DISPLAY '  COMPUTE-INDIVIDUAL-BILL paragraph entered'.
    PERFORM COMPUTE-TUITION.
    PERFORM COMPUTE-UNION-FEE.
    PERFORM COMPUTE-ACTIVITY-FEE.
    PERFORM COMPUTE-SCHOLARSHIP.

COMPUTE-TUITION.
    DISPLAY '  COMPUTE-TUITION paragraph entered'.

COMPUTE-UNION-FEE.
    DISPLAY '  COMPUTE-UNION-FEE paragraph entered'.

COMPUTE-ACTIVITY-FEE.
    DISPLAY '  COMPUTE-ACTIVITY-FEE paragraph entered'.

COMPUTE-SCHOLARSHIP.
    DISPLAY '  COMPUTE-SCHOLARSHIP paragraph entered'.

INCREMENT-UNIVERSITY-TOTALS.
    DISPLAY '  INCREMENT-UNIVERSITY-TOTALS paragraph entered'.

WRITE-DETAIL-LINE.
    DISPLAY '  WRITE-DETAIL-LINE paragraph entered'.

WRITE-UNIVERSITY-TOTALS.
    DISPLAY ' '.
    DISPLAY 'WRITE-UNIVERSITY-TOTALS paragraph entered'.
```

(c) Stubs Program

Figure 5.5   The Tuition Billing Program

```
1          IDENTIFICATION DIVISION.
2          PROGRAM-ID.    TUITION5.
3          AUTHOR.         CAROL VAZQUEZ VILLAR.
4
5          ENVIRONMENT DIVISION.
6          INPUT-OUTPUT SECTION.
7          FILE-CONTROL.
8              SELECT STUDENT-FILE  ASSIGN TO SYSIN
9                  ORGANIZATION IS LINE SEQUENTIAL.
10             SELECT PRINT-FILE    ASSIGN TO SYSOUT
11                 ORGANIZATION IS LINE SEQUENTIAL.
12
13         DATA DIVISION.
14         FILE SECTION.
15         FD  STUDENT-FILE
16             RECORD CONTAINS 27 CHARACTERS.
17         01  STUDENT-RECORD.
18             05  STU-NAME.
19                 10  STU-LAST-NAME   PIC X(15).
20                 10  STU-INITIALS    PIC XX.
21             05  STU-CREDITS         PIC 9(2).
22             05  STU-UNION-MEMBER    PIC X.
23             05  STU-SCHOLARSHIP     PIC 9(4).
24             05  STU-GPA             PIC 9V99.
25
26         FD  PRINT-FILE
27             RECORD CONTAINS 132 CHARACTERS.
28         01  PRINT-LINE              PIC X(132).
29
30         WORKING-STORAGE SECTION.
31         01  DATA-REMAINS-SWITCH     PIC X(2)  VALUE SPACES.
32
33         01  INDIVIDUAL-CALCULATIONS.
34             05  IND-TUITION         PIC 9(4)  VALUE ZEROS.
35             05  IND-ACTIVITY-FEE    PIC 9(2)  VALUE ZEROS.
36             05  IND-UNION-FEE       PIC 9(2)  VALUE ZEROS.
37             05  IND-SCHOLARSHIP     PIC 9(4)  VALUE ZEROS.
38             05  IND-BILL            PIC 9(6)  VALUE ZEROS.
39
40         01  UNIVERSITY-TOTALS.
41             05  UNI-TUITION         PIC 9(6)  VALUE ZEROS.
42             05  UNI-UNION-FEE       PIC 9(4)  VALUE ZEROS.
43             05  UNI-ACTIVITY-FEE    PIC 9(4)  VALUE ZEROS.
44             05  UNI-SCHOLARSHIP     PIC 9(6)  VALUE ZEROS.
45             05  UNI-IND-BILL        PIC 9(6)  VALUE ZEROS.
46
47         01  CONSTANTS-AND-RATES.
48             05  PRICE-PER-CREDIT    PIC 9(3)  VALUE 200.
49             05  UNION-FEE           PIC 9(2)  VALUE 25.
50             05  ACTIVITY-FEES.
```

Figure 5.5   *(continued)*

```
51              10  1ST-ACTIVITY-FEE PIC 99    VALUE 25.
52              10  1ST-CREDIT-LIMIT PIC 99    VALUE 6.
53              10  2ND-ACTIVITY-FEE PIC 99    VALUE 50.
54              10  2ND-CREDIT-LIMIT PIC 99    VALUE 12.
55              10  3RD-ACTIVITY-FEE PIC 99    VALUE 75.
56          05  MINIMUM-SCHOLAR-GPA  PIC 9V9   VALUE 2.5.
57
58      01  HEADING-LINE.
59          05  FILLER              PIC X     VALUE SPACES.
60          05  FILLER              PIC X(12) VALUE 'STUDENT NAME'.
61          05  FILLER              PIC X(10) VALUE SPACES.
62          05  FILLER              PIC X(7)  VALUE 'CREDITS'.
63          05  FILLER              PIC X(2)  VALUE SPACES.
64          05  FILLER              PIC X(7)  VALUE 'TUITION'.
65          05  FILLER              PIC X(2)  VALUE SPACES.
66          05  FILLER              PIC X(9)  VALUE 'UNION FEE'.
67          05  FILLER              PIC X(2)  VALUE SPACES.
68          05  FILLER              PIC X(7)  VALUE 'ACT FEE'.
69          05  FILLER              PIC X(2)  VALUE SPACES.
70          05  FILLER              PIC X(11) VALUE 'SCHOLARSHIP'.
71          05  FILLER              PIC X(2)  VALUE SPACES.
72          05  FILLER              PIC X(10) VALUE 'TOTAL BILL'.
73          05  FILLER              PIC X(48) VALUE SPACES.
74
75      01  DETAIL-LINE.
76          05  FILLER              PIC X     VALUE SPACES.
77          05  DET-LAST-NAME       PIC X(15).
78          05  FILLER              PIC X(2)  VALUE SPACES.
79          05  DET-INITIALS        PIC X(2).
80          05  FILLER              PIC X(5)  VALUE SPACES.
81          05  DET-CREDITS         PIC 9(2).
82          05  FILLER              PIC X(6)  VALUE SPACES.
83          05  DET-TUITION         PIC 9(6).
84          05  FILLER              PIC X(7)  VALUE SPACES.
85          05  DET-UNION-FEE       PIC 9(3).
86          05  FILLER              PIC X(6)  VALUE SPACES.
87          05  DET-ACTIVITY-FEE    PIC 9(3).
88          05  FILLER              PIC X(8)  VALUE SPACES.
89          05  DET-SCHOLARSHIP     PIC 9(5).
90          05  FILLER              PIC X(6)  VALUE SPACES.
91          05  DET-IND-BILL        PIC 9(6).
92          05  FILLER              PIC X(49) VALUE SPACES.
93
94      01  DASH-LINE.
95          05  FILLER              PIC X(31) VALUE SPACES.
96          05  FILLER              PIC X(8)  VALUE ALL '-'.
97          05  FILLER              PIC X(2)  VALUE SPACES.
98          05  FILLER              PIC X(8)  VALUE ALL '-'.
99          05  FILLER              PIC X(2)  VALUE SPACES.
100         05  FILLER              PIC X(7)  VALUE ALL '-'.
```

Figure 5.5 *(continued)*

```
101              05  FILLER               PIC X(6)  VALUE SPACES.
102              05  FILLER               PIC X(7)  VALUE ALL '-'.
103              05  FILLER               PIC X(5)  VALUE SPACES.
104              05  FILLER               PIC X(7)  VALUE ALL '-'.
105              05  FILLER               PIC X(49) VALUE SPACES.
106
107          01  TOTAL-LINE.
108              05  FILLER               PIC X(8)  VALUE SPACES.
109              05  FILLER               PIC X(17)
110                      VALUE 'UNIVERSITY TOTALS'.
111              05  FILLER               PIC X(8)  VALUE SPACES.
112              05  TOT-TUITION          PIC 9(6).
113              05  FILLER               PIC X(6)  VALUE SPACES.
114              05  TOT-UNION-FEE        PIC 9(4).
115              05  FILLER               PIC X(5)  VALUE SPACES.
116              05  TOT-ACTIVITY-FEE     PIC 9(4).
117              05  FILLER               PIC X(7)  VALUE SPACES.
118              05  TOT-SCHOLARSHIP      PIC 9(6).
119              05  FILLER               PIC X(6)  VALUE SPACES.
120              05  TOT-IND-BILL         PIC 9(6).
121              05  FILLER               PIC X(49) VALUE SPACES.
122
123          PROCEDURE DIVISION.
124          PREPARE-TUITION-REPORT.
125              OPEN INPUT STUDENT-FILE
126                   OUTPUT PRINT-FILE.
127              PERFORM WRITE-HEADING-LINE.
128              PERFORM READ-STUDENT-FILE.              ── Initial (priming) READ statement
129              PERFORM PROCESS-STUDENT-RECORD
130                  UNTIL DATA-REMAINS-SWITCH = 'NO'.
131              PERFORM WRITE-UNIVERSITY-TOTALS.
132              CLOSE STUDENT-FILE
133                    PRINT-FILE.
134              STOP RUN.
135
136          WRITE-HEADING-LINE.
137              MOVE HEADING-LINE TO PRINT-LINE.
138              WRITE PRINT-LINE
139                  AFTER ADVANCING PAGE.
140              MOVE SPACES TO PRINT-LINE.
141              WRITE PRINT-LINE.
142
143          READ-STUDENT-FILE.
144              READ STUDENT-FILE
145                  AT END MOVE 'NO' TO DATA-REMAINS-SWITCH
146              END-READ.
147
148          PROCESS-STUDENT-RECORD.
149              PERFORM COMPUTE-INDIVIDUAL-BILL.
150              PERFORM INCREMENT-UNIVERSITY-TOTALS
151              PERFORM WRITE-DETAIL-LINE.
```

Figure 5.5   *(continued)*

```
152          PERFORM READ-STUDENT-FILE.
153
154      COMPUTE-INDIVIDUAL-BILL.
155          PERFORM COMPUTE-TUITION.
156          PERFORM COMPUTE-UNION-FEE.
157          PERFORM COMPUTE-ACTIVITY-FEE.
158          PERFORM COMPUTE-SCHOLARSHIP.
159          COMPUTE IND-BILL = IND-TUITION + IND-UNION-FEE +
160              IND-ACTIVITY-FEE - IND-SCHOLARSHIP.
161
162      COMPUTE-TUITION.
163          COMPUTE IND-TUITION = PRICE-PER-CREDIT * STU-CREDITS.
164
165      COMPUTE-UNION-FEE.
166          IF STU-UNION-MEMBER = 'Y'
167              MOVE UNION-FEE TO IND-UNION-FEE
168          ELSE
169              MOVE ZERO TO IND-UNION-FEE
170          END-IF.
171
172      COMPUTE-ACTIVITY-FEE.
173          EVALUATE TRUE
174              WHEN STU-CREDITS <= 1ST-CREDIT-LIMIT
175                  MOVE 1ST-ACTIVITY-FEE TO IND-ACTIVITY-FEE
176              WHEN STU-CREDITS > 1ST-CREDIT-LIMIT
177                  AND STU-CREDITS <= 2ND-CREDIT-LIMIT
178                      MOVE 2ND-ACTIVITY-FEE TO IND-ACTIVITY-FEE
179              WHEN STU-CREDITS > 2ND-CREDIT-LIMIT
180                  MOVE 3RD-ACTIVITY-FEE TO IND-ACTIVITY-FEE
181              WHEN OTHER
182                  DISPLAY 'INVALID CREDITS FOR: ' STU-NAME
183          END-EVALUATE.
184
185      COMPUTE-SCHOLARSHIP.
186          IF STU-GPA > MINIMUM-SCHOLAR-GPA
187              MOVE STU-SCHOLARSHIP TO IND-SCHOLARSHIP
188          ELSE
189              MOVE ZERO TO IND-SCHOLARSHIP
190          END-IF.
191
192      INCREMENT-UNIVERSITY-TOTALS.
193          ADD IND-TUITION      TO UNI-TUITION.
194          ADD IND-UNION-FEE     TO UNI-UNION-FEE.
195          ADD IND-ACTIVITY-FEE TO UNI-ACTIVITY-FEE.
196          ADD IND-SCHOLARSHIP   TO UNI-SCHOLARSHIP.
197          ADD IND-BILL         TO UNI-IND-BILL.
198
199      WRITE-DETAIL-LINE.
200          MOVE STU-LAST-NAME TO DET-LAST-NAME.
201          MOVE STU-INITIALS TO DET-INITIALS.
202          MOVE STU-CREDITS TO DET-CREDITS.
```

Last statement of performed paragraph is a second READ

IF statement ends with END-IF scope terminator and implements selection structure

EVALUATE statement implements case structure

Comparison done on numeric fields with implied decimal places

Figure 5.5 *(continued)*

```
203            MOVE IND-TUITION TO DET-TUITION.
204            MOVE IND-UNION-FEE TO DET-UNION-FEE.
205            MOVE IND-ACTIVITY-FEE TO DET-ACTIVITY-FEE.
206            MOVE IND-SCHOLARSHIP TO DET-SCHOLARSHIP.
207            MOVE IND-BILL TO DET-IND-BILL.
208            MOVE DETAIL-LINE TO PRINT-LINE.
209            WRITE PRINT-LINE
210                AFTER ADVANCING 1 LINE.
211
212        WRITE-UNIVERSITY-TOTALS.
213            MOVE DASH-LINE TO PRINT-LINE.
214            WRITE PRINT-LINE.
215            MOVE UNI-TUITION TO TOT-TUITION.
216            MOVE UNI-UNION-FEE TO TOT-UNION-FEE.
217            MOVE UNI-ACTIVITY-FEE TO TOT-ACTIVITY-FEE.
218            MOVE UNI-SCHOLARSHIP TO TOT-SCHOLARSHIP.
219            MOVE UNI-IND-BILL TO TOT-IND-BILL.
220            MOVE TOTAL-LINE TO PRINT-LINE.
221            WRITE PRINT-LINE
222                AFTER ADVANCING 1 LINE.
```

— Building a print line

copied directly from Figure 4.10. The completed program appears somewhat formidable the first time you see it, but it has been developed over the last three chapters, and you should have no difficulty in following it. We suggest you take it in pieces and review sections of the text as you need them with respect to the following:

1. The Identification Division in lines 1–3 contains only the PROGRAM-ID and AUTHOR paragraphs.

2. The Environment Division in lines 5–11 contains the SELECT statements for the two required files.

3. The FD's in lines 15–16 and 26–28 correspond to the SELECT statements in the Environment Division.

4. The description for the incoming data in lines 17–24 matches the program specifications of Chapter 3.

5. Separate 01 entries are defined for individual and total calculations (lines 33–38 and 40–45); also data names for the constants and rates are established in lines 47–56.

6. Heading, detail, dashed, and total lines are described separately in WORKING-STORAGE (lines 58–73, 75–92, 94–105, and 107–121, respectively); note the use of VALUE clauses to initialize the various print lines.

7. The paragraphs in the Procedure Division correspond one to one with the blocks in the hierarchy chart of Figure 5.4a.

8. An initial READ statement in line 128 is followed by the PERFORM statement in lines 129 and 130 to execute PROCESS-STUDENT-RECORD (lines 148–152) until there are no more records. The last statement of the performed paragraph is a second READ statement. The combination of these statements implements the overall logic in the pseudocode of Figure 5.4b.

9.　An EVALUATE statement in lines 173–183 computes the activity fee according to the number of credits taken.

10.　Separate paragraphs in the Procedure Division compute an individual bill (lines 154–160), increment university totals (lines 192–197), and write a detail line (lines 199–210).

11.　Multiple MOVE statements are required within the paragraph to write a detailed line (lines 199–210), with each statement moving a computed value (such as IND-TUITION) to the corresponding entry in the print line (DET-TUITION). The need for both data names will be more apparent after the material on editing in Chapter 7. The paragraph to write university totals requires similar treatment.

12.　Multiple ADD statements are needed within the paragraph to increment university totals (lines 193–197). Each total is stored in a separate field and thus must be incremented separately.

Figure 5.6　Test Data and Output

```
                          SMITH          JB15Y0000230
                          JAMES          HR15 0500245
                          BAKER          SR09 0500350
                          PART-TIMER     JR03Y0000300
                          JONES          PL15Y0000280
                          HEAVYWORKER    HM18 0000200
                          LEE            BL18 0000335
                          CLARK          JC06 0000310
                          GROSSMAN       SE07 0000215
                          FRANKEL        LF10 0000350
                          BENWAY         CT03 0250395
                          KERBEL         NB04 0000100
```

(a) Test Data

STUDENT NAME		CREDITS	TUITION	UNION FEE	ACT FEE	SCHOLARSHIP	TOTAL BILL
SMITH	JB	15	003000	025	075	00000	003100
JAMES	HR	15	003000	000	075	00000	003075
BAKER	SR	09	001800	000	050	00500	001350
PART-TIMER	JR	03	000600	025	025	00000	000650
JONES	PL	15	003000	025	075	00000	003100
HEAVYWORKER	HM	18	003600	000	075	00000	003675
LEE	BL	18	003600	000	075	00000	003675
CLARK	JC	06	001200	000	025	00000	001225
GROSSMAN	SE	07	001400	000	050	00000	001450
FRANKEL	LF	10	002000	000	050	00000	002050
BENWAY	CT	03	000600	000	025	00250	000375
KERBEL	NB	04	000800	000	025	00000	000825
			--------	--------	-------	-------	-------
UNIVERSITY TOTALS			024600	0075	0625	000750	024550

(b) Output

Test Data

The test data and associated output are shown in Figures 5.6a and 5.6b, respectively. The test data are identical to those used in the original stubs program; the output, however, is different and reflects the expanded Procedure Division of Figure 5.5. Note, too, the correspondence between individual records in the input data file and the associated lines in the printed report.

Observe, for example, that JB Smith, JR Part-Timer, and PL Jones each have a Y in column 20 of their input records, and that these are the only individuals who are charged a Union Fee. In similar fashion, James, Baker, and Benway are the only students with potential scholarships in the incoming data; James, however, does not have the requisite average and so he does not receive a scholarship. The student file has 12 records, and hence 12 students appear in the printed report.

In retrospect, the output produced isn't very pretty as it is unformatted and contains extraneous zeros throughout. (Editing is presented in Chapter 7 together with a final version of the program.)

Hierarchy Chart

The hierarchy chart was introduced initially as a design aid and developed before the program was written; it is also used as a documentation technique after coding is completed to better understand the overall program structure. The hierarchy chart depicts the functions inherent in a program, and is closely tied to the paragraphs in the Procedure Division. Observe therefore, the properties of the hierarchy chart in Figure 5.4a as they relate to the COBOL program in Figure 5.5.

1. Every box (module) in the hierarchy chart corresponds to a paragraph in the COBOL program. There are twelve different modules (the READ appears twice) in the hierarchy chart, and twelve paragraphs in the program.

2. Each paragraph in the COBOL program contains as many PERFORM statements as there are modules in the next lower level of the hierarchy chart. Thus the paragraph at the highest level, PREPARE-TUITION-REPORT, contains four PERFORM statements, one for each subordinate paragraph.

3. A paragraph can be entered only from the paragraph directly above it and must eventually return control to that paragraph. Hence, PROCESS-STUDENT-RECORDS is entered via a PERFORM statement in PREPARE-TUITION-REPORT. PROCESS-STUDENT-RECORDS in turn invokes four lower level paragraphs, each of which returns control to PROCESS-STUDENT-RECORDS, which eventually returns control to PREPARE-TUITION-REPORT.

4. Every module in a hierarchy chart (paragraph within a program) should be dedicated to a single function. The nature of that function should be apparent from the module's name and should consist of a verb, one or two adjectives, and an object.

Remember, too, that a hierarchy chart is very different from flowcharts or pseudocode. A hierarchy chart shows what has to be done, but not when; it contains no decision-making logic. Flowcharts and pseudocode, on the other hand, specify when and if a given block of code is executed. We say that hierarchy charts are *functional* in nature; they contain the tasks necessary to accomplish the specifications but do not indicate an order for execution. Pseudocode and flowcharts are *procedural* and specify logic.

COBOL Program Skeleton

Our objective is for you to write meaningful COBOL programs, not to memorize what must appear to be an endless list of rules. You must eventually remember certain things, but we have found the best approach is to pattern your first few COBOL programs after existing examples such as the tuition billing program. Everything you need to get started is contained in that program (Figure 5.5) if you will look at it carefully. As a further aid, Figure 5.7 contains a skeleton outline of a COBOL program and some helpful hints. Consider:

1. The four divisions must appear in the order: Identification, Environment, Data, and Procedure. Division headers begin in the A margin and always appear on a line by themselves.

2. The Environment and Data Divisions contain sections with fixed names. The Identification Division does not contain any sections. (The Procedure Division may contain programmer-defined sections; however, this is usually not done in beginning programs.)

3. The Data Division is the only division without paragraph names. In the Identification and Environment Divisions, the paragraph names are fixed. In the Procedure Division they are determined by the programmer. Paragraph names begin in the A margin.

4. Any entry not required to begin in the A margin begins in the B margin—that is, in or past column 12.

5. The program executes instructions sequentially, as they appear in the Procedure Division, unless a transfer-of-control statement such as PERFORM is encountered.

6. Every file must be opened and closed. A file name will appear in at least four statements: SELECT, FD, OPEN, and CLOSE. The READ statement also contains the file name of an input file, whereas the WRITE statement contains the record name of an output file.

Limitations OF COBOL-74

Scope terminators (e.g., END-IF, and END-READ) did not exist in COBOL 74; hence all scope terminators in Figure 5.5 must be removed for the program to compile under COBOL-74. The advantage of including scope terminators is explained further in Chapter 7.

The EVALUATE statement is also new to COBOL-85 and hence an alternative way to compute the activity fee (e.g., multiple IF statements) is required to develop the program under the older compiler.

The word TO is permitted as an optional reserved word in the GIVING form of the ADD statement in COBOL-85; it was not allowed in COBOL-74. THEN is an optional reserved word in the IF statement in COBOL-85 but was not allowed in COBOL-74.

Figure 5.7 Skeleton Outline of a COBOL Program

```
IDENTIFICATION DIVISION.
PROGRAM-ID.          PROGNAME.
AUTHOR.              JOHN DOE.


ENVIRONMENT DIVISION.
INPUT-OUTPUT SECTION.
FILE-CONTROL.
    SELECT INPUT-FILE   ASSIGN TO SYSIN
        ORGANIZATION IS LINE SEQUENTIAL.
    SELECT PRINT-FILE   ASSIGN TO SYSOUT
        ORGANIZATION IS LINE SEQUENTIAL.          ── Select statements for input and output files


DATA DIVISION.
FILE SECTION.
FD  INPUT-FILE
    RECORD CONTAINS 80 CHARACTERS.
01  INPUT-RECORD             PIC X(80).


FD  PRINT-FILE
    RECORD CONTAINS 132 CHARACTERS.
01  PRINT-LINE               PIC X(132).

                                                   ── Controls performed paragraph
WORKING-STORAGE SECTION
01  DATA-REMAINS-SWITCH      PIC X(2)   VALUE SPACES.
01  HEADING-LINE.
    .
      .
        .
01  DETAIL-LINE.
    .
      .
        .
01  TOTAL-LINE.
    .
      .
        .


PROCEDURE DIVISION.
MAINLINE.
    OPEN INPUT INPUT-FILE
        OUTPUT PRINT-FILE.                         ── Housekeeping consists of opening files
    READ INPUT-FILE                                   and the initial READ
        AT END MOVE 'NO' TO DATA-REMAINS-SWITCH
    END-READ.
    PERFORM PROCESS-RECORDS
        UNTIL DATA-REMAINS-SWITCH = 'NO'.
    CLOSE INPUT-FILE
        PRINT-FILE.
    STOP RUN.                                      ── Termination includes closing files and STOP RUN

PROCESS-RECORDS.
    .
      .
        .
    READ INPUT-FILE                                ── Last line of performed paragraph is a second READ
        AT END MOVE 'NO' TO DATA-REMAINS-SWITCH
    END-READ.
```

SUMMARY

Points to Remember

■ The READ statement typically appears twice in a COBOL program; as an initial (priming) read, and as the last statement of a performed paragraph to process a file until its records are exhausted.

■ The PERFORM statement may be used with or without an UNTIL clause; the latter is used to implement a loop.

■ The IF statement may be used with or without an ELSE clause; indentation is optional, but strongly suggested, in order to clarify intent.

■ The EVALUATE statement implements the case structure and is used instead of multiple IF statements.

■ The MOVE statement has several precisely defined rules, which govern the use of sending and receiving fields of different lengths and/or data types.

■ Arithmetic is done in one of two ways: either through individual statements such as ADD, SUBTRACT, MULTIPLY, and DIVIDE, or through a COMPUTE statement which combines multiple operations.

■ Parentheses may clarify and/or alter the normal sequence of operations; exponentiation, multiplication or division, addition or subtraction (and from left to right, if a tie).

■ The hierarchy chart can be used as a design aid before a program is written, and as a documentation technique afterward.

Key Words and Concepts

Assumed (implied) decimal point	Hierarchy of operations
Decimal alignment	Indentation
Design aid	Priming (initial) read
Documentation	Pseudocode
Exponentiation	Receiving (destination) field
Group move	Scope terminator
Hierarchy chart	Source (sending) field

COBOL Elements

ADD	END-COMPUTE	EVALUATE	READ
ADVANCING	END-DIVIDE	GIVING	ROUNDED
CLOSE	END-EVALUATE	IF	SIZE ERROR
COMPUTE	END-IF	MOVE	STOP RUN
DIVIDE	END-MULTIPLY	MULTIPLY	SUBTRACT
ELSE	END-READ	OPEN	UNTIL
END-ADD	END-SUBTRACT	PERFORM	WRITE

F i l l - i n

1. The _____ statement permits multiple arithmetic operations in a single statement.

2. Most arithmetic statements have _____ distinct formats.

3. Specification of the _____ clause causes a calculation to be carried to one more place than is specified in the result field.

4. Exponentiation is indicated by _____.

5. In the absence of parentheses exponentiation comes (before/after) multiplication.

6. If both multiplication and division are present, computation proceeds from _____ to _____.

7. The IF statement (does/does not) require an ELSE clause.

8. The effect of an IF statement is terminated by the presence of a _____ or the presence of an _____ clause.

9. _____ is normally the last statement that is executed in any COBOL program.

10. A typical COBOL program usually has _____ distinct READ statements.

11. A file containing *N* records is generally read _____ times.

12. In COBOL, one reads a _____ and writes a _____.

13. Specification of _____ _____ _____ in a WRITE statement causes the next line of output to begin on top of a new page.

14. The type of file—that is, INPUT or OUTPUT—appears in an _____, but not in a _____ statement.

15. When an alphanumeric field is moved to an alphanumeric field, data are moved _____ character at a time, from _____ to _____.

16. If a five position alphanumeric field is moved to a four position alphanumeric field, the low order character is _____.

17. A numeric move always maintains _____ _____.

18. A PERFORM UNTIL statement always tests the condition (before/after) performing the designated paragraph.

19. A numeric field (may/may not) be moved to an alphabetic field.

20. If a numeric field with PIC 999 is moved to a numeric field with PIC 99, the (most/least) significant digit will be truncated.

21. The _____ _____ option is available for all arithmetic statements and indicates when the result of a computation is larger than its designated PICTURE clause.

22. The _____ statement has been introduced to express a multibranch situation.

True/False

1. One ADD instruction can change the value of more than one data name.

2. Both GIVING and TO may be present in the same ADD instruction.

3. A valid ADD instruction may contain neither GIVING nor TO.

4. Both FROM and GIVING may appear in the same SUBTRACT instruction.

5. The use of GIVING is optional in the MULTIPLY statement.

6. The reserved word INTO must appear in a DIVIDE statement.

7. In the DIVIDE statement, the dividend is always identifier-1.

8. Multiplication and division can be performed in the same MULTIPLY statement.

9. Multiplication and addition can be performed in the same COMPUTE statement.

10. In a COMPUTE statement with no parentheses, multiplication is always done before subtraction.

11. In a COMPUTE statement with no parentheses, multiplication is always done before division.

12. Parentheses are sometimes required in a COMPUTE statement.

13. The COMPUTE statement changes the value of only one data name.

14. The IF statement must always contain the ELSE option.

15. The PERFORM statement transfers control to a paragraph elsewhere in the program.

16. A program may contain more than one STOP RUN statement.

17. STOP RUN must be the last statement in the Procedure Division.

18. The ADVANCING option is mandatory in the WRITE statement.

19. The READ statement contains a record name.

20. The WRITE statement contains a record name.

21. The OPEN and CLOSE statements are optional.

22. The END-IF scope terminator has little effect in an IF statement.

23. An IF statement can cause the execution of several other statements.

24. If the ELSE clause is satisfied in an IF statement, it can cause execution of several statements.

25. The ROUNDED clause is required in the COMPUTE statement.

26. The SIZE ERROR option is allowed only in the COMPUTE statement.

27. The SIZE ERROR option is required in the COMPUTE statement.

28. The EVALUATE statement facilitates implementation of the case construct.

P r o b l e m s

1. Some of the following arithmetic statements are invalid. Identify those, and state why they are unacceptable.

   a. ADD A B C.
   b. SUBTRACT 10 FROM A B.
   c. SUBTRACT A FROM 10.
   d. ADD A TO B GIVING C.
   e. SUBTRACT A ROUNDED FROM B ROUNDED GIVING C.
   f. MULTIPLY A BY 10.
   g. MULTIPLY 10 BY A ROUNDED.
   h. MULTIPLY A BY 10 GIVING B C.
   i. DIVIDE A BY B.
   j. DIVIDE A INTO B.
   k. DIVIDE A INTO B GIVING C.
   l. DIVIDE B BY A GIVING C.
   m. COMPUTE X ROUNDED = A + B.
   n. COMPUTE X = 2(A + B).
   o. COMPUTE V = 20 / A - C.

2. Complete the table below. In each instance, refer to the *initial* values of A, B, C, and D.

Data Name	A	B	C	D
Value before execution	4	8	12	2
Value after execution of				
a. ADD 1 TO D B.				
b. ADD A B C GIVING D.				
c. ADD A B C TO D.				
d. SUBTRACT A B FROM C.				
e. SUBTRACT A B FROM C GIVING D.				
f. MULTIPLY A BY B C.				
g. MULTIPLY B BY A.				
h. DIVIDE A INTO C.				
i. DIVIDE C BY B GIVING D REMAINDER A.				
j. COMPUTE D = A + B / 2 * D.				
k. COMPUTE D = (A + B) / (2 * D).				
l. COMPUTE D = A + B / (2 * D).				
m. COMPUTE D = (A + B) / 2 * D.				
n. COMPUTE D = A + (B / 2) * D.				

3. Indicate the logical errors inherent in the following COBOL fragment:

```
FILE SECTION.
FD  EMPLOYEE-FILE
    .
        .
            .
FD  PRINT-FILE
    .
        .
            .
WORKING-STORAGE SECTION.
01  END-OF-FILE-SWITCH        PIC X(3)        VALUE 'YES'.
    .
        .
            .
PROCEDURE DIVISION.
PREPARE-EMPLOYEE-REPORT.
    MOVE HEADING-LINE TO PRINT-LINE.
    WRITE PRINT-LINE
        AFTER ADVANCING PAGE.
    OPEN INPUT EMPLOYEE-FILE
        OUTPUT PRINT-FILE.
    PERFORM PROCESS-RECORDS
        UNTIL END-OF-FILE-SWITCH = 'YES'.
    CLOSE EMPLOYEE-FILE.
    STOP RUN.
PROCESS-RECORDS.
    READ EMPLOYEE-FILE
        AT END MOVE 'YES' TO END-OF-FILE-SWITCH
    END-READ.
    .
        .
            .
```

4. Some of the following statements are invalid. Indicate those, and state why they are invalid. (Assume FILE-ONE and FILE-TWO are file names and RECORD-ONE is a record name.)

   a. OPEN INPUT RECORD-ONE.
   b. OPEN INPUT FILE-ONE OUTPUT FILE-TWO.
   c. OPEN INPUT FILE-ONE.
   d. CLOSE OUTPUT FILE-ONE.
   e. READ FILE-ONE.
   f. READ FILE-ONE AT END PERFORM END-OF-JOB-ROUTINE.
   g. READ RECORD-ONE AT END PERFORM END-OF-JOB.
   h. WRITE RECORD-ONE.
   i. WRITE RECORD-ONE AFTER ADVANCING TWO LINES.
   j. WRITE RECORD-ONE BEFORE ADVANCING TWO LINES.
   k. CLOSE FILE-ONE FILE-TWO.
   l. WRITE FILE-ONE.
   m. WRITE RECORD-ONE AFTER ADVANCING PAGE.

5. Write COBOL COMPUTE statements to accomplish the intended logic:

   a. $x = a + b + c$

   b. $x = \dfrac{a + bc}{2}$

   c. $x = a^2 + b^2 + c^2$

   d. $x = \dfrac{a + b}{2} - c$

   e. $x = a + b$

   f. $x = \sqrt{\dfrac{a^2 + b^2}{2c}}$

   g. $f = p(1 + i)^n$

   h. $f = \dfrac{\left((1 + i)^n - 1\right)}{i}$

   i. $x = \dfrac{(a + b)^c}{(d + e)^f}$

6. Given the following Procedure Division:

```
PROCEDURE DIVISION.
FIRST-PARAGRAPH.
    MOVE ZEROS TO FIELD-A FIELD-B.
    PERFORM SECOND-PARAGRAPH.
    PERFORM THIRD-PARAGRAPH.
    PERFORM SECOND-PARAGRAPH.
    STOP RUN.
SECOND-PARAGRAPH.
    ADD 10 TO FIELD-A.
    ADD 20 TO FIELD-B.
THIRD-PARAGRAPH.
    MULTIPLY FIELD-A BY FIELD-B GIVING FIELD-C.
    DIVIDE FIELD-A INTO FIELD-B GIVING FIELD-D.
```

   a. What are the final values for FIELD-A, FIELD-B, FIELD-C, and FIELD-D?

   b. How many times is each paragraph executed?

7. Complete the following table, showing the contents of the receiving field.

	SENDING FIELD		RECEIVING FIELD	
	Picture	**Contents**	**Picture**	**Contents**
a.	X(4)	H O P E	X(4)	
b.	X(4)	H O P E	9(4)	
c.	X(4)	H O P E	X(3)	
d.	X(4)	H O P E	X(5)	
e.	9(4)	6 7 8 9	X(4)	
f.	9(4)	6 7 8 9	9(3)	
g.	9(4)	6 7 8 9	9(5)	
h.	999V9	6 7 8 9	9(4)	
i.	999V9	6 7 8 9	9(4)V9	
j.	999V9	6 7 8 9	9(3)V99	
j.	999V9	6 7 8 9	99V99	

8. Supply Procedure Division statements as indicated:

   a. Code two equivalent statements, an ADD and a COMPUTE, to add 1 to the counter NUMBER-QUALIFIED-EMPLOYEES.

   b. Code a COBOL statement to add the contents of five fields, MONDAY-SALES, TUESDAY-SALES, WEDNESDAY-SALES, THURSDAY-SALES, and FRIDAY-SALES, storing the result in WEEKLY-SALES.

   c. Code a COBOL statement to subtract the fields FED-TAX, STATE-TAX, FICA, and VOLUNTARY-DEDUCTIONS, from GROSS-PAY, and put the result in NET-PAY.

   d. Code a single COBOL statement to calculate NET-AMOUNT-DUE, which is equal to the GROSS-SALE minus a 2% discount.

   e. Recode part (d), using two statements (a MULTIPLY and a SUBTRACT).

   f. Code a COBOL statement to compute GROSS-PAY, which is equal to HOURS-WORKED times HOURLY-RATE.

   g. Code a single COBOL statement to compute GROSS-PAY, which is equal to REG-HOURS-WORKED times HOURLY-RATE plus OVERTIME-HOURS times HOURLY-RATE times 1.5.

   h. Code a COBOL statement to determine AVERAGE-SALARY by dividing TOTAL-SALARY by NUMBER-OF-EMPLOYEES.

   i. Code a COBOL Compute statement equivalent to the algebraic formula.

   $$x = \frac{(a+b)c}{de}$$

   j. Code a COBOL Compute statement equivalent to the algebraic formula.

   $$x = \frac{-b + \sqrt{b^2 - 4ac}}{2a}$$

9. Write Procedure Division code for the flowchart in Figure 5.8.

Figure 5.8 Flowcharts for Problem 9

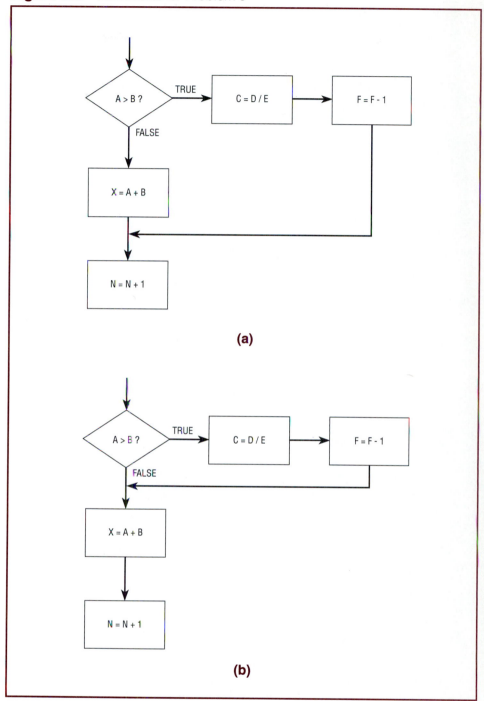

(a)

(b)

6

Debugging

CHAPTER OUTLINE

Overview
Errors in Compilation
    Common Compilation Errors
Errors in Execution
    File Status Codes
    Run-Time Errors
    Logic Errors
Tips for Debugging
    DISPLAY Statement
The Structured Walkthrough
Summary
Fill-in
True/False
Problems

OBJECTIVES

After reading this chapter you will be able to:

■ Distinguish between errors in compilation and execution; correct typical compilation errors.

■ Use the DISPLAY statement as a debugging tool.

■ Explain how an interactive debugger can be used to find and correct execution errors.

■ Describe the use of file status codes in correcting data management errors.

■ Explain what is meant by a structured walkthrough; be able to participate as reviewer, reviewee, moderator, or secretary.

OVERVIEW

Very few computer programs run successfully on the first attempt. Indeed, the programmer is realistically expected to make errors, and an important test of a good programmer is not whether he or she makes mistakes, but how quickly he or she is able to detect and correct the errors. Since this process is such an integral part of programming, an entire chapter is devoted to debugging. We consider errors in both compilation and execution.

Compilation errors occur during the translation of COBOL to machine language and are caused by a mistake in COBOL syntax, for example, a missing period or an entry in a wrong column. Execution errors result after the program has been translated to machine language and produce results that are different from what the programmer expected or intended.

Compilation errors are easy to find because the compiler produces an explicit error message. Execution errors are more difficult to detect and may require the use of additional debugging tools, such as the insertion of DISPLAY statements into a program and/or the use of an interactive debugger. The chapter also considers the structured walkthrough as a means of reducing errors before they occur.

Errors in Compilation

Compilation is the process of translating a source (COBOL) program into machine language. Any mistake in COBOL syntax causes the compiler to make an assumption in the interpretation of the statement in which the error occurs, or, worse yet, makes it impossible for the compiler to interpret the statement at all. Either way a *compilation error* results.

Some errors are less severe than others; for example, the compiler is generally able to guess the programmer's intent when periods are omitted in the Data Division, whereas it is unable to decipher a misspelled reserved word. Accordingly, most compilers provide different levels of ***compiler diagnostics*** (error messages) according to the severity of the error. Fujitsu COBOL97, for example, produces five types of error messages, which are listed in order of increasing severity. Other compilers have similar classifications. Consider:

5 types of Red Lines that come Out as errors

I	Informational Diagnostics	Indicates a coding inefficiency or other condition (for example, an incompatibility with the ANS standard). The program will compile correctly.
W	Warning Diagnostics	The statement is syntactically correct, but the source of a potential problem. A program can compile and execute with several W-level diagnostics present; however, ignoring these messages could lead to errors in execution.
E	Error Diagnostics	The statement is incorrect as written, and requires the compiler to make an assumption in order to complete the compilation. You may wish to correct the program in case the compiler's assumption is not what you intended.
S	Serious Diagnostics	A serious error in that the compiler cannot make corrections and therefore cannot generate object instructions. Any statement flagged as an S-level error is ignored and treated as if it were not present in the program.
U	Unrecoverable Diagnostics	An error of such severity that the compiler does not know what to do and cannot continue. U-level diagnostics are extremely rare, and you practically have to submit a Visual BASIC program to the COBOL compiler to cause a U-level message.

When the computer freezes up

The COBOL compiler tends to rub salt in a wound in the sense that an error in one statement can cause error messages in other statements that appear correct. For example, should you have an S-level error in a SELECT statement, the compiler will flag the error, ignore the SELECT statement, and then flag any other statements that reference that file even though those other statements are correct.

Often simple mistakes such as omitting a line or misspelling a reserved word can lead to a long and sometimes confusing set of error messages. The only consolation is that compiler errors can disappear as quickly as they occurred. Correction of the misspelled word or insertion of the missing statement will often eliminate several errors at once.

Proficiency in debugging comes from experience—the more programs you write, the better you become. You may correct the errors in the order they appear (our preference), or in the order of severity (from Unrecoverable, Serious, Error, Warning, to Informational), or even haphazardly as you find them. Whichever way you choose, try to find the mistakes as quickly as possible and without wasting time. Moreover, don't spend too much time on any single error; instead, if you are stuck, skip the error temporarily and continue to the next, eliminating as many errors as you can before you recompile.

Figure 6.1   Tuition Billing Program with Compilation Errors

```
1       IDENTIFICATION DIVISION.
2       PROGRAM-ID.    TUIT6COM.
3       AUTHOR.        CAROL VAZQUEZ VILLAR.
4
5       ENVIRONMENT DIVISION.
6       INPUT-OUTPUT SECTION.
7       FILE-CONTROL.
8           SELECT STUDENT-FILE   ASSIGN TO SYSIN
9               ORGANIZATION IS LINE SEQUENTIAL.
10          SELECT PRINT-FILE     ASSIGN TO SYSOUT
11              ORGANIZATION IS LINE SEQUENTIAL.
12
13      DATA DIVISION.
14      FILE SECTION.
15      FD  STUDENT-FILE
16          RECORD CONTAINS 27 CHARACTERS.
17      01  STUDENT-RECORD.
18          05  STU-NAME.
19              10  STU-LAST-NAME    PIC X(15).
20              10  STU-INITIALS     PIC XX.
21          05  STU-CREDITS          PIC 9(2).
22          05  STU-UNION-MEMBER     PIC X.
23          05  STU-SCHOLARSHIP      PIC 9(4).
24          05  STU-GPA              PIC 9V99.
25
26      FD  PRINT-FILE
27          RECORD CONTAINS 132 CHARACTERS.
28      01  PRINT-LINE               PIC X(132).
29
30      WORKING-STORAGE SECTION.
31      01  DATA-REMAINS-SWITCH      PIC X(2)  VALUE SPACES.
32
33      01  INDIVIDUAL-CALCULATIONS.
34          05  IND-TUITION          PIC 9(4)  VALUE ZEROS.
35          05  IND-ACTIVITY-FEE     PIC 9(2)  VALUE ZEROS.
36          05  IND-UNION-FEE        PIC 9(2)  VALUE ZEROS.
37          05  IND-SCHOLARSHIP      PIC 9(3)  VALUE ZEROS.
38          05  IND-BILL             PIC 9(6)  VALUE ZEROS.
39
40      01  UNIVERSITY-TOTALS.
41          05  UNI-TUITION          PIC 9(6)  VALUE ZEROS.
42          05  UNI UNION FEE        PIC 9(4)  VALUE ZEROS.
```

Hyphens missing (annotation pointing to line 42, UNI UNION FEE)

Figure 6.1 *(continued)*

```
43        05  UNI-ACTIVITY-FEE   PIC 9(4)   VALUE ZEROS.
44        05  UNI-SCHOLARSHIP    PIC X(6)   VALUE ZEROS.
45        05  UNI-IND-BILL       PIC 9(6)   VALUE ZEROS.
46
47     01 CONSTANTS-AND-RATES.
48        05  PRICE-PER-CREDIT   PIC 9(3)   VALUE 200.
49        05  UNION-FEE          PIC 9(2)   VALUE 25.
50        05  ACTIVITY-FEES.
51            10  1ST-ACTIVITY-FEE PIC 99    VALUE 25.
52            10  1ST-CREDIT-LIMIT PIC 99    VALUE 6.
53            10  2ND-ACTIVITY-FEE PIC 99    VALUE 50.
54            10  2ND-CREDIT-LIMIT PIC 99    VALUE 12.
55            10  3RD-ACTIVITY-FEE PIC 99    VALUE 75.
56        05  MINIMUM-SCHOLAR-GPA PIC 9V9    VALUE 2.5.
57
58     01 HEADING-LINE.
59        05  FILLER             PIC X      VALUE SPACES.
60        05  FILLER             PIC X(12) VALUE 'STUDENT NAME'.
61        05  FILLER             PIC X(10) VALUE SPACES
62        05  FILLER             PIC X(7)  VALUE 'CREDITS'.
63        05  FILLER             PIC X(2)  VALUE SPACES.
64        05  FILLER             PIC X(7)  VALUE 'TUITION'.
65        05  FILLER             PIC X(2)  VALUE SPACES.
66        05  FILLER             PIC X(9)  VALUE 'UNION FEE'.
67        05  FILLER             PIC X(2)  VALUE SPACES.
68        05  FILLER             PIC X(7)  VALUE 'ACT FEE'.
69        05  FILLER             PIC X(2)  VALUE SPACES.
70        05  FILLER             PIC X(11) VALUE 'SCHOLARSHIP'.
71        05  FILLER             PIC X(2)  VALUE SPACES.
72        05  FILLER             PIC X(10) VALUE 'TOTAL BILL'.
73        05  FILLER             PIC X(48) VALUE SPACES.
74
75     01 DETAIL-LINE.
76        05  FILLER             PIC X      VALUE SPACES.
77        05  DET-LAST-NAME      PIC X(15).
78        05  FILLER             PIC X(2)  VALUE SPACES.
79        05  DET-INITIALS       PIC X(2).
80        05  FILLER             PIC X(5)  VALUE SPACES.
81        05  STU-CREDITS        PIC 9(2).
82        05  FILLER             PIC X(6)  VALUE SPACES.
83        05  DET-TUITION        PIC 9(6).
84        05  FILLER             PIC X(7)  VALUE SPACES.
85        05  DET-UNION-FEE      PIC 9(3).
86        05  FILLER             PIC X(6)  VALUE SPACES.
87        05  DET-ACTIVITY-FEE   PIC 9(3).
88        05  FILLER             PIC X(8)  VALUE SPACES.
89        05  DET-SCHOLARSHIP    PIC 9(5).
90        05  FILLER             PIC X(6)  VALUE SPACES.
91        05  DET-IND-BILL       PIC 9(6).
92        05  FILLER             PIC X(49) VALUE SPACES.
```

Alphanumeric picture is not permitted for numeric calculation (annotation pointing to line 44)

Period missing (annotation pointing to line 61)

Should be DET-CREDITS (annotation pointing to line 81, STU-CREDITS)

Figure 6.1 *(continued)*

```
93
94      01   DASH-LINE.
95           05   FILLER            PIC X(31) VALUE SPACES.
96           05   FILLER            PIC X(8)  VALUE ALL '-'.
97           05   FILLER            PIC X(2)  VALUE SPACES.
98           05   FILLER            PIC X(8)  VALUE ALL '-'.
99           05   FILLER            PIC X(2)  VALUE SPACES.
100          05   FILLER            PIC X(7)  VALUE ALL '-'.
101          05   FILLER            PIC X(6)  VALUE SPACES.
102          05   FILLER            PIC X(7)  VALUE ALL '-'.
103          05   FILLER            PIC X(5)  VALUE SPACES.
104          05   FILLER            PIC X(7)  VALUE ALL '-'.
105          05   FILLER            PIC X(49) VALUE SPACES.
106
107     01   TOTAL-LINE.
108          05   FILLER            PIC X(8)  VALUE SPACES.
109          05   FILLER            PIC X(17)
110                   VALUE 'UNIVERSITY TOTALS'.
111          05   FILLER            PIC X(8)  VALUE SPACES.
112          05   TOT-TUITION       PIC 9(6).
113          05   FILLER            PIC X(6)  VALUE SPACES.
114          05   TOT-UNION-FEE     PIC 9(4).
115          05   FILLER            PIC X(5)  VALUE SPACES.
116          05   TOT-ACTIVITY-FEE  PIC 9(4).
117          05   FILLER            PIC X(7)  VALUE SPACES.
118          05   TOT-SCHOLARSHIP   PIC 9(6).
119          05   FILLER            PIC X(6)  VALUE SPACES.
120          05   TOT-IND-BILL      PIC 9(6).
121          05   FILLER            PIC X(49) VALUE SPACES.
122
123     PROCEDURE DIVISION.
124     START.
125         OPEN INPUT STUDENT-FILE
126             OUTPUT PRINT-FILE.
127         PERFORM WRITE-HEADING-LINE.
128         PERFORM READ-STUDENT-FILE.
129         PERFORM PROCESS-STUDENT-RECORD
130             UNTIL DATA-REMAINS-SWITCH = 'NO'.
131         PERFORM WRITE-UNIVERSITY-TOTALS.
132         CLOSE STUDENT-FILE
133             PRINT-FILE.
134         STOP RUN.
135
136     WRITE-HEADING-LINE.
137         MOVE HEADING-LINE TO PRINT-LINE.
138         WRITE PRINT-LINE
139             AFTER ADVANCING PAGE.
140         MOVE SPACES TO PRINT-LINE.
141         WRITE PRINT-LINE.
142
```

— Reserved word used as paragraph name (annotation pointing to line 124 `START.`)

Figure 6.1   *(continued)*

```
143        READ-STUDENT-FILE.                                    Should be STUDENT-FILE
144            READ STUDNET-FILE
145                AT END MOVE 'NO' TO DATA-REMAINS-SWITCH
146            END-READ.
147
148        PROCESS-STUDENT-RECORD.
149            PERFORM COMPUTE-INDIVIDUAL-BILL.
150            PERFORM INCREMENT-UNIVERSITY-TOTALS
151            PERFORM WRITE-DETAIL-LINE.
152            PERFORM READ-STUDENT-FILE.
153
154        COMPUTE-INDIVIDUAL-BILL.
155            PERFORM COMPUTE-TUITION.
156            PERFORM COMPUTE-UNION-FEE.                  FEE extends past column 72
157            PERFORM COMPUTE-ACTIVITY-FEE.
158            PERFORM COMPUTE-SCHOLARSHIP.
159            COMPUTE IND-BILL = IND-TUITION + IND-UNION-FEE + IND-ACTIVITY-FEE
160                              - IND-SCHOLARSHIP.
161
162        COMPUTE-TUITION.
163            COMPUTE IND-TUITION =PRICE-PER-CREDIT * STU-CREDITS.
164
165        COMPUTE-UNION-FEE.
166            IF STU-UNION-MEMBER = 'Y'
167                MOVE UNION-FEE TO IND-UNION-FEE
168            ELSE                                              Missing space after =
169                MOVE ZERO TO IND-UNION-FEE
170            END-IF.
171
172        COMPUTE-ACTIVITY-FEE.                    Multiple definition in lines 21 and 81
173            EVALUATE TRUE
174                WHEN STU-CREDITS <= 1ST-CREDIT-LIMIT
175                    MOVE 1ST-ACTIVITY-FEE TO IND-ACTIVITY-FEE
176                WHEN STU-CREDITS > 1ST-CREDIT-LIMIT
177                    AND STU-CREDITS <= 2ND-CREDIT-LIMIT
178                        MOVE 2ND-ACTIVITY-FEE TO IND-ACTIVITY-FEE
179                WHEN STU-CREDITS > 2ND-CREDIT-LIMIT
180                    MOVE 3RD-ACTIVITY-FEE TO IND-ACTIVITY-FEE
181                WHEN OTHER
182                    DISPLAY 'INVALID CREDITS FOR: ' STU-NAME
183            END-EVALUATE.
184
185        COMPUTE-SCHOLARSHIP.
186            IF STU-GPA > MINIMUM-SCHOLAR-GPA
187                MOVE STU-SCHOLARSHIP TO IND-SCHOLARSHIP
188            ELSE
189                MOVE ZERO TO IND-SCHOLARSHIP      Inconsistent PIC clauses in lines 23 and 37
190            END-IF.
191
192        INCREMENT-UNIVERSITY-TOTALS.
```

Figure 6.1   *(continued)*

```
193          ADD IND-TUITION      TO UNI-TUITION.
194          ADD IND-UNION-FEE     TO UNI-UNION-FEE.
195          ADD IND-ACTIVITY-FEE  TO UNI-ACTIVITY-FEE.
196          ADD IND-SCHOLARSHIP   TO UNI-SCHOLARSHIP.
197          ADD IND-BILL          TO UNI-IND-BILL.
198
199      WRITE-DETAIL-LINE.
200          MOVE STU-LAST-NAME TO DET-LAST-NAME.
201          MOVE STU-INITIALS TO DET-INITIALS.
202          MOVE STU-CREDITS TO DET-CREDITS.
203          MOVE IND-TUITION TO DET-TUITION.
204          MOVE IND-UNION-FEE TO DET-UNION-FEE.
205          MOVE IND-ACTIVITY-FEE TO DET-ACTIVITY-FEE.
206          MOVE IND-SCHOLARSHIP TO DET-SCHOLARSHIP.
207          MOVE IND-BILL TO DET-IND-BILL.
208          MOVE DETAIL-LINE TO PRINT-LINE.
209          WRITE PRINT-FILE
210              AFTER ADVANCING 1 LINE.
211
212      WRITE-UNIVERSITY-TOTALS.
213          MOVE DASH-LINE TO PRINT-LINE.
214          WRITE PRINT-LINE.
215          MOVE UNI-TUITION TO TOT-TUITION.
216          MOVE UNI-UNION-FEE TO TOT-UNION-FEE.
217          MOVE UNI-ACTIVITY-FEE TO TOT-ACTIVITY-FEE.
218          MOVE UNI-SCHOLARSHIP TO TOT-SCHOLARSHIP.
219          MOVE UNI-IND-BILL TO TOT-IND-BILL.
220          MOVE TOTAL-LINE TO PRINT-LINE.
221          WRITE PRINT-LINE
222              AFTER ADVANCING 1 LINE.
```

Put hyphens in Working-Storage definition line 42
PIC X(6) used in definition
Multiple definitions in lines 21 and 81
Not defined in detail line
Should be PRINT-LINE

To give you a better feel of what to expect from your programs, we have taken the tuition billing program from Chapter 5 and deliberately changed several of the statements to cause compilation errors as shown in Figures 6.1 and 6.2. Each message in Figure 6.2 references a statement line number and error level and contains a brief explanation of the error. Some of the errors will be immediately obvious; others may require you to seek help. As you progress through this book and gain practical experience, you will become increasingly self-sufficient.

Figure 6.2   Compilation Errors

```
** DIAGNOSTIC MESSAGE ** (TUIT6COM)
TUIT6COM.CBL 42: JMN1123I-S  INVALID WORD 'UNION' IS FOUND. IGNORED UNTIL NEXT VALID PARAGRAPH,
SECTION OR DIVISION.
TUIT6COM.CBL 61: JMN1103I-W  PERIOD IS MISSING. ASSUMED TO BE CODED.
TUIT6COM.CBL 124: JMN2516I-S  '. ' IN START STATEMENT MUST BE FILE OTHER THAN SORT-MERGE FILE.
TUIT6COM.CBL 124: JMN1004I-W  RESERVED WORD 'START' MUST START IN AREA B. ASSUMED TO START IN
AREA B.
```

Meaning of Errors on pg 141 (handwritten)

Figure 6.2 Compilation Errors *(continued)*

```
TUIT6COM.CBL 144: JMN2503I-S  USER WORD 'STUDNET-FILE' IS UNDEFINED.
TUIT6COM.CBL 146: JMN2510I-S  NO CORRESPONDING 'END-READ' IS SPECIFIED. 'END-READ' IS IGNORED.
TUIT6COM.CBL 163: JMN2504I-S  USER WORD 'STU-CREDITS' IS MULTI-DEFINED.
TUIT6COM.CBL 163: JMN2565I-S  INVALID OPERAND IS SPECIFIED IN ARITHMETIC EXPRESSION. ARITHMETIC
EXPRESSION IGNORED.
TUIT6COM.CBL 163: JMN2557I-S  FORMAT OF COMPUTE STATEMENT IS INCOMPLETE.
TUIT6COM.CBL 163: JMN1041I-W  SEPARATOR MUST FOLLOW CHARACTER STRING. SEPARATOR ASSUMED.
TUIT6COM.CBL 174: JMN2504I-S  USER WORD 'STU-CREDITS' IS MULTI-DEFINED.
TUIT6COM.CBL 174: JMN2539I-S  NUMBER OF SELECTION OBJECTS IS MORE THAN NUMBER OF SELECTION SUBJECTS.
THEIR NUMBERS MUST BE EQUAL. EXCESS SELECTION OBJECTS IGNORED.
TUIT6COM.CBL 176: JMN2504I-S  USER WORD 'STU-CREDITS' IS MULTI-DEFINED.
TUIT6COM.CBL 176: JMN2539I-S  NUMBER OF SELECTION OBJECTS IS MORE THAN NUMBER OF SELECTION SUBJECTS.
THEIR NUMBERS MUST BE EQUAL. EXCESS SELECTION OBJECTS IGNORED.
TUIT6COM.CBL 179: JMN2504I-S  USER WORD 'STU-CREDITS' IS MULTI-DEFINED.
TUIT6COM.CBL 179: JMN2539I-S  NUMBER OF SELECTION OBJECTS IS MORE THAN NUMBER OF SELECTION SUBJECTS.
THEIR NUMBERS MUST BE EQUAL. EXCESS SELECTION OBJECTS IGNORED.
TUIT6COM.CBL 194: JMN2503I-S  USER WORD 'UNI-UNION-FEE' IS UNDEFINED.
TUIT6COM.CBL 194: JMN2557I-S  FORMAT OF ADD STATEMENT IS INCOMPLETE.
TUIT6COM.CBL 196: JMN3062I-S  OPERAND 'UNI-SCHOLARSHIP' IN ADD STATEMENT MUST BE NUMERIC ITEM.
TUIT6COM.CBL 202: JMN2504I-S  USER WORD 'STU-CREDITS' IS MULTI-DEFINED.
TUIT6COM.CBL 209: JMN2589I-S  'PRINT-FILE' IN WRITE STATEMENT MUST NOT BE RECORD-NAME OR SORT-MERGE
FILE.
TUIT6COM.CBL 216: JMN2503I-S  USER WORD 'UNI-UNION-FEE' IS UNDEFINED.
STATISTICS: HIGHEST SEVERITY CODE=S. PROGRAM UNIT=1
BUILD INTERRUPTED
```

(handwritten annotation right of arithmetic lines) *space b/g after symbols eg < > + - etc*

(handwritten annotation right of ADD statement line) *['as in the program, itts an X instead of a no,]*

Let us examine the errors:

42: JMN1123I-S INVALID WORD 'UNION' IS FOUND. IGNORED UNTIL NEXT VALID PARAGRAPH, SECTION OR DIVISION.

This error results from the first omitted hyphen in the definition of UNI-UNION-FEE in line 42; that is, the compiler does not know how to handle what it thinks are two data names in a row (UNI and UNION), hence the error. In this case, the compiler found an S-level error and ignored the rest of the statement. Thus, the compiler did not detect the missing hyphen between UNION and FEE. If only the first hyphen is inserted and the program recompiled, the compiler will then discover that the second hyphen is missing. Sometimes, one syntax error hides other errors.

Correction: Insert hyphens to read UNI-UNION.

61: JMN1103I-W PERIOD IS MISSING. ASSUMED TO BE CODED.

A level number must follow a completed statement, but the period ending line 61 has been removed. In this instance, the compiler assumes that the period is present, so no harm is done, but it is poor programming to permit such W-level diagnostics to remain. Moreover, a missing period can be very damaging in some situations.

Correction: Insert a period at the end of line 61.

124: JMN2516I-S '. ' IN START STATEMENT MUST BE FILE OTHER THAN SORT-MERGE FILE.

124: JMN1004I-S RESERVED WORD 'START' MUST START IN AREA B. ASSUMED TO START IN AREA B.

The error in line 124 is a subtle one that typically sends the beginner for help. START is intended as a paragraph name, and paragraph names must begin in the A-margin, so what's the problem? The difficulty is that START is a reserved word and cannot be used as a paragraph name.

Correction: Choose another name, for example, START-THE-PROGRAM.

```
144: JMN2503I-S  USER WORD 'STUDNET-FILE' IS UNDEFINED.
```

The compiler was expecting a valid file name but didn't find one because line 144 references STUD*NET*-FILE rather than STUDENT-FILE. *You* know they are the same, but the compiler does not and hence the error.

Correction: Change the file name to STUDENT-FILE in statement 144.

```
146: JMN2510I-S  NO CORRESPONDING 'END-READ' IS SPECIFIED. 'END-READ' IS
IGNORED.
```

This error will disappear with the correction to the previous READ statement.

Correction: None required beyond the correction to line 144.

```
163: JMN2504I-S  USER WORD 'STU-CREDITS' IS MULTI-DEFINED.
163: JMN2565I-S  INVALID OPERAND IS SPECIFIED IN ARITHMETIC EXPRESSION.
ARITHMETIC EXPRESSION IGNORED.
163: JMN2557I-S  FORMAT OF COMPUTE STATEMENT IS INCOMPLETE.
163: JMN1041I-W  SEPARATOR MUST FOLLOW CHARACTER STRING. SEPARATOR
ASSUMED.
```

These four error messages refer to two problems. The first message points out that STU-CREDITS is defined multiple times. We discuss this situation below. The remaining three messages are generated because there is no blank between the "=" and PRICE-PER-CREDIT. All relational symbols, as well as all arithmetic operators, must be preceded and followed by a blank.

Correction: Insert a space after the "=".

```
174: JMN2504I-S  USER WORD 'STU-CREDITS' IS MULTI-DEFINED.
174: JMN2539I-S  NUMBER OF SELECTION OBJECTS IS MORE THAN NUMBER OF
SELECTION SUBJECTS.  THEIR NUMBERS MUST BE EQUAL. EXCESS SELECTION OBJECTS
IGNORED.
176: JMN2504I-S  USER WORD 'STU-CREDITS' IS MULTI-DEFINED.
176: JMN2539I-S  NUMBER OF SELECTION OBJECTS IS MORE THAN NUMBER OF
SELECTION SUBJECTS.  THEIR NUMBERS MUST BE EQUAL. EXCESS SELECTION OBJECTS
IGNORED.
179: JMN2504I-S  USER WORD 'STU-CREDITS' IS MULTI-DEFINED.
179: JMN2539I-S  NUMBER OF SELECTION OBJECTS IS MORE THAN NUMBER OF
SELECTION SUBJECTS.  THEIR NUMBERS MUST BE EQUAL. EXCESS SELECTION OBJECTS
IGNORED.
```

A multi-defined error message implies that two or more data names are the same. In this instance STU-CREDITS is defined in line 21 and again in line 81 (the latter should be DET-CREDITS), and the compiler does not know which is which.

Correction: Restore uniqueness to the data name in line 81 by changing STU-CREDITS to DET-CREDITS. This action will also eliminate the first error message for line 163.

```
194: JMN2503I-S  USER WORD 'UNI-UNION-FEE' IS UNDEFINED.
194: JMN2557I-S  FORMAT OF ADD STATEMENT IS INCOMPLETE.
```

The error message references UNI-UNION-FEE as an undefined symbol and is another example of how one error can cause several others. Hyphens were omitted in the definition of UNI-UNION-FEE in line 42, and thus (as far as the compiler is concerned) the data name UNI-UNION-FEE does not exist. Because

UNI-UNION-FEE does not exist, the ADD statement has no place to put its results. Thus, the compiler states that the ADD statement is incomplete.

Correction: This diagnostic will disappear with the correction to line 42.

```
    196: JMN3062I-S  OPERAND 'UNI-SCHOLARSHIP' IN ADD STATEMENT MUST BE NUMERIC
ITEM.
```

Arithmetic is permitted only on numeric data names. UNI-SCHOLARSHIP, however, was defined in line 44 as an alphanumeric rather than a numeric data name, and hence the error.

Correction: Change the PICTURE clause in line 44 from X(6) to 9(6).

```
    202: JMN2504I-S  USER WORD 'STU-CREDITS' IS MULTI-DEFINED.
```

This error is identical to the earlier nonunique message from lines 163, 174, 176, 177, and 179.

Correction: This error will disappear after changing STU-CREDITS to DET-CREDITS in line 81.

```
    209: JMN2589I-S  'PRINT-FILE' IN WRITE STATEMENT MUST NOT BE RECORD-NAME OF
SORT-MERGE FILE.
```

A WRITE statement, such as the one in line 209, requires a record name rather than a file name.

Correction: Change line 209 to WRITE PRINT-LINE instead of WRITE PRINT-FILE.

```
    216: JMN2503I-S  USER WORD 'UNI-UNION-FEE' IS UNDEFINED.
```

This error is identical to the one in line 194 and is due to the omitted hyphens in the definition of UNI-UNION-FEE.

Correction: None required beyond the previous correction to line 42.

These are all of the compilation errors detected by COBOL97. This program example was prepared for an earlier edition of the book and a different compiler. In making the conversion to COBOL97, we found two errors it did not detect. The first was in line 159, where IND-ACTIVITY-FEE extends beyond column 72. COBOL97 allows code to be written beyond column 72. Thus, line 159 compiled properly. This feature overcomes an unnecessary restriction imposed by earler compilers. However, you must be aware that most COBOL compilers do have this restriction.

The second error COBOL97 did not detect was in line 187. The MOVE statement moves the value of STU-SCHOLARSHIP—a 9(4) field) to a 9(3) field. When the sending field is larger than the receiving field, the leftmost digit may be lost. This error may result in computation errors. Some compilers issue an I- or W-level warning for this condition. COBOL97 does not.

Common Compilation Errors

Compilation errors are a fact of life. Don't be discouraged if you have many compilation errors in your first few attempts, and don't be surprised if you have several pages of diagnostics. Remember that a single error in a COBOL program can result in many error messages, and that several errors often can be made to disappear with one correction. Before leaving the subject, it is worthwhile to review a list of common errors and suggested ways to avoid them:

Nonunique data names. This error occurs because the same data name is defined in two different records or twice within the same record. For example, CREDITS might be specified as an input field in STUDENT-FILE and again as output in a detail line. You can avoid the problem by prefixing every data name within a record by a unique prefix as shown below:

```
01  STUDENT-RECORD
    05  STU-NAME
        10  STU-LAST-NAME
        10  STU-INITIALS
    05  STU-CREDITS
    05  STU-UNION-MEMBER
    05  STU-SCHOLARSHIP
    05  STU-GPA
```

Omitted (or extra) periods. Every COBOL sentence should have a period. Omission in the first three divisions often results in the compiler's assumption of a period where one belongs, and such errors are generally harmless. The effect is far more serious in the Procedure Division, where missing and/or extra periods affect the generated logic.

Omitted space before or after an arithmetic operator. The arithmetic operators, **, *, /, +, and – all require a space before and after (a typical error for BASIC programmers, since the space is not required in that language).

Invalid picture clause for numeric entry. All data names used in arithmetic statements must have numeric picture clauses consisting of 9's, an implied decimal point, and an optional sign.

Conflicting picture and value clause. Numeric pictures must have numeric values (no quotes); nonnumeric pictures must have nonnumeric values (enclosed in quotes). Both entries below are *invalid*.

```
05  TOTAL   PIC 9(3)  VALUE '123'.
05  TITLE   PIC X(3)  VALUE 123.
```

Inadvertent use of COBOL reserved words. COBOL has a list of some 300 reserved words that can be used only in their designated sense; any other use results in one or several diagnostics. Some reserved words are obvious, for example, WORKING-STORAGE, IDENTIFICATION, ENVIRONMENT, DATA, and PROCEDURE. Others—such as CODE, DATE, START, and REPORT—are less obvious. Instead of memorizing the list or continually referring to it, we suggest this simple rule of thumb: *Always use a hyphen in every data name you create.* This will work more than 99% of the time.

Conflicting RECORD CONTAINS clause and FD record description. This is a common error, even for established programmers. It can stem from careless addition in that the sum of the pictures in the FD does not equal the number of characters in the RECORD CONTAINS clause. It can also result from other errors within the Data Division, for example, when an entry containing a PICTURE clause is flagged. (Remember that if an E-level diagnostic occurs, that entry will be ignored, and the count is thrown off.)

Receiving field too small to accommodate sending field. This is an extremely common error, often associated with edited pictures (editing is discussed in Chapter 7). Consider the entries:

```
05  PRINT-TOTAL-PAY    PIC $$,$$$.
05  WS-TOTAL-PAY       PIC 9(5).
```

```
MOVE WS-TOTAL-PAY TO PRINT-TOTAL-PAY.
```

The MOVE statement would generate the warning that the receiving field may be too small to accommodate the sending field. The greatest possible value for WS-TOTAL-PAY is 99,999; the largest possible value that could be printed by PRINT-TOTAL-PAY is $9,999. Even though the picture for the print field contains five $'s, one $ must always be printed along with the numeric characters, hence the warning.

Omitted (or extra) hyphens in a data name. This is a careless error, but one that occurs too often. If, for example, we define PRINT-TOTAL-PAY in the Data Division and then reference PRINT TOTAL-PAY in the Procedure Division, the compiler catches the inconsistency. It doesn't state that a hyphen was omitted, but indicates that PRINT and TOTAL-PAY are undefined.

A related error is the insertion of extra hyphens where they don't belong, for example, WORKING-STORAGE-SECTION or DATA-DIVISION.

Misspelled data names or reserved words. Too many COBOL students are poor spellers. Sound strange? How do you spell *environment*? One or many errors can result, depending on which word was spelled incorrectly.

Reading a record name or writing a file name. The COBOL rule is very simple—read a file and write a record—but many people get it confused. Consider:

```
FD  STUDENT-FILE
        DATA RECORD IS STUDENT-RECORD.

FD  PRINT-FILE
        DATA RECORD IS PRINT-RECORD.

Correct entries:
        READ STUDENT-FILE . . .
        WRITE PRINT-RECORD . . .

Incorrect entries:
        READ STUDENT-RECORD . . .
        WRITE PRINT-FILE . . .
```

Going past column 72. This error can cause any of the preceding errors as well as a host of others. A COBOL statement must end in column 72 or before; columns 73–80 are left blank or used for program identification. (The 72-column restriction does not apply to data.)

Errors in Execution

After a program has been successfully compiled, it can proceed to execution, and therein lies the strength and weakness of the computer. The primary attractiveness of the machine is its ability to perform its task quickly; its weakness stems from the fact that it does exactly what it has been instructed to do. The machine cannot think for itself; the programmer must think for the machine. If you were to inadvertently instruct the computer to compute tuition by charging $20 instead of $200 per credit, then that is what it would do.

To give you an idea of what can happen, we have deliberately altered the original tuition billing program of Chapter 5 and created a new program, shown in Figure 6.3. Incorporated into this program are two types of errors: run-time errors and logic errors. Run-time errors prevent the program from carrying out its task even though the program compiled properly. Logic errors do not stop the program, but they cause invalid output from the program.

Figure 6.3 Tuition Billing Program with Execution Errors

```
1       IDENTIFICATION DIVISION.
2       PROGRAM-ID.    TUIT6EXE.
3       AUTHOR.        CAROL VAZQUEZ VILLAR.
4
```

Figure 6.3 *(continued)*

```
 5      ENVIRONMENT DIVISION.
 6      INPUT-OUTPUT SECTION.
 7      FILE-CONTROL.
 8          SELECT STUDENT-FILE   ASSIGN TO SYSIN
 9              ORGANIZATION IS LINE SEQUENTIAL.
10          SELECT PRINT-FILE     ASSIGN TO SYSOUT
11              ORGANIZATION IS LINE SEQUENTIAL.
12
13      DATA DIVISION.
14      FILE SECTION.
15      FD  STUDENT-FILE
16          RECORD CONTAINS 27 CHARACTERS.
17      01  STUDENT-RECORD.
18          05  STU-NAME.
19              10  STU-LAST-NAME   PIC X(15).
20              10  STU-INITIALS    PIC XX.
21          05  STU-CREDITS         PIC 9(2).
22          05  STU-UNION-MEMBER    PIC X.
23          05  STU-SCHOLARSHIP     PIC 9(4).
24          05  STU-GPA             PIC 999.              ————— Implied decimal place missing
25
26      FD  PRINT-FILE
27          RECORD CONTAINS 132 CHARACTERS.
28      01  PRINT-LINE              PIC X(132).
29
30      WORKING-STORAGE SECTION.
31      01  DATA-REMAINS-SWITCH     PIC X(2)  VALUE SPACES.
32
33      01  INDIVIDUAL-CALCULATIONS.
34          05  IND-TUITION         PIC 9(4)  VALUE ZEROS.
35          05  IND-ACTIVITY-FEE    PIC 9(2)  VALUE ZEROS.
36          05  IND-UNION-FEE       PIC 9(2)  VALUE ZEROS.
37          05  IND-SCHOLARSHIP     PIC 9(4)  VALUE ZEROS.
38          05  IND-BILL            PIC 9(6)  VALUE ZEROS.
39
40      01  UNIVERSITY-TOTALS.
41          05  UNI-TUITION         PIC 9(6)  VALUE ZEROS.
42          05  UNI-UNION-FEE       PIC 9(4)  VALUE ZEROS.
43          05  UNI-ACTIVITY-FEE    PIC 9(4)  VALUE ZEROS.
44          05  UNI-SCHOLARSHIP     PIC 9(6)  VALUE ZEROS.
45          05  UNI-IND-BILL        PIC 9(6)  VALUE ZEROS.
46
47      01  CONSTANTS-AND-RATES.
48          05  PRICE-PER-CREDIT    PIC 9(3)  VALUE 200.
49          05  UNION-FEE           PIC 9(2)  VALUE 25.
50          05  ACTIVITY-FEES.
51              10  1ST-ACTIVITY-FEE PIC 99   VALUE 25.
52              10  1ST-CREDIT-LIMIT PIC 99   VALUE 6.
```

Figure 6.3 *(continued)*

```
53                 10  2ND-ACTIVITY-FEE PIC 99     VALUE 50.
54                 10  2ND-CREDIT-LIMIT PIC 99     VALUE 12.
55                 10  3RD-ACTIVITY-FEE PIC 99     VALUE 75.
56             05  MINIMUM-SCHOLAR-GPA  PIC 9V9    VALUE 2.5.
57
58         01  HEADING-LINE.
59             05  FILLER            PIC X     VALUE SPACES.
60             05  FILLER            PIC X(12) VALUE 'STUDENT NAME'.
61             05  FILLER            PIC X(10) VALUE SPACES.
62             05  FILLER            PIC X(7)  VALUE 'CREDITS'.
63             05  FILLER            PIC X(2)  VALUE SPACES.
64             05  FILLER            PIC X(7)  VALUE 'TUITION'.
65             05  FILLER            PIC X(2)  VALUE SPACES.
66             05  FILLER            PIC X(9)  VALUE 'UNION FEE'.
67             05  FILLER            PIC X(2)  VALUE SPACES.
68             05  FILLER            PIC X(7)  VALUE 'ACT FEE'.
69             05  FILLER            PIC X(2)  VALUE SPACES.
70             05  FILLER            PIC X(11) VALUE 'SCHOLARSHIP'.
71             05  FILLER            PIC X(2)  VALUE SPACES.
72             05  FILLER            PIC X(10) VALUE 'TOTAL BILL'.
73             05  FILLER            PIC X(48) VALUE SPACES.
74
75         01  DETAIL-LINE.
76             05  FILLER            PIC X     VALUE SPACES.
77             05  DET-LAST-NAME     PIC X(15).
78             05  FILLER            PIC X(2)  VALUE SPACES.
79             05  DET-INITIALS      PIC X(2).
80             05  FILLER            PIC X(5)  VALUE SPACES.
81             05  DET-CREDITS       PIC 9(2).
82             05  FILLER            PIC X(6)  VALUE SPACES.
83             05  DET-TUITION       PIC 9(6).
84             05  FILLER            PIC X(7)  VALUE SPACES.
85             05  DET-UNION-FEE     PIC 9(3).
86             05  FILLER            PIC X(6)  VALUE SPACES.
87             05  DET-ACTIVITY-FEE  PIC 9(3).
88             05  FILLER            PIC X(8)  VALUE SPACES.
89             05  DET-SCHOLARSHIP   PIC 9(5).
90             05  FILLER            PIC X(6)  VALUE SPACES.
91             05  DET-IND-BILL      PIC 9(6).
92             05  FILLER            PIC X(49) VALUE SPACES.
93
94         01  DASH-LINE.
95             05  FILLER            PIC X(31) VALUE SPACES.
96             05  FILLER            PIC X(8)  VALUE ALL '-'.
97             05  FILLER            PIC X(2)  VALUE SPACES.
98             05  FILLER            PIC X(8)  VALUE ALL '-'.
99             05  FILLER            PIC X(2)  VALUE SPACES.
100            05  FILLER            PIC X(7)  VALUE ALL '-'.
```

Figure 6.3   *(continued)*

```
101              05   FILLER              PIC X(6)  VALUE SPACES.
102              05   FILLER              PIC X(7)  VALUE ALL '-'.
103              05   FILLER              PIC X(5)  VALUE SPACES.
104              05   FILLER              PIC X(7)  VALUE ALL '-'.
105              05   FILLER              PIC X(49) VALUE SPACES.
106
107         01   TOTAL-LINE.
108              05   FILLER              PIC X(8)  VALUE SPACES.
109              05   FILLER              PIC X(17)
110                        VALUE 'UNIVERSITY TOTALS'.
111              05   FILLER              PIC X(8)  VALUE SPACES.
112              05   TOT-TUITION         PIC 9(6).
113              05   FILLER              PIC X(6)  VALUE SPACES.
114              05   TOT-UNION-FEE       PIC 9(4).
115              05   FILLER              PIC X(5)  VALUE SPACES.
116              05   TOT-ACTIVITY-FEE    PIC 9(4).
117              05   FILLER              PIC X(7)  VALUE SPACES.
118              05   TOT-SCHOLARSHIP     PIC 9(6).
119              05   FILLER              PIC X(6)  VALUE SPACES.
120              05   TOT-IND-BILL        PIC 9(6).
121              05   FILLER              PIC X(49) VALUE SPACES.
122
123         PROCEDURE DIVISION.
124         PREPARE-TUITION-REPORT.
125             OPEN INPUT STUDENT-FILE
126                  OUTPUT PRINT-FILE.
127             PERFORM WRITE-HEADING-LINE.
128             PERFORM READ-STUDENT-FILE.
129             PERFORM PROCESS-STUDENT-RECORD
130                  UNTIL DATA-REMAINS-SWITCH = 'NO'.
131             PERFORM WRITE-UNIVERSITY-TOTALS.
132             CLOSE STUDENT-FILE
133                  PRINT-FILE.
134             STOP RUN.
135
136         WRITE-HEADING-LINE.
137             MOVE HEADING-LINE TO PRINT-LINE.
138             WRITE PRINT-LINE
139                 AFTER ADVANCING PAGE.
140             MOVE SPACES TO PRINT-LINE.
141             WRITE PRINT-LINE.
142
143         READ-STUDENT-FILE.
144             READ STUDENT-FILE
145                 AT END MOVE 'NO' TO DATA-REMAINS-SWITCH
```

Figure 6.3 *(continued)*

```
146            END-READ.
147
148        PROCESS-STUDENT-RECORD.                    ── READ statement incorrectly placed
149            PERFORM READ-STUDENT-FILE.
150            PERFORM COMPUTE-INDIVIDUAL-BILL.
151            PERFORM INCREMENT-UNIVERSITY-TOTALS
152            PERFORM WRITE-DETAIL-LINE.
153
154        COMPUTE-INDIVIDUAL-BILL.
155            PERFORM COMPUTE-TUITION.
156            PERFORM COMPUTE-UNION-FEE.
157            PERFORM COMPUTE-ACTIVITY-FEE.
158            PERFORM COMPUTE-SCHOLARSHIP.
159            COMPUTE IND-BILL = IND-TUITION + IND-UNION-FEE +
160                IND-ACTIVITY-FEE - IND-SCHOLARSHIP.
161
162        COMPUTE-TUITION.
163            COMPUTE IND-TUITION = PRICE-PER-CREDIT * STU-CREDITS.
164
165        COMPUTE-UNION-FEE.
166            IF STU-UNION-MEMBER = 'Y'                ── Order of IF statement is reversed
167               MOVE ZERO TO IND-UNION-FEE
168            ELSE
169               MOVE UNION-FEE TO IND-UNION-FEE
170            END-IF.
171
172        COMPUTE-ACTIVITY-FEE.
173            EVALUATE TRUE
174                WHEN STU-CREDITS <= 1ST-CREDIT-LIMIT
175                    MOVE 1ST-ACTIVITY-FEE TO IND-ACTIVITY-FEE
176                WHEN STU-CREDITS > 1ST-CREDIT-LIMIT
177                    AND STU-CREDITS <= 2ND-CREDIT-LIMIT
178                        MOVE 2ND-ACTIVITY-FEE TO IND-ACTIVITY-FEE
179                WHEN STU-CREDITS > 2ND-CREDIT-LIMIT
180                    MOVE 3RD-ACTIVITY-FEE TO IND-ACTIVITY-FEE
181                WHEN OTHER
182                    DISPLAY 'INVALID CREDITS FOR: ' STU-NAME
183            END-EVALUATE.
184
185        COMPUTE-SCHOLARSHIP.
186            IF STU-GPA > MINIMUM-SCHOLAR-GPA
187               MOVE STU-SCHOLARSHIP TO IND-SCHOLARSHIP
188            ELSE
189               MOVE ZERO TO IND-SCHOLARSHIP
```

Figure 6.3   *(continued)*

```
190           END-IF.
191
192       INCREMENT-UNIVERSITY-TOTALS.
193           ADD IND-TUITION       TO UNI-TUITION.
194           ADD IND-ACTIVITY-FEE TO UNI-ACTIVITY-FEE.
195           ADD IND-SCHOLARSHIP   TO UNI-SCHOLARSHIP.
196           ADD IND-BILL          TO UNI-IND-BILL.
197
198       WRITE-DETAIL-LINE.
199           MOVE STU-LAST-NAME TO DET-LAST-NAME.
200           MOVE STU-INITIALS TO DET-INITIALS.
201           MOVE STU-CREDITS TO DET-CREDITS.
202           MOVE IND-TUITION TO DET-TUITION.
203           MOVE IND-UNION-FEE TO DET-UNION-FEE.
204           MOVE IND-ACTIVITY-FEE TO DET-ACTIVITY-FEE.
205           MOVE IND-SCHOLARSHIP TO DET-SCHOLARSHIP.
206           MOVE IND-BILL TO DET-IND-BILL.
207           MOVE DETAIL-LINE TO PRINT-LINE.
208           WRITE PRINT-LINE
209              AFTER ADVANCING 1 LINE.
210
211       WRITE-UNIVERSITY-TOTALS.
212           MOVE DASH-LINE TO PRINT-LINE.
213           WRITE PRINT-LINE.
214           MOVE UNI-TUITION TO TOT-TUITION.
215           MOVE UNI-UNION-FEE TO TOT-UNION-FEE.
216           MOVE UNI-ACTIVITY-FEE TO TOT-ACTIVITY-FEE.
217           MOVE UNI-SCHOLARSHIP TO TOT-SCHOLARSHIP.
218           MOVE IND-BILL TO TOT-IND-BILL.
219           MOVE TOTAL-LINE TO PRINT-LINE.
220           WRITE PRINT-LINE
221              AFTER ADVANCING 1 LINE.
```

ADD statement is missing for UNI-UNION-FEE — (annotation pointing to lines 193–196)

Wrong field is moved to print line — (annotation pointing to line 218)

Run-Time Errors

Input/output operations occur throughout the execution of a COBOL program and are frequently a source of run-time errors. A common error is misspelling a file name. Figures 6.4a and 6.4b show the messages that occur when this happens. The message in Figure 6.4a is very cryptic, but it is saying that the program cannot open the SYSIN file. The program cannot find a file with the specified name. Figure 6.4b's message is not much better. This message says that the program cannot continue to run.

Look carefully at the SYSIN statement in the Environmental Variables dialog box shown in Figure 6.4c. There is a subtle and maddening error here. The word TUITI0N is spelled with a"zero" and not an "oh." These two characters look very much alike to us, but the computer detects the difference. Therefore, while we think that the program should find TUITI0N.DAT, the program is actually looking for TUITI0N.DAT.

You can correct the error by highlighting the SYSIN statement. This causes a copy of the statement to appear in the Environmental Variables Information text

Figure 6.4 File Status Errors

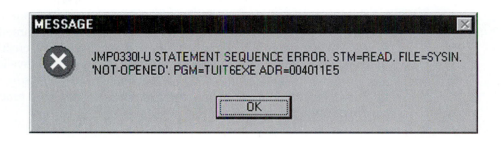

(a) File not opened error message

(b) Forced termination message.

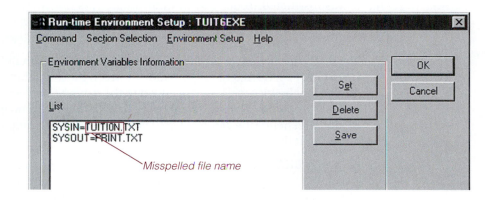

(c) Misspelled file name.

box. Correct the spelling and click on the Set button. You may also want to save your correction by clicking on the Save button. Misspelled file names are likely to be your most common run-time error using COBOL97.

Another common run-time error may cause COBOL programs to fail. This error occurs when a program encounters a space or letter in a numeric field. Since numeric fields can include numeric digits, many programs will immediately stop if they detect this condition. Mainframe programs are particularly sensitive to invalid characters in numeric fields. COBOL97, however, is tolerant of invalid characters. Thus, programs compiled by COBOL97 probably will not stop under these conditions. Nevertheless, when building data files, it is *not* good practice to allow spaces in numeric fields.

Logic Errors

There are several subtle errors in Figure 6.5:

1. The university total for union fees is zero rather than a computed amount.

2. The sum of the individual fills in the total line appears as 850 (the amount for the last record), rather than a running total of 24550.

3. The union fees are reversed for each student. For example, James and Baker are charged $25 when they should be charged nothing; conversely, Part-Timer and Jones are charged nothing when their fee is $25.

4. The last record for NB Kerbel is processed twice; a related error is that the first record for Smith was omitted.

5. James was erroneously awarded a scholarship of $500; James, however, does not qualify, because his average is below 2.5.

We emphasize that these logic errors are not contrived but are typical of students and beginning programmers. Even the accomplished practitioner can be guilty of similar errors when rushed or careless. Realize also that logic errors occur without fanfare. There are no compiler diagnostics or run-time error messages to warn of impending trouble. The program has compiled cleanly and runs smoothly to the end; there is nothing to indicate a problem.

The errors in Figure 6.3 are errors in execution, rather than in compilation. The program compiled cleanly because it is *syntactically correct*, but it executed improperly because it is *logically incorrect*. Nevertheless, the program did precisely what it was instructed to do, which, unfortunately, is not what the programmer wanted it to do. It is necessary, therefore, to find the source of each logic error, as discussed below.

1. The totals for the university are computed in the paragraph INCREMENT-UNIVERSITY-TOTALS (lines 192–196), in which the individual amounts for the student being processed are added to the running university totals. Note, however, that the ADD statement for UNI-UNION-FEE is conspicuously absent, and hence the value of UNI-UNION-FEE remains unchanged throughout the program.

2. UNI-IND-BILL is defined in line 45 and correctly incremented for each record in line 196; so far, so good. However, when the total line is built in line 218, IND-BILL rather than UNI-IND-BILL is moved to TOT-IND-BILL, causing the individual last bill (for Kerbel) to be printed as the total.

3. IND-UNION-FEE is calculated in a simple IF statement in lines 166–170, in which the IF and ELSE clauses are reversed; that is, the union fee is $25 for

students who belong to the union as indicated by a Y in the appropriate incoming field.

4. The *correct* implementation to process a file requires an initial (priming) READ in the paragraph PREPARE-TUITION-REPORT, as well as a second READ statement as the *last* statement in the PROCESS-STUDENT-RECORD. The errors for Kerbel and Smith occur because the latter READ statement was *incorrectly* moved to the beginning of the performed routine.

   To understand the effect of the misplaced statement, consider a file with two records. The first record is read by the initial READ statement, after which the paragraph PROCESS-STUDENT-RECORD is entered. The second READ statement (incorrectly placed at the beginning of the paragraph) overwrites the first record without processing it. Thus, the first record is effectively lost.

   Moreover, when the last statement in PROCESS-STUDENT-RECORD is executed, the end of file has not yet been reached. This in turn causes PROCESS-STUDENT-RECORD to be executed a *second* time, although there are not any more records. The end of file is sensed immediately in line 149, but the PERFORM is not terminated until line 152, so that the intermediate statements are executed a second time for the last record.

5. The definition of STU-GPA in line 24 incorrectly omits the implied decimal point in the PICTURE clause. Hence, incoming averages will be interpreted as ten times their true value (i.e., 2.5 will be stored as 25). Thus, all students will have an average greater than 2.5, and hence all students with potential scholarships receive them.

Tips for Debugging

It was easy to find the execution errors just discussed because we created them in the first place, and hence we knew exactly where to look. In practice, it is not so easy. Fortunately, COBOL97 provides some powerful tools to help with debugging programs. Appendix A provides some useful exercises and one specifically devoted to debugging. However, we can provide a few tips here as well.

1. Step through the program using the Step Into Button. This button allows you to move through the program one line at a time. As you move through the program, you can find the current value of any field by moving your cursor over that field. A little window appears to show the value.

2. Use breakpoints to stop the program at critical junctures in the program. You can set the breakpoints by right-clicking on the line of code and choosing the Set Breakpoint option as shown in Figure 6.6a. By setting a breakpoint, you can run the program at full speed until it encounters the breakpoint. The program stops at that point, and you can proceed one step at a time through the problem code.

3. Set Watches on critical data fields. Highlight the desired field, then right-click to bring up a menu as shown in Figure 6.6b. Choose Watch Data for tracking the field's values as the program runs.

Figure 6.5 Tuition Billing Report Comparisons—Invalid and Valid

4 *Smith is missing*   3 *Union fees are reversed*

STUDENT NAME		CREDITS	TUITION	UNION FEE	ACT FEE	SCHOLARSHIP	TOTAL BILL
							5 *Should not have a scholarship*
JAMES	HR	15	003000	025	075	00500	002600
BAKER	SR	09	001800	025	050	00500	001375
PART-TIMER	JR	03	000600	000	025	00000	000625
JONES	PL	15	003000	000	075	00000	003075
HEAVYWORKER	HM	0	000000	025	025	00000	000050
LEE	BL	18	003600	025	075	00000	003700
CLARK	JC	06	001200	025	025	00000	001250
GROSSMAN	SE	07	001400	025	050	00000	001475
FRANKEL	LF	10	002000	025	050	00000	002075
BENWAY	CT	03	000600	025	025	00250	000400
KERBEL	NB	04	000800	025	025	00000	000850
KERBEL	NB	04	000800	025	025	00000	000850
			--------	--------	-------	-------	-------
UNIVERSITY TOTALS			018800	0000	0625	001250	000850

2 *Total is incorrect*

4 *Last student appears twice*   1 *Union fee was not summed*

(a) Invalid Output

STUDENT NAME		CREDITS	TUITION	UNION FEE	ACT FEE	SCHOLARSHIP	TOTAL BILL
SMITH	JB	15	003000	025	075	00000	003100
JAMES	HR	15	003000	000	075	00000	003075
BAKER	SR	09	001800	000	050	00500	001350
PART-TIMER	JR	03	000600	025	025	00000	000650
JONES	PL	15	003000	025	075	00000	003100
HEAVYWORKER	HM	18	003600	000	075	00000	003675
LEE	BL	18	003600	000	075	00000	003675
CLARK	JC	06	001200	000	025	00000	001225
GROSSMAN	SE	07	001400	000	050	00000	001450
FRANKEL	LF	10	002000	000	050	00000	002050
BENWAY	CT	03	000600	000	025	00250	000375
KERBEL	NB	04	000800	000	025	00000	000825
			--------	--------	-------	-------	-------
UNIVERSITY TOTALS			024600	0075	0625	000750	024550

(b) Valid Output (from Chapter 5)

Figure 6.6 Debugging Tools

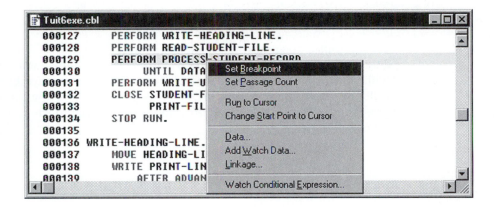

(a) Set Breakpoint

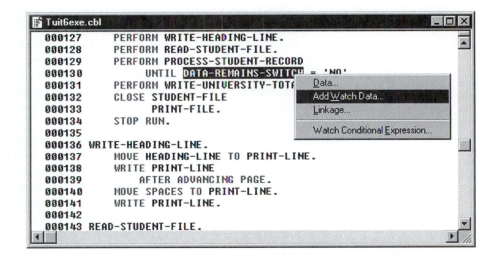

(b) Add Watch to Data

DISPLAY Statement

It is often helpful to display intermediate results of a program as the program is being executed. One way to accomplish this is through the insertion of **DISPLAY** statements at strategic points in the program. The statement enables you to print the value of one or more data names and/or one or more literals without having to format a record description. Consider:

$$\underline{\text{DISPLAY}} \left\{ \begin{array}{l} \text{identifier-1} \\ \text{literal-1} \end{array} \right\} \left[\begin{array}{l} \text{identifier-2} \\ \text{literal-2} \end{array} \right] \dots$$

The DISPLAY statement produces the contents of each item listed in the order shown. For example,

1. DISPLAY STUDENT-RECORD.

2. DISPLAY 'Record being processed: ' STUDENT-RECORD.

3. DISPLAY 'COMPUTE-TUITION paragraph is entered'

4. DISPLAY 'Student data: ' STU-NAME STU-CREDITS.

Examples one and two both display the value of the data name STUDENT-RECORD; the second example, however, precedes the data name with a literal to facilitate interpretation of the output. Example three displays just a literal but could be used (in conjunction with similar DISPLAY statements in other paragraphs) to show the flow of program execution. Example four displays a literal and two data names.

The Structured Walkthrough

Although it is reasonable to expect errors, the programmer is also expected (reasonably) to find and correct them. Until recently, error detection and correction was a lonely activity. A programmer was encouraged to **desk check**—that is, read and reread the code—in an attempt to discern logical errors before they occurred. Desk checking is still an important activity, but it is frequently supplemented by a newer technique, the **structured walkthrough**.

The walkthrough brings the evaluation into the open. It requires a programmer to have his or her work reviewed formally and periodically by a peer group. The theory is simple—a programmer is too close to his or her work to see potential problems adequately and evaluate them objectively. The purpose of the walkthrough is to ensure that all specifications are met, and that the logic and its COBOL implementation are correct.

The earlier an error is found, the easier it is to correct and thus the single most important objective of a walkthrough is *early error detection*. Walkthroughs occur at several stages during a project, beginning in the analysis phase, where the purpose is to ensure that the systems analyst has understood the user's requirements. Walkthroughs occur again during the design phase, after the programmer has developed a hierarchy chart and/or associated pseudocode. Finally, walkthroughs occur during the implementation phase, during which the programmer presents actual code prior to testing.

Walkthroughs are scheduled by the person being reviewed, who also selects the reviewers. The programmer distributes copies of the work (for example, a hierarchy chart, pseudocode, or a COBOL program) prior to the session. Reviewers are supposed to study the material in advance so that they can discuss it intelligently. At the walkthrough itself, the programmer presents the material objectively, concisely, and dispassionately. He or she should encourage discussion and be genuinely glad when errors are discovered.

One of the reviewers should function as a **moderator** to keep the discussion on track. Another should act as a **secretary** and maintain an **action list** of problems uncovered during the session. At the end of the walkthrough the action list is given to the programmer, who in turn is expected to correct the errors and notify attendees accordingly. The objective of the walkthrough is to find errors, not to correct them. The latter is accomplished by the programmer upon receipt of the action list.

The preceding discussion may read well in theory, but programmers often dislike the walkthrough concept. The probable reason is that they dislike having their work reviewed and regard criticism of code as a personal affront, intended or otherwise. This attitude is natural and stems from years of working as individuals.

In addition, walkthroughs can and have become unpleasant and ego-deflating experiences. "Structured walkover" and "stomp through" are terms that have been applied to less-than-successful sessions. Only if the atmosphere is kept open and nondefensive, only if the discussion is restricted to major problems rather than trivial errors, and only if personality clashes are avoided can the walkthrough be an effective technique. To have any chance of success, programmers who function as both reviewer and reviewee must adhere to the following guidelines:

1. *The program, and not the programmer, is reviewed.* Structured walkthroughs are intended to find programming problems; they will not be used by management as an evaluation tool. No one should keep count of how many errors are found in an individual's work or how many errors one finds in someone else's. It is quite logical, therefore, to exclude the project manager—that is, the individual in charge of salaries and promotions—from review sessions.

2. *Emphasis is on error detection, not correction.* It is assumed that the individual being reviewed will take the necessary corrective action. Reviewers should not harp on errors by discussing how to correct them; indeed, no corrections whatever are made during a walkthrough.

3. *Everyone, from senior analyst to trainee, has his or her work reviewed.* This avoids singling out an individual and further removes any stigma from having one's work reviewed. It also promotes the give-and-take atmosphere that is so vital to making the concept work.

4. *A list of well-defined objectives for each session should be specified in advance.* Adherence to this guideline keeps the discussion on track and helps to guarantee productive discussions. Another guideline is to impose a predetermined time limit, from half an hour to two hours. Walkthroughs will eventually cease to be productive and degenerate into a discussion of last night's ball game, the new manager, the latest rumor, or some other "hot" topic. The situation should be anticipated and avoided, perhaps by scheduling walkthroughs an hour before lunch. If all of the walkthrough's objectives have not been met when the deadline is reached, schedule a second session.

5. *Participation must be encouraged and demanded from the reviewers.* A walkthrough will indeed become a waste of time if no one has anything to say. Let it be known in advance that each reviewer will be expected to make at least two comments, one positive and one negative. Alternatively, require each reviewer to come to the session with a list of at least three questions.

SUMMARY

*Points to Remember

■ Compilation errors occur in the translation of COBOL to machine language and result from a violation of COBOL syntax—for example, a misspelled data name or an entry in the wrong column.

■ Run time and execution errors develop after compilation has taken place, and are caused by improper logic and/or improper COBOL implementation of valid logic.

■ A program may compile cleanly and be logically correct, yet still fail to execute if there are problems with the associated data files. Run time errors will occur and generate error messages to help determine the cause of such data management errors.

■ Sometimes data file problems are not the fault of the program, but are from the data file itself. The most common problem occurs when a numeric field includes spaces rather than zeroes.

■ COBOL97 provides many tools for debugging and can be quite helpful in tracking both syntax and logic errors.

■ A structured walkthrough is an open evaluation of an individual's work by a group of his or her peers, with the primary objective of detecting errors as soon as possible in the development cycle.

Key Words and Concepts

Action list   Execution error
Compilation error   File status codes
Compiler option   Interactive debugger
Cross-reference listing   Moderator
Debugging   Run-time error
Desk checking   Secretary
Early error detection   Structured walkthrough

COBOL Element

DISPLAY

F i l l - i n

1. _____ errors occur in the translation of COBOL to machine language.

2. _____ errors occur after a program has been successfully translated to machine language.

3. Incorrect translation of valid pseudocode into COBOL will most likely produce _____ errors.

4. Misspelling a reserved word will most likely produce a _____ error.

5. If a program _____ cleanly, it means only that the program has been successfully translated into machine language.

6. _____ errors are accompanied by some type of error message, whereas _____ errors are frequently undetected by the computer.

7. The process of peer review is known as a _____ _____.

8. The errors that are detected during a _____ _____ are entered on an _____ _____, which is maintained by the secretary.

9. The emphasis in a structured walkthrough is on error _____, not error _____.

10. One suggestion for conducting successful walkthroughs is to remember that the _____, and not the _____, is reviewed.

11. _____ _____ _____ cause a program to stop processing even though it is syntactically correct.

12. _____ _____ _____ are helpful in detecting errors in execution that pertain to data management.

True/False

1. If a program compiles with no diagnostics, it must execute correctly.

2. If a program compiles with warning diagnostics, execution will be suppressed.

3. If a program contains logical errors but not syntactical errors, the compiler will print appropriate warnings.

4. A COBOL program is considered data by the COBOL compiler.

5. An error in one COBOL statement can cause errors in several other, apparently unrelated, statements.

6. There are several different levels (of severity) of compilation errors.

7. Paragraph names begin in the A margin.

8. Spaces are required before and after arithmetic symbols.

9. Spaces are required before and after punctuation symbols.

10. A data name that appears in a COMPUTE statement can be defined with a picture of X's.

11. Data names may contain blanks.

12. The contents of columns 73–80 are ignored by the compiler.

13. In a COBOL program one reads a record name and writes a file name.

14. The emphasis in a structured walkthrough is on error detection rather than error correction.

15. Walkthroughs should be held for trainees only, as these are the individuals most likely to make mistakes.

16. Managers typically do not attend walkthroughs.

17. A walkthrough generally takes a minimum of two hours.

18. Walkthroughs should be restricted to the coding phase of a project.

Problems

1. Has your work ever been the subject of a structured walkthrough? Was the experience helpful or a waste of time, or worse? Are you looking forward to your next walkthrough?

2. Do you agree with banning managers from walkthroughs? Is it possible that the role of moderator in a walkthrough might best be filled by the project manager?

3. Do you agree with the authors' suggestions for successful walkthroughs? Are there any guidelines you wish to add to the list? To remove from the list?

4. Identify the syntactical errors in the COBOL fragment in Figure 6.8.

5. Identify the logical errors in the COBOL fragment in Figure 6.9. (Assume there are no other READ statements in the program.)

6. The COBOL fragment in Figure 6.10a is taken from a program that compiled cleanly but failed to execute. The error message is in Figure 6.10b. Explain the problem.

Figure 6.8 COBOL Fragment for Problem 4

```
IDENTIFICATION DIVISION.
PROGRAM ID.  ERRORS.
ENVIRONMENT DIVISION.
INPUT-OUTPUT SECTION.
SELECT EMPLOYEE-FILE   ASSIGN TO SYSIN
    ORGANIZATION IS LINE SEQUENTIAL.
DATA DIVISION.
FILE SECTION.
FD  EMPLOYEE-FILE
    RECORD CONTAINS 50 CHARACTERS
    DATA RECORD IS EMPLOYEE-RECORD.
    EMPLOYEE-RECORD.
    05  EMP-NAME                PIC X(20).
    05  EMP-NUMBER              PIC X(9).
    05  FILLER                  PIC X(20).
WORKING STORAGE SECTION.
10  END-OF-FILE-SWITCH          PIC X(3)    VALUE BLANKS.
```

Figure 6.9 COBOL Fragment for Problem 5

```
WORKING-STORAGE SECTION.
01  END-OF-FILE-SWITCH    PIC X(3)    VALUE 'YES'.
 .
   .
PROCEDURE DIVISION.
MAINLINE.
 .
   .
   PERFORM PROCESS-RECORDS
       UNTIL END-OF-FILE-SWITCH = 'YES'
 .
   .
PROCESS-RECORDS.
   READ EMPLOYEE-FILE
       AT END MOVE 'YES' TO END-OF-FILE-SWITCH
   END-READ.
```

Figure 6.10   COBOL Fragment for Problem 6

```
              SELECT STUDENT-FILE   ASSIGN TO SYSIN
                  ORGANIZATION IS LINE SEQUENTIAL.
              SELECT PRINT-FILE     ASSIGN TO SYSOUT
                  ORGANIZATION IS LINE SEQUENTIAL.
            .

            .
      PROCEDURE DIVISION.
      PREPARE-SENIOR-REPORT.
          READ STUDENT-FILE
              AT END MOVE 'NO' TO DATA-REMAINS-SWITCH
          END-READ.
          OPEN INPUT  STUDENT-FILE
              OUTPUT PRINT-FILE.
          PERFORM WRITE-HEADING-LINE.
          PERFORM PROCESS-RECORDS
              UNTIL DATA-REMAINS-SWITCH = 'NO'.
          CLOSE STUDENT-FILE
              PRINT-FILE.
          STOP RUN.
```

(a) COBOL Fragments

(b) Not opened error message

7

Editing and Coding Standards

CHAPTER OUTLINE

Overview

Editing

    The Decimal Point

    Zero Suppression

    Dollar Signs

    Commas

    Asterisks for Check Protection

    Insertion Characters

    Synopsis

Signed Numbers

    CR and DB

    Plus and Minus Signs

BLANK WHEN ZERO Clause

The Tuition Billing Program Revisited

Coding Standards

    Data Division

    Procedure Division

    Both Divisions

Programming Tip: Avoid Literals

Programming Tip: Use Scope Terminators

A Well-Written Program

Summary

Fill-in

True/False

Problems

OBJECTIVES

After reading this chapter you will be able to:

■ List the complete set of COBOL editing characters.

■ Differentiate between a numeric field and a numeric-edited field; predict the results when a numeric field is moved to a numeric-edited field.

■ Understand the difference between an implied decimal point and an actual decimal point; state the role of each in editing.

■ Describe the rules for signed numbers and the editing characters +, –, CR, and DB.

■ Describe the rationale for coding standards that go beyond the syntactical requirements of COBOL.

OVERVIEW

The chapter introduces editing—the ability to dress up printed reports by inserting dollar signs, decimal points, and so on, into numeric fields prior to printing. The chapter also introduces the concept of signed numbers and the use of CR and DB, or a plus and minus sign, to indicate positive or negative results. All of this material is incorporated into the tuition billing program from Chapter 5.

The second half of the chapter develops the rationale for coding standards, or requirements imposed by an installation to increase the readability (and maintainability) of COBOL programs. We present a series of typical standards and show how they are incorporated into existing programs.

Editing

The importance of editing is best demonstrated by comparing outputs from two programs. Figure 7.1a contains the original (unedited) output produced by the tuition billing program of Chapter 5. Figure 7.1b contains edited output, produced by a modified version of the program, which is presented later in the chapter. The last line of Figure 7.1b displays a new student, Lucky One, whose scholarship grant exceeds the total amount of his bill, producing a credit of $150. (Lucky One is not shown in Figure 7.1a as the original program did not address signed numbers.) The superiority of the edited output speaks for itself.

The ***editing characters*** of Table 7.1 enable the kind of output shown in Figure 7.1b. Editing is achieved by incorporating these characters into the various PICTURE clauses within a COBOL program.

The editing characters are not associated with the numeric fields used in computations, as these fields may contain only digits, an implied decimal point, and an optional sign. Additional data names, known as ***numeric-edited fields***, are necessary within the program, and it is the picture clauses for the latter that contain editing characters from Table 7.1. In other words, arithmetic is performed on numeric fields, whose computed values are subsequently moved to numeric-edited fields, and the latter are printed.

Figure 7.1 Comparison of Outputs

STUDENT NAME		CREDITS	TUITION	UNION FEE	ACT FEE	SCHOLARSHIP	TOTAL BILL
SMITH	JB	15	003000	025	075	00000	003100
JAMES	HR	15	003000	000	075	00000	003075
BAKER	SR	09	001800	000	050	00500	001350
PART-TIMER	JR	03	000600	025	025	00000	000650
JONES	PL	15	003000	025	075	00000	003100
HEAVYWORKER	HM	18	003600	000	075	00000	003675
LEE	BL	18	003600	000	075	00000	003675
CLARK	JC	06	001200	000	025	00000	001225
GROSSMAN	SE	07	001400	000	050	00000	001450
FRANKEL	LF	10	002000	000	050	00000	002050
BENWAY	CT	03	000600	000	025	00250	000375
KERBEL	NB	04	000800	000	025	00000	000825
UNIVERSITY TOTALS			024600	0075	0625	000750	024550

(a) Without Editing

STUDENT NAME		CREDITS	TUITION	UNION FEE	ACT FEE	SCHOLARSHIP	TOTAL BILL
SMITH	JB	15	$3,000	$25	$75		$3,100
JAMES	HR	15	$3,000		$75		$3,075
BAKER	SR	9	$1,800		$50	$500	$1,350
PART-TIMER	JR	3	$600	$25	$25		$650
JONES	PL	15	$3,000	$25	$75		$3,100
HEAVYWORKER	HM	18	$3,600		$75		$3,675
LEE	BL	18	$3,600		$75		$3,675
CLARK	JC	6	$1,200		$25		$1,225
GROSSMAN	SE	7	$1,400		$50		$1,450
FRANKEL	LF	10	$2,000		$50		$2,050
BENWAY	CT	3	$600		$25	$250	$375
KERBEL	NB	4	$800		$25		$825
LUCKY ONE	FR	9	$1,800		$50	$2000	$150CR
UNIVERSITY TOTALS			$26,400	$75	$675	$2,750	$24,400

Student has been added to the original data

(a) With Editing

TABLE 7.1 Editing Characters

CHARACTER	MEANING	CHARACTER	MEANING
.	Actual decimal point	B	Blank
Z	Zero suppression	/	Slash
$	Dollar sign	CR	Credit character
,	Comma	DB	Debit character
*	Check protection	+	Plus sign
0	Zero	−	Minus sign

The relationship between numeric fields and numeric-edited fields is illustrated in Figure 7.2, which depicts the calculation of tuition as credits times the rate ($200 per credit). The incoming student record contains the field STU-CREDITS, with the calculated result defined in Working-Storage as IND-TUITION. The two fields are numeric, and do not contain any editing characters.

On the other hand, DETAIL-LINE contains two numeric-edited fields (DET-CREDITS and DET-TUITION), each of which holds one or more editing characters from Table 7.1. It is not necessary for you to know the precise function of the various editing characters at this time; you need only perceive the difference between numeric and numeric-edited fields.

The calculations within Figure 7.2 are done with the numeric fields (IND-TUITION and STU-CREDITS). Then, just prior to printing, the values in the numeric fields are moved to the corresponding numeric-edited fields, which are printed.

Let us consider the various editing characters from Table 7.1, in turn.

The Decimal Point

The *actual decimal point* is the most basic editing character. In reviewing this and other examples, it is essential that you remember that *any move of a numeric field to a numeric-edited field maintains decimal alignment*. Consider:

```
05  FIELD-A          PIC 9V99.
05  FIELD-A-EDITED   PIC 9.99.
```

FIELD-A is a numeric field, with two digits after an *implied* decimal point. FIELD-A-EDITED is a numeric-edited field containing an *actual* decimal point. All calculations are done using FIELD-A, which is moved to FIELD-A-EDITED prior to printing by means of the statement MOVE FIELD-A TO FIELD-A-EDITED. Thus:

	FIELD-A	FIELD-A-EDITED
Before move:	7 8 3	9 . 9 9
After execution:	7 8 3	7 . 8 3

The decimal point requires a position in FIELD-A-EDITED, but not in FIELD-A; that is, FIELD-A-EDITED is a *four*-position field, whereas FIELD-A requires only *three* positions.

Zero Suppression

One of the simplest editing requirements is to eliminate high-order (insignificant) zeros. For example, consider a numeric field defined with a PICTURE clause of 9(5), but whose value is 00120; in other words the two high-order positions contain insignificant zeros. It is likely that you would prefer the printed output to appear as 120, rather than 00120, which is accomplished by the statement MOVE FIELD-B TO FIELD-B-EDITED as shown:

```
05  FIELD-B          PIC 9(5).
05  FIELD-B-EDITED   PIC ZZZZ9
```

	FIELD-B	FIELD-B-EDITED
Before move:	0 0 1 2 0	Z Z Z Z 9
After execution:	0 0 1 2 0	1 2 0

Figure 7.2 Numeric and Numeric-Edited Fields

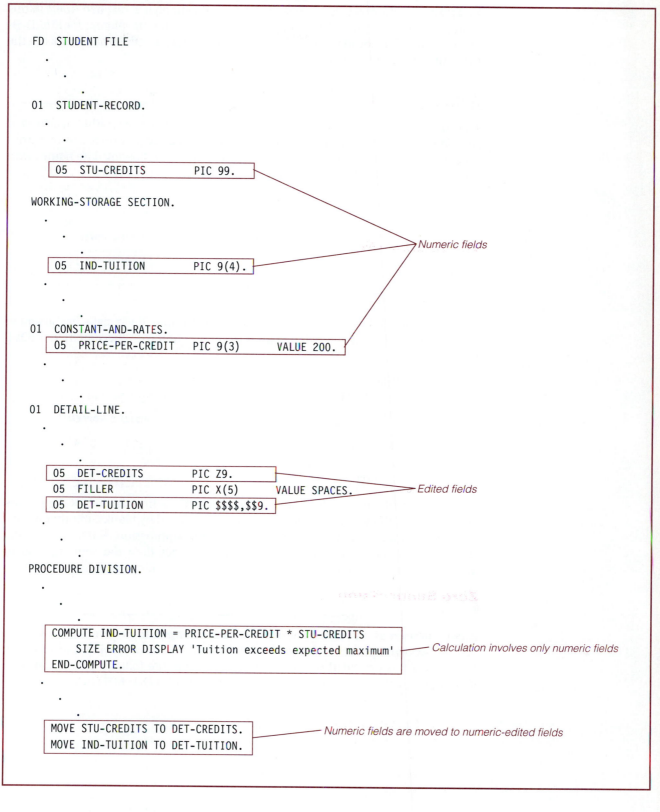

```
FD  STUDENT FILE
     .
        .
           .
01  STUDENT-RECORD.
     .
        .
           .
        05  STU-CREDITS        PIC 99.
WORKING-STORAGE SECTION.
     .
        .
           .
        05  IND-TUITION        PIC 9(4).
     .
        .
           .
01  CONSTANT-AND-RATES.
        05  PRICE-PER-CREDIT   PIC 9(3)       VALUE 200.
     .
        .
           .
01  DETAIL-LINE.
     .
        .
           .
        05  DET-CREDITS        PIC Z9.
        05  FILLER             PIC X(5)    VALUE SPACES.
        05  DET-TUITION        PIC $$$$,$$9.
     .
        .
           .
PROCEDURE DIVISION.
     .
        .
           .
        COMPUTE IND-TUITION = PRICE-PER-CREDIT * STU-CREDITS
            SIZE ERROR DISPLAY 'Tuition exceeds expected maximum'
        END-COMPUTE.
     .
        .
           .
        MOVE STU-CREDITS TO DET-CREDITS.
        MOVE IND-TUITION TO DET-TUITION.
```

Numeric fields

Edited fields

Calculation involves only numeric fields

Numeric fields are moved to numeric-edited fields

The editing character **Z** indicates *zero suppression*, and prevents the printing of leading zeros. However, as soon as the first significant digit is reached (the 1 in this example), all subsequent digits are printed. Note, too, that the picture for FIELD-B-EDITED has a 9 as the low-order character, to print a zero, rather than blank out the field entirely, in the event of a zero value.

Dollar Signs

The dollar sign is used as an editing character in one of two ways, either in a *fixed* or *floating* position. A single dollar sign in the numeric-edited picture will always print the dollar sign in the same (fixed) position. Consider the following data names with the statement MOVE FIELD-C TO FIELD-C-EDITED:

```
05  FIELD-C          PIC 9(4).
05  FIELD-C-EDITED   PIC $ZZZ9.
```

	FIELD-C	FIELD-C-EDITED
Before move:	0 0 4 3	$ Z Z Z 9
After execution:	0 0 4 3	$ 4 3

A floating dollar sign is obtained by using multiple dollar signs in the edited field. Consider the following data names in conjunction with the statement MOVE FIELD-D TO FIELD-D-EDITED:

```
05  FIELD-D          PIC 9(4).
05  FIELD-D-EDITED   PIC $$$$9.
```

	FIELD-D	FIELD-D-EDITED
Before move:	0 0 2 3	$ $ $ $ 9
After execution:	0 0 2 3	$ 2 3

A single (floating) dollar sign is printed before the first significant digit in the edited field, with the leading zero digits, if any, replaced by blanks. In other words, the floating dollar sign has the same effect as zero suppression. Note, too, that the receiving field must be at least one character longer than the sending field to accommodate the dollar sign; otherwise, a compiler warning results.

Comma

A *comma* used as an editing character causes a comma to be printed, provided a significant digit appears to the left of the comma. The comma will be suppressed, however, if it is preceded by leading zeros. Consider the following data names in conjunction with the statement MOVE FIELD-E TO FIELD-E-EDITED:

```
05  FIELD-E          PIC 9(4).
05  FIELD-E-EDITED   PIC $$,$$9.
```

	FIELD-E	FIELD-E-EDITED
Before move:	8 7 6 5	$ $, $ $ 9
After execution:	8 7 6 5	$ 8 , 7 6 5

The comma is printed in the indicated position. Suppose, however, that the contents of the sending field are less than 1,000, and that the statement MOVE FIELD-F TO FIELD-F-EDITED is executed in conjunction with the fields:

```
05  FIELD-F          PIC 9(4).
05  FIELD-F-EDITED   PIC $$,$$9.
```

	FIELD-F	FIELD-F-EDITED
Before move:	0 0 8 7	$ $, $ $ 9
After execution:	0 0 8 7	. $ 8 7

The comma is suppressed because it was not preceded by a significant digit. Observe also how the comma is used in conjunction with a floating dollar sign.

Asterisks for Check Protection

The *asterisk* is used as a fill character to avoid blanks between a fixed dollar sign and the first significant digit as in $****87. Consider the following fields in conjunction with the statement MOVE FIELD-G TO FIELD-G-EDITED:

```
05  FIELD-G          PIC 9(5).
05  FIELD-G-EDITED   PIC $**,**9.
```

	FIELD-G	FIELD-G-EDITED
Before move:	0 0 0 8 7	$ * * , * * 9
After execution:	0 0 0 8 7	$ * * * * 8 7

The dollar sign will print in its fixed position, with asterisks replacing leading zeros. The use of the asterisk as a fill character is commonly referred to as *check protection.*

Insertion Characters

The slash, blank, and zero (/, B, and 0, respectively) are *insertion characters*, meaning that they are printed exactly where they appear in an edited field. Consider the following fields together with the statement MOVE FIELD-H TO FIELD-H-EDITED:

```
05  FIELD-H          PIC 9(8).
05  FIELD-H-EDITED   PIC 99/99/9999.
```

	FIELD-H	FIELD-H-EDITED
Before move:	0 3 1 6 2 0 0 0	9 9 / 9 9 / 9 9 9 9
After execution:	0 3 1 6 2 0 0 0	9 9 / 9 9 / 2 0 0 0

FIELD-H-EDITED is an eight-position field and is typical of how a date field may be edited. Blanks and zeros may be inserted in similar fashion. Note, however, that the hyphen is *not* an insertion character and cannot be used to place hyphens within a social security number.

Synopsis

Table 7.2 provides an effective review of the editing characters covered so far. Each entry in the table shows the result of a MOVE statement of a numeric source field to a numeric-edited receiving field. All of the examples maintain decimal alignment as required. (The Ƅ which appears in several examples indicates a space.)

TABLE 7.2   Review of Editing Characters

	SOURCE FIELD		RECEIVING FIELD	
	Picture	**Value**	**Picture**	**Edited Result**
a.	9(4)	0678	Z(4)	⸱678
b.	9(4)	0678	$9(4)	$0678
c.	9(4)	0678	$Z(4)	$⸱678
d.	9(4)V99	123456	9(4).99	1234.56
e.	9(4)V99	123456	$9(4).99	$1234.56
f.	9(4)V99	123456	$9,999.99	$1,234.56
g.	9(4)	0008	$$,$$$9	⸱⸱⸱⸱⸱$8
h.	9(4)V9	12345	9(4)	1234
i.	9(4)V9	12345	9(4).99	1234.50
j.	9(5)	00045	$****9	$***45
k.	9(9)	123456789	999B99B9999	123⸱45⸱6789
l.	9(4)	1234	$$,$$9.00	$1,234.00
m.	9(6)	080594	99/99/99	08/05/94
n.	9(6)	080594	Z9/99/99	⸱8/05/94

Signed Numbers

Thus far we have considered only positive numbers, a rather unrealistic limitation. Numeric fields with negative values require an **S** in their PICTURE clause to indicate a *signed field*, that is, a field that may contain either positive or negative values. If the sign (the S in the PICTURE clause) is omitted, the value of the data name will always be converted to a positive number, regardless of the result of the computation. Consider:

```
05  FIELD-A      PIC S99    VALUE -20.
05  FIELD-B      PIC 99     VALUE 15.
05  FIELD-C      PIC S99    VALUE -20.
05  FIELD-D      PIC 99     VALUE 15.
      .
        .
          .
    ADD FIELD-B TO FIELD-A.
        ADD FIELD-C TO FIELD-D.
```

Numerically, the sum of –20 and +15 is –5, and there is no problem when the result is stored in FIELD-A as in the first command. In the second command, however, the sum is stored in FIELD-D (an unsigned field), and thus it will assume a value of +5. Accordingly many programmers adopt the habit of always using signed fields to avoid any difficulty. Signed numbers require additional editing characters.

CR and DB

Financial statements use either the credit (**CR**) or debit (**DB**) character to indicate a negative number. In other words, the representation of a negative number can be either CR or DB, and depends entirely on the accounting system in use; some systems use CR, whereas others will use DB.

Table 7.3 contains four examples that should clarify the matter. In each instance, CR or DB appears only when the sending field is negative [examples (b) and (d)]. If the source field is positive or zero, CR and/or DB are replaced by blanks. The essential point is that COBOL treats CR and DB identically, and the determination of which negative indicator to use depends on the accounting system.

TABLE 7.3   CR and DB Editing Characters

	SOURCE FIELD		RECEIVING FIELD	
	Picture	**Value**	**Picture**	**Edited Result**
a.	S9(5)	98765	$$$,999CR	$98,765
b.	S9(5)	−98765	$$$,999CR	$98,765CR
c.	S9(5)	98765	$$$,999DB	$98,765
d.	S9(5)	−98765	$$$,999DB	$98,765DB

Plus and Minus Signs

Table 7.4 illustrates the use of plus and minus signs. The repetition of a (plus or minus) sign within the edited PICTURE clause denotes a *floating* (plus or minus) *sign*, which will appear in the printed field immediately to the left of the first significant digit. A single (plus or minus) sign, however, indicates a *fixed* (plus or minus) *sign*, which prints in the indicated position.

Specification of a (fixed or floating) plus sign displays the sign of the edited field if the number is positive, negative, or zero [examples (a), (b), and (c)]. Specification of a minus sign, however, displays the sign only when the edited result is negative. The receiving field must be at least one character longer than the sending field to accommodate the sign; otherwise, a compiler warning results.

TABLE 7.4   Floating Plus and Minus Sign

	SOURCE FIELD		RECEIVING FIELD	
	Picture	**Value**	**Picture**	**Edited Result**
a.	S9(4)	1234	++,+++	+1,234
b.	S9(4)	0123	++,+++	ƀƀ+123
c.	S9(4)	−1234	++,+++	−1,234
d.	S9(4)	1234	--,---	ƀ1,234
e.	S9(4)	0123	--,---	ƀƀƀ123
f.	S9(4)	−1234	--,---	−1,234
g.	S9(4)	1234	ZZ,ZZ9+	ƀ1,234+
h.	S9(4)	−1234	ZZ,ZZ9+	ƀ1,234−

BLANK WHEN ZERO Clause

The **BLANK WHEN ZERO** clause produces a blank field when the associated numeric value is zero. Although the same effect can be achieved with certain editing strings, such as ZZZZZ or $$$$$, there are times when the clause is essential. A field with dollars and cents—for example, $$$9.99, formatted to print a digit immediately to the left of the decimal point—will print $0.00. In similar fashion it might be desirable to blank out a date field with PIC Z9/Z9/Z9 if the values are unavailable. The inclusion of BLANK WHEN ZERO at the end of the PICTURE clause in all three instances will accomplish the desired result.

The Tuition Billing Program Revisited

We return once more to Figure 7.1, the example with which we began the chapter. The earlier version of the tuition billing program in Chapter 5 did not include editing characters, and so produced the output in Figure 7.1a. Now we incorporate the material just presented into a revised version of the program to produce the edited output of Figure 7.1b.

The necessary changes are highlighted in Figure 7.3, which compares edited and unedited PICTURE clauses. The changes affect only the detail (7.3a) and total

Figure 7.3   Edited versus Unedited PICTURE Clauses

```
                            Edited Fields                    Unedited Fields

01  DETAIL-LINE.
    05  FILLER           PIC X        VALUE SPACES.    PIC X      VALUE SPACES.
    05  DET-LAST-NAME    PIC X(15).                    PIC X(15).
    05  FILLER           PIC X(2)     VALUE SPACES.    PIC X(2)   VALUE SPACES.
    05  DET-INITIALS     PIC X(2).                     PIC X(2).
    05  FILLER           PIC X(5)     VALUE SPACES.    PIC X(5)   VALUE SPACES.
    05  DET-CREDITS      PIC Z9.                       PIC 9(2).
    05  FILLER           PIC X(4)     VALUE SPACES.    PIC X(6)   VALUE SPACES.
    05  DET-TUITION      PIC $$$$,$$9.                 PIC 9(6).
    05  FILLER           PIC X(6)     VALUE SPACES.    PIC X(7)   VALUE SPACES.
    05  DET-UNION-FEE    PIC $$$9     BLANK WHEN ZERO. PIC 9(3).
    05  FILLER           PIC X(5)     VALUE SPACES.    PIC X(6)   VALUE SPACES.
    05  DET-ACTIVITY-FEE PIC $$$9     BLANK WHEN ZERO. PIC 9(3).
    05  FILLER           PIC X(6)     VALUE SPACES.    PIC X(8)   VALUE SPACES.
    05  DET-SCHOLARSHIP  PIC $$,$$$9  BLANK WHEN ZERO  PIC 9(5).
    05  FILLER           PIC X(4)     VALUE SPACES.    PIC X(6)   VALUE SPACES.
    05  DET-IND-BILL     PIC $$$$,$$9CR.               PIC 9(6).
    05  FILLER           PIC X(47)    VALUE SPACES.    PIC X(49)  VALUE SPACES.
```

(a) Detail Line

```
01  TOTAL-LINE.
    05  FILLER           PIC X(8)     VALUE SPACES.    PIC X(8)   VALUE SPACES.
    05  FILLER           PIC X(17)                     PIC X(17)
              VALUE 'UNIVERSITY TOTALS'.                    VALUE 'UNIVERSITY TOTALS'.
    05  FILLER           PIC X(6)     VALUE SPACES.    PIC X(8)   VALUE SPACES.
    05  TOT-TUITION      PIC $$$$,$$9.                 PIC 9(6).
    05  FILLER           PIC X(2)     VALUE SPACES.    PIC X(6)   VALUE SPACES.
    05  TOT-UNION-FEE    PIC $$$$,$$9.                 PIC 9(4).
    05  FILLER           PIC X        VALUE SPACES.    PIC X(5)   VALUE SPACES.
    05  TOT-ACTIVITY-FEE PIC $$$$,$$9.                 PIC 9(4).
    05  FILLER           PIC X(5)     VALUE SPACES.    PIC X(7)   VALUE SPACES.
    05  TOT-SCHOLARSHIP  PIC $$$$,$$9.                 PIC 9(6).
    05  FILLER           PIC X(4)     VALUE SPACES.    PIC X(6)   VALUE SPACES.
    05  TOT-IND-BILL     PIC $$$$,$$9CR.               PIC 9(6).
    05  FILLER           PIC X(47)    VALUE SPACES.    PIC X(49)  VALUE SPACES.
```

(b) Total Line

(7.3b) lines. Computations are made within the program using the unedited PICTURE clauses found in INDIVIDUAL-CALCULATIONS and UNIVERSITY-TOTALS, then moved to edited PICTURE clauses found in DETAIL-LINE and TOTAL-LINE, respectively.

All of the calculations and editing are accomplished as illustrated earlier in Figure 7.2. The computed value of tuition, for example, is stored in the data name IND-TUITION with PIC 9(6), then moved to the edited field DET-TUITION with a PIC \$\$\$\$,\$\$9 prior to printing.

Observe the presence of a CR within the PICTURE clauses for both DET-IND-BILL and TOT-IND-BILL in Figures 7.3a and 7.3b, respectively. The CR is blanked out when students owe money to the university, but appears when the student is due a credit (Lucky One in Figure 7.1b). Note, too, the various BLANK WHEN ZERO clauses throughout Figure 7.3, which produce the more appealing edited output of Figure 7.1b contrasted to the zeros in Figure 7.1a.

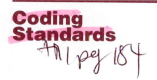

Coding Standards

All pg 184

A good program is easily read and maintained by someone other than the author. Indeed, continuing success in a commercial installation depends on someone other than the author being able to maintain a program. Most installations impose a set of **coding standards**, such as those described here, which go beyond the requirements of the COBOL compiler. These standards are optional for the student, but typical of what is required in the real world.

The next several pages suggest a series of coding standards for you to use. However, there are no absolute truths—no right or wrong—insofar as programming style is concerned. Different programmers develop slightly or even radically different styles that are consistent with the rules of COBOL and with the programmer's objective. The discussion that follows reflects the viewpoint of the authors and is necessarily subjective.

We begin with suggestions for the Data Division.

Data Division

Choose meaningful names. Avoid taking the easy way out with two- or three-character data names. It is impossible for the maintenance programmer, or even the original author, to determine the meaning of abbreviated data names. The usual student response is that this adds unnecessarily to the burden of writer's cramp. Initial coding, however, takes only 5–10% of the total time associated with a program (maintenance, testing, and debugging take the vast majority), and the modest increase in coding time is more than compensated by improvements in the latter activities.

Prefix all data names within the same FD or 01 with two or three characters unique to the FD; for example, OM-LAST-NAME, OM-BIRTH-DATE. The utility of this guideline becomes apparent in the Procedure Division if it is necessary to refer back to the definition of a data name.

Begin all PICTURE clauses in the same column. Usually in columns 36–48, but the choice is arbitrary. Do not be unduly disturbed if one or two entries stray from the designated column, because of long data names and/or indentation of level numbers.

Choose one form of the PICTURE clause. Choose PIC, PIC IS, PICTURE, or PICTURE IS and follow it consistently. PIC is the shortest and is as good as any.

PROGRAMMING TIP
Avoid Literals

The constant (literal) portion of a print line should be defined in Working-Storage, rather than moved to the print line in the Procedure Division. Consider the following:

Poor Code:

```
      MOVE 'STUDENT NAME      SOC SEC NUM  CREDITS  TUITION
  −   'SCHOLARSHIP FEES' TO PRINT-LINE.
```

Hyphen required to continue nonnumeric literal

```
      WRITE PRINT-LINE.
```

Improved Code:

```
      01   HEADING-LINE.
           05                   PIC X(12)      VALUE 'STUDENT NAME'
           05                   PIC X(10)      VALUE SPACES.
           05                   PIC X(11)      VALUE 'SOC SEC NUM'.
           05                   PIC X(2)       VALUE SPACES.
           05                   PIC X(7)       VALUE 'CREDITS'.
           05                   PIC X(2)       VALUE SPACES.
           05                   PIC X(7)       VALUE 'TUITION'.
           05                   PIC X(3)       VALUE SPACES.
           05                   PIC X(11)      VALUE 'SCHOLARSHIP'.
           05                   PIC X(2)       VALUE SPACES.
           05                   PIC X(4)       VALUE 'FEES'.

           WRITE PRINT-LINE FROM HEADING-LINE.
```

The poor code illustrates continuation of a nonnumeric literal. The first line begins with an apostrophe before **STUDENT NAME** and ends *without* a closing apostrophe in column 72. The continued line contains a hyphen in column 7, and both a beginning and ending apostrophe.

The improved code may appear unnecessarily long in contrast to the poor code. However, it is an unwritten law that users will change column headings, and/or spacing at least twice before being satisfied. Such changes are easily accommodated in the improved code but often tedious in the original solution. Assume, for example, that four spaces are required between **CREDITS** and **TUITION**, rather than the two that are there now. Modification of the poor code requires that both lines in the **MOVE** statement be completely rewritten, whereas only a PICTURE clause changes in the improved version. Note, too, that the improved code can be rewritten to reduce the number of **FILLER** entries, and also to eliminate the word FILLER, as shown below.

```
      01   HEADING-LINE.
           05                   PIC X(22)      VALUE 'STUDENT NAME'.
           05                   PIC X(13)      VALUE 'SOC SEC NUM'.
           05                   PIC X(9)       VALUE 'CREDITS'.
           05                   PIC X(10)      VALUE 'TUITION'.
           05                   PIC X(13)      VALUE 'SCHOLARSHIP'.
           05                   PIC X(4)       VALUE 'FEES'.
```

In this example each **VALUE** clause contains fewer characters than the associated **PICTURE** clause. Accordingly, alignment is from left to right, with the extra (low-order) positions padded with blanks.

Indent successive level numbers under a 01 consistently. For example, two or four columns. Leave gaps between adjacent levels (for example, 01, 05, 10, 15 or 01, 04, 08, 12) instead of using consecutive numbers; that is, avoid 01, 02, 03 (as discussed in Chapter 4). Use the same level numbers from FD to FD to maintain consistency within a program.

Avoid 77-level entries. 77-level entries have not been mentioned in the text, because current programming practice argues for their elimination. Nevertheless, they are apt to be found in existing programs and are discussed now for that reason.

A 77-level entry was originally defined as an independent data name with no relationship to any other data name in a program. (77-level entries are coded as elementary items in Working-Storage.) However, few if any data names are truly independent, and 77-level entries should be avoided for that reason. The authors, for example, have gotten along quite nicely by grouping related entries under a common 01 description. Consider the following:

Poor Code:

```
77  TUITION           PIC 9(4)V99    VALUE ZEROS.
77  ACTIVITY-FEE      PIC 9(2)       VALUE ZEROS.
77  UNION-FEE         PIC 9(2)       VALUE ZEROS.
```

Improved Code:

```
01  INDIVIDUAL-CALCULATIONS.
    05  IND-TUITION       PIC 9(4)V99    VALUE ZEROS.
    05  IND-ACTIVITY-FEE  PIC 9(2)       VALUE ZEROS.
    05  IND-UNION-FEE     PIC 9(2)       VALUE ZEROS.
```

The improved code also uses a common prefix, which reflects the similarities among the related items. There is simply no reason to use the older approach of independent data items.

Procedure Division

Develop functional paragraphs. Every statement in a paragraph should be related to the overall function of that paragraph, which in turn should be reflected in the paragraph name. A well-chosen name will consist of a verb, one or two adjectives, and an object; for example, READ-STUDENT-FILE, WRITE-HEADING-LINE, and so on. If a paragraph cannot be named in this manner, it is probably not functional, and consideration should be given to redesigning the program and/or paragraph.

Sequence paragraph names. Programmers and managers alike accept the utility of this guideline to locate paragraphs in the Procedure Division quickly. However, there is considerable disagreement on just what sequencing scheme to use: all numbers, a single letter followed by numbers, and so on. We make no strong argument for one scheme over another, other than to insist that a consistent sequencing rule be followed. Some examples are A010-WRITE-NEW-MASTER-RECORD and 100-PRODUCE-ERROR-REPORT.

Avoid commas. The compiler treats a comma as noise; it has no effect on the generated object code. Many programmers have acquired the habit of inserting commas to increase readability. Though this works rather well with prose, it can have just the opposite effect in COBOL, because of blurred print chains, which make it difficult to distinguish a comma from a period. The best solution is to try to avoid commas altogether.

Use scope terminators. END-IF (see programming tip on page 182) is one of several scope terminators included in COBOL-85 that should be used whenever possible to

PROGRAMMING TIP
Use Scope Terminators

Scope terminators are one of the most powerful enhancements in COBOL-85, and in the opinion of the authors, justify in and of themselves, conversion to the new standard. In its simplest role a scope terminator is used in place of a period to end a conditional statement—for example, **END-IF** to terminate an **IF** statement. (A scope terminator and a period should not appear together unless the period also ends the sentence.)

One of the most important reasons for using scope terminators is that they eliminate the very subtle *column 73* problem which has always existed, and which is depicted below. The intended logic is straightforward, and is supposed to apply a discount of two percent on an order of $2,000 or more. The amount due (**NET**) is equal to the amount ordered less the discount (if any).

COBOL code

```
IF AMOUNT-ORDERED-THISWEEK < 2000
    MOVE ZEROS TO CUSTOMER-DISCOUNT
ELSE
    COMPUTE CUSTOMER-DISCOUNT = AMOUNT-ORDERED-THISWEEK * .02.
COMPUTE NET = AMOUNT-ORDERED-THISWEEK - CUSTOMER-DISCOUNT.
```

The period is in column 73

COMPUTE statement inadvertently taken as part of the ELSE clause

Output

Amount ordered	Discount	Net
3000	60	2940
4000	80	3920
1000	0	3920
5000	100	4900
1500	0	4900

Net amount is incorrect and equal to the value of the previous order

The COBOL statements appear correct, yet the output is wrong! In particular, *the net amounts are wrong for any order less than $2,000* (but valid for orders of $2,000 or more). The net amount for orders less than $2,000 equals the net for the previous order (that is, the net for an order of $1,000 is incorrectly printed as $3,920, which was the correct net for the preceding order of $4,000). The net amount for an order of $1,500 was printed as $4,900, and so on. Why?

The only possible explanation is that the **COMPUTE NET** statement is not executed for net amounts less than $2,000. The only way that can happen is if the **COMPUTE NET** statement is taken as part of the **ELSE** clause, and that can happen only if the **ELSE** is not terminated by a period. The period is present, however, so we are back at ground zero—or are we? *The period is present, but in column 73, which is ignored by the compiler.* Hence the visual code does not match the compiler interpretation, and the resulting output is incorrect. Replacing the period by the **END-IF** delimiter will eliminate this and similar errors in the future. (Remember, a period may appear *at the end of the sentence* after the **END-IF** terminator.)

terminate a conditional statement. The END-READ terminator should be used in similar fashion to end the conditional AT END clause in the READ statement.

Indent. Virtually all programmers indent successive level numbers in the Data Division, yet many of these same individuals do not apply a similar principle in the Procedure Division. The readability of a program is enhanced significantly by indenting subservient clauses under the main statements. Some examples:

```
READ STUDENT-FILE
    AT END MOVE 'NO' TO DATA-REMAINS-SWITCH
END-READ.


PERFORM 0020-PROCESS-A-RECORD
    UNTIL DATA-REMAINS-SWITCH   = 'NO'.


IF STU-UNION-MEMBER = 'Y'
    MOVE UNION-FEE TO IND-UNION-FEE
ELSE
    MOVE ZERO TO IND-UNION-FEE
END-IF.


COMPUTE IND-TUITION = PRICE-PER-CREDIT * STU-CREDITS
    SIZE ERROR DISPLAY 'Size error for individual tuition'
END-COMPUTE.
```

Both Divisions

Space attractively. The adoption of various spacing conventions can go a long way toward improving the appearance of a program. The authors believe very strongly in the insertion of blank lines throughout a program to highlight important statements. Specific suggestions include a blank line before all paragraphs, FDs, and 01 entries.

You can also force various portions of a listing to begin on a new page, by putting a slash in column 7 of a separate statement.

Avoid constants. A significant portion of maintenance programming (and headaches) could be avoided if a program is written with an eye toward change. Consider:

Poor Code:
```
COMPUTE IND-TUITION = 200 * STU-CREDITS.
```

Improved Code:
```
WORKING-STORAGE SECTION.
01  CONSTANTS-AND-RATES.
    05  PRICE-PER-CREDIT        PIC 9(4)     VALUE 200.
  .
    .
      .
PROCEDURE DIVISION.
  .
    .
      .
        COMPUTE IND-TUITION = PRICE-PER-CREDIT * STU-CREDITS.
```

The improved code is easy to modify when (not if) the tuition rate changes as the only required modification is to the VALUE clause in Working Storage. The poor code requires changes to the appropriate Procedure Division statement(s), and if the constant 200 appears more than once in the Procedure Division, it is very easy to miss some of the statements in which the change is required. There is less possibility for error in the improved code.

Don't overcomment. Contrary to popular belief, the mere presence of comments does not ensure a well-documented program, and poor comments are sometimes worse than no comments at all. The most common fault is redundancy with the source code. Consider:

```
*     CALCULATE  NET PAY
      COMPUTE NET-PAY = GROSS-PAY - FED-TAX - VOL-DEDUCT.
```

The comment detracts from the readability of the statement because it breaks the logical flow as you read the Procedure Division. Worse than redundant, comments may be obsolete or inconsistent with the associated code, as is the case when program statements are changed during maintenance, and the comments are not correspondingly altered.

The authors certainly do not advocate the elimination of comments altogether, but argue simply that care, more than is commonly exercised, should be applied to developing them. One guideline is to provide a comment whenever the purpose of a program statement is not immediately obvious. Imagine, for example, that you are turning the program over to someone else for maintenance, and insert a comment whenever you would explain a statement to the other person. Comments should be used only to show *why* you are doing something, rather than *what* you are doing. Assume that the maintenance programmer is as competent in COBOL as you are; avoid using comments to explain how a particular COBOL statement works.

A Well-Written Program

Figure 7.4 is our final pass at the tuition billing program, with attention drawn to the application of the coding standards just developed. All data names within a 01 entry are given a common prefix: STU for entries in STUDENT-RECORD (lines 17–24), IND for data names under INDIVIDUAL-CALCULATIONS (lines 34–38), and so on. This guideline applies equally well to record descriptions in both the File and Working-Storage Sections.

Blank lines highlight 01 entries in the Data Division and paragraph headers in the Procedure Division. All PICTURE clauses are vertically aligned. Indentation is stressed in the Procedure Division with subservient clauses four columns under the associated statements.

Paragraph headers are sequenced and functional in nature. All statements within a paragraph pertain to the function of that paragraph, as indicated by its name. We have chosen a three-digit numerical sequencing scheme, in which the first digit reflects the hierarchy chart level and the remaining two digits reflect the order in which the paragraphs are performed.

Figure 7.4 A Well-Written COBOL Program

```
 1          IDENTIFICATION DIVISION.
 2          PROGRAM-ID.    TUITION7.
 3          AUTHOR.        CAROL VAZQUEZ VILLAR.
 4
 5          ENVIRONMENT DIVISION.
 6          INPUT-OUTPUT SECTION.
 7          FILE-CONTROL.
 8              SELECT STUDENT-FILE  ASSIGN TO SYSIN
 9                  ORGANIZATION IS LINE SEQUENTIAL.
10              SELECT PRINT-FILE    ASSIGN TO SYSOUT
11                  ORGANIZATION IS LINE SEQUENTIAL.
12
13          DATA DIVISION.
14          FILE SECTION.
15          FD  STUDENT-FILE
16              RECORD CONTAINS 27 CHARACTERS.
17          01  STUDENT-RECORD.
18              05  STU-NAME.
19                  10  STU-LAST-NAME    PIC X(15).
20                  10  STU-INITIALS     PIC XX.
21              05  STU-CREDITS          PIC 9(2).
22              05  STU-UNION-MEMBER     PIC X.
23              05  STU-SCHOLARSHIP      PIC 9(4).
24              05  STU-GPA              PIC 9V99.
25
26          FD  PRINT-FILE
27              RECORD CONTAINS 132 CHARACTERS.
28          01  PRINT-LINE               PIC X(132).
29
30          WORKING-STORAGE SECTION.
31          01  DATA-REMAINS-SWITCH      PIC X(2)     VALUE SPACES.
32
33          01  INDIVIDUAL-CALCULATIONS.
34              05  IND-TUITION          PIC 9(4)     VALUE ZEROS.
35              05  IND-ACTIVITY-FEE     PIC 9(2)     VALUE ZEROS.
36              05  IND-UNION-FEE        PIC 9(2)     VALUE ZEROS.
37              05  IND-SCHOLARSHIP      PIC 9(4)     VALUE ZEROS.
38              05  IND-BILL             PIC S9(6)    VALUE ZEROS.
39
40          01  UNIVERSITY-TOTALS.
41              05  UNI-TUITION          PIC 9(6)     VALUE ZEROS.
42              05  UNI-UNION-FEE        PIC 9(4)     VALUE ZEROS.
43              05  UNI-ACTIVITY-FEE     PIC 9(4)     VALUE ZEROS.
44              05  UNI-SCHOLARSHIP      PIC 9(6)     VALUE ZEROS.
45              05  UNI-IND-BILL         PIC S9(6)    VALUE ZEROS.
46
47          01  CONSTANTS-AND-RATES.
48              05  PRICE-PER-CREDIT     PIC 9(3)     VALUE 200.
49              05  UNION-FEE            PIC 9(2)     VALUE 25.
50              05  ACTIVITY-FEES.
```

— *Data names within 01 have common prefix*

— *Blank lines appear before 01 entries*

Figure 7.4   *(continued)*

```
51              10  1ST-ACTIVITY-FEE PIC 99        VALUE 25.
52              10  1ST-CREDIT-LIMIT PIC 99        VALUE 6.
53              10  2ND-ACTIVITY-FEE PIC 99        VALUE 50.
54              10  2ND-CREDIT-LIMIT PIC 99        VALUE 12.
55              10  3RD-ACTIVITY-FEE PIC 99        VALUE 75.
56          05  MINIMUM-SCHOLAR-GPA  PIC 9V9       VALUE 2.5.
57
58      01  HEADING-LINE.
59          05  FILLER            PIC X          VALUE SPACES.
60          05  FILLER            PIC X(12)      VALUE 'STUDENT NAME'.
61          05  FILLER            PIC X(10)      VALUE SPACES.
62          05  FILLER            PIC X(7)       VALUE 'CREDITS'.
63          05  FILLER            PIC X(2)       VALUE SPACES.
64          05  FILLER            PIC X(7)       VALUE 'TUITION'.
65          05  FILLER            PIC X(2)       VALUE SPACES.
66          05  FILLER            PIC X(9)       VALUE 'UNION FEE'.
67          05  FILLER            PIC X(2)       VALUE SPACES.
68          05  FILLER            PIC X(7)       VALUE 'ACT FEE'.
69          05  FILLER            PIC X(2)       VALUE SPACES.
70          05  FILLER            PIC X(11)      VALUE 'SCHOLARSHIP'.
71          05  FILLER            PIC X(2)       VALUE SPACES.
72          05  FILLER            PIC X(10)      VALUE 'TOTAL BILL'.
73          05  FILLER            PIC X(48)      VALUE SPACES.
74
75      01  DETAIL-LINE.
76          05  FILLER            PIC X          VALUE SPACES.
77          05  DET-LAST-NAME     PIC X(15).
78          05  FILLER            PIC X(2)       VALUE SPACES.
79          05  DET-INITIALS      PIC X(2).
80          05  FILLER            PIC X(5)       VALUE SPACES.
81          05  DET-CREDITS       PIC Z9.
82          05  FILLER            PIC X(4)       VALUE SPACES.
83          05  DET-TUITION       PIC $$$$,$$9.
84          05  FILLER            PIC X(6)       VALUE SPACES.
85          05  DET-UNION-FEE     PIC $$$9       BLANK WHEN ZERO.
86          05  FILLER            PIC X(5)       VALUE SPACES.
87          05  DET-ACTIVITY-FEE  PIC $$$9       BLANK WHEN ZERO.
88          05  FILLER            PIC X(6)       VALUE SPACES.
89          05  DET-SCHOLARSHIP   PIC $$,$$$9 BLANK WHEN ZERO.
90          05  FILLER            PIC X(4)       VALUE SPACES.
91          05  DET-IND-BILL      PIC $$$$,$$9CR.
92          05  FILLER            PIC X(47)      VALUE SPACES.
93
94      01  DASH-LINE.
95          05  FILLER            PIC X(31)      VALUE SPACES.
96          05  FILLER            PIC X(8)       VALUE ALL '-'.
97          05  FILLER            PIC X(2)       VALUE SPACES.
98          05  FILLER            PIC X(8)       VALUE ALL '-'.
99          05  FILLER            PIC X(2)       VALUE SPACES.
100         05  FILLER            PIC X(7)       VALUE ALL '-'.
```

Figure 7.4 *(continued)*

```
101          05  FILLER           PIC X(6)     VALUE SPACES.
102          05  FILLER           PIC X(7)     VALUE ALL '-'.
103          05  FILLER           PIC X(5)     VALUE SPACES.
104          05  FILLER           PIC X(7)     VALUE ALL '-'.
105          05  FILLER           PIC X(49)    VALUE SPACES.
106
107      01  TOTAL-LINE.
108          05  FILLER           PIC X(8)     VALUE SPACES.
109          05  FILLER           PIC X(17)
110                  VALUE 'UNIVERSITY TOTALS'.
111          05  FILLER           PIC X(6)     VALUE SPACES.
112          05  TOT-TUITION      PIC $$$$,$$9.
113          05  FILLER           PIC X(2)     VALUE SPACES.
114          05  TOT-UNION-FEE    PIC $$$$,$$9.
115          05  FILLER           PIC X        VALUE SPACES.
116          05  TOT-ACTIVITY-FEE PIC $$$$,$$9.
117          05  FILLER           PIC X(5)     VALUE SPACES.
118          05  TOT-SCHOLARSHIP  PIC $$$$,$$9.
119          05  FILLER           PIC X(4)     VALUE SPACES.
120          05  TOT-IND-BILL     PIC $$$$,$$9CR.
121          05  FILLER           PIC X(47)    VALUE SPACES.
122
123      PROCEDURE DIVISION.
124      100-PREPARE-TUITION-REPORT.
125          OPEN INPUT STUDENT-FILE
126               OUTPUT PRINT-FILE.
127          PERFORM 210-WRITE-HEADING-LINE.
128          PERFORM 230-READ-STUDENT-FILE.
129          PERFORM 260-PROCESS-STUDENT-RECORD
130              UNTIL DATA-REMAINS-SWITCH = 'NO'.
131          PERFORM 290-WRITE-UNIVERSITY-TOTALS.
132          CLOSE STUDENT-FILE
133                PRINT-FILE.
134          STOP RUN.
135
136      210-WRITE-HEADING-LINE.
137          MOVE HEADING-LINE TO PRINT-LINE.
138          WRITE PRINT-LINE
139              AFTER ADVANCING PAGE.
140          MOVE SPACES TO PRINT-LINE.
141          WRITE PRINT-LINE.
142
143      230-READ-STUDENT-FILE.
144          READ STUDENT-FILE
145              AT END MOVE 'NO' TO DATA-REMAINS-SWITCH
146          END-READ.
147
148      260-PROCESS-STUDENT-RECORD.
149          PERFORM 310-COMPUTE-INDIVIDUAL-BILL.
150          PERFORM 330-INCREMENT-UNIVER-TOTALS
```

Data names within 01 have common prefix

Subservient Procedure Division clauses are indented

Figure 7.4   *(continued)*

```
151            PERFORM 360-WRITE-DETAIL-LINE.
152            PERFORM 230-READ-STUDENT-FILE.
153
154        290-WRITE-UNIVERSITY-TOTALS.
155            MOVE DASH-LINE TO PRINT-LINE.
156            WRITE PRINT-LINE.
157            MOVE UNI-TUITION TO TOT-TUITION.
158            MOVE UNI-UNION-FEE TO TOT-UNION-FEE.
159            MOVE UNI-ACTIVITY-FEE TO TOT-ACTIVITY-FEE.
160            MOVE UNI-SCHOLARSHIP TO TOT-SCHOLARSHIP.
161            MOVE UNI-IND-BILL TO TOT-IND-BILL.
162            MOVE TOTAL-LINE TO PRINT-LINE.
163            WRITE PRINT-LINE
164                AFTER ADVANCING 1 LINE.
165
166        310-COMPUTE-INDIVIDUAL-BILL.
167            PERFORM 410-COMPUTE-TUITION.
168            PERFORM 430-COMPUTE-UNION-FEE.
169            PERFORM 460-COMPUTE-ACTIVITY-FEE.
170            PERFORM 490-COMPUTE-SCHOLARSHIP.
171            COMPUTE IND-BILL = IND-TUITION + IND-UNION-FEE +
172                IND-ACTIVITY-FEE - IND-SCHOLARSHIP.
173
174        330-INCREMENT-UNIVER-TOTALS.
175            ADD IND-TUITION      TO UNI-TUITION.
176            ADD IND-UNION-FEE    TO UNI-UNION-FEE.
177            ADD IND-ACTIVITY-FEE TO UNI-ACTIVITY-FEE.
178            ADD IND-SCHOLARSHIP  TO UNI-SCHOLARSHIP.
179            ADD IND-BILL         TO UNI-IND-BILL.
180
181        360-WRITE-DETAIL-LINE.
182            MOVE STU-LAST-NAME TO DET-LAST-NAME.
183            MOVE STU-INITIALS TO DET-INITIALS.
184            MOVE STU-CREDITS TO DET-CREDITS.
185            MOVE IND-TUITION TO DET-TUITION.
186            MOVE IND-UNION-FEE TO DET-UNION-FEE.
187            MOVE IND-ACTIVITY-FEE TO DET-ACTIVITY-FEE.
188            MOVE IND-SCHOLARSHIP TO DET-SCHOLARSHIP.
189            MOVE IND-BILL TO DET-IND-BILL.
190            MOVE DETAIL-LINE TO PRINT-LINE.
191            WRITE PRINT-LINE
192                AFTER ADVANCING 1 LINE.
193
194        410-COMPUTE-TUITION.
195            COMPUTE IND-TUITION = PRICE-PER-CREDIT * STU-CREDITS.
196
197        430-COMPUTE-UNION-FEE.
198            IF STU-UNION-MEMBER = 'Y'
199                MOVE UNION-FEE TO IND-UNION-FEE
200            ELSE
```

Paragraph names are functional, i.e., verb, adjective, object

Continued line is indented

Paragraph names are functional, i.e., verb, adjective, object

IF/ELSE statement indented and ends with END-IF scope terminator

Figure 7.4 *(continued)*

```
201          MOVE ZERO TO IND-UNION-FEE
202       END-IF.
203
204    460-COMPUTE-ACTIVITY-FEE.
205       EVALUATE TRUE
206          WHEN STU-CREDITS <= 1ST-CREDIT-LIMIT
207             MOVE 1ST-ACTIVITY-FEE TO IND-ACTIVITY-FEE
208          WHEN STU-CREDITS > 1ST-CREDIT-LIMIT
209             AND STU-CREDITS <= 2ND-CREDIT-LIMIT
210                MOVE 2ND-ACTIVITY-FEE TO IND-ACTIVITY-FEE
211          WHEN STU-CREDITS > 2ND-CREDIT-LIMIT
212             MOVE 3RD-ACTIVITY-FEE TO IND-ACTIVITY-FEE
213          WHEN OTHER
214             DISPLAY 'INVALID CREDITS FOR: ' STU-NAME
215       END-EVALUATE.
216
217    490-COMPUTE-SCHOLARSHIP.
218       IF STU-GPA > MINIMUM-SCHOLAR-GPA
219          MOVE STU-SCHOLARSHIP TO IND-SCHOLARSHIP
220       ELSE
221          MOVE ZERO TO IND-SCHOLARSHIP
222       END-IF.
```

IF/ELSE statement indented and ends with END-IF scope terminator

S U M M A R Y

Points to Remember

- A numeric field contains digits, an (optional) implied decimal point, and/or an optional sign. A numeric-edited field may contain any editing character. All calculations in a COBOL program are done on numeric fields, whose computed values are moved to numeric-edited fields prior to printing.

- Any move involving a numeric field and a numeric-edited field maintains decimal alignment.

- Only a signed numeric field can hold a negative value; that is, a numeric field cannot retain a negative value unless it has been defined with an S in its PICTURE clause.

- Coding standards are intended to improve the readability and maintainability of COBOL programs. They are imposed by individual installations and go beyond the requirements of COBOL.

Key Words and Concepts

Actual decimal point	Implied decimal point
Check protection	Indentation
Coding standards	Insertion characters
CR	Maintainability
DB	Numeric field
Decimal alignment	Numeric-edited field
Editing	Prefixing data names
Editing characters	Readability
Fixed dollar sign	Receiving field
Floating dollar sign	Sequencing paragraph names
Floating minus sign	Signed numbers
Floating plus sign	Source (sending) field
Functional paragraph	Zero suppression

COBOL Element

BLANK WHEN ZERO

F i l l - i n

1. _____ _____ are a set of rules unique to each installation, which go beyond the rules of COBOL, to improve the readability of a COBOL program.

2. The editing characters, _____ and _____, will appear if and only if the sending field is _____ and are suppressed otherwise.

3. The presence of multiple dollar signs in the PICTURE clause of an edited field indicates a _____ dollar sign, whereas a single dollar sign indicates a _____ dollar sign.

4. The _____ is the character used for check protection.

5. The PICTURE clause of a numeric field may consist of 9's, a _____ to indicate an implied decimal point, and the letter _____ to indicate a signed field.

6. Continuation of a _____ literal requires a _____ in column _____.

7. A well-chosen paragraph name consists of a _____, _____, and _____ to indicate the function of that paragraph.

8. All data names within the same 01 record should begin with a common _____.

9. _____ of COBOL statements within the B margin does not affect compiler interpretation but goes a long way toward improving the readability of a program.

10. _____ _____ may be left before 01 records and paragraph names to enhance readability.

11. If a numeric field is defined without an S in its PICTURE clause, the field will never assume a _____ value.

12. All calculations in a COBOL program are performed on (numeric/numeric-edited) fields.

True/False

1. Indentation within the B margin affects compiler interpretation.

2. Blank lines are not permitted within a COBOL program.

3. The COBOL coding standards for AT&T and IBM are apt to be identical.

4. COBOL requires that paragraph names be sequenced.

5. Data names should be as short as possible to cut down on the coding effort.

6. Indentation in COBOL is a waste of time.

7. A well-commented COBOL program should contain half as many comment lines as Procedure Division statements.

8. All continued statements require a hyphen in column 7.

9. COMPUTE-AND-WRITE is a good paragraph name.

10. Heading, detail, and total lines may be established as separate 01 entries in Working-Storage.

11. Every PICTURE clause requires a corresponding VALUE clause.

12. Arithmetic may be done on numeric-edited fields.

13. A positive field should always be defined with a CR in its PICTURE clause, whereas a negative field requires DB.

14. A single numeric-edited field may contain a dollar sign, comma, decimal point, asterisk, and the character string CR in its PICTURE clause.

15. The same numeric-edited field may contain both CR and DB in its PICTURE clause.

16. Hyphens may be used as insertion characters in a social security number.

17. Slashes may be used as insertion characters in a date.

18. The presence of CR or DB in a numeric-edited field implies that the sending field is signed.

19. Zero is a valid insertion character.

Problems

1. Supply PICTURE clauses for the receiving fields needed to accomplish the following:
   a. A floating dollar sign, omission of cents, printing (or suppression) of commas as appropriate, and a maximum value of $9,999,999.
   b. A fixed dollar sign, asterisk fill for insignificant leading zeros, printing (or suppression) of commas as appropriate, a maximum value of $9,999, and a trailing DB if the sending field is negative.

   c. A fixed dollar sign, zero suppression of insignificant leading zeros, omission of commas in all instances, and a maximum value of $99,999.99.

   d. A floating dollar sign, printing (or suppression) of commas as appropriate, a maximum value of $9,999.00, and a trailing CR if the sending field is negative.

2. Show the value of the edited result for each of the following entries:

	SOURCE FIELD		RECEIVING FIELD	
	Picture	Value	Picture	Edited Result
a.	9(6)	123456	9(6)	_____
b.	9(6)	123456	9(8)	_____
c.	9(6)	123456	9(6).99	_____
d.	9(4)V99	123456	9(6)	_____
e.	9(4)V99	123456	9(4)	_____
f.	9(4)V99	123456	$$$$$9.99	_____
g.	9(4)V99	123456	$$$,$$9.99	_____
h.	9(6)	123456	$$$$,$$9.99	_____
i.	9(6)	123456	Z(8)	_____
j.	9(4)V99	123456	$ZZZ,ZZZ.99	_____

3. Show the edited results for each entry:

	SOURCE FIELD		RECEIVING FIELD	
	Picture	Value	Picture	Edited Result
a.	S9(4)V99	45600	$$$$$.99CR	_____
b.	S9(4)V99	45600	$$,$$$.99DB	_____
c.	S9(4)	4567	$$,$$$.00	_____
d.	S9(6)	122577	99B99B99	_____
e.	S9(6)	123456	++++,+++	_____
f.	S9(6)	-123456	++++,+++	_____
g.	S9(6)	123456	----,---	_____
h.	S9(6)	-123456	----,---	_____
i.	9(4)V99	567890	$$$$,$$$.99	_____
j.	9(4)V99	567890	$ZZZ,ZZZ.99	_____
k.	9(4)V99	567890	$***,***.99	_____

4. What, if anything, is wrong (either syntactically or logically) with the following PICTURE clauses?

   a. $,$$$,$$9.99

   b. 999999999

   c. $$$$,$$$,$$$

   d. $ZZZ.ZZ

   e. $999V99

   f. $999,999,999.99

   g. $$$$$,$$9.99

5. Do you agree with all of the coding standards suggested by the authors? Can you suggest any others? Do you think the imposition of coding standards within an installation impinges on the creativity of individual programmers? Are coding standards worth the extra time and trouble they require?

6. Consider the following code:

```
01  AMOUNT-REMAINING           PIC 9(3)      VALUE 100.
01  WS-INPUT-AREA.
    05  QUANTITY-SHIPPED       PIC 99.
    05  REST-OF-A-RECORD       PIC X(50).
    .
        .
            .
    READ TRANSACTION-FILE INTO WS-INPUT-AREA
        AT END MOVE 'YES' TO EOF-SWITCH
    END-READ.
    PERFORM PROCESS-TRANSACTIONS
        UNTIL EOF-SWITCH = 'YES'.
    .
        .
            .

PROCESS-TRANSACTIONS.
    SUBTRACT QUANTITY-SHIPPED FROM AMOUNT-REMAINING.
    READ TRANSACTION-FILE INTO WS-INPUT-AREA
        AT END MOVE 'YES' TO EOF-SWITCH
    END-READ.
```

   a. Why will AMOUNT-REMAINING never be less than zero?

   b. What will be the final value of AMOUNT-REMAINING, given successive values of 30, 50, 25, and 15 for QUANTITY-SHIPPED?

8

Data Validation

CHAPTER OUTLINE

Overview

System Concepts: Data Validation

The IF Statement

    Relational Condition

    Class Test

    Sign Test

    Condition-Name Test (88-Level Entries)

    Compound Test

        Hierarchy of Operations

    Implied Conditions

    Nested IFs

    NEXT SENTENCE

ACCEPT Statement

    Calculations Involving Dates

Stand-Alone Edit Program

    Programming Specifications

    Error Messages

    Pseudocode

    Hierarchy Chart

    The Completed Program

Limitations of COBOL-74

Summary

Fill-in

True/False

Problems

O B J E C T I V E S

After reading this chapter you will be able to:

■ Describe the importance of data validation and its implementation in a stand-alone edit program.

■ Define the following validity tests: numeric test, alphabetic test, consistency check, sequence check, completeness check, date check, and subscript check.

■ Describe the various types of conditions in an IF statement.

■ Define a nested IF; indicate guidelines for proper indentation in coding such statements.

■ Describe the advantages of the END-IF scope terminator; show how the scope terminator eliminates the need for the NEXT SENTENCE clause.

■ Obtain the date (calendar and Julian) and time of execution; implement date checking in a program to ensure that the day and month are consistent.

O V E R V I E W

This chapter introduces the concept of data validation, the process of ensuring that data entered into a system is as error-free as possible. It begins by describing various types of error checking, then focuses on the IF statement, the means by which data validation is implemented in COBOL. We cover the different types of conditions that exist within an IF statement (relation, class, sign, and condition name), the concept of a nested IF, and the importance of the END-IF scope terminator.

The second half of the chapter develops a stand-alone edit program to illustrate the implementation of data validation. The program is designed to process a file of incoming transactions, reject invalid transactions with appropriate error messages, and write valid transactions to an output file. The latter is then input to a reporting (or other) program.

Systems Concepts: Data Validation

A well-written program is not limited to merely computing answers, but must also validate the data on which those answers are based. Failure to do so results in programs that produce meaningless or inaccurate information, a situation described by the cliché GIGO (Garbage In, Garbage Out). It is the job of the programmer or analyst to ensure that a system remains as error-free as possible and that the "garbage" does not enter the system in the first place.

Incoming data may be validated within the program in which it is used or in a separate stand-alone edit program. The essential point is that incoming data *must* be checked; when and how this is done is of secondary importance. The following are typical types of data validation:

Numeric test. Ensures that a numeric field contains numeric data. Commas, dollar signs, decimal points, blanks, or other alphabetic characters are not numeric, and will cause problems in execution.

Alphabetic test. Analogous to a numeric test, except that alphabetic fields should contain only alphabetic data. Any errors detected here are typically less serious than for numeric fields.

Reasonableness (limit or range) check. Ensures that a number is within expected limits; that is, that a value does not exceed a designated upper or lower extreme.

Consistency check. Verifies that the values in two or more fields are consistent, for example, salary and job title. Other examples of consistency checks are an individual's credit rating and the amount of credit a bank is willing to extend, or (as used by the Internal Revenue Service) an individual's reported income and the zip code.

Existing code check. One of the most important tests, the omission of which produces countless errors. Consider:

```
IF SEX = 'M'
    ADD 1 TO NUMBER-OF-MEN
ELSE
    ADD 1 TO NUMBER-OF-WOMEN
END-IF.
```

It is decidedly poor practice to assume that an incoming record is female if it is not male. Both codes should be explicitly checked, and if neither occurs, a suitable error should be printed.

Sequence check. Ensures that incoming records are in proper order. It can also be used when one record is continued over several lines to ensure that the lines within a record are in proper sequence.

Completeness check. Verifies that data in all required fields are present; this check is normally used when new records are added to a file.

Date check. Ensures that an incoming date is acceptable—for example, that the day is from 1 to 31, the month from 1 to 12, and the year within a designated period, often just the current year. A further check is that the month and day are consistent with one another—for example, a date of April 31 is invalid.

Subscript check. Validates that a subscript or index is within a table's original definition. (Table processing is discussed fully in Chapter 11.)

Diligent application of data validation (sometimes referred to as defensive programming) minimizes the need for subsequent debugging. It assumes that errors will occur and takes steps to make them apparent to the programmer and/or user *before* a program terminates. Is it worth the extra time? Emphatically yes, especially if you have ever been called at two in the morning to hear that your program "bombed" because of invalid data.

The IF Statement

The importance of the *IF* statement is obvious, yet the large number of options make it one of the more difficult statements to master. Essential to any IF statement, however, is the condition, the portion of the statement that is evaluated as either true or false. Four types of conditions are possible: relational, class, sign, and condition-name, each of which is discussed in a separate section.

Relational Condition

The **relational condition** is the most common type of condition and has appeared throughout the book. As you already know there is considerable variation in the way the relational operator may be expressed. In all instances, however, the condition compares the quantities on either side of the relational operator to determine whether (or not) the condition is true.

The data type of the quantities being compared must be the same; for example, a numeric data item must be compared to a numeric literal and a nonnumeric data item to a nonnumeric literal. Failure to do so produces a syntax error during compilation. The relational condition is illustrated in Figure 8.1.

Figure 8.1   The Relational Condition

```
                    ┌ IS [NOT] GREATER THAN              ┐
                    │ IS [NOT] >                         │
                    │ IS [NOT] LESS THAN                 │
       ┌identifier-1┐│ IS [NOT] <                        │┌identifier-2┐
    IF {literal-1   }│ IS [NOT] EQUAL TO                 }{literal-2   }
       └expression-1┘│ IS [NOT] =                        │└expression-2┘
                    │ IS [NOT] GREATER THAN OR EQUAL TO  │
                    │ IS [NOT] >=                        │
                    │ IS [NOT] LESS THAN OR EQUAL TO     │
                    └ IS [NOT] <=                        ┘
```

(a) Syntax

```
05   NUMERIC-FIELD            PIC 9(5).
05   ALPHANUMERIC-FIELD       PIC X(5).
     .
       .
         .
IF NUMERIC-FIELD = 10 . . .            (valid entry)
IF NUMERIC-FIELD = '10' . . .          (invalid entry)
IF ALPHANUMERIC-FIELD = 10 . . .       (invalid entry)
IF ALPHANUMERIC-FIELD = '10' . . .     (valid entry)
```

(b) Examples

Class Test

The ***class test*** ensures that a field contains numeric or alphabetic data in accordance with its PICTURE clause. A valid numeric field will contain only the digits 0 to 9 (a sign is optional); blanks, decimal points, commas, and other editing characters are not valid as numeric characters. A valid alphabetic field will contain the letters A to Z (upper or lower case) and/or blanks. An alphanumeric field may contain any character; letters, numbers, and/or special characters.

The class test cannot be used indiscriminately; that is, a numeric test cannot be used for data names defined as alphabetic, nor can an alphabetic test be used for numeric data names. Either test, however, may be performed on alphanumeric items. The class test is illustrated in Figure 8.2

Figure 8.2 The Class Test

```
                                        ┌ NUMERIC          ┐
                                        │ ALPHABETIC       │
            IF identifier IS [NOT]      │ ALPHABETIC-UPPER │
                                        └ ALPHABETIC-LOWER ┘
```

(a) Syntax

```
05  NUMERIC-FIELD               PIC 9(5).
05  ALPHABETIC-FIELD            PIC A(5).
    .
      .
        .

IF NUMERIC-FIELD IS NUMERIC
    PERFORM DO-ARITHMETIC-CALCULATIONS
END-IF.

IF NUMERIC-FIELD IS NOT NUMERIC
    DISPLAY 'ERROR - NUMERIC FIELD CONTAINS INVALID DATA'
END-IF.

IF ALPHABETIC-FIELD IS ALPHABETIC
    DISPLAY 'ALPHABETIC FIELD CONTAINS UPPER AND/OR LOWER CASE LETTERS'
END-IF.

IF ALPHABETIC-FIELD IS NOT ALPHABETIC
    DISPLAY 'ALPHABETIC FIELD CONTAINS NON-ALPHABETIC DATA'
END-IF.
```

(b) Examples

Figure 8.3   The Sign Test

$$\text{\underline{IF}} \left\{ \begin{array}{l} \text{identifier} \\ \text{arithmetic expression} \end{array} \right\} \text{IS} \left[\underline{\text{NOT}}\right] \left\{ \begin{array}{l} \underline{\text{POSITIVE}} \\ \underline{\text{NEGATIVE}} \\ \underline{\text{ZERO}} \end{array} \right\}$$

(a) Syntax

```
IF NET-PAY IS NOT POSITIVE
    PERFORM TOO-MUCH-TAXES
END-IF.

IF CHECK-BALANCE IS NEGATIVE
    PERFORM OVERDRAWN
END-IF.
```

(b) Examples

Sign Test

The *sign test* determines whether a numeric field is positive, negative, or zero. The test is of limited value and could in fact be replaced with the equivalent relational condition. Nevertheless, the sign test is illustrated in Figure 8.3.

Condition-Name Test

A *condition name* (88-level entry) is a special way of writing a relational condition that makes it (the condition) easier to read. Condition names are defined in the Data Division, then referenced in the Procedure Division as shown in Figure 8.4. Condition names are used for elementary items only.

The definition of a condition name in the Data Division simplifies subsequent coding in the Procedure Division; for example, IF FRESHMAN is equivalent to IF YEAR-CODE = 1. 88-level entries provide improved documentation in that IF FRESHMAN is inherently clearer than IF YEAR-CODE = 1.

The use of an 88-level entry also allows multiple codes to be grouped under a single data name; for example, VALID-CODES is defined as any value from 1 to 8. This in turn makes it possible to test for an invalid code with a simple IF statement as shown in Figure 8.4b. Note, too, that condition names permit a given value to appear under more than one classification; for example, records containing a 3 belong to JUNIOR, UPPER-CLASSMAN, and VALID-CODES.

Compound Test

Any two simple tests may be combined to form a *compound test* through the logical operators AND and OR. AND implies that both conditions must be satisfied for the IF to be considered true, whereas OR requires that only one of the conditions be satisfied. A flowchart is shown in Figure 8.5a depicting the AND condition. It requires that *both* A be greater than B *and* C be greater than D in order to proceed to TRUE. If either of these tests fails, the compound condition is judged false. The general format is:

$$\text{\underline{IF}} \ \text{condition-1} \ \left\{ \begin{array}{l} \underline{\text{AND}} \\ \underline{\text{OR}} \end{array} \right\} \ \text{condition-2} \right\} \ . \ . \ .$$

Figure 8.4   Condition Names (88-level entries)

$$88 \text{ data-name } \begin{Bmatrix} \underline{\text{VALUE}} \text{ IS} \\ \underline{\text{VALUES}} \text{ ARE} \end{Bmatrix} \begin{Bmatrix} \text{literal-1} \begin{bmatrix} \begin{Bmatrix} \underline{\text{THROUGH}} \\ \underline{\text{THRU}} \end{Bmatrix} \text{literal-2} \end{bmatrix} \end{Bmatrix} \dots$$

(a) Syntax

```
05  YEAR-CODE          PIC 9.
    88  FRESHMAN            VALUE 1.
    88  SOPHOMORE           VALUE 2.
    88  JUNIOR              VALUE 3.
    88  SENIOR              VALUE 4.
    88  GRAD-STUDENT        VALUES ARE 5 THRU 8.
    88  UNDER-CLASSMAN      VALUES ARE 1, 2.
    88  UPPER-CLASSMAN      VALUES ARE 3, 4.
    88  VALID-CODES         VALUES ARE 1 THRU 8.
.
  .
    .


IF FRESHMAN
    PERFORM WELCOME-NEW-STUDENTS
END-IF.


IF VALID-CODES
    PERFORM PROCESS-STUDENT-RECORD
ELSE
    DISPLAY 'INCOMING YEAR CODE IS IN ERROR'
END-IF.
```

(b) Examples

Figure 8.5b contains a flowchart for a compound OR in which only one of two conditions needs to be met for the condition to be considered true. Thus, if either A is greater than B or C is greater than D, processing is directed to TRUE.

Hierarchy of Operations

IF statements containing compound conditions can become difficult to interpret; for example, in the statement,

```
IF X > Y OR X = Z AND X < W ...
```

which takes precedence, AND or OR? To provide an unequivocal evaluation of compound conditions, the following hierarchy for evaluation is established:

1. Arithmetic expressions

2. Relational operators

3. NOT condition

4. AND (from left to right if more than one)

5. OR (from left to right if more than one)

Figure 8.5   Compound Conditions

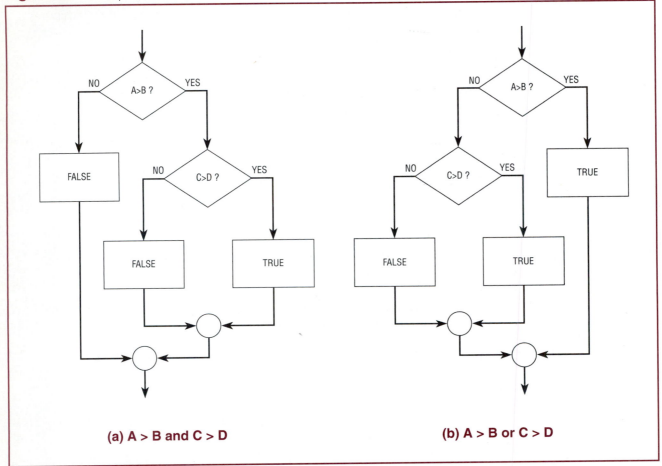

(a) A > B and C > D   (b) A > B or C > D

Thus, for the preceding statement to be true, either

```
X > Y
```

or

```
X = Z and X < W
```

Parentheses can (and should) be used to clarify the programmer's intent and the preceding statement is made clearer if it is rewritten as

```
IF X > Y OR (X = Z AND X < W) . . .
```

Parentheses can also *alter* the outcome in that the expression in parentheses is evaluated first. The following statement is *logically different* from the original statement:

```
IF (X > Y OR X = Z) AND X < W . . .
```

In this example the condition in parentheses (X > Y OR X = Z) is evaluated first, after which X is compared to W. Both conditions (the one in parentheses and X < W) must be true for the compound condition to be considered true.

Implied Conditions

The simple conditions within a compound condition often have the same subject as in the statement:

```
IF SALARY > 30000 AND SALARY < 40000
```

A more concise way of expressing this logic is with an ***implied condition***, which requires only the first occurrence of the subject; that is,

```
IF SALARY > 30000 AND < 40000
```

is equivalent to the earlier entry. If both the subject and relational operator are the same, then only the first occurrence of both needs to be written; that is,

```
IF DEPARTMENT = 10 OR 20
```

is equivalent to

```
IF DEPARTMENT = 10 OR DEPARTMENT = 20
```

Implied conditions are often confusing and the following are provided as additional examples:

```
IF X = Y OR Z        is equivalent to IF X = Y OR X = Z
IF A = B OR C OR D   is equivalent to IF A = B OR A = C OR A = D
IF A = B AND C       is equivalent to IF A = B AND A = C
```

Nested IFs

The general format of the IF statement is:

```
IF identifier IS [NOT]  { NUMERIC
                          ALPHABETIC
                          ALPHABETIC-UPPER
                          ALPHABETIC-LOWER }
```

A ***nested IF*** results when either statement-1 or statement-2 is itself another IF statement, that is, when there are two or more IFs in one sentence. For example, consider

```
IF A > B
    IF C > D
        MOVE S TO W
        MOVE X TO Y
    ELSE
        ADD 1 TO Z
    END-IF
END-IF.
```

The ELSE clause is associated with the closest previous IF that is not already paired with another ELSE. Hence, in this example, Z is incremented by 1 if A is greater than B, but C is not greater than D. If, however, A is not greater than B, control passes to the statement immediately following the period with no further action being taken. (The END-IF scope terminator is optional in both instances, but is included as per our coding standard of Chapter 7 of always specifying the scope terminator.)

Figure 8.6 shows a flowchart and corresponding COBOL code to determine the largest of three quantities A, B, and C. (They are assumed to be unequal numbers.) Observe how the true and false branches of each decision block meet in a single exit point and how this corresponds to the COBOL code. Notice also how the indentation

Figure 8.6 Nested IF Statements

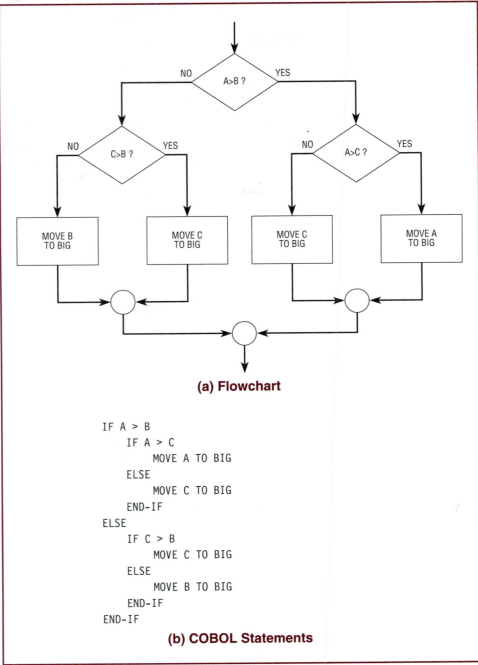

(a) Flowchart

```
IF A > B
    IF A > C
        MOVE A TO BIG
    ELSE
        MOVE C TO BIG
    END-IF
ELSE
    IF C > B
        MOVE C TO BIG
    ELSE
        MOVE B TO BIG
    END-IF
END-IF
```

(b) COBOL Statements

in the COBOL statement facilitates interpretation of the statement. (The compiler pays no attention to the indentation, which is done strictly for programmer convenience.)

We advocate careful attention to indentation and recommend the following guidelines:

1. Each nested IF should be indented four columns from the previous IF.

2. ELSE should appear on a line by itself directly under its associated IF.

3. Detail lines should be indented four columns under both IF and ELSE.

4. The END-IF scope terminator should always be used and appear on a line by itself directly under its associated IF.

These guidelines were used in Figure 8.6.

NEXT SENTENCE

The **NEXT SENTENCE** clause directs control to the statement following the period in an IF statement. It was an essential clause in COBOL-74 to implement certain types of nested IF statements, but is no longer needed due to the the END-IF scope terminator in COBOL-85. The use of NEXT SENTENCE is compared to the scope terminator in Figure 8.7. (COBOL 2002 does not allow NEXT SENTENCE. Replace NEXT SENTENCE with CONTINUE.)

Figure 8.7   Nested IF Statements/II

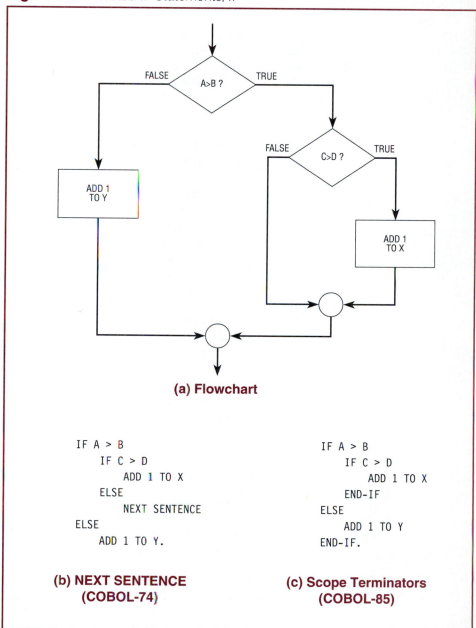

(a) Flowchart

```
IF A > B
    IF C > D
        ADD 1 TO X
    ELSE
        NEXT SENTENCE
ELSE
    ADD 1 TO Y.
```

```
IF A > B
    IF C > D
        ADD 1 TO X
    END-IF
ELSE
    ADD 1 TO Y
END-IF.
```

(b) NEXT SENTENCE
(COBOL-74)

(c) Scope Terminators
(COBOL-85)

The intended logic is to add 1 to X if A is greater than B and C is greater than D; if, however, A is greater than B, but C is not greater than D, no further action is to be taken. The NEXT SENTENCE clause in Figure 8.7b terminates the IF statement if the second condition (C > D) is not met. The identical effect is achieved by the END-IF scope terminator in Figure 8.7c.

ACCEPT Statement

The **ACCEPT** statement is used to obtain the day of the week, date, and/or time of program execution. Consider:

$$\underline{\text{ACCEPT}} \text{ identifier-1} \underline{\text{ FROM}} \left\{ \begin{array}{l} \underline{\text{DAY-OF-WEEK}} \\ \underline{\text{DATE}} \\ \underline{\text{DAY}} \\ \underline{\text{TIME}} \end{array} \right\}$$

Identifier-1 is a programmer-defined work area that holds the information being accepted such as the DAY-OF-WEEK, DATE, DAY, or TIME. The DAY-OF-WEEK is returned as a single digit, from one to seven inclusive, corresponding to Monday through Sunday. (See Figure 9.8 in the next chapter.) DATE and DAY both reflect the current date, but in different formats. Specification of DATE places a six-digit numeric field into identifier-1 in the form *yymmdd;* the first two digits contain year; the next two, month; and the last two, the day of the month; for example, 930316, denotes March 16, 1993.

Specification of DAY, rather than DATE, returns a five-digit numeric field to the work area. The first two digits represent year and the last three the day of the year, numbered from 1 to 365 (366 in a leap year). March 16, 1999, would be represented as 99075, but March 16, 2000, as 00076, since 2000 is a leap year.

In both DAY and DATE representations, only the last two digits of the year are specified. This characteristic has led to the so-called Year 2000 problem. Chapter 19 discusses the problem and provides alternate methods for dealing with dates. Appendix E discusses an Intrinsic Function that can replace ACCEPT . . . FROM DATE. CURRENT-DATE returns the system date in *yyyymmddhhmmsshh* format. There is no CURRENT-DAY function to replace ACCEPT . . . FROM DAY. However, Appendix E includes other functions that are able to convert date formats from one type to another.

We present ACCEPT . . . FROM DATE and ACCEPT . . . FROM DAY because they are part of many COBOL programs.

TIME returns an eight-digit numeric field, *hhmmsshh,* in a 24-hour system. It contains the number of elapsed hours, minutes, seconds, and hundredths of seconds after midnight, in that order, from left to right. 10:15 A.M. would return as 10150000, 10:15 P.M. as 22150000.

Calculations Involving Dates

Once the date of execution is obtained, it can be used for various types of date validation such as checking that an employee's hire date is within the current year. It can also be used in various calculations, for example, to compute an employee's age, or to determine which accounts haven't been paid in 30 days. Figure 8.8 illustrates how an employee's age may be calculated from the date of execution and the employee's birth date.

You should verify that the COMPUTE statement in Figure 8.8 works as intended, and further that it works for all combinations of data. This is best accomplished by "playing computer" and plugging in numbers. Accordingly, consider two examples:

Figure 8.8 The ACCEPT Statement

```
WORKING-STORAGE SECTION.

01  EMPLOYEE-RECORD.
    .
      .

    05  EMP-DATE-OF-BIRTH.
        10  EMP-BIRTH-MONTH        PIC 99.
        10  EMP-BIRTH-YEAR         PIC 99.

01  EMPLOYEE-AGE                    PIC 99V99.

01  DATE-WORK-AREA.
    05  TODAYS-YEAR                 PIC 99.
    05  TODAYS-MONTH               PIC 99.
    05  TODAYS-DAY                  PIC 99.
    .
      .


PROCEDURE DIVISION.
    .
      .
    ACCEPT DATE-WORK-AREA FROM DATE.
    .
      .


    COMPUTE EMPLOYEE-AGE = TODAYS-YEAR - EMP-BIRTH-YEAR
        + (TODAYS-MONTH - EMP-BIRTH-MONTH) / 12.
```

Example 8.1

```
Date of birth: 3/73
Date of execution: 6/93
Expected age: 20 1/4
Calculation: 93 - 73 + (6 - 3)/12 = 20 + 3/12 = 20.25
```

Example 8.2

```
Date of birth: 9/73
Date of execution: 6/93
Expected age: 19 3/4
Calculation: 93 - 73 + (6 - 9)/12 = 20 + -3/12 = 19.75
```

The calculations are correct, and they work for both combinations of data; it doesn't matter whether the month of execution is before or after the birth month. (For simplicity only month and year were used in the calculation of age.) For these calculations to work over the transition to 2000, years must be specified in *yyyy* format.

The Stand-Alone Edit Program

The validation of incoming data is often done in a stand-alone edit program as opposed to the reporting program that processes the data. The sequence is shown in Figure 8.9. A transaction file is input to the edit program, which checks each incoming record for validity. Invalid transactions are rejected with an appropriate

Figure 8.9 The Stand-Alone Edit Program

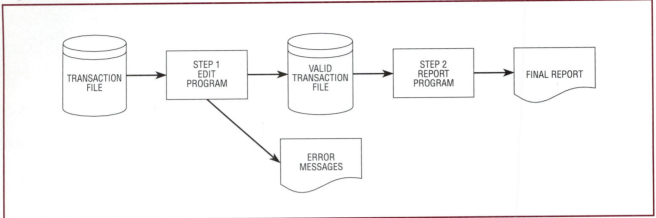

error message(s), whereas valid transactions are written to an output file. The valid transaction file (i.e., the output file from the edit program) is then input to a reporting program.

The flowchart in Figure 8.9 serves as an effective blueprint for the *combination* of programs that are developed in this chapter and the next. The programs are related to one another in that the output of the edit program in this chapter will be input to the reporting program in Chapter 9. Specifications for the edit program are given below, whereas the requirements of the reporting program are presented in Chapter 9.

Like many programs written during the 1970s, 80s, and early 90s, the following program suffers from the Year 2000 bug. In other words, once the system date goes past January 1, 2000, the date validation routine will fail. Can you see why?

We have chosen to let the program stand as we presented it in the past—for two reasons. First, the program demonstrates the mind set of COBOL programmers in earlier days (even COBOL text writers). Second, it gives an opportunity for you to correct the program. Therefore, we have included a problem at the end of the chapter to make this program Year 2000 compliant.[1]

Programming Specifications

Program Name: Car Rental Validation

Narrative: The specifications describe a stand-alone edit program for car rental transactions, each of which is subject to multiple validity checks. Invalid transactions are to be rejected with appropriate error message(s), whereas valid transactions are to be written in their entirety to an output file; the latter will be input to a reporting program developed in the next chapter.

Input File(s): RENTAL-RECORD-FILE

Input Record Layout:
```
01  RENTAL-RECORD-IN.
    05  REN-CONTRACT-NO        PIC 9(6).
    05  REN-NAME.
        10  REN-LAST-NAME      PIC X(15).
        10  REN-FIRST-NAME     PIC X(10).
        10  REN-INITIAL        PIC X.
```

---

[1]Your data files include a project called Val2000.prj that contains a Year 2000 compliant version of the program.

```
            05  REN-RETURNED-DATE.
                10  REN-RETURNED-YEAR      PIC 9(2).
                10  REN-RETURNED-MONTH     PIC 9(2).
                10  REN-RETURNED-DAY       PIC 9(2).
            05  REN-CAR-TYPE               PIC X.
            05  REN-DAYS-RENTED            PIC 99.
            05  REN-MILEAGE.
                10  REN-MILES-IN           PIC 9(6).
                10  REN-MILES-OUT          PIC 9(6).
                10  REN-MILEAGE-RATE       PIC 99.
            05  REN-INSURANCE              PIC X.
```

Test Data: See Figure 8.10a (Four errors are identified.)

Report Layout: See Figure 8.10b

Processing Requirements:

1. Read a file of car rental records.

2. Validate each input record for all of the following:

   a. A numeric contract number; print the message *Nonnumeric Contract Number* for any nonnumeric contract.

   b. The presence of both a first and last name; print the message *Missing last name* or *Missing first name* for a record missing either field. A middle initial is not required, but if present, the initial must be alphabetic; print the message *Nonalphabetic initial* as appropriate.

   c. A valid car type where the code is one of five values; E, C, M, F, or L. Print the message *Car type must be: E, C, M, F, or L* for any record with an invalid car type.

   d. Valid dates:

Figure 8.10 Transaction Files and Error Reports

```
                                                            ── 1 Invalid date
123459BAKER       ROBERT     G930431F0500670000664025X
987651BROWN       PETER      G930112M1000353000352000N
999999JONES       TOM        J931309E35004500004600D5Y    ── 2 Inconsistent mileage
987655BROWNING    PAULA      J931024007002400002525000Y
999777ELSINOR     TERRY      R921126F0500168000159005N
655443FITZPATRICK DAN        T930532L07010000000987000C
987654SMITH       PAUL       G921213M03005100005005020Y
        PINNOCK              1931012F100034240033100N     ── 3 Nonnumeric mileage
X93477BUTLER      JOHN       H930631C0000423000419075N
354679KERBEL      NORMAN     X930331E1000340000324300Y
264805CLARK       JANE       S921101F0700561500551200N    ── 4 Invalid car type
846440            SAM        921231XI500182300169802N
233432BEINHORN    CATHY      B921122M0200123400113402Y
556564HUMMER      MARGO      R920815C0800234500123403Y
677844MCDONALD    JAMES      930123C0500423500402300N
886222VOGEL       JANICE     D930518F1200634500612302Y
008632TOWER       DARREN     R930429L0900700200689300N
```

(a) Transaction File

Figure 8.10 *(continued)*

```
                    ERROR REPORT AS OF 07/03/93


CONTRACT #   LAST NAME        ERROR MESSAGE & FIELD                 CONTENTS


  123459     BAKER            INVALID DAY                  1 ──  04/31
  123459     BAKER            INSURANCE CODE MUST BE Y OR N         X


  987651     BROWN            MILES DRIVEN UNREASONABLY LOW       DAYS: 10  MILES: 000010


  999999     JONES            MONTH MUST BE BETWEEN 1 AND 12        13
  999999     JONES            MILEAGE IN LESS THAN MILEAGE OUT  2 ── IN: 004500 OUT: 004600
  999999     JONES            NON-NUMERIC MILEAGE RATE              05


  987655     BROWNING         CAR TYPE MUST BE:  E, C, M, F, OR L   0
  987655     BROWNING         DATE HAS NOT YET OCCURRED             10/24/93
  987655     BROWNING         NON-NUMERIC MILES IN                  002400


  655443     FITZPATRICK      INVALID DAY                           05/32
  655443     FITZPATRICK      INSURANCE CODE MUST BE Y OR N         C


             PINNOCK          NON-NUMERIC CONTRACT NUMBER
             PINNOCK          MISSING FIRST NAME
             PINNOCK          NON ALPHABETIC INITIAL                1
             PINNOCK          DATE HAS NOT YET OCCURRED             10/12/93
             PINNOCK          NON-NUMERIC MILES OUT             3 ── 003310


  X93477     BUTLER           NON-NUMERIC CONTRACT NUMBER           X93477
  X93477     BUTLER           INVALID DAY                           06/31
  X93477     BUTLER           DAYS RENTED MUST BE > ZERO            00
  X93477     BUTLER           MILEAGE RATE OUT OF RANGE             75


  846440                      NON-NUMERIC CONTRACT NUMBER           846440
  846440                      MISSING LAST NAME
  846440                      CAR TYPE MUST BE:  E, C, M, F, OR L  4 ── X
  846440                      DAYS RENTED MUST BE NUMERIC           I5
  846440                      MILES DRIVEN UNREASONABLY LOW        DAYS: I5  MILES: 000125
```

(b) Error Report

```
999777ELSINOR     TERRY    R921126F0500168000159005N
987654SMITH       PAUL     G921213M0300510000500502Y
354679KERBEL      NORMAN   X930331E1000340000324300Y
264805CLARK       JANE     S921101F0700561500551200N
233432BEINHORN    CATHY    B921122M0200123400113402Y
556564HUMMER      MARGO    R920815C0800234500123403Y
677844MCDONALD    JAMES     930123C0500423500402300N
886222VOGEL       JANICE   D930518F1200634500612302Y
008632TOWER       DARREN   R930429L0900700200689300N
```

(c) Valid Transaction File

(1) A valid month; that is, a month must be from 1 to 12; print the message *Month must be between 1 and 12* for any invalid month.

(2) A valid day; that is, the day cannot exceed the maximum days in the corresponding month; print the message *Invalid Day* for any date that is inconsistent with the month—for example, April 31.

(3) A valid date; that is, a date that is less than or equal to the system date; print the message *Date has not yet occurred* for any date in the future.

e. A valid number of days rented where the number of days is numeric, is greater than zero, and less than or equal to 35. Print appropriate error messages for any condition that is not met; e.g., *Days rented must be numeric*, *Days rented must be > zero*, or *Refer to Long-Term Leasing*.

f. Valid values for the mileage in and out:

(1) The values for both miles in and miles out must be numeric; print the message *Nonnumeric miles in* or *nonnumeric miles out*, respectively.

(2) The mileage reported when the car is turned in cannot be less than the mileage when the car was taken out; print the message *Mileage in less than mileage out* as appropriate.

(3) The number of miles driven must pass a reasonableness test of 10 miles or more per day; Display the message, *Miles driven unreasonably low* as appropriate.

g. The mileage rate must be numeric and less than or equal to 50 cents per day; print the message *Mileage rate out of range* for an invalid rate.

h. The value of the insurance field must be either Y or N; print the message *Insurance code must be Y or N* for an invalid value.

3. Any record that fails any validity test is to be rejected and omitted from the valid record file. It is quite possible that a given record may contain more than one error, and all errors are to be printed except where noted.

4. Valid records are to be written to a file.

Error Messages

The utility of a data validation program is determined by the number of potential errors that it can detect as well as the clarity of the resulting error messages. A truly useful program must check for a variety of errors and explain to the user the nature of any errors that are detected. These concepts are illustrated in Figure 8.10. The incoming transaction file is shown in Figure 8.10a, the associated error messages (in conjunction with the programming specifications) in Figure 8.10b, and the valid transaction file in Figure 8.10c.

The transaction file in Figure 8.10a is named CARS.DAT and is set as the default input file for the VALCARS8 project. The valid transaction file in Figure 8.10c is VALCARS.DAT. Exercise 6 of Appendix A shows how to change the input file using Environmental Variables.

The individual error messages are fully descriptive and list both the contract number and last name of the associated transaction. In addition, the contents of the erroneous field(s) are shown to the right of the error message, making it even easier to correct the invalid transaction. Note, too, that the program can also detect *multiple* errors for the same transaction; for example, three errors are identified in the single transaction for Jones.

Pseudocode

The pseudocode in Figure 8.11 begins with statements to obtain the date of execution, write the heading for the error report, and read the first record. The main loop of the program is executed next and does the following:

Figure 8.11   Pseudocode

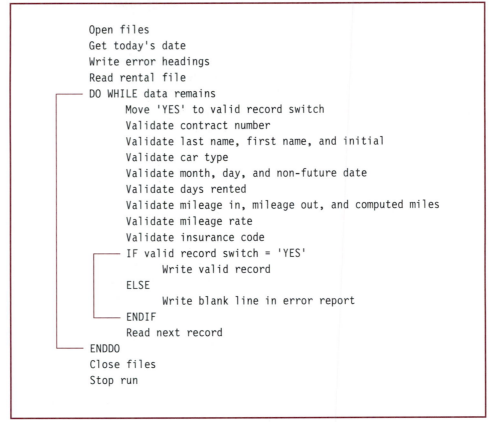

```
              Open files
              Get today's date
              Write error headings
              Read rental file
          ┌─ DO WHILE data remains
          │         Move 'YES' to valid record switch
          │         Validate contract number
          │         Validate last name, first name, and initial
          │         Validate car type
          │         Validate month, day, and non-future date
          │         Validate days rented
          │         Validate mileage in, mileage out, and computed miles
          │         Validate mileage rate
          │         Validate insurance code
          │     ┌─ IF valid record switch = 'YES'
          │     │       Write valid record
          │     │  ELSE
          │     │       Write blank line in error report
          │     └─ ENDIF
          │         Read next record
          └─ ENDDO
              Close files
              Stop run
```

1. The incoming transaction is assumed to be valid by moving 'YES' to a valid-record-switch.

2. The incoming transaction is subject to all of the individual validity checks, any one of which can set the valid-record-switch to 'NO'. Note, too, that since each transaction record is subject to *every* validity check, multiple errors can be detected for a single transaction.

3. The valid-record-switch is checked to see if the record is still valid, and if so, the transaction is written to the valid record file. If, on the other hand, the record is no longer valid, a blank line is written to the error report, which double spaces between the error messages for one transaction and the next.

4. The next record is read and the loop continues until the transaction file is exhausted.

The pseudocode is concise in that the specific nature of each error check is not shown; nevertheless it (the pseudocode) is an effective aid in writing the program.

Hierarchy Chart

The hierarchy chart for the data validation program is shown in Figure 8.12. The module CREATE-VALID-FILE sits at the top of the hierarchy chart and invokes four subordinates, one of which is PROCESS-RENTAL-RECORDS, which implements the main loop of the program.

PROCESS-RENTAL-RECORDS in turn has three subordinates, VALIDATE-RENTAL-RECORD to perform the individual error checks, WRITE-VALID-RECORD

Figure 8.12 Hierarchy Chart for Validation Program

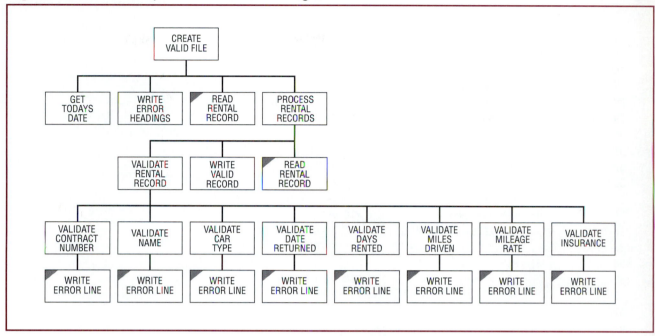

Figure 8.13 Data Validation Program

```
 1        IDENTIFICATION DIVISION.
 2        PROGRAM-ID.      VALCARS8.
 3        AUTHOR.          CVV.
 4
 5        ENVIRONMENT DIVISION.
 6        INPUT-OUTPUT SECTION.
 7        FILE-CONTROL.
 8            SELECT RENTAL-FILE    ASSIGN TO SYSIN
 9                ORGANIZATION IS LINE SEQUENTIAL.
10            SELECT VALID-RENTAL-FILE    ASSIGN TO SYSOUT
11                ORGANIZATION IS LINE SEQUENTIAL.
12            SELECT ERROR-FILE     ASSIGN TO SYSPRINT
13                ORGANIZATION IS LINE SEQUENTIAL.
14
15        DATA DIVISION.
16        FILE SECTION.
17        FD  RENTAL-FILE
18            RECORD CONTAINS 56 CHARACTERS.
19        01  RENTAL-RECORD.
20            05  REN-CONTRACT-NO        PIC 9(6).
21            05  REN-NAME.
22                10  REN-LAST-NAME      PIC X(15).
23                10  REN-FIRST-NAME     PIC X(10).
```

Figure 8.13 *(continued)*

```
24              10  REN-INITIAL           PIC X.
25          05  REN-RETURNED-DATE.
26              10  REN-RETURNED-YEAR      PIC 9(2).
27              10  REN-RETURNED-MONTH     PIC 9(2).
28                  88  VALID-MONTHS           VALUES 1 THRU 12.
29                  88  FEBRUARY               VALUE 2.
30                  88  30-DAY-MONTH           VALUES 4 6 9 11.
31                  88  31-DAY-MONTH           VALUES 1 3 5 7 8 10 12.
32              10  REN-RETURNED-DAY      PIC 9(2).
33          05  REN-CAR-TYPE             PIC X.
34              88  VALID-CAR-TYPES           VALUES 'E' 'C' 'M' 'F' 'L'.
35          05  REN-DAYS-RENTED          PIC 99.
36              88  ZERO-DAYS-RENTED         VALUE  0.
37              88  VALID-DAYS-RENTED        VALUES 1 THRU 35.
38          05  REN-MILEAGE.
39              10  REN-MILES-IN          PIC 9(6).
40              10  REN-MILES-OUT         PIC 9(6).
41              10  REN-MILEAGE-RATE      PIC 99.
42                  88  VALID-MILEAGE-RATES  VALUES 00 THRU 50.
43          05  REN-INSURANCE            PIC X.
44              88  VALID-INSURANCE          VALUES 'Y' 'N'.
45
46      FD  VALID-RENTAL-FILE
47          RECORD CONTAINS 56 CHARACTERS.
48      01  VALID-RENTAL-RECORD         PIC X(56).
49
50      FD  ERROR-FILE
51          RECORD CONTAINS 132 CHARACTERS.
52      01  ERROR-RECORD                PIC X(132).
53
54      WORKING-STORAGE SECTION.
55      01  PROGRAM-SWITCHES.
56          05  NO-DATA-REMAINS-SWITCH   PIC XXX VALUE SPACES.
57              88 NO-DATA-REMAINS           VALUE 'NO'.
58          05  VALID-RECORD-SWITCH      PIC X(3).
59              88  VALID-RECORD             VALUE 'YES'.
60
61      01  VALIDATION-CONSTANTS-AND-CALCS.
62          05  MILES-PER-DAY-FACTOR    PIC 99  VALUE 10.
63          05  EXPECTED-MILES          PIC 9(6).
64          05  ACTUAL-MILES            PIC 9(6).
65
66      01  ERROR-REASONS.
67          05  NON-NUMERIC-CONTRACT-MSG  PIC X(40)
68                  VALUE 'NON-NUMERIC CONTRACT NUMBER'.
69          05  LAST-NAME-MSG           PIC X(40)
70                  VALUE 'MISSING LAST NAME'.
71          05  FIRST-NAME-MSG          PIC X(40)
72                  VALUE 'MISSING FIRST NAME'.
73          05  INITIAL-MSG             PIC X(40)
```

88-level entries define valid values

Table of error messages

Figure 8.13 *(continued)*

```
74                       VALUE 'NON ALPHABETIC INITIAL'.
75          05  CAR-TYPE-MSG            PIC X(40)
76                  VALUE 'CAR TYPE MUST BE:  E, C, M, F, OR L'.
77          05  MONTH-MSG               PIC X(40)
78                  VALUE 'MONTH MUST BE BETWEEN 1 AND 12'.
79          05  DAY-MSG                 PIC X(40)
80                  VALUE 'INVALID DAY'.
81          05  FUTURE-DATE-MSG         PIC X(40)
82                  VALUE 'DATE HAS NOT YET OCCURRED'.
83          05  NON-NUM-DAYS-RENTED-MSG PIC X(40)
84                  VALUE 'DAYS RENTED MUST BE NUMERIC'.
85          05  ZERO-DAYS-MSG           PIC X(40)
86                  VALUE 'DAYS RENTED MUST BE > ZERO'.
87          05  LEASING-MSG             PIC X(40)
88                  VALUE 'REFER TO LONG-TERM LEASING'.
89          05  NON-NUM-MILES-IN-MSG    PIC X(40)
90                  VALUE 'NON-NUMERIC MILES IN'.
91          05  NON-NUM-MILES-OUT-MSG   PIC X(40)
92                  VALUE 'NON-NUMERIC MILES OUT'.
93          05  LESS-THAN-MILES-MSG     PIC X(40)
94                  VALUE 'MILEAGE IN LESS THAN MILEAGE OUT' .
95          05  INVALID-MILES-MSG       PIC X(40)
96                  VALUE 'MILES DRIVEN UNREASONABLY LOW'.
97          05  NON-NUM-RATE-MSG        PIC X(40)
98                  VALUE 'NON-NUMERIC MILEAGE RATE'.
99          05  MILEAGE-RATE-MSG        PIC X(40)
100                 VALUE 'MILEAGE RATE OUT OF RANGE'.
101         05  INSURANCE-MSG           PIC X(40)
102                 VALUE 'INSURANCE CODE MUST BE Y OR N'.
103
104     01  TODAYS-DATE.
105         05  TODAYS-YEAR             PIC 99.
106         05  TODAYS-MONTH            PIC 99.
107         05  TODAYS-DAY              PIC 99.
108
109     01  HEADING-ERROR-LINE-ONE.
110         05  FILLER                  PIC X(26) VALUE SPACES.
111         05  FILLER                  PIC X(19)
112                 VALUE 'ERROR REPORT AS OF '.
113         05  HDG-DATE.
114             10  HDG-MONTH           PIC 99/.
115             10  HDG-DAY             PIC 99/.
116             10  HDG-YEAR            PIC 99.
117         05  FILLER                  PIC X(79) VALUE SPACES.
118
119     01  HEADING-ERROR-LINE-TWO.
120         05  FILLER                  PIC X(10) VALUE 'CONTRACT #'.
121         05  FILLER                  PIC XX    VALUE SPACES.
122         05  FILLER                  PIC X(9)  VALUE 'LAST NAME'.
123         05  FILLER                  PIC X(8)  VALUE SPACES.
```

Table of error messages

Figure 8.13   *(continued)*

```
124        05  FILLER                  PIC X(21)
125              VALUE 'ERROR MESSAGE & FIELD'.
126        05  FILLER                  PIC X(21) VALUE SPACES.
127        05  FILLER                  PIC X(8)  VALUE 'CONTENTS'.
128        05  FILLER                  PIC X(46) VALUE SPACES.
129
130    01  ERROR-LINE.
131        05  FILLER                  PIC XX    VALUE SPACES.
132        05  ERR-CONTRACT-NO         PIC 9(6).
133        05  FILLER                  PIC X(4)  VALUE SPACES.
134        05  ERR-LAST-NAME           PIC X(15).
135        05  FILLER                  PIC XX    VALUE SPACES.
136        05  ERR-MESSAGE             PIC X(40).
137        05  FILLER                  PIC XX    VALUE SPACES.
138        05  ERR-CONTENTS            PIC X(23).
139        05  FILLER                  PIC X(38) VALUE SPACES.
140
141    01  ERROR-DETAILS.
142        05  ERR-MILES-IN-OUT.
143            10  FILLER              PIC X(4) VALUE 'IN: '.
144            10  ERR-MILES-IN        PIC 9(6).
145            10  FILLER              PIC X(6) VALUE ' OUT: '.
146            10  ERR-MILES-OUT       PIC 9(6).
147        05  ERR-RETURNED-DATE.
148            10  ERR-RETURNED-MONTH-DAY.
149                15  ERR-RETURNED-MONTH   PIC 99.
150                15  ERR-RETURNED-DAY     PIC /99.
151            10  ERR-RETURNED-YEAR        PIC /99.
152        05  ERR-EXPECTED-MILES.
153            10  FILLER              PIC X(6) VALUE 'DAYS: '.
154            10  ERR-DAYS-RENTED     PIC 99.
155            10  FILLER              PIC X(9) VALUE '  MILES: '.
156            10  ERR-MILES           PIC 9(6).
157
158    PROCEDURE DIVISION.
159    000-CREATE-VALID-RENTAL-FILE.
160        OPEN INPUT   RENTAL-FILE
161             OUTPUT VALID-RENTAL-FILE
162                    ERROR-FILE.
163        PERFORM 100-GET-TODAYS-DATE.
164        PERFORM 200-WRITE-ERROR-HEADINGS.
165        PERFORM 300-READ-RENTAL-RECORD.
166        PERFORM 400-PROCESS-RENTAL-RECORDS
167            UNTIL NO-DATA-REMAINS.
168        CLOSE RENTAL-FILE
169              VALID-RENTAL-FILE
170              ERROR-FILE.
171        STOP RUN.
172
173    100-GET-TODAYS-DATE.
```

Separate output files for error messages and valid records

Figure 8.13 *(continued)*

```
174             ACCEPT TODAYS-DATE FROM DATE.
175             MOVE TODAYS-MONTH TO HDG-MONTH.
176             MOVE TODAYS-DAY TO HDG-DAY.
177             MOVE TODAYS-YEAR TO HDG-YEAR.
178
179         200-WRITE-ERROR-HEADINGS.
180             MOVE HEADING-ERROR-LINE-ONE TO ERROR-RECORD.
181             WRITE ERROR-RECORD
182                 AFTER ADVANCING PAGE.
183             MOVE HEADING-ERROR-LINE-TWO TO ERROR-RECORD
184             WRITE ERROR-RECORD
185                 AFTER ADVANCING 2 LINES.
186             MOVE SPACES TO ERROR-RECORD.
187             WRITE ERROR-RECORD.
188
189         300-READ-RENTAL-RECORD.
190             READ RENTAL-FILE
191                 AT END MOVE 'NO' TO NO-DATA-REMAINS-SWITCH
192             END-READ.
193
194         400-PROCESS-RENTAL-RECORDS.
195             MOVE 'YES' TO VALID-RECORD-SWITCH.
196             PERFORM 500-VALIDATE-RENTAL-RECORD.
197             PERFORM 600-WRITE-VALID-RECORD.
198             PERFORM 300-READ-RENTAL-RECORD.
199
200         500-VALIDATE-RENTAL-RECORD.
201             PERFORM 510-VALIDATE-CONTRACT-NO.
202             PERFORM 520-VALIDATE-NAME.
203             PERFORM 530-VALIDATE-CAR-TYPE.
204             PERFORM 540-VALIDATE-DATE-RETURNED.
205             PERFORM 550-VALIDATE-DAYS-RENTED.
206             PERFORM 560-VALIDATE-MILES-DRIVEN
207             PERFORM 570-VALIDATE-MILEAGE-RATE.
208             PERFORM 580-VALIDATE-INSURANCE.
209
210         510-VALIDATE-CONTRACT-NO.
211             IF REN-CONTRACT-NO NOT NUMERIC
212                 MOVE NON-NUMERIC-CONTRACT-MSG TO ERR-MESSAGE
213                 MOVE REN-CONTRACT-NO TO ERR-CONTENTS
214                 PERFORM 599-WRITE-ERROR-LINE
215             END-IF.
216
217         520-VALIDATE-NAME.
218             IF REN-LAST-NAME = SPACES
219                 MOVE LAST-NAME-MSG TO ERR-MESSAGE
220                 MOVE SPACES TO ERR-CONTENTS
221                 PERFORM 599-WRITE-ERROR-LINE
222             END-IF.
223             IF REN-FIRST-NAME = SPACES
```

Obtain system date

Incoming records are assumed to be valid

Class test for numeric data

Figure 8.13   *(continued)*

```
224                 MOVE FIRST-NAME-MSG TO ERR-MESSAGE
225                 MOVE SPACES TO ERR-CONTENTS
226                 PERFORM 599-WRITE-ERROR-LINE
227             END-IF.
228             IF REN-INITIAL NOT ALPHABETIC
229                 MOVE INITIAL-MSG TO ERR-MESSAGE
230                 MOVE REN-INITIAL TO ERR-CONTENTS
231                 PERFORM 599-WRITE-ERROR-LINE
232             END-IF.
233
234         530-VALIDATE-CAR-TYPE.
235             IF NOT VALID-CAR-TYPES
236                 MOVE CAR-TYPE-MSG TO ERR-MESSAGE
237                 MOVE REN-CAR-TYPE TO ERR-CONTENTS
238                 PERFORM 599-WRITE-ERROR-LINE
239             END-IF.
240
241         540-VALIDATE-DATE-RETURNED.
242             IF VALID-MONTHS
243                 IF 30-DAY-MONTH AND REN-RETURNED-DAY <= 30 OR
244                     31-DAY-MONTH AND REN-RETURNED-DAY <= 31 OR
245                    FEBRUARY AND REN-RETURNED-DAY <= 29
246                 IF REN-RETURNED-DATE > TODAYS-DATE
247                     MOVE FUTURE-DATE-MSG TO ERR-MESSAGE
248                     MOVE REN-RETURNED-MONTH TO ERR-RETURNED-MONTH
249                     MOVE REN-RETURNED-DAY TO ERR-RETURNED-DAY
250                     MOVE REN-RETURNED-YEAR TO ERR-RETURNED-YEAR
251                     MOVE ERR-RETURNED-DATE TO ERR-CONTENTS
252                     PERFORM 599-WRITE-ERROR-LINE
253                 END-IF
254             ELSE
255                 MOVE DAY-MSG TO ERR-MESSAGE
256                 MOVE REN-RETURNED-MONTH TO ERR-RETURNED-MONTH
257                 MOVE REN-RETURNED-DAY TO ERR-RETURNED-DAY
258                 MOVE ERR-RETURNED-MONTH-DAY TO ERR-CONTENTS
259                 PERFORM 599-WRITE-ERROR-LINE
260             END-IF
261             ELSE
262                 MOVE MONTH-MSG TO ERR-MESSAGE
263                 MOVE REN-RETURNED-MONTH TO ERR-CONTENTS
264                 PERFORM 599-WRITE-ERROR-LINE
265             END-IF.
266
267         550-VALIDATE-DAYS-RENTED.
268             IF REN-DAYS-RENTED NOT NUMERIC
269                 MOVE NON-NUM-DAYS-RENTED-MSG TO ERR-MESSAGE
270                 MOVE REN-DAYS-RENTED TO ERR-CONTENTS
271                 PERFORM 599-WRITE-ERROR-LINE
272             ELSE
273                 IF ZERO-DAYS-RENTED
```

Class test for alphabetic data

Nested IF to implement date validation

Figure 8.13   *(continued)*

```
274                   MOVE ZERO-DAYS-MSG TO ERR-MESSAGE
275                   MOVE REN-DAYS-RENTED TO ERR-CONTENTS
276                   PERFORM 599-WRITE-ERROR-LINE
277               ELSE
278                   IF NOT VALID-DAYS-RENTED
279                       MOVE LEASING-MSG TO ERR-MESSAGE
280                       MOVE REN-DAYS-RENTED TO ERR-CONTENTS
281                       PERFORM 599-WRITE-ERROR-LINE
282                   END-IF
283               END-IF
284           END-IF.
285
286       560-VALIDATE-MILES-DRIVEN.
287           IF REN-MILES-IN NOT NUMERIC
288               MOVE NON-NUM-MILES-IN-MSG TO ERR-MESSAGE
289               MOVE REN-MILES-IN TO ERR-CONTENTS
290               PERFORM 599-WRITE-ERROR-LINE
291           ELSE
292               IF REN-MILES-OUT NOT NUMERIC
293                   MOVE NON-NUM-MILES-OUT-MSG TO ERR-MESSAGE
294                   MOVE REN-MILES-OUT TO ERR-CONTENTS
295                   PERFORM 599-WRITE-ERROR-LINE
296               ELSE
297                   IF REN-MILES-IN < REN-MILES-OUT
298                       MOVE LESS-THAN-MILES-MSG TO ERR-MESSAGE
299                       MOVE REN-MILES-IN TO ERR-MILES-IN
300                       MOVE REN-MILES-OUT TO ERR-MILES-OUT
301                       MOVE ERR-MILES-IN-OUT TO ERR-CONTENTS
302                       PERFORM 599-WRITE-ERROR-LINE
303                   ELSE
304                       COMPUTE EXPECTED-MILES =
305                           MILES-PER-DAY-FACTOR * REN-DAYS-RENTED
306                           SIZE ERROR DISPLAY 'SIZE ERROR EXPECT MILES'
307                       END-COMPUTE
308                       COMPUTE ACTUAL-MILES =
309                           REN-MILES-IN - REN-MILES-OUT
310                           SIZE ERROR DISPLAY 'SIZE ERROR ACTUAL MILES'
311                       END-COMPUTE
312                       IF ACTUAL-MILES < EXPECTED-MILES
313                           MOVE INVALID-MILES-MSG TO ERR-MESSAGE
314                           MOVE REN-DAYS-RENTED TO ERR-DAYS-RENTED
315                           MOVE ACTUAL-MILES TO ERR-MILES
316                           MOVE ERR-EXPECTED-MILES TO ERR-CONTENTS
317                           PERFORM 599-WRITE-ERROR-LINE
318                       END-IF
319                   END-IF
320               END-IF
321           END-IF.
322
323       570-VALIDATE-MILEAGE-RATE.
```

SIZE ERROR clause in anticipation of unexpectedly large fields

Figure 8.13 *(continued)*

```
324          IF REN-MILEAGE-RATE NOT NUMERIC
325              MOVE NON-NUM-RATE-MSG TO ERR-MESSAGE
326              MOVE REN-MILEAGE-RATE TO ERR-CONTENTS
327              PERFORM 599-WRITE-ERROR-LINE
328          ELSE
329              IF NOT VALID-MILEAGE-RATES
330                  MOVE MILEAGE-RATE-MSG TO ERR-MESSAGE
331                  MOVE REN-MILEAGE-RATE TO ERR-CONTENTS
332                  PERFORM 599-WRITE-ERROR-LINE
333              END-IF
334          END-IF.
335
336      580-VALIDATE-INSURANCE.
337          IF NOT VALID-INSURANCE
338              MOVE INSURANCE-MSG TO ERR-MESSAGE
339              MOVE REN-INSURANCE TO ERR-CONTENTS
340              PERFORM 599-WRITE-ERROR-LINE
341          END-IF.
342
343      599-WRITE-ERROR-LINE.
344          MOVE 'NO ' TO VALID-RECORD-SWITCH.
345          MOVE REN-CONTRACT-NO TO ERR-CONTRACT-NO.
346          MOVE REN-LAST-NAME TO ERR-LAST-NAME.        Common error routine sets switch to indicate
347          MOVE ERROR-LINE TO ERROR-RECORD.            invalid record and write error message
348          WRITE ERROR-RECORD.
349
350      600-WRITE-VALID-RECORD.
351          IF VALID-RECORD
352              MOVE RENTAL-RECORD TO VALID-RENTAL-RECORD
353              WRITE VALID-RENTAL-RECORD
354          ELSE                                        Valid transactions are written to a
355              MOVE SPACES TO ERROR-RECORD             valid file, the ELSE clause writes a
356              WRITE ERROR-RECORD                      blank line before each group of
357          END-IF.                                     invalid transactions
```

to write valid transactions to the output file, and READ-RENTAL-RECORD to read the next transaction. Each of the required validity checks is implemented in its own module, and all of these modules call a common routine to write an error message.

The Completed Program

The completed program is shown in Figure 8.13. It is considerably longer than the tuition billing program of the previous chapters, but nonetheless straightforward and easy to follow. The logic in the program parallels that of the pseudocode just developed, whereas the paragraphs in the Procedure Division correspond one to one with the modules in the hierarchy chart. The program complies completely with the processing requirements and also illustrates the various COBOL features presented earlier. Consider:

1. The use of condition names within the FD for RENTAL-RECORD (e.g., lines 28–31, 34, 36–37, etc.) to define valid values for the various input fields.

2. A table of error messages in lines 66–102; grouping the error messages in this way makes it easy to determine precisely which error checks are implemented. It also facilitates uniform formatting of the various error messages.

3. The ACCEPT statement in line 174 to obtain the system date; also the definition of TODAYS-DATE in WORKING-STORAGE to hold the date after it is read.

4. The MOVE statement to initialize VALID-RECORD-SWITCH to 'YES' for each incoming transaction record (line 195). A second MOVE statement in the WRITE-ERROR-LINE paragraph (line 344) to reset the switch to 'NO' if the current transaction fails any one of the validity tests.

5. Various class tests for numeric and alphabetic data as in lines 211 and 228.

6. A nested IF statement in lines 242–265 to implement the various types of date validation. A second nested IF statement in lines 287 through 321 performs the various checks on the incoming, outgoing, and computed mileage.

7. SIZE ERROR clauses within the COMPUTE statements, lines 306 and 310, in anticipation of unexpectedly large fields.

8. The IF statement in lines 351–357 that determines whether the transaction is written to the valid file. Note, too, the ELSE clause within this IF statement, which writes a blank line for every invalid record, which in turn puts a blank line before each group of invalid transactions in the error report.

LIMITATIONS OF COBOL-74

COBOL-85 introduced two additional relational conditions into the IF statement, GREATER THAN OR EQUAL TO and LESS THAN OR EQUAL TO; these conditions were not allowed in COBOL-74, which used NOT LESS THAN as the equivalent of GREATER THAN OR EQUAL TO and NOT GREATER THAN for LESS THAN OR EQUAL TO.

COBOL-85 enables the testing of upper- and/or lowercase letters through expansion of the alphabetic class test. In COBOL-85 the ALPHABETIC test is true for uppercase letters, lowercase letters, and the space character; the ALPHABETIC-UPPER test is true for uppercase letters and the space character; and the ALPHABETIC-LOWER test is true for lowercase letters and the space character. There were no UPPER/LOWER tests in COBOL-74 and the ALPHABETIC test was true only for uppercase letters and space characters.

The most significant change, however, is the introduction of the END-IF scope terminator, which did not exist in COBOL-74. We have already seen how the scope terminator eliminates the column-73 problem in conjunction with a "missing period" (page 182) and how it eliminates the need for the NEXT SENTENCE clause (Figure 8.7). The scope terminator also facilitates the nesting of conditional statements as shown in Figure 8.14.

Consider, for example, the flowchart of Figure 8.14a, and the contrasting implementations in COBOL-85 and COBOL-74 in Figures 8.14b and 8.14c, respectively. The END-IF terminator transforms a conditional statement to an imperative (complete) statement, making it possible to express the required logic as a single IF statement in COBOL-85. By contrast, the COBOL-74 implementation requires an additional PERFORM statement and is more difficult to follow.

Figure 8.14   Limitations of COBOL-74

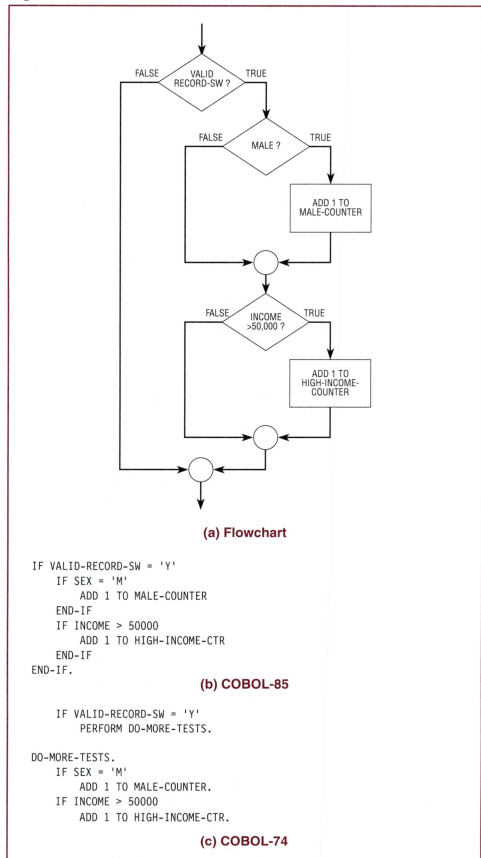

(a) Flowchart

```
IF VALID-RECORD-SW = 'Y'
    IF SEX = 'M'
        ADD 1 TO MALE-COUNTER
    END-IF
    IF INCOME > 50000
        ADD 1 TO HIGH-INCOME-CTR
    END-IF
END-IF.
```

(b) COBOL-85

```
    IF VALID-RECORD-SW = 'Y'
        PERFORM DO-MORE-TESTS.

DO-MORE-TESTS.
    IF SEX = 'M'
        ADD 1 TO MALE-COUNTER.
    IF INCOME > 50000
        ADD 1 TO HIGH-INCOME-CTR.
```

(c) COBOL-74

S U M M A R Y

Points to Remember

■ Data validation is a critical portion of any system, as the output produced by any program is only as good as its input.

■ Data validation is often done in a stand-alone edit program as opposed to the reporting program that processes the data; that is, the valid transaction file produced as output by the edit program becomes the input file to the reporting program.

■ The ACCEPT statement is used to obtain the date of execution for use in implementing various types of date checks.

■ There are four types of conditions in the IF statement: relation, class, sign, and condition name (88-level entries).

■ Any two simple conditions may be combined to form a compound condition using the logical operators AND and OR. An IF statement may also use implied conditions, in which the subject and/or operation is understood.

■ A nested IF statement contains two or more IF statements within a sentence. The scope of the condition in the IF statement is terminated by the ELSE clause, the END-IF scope terminator, and/or a period. The scope terminator is optional but strongly recommended in all instances.

■ Indentation within an IF statement is not required by the compiler but recommended to facilitate the programmer's interpretation.

■ The NEXT SENTENCE clause directs control to the statement immediately following the period and is required (in COBOL-74) to implement certain types of nested conditional statements. The END-IF scope terminator, introduced in COBOL-85, eliminates the need for the NEXT SENTENCE clause in all instances.

Key Words and Concepts

88-level entry	Implied condition
Alphabetic test	Limit check
Class test	Nested IF
Completeness check	Numeric test
Compound test	Range check
Condition name	Reasonableness check
Consistency check	Scope terminator
Data validation	Sequence check
Date check	Sign test
Edit program	Subscript check
Existing code check	

COBOL Elements

ACCEPT	END-IF
AND	IF
DATE	NEXT SENTENCE
DAY	NOT
DAY-OF-WEEK	OR
ELSE	TIME

Fill-in

1. Incoming data should be _____ prior to being used in computations.

2. The valid transaction file produced as output by an edit program is _____ to a reporting program.

3. A _____ test ensures that numeric fields do in fact contain numeric data.

4. A _____ check tests that a value does not exceed a designated upper or lower bound.

5. A _____ check verifies that all required fields are present.

6. In evaluating a compound condition, AND comes (before/after) OR.

7. A condition name is also known as an _____-level entry.

8. The _____ _____ clause directs control to the statement immediately following the period.

9. The _____ scope terminator eliminates the need for the NEXT SENTENCE clause.

10. The statement, ACCEPT DATE-WORK-AREA FROM DATE requires specification of a user-defined work area in the form, _____.

True/False

1. Output from a reporting program is typically input to an edit program.

2. The numeric class test can be applied to alphanumeric data.

3. The alphabetic class test can be applied to alphanumeric data.

4. The numeric class test can be applied to alphabetic data.

5. The alphabetic class test can be applied to numeric data.

6. A nested IF statement contains two or more IF statements within a single sentence.

7. The NEXT SENTENCE clause may be associated with either an IF or an ELSE.

8. The END-IF scope terminator eliminates the need for a NEXT SENTENCE clause.

9. The ACCEPT statement is used to obtain the date of execution.

10. DATE is a COBOL reserved word, containing the date of execution in the form yymmdd.

11. DAY and DATE produce the same results.

12. TIME returns a six-digit numeric field, indicating the time of program execution.

P r o b l e m s

1. Recode the following statements to include scope terminators and proper indentation with the ELSE clause indented under the relevant IF.

   a. IF A > B, IF C > D, MOVE E TO F,
      ELSE MOVE G TO H.

   b. IF A > B, IF C > D, MOVE E TO F,
      ELSE MOVE G TO H, ELSE MOVE X TO Y.

   c. IF A > B, IF C > D, MOVE E TO F,
      ADD 1 TO E, ELSE MOVE G TO H,
      ADD 1 TO G.

   d. IF A > B, MOVE X TO Y, MOVE Z TO W,
      ELSE IF C > D MOVE 1 TO N,
      ELSE MOVE 2 TO Y, ADD 3 TO Z.

2. Given the nested IF statement:

```
IF SEX = 'M'
    PERFORM PROCESS-MALE-RECORD
ELSE
    IF SEX = 'F'
        PERFORM PROCESS-FEMALE-RECORD
    ELSE
        PERFORM WRITE-ERROR-MESSAGE
    END-IF
END-IF.
```

   and the logically equivalent code:

```
IF SEX = 'M'
    PERFORM PROCESS-MALE-RECORD
END-IF.
IF SEX = 'F'
    PERFORM PROCESS-FEMALE-RECORD
END-IF.
IF SEX NOT = 'M' AND SEX NOT = 'F'
    PERFORM WRITE-ERROR-MESSAGE
END-IF.
```

   a. Discuss the relative efficiency of the two alternatives.

   b. What would be the effect of changing AND to OR in the third IF of the second set of statements?

   c. What would be the effect of removing the word ELSE wherever it occurs in the first set of IF statements?

3. Are the two IF statements logically equivalent?

   Statement 1:

```
IF A > B
    IF C > D
        ADD 1 TO X
    ELSE
        ADD 1 TO Y
    END-IF
END-IF.
```

Statement 2:

```
IF A > B AND C > D
    ADD 1 TO X
ELSE
    ADD 1 TO Y
END-IF.
```

Try the following sets of values to aid in answering the question:

a. A = 5, B = 1, C = 10, D = 15.

b. A = 1, B = 5, C = 10, D = 15.

4. Company XYZ has four corporate functions: manufacturing, marketing, financial, and administrative. Each function in turn has several departments, as shown:

Function	Departments
MANUFACTURING	10, 12, 16-30, 41, 56
MARKETING	6-9, 15, 31-33
FINANCIAL	60-62, 75
ADMINISTRATIVE	1-4, 78

Establish condition-name entries so that, given a value of EMPLOYEE-DEPARTMENT, you can determine the function. Include an 88-level entry, VALID-CODES, to verify that the incoming department is indeed a valid department (any department number not shown is invalid).

5. Given the following COBOL definitions:

```
05  LOCATION-CODE      PIC 99.
    88  NEW-YORK           VALUE 10.
    88  BOSTON            VALUE 20.
    88  CHICAGO           VALUE 30.
    88  DETROIT           VALUE 40.
    88  NORTH-EAST        VALUES 10 20.
```

Are the following entries valid as the condition portion of an IF statement?

a. IF LOCATION-CODE = '10'

b. IF LOCATION-CODE = 40

c. IF NEW-YORK

d. IF LOCATION-CODE = 10 OR 20 OR 30

e. IF NEW-YORK OR BOSTON OR CHICAGO

f. IF DETROIT = 40

Would the following be valid examples of MOVE statements?

g. MOVE 20 TO BOSTON.

h. MOVE 20 TO LOCATION-CODE.

i. MOVE '20' TO LOCATION-CODE.

6. Given the following pairs of IF statements, indicate whether the statements in each pair have the same effect:

a. IF A > B OR C > D AND E = F
    IF A > B OR (C > D AND E = F)

b. IF A > B OR C > D AND E = F
    IF (A > B OR C > D) AND E = F

c. IF A > B OR A > C OR A > D
    IF A> B OR C OR D

d. IF A > B
    IF A NOT < B OR A NOT = B

7. Consider the following code, intended to calculate an individual's age from a stored birth date and the date of execution.

```
01  EMPLOYEE-RECORD.
    05  EMP-BIRTH-DATE.
        10  BIRTH-MONTH   PIC 99.
        10  BIRTH-YEAR    PIC 99.
01  DATE-WORK-AREA.
    05  TODAYS-MONTH      PIC 99.
    05  TODAYS-DAY        PIC 99.
    05  TODAYS-YEAR       PIC 99.

PROCEDURE DIVISION.
    ACCEPT DATE-WORK-AREA FROM DATE.
    .
      .
        .
    COMPUTE EMPLOYEE-AGE = TODAYS-YEAR - BIRTH-YEAR
            + TODAYS-MONTH - BIRTH-MONTH.
```

There are two distinct reasons why the code will not work as intended. Find and correct the errors.

8. Implement the logic in Figure 8.15 with and without scope terminators, corresponding to the implementations in COBOL-74 and COBOL-85. Do you see any distinct advantages to the latter compiler?

Figure 8.15   Flowcharts for Problem 8

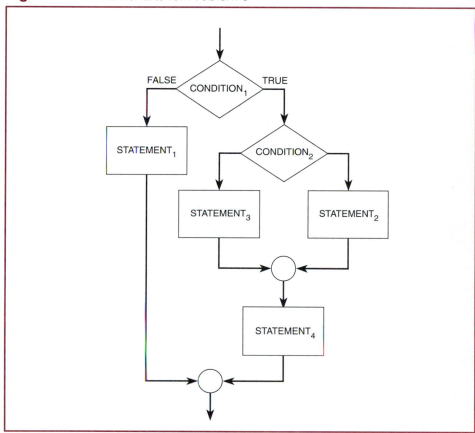

9. Change the VALCARS8 program to become Year 2000 compliant. You may want to apply a simple "windowing technique" to determine the century in which a date falls. For example, you might consider any year less than "90" to occur after 2000 and any year from 90 to 99 to occur in the twentieth century. Thus, "98" should be treated as "1998." Chapter 19 discusses the Year 2000 problem and provides other ways of solving the problem.

More About the Procedure Division

CHAPTER OUTLINE

Overview
PERFORM
    TEST BEFORE/TEST AFTER
    In-line Perform
    Performing Sections
    PERFORM THRU
    Programming Tip: Perform Paragraphs, Not Sections
READ
    False-Condition Branch
    READ INTO
WRITE FROM
INITIALIZE
String Processing
    INSPECT
    STRING
    UNSTRING
    Reference Modification
ACCEPT
Duplicate Data Names
    Qualification
    MOVE CORRESPONDING
The Car Billing Program
    Programming Specifications
    Program Design
    The Completed Program
Limitations of COBOL-74
Summary
Fill-in
True/False
Problems

O B J E C T I V E S

After reading this chapter you will be able to:

■ Differentiate between the DO WHILE and DO UNTIL structures; describe how each is implemented in conjunction with a PERFORM statement.

■ Define an in-line perform and a false-condition branch; explain how the combination of these features eliminates the need for a priming read statement.

■ Differentiate between a paragraph and a section.

■ Code the READ INTO and WRITE FROM statements in the Procedure Division.

■ Use the INITIALIZE statement.

■ Perform basic string processing operations through use of the INSPECT, STRING, and UNSTRING statements.

■ Define a duplicate data name and use qualification to eliminate ambiguity; describe the use of the MOVE CORRESPONDING statement.

O V E R V I E W

This chapter completes the two-program sequence begun in Chapter 8 by developing the reporting program for the valid transaction file. The program is also intended to illustrate a series of advanced Procedure Division statements that are presented in the chapter. Many of the statements are new to COBOL-85 and were not available in COBOL-74.

We begin with the PERFORM statement and include material on the TEST BEFORE and TEST AFTER clauses which correspond to the DO WHILE and DO UNTIL constructs of structured programming. The in-line perform is presented, as is the THROUGH clause, to perform multiple paragraphs; the use of sections in lieu of paragraphs is also covered. The READ INTO and WRITE FROM clauses are introduced to combine the effects of a MOVE statement with the indicated I/O operation. The ACCEPT statement is expanded to include the DAY-OF-WEEK clause, and the INITIALIZE statement establishes values for multiple data names in a single statement. The INSPECT, STRING, and UNSTRING statements are introduced to implement string processing operations. Duplicate data names, qualification, and the MOVE CORRESPONDING statement are introduced as well.

The program at the end of the chapter is designed very differently from the programs presented thus far as it uses an in-line perform and a false-condition branch to eliminate the priming read used in earlier programs. The program also makes extensive use of scope terminators throughout the Procedure Division.

Perform

A simple form of the PERFORM statement has been used throughout the text to implement the iteration construct of structured programming:

        PERFORM procedure-name UNTIL condition

The condition in the UNTIL clause is tested *before* the procedure is executed, and if the condition is not met, control is transferred to the designated procedure. When the procedure has completed execution, the condition is retested, and if it (the condition) is still not met, the procedure is executed a second time. The process continues indefinitely until the condition is finally satisfied.

In actuality the PERFORM statement is considerably more complex with many additional options. Consider:

$$
\text{PERFORM} \left[\text{procedure-name-1} \left[\left\{ \begin{array}{c} \text{THROUGH} \\ \text{THRU} \end{array} \right\} \text{procedure-name-2} \right] \right]
$$

$$
\left[\text{WITH } \underline{\text{TEST}} \left\{ \begin{array}{c} \underline{\text{BEFORE}} \\ \text{AFTER} \end{array} \right\} \right] \underline{\text{UNTIL}} \text{ condition-1}
$$

$$
\left[\text{imperative-statement-1 } \underline{\text{END-PERFORM}} \right]
$$

TEST BEFORE/TEST AFTER

The optional TEST BEFORE/TEST AFTER clause is explained in conjunction with Figure 9.1. Figure 9.1a depicts the DO WHILE structure that has been used

Figure 9.1 The Iteration Structure

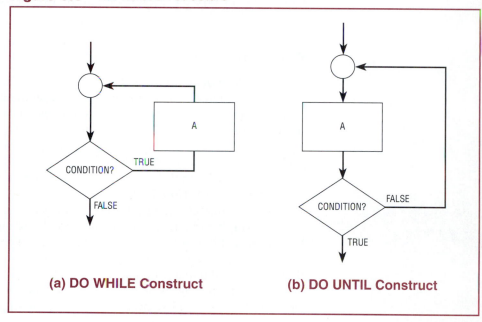

(a) DO WHILE Construct   **(b) DO UNTIL Construct**

throughout the book, while Figure 9.1b illustrates the slightly different DO UNTIL structure. The difference between the two (aside from the semantics of switching the true and false branches) pertains to the sequence in which the condition and statement are executed.

The DO WHILE structure of Figure 9.1a tests the condition *before* executing Block A; the DO UNTIL structure in Figure 9.1b tests the condition *after* executing Block A. The DO WHILE structure does not execute Block A if the condition is initially false, whereas DO UNTIL guarantees that Block A is executed at least once.

The PERFORM statement includes the TEST BEFORE and TEST AFTER phrases, corresponding to a DO WHILE and DO UNTIL, respectively. Specification of TEST BEFORE tests the condition before performing the procedure, and corresponds to the DO WHILE. Specification of TEST AFTER performs the procedure and then tests the condition, and corresponds to a DO UNTIL. Omission of both TEST BEFORE and TEST AFTER (as has been done throughout the text) defaults to TEST BEFORE.

In-line PERFORM

The procedure-name is enclosed within brackets within the syntax of the PERFORM statement and thus is an *optional* entry. Omission of the procedure name produces an **in-line perform,** where the statements to be executed appear immediately below the PERFORM statement itself, as opposed to the out-of-line execution of a designated procedure elsewhere in the program. For example:

```
PERFORM
    Statement 1
    Statement 2
    .
    . Other statements to be executed
    .
END-PERFORM
```

An in-line perform functions just as a regular PERFORM, except that the statements to be executed are contained entirely within the statement—that is, between PERFORM and END-PERFORM. Omission of the procedure name (that is, specification of an in-line perform) requires the END-PERFORM delimiter; conversely, the END-PERFORM may *not* be specified in conjunction with performing a paragraph.

Performing Sections

The procedure name in the PERFORM statement can be either a **paragraph** or a **section**. A paragraph consists of one or more sentences, whereas a section is made up of one or more paragraphs. Paragraph headers are required to begin in the A-margin (columns 8–11), whereas sentences begin in the B-margin (columns 12–72). The compiler recognizes the end of one paragraph when it senses the beginning of the next paragraph—that is, when it finds the next entry in the A-margin. Section headers also begin in the A-margin and are distinguished from paragraph headers by the reserved word SECTION.

When a paragraph is performed, control is transferred to the first sentence in that paragraph and remains in that paragraph until the next paragraph is reached. In similar fashion, if the procedure name in a PERFORM statement refers to a section (rather than a paragraph), control is transferred to the first paragraph in that section and remains in that section until the next section is reached.

The authors suggest that you avoid sections altogether (see tip on page 233); the material is included here because sections appear in many older COBOL programs.

PROGRAMMING TIP

Perform Paragraphs, Not Sections

The motivation behind this guideline is best demonstrated by example. Given the following Procedure Division, what will be the final value of X?

```
PROCEDURE DIVISION.

MAINLINE SECTION.
     MOVE ZERO TO X.
     PERFORM A.
     PERFORM B.
     PERFORM C.
     PERFORM D.
     STOP RUN.

A SECTION.
     ADD 1 TO X.
B.
     ADD 1 TO X.
C.
     ADD 1 TO X.
D.
     ADD 1 TO X.
```

The correct answer is 7, not 4. A common error made by many programmers is a misinterpretation of the statement **PERFORM A**. Since **A** is a *section* and not a *paragraph*, the statement **PERFORM A** invokes *every* paragraph in that section, namely, paragraphs B, C, and D, in addition to the unnamed paragraph immediately after the section header.

A **PERFORM** statement specifies a *procedure*, which is *either* a section *or* a paragraph, yet there is no way of telling the nature of the procedure from the **PERFORM** statement itself. Consequently, when a section is specified as a procedure, the unfortunate result is too often execution of unintended code. Can't happen? Did you correctly compute the value of **X**?

PERFORM THRU

The THROUGH (THRU) clause executes all statements *between* the specified procedure names. The procedures may be paragraphs or sections, but procedure-name-1 must be physically before procedure-name-2 within the COBOL program.

A common practice is to make procedure-name-2 a single-sentence paragraph consisting of the word EXIT. The EXIT statement causes no action to be taken; its function is to delineate the end of the PERFORM. Consider:

```
PERFORM PROCESS-RECORDS THRU PROCESS-RECORDS-EXIT.
     .
      .
       .
PROCESS-RECORDS.
     .
      .
       .
```

```
PROCESS-RECORDS-EXIT.
    EXIT.
```

The only practical reason to use a PERFORM THRU statement with an EXIT paragraph is to enable *downward* branching to the EXIT statement depending on a condition within the paragraph. Although an argument could be made for this usage in limited instances, the need for such statements as GO TO PROCESS-RECORDS-EXIT should generally be avoided.

Read

The READ statement includes two important clauses—INTO and NOT AT END—that were not previously presented. Consider:

```
READ file-name RECORD [ INTO identifier ]
    [AT END imperative-statement-1]
    [NOT AT END imperative-statement-2]
[END-READ]
```

Figure 9.2   Structure of a COBOL Program

```
        READ INPUT-FILE
            AT END MOVE 'NO' TO DATA-REMAINS-SWITCH.
        PERFORM PROCESS-RECORDS
            UNTIL DATA-REMAINS-SWITCH = 'NO'.


    PROCESS-RECORDS.
        .
        .
                            Procedure Division statements to process the current record
        .
        READ INPUT-FILE
            AT END MOVE 'NO' TO DATA-REMAINS-SWITCH.


                        (a) Priming Read


    PERFORM UNTIL DATA-REMAINS-SWITCH = 'NO'
        READ INPUT-FILE
            AT END
                MOVE 'NO' TO DATA-REMAINS-SWITCH
            NOT AT END
                .
                .               Procedure Division statements to process the current record
                .
        END-READ
    END-PERFORM.


                (b) False Condition Branch with In-line Perform
```

False-Condition Branch

The **NOT AT END** clause specifies an action for the false branch of a conditional statement; it is commonly used is in conjunction with a scope terminator and an in-line perform to eliminate the priming read, as shown in Figure 9.2.

The choice between the priming read in Figure 9.2a and the equivalent logic in Figure 9.2b is one of personal preference. The earlier listings (e.g., the tuition billing program in Chapter 5) used the priming read because it was required in COBOL-74 as the earlier compiler had neither the false-condition branch nor the in-line perform. Many programmers are, in fact, so accustomed to the priming read that they continue to use it even though it is no longer necessary. We prefer the in-line perform and false-condition branch, but both techniques are equally acceptable.

READ INTO

The **READ INTO** phrase causes the input record to be stored in two places: in the I/O area of the designated file *and* in the identifier name specified in the INTO phrase in Working-Storage. The statement is illustrated in Figure 9.3, where the input data are available in both EMPLOYEE-RECORD and WS-EMPLOYEE-RECORD. READ INTO is equivalent to the combination of a READ statement and a MOVE statement as shown:

```
READ EMPLOYEE-FILE
    AT END
        MOVE 'NO' TO DATA-REMAINS-SWITCH
    NOT AT END
```

Figure 9.3 The READ INTO Statement

```
FD  EMPLOYEE-FILE
    DATA RECORD IS EMPLOYEE-RECORD.
01  EMPLOYEE-RECORD          PIC X(60).
        .
            .
                .

WORKING-STORAGE SECTION.
01  FILLER                   PIC X(14)    VALUE 'WS BEGINS HERE'.
01  WS-EMPLOYEE-RECORD.
    05  EMP-NAME             PIC X(25).
            .
                .
                    .

PROCEDURE DIVISION.
        .
            .
                .
        READ EMPLOYEE-FILE INTO WS-EMPLOYEE-RECORD
            AT END
                MOVE 'NO' TO DATA-REMAINS-SWITCH
            NOT AT END
                PERFORM PROCESS-THIS-RECORD
        END-READ.
```

```
            PERFORM PROCESS-THIS-RECORD
        END-READ.
        MOVE EMPLOYEE-RECORD TO WS-EMPLOYEE-RECORD.
```

The advantage of the READ INTO statement is in debugging. If a program ends prematurely, the first task is to identify the record being processed at the instant the problem occurred. The FD area is difficult to find, and identification of the specific logical record is further complicated by considerations of blocking. Working-Storage, however, is easy to find because of the literal WS BEGINS HERE. The technique is not sophisticated, but it does work. Once Working-Storage is found, you can identify the record in question as well as the values of all other data names defined in Working-Storage.

Write From

The **WRITE FROM** statement is analogous to READ INTO in that it combines the effects of a MOVE and a WRITE into a single statement. The general format of the WRITE statement is:

```
WRITE record-name [FROM identifier-1]

⎡ ⎧BEFORE⎫            ⎧⎧identifier-2⎫ ⎡LINE ⎤⎫ ⎤
⎢ ⎨      ⎬ ADVANCING  ⎨⎨integer     ⎬ ⎢     ⎥⎬ ⎥
⎢ ⎩AFTER ⎭            ⎨⎩mnemonic-name⎭ ⎣LINES⎦⎬ ⎥
⎣                     ⎩PAGE                  ⎭ ⎦
```

A single WRITE FROM statement, for example,

```
WRITE PRINT-LINE FROM HEADING-LINE
    AFTER ADVANCING PAGE.
```

is equivalent to the combination of a MOVE and a WRITE statement:

```
MOVE HEADING-LINE TO PRINT-LINE.
WRITE PRINT-LINE
    AFTER ADVANCING PAGE.
```

WRITE FROM can be used throughout a program to write heading, detail, and total lines.

Initialize

The **INITIALIZE** statement sets multiple data names to initial values in a single statement. Consider:

```
INITIALIZE [identifier-1] . . .

⎡            ⎧ALPHABETIC        ⎫                            ⎤
⎢            ⎪ALPHANUMERIC      ⎪          ⎧identifier-2⎫    ⎥
⎢ REPLACING  ⎨NUMERIC           ⎬ DATA BY  ⎨            ⎬ ...⎥ ...
⎢            ⎪ALPHANUMERIC-EDITED⎪         ⎩literal-1   ⎭    ⎥
⎣            ⎩NUMERIC-EDITED    ⎭                            ⎦
```

The brackets indicate that all parameters are optional; that is, INITIALIZE in and of itself is a valid statement that initializes all numeric items in a program to zeros, and all nonnumeric items to spaces. You can also restrict the INITIALIZE statement to one (data name or more,) initialize only specific categories of data names, and/or initialize to values other than zeros or spaces. Thus given the COBOL fragment:

```
01  GROUP-ITEM.
    05  NUMERIC-FIELD-1          PIC 9(4).
    05  NUMERIC-FIELD-2          PIC 9(4).
    05  ALPHANUMERIC-FIELD-1     PIC X(15).
    05  ALPHANUMERIC-FIELD-2     PIC X(20).
```

The statement INITIALIZE GROUP-ITEM is equivalent to:

```
MOVE ZEROS TO NUMERIC-FIELD-1.
MOVE ZEROS TO NUMERIC-FIELD-2.
MOVE SPACES TO ALPHANUMERIC-FIELD-1.
MOVE SPACES TO ALPHANUMERIC-FIELD-2.
```

In similar fashion, INITIALIZE GROUP-ITEM REPLACING NUMERIC BY ZERO is equivalent to:

```
MOVE ZEROS TO NUMERIC-FIELD-1.
MOVE ZEROS TO NUMERIC-FIELD-2.
```

And finally, INITIALIZE GROUP-ITEM REPLACING ALPHANUMERIC BY SPACES is equivalent to:

```
MOVE SPACES TO ALPHANUMERIC-FIELD-1.
MOVE SPACES TO ALPHANUMERIC-FIELD-2.
```

String Processing

It is often necessary to operate on individual characters within a field, when the field is alphanumeric. Operations of this type are called *string processing* operations, and are accomplished with the INSPECT, STRING, and UNSTRING statements in COBOL. Each of these statements is discussed in detail.

INSPECT

The INSPECT statement is a convenient way to replace one character (or character string) with another. Consider:

```
INSPECT identifier-1 REPLACING

  CHARACTERS BY  {identifier-2}  [{BEFORE}  INITIAL {identifier-3}] ...
                 {literal-1  }    {AFTER }          {literal-2  }

  {ALL    }  {identifier-4}     {identifier-5}   [{BEFORE}           {identifier-6}]
  {LEADING}  {literal-3  }  BY  {literal-4  }     {AFTER }  INITIAL  {literal-5  }  ...
  {FIRST  }
```

The INSPECT statement can be used with the editing characters of Chapter 7 as illustrated in Figure 9.4. Assume, for example, that social security number is stored as a nine-position field (with no hyphens) in the input record, but is to appear with hyphens in the printed report. The MOVE statement transfers the incoming social security number to an 11-position field containing two blanks

Figure 9.4   The INSPECT Statement

```
      01   RECORD-IN.
           05   SOC-SEC-NUM              PIC 9(9).
            .
              .
                .
      01   PRINT-LINE.
           05   SOC-SEC-NUM-OUT          PIC 999B99B9999.
            .
              .
                .
      PROCEDURE DIVISION.
            .
              .
                .
           MOVE SOC-SEC-NUM TO SOC-SEC-NUM-OUT.
           INSPECT SOC-SEC-NUM-OUT REPLACING ALL ' ' BY '-'.
```

(denoted by B in the PICTURE clause). The INSPECT statement replaces every occurrence of a blank in SOC-SEC-NUM-OUT by the desired hyphen.

Another frequent use of the INSPECT statement is the elimination of leading blanks in numeric fields. (Numeric fields in COBOL should not contain anything other than the digits 0 to 9 and a sign over the rightmost (low-order) position.) Leading blanks can be replaced with zeros as follows:

```
   INSPECT FIELD-WITH-BLANKS REPLACING LEADING ' ' BY '0'.
```

STRING

The STRING statement joins (concatenates) one or more fields and/or one or more literals into a single field. Thus a STRING statement has the same effect as a series of MOVE statements, except that the destination fields are one and the same. An abbreviated form of the COBOL notation for the STRING follows:

$$\underline{\text{STRING}} \quad \begin{Bmatrix} \text{identifier-1} \\ \text{literal-1} \end{Bmatrix} \begin{bmatrix} \text{identifier-2} \\ \text{literal-2} \end{bmatrix} \; \ldots \; \underline{\text{DELIMITED}} \text{ BY} \begin{Bmatrix} \text{identifier-3} \\ \text{literal-3} \\ \underline{\text{SIZE}} \end{Bmatrix} \; \ldots$$

$$\underline{\text{INTO}} \text{ identifier-4} \begin{bmatrix} \text{WITH } \underline{\text{POINTER}} \text{ identifier-5} \end{bmatrix}$$

$$\begin{bmatrix} \text{END-STRING} \end{bmatrix}$$

The above notation can be simplified, for our discussion, in the following manner:

```
   STRING sending item INTO receiving field
```

A sending item may be either an identifier or a literal. Each sending item must be accompanied by a delimiting clause, which indicates when to stop moving characters from the sending field. The delimiter can take one of three forms:

1. An identifier name that contains the delimiting character(s),

2. A figurative literal or constant whose value is the delimiting character(s), or

3. SIZE, which transfers the entire contents of the sending item.

The delimiting character(s) itself is *not* transferred. Figure 9.5 contains an example of the STRING statement in which the components of an individual's name are stored separately, then put together to form a single character string. The application is not unusual in that a program often requires a person's name in two formats. It is easy, for example, to visualize the name (John H. Smith) as a single entity as it might appear on an address label. You would not, however, want to store the name as a single field as that would preclude the ability to obtain an alphabetical

Figure 9.5   The STRING Statement

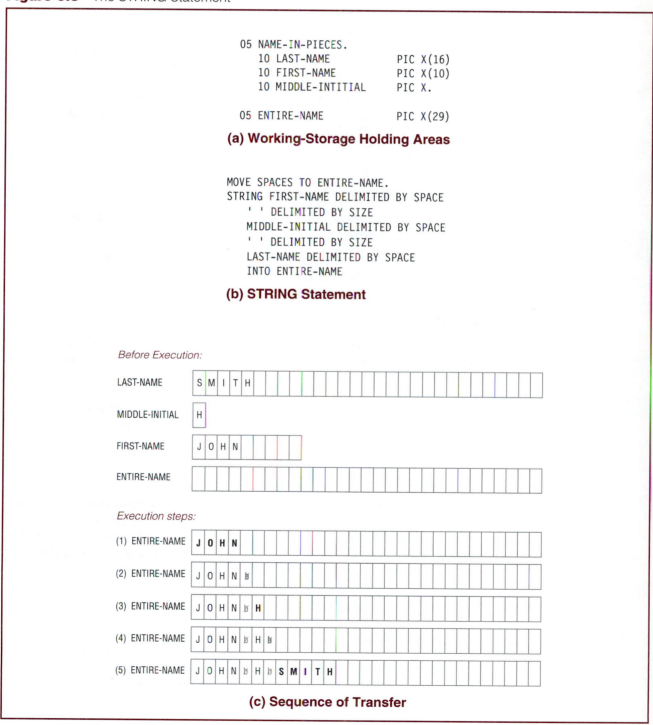

```
          05 NAME-IN-PIECES.
             10 LAST-NAME          PIC X(16)
             10 FIRST-NAME         PIC X(10)
             10 MIDDLE-INITITAL    PIC X.

          05 ENTIRE-NAME           PIC X(29)
```

(a) Working-Storage Holding Areas

```
          MOVE SPACES TO ENTIRE-NAME.
          STRING FIRST-NAME DELIMITED BY SPACE
              ' ' DELIMITED BY SIZE
              MIDDLE-INITIAL DELIMITED BY SPACE
              ' ' DELIMITED BY SIZE
              LAST-NAME DELIMITED BY SPACE
              INTO ENTIRE-NAME
```

(b) STRING Statement

Before Execution:

LAST-NAME | S | M | I | T | H |

MIDDLE-INITIAL | H |

FIRST-NAME | J | O | H | N |

ENTIRE-NAME | (empty)

Execution steps:

(1) ENTIRE-NAME | J | O | H | N |

(2) ENTIRE-NAME | J | O | H | N | ␢ |

(3) ENTIRE-NAME | J | O | H | N | ␢ | H |

(4) ENTIRE-NAME | J | O | H | N | ␢ | H | ␢ |

(5) ENTIRE-NAME | J | O | H | N | ␢ | H | ␢ | S | M | I | T | H |

(c) Sequence of Transfer

list on last name; that is you must have access to last name as a separate entity, in order to alphabetize a list. (See problem 3.)

The Data Division entries in Figure 9.5a define NAME-IN-PIECES to hold the individual fields, and ENTIRE-NAME to hold the concatenated result. Five distinct steps are required to string the individual fields together to form a single name:

1. Move FIRST-NAME to ENTIRE-NAME.

2. Move a space to ENTIRE-NAME after the first name.

3. Move MIDDLE-INITIAL to ENTIRE-NAME after the space.

4. Move a space to ENTIRE-NAME after the initial.

5. Move LAST-NAME to ENTIRE-NAME after the second space.

The STRING statement in Figure 9.5b accomplishes all five tasks and is illustrated in Figure 9.5c. The STRING statement executes as follows:

1. The characters in the FIRST-NAME field are moved (from left to right) to ENTIRE-NAME until a space is encountered (the delimiter), or the entire contents of FIRST-NAME are transferred.

2. The literal ' ' (delimiter is SIZE) is moved to the position following the last character of FIRST-NAME.

3. The MIDDLE-INITIAL is moved.

4. The literal ' ' (delimiter is SIZE) is moved to the position following the MIDDLE-INITIAL.

5. Finally, each character in LAST-NAME is moved until either a space is encountered (the delimiter), or the entire field is transferred.

UNSTRING

The UNSTRING statement breaks a concatenated field into its components and is the opposite of the STRING statement. An abbreviated form of the COBOL notation for the UNSTRING follows:

$$\underline{\text{UNSTRING}} \text{ identifier-1} \left[\underline{\text{DELIMITED}} \text{ BY} \begin{Bmatrix} \text{identifier-2} \\ \text{literal-1} \end{Bmatrix} \left[\underline{\text{OR}} \begin{Bmatrix} \text{identifier-3} \\ \text{literal-2} \end{Bmatrix} \right] \right] \dots$$

$$\underline{\text{INTO}} \text{ identifier-4}$$

$$\left[\underline{\text{END-UNSTRING}} \right]$$

We reverse the previous example and divide ENTIRE-NAME into its three components, FIRST-NAME, MIDDLE-INITIAL, and LAST-NAME, as shown in Figure 9.6. The UNSTRING statement operates from left to right on ENTIRE-NAME, moving characters into FIRST-NAME until a space is encountered, then into MIDDLE-INITIAL, and finally into LAST-NAME.

Reference Modification

Reference modification enables you to address a character string that was not explicitly defined—that is, a character string within an existing data name. This is done by specifying the leftmost (starting) position of the string within the data name and the length of the string, separating the parameters by a colon. The format for reference modification is shown below and is illustrated in Figure 9.7.

```
data-name (leftmost position: [length])
```

Figure 9.6   The UNSTRING Statement

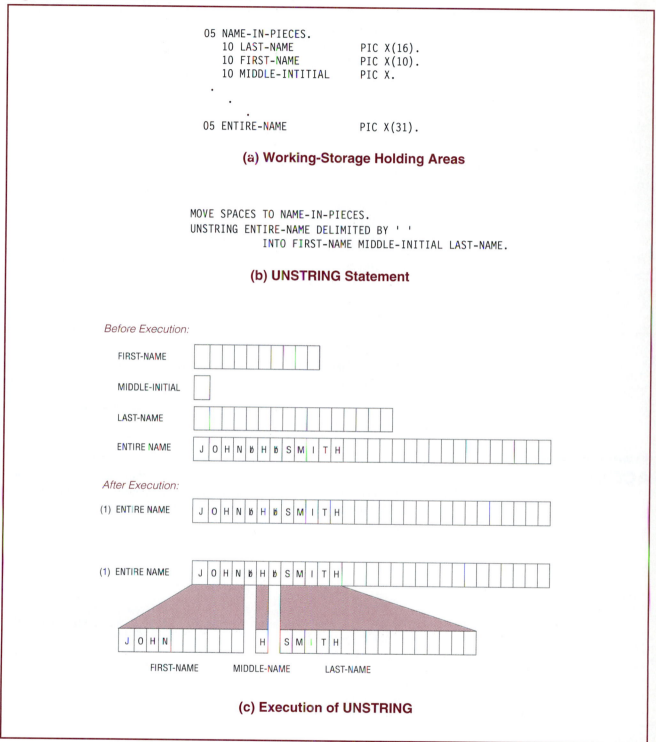

```
                    05 NAME-IN-PIECES.
                       10 LAST-NAME          PIC X(16).
                       10 FIRST-NAME         PIC X(10).
                       10 MIDDLE-INTITIAL    PIC X.
                      .
                       .
                        .
                    05 ENTIRE-NAME           PIC X(31).
```

(a) Working-Storage Holding Areas

```
               MOVE SPACES TO NAME-IN-PIECES.
               UNSTRING ENTIRE-NAME DELIMITED BY ' '
                          INTO FIRST-NAME MIDDLE-INITIAL LAST-NAME.
```

(b) UNSTRING Statement

(c) Execution of UNSTRING

In Figure 9.7 TELEPHONE-NUMBER is defined as a 10 position field within an incoming record. Portions of this field are then moved to EDITED-PHONE-NUMBER through reference modification; for example, TELEPHONE-NUMBER (4:3) refers to positions 4, 5, and 6 within TELEPHONE-NUMBER. The specification of length is optional, and its omission defaults to the end of the data name; i.e., TELEPHONE-NUMBER (7:4) and TELEPHONE-NUMBER (7:) are equivalent.

Figure 9.7   Reference Modification

```
01  INCOMING-RECORD.
     .
       .
         .
    05  TELEPHONE-NUMBER        PIC X(10).
     .
       .
         .


01  EDITED-PHONE-NUMBER.
    05  FILLER                  PIC X     VALUE '('.
    05  AREA-CODE               PIC X(3).
    05  FILLER                  PIC X     VALUE ')'.
    05  EXCHANGE                PIC X(3).
    05  FILLER                  PIC X     VALUE '-'.
    05  DIGITS                  PIC X(4).
     .
       .
         .


    MOVE TELEPHONE-NUMBER (1:3) TO AREA-CODE.
    MOVE TELEPHONE-NUMBER (4:3) TO EXCHANGE.
    MOVE TELEPHONE-NUMBER (7:4) TO DIGITS.
```

ACCEPT

The **ACCEPT** statement was introduced in Chapter 8 to obtain the date of execution and implement various forms of date validation. The statement is expanded in this chapter to include the day of the week as well as the date. Consider:

$$\underline{\text{ACCEPT}}\ \text{identifier-1}\ \underline{\text{FROM}}\ \left\{\begin{array}{l}\underline{\text{DAY-OF-WEEK}}\\ \underline{\text{DATE}}\\ \underline{\text{DAY}}\\ \underline{\text{TIME}}\end{array}\right\}$$

The DAY-OF-WEEK clause returns an integer from 1 to 7 representing the day according to the following table:

Integer	Day
1	Monday
2	Tuesday
3	Wednesday
4	Thursday
5	Friday
6	Saturday
7	Sunday

The ACCEPT statement is illustrated in Figure 9.8. The user defines a data name in Working-Storage—for example, DAY-CODE-VALUE in Figure 9.8a—then accepts

Figure 9.8 The ACCEPT Statement

```
01  DAY-CODE-VALUE              PIC 9.


01  TODAYS-DATE.
    05  TODAYS-YEAR             PIC 99.
    05  TODAYS-MONTH            PIC 99.
    05  TODAYS-DAY              PIC 99.


01  HDG-LINE.
    05  HDG-DAY-OF-WEEK         PIC X(9).
    05  FILLER                  PIC XX    VALUE ', '.
    05  HDG-DATE                PIC X(8).
```

(a) Working-Storage Entries

```
ACCEPT DAY-CODE-VALUE FROM DAY-OF-WEEK.
EVALUATE DAY-CODE-VALUE
    WHEN 1 MOVE '   Monday' TO HDG-DAY-OF-WEEK
    WHEN 2 MOVE '  Tuesday' TO HDG-DAY-OF-WEEK
    WHEN 3 MOVE 'Wednesday' TO HDG-DAY-OF-WEEK
    WHEN 4 MOVE ' Thursday' TO HDG-DAY-OF-WEEK
    WHEN 5 MOVE '   Friday' TO HDG-DAY-OF-WEEK
    WHEN 6 MOVE ' Saturday' TO HDG-DAY-OF-WEEK
    WHEN 7 MOVE '   Sunday' TO HDG-DAY-OF-WEEK
END-EVALUATE.
```

(b) DAY-OF-WEEK Clause

```
ACCEPT TODAYS-DATE FROM DATE.
STRING TODAYS-MONTH '/' TODAYS-DAY '/' TODAYS-YEAR
    DELIMITED BY SIZE INTO HDG-DATE
END-STRING.
```

(c) DATE Clause

the value from DAY-OF-WEEK into that data name. The subsequent EVALUATE statement expands the one-position code to a literal day.

The DATE and DAY clauses were described in Chapter 8 and represent the date (in the form yymmdd) and Julian date (in the form yyddd), respectively. The DATE clause is illustrated in Figure 9.8c for purposes of review.

Duplicate Data Names

Most programs require that the output contain some of the input, for example, name and social security number. COBOL permits the definition of *duplicate data names* in the Data Division, provided all Procedure Division references to duplicate names use the appropriate *qualification*. We prefer *not* to use duplicate names because they violate the prefix coding standard discussed in Chapter 7, but they are used in older programs, and are covered here for completeness.

Qualification

The Data Division entries in Figure 9.9a contain several data names that appear in both STUDENT-RECORD and PRINT-LINE—for example, CREDITS—and any Procedure Division reference to CREDITS will produce a compiler error indicating a *nonunique data name.* This is because the compiler cannot determine which CREDITS (in STUDENT-RECORD or PRINT-LINE) is referenced. One solution is

Figure 9.9 Duplicate Data Names

```
01   STUDENT-RECORD.
     05   STUDENT-NAME            PIC X(20).
     05   SOCIAL-SECURITY-NUM     PIC 9(9).
     05   STUDENT-ADDRESS.
          10   STREET             PIC X(15).
          10   CITY-STATE         PIC X(15).
     05   ZIP-CODE                PIC X(5).
     05   CREDITS                 PIC 9(3).
     05   MAJOR                   PIC X(10).
     05   FILLER                  PIC X(3).
          .
            .
              .
01   PRINT-LINE.
     10   STUDENT-NAME            PIC X(20).
     10   FILLER                  PIC XX.
     10   CREDITS                 PIC ZZ9.
     10   FILLER                  PIC XX.
     10   TUITION                 PIC $$,$$9.99.
     10   FILLER                  PIC XX.
     10   STUDENT-ADDRESS.
          15   STREET             PIC X(15).
          15   CITY-STATE         PIC X(15).
          15   ZIP-CODE           PIC X(5).
     10   FILLER                  PIC XX.
     10   SOCIAL-SECURITY-NUM     PIC 999B99B9999.
     10   FILLER                  PIC X(47).
```

(a) Duplicate Data Names

```
MOVE CORRESPONDING STUDENT-RECORD TO PRINT-LINE.
```

(b) MOVE CORRESPONDING Statement

```
MOVE STUDENT-NAME OF STUDENT-RECORD
     TO STUDENT-NAME OF PRINT-LINE.
MOVE SOCIAL-SECURITY-NUM OF STUDENT-RECORD
     TO SOCIAL-SECURITY-NUM OF PRINT-LINE.
MOVE STREET OF STUDENT-RECORD
     TO STREET OF PRINT-LINE.
MOVE CITY-STATE OF STUDENT-RECORD
     TO CITY-STATE OF PRINT-LINE.
MOVE CREDITS OF STUDENT-RECORD
     TO CREDITS OF PRINT-LINE.
```

(c) Equivalent MOVE Statements

to *qualify* the data name, using **OF** or **IN,** and refer to CREDITS OF STUDENT-RECORD or CREDITS IN STUDENT-RECORD.

Qualification is sometimes necessary over several levels. For example, the use of STREET OF STUDENT-ADDRESS in the statement below is still ambiguous.

```
MOVE STREET OF STUDENT-ADDRESS TO OUTPUT-AREA.
```

The qualifier STUDENT-ADDRESS appears in both 01 records and thus the ambiguity was not resolved. Two levels of qualification are necessary to make the intent clear:

```
MOVE STREET OF STUDENT-ADDRESS OF STUDENT-RECORD TO OUTPUT-AREA.
```

Alternatively, you could skip the intermediate level and rewrite the statement as:

```
MOVE STREET IN STUDENT-RECORD TO OUTPUT-AREA.
```

OF and IN can be used interchangeably. Duplicate data names offer the advantage of not having to invent different names for the same item—for example, an employee name appearing in both an input record and output report. They also permit use of the MOVE CORRESPONDING statement which is *not* recommended by the authors, but which is covered for completeness.

MOVE CORRESPONDING

The syntax of the MOVE CORRESPONDING statement is:

$$\text{MOVE} \left\{ \begin{array}{l} \underline{\text{CORRESPONDING}} \\ \underline{\text{CORR}} \end{array} \right\} \text{ identifier-1 } \underline{\text{TO}} \text{ identifier-2}$$

The MOVE CORRESPONDING statement in Figure 9.9b is the equivalent of the individual MOVE statements in Figure 9.9c; that is, the single MOVE CORRESPONDING statement has the same effect as the five individual MOVE statements. The CORRESPONDING option searches every data name in STUDENT-RECORD for a matching (duplicate) data name in PRINT-LINE, then generates an individual MOVE statement whenever a match is found. It is very convenient because you have to code only the single MOVE CORRESPONDING statement.

The level numbers of the duplicate data names in Figure 9.9a do not have to match for a move to be generated—only the data names must be the same. The order of the data names in the 01 records is also immaterial; for example, SOCIAL-SECURITY-NUM is the second field in STUDENT-RECORD, and the next to last in PRINT-LINE. Two other conditions must be satisfied, however, in order for a move to be generated:

1. At least one item in each pair of CORRESPONDING items must be an elementary item; that is, STUDENT-ADDRESS of STUDENT-RECORD is not moved to STUDENT-ADDRESS of PRINT-LINE. (The elementary items STREET and CITY-STATE are moved instead.)

2. Corresponding elementary items are moved only if they have the same name and qualification, up to but not including identifier-1 and identifier-2. ZIP-CODE, for example, belongs directly to STUDENT-RECORD, but has an intermediate qualifier (STUDENT-ADDRESS) in PRINT-LINE, and thus ZIP-CODE is not moved.

The Car Billing Program

Our fundamental approach throughout the text is to learn by doing. To that end we have developed a complete COBOL program that incorporates the various statements presented in the chapter. Specifications follow in the usual format.

Programming Specifications

Program Name: Car Billing Program

Narrative: This program processes the file of valid car rental records that was created in the validation program of Chapter 8 to produce a report reflecting the amounts owed by individual customers.

Input File(s):

```
RENTAL-FILE
01  RENTAL-RECORD-IN.
    05  REN-CONTRACT-NO          PIC 9(6).
    05  REN-NAME.
        10  REN-LAST-NAME        PIC X(15).
        10  REN-FIRST-NAME       PIC X(10).
        10  REN-INITIAL          PIC X.
    05  REN-RETURNED-DATE.
        10  REN-RETURNED-YEAR    PIC 9(2).
        10  REN-RETURNED-MONTH   PIC 9(2).
        10  REN-RETURNED-DAY     PIC 9(2).
    05  REN-CAR-TYPE             PIC X.
    05  REN-DAYS-RENTED          PIC 99.
    05  REN-MILEAGE.
        10  REN-MILES-IN         PIC 9(6).
        10  REN-MILES-OUT        PIC 9(6).
        10  REN-MILEAGE-RATE     PIC V99.
    05  REN-INSURANCE            PIC X.
```

Test Data: The input file used by this program was created by the data validation program of Chapter 8 and was shown earlier as Figure 8.10c. The data are repeated below for convenience:

```
999777ELSINOR        TERRY     R921126F0500168000159005N
987654SMITH          PAUL      G921213M0300510000500502Y
354679KERBEL         NORMAN    X930331E1000340000324300Y
264805CLARK          JANE      S921101F0700561500551200N
233432BEINHORN       CATHY     B921122M0200123400113402Y
556564HUMMER         MARGO     R920815C0800234500123403Y
677844MCDONALD       JAMES      930123C0500423500402300N
886222VOGEL          JANICE    D930518F1200634500612302Y
008632TOWER          DARREN    R930429L0900700200689300N
```

Report Layout: See Figure 9.10.

Processing Requirements: 1. Read the file of valid car rental records that was produced by the editing program of Chapter 8. No further validation is required in this program.

2. Calculate the amount due for each incoming record as a function of car type, days rented, miles driven, mileage rate, and insurance.

   a. The mileage rate is different for each customer and appears as a field in the incoming record; the mileage total is the mileage rate times the number of miles driven.

   b. The daily rate is a function of the type of car rented. Economy cars cost $15 a day, compact cars $20 a day, mid-size cars $24 a day, full-size cars $28 a day, and luxury cars $35 a day. The daily total is the daily rate times the number of days rented.

   c. Insurance is optional and is indicated by a 'Y' in the appropriate position in the incoming record. Insurance is $10.50 a day (for customers who choose it), regardless of the type of car rented.

   d. A customer's total bill consists of the mileage total, daily total, and insurance total as described in parts (a), (b), and (c).

3. A heading is required at the top of every page, as shown in Figure 9.10. Detail lines are to be double-spaced and limited to five per page.

4. A total line for all computed fields is required at the end of the report.

Figure 9.10 Car Rental Report

```
          Mavis Car Rental Report              Saturday - 07/03/93                        Page  2

Contract                      Date   Car  Days  Rental  Miles  Mileage Mileage Insurance  Amount
Number   Name               Returned Type Rented Total  Driven  Rate   Total    Total      Due

5-565-64  HUMMER, MARGO R.   08/15/92  C    8    160.00  1,111   .03    33.33    84.00     277.33

6-778-44  MCDONALD, JAMES    01/23/93  C    5    100.00   212    .00     0.00              100.00

8-862-22  VOGEL, JANICE D.   05/18/93  F    12   336.00   222    .02     4.44   126.00     466.44
```

```
          Mavis Car Rental Report           Saturday - 07/03/93                   Page  1

Contract                  Date   Car  Days  Rental  Miles  Mileage Mileage Insurance  Amount
Number   Name           Returned Type Rented Total  Driven  Rate   Total    Total      Due

9-997-77  ELSINOR, TERRY R.  11/26/92  F    5    140.00   90    .05     4.50              144.50

9-876-54  SMITH, PAUL G.     12/13/92  M    3     72.00   95    .02     1.90    31.50     105.40

3-546-79  KERBEL, NORMAN X.  03/31/93  E    10   150.00  157    .00     0.00   105.00     255.00

2-648-05  CLARK, JANE S.     11/01/92  F    7    196.00  103    .00     0.00              196.00

2-334-32  BEINHORN, CATHY B. 11/22/92  M    2     48.00  100    .02     2.00    21.00      71.00
```

```
                                                                                    315.00

                                                                                  ----------
                                                                                  $1,930.67
```

Program Design

The car billing program has two objectives: to complete the two-program sequence begun in Chapter 8 and to illustrate the Procedure Division statements presented in this chapter. Both objectives impact the design of the pseudocode and associated hierarchy chart.

The hierarchy chart in Figure 9.11 is written *without* the priming read of earlier programs. The highest-level module, PREPARE-RENTAL-REPORT, has three subordinates: GET-TODAYS-DATE, PROCESS-RENTAL-RECORDS, and WRITE-RENTAL-TOTALS. PROCESS-RENTAL-RECORDS in turn is the driving module of the program and performs four lower-level paragraphs: COMPUTE-INDIVIDUAL-BILL, WRITE-HEADING-LINES, WRITE-DETAIL-LINE, and INCREMENT-RENTAL-TOTALS. COMPUTE-INDIVIDUAL-BILL has three subordinate modules, COMPUTE-MILEAGE-TOTAL, COMPUTE-DAILY-TOTAL, and COMPUTE-INSURANCE-TOTAL to compute the components of a customer's bill.

The paragraph WRITE-HEADING-LINES is subordinate to PROCESS-RENTAL-RECORDS, which differs from an earlier hierarchy chart (page 119) that placed the heading routine on a higher level. The earlier structure, however, produced only a single heading at the start of processing, whereas the current requirement is to produce a heading at the top of every page; hence the heading routine will be executed several times and is subordinate to processing a record.

The pseudocode in Figure 9.12 takes advantage of the in-line perform and false-condition branch to eliminate the priming read used in earlier examples. The pseudocode also implements the required page heading routine by initializing the line counter to six and testing its value prior to writing each detail line. The heading

Figure 9.11   Hierarchy Chart

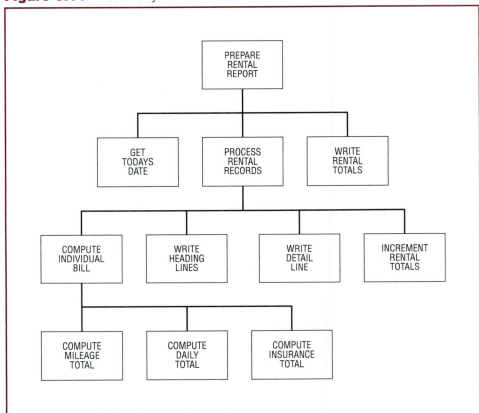

Figure 9.12   Pseudocode

```
        Open Files
        Get today's date
      ┌ DO WHILE data remains
      │        ┌ Read Rental File
      │        │       AT END
      │        │           Indicate no more data
      │        │       NOT AT END
      │        │           Initialize individual calculations
      │        │           Compute miles driven = miles in - miles out
      │        │         ┌ DO CASE
      │        │         │      Car Type E - Move economy rate to mileage rate
      │        │         │      Car Type C - Move compact rate to mileage rate
      │        │         │      Car Type M - Move midsize to mileage rate
      │        │         │      Car Type F - Move fullsize rate to mileage rate
      │        │         │      Car Type L - Move luxury rate to mileage rate
      │        │         └ END CASE
      │        │           Compute mileage total = miles driven * mileage rate
      │        │           Compute daily total = days rented * daily rate
      │        │         ┌ IF insurance taken
      │        │         │      Compute insurance = insurance rate * days rented
      │        │         └ END-IF
      │        │           Compute total bill = mileage amount + daily amount + insurance
      │        │         ┌ IF line count greater than 5
      │        │         │      Initialize line count to 1
      │        │         │      Increment page count
      │        │         │      Write heading lines
      │        │         └ END-IF
      │        │           Write detail line
      │        │           Add 1 to line count
      │        │           Increment rental totals
      │        └ END READ
      └ ENDDO
        Write rental totals
        Close files
        Stop run
```

will be written prior to the first detail record because it (the line counter) is greater than five (the desired number of lines per page). The line counter is then reset to one so that the heading will be produced for every fifth record.

The Completed Program

The completed program in Figure 9.13 illustrates many of the statements presented in the chapter. The logic of the program is straightforward and parallels the pseudocode just discussed. Several features of the program merit attention:

1. The combination of the in-line perform and false-condition branch (lines 209–216) to eliminate the priming read used in all previous programs.

Figure 9.13   The Completed Program

```
1        IDENTIFICATION DIVISION.
2        PROGRAM-ID.        CARSRPT.
3        AUTHOR.            CVV.
4
5        ENVIRONMENT DIVISION.
6        INPUT-OUTPUT SECTION.
7        FILE-CONTROL.
8           SELECT RENTAL-FILE   ASSIGN TO SYSIN
9               ORGANIZATION IS LINE SEQUENTIAL.
10          SELECT PRINT-FILE    ASSIGN TO SYSOUT
11              ORGANIZATION IS LINE SEQUENTIAL.
12
13       DATA DIVISION.
14       FILE SECTION.
15       FD  RENTAL-FILE
16           RECORD CONTAINS 56 CHARACTERS.
17       01  RENTAL-RECORD            PIC X(56).
18
19       FD  PRINT-FILE
20           RECORD CONTAINS 132 CHARACTERS.
21       01  PRINT-LINE              PIC X(132).
22
23       WORKING-STORAGE SECTION.
24       01  FILLER                  PIC X(14)
25               VALUE 'WS BEGINS HERE'.
26
27       01  RENTAL-RECORD-IN.
28           05  REN-CONTRACT-NO      PIC 9(6).
29           05  REN-NAME.
30               10  REN-LAST-NAME    PIC X(15).
31               10  REN-FIRST-NAME   PIC X(10).
32               10  REN-INITIAL      PIC X.
33           05  REN-RETURNED-DATE.
34               10  REN-RETURNED-YEAR   PIC 9(2).
35               10  REN-RETURNED-MONTH  PIC 9(2).
36               10  REN-RETURNED-DAY    PIC 9(2).
37           05  REN-CAR-TYPE        PIC X.
38           05  REN-DAYS-RENTED     PIC 99.
39           05  REN-MILEAGE.
40               10  REN-MILES-IN     PIC 9(6).
41               10  REN-MILES-OUT    PIC 9(6).
42               10  REN-MILEAGE-RATE PIC V99.
43           05  REN-INSURANCE       PIC X.
44
45       01  PROGRAM-SWITCHES.
46           05  DATA-REMAINS-SWITCH  PIC XX   VALUE SPACES.
47           05  NAME-POINTER         PIC 999 VALUE 1.
48
49       01  PAGE-AND-LINE-COUNTERS.
50           05  LINE-COUNT           PIC 9(2)     VALUE 6.
```

Definition of line counter in conjunction with heading routine

Figure 9.13   *(continued)*

```
51        05  PAGE-COUNT              PIC 9(2)      VALUE ZEROS.        Definition of page counters
52        05  LINES-PER-PAGE          PIC 9(2)      VALUE 5.           in conjunction with heading
53                                                                      routine
54    01  DAILY-RATES.
55        05  ECONOMY-RATE            PIC 9(3)V99   VALUE 15.
56        05  COMPACT-RATE            PIC 9(3)V99   VALUE 20.
57        05  MID-RATE                PIC 9(3)V99   VALUE 24.
58        05  FULL-RATE               PIC 9(3)V99   VALUE 28.
59        05  LUXURY-RATE             PIC 9(3)V99   VALUE 35.
60        05  INSURANCE-RATE          PIC 99V99     VALUE 10.50.
61
62    01  IND-BILL-INFORMATION.
63        05  IND-MILES-DRIVEN        PIC 9(5).
64        05  IND-DAILY-RATE          PIC 9(3)V99.
65        05  IND-DAILY-TOTAL         PIC 9(4)V99.
66        05  IND-MILEAGE-TOTAL       PIC 9(3)V99.
67        05  IND-INSURANCE-TOTAL     PIC 9(3)V99.
68        05  IND-AMOUNT-DUE          PIC 9(4)V99.
69
70    01  TOTALS-FOR-REPORT.
71        05  TOTAL-DAYS-RENTED       PIC 9(4)      VALUE ZEROES.
72        05  TOTAL-DAILY-RENTAL      PIC 9(6)V99   VALUE ZEROES.
73        05  TOTAL-MILES-DRIVEN      PIC 9(6)      VALUE ZEROES.
74        05  TOTAL-MILEAGE           PIC 9(4)V99   VALUE ZEROES.
75        05  TOTAL-INSURANCE         PIC 9(4)V99   VALUE ZEROES.
76        05  TOTAL-AMOUNT-DUE        PIC 9(6)V99   VALUE ZEROES.
77
78    01  TODAYS-DATE-AREA.
79        05  TODAYS-YEAR             PIC 99.
80        05  TODAYS-MONTH            PIC 99.
81        05  TODAYS-DAY              PIC 99.
82
83    01  DAY-CODE-VALUE              PIC 9.
84
85    01  HEADING-LINE-ONE.
86        05  FILLER                  PIC X(20)  VALUE SPACES.
87        05  FILLER                  PIC X(25)
88                    VALUE 'Mavis Car Rental Report'.
89        05  FILLER                  PIC X(16)  VALUE SPACES.
90        05  HDG-DAY                 PIC X(9).
91        05  FILLER                  PIC X(3)   VALUE ' - '.
92        05  HDG-DATE                PIC X(8).
93        05  FILLER                  PIC X(41)  VALUE SPACES.
94        05  FILLER                  PIC X(5)   VALUE 'Page '.
95        05  HDG-PAGE-NUMBER         PIC Z9.
96        05  FILLER                  PIC X(3)   VALUE SPACES.
97
98    01  HEADING-LINE-TWO.
99        05  FILLER                  PIC X(8)  VALUE 'Contract'.
100       05  FILLER                  PIC X(38) VALUE SPACES.
```

Figure 9.13 *(continued)*

```
101         05  FILLER              PIC X(4)   VALUE 'Date'.
102         05  FILLER              PIC X(5)   VALUE SPACES.
103         05  FILLER              PIC X(3)   VALUE 'Car'.
104         05  FILLER              PIC X(3)   VALUE SPACES.
105         05  FILLER              PIC X(4)   VALUE 'Days'.
106         05  FILLER              PIC X(6)   VALUE SPACES.
107         05  FILLER              PIC X(6)   VALUE 'Rental'.
108         05  FILLER              PIC X(4)   VALUE SPACES.
109         05  FILLER              PIC X(5)   VALUE 'Miles'.
110         05  FILLER              PIC X(2)   VALUE SPACES.
111         05  FILLER              PIC X(7)   VALUE 'Mileage'.
112         05  FILLER              PIC X(2)   VALUE SPACES.
113         05  FILLER              PIC X(7)   VALUE 'Mileage'.
114         05  FILLER              PIC X(2)   VALUE SPACES.
115         05  FILLER              PIC X(9)   VALUE 'Insurance'.
116         05  FILLER              PIC X(6)   VALUE SPACES.
117         05  FILLER              PIC X(6)   VALUE 'Amount'.
118         05  FILLER              PIC X(5)   VALUE SPACES.
119
120     01  HEADING-LINE-THREE.
121         05  FILLER              PIC X      VALUE SPACES.
122         05  FILLER              PIC X(6)   VALUE 'Number'.
123         05  FILLER              PIC X(4)   VALUE SPACES.
124         05  FILLER              PIC X(4)   VALUE 'Name'.
125         05  FILLER              PIC X(29)  VALUE SPACES.
126         05  FILLER              PIC X(8)   VALUE 'Returned'.
127         05  FILLER              PIC X(2)   VALUE SPACES.
128         05  FILLER              PIC X(4)   VALUE 'Type'.
129         05  FILLER              PIC X(2)   VALUE SPACES.
130         05  FILLER              PIC X(6)   VALUE 'Rented'.
131         05  FILLER              PIC X(6)   VALUE SPACES.
132         05  FILLER              PIC X(5)   VALUE 'Total'.
133         05  FILLER              PIC X(3)   VALUE SPACES.
134         05  FILLER              PIC X(6)   VALUE 'Driven'.
135         05  FILLER              PIC X(4)   VALUE SPACES.
136         05  FILLER              PIC X(4)   VALUE 'Rate'.
137         05  FILLER              PIC X(4)   VALUE SPACES.
138         05  FILLER              PIC X(5)   VALUE 'Total'.
139         05  FILLER              PIC X(6)   VALUE SPACES.
140         05  FILLER              PIC X(5)   VALUE 'Total'.
141         05  FILLER              PIC X(9)   VALUE SPACES.
142         05  FILLER              PIC X(3)   VALUE 'Due'.
143         05  FILLER              PIC X(6)   VALUE SPACES.
144
145     01  DETAIL-LINE.
146         05  DET-CONTRACT-NO     PIC 9B999B99.
147         05  FILLER              PIC X(3)   VALUE SPACES.
148         05  DET-NAME            PIC X(30).
149         05  FILLER              PIC X(3)   VALUE SPACES.
150         05  DET-RETURN-DATE     PIC X(8).
```

Blanks are replaced in the INSPECT statement of line 302

Figure 9.13   *(continued)*

```
151          05  FILLER                PIC X(4)   VALUE SPACES.
152          05  DET-CAR-TYPE          PIC X.
153          05  FILLER                PIC X(5)   VALUE SPACES.
154          05  DET-DAYS-RENTED       PIC Z9.
155          05  FILLER                PIC X(5)   VALUE SPACES.
156          05  DET-DAILY-TOTAL       PIC Z,ZZ9.99.
157          05  FILLER                PIC X(3)   VALUE SPACES.
158          05  DET-MILES-DRIVEN      PIC ZZ,ZZ9.
159          05  FILLER                PIC X(5)   VALUE SPACES.
160          05  DET-MILEAGE-RATE      PIC .99.
161          05  FILLER                PIC X(5)   VALUE SPACES.
162          05  DET-MILEAGE-TOTAL     PIC ZZ9.99.
163          05  FILLER                PIC X(4)   VALUE SPACES.
164          05  DET-INSURANCE-TOTAL   PIC ZZ9.99 BLANK WHEN ZERO.
165          05  FILLER                PIC X(4)   VALUE SPACES.
166          05  DET-AMOUNT-DUE        PIC Z,ZZ9.99.
167          05  FILLER                PIC X(5)   VALUE SPACES.
168
169      01  TOTAL-DASH-LINE.
170          05  FILLER                PIC X(59)  VALUE SPACES.
171          05  FILLER                PIC X(5)   VALUE ALL '-'.
172          05  FILLER                PIC X(3)   VALUE SPACES.
173          05  FILLER                PIC X(10)  VALUE ALL '-'.
174          05  FILLER                PIC XX     VALUE SPACES.
175          05  FILLER                PIC X(7)   VALUE ALL '-'.
176          05  FILLER                PIC X(11)  VALUE SPACES.
177          05  FILLER                PIC X(8)   VALUE ALL '-'.
178          05  FILLER                PIC XX     VALUE SPACES.
179          05  FILLER                PIC X(8)   VALUE ALL '-'.
180          05  FILLER                PIC XX     VALUE SPACES.
181          05  FILLER                PIC X(10)  VALUE ALL '-'.
182          05  FILLER                PIC X(5)   VALUE SPACES.
183
184      01  TOTAL-LINE.
185          05  FILLER                PIC XX     VALUE SPACES.
186          05  FILLER                PIC X(6)   VALUE 'Totals'.
187          05  FILLER                PIC X(51)  VALUE SPACES.
188          05  TOT-DAYS-RENTED       PIC Z,ZZ9.
189          05  FILLER                PIC X(2)   VALUE SPACES.
190          05  TOT-DAILY-RENTAL      PIC $$$$,$$9.99.
191          05  FILLER                PIC XX     VALUE SPACES.
192          05  TOT-MILES-DRIVEN      PIC ZZZ,ZZ9.
193          05  FILLER                PIC X(9)   VALUE SPACES.
194          05  TOT-MILEAGE           PIC $$$,$$9.99.
195          05  FILLER                PIC X      VALUE SPACES.
196          05  TOT-INSURANCE         PIC $$,$$9.99.
197          05  FILLER                PIC X      VALUE SPACES.
198          05  TOT-AMOUNT-DUE        PIC $$$$,$$9.99.
199          05  FILLER                PIC X(5)   VALUE SPACES.
200
```

Figure 9.13   *(continued)*

```
201        01  FILLER                    PIC X(12)
202                VALUE 'WS ENDS HERE'.
203
204        PROCEDURE DIVISION.
205        000-PREPARE-RENTAL-REPORT.
206           OPEN INPUT  RENTAL-FILE
207                OUTPUT PRINT-FILE.
208           PERFORM 100-GET-TODAYS-DATE.
209           PERFORM UNTIL DATA-REMAINS-SWITCH = 'NO'
210              READ RENTAL-FILE INTO RENTAL-RECORD-IN
211                 AT END
212                    MOVE 'NO' TO DATA-REMAINS-SWITCH
213                 NOT AT END
214                    PERFORM 200-PROCESS-RENTAL-RECORDS
215              END-READ
216           END-PERFORM.
217           PERFORM 700-WRITE-RENTAL-TOTALS.
218           CLOSE RENTAL-FILE
219                 PRINT-FILE.
220           STOP RUN.
221
222        100-GET-TODAYS-DATE.
223           ACCEPT TODAYS-DATE-AREA FROM DATE.
224           STRING TODAYS-MONTH '/' TODAYS-DAY  '/' TODAYS-YEAR
225              DELIMITED BY SIZE INTO HDG-DATE
226           END-STRING.
227           ACCEPT DAY-CODE-VALUE FROM DAY-OF-WEEK.
228           EVALUATE DAY-CODE-VALUE
229              WHEN 1 MOVE '   Monday' TO HDG-DAY
230              WHEN 2 MOVE '  Tuesday' TO HDG-DAY
231              WHEN 3 MOVE 'Wednesday' TO HDG-DAY
232              WHEN 4 MOVE ' Thursday' TO HDG-DAY
233              WHEN 5 MOVE '   Friday' TO HDG-DAY
234              WHEN 6 MOVE ' Saturday' TO HDG-DAY
235              WHEN 7 MOVE '   Sunday' TO HDG-DAY
236           END-EVALUATE.
237
238        200-PROCESS-RENTAL-RECORDS.
239           PERFORM 300-COMPUTE-IND-BILL.
240           IF LINE-COUNT > LINES-PER-PAGE
241              PERFORM 400-WRITE-HEADING-LINES
242           END-IF.
243           PERFORM 500-WRITE-DETAIL-LINE.
244           PERFORM 600-INCREMENT-TOTALS.
245
246        300-COMPUTE-IND-BILL.
247           INITIALIZE IND-BILL-INFORMATION.
248           PERFORM 320-COMPUTE-MILEAGE-TOTAL.
249           PERFORM 340-COMPUTE-DAILY-TOTAL.
250           PERFORM 360-COMPUTE-INSURANCE-TOTAL.
```

In-line perform and false-condition branch drive program

ACCEPT statement obtains date of execution

Scope terminators are used throughout the Procedure Division

INITIALIZE statement resets initial values

Figure 9.13 *(continued)*

```
251          COMPUTE IND-AMOUNT-DUE ROUNDED
252             = IND-MILEAGE-TOTAL + IND-DAILY-TOTAL
253                + IND-INSURANCE-TOTAL
254             SIZE ERROR DISPLAY 'SIZE ERROR ON AMOUNT DUE FOR '
255                REN-CONTRACT-NO
256          END-COMPUTE.
257
258      320-COMPUTE-MILEAGE-TOTAL.
259          COMPUTE IND-MILES-DRIVEN
260             = REN-MILES-IN - REN-MILES-OUT
261          END-COMPUTE.
262          COMPUTE IND-MILEAGE-TOTAL ROUNDED
263             = IND-MILES-DRIVEN * REN-MILEAGE-RATE
264             SIZE ERROR
265                DISPLAY 'COMPUTED BILL EXCESSIVELY LARGE'
266          END-COMPUTE.
267
268      340-COMPUTE-DAILY-TOTAL.
269          EVALUATE REN-CAR-TYPE
270             WHEN 'E' MOVE ECONOMY-RATE TO IND-DAILY-RATE
271             WHEN 'C' MOVE COMPACT-RATE TO IND-DAILY-RATE
272             WHEN 'M' MOVE MID-RATE TO IND-DAILY-RATE
273             WHEN 'F' MOVE FULL-RATE TO IND-DAILY-RATE
274             WHEN 'L' MOVE LUXURY-RATE TO IND-DAILY-RATE
275             WHEN OTHER MOVE ZEROES TO IND-DAILY-RATE
276          END-EVALUATE.
277          MULTIPLY IND-DAILY-RATE BY REN-DAYS-RENTED
278             GIVING IND-DAILY-TOTAL
279             SIZE ERROR DISPLAY 'SIZE ERROR ON RENTAL TOTAL'
280          END-MULTIPLY.
281
282      360-COMPUTE-INSURANCE-TOTAL.
283          IF REN-INSURANCE = 'Y'
284             MULTIPLY INSURANCE-RATE BY REN-DAYS-RENTED
285                GIVING IND-INSURANCE-TOTAL
286                SIZE ERROR DISPLAY 'SIZE ERROR ON INSURANCE TOTAL'
287             END-MULTIPLY
288          END-IF.
289
290      400-WRITE-HEADING-LINES.
291          MOVE 1 TO LINE-COUNT.
292          ADD 1 TO PAGE-COUNT.
293          MOVE PAGE-COUNT TO HDG-PAGE-NUMBER.
294          WRITE PRINT-LINE FROM HEADING-LINE-ONE
295             AFTER ADVANCING PAGE.
296          WRITE PRINT-LINE FROM HEADING-LINE-TWO
297             AFTER ADVANCING 2 LINES.
298          WRITE PRINT-LINE FROM HEADING-LINE-THREE.
299
300      500-WRITE-DETAIL-LINE.
```

SIZE ERROR clause is used within COMPUTE statement

EVALUATE statement determines daily rate

Indentation increases readability

Figure 9.13   *(continued)*

```
301          MOVE REN-CONTRACT-NO TO DET-CONTRACT-NO.
302          INSPECT DET-CONTRACT-NO REPLACING ALL ' ' BY '-'.
303          MOVE 1 TO NAME-POINTER.
304          MOVE SPACES TO DET-NAME.
305          STRING REN-LAST-NAME DELIMITED BY ' '
306              ', ' DELIMITED BY SIZE
307              REN-FIRST-NAME DELIMITED BY ' '
308              INTO DET-NAME POINTER NAME-POINTER
309          END-STRING.
310          IF REN-INITIAL NOT = SPACES
311              STRING ' ' REN-INITIAL '.' DELIMITED BY SIZE
312                  INTO DET-NAME POINTER NAME-POINTER
313              END-STRING
314          END-IF.
315          STRING REN-RETURNED-MONTH '/' REN-RETURNED-DAY '/'
316              REN-RETURNED-YEAR DELIMITED BY SIZE
317              INTO DET-RETURN-DATE
318          END-STRING.
319          MOVE REN-CAR-TYPE TO DET-CAR-TYPE.
320          MOVE REN-DAYS-RENTED TO DET-DAYS-RENTED.
321          MOVE IND-DAILY-TOTAL TO DET-DAILY-TOTAL.
322          MOVE IND-MILES-DRIVEN TO DET-MILES-DRIVEN.
323          MOVE REN-MILEAGE-RATE TO DET-MILEAGE-RATE.
324          MOVE IND-MILEAGE-TOTAL TO DET-MILEAGE-TOTAL.
325          MOVE IND-INSURANCE-TOTAL TO DET-INSURANCE-TOTAL.
326          MOVE IND-MILEAGE-TOTAL TO DET-MILEAGE-TOTAL.
327          MOVE IND-AMOUNT-DUE TO DET-AMOUNT-DUE.
328          WRITE PRINT-LINE FROM DETAIL-LINE
329              AFTER ADVANCING 2 LINES.
330          ADD 1 TO LINE-COUNT.
331
332      600-INCREMENT-TOTALS.
333          ADD REN-DAYS-RENTED TO TOTAL-DAYS-RENTED
334              SIZE ERROR DISPLAY 'SIZE ERROR ON TOTAL DAYS RENTED'
335          END-ADD.
336          ADD IND-DAILY-TOTAL TO TOTAL-DAILY-RENTAL
337              SIZE ERROR DISPLAY 'SIZE ERROR ON TOTAL RENTAL'
338          END-ADD.
339          ADD IND-MILES-DRIVEN TO TOTAL-MILES-DRIVEN
340              SIZE ERROR DISPLAY 'SIZE ERROR ON TOTAL MILES DRIVEN'
341          END-ADD.
342          ADD IND-MILEAGE-TOTAL TO TOTAL-MILEAGE
343              SIZE ERROR DISPLAY 'SIZE ERROR ON TOTAL MILEAGE'
344          END-ADD.
345          ADD IND-INSURANCE-TOTAL TO TOTAL-INSURANCE
346              SIZE ERROR DISPLAY 'SIZE ERROR ON TOTAL INSURANCE'
347          END-ADD.
348          ADD IND-AMOUNT-DUE TO TOTAL-AMOUNT-DUE
349              SIZE ERROR DISPLAY 'SIZE ERROR ON TOTAL AMOUNT DUE'
350          END-ADD.
351
```

STRING statement joins last name and first name

Line counter is incremented

Figure 9.13 *(continued)*

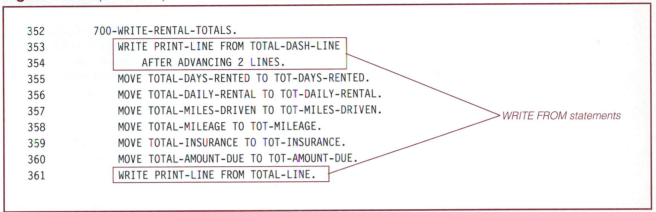

```
352        700-WRITE-RENTAL-TOTALS.
353            WRITE PRINT-LINE FROM TOTAL-DASH-LINE
354                AFTER ADVANCING 2 LINES.
355            MOVE TOTAL-DAYS-RENTED TO TOT-DAYS-RENTED.
356            MOVE TOTAL-DAILY-RENTAL TO TOT-DAILY-RENTAL.
357            MOVE TOTAL-MILES-DRIVEN TO TOT-MILES-DRIVEN.
358            MOVE TOTAL-MILEAGE TO TOT-MILEAGE.
359            MOVE TOTAL-INSURANCE TO TOT-INSURANCE.
360            MOVE TOTAL-AMOUNT-DUE TO TOT-AMOUNT-DUE.
361            WRITE PRINT-LINE FROM TOTAL-LINE.
```

WRITE FROM statements

(A period may not be present after the END-READ scope terminator because it is nested within the in-line perform statement. See problem 2 at the end of the chapter.)

2. The use of scope terminators throughout the Procedure Division—for example, END-READ in line 215, END-COMPUTE in lines 256 and 266, and END-IF in lines 242, 288, and 314.

3. The establishment of a heading routine (lines 290–298) and the associated definition of counters in Working-Storage, LINE-COUNT and PAGE-COUNT in lines 50 and 51. LINE-COUNT is tested prior to writing a detail line (lines 240–242). Since it was initialized to six (a value greater than the desired number of detail lines per page), a heading is written prior to the first detail record. The heading routine resets the line counter (line 291), which is subsequently incremented after every detail line is written (line 330). The page counter is also incremented in the heading routine (line 292), so that the page number can appear on the top of every page in the report.

4. The ACCEPT statement (line 223) to obtain the date of execution and again to accept the corresponding day of the week (line 227). The EVALUATE statement of lines 228–236 converts the numeric DAY-OF-WEEK code to its literal equivalent.

5. The INITIALIZE statement in line 247 to initialize the six data names defined under IND-BILL-INFORMATION.

6. The READ INTO statement in line 210 and the associated WS BEGINS HERE literal at the start of Working-Storage (lines 24–25) to facilitate debugging. The WRITE FROM statement is used throughout the Procedure Division with various print lines.

7. The indentation of subservient clauses throughout the Procedure Division to enhance the readability of the program. AT END and NOT AT END are indented under READ, AFTER ADVANCING is indented under WRITE, and so on. Blank lines are used throughout the program and appear before 01 entries in the Data Division and before paragraph headers in the Procedure Division.

8. The STRING statements in lines 305–309 and 311–313; the latter statements use the POINTER phrase to place the middle initial (if one is present) after the first name.

LIMITATIONS OF COBOL-74

The chapter focused on advanced statements in the Procedure Division, many of which were not available in COBOL-74. The most significant enhancements include scope terminators, the in-line perform, and false-condition branch, all of which are new to COBOL-85. The TEST BEFORE and TEST AFTER clauses are also new, as are the INITIALIZE statement and DAY-OF-WEEK clause.

The statements for string processing (INSPECT, STRING, and UNSTRING) were previously available in COBOL-74; reference modification, however, is new to COBOL-85. Duplicate data names, qualification, and the MOVE CORRESPONDING statement are unchanged from the earlier compiler.

SUMMARY

Points to Remember

- The PERFORM statement contains the optional TEST BEFORE and TEST AFTER clauses, corresponding to the DO WHILE and DO UNTIL iteration structures.

- The combination of an in-line PERFORM and false-condition branch within the READ statement eliminates the need for a priming read.

- The procedure-name in a PERFORM statement may be either a paragraph or a section. The THRU clause enables the execution of multiple procedures, which typically include an EXIT paragraph.

- READ INTO and WRITE FROM combine the effects of a MOVE statement with the indicated I/O operation. READ INTO is also used in conjunction with the literal WS BEGINS HERE to facilitate debugging.

- String processing is accomplished through the INSPECT, STRING, and UNSTRING statements, which provide flexibility in character manipulation.

- The ACCEPT statement includes the DAY and DAY-OF-WEEK clauses to obtain the date and corresponding day of the week on which a program executes.

- The INITIALIZE statement sets multiple data names to initial values in a single statement.

- Duplicate data names may be defined (but are *not* recommended) provided all Procedure Division references to the duplicate names use appropriate qualification. The MOVE CORRESPONDING statement is the equivalent of several individual MOVE statements.

Key Words and Concepts

DO UNTIL structure   Procedure name
DO WHILE structure   Qualification
Duplicate (nonunique) datanames   Reference modification
False-condition branch   Section
In-line perform   String processing

COBOL Elements

ACCEPT   OF
DAY   PERFORM THRU
DAY-OF-WEEK   PERFORM UNTIL
EXIT   READ INTO
IN   STRING
INITIALIZE   TEST AFTER
INSPECT   TEST BEFORE
MOVE CORRESPONDING   UNSTRING
NOT AT END   WRITE FROM

F i l l - i n

1. The READ INTO statement causes each incoming record to be moved to
   _____ areas.

2. The WRITE FROM statement is the equivalent of two statements, a _____
   and a _____.

3. A _____ consists of one or more paragraphs.

4. The _____ statement causes no action to be taken and is often used to
   delineate the end of a PERFORM THRU statement.

5. Nonunique data names within a COBOL program may be _____ using
   the reserved words _____ or _____.

6. The _____ statement is a convenient way to replace leading blanks in a
   field with zeros.

7. String processing operations are accomplished through the _____,
   _____, and _____ statements.

8. The READ statement includes an optional false-condition branch implemented by
   the _____ _____ _____ clause.

9. The DO WHILE and DO UNTIL constructs of structured programming are
   implemented with the TEST _____ and TEST _____ clauses
   in the PERFORM statement.

10. _____ _____ makes it possible to address a string of
    characters contained within another string.

11. Omission of the procedure name in a PERFORM statement creates an _____ perform.

12. The _____ statement enables the initialization of multiple data types in a single statement.

True/False

1. The INSPECT statement facilitates the elimination of leading blanks.

2. A paragraph consists of one or more sections.

3. A PERFORM statement must include a procedure (paragraph or section) name.

4. Qualification over a single level will always remove ambiguity of duplicate data names.

5. The CORRESPONDING option is required if duplicate data names are used.

6. The STRING statement is used to combine several fields together.

7. For the CORRESPONDING option to work, both duplicate names must be at the same level.

8. The UNSTRING statement is used to separate a field into a maximum of three distinct fields.

9. The EXIT statement is required to delineate the end of a performed routine.

10. A PERFORM statement must specify either TEST BEFORE or TEST AFTER.

11. The READ statement may include both an AT END and a NOT AT END clause.

12. The READ statement must be terminated by an END-READ scope terminator.

Problems

1. Given the code:

```
PROCEDURE DIVISION.
MAINLINE SECTION.
FIRST-PARAGRAPH.
    PERFORM SEC-A.
    PERFORM PAR-C THRU PAR-E.
    MOVE 1 TO N.
    PERFORM PAR-G
        WITH TEST AFTER
        UNTIL N > 2.
    STOP RUN.
SEC-A SECTION.
    ADD 1 TO X.
    ADD 1 TO Y.
    ADD 1 TO Z.
PAR-B.
    ADD 2 TO X.
PAR-C.
    ADD 10 TO X.
```

```
PAR-D.
    ADD 10 TO Y
    ADD 20 TO Z.
PAR-E.
    EXIT.
PAR-F.
    MOVE 2 TO N.
PAR-G.
    ADD 1 TO N
    ADD 5 TO X.
```

   a. How many times is each paragraph executed?

   b. What are the final values of X, Y, and Z? (Assume they were all initialized to 0.)

   c. What would happen if the statement ADD 1 TO N were removed from PAR-G?

2. Figure 9.14a contains a slightly modified version of the first paragraph in the car reporting program in which two periods have been added to produce the indicated compilation errors. Indicate the erroneous periods and explain why they produce the error messages.

Figure 9.14 COBOL Listing for Problem 2

```
204        PROCEDURE DIVISION.
205        000-PREPARE-RENTAL-REPORT.
206           OPEN INPUT   RENTAL-FILE
207                 OUTPUT PRINT-FILE.
208           PERFORM 100-GET-TODAYS-DATE.
209           PERFORM UNTIL DATA-REMAINS-SWITCH = 'NO'
210              READ RENTAL-FILE INTO RENTAL-RECORD-IN
211                 AT END
212                    MOVE 'NO' TO DATA-REMAINS-SWITCH.
213                 NOT AT END
214                    PERFORM 200-PROCESS-RENTAL-RECORDS.
215              END-READ.
216           END-PERFORM.
217           PERFORM 700-WRITE-RENTAL-TOTALS.
218           CLOSE RENTAL-FILE
219                 PRINT-FILE.
220           STOP RUN.
```

(a) Modified Procedure Division

```
209 W Explicit scope terminator END- 'PERFORM' assumed present
213 E AT END exception only valid for READ or SEARCH verbs
215 E No corresponding active scope for 'END-READ'
216 E No corresponding active scope for 'END-PERFORM'
```

(b) Error Messages

3. Is the following list of names in alphabetical order?

   ```
   Joel Stutz
   Maryann Barber
   Shelly Parker
   ```

   Your answer depends on the record layout, that is, whether Name is a single field or whether Last Name, First Name, and Middle Initial are defined as individual fields. Can you see the need to define separate fields for these items? Can you appreciate the utility of the STRING statement to concatenate the fields together when necessary?

4. Given the following Data Division entries:

   ```
   01   EMPLOYEE-RECORD.
        05   EMP-NAME.
             10   EMP-LAST-NAME        PIC X(16).
             10   EMP-FIRST-NAME       PIC X(10).
             10   EMP-MIDDLE-INITIAL   PIC X.
        05   ADDRESS.
             10   EMP-STREET-ADDRESS   PIC X(20).
             10   EMP-CITY             PIC X(20).
             10   EMP-STATE            PIC XX.
             10   EMP-ZIP              PIC X(5).
   ```

   Write the necessary STRING statements to create a mailing label with the format:
   First-Name Middle-Initial Last-Name
   Street-Address
   City, State Zip

5. Given the following COBOL fragment:

   ```
   01   DATE-WORK-AREA-1.
        05   YEAR-1        PIC 99.
        05   MONTH-1       PIC 99.
        05   DAY-1         PIC 99.
   01   DATE-WORK-AREA-2.
        05   YEAR-2        PIC 99.
        05   DAY-2         PIC 999.
   01   DATE-WORK-AREA-3.
        05   DAY-3         PIC 9.


             .
               .
                 .


        ACCEPT DATE-WORK-AREA-1 FROM DATE.
        ACCEPT DATE-WORK-AREA-2 FROM DAY.
        ACCEPT DATE-WORK-AREA-3 FROM DAY-OF-WEEK.
   ```

   Indicate the stored values of each of the elementary items in the program. Assume a date of execution of March 16, 1993 (a Tuesday).

6. Given the following COBOL fragment:

```
01  DATE-WORK-AREA            PIC X(6).
01  EDITED-DATE.
    05  EDIT-MONTH            PIC XX.
    05  FILLER                PIC X     VALUE '/'.
    05  EDIT-DAY              PIC XX.
    05  FILLER                PIC X     VALUE '/'
    05  EDIT-YEAR             PIC XX.

            .
              .
                .

    ACCEPT DATE-WORK-AREA FROM DATE.
    MOVE DATE-WORK-AREA (3:2) TO EDIT-MONTH.
    MOVE DATE-WORK-AREA (5:2) TO EDIT-DAY.
    MOVE DATE-WORK-AREA (1:2) TO EDIT-YEAR.
```

Indicate the stored values of EDIT-MONTH, EDIT-DAY, and EDIT-YEAR. (Assume the same date as in the previous problem.)

7. Given the following COBOL definition:

```
01  GROUP-ITEM
    05  NUMERIC-FIELD-1          PIC 9(4).
    05  NUMERIC-FIELD-2          PIC 9(4).
    05  ALPHANUMERIC-FIELD-1     PIC X(15).
    05  ALPHANUMERIC-FIELD-2     PIC X(20).
```

What difference (if any) is there between the following statements?

a. INITIALIZE.
   and
   INITIALIZE GROUP-ITEM.

b. INITIALIZE GROUP-ITEM.
   and
   INITIALIZE GROUP-ITEM
       REPLACING NUMERIC DATA BY ZERO
                 ALPHANUMERIC DATA BY SPACES.

c. INITIALIZE GROUP-ITEM.
   and
   MOVE ZEROS TO NUMERIC-FIELD-1 NUMERIC-FIELD-2.
   MOVE SPACES TO ALPHANUMERIC-FIELD-1 ALPHANUMERIC-FIELD-2.

10

Screen I-O

CHAPTER OUTLINE

Overview
ACCEPT
  Programming Tip: The Use of COBOL Constants
DISPLAY
The Tuition Billing Program Revisited
  Programming Specifications
  Hierarchy Chart
  Pseudocode
  The Completed Program
  Programming Tip: The Hidden Power of the Alt Key
Car Validation and Billing Program
  Programming Specifications
  The Screen Section
  Hierarchy Chart
  Pseudocode
  The Completed Program
Limitations of COBOL-74
Summary
Fill-in
True/False
Problems

OBJECTIVES

After reading this chapter you will be able to:

- Discuss the concept of screen I-O versus the file-oriented approach of earlier chapters.

- Describe the ACCEPT and DISPLAY statements; discuss at least three optional clauses for each statement.

- Describe the SCREEN SECTION and indicate why its use may be preferable to individual ACCEPT and DISPLAY statements.

- Differentiate between the background and foreground colors; implement a color scheme using ACCEPT and DISPLAY statements and/or the Screen Section.

- Describe how interactive data validation is implemented in a screen I-O program; contrast this technique to the batch-oriented procedure in Chapter 8.

OVERVIEW

The proliferation of the PC has increased the importance of screen I-O, whereby input to a program is received from the keyboard and output is displayed on the monitor. The specific options (color, highlighting, positioning, and so on) vary according to the particular keyboard or monitor (display terminal) and are *not* part of the COBOL-85 standard. Virtually all compilers, however, include these capabilities as an *extension* to the 85 standard, and hence we do our best to describe them in general fashion. The syntax is that of COBOL97 which accompanies the text. This syntax meets the X-Open standard. In this chapter we show the traditional screen I-O capabilities of COBOL. We recognize, however, that the character-based screens that result seem somewhat primitive compared to the Windows interfaces of other languages. Modern COBOL compilers with their assorted tools provide ways to generate Windows interfaces to COBOL. We do not attempt to demonstrate any of those tools, since they are proprietary and not yet standard extensions to COBOL. However, in Appendix B you can see how to build a Windows interface using Visual Basic and link it to a COBOL program.

The chapter begins with the ACCEPT and DISPLAY statements that are used for low-volume input and output and that reference specific line and column positions. Both statements contain an abundance of optional clauses that are illustrated in a final version of the tuition-billing program that first appeared in Chapter 5.

The second half of the chapter focuses on the Screen Section to define an entire screen as opposed to individual lines. We combine the data validation and reporting programs of Chapters 8 and 9 to produce an interactive program that validates data as it is entered, and produces an on-screen result.

Accept

The **ACCEPT** statement enables data to be entered in specific positions according to a precise format. The statement contains a required identifier—that is, a data name to hold the input data, followed by optional clauses that can be entered in any order.

As indicated, the specific implementation for screen I-O is not defined in the COBOL-85 standard, but has been proposed as an extension to that standard. Our examples follow the syntax of COBOL97 that accompanies this text. Consider:

```
ACCEPT identifier [AT]

   [LINE NUMBER {identifier-1}]  [{COLUMN}  NUMBER {identifier-2}]
                {integer-1  }     {COL   }         {integer-2  }

   [WITH [AUTO] [BACKGROUND-COLOR IS integer-3] [BELL] [BLINK]

   [FOREGROUND-COLOR IS integer-4] [HIGHLIGHT] [SECURE] [REVERSE-VIDEO]

   [{LEFT-JUSTIFY }  {SPACE-FILL}  [TRAILING SIGN] [UNDERLINE] [UPDATE]]
    {RIGHT-JUSTIFY}  {ZERO-FILL }
```

The **LINE** and **COLUMN** clauses provide the location for the data. (The typical screen displays 25 lines of 80 columns.) Both clauses are optional with default actions as follows. Omission of the LINE clause defaults to line one if a previous screen element has not been defined, or to the existing line otherwise. Omission of the COLUMN clause defaults to column one if the LINE clause is also specified, and to the next column (after the last screen element) if the LINE clause is also omitted.

The **BACKGROUND-COLOR** and **FOREGROUND-COLOR** clauses specify the colors of the field, the FOREGROUND-COLOR being the color of the text. Any of the eight colors specified in Table 10.1 may be used. COBOL97 requires that an integer or a **SYMBOLIC-CONSTANT** be used to designate the color. (See the Programming Tip on how to establish SYMBOLIC-CONSTANTS.) The default color for the background is black, with white as the default for the foreground.

P R O G R A M M I N G   T I P

Special Names Section and Symbolic Constants to Specify Color Names

In Fujitsu's version of the Screen Section, the ACCEPT and DISPLAY verbs require the use of an integer literal to specify BACKGROUND-COLOR and FOREGROUND-COLOR. Specifying colors by number and not by name can be confusing. Fortunately, COBOL provides a way to associate a name with a value. The Configuration Section of the Environment Division allows for a paragraph called **SPECIAL-NAMES**. This paragraph allows the assignment of names to particular values using the **SYMBOLIC CONSTANT** clause. The following example shows how to assign color names to integer values.

```
ENVIRONMENT DIVISION.
CONFIGURATION SECTION.
SPECIAL-NAMES.
SYMBOLIC CONSTANT

        BLACK                       IS    0
        BLUE                        IS    1
        GREEN                       IS    2
        CYAN                        IS    3
        RED                         IS    4
        MAGENTA                     IS    5
        BROWN                       IS    6
        WHITE                       IS    7.
```
The Symbolic Constant clause does not take a period until all of the constants are specified. Hence, the period comes after the definition of WHITE.

TABLE 10.1   Foreground and Background Colors

Integer	Color
0	Black
1	Blue
2	Green
3	Cyan
4	Red
5	Magenta
6	Brown
7	White

The **AUTO** clause terminates the ACCEPT statement when the last character in the data item has been entered; the user does not have to press the return key for processing to continue. If, however, multiple data names are entered into the same ACCEPT statement, the AUTO clause moves the cursor to the first character of the next item.

The **HIGHLIGHT**, **REVERSE-VIDEO**, **BLINK**, and **UNDERLINE** clauses are used for emphasis, and their intended effects are apparent: BLINK causes characters to blink on and off, UNDERLINE underlines each character as it is displayed on the screen, and HIGHLIGHT displays a field at its highest intensity. The REVERSE-VIDEO clause displays light characters on a dark background; that is, the characters are dark and the area surrounding the characters is light. The **BELL** clause sounds the system's audio tone when the referenced data item is processed during the execution of the ACCEPT statement.

The **ZERO-FILL** option displays a numeric item with high-order zeros, whereas the (default) **SPACE-FILL** clause displays data with zero suppression. The **RIGHT-JUSTIFY** clause makes operator-keyed characters align in the rightmost character position of the field and is for elementary items only. **LEFT-JUSTIFY** (the default) is for documentation only and has no effect. The SPACE-FILL, ZERO-FILL, LEFT-JUSTIFY, and RIGHT-JUSTIFY clauses are allowed only for elementary items.

The **UPDATE** option displays the initial value of the data item before the operator is prompted for new input, and if no new data are entered, the initial data are treated as though they were operator keyed. UPDATE is not allowed for a numeric-edited item.

The **SECURE** clause prevents the accepted data item from appearing on the screen and is useful in implementing *password protection* and/or other security considerations.

Display

The **DISPLAY** statement was introduced in Chapter 3 in conjunction with top-down testing and referenced again in Chapter 6 for use in debugging. In both instances the simplest form of the statement was used at strategic points in a program, to display messages and/or intermediate results to help monitor program execution. The DISPLAY statement also has many additional options to enhance its output. Consider:

$$\underline{\text{DISPLAY}} \begin{Bmatrix} \text{identifier-1} \\ \text{literal-1} \end{Bmatrix}$$

$$\left[\text{AT } \underline{\text{LINE}} \text{ NUMBER} \begin{Bmatrix} \text{identifier-2} \\ \text{integer-1} \end{Bmatrix} \right] \left[\underline{\text{COLUMN}} \text{ NUMBER} \begin{Bmatrix} \text{identifier-3} \\ \text{integer-2} \end{Bmatrix} \right]$$

$$\left[\underline{\text{WITH}} \left[\underline{\text{BACKGROUND-COLOR}} \text{ IS integer-3} \right] \left[\underline{\text{BELL}} \right] \left[\underline{\text{BLINK}} \right] \right.$$

$$\left[\underline{\text{FOREGROUND-COLOR}} \text{ IS integer-4} \right] \left[\underline{\text{HIGHLIGHT}} \right] \left[\underline{\text{REVERSE-VIDEO}} \right]$$

$$\left. \left[\underline{\text{UNDERLINE}} \right] \left[\text{BLANK} \begin{Bmatrix} \underline{\text{SCREEN}} \\ \underline{\text{LINE}} \end{Bmatrix} \right] \right]$$

Many of the clauses in the DISPLAY statement have been explained in conjunction with the ACCEPT statement; for example, you can use the LINE and COLUMN clauses to control the specific position where the displayed output is to appear. You can also emphasize the displayed message by blinking, beeping, underlining, or reverse video. You can (on a color monitor) implement a variety of color schemes for both the foreground (text) and background.

The DISPLAY statement also enables you to clear all or a portion of the screen prior to displaying a data element. The **BLANK SCREEN** clause clears the entire screen and leaves the cursor positioned in line 1, column 1. The **BLANK LINE** clause blanks the associated line beginning in column 1 unless a column is specified. Specification of either entry, BLANK SCREEN or BLANK LINE, also reactivates the default background and foreground colors.

The Tuition Billing Program Revisited

The tuition-billing program has appeared several times throughout the text. It was first presented in Chapter 3 in conjunction with structured methodology, used in Chapters 4 and 5 to introduce basic COBOL statements, and expanded in Chapter 7 to include editing characters. We continue now with one final version to illustrate screen I-O, whereby student data are accepted for one student at a time, after which the computed bill (for that student) is displayed on the monitor.

The programming specifications parallel the original problem statement on page 49 with minor modifications to reflect the interactive nature of screen I-O. Thus, unlike the original file-based program, which processed students until the input file was exhausted, the screen-based program accepts data for one student at a time, then asks the user whether data for another student are to be entered. The screen I-O program also imposes the requirement for a valid password prior to processing the first student, and it eliminates the calculation of university totals. The formal specifications follow in the usual format.

Programming Specifications

Program Name: Tuition Billing Program (Screen Version)

Narrative: This program modifies the specifications for the original tuition billing program to accommodate screen I-O. Incoming records are to be entered one at a time via the keyboard with computed results for each student displayed as they are calculated.

Screen Layouts: The password is to be masked and entered as per the screen in Figure 10.1a, student data are to be entered according to the screen in Figure 10.1b, and the computed results displayed as in Figure 10.1c.

Processing Requirements:

1. Develop an *interactive program* to accept student data, then compute and display the student's bill. The program is to execute continually until it receives a response indicating that no more students are to be processed.

2. The program is to check for a valid password prior to accepting data for the first student. (The password is COBOL in either all upper- or all lowercase letters) The user is allowed a maximum of two tries to enter the password correctly, after which the program is to terminate with an appropriate error message.

3. The specifications for computing an individual student's bill are the same as in the original program:
   a. Compute the individual bill as the sum of tuition, union fee, and activity fee, minus a scholarship (if any).
   b. The tuition is $200 per credit.
   c. The union fee is $25.
   d. The activity fee is based on the number of credits taken:

ACTIVITY FEE	CREDITS
$25	6 or less
$50	7–12
$75	more than 12

   e. Award a scholarship equal to the amount in the incoming record if the GPA is greater than 2.5.

4. The requirement to compute university totals has been deleted.

Figure 10.1 Tuition Billing Program (Screen I-O)

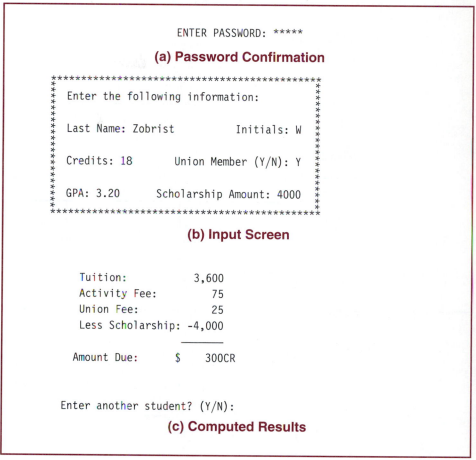

```
                        ENTER PASSWORD: *****
```
(a) Password Confirmation

```
**********************************************
*                                            *
*  Enter the following information:          *
*                                            *
*                                            *
*  Last Name: Zobrist        Initials: W     *
*                                            *
*                                            *
*  Credits: 18       Union Member (Y/N): Y   *
*                                            *
*                                            *
*  GPA: 3.20      Scholarship Amount: 4000   *
*                                            *
**********************************************
```
(b) Input Screen

```
     Tuition:            3,600
     Activity Fee:          75
     Union Fee:             25
     Less Scholarship:  -4,000
                        _____

     Amount Due:      $    300CR



   Enter another student? (Y/N):
```
(c) Computed Results

Hierarchy Chart

The hierarchy chart for the screen version of the tuition billing program is shown in Figure 10.2. The highest-level module, PROCESS-STUDENT-DATA, has four subordinates: PROCESS-PASSWORD, INPUT-STUDENT-INFO, COMPUTE-INDIVIDUAL-BILL, and DISPLAY-STUDENT-BILL. COMPUTE-STUDENT-BILL has four subordinates of its own: COMPUTE-TUITION, COMPUTE-UNION-FEE, COMPUTE-ACTIVITY-FEE, and COMPUTE-SCHOLARSHIP, all of which appeared in the original hierarchy chart.

The requirement to compute university totals has been dropped from the programming specifications, and thus the modules associated with this function that appeared in the original hierarchy chart (Figure 3.3) have been dropped from the current version.

Pseudocode

The pseudocode in Figure 10.3 contains two iterative structures, a DO UNTIL associated with obtaining the password, and a DO WHILE to process student data. The difference between the two is significant and was explained previously in Chapter 9 (see Figure 9.1). Recall, therefore, that the DO UNTIL structure tests the condition *after* executing the indicated statements and thus ensures that those statements are executed at least once. A DO WHILE, however, tests the condition *before* executing the statements, and hence the indicated statements need not be executed at all.

Figure 10.2   Hierarchy Chart for Tuition Billing Program (Screen Version)

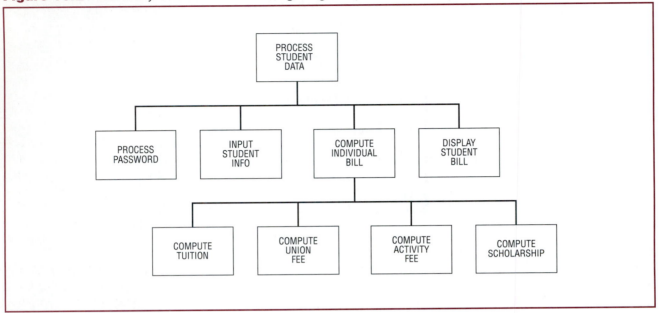

Figure 10.3   Pseudocode for Tuition Billing Program (Screen Version)

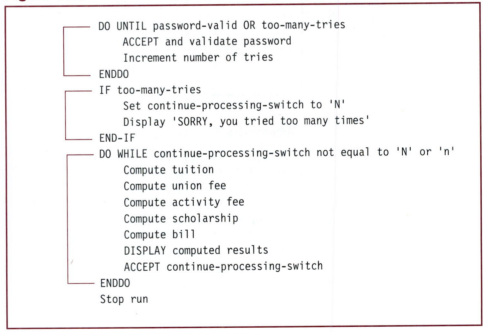

```
DO UNTIL password-valid OR too-many-tries
    ACCEPT and validate password
    Increment number of tries
ENDDO
IF too-many-tries
    Set continue-processing-switch to 'N'
    Display 'SORRY, you tried too many times'
END-IF
DO WHILE continue-processing-switch not equal to 'N' or 'n'
    Compute tuition
    Compute union fee
    Compute activity fee
    Compute scholarship
    Compute bill
    DISPLAY computed results
    ACCEPT continue-processing-switch
ENDDO
Stop run
```

The user must be given *at least* one try to enter the password and hence the DO UNTIL structure is used to accept and validate (reject) the user's entry. If the user fails to enter the correct password within the allocated number of tries, the continue-processing-switch will be set to 'N', which prevents the execution of statements within the DO WHILE loop; that is, the program terminates without processing a student record.

The Completed Program

The completed program is shown in Figure 10.4 and reflects the hierarchy chart and pseudocode just discussed. It is different from all previous programs in that input is received from the keyboard and output is displayed on the monitor. Thus, there are no files in this program, and hence no need for an Environment Division (and the associated SELECT statements), or for the File Section in the Data Division. The absence of all files also means that the Procedure Division does not contain the familiar OPEN, CLOSE, READ, and WRITE statements that were present in all previous programs.

All I-O is screen based and accomplished through ACCEPT and DISPLAY statements with LINE and COLUMN clauses to control the location of the displayed fields. Different colors are used for different areas of the screen as implemented through the COLOR clauses that appear throughout the program; the available colors are defined as data names in lines 9–16, then referenced as necessary in the various ACCEPT and DISPLAY statements.

The imposition of a password is accomplished through the in-line PERFORM statement in lines 73–82, which uses the TEST AFTER clause to give the user two chances to enter the password correctly. The SECURE clause, in the ACCEPT statement of lines 80 and 81, prevents the user's response from appearing on the screen, and the AUTO clause saves the user from having to press the return key. The BLANK SCREEN clause in line 77 clears the screen before requesting the password. The program accepts either COBOL or cobol as a valid password according to the 88-level entry in line 31; it will not, however, recognize a combination of upper- and lowercase letters.

Once a valid password has been entered, the program processes students one at a time through the in-line PERFORM statement in lines 65–69, which invokes three lower-level paragraphs for each student: 200-INPUT-STUDENT-INFO, 310-COMPUTE-INDIVIDUAL-BILL, and 500-DISPLAY-STUDENT-BILL. The latter paragraph ends by obtaining the user response regarding another student (lines 183–185). Note, too, the provision for both upper- and lowercase data entry as the CONTINUE-PROCESSING-SWITCH in line 65 is compared to both 'N' and 'n'.

The COBOL EVALUATE statement is much more powerful than CASE statements in other languages. Most languages can test a condition for only one variable at a time. The EVALUATE statement allows testing of several conditions at once. The ALSO clause separates the conditions in the EVALUATE portion and in the WHEN portion of the statement. Consider the following code portion from SCRNCARS.

```
EVALUATE REN-RETURNED-DAY     ALSO TRUE
    WHEN 1 THRU 29             ALSO ANY
        PERFORM 498-CLEAR-ERRORS
    WHEN 30 THRU 31            ALSO 31-DAY-MONTH
        PERFORM 498-CLEAR-ERRORS
    WHEN 30                    ALSO 30-DAY-MONTH
        PERFORM 498-CLEAR-ERRORS
    WHEN OTHER
        MOVE DAY-MSG TO ERROR-MESSAGE
        PERFORM 499-DISPLAY-ERROR-MESSAGE
END-EVALUATE
```

In this code segment, the program tests for valid days in a month (to keep things simple, we do not test for leap years). The first condition tested is the value of REN-RETURN-DAY. The second condition follows the ALSO and tests whether a second condition is TRUE. Look at the first WHEN clause. The code tests to see if the return day is between 1 and 29. For our purposes, days in that range are valid for all months. Thus, if the day is within the range, we do not have to test a second condition and the ANY operator gives an automatic TRUE.

The second WHEN tests for valid days in a 31-day month. Here the range of 30 through 31 is specified (1 to 29 were processed in the first WHEN statement). The second condition uses the 88-level condition 31-DAY-MONTH to assure that the day is valid for a 31-day month. In other words, the day has to be either 30 or 31 and the month has to have up to 31 days.

If the day and month combination fails both of the previous tests, the third WHEN tests for the day value 30 and a 30-day month.

Finally, if all tests fail, the WHEN OTHER condition handles error processing.

Proper use of the EVALUATE statement can reduce the need for complex and nested IF statements.

Figure 10.4 Screen Version of Tuition Billing Program

```
1          IDENTIFICATION DIVISION.
2          PROGRAM-ID.    SCRNTUIT.
3          AUTHOR.        CAROL VAZQUEZ VILLAR.
4
5          ENVIRONMENT DIVISION.
6          CONFIGURATION SECTION.
7          SPECIAL-NAMES.
8              SYMBOLIC CONSTANT.
9                  BLACK              IS 0
10                 BLUE               IS 1
11                 GREEN              IS 2
12                 CYAN               IS 3
13                 RED                IS 4
14                 MAGENTA            IS 5
15                 BROWN              IS 6
16                 WHITE              IS 7
17
18         DATA DIVISION.
19         WORKING-STORAGE SECTION.
20         01  STUDENT-DATA.
21             05  STU-NAME.
22                 10  STU-LAST-NAME    PIC X(15).
23                 10  STU-INITIALS     PIC XX.
24             05  STU-CREDITS          PIC 9(2).
25             05  STU-UNION-MEMBER     PIC X.
26             05  STU-SCHOLARSHIP      PIC 9(4).
27             05  STU-GPA              PIC 9V99.
28
29         01  PASSWORD-VARIABLES.
30             05  PASSWORD-ENTERED     PIC X(5).
31                 88  VALID-PASSWORD              VALUE 'COBOL' 'cobol'.
32             05  TRIES-COUNTER        PIC 9.
33                 88  TOO-MANY-TRIES              VALUE 3.
34
35         01  CONTINUE-PROCESSING-SWITCH PIC X    VALUE 'Y'.
36
37         01  INDIVIDUAL-CALCULATIONS.
38             05  IND-TUITION          PIC 9(4)  VALUE ZEROS.
39             05  IND-ACTIVITY-FEE     PIC 9(2)  VALUE ZEROS.
40             05  IND-UNION-FEE        PIC 9(2)  VALUE ZEROS.
41             05  IND-SCHOLARSHIP      PIC 9(4)  VALUE ZEROS.
42             05  IND-BILL             PIC S9(6) VALUE ZEROS.
43
44         01  DISPLAY-CALCULATIONS.
45             05  DIS-TUITION          PIC Z,ZZ9.
46             05  DIS-ACTIVITY-FEE     PIC Z9.
47             05  DIS-UNION-FEE        PIC Z9.
48             05  DIS-SCHOLARSHIP      PIC Z,ZZ9.
49             05  DIS-BILL             PIC $ZZZ,ZZ9CR.
50
```

Colors are given mnemonic names for subsequent reference in Procedure Division

Figure 10.4 *(continued)*

```
51      01  CONSTANTS-AND-RATES.
52          05  PRICE-PER-CREDIT        PIC 9(3)  VALUE 200.
53          05  UNION-FEE               PIC 9(2)  VALUE 25.
54          05  ACTIVITY-FEES.
55              10  1ST-ACTIVITY-FEE    PIC 99    VALUE 25.
56              10  1ST-CREDIT-LIMIT    PIC 99    VALUE 6.
57              10  2ND-ACTIVITY-FEE    PIC 99    VALUE 50.
58              10  2ND-CREDIT-LIMIT    PIC 99    VALUE 12.
59              10  3RD-ACTIVITY-FEE    PIC 99    VALUE 75.
60          05  MINIMUM-SCHOLAR-GPA     PIC 9V9   VALUE 2.5.
61
62      PROCEDURE DIVISION.
63      000-PROCESS-STUDENT-DATA.
64          PERFORM 100-PROCESS-PASSWORD.
65          PERFORM UNTIL CONTINUE-PROCESSING-SWITCH = 'N' OR 'n'
66              PERFORM 200-INPUT-STUDENT-INFO
67              PERFORM 310-COMPUTE-INDIVIDUAL-BILL
68              PERFORM 500-DISPLAY-STUDENT-BILL
69          END-PERFORM.
70          STOP RUN.
71
72      100-PROCESS-PASSWORD.
73          PERFORM WITH TEST AFTER
74              VARYING TRIES-COUNTER FROM 1 BY 1
75              UNTIL VALID-PASSWORD OR TOO-MANY-TRIES
76                  DISPLAY 'ENTER PASSWORD: ' LINE 12 COLUMN 30
77                      WITH BLANK SCREEN
78                      FOREGROUND-COLOR BLACK
79                      BACKGROUND-COLOR WHITE
80                  ACCEPT PASSWORD-ENTERED LINE 12 COLUMN 46
81                      WITH REVERSE-VIDEO AUTO SECURE
82          END-PERFORM.
83          IF TOO-MANY-TRIES
84              MOVE 'N' TO CONTINUE-PROCESSING-SWITCH
85              DISPLAY 'SORRY, You tried too many times'
86                  LINE 24 COLUMN 22 WITH BLINK
87                  FOREGROUND-COLOR WHITE
88                  BACKGROUND-COLOR RED
89          END-IF.
90
91      200-INPUT-STUDENT-INFO.
92          DISPLAY ' ********************************************
93              AT LINE  2 COLUMN 5 WITH BLANK SCREEN HIGHLIGHT
94              FOREGROUND-COLOR CYAN
95              BACKGROUND-COLOR BLUE.
96          DISPLAY '* Enter the following information:          *'
97              AT LINE  3 COLUMN 5.
98          DISPLAY '*                                          *'
99              AT LINE  4 COLUMN  5.
100         DISPLAY '* Last Name:                    Initials:  *'
```

In-line PERFORM statement drives program (pointing to lines 65–69)

TEST AFTER clause ensures that in-line statements are executed at least once (pointing to lines 73–82)

Use of color in screen output (pointing to lines 87–88)

Figure 10.4 *(continued)*

```
101                AT LINE  5 COLUMN  5.
102          DISPLAY '*                                      *'
103                AT LINE  6 COLUMN  5.
104          DISPLAY '* Credits:         Union Member (Y/N):   *'
105                AT LINE  7 COLUMN  5.
106          DISPLAY '*                                      *'
107                AT LINE  8 COLUMN  5.
108          DISPLAY '*    GPA:             Scholarship Amount:   *'
109                AT LINE  9 COLUMN  5.
110          DISPLAY '******************************************'
111                AT LINE 10 COLUMN  5.
112          ACCEPT STU-LAST-NAME AT LINE 5 COLUMN 18.
113                WITH REVERSE-VIDEO.
114          ACCEPT STU-INITIALS AT LINE 5 COLUMN 45.
115          ACCEPT STU-CREDITS AT LINE 7 COLUMN 16.
116          ACCEPT STU-UNION-MEMBER AT LINE 7 COLUMN 45 WITH AUTO.
117          ACCEPT STU-GPA AT LINE 9 COLUMN 16 WITH AUTO.
118          ACCEPT STU-SCHOLARSHIP AT LINE 9 COLUMN 45.
119
120      310-COMPUTE-INDIVIDUAL-BILL.
121          PERFORM 410-COMPUTE-TUITION.
122          PERFORM 430-COMPUTE-UNION-FEE.
123          PERFORM 460-COMPUTE-ACTIVITY-FEE.
124          PERFORM 490-COMPUTE-SCHOLARSHIP.
125          COMPUTE IND-BILL = IND-TUITION + IND-UNION-FEE +
126              IND-ACTIVITY-FEE - IND-SCHOLARSHIP
127              SIZE ERROR DISPLAY 'SIZE ERROR FOR INDIVIDUAL BILL'
128          END-COMPUTE.
129
130      410-COMPUTE-TUITION.
131          COMPUTE IND-TUITION = PRICE-PER-CREDIT * STU-CREDITS
132              SIZE ERROR DISPLAY 'SIZE ERROR FOR INDIVIDUAL TUITION'
133          END-COMPUTE.
134
135      430-COMPUTE-UNION-FEE.
136          IF STU-UNION-MEMBER = 'Y' or 'y'
137              MOVE UNION-FEE TO IND-UNION-FEE
138          ELSE
139              MOVE ZERO TO IND-UNION-FEE
140          END-IF.
141
142      460-COMPUTE-ACTIVITY-FEE.
143          EVALUATE TRUE
144              WHEN STU-CREDITS <= 1ST-CREDIT-LIMIT
145                  MOVE 1ST-ACTIVITY-FEE TO IND-ACTIVITY-FEE
146              WHEN STU-CREDITS > 1ST-CREDIT-LIMIT
147                  AND STU-CREDITS <= 2ND-CREDIT-LIMIT
148                      MOVE 2ND-ACTIVITY-FEE TO IND-ACTIVITY-FEE
149              WHEN STU-CREDITS > 2ND-CREDIT-LIMIT
150                  MOVE 3RD-ACTIVITY-FEE TO IND-ACTIVITY-FEE
```

IF statement checks for upper and lower case

Figure 10.4   *(continued)*

```
151             WHEN OTHER
152                 DISPLAY 'INVALID CREDITS FOR: ' STU-NAME
153         END-EVALUATE.
154
155     490-COMPUTE-SCHOLARSHIP.
156         IF STU-GPA > MINIMUM-SCHOLAR-GPA
157             MOVE STU-SCHOLARSHIP TO IND-SCHOLARSHIP
158         ELSE
159             MOVE ZERO TO IND-SCHOLARSHIP
160         END-IF.
161
162     500-DISPLAY-STUDENT-BILL.
163         MOVE IND-TUITION TO DIS-TUITION.
164         DISPLAY 'Tuition:' AT LINE 12 COLUMN 10.
165         DISPLAY DIS-TUITION AT LINE 12 COLUMN 29.
166
167         MOVE IND-ACTIVITY-FEE TO DIS-ACTIVITY-FEE.
168         DISPLAY 'Activity Fee:' AT LINE 13 COLUMN 10.
169         DISPLAY DIS-ACTIVITY-FEE AT LINE 13 COLUMN 32.
170
171         MOVE IND-UNION-FEE TO DIS-UNION-FEE.
172         DISPLAY 'Union Fee:' AT LINE 14 COLUMN 10.
173         DISPLAY DIS-UNION-FEE AT LINE 14 COLUMN 32.
174
175         MOVE IND-SCHOLARSHIP TO DIS-SCHOLARSHIP.
176         DISPLAY 'Less Scholarship: -' AT LINE 15 COLUMN 10.
177         DISPLAY DIS-SCHOLARSHIP AT LINE 15 COLUMN 29.
178
179         DISPLAY '--------' AT LINE 16 COLUMN 27.
180         MOVE IND-BILL TO DIS-BILL.
181         DISPLAY 'Amount Due:' AT LINE 17 COLUMN  9.
182         DISPLAY DIS-BILL AT LINE 17 COLUMN 26.
183         DISPLAY 'Enter another student? (Y/N):'
184             AT LINE 20 COLUMN 7.
185         ACCEPT CONTINUE-PROCESSING-SWITCH AT LINE 20 COLUMN 37.
```

LINE and COLUMN clause controls screen output

Obtains response for next student

Car Validation and Billing Program

The concept of *data validation* was introduced in Chapter 8 in the form of a stand-alone edit program that processed a file of incoming transactions, rejected invalid transactions with appropriate error message(s), and wrote valid transactions to a new file; the latter was then input to a reporting program that was developed in Chapter 9. This chapter combines the data validation and reporting programs into a single program to validate data as they are entered and produce an on-screen result.

   The biggest difference between this program and its predecessor(s) is that the data are validated *interactively* as they are entered, as opposed to the *batch-oriented* approach in Chapter 8. The advantage of the interactive program is that the user is given the opportunity to correct the invalid transaction at the time the error is detected, as opposed to receiving a report listing the errors. Realize, however, that interactive (screen-based) programs are restricted to low-volume applications and that their execution is far more time consuming than programs that are file-driven. Specifications follow in the usual format.

Programming Specifications

Program Name: Car Validation and Billing Program (Screen Version)

Narrative: This program combines the specifications for data validation and reporting as presented earlier in Chapters 8 and 9. The fields in each incoming transaction are accepted and validated one at time, after which the bill is computed and displayed on the screen. Valid transactions are also written to an output file.

Screen Layout: See Figure 10.5 (page 280).

Processing Requirements:

1. Develop an interactive program to accept and validate car rental data, then compute and display the associated bill. The program is to execute continually until it receives a response indicating that no more records are to be processed.

2. Each incoming field is to be validated as it is entered; that is, the user cannot move to the next field until valid data have been entered in the current field. The requirements for validation were presented in Chapter 8 and are summarized below. Each transaction is to be checked for the following:

   a. A numeric contract number.

   b. The presence of both a first and last name; a middle initial is not required, but if present, the initial must be alphabetic.

   c. A valid car type where the code is one of five values; E, C, M, F, or L.

   d. A valid date in which the month is between 1 and 12, the day is consistent with the month (e.g., April 31 should be rejected), and the date is less than or equal to the system date.

   e. A valid number of days rented that is greater than zero and less than or equal to 35.

   f. Numeric values for the mileage in and out; and further, that the mileage reported when the car is turned in is greater than the mileage when the car was taken out. The number of miles driven must also pass a reasonableness test of 10 miles or more per day

   g. A numeric mileage rate less than or equal to 50 cents per day.

   h. An insurance field of either Y or N.

3. Write the validated transaction to a file as per the original program in Chapter 8.

4. Calculate the customer's bill after all fields have been validated. The amount due is a function of car type, days rented, miles driven, mileage rate, and insurance.

   a. The mileage rate is different for each customer and appears as a field in the incoming transaction; the mileage total is the mileage rate times the number of miles driven.

   b. The daily rate is a function of the type of car rented. Economy cars cost $15 a day, compact cars $20 a day, mid-size cars $24 a day, full-size cars $28 a day, and luxury cars $35 a day. The daily total is the daily rate times the number of days rented.

   c. Insurance is optional at $10.50, regardless of the type of car rented.

d. A customer's total bill consists of the mileage total, daily total, and insurance total as described in parts (a), (b), and (c).

5. Display the computed bill on the screen as per the screen layout of Figure 10.5.

6. The requirement to compute totals has been deleted.

The Screen Section

The tuition billing program illustrated the use of ACCEPT and DISPLAY statements within the Procedure Division. This approach is useful to display individual lines and/or to accept a limited number of fields as input, but awkward when you need to fill an entire screen. A second limitation of individual ACCEPT and DISPLAY statements is that they are scattered throughout the Procedure Division, making it difficult to reproduce consistent screens from program to program within a system.

The **Screen Section** specifies the characteristics of an entire screen in the Data Division, then accepts or displays that screen in a single statement in the Procedure Division. The Screen Section is physically the *last* section in the Data Division, and its structure is similar to that of the File and/or Working-Storage Sections. Consider:

$$
\text{level-number} \left\{ \begin{array}{l} \text{screen-name} \\ \text{FILLER} \end{array} \right\} \left[\text{BLANK} \left\{ \begin{array}{l} \underline{\text{SCREEN}} \\ \underline{\text{LINE}} \end{array} \right\} \right] \left[\text{BELL} \right] \left[\text{BLINK} \right]
$$

$$
\left[\text{HIGHLIGHT} \right] \left[\text{REVERSE-VIDEO} \right] \left[\underline{\text{UNDERLINE}} \right]
$$

$$
\left[\underline{\text{BACKGROUND}} \ \text{COLOR IS} \left\{ \begin{array}{l} \text{integer-1} \\ \text{data-name-1} \end{array} \right\} \right] \left[\underline{\text{FOREGROUND}} - \text{COLOR IS} \left\{ \begin{array}{l} \text{integer-2} \\ \text{data-name-2} \end{array} \right\} \right]
$$

$$
\left[\underline{\text{LINE}} \ \text{NUMBER} \left\{ \begin{array}{l} \text{identifier-1} \\ \text{integer-3} \end{array} \right\} \right] \left[\underline{\text{COLUMN}} \ \text{NUMBER} \left\{ \begin{array}{l} \text{identifier-2} \\ \text{integer-4} \end{array} \right\} \right]
$$

$$
\left[\underline{\text{VALUE}} \ \text{IS literal-1} \right]
$$

$$
\left\{ \begin{array}{l} \underline{\text{PICTURE}} \\ \underline{\text{PIC}} \end{array} \right\} \ \text{IS} \left\{ \begin{array}{l} \text{FROM identifier-4 TO identifier-5} \\ \underline{\text{USING}} \ \text{identifier-6} \end{array} \right\}
$$

$$
\left[\underline{\text{AUTO}} \right] \left[\underline{\text{SECURE}} \right]
$$

An appreciation for the Screen Section can best be gained by viewing sample screens and the associated COBOL entries. Consider now Figure 10.5, which displays three screens from the car validation and billing program to be developed later in the chapter. Figure 10.5a displays the opening screen, consisting entirely of prompts for the various fields. Figure 15.5b displays a completed screen for Janice Vogel with valid entries in all fields, and Figure 10.5c displays the computed results.

The screens are produced in the sequence shown; that is, the system displays the opening screen of Figure 10.5a and the user enters the fields one at a time. Each field is validated as it is entered; the user cannot move to the next field until he or she has entered a valid value for the current field. Once all fields have been entered the system computes the bill and displays the results.

An abbreviated Screen Section, extracted from the completed program at the end of the chapter, is shown in Figure 10.6. The entries in the Screen Section are similar to those in the File or Working-Storage Section; that is, they consist of group items divided into elementary items. The entry at the 01 level must specify a screen-name—for example, OPENING-SCREEN and UPDATE-SCREEN in Figure 10.6. The

Figure 10.5   Screen Layouts

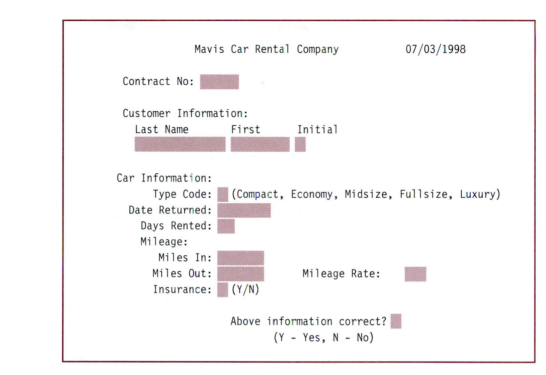

(a) Opening Screen (No Data Entered)

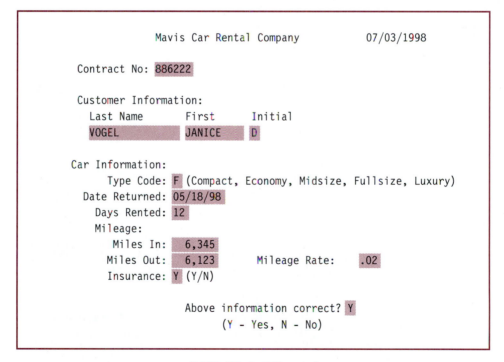

(b) Validated Record

Figure 10.5 *(continued)*

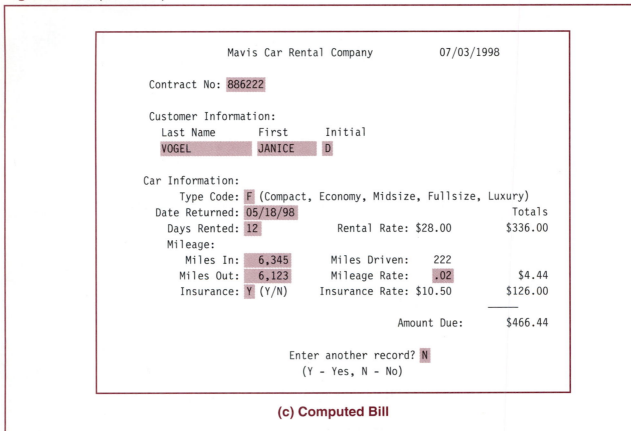

                    Mavis Car Rental Company   07/03/1998

         Contract No: 886222

         Customer Information:
           Last Name   First   Initial
           VOGEL   JANICE   D

         Car Information:
                 Type Code: F (Compact, Economy, Midsize, Fullsize, Luxury)
               Date Returned: 05/18/98   Totals
               Days Rented: 12   Rental Rate: $28.00 $336.00
               Mileage:
                 Miles In: 6,345   Miles Driven: 222
                 Miles Out: 6,123   Mileage Rate: .02 $4.44
                 Insurance: Y (Y/N)   Insurance Rate: $10.50 $126.00
                                                                 _____

                                                 Amount Due: $466.44

                            Enter another record? N
                            (Y - Yes, N - No)

(c) Computed Bill

Figure 10.6 Abbreviated Screen Section

```
SCREEN SECTION.
01  OPENING-SCREEN
    BLANK SCREEN
    BACKGROUND-COLOR BLUE  FOREGROUND-COLOR WHITE.
    05  SCREEN-PROMPTS.
      .

        .
        10  LINE  3 COLUMN  7  VALUE 'Contract No:'.
        10  LINE  5 COLUMN  7  VALUE 'Customer Information:'.
        10  LINE  6 COLUMN  9  VALUE 'Last Name'.
        10           COLUMN 25  VALUE 'First'.
        10           COLUMN 36  VALUE 'Initial'.
        10  LINE  9 COLUMN  6  VALUE 'Car Information:'.
        10  LINE 10 COLUMN 12  VALUE 'Type Code:'.

        .
    05  SCREEN-INPUTS.
        10  SCR-CONTRACT-NO    PIC 9(6) USING REN-CONTRACT-NO
            LINE  3 COLUMN 20  REVERSE-VIDEO.
```

Figure 10.6 *(continued)*

```
           10  SCR-LAST-NAME     PIC X(15) USING REN-LAST-NAME
               LINE  7 COLUMN  9  REVERSE-VIDEO.
           10  SCR-FIRST-NAME    PIC X(10) USING REN-FIRST-NAME
               LINE  7 COLUMN 25  REVERSE-VIDEO.
           10  SCR-INITIAL       PIC X     USING REN-INITIAL
               LINE  7 COLUMN 36  REVERSE-VIDEO.
           10  SCR-CAR-TYPE      PIC X     USING REN-CAR-TYPE
               LINE 10 COLUMN 23  REVERSE-VIDEO AUTO.

            .
            .
    01  UPDATE-SCREEN.
        05  LINE 11 COLUMN 67        VALUE 'Totals' HIGHLIGHT.
        05  LINE 12 COLUMN 38        VALUE 'Rental Rate:' HIGHLIGHT.
        05  UPD-DAILY-RATE           PIC $$$9.99   FROM IND-DAILY-RATE
            LINE 12 COLUMN 50        HIGHLIGHT.
        05  UPD-DAILY-TOTAL          PIC $$$,$$9.99 FROM IND-DAILY-TOTAL
                    COLUMN 63        HIGHLIGHT.
        05  LINE 14 COLUMN 37        VALUE 'Miles Driven:' HIGHLIGHT.
        05  UPD-MILES-DRIVEN         PIC ZZZ,ZZ9   FROM IND-MILES-DRIVEN
                    COLUMN 50        HIGHLIGHT.
        05  UPD-MILEAGE-TOTAL        PIC $$,$$9.99
                                     FROM IND-MILEAGE-TOTAL
            LINE 15 COLUMN 64        HIGHLIGHT.
        05  LINE 16 COLUMN 35        VALUE 'Insurance Rate:' HIGHLIGHT.
        05  UPD-INSURANCE-RATE       PIC $$9.99 FROM INSURANCE-RATE
            LINE 16 COLUMN 51        HIGHLIGHT.
        05  UPD-INSURANCE-TOTAL      PIC $$,$$9.99
                                     FROM IND-INSURANCE-TOTAL
                    COLUMN 64        HIGHLIGHT.
        05  LINE 17 COLUMN 63        VALUE '----------' HIGHLIGHT.
        05  LINE 18 COLUMN 48        VALUE 'Amount Due: ' HIGHLIGHT.
        05  UPD-AMOUNT-DUE           PIC $$$$,$$9.99 FROM IND-AMOUNT-DUE
                    COLUMN 62        HIGHLIGHT.
```

BLANK SCREEN clause should be specified at the 01-level. The screen (data) name is optional at any other level. For example, the first 05-level entry includes a data name, SCREEN-PROMPTS, which is divided into multiple elementary items, each of which omits the data name.

If a screen (data) name or FILLER is specified, then it must be the first word following the level name. The remaining clauses can appear in any order, but each elementary item must contain at least one of the following clauses: BELL, BLANK LINE, BLANK SCREEN, COLUMN, LINE, PICTURE, or VALUE. (The VALUE and PICTURE clauses are mutually exclusive in the Screen Section.) Any clause that appears on a group item applies to all elementary items within the group where it is allowed. If the same clause is specified at multiple levels in the hierarchy, the *lowest* level takes effect. The various optional clauses are illustrated in Figure 10.6 and function as explained previously in conjunction with the ACCEPT and DISPLAY statements.

Note, too, the correspondence between the line and column positioning within SCREEN-PROMPTS and SCREEN-INPUT; for example, a prompt for 'Contract No:' appears on line 3 and extends from column 7 to 18; the data name SCR-CONTRACT-NO is subsequently accepted in column 20 on the same line. The action of the LINE and COLUMN clauses is the same as with individual ACCEPT and DISPLAY statements: omission of the LINE clause defaults to the same line as the previously specified element. Thus the prompt for last name is displayed on line 6, column 9 followed by the prompt for first name in column 25 of the same line, followed by the initial in column 36 of the same line.

The Screen Section makes possible the definition of multiple screens within the same program as implied by the screen in Figure 10.5c, in which the computed results are displayed on the same (expanded) screen as the original inputs. Thus the Screen Section in Figure 10.6 contains a second 01 entry, UPDATE-SCREEN, with multiple entries that display both text and computed information; the latter is displayed after all data have been entered and the bill has been computed.

The **TO** clause in a screen description entry indicates an input field; the **FROM** clause indicates an output field. The **USING** clause—for example, USING REN-CONTRACT-NO—is equivalent to the combination of FROM and TO clauses each specifying the same data name. In this instance the screen input in line 3, column 20 is accepted from and/or moved to the data name SCR-CONTRACT-NO, which is defined elsewhere in the Data Division.

Hierarchy Chart

The hierarchy chart in Figure 10.7 combines the functions of the data validation and reporting programs of Chapters 8 and 9. The second-level module, PROCESS-RENTAL-RECORDS, effectively drives the program and contains subordinates to VALIDATE-RENTAL-RECORD, COMPUTE-IND-BILL, WRITE-VALID-RECORD, and INPUT-SCREEN-CONFIRM.

The validation module, VALIDATE-RENTAL-RECORD, contains a lower-level module for every validity check (identical to those in Chapter 8), each of which calls a common routine that displays the indicated error message or clears the error line. The computation module, COMPUTE-IND-BILL, has three subordinates of its own: COMPUTE-MILEAGE-TOTAL, COMPUTE-DAILY-TOTAL, and COMPUTE-INSURANCE-TOTAL. The remaining modules under PROCESS-RENTAL-RECORDS write the validated record, then determine whether another record is to be processed.

Pseudocode

The pseudocode in Figure 10.8 is driven by an overall loop to process transactions until the user elects to quit. Each new transaction begins with validation of individual fields, which continues until the user indicates that the entire screen is accurate; that is, the user is given the opportunity to change any field that has been previously validated. Within this loop, each field is validated interactively; that is, the user cannot enter the next field until the current field has been accepted as valid.

Once all fields have been entered and validated, the program moves to the computation of the bill according to the specifications presented earlier. The computed bill is displayed on the screen, the validated record is written to a valid record file, and the user is given the opportunity to process another transaction.

Figure 10.7 Hierarchy Chart

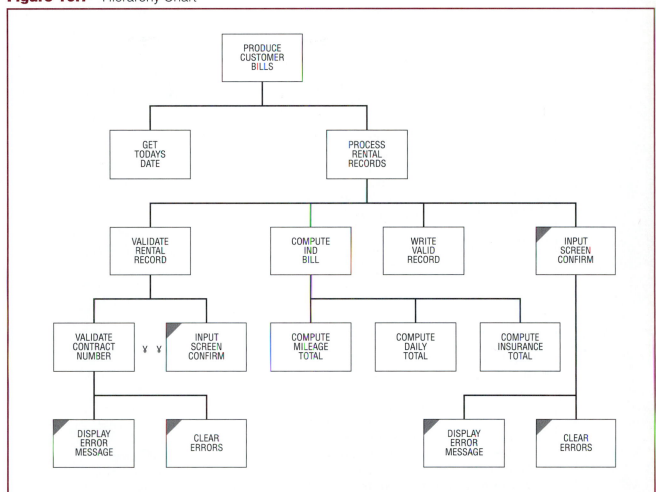

Figure 10.8 Pseudocode for Car Validation and Billing Program (Screen Version)

```
Open valid-rental-file
Get today's date
DO WHILE another record is desired
    DO UNTIL information correct
        DO UNTIL valid-field-switch = spaces
            Accept contract number
            IF contract number = zeros
                Display 'Contract number must not be zero'
                Move 'NO' to valid-field-switch
            ELSE
                Move spaces to valid-field-switch
            ENDIF
        ENDDO
```

Figure 10.8   *(continued)*

```
            DO UNTIL valid-field-switch = spaces
                Accept last-name
                IF last-name = spaces
                    Display 'Error - Missing last name'
                    Move 'NO' to valid-field-switch
                ELSE
                    Move spaces to valid-field-switch
                ENDIF
            ENDDO
                . . . Validation checks for remaining fields
            Display information correct message
            DO UNTIL valid confirmation ("Y", "y", "N", or "n")
                Accept confirm-switch
                IF valid confirmation
                    Clear previous error message
                ELSE
                    Display 'Must be "Y" or "N"'
                ENDIF
            ENDDO
        ENDDO
        Compute miles driven = miles in - miles out
        DO CASE
            Car Type E - Move economy rate to mileage rate
            Car Type C - Move compact rate to mileage rate
            Car Type M - Move midsize to mileage rate
            Car Type F - Move fullsize rate to mileage rate
            Car Type L - Move luxury rate to mileage rate
        END CASE
        Compute mileage total = miles driven * mileage rate
        Compute daily total = days rented * daily rate
        IF insurance taken
            Compute insurance = insurance rate * days rented
        END-IF
        Compute total bill = mileage amount + daily amount + insurance
        Display computed bill
        Write valid record to valid record file
        Display Another record message
        DO UNTIL valid confirmation ("Y", "y", "N", or "n")
            Accept confirm-switch
            IF valid confirmation
                Clear previous error message
            ELSE
                Display 'Must be "Y" or "N"'
            ENDIF
        ENDDO
    ENDDO
    Close valid-rental-file
    Stop run
```

The Completed Program

The completed program is shown in Figure 10.9 and includes many statements from the earlier programs in Chapters 8 and 9. The most significant difference is that I-O is screen based, with transactions entered via the keyboard and computed results displayed on the monitor, as provided through the extended Screen Section (lines 145–256). The program also creates a VALID-RENTAL-FILE as output, illustrating that the same program can contain both a File Section and a Screen Section.

Figure 10.9 Car Validation and Billing Program

```
1           IDENTIFICATION DIVISION.
2           PROGRAM-ID.     SCRNCARS.
3           AUTHOR.         CVV.
4
5           ENVIRONMENT DIVISION.
6           CONFIGURATION SECTION.
7           SPECIAL-NAMES.
8               SYMBOLIC CONSTANT.
9                   BLACK           IS 0
10                  BLUE            IS 1
11                  GREEN           IS 2
12                  CYAN            IS 3
13                  RED             IS 4
14                  MAGENTA         IS 5
15                  BROWN           IS 6
16                  WHITE           IS 7
17
18          INPUT-OUTPUT SECTION.
19          FILE-CONTROL.
20              SELECT VALID-RENTAL-FILE     ASSIGN TO SYSOUT
21                  ORGANIZATION IS LINE SEQUENTIAL.
22
23          DATA DIVISION.
24          FILE SECTION.
25          FD  VALID-RENTAL-FILE.
26          01  VALID-RENTAL-RECORD      PIC X(57).
27
28          WORKING-STORAGE SECTION.
29          01  RENTAL-RECORD-IN.
30              05  REN-CONTRACT-NO       PIC 9(6).
31              05  REN-NAME.
32                  10  REN-LAST-NAME     PIC X(15).
33                  10  REN-FIRST-NAME    PIC X(10).
34                  10  REN-INITIAL       PIC X.
35              05  REN-RETURNED-DATE.
36                  10  REN-RETURNED-CENT    PIC 9(2).                Allows for Y2K
37                  10  REN-RETURNED-YEAR    PIC 9(2).
38                      88  TWENTIETH-CENTURY       VALUES 90 THRU 99.
39                  10  REN-RETURNED-MONTH   PIC 9(2).
40                      88  VALID-MONTHS          VALUES 1 THRU 12.
41                      88  FEBRUARY              VALUE 2.
```

Figure 10.9   *(continued)*

```
42                   88  30-DAY-MONTH          VALUES 4 6 9 11.
43                   88  31-DAY-MONTH          VALUES 1 3 5 7 8 10 12.
44              10  REN-RETURNED-DAY    PIC 9(2).
45          05  REN-CAR-TYPE           PIC X.
46              88  VALID-CAR-TYPES       VALUES 'E' 'C' 'M' 'F' 'L'.
47          05  REN-DAYS-RENTED        PIC 99.
48              88  ZERO-DAYS-RENTED      VALUE  0.
49              88  VALID-DAYS-RENTED     VALUES 1 THRU 35.
50          05  REN-MILEAGE.
51              10  REN-MILES-IN       PIC 9(6).
52              10  REN-MILES-OUT      PIC 9(6).
53              10  REN-MILEAGE-RATE   PIC V99.
54                  88  VALID-MILEAGE-RATES   VALUES 00 THRU .50.
55          05  REN-INSURANCE          PIC X.
56              88  VALID-INSURANCE       VALUE 'Y' 'y' 'N' 'n'.
57              88  INSURANCE             VALUE 'Y' 'y'.
58
59      01  PROGRAM-SWITCHES-AND-CONSTANTS.
60          05  MILES-PER-DAY-FACTOR   PIC 99   VALUE 10.
61          05  VALID-FIELD-SWITCH     PIC XX.
62              88  VALID-FIELD           VALUE SPACES.
63          05  CONFIRM-SWITCH         PIC X   VALUE SPACES.
64              88  INFO-CORRECT          VALUE 'Y' 'y'.
65              88  NO-MORE-RECORDS       VALUE 'N' 'n'.
66              88  VALID-CONFIRMED       VALUE 'N' 'n' 'Y' 'y'.
67          05  CENTURY-PREFIXES.
68              10  NINETEEN       PIC 99 VALUE 19.
69              10  TWENTY         PIC 99 VALUE 20.
70
71      01  TODAYS-DATE-INFORMATION.
72          05  TODAYS-FULL-DATE.
73              10  TODAYS-CENT        PIC 99.
74              10  TODAYS-DATE.
75                  15  TODAYS-YEAR    PIC 99.
76                      88  TODAY-IS-20TH    VALUE 90 THRU 99.
77                  15  TODAYS-MONTH   PIC 99.
78                  15  TODAYS-DAY     PIC 99.
79          05  SCREEN-DATE            PIC X(10).
80
81      01  CONFIRM-MESSAGES.
82          05  CONFIRM-MESSAGE        PIC X(27).
83          05  INFO-CORRECT-MESSAGE   PIC X(27)
84              VALUE 'Above information correct? '.
85          05  ANOTHER-RECORD-MESSAGE  PIC X(27)
86              VALUE '    Enter Another Record? '.
87
88      01  ERROR-MESSAGES.
89          05  ERROR-MESSAGE         PIC X(40).
90          05  ZERO-CONTRACT-NO-MSG  PIC X(40)
91              VALUE '   CONTRACT NUMBER MUST NOT BE ZERO'.
92          05  LAST-NAME-MSG         PIC X(40)
93              VALUE '          MISSING LAST NAME'.
```

User may enter upper- or lowercase response

Allows for Y2K

Table of error messages established in Working-Storage

Figure 10.9 *(continued)*

```
94          05  FIRST-NAME-MSG        PIC X(40)
95              VALUE '         MISSING FIRST NAME'.
96          05  INITIAL-MSG           PIC X(40)
97              VALUE '         NON ALPHABETIC INITIAL'.
98          05  CAR-TYPE-MSG          PIC X(40)
99              VALUE '  CAR TYPE MUST BE:  E, C, M, F, OR L'.
100         05  MONTH-MSG             PIC X(40)
101             VALUE '    MONTH MUST BE BETWEEN 1 AND 12'.
102         05  DAY-MSG               PIC X(40)
103             VALUE '            INVALID DAY'.
104         05  FUTURE-DATE-MSG       PIC X(40)
105             VALUE '      DATE HAS NOT YET OCCURRED'.
106         05  NON-NUM-DAYS-RENTED-MSG PIC X(40)
107             VALUE '     DAYS RENTED MUST BE NUMERIC'.
108         05  ZERO-DAYS-MSG         PIC X(40)
109             VALUE '      DAYS RENTED MUST BE > ZERO'.
110         05  LEASING-MSG           PIC X(40)
111             VALUE '      REFER TO LONG-TERM LEASING'.
112         05  NON-NUM-MILES-IN-MSG  PIC X(40)
113             VALUE '         NON-NUMERIC MILES IN'.
114         05  NON-NUM-MILES-OUT-MSG PIC X(40)
115             VALUE '         NON-NUMERIC MILES OUT'.
116         05  LESS-THAN-MILES-MSG   PIC X(40)
117             VALUE '   MILEAGE IN LESS THAN MILEAGE OUT' .
118         05  INVALID-MILES-MSG     PIC X(40)
119             VALUE '     MILES DRIVEN UNREASONABLY LOW'.
120         05  NON-NUM-RATE-MSG      PIC X(40)
121             VALUE '       NON-NUMERIC MILEAGE RATE'.
122         05  MILEAGE-RATE-MSG      PIC X(40)
123             VALUE '       MILEAGE RATE OUT OF RANGE'.
124         05  INSURANCE-MSG         PIC X(40)
125             VALUE '    INSURANCE CODE MUST BE Y OR N'.
126         05  YES-NO-MSG            PIC X(40)
127             VALUE '           MUST BE "Y" OR "N"'.
128
129     01  DAILY-RATES.
130         05  ECONOMY-RATE          PIC 9(3)V99  VALUE 15.
131         05  COMPACT-RATE          PIC 9(3)V99  VALUE 20.
132         05  MID-RATE              PIC 9(3)V99  VALUE 24.
133         05  FULL-RATE             PIC 9(3)V99  VALUE 28.
134         05  LUXURY-RATE           PIC 9(3)V99  VALUE 35.
135         05  INSURANCE-RATE        PIC 99V99    VALUE 10.50.
136
137     01  IND-BILL-INFORMATION.
138         05  IND-MILES-DRIVEN      PIC 9(6).
139         05  IND-DAILY-RATE        PIC 9(3)V99.
140         05  IND-DAILY-TOTAL       PIC 9(5)V99.
141         05  IND-MILEAGE-TOTAL     PIC 9(4)V99.
142         05  IND-INSURANCE-TOTAL   PIC 9(4)V99.
143         05  IND-AMOUNT-DUE        PIC 9(6)V99.
144
145     SCREEN SECTION.                            ——— Screen Section follows Working-Storage Section
```

Figure 10.9 *(continued)*

```
146       01  OPENING-SCREEN.
147           BLANK SCREEN
148           BACKGROUND-COLOR BLUE   FOREGROUND-COLOR WHITE.
149           05  SCREEN-PROMPTS.
150               10  LINE   1 BLANK LINE.
151               10           COLUMN 20  VALUE 'Mavis Car Rental Company'
152                            BACKGROUND-COLOR MAGENTA
153                            FOREGROUND-COLOR GREEN.
154               10  SCR-DATE          PIC X(10) FROM SCREEN-DATE
155                        COLUMN 55  BACKGROUND-COLOR MAGENTA
156                                   FOREGROUND-COLOR GREEN.
157               10  LINE   3 COLUMN   7  VALUE 'Contract No:'.
158               10  LINE   5 COLUMN   7  VALUE 'Customer Information:'.
159               10  LINE   6 COLUMN   9  VALUE 'Last Name'.
160               10           COLUMN 25  VALUE 'First'.
161               10           COLUMN 36  VALUE 'Initial'.
162               10  LINE   9 COLUMN   6  VALUE 'Car Information:'.
163               10  LINE  10 COLUMN  12  VALUE 'Type Code:'.
164               10           COLUMN 25
165                   VALUE '(Compact, Economy, Midsize, Fullsize, Luxury)'
166                                   FOREGROUND-COLOR CYAN.
167               10           COLUMN 26  VALUE 'C' HIGHLIGHT.
168               10           COLUMN 35  VALUE 'E' HIGHLIGHT.
169               10           COLUMN 44  VALUE 'M' HIGHLIGHT.
170               10           COLUMN 53  VALUE 'F' HIGHLIGHT.
171               10           COLUMN 63  VALUE 'L' HIGHLIGHT.
172               10  LINE  11 COLUMN   8  VALUE 'Date Returned:'.
173               10           COLUMN 23  VALUE 'mm/dd/yy'
174                                   FOREGROUND-COLOR WHITE.
175               10  LINE  12 COLUMN  10  VALUE 'Days Rented:'.
176               10  LINE  13 COLUMN  10  VALUE 'Mileage:'.
177               10  LINE  14 COLUMN  13  VALUE 'Miles In:'.
178               10  LINE  15 COLUMN  12  VALUE 'Miles Out:'.
179               10           COLUMN 37  VALUE 'Mileage Rate:'.
180               10  LINE  16 COLUMN  12  VALUE 'Insurance:'.
181               10           COLUMN 25  VALUE '(Y/N)'
182                                   FOREGROUND-COLOR CYAN.
183
184           05  SCREEN-INPUTS.
185               10  SCR-CONTRACT-NO    PIC 9(6) USING REN-CONTRACT-NO
186                       LINE   3 COLUMN 20  REVERSE-VIDEO
187                       BLANK WHEN ZERO.
188               10  SCR-LAST-NAME      PIC X(15) USING REN-LAST-NAME
189                       LINE   7 COLUMN   9  REVERSE-VIDEO.
190               10  SCR-FIRST-NAME     PIC X(10) USING REN-FIRST-NAME
191                       LINE   7 COLUMN 25  REVERSE-VIDEO.
192               10  SCR-INITIAL        PIC X     USING REN-INITIAL
193                       LINE   7 COLUMN 36  REVERSE-VIDEO.
194               10  SCR-CAR-TYPE       PIC X     USING REN-CAR-TYPE
195                       LINE  10 COLUMN 23  REVERSE-VIDEO AUTO.
196               10  SCR-RETURNED-MONTH PIC ZZ  USING REN-RETURNED-MONTH
197                       LINE  11 COLUMN 23  REVERSE-VIDEO AUTO.
```

Omitted LINE clause causes all three entries on line 6

Figure 10.9   *(continued)*

```
198              10  SCR-RETURNED-DAY    PIC ZZ    USING REN-RETURNED-DAY
199                  LINE 11 COLUMN 26   REVERSE-VIDEO AUTO.
200              10  SCR-RETURNED-YEAR   PIC 99    USING REN-RETURNED-YEAR
201                  LINE 11 COLUMN 29   REVERSE-VIDEO AUTO.
202              10  SCR-DAYS-RENTED     PIC ZZ    USING REN-DAYS-RENTED
203                  LINE 12 COLUMN 23   REVERSE-VIDEO AUTO.
204              10  SCR-MILES-IN        PIC ZZZ,ZZZ USING REN-MILES-IN
205                  LINE 14 COLUMN 23   REVERSE-VIDEO.
206              10  SCR-MILES-OUT       PIC ZZZ,ZZZ USING REN-MILES-OUT
207                  LINE 15 COLUMN 23   REVERSE-VIDEO.
208              10  LINE 15 COLUMN 54   REVERSE-VIDEO VALUE '.'.
209              10  SCR-MILEAGE-RATE    PIC V99   USING REN-MILEAGE-RATE
210                  LINE 15 COLUMN 55   REVERSE-VIDEO.
211              10  SCR-INSURANCE       PIC X     USING REN-INSURANCE
212                  LINE 16 COLUMN 23   REVERSE-VIDEO AUTO.
213          05  LINE 24 BLANK LINE.
214          05  LINE 25 BLANK LINE.
215
216      01  UPDATE-SCREEN.
217          05  LINE 11 COLUMN 67       VALUE 'Totals' HIGHLIGHT.
218          05  LINE 12 COLUMN 38       VALUE 'Rental Rate:' HIGHLIGHT.
219          05  UPD-DAILY-RATE          PIC $$$9.99   FROM IND-DAILY-RATE
220              LINE 12 COLUMN 50       HIGHLIGHT.
221          05  UPD-DAILY-TOTAL         PIC $$$,$$9.99 FROM IND-DAILY-TOTAL
222                  COLUMN 63           HIGHLIGHT.
223          05  LINE 14 COLUMN 37       VALUE 'Miles Driven:' HIGHLIGHT.
224          05  UPD-MILES-DRIVEN        PIC ZZZ,ZZ9   FROM IND-MILES-DRIVEN
225                  COLUMN 50           HIGHLIGHT.
226          05  UPD-MILEAGE-TOTAL       PIC $$,$$9.99
227                                      FROM IND-MILEAGE-TOTAL
228              LINE 15 COLUMN 64       HIGHLIGHT.
229          05  LINE 16 COLUMN 35       VALUE 'Insurance Rate:' HIGHLIGHT.
230          05  UPD-INSURANCE-RATE      PIC $$9.99 FROM INSURANCE-RATE
231              LINE 16 COLUMN 51       HIGHLIGHT.
232          05  UPD-INSURANCE-TOTAL     PIC $$,$$9.99
233                                      FROM IND-INSURANCE-TOTAL
234                  COLUMN 64           HIGHLIGHT.
235          05  LINE 17 COLUMN 63       VALUE '----------' HIGHLIGHT.
236          05  LINE 18 COLUMN 48       VALUE 'Amount Due: ' HIGHLIGHT.
237          05  UPD-AMOUNT-DUE          PIC $$$$,$$9.99 FROM IND-AMOUNT-DUE
238                  COLUMN 62           HIGHLIGHT.
239
240      01  ERROR-LINE.
241          05  LINE 25 BLANK LINE BACKGROUND-COLOR RED.
242          05                          PIC X(40) FROM ERROR-MESSAGE
243                  COLUMN 20           HIGHLIGHT BLINK BEEP
244              FOREGROUND-COLOR WHITE  BACKGROUND-COLOR RED.
245
246      01  CONFIRM-SCREEN.
247          05  LINE 24 BLANK LINE      BACKGROUND-COLOR MAGENTA.
248          05                          PIC X(27) FROM CONFIRM-MESSAGE
249              LINE 24 COLUMN 25
```

— Screen name is displayed in line 283

Figure 10.9 (continued)

```
250              BACKGROUND-COLOR MAGENTA FOREGROUND-COLOR GREEN.
251         05                  PIC X USING CONFIRM-SWITCH
252            LINE 24 COLUMN 52     BLINK AUTO
253            BACKGROUND-COLOR MAGENTA FOREGROUND-COLOR GREEN.
254         05  LINE 25 BLANK LINE BACKGROUND-COLOR MAGENTA.
255         05  LINE 25 COLUMN 32     VALUE '(Y - Yes, N - No)'
256            BACKGROUND-COLOR MAGENTA FOREGROUND-COLOR GREEN.
257
258    PROCEDURE DIVISION.
259    000-CREATE-VALID-RENTAL-FILE.
260        OPEN OUTPUT VALID-RENTAL-FILE.
261        PERFORM 100-GET-TODAYS-DATE.
262        PERFORM 200-INPUT-RENTAL-RECORDS
263            UNTIL NO-MORE-RECORDS.
264        CLOSE VALID-RENTAL-FILE.
265        STOP RUN.
266
267    100-GET-TODAYS-DATE.
268        ACCEPT TODAYS-DATE FROM DATE.
269        IF TODAY-IS-20TH
270            MOVE NINETEEN TO TODAYS-CENT
271        ELSE
272            MOVE TWENTY TO TODAYS-CENT
273        END-IF
274        STRING TODAYS-MONTH '/' TODAYS-DAY '/' TODAYS-CENT
275            TODAYS-YEAR
276            DELIMITED BY SIZE INTO SCREEN-DATE.
277
278    200-INPUT-RENTAL-RECORDS.
279        INITIALIZE RENTAL-RECORD-IN.
280        PERFORM 400-VALIDATE-RENTAL-RECORD WITH TEST AFTER
281            UNTIL INFO-CORRECT.
282        PERFORM 500-COMPUTE-IND-BILL.
283        DISPLAY UPDATE-SCREEN.
284        PERFORM 600-WRITE-VALID-RECORD.
285        MOVE ANOTHER-RECORD-MESSAGE TO CONFIRM-MESSAGE.
286        PERFORM 700-INPUT-SCREEN-CONFIRM.
287
288    400-VALIDATE-RENTAL-RECORD.
289        DISPLAY OPENING-SCREEN.
290        PERFORM 410-VALIDATE-CONTRACT-NO.
291        PERFORM 420-VALIDATE-NAME.
292        PERFORM 430-VALIDATE-CAR-TYPE.
293        PERFORM 440-VALIDATE-DATE-RETURNED
294            WITH TEST AFTER UNTIL VALID-FIELD.
295        PERFORM 450-VALIDATE-DAYS-RENTED.
296        PERFORM 460-VALIDATE-MILES-DRIVEN.
297        PERFORM 470-VALIDATE-MILEAGE-RATE.
298        PERFORM 480-VALIDATE-INSURANCE.
299        MOVE INFO-CORRECT-MESSAGE TO CONFIRM-MESSAGE.
300        PERFORM 700-INPUT-SCREEN-CONFIRM.
301
302    410-VALIDATE-CONTRACT-NO.
```

Combination of foreground and background colors for emphasis

Window technique for Y2K

DISPLAY statement references 01 entry in Screen Section

Figure 10.9 *(continued)*

```
303            PERFORM WITH TEST AFTER UNTIL VALID-FIELD
304                ACCEPT SCR-CONTRACT-NO
305                IF REN-CONTRACT-NO = ZEROES
306                    MOVE ZERO-CONTRACT-NO-MSG TO ERROR-MESSAGE
307                    PERFORM 499-DISPLAY-ERROR-MESSAGE
308                ELSE
309                    PERFORM 498-CLEAR-ERRORS
310                END-IF
311            END-PERFORM.
312
313        420-VALIDATE-NAME.
314            PERFORM WITH TEST AFTER UNTIL VALID-FIELD
315                ACCEPT SCR-LAST-NAME
316                IF REN-LAST-NAME = SPACES
317                    MOVE LAST-NAME-MSG TO ERROR-MESSAGE
318                    PERFORM 499-DISPLAY-ERROR-MESSAGE
319                ELSE
320                    PERFORM 498-CLEAR-ERRORS
321                END-IF
322            END-PERFORM.
323            PERFORM WITH TEST AFTER UNTIL VALID-FIELD
324                ACCEPT SCR-FIRST-NAME
325                IF REN-FIRST-NAME = SPACES
326                    MOVE FIRST-NAME-MSG TO ERROR-MESSAGE
327                    PERFORM 499-DISPLAY-ERROR-MESSAGE
328                ELSE
329                    PERFORM 498-CLEAR-ERRORS
330                END-IF
331            END-PERFORM.
332            PERFORM WITH TEST AFTER UNTIL VALID-FIELD
333                ACCEPT SCR-INITIAL
334                IF REN-INITIAL NOT ALPHABETIC
335                    MOVE INITIAL-MSG TO ERROR-MESSAGE
336                    PERFORM 499-DISPLAY-ERROR-MESSAGE
337                ELSE
338                    PERFORM 498-CLEAR-ERRORS
339                END-IF
340            END-PERFORM.
341
342        430-VALIDATE-CAR-TYPE.
343            PERFORM WITH TEST AFTER UNTIL VALID-FIELD
344                ACCEPT SCR-CAR-TYPE
345                IF NOT VALID-CAR-TYPES
346                    MOVE CAR-TYPE-MSG TO ERROR-MESSAGE
347                    PERFORM 499-DISPLAY-ERROR-MESSAGE
348                ELSE
349                    PERFORM 498-CLEAR-ERRORS
350                END-IF
351            END-PERFORM.
352
353        440-VALIDATE-DATE-RETURNED.
354            PERFORM WITH TEST AFTER UNTIL VALID-FIELD
355                PERFORM WITH TEST AFTER UNTIL VALID-FIELD
```

TEST AFTER clause ensures that in-line statements are executed at least once (lines 314–322)

TEST AFTER clause ensures that in-line statements are executed at least once (lines 343–351)

Nested PERFORMS (lines 354–355)

Figure 10.9 *(continued)*

```
356            ACCEPT SCR-RETURNED-MONTH
357            IF VALID-MONTHS
358                PERFORM 498-CLEAR-ERRORS
359            ELSE
360                MOVE MONTH-MSG TO ERROR-MESSAGE
361                PERFORM 499-DISPLAY-ERROR-MESSAGE
362            END-IF
363        END-PERFORM.
364        PERFORM WITH TEST AFTER UNTIL VALID-FIELD
365            ACCEPT SCR-RETURNED-DAY
366            EVALUATE REN-RETURNED-DAY      ALSO TRUE
367              WHEN 1 THRU 29               ALSO ANY
368                  PERFORM 498-CLEAR-ERRORS
369              WHEN 30 THRU 31              ALSO 31-DAY-MONTH
370                  PERFORM 498-CLEAR-ERRORS
371              WHEN 30                      ALSO 30-DAY-MONTH
372                  PERFORM 498-CLEAR-ERRORS
373            WHEN OTHER
374                MOVE DAY-MSG TO ERROR-MESSAGE
375                PERFORM 499-DISPLAY-ERROR-MESSAGE
376            END-EVALUATE
377        END-PERFORM.
378            ACCEPT SCR-RETURNED-YEAR
379            IF TWENTIETH-CENTURY
380                MOVE NINETEEN TO REN-RETURNED-CENT
381            ELSE
382                MOVE TWENTY TO REN-RETURNED-CENT
383            END-IF
384            IF REN-RETURNED-DATE > TODAYS-FULL-DATE
385                MOVE FUTURE-DATE-MSG TO ERROR-MESSAGE
386                PERFORM 499-DISPLAY-ERROR-MESSAGE
387            ELSE
388                PERFORM 498-CLEAR-ERRORS
389            END-IF
390        END-PERFORM.
391
392    450-VALIDATE-DAYS-RENTED.
393        PERFORM WITH TEST AFTER UNTIL VALID-FIELD
394            ACCEPT SCR-DAYS-RENTED
395            IF ZERO-DAYS-RENTED
396                MOVE ZERO-DAYS-MSG TO ERROR-MESSAGE
397                PERFORM 499-DISPLAY-ERROR-MESSAGE
398            ELSE
399              IF NOT VALID-DAYS-RENTED
400                  MOVE LEASING-MSG TO ERROR-MESSAGE
401                  PERFORM 499-DISPLAY-ERROR-MESSAGE
402              ELSE
403                  PERFORM 498-CLEAR-ERRORS
404              END-IF
405            END-IF
406        END-PERFORM.
407
408    460-VALIDATE-MILES-DRIVEN.
```

EVALUATE statement tests day and month

Y2K correction

Figure 10.9 *(continued)*

```
409              PERFORM WITH TEST AFTER UNTIL VALID-FIELD
410                  ACCEPT SCR-MILES-IN
411                  ACCEPT SCR-MILES-OUT
412                  IF REN-MILES-IN < REN-MILES-OUT
413                      MOVE LESS-THAN-MILES-MSG TO ERROR-MESSAGE
414                      PERFORM 499-DISPLAY-ERROR-MESSAGE
415                  ELSE
416                      IF REN-MILES-IN - REN-MILES-OUT <
417                          MILES-PER-DAY-FACTOR * REN-DAYS-RENTED
418                              MOVE INVALID-MILES-MSG TO ERROR-MESSAGE
419                              PERFORM 499-DISPLAY-ERROR-MESSAGE
420                      ELSE
421                              PERFORM 498-CLEAR-ERRORS
422                      END-IF
423                  END-IF
424              END-PERFORM.
425
426          470-VALIDATE-MILEAGE-RATE.
427              PERFORM WITH TEST AFTER UNTIL VALID-FIELD
428                  ACCEPT SCR-MILEAGE-RATE
429                  IF NOT VALID-MILEAGE-RATES
430                      MOVE MILEAGE-RATE-MSG TO ERROR-MESSAGE
431                      PERFORM 499-DISPLAY-ERROR-MESSAGE
432                  ELSE
433                      PERFORM 498-CLEAR-ERRORS
434                  END-IF
435              END-PERFORM.
436
437          480-VALIDATE-INSURANCE.
438              PERFORM WITH TEST AFTER UNTIL VALID-FIELD
439                  ACCEPT SCR-INSURANCE
440                  IF NOT VALID-INSURANCE
441                      MOVE INSURANCE-MSG TO ERROR-MESSAGE
442                      PERFORM 499-DISPLAY-ERROR-MESSAGE
443                  ELSE
444                      PERFORM 498-CLEAR-ERRORS
445                  END-IF
446              END-PERFORM.
447
448          498-CLEAR-ERRORS.
449              INITIALIZE VALID-FIELD-SWITCH.
450              DISPLAY ' ' LINE 25 WITH BLANK LINE.
451
452          499-DISPLAY-ERROR-MESSAGE.
453              MOVE 'NO' TO VALID-FIELD-SWITCH.
454              DISPLAY ERROR-LINE.
455
456          500-COMPUTE-IND-BILL.
457              PERFORM 520-COMPUTE-MILEAGE-TOTAL.
458              PERFORM 540-COMPUTE-DAILY-TOTAL.
459              PERFORM 560-COMPUTE-INSURANCE-TOTAL.
460              COMPUTE IND-AMOUNT-DUE ROUNDED
461                  = IND-MILEAGE-TOTAL + IND-DAILY-TOTAL
```

TEST AFTER clause ensures that in-line statements are executed at least once

Figure 10.9 *(continued)*

```
462              + IND-INSURANCE-TOTAL
463         SIZE ERROR DISPLAY 'SIZE ERROR ON AMOUNT DUE FOR '
464            REN-CONTRACT-NO
465     END-COMPUTE.
466
467  520-COMPUTE-MILEAGE-TOTAL.
468     COMPUTE IND-MILES-DRIVEN
469        = REN-MILES-IN - REN-MILES-OUT
470     END-COMPUTE.
471     COMPUTE IND-MILEAGE-TOTAL ROUNDED
472        = IND-MILES-DRIVEN * REN-MILEAGE-RATE
473        SIZE ERROR
474           DISPLAY 'COMPUTED BILL EXCESSIVELY LARGE'
475     END-COMPUTE.
476
477  540-COMPUTE-DAILY-TOTAL.
478     EVALUATE REN-CAR-TYPE
479        WHEN 'E' MOVE ECONOMY-RATE TO IND-DAILY-RATE
480        WHEN 'C' MOVE COMPACT-RATE TO IND-DAILY-RATE
481        WHEN 'M' MOVE MID-RATE TO IND-DAILY-RATE
482        WHEN 'F' MOVE FULL-RATE TO IND-DAILY-RATE
483        WHEN 'L' MOVE LUXURY-RATE TO IND-DAILY-RATE
484        WHEN OTHER MOVE ZEROES TO IND-DAILY-RATE
485     END-EVALUATE.
486     MULTIPLY IND-DAILY-RATE BY REN-DAYS-RENTED
487        GIVING IND-DAILY-TOTAL
488        SIZE ERROR DISPLAY 'SIZE ERROR ON RENTAL TOTAL'
489     END-MULTIPLY.
490
491  560-COMPUTE-INSURANCE-TOTAL.
492     IF INSURANCE
493        MULTIPLY INSURANCE-RATE BY REN-DAYS-RENTED
494           GIVING IND-INSURANCE-TOTAL
495           SIZE ERROR DISPLAY 'SIZE ERROR ON INSURANCE TOTAL'
496        END-MULTIPLY
497     ELSE
498        MOVE ZEROES TO IND-INSURANCE-TOTAL
499     END-IF.
500
501  600-WRITE-VALID-RECORD.
502     WRITE VALID-RENTAL-RECORD FROM RENTAL-RECORD-IN.
503
504  700-INPUT-SCREEN-CONFIRM.
505     DISPLAY CONFIRM-SCREEN.
506     PERFORM WITH TEST AFTER UNTIL VALID-CONFIRMED
507        ACCEPT CONFIRM-SCREEN
508        IF VALID-CONFIRMED
509           PERFORM 498-CLEAR-ERRORS
510        ELSE
511           MOVE YES-NO-MSG TO ERROR-MESSAGE
512           PERFORM 499-DISPLAY-ERROR-MESSAGE
513        END-IF
514     END-PERFORM.
```

EVALUATE statement determines daily rate

Indentation increases readability

The requirements for the validation of individual fields parallel those in Chapter 8, and thus the table of error messages (lines 88–127) is repeated from the validation program. The validation process is different, however, as each field is checked interactively, so that the user cannot move to the next field until a valid value has been entered for the current field.

Consider, for example, the validation of car type in lines 342–351. The TEST AFTER clause guarantees that the performed statements are executed at least once; that is, the car type is accepted into SCR-CAR-TYPE (defined in lines 194–195), then tested by the IF statement in lines 345–350. A valid car type will reset VALID-FIELD-SWITCH to 'NO', which in turn satisfies the condition in the PERFORM statement in line 343. An invalid response, however, displays the appropriate error message, then requests a new response from the user. A similar process is followed for the other fields in each transaction. Notice the nested loops in 440-VALIDATE-DATE-RETURNED (lines 353-390). This routine validates each portion of the date and allows correction if any part is incorrect. The routine also adjusts the year to handle dates past 1999. An appreciation for the interactive nature of the program can best be gained by executing the program as it exists on the accompanying data disk.

The remainder of the Procedure Division is straightforward with applicable paragraphs copied from the earlier programs—for example, COMPUTE-MILEAGE-TOTAL, COMPUTE-DAILY-TOTAL, and COMPUTE-INSURANCE-TOTAL.

LIMITATIONS OF COBOL-74

The Screen Section and extended options of the ACCEPT and DISPLAY statements are *not* included in either the COBOL-74 or COBOL-85 standard, and thus there are no limitations per se in the earlier compiler. In other words, any differences that do exist are due to vendor-specific extensions, which vary significantly from compiler to compiler.

SUMMARY

Points to Remember

- The extended screen handling capabilities in the Screen Section and the ACCEPT and DISPLAY statements are not part of the COBOL-85 standard. The examples in this chapter follow the syntax of the Classroom COBOL compiler that accompanies the text, which conforms to the X-Open standard.

- The ACCEPT and DISPLAY statements display individual lines and/or accept a limited number of fields as input. Both statements contain an abundance of optional clauses, the functions of which are generally apparent from the clause itself: BLINK, BEEP, BACKGROUND-COLOR, FOREGROUND-COLOR, and so forth.

- The Screen Section facilitates the production of uniform screens within a system as an entire screen may be easily copied from one program to the next. This is in contrast to individual ACCEPT and DISPLAY statements that are scattered throughout the Procedure Division.

■   The format of the Screen Section parallels that of the File and Working-Storage sections in the Data Division; that is, it consists of 01-level entries that are further divided into group and elementary items. The Screen Section must be the last section in the Data Division.

■   Data validation may be implemented interactively through an in-line perform and through TEST AFTER clauses, which accept a data name, perform the indicated validation, then repeat the process until a valid field has been entered.

Key Words and Concepts

Alt key	Interactive program
ASCII characters	Password protection
Background color	Prompt
Batch-oriented program	Reversed video
Data validation	Screen attribute
Foreground color	Screen-name

COBOL Elements

ACCEPT	HIGHLIGHT
AUTO	LINE
BACKGROUND-COLOR	REVERSE-VIDEO
COLUMN	SCREEN SECTION
DISPLAY	SECURE
FOREGROUND-COLOR	TO
FROM	USING

Fill-in

1. The Screen Section (_____) part of the COBOL-85 standard.

2. The typical screen displays _____ lines of _____ columns each.

3. The _____ clause in the ACCEPT statement prevents the user's response from being displayed on the monitor.

4. The LINE and COLUMN clauses (_____) required in the ACCEPT and/or DISPLAY statements

5. The Screen Section is the (_____) section in the Data Division.

6. The _____ key, in conjunction with the numeric keyboard, can be used to enter any of the 256 _____ characters into a program.

7. In general, the foreground and background colors (_____) be the same.

8. The (_____) statement is often used in conjunction with top-down testing and/or debugging.

9. An in-line PERFORM statement, coupled with the (_____) clause, is used to implement interactive data validation.

10. The _____ _____ facilitates the production of uniform screens within a system in that its entries can be easily copied from program to program.

11. Screen I-O makes possible the implementation of (_____) programs.

12. An in-line perform, in conjunction with the TEST AFTER clause, can be used to _____ a field as it is entered.

True/False

1. The same COBOL program cannot contain a Screen Section and a File Section.

2. The File Section is required in every program.

3. The LINE and/or COLUMN clauses are required in the DISPLAY statement.

4. The Screen Section is required in all programs that display output on the monitor.

5. The ACCEPT and DISPLAY statements are used for low-volume output.

6. The options and syntax for screen I-O are unlikely to change from one compiler to the next.

7. Text is typically displayed on screens in which the foreground and background colors are the same.

8. COBOL-85 makes little provision for screen I-O, and thus its implementation varies greatly from compiler to compiler.

9. The optional clauses in the ACCEPT statement can appear in any order.

10. Interactive data validation cannot be implemented in programs with extensive screen I-O.

Problems

1. Which clause is used to implement the following in an ACCEPT and/or DISPLAY statement?
   a. Invert the specified or default background and foreground colors
   b. Prevent the referenced field from being displayed on the screen
   c. Require that at least one character is entered in the referenced field
   d. Automatically position the cursor to the first character of the next field after the last character of the current field has been entered
   e. Clear the screen before accepting (displaying) a data element
   f. Emphasize the displayed field (multiple clauses are acceptable)

2. Indicate the exact effect of each of the following DISPLAY statements. Note, however, that some of the statements are invalid syntactically, in which case you should indicate the nature of the error. Other statements are valid syntactically, but most probably do not do what the programmer intended.

    a. DISPLAY

    b. DISPLAY 'COMPUTE-TUITION paragraph is entered'

    c. DISPLAY 'TUITION = IND-TUITION'

    d. DISPLAY 'TUITION = ', IND-TUITION

    e. DISPLAY 'Initials: AT LINE 5 COLUMN 5'

    f. DISPLAY 'Initials:' AT LINE 5 COLUMN 5

    g. The two statements, DISPLAY 'Less Scholarship' AT LINE 15 COLUMN 10 followed by DISPLAY 'Amount due' AT LINE 15 COLUMN 16

3. Modify the tuition billing program to accommodate the following:

    a. A new password, RTG, which should be accepted as valid in all uppercase, all lowercase, or any combination of upper- and lowercase letters.

    b. Data validation as you see fit; the program as presently written does no validation whatsoever. Suggest and implement validation checks for at least three fields.

    c. Display a total screen at the conclusion of processing that contains the number of students processed and the corresponding totals for total tuition, total activity fee, total union fee, total scholarship awarded, and the total amount due.

    d. Create a valid record file as output—that is, a file containing the valid student records that could be input into the edited version of the tuition billing program in Chapter 7.

4. Answer the following with respect to the car validation and billing program:

    a. Is the program case-sensitive; that is, is there any difference between entering an upper- or lowercase C to denote a compact car?

    b. What changes (if any) have to be made to VALUE clauses in the Data Division to make the program case-insensitive for car type?

    c. What changes (if any) have to be made in the Procedure Division to support those made in the Data Division in part (b)?

    d. What other changes (if any) are needed to make the program case-insensitive to other data names?

5. The car validation and billing program makes extensive use of the in-line PERFORM statement to validate data as it is entered.

    a. What is the minimum number of times the statements within an in-line perform (e.g., lines 303–311) will be executed?

    b. Do the PERFORM statements (e.g., lines 303–311) implement a DO WHILE or a DO UNTIL structure?

    c. What is the effect (if any) of substituting TEST BEFORE for TEST AFTER in line 303?

    d. What is the effect (if any) of removing the TEST clause in line 303?

Introduction to Tables

CHAPTER OUTLINE

Overview
Introduction to Tables
    OCCURS Clause
    Processing a Table
    PERFORM VARYING
A Second Example
    Problems with the OCCURS Clause
    Rules for Subscripts
    Relative Subscripting
    USAGE Clause
    OCCURS DEPENDING ON
The Student Transcript Program
    Programming Specifications
    Program Design
    The Completed Program
Indexes versus Subscripts
    The SET Statement
Limitations of COBOL-74
Summary
Fill-in
True/False
Problems

OBJECTIVES

After reading this chapter you will be able to:

■ Define a table and describe its use in programming.

■ Use the OCCURS (at either the group or elementary level) to implement a table in COBOL.

■ Use the PERFORM VARYING statement to process a table.

■ Distinguish between fixed and variable length records; use the OCCURS DEPENDING ON clause to implement a variable length table.

■ State the purpose of the USAGE clause.

■ Differentiate between a subscript and an index.

OVERVIEW

This is the first of three chapters that deal exclusively with tables, a topic of major importance in any programming language. A table is a grouping of similar data whose values are stored in consecutive storage locations and assigned a single data name. Any reference to an individual element within a table is accomplished by a subscript or an index.

The present chapter introduces the basic statements for table processing. We begin with the OCCURS clause to define a table and show how it can be used at both the group and elementary levels. We discuss the DEPENDING ON phrase to specify a variable-length table and the concept of relative subscripting. We cover the PERFORM VARYING statement to process the elements in a table by repeatedly executing a paragraph or a series of in-line statements. We also differentiate between an index that is specified in an INDEXED BY clause and a subscript defined in Working-Storage. All of this material is summarized by the illustrative program at the end of the chapter.

Introduction to Tables

The motivation for using a table comes from examination of Figure 11.1. Let us assume that a company tabulates its sales on a monthly basis and that the sales of each month are to be referenced within a COBOL program. Without tables, as in the brute force approach of Figure 11.1a, 12 different data names are required: JAN-SALES, FEB-SALES, and so on. A table, however, enables you to define a single data name such as SALES, then subsequently refer to individual months by an appropriate subscript. SALES (2), for example, refers to the sales for the second month, February.

Figure 11.1 The Table Concept

```
01  ANNUAL-SALES-DATA.
    05  JAN-SALES        PIC 9(6).
    05  FEB-SALES        PIC 9(6).
    05  MAR-SALES        PIC 9(6).
    05  APR-SALES        PIC 9(6).
    05  MAY-SALES        PIC 9(6).
    05  JUN-SALES        PIC 9(6).
    05  JUL-SALES        PIC 9(6).
    05  AUG-SALES        PIC 9(6).
    05  SEP-SALES        PIC 9(6).
    05  OCT-SALES        PIC 9(6).
    05  NOV-SALES        PIC 9(6).
    05  DEC-SALES        PIC 9(6).
```

(a) Brute Force

```
01  ANNUAL-SALES-DATA.
    05  SALES  OCCURS  12  TIMES         PIC 9(6).
```

(b) OCCURS Clause

ANNUAL-SALES-DATA			
SALES (1)	SALES (2)		SALES (3)
		• • •	

(c) Storage Schematic

OCCURS Clause

The **OCCURS** clause defines the number of entries in a table and is covered in detail later in the chapter. For the time being, however, we consider only its simplest form:

```
OCCURS integer TIMES
```

The OCCURS clause is illustrated in Figure 11.1b to define a table of 12 elements, with each element in the table having the identical format; that is, each element is a six-position numeric field. The entire table takes a total of 72 positions (12 entries x 6 positions per entry), as shown in the schematic of Figure 11.1c. As indicated, individual entries in the table are referenced by the table name, SALES, and an appropriate subscript—for example, SALES (1) to refer to the first element (January sales), SALES (2) to refer to the second element (February sales), and so on.

The OCCURS clause is not permitted at the 01 level and thus the sales table was defined under the entry ANNUAL-SALES-DATA in Figure 11.1b. The 12 elements may be referenced collectively by the data name ANNUAL-SALES-DATA although such a reference is unlikely to be used.

Processing a Table

After a table has been defined, we shall want to sum the 12 monthly totals to produce an annual total. There are several approaches, the first of which is brute force:

```
COMPUTE ANNUAL-TOTAL
     = SALES (1) + SALES (2) + SALES (3)
     + SALES (4) + SALES (5) + SALES (6)
     + SALES (7) + SALES (8) + SALES (9)
     + SALES (10) + SALES (11) + SALES (12)
END-COMPUTE.
```

This technique is cumbersome to code, and defeats the purpose of defining the table in the first place, but it does explicitly illustrate the concept of table processing. Fortunately, however, there is a better way through the PERFORM VARYING statement.

PERFORM VARYING

The **PERFORM VARYING** statement causes repeated execution of a designated procedure or series of in-line statements and is the most common means of processing a table. Consider:

```
PERFORM [procedure-name-1]

     [WITH TEST {BEFORE / AFTER}]

     VARYING identifier-1 FROM {literal-1 / identifier-2} BY {literal-2 / identifier-3}

     UNTIL condition-1

     [imperative-statement-1 END-PERFORM]
```

The TEST BEFORE/TEST AFTER clause is new to COBOL-85 and was explained in Chapter 9. The clause is optional and typically omitted; the default is TEST BEFORE and corresponds to the COBOL-74 implementation.

The PERFORM VARYING statement (with test before) *initializes* a variable, *tests a condition*, and if the condition is not satisfied, enters a loop to *execute* a procedure, *increment* a variable, and *retest* the condition (condition-1). The loop is executed repeatedly until the condition is finally satisfied, at which point the PERFORM VARYING statement ends, and control passes to the next sequential statement in the program. The sequence just described is illustrated in Figure 11.2 and is restated below:

1. Identifier-1 is initialized to the value in the **FROM** clause

2. Condition-1 is evaluated and is either true or false:

    a. If the condition is true, the PERFORM VARYING is terminated and control passes to the next sequential statement.

    b. If the condition is false, procedure-name-1 or imperative-statement-1 is executed, after which identifier-1 is incremented with the value in the **BY** clause. Condition-1 is reevaluated as either true or false with subsequent action as just described.

Figure 11.2   PERFORM VARYING (with TEST BEFORE)

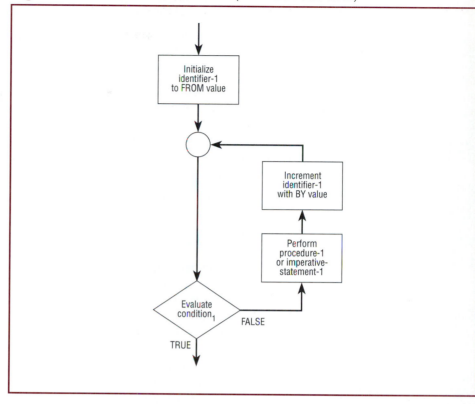

The condition in the PERFORM VARYING statement typically includes a greater than sign, rather than an equal sign, to execute the designated procedure an integer number of times; for example, the statement

```
PERFORM COMPUTE-PAYMENT
     VARYING SUBSCRIPT FROM 1 BY 1
          UNTIL SUBSCRIPT > 3
```

executes the procedure COMPUTE-PAYMENT three times. The sequence is explained as follows:

1. SUBSCRIPT is initially set to 1 and the condition SUBSCRIPT > 3 is evaluated. The condition is not true, so the designated procedure, COMPUTE-PAYMENT, is executed the first time.

2. SUBSCRIPT is incremented to 2 and the condition is retested. The condition is still not satisfied, so COMPUTE-PAYMENT is executed a second time.

3. SUBSCRIPT is incremented to 3, but the condition is still false—*3 is not greater than 3*—and hence COMPUTE-PAYMENT is executed a third (and final) time.

4. SUBSCRIPT is incremented to 4, satisfying the condition in the UNTIL clause and terminating the PERFORM statement. (Note that, had the condition been specified as SUBSCRIPT = 3, COMPUTE-PAYMENT would have been executed only twice.)

Extending this reasoning to the general case of executing a procedure N times requires a statement of the form:

```
PERFORM PARAGRAPH
    VARYING SUBSCRIPT FROM 1 BY 1
        UNTIL SUBSCRIPT > N.
```

The data name used to monitor execution—for example, SUBSCRIPT—must be explicitly defined in Working-Storage.

The PERFORM VARYING statement is illustrated a final time in Figure 11.3. The choice between performing a paragraph as in Figure 11.3a, or using an in-line perform as in Figure 11.3b, is one of personal preference. Both techniques are equally acceptable and achieve identical results.

Figure 11.3   Processing a Table

```
        MOVE ZERO TO ANNUAL-TOTAL.
        PERFORM INCREMENT-ANNUAL-TOTAL
            VARYING SALES-SUB FROM 1 BY 1
                UNTIL SALES-SUB > 12.
            .
            .
            .
    INCREMENT-ANNUAL-TOTAL.
        ADD SALES (SALES-SUB) TO ANNUAL-TOTAL.
```

(a) Performing a Paragraph

```
        MOVE ZERO TO ANNUAL-TOTAL.
        PERFORM
            VARYING SALES-SUB FROM 1 BY 1
                UNTIL SALES-SUB > 12
            ADD SALES (SALES-SUB) TO ANNUAL-TOTAL
        END-PERFORM.
```

(b) In-line Perform

A Second Example

Let us consider a second example in which three sets of salary data are kept for each employee; that is, each employee record contains the employee's present salary and date on which it became effective, the previous salary and date, and the second previous salary and date. (Not all employees have all three salaries.)

It is, of course, possible to develop unique data names for each occurrence of salary information, for example,

```
05  SALARY-DATA.
    10  PRESENT-SALARY                 PIC 9(6).
    10  PRESENT-SALARY-DATE            PIC 9(6).
    10  PREVIOUS-SALARY                PIC 9(6).
    10  PREVIOUS-SALARY-DATE           PIC 9(6).
    10  SECOND-PREVIOUS-SALARY         PIC 9(6).
    10  SECOND-PREVIOUS-SALARY-DATE    PIC 9(6).
```

Figure 11.4   OCCURS Clause at the Group Level

```
05  SALARY-DATA OCCURS 3 TIMES.
    10  SALARY          PIC 9(6).
    10  SAL-DATE        PIC 9(6).
```

(a) COBOL Statements

SALARY-DATA(1)		SALARY-DATA(2)		SALARY-DATA(3)	
SALARY (1)	SAL-DATE(1)	SALARY (2)	SAL-DATE(2)	SALARY (3)	SAL-DATE(3)

(b) Storage Schematic

Figure 11.5   OCCURS Clause at the Elementary Level

```
05  SALARY-DATA.
    10  SALARY       OCCURS  3  TIMES    PIC 9(6).
    10  SAL-DATE     OCCURS  3  TIMES    PIC 9(6).
```

(a) COBOL Statements

SALARY-DATA					
SALARY (1)	SALARY (2)	SALARY (3)	SAL-DATE(1)	SAL-DATE(2)	SAL-DATE(3)

(b) Storage Schematic

What if, however, it were suddenly decided that four, five, or even ten levels of historical data were required? The situation is neatly circumvented by establishing a table that enables the programmer to define logically similar elements under a common name, and to reference the desired entry subsequently by an appropriate subscript. Hence SALARY (1) denotes the present salary, SALARY (2) the previous salary, SALARY (3) the second previous salary, and so on. Figure 11.4 shows the COBOL statements and corresponding storage allocation for such a scheme.

Figure 11.4 depicts a total of 36 storage positions for the table SALARY-DATA, with the OCCURS clause at the group level. Positions 1–6 refer to SALARY (1), positions 7–12 refer to SAL-DATE (1), and positions 1–12 collectively to SALARY-DATA (1). In a similar fashion, positions 13–18 refer to SALARY (2), positions 19–24 to SAL-DATE (2), and positions 13–24 collectively to SALARY-DATA (2). Whenever a subscript is used, it is enclosed in parentheses.

Figure 11.5 contains an alternate implementation with two OCCURS clauses at the elementary level. A total of 36 storage positions are still assigned to the table, but the storage allocation is different; i.e., positions 1–6 contain SALARY (1), positions 7–12 contain SALARY (2), and positions 13–18 contain SALARY (3). In similar fashion, positions 19–24 correspond to SAL-DATE (1), positions 25–30 to SAL-DATE (2), and positions 31–36 to SAL-DATE (3). Either arrangement, Figure 11.4 or Figure 11.5, is appropriate; the choice is up to the programmer.

Problems with the OCCURS Clause

The most common error associated with tables is the omission of a subscript where one is required, or the inclusion of a subscript where it is not needed. The rule is very simple. *Any data name that has been defined with an OCCURS clause, or any data name subservient to a group item containing an OCCURS clause, must always be referenced with a subscript.* Failure to do so results in a compilation error. Thus all of the following are valid references with respect to the table definition of Figure 11.4: SALARY-DATA (2), SALARY (2), and SAL-DATE (2).

In the table definition of Figure 11.5, however, the OCCURS clause exists at the elementary, rather than the group, level. SALARY-DATA is referenced *without* a subscript and refers collectively to the 30 bytes in the table. SALARY and SAL-DATE are both defined with OCCURS clauses and require subscripts: SALARY (2) and SAL-DATE (2), for example.

The compiler checks only for the existence of a subscript, but not its value; for example, the entry SALARY (20) is syntactically correct in that a subscript is present, but logically incorrect as the OCCURS clause defines only three elements. The error would not be detected during compilation; it would pose a problem during execution as it references an invalid storage location with unpredictable results. Some compilers offer the option of including a ***subscript check*** whereby an error message will be produced during execution if an invalid subscript is referenced.

Rules for Subscripts

COBOL subscripts may be either variable or constant, but in either case must adhere to the following:

1. At least one space is required between the data name and the left parenthesis.

Valid:	SALES (2)
Invalid:	SALES(SUB)
Invalid:	SALES(2)

2. A space may not follow the left parenthesis nor precede the right parenthesis.

Valid:	SALES (SUB)
Valid:	SALES (2)
Invalid:	SALES(2)
Invalid:	SALES(2)

3. A subscript can be a data name or a numeric literal with an integer value. Relative subscripting—that is, a data name plus or minus an integer—is also permitted.

Valid:	SALES (SUB + 1)
Invalid:	SALES (1.2)

Relative Subscripting

Relative subscripting—that is, the ability to add or subtract an integer from a subscript—is a tremendous convenience in certain situations. The report in Figure

Figure 11.6   Relative Subscripting

```
        CURRENT SALARY      EFFECTIVE DATE      PERCENT INCREASE
            $46,000             09/1998              15.0%
            $40,000             09/1997              11.1%
            $36,000             09/1996              12.5%
            $32,000             09/1995
```

(a) Salary History

```
PERFORM VARYING SUB FROM 1 BY 1
    UNTIL SUB > 3 OR SALARY (SUB + 1) = 0
        COMPUTE PCT-SALARY-INC (SUB)
            = 100 * ((SALARY (SUB) - SALARY (SUB + 1))
            / SALARY (SUB + 1)
        END-COMPUTE
END-PERFORM.
```

(b) Computation of Percent Salary Increase

11.6a displays four levels of salary, the date on which each salary became effective, and the associated percent increase for each pair of salaries. (The percent increase is not calculated for the last salary.) Percent increase is computed according to the general formula:

$$\text{Percent Salary Increase} = \frac{\text{New Salary} - \text{Old Salary}}{\text{Old Salary}} \times 100$$

The current salary of $46,000 in Figure 11.6a reflects a 15 percent increase over the previous salary of $40,000 and was computed as follows:

$$\text{Percent Salary Increase} = \frac{46,000 - 40,000}{40,000} \times 100 = .15$$

The percent salary increase is a repetitive calculation that is required for each pair of salaries stored within the salary table. One (tedious) approach is to use a different formula for each pair of salaries—that is, one formula to reference SALARY (1) and SALARY (2), a second formula to reference SALARY (2) and SALARY (3), and so on. A more elegant solution is to develop a general formula that references SALARY (SUB) and SALARY (SUB + 1) as shown in Figure 11.6b.

The COMPUTE statement is executed three times if all four salaries are present. Newer employees will not have a complete salary history, however, and hence the second condition in the UNTIL clause will cease execution if an earlier salary is not present; that is, the latter condition prevents a division by zero when an earlier salary is not available.

USAGE Clause

The **USAGE** clause is intended to make a program more efficient. The clause is entirely optional as the presence (or absence) of a USAGE clause does not alter the logic of a program, but affects only the generated object code. A true understanding, therefore, requires a knowledge of assembler fundamentals which is beyond the present discussion. Suffice it to say that subscripts are best defined with a USAGE clause in one of four equivalent formats as follows:

```
05  SUBSCRIPT-1    PIC S9(4)    USAGE IS COMPUTATIONAL.
05  SUBSCRIPT-2    PIC S9(4)    COMPUTATIONAL.
05  SUBSCRIPT-3    PIC S9(4)    USAGE IS COMP.
05  SUBSCRIPT-4    PIC S9(4)    COMP.
```

OCCURS DEPENDING ON

We began the chapter with the simplest form of the OCCURS clause to define a table. The clause has several additional options, however, as shown below:

$$\underline{OCCURS} \begin{Bmatrix} \text{integer-1 } \underline{TO} \text{ integer-2 TIMES } [\underline{DEPENDING} \text{ ON data-name-1}] \\ \text{integer-2 TIMES} \end{Bmatrix}$$

$$\left[\begin{Bmatrix} \underline{ASCENDING} \\ \underline{DESCENDING} \end{Bmatrix} \text{KEY IS data-name-2 } [\text{data-name-3}] \ldots \right]$$

$$[\underline{INDEXED} \text{ BY index-name-1 } [\text{index-name-2}] \ldots]$$

The DEPENDING ON clause defines a *variable-length table.* This in turn produces a *variable-length record*, which is reflected in the RECORD CONTAINS clause of the FD as shown in Figure 11.7.

The records in STUDENT-TRANSCRIPT-FILE will vary in length from 42 to 1,131 characters, depending on the number of courses a student has completed. The minimum record length is 42 characters; 30 for name, 10 for major, and 2 for the number of courses. The records for incoming freshmen will contain the minimum 42 characters, whereas the records for upperclassmen contain an additional 11 bytes for every completed course. An arbitrary maximum of 99 courses is permitted in a record.

The advantage of *variable-length records* is that they allocate only as much space as necessary in the storage medium. *Fixed-length records*, on the other hand, assign the same (maximum) amount of disk space to every record in the file.

Figure 11.7 Variable-length Records

```
FD  STUDENT-TRANSCRIPT-FILE
    RECORD CONTAINS 42 TO 1131 CHARACTERS
    DATA RECORD IS STUDENT-RECORD.
01  STUDENT-RECORD.
    05  ST-NAME                              PIC X(30).
    05  ST-MAJOR                             PIC X(10).
    05  ST-COURSES-COMPLETED                 PIC 99.
    05  ST-COURSE-GRADE OCCURS 0 TO 99 TIMES
        DEPENDING ON ST-COURSES-COMPLETED.
        10  ST-COURSE-NUMBER                 PIC 9(6).
        10  ST-GRADE                         PIC X.
        10  ST-COURSE-DATE                   PIC 9(4).
```

What, then, is the maximum number of courses? Is it five per semester, times 8 semesters, or 40 courses? What about the student who fails a course or the one with two majors, or the one who remains in the university to pursue a master's or doctoral degree? Perhaps we should allocate space for 100 courses, just to be safe. If we do, every student record will require 1,100 bytes (11 bytes per course times 100 courses). But at any given time the average student probably has completed twenty or fewer courses (that is, there are freshmen, sophomores, juniors, and seniors in the file), and hence most records would require only 220 (20 x 11) or fewer characters. In other words, approximately 900 bytes per record would be wasted in the storage medium. Multiply this by the number of students in the university, and you can quickly see the inefficiency of fixed-length records in certain applications.

Variable-length records, on the other hand, allow only as much space in each record as is actually required. Each variable-length record contains a specific field from which the length of the record can be calculated—for example, the number of completed courses, which becomes the data name specified in the OCCURS DEPENDING ON clause.

The INDEXED BY clause is covered later in this chapter (on page 321). The ASCENDING/DESCENDING KEY clause is presented in Chapter 12 in conjunction with table lookups.

The Student Transcript Program

We are ready to incorporate the basic material on table processing into an illustrative program. Specifications follow in the usual format.

Programming Specifications

Program Name: Student Transcript Program

Narrative: This program processes a file of student records to produce a set of student transcripts. Each incoming record contains a variable-length table with the student's grades from the preceding semester. The program computes the grade point average for every student, prints individual transcripts for each student, and produces a table of students on the dean's list at the end of processing.

Input File(s): STUDENT-FILE

Input Record Layout:
```
01  STUDENT-RECORD.
    05  ST-NAME                        PIC X(19).
    05  ST-NUMBER-OF-COURSES           PIC 99.
    05  ST-COURSE-INFO OCCURS 1 TO 8 TIMES
        DEPENDING ON ST-NUMBER-OF-COURSES.
        10  ST-COURSE-NUMBER           PIC X(3).
        10  ST-COURSE-GRADE            PIC X.
        10  ST-COURSE-CREDITS          PIC 9.
```

Test Data: See Figure 11.8a.

Report Layout: See Figure 11.8b and 11.8c.

Processing Requirements: 1. Read a file of student records.

Figure 11.8 Test Data and Required Output

```
BENJAMIN, L      05111A3222A2333A3444A3555B3
BORROW, J        04666B3777B3888B3999B4
MILGROM, M       06123C4456C4789C4012C4345C3678C4
```

(a) Test Data

```
NAME:BENJAMIN, L              OFFICIAL TRANSCRIPT

       COURSE # CREDITS  GRADE
         111       3       A
         222       2       A
         333       3       A
         444       3       A
         555       3       B

          AVERAGE: 3.79    *DEANS LIST*


NAME:BORROW, J                OFFICIAL TRANSCRIPT

       COURSE # CREDITS  GRADE
         666       3       B
         777       3       B
         888       3       B
         999       4       B

          AVERAGE: 3.00


NAME:MILGROM, M               OFFICIAL TRANSCRIPT

       COURSE # CREDITS  GRADE
         123       4       C
         456       4       C
         789       4       C
         012       4       C
         345       3       C
         678       4       C

          AVERAGE: 2.00
```

(b) Individual Transcripts

```
             STUDENTS ON THE DEANS LIST

                  TOTAL    TOTAL    QUALITY
   NAME          COURSES  CREDITS   POINTS    GPA

   BENJAMIN, L      5        14        53     3.79
```

(c) The Dean's List

Figure 11.9   Calculation of Grade Point Average

```
              COURSE              COURSE GRADE        COURSE CREDITS
        Course Number 1               A                    2
        Course Number 2               B                    4
```

(a) Hypothetical Grades

```
SUB   GRADE(SUB)   CREDITS(SUB)   MULTIPLIER   TOTAL-QUALITY-POINTS   TOTAL-CREDITS
 1        A             2             4              8 (0 + 2*4)            2
 2        B             4             3             20 (8 + 4*3)            6
```

(b) Incrementing Counters

```
GRADE-POINT-AVERAGE = TOTAL-QUALITY-POINTS / TOTAL-CREDITS = 20 / 6 = 3.33
```

(c) Calculation of Grade Point Average

2. For every record read,

   a. Calculate the grade point average (GPA) according to a four-point scale with grades of A, B, C, D, and F, worth 4, 3, 2, 1, and 0, respectively. Courses are weighted according to their credit value in computing the GPA. The number of quality points for a given course is equal to the number of credits for that course times the numeric value of that grade. The GPA is equal to the total number of quality points (for all courses) divided by the total number of credits. The computation of the GPA is further illustrated in Figure 11.9.

   b. Print the student's name, list of courses with associated grades, and computed grade point average according to the format in Figure 11.8b. Every transcript is to begin on a new page.

   c. Determine whether the student qualifies for the dean's list, which requires a GPA of 3.5 or higher; if so, print the dean's list designation on the last line of the transcript.

3. Print a list of all students on the dean's list at the end of processing as shown in Figure 11.8c.

Program Design

The development of this (or any other) program begins with a hierarchy chart that includes all necessary functions to implement the processing requirements. The output in Figure 11.8 shows individual transcripts and a composite dean's list, both of which represent major tasks to be fully expanded; thus the highest-level module in the hierarchy chart will have two subordinates, CREATE-TRANSCRIPT and WRITE-DEANS-LIST, corresponding to the major functions. Each of these is expanded further as shown in the hierarchy chart of Figure 11.10.

The CREATE-TRANSCRIPT module has four subordinates: WRITE-TRANS-HEADING, PROCESS-COURSES, WRITE-GPA, and ADD-TO-DEANS-LIST. PROCESS-COURSES, in turn, has two subordinates: INCREMENT-COUNTERS and WRITE-DETAIL-LINE. WRITE-DEANS-LIST also has two subordinates: WRITE-DEANS-LIST-HEADING and WRITE-DEANS-LIST-DETAILS. The hierarchy chart is straightforward and easy to follow with the functions of all modules readily apparent from the module names.

Figure 11.10 Hierarchy Chart for Transcript Program

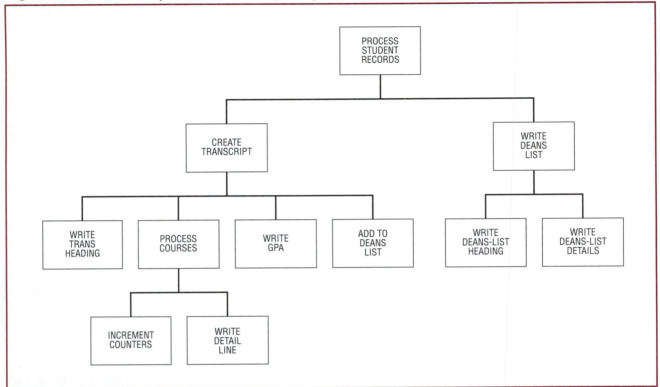

The pseudocode in Figure 11.11 uses an in-line perform to eliminate the priming read used in earlier programs. The false-condition branch in the read statement drives the program and contains the logic to compute an individual's grade point average, produce the transcript, and determine whether the individual qualifies for the dean's list.

The processing of each incoming record focuses on the production of a transcript, a process that begins with the initialization of two counters, for total quality points and total credits, respectively. Next, an inner loop is executed for every course in the current record, to determine the appropriate multiplier for the course (4 for an A, 3 for a B, and so on), to increment the counters for quality points and credits, and to write the detail line. This loop terminates after all courses (for one student) have been processed, after which the grade point average is computed by dividing the total quality points by the total number of credits.

The pseudocode next determines whether the student qualifies for the dean's list, and if so, increments the number of students on the dean's list, then moves the student's data to the appropriate place in a dean's list table. The table containing the students on the dean's list is written at the end of processing.

The Completed Program

The completed program is shown in Figure 11.12. The paragraphs in the Procedure Division correspond one to one with the modules in the hierarchy chart, and its logic in the program parallels that of the pseudocode just developed. The program complies with the processing requirements and also illustrates the various COBOL features presented earlier. Note the following:

Figure 11.11   Pseudocode for Transcript Program

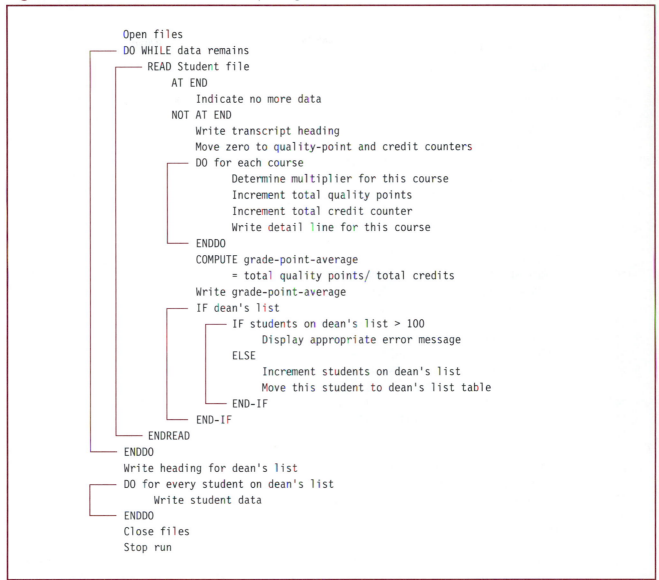

```
            Open files
        ┌── DO WHILE data remains
        │   ┌── READ Student file
        │   │       AT END
        │   │           Indicate no more data
        │   │       NOT AT END
        │   │           Write transcript heading
        │   │           Move zero to quality-point and credit counters
        │   │       ┌── DO for each course
        │   │       │       Determine multiplier for this course
        │   │       │       Increment total quality points
        │   │       │       Increment total credit counter
        │   │       │       Write detail line for this course
        │   │       └── ENDDO
        │   │           COMPUTE grade-point-average
        │   │               = total quality points/ total credits
        │   │           Write grade-point-average
        │   │   ┌── IF dean's list
        │   │   │       ┌── IF students on dean's list > 100
        │   │   │       │       Display appropriate error message
        │   │   │       ELSE
        │   │   │       │       Increment students on dean's list
        │   │   │       │       Move this student to dean's list table
        │   │   │       └── END-IF
        │   │   └── END-IF
        │   └── ENDREAD
        └── ENDDO
            Write heading for dean's list
        ┌── DO for every student on dean's list
        │       Write student data
        └── ENDDO
            Close files
            Stop run
```

1. The OCCURS DEPENDING ON clause in lines 21 and 22 defines a variable-length table for the number of courses, which in turn produces a variable-length record in lines 15–17 of the FD for STUDENT-FILE.

2. The definition of two subscripts in Working-Storage—COURSE-SUB and DEAN-SUB—both of which contain the (USAGE IS) COMP clause for efficiency.

3. The in-line PERFORM statement of lines 133–140, coupled with the false-condition branch in the READ statement, drives the program by performing the paragraph 200-CREATE-TRANSCRIPT (lines 146–159) for every record in the file. This critical paragraph computes the grade point average, produces the transcript, and determines whether the student qualifies for the dean's list.

Figure 11.12   The Student Transcript Program

```
1        IDENTIFICATION DIVISION.
2        PROGRAM-ID.    TRANSCRP.
3        AUTHOR.        ROBERT GRAUER.
4
5        ENVIRONMENT DIVISION.
6        INPUT-OUTPUT SECTION.
7        FILE-CONTROL.
8           SELECT STUDENT-FILE  ASSIGN TO SYSIN
9               ORGANIZATION IS LINE SEQUENTIAL.
10          SELECT PRINT-FILE    ASSIGN TO SYSOUT
11              ORGANIZATION IS LINE SEQUENTIAL.
12
13       DATA DIVISION.
14       FILE SECTION.
15       FD  STUDENT-FILE
16           RECORD CONTAINS 26 TO 61 CHARACTERS
17           DATA RECORD IS STUDENT-RECORD.
18       01  STUDENT-RECORD.
19           05  ST-NAME                PIC X(19).
20           05  ST-NUMBER-OF-COURSES   PIC 99.
21           05  ST-COURSE-INFO OCCURS 1 TO 8 TIMES
22               DEPENDING ON ST-NUMBER-OF-COURSES.
23               10  ST-COURSE-NUMBER   PIC X(3).
24               10  ST-COURSE-GRADE    PIC X.
25               10  ST-COURSE-CREDITS  PIC 9.
26
27       FD  PRINT-FILE
28           RECORD CONTAINS 132 CHARACTERS
29           DATA RECORD IS PRINT-LINE.
30       01  PRINT-LINE                 PIC X(132).
31
32       WORKING-STORAGE SECTION.
33       01  SUBSCRIPTS.
34           05  COURSE-SUB             PIC S9(4)              COMP.
35           05  DEAN-SUB               PIC 9(3)    VALUE ZERO COMP.
36
37       01  SWITCHES-AND-COUNTERS.
38           05  END-OF-FILE-SWITCH     PIC X(3)    VALUE 'NO '.
39           05  STUDENTS-ON-DEANS-LIST PIC 9(3)    VALUE ZERO.
40
41       01  INDIVIDUAL-GPA-VARIABLES.
42           05  IND-TOTAL-CREDITS      PIC 999.
43           05  IND-TOTAL-QUAL-POINTS  PIC 999.
44           05  IND-MULTIPLIER         PIC 9.
45           05  IND-GRADE-POINT-AVERAGE PIC S9V99.
46               88  DEANS-LIST                     VALUES 3.5 THRU 4.
47
48       01  DEANS-LIST-TABLE.
49           05  DEANS-LIST-INFO OCCURS 100 TIMES.
50               10  DL-NAME            PIC X(19).
```

Definition of variable-length table (pointing to lines 21–22)

COMPUTATIONAL clause increases efficiency of compiled program (pointing to COMP. on lines 34–35)

Figure 11.12 *(continued)*

```
51                  10  DL-COURSES          PIC 99.
52                  10  DL-CREDITS          PIC 999.
53                  10  DL-QUAL-POINTS      PIC 999.
54                  10  DL-GPA              PIC S9V99.
55
56          01  TRANS-HEADING-LINE-ONE.
57              05  FILLER                  PIC X(6)    VALUE ' NAME:'.
58              05  HDG-NAME                PIC X(15).
59              05  FILLER                  PIC X(10)   VALUE SPACES.
60              05  FILLER                  PIC X(19)
61                          VALUE 'OFFICIAL TRANSCRIPT'.
62              05  FILLER                  PIC X(82) VALUE SPACES.
63
64          01  TRANS-HEADING-LINE-TWO.
65              05  FILLER                  PIC X(10)   VALUE SPACES.
66              05  FILLER                  PIC X(9)    VALUE 'COURSE # '.
67              05  FILLER                  PIC X(9)    VALUE 'CREDITS  '.
68              05  FILLER                  PIC X(5)    VALUE 'GRADE'.
69              05  FILLER                  PIC X(99)   VALUE SPACES.
70
71          01  DETAIL-LINE.
72              05  FILLER                  PIC X(13)   VALUE SPACES.
73              05  DET-COURSE              PIC X(3).
74              05  FILLER                  PIC X(9)    VALUE SPACES.
75              05  DET-CREDITS             PIC 9.
76              05  FILLER                  PIC X(5)    VALUE SPACES.
77              05  DET-GRADE               PIC X.
78              05  FILLER                  PIC X(100) VALUE SPACES.
79
80          01  LAST-LINE.
81              05  FILLER                  PIC X(16)   VALUE SPACES.
82              05  FILLER                  PIC X(9)    VALUE 'AVERAGE: '.
83              05  LAST-GPA                PIC 9.99.
84              05  FILLER                  PIC X(4)    VALUE SPACES.
85              05  LAST-DEANS-LIST         PIC X(12)   VALUE SPACES.
86              05  FILLER                  PIC X(87)   VALUE SPACES.
87
88          01  DEANS-LIST-HEADING-LINE-ONE.
89              05  FILLER                  PIC X(20)   VALUE SPACES.
90              05  FILLER                  PIC X(26)
91                          VALUE 'STUDENTS ON THE DEANS LIST'.
92              05  FILLER                  PIC X(86)   VALUE SPACES.
93
94          01  DEANS-LIST-HEADING-LINE-TWO.
95              05  FILLER                  PIC X(25)   VALUE SPACES.
96              05  FILLER                  PIC X(5)    VALUE 'TOTAL'.
97              05  FILLER                  PIC X(5)    VALUE SPACES.
98              05  FILLER                  PIC X(5)    VALUE 'TOTAL'.
99              05  FILLER                  PIC X(4)    VALUE SPACES.
100             05  FILLER                  PIC X(7)    VALUE 'QUALITY'.
```

Figure 11.12   *(continued)*

```
101              05  FILLER                    PIC X(81)  VALUE SPACES.
102
103      01  DEANS-LIST-HEADING-LINE-THREE.
104              05  FILLER                    PIC X      VALUE SPACES.
105              05  FILLER                    PIC X(4)   VALUE 'NAME'.
106              05  FILLER                    PIC X(19)  VALUE SPACES.
107              05  FILLER                    PIC X(7)   VALUE 'COURSES'.
108              05  FILLER                    PIC X(3)   VALUE SPACES.
109              05  FILLER                    PIC X(7)   VALUE 'CREDITS'.
110              05  FILLER                    PIC X(4)   VALUE SPACES.
111              05  FILLER                    PIC X(6)   VALUE 'POINTS'.
112              05  FILLER                    PIC X(5)   VALUE SPACES.
113              05  FILLER                    PIC X(3)   VALUE 'GPA'.
114              05  FILLER                    PIC X(73)  VALUE SPACES.
115
116      01  DEANS-LIST-DETAIL-LINE.
117              05  FILLER                    PIC X      VALUE SPACES.
118              05  DL-DET-NAME               PIC X(19).
119              05  FILLER                    PIC X(7)   VALUE SPACES.
120              05  DL-DET-TOT-COURSES        PIC Z9.
121              05  FILLER                    PIC X(7)   VALUE SPACES.
122              05  DL-DET-TOT-CREDITS        PIC ZZ9.
123              05  FILLER                    PIC X(8)   VALUE SPACES.
124              05  DL-DET-TOT-QUAL-POINTS    PIC ZZ9.
125              05  FILLER                    PIC X(6)   VALUE SPACES.
126              05  DL-DET-GPA                PIC 9.99.
127              05  FILLER                    PIC X(72)  VALUE SPACES.
128
129      PROCEDURE DIVISION.
130      100-PROCESS-STUDENT-RECORDS.
131          OPEN INPUT  STUDENT-FILE
132               OUTPUT PRINT-FILE.
133          PERFORM UNTIL END-OF-FILE-SWITCH = 'YES'
134              READ STUDENT-FILE
135                  AT END
136                      MOVE 'YES' TO END-OF-FILE-SWITCH
137                  NOT AT END
138                      PERFORM 200-CREATE-TRANSCRIPT
139              END-READ
140          END-PERFORM.
141          PERFORM 300-WRITE-DEANS-LIST.
142          CLOSE STUDENT-FILE
143                PRINT-FILE.
144          STOP RUN.
145
146      200-CREATE-TRANSCRIPT.
147          PERFORM 210-WRITE-TRANS-HEADING.
148          MOVE ZERO TO IND-TOTAL-QUAL-POINTS IND-TOTAL-CREDITS.
149          PERFORM 220-PROCESS-COURSES
150              VARYING COURSE-SUB FROM 1 BY 1
151                  UNTIL COURSE-SUB > ST-NUMBER-OF-COURSES.
```

In-line PERFORM statement and false-condition branch drives the program

PERFORM VARYING statement processes all entries in course table

Figure 11.12 *(continued)*

```
152          COMPUTE IND-GRADE-POINT-AVERAGE ROUNDED
153              = IND-TOTAL-QUAL-POINTS / IND-TOTAL-CREDITS
154              SIZE ERROR DISPLAY 'SIZE ERROR ON GPA'
155          END-COMPUTE.
156          PERFORM 250-WRITE-GPA.
157          IF DEANS-LIST
158              PERFORM 260-ADD-TO-DEANS-LIST
159          END-IF.
160
161      210-WRITE-TRANS-HEADING.
162          MOVE ST-NAME TO HDG-NAME.
163          WRITE PRINT-LINE FROM TRANS-HEADING-LINE-ONE
164              AFTER ADVANCING PAGE.
165          WRITE PRINT-LINE FROM TRANS-HEADING-LINE-TWO
166              AFTER ADVANCING 2 LINES.
167
168      220-PROCESS-COURSES.
169          PERFORM 230-INCREMENT-COUNTERS.
170          PERFORM 240-WRITE-DETAIL-LINE.
171
172      230-INCREMENT-COUNTERS.
173          EVALUATE ST-COURSE-GRADE (COURSE-SUB)
174             WHEN 'A'
175                 MOVE 4 TO IND-MULTIPLIER
176             WHEN 'B'
177                 MOVE 3 TO IND-MULTIPLIER
178             WHEN 'C'
179                 MOVE 2 TO IND-MULTIPLIER
180             WHEN 'D'
181                 MOVE 1 TO IND-MULTIPLIER
182             WHEN OTHER
183                 MOVE 0 TO IND-MULTIPLIER
184                 DISPLAY 'INVALID COURSE GRADE'
185          END-EVALUATE.
186          COMPUTE IND-TOTAL-QUAL-POINTS = IND-TOTAL-QUAL-POINTS
187              + ST-COURSE-CREDITS (COURSE-SUB) * IND-MULTIPLIER
188              SIZE ERROR DISPLAY 'SIZE ERROR ON TOTAL QUALITY POINTS'
189          END-COMPUTE.
190          ADD ST-COURSE-CREDITS (COURSE-SUB) TO IND-TOTAL-CREDITS
191              SIZE ERROR DISPLAY 'SIZE ERROR ON TOTAL CREDITS'
192          END-ADD.
193
194      240-WRITE-DETAIL-LINE.
195          MOVE ST-COURSE-NUMBER (COURSE-SUB) TO DET-COURSE.
196          MOVE ST-COURSE-CREDITS (COURSE-SUB) TO DET-CREDITS.
197          MOVE ST-COURSE-GRADE (COURSE-SUB) TO DET-GRADE.
198          WRITE PRINT-LINE FROM DETAIL-LINE.
199
200      250-WRITE-GPA.
201          MOVE IND-GRADE-POINT-AVERAGE TO LAST-GPA.
```

COURSE-SUB varies during execution of WRITE-DETAIL-LINE

Figure 11.12   *(continued)*

```
202          IF DEANS-LIST
203              MOVE '*DEANS LIST*' TO LAST-DEANS-LIST
204          ELSE
205              MOVE SPACES TO LAST-DEANS-LIST
206          END-IF.
207          WRITE PRINT-LINE FROM LAST-LINE
208              AFTER ADVANCING 2 LINES.
209
210      260-ADD-TO-DEANS-LIST.
211          IF STUDENTS-ON-DEANS-LIST > 100
212              DISPLAY 'DEAN LIST TABLE EXCEEDED'
213          ELSE
214              ADD 1 TO STUDENTS-ON-DEANS-LIST
215              ADD 1 TO DEAN-SUB
216              MOVE ST-NAME TO DL-NAME (DEAN-SUB)
217              MOVE ST-NUMBER-OF-COURSES TO DL-COURSES (DEAN-SUB)
218              MOVE IND-TOTAL-CREDITS TO DL-CREDITS (DEAN-SUB)
219              MOVE IND-TOTAL-QUAL-POINTS TO DL-QUAL-POINTS (DEAN-SUB)
220              MOVE IND-GRADE-POINT-AVERAGE TO DL-GPA (DEAN-SUB)
221          END-IF.
222
223      300-WRITE-DEANS-LIST.
224          PERFORM 310-WRITE-DEANS-LIST-HEADINGS.
225          PERFORM 320-WRITE-DEANS-LIST-DETAILS
226              VARYING DEAN-SUB FROM 1 BY 1
227                  UNTIL DEAN-SUB > STUDENTS-ON-DEANS-LIST.
228
229      310-WRITE-DEANS-LIST-HEADINGS.
230          WRITE PRINT-LINE FROM DEANS-LIST-HEADING-LINE-ONE
231              AFTER ADVANCING PAGE.
232          WRITE PRINT-LINE FROM DEANS-LIST-HEADING-LINE-TWO
233              AFTER ADVANCING 2 LINES.
234          WRITE PRINT-LINE FROM DEANS-LIST-HEADING-LINE-THREE.
235          MOVE SPACES TO PRINT-LINE.
236          WRITE PRINT-LINE.
237
238      320-WRITE-DEANS-LIST-DETAILS.
239          MOVE DL-NAME (DEAN-SUB) TO DL-DET-NAME.
240          MOVE DL-COURSES (DEAN-SUB) TO DL-DET-TOT-COURSES.
241          MOVE DL-CREDITS (DEAN-SUB) TO DL-DET-TOT-CREDITS.
242          MOVE DL-QUAL-POINTS (DEAN-SUB) TO DL-DET-TOT-QUAL-POINTS.
243          MOVE DL-GPA (DEAN-SUB) TO DL-DET-GPA.
244          WRITE PRINT-LINE FROM DEANS-LIST-DETAIL-LINE.
```

Increments number of entries in variable-length table

Produces the dean's list

4. The computation of the grade point average is described as follows:

   a. The counters IND-TOTAL-QUALITY-POINTS and IND-TOTAL-CREDITS are set to zero by the MOVE ZERO statement in line 148.

   b. The PERFORM VARYING statement in lines 149–151 executes the paragraph 220-PROCESS-COURSES, which in turn performs two lower-level paragraphs for every course in the current record, one course at a time.

   c. Each time the paragraph 230-INCREMENT-COUNTERS is executed, the course multiplier is determined (4 for an A, 3 for a B, and so on), after which the cumulative values of the quality points and credits are updated.

   d. The PERFORM VARYING terminates, after which the GPA is determined in lines 152–155.

5. The definition of a counter STUDENTS-ON-DEANS-LIST (line 39) and the definition of the associated DEANS-LIST-TABLE in lines 48–54 to hold data for qualifying students. The IF statement in lines 157–159 determines whether the current student qualifies for the dean's list, then executes paragraph 260-ADD-TO-DEANS-LIST (lines 210–221) to increment the counter and move the student's values to the appropriate place in the table.

6. The PERFORM VARYING statement in lines 225–227 to produce the dean's list based on the number of students (i.e., the final value of STUDENTS-ON-DEANS-LIST) and the entries in the table.

Indexes Versus Subscripts

The transcript program just completed illustrates the basics of table processing, and as such goes a long way toward increasing your proficiency in COBOL. There is, however, a good deal more to learn about tables, and so we return to the syntax of the OCCURS clause shown earlier in the chapter.

The OCCURS clause includes an optional INDEXED BY entry to define an *index* for use with a particular table. An index is conceptually the same as a subscript in that both reference an entry in a table. Indexes, however, produce more efficient object code and are preferred (by some programmers) for that reason. The difference is subtle; an index represents a ***displacement*** (the number of positions into a table), whereas a subscript indicates an occurrence. Consider:

```
05  ST-COURSE-INFO OCCURS 10 TIMES
      INDEXED BY COURSE-INDEX.
    10  ST-COURSE-NUMBER          PIC X(3).
    10  ST-COURSE-GRADE           PIC X.
    10  ST-COURSE-CREDITS         PIC 99.
```

The COBOL statements establish a table with 10 entries which occupy a total of 60 positions in memory. Valid subscripts for ST-COURSE-INFO are 1, 2, 3, . . . 10, because the table entries occur 10 times. The first occurrence of ST-COURSE-INFO is at the start of the table (displacement zero), the second occurrence begins 6 bytes into the table, the third occurrence 12 bytes into the table, and so on. The value of the index is the value of the displacement, that is, the number of positions into a table to the entry in question; hence valid displacements for ST-COURSE-INFO are 0, 6, 12, . . . 54.

Fortunately, you need not be concerned with the actual value (displacement) of an index, and can regard it conceptually as a subscript. In other words, you will indicate index values of 1, 2, 3, and so on, which will be converted by the compiler to internal displacements of 0, 6, 12, and so on. Indexes can not, however, be initialized with a MOVE statement, nor can they be incremented with an ADD statement. The SET statement is used instead.

The SET Statement

The **SET** statement has two formats and is used only with indexes.

Format 1

$$\underline{SET} \begin{Bmatrix} \text{identifier-1} \left[, \text{ identifier-2}\right] \ldots \\ \text{index-name-1} \left[, \text{ index-name-2}\right] \ldots \end{Bmatrix} \underline{TO} \begin{Bmatrix} \text{identifier-3} \\ \text{index-name-3} \\ \text{integer-1} \end{Bmatrix}$$

Format 2

$$\underline{SET} \text{ index-name-4} \left[, \text{ index-name-5}\right] \ldots \begin{Bmatrix} \underline{UP\ BY} \\ \underline{DOWN\ BY} \end{Bmatrix} \begin{Bmatrix} \text{identifier-4} \\ \text{integer-2} \end{Bmatrix}$$

Figures 11.13 and 11.14 compare indexes and subscripts. Figure 11.13a depicts the definition of a table without an index, which in turn requires the definition of a subscript elsewhere in the Data Division. Figure 11.13b uses a PERFORM VARYING statement to manipulate this table (in conjunction with COURSE-SUBSCRIPT), while Figure 11.13c shows the PERFORM TIMES statement to accomplish the same objective. The latter is yet another form of the PERFORM statement and performs the designated procedure (or in-line statement) the indicated number of times. It is less convenient than a comparable PERFORM VARYING statement as the programmer has to vary the subscript (index) explicitly.

Figure 11.14 contains parallel code, except that the table is defined in Figure 11.14a with an index (so there is no need to define a subscript). Figure 11.14b is virtually identical to its predecessor in that the PERFORM VARYING statement can manipulate either subscripts or indexes. Finally, Figure 11.14c shows the alternate (less desirable) way to process the table. Observe, therefore, the use of SET statements to initialize and increment the index (as opposed to the MOVE and ADD statements in Figure 11.13c).

Indexing is not required in COBOL, and thus you can choose between subscripts and indexes in any given application. Indeed, you may wonder why bother with indexes at all, if they provide the same capability as subscripts. The answer is twofold:

1. Indexes provide more efficient object code than subscripts.

2. Indexes are required for SEARCH and SEARCH ALL, two powerful statements that are presented in Chapter 12.

Differences between indexes and subscripts are summarized in Table 11.1.

Table 11.1   Indexes versus Subscripts

Indexes	Subscripts
Defined with a specific table; can be used only with the table with which they are defined	Defined in Working-Storage; the same subscript can be used with multiple tables although this is not recommended
Initialized and incremented via the SET statement; can also be manipulated in PERFORM statements	May not be used with SET statements (MOVE and ADD are used instead); can also be manipulated in PERFORM statements
Provide more efficient object code than subscripts	USAGE IS COMPUTATIONAL makes subscripts more efficient, although indexes are still faster

Figure 11.13 Indexes versus Subscripts (Subscripts)

```
   05  ST-NUMBER-OF-COURSES         PIC 99.
   05  ST-COURSE-INFO OCCURS 1 TO 8 TIMES
           DEPENDING ON ST-NUMBER-OF-COURSES.
       10  ST-COURSE-NUMBER         PIC X(3).
       10  ST-COURSE-GRADE          PIC X.
       10  ST-COURSE-CREDITS        PIC 99.
   .
     .
       .
   05  COURSE-SUBSCRIPT             PIC S9(4)  COMP.
```
— *Subscript defined separately in Working-Storage*

(a) Table Definition

```
PERFORM WRITE-COURSE-DATA
    VARYING COURSE-SUBSCRIPT FROM 1 BY 1
        UNTIL COURSE-SUBSCRIPT > ST-NUMBER-OF-COURSES.
    .
      .
        .
WRITE-COURSE-DATA.
    MOVE ST-COURSE-NUMBER (COURSE-SUBSCRIPT) TO PL-NUMBER.
    MOVE ST-COURSE-GRADE (COURSE-SUBSCRIPT) TO PL-GRADE.
    WRITE PRINT-LINE FROM PRINT-LINE-ONE
        AFTER ADVANCING 1 LINE.
```

(b) PERFORM VARYING

```
    MOVE 1 TO COURSE-SUBSCRIPT.
    PERFORM WRITE-COURSE-DATA ST-NUMBER-OF-COURSES TIMES.
    .
      .
        .
WRITE-COURSE-DATA.
    MOVE ST-COURSE-NUMBER (COURSE-SUBSCRIPT) TO PL-NUMBER.
    MOVE ST-COURSE-GRADE (COURSE-SUBSCRIPT) TO PL-GRADE.
    WRITE PRINT-LINE FROM PRINT-LINE-ONE
        AFTER ADVANCING 1 LINE.
    ADD 1 TO COURSE-SUBSCRIPT.
```

(c) PERFORM TIMES

Figure 11.14 Indexes versus Subscripts (Indexes)

```
05  ST-NUMBER-OF-COURSES          PIC 99.
05  ST-COURSE-INFO OCCURS 1 TO 8 TIMES
    DEPENDING ON ST-NUMBER-OF-COURSES ──────── Index is defined with table
    INDEXED BY COURSE-INDEX.
    10  ST-COURSE-NUMBER          PIC X(3).
    10  ST-COURSE-GRADE           PIC X.
    10  ST-COURSE-CREDITS         PIC 99.
```

(a) Table Definition

```
PERFORM WRITE-COURSE-DATA
    VARYING COURSE-INDEX FROM 1 BY 1
        UNTIL COURSE-INDEX > ST-NUMBER-OF-COURSES.
.
   .
      .

WRITE-COURSE-DATA.
    MOVE ST-COURSE-NUMBER (COURSE-INDEX) TO PL-NUMBER.
    MOVE ST-COURSE-GRADE (COURSE-INDEX) TO PL-GRADE.
    WRITE PRINT-LINE FROM PRINT-LINE-ONE
        AFTER ADVANCING 1 LINE.
```

(b) PERFORM VARYING

```
                               ──────── Index is initialized by a SET statement
SET COURSE-INDEX TO 1.
PERFORM WRITE-COURSE-DATA ST-NUMBER-OF-COURSES TIMES.
.
   .
      .

WRITE-COURSE-DATA.
    MOVE ST-COURSE-NUMBER (COURSE-INDEX) TO PL-NUMBER.
    MOVE ST-COURSE-GRADE (COURSE-INDEX) TO PL-GRADE.
    WRITE PRINT-LINE FROM PRINT-LINE-ONE
        AFTER ADVANCING 1 LINE.
    SET COURSE-INDEX UP BY 1.
```

(c) PERFORM TIMES

LIMITATIONS OF COBOL-74

COBOL-85 introduced several minor changes in conjunction with table processing. The new compiler allows seven levels of subscripting as opposed to the earlier limit of three, but given that the typical programmer seldom uses three-level tables, this extension is of little practical benefit. (Multiple-level tables are covered in Chapter 13.) The OCCURS DEPENDING ON clause may specify a value of zero, whereas at least one occurrence was required in COBOL-74.

A more significant change is the introduction of relative subscripting (as explained in Figure 11.6), enabling the reference DATA-NAME (SUBSCRIPT ± integer). Relative subscripting was not permitted in COBOL-74 (although relative indexing was).

S U M M A R Y

Points to Remember

■ A table is a grouping of similar data whose values are stored in contiguous storage locations and assigned a single name. Tables are implemented in COBOL through the OCCURS clause with subscripts or indexes used to reference individual items in a table. The OCCURS DEPENDING ON clause implements a variable-length table.

■ An index is conceptually the same as a subscript but provides more efficient object code. Indexes are manipulated with the SET statement, whereas subscripts are initialized with a MOVE statement and incremented with an ADD statement.

■ The PERFORM VARYING statement manipulates an index or a subscript to execute a procedure or series of in-line statements. Omission of the TEST BEFORE and TEST AFTER clauses defaults to TEST BEFORE and corresponds to the COBOL-74 implementation.

■ The PERFORM TIMES statement also provides for repeated execution of a procedure or in-line statement, but requires the programmer to explicitly vary the value of the subscript or index.

■ The optional USAGE IS COMPUTATIONAL clause is used to improve the efficiency of a program's generated object code, but does not affect its logic.

Key Words and Concepts

Displacement	Subscript
Fixed-length record	Table
Index	Variable-length record
Relative indexing	Variable-length table
Relative subscripting	

COBOL Elements

BY	PERFORM VARYING
FROM	SET
INDEXED BY	TEST AFTER
OCCURS	TEST BEFORE
OCCURS DEPENDING ON	UNTIL
PERFORM TIMES	USAGE IS COMPUTATIONAL

Fill-in

1. A table is defined through the _____ clause.

2. Entries in a table may be referenced by either a _____ or an
   _____.

3. A _____ length table is defined by the _____
   _____ _____ clause.

4. The USAGE clause is a (required/optional) entry for a subscript.

5. A table (must/may) be defined with an index.

6. (Subscripts/indexes) are manipulated with a SET statement.

7. Arithmetic (is/is not) permitted for subscripts and indexes.

8. _____ levels of subscripting are permitted in COBOL-85.

9. The TEST BEFORE clause (changes/does not change) the effect of a PERFORM
   VARYING statement.

10. The OCCURS DEPENDING ON, ASCENDING/DESCENDING KEY, and INDEXED
    BY clauses are (optional/required) entries in an OCCURS clause.

True/False

1. Tables are established by a DIMENSION statement.

2. The same entry may not contain both an OCCURS clause and a PICTURE clause.

3. When using subscripts, a space is required between a data name and the left
   parenthesis.

4. The USAGE clause is required when defining a subscript in Working-Storage.

5. The entry DATA-NAME (0) would not cause a compilation error, provided that an
   OCCURS clause had been used in the associated definition.

6. The same subscript can be used to reference different tables.

7. The same index can be used to reference different tables

8. A subscript may be a constant or a variable.

9. All records in the same file must be the same length.

10. The SET statement is used to manipulate subscripts or indexes.

11. An index may be modified by either an ADD or a MOVE statement.

12. The PERFORM VARYING statement may manipulate both subscripts and indexes.

Problems

1. Indicate which entries are incorrectly subscripted. Assume that SUB1 has been set to 5, and that the following entry applies:

   ```
   05 SALES-TABLE OCCURS 12 TIMES PIC 9(5).
   ```
   a. SALES-TABLE (1)
   b. SALES-TABLE (15)
   c. SALES-TABLE (0)
   d. SALES-TABLE (SUB1)
   e. SALES-TABLE(SUB1)
   f. SALES-TABLE (5)
   g. SALES-TABLE (SUB1, SUB2)
   h. SALES-TABLE (3)
   i. SALES-TABLE (3)
   j. SALES-TABLE (SUB1 + 1)

2. How many times will PARAGRAPH-A be executed by each of the following PERFORM statements?

   ```
   a. PERFORM PARAGRAPH-A
         VARYING SUBSCRIPT FROM 1 BY 1
            UNTIL SUBSCRIPT > 5.

   b. PERFORM PARAGRAPH-A
         VARYING SUBSCRIPT FROM 1 BY 1
            WITH TEST BEFORE
               UNTIL SUBSCRIPT > 5.

   c. PERFORM PARAGRAPH-A
         VARYING SUBSCRIPT FROM 1 BY 1
            WITH TEST AFTER
               UNTIL SUBSCRIPT > 5.

   d. PERFORM PARAGRAPH-A
         VARYING SUBSCRIPT FROM 1 BY 1
            UNTIL SUBSCRIPT = 5.

   e. PERFORM PARAGRAPH-A
         VARYING SUBSCRIPT FROM 1 BY 1
            WITH TEST BEFORE
                  UNTIL SUBSCRIPT = 5.
   ```

```
f.  PERFORM PARAGRAPH-A
        VARYING SUBSCRIPT FROM 1 BY 1
            WITH TEST AFTER
                UNTIL SUBSCRIPT = 5.
```

3. Given the following Working-Storage entries:

```
01  SAMPLE-TABLES.
    05  FIRST-TABLE OCCURS 10 TIMES
        INDEXED BY FIRST-INDEX.
        10  FIRST-TABLE-ENTRY       PIC X(5).
    05  SECOND-TABLE OCCURS 10 TIMES
        INDEXED BY SECOND-INDEX.
        10  SECOND-TABLE-ENTRY      PIC X(5).

01  SUBSCRIPT-ENTRIES.
    05  FIRST-SUBSCRIPT             PIC 9(4).
    05  SECOND-SUBSCRIPT            PIC 9(4).
```

Indicate whether the following table references are valid syntactically.

a. FIRST-TABLE-ENTRY (FIRST-INDEX)

b. FIRST-TABLE-ENTRY (FIRST-SUBSCRIPT)

c. SECOND-TABLE-ENTRY (FIRST-INDEX)

d. SECOND-TABLE-ENTRY (SECOND-INDEX)

e. SECOND-TABLE-ENTRY (FIRST-SUBSCRIPT)

f. SECOND-TABLE-ENTRY (SECOND-SUBSCRIPT)

g. FIRST-TABLE-ENTRY (FIRST-INDEX + 1)

h. FIRST-TABLE-ENTRY (FIRST-SUBSCRIPT + 1)

Indicate whether the following Procedure Division statements are valid.

i. MOVE 1 TO FIRST-SUBSCRIPT

j. SET FIRST-SUBSCRIPT TO 1

k. MOVE 1 TO FIRST-INDEX

l. SET FIRST-INDEX TO 1

m. SET FIRST-INDEX UP BY 1

n. ADD 1 TO FIRST-INDEX

4. Use the general format of the OCCURS clause to determine whether the following are valid entries (the level number has been omitted in each instance):

```
a. TABLE-ENTRY OCCURS 4 TIMES.

b. TABLE-ENTRY OCCURS 4.

c. TABLE-ENTRY OCCURS 3 TO 30 TIMES
       DEPENDING ON NUMBER-OF-TRANS.

d. TABLE-ENTRY OCCURS 5 TIMES
       INDEXED BY TABLE-INDEX.

e. TABLE-ENTRY OCCURS 5 TIMES
       SUBSCRIPTED BY TABLE-SUBSCRIPT.
```

f. TABLE-ENTRY OCCURS 5 TO 50 TIMES
   DEPENDING ON NUMBER-OF-TRANSACTIONS
   INDEXED BY TABLE-INDEX.

g. TABLE-ENTRY OCCURS 6 TIMES
   ASCENDING KEY TABLE-CODE
   INDEXED TABLE-INDEX.

h. TABLE-ENTRY OCCURS 6 TIMES
   ASCENDING KEY TABLE-CODE-1
   DESCENDING KEY TABLE-CODE-2 INDEXED BY TABLE-INDEX.

5. How many storage positions are allocated for each of the following table definitions? Show an appropriate schematic indicating storage assignment for each table.

   a. 01 STATE-TABLE.
          05 STATE-NAME OCCURS 50 TIMES   PIC X(15).
          05 STATE-POPULATION OCCURS 50 TIMES   PIC 9(8).

   b. 01 STATE-TABLE.
          05 NAME-POPULATION OCCURS 50 TIMES.
              10 STATE-NAME   PIC X(15).
              10 STATE-POPULATION   PIC 9(8).

6. Show Procedure Division statements to determine the largest and smallest population in POPULATION-TABLE. (Assume the table has been initialized elsewhere.) Move these values to BIGGEST and SMALLEST, respectively. Move the state names to BIG-STATE and SMALL-STATE, respectively. POPULATION-TABLE is defined as follows:

   01 POPULATION-TABLE.
       05 POPULATION-AND-NAME OCCURS 50 TIMES
           INDEXED BY POP-INDEX.
           10 POPULATION   PIC 9(8).
           10 STATE-NAME   PIC X(15).

Table Lookups

CHAPTER OUTLINE

Overview
System Concepts
    Types of Codes
    Characteristics of Codes
    Sequential Table Lookup
    Binary Table Lookup
    Positional Organization and Direct Lookups
Initializing a Table
    Hard Coding
    Input-loaded Tables
Programming Tip—Restrict Subscripts and Switches to a Single Use
Table Lookups
    PERFORM VARYING Statement
    SEARCH Statement
    SEARCH ALL Statement
    Direct Lookup
    Range-Step Tables
A Complete Example
    Programming Specifications
    Program Design
    The Completed Program
Limitations of COBOL-74
Summary
Fill-in
True/False
Problems

O B J E C T I V E S

After reading this chapter you will be able to:

■ Define a table lookup and describe why it is used.

■ Distinguish between a numeric, alphabetic, and alphanumeric code; describe several attributes of a good coding system.

■ Distinguish between a sequential table lookup, a binary table lookup, and direct access to table entries.

■ Distinguish between a table that is hard coded versus one that is input loaded.

■ State the purpose of the VALUE, OCCURS, and REDEFINES clauses as they pertain to table definition and initialization.

■ Define a range-step table.

■ Code SEARCH and SEARCH ALL statements to implement table lookups.

O V E R V I E W

One-level tables, subscripts, and indexes were introduced in Chapter 11. This chapter extends that information to include table lookups—the conversion of incoming data from a concise, coded format to a descriptive and more meaningful result.

The System Concepts section begins with a discussion of codes, then proceeds to techniques for table organization, table initialization, and table lookups. The body of the chapter covers the COBOL implementation of the conceptual material, and includes the REDEFINES, VALUE, and OCCURS clauses, and the SEARCH and SEARCH ALL statements. All of this material is effectively summarized in a COBOL program at the end of the chapter.

System Concepts

Figure 12.1 depicts a table of student major *codes* and the associated descriptions. Records in the storage medium contain a two-position code, whereas printed reports display the descriptive (expanded) value. The conversion is accomplished through a *table lookup*, with the obvious advantage that less space is required to store codes rather than descriptive values. (Consider the implications for large files with thousands, perhaps millions of records.)

A second, perhaps more important, reason for using codes is to assign records to consistent classes. It is a simple matter for a data-entry clerk to look up a *unique* code for a Computer Information Systems major (e.g., 24 in Figure 12.1), and different clerks will always obtain the same code for the same major. It is far less likely that different clerks will always use identical spellings for a given major; even the same individual is apt to use different spellings at different times, especially when one begins to abbreviate. By assigning a code, rather than a descriptive value, individuals

Figure 12.1   Table of Major Codes

02	ART HISTORY
04	BIOLOGY
19	CHEMISTRY
21	CIVIL ENGINEERING
24	COMP INF SYS
32	ECONOMICS
39	FINANCE
43	MANAGEMENT
49	MARKETING
54	STATISTICS

with the same major will have a common identifying characteristic that can be subsequently processed by a program.

Types of Codes

The codes in a table may be *numeric, alphabetic,* or *alphanumeric.* A numeric code consists entirely of digits; for example, the zip code is a numeric code familiar to all Americans. A three-digit numeric code has 1,000 possible values (from 0 through 999). In similar fashion, four- and five-digit numeric codes have 10,000 and 100,000 values, respectively.

Alphabetic codes contain only letters—for example, state abbreviations. A two-position alphabetic code has 676 possible values. (Each character can assume one of 26 values, A through Z. Thus, a two-position alphabetic code has $26 \times 26 = 26^2$ = 676 possible values. In similar fashion, a three-position alphabetic code has $26^3 = 17,576$ possible values.)

Alphanumeric codes contain both letters and numbers—for example, license plates. Alphanumeric codes offer the advantage of providing a greater number of combinations than either pure numeric or pure alphabetic codes. A three-digit numeric code has 1,000 (10^3) variations, a three-digit alphabetic code has 17,576 (26^3) possibilities, but a three-position alphanumeric code (in which each character can be either a letter or number) has 46,656 (36^3) choices. Table 12.1 summarizes the various types of codes.

TABLE 12.1   Types of Table Codes

CODE TYPE	SYMBOLS Used	Number of Possible Values 1 Position	2 Positions	n Positions
Numeric	0–9	$10^1 = 10$	$10^2 = 100$	10^n
Alphabetic	A–Z	$26^1 = 26$	$26^2 = 676$	26^n
Alphanumeric	A–Z, 0–9	$36^1 = 36$	$36^2 = 1,296$	36^n

Characteristics of Codes

A good coding system is *precise, mnemonic,* and *expandable.* A precise code is unique; that is, it should not be possible to select alternative choices from a table of codes for a given entry. Indeed, codes are often assigned because the original attribute is not unique. Universities, for example, assign student numbers because different students may have the same name.

Good codes are mnemonic, that is, easy to remember. State abbreviations are alphabetic rather than numeric for this reason. Thus NY and TX are inherently easier to learn as abbreviations for New York and Texas than random two-digit numbers.

A coding system should also be expandable so that future additions can be easily handled. It is poor design, for example, to allocate only two positions in a record for a numeric branch office code, if 98 unique branch offices already exist.

Sequential Table Lookup

A *table lookup* occurs when an incoming code is compared to entries in a table in order to convert the code to an expanded value. In a *sequential* table lookup the entries in the table are checked in order, as shown in Figure 12.2.

Figure 12.2   Sequential Table Lookup

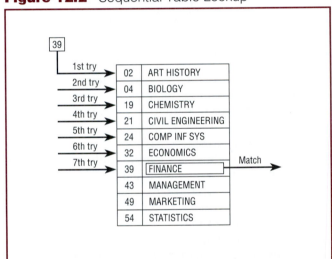

Assume, for example, an incoming code of 39. A sequential lookup begins with the first entry, then the second entry, and so on until a match is found or the table is exhausted. In this instance, 7 tries are required. On the average, a sequential table lookup requires N/2 tries (where N is the number of entries in the table) to find a match, assuming that each entry is equally likely.

The codes in Figure 12.2 were arranged sequentially. An alternative form of table organization, by *frequency of occurrence*, is sometimes used to reduce the number of trials needed to find a match in a sequential lookup. Assume, for example, that Computer Information Systems is the most common major, followed by Management. It is reasonable, therefore, to list these majors first and second in the table. In other words, majors are listed according to the likelihood of finding a match, rather than by a strict numeric sequence. The codes in the table are still examined in order, but the table itself has been rearranged.

Many tables follow a so-called 80/20 rule; that is, 80% of the matches come from 20% of the entries. (For example, 80% of the questions raised in class may come from 20% of the students; 80% of the United States population lives in 20% of the states, and so on. The numbers 80 and 20 are approximate, but the concept is valid over a surprising number of applications.)

Organization by frequency of occurrence requires a knowledge of code probabilities that is often unavailable. Sequential organization is therefore more common.

Binary Table Lookup

A binary lookup makes the number of comparisons relatively independent of where in the table the match occurs, but requires that the entries in the table be in sequence (either ascending or descending). The action of a binary lookup is illustrated in Figure 12.3.

Figure 12.3 Binary Lookup

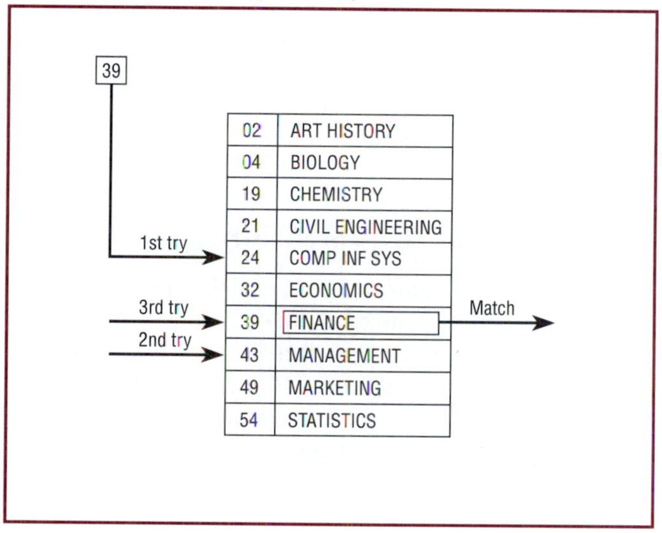

A binary search begins in the *middle* of the table, for example, at the fifth entry in Figure 12.3, and eliminates half the table with every comparison. The search then proceeds as follows:

1. Is the value of the incoming entry (the code you want to find) greater than the middle entry in the table? The answer is yes in this example in that 39 (the incoming code) is greater than 24 (the value of the middle entry). The search algorithm therefore eliminates table entries one through five.

2. There are five remaining entries (positions 6–10) that could yet contain a value equal to the incoming code. The middle (eighth) entry is selected and the comparison is made again; that is, is the value of incoming code 39 greater than the value of the eighth (middle) entry of 43? It isn't, which eliminates table entries eight through 10.

3. There are two remaining entries (positions 6–7). The middle (seventh) entry is selected, and its value of 39 matches that of the incoming code. The search is terminated.

A total of three comparisons was required to match the incoming code, 39. (If 32 had been the incoming entry, four comparisons would have been needed, but this is the *maximum* number that would ever be required for a 10-position table.) A sequential lookup, on the other hand, required seven comparisons until a match was found on 39.

If all 10 entries in a table have an equal chance of occurring, the *average* number of comparisons for a sequential search on a table of 10 entries is five. This is greater than the *maximum* number for a binary search. Indeed, as table size increases, the advantage of the binary search increases dramatically. Table 12.2 shows the maximum number of comparisons for tables with 8 to 4,095 entries.

TABLE 12.2 Required Number of Comparisons for Binary Search

Number of Elements		Maximum Number of Comparisons
8–15	(less than 2^4)	4
16–31	(less than 2^5)	5
32–63	(less than 2^6)	6
64–127	(less than 2^7)	7
128–255	(less than 2^8)	8
256–511	(less than 2^9)	9
512–1023	(less than 2^{10})	10
1024–2047	(less than $2^{11)}$)	11
2048–4095	(less than 2^{12})	12

Positional Organization and Direct Lookups

A *positional table* is a sequential table with a *consecutive* set of numeric codes. It permits immediate retrieval of a table value at the expense of unused storage space. Figure 12.4 depicts positional organization and the associated *direct lookup*.

The table in Figure 12.4 is considerably larger than the sequential table in Figures 12.2 and 12.3. Fifty-four entries are present in Figure 12.4, as opposed to 10 in the earlier tables. Observe also that codes are not stored in a positional table; that is, the value of the associated code is the position of the descriptive value within the table. Hence, ART HISTORY is stored in the second position and has an associated code of 2; BIOLOGY is stored in the fourth position with an associated code of 4; and so forth. As can be seen, this arrangement results in considerable empty (wasted) space, as only 10 of the 54 table entries contain descriptive values.

The advantage of a positional table is that a match is found immediately; for example, to obtain the descriptive value for an incoming code of 39, you go *directly* to the 39th entry in the table. (Prudent practice dictates that the programmer ensure the incoming code is valid, that is, within the table's range, before attempting a direct lookup.)

Initializing a Table

A table is initialized in one of two ways, by hard coding it into a program, or by reading its values from a file. (A table may also be initialized through the COPY statement, which is presented in Chapter 16.) Both techniques are discussed in detail.

Hard Coding

A table may be **hard-coded** directly in a program as shown in Figure 12.5. This is accomplished through a combination of the VALUE, OCCURS, and REDEFINES clauses, which are explained below:

VALUE   Assigns an initial value to a specified area in memory.

REDEFINES   Assigns another name to previously allocated memory locations.

Figure 12.4   Positional Organization and Direct Lookup

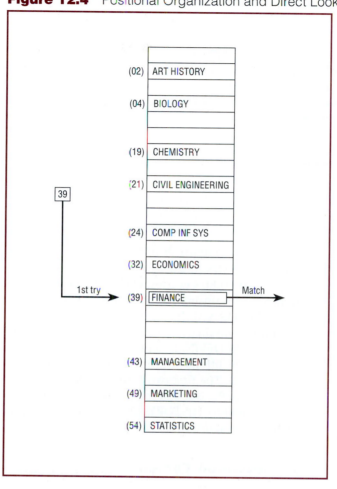

Figure 12.5   Initialization via Hard Coding

```
01   MAJOR-VALUE.
     05   FILLER          PIC X(14)     VALUE '02ART HISTORY'.
     05   FILLER          PIC X(14)     VALUE '04BIOLOGY'.
     05   FILLER          PIC X(14)     VALUE '19CHEMISTRY'.
     05   FILLER          PIC X(14)     VALUE '21CIVIL ENG'.
     05   FILLER          PIC X(14)     VALUE '24COMP INF SYS'.
     05   FILLER          PIC X(14)     VALUE '32ECONOMICS'.
     05   FILLER          PIC X(14)     VALUE '39FINANCE'.
     05   FILLER          PIC X(14)     VALUE '43MANAGEMENT'.
     05   FILLER          PIC X(14)     VALUE '49MARKETING'.
     05   FILLER          PIC X(14)     VALUE '54STATISTICS'.

01   MAJOR-TABLE REDEFINES MAJOR-VALUE.
     05   MAJORS OCCURS 10 TIMES.
          10   MAJOR-CODE   PIC 9(2).
          10   EXP-MAJOR    PIC X(12).
```

Figure 12.6　Table Initialization (Storage Schematic)

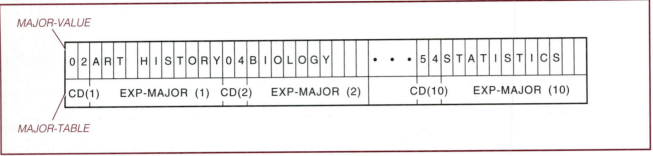

OCCURS　　Establishes a table, that is, permits different locations to be referenced by the same data name, but with different subscripts.

The need for the VALUE and OCCURS clauses is somewhat intuitive, whereas the REDEFINES clause is more obscure. The 01 entry MAJOR-VALUE contains 10 successive FILLER entries, each with a different VALUE clause, which collectively initialize 140 consecutive positions with the indicated values. The first two positions under MAJOR-VALUE contain 02, positions 3–14 contain ART HISTORY, positions 15 and 16 contain 04, positions 17–28 contain BIOLOGY, and so on.

The REDEFINES clause assigns a different name (MAJOR-TABLE) to these same 140 positions, and the subsequent OCCURS clause creates a table with 10 occurrences. The first two positions in the table are designated MAJOR-CODE (1) and contain 02, the first major code. Positions 3–14 are known as EXP-MAJOR (1) and contain ART HISTORY, and so on. The conceptual view of these storage locations is shown in Figure 12.6.

Input-loaded Tables

Initialization of a table through hard coding is a commonly used technique, but one that presents problems in program maintenance when the table changes. Any change to a hard-coded table requires a corresponding change in the program, which in turn requires that the program be recompiled and retested. Moreover, if the same table is used in multiple programs, then the same change has to be made in *every* program that uses the table, a time-consuming and error-prone procedure.

A better technique is to initialize the table dynamically, by reading values from a file when the program is executed. This is known as an ***input-loaded table*** and is illustrated in Figure 12.7. The Data Division entries in Figure 12.7a establish space for the variable-length major table without assigning values; the latter is accomplished at execution time by the Procedure Division entries in Figure 12.7b. (The statements in Figure 12.7b use the in-line PERFORM statement and false-condition branch of the READ statement to process a file until its records are exhausted.)

The process is further illustrated by Figure 12.8, in which records from the external file (containing the table codes and descriptive values) are read one at a time and moved to the appropriate table entries. The first record in MAJOR-CODE-FILE contains the first code and descriptive value, 02 and ART HISTORY, respectively, which are moved into MAJOR-CODE (1) and EXP-MAJOR (1). Subsequent table values are moved in similar fashion.

The advantage of an input-loaded table (over one that is hard coded) is that any change to the table is accommodated by modifying the file that contains the table values. The program (or programs) that access that table are unaffected.

Figure 12.7   Input-Loaded Table

```
        FD  MAJOR-CODE-FILE
            RECORD CONTAINS 14 CHARACTERS
            DATA RECORD IS MAJOR-CODE-RECORD.
        01  MAJOR-CODE-RECORD.
            05  INCOMING-FILE-CODE    PIC 9(2).
            05  INCOMING-FILE-NAME    PIC X(12).
                .
                  .
                    .
        WORKING-STORAGE SECTION.
        01  MAJOR-TABLE.
            05  MAJORS OCCURS 1 TO 10 TIMES
                DEPENDING ON NUMBER-OF-MAJORS
                INDEXED BY MAJOR-INDEX.
                10  MAJOR-CODE        PIC 9(2).
                10  EXP-MAJOR         PIC X(12).

        01  NUMBER-OF-MAJORS          PIC 99    VALUE ZERO.
```

(a) Data Division Entries

```
        OPEN INPUT MAJOR-CODE-FILE.
        PERFORM VARYING MAJOR-INDEX FROM 1 BY 1
            UNTIL MAJOR-INDEX > 10
              OR END-OF-MAJOR-FILE = 'YES'
            READ MAJOR-CODE-FILE
                AT END
                    MOVE 'YES' TO END-OF-MAJOR-FILE
                NOT AT END
                    ADD 1 TO NUMBER-OF-MAJORS
                    MOVE INCOMING-FILE-CODE TO MAJOR-CODE (MAJOR-INDEX)
                    MOVE INCOMING-FILE-NAME TO EXP-MAJOR (MAJOR-INDEX)
            END-READ
        END-PERFORM.
        IF MAJOR-INDEX > 10
            DISPLAY 'MAJOR TABLE TOO SMALL'
        END-IF.
        CLOSE MAJOR-CODE-FILE.
```

(b) In-Line Perform

Table Lookups

Once a table has been established, the table lookup procedure is coded in the Procedure Division. We illustrate four alternative COBOL techniques: PERFORM VARYING, SEARCH, SEARCH ALL, and Direct Access to table entries.

Figure 12.8 Input-Loaded Tables

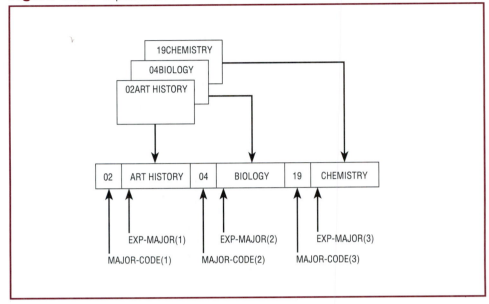

PERFORM VARYING Statement

Figure 12.9 contains the COBOL statements to implement the sequential table lookup of Figure 12.2. Entries in the table are compared sequentially to the incoming code ST-MAJOR-CODE with one of two outcomes. Either a match is found, in which case the corresponding descriptive value is moved to the output area, or the incoming code is not in the major table, which produces an appropriate error message.

The check for an invalid code is accomplished by comparing the value of the subscript WS-MAJOR-SUB, to the number of entries in the table. This type of error checking is extremely important and is one way of distinguishing between professional work and sloppy coding. (What would happen if the check were not included and an unknown code did appear?) Observe also the need to initialize both switches prior to the lookup, and how the switches are reset when the search is terminated.

SEARCH Statement

The SEARCH statement implements a sequential table lookup and is easier to use than the corresponding PERFORM VARYING statement. SEARCH has the following syntax:

$$\underline{\text{SEARCH}} \ \text{identifier-1} \left[\underline{\text{VARYING}} \begin{Bmatrix} \text{index-name-1} \\ \text{identifier} \end{Bmatrix} \right]$$

$$\left[\text{AT} \ \underline{\text{END}} \ \text{imperative-statement-1} \right]$$

$$\underline{\text{WHEN}} \ \text{condition-1} \begin{Bmatrix} \text{imperative-statement-2} \\ \underline{\text{NEXT}} \ \underline{\text{SENTENCE}} \end{Bmatrix}$$

$$\left[\underline{\text{WHEN}} \ \text{condition-2} \begin{Bmatrix} \text{imperative-statement-3} \\ \underline{\text{NEXT}} \ \underline{\text{SENTENCE}} \end{Bmatrix} \right] \dots$$

$$\left[\underline{\text{END-SEARCH}} \right]$$

Figure 12.9 Sequential Lookup with PERFORM VARYING

```
WORKING-STORAGE SECTION.

01  TABLE-PROCESSING-ELEMENTS.
    05  WS-MAJOR-SUB            PIC S9(4)    USAGE IS COMP.
    05  WS-FOUND-MAJOR-SWITCH   PIC X(3)     VALUE 'NO'
    05  WS-END-OF-TABLE-SWITCH  PIC X(3)     VALUE 'NO'.

01  MAJOR-VALUE.
    05  FILLER                  PIC X(14)    VALUE '02ART HISTORY'.
    05  FILLER                  PIC X(14)    VALUE '04BIOLOGY'.
    05  FILLER                  PIC X(14)    VALUE '19CHEMISTRY'.
    05  FILLER                  PIC X(14)    VALUE '21CIVIL ENG'.
    05  FILLER                  PIC X(14)    VALUE '24COMP INF SYS'.
    05  FILLER                  PIC X(14)    VALUE '32ECONOMICS'.
    05  FILLER                  PIC X(14)    VALUE '39FINANCE'.
    05  FILLER                  PIC X(14)    VALUE '43MANAGEMENT'.
    05  FILLER                  PIC X(14)    VALUE '49MARKETING'.
    05  FILLER                  PIC X(14)    VALUE '54STATISTICS'.

01  MAJOR-TABLE REDEFINES MAJOR-VALUE.
    05  MAJORS OCCURS 10 TIMES.
        10  MAJOR-CODE          PIC 9(2).
        10  EXP-MAJOR           PIC X(12).
    .
      .
        .

PROCEDURE DIVISION.
    MOVE 'NO' TO WS-FOUND-MAJOR-SWITCH  WS-END-OF-TABLE-SWITCH.
    PERFORM FIND-MAJOR
        VARYING WS-MAJOR-SUB FROM 1 BY 1
            UNTIL WS-END-OF-TABLE-SWITCH = 'YES'
                OR WS-FOUND-MAJOR-SWITCH = 'YES'.
    .
      .
        .

FIND-MAJOR.
    IF WS-MAJOR-SUB > 10
        MOVE 'YES' TO WS-END-OF-TABLE-SWITCH
        MOVE 'UNKNOWN' TO HDG-MAJOR
    ELSE
        IF ST-MAJOR-CODE = MAJOR-CODE (WS-MAJOR-SUB)
            MOVE 'YES' TO WS-FOUND-MAJOR-SWITCH
            MOVE EXP-MAJOR (WS-MAJOR-SUB) TO HDG-MAJOR
        END-IF
    END-IF.
```

Restrict Subscripts and Switches to a Single Use

Data names defined as switches and/or subscripts should be restricted to a single use. Consider:

Poor Code

```
01    SUBSCRIPT                     PIC S9(4)    COMP.
01    EOF-SWITCH                    PIC X(3)     VALUE SPACES.


      PERFORM INITIALIZE-TITLE-FILE
          UNTIL EOF-SWITCH = 'YES'.
      MOVE SPACES TO EOF-SWITCH.
      PERFORM PROCESS-EMPLOYEE-RECORDS
          UNTIL EOF-SWITCH = 'YES'.
      PERFORM COMPUTE-SALARY-HISTORY
          VARYING SUBSCRIPT FROM 1 BY 1
              UNTIL SUBSCRIPT > 3.
      PERFORM FIND-MATCH-TITLE
          VARYING SUBSCRIPT FROM 1 BY 1
              UNTIL SUBSCRIPT > 100.
```

Improved Code

```
01    PROGRAM-SUBSCRIPTS.
      05 TITLE-SUBSCRIPT            PIC S9(4)    COMP.
      05 SALARY-SUBSCRIPT           PIC S9(4)    COMP.
01    END-OF-FILE-SWITCHES.
      05 END-OF-TITLE-FILE-SWITCH   PIC X(3)     VALUE SPACES.
      05 END-OF-EMPLOYEE-FILE-SWITCH PIC X(3)    VALUE SPACES.

      PERFORM INITIALIZE-TITLE-FILE
          UNTIL END-OF-TITLE-FILE-SWITCH = 'YES'.
      PERFORM PROCESS-EMPLOYEE-RECORDS
          UNTIL END-OF-EMPLOYEE-FILE-SWITCH = 'YES'.
      PERFORM COMPUTE-SALARY-HISTORY
          VARYING SALARY-SUBSCRIPT FROM 1 BY 1
              UNTIL SALARY-SUBSCRIPT > 3.
      PERFORM FIND-MATCHING-TITLE
          VARYING TITLE-SUBSCRIPT FROM 1 BY 1
              UNTIL TITLE-SUBSCRIPT > 100.
```

At the very least, the improved code offers superior documentation. By restricting data names to a single use, one automatically avoids such nondescript entries as EOF-SWITCH or SUBSCRIPT. Of greater impact, the improved code is more apt to be correct in that a given data name is modified or tested in fewer places within a program. Finally, if bugs do occur, the final values of the unique data names (TITLE-SUBSCRIPT and SALARY-SUBSCRIPT) will be of much greater use than the single value of SUBSCRIPT.

Identifier-1 in the SEARCH statement designates a table that contains both the OCCURS and INDEXED BY clauses. AT END is optional, but strongly recommended, to detect invalid or unknown codes. The WHEN clause specifies both a condition and an imperative sentence; the latter is executed when the condition is satisfied (that is, when a match is found.) Control passes to the statement immediately following the SEARCH statement after the WHEN condition is satisfied or the AT END clause is reached. (The VARYING option is covered in Chapter 13.)

The SEARCH statement is illustrated in Figure 12.10 (which implements the identical logic of Figure 12.9). The table definition includes the INDEXED BY clause, which is required by the SEARCH statement, and establishes values through hard coding.

The SEARCH statement compares, in sequence, entries in the MAJORS table to ST-MAJOR-CODE. If no match is found (that is, if the AT END condition is

Figure 12.10 SEARCH Statement (Sequential Lookup)

```
01  MAJOR-VALUE.
    05  FILLER          PIC X(14)    VALUE '02ART HISTORY'.
    05  FILLER          PIC X(14)    VALUE '04BIOLOGY'.
    05  FILLER          PIC X(14)    VALUE '19CHEMISTRY'.
    05  FILLER          PIC X(14)    VALUE '21CIVIL ENG'.
    05  FILLER          PIC X(14)    VALUE '24COMP INF SYS'.
    05  FILLER          PIC X(14)    VALUE '32ECONOMICS'.
    05  FILLER          PIC X(14)    VALUE '39FINANCE'.
    05  FILLER          PIC X(14)    VALUE '43MANAGEMENT'.
    05  FILLER          PIC X(14)    VALUE '49MARKETING'.
    05  FILLER          PIC X(14)    VALUE '54STATISTICS'.

01  MAJOR-TABLE REDEFINES MAJOR-VALUE.
    05  MAJORS OCCURS 10 TIMES
        INDEXED BY MAJOR-INDEX.        ─── INDEXED BY clause required
        10  MAJOR-CODE  PIC 9(2).          in table definition
        10  EXP-MAJOR   PIC X(12).
    .
      .
        .

PROCEDURE DIVISION.
    .
      .

        .
    SET MAJOR-INDEX TO 1.              ─── SET statement establishes
    SEARCH MAJORS                         starting point
        AT END
            MOVE 'UNKNOWN' TO HDG-MAJOR
        WHEN ST-MAJOR-CODE = MAJOR-CODE (MAJOR-INDEX)
            MOVE EXP-MAJOR (MAJOR-INDEX) TO HDG-MAJOR
    END-SEARCH.
```

reached), then UNKNOWN is moved to HDG-MAJOR. However, if a match does occur, [that is, if ST-MAJOR-CODE = MAJOR-CODE (MAJOR-INDEX)], the appropriate major is moved to HDG-MAJOR. The search is terminated, and control passes to the statement following the SEARCH.

The statement SET MAJOR-INDEX TO 1 is necessary to indicate the point in the table where the search is to begin, and appears before the SEARCH statement. Recall also that the SET statement must be used to modify an index; that is, it is *incorrect* to say MOVE 1 TO MAJOR-INDEX.

SEARCH ALL Statement

The SEARCH ALL statement implements a binary lookup, and is presented below:

```
SEARCH ALL identifier-1

    [AT END imperative-statement-1]

    WHEN condition-1 {imperative-statement-2}
                     {NEXT SENTENCE         }

[END SEARCH]
```

As with a sequential search statement, SEARCH ALL requires the associated table be defined with an index. In addition, *the codes in the table must be in sequence* (either ascending or descending).

The implementation of a binary search is shown in Figure 12.11, and is very similar in appearance to Figure 12.10. Observe, however, the KEY clause in the table definition to indicate the sequence in which codes appear. (In the event that codes in the table are out of sequence, COBOL will not indicate an explicit error, but the results of the search will be incorrect.) Note too that since SEARCH ALL determines its own starting position in the table, a SET statement is not used in conjunction with a binary lookup. The differences between SEARCH and SEARCH ALL are summarized in Table 12.3.

TABLE 12.3   SEARCH versus SEARCH ALL

SEARCH	SEARCH ALL
Implements a sequential lookup	Implements a binary lookup
Requires a SET statement prior to SEARCH, to establish the initial position in the table	Does not require an initial SET statement (calculates its own starting position)
Does not require codes in the table to be in any special sequence	Requires codes to be in (ascending or descending) sequence on the associated KEY clause in the table definition
Contains an optional VARYING clause (See Figure 13.18)	Does not contain a VARYING clause
May specify more than one WHEN clause	Restricted to a single WHEN clause

Direct Lookup

A positional table results in wasted space but permits a far faster table lookup in that you go *directly* to the appropriate table entry. Implementation of a direct lookup is shown in Figure 12.12.

Figure 12.11 SEARCH ALL Statement (Binary Lookup)

```
01  MAJOR-VALUE.
    05  FILLER          PIC X(14)    VALUE '02ART HISTORY'.
    05  FILLER          PIC X(14)    VALUE '04BIOLOGY'.
    05  FILLER          PIC X(14)    VALUE '19CHEMISTRY'.
    05  FILLER          PIC X(14)    VALUE '21CIVIL ENG'.
    05  FILLER          PIC X(14)    VALUE '24COMP INF SYS'.
    05  FILLER          PIC X(14)    VALUE '32ECONOMICS'.
    05  FILLER          PIC X(14)    VALUE '39FINANCE'.
    05  FILLER          PIC X(14)    VALUE '43MANAGEMENT'.
    05  FILLER          PIC X(14)    VALUE '49MARKETING'.
    05  FILLER          PIC X(14)    VALUE '54STATISTICS'.

01  MAJOR-TABLE REDEFINES MAJOR-VALUE.
    05  MAJORS OCCURS 10 TIMES
        ASCENDING KEY IS MAJOR-CODE          ──── ASCENDING KEY required
        INDEXED BY MAJOR-INDEX.                        for binary search
        10  MAJOR-CODE   PIC 9(2).
        10  EXP-MAJOR    PIC X(12).
          .
          .
          .

PROCEDURE DIVISION.
      .
      .
      .
    SEARCH ALL MAJORS
        AT END
            MOVE 'UNKNOWN' TO HDG-MAJOR
        WHEN MAJOR-CODE (MAJOR-INDEX) = ST-MAJOR-CODE
            MOVE EXP-MAJOR (MAJOR-INDEX) TO HDG-MAJOR
    END-SEARCH.
```

The codes themselves are not stored in the table of descriptive values as the *position* of an entry within the table corresponds to its associated code. The direct lookup is in essence a single MOVE statement in which the descriptive value in the indicated table position is chosen. The associated IF statement ensures that the incoming code lies within the range of the table.

Range-Step Tables

A *range-step table* is used when the same table value is applicable to multiple search arguments—that is, when there is no longer a one-to-one correspondence between a table value and the search argument. The computation of federal income tax is a well-known example as the same tax rate is applied to an entire tax bracket; that is, there is one tax rate for all incomes less than $20,000, a different rate for incomes between $20,000 and $40,000, and so on.

The scholarship table in Figure 12.13a is another example of a range-step table in which the amount of financial aid depends on a student's grade point

Figure 12.12   Direct Access to Table Entries

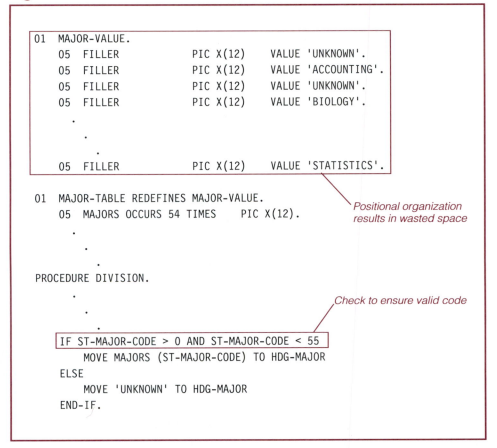

```
01  MAJOR-VALUE.
    05  FILLER          PIC X(12)    VALUE 'UNKNOWN'.
    05  FILLER          PIC X(12)    VALUE 'ACCOUNTING'.
    05  FILLER          PIC X(12)    VALUE 'UNKNOWN'.
    05  FILLER          PIC X(12)    VALUE 'BIOLOGY'.
                .
                  .
                    .
    05  FILLER          PIC X(12)    VALUE 'STATISTICS'.


01  MAJOR-TABLE REDEFINES MAJOR-VALUE.
    05  MAJORS OCCURS 54 TIMES    PIC X(12).
                .
                  .
                    .
PROCEDURE DIVISION.
                .
                  .
                    .
    IF ST-MAJOR-CODE > 0 AND ST-MAJOR-CODE < 55
        MOVE MAJORS (ST-MAJOR-CODE) TO HDG-MAJOR
    ELSE
        MOVE 'UNKNOWN' TO HDG-MAJOR
    END-IF.
```

*Positional organization
results in wasted space*

Check to ensure valid code

Figure 12.13   Range-step Table

Grade Point Average	Scholarship Percentage
3.75 - 4.00	100
3.50 - 3.74	75
3.25 - 3.49	50
3.00 - 3.24	33
2.75 - 2.99	25
2.50 - 2.74	15

(a) Scholarship Table

average. Students with a GPA between 2.50 and 2.74 receive a scholarship of 15%, students with a GPA between 2.75 and 2.99 an award of 25%, and so on.

The COBOL implementation is shown in Figure 12.13b. The scholarship table is hard coded and parallels the earlier example in Figure 12.5. The GPA table includes the minimum grade point average and corresponding scholarship amount for each of the six table entries. (There is no need to include the corresponding maximum grade point average).

Figure 12.13 *(continued)*

```
01  SCHOLARSHIP-TABLE.
    05  GPA-SCHOLARSHIP-PERCENTAGES.
        10  FILLER            PIC X(6)    VALUE '375100'.
        10  FILLER            PIC X(6)    VALUE '350075'.
        10  FILLER            PIC X(6)    VALUE '325050'.
        10  FILLER            PIC X(6)    VALUE '300033'.
        10  FILLER            PIC X(6)    VALUE '275025'.
        10  FILLER            PIC X(6)    VALUE '250015'.
    05  GPA-TABLE REDEFINES GPA-SCHOLARSHIP-PERCENTAGES
            OCCURS 6 TIMES
            INDEXED BY GPA-INDEX.
        10  GPA-MINIMUM       PIC 9V99.
        10  SCHOLARSHIP-PCT   PIC 999.
    .
  .
    .

    SET GPA-INDEX TO 1.
    SEARCH GPA-TABLE
        AT END                                    Range-step table
            MOVE ZERO TO SCHOLARSHIP-AWARD        uses a >= condition
        WHEN STUDENT-GPA >= GPA-MINIMUM (GPA-INDEX)
            MOVE SCHOLARSHIP-PCT (GPA-INDEX) TO SCHOLARSHIP-AWARD
    END-SEARCH.
```

(b) COBOL Implementation

The SEARCH statement implements a sequential search similar to the earlier example in Figure 12.10. Note, however, that the WHEN condition uses a greater than or equal condition in accordance with the definition of the range-step table.

A Complete Example

We are ready now to incorporate the material on table lookups and initialization procedures into a complete example. Specifications are as follows:

Programming Specifications

Program Name: Tables

Narrative: This program fully illustrates table processing. Two distinct means for initialization (hard coding and input loaded tables) are shown, as are three techniques for table lookups (sequential, binary, and direct access to table entries).

Input File(s): EMPLOYEE-FILE

TITLE-FILE

Employee Record:

COLUMNS	FIELD	PICTURE
1–20	Name	X(20)
21–24	Title Code	X(4)
25–27	Location Code	X(3)
28	Education Code	9
29–34	Employee Salary	9(6)

Title Record:

COLUMNS	FIELD	PICTURE
1–4	Title Code	X(4)
5–19	Descriptive Value	X(15)

Test Data: See Figure 12.14a for TITLE-FILE. See Figure 12.14b for EMPLOYEE-FILE.

Report Layout: See Figure 12.14c.

Processing Requirements:

1. Process an employee file, with each record containing the employee's salary as well as *coded* data on an employee's location, education, and title.

2. The table of location codes is to be hard-coded into the program and expanded via a sequential search. Location codes and their descriptive values are shown below:

Code	City
ATL	Atlanta
BOS	Boston
CHI	Chicago
DET	Detroit
KC	Kansas City
LA	Los Angeles
MIN	Minneapolis
NY	New York
PHI	Philadelphia
SF	San Francisco

3. The education codes are to be stored in a positional table and expanded via a direct lookup. Education codes and their descriptive values are shown below:

Code	Education
1	Some high school
2	High school diploma
3	Two-year degree
4	Four-year degree
5	Some graduate work
6	Master's degree
7	Doctorate degree
8	Other

4. The table of title codes is to be read from a file and expanded via a binary search. The title codes and their descriptive values were shown earlier in Figure 12.14a.

5. The amount of life insurance is determined by the employee's salary according to the following range-step table:

Figure 12.14 Test Data and Report

```
1000PROGRAMMER
1500DATA BASE
2000OPERATOR
2999SYSTEMS ANALYST
3499DATA DICTIONARY
```

(a) Title File

```
JACKIE CLARK      2999CHI4025000
MARGOT HUMMER     1000LA 6080000
PERCY GARCIA      2999IND3015000
CATHY BENWAY      3499ATL5110000
LOUIS NORIEGA     0100NC 9035000
JUD MCDONALD      1500ATL3065000
NELSON KERBEL     1000PHI3038000
```

(b) Employee File

EMPLOYEE	LOCATION	TITLE	EDUCATION	SALARY	LIFE INS
JACKIE CLARK	CHICAGO	SYSTEMS ANALYST	4YR DEGREE	$25,000	$80,000
MARGOT HUMMER	LOS ANGELES	PROGRAMMER	MASTERS	$80,000	$250,000
PERCY GARCIA	UNKNOWN	SYSTEMS ANALYST	2YR DEGREE	$15,000	$40,000
CATHY BENWAY	ATLANTA	DATA DICTIONARY	SOME GRAD	$110,000	$500,000
LOUIS NORIEGA	UNKNOWN	UNKNOWN	UNKNOWN	$35,000	$80,000
JUD MCDONALD	ATLANTA	DATA BASE	2YR DEGREE	$65,000	$175,000
NELSON KERBEL	PHILADELPHIA	PROGRAMMER	2YR DEGREE	$38,000	$80,000

(c) Report

Salary Range	Life Insurance
<= $ 20,000	$ 40,000
$ 20,001–$ 40,000	$ 80,000
$ 40,001–$ 75,000	$ 175,000
$ 75,001–$ 100,000	$ 250,000
$ 100,001–$ 200,000	$ 500,000

6. Print a detail line for each employee with descriptive information for location, education, title, and life insurance. Single-space this report.

Program Design

The hierarchy chart for the table lookup is shown in Figure 12.15. The highest-level module, PRODUCE-EMPLOYEE-REPORT, contains three subordinates to initialize the title table (the specifications called for an input-loaded table), write a heading

Figure 12.15   Hierarchy Chart for Table-Lookup Program

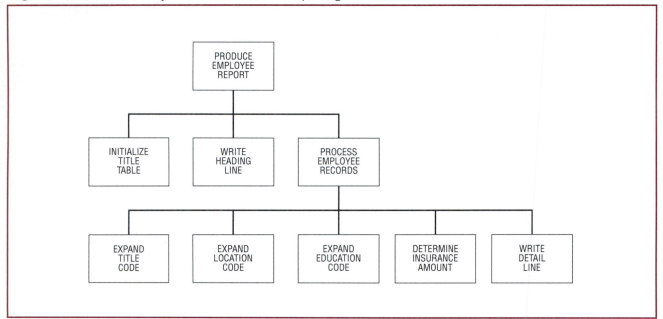

line, and process employee records; the latter includes four lower modules for the four table lookups.

The associated pseudocode is shown in Figure 12.16 and uses the in-line perform and false-condition branch first to process both the title and employee files. The title file is processed first and includes a check to ensure that the size of the title table is not exceeded. After the last record from the title file has been read, the employee file is opened and processed in its entirety. Each incoming employee record has its title, location, and education codes expanded, the amount of insurance determined, and a detail line written.

The Completed Program

The completed program is shown in Figure 12.17. The paragraphs in the Procedure Division correspond one to one with the modules in the hierarchy chart, and its logic in the program parallels that of the pseudocode just developed. The program complies with the processing requirements and also illustrates the various COBOL features presented earlier. Note the following:

1. The use of three SELECT statements for EMPLOYEE-FILE, PRINT-FILE, and TITLE-FILE; the latter is used to dynamically load the title table.

2. Omission of all optional clauses in the FD entries in the Data Division; that is, the FD contains only the file name. The optional reserved word FILLER is also omitted throughout the Data Division (see Limitations of COBOL-74 on page 357).

3. The use of READ INTO and WRITE FROM throughout the Procedure Division; this is not a requirement of table processing per se, but a coding style used throughout the text.

4. The definition of the location table in lines 43–59 through combination of the VALUES, OCCURS, and REDEFINES clauses. The location table includes the INDEXED BY clause as required by the SEARCH statement in lines 190–196.

Figure 12.16 Pseudocode for Table-Lookup Program

```
              Open title file
         ┌─── DO WHILE title data remains or title table not exceeded
         │  ┌─── READ title file
         │  │         AT END
         │  │             Indicate no more title data
         │  │         NOT AT END
         │  │             Increment number of titles in table
         │  │             Move incoming title to current position in table
         │  └─── ENDREAD
         └─── ENDDO
         ┌─── IF title table exceeded
         │        Display error message
         └─── ENDIF
              Close title file
              Open employee file and print file
         ┌─── DO WHILE employee data remains
         │  ┌─── READ employee file
         │  │         AT END
         │  │             Indicate no more data
         │  │         NOT AT END
         │  │             Expand title code
         │  │             Expand location code
         │  │             Expand education code
         │  │             Determine insurance amount
         │  │             Write detail line
         │  └─── ENDREAD
         └─── ENDDO
              Close employee file and print file
              Stop run
```

Figure 12.17 Table-Lookup Program

```
 1       IDENTIFICATION DIVISION.
 2       PROGRAM-ID.    TABLES.
 3       AUTHOR.        ROBERT GRAUER
 4
 5       ENVIRONMENT DIVISION.
 6       INPUT-OUTPUT SECTION.
 7       FILE-CONTROL.
 8          SELECT EMPLOYEE-FILE   ASSIGN TO SYSIN
 9             ORGANIZATION IS LINE SEQUENTIAL.
10          SELECT PRINT-FILE      ASSIGN TO SYSPRINT
11             ORGANIZATION IS LINE SEQUENTIAL.
12          SELECT TITLE-FILE      ASSIGN TO TITLFILE
13             ORGANIZATION IS LINE SEQUENTIAL.
14
15       DATA DIVISION.
```

Separate file is used to initialize title table

Figure 12.17   *(continued)*

```
16        FILE SECTION.
17        FD  TITLE-FILE.
18        01  TITLE-IN              PIC X(19).
19
20        FD  EMPLOYEE-FILE.
21        01  EMPLOYEE-RECORD       PIC X(34).
22
23        FD  PRINT-FILE.
24        01  PRINT-LINE            PIC X(132).
25
26        WORKING-STORAGE SECTION.
27        01                        PIC X(14)
28            VALUE 'WS BEGINS HERE'.
29
30        01  PROGRAM-SWITCHES-AND-COUNTERS.
31            05  END-OF-TITLE-FILE   PIC X(3)   VALUE 'NO '.
32            05  END-OF-EMP-FILE     PIC X(3)   VALUE 'NO '.
33            05  NUMBER-OF-TITLES    PIC 999    VALUE ZEROS.
34
35        01  TITLE-TABLE.
36            05  TITLES OCCURS 1 TO 999 TIMES
37                DEPENDING ON NUMBER-OF-TITLES
38                ASCENDING KEY IS TITLE-CODE
39                INDEXED BY TITLE-INDEX.
40                10  TITLE-CODE     PIC X(4).
41                10  TITLE-NAME     PIC X(15).
42
43        01  LOCATION-VALUE.
44            05                     PIC X(16)  VALUE 'ATLATLANTA'.
45            05                     PIC X(16)  VALUE 'BOSBOSTON'.
46            05                     PIC X(16)  VALUE 'CHICHICAGO'.
47            05                     PIC X(16)  VALUE 'DETDETROIT'.
48            05                     PIC X(16)  VALUE 'KC KANSAS CITY'.
49            05                     PIC X(16)  VALUE 'LA LOS ANGELES'.
50            05                     PIC X(16)  VALUE 'MINMINNEAPOLIS'.
51            05                     PIC X(16)  VALUE 'NY NEW YORK'.
52            05                     PIC X(16)  VALUE 'PHIPHILADELPHIA'.
53            05                     PIC X(16)  VALUE 'SF SAN FRANCISCO'.
54
55        01  LOCATION-TABLE REDEFINES LOCATION-VALUE.
56            05  LOCATIONS OCCURS 10 TIMES
57                INDEXED BY LOCATION-INDEX.
58                10  LOCATION-CODE  PIC X(3).
59                10  LOCATION-NAME  PIC X(13).
60
61        01  EDUCATION-TABLE.
62            05  EDUCATION-VALUES.
63                10                 PIC X(10)     VALUE 'SOME HS'.
64                10                 PIC X(10)     VALUE 'HS DIPLOMA'.
```

Different switches are defined for different files

ASCENDING KEY clause required for subsequent binary search

Location table is initialized through combination of OCCURS, VALUES, and REDEFINES clauses

Figure 12.17   *(continued)*

```
65                     10                 PIC X(10)    VALUE '2YR DEGREE'.
66                     10                 PIC X(10)    VALUE '4YR DEGREE'.
67                     10                 PIC X(10)    VALUE 'SOME GRAD'.
68                     10                 PIC X(10)    VALUE 'MASTERS'.
69                     10                 PIC X(10)    VALUE 'PH. D.'.
70                     10                 PIC X(10)    VALUE 'OTHER'.
71             05  EDU-NAME REDEFINES EDUCATION-VALUES
72                    OCCURS 8 TIMES   PIC X(10).
73
74         01  SALARY-INSURANCE-TABLE.
75             05  INSURANCE-VALUES.
76                     10                 PIC X(12)    VALUE '020000040000'.
77                     10                 PIC X(12)    VALUE '040000080000'.
78                     10                 PIC X(12)    VALUE '075000175000'.
79                     10                 PIC X(12)    VALUE '100000250000'.
80                     10                 PIC X(12)    VALUE '200000500000'.
81             05  INSURANCE-TABLE REDEFINES INSURANCE-VALUES
82                    OCCURS 5 TIMES
83                    INDEXED BY INSURANCE-INDEX.
84                 10  SALARY-MAXIMUM   PIC 9(6).
85                 10  INSURANCE-AMOUNT PIC 9(6).
86
87         01  HEADING-LINE.
88             05                         PIC X(2)     VALUE SPACES.
89             05                         PIC X(10)    VALUE 'EMPLOYEE'.
90             05                         PIC X(10)    VALUE SPACES.
91             05                         PIC X(8)     VALUE 'LOCATION'.
92             05                         PIC X(7)     VALUE SPACES.
93             05                         PIC X(5)     VALUE 'TITLE'.
94             05                         PIC X(12)    VALUE SPACES.
95             05                         PIC X(10)    VALUE 'EDUCATION'.
96             05                         PIC X(4)     VALUE SPACES.
97             05                         PIC X(6)     VALUE 'SALARY'.
98             05                         PIC X(3)     VALUE SPACES.
99             05                         PIC X(8)     VALUE 'LIFE INS'.
100            05                         PIC X(47)    VALUE SPACES.
101
102        01  DASHED-LINE.
103            05                         PIC X(85)    VALUE ALL '-'.
104            05                         PIC X(47)    VALUE SPACES.
105
106        01  DETAIL-LINE.
107            05  DET-NAME               PIC X(20).
108            05                         PIC XX       VALUE SPACES.
109            05  DET-LOCATION           PIC X(13).
110            05                         PIC XX       VALUE SPACES.
111            05  DET-TITLE              PIC X(15).
112            05                         PIC XX       VALUE SPACES.
113            05  DET-EDUCATION          PIC X(10).
114            05                         PIC XXX      VALUE SPACES.
```

FILLER optional in COBOL-85

Figure 12.17   *(continued)*

```
115          05  DET-SALARY          PIC $$$$,$$$.
116          05                      PIC XX          VALUE SPACES.
117          05  DET-INSURANCE       PIC $$$$,$$$.
118          05                      PIC X(47)       VALUE SPACES.
119
120      01  WS-EMPLOYEE-RECORD.
121          05  EMP-NAME            PIC X(20).
122          05  EMP-TITLE-CODE      PIC X(4).
123          05  EMP-LOC-CODE        PIC X(3).
124          05  EMP-EDUC-CODE       PIC 9.
125          05  EMP-SALARY          PIC 9(6).
126
127      01  WS-TITLE-RECORD.
128          05  TITLE-IN-CODE       PIC X(4).
129          05  TITLE-IN-NAME       PIC X(15).
130
131      PROCEDURE DIVISION.
132      100-PRODUCE-EMPLOYEE-REPORT.
133          PERFORM 200-INITIALIZE-TITLE-TABLE.
134          OPEN INPUT EMPLOYEE-FILE
135               OUTPUT PRINT-FILE.
136          PERFORM 300-WRITE-HEADING-LINES.
137          PERFORM UNTIL END-OF-EMP-FILE = 'YES'
138              READ EMPLOYEE-FILE INTO WS-EMPLOYEE-RECORD
139                  AT END
140                      MOVE 'YES' TO END-OF-EMP-FILE
141                  NOT AT END
142                      PERFORM 400-PROCESS-EMPLOYEE-RECORDS
143              END-READ
144          END-PERFORM.
145          CLOSE EMPLOYEE-FILE
146                PRINT-FILE.
147          STOP RUN.
148
149      200-INITIALIZE-TITLE-TABLE.
150          OPEN INPUT TITLE-FILE.
151          PERFORM VARYING TITLE-INDEX FROM 1 BY 1
152              UNTIL END-OF-TITLE-FILE = 'YES'
153                  OR TITLE-INDEX > 999
154              READ TITLE-FILE INTO WS-TITLE-RECORD
155                  AT END
156                      MOVE 'YES' TO END-OF-TITLE-FILE
157                  NOT AT END
158                      ADD 1 TO NUMBER-OF-TITLES
159                      MOVE TITLE-IN-CODE TO TITLE-CODE (TITLE-INDEX)
160                      MOVE TITLE-IN-NAME TO TITLE-NAME (TITLE-INDEX)
161              END-READ
162          END-PERFORM.
163          IF TITLE-INDEX > 999
164              DISPLAY 'SIZE OF TITLE TABLE IS EXCEEDED'
```

Title table is initialized dynamically — (line 133)

Checks that table size is not exceeded — (line 153)

Figure 12.17 (continued)

```
165            END-IF.
166            CLOSE TITLE-FILE.
167
168        300-WRITE-HEADING-LINES.
169            WRITE PRINT-LINE FROM HEADING-LINE
170                AFTER ADVANCING PAGE.
171            WRITE PRINT-LINE FROM DASHED-LINE
172                AFTER ADVANCING 1 LINE.
173
174        400-PROCESS-EMPLOYEE-RECORDS.
175            PERFORM 420-EXPAND-TITLE-CODE.
176            PERFORM 430-EXPAND-LOCATION-CODE.
177            PERFORM 440-EXPAND-EDUCATION-CODE.
178            PERFORM 450-DETERMINE-INSURANCE-AMOUNT.
179            PERFORM 470-WRITE-DETAIL-LINE.
180
181        420-EXPAND-TITLE-CODE.
182            SEARCH ALL TITLES
183                AT END
184                    MOVE 'UNKNOWN' TO DET-TITLE
185                WHEN TITLE-CODE (TITLE-INDEX) = EMP-TITLE-CODE       Binary search
186                    MOVE TITLE-NAME (TITLE-INDEX) TO DET-TITLE
187            END-SEARCH.
188
189        430-EXPAND-LOCATION-CODE.
190            SET LOCATION-INDEX TO 1.
191            SEARCH LOCATIONS
192                AT END
193                    MOVE 'UNKNOWN' TO DET-LOCATION
194                WHEN EMP-LOC-CODE = LOCATION-CODE (LOCATION-INDEX)     Sequential search
195                    MOVE LOCATION-NAME (LOCATION-INDEX) TO DET-LOCATION
196            END-SEARCH.
197
198        440-EXPAND-EDUCATION-CODE.
199            IF EMP-EDUC-CODE < 1 OR > 8
200                MOVE 'UNKNOWN' TO DET-EDUCATION
201            ELSE
202                MOVE EDU-NAME (EMP-EDUC-CODE) TO DET-EDUCATION       Direct access to table entries
203            END-IF.
204
205        450-DETERMINE-INSURANCE-AMOUNT.
206            IF EMP-SALARY IS NUMERIC
207                SET INSURANCE-INDEX TO 1
208                SEARCH INSURANCE-TABLE
209                    AT END
210                        MOVE ZERO TO DET-INSURANCE
211                    WHEN EMP-SALARY <= SALARY-MAXIMUM (INSURANCE-INDEX)   Range-step table
212                        MOVE INSURANCE-AMOUNT (INSURANCE-INDEX)           uses <= condition
213                            TO DET-INSURANCE
214                END-SEARCH
```

Figure 12.17 *(continued)*

```
215          ELSE
216              DISPLAY 'INCOMING SALARY NOT NUMERIC'
217              MOVE ZERO TO DET-INSURANCE
218          END-IF.
219
220      470-WRITE-DETAIL-LINE.
221          MOVE SPACES TO PRINT-LINE.
222          MOVE EMP-NAME TO DET-NAME.
223          MOVE EMP-SALARY TO DET-SALARY.
224          WRITE PRINT-LINE FROM DETAIL-LINE
225              AFTER ADVANCING 1 LINE.
```

5. The definition of the education table (lines 61–72) as a positional table; that is, the education codes themselves (1, 2, ... ,8) are *not* entered in the table, and the incoming employee education code is expanded via direct access to a table entry in the MOVE statement of line 202. (The IF statement in line 199 is executed prior to the MOVE to ensure a valid education code.)

6. The definition of the insurance table (lines 74–85), which includes an INDEXED BY clause as required by the subsequent SEARCH statement. Note, too, the WHEN clause in line 211 includes a less than or equal condition consistent with the implementation of a range-step table.

7. The definition of the title table as input loaded in lines 35–41; that is, the OCCURS clause merely allocates spaces for the table but does not assign values to it; the latter is done dynamically in lines 150–166 of the Procedure Division. Note, too, the inclusion of the INDEXED BY and ASCENDING KEY clauses that are required by the SEARCH ALL statement in lines 182–187.

The flow in the Procedure Division is straightforward and easy to follow. The PERFORM statement in line 133 initializes the title table, after which the employee and print files are opened and a heading line is written. The combination of the in-line perform and false-condition branch in lines 137 through 144 processes employee records until the file is exhausted.

The optional END-SEARCH scope terminator is new to COBOL-85 and terminates the conditional portion of the SEARCH and SEARCH ALL statements.

The word FILLER is optional, making possible Data Division entries of the form:

```
01  MAJOR-VALUE.
    05              PIC X(14)    VALUE '02ART HISTORY'.
    05              PIC X(14)    VALUE '04BIOLOGY'.
    05              PIC X(14)    VALUE '19CHEMISTRY'.
              .
          .
       .
```

The entries look strange initially, but make perfect sense when you realize that data names defined as FILLER are not referenced in the Procedure Division; that is, omission of the word FILLER has no effect on the remainder of a program.

S U M M A R Y

Points to Remember

- Codes may be alphabetic, numeric, or alphanumeric. A good coding system will be precise, mnemonic, and expandable.

- The VALUE, OCCURS, and REDEFINES clauses are used in combination to define and initialize a table within a COBOL program.

- A table lookup may be implemented sequentially, in binary fashion, or through direct access to table entries.

- A range-step table occurs when there is no one-to-one correspondence between a table value and the search argument.

- Tables may be initialized through hard coding or dynamically loaded at execution time.

- A SEARCH statement is used to implement a sequential lookup. The statement requires the INDEXED BY clause in the table definition.

- A SEARCH ALL statement is used to implement a binary lookup. The statement requires the INDEXED BY and KEY clauses in the table definition, and requires the keys in the table to be in either ascending or descending sequence.

Key Words and Concepts

Alphabetic code	Numeric code
Alphanumeric code	Positional organization
Binary table lookup	Precise code
Direct access to table entries	Range-step table
Hard coding	Sequential table lookup
Index	Subscript
Input-loaded table	Table lookup
Mnemonic code	

COBOL Elements

ASCENDING KEY	REDEFINES
AT END	SEARCH
DESCENDING KEY	SEARCH ALL
END-SEARCH	SET
INDEXED BY	VALUE
OCCURS	WHEN
PERFORM VARYING	

Fill-in

1. A two-position numeric code has _____ combinations; a two-position alphabetic code has _____; and a two-position alphanumeric code has _____.

2. A _____ table lookup does not require its entries to be in any special order, whereas a binary table lookup requires that the entries be in either _____ or _____ sequence.

3. If a table is _____ _____, then the program in which it is found must be recompiled in order to change the table.

4. An _____ _____ table makes it possible to change entries in the table without recompiling the program.

5. Direct access to table entries is possible only if the table has _____ organization.

6. A sequential table lookup in a table of 500 elements could require as many as _____ tries, whereas a binary lookup for the same table would take no more than _____ tries.

7. The _____ clause gives another name to previously allocated space.

8. A sequential table lookup is implemented by the _____ statement, whereas a binary lookup is implemented by _____ _____.

9. The ASCENDING/DESCENDING _____ clause is required in the table definition if a binary table lookup is to be implemented.

10. The _____ statement appears before a sequential search, but is not used prior to a binary search.

11. The _____ clause is required in a table's definition if either a sequential or binary search is used.

12. The REDEFINES clause (<u>must/may</u>) be used when initializing a table.

13. If the wrong number of subscripts are used with a particular data name, a (<u>compilation/execution</u>) error will result.

14. A SET statement (<u>is/is not</u>) used before a SEARCH ALL statement, as the binary algorithm calculates its own starting position.

15. A _____ _____ table occurs when there is no longer a one-to-one correspondence between a table value and the search argument.

True/False

1. A binary search over a table of 500 elements requires 9 or fewer comparisons.

2. A sequential search over a table of 500 elements could require 500 comparisons.

3. Direct access to table entries requires no comparisons.

4. The SEARCH statement requires an index.

5. SEARCH ALL denotes a binary search.

6. There are no additional requirements of table organization in order to implement a binary rather than a sequential search.

7. An index (that is, displacement) of zero refers to the first element in a table.

8. A subscript of zero refers to the first element in a table.

9. An index cannot be manipulated by a MOVE statement.

10. PERFORM VARYING can manipulate both indexes and subscripts.

11. A SEARCH statement can contain only a single WHEN clause.

12. The ASCENDING (DESCENDING) KEY clause is required whenever the SEARCH statement is applied to a table.

13. The INDEXED BY clause is required whenever the SEARCH statement is applied to a table.

14. The same index can be applied to many tables.

15. The same subscript can be applied to many tables.

16. An index and a subscript can be applied to the same table.

17. The REDEFINES clause provides another name for previously allocated space.

18. The REDEFINES clause must be used in initializing a table.

19. A binary search could be applied to a table if its elements were arranged in descending (rather than ascending) sequence.

20. A numeric code of four digits provides a greater number of possibilities than a three-digit alphabetic code.

21. Codes are used for reasons other than to conserve space.

22. Alphabetic codes are more likely to be mnemonic than numeric codes.

23. Numeric codes, such as Social Security numbers, should not be unique to accommodate individuals with the same last name.

24. Positionally organized tables require the first code to begin at 1.

25. Positionally organized tables require numeric codes.

26. Positionally organized tables often result in large amounts of wasted space.

27. A range-step table requires a one-to-one correspondence between the table value and search argument.

28. The federal income tax table is an example of a range-step table.

Problems

1. How many unique codes can be developed from a four-position numeric code? From a four-position alphabetic code? From a four-position alphanumeric code?

2. Ask a friend to pick a number from 1 to 2,000. What is the maximum number of guesses required to find the number if

   a. a binary search is used?

   b. a sequential search is used?

   Answer parts (a) and (b), if the selected number is between 1 and 4,000.

3. What, if anything, is wrong with the following table definition?

```
01  MONTH-TABLE.
    05  MONTH OCCURS 12 TIMES          PIC X(4).
    05  MONTH-VALUES REDEFINES MONTH   PIC X(36)
        VALUE 'JANFEBMARAPRMAYJUNJULAUGSEPOCTNOVDEC'.
```

4. The DAY-OF-WEEK phrase was introduced in Chapter 9 (page 242) to obtain a one-position code corresponding to the day of the week. An alternate way of expanding the code (as opposed to the EVALUATE statement in Chapter 9) is to use a positional table and direct lookup.

   a. Use the data names in Figure 12.18 to write the appropriate ACCEPT statement.

   b. Write the necessary statements to implement a direct lookup on the table of Figure 12.18.

Figure 12.18 DAY-OF-WEEK Table

```
01  DAY-CODE-VALUE        PIC 9.

01  DAY-HEADING.
    05  FILLER            PIC X(9)     VALUE 'TODAY IS '.
    05  TODAYS-DAY        PIC X(9).

01  DAY-OF-WEEK-VALUE.
    05  FILLER            PIC X(9)     VALUE 'MONDAY'.
    05  FILLER            PIC X(9)     VALUE 'TUESDAY'.
    05  FILLER            PIC X(9)     VALUE 'WEDNESDAY'.
    05  FILLER            PIC X(9)     VALUE 'THURSDAY'.
    05  FILLER            PIC X(9)     VALUE 'FRIDAY'.
    05  FILLER            PIC X(9)     VALUE 'SATURDAY'.
    05  FILLER            PIC X(9)     VALUE 'SUNDAY'.

01  DAY-OF-WEEK-TABLE REDEFINES MAJOR-VALUE.
    05  DAY OCCURS 7 TIMES    PIC X(9).
```

5. Given the following table definition:

```
01  LOCATION-VALUE.
    05  FILLER            PIC X(16)  VALUE '010ATLANTA'.
    05  FILLER            PIC X(16)  VALUE '020BOSTON'.
    05  FILLER            PIC X(16)  VALUE '030CHICAGO'.
    05  FILLER            PIC X(16)  VALUE '040DETROIT'.
    05  FILLER            PIC X(16)  VALUE '050KANSAS CITY'.
    05  FILLER            PIC X(16)  VALUE '060LOS ANGELES'.
    05  FILLER            PIC X(16)  VALUE '070NEW YORK'.
    05  FILLER            PIC X(16)  VALUE '080PHILADELPHIA'.
    05  FILLER            PIC X(16)  VALUE '090SAN FRANCISCO'.
    05  FILLER            PIC X(16)  VALUE '045DENVER'.
01  LOCATION-TABLE REDEFINES LOCATION-VALUE.
    05  LOCATION OCCURS 10 TIMES
        ASCENDING KEY IS LOCATION-CODE
        INDEXED BY LOCATION-INDEX.
        10  LOCATION-CODE   PIC X(3).
        10  LOCATION-NAME   PIC X(13).
```

and the following Procedure Division code:

```
SET LOCATION-INDEX TO 1.
SEARCH LOCATION
    AT END
        DISPLAY '*ERROR IN SEQUENTIAL SEARCH FOR DENVER'
    WHEN LOCATION-CODE (LOCATION-INDEX) = '045'
        DISPLAY 'SEQUENTIAL SEARCH OK FOR DENVER'
END-SEARCH.
SEARCH LOCATION
    AT END
        DISPLAY '*ERROR IN SEQUENTIAL SEARCH FOR NEW YORK'
    WHEN LOCATION-CODE (LOCATION-INDEX) = '070'
        DISPLAY 'SEQUENTIAL SEARCH OK FOR NEW YORK'
END-SEARCH.
```

a. Indicate the output that will be produced.

b. Code a binary search statement to expand code 045 for Denver. Do you expect any trouble in the execution of that statement?

Multilevel Tables

CHAPTER OUTLINE

Overview
System Concepts
COBOL Implementation
One-Level Tables
    PERFORM VARYING
Two-Level Tables
    Errors in Compilation
    PERFORM VARYING
A Sample Program
    Programming Specifications
    Program Design
    The Completed Program
Three-Level Tables
    PERFORM VARYING
A Sample Program
    Programming Specifications
    The Completed Program
Table Lookups
A Calorie Counter's Delight
    Programming Specifications
    Range-Step Tables
    The Completed Program
Limitations of COBOL-74
Summary
Fill-in
True/False
Problems

OBJECTIVES

After reading this chapter you will be able to:

■ Describe a conceptual (user's) view of one-, two-, and three-level tables; implement (that is, define and initialize) one-, two-, and three-level tables in COBOL.

■ Differentiate between the VALUE, OCCURS, and REDEFINES clauses as they relate to table definition and initialization.

■ Distinguish between errors in compilation versus errors in execution; give an example of each as it pertains to multilevel table processing.

■ Explain the operation of a PERFORM VARYING statement; develop suitable examples to process tables in one, two, and three dimensions.

■ Use the VARYING option of the SEARCH statement; nest SEARCH statements within one another for multilevel-table lookups.

OVERVIEW

COBOL-85 allows multilevel tables of up to seven dimensions as opposed to the earlier limit of three in COBOL-74. Most applications do not require anything beyond a three-level table, and thus our coverage is limited to two- and three-level tables. The underlying concepts are identical regardless of a table's complexity, and hence our approach to multilevel tables will be a simple extension of the single-level problem.

We begin with a one-level example and develop it completely. This material reviews some discussion from the previous chapter, but is included nonetheless, in order to build the parallel between one-, two-, and three-level examples. Our presentation reexamines the OCCURS, VALUE, and REDEFINES clauses in the Data Division, and the PERFORM VARYING statement in the Procedure Division. We then extend the discussion to two and three dimensions and present complete programs to illustrate all statements.

The chapter concludes with a third program to implement table lookups in a multilevel table. The example introduces the VARYING option of the SEARCH statement and also nests SEARCH statements within one another.

System Concepts

Figure 13.1a depicts the user's view of a table of starting salaries within a company. In this example, an employee starts at one of 10 salaries, depending on the responsibility level for his or her job. A junior account executive, for example, may be designated as having a responsibility level of 1, whereas a divisional manager may be assigned level 10. The 10 salaries together comprise a salary table, with individual values designated by a subscript. The starting salary at responsibility level four, for example, is $30,000.

Figure 13.1 Multilevel Tables

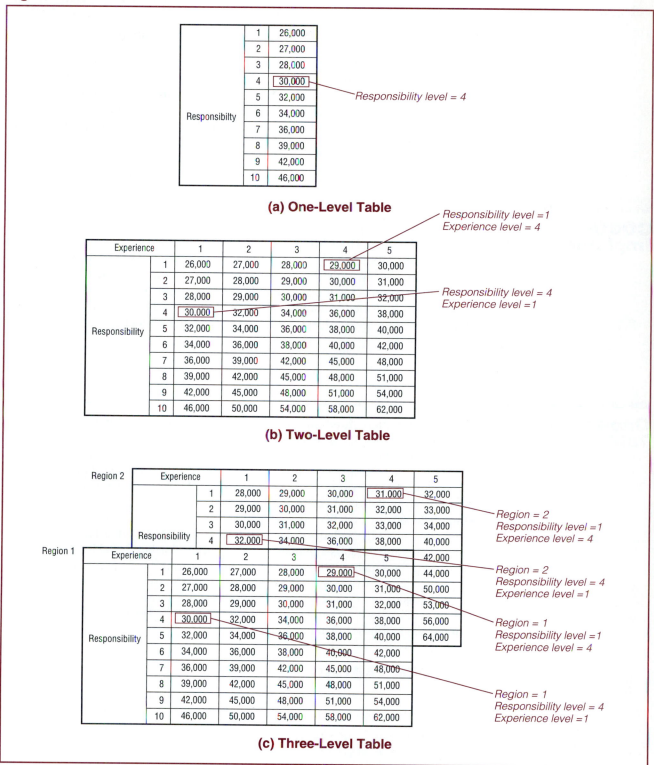

(a) One-Level Table

(b) Two-Level Table

(c) Three-Level Table

Figure 13.1b extends the user's view to two dimensions, in which salary is a function of two variables, responsibility and experience. The additional variable enables individuals with the same responsibility to be assigned different salaries, depending on experience. An individual at responsibility level four, for example, earns one of five salaries ($30,000, $32,000, $34,000, $36,000, or $38,000), depending on his or her experience level (which varies from one to five, respectively.) Two subscripts are necessary to designate a specific value in a two-level table; it should be apparent that the order of the subscripts is important; that is, the entry in row 4, column 1 ($30,000) is different from the entry in row 1, column 4 ($29,000).

Figure 13.1c extends the user's view to a third dimension, region, in which salary is a function of three variables; region (based on cost of living), responsibility, and experience. Any reference to a specific entry in a three-level table requires three subscripts, and again the order is important. Look again at Figure 13.1c and verify that the salary for region 1, responsibility 4, and experience 1 is $30,000, while the entry in region 2, responsibility 4, and experience 1 is $32,000.

COBOL Implementation

A table is initialized either by hard-coding it in a program or by dynamically loading it at execution time. Once initialized, the entries in a table can be accessed through a PERFORM VARYING or SEARCH statement, and these statements are applicable to tables in one, two, or three dimensions. We have, however, for the sake of simplicity, chosen to focus on hard-coding and the PERFORM VARYING statement. As previously indicated, our approach will be to develop the material for the simplest application (one-level tables), and then extend the concepts to two and three dimensions.

One-Level Tables

Figure 13.2 depicts three different views of the one-level table shown earlier in Figure 13.1. Figure 13.2a repeats the user's view in which salary is a function of responsibility, Figure 13.2b contains the COBOL statements to define and initialize the table in COBOL, and Figure 13.2c shows the resulting storage allocation.

Figure 13.2b creates the 01 entry SALARY-VALUES with 10 successive VALUE clauses that initialize 50 consecutive locations in memory. The first five locations contain 26000, the next five contain 27000, and so on.

The REDEFINES clause assigns another name, SALARY-TABLE, to these same 50 locations, and the subsequent OCCURS clause establishes the table. (The OCCURS clause cannot appear on the 01 level and hence SALARY is defined under SALARY-TABLE.) The first five positions in SALARY-VALUES are renamed SALARY (1) and contain 26000, the starting salary for responsibility level one. The next five positions are renamed SALARY (2) and contain 27000, and so on. The conceptual view of the storage allocation is shown in Figure 13.2c.

PERFORM VARYING

The PERFORM VARYING statement (explained previously in Chapter 11) processes the elements in a table. For example, the statement

```
PERFORM WRITE-STARTING-SALARY
    VARYING RESPONSIBILITY-SUB FROM 1 BY 1
        UNTIL RESPONSIBILITY-SUB > 10
```

executes the procedure WRITE-STARTING-SALARY 10 times, changing the value of RESPONSIBILITY-SUB each time the procedure is executed. The PERFORM VARYING statement initializes (increments) a subscript (index), tests a condition, then performs the designated procedure, depending on whether the condition is true. In the example, RESPONSIBILITY-SUB is initialized to 1, and the condition

Figure 13.2 One-level Table

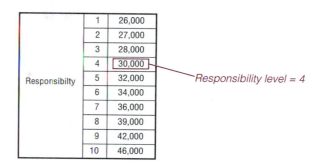

(a) User's View

```
01  SALARY-VALUES.
      05  FILLER    PIC X(5)    VALUE '26000'.
      05  FILLER    PIC X(5)    VALUE '27000'.
      05  FILLER    PIC X(5)    VALUE '28000'.
      05  FILLER    PIC X(5)    VALUE '30000'.
      05  FILLER    PIC X(5)    VALUE '32000'.
      05  FILLER    PIC X(5)    VALUE '34000'.
      05  FILLER    PIC X(5)    VALUE '36000'.
      05  FILLER    PIC X(5)    VALUE '39000'.
      05  FILLER    PIC X(5)    VALUE '42000'.
      05  FILLER    PIC X(5)    VALUE '46000'.


01  SALARY-TABLE REDEFINES SALARY-VALUES.
      05  SALARY OCCURS 10 TIMES        PIC 9(5).
```

(b) Initialization via the REDEFINES and VALUES Clauses

SALARY-TABLE									
SALARY (1)	SALARY (2)	SALARY (3)	SALARY (4)	SALARY (5)	SALARY (6)	SALARY (7)	SALARY (8)	SALARY (9)	SALARY (10)
2 6 0 0 0	2 7 0 0 0	2 8 0 0 0	3 0 0 0 0	3 2 0 0 0	3 4 0 0 0	3 6 0 0 0	3 9 0 0 0	4 2 0 0 0	4 6 0 0 0
SALARY-VALUES									

(c) Storage Schematic

RESPONSIBILITY-SUB > 10 is evaluated. The condition is not satisfied, so the designated procedure, WRITE-STARTING-SALARY, is executed for the first time. RESPONSIBILITY-SUB is incremented to 2, and the condition is retested. The condition is still false, so WRITE-STARTING-SALARY is executed a second time. The loop (testing, executing, and incrementing) continues for values of RESPONSIBILITY-SUB of 3, 4, 5, and so on, until RESPONSIBILITY-SUB reaches 10. Even then the condition is still not satisfied, because *10 is **not** greater than 10*, and so WRITE-STARTING-SALARY is executed a tenth (and last) time. RESPONSIBILITY-SUB is incremented to 11, the condition is finally satisfied (11 > 10), and the PERFORM VARYING is terminated.

Two-Level Tables

All of this material is easily extended to two levels as shown in Figure 13.3. Figure 13.3a repeats the user's view of the table in which salary is a function of both responsibility and experience, Figure 13.3b shows the COBOL definition and initialization, and Figure 13.3c depicts the storage allocation.

Figure 13.3 Two-level Tables

Experience	1	2	3	4	5
1	26,000	27,000	28,000	29,000	30,000
2	27,000	28,000	29,000	30,000	31,000
3	28,000	29,000	30,000	31,000	32,000
4	30,000	32,000	34,000	36,000	38,000
5	32,000	34,000	36,000	38,000	40,000
6	34,000	36,000	38,000	40,000	42,000
7	36,000	39,000	42,000	45,000	48,000
8	39,000	42,000	45,000	48,000	51,000
9	42,000	45,000	48,000	51,000	54,000
10	46,000	50,000	54,000	58,000	62,000

Responsibility (rows)

Responsibility level = 1, Experience level = 4
Responsibility level = 4, Experience level = 1

(a) User's View

```
01 SALARY-VALUES.
    05 FILLER  PIC X(25)   VALUE '2600027000280002900030000'.
    05 FILLER  PIC X(25)   VALUE '2700028000290003000031000'.
    05 FILLER  PIC X(25)   VALUE '2800029000300003100032000'.
    05 FILLER  PIC X(25)   VALUE '3000032000340003600038000'.
    05 FILLER  PIC X(25)   VALUE '3200034000360003800040000'.
    05 FILLER  PIC X(25)   VALUE '3400036000380004000042000'.
    05 FILLER  PIC X(25)   VALUE '3600039000420004500048000'.
    05 FILLER  PIC X(25)   VALUE '3900042000450004800051000'.
    05 FILLER  PIC X(25)   VALUE '4200045000480005100054000'.
    05 FILLER  PIC X(25)   VALUE '4600050000540005800062000'.

01 SALARY-TABLE REDEFINES SALARY-VALUES.
    05 RESPONSIBILITY OCCURS 10 TIMES.
       10  EXPERIENCE OCCURS 5 TIMES.
          15  SALARY            PIC 9(5).
```

(b) Initialization via the REDEFINES and VALUES Clauses

(c) Storage Schematic

Establishment of a two-level table requires two OCCURS clauses, each at a different level, in the table definition as shown:

```
01  SALARY-TABLE.
   05  RESPONSIBILITY  OCCURS 10 TIMES.
      10  EXPERIENCE  OCCURS  5 TIMES.
         15  SALARY                PIC 9(5).
```

The above entries establish a 50-element table (10 rows and 5 columns) with each element assigned five memory locations (according to the PICTURE clause). There are a total of 250 memory locations (10 x 5 x 5) allocated to the table as shown in Figure 13.3c. The first 25 locations contain the salaries for the five experience levels at the first responsibility level. Locations 1–5 contain the salary at responsibility level 1, experience level 1; locations 6–10 contain the salary at responsibility level 1, experience level 2; and so on. In similar fashion, locations 26–50 refer to the salaries for the five experience levels at responsibility level 2; locations 51–75 to the salaries at the five experience levels for responsibility level 3; and so on.

As in the one-level example, the table is initialized through combination of the OCCURS, VALUE, and REDEFINES clauses. This time, however, each VALUE clause fills an entire row (consisting of five experience levels or 25 positions in all). The first VALUE clause fills the first 25 locations (corresponding to the five experience levels for responsibility one), the second VALUE clause fills locations 26–50 (the five experience levels for responsibility two), and so on. The order of the VALUE clauses is critical and coincides with Figure 13.3a. The resulting storage allocation is shown in Figure 13.3c and further clarifies the discussion.

Errors in Compilation

Newcomers to multilevel tables find it all too easy to use the wrong number of subscripts, specify subscripts in improper sequence, and/or supply an invalid subscript value (that is, a value beyond the definition in the OCCURS clause.) The rule is very simple, namely that the number of subscripts is equal to the number of OCCURS clauses used to define the entry and further, that the order of subscripts corresponds to the order of the OCCURS clauses.

Consider again the table definition in Figure 13.3b, observing that SALARY is subordinate to EXPERIENCE, that EXPERIENCE is subordinate to RESPONSIBILITY, and that both RESPONSIBILITY and EXPERIENCE were defined with an OCCURS clause. In other words an OCCURS clause appears in *both* group items prior to the definition of SALARY, and thus *two* subscripts will be required for all Procedure Division references to SALARY. Any reference to SALARY that does not include two subscripts will be flagged during compilation. SALARY (1,4) is a valid reference to indicate the element in row 1, column 4 of the two-level table; SALARY (1) is *invalid* and will be flagged accordingly.

The compiler, however, is concerned only with syntax (namely that the proper number of subscripts is supplied), and not with the values of those subscripts. In other words, a reference to SALARY (20, 20) would not produce a compilation error, because it contains two subscripts and is syntactically valid. It would, however, cause problems during execution as the subscript values are inconsistent with the table definition. (The execution results are unpredictable.)

COBOL also allows reference to data names at different **hierarchical levels** of a table (although such reference may not make sense logically). Thus the definition of a two-dimensional table automatically allows reference to other one-dimensional tables. Refer again to the storage schematic of Figure 13.3c and/or the examples below to clarify the issue.

SALARY (6, 5)	A valid entry in all respects, which refers to salary responsibility level 6, experience level 5. The data name SALARY must always be referenced with two subscripts.
SALARY (5, 6)	Syntactically correct in that SALARY has two subscripts. The entry will compile cleanly but will cause problems in execution because it refers to responsibility and experience levels of 5 and 6, respectively, which are inconsistent with the table definition.
SALARY-TABLE	Refers to the entire table of 50 elements (250 locations). SALARY-TABLE is referenced without any subscripts.
RESPONSIBILITY (1)	Refers collectively to the five experience levels for the first level of salary responsibility; RESPONSIBILITY is referenced with a single subscript.
EXPERIENCE (6, 5)	A valid entry equivalent to SALARY (6,5); the entries are equivalent because SALARY is the only elementary item defined under the group item EXPERIENCE.

PERFORM VARYING

The PERFORM VARYING statement was introduced in Chapter 11 in conjunction with processing a one-level table. Its syntax is easily extended to process a two-level table as shown below. Consider:

$$\text{PERFORM } [\text{procedure-name-1}] \left[\text{WITH } \underline{\text{TEST}} \left\{ \begin{array}{l} \underline{\text{BEFORE}} \\ \underline{\text{AFTER}} \end{array} \right\} \right]$$

$$\underline{\text{VARYING}} \left\{ \begin{array}{l} \text{identifier-1} \\ \text{index-name-1} \end{array} \right\} \underline{\text{FROM}} \left\{ \begin{array}{l} \text{identifier-2} \\ \text{index-name-2} \\ \text{literal-1} \end{array} \right\} \underline{\text{BY}} \left\{ \begin{array}{l} \text{literal-2} \\ \text{identifier-3} \end{array} \right\}$$

$$\underline{\text{UNTIL}} \text{ condition-1}$$

$$\left[\underline{\text{AFTER}} \left\{ \begin{array}{l} \text{identifier-4} \\ \text{literal-3} \end{array} \right\} \underline{\text{FROM}} \left\{ \begin{array}{l} \text{identifier-5} \\ \text{index-name-3} \\ \text{literal-4} \end{array} \right\} \underline{\text{BY}} \left\{ \begin{array}{l} \text{identifier-6} \\ \text{literal-5} \end{array} \right\} \right.$$

$$\left. \underline{\text{UNTIL}} \text{ condition-2} \right] \ldots$$

$$[\text{imperative-statement-1 } \underline{\text{END PERFORM}}]$$

The PERFORM VARYING statement accommodates a two-level table through inclusion of the **AFTER** clause that varies two subscripts (indexes) simultaneously. As in the case of a one-level table, the TEST BEFORE/TEST AFTER clause is optional and is typically omitted; the default is TEST BEFORE and corresponds to the COBOL-74 implementation.

The PERFORM VARYING statement executes a designated procedure as in Figure 13.4a, or the statements in an in-line perform as in Figure 13.4b. Either way two subscripts are used as shown in Figure 13.4c. RESPONSIBILITY-SUB is varied from 1 to 10, in conjunction with EXPERIENCE-SUB changing from 1 to 5, so that the performed statements are executed 50 times in all.

The *bottom* subscript (EXPERIENCE-SUB in this example) is varied first. Thus RESPONSIBILITY-SUB is initially set to 1 while EXPERIENCE-SUB is varied from 1 to 5. RESPONSIBILITY-SUB is then incremented to 2, while EXPERIENCE-SUB

Figure 13.4 PERFORM VARYING with Two Subscripts

```
     PERFORM INITIALIZE-SALARIES
         VARYING RESPONSIBILITY-SUB FROM 1 BY 1
             UNTIL RESPONSIBILITY-SUB > 10
         AFTER EXPERIENCE-SUB FROM 1 BY 1
             UNTIL EXPERIENCE-SUB > 5.
     .
      .
       .
 INITIALIZE-SALARIES.
     MOVE ZERO TO SALARY (RESPONSIBILITY-SUB, EXPERIENCE-SUB).
```

(a) Performing a Paragraph

```
 PERFORM
         VARYING RESPONSIBILITY-SUB FROM 1 BY 1
             UNTIL RESPONSIBILITY-SUB > 10
         AFTER EXPERIENCE-SUB FROM 1 BY 1
             UNTIL EXPERIENCE-SUB > 5
                 MOVE ZERO TO SALARY (RESPONSIBILITY-SUB, EXPERIENCE-SUB)
 END-PERFORM.
```

(b) In-Line Perform

Responsibility Subscript	Experience Subscript
1	1
1	2
1	3
1	4
1	5

RESPONSIBILITY-SUB is set to 1 while EXPERIENCE-SUB varies from 1 to 5

2	1
2	2
2	3
2	4
2	5

RESPONSIBILITY-SUB is set to 2 while EXPERIENCE-SUB varies from 1 to 5

10	1
10	2
10	3
10	4
10	5

RESPONSIBILITY-SUB reaches 10 and EXPERIENCE-SUB varies from 1 to 5

(c) Variation of Subscripts

Figure 13.5   Varying Column and/or Row Subscripts

Question: What is the average salary for responsibility level three?
Answer: Sum the five salaries in row three of the salary table, then divide that total by five.

```
MOVE ZERO TO TOTAL-SALARY.
PERFORM
    VARYING EXPERIENCE-SUB FROM 1 BY 1
        UNTIL EXPERIENCE-SUB > 5
            ADD SALARY (3, EXPERIENCE-SUB) TO TOTAL-SALARY
END-PERFORM.
COMPUTE AVERAGE-SALARY = TOTAL-SALARY / 5.
```

(a) Varying a Column Subscript

Question: What is the average salary for experience level four?
Answer: Sum the 10 salaries in column four of the salary table, then divide that total by 10.

```
MOVE ZERO TO TOTAL-SALARY.
PERFORM
    VARYING RESPONSIBILITY-SUB FROM 1 BY 1
        UNTIL EXPERIENCE-SUB > 10
            ADD SALARY (RESPONSIBILITY-SUB, 4) TO TOTAL-SALARY
END-PERFORM.
COMPUTE AVERAGE-SALARY = TOTAL-SALARY / 10.
```

(b) Varying a Row Subscript

Question: What is the average salary over all responsibility and experience levels?
Answer: Sum all 50 salaries in the table, then divide that total by 50.

```
MOVE ZERO TO TOTAL-SALARY.
PERFORM
    VARYING RESPONSIBILITY-SUB FROM 1 BY 1
        UNTIL RESPONSIBILITY-SUB > 10
    AFTER EXPERIENCE-SUB FROM 1 BY 1
        UNTIL EXPERIENCE-SUB > 5
            ADD SALARY (RESPONSIBILITY-SUB, EXPERIENCE-SUB) TO TOTAL-SALARY
END-PERFORM.
COMPUTE AVERAGE-SALARY = TOTAL-SALARY / 50.
```

(c) Varying Both Subscripts

is again varied from 1 to 5. The process continues until all 50 combinations have been reached.

It is not necessary to always vary both subscripts in a two-level table; that is, you can hold the row constant and vary the column, or keep the column constant and vary the row. Indeed, different types of information are obtained according to the subscript that is used. Figure 13.5a, for example, varies the column subscript (EXPERIENCE-SUB) while keeping the row constant, to obtain the average starting salary at the third responsibility level. In similar fashion, Figure 13.5b varies the row subscript (RESPONSIBILITY-SUB) while keeping the column constant, to obtain the average starting salary for the fourth experience level. Figure 13.5c varies both subscripts to compute the average salary over all 50 row-column combinations.

A Sample Program

We incorporate the material on two-level tables into a COBOL program. Specifications follow in the usual format.

Programming Specifications

Program Name:　Two-Level Tables

Narrative:　This program illustrates the definition, initialization, and processing of two-level tables, building directly on the examples just presented. The specifications call for the processing of an employee file and the printing of each individual's salary, based on his or her responsibility and experience. In addition, the number of employees in each responsibility/experience combination is to be computed.

Input File(s):　EMPLOYEE-FILE

Input Record Layout:

```
01   EMPLOYEE-RECORD.
     05   EMP-NAME                          PIC X(15).
     05   EMP-SALARY-DETERMINANTS.
          10   EMP-RESP                     PIC 99.
          10   FILLER                       PIC X.
          10   EMP-EXP                      PIC 99.
          10   FILLER                       PIC X(3).
     05   FILLER                            PIC X(5).
```

Test Data:

```
ADAMS          04 01
BAKER          01 04
BROWN          08 02
CHARLES        09 02
DAVIDSON       09 04
DAVIS          10 04
EPSTEIN        04 05
FRANKEL        03 03
GOODMAN        03 03
GULFMAN        03 05
HATHAWAY       07 02
INGLES         03 01
JACKSON        06 03
JORDAN         06 03
KING           07 02
LIPMAN         07 01
LOWELL         01 04
```

Report Layout: See Figure 13.6.

Processing Requirements: 1. Read a file of employee records, and for each record:

    a. Determine the employee's starting salary as a function of responsibility and experience.

    b. Print a detail line for this employee showing his or her name and starting salary.

2. Compute the number of employees for each responsibility-experience combination. This requires creation of a 10-by-5 table to store the number of individuals in each responsibility-experience combination, and implies that as each employee record is

Figure 13.6   Output of Two-Level Program

```
                    STARTING SALARIES OF ALL NEW EMPLOYEES


                        ADAMS              $30,000
                        BAKER              $29,000
                        BROWN              $42,000
                        CHARLES            $45,000
                        DAVIDSON           $51,000
                        DAVIS              $58,000
                        EPSTEIN            $38,000
                        FRANKEL            $30,000
                        GOODMAN            $30,000
                        GULFMAN            $32,000
                        HATHAWAY           $39,000
                        INGLES             $28,000
                        JACKSON            $38,000
                        JORDAN             $38,000
                        KING               $39,000
                        LIPMAN             $36,000
                        LOWELL             $29,000
```

(a) Detail Report

```
                    STARTING SALARY SUMMARY REPORT
```

		EXPERIENCE			
RESPONSIBILITY	1	2	3	4	5
1	0	0	0	2	0
2	0	0	0	0	0
3	1	0	2	0	1
4	1	0	0	0	1
5	0	0	0	0	0
6	0	0	2	0	0
7	1	2	0	0	0
8	0	1	0	0	0
9	0	1	0	1	0
10	0	0	0	1	0

(b) Summary Report

read, the corresponding table entry (the particular responsibility-experience combination) has to be incremented by one.

3. When all employees have been processed, print the table containing the number of employees in each category as shown in Figure 13.6b.

Program Design

The report layout in Figure 13.6 requires both a ***detail report*** containing a line for every employee, as well as a ***summary report*** displaying the total number of employees in each of the 50 responsibility-experience combinations. The program will evaluate each incoming record to determine in which of the 50 categories the employee fits, then increment the appropriate counter. At the conclusion of processing—after all employee records have been read—the table of 50 totals will be printed as the summary report.

The functions needed in the eventual program are shown in the expanded hierarchy chart of Figure 13.7. The purpose of the individual modules should be apparent from the module name and/or the eventual COBOL program (shown later in the chapter).

The pseudocode in Figure 13.8 is succinct and is restricted to the basic building blocks of structured programming. The initial statements open the files and write an appropriate heading. The program is driven by a loop that determines the appropriate responsibility/experience combination for each employee record, writes the detail line, and increments the appropriate counter. The summary report is written after this loop has ended (when all employee records have been processed).

The Completed Program

Much of the completed program in Figure 13.9 is already familiar as it repeats the COBOL statements used in the explanation of two-level tables. The COBOL statements to define the salary table (lines 42–57), appeared earlier in Figure 13.3b and were discussed fully at that time. A second two-level table, for the number of employees in each category, is defined in lines 59–62; the definition uses the OCCURS

Figure 13.7 Hierarchy Chart for Two-Level Program

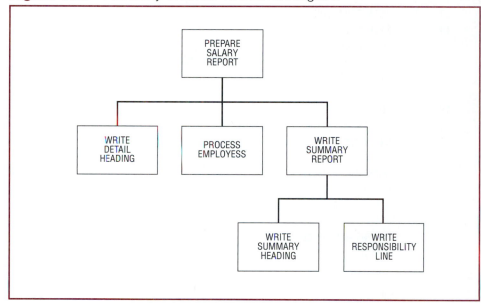

Figure 13.8 Pseudocode for Two-Level Program

```
            Open files
            Write heading lines
        ┌── DO WHILE data remains
        │   ┌── READ employee file
        │   │       AT END
        │   │           Indicate no more data
        │   │       NOT AT END
        │   │           Determine responsibility/experience combination
        │   │           Increment number of employees in that combination
        │   │           Write detail line
        │   └── END-READ
        └── ENDDO
            Write summary report
            Close files
            Stop run
```

Figure 13.9 Two-Level Program

```
1        IDENTIFICATION DIVISION.
2        PROGRAM-ID.    2LVTABLE.
3        AUTHOR.        ROBERT T. GRAUER.
4
5        ENVIRONMENT DIVISION.
6        INPUT-OUTPUT SECTION.
7        FILE-CONTROL.
8            SELECT EMPLOYEE-FILE    ASSIGN TO SYSIN
9                                    ORGANIZATION IS LINE SEQUENTIAL.
10           SELECT PRINT-FILE       ASSIGN TO SYSOUT
11                                   ORGANIZATION IS LINE SEQUENTIAL.
12
13       DATA DIVISION.
14       FILE SECTION.
15       FD  EMPLOYEE-FILE
16           DATA RECORD IS EMPLOYEE-RECORD.
17       01  EMPLOYEE-RECORD                 PIC X(23).
18
19       FD  PRINT-FILE
20           DATA RECORD IS PRINT-LINE.
21       01  PRINT-LINE                      PIC X(132).
22
23       WORKING-STORAGE SECTION.
24       01  FILLER                          PIC X(14)
25               VALUE 'WS BEGINS HERE'.
26
27       01  WS-EMPLOYEE-RECORD.
28           05  EMP-NAME                    PIC X(15).
```

Figure 13.9 *(continued)*

```
29            05   EMP-SALARY-DETERMINANTS.
30                 10   EMP-RESP            PIC 99.
31                 10   FILLER              PIC X.
32                 10   EMP-EXP             PIC 99.
33                 10   FILLER              PIC X(3).
34
35       01   PROGRAM-SUBSCRIPTS.
36            05   RESP-SUB                 PIC S9(4) COMP.
37            05   EXP-SUB                  PIC S9(4) COMP.
38
39       01   WS-END-OF-DATA-SWITCH         PIC X(3)     VALUE SPACES.
40            88   END-OF-DATA                           VALUE 'YES'.
41
42       01   SALARY-VALUES.
43            05   FILLER  PIC X(25)   VALUE '2600027000280002900030000'.
44            05   FILLER  PIC X(25)   VALUE '2700028000290003000031000'.
45            05   FILLER  PIC X(25)   VALUE '2800029000300003100032000'.
46            05   FILLER  PIC X(25)   VALUE '3000032000340003600038000'.
47            05   FILLER  PIC X(25)   VALUE '3200034000360003800040000'.
48            05   FILLER  PIC X(25)   VALUE '3400036000380004000042000'.
49            05   FILLER  PIC X(25)   VALUE '3600039000420004500048000'.
50            05   FILLER  PIC X(25)   VALUE '3900042000450004800051000'.
51            05   FILLER  PIC X(25)   VALUE '4200045000480005100054000'.
52            05   FILLER  PIC X(25)   VALUE '4600050000540005800062000'.
53
54       01   SALARY-TABLE REDEFINES SALARY-VALUES.
55            05   RESPONSIBILITY OCCURS 10 TIMES.
56                 10   EXPERIENCE OCCURS 5 TIMES.
57                      15   SALARY              PIC 9(5).
58
59       01   NUMBER-OF-EMPLOYEES-TABLE.
60            05   NUMBER-RESPONSIBILITY OCCURS 10 TIMES.
61                 10   NUMBER-EXPERIENCE OCCURS 5 TIMES.
62                      15   NUMB-EMP     PIC 99     VALUE ZERO.
63
64       01   DETAIL-REPORT-HEADING-LINE.
65            05   FILLER                 PIC X(9)    VALUE SPACES.
66            05   FILLER                 PIC X(39)
67                 VALUE 'STARTING SALARIES OF ALL NEW EMPLOYEES'.
68            05   FILLER                 PIC X(82)   VALUE SPACES.
69
70       01   DETAIL-LINE-1.
71            05   FILLER                 PIC X(12)   VALUE SPACES.
72            05   DET-EMP-NAME           PIC X(15).
73            05   FILLER                 PIC X(4)    VALUE SPACES.
74            05   DET-SALARY             PIC $99,999.
75            05   FILLER                 PIC X(94)   VALUE SPACES.
76
77       01   SUMMARY-REPORT-HEADING-LINE-1.
78            05   FILLER                 PIC X(24)   VALUE SPACES.
```

Used as subscripts into summary table

Two-level salary is hard coded

Two-level summary table is defined and initialized to zero

Figure 13.9 *(continued)*

```
 79            05  FILLER              PIC X(39)
 80                    VALUE 'STARTING SALARY SUMMARY REPORT'.
 81            05  FILLER              PIC X(69)  VALUE SPACES.
 82
 83        01  SUMMARY-REPORT-HEADING-LINE-2.
 84            05  FILLER              PIC X(36)  VALUE SPACES.
 85            05  FILLER              PIC X(10)  VALUE 'EXPERIENCE'.
 86            05  FILLER              PIC X(86)  VALUE SPACES.
 87
 88        01  SUMMARY-REPORT-HEADING-LINE-3.
 89            05  FILLER              PIC X(5)   VALUE SPACES.
 90            05  FILLER              PIC X(14)  VALUE 'RESPONSIBILITY'.
 91            05  FILLER              PIC X(48)
 92                    VALUE '      1        2        3        4        5'.
 93            05  FILLER              PIC X(65)  VALUE SPACES.
 94
 95        01  SUMMARY-LINE-1.
 96            05  FILLER              PIC X(9).
 97            05  SUMMARY-RESPONSIBILITY PIC Z(4).
 98            05  FILLER              PIC X(4)   VALUE SPACES.
 99            05  SUMMARY-TOTAL-VALUES OCCURS 5 TIMES.
100                10  FILLER          PIC X(4).
101                10  SUMMARY-NUMBER  PIC Z(4)9.
102            05  FILLER              PIC X(70).
103
104        PROCEDURE DIVISION.
105        100-PREPARE-SALARY-REPORT.
106            OPEN INPUT EMPLOYEE-FILE
107                 OUTPUT PRINT-FILE.
108            PERFORM 200-WRITE-DETAIL-REPORT-HDG.
109            PERFORM UNTIL END-OF-DATA
110                READ EMPLOYEE-FILE INTO WS-EMPLOYEE-RECORD
111                    AT END
112                        MOVE 'YES' TO WS-END-OF-DATA-SWITCH
113                    NOT AT END
114                        PERFORM 300-PROCESS-EMPLOYEES
115                END-READ
116            END-PERFORM.
117            PERFORM 400-WRITE-SUMMARY-REPORT.
118            CLOSE EMPLOYEE-FILE
119                  PRINT-FILE.
120            STOP RUN.
121
122        200-WRITE-DETAIL-REPORT-HDG.
123            WRITE PRINT-LINE FROM DETAIL-REPORT-HEADING-LINE
124                AFTER ADVANCING PAGE.
125            MOVE SPACES TO PRINT-LINE.
126            WRITE PRINT-LINE.
127
128        300-PROCESS-EMPLOYEES.
```

Program driven by in-line PERFORM and False-Condition Branch

Figure 13.9 *(continued)*

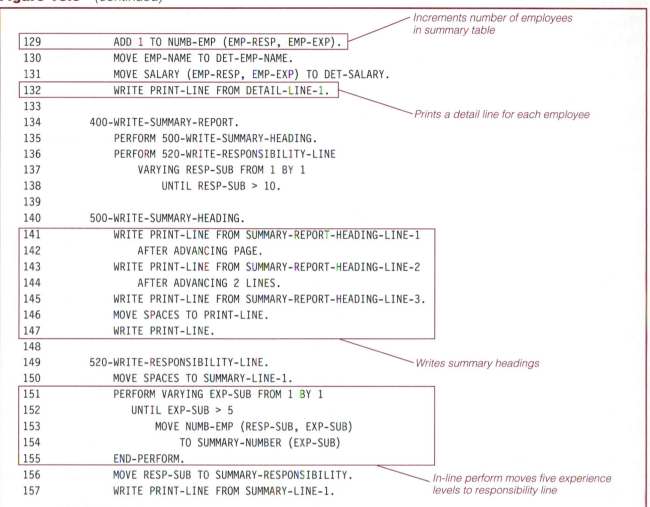

```
129           ADD 1 TO NUMB-EMP (EMP-RESP, EMP-EXP).          ── Increments number of employees
130           MOVE EMP-NAME TO DET-EMP-NAME.                      in summary table
131           MOVE SALARY (EMP-RESP, EMP-EXP) TO DET-SALARY.
132           WRITE PRINT-LINE FROM DETAIL-LINE-1.
133
134       400-WRITE-SUMMARY-REPORT.                            ── Prints a detail line for each employee
135           PERFORM 500-WRITE-SUMMARY-HEADING.
136           PERFORM 520-WRITE-RESPONSIBILITY-LINE
137               VARYING RESP-SUB FROM 1 BY 1
138                   UNTIL RESP-SUB > 10.
139
140       500-WRITE-SUMMARY-HEADING.
141           WRITE PRINT-LINE FROM SUMMARY-REPORT-HEADING-LINE-1
142               AFTER ADVANCING PAGE.
143           WRITE PRINT-LINE FROM SUMMARY-REPORT-HEADING-LINE-2
144               AFTER ADVANCING 2 LINES.
145           WRITE PRINT-LINE FROM SUMMARY-REPORT-HEADING-LINE-3.
146           MOVE SPACES TO PRINT-LINE.
147           WRITE PRINT-LINE.
148
149       520-WRITE-RESPONSIBILITY-LINE.                       ── Writes summary headings
150           MOVE SPACES TO SUMMARY-LINE-1.
151           PERFORM VARYING EXP-SUB FROM 1 BY 1
152               UNTIL EXP-SUB > 5
153                   MOVE NUMB-EMP (RESP-SUB, EXP-SUB)
154                       TO SUMMARY-NUMBER (EXP-SUB)
155           END-PERFORM.
156           MOVE RESP-SUB TO SUMMARY-RESPONSIBILITY.        ── In-line perform moves five experience
157           WRITE PRINT-LINE FROM SUMMARY-LINE-1.              levels to responsibility line
```

clauses to allocate space for the table, but omits the REDEFINES clause, because (unlike the salary table) the number of employees is computed during processing. The 50 elements in the table are initialized to zero by the VALUE ZERO clause in line 62. (See limitations of COBOL-74 at the end of the chapter.)

The Procedure Division follows both the hierarchy chart and pseudocode. The key to the program is the ADD statement in line 129, which increments the number of employees for the particular responsibility-experience combination. The subscript values in this statement are taken directly from the incoming employee record, which defines EMP-RESP and EMP-EXP in lines 30 and 32, respectively. The detail line for the individual employee is written in lines 130–132.

The summary report is produced after the end of file has been reached by the PERFORM WRITE-SUMMARY-REPORT statement of line 117. The heading lines are written in lines 140–146, after which the paragraph WRITE-RESPONSIBILITY-LINE is executed 10 times (once for each responsibility level) in lines 149–157. The latter paragraph contains its own PERFORM VARYING statement to write each of the five experience totals for each of the 10 responsibility levels.

Three-Level Tables

The material on two-level tables is easily extended to a third dimension. We continue therefore with our two-level example, in which salary is a function of responsibility and experience, but this time add a third determinant, region (due to different costs of living in different areas of the country). Figure 13.10a depicts the user's view showing salary as a function of three variables (region, responsibility, and experience), Figure 13.10b contains the COBOL definition, and Figure 13.10c shows the storage allocation.

Establishment of a three-level table requires three OCCURS clauses in the table definition:

```
01  SALARY-TABLE.
    05  REGION OCCURS 2 TIMES.
        10  RESPONSIBILITY OCCURS 10 TIMES.
            15  EXPERIENCE OCCURS  5 TIMES.
                20  SALARY                    PIC 9(5).
```

These entries establish a 100-element table (2 x 10 x 5) with each element assigned five memory locations (according to the PICTURE clause). Thus there are a total of 500 memory locations allocated to the table as indicated in Figure 13.10c. The first 25 locations refer to the five experience levels at the first responsibility level in the first region; the next 25 locations to the five experience levels at the second responsibility level in the first region, and so on.

As in the two-level example, the table is initialized through combinations of the OCCURS, VALUE, and REDEFINES clauses. Each VALUE clause fills an entire row (consisting of five experience elements or 25 positions in all), with 20 such statements needed to initialize all 500 storage locations. The first VALUE clause fills the first 25 locations (corresponding to the five experience levels for responsibility one in region one), the second VALUE clause fills locations 26–50 (the five experience levels for responsibility two in region one), and so on. The order of the VALUE clauses is critical and coincides with Figure 13.10a. The resulting storage allocation is shown in Figure 13.10c and further clarifies the discussion.

Once again you must be careful to use the correct number of subscripts, as well as specify the subscripts in the proper order. The rule is the same as for two-level tables, namely that the number of subscripts is equal to the number of OCCURS clauses used to define the entry, and further, that the order of the subscripts corresponds to the order of the OCCURS clauses.

Return to the table definition of Figure 13.10b, observing that three OCCURS clauses are associated with SALARY, and hence three subscripts are necessary; that is, SALARY is subordinate to REGION, RESPONSIBILITY, and EXPERIENCE, each of which was defined with its own OCCURS clause. Hence any Procedure Division reference to SALARY must include three subscripts—for example, SALARY (2, 4, 1) to indicate the salary for region 2, responsibility 4, and experience 1.

As is the case with one- and two-level tables, the compiler is concerned only with syntax (that the proper number of subscripts is supplied), and not with the values of those subscripts. A reference to SALARY (3, 1, 1) would not produce a compilation error because it is syntactically valid. It would, however, cause problems during execution because the subscript value for region 3 is inconsistent with the table definition. The execution results are unpredictable.

COBOL also permits reference at different hierarchical levels, so that the definition of a three-level table automatically allows reference to other one- and two-dimensional tables (although such references may not make sense logically). Refer again to the storage schematic in Figure 13.10c and/or the examples below to further clarify this discussion.

Figure 13.10 Three-level Tables

Region 2	Experience		1	2	3	4	5
		1	28,000	29,000	30,000	31,000	32,000
		2	29,000	30,000	31,000	32,000	33,000
		3	30,000	31,000	32,000	33,000	34,000
	Responsibility	4	32,000	34,000	36,000	38,000	40,000

Region = 2
Responsibility level = 1
Experience level = 4

Region 1	Experience		1	2	3	4	5	
		1	26,000	27,000	28,000	29,000	30,000	44,000
		2	27,000	28,000	29,000	30,000	31,000	50,000
		3	28,000	29,000	30,000	31,000	32,000	53,000
		4	30,000	32,000	34,000	36,000	38,000	56,000
	Responsibility	5	32,000	34,000	36,000	38,000	40,000	64,000
		6	34,000	36,000	38,000	40,000	42,000	
		7	36,000	39,000	42,000	45,000	48,000	
		8	39,000	42,000	45,000	48,000	51,000	
		9	42,000	45,000	48,000	51,000	54,000	
		10	46,000	50,000	54,000	58,000	62,000	

Region = 2
Responsibility level = 4
Experience level =1

Region = 1
Responsibility level =1
Experience level = 4

Region = 1
Responsibility level = 4
Experience level =1

(a) User's View

```
01 SALARY-VALUES.
   05 REGION-ONE.
      10      FILLER      PIC X(25)      VALUE '26000270002800029000030000'.
      10      FILLER      PIC X(25)      VALUE '27000280002900003000031000'.
      10      FILLER      PIC X(25)      VALUE '28000290003000031000032000'.
      10      FILLER      PIC X(25)      VALUE '30000320003400036000038000'.
      10      FILLER      PIC X(25)      VALUE '32000340003600038000040000'.
      10      FILLER      PIC X(25)      VALUE '34000360003800040000042000'.
      10      FILLER      PIC X(25)      VALUE '36000390004200045000048000'.
      10      FILLER      PIC X(25)      VALUE '39000420004500048000051000'.
      10      FILLER      PIC X(25)      VALUE '42000450004800051000054000'.
      10      FILLER      PIC X(25)      VALUE '46000500005400058000062000'.
   05 REGION-TWO.
      10  FILLER  PIC X(25)      VALUE '28000290003000031000032000'.
      10  FILLER  PIC X(25)      VALUE '29000300003100032000033000'.
      10  FILLER  PIC X(25)      VALUE '30000310003200033000034000'.
      10  FILLER  PIC X(25)      VALUE '32000340003600038000040000'.
      10  FILLER  PIC X(25)      VALUE '34000360003800040000042000'.
      10  FILLER  PIC X(25)      VALUE '36000380004000042000044000'.
      10  FILLER  PIC X(25)      VALUE '38000410004400047000050000'.
      10  FILLER  PIC X(25)      VALUE '41000440004700050000053000'.
      10  FILLER  PIC X(25)      VALUE '44000470005000053000056000'.
      10  FILLER  PIC X(25)      VALUE '48000520005600060000064000'.

01 SALARY-TABLE REDEFINES SALARY-VALUES.
   05 REGION OCCURS 2 TIMES.
      10 RESPONSIBILITY OCCURS 10 TIMES.
         15 EXPERIENCE OCCURS 5 TIMES.
            20 SALARY          PIC 9(5).
```

(b) Initialization via the REDEFINES and VALUES Clauses

										SALARY-VALUES										
		REGION (1)										REGION (2)								
	RESPONSIBILITY (1)					RESPONSIBILITY (10)						RESPONSIBILITY (1)					RESPONSIBILITY (10)				
Exp 1	Exp 2	Exp 3	Exp 4	Exp 5	...	Exp 1	Exp 2	Exp 3	Exp 4	Exp 5	Exp 1	Exp 2	Exp 3	Exp 4	Exp 5	...	Exp 1	Exp 2	Exp 3	Exp 4	Exp 5
26000	27000	28000	29000	30000	...	46000	50000	54000	58000	62000	26000	27000	28000	29000	30000	...	46000	50000	54000	58000	62000

SALARY-VALUES   SALARY-VALUES

(c) Storage Schematic

SALARY (1, 2, 3)   A valid reference in all respects, which refers to the salary for region 1, responsibility 2, and experience 3. SALARY must always be referenced with three subscripts.

SALARY (2, 12, 7) Syntactically correct in that SALARY has three subscripts. The entry compiles cleanly but will cause problems in execution, because it refers to responsibility and experience levels of 12 and 7, respectively, which are inconsistent with the table definition.

SALARY-TABLE   Refers to the entire table of 100 elements (500 memory locations in all). SALARY-TABLE is referenced without any subscripts.

REGION (1)   Refers collectively to the 10 responsibility levels, each containing five experience levels associated with the first region; REGION is referenced with a single subscript.

RESPONSIBILITY (1, 2)   Refers collectively to the five experience levels for responsibility level 2 for region 1; RESPONSIBILITY is referenced with two subscripts.

EXPERIENCE (1, 2, 3)   A valid entry equivalent to SALARY (1, 2, 3); the entries are equivalent because SALARY is the only elementary item defined under the group item EXPERIENCE.

PERFORM VARYING

The syntax of the PERFORM VARYING statement shows the AFTER clause enclosed in brackets and followed by three dots to indicate the clause can be repeated. Accordingly, three-level tables are processed with a PERFORM VARYING statement that includes two AFTER clauses as shown in Figure 13.11. The statement may execute either a designated procedure as in Figure 13.11a, or a series of in-line statements as in Figure 13.11b.

As in the two-level example, all possible combinations of the three subscripts are executed, causing the designated statements to be executed a total of 100

Figure 13.11 PERFORM VARYING with Three Subscripts

```
PERFORM INITIALIZE-SALARIES
    VARYING REGION-SUB FROM 1 BY 1
        UNTIL REGION-SUB > 2
    AFTER RESPONSIBILITY-SUB FROM 1 BY 1
        UNTIL RESPONSIBILITY-SUB > 10
    AFTER EXPERIENCE-SUB FROM 1 BY 1
        UNTIL EXPERIENCE-SUB > 5.
    .
    .
        .
INITIALIZE-SALARIES.
    MOVE ZERO TO SALARY (REGION-SUB, RESPONSIBILITY-SUB, EXPERIENCE-SUB).
```

(a) Performing a Paragraph

Figure 13.11 *(continued)*

```
PERFORM
     VARYING REGION-SUB FROM 1 BY 1
         UNTIL REGION-SUB > 2
     AFTER RESPONSIBILITY-SUB FROM 1 BY 1
         UNTIL RESPONSIBILITY-SUB > 10
     AFTER EXPERIENCE-SUB FROM 1 BY 1
         UNTIL EXPERIENCE-SUB > 5
             MOVE ZERO TO SALARY (REGION-SUB, RESPONSIBILITY-SUB, EXPERIENCE-SUB)
END-PERFORM.
```

(b) In-Line Perform

Region Subscript	Responsibility Subscript	Experience Subscript	
1	1	1	
1	1	2	REGION-SUB and RESPONSIBILITY-SUB are both set to 1 while EXPERIENCE-SUB varies from 1 to 5
1	1	3	
1	1	4	
1	1	5	
1	2	1	
1	2	2	REGION-SUB remains at 1 while RESPONSIBILITY-SUB is incremented to 2 and EXPERIENCE-SUB is again varied from 1 to 5
1	2	3	
1	2	4	
1	2	5	
1	10	1	
1	10	2	At the 50th iteration, REGION-SUB is still set to 1, but RESPONSIBILITY-SUB has reached 10
1	10	3	
1	10	4	
1	10	5	
2	1	1	
2	1	2	REGION-SUB is incremented to 2, RESPONSIBILITY-SUB is reset to 1 while EXPERIENCE-SUB varies from 1 to 5
2	1	3	
2	1	4	
2	1	5	
2	10	1	
2	10	2	At the 100th iteration, REGION-SUB reaches 2, RESPONSIBILITY-SUB reaches 10 and EXPERIENCE-SUB reaches 5
2	10	3	
2	10	4	
2	10	5	

(c) Variation of Subscripts

$(2 \times 10 \times 5)$ times. The *bottom* subscript (EXPERIENCE-SUB in the example) is varied first, then the middle subscript (RESPONSIBILITY-SUB), and finally the top subscript (REGION-SUB). The sequence in which the 100 combinations are executed is shown in Figure 13.11.

A Sample Program

We incorporate the material on three-level tables into our previous sample COBOL program on two-level tables. The specifications have been updated and are presented in their entirety.

Programming Specifications

Program Name: Three-Level Tables

Narrative: This program extends the example on two-level tables to a third dimension in that salary is now a function of three variables (region, responsibility, and experience). As in the earlier program, a detail report is required showing the salary of each employee. In addition a summary report containing the number of employees in each region/ responsibility/experience combination is to be produced.

Input File(s): EMPLOYEE-FILE

Input Record Layout:
```
01  EMPLOYEE-RECORD.
    05  EMP-NAME                    PIC X(15).
    05  EMP-SALARY-DETERMINANTS.
        10  EMP-RESP                PIC 99.
        10  FILLER                  PIC X.
        10  EMP-EXP                 PIC 99.
        10  FILLER                  PIC X(3).
        10  EMP-REGION              PIC 99.
    05  FILLER                      PIC X(5).
```

Test Data:
```
ADAMS       04 01 01
BAKER       01 04 01
BROWN       08 02 02
CHARLES     09 02 02
DAVIDSON    09 04 02
DAVIS       10 04 01
EPSTEIN     04 05 02
FRANKEL     03 03 01
GOODMAN     03 03 01
GULFMAN     03 05 01
HATHAWAY    07 02 01
INGLES      03 01 01
JACKSON     06 03 01
JORDAN      06 03 01
KING        07 02 01
LIPMAN      07 01 01
LOWELL      01 04 02
```

Report Layout: See Figure 13.12.

Figure 13.12 Output of Three-Level Program

```
                    STARTING SALARIES OF ALL NEW EMPLOYEES
                         ADAMS              $30,000
                         BAKER              $29,000
                         BROWN              $44,000
                         CHARLES            $47,000
                         DAVIDSON           $53,000
                         DAVIS              $58,000
                         EPSTEIN            $40,000
                         FRANKEL            $30,000
                         GOODMAN            $30,000
                         GULFMAN            $32,000
                         HATHAWAY           $39,000
                         INGLES             $28,000
                         JACKSON            $38,000
                         JORDAN             $38,000
                         KING               $39,000
                         LIPMAN             $36,000
                         LOWELL             $31,000
```

(a) Detail Report

```
          STARTING SALARY SUMMARY REPORT - REGION   1
                            EXPERIENCE
    RESPONSIBILITY      1        2        3        4        5
```

RESPONSIBILITY	1	2	3	4	5
1	0	0	0	1	0
2	0	0	0	0	0
3	1	0	2	0	1
4	1	0	0	0	0
5	0	0	0	0	0
6	0	0	2	0	0
7	1	2	0	0	0
8	0	0	0	0	0
9	0	0	0	0	0
10	0	0	0	1	0

```
          STARTING SALARY SUMMARY REPORT - REGION   2
                            EXPERIENCE
    RESPONSIBILITY      1        2        3        4        5
```

RESPONSIBILITY	1	2	3	4	5
1	0	0	0	1	0
2	0	0	0	0	0
3	0	0	0	0	0
4	0	0	0	0	1
5	0	0	0	0	0
6	0	0	0	0	0
7	0	0	0	0	0
8	0	1	0	0	0
9	0	1	0	1	0
10	0	0	0	0	0

(b) Summary Report

Processing Requirements: 1. Read a file of employee records, and for each record:

    a. Determine the employee's starting salary as a function of region, responsibility, and experience.

    b. Print a detail line for this employee showing his or her name and starting salary.

2. Compute the number of employees for each *region-responsibility-experience* combination. This requires creation of a 2 x 10 x 5 table to store the number of individuals in each region-responsibility-experience combination, and implies that as each employee record is read, the corresponding table entry is incremented by one.

3. When all employees have been processed, print the table containing the number of employees in each category as shown in Figure 13.12b.

The Completed Program

The extension of the original program from two to three dimensions is so direct that the hierarchy chart and pseudocode are virtually unchanged. The completed program is shown in Figure 13.13, and should already appear familiar, as it repeats the COBOL statements used in the explanation of three-level tables. The COBOL statements to define the salary table (lines 44–73), appeared earlier in Figure 13.10b and were discussed fully at that time. Observe also the definition of a second

Figure 13.13   Three-Level Program

```
 1        IDENTIFICATION DIVISION.
 2        PROGRAM-ID.    3LVTABLE.
 3        AUTHOR.        ROBERT T. GRAUER.
 4
 5        ENVIRONMENT DIVISION.
 6        INPUT-OUTPUT SECTION.
 7        FILE-CONTROL.
 8            SELECT EMPLOYEE-FILE   ASSIGN TO SYSIN
 9                                   ORGANIZATION IS LINE SEQUENTIAL.
10            SELECT PRINT-FILE      ASSIGN TO SYSOUT
11                                   ORGANIZATION IS LINE SEQUENTIAL.
12
13        DATA DIVISION.
14        FILE SECTION.
15        FD  EMPLOYEE-FILE
16            DATA RECORD IS EMPLOYEE-RECORD.
17        01  EMPLOYEE-RECORD                PIC X(23).
18
19        FD  PRINT-FILE
20            DATA RECORD IS PRINT-LINE.
21        01  PRINT-LINE                     PIC X(132).
22
23        WORKING-STORAGE SECTION.
24        01  FILLER                         PIC X(14)
25                VALUE 'WS BEGINS HERE'.
26
27        01  WS-EMPLOYEE-RECORD.
```

Figure 13.13 *(continued)*

```
28          05   EMP-NAME                    PIC X(15).
29          05   EMP-SALARY-DETERMINANTS.
30              10   EMP-RESP                PIC 99.
31              10   FILLER                  PIC X.
32              10   EMP-EXP                 PIC 99.
33              10   FILLER                  PIC X.
34              10   EMP-REG                 PIC 99.
35
36      01   PROGRAM-SUBSCRIPTS.
37          05   RESP-SUB                    PIC S9(4) COMP.
38          05   EXP-SUB                     PIC S9(4) COMP.
39          05   REG-SUB                     PIC S9(4) COMP.
40
41      01   WS-END-OF-DATA-SWITCH           PIC X(3)   VALUE SPACES.
42          88   END-OF-DATA                            VALUE 'YES'.
43
44      01   SALARY-VALUES.
45          05   REGION-ONE.
46              10   FILLER  PIC X(25)   VALUE '26000270002800029000030000'.
47              10   FILLER  PIC X(25)   VALUE '27000280002900030000031000'.
48              10   FILLER  PIC X(25)   VALUE '28000290003000031000032000'.
49              10   FILLER  PIC X(25)   VALUE '30000320003400036000038000'.
50              10   FILLER  PIC X(25)   VALUE '32000340003600038000040000'.
51              10   FILLER  PIC X(25)   VALUE '34000360003800040000042000'.
52              10   FILLER  PIC X(25)   VALUE '36000390004200045000048000'.
53              10   FILLER  PIC X(25)   VALUE '39000420004500048000051000'.
54              10   FILLER  PIC X(25)   VALUE '42000450004800051000054000'.
55              10   FILLER  PIC X(25)   VALUE '46000500005400058000062000'.
56
57          05   REGION-TWO.
58              10   FILLER  PIC X(25)   VALUE '28000290003000031000032000'.
59              10   FILLER  PIC X(25)   VALUE '29000300003100032000033000'.
60              10   FILLER  PIC X(25)   VALUE '30000310003200033000034000'.
61              10   FILLER  PIC X(25)   VALUE '32000340003600038000040000'.
62              10   FILLER  PIC X(25)   VALUE '34000360003800040000042000'.
63              10   FILLER  PIC X(25)   VALUE '36000380004000042000044000'.
64              10   FILLER  PIC X(25)   VALUE '38000410004400047000050000'.
65              10   FILLER  PIC X(25)   VALUE '41000440004700050000053000'.
66              10   FILLER  PIC X(25)   VALUE '44000470005000053000056000'.
67              10   FILLER  PIC X(25)   VALUE '48000520005600060000064000'.
68
69      01   SALARY-TABLE REDEFINES SALARY-VALUES.
70          05   REGION OCCURS 2 TIMES.
71              10   RESPONSIBILITY OCCURS 10 TIMES.
72                  15   EXPERIENCE OCCURS 5 TIMES.
73                      20   SALARY                PIC 9(5).
74
75      01   NUMBER-OF-EMPLOYEES-TABLE.
76          05   NUMBER-REGION OCCURS 2 TIMES.
77              10   NUMBER-RESPONSIBILITY OCCURS 10 TIMES.
```

Used as subscripts into summary table

Three-level salary table

Figure 13.13   *(continued)*

```
78                      15   NUMBER-EXPERIENCE OCCURS 5 TIMES.
79                          20   NUMB-EMP      PIC 99      VALUE ZERO.
80
81          01   DETAIL-REPORT-HEADING-LINE.
82               05   FILLER              PIC X(9)    VALUE SPACES.
83               05   FILLER              PIC X(39)
84                        VALUE 'STARTING SALARIES OF ALL NEW EMPLOYEES'.
85               05   FILLER              PIC X(82)   VALUE SPACES.
86
87          01   DETAIL-LINE-1.
88               05   FILLER              PIC X(12)   VALUE SPACES.
89               05   DET-EMP-NAME        PIC X(15).
90               05   FILLER              PIC X(4)    VALUE SPACES.
91               05   DET-SALARY          PIC $99,999.
92               05   FILLER              PIC X(94)   VALUE SPACES.
93
94          01   SUMMARY-REPORT-HEADING-LINE-1.
95               05   FILLER              PIC X(24)   VALUE SPACES.
96               05   FILLER              PIC X(39)
97                        VALUE 'STARTING SALARY SUMMARY REPORT - REGION'.
98               05   SUM-REGION-NUMBER   PIC ZZZ9.
99               05   FILLER              PIC X(65)   VALUE SPACES.
100
101         01   SUMMARY-REPORT-HEADING-LINE-2.
102              05   FILLER              PIC X(36)   VALUE SPACES.
103              05   FILLER              PIC X(10)   VALUE 'EXPERIENCE'.
104              05   FILLER              PIC X(86)   VALUE SPACES.
105
106         01   SUMMARY-REPORT-HEADING-LINE-3.
107              05   FILLER              PIC X(5)    VALUE SPACES.
108              05   FILLER              PIC X(14)   VALUE 'RESPONSIBILITY'.
109              05   FILLER              PIC X(48)
110                       VALUE '      1       2       3       4       5'.
111              05   FILLER              PIC X(65)   VALUE SPACES.
112
113         01   SUMMARY-LINE-1.
114              05   FILLER              PIC X(9).
115              05   SUMMARY-RESPONSIBILITY PIC Z(4).
116              05   FILLER              PIC X(4)    VALUE SPACES.
117              05   SUMMARY-TOTAL-VALUES OCCURS 5 TIMES.
118                  10   FILLER          PIC X(4).
119                  10   SUMMARY-NUMBER  PIC Z(4)9.
120              05   FILLER              PIC X(70).
121
122         PROCEDURE DIVISION.
123         100-PREPARE-SALARY-REPORT.
124             OPEN INPUT EMPLOYEE-FILE
125                  OUTPUT PRINT-FILE.
126             PERFORM 200-WRITE-DETAIL-REPORT-HDG.
127             PERFORM UNTIL END-OF-DATA
128                 READ EMPLOYEE-FILE INTO WS-EMPLOYEE-RECORD
```

Figure 13.13 *(continued)*

```
129                  AT END
130                      MOVE 'YES' TO WS-END-OF-DATA-SWITCH
131                  NOT AT END
132                      PERFORM 300-PROCESS-EMPLOYEES
133              END-READ
134          END-PERFORM.
135          PERFORM 400-WRITE-SUMMARY-REPORT
136              VARYING REG-SUB FROM 1 BY 1
137                  UNTIL REG-SUB > 2.
138          CLOSE EMPLOYEE-FILE
139                PRINT-FILE.
140          STOP RUN.
141
142      200-WRITE-DETAIL-REPORT-HDG.
143          WRITE PRINT-LINE FROM DETAIL-REPORT-HEADING-LINE
144              AFTER ADVANCING PAGE.
145          MOVE SPACES TO PRINT-LINE.
146          WRITE PRINT-LINE.
147
148      300-PROCESS-EMPLOYEES.
149          ADD 1 TO NUMB-EMP (EMP-REG, EMP-RESP, EMP-EXP).
150          MOVE EMP-NAME TO DET-EMP-NAME.
151          MOVE SALARY (EMP-REG, EMP-RESP, EMP-EXP) TO DET-SALARY.
152          WRITE PRINT-LINE FROM DETAIL-LINE-1.
153
154      400-WRITE-SUMMARY-REPORT.
155          MOVE REG-SUB TO SUM-REGION-NUMBER.
156          PERFORM 500-WRITE-SUMMARY-HEADING.
157          PERFORM 520-WRITE-RESPONSIBILITY-LINE
158              VARYING RESP-SUB FROM 1 BY 1
159                  UNTIL RESP-SUB > 10.
160
161      500-WRITE-SUMMARY-HEADING.
162          WRITE PRINT-LINE FROM SUMMARY-REPORT-HEADING-LINE-1
163              AFTER ADVANCING PAGE.
164          WRITE PRINT-LINE FROM SUMMARY-REPORT-HEADING-LINE-2
165              AFTER ADVANCING 2 LINES.
166          WRITE PRINT-LINE FROM SUMMARY-REPORT-HEADING-LINE-3.
167          MOVE SPACES TO PRINT-LINE.
168          WRITE PRINT-LINE.
169
170      520-WRITE-RESPONSIBILITY-LINE.
171          MOVE SPACES TO SUMMARY-LINE-1.
172          PERFORM VARYING EXP-SUB FROM 1 BY 1
173              UNTIL EXP-SUB > 5
174                  MOVE NUMB-EMP (REG-SUB, RESP-SUB, EXP-SUB)
175                          TO SUMMARY-NUMBER (EXP-SUB)
176          END-PERFORM.
177          MOVE RESP-SUB TO SUMMARY-RESPONSIBILITY.
178          WRITE PRINT-LINE FROM SUMMARY-LINE-1.
```

Program driven by in-line PERFORM and False Condition Branch

Increments number of employees in summary table

Prints a detail line for each employee

Invoked twice—once for each region

Invoked 10 times—once for each responsibility level

In-line PERFORM moves five experience levels to appropriate region and responsibility three-level table, for the number of employees in each category in lines 75–79; the definition uses the OCCURS clauses to allocate space for the table, but omits the REDEFINES clause, because (unlike the salary table) the number of employees is computed during processing. The 100 elements in the table are initialized to zero by the VALUE ZERO clause in line 79. (See limitations of COBOL-74 at the end of the chapter.)

The Procedure Division of Figure 13.13 follows both the hierarchy chart and pseudocode. The key to the program is the ADD statement of line 149, which increments the number of employees for the particular region/responsibility/ experience combination. The subscript values in this statement are taken directly from the incoming employee record, which define EMP-REG, EMP-RESP, and EMP-EXP. The detail line for the individual employee is created in lines 150–152.

The summary report is produced after the end of file has been reached by the PERFORM statement of lines 135–137, which executes the paragraph WRITE-SUMMARY-REPORT twice, once for each region. The heading lines are written (statements 161–168), after which the paragraph WRITE-RESPONSIBILITY-LINE is executed 10 times (once for each responsibility level) in lines 172–176. The latter paragraph contains its own PERFORM VARYING statement to write the five experience totals for each responsibility level.

Table Lookups

The examples thus far took advantage of a direct lookup in which the table elements were referenced directly by the value of the subscript; that is, the examples used numeric subscripts for responsibility and experience that corresponded directly to the row and column of the table. This is not always true as indicated by the example in Figure 13.14.

The table in Figure 13.14a depicts a user's view in which quarterly sales are recorded for every branch within the corporation. The COBOL implementation in Figure 13.14b establishes BRANCH as a one-level table with 25 rows; it also establishes QUARTERLY-SALES as a two-level table consisting of 25 rows and 4 columns. Any reference to BRANCH-NAME requires a single subscript (index)— for example, BRANCH-NAME (2) to obtain the branch-name in the second row. Any reference to QUARTERLY-SALES requires two subscripts (indexes) to indicate the branch and quarter—for example, QUARTERLY-SALES (2, 1), QUARTERLY-SALES (2, 2), QUARTERLY-SALES (2, 3), and QUARTERLY-SALES (2, 4) to reference the four sales figures for the branch in row two. Figure 13.14c shows the corresponding storage schematic.

Assume now that we want to obtain the annual sales for a specific branch, for example, Boston. An individual could tell at a glance that the data for Boston are in the second row of the table and would know automatically to sum the figures in row two to obtain the annual sales. The computer, however, has to first search the table of branch names to locate the proper row before summing the quarterly sales. The process is illustrated in Figure 13.4d, which contains the Procedure Division statements necessary to obtain the annual sales for Boston.

The SET statement is required prior to a sequential search in order to begin the search in row one of the BRANCH table. The SEARCH statement varies BRANCH-INDEX until a match is found on branch name; the WHEN clause includes a PERFORM VARYING statement that varies QUARTERLY-INDEX from one to four in the appropriate (BRANCH-INDEX) row in order to obtain the annual total. Note, too, the use of scope terminators (END-ADD, END-PERFORM, and END-SEARCH) and how the various statements are nested within one another.

Figure 13.14 Two-Level Table Lookup

Branch Name	1st Quarter	2nd Quarter	3rd Quarter	4th Quarter
Atlanta	$100,000	$200,000	$300,000	$400,000
Boston	$50,000	$150,000	$250,000	$350,000
Chicago	$150,000	$165,000	$400,000	$275,000
.				
.				
.				
San Diego	$25,000	$50,000	$75,000	$100,000

(a) User's View

```
01  SALES-TABLE REDEFINES SALES-DATA.
    05  BRANCH OCCURS 25 TIMES
        INDEXED BY BRANCH-INDEX.
        10  BRANCH-NAME                PIC X(12).
        10  QUARTERLY-SALES    OCCURS 4 TIMES
            INDEXED BY QUARTERLY-INDEX   PIC 9(6).
```

(b) Table Definition

SALES-TABLE							
BRANCH (1)				...	BRANCH (25)		
BRANCH NAME (1)	QUARTERLY SALES (1,1)	...	QUARTERLY SALES (1,4)		BRANCH NAME (25)	QUARTERLY SALES (25,1)	... QUARTERLY SALES (25,4)
PIC X(12)	PIC 9(6)		PIC 9(6)		PIC X(12)	PIC 9(6)	PIC 9(6)

(c) Storage Schematic

```
MOVE ZEROS TO ANNUAL-TOTAL.
SET BRANCH-INDEX TO 1.
SEARCH BRANCH
    AT END
        DISPLAY 'Boston not in table'
    WHEN BRANCH-NAME (BRANCH-INDEX) = 'Boston'
        PERFORM VARYING QUARTERLY-INDEX FROM 1 BY 1
            UNTIL QUARTERLY-INDEX > 4
                ADD QUARTERLY-SALES (BRANCH-INDEX, QUARTERLY-INDEX)
                    TO ANNUAL-TOTAL
                SIZE ERROR
                    DISPLAY 'ANNUAL TOTAL TOO LARGE'
                END-ADD
        END-PERFORM
END-SEARCH.
```

(d) SEARCH Statement

A Calorie Counter's Delight

We come now to our final example, which ties together material from several previous chapters. The specifications call for an interactive program that accepts information from the console and displays the results on the monitor. Specifications follow in the usual format.

Programming Specifications

Program Name: A Calorie Counter's Delight

Narrative: Develop a program that will prompt the operator for an age and weight, then display the number of calories needed to maintain that weight. The table of daily maintenance calories is given in the second processing requirement.

Input File(s):   None; input will be accepted from the console.

Report Layout: None; output will be displayed on the monitor.

Processing Requirements: 1. Prompt the user for age and weight; validate the parameters immediately as they are input and prompt the user continually until valid values are received. Age must be between 18 and 75 years, inclusive; weight between 90 and 165 pounds, inclusive.

2. Display the calories required to maintain the indicated weight according to the table below.

Daily Maintenance Calories Table

| Weight (POUNDS) | | Age Range (YEARS) | | |
From	To	18–35	36–55	56–75
90	99	1,700	1,500	1,300
100	110	1,850	1,650	1,400
111	121	2,000	1,750	1,550
122	128	2,100	1,900	1,600
129	132	2,150	1,950	1,650
133	143	2,300	2,050	1,800
144	154	2,400	2,150	1,850
155	165	2,550	2,300	1,950

3. Ask the user whether s/he wishes to input another set of parameters; if yes, repeat steps one and two above; if not, terminate the program.

Range-Step Tables

The concept of a range-step table was introduced in the previous chapter and is essential to the solution of the present problem. A range-step table occurs when the same table value—for example, 1,700 calories—is applicable to many search arguments—for example, any weight between 90 and 99 pounds coupled with any age between 18 and 35. We need to recognize, therefore, that two range-step tables, for weight and age, are necessary in addition to the calorie maintenance table.

Our solution is shown in Figure 13.15. The user's view of the three tables is shown in Figure 13.15a and the COBOL implementation in Figure 13.15b. The

Figure 13.15 Range-step Tables

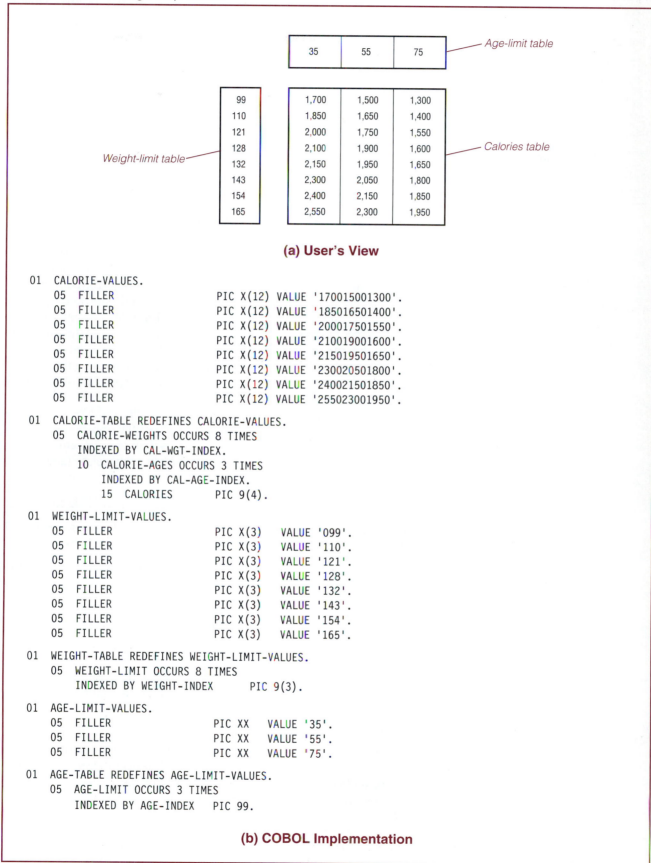

(a) User's View

```
01   CALORIE-VALUES.
     05   FILLER                 PIC X(12) VALUE '170015001300'.
     05   FILLER                 PIC X(12) VALUE '185016501400'.
     05   FILLER                 PIC X(12) VALUE '200017501550'.
     05   FILLER                 PIC X(12) VALUE '210019001600'.
     05   FILLER                 PIC X(12) VALUE '215019501650'.
     05   FILLER                 PIC X(12) VALUE '230020501800'.
     05   FILLER                 PIC X(12) VALUE '240021501850'.
     05   FILLER                 PIC X(12) VALUE '255023001950'.

01   CALORIE-TABLE REDEFINES CALORIE-VALUES.
     05   CALORIE-WEIGHTS OCCURS 8 TIMES
          INDEXED BY CAL-WGT-INDEX.
          10   CALORIE-AGES OCCURS 3 TIMES
               INDEXED BY CAL-AGE-INDEX.
               15   CALORIES      PIC 9(4).

01   WEIGHT-LIMIT-VALUES.
     05   FILLER                 PIC X(3)   VALUE '099'.
     05   FILLER                 PIC X(3)   VALUE '110'.
     05   FILLER                 PIC X(3)   VALUE '121'.
     05   FILLER                 PIC X(3)   VALUE '128'.
     05   FILLER                 PIC X(3)   VALUE '132'.
     05   FILLER                 PIC X(3)   VALUE '143'.
     05   FILLER                 PIC X(3)   VALUE '154'.
     05   FILLER                 PIC X(3)   VALUE '165'.

01   WEIGHT-TABLE REDEFINES WEIGHT-LIMIT-VALUES.
     05   WEIGHT-LIMIT OCCURS 8 TIMES
          INDEXED BY WEIGHT-INDEX      PIC 9(3).

01   AGE-LIMIT-VALUES.
     05   FILLER           PIC XX    VALUE '35'.
     05   FILLER           PIC XX    VALUE '55'.
     05   FILLER           PIC XX    VALUE '75'.

01   AGE-TABLE REDEFINES AGE-LIMIT-VALUES.
     05   AGE-LIMIT OCCURS 3 TIMES
          INDEXED BY AGE-INDEX   PIC 99.
```

(b) COBOL Implementation

Figure 13.16   Hierarchy Chart

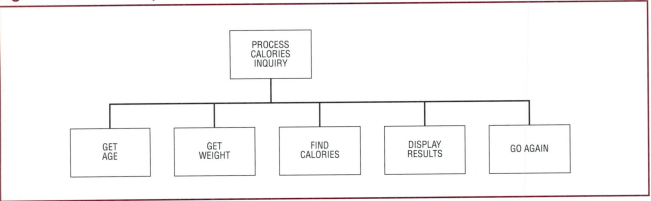

definition of the CALORIE-TABLE is straightforward and uses the OCCURS, VALUE, and REDEFINES clauses as explained earlier. The WEIGHT-LIMIT table stores only the upper limit for each weight class because the ranges overlap from one class to the next—that is, 90–99 pounds, 100–110 pounds, 111–121 pounds, and so on. In similar fashion the age-limit table stores only the upper limit for each age class.

The hierarchy chart in Figure 13.16 contains the modules to get the user's age and weight, determine the number of calories, display the results, then determine whether the entire process is to be repeated. The pseudocode in Figure 13.17 continually prompts the user until a valid age is received, then prompts the user for a valid weight. The *nested search* statement mimics the process a person would follow to determine the number of calories based on weight and age—that is, to search the weight limits in the various rows, then go across the appropriate row to search the age limits for that weight. Note, too, the less than or equal condition in the search argument, which checks only the upper limit in each weight (age) class.

The Completed Program

The completed program is shown in Figure 13.18 and parallels the pseudocode and hierarchy chart just discussed. Several features of the program merit attention.

1. The definition of CALORIE-TABLE in lines 17–32 as a two-level 8 x 3 table; the indexes CAL-WGT-INDEX and CAL-AGE-INDEX are defined with the table to reference the row and column, respectively.

2. The definition of two range-step tables for weight and age limits in lines 34–46 and lines 48–55, and referenced by WEIGHT-INDEX and AGE-INDEX, respectively.

3. The *nested SEARCH statements* in lines 82–94, which identify the row containing the weight limit (from the one-level weight-limit table), the column containing the age limit (from the one-level age-limit table), then reference the corresponding row and column in the calorie table to display the answer.

4. The SET statement in line 81 that initializes WEIGHT-INDEX (from the weight-limit table) *and* CAL-WGT-INDEX (from the two-level calorie table); the **SEARCH VARYING** statement in line 82 manipulates these indexes in conjunction with one another so that when the weight limit is found in the

Figure 13.17 Pseudocode

```
            ┌─ DO WHILE user wants to inquire
            │      Initialize age & weight
            │   ┌─ DO WHILE invalid age
            │   │      Display age prompt
            │   │      Accept age from user
            │   └─ ENDDO
            │   ┌─ DO WHILE invalid weight
            │   │      Display weight prompt
            │   │      Accept weight from user
            │   └─ ENDDO
            │   ┌─ SEARCH weight-limit-table
            │   │      AT END
            │   │          Display invalid weight
            │   │      WHEN user's weight <= table value
            │   │       ┌─ SEARCH age-limit table
            │   │       │      AT END
            │   │       │          Display invalid age
            │   │       │      WHEN user's age <= table value
            │   │       │          MOVE calories (wgt-limt, age-limit) to output
            │   │       └─ END-SEARCH
            │   └─ END-SEARCH
            │      Display required calories
            │      Display prompt to go again
            │      Accept user's response
            └─ ENDDO
               Stop Run
```

Figure 13.18 Calories Program

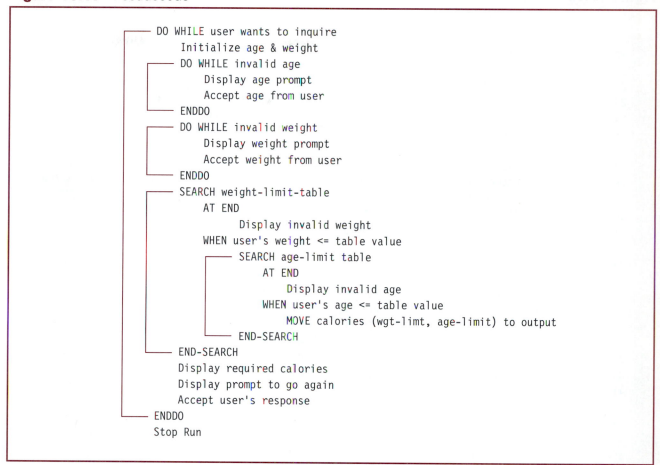

```
1          IDENTIFICATION DIVISION.
2          PROGRAM-ID.    CALORIE.
3          AUTHOR.        CVV.
4
5          DATA DIVISION.
6          WORKING-STORAGE SECTION.
7          01  INDIVIDUAL-DATA.
8              05  IND-AGE          PIC 99.
9                  88  VALID-AGE               VALUE 18 THRU 75.
10             05  IND-WEIGHT       PIC 9(3).
11                 88  VALID-WEIGHT            VALUE 90 THRU 165.
12
13         01  PROGRAM-VARIABLES.
14             05  CALORIES-NEEDED  PIC Z,ZZ9 VALUE ZEROS.
15             05  GO-AGAIN-SWITCH  PIC X.
16
17         01  CALORIE-VALUES.
18             05  FILLER           PIC X(12) VALUE '170015001300'.
```

Definition of two-level table

Figure 13.18   *(continued)*

```
19          05  FILLER              PIC X(12) VALUE '185016501400'.
20          05  FILLER              PIC X(12) VALUE '200017501550'.
21          05  FILLER              PIC X(12) VALUE '210019001600'.
22          05  FILLER              PIC X(12) VALUE '215019501650'.
23          05  FILLER              PIC X(12) VALUE '230020501800'.
24          05  FILLER              PIC X(12) VALUE '240021501850'.
25          05  FILLER              PIC X(12) VALUE '255023001950'.
26
27      01  CALORIE-TABLE REDEFINES CALORIE-VALUES.
28          05  CALORY-WEIGHTS OCCURS 8 TIMES
29              INDEXED BY CAL-WGT-INDEX.
30              10  CALORY-AGES OCCURS 3 TIMES
31                  INDEXED BY CAL-AGE-INDEX.
32                  15  CALORIES      PIC 9(4).
33
34      01  WEIGHT-LIMIT-VALUES.
35          05  FILLER              PIC X(3)   VALUE '099'.
36          05  FILLER              PIC X(3)   VALUE '110'.
37          05  FILLER              PIC X(3)   VALUE '121'.
38          05  FILLER              PIC X(3)   VALUE '128'.
39          05  FILLER              PIC X(3)   VALUE '132'.
40          05  FILLER              PIC X(3)   VALUE '143'.
41          05  FILLER              PIC X(3)   VALUE '154'.
42          05  FILLER              PIC X(3)   VALUE '165'.
43
44      01  WEIGHT-TABLE REDEFINES WEIGHT-LIMIT-VALUES.
45          05  WEIGHT-LIMIT OCCURS 8 TIMES
46              INDEXED BY WEIGHT-INDEX      PIC 9(3).
47
48      01  AGE-LIMIT-VALUES.
49          05  FILLER              PIC XX   VALUE '35'.
50          05  FILLER              PIC XX   VALUE '55'.
51          05  FILLER              PIC XX   VALUE '75'.
52
53      01  AGE-TABLE REDEFINES AGE-LIMIT-VALUES.
54          05  AGE-LIMIT OCCURS 3 TIMES
55              INDEXED BY AGE-INDEX   PIC 99.
56
57      PROCEDURE DIVISION.
58      PROCESS-CALORIE-INQUIRY.
59          PERFORM UNTIL GO-AGAIN-SWITCH = 'n' OR 'N'
60              MOVE ZEROS TO IND-AGE IND-WEIGHT
61              PERFORM GET-AGE
62                  UNTIL VALID-AGE
63              PERFORM GET-WEIGHT
64                  UNTIL VALID-WEIGHT
65              PERFORM FIND-CALORIES
66              PERFORM DISPLAY-RESULTS
67              PERFORM GO-AGAIN
68          END-PERFORM.
69          DISPLAY 'May all your calories be non-fat'.
```

Definition of two-level table

Prompts user continually until valid age and weight are entered

Figure 13.18 *(continued)*

```
70            STOP RUN.
71
72        GET-AGE.
73            DISPLAY 'Enter Age (18-75): ' NO ADVANCING.
74            ACCEPT IND-AGE.
75
76        GET-WEIGHT.
77            DISPLAY 'Enter Weight (90-165): ' NO ADVANCING.
78            ACCEPT IND-WEIGHT.
79
80        FIND-CALORIES.
81            SET WEIGHT-INDEX CAL-WGT-INDEX TO 1.
82            SEARCH WEIGHT-LIMIT VARYING CAL-WGT-INDEX
83                AT END
84                    DISPLAY 'Weight not found in table'
85                WHEN IND-WEIGHT <= WEIGHT-LIMIT (WEIGHT-INDEX)
86                    SET AGE-INDEX CAL-AGE-INDEX TO 1
87                    SEARCH AGE-LIMIT VARYING CAL-AGE-INDEX
88                        AT END
89                            DISPLAY 'Age not found in table'
90                        WHEN IND-AGE <= AGE-LIMIT (AGE-INDEX)
91                            MOVE CALORIES (CAL-WGT-INDEX, CAL-AGE-INDEX)
92                            TO CALORIES-NEEDED
93                    END-SEARCH
94            END-SEARCH.
95
96        DISPLAY-RESULTS.
97            DISPLAY ' '.
98            DISPLAY CALORIES-NEEDED ' calories/day will maintain '
99            'a weight of ' IND-WEIGHT ' pounds at age ' IND-AGE.
100           DISPLAY ' '.
101
102       GO-AGAIN.
103           DISPLAY 'Go again? (Y/N) ' NO ADVANCING.
104           ACCEPT GO-AGAIN-SWITCH.
```

Nested SEARCH statements use VARYING option

first table, the corresponding row is set in the second table. The SET statement in line 86 and the SEARCH VARYING statement in line 87 function in similar fashion for the age limit and corresponding column in the calorie table.

5. The MOVE statement in line 91 is a direct lookup that uses values of CAL-WGT-INDEX and CAL-AGE-INDEX established by the nested SEARCH statements.

6. The various ACCEPT and DISPLAY statements throughout the program that utilize screen I-O.

LIMITATIONS OF COBOL-74

Seven levels of subscripting are permitted in COBOL-85 as opposed to the earlier limit of three; most applications, however, do not require even three-level tables.

COBOL-85 facilitates the initialization of a table in which all elements have the same value by allowing the VALUE clause to be specified in the same entry as an OCCURS clause. (The technique was illustrated in lines 61–62 of Figure 13.9.) This was not permitted in COBOL-74, which required a PERFORM VARYING statement or REDEFINES clause to achieve the same result.

The optional END-SEARCH scope terminator is new to COBOL-85 and terminates the conditional portion of the SEARCH and SEARCH ALL statements; the scope terminator makes it possible to nest SEARCH statements.

SUMMARY

Points to Remember

- Multilevel tables of up to seven levels are possible in COBOL-85 although most applications use tables of only one, two, or three dimensions.

- The entries in multiple-level tables may be referenced in different hierarchical levels. The number of subscripts (indexes) needed is equal to the number of OCCURS clauses in the entry definition.

- Tables at any level may be initialized through a combination of the OCCURS, VALUES, and REDEFINES clauses. The OCCURS clause allocates space for the table, the VALUE clause places data in these locations, and the REDEFINES clause assigns another name to previously allocated space.

- Multilevel tables can be manipulated by using the PERFORM VARYING statement with the addition of the appropriate AFTER clause(s). The bottom subscript (index) is always manipulated first.

- The SEARCH VARYING statement manipulates the indexes in two tables in conjunction with one another; the technique is often used with range-step tables, in which the table arguments are stored in a separate table.

Key Words and Concepts

Compilation error	Range-step table
Detail report	Summary report
Execution error	Three-level table
Hierarchical level	Two-level table
Nested search statement	User view

COBOL Elements

AFTER	REDEFINES
BY	SEARCH VARYING
END-SEARCH	UNTIL
OCCURS	VALUE
PERFORM VARYING	

Fill-in

1. A two-level table requires two _____ clauses in its definition.

2. In a PERFORM VARYING statement with two subscripts, the (bottom/top) subscript is varied first.

3. COBOL-85 permits a maximum of _____ subscripts.

4. If a Procedure Division reference is made to FIELD-ONE (SUB1, SUB2), SUB1 refers to the _____ level OCCURS clause, whereas SUB2 refers to the _____ level OCCURS clause.

5. In COBOL-74 a VALUE clause (may/may not) be used in conjunction with an _____ clause to initialize a table, and so a _____ clause is used as well.

6. The statement:
```
PERFORM PARAGRAPH-A
    VARYING SUB1 FROM 1 BY 1 UNTIL SUB1 > 5
        AFTER SUB2 FROM 1 BY 1 UNTIL SUB2 > 6.
```

will perform PARAGRAPH-A a total of _____ times.

7. The PERFORM statement of question 6 begins execution by setting SUB1 to 1, and varying SUB2 from _____ to _____, after which SUB1 will be incremented to _____, and SUB2 will again vary from _____ to _____.

8. Given the COBOL definition:
```
01  CORPORATION.
    05  REGION  OCCURS 4 TIMES.
        10  STATE  OCCURS 5 TIMES.
            15  CITY  OCCURS 6 TIMES  PIC 9(6).
```

A total of _____ elements are present in the table.

9. Answer with respect to the table of question 8. Any reference to REGION requires _____ subscript(s), a reference to STATE requires _____ subscript(s), and a reference to CITY requires _____ subscript(s).

True/False

1. A maximum of seven OCCURS clauses in a given table is permitted in COBOL-85.

2. A given entry may contain both an OCCURS clause and a PICTURE clause.

3. A given entry may contain both an OCCURS clause and a VALUE clause.

4. The REDEFINES clause is required whenever a table is initialized.

5. A PERFORM VARYING statement may vary indexes as well as subscripts.

6. Referencing a data name with two subscripts, when only a single OCCURS clause appears in the table definition, produces a compilation error.

7. Referencing a data name with a subscript value of 50, when the OCCURS clause indicates only 10 entries, produces a compilation error.

8. SEARCH statements may be nested.

9. The VARYING, FROM, BY, and AFTER clauses are mandatory in a PERFORM statement.

10. A PERFORM VARYING statement will always execute the designated procedure at least once.

Problems

1. Write out the 12 pairs of values that will be assumed by SUB-1 and SUB-2 as a result of the statement:
```
PERFORM 10-PROCESS-TABLE
    VARYING SUB-1 FROM 1 BY 1
        UNTIL SUB-1 > 4
    AFTER SUB-2 FROM 1 BY 1
        UNTIL SUB-2 > 3.
```

2. Indicate the 24 sets of values that will be assumed by SUB-1, SUB-2, and SUB-3 as a result of the following statement. Remember that the bottom subscript is varied first.
```
PERFORM 10-PROCESS-TABLE
    VARYING SUB-1 FROM 1 BY 1
        UNTIL SUB-1 > 3
    AFTER SUB-2 FROM 1 BY 1
        UNTIL SUB-2 > 2
    AFTER SUB-3 FROM 1 BY 1
        UNTIL SUB-3 > 4.
```

3. Given the following table definition:
```
01  CORPORATE-DATA.
    05  COMPANY OCCURS 10 TIMES.
        10  DIVISION-NAME           PIC X(15).
        10  YEARLY-FINANCIAL-DATA OCCURS 4 TIMES.
            15  REVENUE             PIC 9(7).
            15  NET-INCOME          PIC 9(7).
```

    a. Indicate an appropriate storage schematic.

    b. State whether the following are valid or invalid references, and if invalid, indicate whether the problem occurs during compilation or execution:

        i.   CORPORATE-DATA

        ii.   COMPANY

        iii. COMPANY (8)

        iv.   DIVISION-NAME (8)

        v.   DIVISION-NAME (12)

      vi. YEARLY-FINANCIAL-DATA (4)

     vii. REVENUE (10, 4)

    viii. NET-INCOME (10,4)

     ix. REVENUE (4, 10)

4. A corporation monitors monthly sales for its six branch offices according to the following table definition:

```
01  CORPORATE-SALES-TABLE.
    05  BRANCH-OFFICE OCCURS 6 TIMES.
        10  BRANCH-NAME            PIC X(10).
        10  MONTHS OCCURS 12 TIMES.
            15  SALES-AMOUNT      PIC 9(6).
```

  a. Indicate the appropriate storage schematic.

  b. Write a PERFORM VARYING statement to determine the annual sales for the third branch office.

  c. Write a PERFORM VARYING statement to determine the corporate sales for May.

  d. Write a PERFORM VARYING statement to determine the corporate sales for the entire year.

  e. Develop an FD, corresponding record description, and associated Procedure Division statements, to read the data for CORPORATE-SALES-TABLE from a file of six records; that is, each incoming record has the 12 monthly sales for a particular branch office.

  f. Develop an FD, corresponding record description, and associated Procedure Division statements, to read the data for CORPORATE-SALES-TABLE from a file of 12 records; that is, each incoming record has the six branch office amounts for a particular month.

5. Your professor has two sections of COBOL. Each section has 40 students. Each student is expected to submit six projects and take three examinations. Develop a file structure suitable to all of this data in a single table.

6. The following table was suggested to tabulate enrollments for the various colleges within a university. Each college, such as the College of Engineering, has multiple majors: Mechanical Engineering, Electrical Engineering, and so on.

```
01  ENROLLMENT-DATA.
    05  COLLEGE OCCURS 3 TIMES.
        10  MAJOR OCCURS 50 TIMES.
            15  YEAR OCCURS 4 TIMES.
                20  NUMBER-OF-STUDENTS    PIC 9(4).
```

  a. Indicate an appropriate storage schematic.

  b. State whether the following are valid or invalid references, and if invalid, indicate whether the problem occurs during compilation or execution:

       i. ENROLLMENT-DATA

      ii. COLLEGE (1)

     iii. MAJOR (1)

     iv. YEAR (1)

      v. NUMBER-OF-STUDENTS (1)

     vi. NUMBER-OF-STUDENTS (1, 2, 3)

    vii. NUMBER-OF-STUDENTS (4, 5, 6)

c. Write PERFORM VARYING statements to determine:

    i. The total number of students in the university.

    ii. The total number of seniors in the first college.

    iii. The total number of students in the first major of the first college.

    iv. The total number of freshmen (year 1) in the first college.

    v. The total number of freshmen in the university.

14 Sorting

CHAPTER OUTLINE

Overview
System Concepts
Collating Sequence
Embedded Sign
COBOL Implementation
SORT Statement
SD (Sort Description)
RELEASE and RETURN
Programming Specifications
USING/GIVING Option
INPUT PROCEDURE/OUTPUT PROCEDURE Option
Comparing Options
MERGE Statement
Limitations of COBOL-74
Summary
Fill-in
True/False
Problems

OBJECTIVES

After reading this chapter you will be able to:

■ Distinguish between an internal sort, a utility sort, and the COBOL SORT statement.

■ Differentiate between an ascending and a descending sort; between major, intermediate, and minor keys; and between primary, secondary, and tertiary keys.

■ Define collating sequence; discuss the most significant differences between EBCDIC and ASCII and how the collating sequence affects fields with an embedded sign.

■ Explain the syntax of the COBOL SORT statement, and the supporting RELEASE, RETURN, and SD statements.

■ Explain the use of INPUT PROCEDURE to sort on a calculated field, and/or to selectively pass records to the sort work file.

■ Distinguish between a merge and a sort.

OVERVIEW

Sorting (the rearrangement of data) is one of the most frequent operations in data processing, making it possible to present data in a variety of sequences according to the analysis required. Transactions may be listed alphabetically, alphabetically by location, in ascending or descending sequence by account balance, and so on. The sorting procedure itself is accomplished in one of three ways:

1. An internal sort, in which the programmer develops his or her own logic within the application program. (This approach is typically not used by the COBOL programmer.)

2. A utility sort, in which an independent sort program is executed outside of the application program as a separate step.

3. The COBOL SORT statement, in which control is passed to the independent sort program from within the COBOL program. (Our discussion deals exclusively with this approach.)

We begin the chapter by developing the general concepts associated with sorting, then present the necessary statements to implement sorting within a COBOL program. We develop two parallel programs to illustrate variations within the SORT statement and conclude with a brief discussion of merging, which is a special case of sorting.

System Concepts

A ***sort key*** is a field within a record that determines how the file is to be arranged. Several keys may be specified in a single sort, as in the case of a departmental census in which employees are to appear alphabetically within department. In other words, the file is to be rearranged (that is, sorted) so that all employees in the same department appear together, and further, so that employees in the same department appear alphabetically. Department is a more important key than employee name; thus department is considered the ***major key*** and employee name the ***minor key***. (Other, equally correct, terminology refers to department as the ***primary key*** and name as the ***secondary key***.)

Sorting is done in one of two sequences: ***ascending*** (low to high) or ***descending*** (high to low). Listing employees in increasing order of salary is an example of an ascending sort, whereas listing them in decreasing order (that is, with the highest salary first) represents a descending sort. *Any sort on an alphabetic field, (employee name, for example) is always perceived as an ascending sort.* (An ascending sort is assumed if the sequence is not specified.)

To be absolutely sure of this terminology, consider Figure 14.1. Figure 14.1a lists unsorted data for 12 students. Figure 14.1b displays these records after they have been sorted by name only. Figure 14.1c shows a primary sort on year (descending) and a secondary sort on name. Thus, all students in year four are listed first (in alphabetical order), then all students in year three, and so on. Finally, Figure 14.1d illustrates primary, secondary, and tertiary sorts. All business majors are listed first, then all engineering majors, and finally all liberal arts majors. Within each major, students are listed by year in descending order and are also listed alphabetically within year.

Collating Sequence

The sequencing of numeric items is done strictly according to their algebraic values; for example, -10 is less than $+5$, which is less than $+10$. The length of a numeric field does not enter into the comparison; for example, a four-digit integer field equal to 0099 is less than a three-digit field equal to 100.

The sequencing of alphabetic and/or alphanumeric fields is more subtle with fields of different length—for example, GREEN and GREENFIELD. The sorting algorithm compares the two names one character at a time, from left to right and determines that the first five letters, G, R, E, E, and N, are the same in both names. The shorter field (GREEN in the example) is then extended with blanks so that comparison may continue. A blank, however, is always considered smaller than any other letter, so that GREEN will be placed ahead of GREENFIELD.

The sorting of alphanumeric fields is further complicated when the sort key contains letters and numbers. Comparison still proceeds from left to right, but which alphanumeric key should come first, 111 or AAA? Surprisingly, either answer could be correct, depending on the ***collating sequence*** in effect. Collating sequence is defined as the ordered list (from low to high) of all valid characters and is a function of manufacturer; IBM mainframes use **EBCDIC,** whereas almost every other computer, including the PC, uses **ASCII.** Both sequences are shown in Figure 14.2 for selected characters.

As can be seen from Figure 14.2, the number one 1 comes *after* the letter A in EBCDIC, but *before* the letter A in ASCII. In other words, in an alphanumeric sort key of 111 will precede a key of AAA under the ASCII collating sequence, but follow it under EBCDIC. It is imperative, therefore, that you be aware of the collating sequence in effect when alphanumeric keys are specified. This is especially true in a

Figure 14.1 Sorting Vocabulary

Primary Key: Name (Ascending)

NAME	YEAR	MAJOR		NAME	YEAR	MAJOR
Smith	1	Liberal arts		Adams	3	Business
Jones	4	Engineering		Benjamin	4	Business
Adams	3	Business		Crawford	2	Engineering
Howe	2	Liberal arts		Deutsch	4	Business
Frank	1	Engineering		Epstein	2	Engineering
Epstein	2	Engineering		Frank	1	Engineering
Zev	4	Business		Grauer	3	Liberal arts
Benjamin	4	Business		Howe	2	Liberal arts
Grauer	3	Liberal arts		Jones	4	Engineering
Crawford	2	Engineering		Makoske	1	Business
Deutsch	4	Business		Smith	1	Liberal arts
Makoske	1	Business		Zev	4	Business

(a) Unsorted Data   **(b) Sorted Data, One Key**

Primary Key: Year (Descending)
Secondary Key: Name (Ascending)

Primary Key: Major (Ascending)
Secondary Key: Year (Descending)
Tertiary Key: Name (Ascending)

NAME	YEAR	MAJOR		NAME	YEAR	MAJOR
Benjamin	4	Business		Benjamin	4	Business
Deutsch	4	Business		Deutsch	4	Business
Jones	4	Engineering		Zev	4	Business
Zev	4	Business		Adams	3	Business
Adams	3	Business		Makoske	1	Business
Grauer	3	Liberal arts		Jones	4	Engineering
Crawford	2	Engineering		Crawford	2	Engineering
Epstein	2	Engineering		Epstein	2	Engineering
Howe	2	Liberal arts		Frank	1	Engineering
Frank	1	Engineering		Grauer	3	Liberal arts
Makoske	1	Business		Howe	2	Liberal arts
Smith	1	Liberal arts		Smith	1	Liberal arts

(c) Sorted Data, Two Keys   **(d) Sorted Data, Three Keys**

multivendor environment, as when on-site mini- or microcomputers offload to an
IBM mainframe.

Embedded Sign

The collating sequence has yet an additional consequence with signed numeric
fields. Arithmetic operations require positive and negative numbers, and hence,
when we do arithmetic with pencil and paper, we precede the numbers with plus

Figure 14.2 EBCDIC and ASCII Collating Sequences

EBCDIC		ASCII	
	(space)		(space)
.	(period)	"	(quotation mark)
<	(less than)	$	(currency symbol)
(	(left parenthesis)	'	(apostrophe)
+	(plus symbol)	(	(left parenthesis)
$	(currency symbol)	)	(right parenthesis)
*	(asterisk)	*	(asterisk)
)	(right parenthesis)	+	(plus symbol)
;	(semicolon)	,	(comma)
–	(hyphen, minus symbol)	–	(hyphen, minus symbol)
/	(slash)	.	(period, decimal point)
,	(comma)	/	(slash)
>	(greater than)		0 through 9
'	(apostrophe)	;	(semicolon)
=	(equal sign)	<	(less than)
"	(quotation mark)	=	(equal sign)
	a through z (lower case)	>	(greater than)
	A through Z (upper case)		A through Z (upper case)
	0 through 9		a through z (lower case)

Figure 14.3 Embedded Signs (ASCII versus EBCDIC)

Digit	Character	Digit	Character	Digit	Character	Digit	Character
+1	1	−1	Q	+1	A	−1	J
+2	2	−2	R	+2	B	−2	K
+3	3	−3	S	+3	C	−3	L
+4	4	−4	T	+4	D	−4	M
+5	5	−5	U	+5	E	−5	N
+6	6	−6	V	+6	F	−6	O
+7	7	−7	W	+7	G	−7	P
+8	8	−8	X	+8	H	−8	Q
+9	9	−9	Y	+9	I	−9	R
+0	0	−0	P	+0	{	−0	}

(a) ASCII   **(b) EBCDIC**

and minus signs. The computer, however, embeds the sign within the low-order digit of the number according to the table in Figure 14.3. The advantage of an *embedded sign* is that a position is saved in the storage medium; for example, only one position is needed for a single-digit numeric field versus two (one for the digit and one for the sign) if the sign were stored separately.

Figure 14.4 Embedded Signs (ASCII versus EBCDIC)/II

Name	Account Balance
John Doe	$1,005
Mary Smith	$1,005CR
Frank Coulter	$2,000
Erik Parker	$2,000CR

(a) Report

John Doe	1005
Mary Smith	100U
Frank Coulter	2000
Erik Parker	200Z

(b) Data (ASCII)

John Doe	100E
Mary Smith	100N
Frank Coulter	200{
Erik Parker	200}

(c) Data (EBCDIC)

The effect of the collating sequence is seen in Figure 14.4. Figure 14.4a contains a simple report in which John Doe and Mary Smith have positive and negative balances of $1,005. The data that produce the report are shown in Figure 14.4b for ASCII and in Figure 14.4c for EBCDIC. The record for Mary Smith contains a "U" in the lower-order digit under ASCII according to the character for -5 in Figure 14.3a, but an upper case N under EBCDIC as indicated in Figure 14.3b.

The optional **SIGN** clause (entered after the PICTURE clause) makes it possible to embed the sign as the leading rather than the trailing character, and/or to establish a separate position for the sign. Consider:

$$\left[\left[\underline{SIGN} \ IS\right] \left\{ \begin{array}{l} \underline{LEADING} \\ \underline{TRAILING} \end{array} \right\} \left[\underline{SEPARATE} \ CHARACTER\right] \right]$$

The vast majority of applications, however, embed the sign as the trailing character (the default action taken by COBOL) as was illustrated in Figure 14.4.

Cobol Implementation

The COBOL requirements for implementing a sort center on the SORT statement. In addition, you must be familiar with an SD (sort description) and with the RELEASE and RETURN statements.

SORT Statement

The syntax for the **SORT** statement is as follows:

```
SORT file-name-1

     {    {DESCENDING}                     }
     {ON  {         } KEY {data-name-1} ...} ...
     {    {ASCENDING }                     }

     [WITH DUPLICATES IN ORDER]

     [COLLATING SEQUENCE IS alphabet-name]

     {INPUT PROCEDURE IS procedure-name-1  [{THRU   }                ]}
     {                                     [{       } procedure-name-2]}
     {USING {fine-name-2}                  [{THROUGH}                ]}

     {OUTPUT PROCEDURE IS procedure-name-3 [{THRU   }                ]}
     {                                     [{       } procedure-name-4]}
     {GIVING {file-name-3}                 [{THROUGH}                ]}
```

Multiple sort keys are listed in the order of importance, with the major (primary) key listed first. Thus, the statement:

```
SORT STUDENT-FILE
    ASCENDING KEY STUDENT-MAJOR
    DESCENDING KEY YEAR-IN-SCHOOL
    ASCENDING KEY STUDENT-NAME
```

corresponds to the order of the keys in Figure 14.1d. (STUDENT-MAJOR is the primary key, YEAR-IN-SCHOOL is the secondary key, and STUDENT-NAME is the tertiary key.) As can be seen from the general syntax, KEY is an optional reserved word, so that the preceding statement could have been written as:

```
SORT STUDENT-FILE
    ASCENDING STUDENT-MAJOR
    DESCENDING YEAR-IN-SCHOOL
    ASCENDING STUDENT-NAME
```

When consecutive keys have the same sequence (both ascending or both descending), ASCENDING (or DESCENDING) need not be repeated. Hence, if it were necessary to obtain a master list of students in ascending order by year in school, and alphabetically within year, you could code:

```
SORT STUDENT-FILE
    ASCENDING YEAR-IN-SCHOOL
              STUDENT-NAME
```

The **WITH DUPLICATES IN ORDER** phrase in the SORT statement ensures that the sequence of records with duplicate keys in the output file will be identical to the sequence of the records in the input file. The phrase is illustrated in Figure 14.9, which appears later in the chapter.

The **COLLATING SEQUENCE** clause allows you to change the collating sequence; that is, you can specify ASCII on an IBM mainframe or EBCDIC on a PC. (Implementation of an alternate collating sequence is less than straightforward, and you should consult an appropriate vendor manual if you wish to use one.)

The SORT statement requires a choice between **INPUT PROCEDURE** and **USING,** and between **OUTPUT PROCEDURE** and **GIVING,** resulting in four possible combinations: USING/GIVING, USING/OUTPUT PROCEDURE, INPUT PROCEDURE/GIVING, and INPUT PROCEDURE/OUTPUT PROCEDURE. The choice between the different options depends on the specific application. (The chapter contains two listings for USING/GIVING and INPUT PROCEDURE/OUTPUT PROCEDURE.)

The difference between USING and INPUT PROCEDURE is that INPUT PROCEDURE requires the programmer to do the I/O to and from the sort utility, whereas the USING option does the I/O automatically. INPUT PROCEDURE is thus a more general technique in that it permits sorting on a ***calculated field***, a field not contained in the input record. Assume, for example, that an employee record contains the present and previous salary, but not the percent of salary increase. The USING option can sort on either salary, but not on the salary increase because the latter is a calculated field that it is not present in the input record.

The INPUT PROCEDURE also allows you to *selectively* pass records to the sort utility, a desirable practice in instances where only some of the records in an input file are to appear in a subsequent report. Sorting is time consuming and thus, it is highly inefficient to sort an entire file only to eliminate records after sorting. It is far better to select the records prior to the sort by using the INPUT PROCEDURE.

The difference between OUTPUT PROCEDURE and GIVING is the status of the sorted file. The OUTPUT PROCEDURE uses a *temporary* work file, which disappears after the program ends so that the results of the sort are lost. The GIVING option creates a *permanent* file containing the sorted results that remains after the program has ended.

SD (Sort Description)

The first file in the SORT statement references the ***sort work file*** that was previously defined in an **SD** (**S**ort **D**escription) statement in the Data Division. The SD is analogous to an FD except that it refers to a sort work file, rather than an ordinary file used for I/O. The SD has the general syntax:

```
SD file-name-1

    [RECORD CONTAINS [integer-1 TO] integer-2 CHARACTERS]

    [DATA {RECORD IS    } {data-name-1} . . .]
          {RECORDS ARE  }
```

RELEASE and RETURN

The **RELEASE** and **RETURN** statements are required in the INPUT and OUTPUT PROCEDURE, respectively. The RELEASE statement is analogous to a WRITE statement and writes a record to the sort work file (the file defined in the SD).

```
RELEASE record-name [FROM identifier]
```

The RELEASE statement appears in the INPUT PROCEDURE. The RETURN statement, on the other hand, is analogous to a READ statement and appears in the OUTPUT PROCEDURE. It has the format:

```
        RETURN file-name [INTO identifier]

          [AT END imperative-statement-1]

          [NOT AT END imperative-statement-2]

      [END-RETURN]
```

The RETURN statement reads a record from the sort work file (the file defined in the SD) for subsequent processing in the program.

The SORT statement and its related statements can be integrated into any COBOL program. We proceed to develop a typical application, with specifications in the usual format. In actuality we present two separate programs, to illustrate both the INPUT PROCEDURE/OUTPUT PROCEDURE and USING/GIVING options of the SORT statement.

Programming Specifications

Program Name: Sort Programs

Narrative: The specifications call for *two* programs to illustrate the USING/GIVING and INPUT PROCEDURE/OUTPUT PROCEDURE options of the SORT statement. The programs use the same data file but produce different reports.

Input File(s): SALES-FILE

Input Record Layout:
```
01  SALES-RECORD-IN.
    05  SR-ACCOUNT-NUMBER        PIC 9(6).
    05  FILLER                   PIC X.
    05  SR-NAME                  PIC X(15).
    05  SR-SALES                 PIC S9(4).
    05  FILLER                   PIC XX.
    05  SR-COMMISSION-PERCENT    PIC V99.
    05  FILLER                   PIC XX.
    05  SR-LOCATION              PIC X(15).
    05  SR-REGION                PIC X(11).
```

Test Data: See Figure 14.5.

Report Layout: See Figure 14.6a and 14.6b. The report layout—the heading, detail, and total lines—is the same for both programs, but the contents of the reports—the specific records as well as the sequence of those records—are different.

Processing Requirements:

1. Develop two parallel programs, each of which processes a file of sales records and computes the commission due for each incoming transaction. The amount of the commission is equal to the sales amount times the commission percentage.

2. The first program is to use the USING/GIVING option to produce a master list of *all* incoming records. The records are to be in sequence by region, location, and name as shown in Figure 14.6a.

3. The second program is to use the INPUT PROCEDURE/OUTPUT PROCEDURE option and list only the transactions with a commission greater than $100. The records are to appear in decreasing order of commission as shown in Figure 14.6b.

Figure 14.5 Test Data (ASCII Format)

```
000069 BENWAY       023Q 10  CHICAGO        MIDWEST
000100 HUMMER       010W 05  CHICAGO        MIDWEST
000101 CLARK        1500 10  TRENTON        NORTHEAST
000104 CLARK        0500 03  TRENTON        NORTHEAST
100000 JOHNSON      030S 06  ST. PETERSBURG SOUTHEAST
130101 CLARK        3200 20  TRENTON        NORTHEAST
203000 HAAS         8900 05  ST. LOUIS      MIDWEST
248545 JOHNSON      0345 14  ST. PETERSBURG SOUTHEAST
277333 HAAS         009X 08  ST. LOUIS      MIDWEST
400000 JOHNSON      070Y 08  ST. PETERSBURG SOUTHEAST
444333 ADAMS        100V 01  NEW YORK       NORTHEAST
444444 FEGEN        0100 02  ST. PETERSBURG SOUTHEAST
475365 HAAS         0333 05  ST. LOUIS      MIDWEST
476236 FEGEN        037V 03  ST. PETERSBURG SOUTHEAST
476530 BENWAY       023U 05  CHICAGO        MIDWEST
555555 FEGEN        0304 05  ST. PETERSBURG SOUTHEAST
555666 ADAMS        2003 20  NEW YORK       NORTHEAST
576235 CLARK        0100 03  TRENTON        NORTHEAST
583645 KARLSTROM    0145 04  BALTIMORE      NORTHEAST
649356 HUMMER       0345 05  CHICAGO        MIDWEST
694446 HUMMER       0904 10  CHICAGO        MIDWEST
700039 MARCUS       0932 10  BALTIMORE      NORTHEAST
750020 MARCUS       0305 05  BALTIMORE      NORTHEAST
800396 KARLSTROM    3030 09  BALTIMORE      NORTHEAST
878787 JOHNSON      1235 12  ST. PETERSBURG SOUTHEAST
987654 ADAMS        2005 10  NEW YORK       NORTHEAST
988888 BENWAY       0450 01  CHICAGO        MIDWEST
999340 BENWAY       0334 30  CHICAGO        MIDWEST
```

Figure 14.6 Sorted Reports

```
                    SALES ACTIVITY REPORT          04/21/99          PAGE   1

    REGION      LOCATION        NAME        ACCOUNT #        SALES    COMMISSION
    MIDWEST     CHICAGO         BENWAY         000069    $   231-     $   23-
    MIDWEST     CHICAGO         BENWAY         476530    $   235-     $   12-
    MIDWEST     CHICAGO         BENWAY         988888    $   450      $    5
    MIDWEST     CHICAGO         BENWAY         999340    $   334      $  100
    MIDWEST     CHICAGO         HUMMER         000100    $   107-     $    5-
    MIDWEST     CHICAGO         HUMMER         649356    $   345      $   17
    MIDWEST     CHICAGO         HUMMER         694446    $   904      $   90
    MIDWEST     ST. LOUIS       HAAS           203000    $8,900       $  445
    MIDWEST     ST. LOUIS       HAAS           277333    $    98-     $    8-
    MIDWEST     ST. LOUIS       HAAS           475365    $   333      $   17
```

(a) By Region, Location, and Name (All Records)

Figure 14.6 *(continued)*

```
                    SALES ACTIVITY REPORT        04/21/99         PAGE  3

      REGION      LOCATION         NAME        ACCOUNT #      SALES    COMMISSION
      NORTHEAST   TRENTON          CLARK        576235     $  100      $    3
      SOUTHEAST   ST. PETERSBURG   FEGEN        444444     $  100      $    2
      SOUTHEAST   ST. PETERSBURG   FEGEN        476236     $  376-     $   11-
      SOUTHEAST   ST. PETERSBURG   FEGEN        555555     $  304      $   15
      SOUTHEAST   ST. PETERSBURG   JOHNSON      100000     $  303-     $   18-
      SOUTHEAST   ST. PETERSBURG   JOHNSON      248545     $  345      $   48
                                                                           57-
                                                                          148

                                                                        2,540
```

```
                    SALES ACTIVITY REPORT        04/21/99         PAGE  2

    REGION      LOCATION        NAME        ACCOUNT #       SALES    COMMISSION
    NORTHEAST   BALTIMORE       KARLSTROM     583645     $   145      $     6
    NORTHEAST   BALTIMORE       KARLSTROM     800396     $3,030       $   273
    NORTHEAST   BALTIMORE       MARCUS        700039     $   932      $    93
    NORTHEAST   BALTIMORE       MARCUS        750020     $   305      $    15
    NORTHEAST   NEW YORK        ADAMS         444333     $1,005-      $    10-
    NORTHEAST   NEW YORK        ADAMS         555666     $2,003       $   401
    NORTHEAST   NEW YORK        ADAMS         987654     $2,005       $   201
    NORTHEAST   TRENTON         CLARK         000101     $1,500       $   150
    NORTHEAST   TRENTON         CLARK         000104     $   500      $    15
    NORTHEAST   TRENTON         CLARK         130101     $3,200       $   640
```

(a) By Region, Location, and Name (All Records)

```
                    SALES ACTIVITY REPORT        04/21/99         PAGE  1

    REGION      LOCATION        NAME        ACCOUNT #       SALES    COMMISSION
    NORTHEAST   TRENTON         CLARK         130101     $3,200       $   640
    MIDWEST     ST. LOUIS       HAAS          203000     $8,900       $   445
    NORTHEAST   NEW YORK        ADAMS         555666     $2,003       $   401
    NORTHEAST   BALTIMORE       KARLSTROM     800396     $3,030       $   273
    NORTHEAST   NEW YORK        ADAMS         987654     $2,005       $   201
    NORTHEAST   TRENTON         CLARK         000101     $1,500       $   150
    SOUTHEAST   ST. PETERSBURG  JOHNSON       878787     $1,235       $   148

               *** COMPANY TOTAL =        $ 21,873       $  2,258
```

(b) By Decreasing Commision (Commission > $100)

USING/GIVING Option

The specifications are similar to those of any other reporting program that requires a combination of heading, detail, and total lines. The hierarchy chart and pseudocode for the USING/GIVING option are shown in Figures 14.7 and 14.8, respectively. The hierarchy chart contains many of the modules found in earlier programs—for example, GET-TODAYS-DATE, WRITE-HEADING-LINES, and WRITE-DETAIL-LINE. In addition, it contains the module SORT-SALES-FILE to sequence records in the sales file.

Figure 14.7 Hierarchy Chart (USING/GIVING)

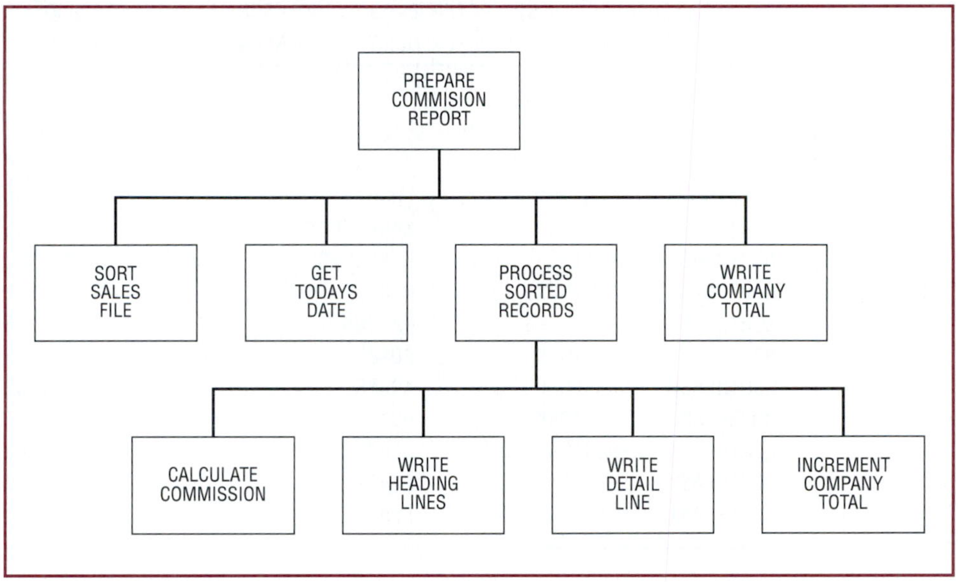

Figure 14.8 Pseudocode (USING/GIVING)

```
Sort Sales File
Open Sorted Sales File, Print File
Get today's date
DO WHILE sorted data remains
    READ Sorted Sales File
        AT END
            Indicate no more data
        NOT AT END
            Calculate commission
            IF line count greater than lines per page
                Initialize line count to 1
                Increment page count
                Write heading lines
            END-IF
            Write detail line
            Increment company total
    END READ
ENDDO
Write company total
Close files
Stop run
```

The pseudocode in Figure 14.8 contains a sort statement prior to the main loop, which contains the in-line perform and false-condition branch used in all other programs. The sales commission is calculated for each incoming record, a detail line is written, and the company total is incremented. The pseudocode also contains the logic to implement a page heading routine as explained previously in Chapter 9.

The USING/GIVING format is illustrated in Figure 14.9. The SORT statement in lines 149–155 references three files—SORT-WORK-FILE, SALES-FILE, and, SORTED-SALES-FILE—each of which has the identical record layout. The SORT statement implicitly opens SALES-FILE and reads every record in that file, releasing each record as it is read to the sort work file. It then sequences the sort work file according to designated keys and writes the newly ordered file to SORTED-SALES-FILE. The programmer does not open or close SORT-WORK-FILE or SALES-FILE as this is done by the SORT statement.

Figure 14.9   SORT Program (USING/GIVING)

```
1          IDENTIFICATION DIVISION.
2          PROGRAM-ID.    SORT1.
3          AUTHOR.        CVV.
4
5          ENVIRONMENT DIVISION.
6          INPUT-OUTPUT SECTION.
7          FILE-CONTROL.
8              SELECT SALES-FILE    ASSIGN TO SYSIN
9                  ORGANIZATION IS LINE SEQUENTIAL.
10             SELECT PRINT-FILE    ASSIGN TO SYSOUT
11                 ORGANIZATION IS LINE SEQUENTIAL.
12             SELECT SORT-WORK-FILE                          ── Sort work file is defined in ordinary SELECT statement
13                 ASSIGN TO SORTWK01.
14             SELECT SORTED-SALES-FILE ASSIGN TO SORTED
15                 ORGANIZATION IS LINE SEQUENTIAL.
16
17         DATA DIVISION.
18         FILE SECTION.
19         FD  SALES-FILE
20             RECORD CONTAINS 58 CHARACTERS
21             DATA RECORD IS SALES-RECORD.
22         01  SALES-RECORD              PIC X(58).
23
24         FD  PRINT-FILE
25             RECORD CONTAINS 132 CHARACTERS
26             DATA RECORD IS PRINT-LINE.
27         01  PRINT-LINE               PIC X(132).
28
29         SD  SORT-WORK-FILE                                 ── Sort work file is defined in an SD
30             RECORD CONTAINS 58 CHARACTERS
31             DATA RECORD IS SORT-RECORD.
32         01  SORT-RECORD.                                   ── Sort keys present in incoming record
33             05  SORT-ACCOUNT-NUMBER    PIC 9(6).
```

Figure 14.9   *(continued)*

```
34              05  FILLER               PIC X.              Sort keys present in incoming record
35              05  SORT-NAME            PIC X(15).
36              05  FILLER               PIC X(10).
37              05  SORT-LOCATION        PIC X(15).
38              05  SORT-REGION          PIC X(11).
39
40      FD  SORTED-SALES-FILE
41          RECORD CONTAINS 58 CHARACTERS
42          DATA RECORD IS SORTED-SALES-RECORD.
43      01  SORTED-SALES-RECORD      PIC X(58).
44
45      WORKING-STORAGE SECTION.
46      01  FILLER                   PIC X(14)
47              VALUE 'WS BEGINS HERE'.
48
49      01  SALES-RECORD-IN.
50          05  SR-ACCOUNT-NUMBER    PIC 9(6).
51          05  FILLER               PIC X.
52          05  SR-NAME              PIC X(15).
53          05  SR-SALES             PIC S9(4).
54          05  FILLER               PIC XX.
55          05  SR-COMMISSION-PERCENT PIC V99.
56          05  FILLER               PIC XX.
57          05  SR-LOCATION          PIC X(15).
58          05  SR-REGION            PIC X(11).
59
60      01  TODAYS-DATE-AREA.
61          05  TODAYS-YEAR          PIC 99.
62          05  TODAYS-MONTH         PIC 99.
63          05  TODAYS-DAY           PIC 99.
64
65      01  PROGRAM-SWITCHES.
66          05  DATA-REMAINS-SWITCH  PIC X(3)     VALUE 'YES'.
67              88  NO-DATA-REMAINS               VALUE 'NO'.
68
69      01  PAGE-AND-LINE-COUNTERS.
70          05  LINE-COUNT           PIC 9(2)     VALUE 11.
71          05  PAGE-COUNT           PIC 9(2)     VALUE ZEROS.
72          05  LINES-PER-PAGE       PIC 9(2)     VALUE 10.
73
74      01  INDIVIDUAL-CALCULATIONS.
75          05  IND-COMMISSION       PIC S9(4).
76
77      01  COMPANY-TOTALS.
78          05  COMPANY-SALES-TOT    PIC S9(6)    VALUE ZEROES.
79          05  COMPANY-COMM-TOT     PIC S9(6)    VALUE ZEROES.
80
81      01  HDG-LINE-ONE.
82          05  FILLER               PIC X(25)    VALUE SPACES.
83          05  FILLER               PIC X(21)
```

Figure 14.9 *(continued)*

```
84                  VALUE 'SALES ACTIVITY REPORT'.
85          05  FILLER              PIC X(8)    VALUE SPACES.
86          05  HDG-DATE            PIC X(8).
87          05  FILLER              PIC X(10)   VALUE SPACES.
88          05  FILLER              PIC X(5)    VALUE 'PAGE '.
89          05  HDG-PAGE            PIC Z9.
90          05  FILLER              PIC X(53)   VALUE SPACES.
91
92      01  HDG-LINE-TWO.
93          05  FILLER              PIC X(7)    VALUE ' REGION'.
94          05  FILLER              PIC X(5)    VALUE SPACES.
95          05  FILLER              PIC X(8)    VALUE 'LOCATION'.
96          05  FILLER              PIC X(11)   VALUE SPACES.
97          05  FILLER              PIC X(4)    VALUE 'NAME'.
98          05  FILLER              PIC X(10)   VALUE SPACES.
99          05  FILLER              PIC X(11)   VALUE 'ACCOUNT # '.
100         05  FILLER              PIC X(5)    VALUE SPACES.
101         05  FILLER              PIC X(5)    VALUE 'SALES'.
102         05  FILLER              PIC X(3)    VALUE SPACES.
103         05  FILLER              PIC X(10)   VALUE 'COMMISSION'.
104         05  FILLER              PIC X(53)   VALUE SPACES.
105
106     01  DETAIL-LINE.
107         05  DET-REGION          PIC X(11).
108         05  FILLER              PIC X       VALUE SPACES.
109         05  DET-LOCATION        PIC X(15).
110         05  FILLER              PIC X(3)    VALUE SPACES.
111         05  DET-NAME            PIC X(15).
112         05  FILLER              PIC X(2)    VALUE SPACES.
113         05  DET-ACCOUNT-NUMBER  PIC 9(6).
114         05  FILLER              PIC X(5)    VALUE SPACES.
115         05  DET-SALES           PIC $Z,ZZ9-.
116         05  FILLER              PIC X(7)    VALUE SPACES.
117         05  DET-COMMISSION      PIC $Z,ZZ9-.
118         05  FILLER              PIC X(50)   VALUE SPACES.
119
120     01  COMPANY-TOTAL-LINE.
121         05  FILLER              PIC X(31)   VALUE SPACES.
122         05  FILLER              PIC X(25)
123                 VALUE '*** COMPANY TOTAL = '.
124         05  COMPANY-SALES-TOTAL PIC $Z(3),ZZ9-.
125         05  FILLER              PIC X(5)    VALUE SPACES.
126         05  COMPANY-COMM-TOTAL  PIC $Z(3),ZZ9-.
127         05  FILLER              PIC X(51)   VALUE SPACES.
128
129     PROCEDURE DIVISION.
130     100-PREPARE-COMMISSION-REPORT.
131         PERFORM 210-SORT-SALES-RECORDS.
132         OPEN INPUT SORTED-SALES-FILE          ──── Opens the sorted file to produce report
133              OUTPUT PRINT-FILE.
```

Figure 14.9   *(continued)*

```
134              PERFORM 230-GET-TODAYS-DATE.
135              PERFORM UNTIL NO-DATA-REMAINS
136                  READ SORTED-SALES-FILE INTO SALES-RECORD-IN
137                      AT END
138                          MOVE 'NO' TO DATA-REMAINS-SWITCH
139                      NOT AT END
140                          PERFORM 250-PROCESS-SORTED-RECORDS
141                  END-READ
142              END-PERFORM.
143              PERFORM 290-WRITE-COMPANY-TOTAL.
144              CLOSE SORTED-SALES-FILE
145                    PRINT-FILE.
146              STOP RUN.
147
148          210-SORT-SALES-RECORDS.
149              SORT SORT-WORK-FILE
150                  ASCENDING KEY SORT-REGION
151                                SORT-LOCATION
152                                SORT-NAME
153                  WITH DUPLICATES IN ORDER
154                  USING SALES-FILE
155                  GIVING SORTED-SALES-FILE.
156
157          230-GET-TODAYS-DATE.
158              ACCEPT TODAYS-DATE-AREA FROM DATE.
159              STRING TODAYS-MONTH '/' TODAYS-DAY '/' TODAYS-YEAR
160                  DELIMITED BY SIZE INTO HDG-DATE.
161
162          250-PROCESS-SORTED-RECORDS.
163              PERFORM 310-CALCULATE-COMMISSION.
164              IF LINE-COUNT > LINES-PER-PAGE
165                  PERFORM 330-WRITE-HEADING-LINES
166              END-IF.
167              PERFORM 350-WRITE-DETAIL-LINE.
168              PERFORM 370-INCREMENT-COMPANY-TOTAL.
169
170          290-WRITE-COMPANY-TOTAL.
171              MOVE COMPANY-SALES-TOT TO COMPANY-SALES-TOTAL.
172              MOVE COMPANY-COMM-TOT TO COMPANY-COMM-TOTAL.
173              WRITE PRINT-LINE FROM COMPANY-TOTAL-LINE
174                  AFTER ADVANCING 2 LINES.
175
176          310-CALCULATE-COMMISSION.
177              COMPUTE IND-COMMISSION ROUNDED =
178                  SR-SALES * SR-COMMISSION-PERCENT
179                  SIZE ERROR DISPLAY 'SIZE ERROR ON COMMISSION FOR '
180                      SR-NAME
181              END-COMPUTE.
182
183          330-WRITE-HEADING-LINES.
```

All three files must have identical length and record layout

Figure 14.9   *(continued)*

```
184              MOVE 1 TO LINE-COUNT.
185              ADD 1 TO PAGE-COUNT.
186              MOVE PAGE-COUNT TO HDG-PAGE.
187              WRITE PRINT-LINE FROM HDG-LINE-ONE
188                  AFTER ADVANCING PAGE.
189              WRITE PRINT-LINE FROM HDG-LINE-TWO
190                  AFTER ADVANCING 2 LINES.
191
192          350-WRITE-DETAIL-LINE.
193              MOVE SR-REGION TO DET-REGION.
194              MOVE SR-LOCATION TO DET-LOCATION.
195              MOVE SR-NAME TO DET-NAME.
196              MOVE SR-ACCOUNT-NUMBER TO DET-ACCOUNT-NUMBER.
197              MOVE SR-SALES TO DET-SALES.
198              MOVE IND-COMMISSION TO DET-COMMISSION.
199              WRITE PRINT-LINE FROM DETAIL-LINE.
200              ADD 1 TO LINE-COUNT.
201
202          370-INCREMENT-COMPANY-TOTAL.
203              ADD SR-SALES TO COMPANY-SALES-TOT.
204              ADD IND-COMMISSION TO COMPANY-COMM-TOT.
```

Three keys—SORT-REGION, SORT-LOCATION, and SORT-NAME—are specified in lines 150–152 as the primary, secondary, and tertiary key, respectively. The WITH DUPLICATES IN ORDER phrase keeps records with duplicate keys in the same sequence as the input file. Note, therefore, that since the input file in Figure 14.5 is already in sequence by account number, records with the same region, location, and name will be in sequence by account number as well.

After the file has been sorted, control returns to the OPEN statement in line 132, which opens SORTED-SALES-FILE as input and PRINT-FILE as output. The remainder of the Procedure Division reads records from the sorted file in order to produce the report of Figure 14.6a. Its logic parallels that of any other reporting program that produces a combination of heading, detail, and total lines.

INPUT PROCEDURE/ OUTPUT PROCEDURE Option

The hierarchy chart to implement the INPUT PROCEDURE/OUTPUT PROCEDURE option is shown in Figure 14.10. It contains the identical modules as its predecessor for the USING/GIVING option, but the placement of the modules (the subordinate relationships and associated span of control) is significantly different.

The most obvious change is the sort module itself, which sits atop the hierarchy chart in Figure 14.10, but which is subordinate to PREPARE-COMMISSION-REPORT in Figure 14.7. This is because the SORT statement effectively drives the INPUT PROCEDURE/OUTPUT PROCEDURE option as it calls the respective procedures. A second major change is the placement of CALCULATE-COMMISSION, which is subordinate to the sort module in Figure 14.10, because the commission is calculated

Figure 14.10   Hierarchy Chart (INPUT PROCEDURE/OUTPUT PROCEDURE)

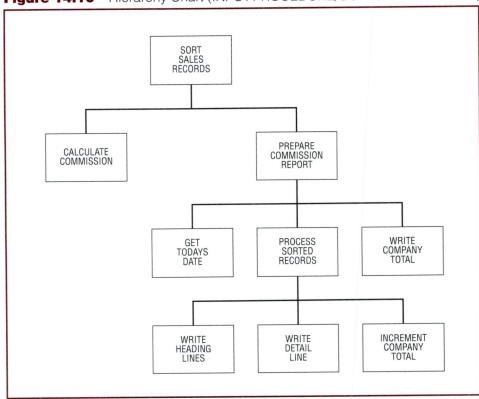

prior to sorting, and only those records with sufficient commission are written to the sort work file. In the earlier hierarchy chart, however, every record in the incoming file appears in the report; the commission is calculated after sorting so that CALCULATE-COMMISSION is subordinate to PROCESS-SORTED-RECORDS.

The pseudocode in Figure 14.11 contains two loops, whereas its predecessor in Figure 14.8 contained only one. This is because the USING/GIVING option does the I/O for the programmer and thus is transparent to the programmer. However, INPUT PROCEDURE/OUTPUT PROCEDURE requires the programmer to do the I/O and this is reflected in the pseudocode. The initial loop opens the (unsorted) sales file, calculates the commission for each incoming record, then selectively releases records to the sort work file. The second loop (which corresponds to the only loop in Figure 14.8) reads records from the sorted file and prepares the report.

The program containing the INPUT PROCEDURE/OUTPUT PROCEDURE format is illustrated in Figure 14.12. Explanation begins with the SORT statement itself, lines 125–128, which references a sort work file defined in an SD in lines 27–37 of the Data Division. SORT-WORK-FILE is to be sorted on SORT-COMMISSION, a calculated field that is not contained in the incoming sales record.

The INPUT PROCEDURE/OUTPUT PROCEDURE involves several implicit transfers of control as follows:

1. Control passes from the SORT statement to the INPUT PROCEDURE, which reads records from an input file and builds the sort work file.

2. When the INPUT PROCEDURE is finished, control passes to the sort utility, which sorts the work file created by the INPUT PROCEDURE.

Figure 14.11   Pseudocode (INPUT PROCEDURE/OUTPUT PROCEDURE)

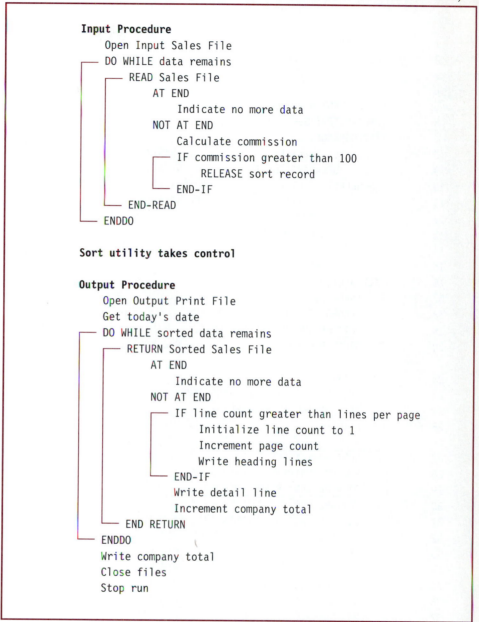

```
Input Procedure
    Open Input Sales File
    DO WHILE data remains
        READ Sales File
            AT END
                Indicate no more data
            NOT AT END
                Calculate commission
                IF commission greater than 100
                    RELEASE sort record
                END-IF
        END-READ
    ENDDO

Sort utility takes control

Output Procedure
    Open Output Print File
    Get today's date
    DO WHILE sorted data remains
        RETURN Sorted Sales File
            AT END
                Indicate no more data
            NOT AT END
                IF line count greater than lines per page
                    Initialize line count to 1
                    Increment page count
                    Write heading lines
                END-IF
                Write detail line
                Increment company total
        END RETURN
    ENDDO
    Write company total
    Close files
    Stop run
```

3. After the sort has taken place, control passes to the OUTPUT PROCEDURE, which reads records from the sorted file in order to produce the required report.

4. When the OUTPUT PROCEDURE is finished, control returns to the statement directly (physically) following the actual SORT statement.

The INPUT PROCEDURE is the paragraph 100-CALCULATE-COMMISSION and extends from lines 131 to 148. It begins by opening SALES-FILE, after which the combination of the in-line PERFORM and false condition branch processes records until the file is empty. The commission is calculated for each incoming record, and

Figure 14.12   SORT Program (INPUT PROCEDURE/OUTPUT PROCEDURE)

```
1        IDENTIFICATION DIVISION.
2        PROGRAM-ID.   SORT2.
3        AUTHOR.       CVV.
4
5        ENVIRONMENT DIVISION.
6        INPUT-OUTPUT SECTION.
7        FILE-CONTROL.
8           SELECT SALES-FILE   ASSIGN TO SYSIN
9               ORGANIZATION IS LINE SEQUENTIAL.
10          SELECT PRINT-FILE   ASSIGN TO SYSOUT
11              ORGANIZATION IS LINE SEQUENTIAL.
12          SELECT SORT-WORK-FILE
13              ASSIGN TO SORTWK01.
14
15       DATA DIVISION.
16       FILE SECTION.
17       FD  SALES-FILE
18           RECORD CONTAINS 57 CHARACTERS
19           DATA RECORD IS SALES-RECORD.
20       01  SALES-RECORD                 PIC X(57).
21
22       FD  PRINT-FILE
23           RECORD CONTAINS 132 CHARACTERS
24           DATA RECORD IS PRINT-LINE.
25       01  PRINT-LINE                   PIC X(132).
26
27       SD  SORT-WORK-FILE
28           RECORD CONTAINS 62 CHARACTERS
29           DATA RECORD IS SORT-RECORD.
30       01  SORT-RECORD.
31           05   SORT-ACCOUNT-NUMBER     PIC 9(6).
32           05   FILLER                  PIC X.
33           05   SORT-NAME               PIC X(15).
34           05   FILLER                  PIC X(10).
35           05   SORT-LOCATION           PIC X(15).
36           05   SORT-REGION             PIC X(11).
37           05   SORT-COMMISSION         PIC S9(4).
38
39       WORKING-STORAGE SECTION.
40       01  FILLER                       PIC X(14)
41               VALUE 'WS BEGINS HERE'.
42
43       01  SALES-RECORD-IN.
44           05   SR-ACCOUNT-NUMBER       PIC 9(6).
45           05   FILLER                  PIC X.
46           05   SR-NAME                 PIC X(15).
47           05   SR-SALES                PIC S9(4).
48           05   FILLER                  PIC XX.
49           05   SR-COMMISSION-PERCENT   PIC V99.
50           05   FILLER                  PIC XX.
51           05   SR-LOCATION             PIC X(15).
```

SD defines sort work file — (annotation pointing to lines 27–29)

Calculated field not found in input record — (annotation pointing to line 37)

Figure 14.12 *(continued)*

```
52              05  SR-REGION               PIC X(11).
53              05  SR-COMMISSION           PIC S9(4).
54
55          01  TODAYS-DATE-AREA.
56              05  TODAYS-YEAR             PIC 99.
57              05  TODAYS-MONTH            PIC 99.
58              05  TODAYS-DAY              PIC 99.
59
60          01  PROGRAM-SWITCHES.
61              05  DATA-REMAINS-SWITCH     PIC X(3)    VALUE 'YES'.
62                  88  NO-DATA-REMAINS                 VALUE 'NO'.
63              05  SORTED-DATA-REMAINS-SW  PIC X(3)    VALUE 'YES'.
64                  88  NO-SORTED-DATA-REMAINS          VALUE 'NO'.
65
66          01  PAGE-AND-LINE-COUNTERS.
67              05  LINE-COUNT              PIC 9(2)    VALUE 11.
68              05  PAGE-COUNT              PIC 9(2)    VALUE ZEROS.
69              05  LINES-PER-PAGE          PIC 9(2)    VALUE 10.
70
71          01  COMPANY-TOTALS.
72              05  COMPANY-SALES-TOT       PIC S9(6)   VALUE ZEROES.
73              05  COMPANY-COMM-TOT        PIC S9(6)   VALUE ZEROES.
74
75          01  HDG-LINE-ONE.
76              05  FILLER                  PIC X(25)  VALUE SPACES.
77              05  FILLER                  PIC X(21)
78                      VALUE 'SALES ACTIVITY REPORT'.
79              05  FILLER                  PIC X(8)   VALUE SPACES.
80              05  HDG-DATE                PIC X(8).
81              05  FILLER                  PIC X(10)  VALUE SPACES.
82              05  FILLER                  PIC X(5)   VALUE 'PAGE '.
83              05  HDG-PAGE                PIC Z9.
84              05  FILLER                  PIC X(53)  VALUE SPACES.
85
86          01  HDG-LINE-TWO.
87              05  FILLER                  PIC X(7)    VALUE ' REGION'.
88              05  FILLER                  PIC X(5)    VALUE SPACES.
89              05  FILLER                  PIC X(8)    VALUE 'LOCATION'.
90              05  FILLER                  PIC X(11)   VALUE SPACES.
91              05  FILLER                  PIC X(4)    VALUE 'NAME'.
92              05  FILLER                  PIC X(10)   VALUE SPACES.
93              05  FILLER                  PIC X(11)   VALUE 'ACCOUNT #'.
94              05  FILLER                  PIC X(5)    VALUE SPACES.
95              05  FILLER                  PIC X(5)    VALUE 'SALES'.
96              05  FILLER                  PIC X(3)    VALUE SPACES.
97              05  FILLER                  PIC X(10)   VALUE 'COMMISSION'.
98              05  FILLER                  PIC X(53)   VALUE SPACES.
99
100         01  DETAIL-LINE.
101             05  DET-REGION              PIC X(11).
102             05  FILLER                  PIC X       VALUE SPACES.
```

Figure 14.12   *(continued)*

```
103        05   DET-LOCATION            PIC X(15).
104        05   FILLER                  PIC X(3)     VALUE SPACES.
105        05   DET-NAME                PIC X(15).
106        05   FILLER                  PIC X(2)     VALUE SPACES.
107        05   DET-ACCOUNT-NUMBER      PIC 9(6).
108        05   FILLER                  PIC X(5)     VALUE SPACES.
109        05   DET-SALES               PIC $Z,ZZ9-.
110        05   FILLER                  PIC X(7)     VALUE SPACES.
111        05   DET-COMMISSION          PIC $Z,ZZ9-.
112        05   FILLER                  PIC X(50)    VALUE SPACES.
113
114   01   COMPANY-TOTAL-LINE.
115        05   FILLER                  PIC X(31)    VALUE SPACES.
116        05   FILLER                  PIC X(25)
117              VALUE '*** COMPANY TOTAL = '.
118        05   COMPANY-SALES-TOTAL     PIC $Z(3),ZZ9-.
119        05   FILLER                  PIC X(5)     VALUE SPACES.
120        05   COMPANY-COMM-TOTAL      PIC $Z(3),ZZ9-.
121        05   FILLER                  PIC X(51)    VALUE SPACES.
122
123   PROCEDURE DIVISION.
124   0000-SORT-SALES-RECORDS.
125       SORT SORT-WORK-FILE
126           DESCENDING KEY SORT-COMMISSION
127           INPUT PROCEDURE 100-CALCULATE-COMMISSION
128           OUTPUT PROCEDURE 200-PREPARE-COMMISSION-REPORT.
129       STOP RUN.
130
131   100-CALCULATE-COMMISSION.
132       OPEN INPUT SALES-FILE.
133       PERFORM UNTIL NO-DATA-REMAINS
134           READ SALES-FILE INTO SALES-RECORD-IN
135               AT END
136                   MOVE 'NO' TO DATA-REMAINS-SWITCH
137               NOT AT END
138                   COMPUTE SR-COMMISSION ROUNDED =
139                       SR-SALES * SR-COMMISSION-PERCENT
140                       SIZE ERROR DISPLAY 'ERROR ON COMMISSION FOR '
141                       SR-NAME
142                   END-COMPUTE
143                   IF SR-COMMISSION > 100
144                       RELEASE SORT-RECORD FROM SALES-RECORD-IN
145                   END-IF
146           END-READ
147       END-PERFORM.
148       CLOSE SALES-FILE.
149
150   200-PREPARE-COMMISSION-REPORT.
151       OPEN OUTPUT PRINT-FILE.
152       PERFORM 230-GET-TODAYS-DATE.
```

Sales are listed by calculated commission
Control returns here after SORT statement
INPUT PROCEDURE
RELEASE statement writes record to work file
Records are conditionally written to work file
OUTPUT procedure

Figure 14.12   *(continued)*

```
153              PERFORM UNTIL NO-SORTED-DATA-REMAINS
154                  RETURN SORT-WORK-FILE INTO SALES-RECORD-IN
155                      AT END
156                          MOVE 'NO' TO SORTED-DATA-REMAINS-SW
157                      NOT AT END
158                          PERFORM 250-PROCESS-SORTED-RECORDS
159                  END-RETURN
160              END-PERFORM.
161              PERFORM 290-WRITE-COMPANY-TOTAL.
162              CLOSE PRINT-FILE.
163
164          230-GET-TODAYS-DATE.
165              ACCEPT TODAYS-DATE-AREA FROM DATE.
166              STRING TODAYS-MONTH '/' TODAYS-DAY '/' TODAYS-YEAR
167                  DELIMITED BY SIZE INTO HDG-DATE.
168
169          250-PROCESS-SORTED-RECORDS.
170              IF LINE-COUNT > LINES-PER-PAGE
171                  PERFORM 330-WRITE-HEADING-LINES
172              END-IF.
173              PERFORM 350-WRITE-DETAIL-LINE.
174              PERFORM 370-INCREMENT-COMPANY-TOTAL.
175
176          290-WRITE-COMPANY-TOTAL.
177              MOVE COMPANY-SALES-TOT TO COMPANY-SALES-TOTAL.
178              MOVE COMPANY-COMM-TOT TO COMPANY-COMM-TOTAL.
179              WRITE PRINT-LINE FROM COMPANY-TOTAL-LINE
180                  AFTER ADVANCING 2 LINES.
181
182          330-WRITE-HEADING-LINES.
183              MOVE 1 TO LINE-COUNT.
184              ADD 1 TO PAGE-COUNT.
185              MOVE PAGE-COUNT TO HDG-PAGE.
186              WRITE PRINT-LINE FROM HDG-LINE-ONE
187                  AFTER ADVANCING PAGE.
188              WRITE PRINT-LINE FROM HDG-LINE-TWO
189                  AFTER ADVANCING 2 LINES.
190
191          350-WRITE-DETAIL-LINE.
192              MOVE SR-REGION TO DET-REGION.
193              MOVE SR-LOCATION TO DET-LOCATION.
194              MOVE SR-NAME TO DET-NAME.
195              MOVE SR-ACCOUNT-NUMBER TO DET-ACCOUNT-NUMBER.
196              MOVE SR-SALES TO DET-SALES.
197              MOVE SR-COMMISSION TO DET-COMMISSION.
198              WRITE PRINT-LINE FROM DETAIL-LINE.
199              ADD 1 TO LINE-COUNT.
200
201          370-INCREMENT-COMPANY-TOTAL.
202              ADD SR-SALES TO COMPANY-SALES-TOT.
203              ADD SR-COMMISSION TO COMPANY-COMM-TOT.
```

RETURN statement reads records from sort work file

only those records with a commission greater than $100 are written (released) to the sort work file. The INPUT PROCEDURE ends by closing SALES-FILE, after which control passes to the sort utility. The sort work file is neither opened nor closed explicitly by the programmer as that is done by the sort utility.

The OUTPUT PROCEDURE is the paragraph 200-PREPARE-COMMISSION-REPORT and extends from lines 150 to 162. It begins by opening PRINT-FILE, after which the combination of the in-line PERFORM and false-condition branch processes records until the sort work file is empty. The report is produced by using many of the identical paragraphs from the earlier program. The OUTPUT PROCEDURE ends by closing PRINT-FILE after which control passes to the STOP RUN statement in line 129 immediately under the SORT statement.

Comparing Options

The differences between the two COBOL programs is highlighted by comparing the generated reports in Figure 14.6. Figure 14.6a was produced by the USING/GIVING option and lists *all records* in sequence by region, location, and name. Figure 14.6b lists a subset of *selected records* in decreasing order of commission, a calculated field. The following are other differences between the two programs:

1. Figure 14.9 sorts on three fields, SORT-REGION, SORT-LOCATION, and SORT-NAME, each of which is contained in the incoming record. Figure 14.12 sorts on SORT-COMMISSION, a calculated field not found in the incoming record.

2. The USING option in Figure 14.9 does the I/O for the programmer; that is, it opens SALES-FILE, reads and writes every record from this file to the sort work file, then closes SALES-FILE when the sort work file has been created.

3. The INPUT PROCEDURE in Figure 14.12 requires the programmer to do the I/O; that is, the programmer has to open SALES-FILE, read records from the input file and write (release) them to the sort work file, then close the input file.

4. The GIVING option in Figure 14.9 creates a permanent file, SORTED-SALES-FILE, that contains the results of the sort; the OUTPUT PROCEDURE in Figure 14.12 creates a temporary work file that disappears when the program terminates. The GIVING option uses an extra file; that is, four files are present in Figure 14.9 versus three in Figure 14.12.

5. The OUTPUT PROCEDURE uses a RETURN statement in lines 154–159 because the sorted records are read from the sort work file. This is in contrast to the READ statement in lines 136–141 of Figure 14.9, which reads records from SORTED-SALES-FILE, an ordinary file defined in an FD.

6. The record lengths in Figure 14.9 of SORT-FILE, SALES-FILE, and SORTED-SALES-FILE, must be the same (58 characters). The record lengths of SORT-FILE and SALES-FILE in Figure 14.12 are different.

Merge Statement

Merging files is a special case of sorting. The **MERGE** statement takes several input files, which have identical record formats and which have been sorted in the same sequence, and combines them into a single output file (device type and blocking may differ for the various files). A merge achieves the same results as sorting, but more efficiently; that is, the several input files to a merge could also be concatenated as a single input file to a sort. The advantage of the merge over a sort is in execution speed; a merge will execute faster because its logic realizes that the several input files are already in order.

The format of the MERGE statement is as follows:

```
MERGE file-name-1

     {     [DESCENDING]                        }
     { ON  [ASCENDING ]  KEY {data-name-1} ... } ...

     [COLLATING SEQUENCE IS alphabet-name]

     USING file-name-2 [file-name-3] ...

     {OUTPUT PROCEDURE IS procedure-name-1  [[THRU   ]               ]}
     {GIVING {file-name-4} ...             [[THROUGH] procedure-name-2]}
```

File-name-1 must be specified in an SD. Rules for ASCENDING (DESCENDING) KEY, COLLATING SEQUENCE, USING/GIVING, and OUTPUT PROCEDURE are identical to those of the SORT statement.

Unlike the SORT statement, however, there is no INPUT PROCEDURE option. In other words you must specify USING, and list all files from which incoming records will be chosen. Hence every record in every file specified in USING will appear in the merged file. However, you do have a choice between GIVING and OUTPUT PROCEDURE.

None of the files specified in a MERGE statement can be open when the statement is executed, as the merge operation implicitly opens them. In similar fashion, the files will be automatically closed by the MERGE.

An example of a MERGE statement is shown below:

```
MERGE WORK-FILE
    ON ASCENDING CUSTOMER-ACCOUNT-NUMBER
        DESCENDING AMOUNT-OF-SALE
    USING
        MONDAY-SALES-FILE
        TUESDAY-SALES-FILE
        WEDNESDAY-SALES-FILE
        THURSDAY-SALES-FILE
        FRIDAY-SALES-FILE
    GIVING
        WEEKLY-SALES-FILE.
```

WORK-FILE is defined in a COBOL SD. WEEKLY-SALES-FILE, MONDAY-SALES-FILE, TUESDAY-SALES-FILE, and so on are each specified in both FD and SELECT statements. These files must be in sequence and are both opened and closed by the merge operation.

The primary key is CUSTOMER-ACCOUNT-NUMBER (ascending), and the secondary key is AMOUNT-OF-SALE (descending). All records with the same account number will be grouped together with the highest sale for each account number listed first. Records with identical keys in one or more input files will be listed in the order in which the files appear in the MERGE statement itself. Hence, in the event of a tie on both account number and amount of sale, Monday's transactions will appear before Tuesday's, and so on.

LIMITATIONS OF COBOL-74

The SORT statement in COBOL-74 is significantly more restrictive than its counterpart in COBOL-85. In particular:

1. The INPUT (OUTPUT) PROCEDURE in COBOL-74 was required to be a *section* rather than a paragraph, which necessitated that other paragraphs in the program be organized into sections as well.
2. The INPUT (OUTPUT) PROCEDURE in COBOL-74 could not transfer control to points outside the designated procedure, requiring the use of a GO TO statement within the procedure. The GO TO statement was directed to an EXIT paragraph at the end of the section.

Both of these restrictions have been removed from COBOL-85 as illustrated in the INPUT PROCEDURE/OUTPUT PROCEDURE example in Figure 14.12. An additional change in COBOL-85 is the introduction of the WITH DUPLICATES IN ORDER phrase, which was not present in the earlier compiler.

S U M M A R Y

Points to Remember

■ Sorting is done in one of two sequences, ascending or descending. Multiple sort keys are listed in order of importance— primary, secondary, and tertiary; or major, intermediate, and minor.

■ Two collating sequences are in common use, EBCDIC (on IBM mainframes) and ASCII (on the PC and other mainframes). The difference is significant when an alphanumeric key is used and/or with an embedded sign in a numeric field.

■ The SORT statement has four combinations: INPUT PROCEDURE/OUTPUT PROCEDURE, USING/GIVING, USING/OUTPUT PROCEDURE, and INPUT PROCEDURE/GIVING.

■ The INPUT PROCEDURE requires the programmer to do the I/O associated with the sort work file, whereas the USING option does the I/O automatically. The advantage of the INPUT PROCEDURE is the ability to sort on a calculated field and/or to selectively pass records to the sort work file.

■ The INPUT PROCEDURE contains a RELEASE statement to transfer (write) records to the sort work file; the OUTPUT PROCEDURE contains a RETURN statement to read the sorted data.

■ The GIVING option specifies a permanent file that remains after the program has ended and that contains the sorted results; the OUTPUT PROCEDURE uses a temporary work file, which is deleted after the program has ended.

■ Regardless of which option is chosen, file-name-1 of the SORT statement must be described in an SD. Further, each key (that is, data name) appearing in the SORT statement must be described in the sort record.

■ If the USING / GIVING option is used, file-name-2 and file-name-3 each require an FD. The record sizes of file names 1, 2, and 3 must all be the same.

Key Words and Concepts

ASCII   Minor key
Ascending sort   Primary key
Calculated field   Secondary key
Collating sequence   Sort key
Descending sort   Sort work file
EBCDIC   Temporary work file
Embedded sign   Tertiary key
Intermediate key   Utility sort program
Major key

COBOL Elements

ASCENDING KEY   RELEASE
DESCENDING KEY   RETURN
DUPLICATES IN ORDER   SD
GIVING   SIGN IS LEADING SEPARATE CHARACTER
INPUT PROCEDURE   SIGN IS TRAILING SEPARATE CHARACTER
MERGE   SORT
OUTPUT PROCEDURE   USING

Fill-in

1. A sort _____ is a field within a record that determines how the file is to be arranged.

2. The most important key is known as the _____ or _____ key.

3. _____ and _____ are widely used collating sequences.

4. If records in a file have been sorted by salary so that the employee with the highest salary appears first, the records are in _____ sequence by salary.

5. If a file has been sorted by state, city within state, and employee within city, then state, city, and name are the _____, _____, and _____ keys, respectively.

6. In a sort on an alphanumeric part number, AAA would precede 111 using the _____ collating sequence, but follow it under _____.

7. The USING option may be used with either _____ or _____ _____.

8. The _____ statement is analogous to WRITE and appears in the _____ _____.

9. A sort work file must be defined in a _____ statement in the Environment Division and in an _____ in the Data Division.

10. An embedded sign (requires/does not require) an extra position within a signed field.

11. The default placement of a sign is as the (leading/trailing) character in a(n) (embedded/separate) position.

12. The _____ _____ may be used to sort on a _____ field, and also to _____ pass records to the sort work file to increase efficiency.

13. The MERGE statement requires that its input files have _____ record layouts.

14. The MERGE statement (does/does not) permit the INPUT PROCEDURE option.

True/False

1. The SORT statement cannot be used on a calculated field.

2. If USING is specified in the SORT statement, then GIVING must also be specified.

3. If INPUT PROCEDURE is specified in the SORT statement, then OUTPUT PROCEDURE is also required.

4. Only one ascending and one descending key are permitted in the SORT statement.

5. Major key and primary key are synonymous.

6. Minor key and secondary key are synonymous.

7. RELEASE and RETURN are associated with the USING/GIVING option.

8. RELEASE is present in the INPUT PROCEDURE.

9. RETURN is specified in the OUTPUT PROCEDURE.

10. If a record is released, it is written to the sort file.

11. If a record is returned, it is read from the sort file.

12. If USING/GIVING is used, the sorted file must contain every record in the input file.

13. If INPUT PROCEDURE/OUTPUT PROCEDURE is used, the sorted file must contain every record in the input file.

14. XYZ will always come before 123 in an alphanumeric sort.

15. ADAMS will always appear before ADAMSON, regardless of collating sequence.

16. The file specified immediately after the word MERGE must be defined in an MD rather than an SD.

17. The MERGE statement can specify INPUT PROCEDURE/OUTPUT PROCEDURE.

18. The MERGE statement can specify USING/GIVING.

19. The MERGE statement can be applied to input files with different record layouts.

20. The sort work file (the file defined in the SD) is a temporary file and does not exist after the COBOL program has finished execution.

P R O B L E M S

1. Given the following data:

Name	Location	Department
Milgrom	New York	1000
Samuel	Boston	2000
Isaac	Boston	2000
Chandler	Chicago	2000
Lavor	Los Angeles	1000
Elsinor	Chicago	1000
Tater	New York	2000
Craig	New York	2000
Borow	Boston	2000
Kenneth	Boston	2000
Renaldi	Boston	1000
Gulfman	Chicago	1000

   Rearrange the data according to the following sorts:

   a. Major field: department (descending); minor field: name (ascending).

   b. Primary field: department (ascending); secondary field: location (ascending); tertiary field: name (ascending).

2. Given the statement

   ```
   SORT SORT-FILE
       ASCENDING KEY STUDENT-MAJOR DESCENDING YEAR-IN-SCHOOL
       ASCENDING STUDENT-NAME
   USING FILE-ONE
   GIVING FILE-TWO.
   ```

   a. What is the major key?

   b. What is the minor key?

   c. Which file will be specified in an SD?

   d. Which file will contain the sorted output?

   e. Which file(s) will be specified in a SELECT?

   f. Which file contains the input data?

   g. Which file must contain the data names STUDENT-NAME, YEAR-IN-SCHOOL, and STUDENT-MAJOR?

3. The following code is intended to sort a file of employee records in order of age, listing the oldest first:

   ```
   FD  EMPLOYEE-FILE
           .
         .
   01  EMPLOYEE-RECORD.
       05  EMP-NAME            PIC X(25).
       05  EMP-BIRTH-DATE.
           10  EMP-BIRTH-MONTH PIC 99.
           10  EMP-BIRTH-YEAR  PIC 9(4).
       05  FILLER             PIC X(51).
   ```

```
01  SORT-RECORD.
    05  FILLER                  PIC X(20).
    05  SORT-BIRTH-DATE.
        10  SORT-BIRTH-MONTH  PIC 99.
        10  SORT-BIRTH-YEAR   PIC 9(4).
    05  FILLER                  PIC X(56).

PROCEDURE DIVISION.
    SORT SORT-FILE
        DESCENDING KEY SORT-BIRTH-MONTH SORT-BIRTH-YEAR
        USING EMPLOYEE-FILE
        GIVING ORDERED-FILE.
```

There are three distinct reasons why the intended code will not work. Find and correct the errors.

4. The registrar has asked for a simple report listing students by year, and alphabetically within year. Thus all freshmen are to appear first, followed by all sophomores, juniors, seniors, and graduate students. The incoming record has the following layout:

```
01  STUDENT-RECORD.
    05  ST-NAME       PIC X(15).
    05  ST-MAJOR      PIC X(15).
    05  ST-YEAR       PIC XX.
    05  ST-CREDITS    PIC 99.
    05  ST-COLLEGE    PIC X(10).
```

The ST-YEAR field uses the codes, FR, SO, JR, SR, and GR for freshman, sophomore, junior, senior, and graduate student, respectively. Develop the Procedure Division code to accomplish the desired sort. (It is not as easy as it looks.)

5. Indicate the form of the SORT statement (USING, INPUT PROCEDURE, GIVING, OUTPUT PROCEDURE) that would most likely be used for the following applications:

   a. Conversion of an incoming inventory file that has its part numbers in ASCII sequence to a new file, having its numbers in EBCDIC sequence.

   b. Preparation of a report to select all graduating seniors (those with completed credits totaling 90 or more), listed in order of decreasing grade point average.

   c. A data-validation program that reads unedited transactions, rejects those with invalid data, and prepares a sorted transaction file containing only valid records.

   d. A program to prepare mailing labels in zip code order from a customer list.

6. Given the statement:

```
MERGE WORK-FILE
    ASCENDING ACCOUNT-NUMBER
    DESCENDING AMOUNT-OF-SALE
USING
    JANUARY-SALES
    FEBRUARY-SALES
    MARCH-SALES
GIVING
    FIRST-QUARTER-SALES.
```

    a. Which file(s) are specified in an SD?

    b. Which file(s) are specified in an FD?

    c. Which file(s) contain the key ACCOUNT-NUMBER?

    d. What is the primary key?

    e. What is the secondary key?

    f. If a record on the JANUARY-SALES file has the identical ACCOUNT-NUMBER as a record on the FEBRUARY-SALES file, which record would come first on the merged file?

    g. If a record on the JANUARY-SALES file has the identical AMOUNT-OF-SALE as a record on the FEBRUARY-SALES file, which record would come first on the merged file?

    h. If a record on the JANUARY-SALES file has the identical AMOUNT-OF-SALE and ACCOUNT-NUMBER as a record on the FEBRUARY-SALES file, which record would come first on the merged file?

7. Given the following COBOL definition:

```
05  TRANSACTION-DATE.
    10  TRANS-MONTH      PIC 99.
    10  TRANS-DAY        PIC 99.
    10  TRANS-YEAR       PIC 99.
```

Write a portion of the SORT statement necessary to put transactions in sequence, with the earliest transaction listed first. Are there any problems in your solution when the century changes? Should you be concerned about those problems now?

8. The registrar requires an alphabetical list of graduating seniors. The report will be generated from the student master file, which contains every student in the school, in social security number sequence.

    Two approaches have been suggested. The first uses the USING/GIVING option to sort the file alphabetically, after which the desired records are selected for inclusion in the report. The second selects the desired records in the INPUT PROCEDURE, after which the file is sorted and the report prepared in the OUTPUT PROCEDURE.

    Both approaches will produce a correct report. Is there any reason to choose one over the other?

Control Breaks

CHAPTER OUTLINE

Overview

System Concepts

Running versus Rolling Totals

One-Level Control Breaks

Programming Specifications

Hierarchy Chart

Pseudocode

The Completed Program

Two-Level Control Breaks

Hierarchy Chart

Pseudocode

The Completed Program

Three-Level Control Breaks

Hierarchy Chart

Pseudocode

The Completed Program

Limitations of COBOL-74

Summary

Fill-in

True/False

Problems

OBJECTIVES

After reading this chapter you will be able to:

■ Define control break; distinguish between a single control break and a multilevel control break.

■ Explain the relationship between sorting and control breaks.

■ Design a hierarchy chart and pseudocode to implement any number of control breaks; evaluate the hierarchy chart with respect to completeness, functionality, and span of control.

■ Use a general purpose algorithm to write a COBOL program for any number of control breaks.

■ Develop COBOL programs for one-, two-, and three-level control breaks.

■ Distinguish between rolling and running totals.

OVERVIEW

This chapter does not introduce any new COBOL per se, but uses the COBOL you already know to present one of the most important applications in data processing, that of control breaks. A control break is defined as a change in a designated field, which in turn requires that the incoming file be in sequence by the designated field. There is, therefore, a close relationship between sorting and control breaks, a relationship that will be stressed throughout the chapter.

The logic associated with control breaks is more complex than many of the examples presented earlier in the text. The difficulty, if any, stems from a rush into coding a program, without giving suitable thought to its design. Accordingly, we emphasize the importance of proper design, and the use of hierarchy charts and pseudocode, to simplify the eventual coding.

Control breaks may be implemented at several levels, just as a file may be sorted on multiple keys. The system concepts section distinguishes between one-, two-, and three-level control breaks, each of which is developed in a separate program.

System Concepts

This chapter continues the example of Chapter 14, beginning with a review of the file in Figure 15.1 (shown previously as Figure 14.5). Six fields are present in every record: account number, salesperson, sales amount, commission percentage, location, and region. The sales amount contains an embedded sign to reflect negative numbers (i.e., returns rather than sales) as previously discussed. Recall, too, that the commission amount is determined by multiplying the commission percentage (contained in the record) by the sales amount.

Figure 15.1 Transaction File (The sales amount shows ASCII rather than EBCDIC characters.)

Acct Num	Salesperson	Sales Amount	Comm Pct	Location	Region
000069	BENWAY	023Q	10	CHICAGO	MIDWEST
000100	HUMMER	010W	05	CHICAGO	MIDWEST
000101	CLARK	1500	10	TRENTON	NORTHEAST
000104	CLARK	0500	03	TRENTON	NORTHEAST
100000	JOHNSON	030S	06	ST. PETERSBURG	SOUTHEAST
130101	CLARK	3200	20	TRENTON	NORTHEAST
203000	HAAS	8900	05	ST. LOUIS	MIDWEST
248545	JOHNSON	0345	14	ST. PETERSBURG	SOUTHEAST
277333	HAAS	009X	08	ST. LOUIS	MIDWEST
400000	JOHNSON	070Y	08	ST. PETERSBURG	SOUTHEAST
444333	ADAMS	100V	01	NEW YORK	NORTHEAST
444444	FEGEN	0100	02	ST. PETERSBURG	SOUTHEAST
475365	HAAS	0333	05	ST. LOUIS	MIDWEST
476236	FEGEN	037V	03	ST. PETERSBURG	SOUTHEAST
476530	BENWAY	023U	05	CHICAGO	MIDWEST
555555	FEGEN	0304	05	ST. PETERSBURG	SOUTHEAST
555666	ADAMS	2003	20	NEW YORK	NORTHEAST
576235	CLARK	0100	03	TRENTON	NORTHEAST
583645	KARLSTROM	0145	04	BALTIMORE	NORTHEAST
649356	HUMMER	0345	05	CHICAGO	MIDWEST
694446	HUMMER	0904	10	CHICAGO	MIDWEST
700039	MARCUS	0932	10	BALTIMORE	NORTHEAST
750020	MARCUS	0305	05	BALTIMORE	NORTHEAST
800396	KARLSTROM	3030	09	BALTIMORE	NORTHEAST
878787	JOHNSON	1235	12	ST. PETERSBURG	SOUTHEAST
987654	ADAMS	2005	10	NEW YORK	NORTHEAST
988888	BENWAY	0450	01	CHICAGO	MIDWEST
999340	BENWAY	0334	30	CHICAGO	MIDWEST

The records in Figure 15.1 are in sequence by account number, so that the transactions associated with any particular salesperson are scattered throughout the file. What if, however, we wanted to know the total sales and/or commission amount for a particular salesperson or for every salesperson? The easiest way to produce such a report would be to sort the file by salesperson so that all of the transactions for each salesperson appear together. It would then be a simple matter to look at all the transactions for Adams in order to compute his total sales and commission, then look at the transactions for Benway, then for Clark, etc. This is precisely what is meant by control break processing.

The records in Figure 15.2a have been sorted by salesperson in order to produce the report of Figure 15.2b. A **control break**, defined as a change in a **control field** (salesperson in the example), occurs when the value of the control field changes from record to record—for example, when we go from the last transaction for Adams to the first transaction for Benway, and again from the last transaction for Benway to the first transaction for Clark. The detection of a control break signals the creation of one or more **control totals,** which in this example would be the sales and commissions for a given salesperson.

Figure 15.2   One-Level Control Break

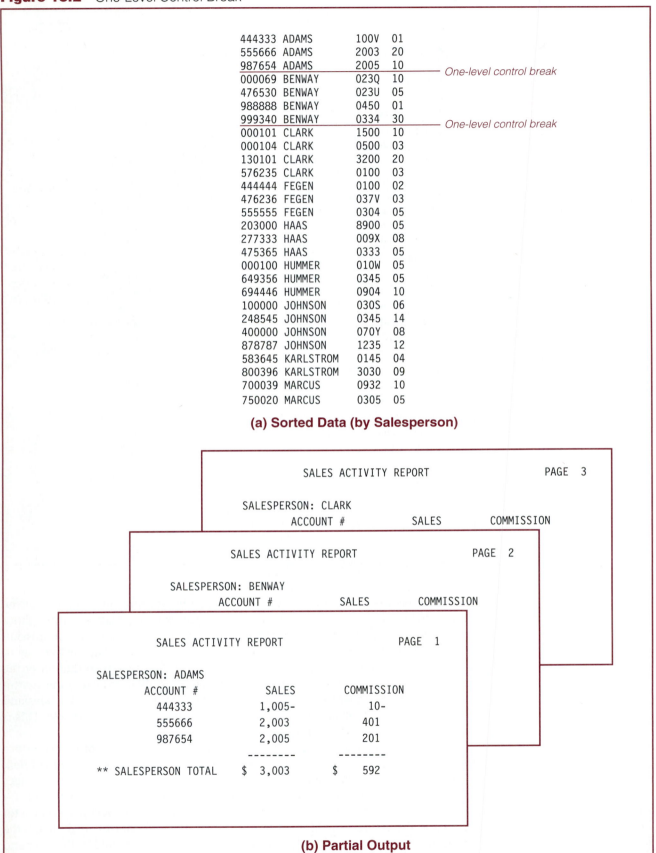

```
444333 ADAMS      100V  01
555666 ADAMS      2003  20
987654 ADAMS      2005  10  ——— One-level control break
000069 BENWAY     023Q  10
476530 BENWAY     023U  05
988888 BENWAY     0450  01
999340 BENWAY     0334  30  ——— One-level control break
000101 CLARK      1500  10
000104 CLARK      0500  03
130101 CLARK      3200  20
576235 CLARK      0100  03
444444 FEGEN      0100  02
476236 FEGEN      037V  03
555555 FEGEN      0304  05
203000 HAAS       8900  05
277333 HAAS       009X  08
475365 HAAS       0333  05
000100 HUMMER     010W  05
649356 HUMMER     0345  05
694446 HUMMER     0904  10
100000 JOHNSON    030S  06
248545 JOHNSON    0345  14
400000 JOHNSON    070Y  08
878787 JOHNSON    1235  12
583645 KARLSTROM  0145  04
800396 KARLSTROM  3030  09
700039 MARCUS     0932  10
750020 MARCUS     0305  05
```

(a) Sorted Data (by Salesperson)

```
              SALES ACTIVITY REPORT                      PAGE  3

         SALESPERSON: CLARK
                 ACCOUNT #          SALES       COMMISSION

          SALES ACTIVITY REPORT                   PAGE  2

      SALESPERSON: BENWAY
              ACCOUNT #        SALES      COMMISSION

     SALES ACTIVITY REPORT                 PAGE  1

SALESPERSON: ADAMS
     ACCOUNT #         SALES        COMMISSION
      444333          1,005-            10-
      555666          2,003            401
      987654          2,005            201
                     --------         --------
** SALESPERSON TOTAL  $  3,003      $    592
```

(b) Partial Output

A ***two-level control break*** is illustrated in Figure 15.3. The data in Figure 15.3a have been sorted by location, and by salesperson within location, in order to produce the report in Figure 15.3b. All salespersons in the same location appear together, as do all transactions for the same salesperson. A one-level control break occurs from Karlstrom to Marcus as salesperson changes, but location does not. A two-level control break occurs from Marcus to Benway, when the values of two control fields, salesperson and location, change simultaneously. The two-level control break produces two sets of control totals: the sales and commission totals for Marcus, as well as the sales and commission totals for all salespersons in Baltimore.

A ***three-level control break*** is shown in Figure 15.4. The data in Figure 15.4a have been sorted by region, location within region, and salesperson within location, in order to produce the report of Figure 15.4b. A one-level control break occurs from Benway to Hummer as salesperson changes, but location and region do not. A two-level control break occurs from Hummer to Haas when salesperson and location change simultaneously but regions remains constant, and a three-level control break occurs from Haas to Karlstrom as all three fields change together.

There is no theoretical limit to the number of control breaks that can be computed; there is a practical limit, however, in that most people lose track after three (or at most four) levels. Regardless of the number of control breaks in effect, the file used to create the control totals must be in sequence according to the designated control fields.

Figure 15.3   Two-Level Control Break

```
583645  KARLSTROM   0145   04   BALTIMORE
800396  KARLSTROM   3030   09   BALTIMORE
                                              ─ One-level control break
700039  MARCUS      0932   10   BALTIMORE
750020  MARCUS      0305   05   BALTIMORE
                                              ─ Two-level control break
000069  BENWAY      023Q   10   CHICAGO
476530  BENWAY      023U   05   CHICAGO
988888  BENWAY      0450   01   CHICAGO
999340  BENWAY      0334   30   CHICAGO
000100  HUMMER      010W   05   CHICAGO
649356  HUMMER      0345   05   CHICAGO
694446  HUMMER      0904   10   CHICAGO
444333  ADAMS       100V   01   NEW YORK
555666  ADAMS       2003   20   NEW YORK
987654  ADAMS       2005   10   NEW YORK
203000  HAAS        8900   05   ST. LOUIS
277333  HAAS        009X   08   ST. LOUIS
475365  HAAS        0333   05   ST. LOUIS
444444  FEGEN       0100   02   ST. PETERSBURG
476236  FEGEN       037V   03   ST. PETERSBURG
555555  FEGEN       0304   05   ST. PETERSBURG
100000  JOHNSON     030S   06   ST. PETERSBURG
248545  JOHNSON     0345   14   ST. PETERSBURG
400000  JOHNSON     070Y   08   ST. PETERSBURG
878787  JOHNSON     1235   12   ST. PETERSBURG
000101  CLARK       1500   10   TRENTON
000104  CLARK       0500   03   TRENTON
130101  CLARK       3200   20   TRENTON
576235  CLARK       0100   03   TRENTON
```

(a) Sorted Data (by Location and Salesperson)

Figure 15.3 *(continued)*

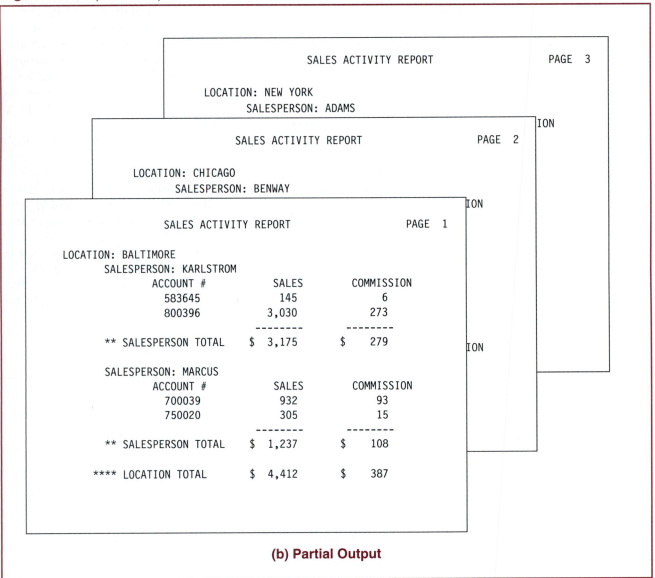

(b) Partial Output

Running versus Rolling Totals

Each of the reports in Figures 15.2 through 15.4 computes totals at one or more levels (at salesperson, location, region, and company), according to the number of control breaks. The company totals are printed at the end of processing and appear on the last page of each report, but are not visible in the individual figures. (The total sales for the company and corresponding commission are $23,906 and $2,540, respectively.)

Consider for a moment how the computations might be accomplished in the one-level report of Figure 15.2b. There is only one way to compute the total for individual salespersons—by initializing the total for each new salesperson to zero, then adding the amount on every transaction for that salesperson to his or her total. There are, however, two ways to compute the company total—by adding the value for every transaction to a ***running company total***, or by waiting for a break on salesperson and then adding, or ***rolling,*** the salesperson total to the company total. The latter is more efficient in that fewer additions are performed.

Similar reasoning applies to the two-level report of Figure 15.3b, in which the location total can be computed two different ways—by adding the value of each incoming transaction to a running location total, or by waiting for a control break on salesperson, then rolling the salesperson total to the location total. In similar fashion, the company total may be obtained in three ways. First, by adding the value of every incoming transaction to a running company total. Second, by rolling the salesperson total into the company total after a one-level break on salesperson. Or third, by rolling the location total into the company total after a two-level break on location. The third approach is the most efficient.

You should be able to extend this logic to the three-level report of Figure 15.4b, which maintains a running total for each salesperson, then rolls the salesperson total into the location total (after a break on salesperson), rolls the location total into the region total (after a break on location), and finally rolls the region total into the company total (after a break on region).

Figure 15.4   Three-Level Control Break

000069	BENWAY	023Q	10	CHICAGO	MIDWEST	
476530	BENWAY	023U	05	CHICAGO	MIDWEST	
988888	BENWAY	0450	01	CHICAGO	MIDWEST	
999340	BENWAY	0334	30	CHICAGO	MIDWEST	*One-level control break*
000100	HUMMER	010W	05	CHICAGO	MIDWEST	
649356	HUMMER	0345	05	CHICAGO	MIDWEST	
694446	HUMMER	0904	10	CHICAGO	MIDWEST	*Two-level control break*
203000	HAAS	8900	05	ST. LOUIS	MIDWEST	
277333	HAAS	009X	08	ST. LOUIS	MIDWEST	
475365	HAAS	0333	05	ST. LOUIS	MIDWEST	*Three-Level control break*
583645	KARLSTROM	0145	04	BALTIMORE	NORTHEAST	
800396	KARLSTROM	3030	09	BALTIMORE	NORTHEAST	
700039	MARCUS	0932	10	BALTIMORE	NORTHEAST	
750020	MARCUS	0305	05	BALTIMORE	NORTHEAST	
444333	ADAMS	100V	01	NEW YORK	NORTHEAST	
555666	ADAMS	2003	20	NEW YORK	NORTHEAST	
987654	ADAMS	2005	10	NEW YORK	NORTHEAST	
000101	CLARK	1500	10	TRENTON	NORTHEAST	
000104	CLARK	0500	03	TRENTON	NORTHEAST	
130101	CLARK	3200	20	TRENTON	NORTHEAST	
576235	CLARK	0100	03	TRENTON	NORTHEAST	
444444	FEGEN	0100	02	ST. PETERSBURG	SOUTHEAST	
476236	FEGEN	037V	03	ST. PETERSBURG	SOUTHEAST	
555555	FEGEN	0304	05	ST. PETERSBURG	SOUTHEAST	
100000	JOHNSON	030S	06	ST. PETERSBURG	SOUTHEAST	
248545	JOHNSON	0345	14	ST. PETERSBURG	SOUTHEAST	
400000	JOHNSON	070Y	08	ST. PETERSBURG	SOUTHEAST	
878787	JOHNSON	1235	12	ST. PETERSBURG	SOUTHEAST	

(a) Sorted Data (by Region, Location, and Salesperson)

Figure 15.4   *(continued)*

```
                           SALES ACTIVITY REPORT                 PAGE   3

        REGION: SOUTHEAST
                LOCATION: ST. PETERSBURG
```

```
                       SALES ACTIVITY REPORT                PAGE  2

    REGION: NORTHEAST
            LOCATION: BALTIMORE
```

```
               SALES ACTIVITY REPORT                PAGE   1

REGION: MIDWEST
        LOCATION: CHICAGO
                SALESPERSON: BENWAY
                        ACCOUNT #           SALES            COMMISSION
                         000069             231-               23-
                         476530             235-               12-
                         988888             450                 5
                         999340             334                100
                                          --------           --------
                ** SALESPERSON TOTAL    $    318        $      70


                SALESPERSON: HUMMER
                        ACCOUNT #           SALES            COMMISSION
                         000100             107-                5-
                         649356             345                17
                         694446             904                90
                                          --------           --------
                ** SALESPERSON TOTAL    $  1,142        $     102


            **** LOCATION TOTAL         $  1,460        $     172

        LOCATION: ST. LOUIS
                SALESPERSON: HAAS
                        ACCOUNT #           SALES            COMMISSION
                         203000            8,900               445
                         277333              98-                8-
                         475365             333                17
                                          --------           --------
                ** SALESPERSON TOTAL    $  9,135        $     454


            **** LOCATION TOTAL         $  9,135        $     454


        ****** REGION TOTAL             $ 10,595        $     626
```

(b) Partial Output

One-Level Control Breaks

The development of the one- (two- and three-) level programs is not difficult given a clear understanding of the requirements and the distinction between running and rolling totals. We begin with the specifications for the one-level program.

Programming Specifications

Program Name: One-Level Control Break

Narrative: The specifications are for the one-level control break program. Changes to the specifications to accommodate two- and three-level control breaks are provided later in the chapter.

Input File(s): SALES-FILE

Input Record Layout:

```
01  SALES-RECORD-IN.
    05  SR-ACCOUNT-NUMBER        PIC 9(6).
    05  FILLER                   PIC X.
    05  SR-NAME                  PIC X(15).
    05  SR-SALES                 PIC S9(4).
    05  FILLER                   PIC XX.
    05  SR-COMMISSION-PERCENT    PIC V99.
    05  FILLER                   PIC XX.
    05  SR-LOCATION              PIC X(15).
    05  SR-REGION                PIC X(11).
```

Test Data: See Figure 15.1.

Report Layout: See Figure 15.2b.

Processing Requirements:

1. Sort the incoming transaction file by salesperson; use the WITH DUPLICATES IN ORDER phrase of the SORT statement to keep the sorted file in sequence by transaction number within salesperson.

2. Process transactions until a control break is encountered on salesperson, then for each new salesperson:

   a. Initialize the total sales and commission for that salesperson to zero.

   b. Print a heading for this salesperson on a new page.

3. Process all transactions for each salesperson as follows:

   a. Compute the commission for each transaction by multiplying the amount of the sale by the commission percentage.

   b. Print a detail line for each transaction containing the account number, sales amount, and computed commission.

   c. Increment the total sales and commissions for that salesperson by the corresponding amounts for this transaction.

4. Print a total line for each salesperson whenever salesperson changes. Print dashes as indicated between the last detail line and the total line.

5. Increment the company totals with the salesperson's accumulated totals as salesperson changes.

6. Print the company totals after all records have been processed.

Hierarchy Chart

The report in Figure 15.2b contains a heading line prior to the first transaction for each salesperson, detail lines containing the sales and commission for the individual transactions, and a total line after all transactions for each salesperson. The company total appears at the end of the report (but is not visible in Figure 15.2b).

All of these functions are recognized in the hierarchy chart of Figure 15.5a, which was developed in stages, beginning at the top and working down to the bottom. The functions at every level in the hierarchy chart are divided into component functions that appear on the next lower-level. The lower-level functions are further subdivided into other functions on a still lower-level, until finally the lowest-level functions cannot be further subdivided.

The module at the top (or first level) of the hierarchy chart, PREPARE-SALES-REPORT, depicts the overall program function. It is divided into four subordinate functions, each of which was taken directly from the programming specifications. These modules are placed on the second level of the hierarchy chart:

1. SORT-TRANSACTION-FILE to sort the transaction file (as indicated in item 1 of the processing requirements)

2. READ-SORTED-SALES-FILE to read a record from the sorted file

3. PROCESS-ONE-SALESPERSON to process each salesperson (from items 2 through 5 of the processing requirements)

4. WRITE-COMPANY-TOTAL to write the company total (from item 6 of the processing requirements)

Each of these modules is considered for further subdivision, but only PROCESS-ONE-SALESPERSON is divided into component functions for the next level. Once again, we use the processing requirements as a guide to determine the subordinate functions for the third level:

1. INITIALIZE-SALESPERSON to initialize the sales and commission amounts for this salesperson (item 2a of the processing requirements)

2. WRITE-SALESPERSON-HEADING to write a heading for each salesperson (item 2b of the processing requirements)

3. PROCESS-ONE-TRANSACTION to process the transaction (item 3 of the processing requirements)

4. WRITE-SALESPERSON-TOTAL to print the salesperson total (item 4 of the processing requirements)

5. INCREMENT-COMPANY-TOTAL to increment the company total (item 5 of the processing requirements)

Each function is evaluated for further subdivision, but only PROCESS-ONE-TRANSACTION is developed further. Repeating the earlier procedure, and again using the processing requirements, we obtain the modules for the fourth and final level:

1. CALCULATE-COMMISSION to calculate the commission for the transaction (item 3a of the processing requirements)

2. WRITE-DETAIL-LINE to write a detail line for each transaction (item 3b of the processing requirements)

3. INCREMENT-SALESPERSON-TOTAL to increment the salesperson's total (item 3c of the processing requirements)

4. READ-SORTED-SALES-FILE to read the next record and avoid an endless loop

Figure 15.5 One-Level Algorithm

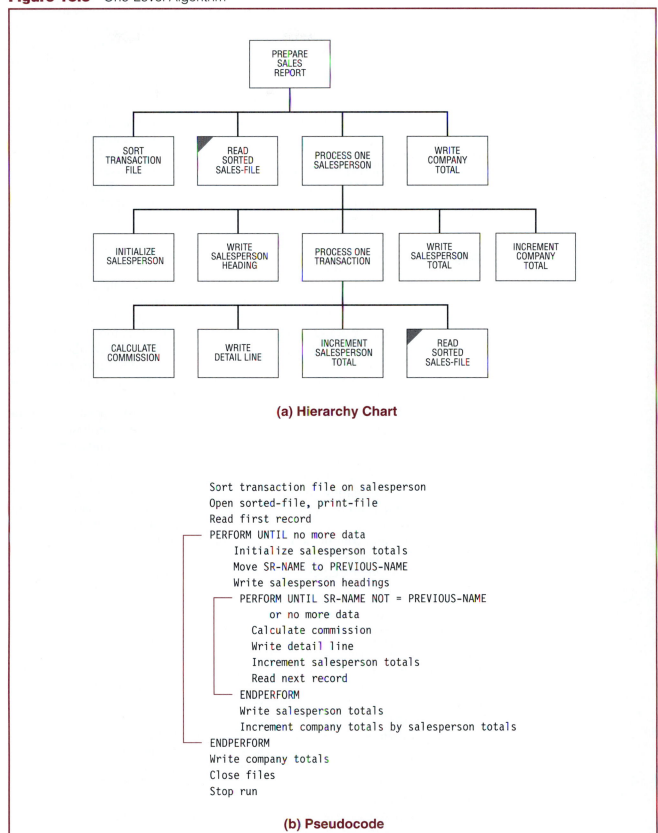

(a) Hierarchy Chart

```
Sort transaction file on salesperson
Open sorted-file, print-file
Read first record
PERFORM UNTIL no more data
    Initialize salesperson totals
    Move SR-NAME to PREVIOUS-NAME
    Write salesperson headings
    PERFORM UNTIL SR-NAME NOT = PREVIOUS-NAME
            or no more data
        Calculate commission
        Write detail line
        Increment salesperson totals
        Read next record
    ENDPERFORM
    Write salesperson totals
    Increment company totals by salesperson totals
ENDPERFORM
Write company totals
Close files
Stop run
```

(b) Pseudocode

The completed hierarchy chart is evaluated according to the criteria presented in Chapter 3—completeness, functionality, and span of control. The hierarchy chart is complete because it contains a module corresponding to every processing requirement. Its modules are functional (i.e., each module accomplishes a single task) as can be implied from the module names that consist of a verb, an adjective or two, and an object—for example, INCREMENT-SALESPERSON-TOTAL or WRITE-DETAIL-LINE.

Finally, the span of control (number of subordinate modules) is reasonably set at three or four throughout the hierarchy chart, and the relationship of the modules to one another appears to be correct. Observe, for example, that WRITE-DETAIL-LINE, INCREMENT-SALESPERSON-TOTAL, and READ-SORTED-SALES-FILE are subordinate to PROCESS-ONE-TRANSACTION, which in turn is subordinate to PROCESS-ONE-SALESPERSON, which is subordinate to PREPARE-SALES-REPORT. There is no other reasonable way to relate these functions, all of which are required to maintain completeness.

Pseudocode

The pseudocode in Figure 15.5b introduces specific COBOL data names, such as SR-NAME and PREVIOUS-NAME, that enable the program to detect a control break. In other words, a COBOL statement cannot simply process records until a control break occurs, but must specify precisely how to determine when the value of salesperson changes. Thus in order to detect a control break, the program compares the name on the record just read to the name on the previous record; that is, it compares SR-NAME to PREVIOUS-NAME, and detects a break when the values are different.

The pseudocode sorts the transaction file according to salesperson, reads the first transaction record, then executes the statements in the outer loop for every salesperson until the entire file has been processed. The (sales and commission) totals for each new salesperson are initialized, then an inner loop is executed until a control break is detected. The inner loop processes all transactions for the current salesperson by calculating the commission amount, writing a detail line, and incrementing the running salesperson totals. The inner loop is terminated by the control break—that is, when SR-NAME is not equal to PREVIOUS-NAME—after which the sales and commission totals for the salesperson are written and rolled into the corresponding company totals.

It is now a simple matter to write the required program.

The Completed Program

The completed program in Figure 15.6 is straightforward and easy to follow, especially after the preceding discussion on hierarchy charts and pseudocode. Note especially the relationship of the hierarchy chart in Figure 15.5a to the paragraphs in the Procedure Division. The modules in the hierarchy chart correspond one to one with the paragraphs in the program. Observe also that each level in the hierarchy chart corresponds to a COBOL PERFORM statement.

The Working-Storage Section contains multiple 01 entries for the various print lines required by the program. There are multiple heading lines, a detail line, and two total lines. Working-Storage also contains separate counters for the salesperson and company totals, as well as a switch, PREVIOUS-NAME, to detect the control break on salesperson.

The SORT statement (lines 151–156) specifies SORT-NAME as the primary key in accordance with the requirements of the control break on salesperson. The

WITH DUPLICATES IN ORDER phrase keeps the transactions for a given salesperson in sequence by account number because the input file (Figure 15.1) was already in sequence by this field.

Figure 15.6 One-Level Control Break Program

```
 1          IDENTIFICATION DIVISION.
 2          PROGRAM-ID.   ONELEVEL.
 3          AUTHOR.        CVV.
 4
 5          ENVIRONMENT DIVISION.
 6          INPUT-OUTPUT SECTION.
 7          FILE-CONTROL.
 8              SELECT SALES-FILE    ASSIGN TO SYSIN
 9                  ORGANIZATION IS LINE SEQUENTIAL.
10              SELECT PRINT-FILE    ASSIGN TO SYSOUT
11                  ORGANIZATION IS LINE SEQUENTIAL.
12              SELECT SORT-WORK-FILE
13                  ASSIGN TO SORTWK01.
14              SELECT SORTED-SALES-FILE   ASSIGN TO SORTED
15                  ORGANIZATION IS LINE SEQUENTIAL.
16
17          DATA DIVISION.
18          FILE SECTION.
19          FD  SALES-FILE
20              RECORD CONTAINS 58 CHARACTERS
21              DATA RECORD IS SALES-RECORD.
22          01  SALES-RECORD                PIC X(58).
23
24          FD  PRINT-FILE
25              RECORD CONTAINS 132 CHARACTERS
26              DATA RECORD IS PRINT-LINE.
27          01  PRINT-LINE                  PIC X(132).
28
29          SD  SORT-WORK-FILE
30              RECORD CONTAINS 58 CHARACTERS
31              DATA RECORD IS SORT-RECORD.
32          01  SORT-RECORD.
33              05  SORT-ACCOUNT-NUMBER     PIC 9(6).
34              05  FILLER                  PIC X.
35              05  SORT-NAME               PIC X(15).
36              05  FILLER                  PIC X(10).
37              05  SORT-LOCATION           PIC X(15).
38              05  SORT-REGION             PIC X(11).
39
40          FD  SORTED-SALES-FILE
41              RECORD CONTAINS 58 CHARACTERS
42              DATA RECORD IS SORTED-SALES-RECORD.
43          01  SORTED-SALES-RECORD         PIC X(58).
```

Figure 15.6   (continued)

```
44
45          WORKING-STORAGE SECTION.
46          01  FILLER                  PIC X(14)
47                  VALUE 'WS BEGINS HERE'.
48
49          01  SALES-RECORD-IN.
50              05  SR-ACCOUNT-NUMBER   PIC 9(6).
51              05  FILLER              PIC X.
52              05  SR-NAME             PIC X(15).
53              05  SR-SALES            PIC S9(4).
54              05  FILLER              PIC XX.
55              05  SR-COMMISSION-PERCENT  PIC V99.
56              05  FILLER              PIC XX.
57              05  SR-LOCATION         PIC X(15).
58              05  SR-REGION           PIC X(11).
59
60          01  PROGRAM-SWITCHES-AND-COUNTERS.
61              05  DATA-REMAINS-SW     PIC X(3)   VALUE 'YES'.
62                  88  NO-DATA-REMAINS            VALUE 'NO'.
63              05  PREVIOUS-NAME       PIC X(15)  VALUE SPACES.
64              05  PAGE-COUNT          PIC 99     VALUE ZEROES.
65
66          01  CONTROL-BREAK-TOTALS.
67              05   INDIVIDUAL-TOTALS.
68                  10  IND-COMMISSION      PIC S9(4).
69              05  SALESPERSON-TOTALS.
70                  10  SALESPERSON-SALES-TOT PIC S9(6).
71                  10  SALESPERSON-COMM-TOT  PIC S9(6).
72              05  COMPANY-TOTALS.
73                  10  COMPANY-SALES-TOT   PIC S9(6)  VALUE ZEROS.
74                  10  COMPANY-COMM-TOT    PIC S9(6)  VALUE ZEROS.
75
76          01  REPORT-HEADING-LINE.
77              05  FILLER              PIC X(25)  VALUE SPACES.
78              05  FILLER              PIC X(21)
79                  VALUE 'SALES ACTIVITY REPORT'.
80              05  FILLER              PIC X(19)  VALUE SPACES.
81              05  FILLER              PIC X(5)   VALUE 'PAGE '.
82              05  HDG-PAGE            PIC Z9.
83              05  FILLER              PIC X(60)  VALUE SPACES.
84
85          01  SALESPERSON-HEADING-LINE-ONE.
86              05  FILLER              PIC X(15)  VALUE SPACES.
87              05  FILLER              PIC X(13)
88                  VALUE 'SALESPERSON: '.
89              05  HDG-NAME            PIC X(15).
90              05  FILLER              PIC X(89)  VALUE SPACES.
91
92          01  SALESPERSON-HEADING-LINE-TWO.
93              05  FILLER              PIC X(23)  VALUE SPACES.
```

Signed fields are used in all computations

Figure 15.6 *(continued)*

```
 94          05  FILLER                  PIC X(11)   VALUE 'ACCOUNT .
 95          05  FILLER                  PIC X(9)    VALUE SPACES.
 96          05  FILLER                  PIC X(5)    VALUE 'SALES'.
 97          05  FILLER                  PIC X(8)    VALUE SPACES.
 98          05  FILLER                  PIC X(10)   VALUE 'COMMISSION'.
 99          05  FILLER                  PIC X(66)   VALUE SPACES.
100
101      01  DETAIL-LINE.
102          05  FILLER                  PIC X(25)   VALUE SPACES.
103          05  DET-ACCOUNT-NUMBER      PIC 9(6).
104          05  FILLER                  PIC X(9)    VALUE SPACES.
105          05  DET-SALES               PIC Z(3),ZZ9-.
106          05  FILLER                  PIC X(7)    VALUE SPACES.
107          05  DET-COMMISSION          PIC Z(3),ZZ9-.
108          05  FILLER                  PIC X(69)   VALUE SPACES.
109
110      01  DASHED-LINE.
111          05  FILLER                  PIC X(40)   VALUE SPACES.
112          05  FILLER                  PIC X(8)    VALUE ALL '-'.
113          05  FILLER                  PIC X(7)    VALUE SPACES.
114          05  FILLER                  PIC X(8)    VALUE ALL '-'.
115          05  FILLER                  PIC X(69)   VALUE SPACES.
116
117      01  SALESPERSON-TOTAL-LINE.
118          05  FILLER                  PIC X(15)   VALUE SPACES.
119          05  FILLER                  PIC X(21)
120              VALUE '** SALESPERSON TOTAL'.
121          05  FILLER                  PIC X(3)    VALUE SPACES.
122          05  SALESPERSON-SALES-TOTAL PIC $Z(3),ZZ9-.
123          05  FILLER                  PIC X(6)    VALUE SPACES.
124          05  SALESPERSON-COMM-TOTAL  PIC $Z(3),ZZ9-.
125          05  FILLER                  PIC X(69)   VALUE SPACES.
126
127      01  COMPANY-TOTAL-LINE.
128          05  FILLER                  PIC X(9)    VALUE SPACES.
129          05  FILLER                  PIC X(22)
130              VALUE '******** COMPANY TOTAL'.
131          05  FILLER                  PIC X(8)    VALUE SPACES.
132          05  COMPANY-SALES-TOTAL     PIC $Z(3),ZZ9-.
133          05  FILLER                  PIC X(6)    VALUE SPACES.
134          05  COMPANY-COMM-TOTAL      PIC $Z(3),ZZ9-.
135          05  FILLER                  PIC X(69)   VALUE SPACES.
136
137      PROCEDURE DIVISION.
138      100-PREPARE-SALES-REPORT.
139          PERFORM 200-SORT-TRANSACTION-FILE.
140          OPEN INPUT SORTED-SALES-FILE
141               OUTPUT PRINT-FILE.
142          PERFORM 220-READ-SORTED-SALES-FILE.
143          PERFORM 240-PROCESS-ONE-SALESPERSON
```

Editing reflects signed fields (lines 105, 107)

Highest-level module in hierarchy chart (line 138)

Figure 15.6   *(continued)*

```
144              UNTIL NO-DATA-REMAINS.
145          PERFORM 260-WRITE-COMPANY-TOTAL.
146          CLOSE SORTED-SALES-FILE
147                PRINT-FILE.
148          STOP RUN.
149
150      200-SORT-TRANSACTION-FILE.
151          SORT SORT-WORK-FILE
152              ASCENDING KEY
153                  SORT-NAME
154              WITH DUPLICATES IN ORDER
155              USING SALES-FILE
156              GIVING SORTED-SALES-FILE.
157
158      220-READ-SORTED-SALES-FILE.
159          READ SORTED-SALES-FILE INTO SALES-RECORD-IN
160              AT END MOVE 'NO' TO DATA-REMAINS-SW
161          END-READ.
162
163      240-PROCESS-ONE-SALESPERSON.
164          PERFORM 300-INITIALIZE-SALESPERSON.
165          PERFORM 320-WRITE-SALESPERSON-HEADING.
166          PERFORM 340-PROCESS-ONE-TRANSACTION
167              UNTIL SR-NAME NOT EQUAL PREVIOUS-NAME
168                    OR NO-DATA-REMAINS.
169          PERFORM 360-WRITE-SALESPERSON-TOTAL.
170          PERFORM 380-INCREMENT-COMPANY-TOTAL.
171
172      260-WRITE-COMPANY-TOTAL.
173          MOVE COMPANY-SALES-TOT TO COMPANY-SALES-TOTAL.
174          MOVE COMPANY-COMM-TOT TO COMPANY-COMM-TOTAL.
175          WRITE PRINT-LINE FROM COMPANY-TOTAL-LINE
176              AFTER ADVANCING 2 LINES.
177
178      300-INITIALIZE-SALESPERSON.
179          MOVE SR-NAME TO PREVIOUS-NAME.
180          INITIALIZE SALESPERSON-TOTALS.
181
182      320-WRITE-SALESPERSON-HEADING.
183          ADD 1 TO PAGE-COUNT.
184          MOVE PAGE-COUNT TO HDG-PAGE.
185          WRITE PRINT-LINE FROM REPORT-HEADING-LINE
186              AFTER ADVANCING PAGE.
187          MOVE SR-NAME TO HDG-NAME.
188          WRITE PRINT-LINE FROM SALESPERSON-HEADING-LINE-ONE
189              AFTER ADVANCING 2 LINES.
190          WRITE PRINT-LINE FROM SALESPERSON-HEADING-LINE-TWO
191              AFTER ADVANCING 1 LINE.
192
193      340-PROCESS-ONE-TRANSACTION.
194          PERFORM 400-CALCULATE-COMMISSION.
```

Sort statement required to place transactions in sequence

Heading written prior to each new salesperson

Detection of control break

Total for this salesperson written after control break is detected

Figure 15.6 *(continued)*

```
195            PERFORM 420-WRITE-DETAIL-LINE.
196            PERFORM 440-INCRMENT-SALESPERSON-TOTAL.
197            PERFORM 220-READ-SORTED-SALES-FILE.
198
199       360-WRITE-SALESPERSON-TOTAL.
200            WRITE PRINT-LINE FROM DASHED-LINE
201                AFTER ADVANCING 1 LINE.
202            MOVE SALESPERSON-SALES-TOT TO SALESPERSON-SALES-TOTAL.
203            MOVE SALESPERSON-COMM-TOT TO SALESPERSON-COMM-TOTAL.
204            WRITE PRINT-LINE FROM SALESPERSON-TOTAL-LINE
205                AFTER ADVANCING 1 LINE.
206            MOVE SPACES TO PRINT-LINE.
207            WRITE PRINT-LINE
208                AFTER ADVANCING 1 LINE.
209
210       380-INCREMENT-COMPANY-TOTAL.
211            ADD SALESPERSON-SALES-TOT TO COMPANY-SALES-TOT.
212            ADD SALESPERSON-COMM-TOT TO COMPANY-COMM-TOT.
213
214       400-CALCULATE-COMMISSION.
215            COMPUTE IND-COMMISSION ROUNDED =
216                SR-SALES * SR-COMMISSION-PERCENT
217                SIZE ERROR DISPLAY 'SIZE ERROR ON COMMISSION FOR '
218                    SR-NAME
219            END-COMPUTE.
220
221       420-WRITE-DETAIL-LINE.
222            MOVE SR-ACCOUNT-NUMBER TO DET-ACCOUNT-NUMBER.
223            MOVE SR-SALES TO DET-SALES.
224            MOVE IND-COMMISSION TO DET-COMMISSION.
225            WRITE PRINT-LINE FROM DETAIL-LINE.
226
227       440-INCRMENT-SALESPERSON-TOTAL.
228            ADD SR-SALES TO SALESPERSON-SALES-TOT.
229            ADD IND-COMMISSION TO SALESPERSON-COMM-TOT.
```

Salesperson totals are rolled into company totals (lines 211–212)

Salesperson totals are accumulated through running totals (lines 228–229)

Two-Level Control Breaks

The reports in Figures 15.2, 15.3, and 15.4 presented a logical progression of one, two, and three control breaks—for salesperson; location and salesperson; and region, location, and salesperson, respectively. This section extends the hierarchy chart, pseudocode, and COBOL program for the one-level application to include a second control break.

Hierarchy Chart

The development of the two-level hierarchy chart is best accomplished as an extension of its existing one-level counterpart. One easy way to anticipate the changes is to compare the one- and two-level reports in Figures 15.2b and 15.3b, then consider the following questions with respect to the hierarchy chart of Figure 15.5a:

1. What additional (i.e., new) modules are necessary?

2. Which existing modules (if any) have to be modified?

3. Which existing modules (if any) have to be deleted?

Every module that appeared in the one-level hierarchy chart will also appear in its two-level counterpart; that is, no modules will be deleted because every function in the one-level application is also required in the two-level example. In addition, several new functions have to be added to accommodate the control break on location. These include:

1. PROCESS-ONE-LOCATION to process all salespersons in one location

2. INITIALIZE-LOCATION to initialize the sales and commission amounts for this location

3. WRITE-LOCATION-HEADING to print a location heading prior to each new location

4. INCREMENT-LOCATION-TOTAL to increment the sales and commission totals for each location

5. WRITE-LOCATION-TOTAL to print the location totals after a control break on location

Changes will also be required in the logic of some existing modules; for example, the module SORT-TRANSACTION-FILE must now reflect a sort on location and salesperson within location. A more subtle change is in WRITE-SALESPERSON-HEADING, which previously began the report for each salesperson on a new page, but which now lists all salespersons in one location on the same page.

The computation of the company total changes as well. The one-level example waited for a control break on salesperson, then rolled the salesperson total into the company total. Although the same approach could be used in the two-level example, it is more efficient to wait for a control break on location, then roll the location total into the company total.

The hierarchy chart for the two-level problem is shown in Figure 15.7a, with the additional and/or modified modules shaded for emphasis. The placement of the new modules is important, and you should notice that the module PROCESS-ONE-LOCATION appears on the second level of the hierarchy chart; this in turn forces the existing module PROCESS-ONE-SALESPERSON, and all of its subordinates, down a level.

Figure 15.7b is subject to the same design considerations as its predecessor, namely, completeness, functionality, and span of control. All design criteria appear satisfactory and the hierarchy chart is finished.

Pseudocode

The pseudocode for the one-level control example is expanded to its two-level counterpart in Figure 15.7b. New and/or modified statements are highlighted to be consistent with the associated hierarchy chart.

The sort statement includes location as an additional key as previously indicated. The major change, however, is the modification of the outer loop to include a series of repetitive statements for each new location that initialize the location totals, write the location heading, and process all salespersons in that location. The detection of a control break on location occurs when SR-LOCATION is unequal to PREVIOUS-LOCATION, and produces the location total, which is then rolled into the company total.

Figure 15.7   Two-Level Algorithm

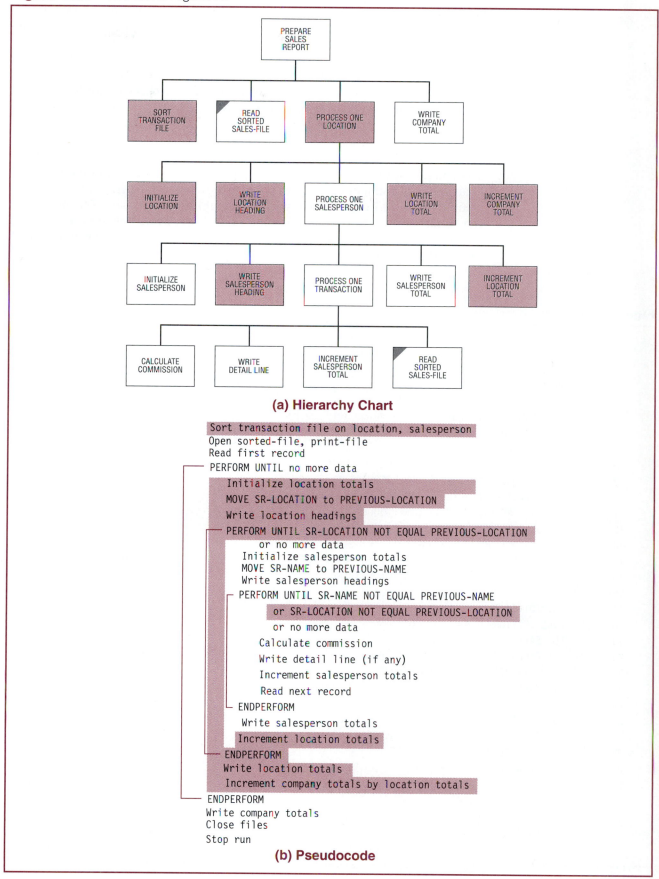

(a) Hierarchy Chart

```
Sort transaction file on location, salesperson
Open sorted-file, print-file
Read first record
PERFORM UNTIL no more data
    Initialize location totals
    MOVE SR-LOCATION to PREVIOUS-LOCATION
    Write location headings
    PERFORM UNTIL SR-LOCATION NOT EQUAL PREVIOUS-LOCATION
            or no more data
        Initialize salesperson totals
        MOVE SR-NAME to PREVIOUS-NAME
        Write salesperson headings
        PERFORM UNTIL SR-NAME NOT EQUAL PREVIOUS-NAME
                or SR-LOCATION NOT EQUAL PREVIOUS-LOCATION
                or no more data
            Calculate commission
            Write detail line (if any)
            Increment salesperson totals
            Read next record
        ENDPERFORM
        Write salesperson totals
        Increment location totals
    ENDPERFORM
    Write location totals
    Increment company totals by location totals
ENDPERFORM
Write company totals
Close files
Stop run
```

(b) Pseudocode

Within each location, there is a second loop (carried over from the one-level application) to process all salespersons in that location. Note, however, the ***compound condition*** in the test for a control break on salesperson that now includes both salesperson and location. This dual test is necessary in the unusual instance where the last salesperson in the current location and the first salesperson in the next location have the same name. (A general rule for the detection of a control break requires a compound condition, which includes a check for the level you are on, as well as any levels above the current level.)

The Completed Program

The completed program is shown in Figure 15.8 and reflects all of the indicated changes. Once again, we call your attention to the relationship between the hierarchy chart in Figure 15.7a and the paragraphs in the Procedure Division. The modules in the hierarchy chart correspond one to one with the paragraphs in the program. Observe also that each level in the hierarchy chart can be matched with a COBOL PERFORM statement.

Figure 15.8   Two-Level Control Break Program

```
1        IDENTIFICATION DIVISION.
2        PROGRAM-ID.    TWOLEVEL.
3        AUTHOR.        CVV.
4
5        ENVIRONMENT DIVISION.
6        INPUT-OUTPUT SECTION.
7        FILE-CONTROL.
8           SELECT SALES-FILE      ASSIGN TO SYSIN
9                ORGANIZATION IS LINE SEQUENTIAL.
10          SELECT PRINT-FILE      ASSIGN TO SYSOUT
11               ORGANIZATION IS LINE SEQUENTIAL.
12          SELECT SORT-WORK-FILE
13               ASSIGN TO SORTWK01.
14          SELECT SORTED-SALES-FILE   ASSIGN TO SORTED
15               ORGANIZATION IS LINE SEQUENTIAL.
16
17       DATA DIVISION.
18       FILE SECTION.
19       FD  SALES-FILE
20           RECORD CONTAINS 58 CHARACTERS
21           DATA RECORD IS SALES-RECORD.
22       01  SALES-RECORD               PIC X(58).
23
24       FD  PRINT-FILE
25           RECORD CONTAINS 132 CHARACTERS
26           DATA RECORD IS PRINT-LINE.
27       01  PRINT-LINE                 PIC X(132).
28
29       SD  SORT-WORK-FILE
30           RECORD CONTAINS 58 CHARACTERS
31           DATA RECORD IS SORT-RECORD.
```

Figure 15.8   *(continued)*

```
32    01   SORT-RECORD.
33         05   SORT-ACCOUNT-NUMBER      PIC 9(6).
34         05   FILLER                   PIC X.
35         05   SORT-NAME                PIC X(15).
36         05   FILLER                   PIC X(10).
37         05   SORT-LOCATION            PIC X(15).
38         05   SORT-REGION              PIC X(11).
39
40    FD   SORTED-SALES-FILE
41         RECORD CONTAINS 58 CHARACTERS
42         DATA RECORD IS SORTED-SALES-RECORD.
43    01   SORTED-SALES-RECORD           PIC X(58).
44
45    WORKING-STORAGE SECTION.
46    01   FILLER                        PIC X(14)
47              VALUE 'WS BEGINS HERE'.
48
49    01   SALES-RECORD-IN.
50         05   SR-ACCOUNT-NUMBER        PIC 9(6).
51         05   FILLER                   PIC X.
52         05   SR-NAME                  PIC X(15).
53         05   SR-SALES                 PIC S9(4).
54         05   FILLER                   PIC XX.
55         05   SR-COMMISSION-PERCENT    PIC V99.
56         05   FILLER                   PIC XX.
57         05   SR-LOCATION              PIC X(15).
58         05   SR-REGION                PIC X(11).
59
60    01   PROGRAM-SWITCHES-AND-COUNTERS.
61         05   DATA-REMAINS-SW          PIC X(3)    VALUE 'YES'.
62              88  NO-DATA-REMAINS                  VALUE 'NO'.
63         05   PREVIOUS-NAME            PIC X(15)   VALUE SPACES.
64         05   PREVIOUS-LOCATION        PIC X(15)   VALUE SPACES.
65         05   PAGE-COUNT               PIC 99      VALUE ZEROES.
66
67    01   CONTROL-BREAK-TOTALS.
68         05   INDIVIDUAL-TOTALS.
69              10  IND-COMMISSION       PIC S9(4).
70         05   SALESPERSON-TOTALS.
71              10  SALESPERSON-SALES-TOT PIC S9(6).
72              10  SALESPERSON-COMM-TOT  PIC S9(6).
73         05   LOCATION-TOTALS.
74              10  LOCATION-SALES-TOT   PIC S9(6).
75              10  LOCATION-COMM-TOT    PIC S9(6).
76         05   COMPANY-TOTALS.
77              10  COMPANY-SALES-TOT    PIC S9(6)   VALUE ZEROS.
78              10  COMPANY-COMM-TOT     PIC S9(6)   VALUE ZEROS.
79
80    01   REPORT-HEADING-LINE.
81         05   FILLER                   PIC X(25)   VALUE SPACES.
```

Used to detect control break on location

Location counters are added to two-level program

Figure 15.8 *(continued)*

```
82        05   FILLER                    PIC X(21)
83               VALUE 'SALES ACTIVITY REPORT'.
84        05   FILLER                    PIC X(19)   VALUE SPACES.
85        05   FILLER                    PIC X(5)    VALUE 'PAGE '.
86        05   HDG-PAGE                  PIC Z9.
87        05   FILLER                    PIC X(60)   VALUE SPACES.
88
89    01  LOCATION-HEADING-LINE.
90        05   FILLER                    PIC X(8)    VALUE SPACES.
91        05   FILLER                    PIC X(10)
92               VALUE 'LOCATION: '.
93        05   HDG-LOCATION              PIC X(19)   VALUE SPACES.
94        05   FILLER                    PIC X(95)   VALUE SPACES.
95
96    01  SALESPERSON-HEADING-LINE-ONE.
97        05   FILLER                    PIC X(15)   VALUE SPACES.
98        05   FILLER                    PIC X(13)
99               VALUE 'SALESPERSON: '.
100       05   HDG-NAME                  PIC X(15).
101       05   FILLER                    PIC X(89)   VALUE SPACES.
102
103   01  SALESPERSON-HEADING-LINE-TWO.
104       05   FILLER                    PIC X(23)   VALUE SPACES.
105       05   FILLER                    PIC X(11)   VALUE 'ACCOUNT # '.
106       05   FILLER                    PIC X(9)    VALUE SPACES.
107       05   FILLER                    PIC X(5)    VALUE 'SALES'.
108       05   FILLER                    PIC X(8)    VALUE SPACES.
109       05   FILLER                    PIC X(10)   VALUE 'COMMISSION'.
110       05   FILLER                    PIC X(66)   VALUE SPACES.
111
112   01  DETAIL-LINE.
113       05   FILLER                    PIC X(25)   VALUE SPACES.
114       05   DET-ACCOUNT-NUMBER        PIC 9(6).
115       05   FILLER                    PIC X(9)    VALUE SPACES.
116       05   DET-SALES                 PIC Z(3),ZZ9-.
117       05   FILLER                    PIC X(7)    VALUE SPACES.
118       05   DET-COMMISSION            PIC Z(3),ZZ9-.
119       05   FILLER                    PIC X(69)   VALUE SPACES.
120
121   01  DASHED-LINE.
122       05   FILLER                    PIC X(40)   VALUE SPACES.
123       05   FILLER                    PIC X(8)    VALUE ALL '-'.
124       05   FILLER                    PIC X(7)    VALUE SPACES.
125       05   FILLER                    PIC X(8)    VALUE ALL '-'.
126       05   FILLER                    PIC X(69)   VALUE SPACES.
127
128   01  SALESPERSON-TOTAL-LINE.
129       05   FILLER                    PIC X(15)   VALUE SPACES.
130       05   FILLER                    PIC X(21)
131               VALUE '** SALESPERSON TOTAL'.
```

Location heading is added to two-level program

Figure 15.8 *(continued)*

```
132          05  FILLER                    PIC X(3)    VALUE SPACES.
133          05  SALESPERSON-SALES-TOTAL   PIC $Z(3),ZZ9-.
134          05  FILLER                    PIC X(6)    VALUE SPACES.
135          05  SALESPERSON-COMM-TOTAL    PIC $Z(3),ZZ9-.
136          05  FILLER                    PIC X(69)   VALUE SPACES.
137
138      01  LOCATION-TOTAL-LINE.
139          05  FILLER                    PIC X(13)   VALUE SPACES.
140          05  FILLER                    PIC X(19)
141              VALUE '**** LOCATION TOTAL'.
142          05  FILLER                    PIC X(7)    VALUE SPACES.
143          05  LOCATION-SALES-TOTAL      PIC $Z(3),ZZ9-.
144          05  FILLER                    PIC X(6)    VALUE SPACES.
145          05  LOCATION-COMM-TOTAL       PIC $Z(3),ZZ9-.
146          05  FILLER                    PIC X(69)   VALUE SPACES.
147
148      01  COMPANY-TOTAL-LINE.
149          05  FILLER                    PIC X(9)    VALUE SPACES.
150          05  FILLER                    PIC X(22)
151              VALUE '******** COMPANY TOTAL'.
152          05  FILLER                    PIC X(8)    VALUE SPACES.
153          05  COMPANY-SALES-TOTAL       PIC $Z(3),ZZ9-.
154          05  FILLER                    PIC X(6)    VALUE SPACES.
155          05  COMPANY-COMM-TOTAL        PIC $Z(3),ZZ9-.
156          05  FILLER                    PIC X(69)   VALUE SPACES.
157
158      PROCEDURE DIVISION.
159      100-PREPARE-SALES-REPORT.
160          PERFORM 200-SORT-TRANSACTION-FILE.
161          OPEN INPUT SORTED-SALES-FILE
162              OUTPUT PRINT-FILE.
163          PERFORM 220-READ-SORTED-SALES-FILE.
164          PERFORM 240-PROCESS-ONE-LOCATION
165              UNTIL NO-DATA-REMAINS.
166          PERFORM 260-WRITE-COMPANY-TOTAL.
167          CLOSE SORTED-SALES-FILE
168              PRINT-FILE.
169          STOP RUN.
170
171      200-SORT-TRANSACTION-FILE.
172          SORT SORT-WORK-FILE
173              ASCENDING KEY
174                  SORT-LOCATION
175                  SORT-NAME
176              WITH DUPLICATES IN ORDER
177              USING SALES-FILE
178              GIVING SORTED-SALES-FILE.
179
180      220-READ-SORTED-SALES-FILE.
181          READ SORTED-SALES-FILE INTO SALES-RECORD-IN
```

Location total line is added to two-level program

Keys in SORT statement match control breaks

Figure 15.8   *(continued)*

```
182              AT END MOVE 'NO' TO DATA-REMAINS-SW
183          END-READ.
184
185      240-PROCESS-ONE-LOCATION.
186          PERFORM 300-INITIALIZE-LOCATION.
187          PERFORM 320-WRITE-LOCATION-HEADING.
188          PERFORM 340-PROCESS-ONE-SALESPERSON
189              UNTIL SR-LOCATION NOT EQUAL PREVIOUS-LOCATION
190                  OR NO-DATA-REMAINS.
191          PERFORM 360-WRITE-LOCATION-TOTAL.
192          PERFORM 380-INCREMENT-COMPANY-TOTAL.
193
194      260-WRITE-COMPANY-TOTAL.
195          MOVE COMPANY-SALES-TOT TO COMPANY-SALES-TOTAL.
196          MOVE COMPANY-COMM-TOT TO COMPANY-COMM-TOTAL.
197          WRITE PRINT-LINE FROM COMPANY-TOTAL-LINE
198              AFTER ADVANCING 2 LINES.
199
200      300-INITIALIZE-LOCATION.
201          MOVE SR-LOCATION TO PREVIOUS-LOCATION.
202          INITIALIZE LOCATION-TOTALS.
203
204      320-WRITE-LOCATION-HEADING.
205          ADD 1 TO PAGE-COUNT.
206          MOVE PAGE-COUNT TO HDG-PAGE.
207          WRITE PRINT-LINE FROM REPORT-HEADING-LINE
208              AFTER ADVANCING PAGE.
209          MOVE SR-LOCATION TO HDG-LOCATION.
210          WRITE PRINT-LINE FROM LOCATION-HEADING-LINE
211              AFTER ADVANCING 2 LINES.
212
213      340-PROCESS-ONE-SALESPERSON.
214          PERFORM 400-INITIALIZE-SALESPERSON.
215          PERFORM 420-WRITE-SALESPERSON-HEADING.
216          PERFORM 440-PROCESS-ONE-TRANSACTION
217              UNTIL SR-NAME NOT EQUAL PREVIOUS-NAME
218                  OR SR-LOCATION NOT EQUAL PREVIOUS-LOCATION
219                  OR NO-DATA-REMAINS.
220          PERFORM 460-WRITE-SALESPERSON-TOTAL.
221          PERFORM 480-INCREMENT-LOCATION-TOTAL.
222
223      360-WRITE-LOCATION-TOTAL.
224          MOVE LOCATION-SALES-TOT TO LOCATION-SALES-TOTAL.
225          MOVE LOCATION-COMM-TOT TO LOCATION-COMM-TOTAL.
226          WRITE PRINT-LINE FROM LOCATION-TOTAL-LINE
227              AFTER ADVANCING 1 LINE.
228          MOVE SPACES TO PRINT-LINE.
229          WRITE PRINT-LINE
230              AFTER ADVANCING 1 LINE.
231
232      380-INCREMENT-COMPANY-TOTAL.
```

Location heading written for each new location — (points to line 187 PERFORM 320-WRITE-LOCATION-HEADING.)

Location total written after control break detected — (points to line 191 PERFORM 360-WRITE-LOCATION-TOTAL.)

Detects control break if salespersons in two locations have the same name — (points to line 218 OR SR-LOCATION NOT EQUAL PREVIOUS-LOCATION)

Figure 15.8 *(continued)*

```
233              ADD LOCATION-SALES-TOT TO COMPANY-SALES-TOT.      ── Location totals are rolled into company totals
234              ADD LOCATION-COMM-TOT TO COMPANY-COMM-TOT.
235
236          400-INITIALIZE-SALESPERSON.
237              MOVE SR-NAME TO PREVIOUS-NAME.
238              INITIALIZE SALESPERSON-TOTALS.
239
240          420-WRITE-SALESPERSON-HEADING.
241              MOVE SR-NAME TO HDG-NAME.
242              WRITE PRINT-LINE FROM SALESPERSON-HEADING-LINE-ONE
243                  AFTER ADVANCING 1 LINE.
244              WRITE PRINT-LINE FROM SALESPERSON-HEADING-LINE-TWO
245                  AFTER ADVANCING 1 LINE.
246
247          440-PROCESS-ONE-TRANSACTION.
248              PERFORM 500-CALCULATE-COMMISSION.
249              PERFORM 520-WRITE-DETAIL-LINE.
250              PERFORM 540-INCRMENT-SALESPERSON-TOTAL.
251              PERFORM 220-READ-SORTED-SALES-FILE.
252
253          460-WRITE-SALESPERSON-TOTAL.
254              WRITE PRINT-LINE FROM DASHED-LINE
255                  AFTER ADVANCING 1 LINE.
256              MOVE SALESPERSON-SALES-TOT TO SALESPERSON-SALES-TOTAL.
257              MOVE SALESPERSON-COMM-TOT TO SALESPERSON-COMM-TOTAL.
258              WRITE PRINT-LINE FROM SALESPERSON-TOTAL-LINE
259                  AFTER ADVANCING 1 LINE.
260              MOVE SPACES TO PRINT-LINE.
261              WRITE PRINT-LINE
262                  AFTER ADVANCING 1 LINE.
263
264          480-INCREMENT-LOCATION-TOTAL.
265              ADD SALESPERSON-SALES-TOT TO LOCATION-SALES-TOT.    ── Salesperson totals are rolled
266              ADD SALESPERSON-COMM-TOT TO LOCATION-COMM-TOT.           into location totals
267
268          500-CALCULATE-COMMISSION.
269              COMPUTE IND-COMMISSION ROUNDED =
270                  SR-SALES * SR-COMMISSION-PERCENT
271                  SIZE ERROR DISPLAY 'SIZE ERROR ON COMMISSION FOR '
272                      SR-NAME
273              END-COMPUTE.
274
275          520-WRITE-DETAIL-LINE.
276              MOVE SR-ACCOUNT-NUMBER TO DET-ACCOUNT-NUMBER.
277              MOVE SR-SALES TO DET-SALES.
278              MOVE IND-COMMISSION TO DET-COMMISSION.
279              WRITE PRINT-LINE FROM DETAIL-LINE.
280
281          540-INCRMENT-SALESPERSON-TOTAL.
282              ADD SR-SALES TO SALESPERSON-SALES-TOT.
283              ADD IND-COMMISSION TO SALESPERSON-COMM-TOT.
```

The Working-Storage Section contains every statement from the previous program plus additional entries to accommodate the second control break. The location heading and total lines are defined in lines 89–94 and 138–146, respectively. There are new counters for the location totals, LOCATION-SALES-TOT, and LOCATION-COMM-TOT, and a new data name, PREVIOUS-LOCATION, to detect the control break on location. The new entries are shaded in the listing for emphasis.

The SORT statement (lines 172–178) specifies two keys, SORT-LOCATION and SORT-NAME, to sort the transaction file by location and salesperson within location. The WITH DUPLICATES IN ORDER phrase keeps the transactions for a given salesperson in sequence by account number since the input file (Figure 15.1) was already in sequence by account number.

The remaining statements in the Procedure Division are straightforward and easy to follow, given the earlier discussion of the hierarchy chart and associated pseudocode. Observe, for example, the paragraph to increment the company totals (lines 232–234), in which location totals are rolled into the company totals. Note, too, the compound condition in the PERFORM statement of lines 216–219 to detect a control break on salesperson.

Three-Level Control Breaks

We return to the reports of Figures 15.2, 15.3, and 15.4, which showed the progression of one-, two-, and three-level control breaks. This time, we will expand the hierarchy chart, pseudocode, and COBOL program from two to three levels.

Hierarchy Chart

The three-level hierarchy chart will be developed as an extension of the existing two-level hierarchy chart. Accordingly, we will compare the two- and three-level reports in Figures 15.3b and 15.4b, then consider the following questions with respect to the existing chart:

1. What additional (i.e., new) modules are necessary?
2. Which existing modules (if any) have to be modified?
3. Which existing modules (if any) have to be deleted?

Every module that appeared in the two-level hierarchy chart will also appear in the three-level version; no modules will be deleted because every function from the two-level example is also required in the three-level example. Several new functions are necessary to accommodate the control break on region. These include:

1. PROCESS-ONE-REGION to process all locations in one region
2. INITIALIZE-REGION to initialize the sales and commission totals for this region
3. WRITE-REGION-HEADING to print a region heading for each new region
4. INCREMENT-REGION-TOTAL to increment the sales and commission totals for each region
5. WRITE-REGION-TOTAL to print region totals after a break on region

Changes will also be required in the logic of some existing modules—for example, a change in SORT-TRANSACTION-FILE to reflect a sort on region, location within region, and salesperson within location. It will also be necessary to change WRITE-LOCATION-HEADING, which previously began the report for each location on a new page, but which now lists all locations in the same region on the same page.

The computation of the company totals also changes. The two-level example waited for a control break on location, then rolled the location total into the company total. The same approach could be used in the three-level example, but it is more efficient to wait for a control break on region, then roll the region total into the company total.

The hierarchy chart for the three-level problem is shown in Figure 15.9a, with the additional and/or modified modules shaded for emphasis. The placement of the new modules is important, and you should notice that the module PROCESS-ONE-REGION appears on the second level of the hierarchy chart, which in turn forces the existing module PROCESS-ONE-LOCATION, and all of its subordinates, down a level.

Figure 15.9b is subject to the same design considerations as its predecessor, namely, completeness, functionality, and span of control. All design criteria appear satisfactory and the hierarchy chart is finished.

Figure 15.9 Three-Level Algorithm

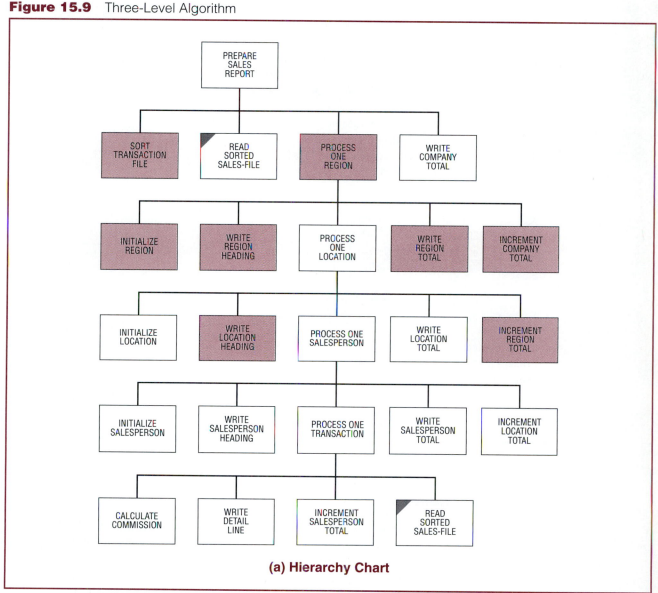

(a) Hierarchy Chart

Figure 15.9   *(continued)*

```
Sort transaction file on region, location, and salesperson
Open sorted-file, print-file
Read first record
PERFORM UNTIL no more data
    Initialize region totals
    MOVE SR-REGION to PREVIOUS-REGION
    Write region heading
    PERFORM UNTIL REGION NOT EQUAL PREVIOUS-REGION
            or no more data
        Initialize location totals
        MOVE SR-LOCATION to PREVIOUS-LOCATION
        Write location heading
        PERFORM UNTIL SR-LOCATION NOT EQUAL PREVIOUS-LOCATION
                or SR-REGION NOT EQUAL PREVIOUS-REGION
                or no more data
            Initialize salesperson totals
            MOVE SR-NAME to PREVIOUS-NAME
            Write salesperson heading
            PERFORM UNTIL SR-NAME NOT EQUAL PREVIOUS-NAME
                    or SR-LOCATION NOT EQUAL PREVIOUS-LOCATION
                    or SR-REGION NOT EQUAL PREVIOUS-REGION
                    or no more data
                Calculate commission
                Write detail line
                Increment salesperson totals
                Read next record
            ENDPERFORM
            Write salesperson totals
            Increment location totals
        ENDPERFORM
        Write location totals
        Increment region totals
    ENDPERFORM
    Write region totals
    Increment company totals by region totals
ENDPERFORM
Write company totals
Close files
Stop run
```

(b) Pseudocode

Pseudocode

The pseudocode for the two-level control break is expanded to its three-level counterpart in Figure 15.9b. New and/or modified statements are highlighted to be consistent with the associated hierarchy chart.

The sort statement includes region as an additional key as previously indicated. The major change, however, is the modification of the outer loop to include a series of repetitive statements for each new region that initialize the region totals, write the region heading, and process all locations in that region. The detection of a control break on region occurs when SR-REGION is unequal to PREVIOUS-REGION, and produces the region total, which is then rolled into the company total.

Within each region, there is a second loop (carried over from the two-level application) to process all locations in that region. A compound condition, that includes location and region, is necessary to detect a control break on location in the unusual instance where the last location in the current region and the first location in the next region have the same name. (This is in accordance with the general rule to detect a control break, which includes a compound condition that checks the level you are on, as well as any levels above the current level. Note, therefore, the compound condition associated with a control break on salesperson that includes salesperson, location, and region.)

The Completed Program

The completed program is shown in Figure 15.10 and reflects all of the indicated changes. Once again, we call your attention to the relationship between the hierarchy chart in Figure 15.9a and the paragraphs in the Procedure Division. The modules in the hierarchy chart correspond one to one with the paragraphs in the program. Observe also that each level in the hierarchy chart can be matched with a COBOL PERFORM statement.

The Working-Storage Section contains every statement from the previous program plus additional entries to accommodate the second control break. The region heading and total lines are defined in lines 93–96 and 157–165, respectively. There are new counters for the region totals, REGION-SALES-TOT, and REGION-COMM-TOT, and a new data name, PREVIOUS-REGION, to detect the control break on region. The new entries are shaded in the listing for emphasis.

The SORT statement (lines 191–198) specifies three keys—SORT-REGION, SORT-LOCATION, and SORT-NAME—to sort the transaction file by region, location within region, and salesperson within location. The WITH DUPLICATES IN ORDER phrase keeps the transactions for a given salesperson in sequence by account number since the input file (Figure 15.1) was already in sequence by account number.

The remaining statements in the Procedure Division are straightforward and easy to follow given the earlier discussion of the hierarchy chart and associated pseudocode. Observe, for example, the paragraph to increment the company totals (lines 249–251), in which region totals are rolled into the company totals. Note, too, the compound condition in the PERFORM statement of lines 236–239 to detect a control break on salesperson.

Figure 15.10 Three-Level Control Break Program

```
1        IDENTIFICATION DIVISION.
2        PROGRAM-ID.   THRLEVEL.
3        AUTHOR.       CVV.
4
5        ENVIRONMENT DIVISION.
```

Figure 15.10   *(continued)*

```
6          INPUT-OUTPUT SECTION.
7          FILE-CONTROL.
8             SELECT SALES-FILE    ASSIGN TO SYSIN
9                 ORGANIZATION IS LINE SEQUENTIAL.
10            SELECT PRINT-FILE    ASSIGN TO SYSOUT
11                ORGANIZATION IS LINE SEQUENTIAL.
12            SELECT SORT-WORK-FILE
13                ASSIGN TO SORTWK01.
14            SELECT SORTED-SALES-FILE   ASSIGN TO SORTED
15                ORGANIZATION IS LINE SEQUENTIAL.
16
17         DATA DIVISION.
18         FILE SECTION.
19         FD   SALES-FILE
20              RECORD CONTAINS 58 CHARACTERS
21              DATA RECORD IS SALES-RECORD.
22         01   SALES-RECORD            PIC X(58).
23
24         FD   PRINT-FILE
25              RECORD CONTAINS 132 CHARACTERS
26              DATA RECORD IS PRINT-LINE.
27         01   PRINT-LINE              PIC X(132).
28
29         SD   SORT-WORK-FILE
30              RECORD CONTAINS 58 CHARACTERS
31              DATA RECORD IS SORT-RECORD.
32         01   SORT-RECORD.
33              05   SORT-ACCOUNT-NUMBER    PIC 9(6).
34              05   FILLER                 PIC X.
35              05   SORT-NAME              PIC X(15).
36              05   FILLER                 PIC X(10).
37              05   SORT-LOCATION          PIC X(15).
38              05   SORT-REGION            PIC X(11).
39
40         FD   SORTED-SALES-FILE
41              RECORD CONTAINS 58 CHARACTERS
42              DATA RECORD IS SORTED-SALES-RECORD.
43         01   SORTED-SALES-RECORD    PIC X(58).
44
45         WORKING-STORAGE SECTION.
46         01   FILLER                 PIC X(14)
47                  VALUE 'WS BEGINS HERE'.
48
49         01   SALES-RECORD-IN.
50              05   SR-ACCOUNT-NUMBER    PIC 9(6).
51              05   FILLER               PIC X.
52              05   SR-NAME              PIC X(15).
```

Figure 15.10 *(continued)*

```
53        05   SR-SALES                 PIC S9(4).
54        05   FILLER                   PIC XX.
55        05   SR-COMMISSION-PERCENT    PIC V99.
56        05   FILLER                   PIC XX.
57        05   SR-LOCATION              PIC X(15).
58        05   SR-REGION                PIC X(11).          ── Region is an additional
59                                                             control field
60    01  PROGRAM-SWITCHES-AND-COUNTERS.
61        05   DATA-REMAINS-SW          PIC X(3)    VALUE 'YES'.
62             88  NO-DATA-REMAINS                  VALUE 'NO'.
63        05   PREVIOUS-NAME            PIC X(15)   VALUE SPACES.
64        05   PREVIOUS-LOCATION        PIC X(15)   VALUE SPACES.
65        05   PREVIOUS-REGION          PIC X(11)   VALUE SPACES.   ── Used to detect control
66        05   PAGE-COUNT               PIC 99      VALUE ZEROES.      break on region
67
68    01  CONTROL-BREAK-TOTALS.
69        05   INDIVIDUAL-TOTALS.
70             10   IND-COMMISSION      PIC S9(4).
71        05   SALESPERSON-TOTALS.
72             10   SALESPERSON-SALES-TOT  PIC S9(6).
73             10   SALESPERSON-COMM-TOT   PIC S9(6).
74        05   LOCATION-TOTALS.
75             10   LOCATION-SALES-TOT  PIC S9(6).
76             10   LOCATION-COMM-TOT   PIC S9(6).               ── Region totals are added to
77        05   REGION-TOTALS.                                      three-level program
78             10   REGION-SALES-TOT    PIC S9(6).
79             10   REGION-COMM-TOT     PIC S9(6).
80        05   COMPANY-TOTALS.
81             10   COMPANY-SALES-TOT   PIC S9(6)   VALUE ZEROS.
82             10   COMPANY-COMM-TOT    PIC S9(6)   VALUE ZEROS.
83
84    01  REPORT-HEADING-LINE.
85        05   FILLER                   PIC X(25)   VALUE SPACES.
86        05   FILLER                   PIC X(21)
87             VALUE 'SALES ACTIVITY REPORT'.
88        05   FILLER                   PIC X(19)   VALUE SPACES.
89        05   FILLER                   PIC X(5)    VALUE 'PAGE '.
90        05   HDG-PAGE                 PIC Z9.
91        05   FILLER                   PIC X(60)   VALUE SPACES.
92
93    01  REGION-HEADING-LINE.
94        05   FILLER                   PIC X(8)    VALUE 'REGION: '.
95        05   HDG-REGION               PIC X(11)   VALUE SPACES.
96        05   FILLER                   PIC X(113)  VALUE SPACES.    ── Region heading is
97                                                                      added to three-level
98    01  LOCATION-HEADING-LINE.                                       program
99        05   FILLER                   PIC X(8)    VALUE SPACES.
```

Figure 15.10 *(continued)*

```
100           05  FILLER                  PIC X(10)
101               VALUE 'LOCATION: '.
102           05  HDG-LOCATION            PIC X(19)   VALUE SPACES.
103           05  FILLER                  PIC X(95)   VALUE SPACES.
104
105       01  SALESPERSON-HEADING-LINE-ONE.
106           05  FILLER                  PIC X(15)   VALUE SPACES.
107           05  FILLER                  PIC X(13)
108               VALUE 'SALESPERSON: '.
109           05  HDG-NAME                PIC X(15).
110           05  FILLER                  PIC X(89)   VALUE SPACES.
111
112       01  SALESPERSON-HEADING-LINE-TWO.
113           05  FILLER                  PIC X(23)   VALUE SPACES.
114           05  FILLER                  PIC X(11)   VALUE 'ACCOUNT .
115           05  FILLER                  PIC X(9)    VALUE SPACES.
116           05  FILLER                  PIC X(5)    VALUE 'SALES'.
117           05  FILLER                  PIC X(8)    VALUE SPACES.
118           05  FILLER                  PIC X(10)   VALUE MMISSION'.
119           05  FILLER                  PIC X(66)   VALUE SPACES.
120
121       01  DETAIL-LINE.
122           05  FILLER                  PIC X(25)   VALUE SPACES.
123           05  DET-ACCOUNT-NUMBER      PIC 9(6).
124           05  FILLER                  PIC X(9)    VALUE SPACES.
125           05  DET-SALES               PIC Z(3),ZZ9-.
126           05  FILLER                  PIC X(7)    VALUE SPACES.
127           05  DET-COMMISSION          PIC Z(3),ZZ9-.
128           05  FILLER                  PIC X(69)   VALUE SPACES.
129
130       01  DASHED-LINE.
131           05  FILLER                  PIC X(40)   VALUE SPACES.
132           05  FILLER                  PIC X(8)    VALUE ALL '-'.
133           05  FILLER                  PIC X(7)    VALUE SPACES.
134           05  FILLER                  PIC X(8)    VALUE ALL '-'.
135           05  FILLER                  PIC X(69)   VALUE SPACES.
136
137       01  SALESPERSON-TOTAL-LINE.
138           05  FILLER                  PIC X(15)   VALUE SPACES.
139           05  FILLER                  PIC X(21)
140               VALUE '** SALESPERSON TOTAL'.
141           05  FILLER                  PIC X(3)    VALUE SPACES.
142           05  SALESPERSON-SALES-TOTAL PIC $Z(3),ZZ9-.
143           05  FILLER                  PIC X(6)    VALUE SPACES.
144           05  SALESPERSON-COMM-TOTAL  PIC $Z(3),ZZ9-.
145           05  FILLER                  PIC X(69)   VALUE SPACES.
146
```

Figure 15.10   *(continued)*

```
147       01  LOCATION-TOTAL-LINE.
148           05  FILLER                PIC X(13)    VALUE SPACES.
149           05  FILLER                PIC X(19)
150               VALUE '**** LOCATION TOTAL'.
151           05  FILLER                PIC X(7)     VALUE SPACES.
152           05  LOCATION-SALES-TOTAL  PIC $Z(3),ZZ9-.
153           05  FILLER                PIC X(6)     VALUE SPACES.
154           05  LOCATION-COMM-TOTAL   PIC $Z(3),ZZ9-.
155           05  FILLER                PIC X(69)    VALUE SPACES.
156
157       01  REGION-TOTAL-LINE.
158           05  FILLER                PIC X(11)    VALUE SPACES.
159           05  FILLER                PIC X(19)
160               VALUE '****** REGION TOTAL'.
161           05  FILLER                PIC X(9)     VALUE SPACES.
162           05  REGION-SALES-TOTAL    PIC $Z(3),ZZ9-.
163           05  FILLER                PIC X(6)     VALUE SPACES.
164           05  REGION-COMM-TOTAL     PIC $Z(3),ZZ9-.
165           05  FILLER                PIC X(69)    VALUE SPACES.
166
167       01  COMPANY-TOTAL-LINE.
168           05  FILLER                PIC X(9)     VALUE SPACES.
169           05  FILLER                PIC X(22)
170               VALUE '******** COMPANY TOTAL'.
171           05  FILLER                PIC X(8)     VALUE SPACES.
172           05  COMPANY-SALES-TOTAL   PIC $Z(3),ZZ9-.
173           05  FILLER                PIC X(6)     VALUE SPACES.
174           05  COMPANY-COMM-TOTAL    PIC $Z(3),ZZ9-.
175           05  FILLER                PIC X(69)    VALUE SPACES.
176
177       PROCEDURE DIVISION.
178       100-PREPARE-SALES-REPORT.
179           PERFORM 200-SORT-TRANSACTION-FILE.
180           OPEN INPUT SORTED-SALES-FILE
181               OUTPUT PRINT-FILE.
182           PERFORM 220-READ-SORTED-SALES-FILE.
183           PERFORM 240-PROCESS-ONE-REGION
184               UNTIL NO-DATA-REMAINS.
185           PERFORM 260-WRITE-COMPANY-TOTAL.
186           CLOSE SORTED-SALES-FILE
187               PRINT-FILE.
188           STOP RUN.
189
190       200-SORT-TRANSACTION-FILE.
191           SORT SORT-WORK-FILE
192               ASCENDING KEY
193                   SORT-REGION
```

Region total line is added to three-level program

Keys in SORT statement match control breaks

Figure 15.10 *(continued)*

```
194              SORT-LOCATION
195              SORT-NAME
196          WITH DUPLICATES IN ORDER
197          USING SALES-FILE
198          GIVING SORTED-SALES-FILE.
199
200      220-READ-SORTED-SALES-FILE.
201          READ SORTED-SALES-FILE INTO SALES-RECORD-IN
202              AT END MOVE 'NO' TO DATA-REMAINS-SW
203          END-READ.
204
205      240-PROCESS-ONE-REGION.
206          PERFORM 300-INITIALIZE-REGION.
207          PERFORM 320-WRITE-REGION-HEADING.
208          PERFORM 340-PROCESS-ONE-LOCATION
209              UNTIL SR-REGION NOT EQUAL PREVIOUS-REGION
210                  OR NO-DATA-REMAINS.
211          PERFORM 360-WRITE-REGION-TOTAL.
212          PERFORM 380-INCREMENT-COMPANY-TOTAL.
213
214      260-WRITE-COMPANY-TOTAL.
215          MOVE COMPANY-SALES-TOT TO COMPANY-SALES-TOTAL.
216          MOVE COMPANY-COMM-TOT TO COMPANY-COMM-TOTAL.
217          WRITE PRINT-LINE FROM COMPANY-TOTAL-LINE
218              AFTER ADVANCING 2 LINES.
219
220      300-INITIALIZE-REGION.
221          MOVE SR-REGION TO PREVIOUS-REGION.
222          INITIALIZE REGION-TOTALS.
223
224      320-WRITE-REGION-HEADING.
225          ADD 1 TO PAGE-COUNT.
226          MOVE PAGE-COUNT TO HDG-PAGE.
227          WRITE PRINT-LINE FROM REPORT-HEADING-LINE
228              AFTER ADVANCING PAGE.
229          MOVE SR-REGION TO HDG-REGION.
230          WRITE PRINT-LINE FROM REGION-HEADING-LINE
231              AFTER ADVANCING 2 LINES.
232
233      340-PROCESS-ONE-LOCATION.
234          PERFORM 400-INITIALIZE-LOCATION.
235          PERFORM 420-WRITE-LOCATION-HEADING.
236          PERFORM 440-PROCESS-ONE-SALESPERSON
237              UNTIL SR-LOCATION NOT EQUAL PREVIOUS-LOCATION
238                  OR SR-REGION NOT EQUAL PREVIOUS-REGION
239                      OR NO-DATA-REMAINS.
240          PERFORM 460-WRITE-LOCATION-TOTAL.
```

Keys in SORT statement match control breaks

Region heading written for each new region

Region total written after control break detected

Figure 15.10 *(continued)*

```
241              PERFORM 480-INCREMENT-REGION-TOTAL.
242
243          360-WRITE-REGION-TOTAL.
244              MOVE REGION-SALES-TOT TO REGION-SALES-TOTAL.
245              MOVE REGION-COMM-TOT TO REGION-COMM-TOTAL.
246              WRITE PRINT-LINE FROM REGION-TOTAL-LINE
247                  AFTER ADVANCING 1 LINE.
248
249          380-INCREMENT-COMPANY-TOTAL.
250              ADD REGION-SALES-TOT TO COMPANY-SALES-TOT.
251              ADD REGION-COMM-TOT TO COMPANY-COMM-TOT.           Region totals are rolled into company totals
252
253          400-INITIALIZE-LOCATION.
254              MOVE SR-LOCATION TO PREVIOUS-LOCATION.
255              INITIALIZE LOCATION-TOTALS.
256
257          420-WRITE-LOCATION-HEADING.
258              MOVE SR-LOCATION TO HDG-LOCATION.
259              WRITE PRINT-LINE FROM LOCATION-HEADING-LINE
260                  AFTER ADVANCING 1 LINE.
261
262          440-PROCESS-ONE-SALESPERSON.
263              PERFORM 500-INITIALIZE-SALESPERSON.
264              PERFORM 520-WRITE-SALESPERSON-HEADING.
265              PERFORM 540-PROCESS-ONE-TRANSACTION
266                  UNTIL SR-NAME NOT EQUAL PREVIOUS-NAME
267                      OR SR-LOCATION NOT EQUAL PREVIOUS-LOCATION
268                          OR SR-REGION NOT EQUAL PREVIOUS-REGION
269                              OR NO-DATA-REMAINS.
270              PERFORM 560-WRITE-SALESPERSON-TOTAL.
271              PERFORM 580-INCREMENT-LOCATION-TOTAL.
272
273          460-WRITE-LOCATION-TOTAL.
274              MOVE LOCATION-SALES-TOT TO LOCATION-SALES-TOTAL.
275              MOVE LOCATION-COMM-TOT TO LOCATION-COMM-TOTAL.
276              WRITE PRINT-LINE FROM LOCATION-TOTAL-LINE
277                  AFTER ADVANCING 1 LINE.
278              MOVE SPACES TO PRINT-LINE.
279              WRITE PRINT-LINE
280                  AFTER ADVANCING 1 LINE.
281
282          480-INCREMENT-REGION-TOTAL.
283              ADD LOCATION-SALES-TOT TO REGION-SALES-TOT.
284              ADD LOCATION-COMM-TOT TO REGION-COMM-TOT.          Location totals are rolled into region totals
285
286          500-INITIALIZE-SALESPERSON.
287              MOVE SR-NAME TO PREVIOUS-NAME.
```

Figure 15.10   *(continued)*

```
288              INITIALIZE SALESPERSON-TOTALS.
289
290      520-WRITE-SALESPERSON-HEADING.
291          MOVE SR-NAME TO HDG-NAME.
292          WRITE PRINT-LINE FROM SALESPERSON-HEADING-LINE-ONE
293              AFTER ADVANCING 1 LINE.
294          WRITE PRINT-LINE FROM SALESPERSON-HEADING-LINE-TWO
295              AFTER ADVANCING 1 LINE.
296
297      540-PROCESS-ONE-TRANSACTION.
298          PERFORM 600-CALCULATE-COMMISSION.
299          PERFORM 620-WRITE-DETAIL-LINE.
300          PERFORM 640-INCREMENT-SALESPERSON-TOTAL.
301          PERFORM 220-READ-SORTED-SALES-FILE.
302
303      560-WRITE-SALESPERSON-TOTAL.
304          WRITE PRINT-LINE FROM DASHED-LINE
305              AFTER ADVANCING 1 LINE.
306          MOVE SALESPERSON-SALES-TOT TO SALESPERSON-SALES-TOTAL.
307          MOVE SALESPERSON-COMM-TOT TO SALESPERSON-COMM-TOTAL.
308          WRITE PRINT-LINE FROM SALESPERSON-TOTAL-LINE
309              AFTER ADVANCING 1 LINE.
310          MOVE SPACES TO PRINT-LINE.
311          WRITE PRINT-LINE
312              AFTER ADVANCING 1 LINE.
313
314      580-INCREMENT-LOCATION-TOTAL.
315          ADD SALESPERSON-SALES-TOT TO LOCATION-SALES-TOT.
316          ADD SALESPERSON-COMM-TOT TO LOCATION-COMM-TOT.
317
318      600-CALCULATE-COMMISSION.
319          COMPUTE IND-COMMISSION ROUNDED =
320              SR-SALES * SR-COMMISSION-PERCENT
321              SIZE ERROR DISPLAY 'SIZE ERROR ON COMMISSION FOR '
322                  SR-NAME
323          END-COMPUTE.
324
325      620-WRITE-DETAIL-LINE.
326          MOVE SR-ACCOUNT-NUMBER TO DET-ACCOUNT-NUMBER.
327          MOVE SR-SALES TO DET-SALES.
328          MOVE IND-COMMISSION TO DET-COMMISSION.
329          WRITE PRINT-LINE FROM DETAIL-LINE.
330
331      640-INCRMENT-SALESPERSON-TOTAL.
332          ADD SR-SALES TO SALESPERSON-SALES-TOT.
333          ADD IND-COMMISSION TO SALESPERSON-COMM-TOT.
```

Salesperson totals are rolled into location totals

PROGRAMMING TIP

How to Write a Control Break Program

The algorithm for one-, two-, and three-level control breaks follows a general pattern that can be adopted for any control break application and/or any number of levels. We suggest, therefore, that you review the hierarchy chart, pseudocode, and/or COBOL programs that were developed in this chapter and see how those examples fit a general pattern.

Start by determining the number of levels in the application, their relative importance (sort order), and corresponding field names. Identify the field names that will be used to detect a control break at each level—for example, **SR-REGION**, **SR-LOCATION**, and **SR-NAME** in the three-level example used in the text.

Modify the hierarchy chart, pseudocode, and COBOL listings from the chapter to accommodate your specific application. Begin with the highest (most important) level and do the following for every level:

1. Initialize the control totals for this level

2. Initialize the field name to detect a control break at this level with the previous value

3. Write the heading for this level (if any)

4. Process this level until the field name at this level is not equal to the previous value

   OR the field name at a higher level is not equal to the previous value

   OR no data remains

5. Write this level's total (if required)

6. Increment the next higher level's total (rolling total)

At the lowest (transaction) level:

1. Perform the necessary calculations (if any)

2. Write a detail line (if any)

3. Increment the lowest level's total (running total)

4. Read the next record

LIMITATIONS OF COBOL-74

There are no specific enhancements in COBOL-85 intended to facilitate the processing of control breaks. Accordingly, all of the listings in this chapter could be made to run under COBOL-74 with only minor modification, such as the removal of the END-READ scope terminator, and the WITH DUPLICATES clause in the sort statement; the latter would require an additional sort key on account number.

SUMMARY

Points to Remember

■ A control break is a change in a designated (control) field; any file used to process control breaks must be in sequence according to the control field.

■ Control breaks may occur at multiple levels; for example, a two-level control break occurs when two control fields change simultaneously; in similar fashion a three-level control break occurs when three control fields change simultaneously.

■ There is no theoretical limit to the number of control breaks; there is a practical limit, however, in that most people lose track after three (or at most four) levels.

■ Programs for one-, two-, and three-level control breaks are developed according to a general algorithm; the importance of a hierarchy chart and pseudocode in the design process cannot be over-emphasized.

■ A running total is incremented by the value of the corresponding field in every transaction; a rolling total is incremented by a lower-level-control total only after a control break has occurred; rolling totals are more efficient than running totals.

Key Words and Concepts

Compound condition	Pseudocode
Control field	Rolling total
Control total	Running total
Control break	Three-level control break
Hierarchy chart	Two-level control break
One-level control break	

Fill-in

1. A _____ in a designated field is known as a _____ _____.

2. Any file used to process control breaks must be in _____ according to the control fields.

3. It (<u>is/is not</u>) possible for data in a given record to produce a control break on more than one field.

4. Control break processing (<u>is/is not</u>) limited to one level.

5. A program's hierarchy chart is best developed (<u>before/after</u>) the program is written.

6. The more significant field in a two-level control break application is known as the _____ field, whereas the less significant field is the _____ field.

7. (Pseudocode/hierarchy charts) depict a program's logic and decision-making sequence.

8. A COBOL program to process control breaks (requires/does not require) the file to be in sequence.

9. Running totals are (more/less) efficient than rolling totals.

10. A _____ total increments the value of a counter after every record.

11. A _____ total increments the value of a counter after a control break.

True/False

1. Control break processing is restricted to a single level.

2. Input to a control break program need not be in any special order.

3. Modules in a hierarchy chart and paragraphs in a COBOL program correspond one to one.

4. A hierarchy chart depicts decision-making logic.

5. Each level in a hierarchy chart corresponds to a COBOL PERFORM statement.

6. A two-level control break occurs when two control fields change simultaneously.

7. A three-level control break implies the occurrence of one- and two-level control breaks as well.

8. A three-level control breaks requires that three control totals be computed at each level.

9. Rolling totals is a more efficient means of computation than running totals

10. A rolling total increments a counter for every transaction.

Problems

1. Return once more to the two-level program in Figure 15.8 and note that the PERFORM statement to detect a break in salesperson (lines 188–190) includes the clause SR-LOCATION NOT EQUAL PREVIOUS-LOCATION. Why? (What would happen if this clause were not present and the last salesperson in one location had the same name as the first salesperson in the next location?) State a generalized rule for the compound condition in PERFORM statements that is needed to detect control breaks.

2. What would be the consequences of omitting the SORT statement in the one-level control break program of Figure 15.6; that is, describe the appearance of the resulting report if the unsorted transaction file of Figure 15.1 were used in lieu of the sorted file in Figure 15.2a. Explain in general terms the consequences of omitting the SORT statement in any of the programs contained in the chapter.

3. The one-level program of Figure 15.6 uses the data names SALESPERSON-SALES-TOT and COMPANY-SALES-TOT to accumulate totals.

   a. Which data name(s) are computed as a *running* total? When, and by what amount, is the total incremented?

   b. Which data name(s) are computed as a *rolling* total? When, and by what amount, is the total incremented?

     c. Repeat parts (a) and (b) for the two-level program of Figure 15.8. Answer for the data names SALESPERSON-SALES-TOT, LOCATION-SALES-TOT, and COMPANY-SALES-TOT.

     d. Repeat parts (a) and (b) for the three-level program of Figure 15.10. Answer for the data names SALESPERSON-SALES-TOT, LOCATION-SALES-TOT, REGION-SALES-TOT, and COMPANY-SALES-TOT.

4. The hypothetical Continental University is composed of multiple colleges, with each college divided into multiple departments. The central administration wants to know the total number of students in a variety of categories and uses a university-wide ENROLLMENT-FILE to compute the desired totals. The following fields are present in each enrollment record: COLLEGE, DEPARTMENT, YEAR, NUMBER-OF-STUDENTS. Identify the control fields and sorting sequence to produce each of the following reports. (Each report is to be treated independently.)

     a. The number of students in each year

     b. The number of students in each department

     c. The number of students in each college

     d. The number of students in each college and within college, the number of students in each department

     e. The number of students in each college and within college, the number of students in each year

Subprograms

CHAPTER OUTLINE

Overview
Subprograms
    Called and Calling Programs
    COPY Statement
    Calling BY CONTENT and BY REFERENCE
INITIAL Clause
A System for Physical Fitness
    Programming Specifications
    Hierarchy Chart
    Pseudocode
The Completed Programs
    Main Program (FITNESS)
    Input Program (INPUTSUB)
    Weight-Range Program (WGTSUB)
    Training Program (TRAINSUB)
    Display Program (DSPLYSUB)
    Time Program (TIMESUB)
The Linkage Editor
    Problems with the Linkage Editor
Limitations of COBOL-74
Summary
Fill-in
True/False
Problems

O B J E C T I V E S

After reading this chapter you will be able to:

■ Define a subprogram and describe its implementation in COBOL.

■ Distinguish between a called and calling program; describe the use of a hierarchy chart to show the relationship of programs within a system.

■ State the purpose of the COPY statement; indicate where it may be used within a program and how it can be used to pass a parameter list.

■ Distinguish between the BY CONTENT and BY REFERENCE clauses as they relate to subprograms.

■ Explain the function of the INITIAL phrase in the PROGRAM-ID paragraph.

■ Describe the purpose of the linkage-editor; explain the meaning of an unresolved external reference.

O V E R V I E W

This chapter introduces the concept of subprograms in order to develop a system of programs associated with physical fitness. Each program is compiled as a separate entity, after which the individual object programs are linked together to produce a single load module. The chapter includes material on all necessary COBOL elements as well as a conceptual discussion on the role of the link program (linkage-editor).

The COBOL presentation begins with the CALL statement and associated parameter list in the calling program, then presents the relationship with data names defined in the LINKAGE SECTION of the called program. It describes the different ways of passing parameters, either BY REFERENCE or BY CONTENT, and introduces the COPY statement as a means of simplifying program development.

The chapter also serves as an effective review of earlier material in that the various subprograms utilize many features from previous chapters. Thus, we once again emphasize the importance of data validation from Chapter 8, illustrate advanced statements from the Procedure Division as covered in Chapter 9, review the screen I/O capabilities presented in Chapter 10, and incorporate material on both one- and two-level tables from Chapters 11 through 13.

Subprograms

The PERFORM statement has been used throughout the text to divide a program into functional paragraphs, each of which is executed as necessary from elsewhere within the program. The individual paragraphs are developed in stages and implemented in hierarchical fashion through top-down testing. The individual paragraphs are, in effect, subroutines that are written, compiled, and executed within the main program.

Alternatively, the performed routines may be developed as independent entities, known as *subprograms,* that are written and compiled separately from the *main (calling) program*. The subprograms within the same system may even be written by different programmers, but they are always executed under control of the main program. Subprograms bring to a system all the advantages of modularity that functional paragraphs bring to a program; for example, a change in one subprogram should not affect the internal workings of another subprogram nor the overall flow of the system. And, like the paragraphs in a program, the subprograms in a system may be developed and tested in top-down fashion.

A subprogram contains the four divisions of a regular program, and in addition, a LINKAGE SECTION in its Data Division to hold the data passed to and from the calling program. Figure 16.1 contains statements extracted from the listings at the end of the chapter to illustrate the use of subprograms. In this example, the calling program contains the logic to accept personal data from a user regarding the individual's height, age, and sex. It passes control to the sub (called) program WGTSUB, which determines the ideal range for the person's weight based on the data received. The CALL statement in the calling program matches the entry in the PROGRAM-ID paragraph of the called program (WGTSUB).

The CALL statement transfers control to the first executable statement in the called program. The CALL statement contains a USING clause, which specifies the data on which the called program is to operate. The called program in turn contains a USING clause in its Procedure Division header, indicating which data it is to receive from the calling program. The data names in either USING clause are known collectively as the *parameter* or *argument list*.

The data names in the two parameter lists can (but need not) be the same, but the order and structure of data names within the list is critical. The first item in the parameter list of the calling program is FITNESS-RECORD, and corresponds to the first item in the parameter list of the called program, which is also called FITNESS-RECORD. In similar fashion, the second and third items in the calling program (WEIGHT-FROM and WEIGHT-TO) correspond to the second and third items in the subroutine (LS-WEIGHT-FROM and LS-WEIGHT-TO). The picture clauses of the individual parameters (arguments) are the same, but the data names are different.

The arguments in the calling program are defined either in the File Section or in Working-Storage, whereas the arguments in the called program must be defined in the *Linkage Section*. The parameters in either program must be defined as 01 or elementary items; that is, group items (other than 01 entries) cannot be passed to a subprogram.

Execution of the CALL statement in the main program transfers control to the first executable statement of the subprogram, which executes exactly as a regular COBOL program; the latter is terminated by an EXIT PROGRAM statement that returns control to the calling program at the statement immediately after the CALL.

Called and Calling Programs

The example in Figure 16.1 included only two programs, one calling program and one called program. More complex arrangements are also possible, for example:

Figure 16.1 COBOL Statements for a Subprogram

```
IDENTIFICATION DIVISION.
PROGRAM-ID.    FITNESS.
    .
    .

DATA DIVISION.
FILE SECTION.
FD  FITNESS-FILE
    DATA RECORD IS FITNESS-RECORD.
01  FITNESS-RECORD.
    05  FULL-NAME           PIC X(19).
    05  HEIGHT              PIC 99.
    05  SEX                 PIC X.
    05  AGE                 PIC 99.
    .

WORKING-STORAGE SECTION.
    .

    05  WEIGHT-FROM         PIC 9(3).
    05  WEIGHT-TO           PIC 9(3).
    .

PROCEDURE DIVISION.
    .

    CALL WGTSUB
        USING FITNESS-RECORD, WEIGHT-FROM, WEIGHT-TO
    END-CALL.
    .
    .
```

Transfers control to first executable statement in called program

(a) Main Program

```
IDENTIFICATION DIVISION.
PROGRAM-ID.    WGTSUB.
    .

LINKAGE SECTION.
01  LS-WEIGHT-FROM          PIC 9(3).
01  LS-WEIGHT-TO            PIC 9(3).
01  FITNESS-RECORD.
    05  FULL-NAME           PIC X(19).
    05  HEIGHT              PIC 99.
    05  SEX                 PIC X.
    05  AGE                 PIC 99.
    .

PROCEDURE DIVISION
    USING FITNESS-RECORD, LS-WEIGHT-FROM, LS-WEIGHT-TO.
    .

    EXIT PROGRAM.
```

Contains the arguments for the subprogram

Returns control to calling program

(b) Subprogram

1. One program can call multiple subprograms; for example, program A can call programs B, C, D, and E.

2. One program can be called from different programs; for example, program F can be called from programs B and C.

3. The same program can be both a called and calling program; for example, program A calls program B, which in turn calls program F. (Program B is both a called and calling program.)

A hierarchy chart depicts the relationship of various programs to one another within a system, just as it shows the relationship of paragraphs within a program. The hierarchy chart in Figure 16.2, for example, illustrates the relationships just expressed. Thus, program A sits at the top of the hierarchy chart and calls programs B, C, D, and E. Program F is shown twice in the hierarchy chart, indicating that it (program F) is called from programs B and C. Programs B and C function as both called and calling programs; they are called from program A and in turn call program F.

Figure 16.2 Called and Calling Programs

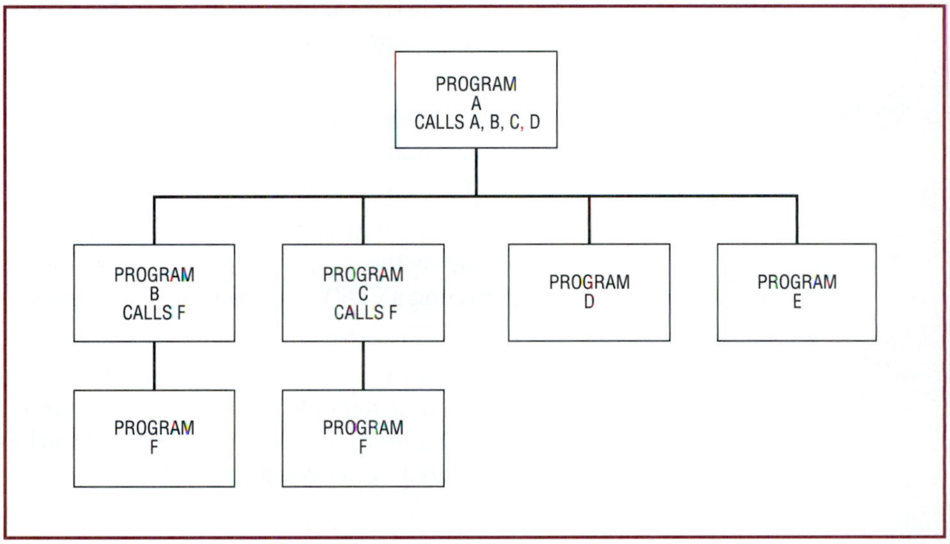

The COPY Statement

The data names used within different programs of the same system are often interrelated because the same file is apt to be referenced by several programs. The **COPY** statement facilitates the development of such programs by allowing the programmer to code a one-line COPY statement, which brings the associated entries into the COBOL program.

Figure 16.3 contains a COPY statement in which the programmer coded the line COPY TRAINCPY in line 27. The COBOL compiler locates the file TRAINCPY, and brings in lines 28–34 as though the programmer had coded them explicitly. The COBOL97 editor does not actually show the COPY files as part of the source listing. We show them here so that you can see how they work.

A COPY statement may be used anywhere within a COBOL program, *except that the text being copied cannot contain another COPY.* The syntax of the COPY statement is simply:

```
COPY text-name
```

Figure 16.3　The COPY Statement

```
27              COPY TRAINCPY.
28C      01 TRAINING-ARGUMENTS.
29C          05  TRAINING-INPUTS.
30C              10  TRAIN-AGE              PIC 99.
31C              10  TRAIN-FITNESS-LEVEL    PIC X.
32C          05  TRAINING-RANGES.
33C              10  TRAIN-OVERALL-RANGE    PIC X(5).
34C              10  TRAIN-FITNESS-RANGE    PIC X(5).
```

where text-name is the name of a file (member, or element) that exists independently of the COBOL program. A COPY statement is not restricted to subprograms; it can be used with any COBOL program. COPY statements offer the following advantages:

1. Individual programmers need not code the extensive Data Division entries that can make COBOL so tedious; a programmer can code a one-line COPY statement, and the compiler will bring the proper entries into the program.

2. Any change that affects multiple programs is made only once, in the library version of the COPY element. Subsequent compilations of all programs containing a COPY statement for that element will automatically bring in the updated version.

3. Programming errors are reduced through standardization and common definition of data elements. All fields within a record description (or other copied element) in one program will always be correct and consistent with the definition in other programs using the same copied element.

Calling BY CONTENT and BY REFERENCE

One of the most important principles of structured design is program independence, which minimizes (eliminates) the effect one program has on another. The optional **USING BY CONTENT** phrase prevents the values of parameters created in the calling program from being changed by the called program. Consider:

```
CALL program  [USING {[BY REFERENCE] identifier-2 . . .} . . .]
                     {BY CONTENT     identifier-3 . . .}

[END-CALL]
```

and an example:

```
CALL 'SUBRIN'  USING FIELD-A
   BY CONTENT FIELD-B FIELD-C
   BY REFERENCE FIELD-D.
```

The CALL statement passes four arguments, FIELD-A, FIELD-B, FIELD-C, and FIELD-D, to a subprogram that manipulates any or all of these parameters (referring to them by its own data names as defined in its LINKAGE SECTION). However, the USING BY CONTENT phrase will restore the values of FIELD-B and FIELD-C to their initial values when control is returned to the calling program, despite any changes made to the corresponding parameters by the called program.

The order of arguments in the **CALL USING** and **PROCEDURE DIVISION USING** clauses of the calling and called programs is critical. You can reduce the chance for error by using a **COPY** clause to pass parameters as shown. Consider:

Poor Code:

```
CALL 'WGTSUB'
    USING HEIGHT, SEX, AGE, WEIGHT-FROM, WEIGHT-TO
END-CALL.


PROCEDURE DIVISION
    USING LS-HEIGHT, LS-SEX, LS-AGE, LS-WGT-FROM, LS-WGT-TO.
```

Improved Code:

```
    COPY WGTLST.
01 WEIGHT-TABLE-ARGUMENTS.
    05  WT-HEIGHT      PIC 99.
    05  WT-SEX         PIC X.
    05  WT-AGE         PIC 99.
    05  WT-FROM        PIC 9(3).
    05  WT-TO          PIC 9(3).


    CALL 'WGTSUB'
        USING WEIGHT-TABLE-ARGUMENTS
    END-CALL.

LINKAGE SECTION.
    COPY WGTLST.
01 WEIGHT-TABLE-ARGUMENTS.
    05  WT-HEIGHT      PIC 99.
    05  WT-SEX         PIC X.
    05  WT-AGE         PIC 99.
    05  WT-FROM        PIC 9(3).
    05  WT-TO          PIC 9(3).


    PROCEDURE DIVISION
        USING WEIGHT-TABLE-ARGUMENTS.
```

Use of the single **01** parameter facilitates coding in the **USING** clauses and also makes them immune to change. Use of the same **COPY** member in both programs eliminates any problem with listing arguments in the wrong order or inconsistent definition through different pictures.

No such restriction is placed on the value of FIELD-A, which will retain any value computed in the called program. The value of FIELD-D will also reflect changes made by the called program, as it (FIELD-D) was specified in a **USING BY REFERENCE** phrase; that is, USING BY REFERENCE is equivalent to a CALL statement with neither phrase.

INITIAL Clause

The **INITIAL** clause in the PROGRAM-ID paragraph restores a program to its initial state each time it is called; that is, all data names in Working-Storage are reset to their original values via any VALUE clauses that are present. Consider:

```
PROGRAM-ID. program-name [IS INITIAL PROGRAM].
```

The INITIAL clause makes it possible to start with an original (unmodified) copy of a called program every time it is executed. Alternatively, omission of the phrase causes every execution of a called program to begin with the values established in the latest (previous) execution.

A System for Physical Fitness

The material on subprograms will be incorporated into a system for physical fitness that obtains input from a user, determines various aspects of the individual's fitness, then displays the results at the end of processing. The individual programs illustrate the transfer of control and passing of parameters between a called and calling program, and also review COBOL material from earlier chapters as described in the chapter overview.

Programming Specifications

Program Name: Physical Fitness System

Narrative: The specifications call for a series of programs that constitute a system for physical fitness. A screen I/O program will accept and verify various inputs from a user, such as age, sex, and height, then pass control to a series of subprograms to compute the desired weight and target heart range at different levels of fitness.

Input Files: There are no input or output files as all data are entered and displayed interactively via screen I/O. Figure 16.4 contains a sample screen for a hypothetical individual named Mr. Fit. The inputs provided by Mr. Fit are highlighted in the top half of the screen. The diagnostic messages produced by the system show Mr. Fit's weight of 185 to be within the desired range for his age, sex, and height. The system also suggests a target (10-second) heart rate (after exercise) between 27 and 30 in accordance with his advanced fitness level.

Processing Requirements: 1. Develop a series of programs that constitute a system for physical fitness as described below:

   a. A main program to govern the overall system and pass control to various subprograms as appropriate

   b. A subprogram to accept and validate an individual's personal data

   c. A subprogram to compute a goal weight based on an individual's sex, height, and age.

   d. A subprogram to compute a target heart rate (after sustained cardiovascular exercise) based on age and fitness level

   e. A subprogram to display the computed results for weight and target heart rate

2. The main program is to control the overall system by passing (receiving) control from the various subprograms. The system is to execute continually—that is, for multiple individuals—until it receives a response that no one else wishes to use the system.

3. The input program is to accept the following fields as indicated in Figure 16.4: Name, Age, Sex, Weight, Height, and Fitness level. Validation checks are required as follows:

   a. A name must be entered

   b. Age must be 18 or higher

   c. Sex must be male or female; the system should accept both upper- and lowercase letters as valid characters.

   d. Height is to be entered in inches and must be consistent with the tables available to the system; valid male heights are between 60 and 76 inches; valid female heights must be between 54 and 74 inches.

   e. The fitness level should be entered as a single letter, B, I, or A, corresponding to Beginner, Intermediate, or Advanced. The system should accept both upper- and lowercase letters as valid characters.

   The input program is to display appropriate prompts and error messages for each of these fields. In addition, it should also display the current time as shown in the upper right portion of Figure 16.4.

4. The goal weight is determined from a person's sex, height, and age as shown in the tables of Figure 16.5.

5. The minimum and maximum target (training) heart ranges, expressed for a 10-second period after exercise, are determined from an individual's age according to the formulas:

```
Minimum target (10 seconds) = .60 * (220 - AGE) / 6
Maximum target (10 seconds) = .90 * (220 - AGE) / 6
```

   The target range can also be adjusted according to the individual's fitness level and the range between the maximum and minimum values; that is, those at a beginner's level of fitness should aim for a target heart range in the lower third of the interval, those with intermediate fitness in the middle third, and those at an advanced level in the upper third.

Figure 16.4   Fitness Screen

```
        Personal Fitness Evaluation                      11:53:10

    Full Name: Mr. Fit

    Age: 22           Weight: 185        Fitness Level: A
    Sex (M/F): M      Height: 74          B - Beginner
                                          I - Intermediate
                                          A - Advanced

    Your Goal Weight Range: 163-196
      CONGRATULATIONS! You are within the range

    Training Heart Rate Range Information (10 Second)
      Overall Heart Rate Range: 20-30
      Adjusted for Fitness Level: 27-30


        Another Person (Y/N):
```

Figure 16.5   Table of Goal Weights

Height (in inches)	Age (in years)				
	18	**19-20**	**21-22**	**23-24**	**25 & Over**
54	83-99	84-101	85-103	86-104	88-106
55	84-100	85-102	86-104	88-105	90-107
56	86-101	87-103	88-105	90-106	92-108
57	89-102	90-104	91-106	92-108	94-110
58	91-105	92-106	93-109	94-111	96-113
59	93-109	94-111	95-113	96-114	99-116
60	96-112	97-113	98-115	100-117	102-119
61	100-116	101-117	102-119	103-121	105-122
62	104-119	105-121	106-123	107-125	108-126
63	106-125	107-126	108-127	109-129	111-130
64	109-130	110-131	111-132	112-134	114-135
65	112-133	113-134	114-136	116-138	118-139
66	116-137	117-138	118-140	120-142	122-143
67	121-140	122-142	123-144	124-146	126-147
68	123-144	124-146	126-148	128-150	130-150
69	130-148	131-150	132-152	133-154	134-155
70	134-151	135-154	136-156	137-158	138-159
71	138-155	139-158	140-160	141-162	142-163
72	142-160	143-162	144-164	145-166	146-167
73	146-164	147-166	148-168	149-170	150-171
74	150-168	151-170	152-172	153-174	154-175

(a) Goal Weights for Women

Height (in inches)	Age (in years)				
	18	**19-20**	**21-22**	**23-24**	**25 & Over**
60	109-122	110-133	112-135	114-137	115-138
61	112-126	113-136	115-138	117-140	118-141
62	115-130	116-139	118-140	120-142	121-144
63	118-135	119-143	121-145	123-147	124-148
64	120-145	122-147	124-149	126-151	127-152
65	124-149	125-151	127-153	129-155	130-156
66	128-154	129-156	131-158	133-160	134-161
67	132-159	133-161	134-158	136-165	138-166
68	135-163	136-165	138-167	140-169	142-170
69	140-163	141-169	142-171	144-173	146-174
70	143-170	144-173	146-175	148-178	150-179
71	147-177	148-179	150-181	152-183	154-184
72	151-180	152-184	154-186	156-188	158-189
73	155-187	156-189	158-190	160-193	162-194
74	160-192	161-194	163-196	165-198	167-199
75	165-198	166-199	168-201	170-203	172-204
76	170-202	171-204	173-206	175-208	177-209

(b) Goal Weights for Men

Hierarchy Chart

The hierarchy chart has been used throughout the text to indicate the required functions within a COBOL program. It can also be used to indicate the relationship of programs within a system as shown in Figure 16.6.

Figure 16.6   Hierarchy Chart of the Overall System

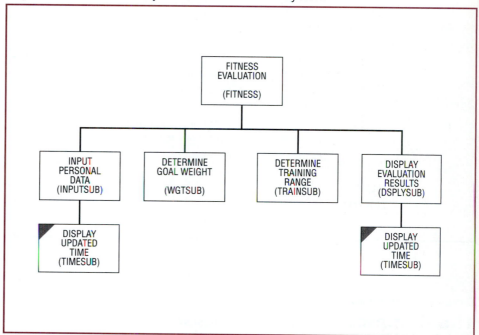

The module at the top of the hierarchy chart, FITNESS-EVALUATION, is the main program for the overall system; it has four subordinates (subprograms) in accordance with the processing specifications: INPUT-PERSONAL-DATA, DETERMINE-GOAL-WEIGHT, DETERMINE-TRAINING-RANGE, and DISPLAY-EVALUATION-RESULTS. (The entries in parentheses correspond to the name of the program as it appears in the PROGRAM-ID paragraph.) A sixth program, DISPLAY-UPDATED-TIME, is subordinate to the programs to accept and display the data.

Pseudocode

The logic for the overall system (main program) is contained in the pseudocode of Figure 16.7. The main program is driven by a single loop to process multiple individuals (as per the second processing specification) until a negative response is received regarding continuation. This is consistent with the corresponding prompt at the bottom of Figure 16.4, which asks whether there is another user.

The logic within the loop is straightforward and passes control from one subprogram to the next in sequential fashion. Note, however, the requirement to establish a parameter list prior to calling each subprogram, and further, how the parameter lists for the different subprograms contain different variables. Observe also that the parameter list for the last program references *another-person-switch*, which determines whether execution is to continue.

Figure 16.7   Pseudocode

```
      ┌── DO WHILE user wants to continue

               CALL INPUTSUB subprogram to get personal information

               Establish parameter list (height, age, sex, weight-from, weight-to)
                   for WGTSUB program
               Call WGTSUB program to determine weight goals

               Establish parameter list (age, fitness-level, overall-range,
                   fitness-range) for TRAINSUB program
               Call TRAINSUB program to determine training ranges

               Establish parameter list (training ranges, weight-goals,
                   another-person-switch) for DSPLYSUB program
               Call DSPLYSUB program to display results and request continuation

      └── ENDDO
           Stop run
```

The Completed Programs

The next several pages contain listings for the completed programs according to the description in Table 16.1. We have, however, in the interest of space, omitted the pseudocode and hierarchy chart for the individual programs.

Main Program (FITNESS)

The main program in Figure 16.8 contains neither an Environment Division nor a File Section as all input/output operations are accomplished via the screen. The Working-Storage Section consists largely of four COPY statements corresponding to the parameter lists for each of the four called programs. The programmer codes a single statement, such as COPY INPUTREC in line 10. The compiler locates the file INPUTREC and brings in lines 11 through 26 as though the programmer had coded them explicitly.

The mainline paragraph in lines 69–76 corresponds exactly to the pseudocode in Figure 16.7. The INITIALIZE statement in line 79 clears the parameters passed to the input program and is necessary so that the input values from one user are not carried over to the next user. The CALL statement in lines 80–82 transfers control to the input subprogram, using a single parameter, INPUT-INFORMATION, which is copied into both programs.

A different parameter list is created immediately prior to calling each of the remaining subprograms; for example, lines 85–87 move the data names for age, height, and sex—obtained from the input subprogram—to the corresponding data names in the parameter list for the weight program. Observe also how the CALL statement uses a single 01 entry, WEIGHT-ARGUMENTS, as the parameter list and further, how the entry is copied into the program (line 40). The same technique is used prior to the CALL statement for the training program in lines 95–97, and prior to the CALL statement for the final display program in lines 105–107.

Table 16.1 Physical Fitness System

PROGRAM-ID	Called/Calling Programs	Figure #	Description
FITNESS	Calls INPUTSUB, WGTSUB, TRAINSUB, and DSPLYSUB	Figure 16.8	The main program governs the overall system; it passes control to the input subprogram, which accepts input from the user, passes control to the weight and training programs, then passes control to the display subprogram that displays the calculated results. The main program executes continually until the user elects to exit.
INPUTSUB	Called from FITNESS; calls TIMESUB	Figure 16.9	The input subprogram obtains all required inputs from the user (name, age, sex, height, and fitness level), validating each field as it is entered. The program reviews the screen section that was first presented in Chapter 10.
WGTSUB	Called from FITNESS	Figure 16.10	The weight subprogram accepts an individual's sex, height, and age, then determines a range for the person's desired weight. The program reviews two-level tables as presented in Chapter 12.
TRAINSUB	Called from FITNESS	Figure 16.11	The training subprogram determines an individual's target heart rate according to age and fitness level. The program reviews various Procedure Division statements and scope terminators from earlier chapters.
DSPLYSUB	Called from FITNESS; calls TIMESUB	Figure 16.12	The display subprogram updates the original screen created by the input program, using various options for the ACCEPT and DISPLAY statements, thus reviewing additional material from Chapter 10.
TIMESUB	Called from INPUTSUB and DSPLYSUB	Figure 16.13	The time subprogram is included to show that a subprogram need not contain a Linkage Section, and further that it can be called from multiple calling programs. It also illustrates the means of obtaining the current time from the system and reference modification.

Figure 16.8 Fitness Program

```
1       IDENTIFICATION DIVISION.
2       PROGRAM-ID.      FITNESS.
3       AUTHOR.          CVV.
4
5       DATA DIVISION.
6       WORKING-STORAGE SECTION.
7       01  FILLER                  PIC X(36)
8           VALUE 'WS BEGINS HERE FOR FITNESS PROGRAM'.
9
```

Figure 16.8   *(continued)*

```
 10              COPY INPUTREC.
STCPY>      01  INPUT-INFORMATION.
 12              05  INP-FULL-NAME           PIC X(30).
 13                  88  MISSING-NAME                VALUE SPACES.
 14              05  INP-AGE                 PIC 99.
 15                  88  INVALID-AGES                VALUES 0 THRU 17.
 16              05  INP-SEX                 PIC X.
 17                  88  VALID-SEX                   VALUES 'M' 'm' 'F' 'f'.
 18                  88  MALE                        VALUES 'M' 'm'.
 19                  88  FEMALE                      VALUES 'F' 'f'.
 20              05  INP-HEIGHT              PIC 99.
 21              05  INP-WEIGHT              PIC 9(3).
 22                  88  INVALID-WEIGHTS
 23                      VALUES 0 THRU 70 500 THRU 999.
 24              05  INP-FITNESS-LEVEL       PIC X.
 25                  88  VALID-FITNESS-LEVELS
EDCPY>                  VALUES 'B' 'I' 'A' 'b' 'i' 'a'.
 27
 28              COPY TRAINCPY.
STCPY>      01  TRAINING-ARGUMENTS.
 30              05  TRAINING-INPUTS.
 31                  10  TRAIN-AGE           PIC 99.
 32                  10  TRAIN-FITNESS-LEVEL PIC X.
 33                      88  BEGINNER                VALUE 'B' 'b'.
 34                      88  INTERMEDIATE            VALUE 'I' 'i'.
 35                      88  ADVANCED                VALUE 'A' 'a'.
 36              05  TRAINING-RANGES.
 37                  10  TRAIN-OVERALL-RANGE PIC X(5).
EDCPY>              10  TRAIN-FITNESS-RANGE PIC X(5).
 39
 40              COPY WGTCOPY.
STCPY>      01  WEIGHT-ARGUMENTS.
 42              05  WEIGHT-TABLE-INPUTS.
 43                  10  WGT-HEIGHT          PIC 99.
 44                  10  WGT-AGE             PIC 99.
 45                  10  WGT-SEX             PIC X.
 46                      88  MALE                    VALUE 'M' 'm'.
 47                      88  FEMALE                  VALUE 'F' 'f'.
 48              05  WEIGHT-GOALS.
 49                  10  GOAL-WGT-FROM       PIC 999.
EDCPY>              10  GOAL-WGT-TO         PIC 999.
 51
 52              COPY DISPCPY.
STCPY>      01  DISPLAY-ARGUMENTS.
 54              05  DISP-TRAINING-RANGES.
 55                  10  DISP-TRAIN-OVERALL-RANGE  PIC X(5).
 56                  10  DISP-TRAIN-FITNESS-RANGE  PIC X(5).
 57              05  DISP-WEIGHT-GOALS.
 58                  10  DISP-GOAL-WGT-FROM  PIC ZZ9.
 59                  10  DISP-GOAL-WGT-TO    PIC ZZ9.
```

Record description is copied into program

Lowercase responses are accepted

Start of COPY AREA

End of COPY AREA

Figure 16.8 *(continued)*

```
60              05  DISP-INPUT-WEIGHT           PIC 9(3).
61              05  ANOTHER-PERSON-SWITCH       PIC X  VALUE SPACES.
62                  88  NO-MORE-PERSONS             VALUE 'N' 'n'.
EDCPY>              88  VALID-ANOTHER               VALUE 'N' 'n' 'Y' 'y'.
64
65          01  FILLER                      PIC X(32)
66                  VALUE 'WS ENDS HERE FOR FITNESS PROGRAM'.
67
68          PROCEDURE DIVISION.
69          000-FITNESS-EVALUATION.
70              PERFORM UNTIL NO-MORE-PERSONS
71                  PERFORM 100-INPUT-PERSONAL-DATA
72                  PERFORM 200-GOAL-WEIGHT-RANGE
73                  PERFORM 300-TRAIN-RATE-RANGE
74                  PERFORM 400-DISPLAY-RESULTS
75              END-PERFORM.
76              STOP RUN.
77
78          100-INPUT-PERSONAL-DATA.
79              INITIALIZE INPUT-INFORMATION.
80              CALL 'INPUTSUB'
81                  USING INPUT-INFORMATION
82              END-CALL.
83
84          200-GOAL-WEIGHT-RANGE.
85              MOVE INP-AGE TO WGT-AGE.
86              MOVE INP-HEIGHT TO WGT-HEIGHT.
87              MOVE INP-SEX TO WGT-SEX.
88              CALL 'WGTSUB'
89                  USING WEIGHT-ARGUMENTS
90              END-CALL.
91
92          300-TRAIN-RATE-RANGE.
93              MOVE INP-AGE TO TRAIN-AGE.
94              MOVE INP-FITNESS-LEVEL TO TRAIN-FITNESS-LEVEL.
95              CALL 'TRAINSUB'
96                  USING TRAINING-ARGUMENTS
97              END-CALL.
98
99          400-DISPLAY-RESULTS.
100             MOVE TRAIN-OVERALL-RANGE TO DISP-TRAIN-OVERALL-RANGE.
101             MOVE TRAIN-FITNESS-RANGE TO DISP-TRAIN-FITNESS-RANGE.
102             MOVE GOAL-WGT-FROM TO DISP-GOAL-WGT-FROM.
103             MOVE GOAL-WGT-TO TO DISP-GOAL-WGT-TO.
104             MOVE INP-WEIGHT TO DISP-INPUT-WEIGHT.
105             CALL 'DSPLYSUB'
106                 USING DISPLAY-ARGUMENTS
107             END-CALL.
```

CALL statement transfers control to called (sub)program

CALL statement transfers control to called (sub)program

Input Program (INPUTSUB)

The input program in Figure 16.9 reviews data validation and screen I/O as presented in Chapter 10. It also functions as a subprogram, and hence the Linkage Section in lines 46–63 which defines the data names passed from the calling (fitness) program. Note the relationship between the CALL statement in the calling program (lines 80–82 in Figure 16.8) and the Procedure Division header in line 113 of this program, both of which contain the 01 entry, INPUT-INFORMATION. The latter is copied into both programs in accordance with the programming tip on page 481.

The input program also contains a second COPY statement, COPY COLORCPY, to define the various colors available with screen I/O. The Screen Section defines an input screen consistent with the display shown earlier in Figure 16.4; it also utilizes various features of screen I/O (line and column positioning, reverse video, and underlining) as presented in Chapter 10.

The Procedure Division accepts and validates the input parameters, one at a time, in accordance with the table of error messages defined in lines 30–41. Each parameter is processed in a separate paragraph, which utilizes the DO UNTIL (TEST AFTER) construct described earlier in Chapters 9 and 10.

Figure 16.9   Input Subprogram

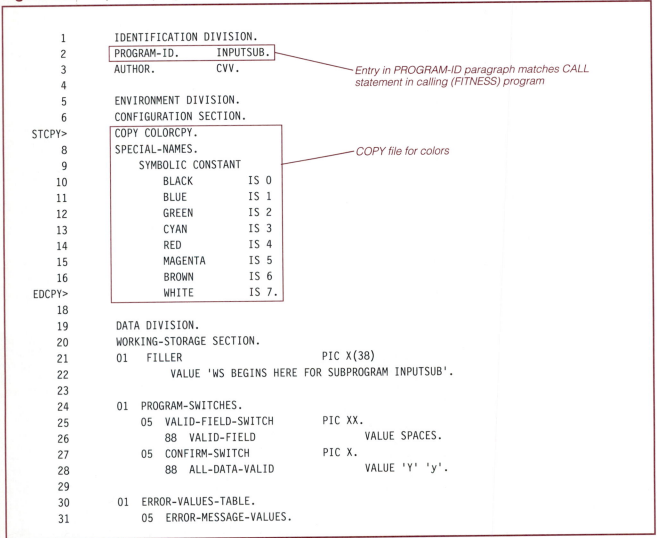

```
     1          IDENTIFICATION DIVISION.
     2          PROGRAM-ID.      INPUTSUB.                    ── Entry in PROGRAM-ID paragraph matches CALL
     3          AUTHOR.          CVV.                            statement in calling (FITNESS) program
     4
     5          ENVIRONMENT DIVISION.
     6          CONFIGURATION SECTION.
STCPY>          COPY COLORCPY.
     8          SPECIAL-NAMES.                               ── COPY file for colors
     9              SYMBOLIC CONSTANT
    10                  BLACK        IS 0
    11                  BLUE         IS 1
    12                  GREEN        IS 2
    13                  CYAN         IS 3
    14                  RED          IS 4
    15                  MAGENTA      IS 5
    16                  BROWN        IS 6
EDCPY>                  WHITE        IS 7.
    18
    19          DATA DIVISION.
    20          WORKING-STORAGE SECTION.
    21          01   FILLER                      PIC X(38)
    22                  VALUE 'WS BEGINS HERE FOR SUBPROGRAM INPUTSUB'.
    23
    24          01   PROGRAM-SWITCHES.
    25              05   VALID-FIELD-SWITCH      PIC XX.
    26                  88  VALID-FIELD              VALUE SPACES.
    27              05   CONFIRM-SWITCH          PIC X.
    28                  88  ALL-DATA-VALID           VALUE 'Y' 'y'.
    29
    30          01   ERROR-VALUES-TABLE.
    31              05   ERROR-MESSAGE-VALUES.
```

Figure 16.9 *(continued)*

```
32              10  PIC X(30) VALUE '      Name must be Entered'.
33              10  PIC X(30) VALUE '       Age must be over 17'.
34              10  PIC X(30) VALUE '      Sex must be M or F'.
35              10  PIC X(30) VALUE '  Weight must be > 70 & < 500'.
36              10  PIC X(30) VALUE '  Male Height must be 60"-76"'.
37              10  PIC X(30) VALUE ' Female Height must be 54"-74"'.
38              10  PIC X(30) VALUE 'Fitness Level must be B I or A'.
39          05  ERROR-MESSAGE-TABLE REDEFINES ERROR-MESSAGE-VALUES.
40              10  ERROR-MESSAGE OCCURS 7 TIMES
41                  INDEXED BY ERROR-INDEX PIC X(30).
42
43      01  FILLER                    PIC X(36)
44              VALUE 'WS ENDS HERE FOR SUBPROGRAM INPUTSUB'.
45
46      LINKAGE SECTION.                 ── Linkage Section contains arguments of called program
STCPY>  COPY INPUTREC.
48      01  INPUT-INFORMATION.
49          05  INP-FULL-NAME         PIC X(30).
50              88  MISSING-NAME          VALUE SPACES.
51          05  INP-AGE               PIC 99.
52              88  INVALID-AGES          VALUES 0 THRU 17.
53          05  INP-SEX               PIC X.
54              88  VALID-SEX             VALUES 'M' 'm' 'F' 'f'.
55              88  MALE                  VALUES 'M' 'm'.
56              88  FEMALE                VALUES 'F' 'f'.
57          05  INP-HEIGHT            PIC 99.
58          05  INP-WEIGHT            PIC 9(3).
59              88  INVALID-WEIGHTS
60                  VALUES 0 THRU 70 500 THRU 999.
61          05  INP-FITNESS-LEVEL     PIC X.
62              88  VALID-FITNESS-LEVELS
EDCPY>              VALUES 'B' 'I' 'A' 'b' 'i' 'a'.
64                                      ── Must be the last section in the Data Division
65      SCREEN SECTION.
66      01  INPUT-SCREEN.
67          05  BLANK SCREEN FOREGROUND-COLOR WHITE
68                           BACKGROUND-COLOR BLUE.
69          05  SCREEN-PROMPTS.
70              10  LINE  1 COLUMN 9
71                  VALUE 'Personal Fitness Evaluation'.
72              10  LINE  3 COLUMN  4  VALUE 'Full Name:'.
73              10  LINE  5 COLUMN  4  VALUE 'Age:'.
74              10  LINE  5 COLUMN 22  VALUE 'Weight:'.
75              10  LINE  5 COLUMN 44  VALUE 'Fitness Level:'.
76              10  LINE  6 COLUMN  4  VALUE 'Sex (M/F):'.
77              10  LINE  6 COLUMN 22  VALUE 'Height:'.
78              10  LINE  6 COLUMN 45  VALUE 'B - Beginner    '
79                  FOREGROUND-COLOR BLACK BACKGROUND-COLOR CYAN.
80              10  LINE  7 COLUMN 45  VALUE 'I - Intermediate'
81                  FOREGROUND-COLOR BLACK BACKGROUND-COLOR CYAN.
```

Figure 16.9   *(continued)*

```
82          10  LINE  8 COLUMN 45   VALUE 'A - Advanced     '
83              FOREGROUND-COLOR BLACK BACKGROUND-COLOR CYAN.
84
85      05  SCREEN-INPUTS.
86          10  SCR-FULL-NAME    LINE  3 COLUMN 15   PIC X(30)
87              USING INP-FULL-NAME REVERSE-VIDEO.
88          10  SCR-AGE          LINE  5 COLUMN  9   PIC 99
89              USING INP-AGE REVERSE-VIDEO REQUIRED AUTO.
90          10  SCR-WEIGHT       LINE  5 COLUMN 30   PIC 999
91              USING INP-WEIGHT REVERSE-VIDEO REQUIRED AUTO.
92          10  SCR-FITNESS-LEVEL LINE  5 COLUMN 59  PIC X
93              USING INP-FITNESS-LEVEL REVERSE-VIDEO AUTO.
94          10  SCR-SEX          LINE  6 COLUMN 15   PIC X
95              USING INP-SEX    REVERSE-VIDEO AUTO.
96          10  SCR-HEIGHT       LINE  6 COLUMN 30   PIC 99
97              USING INP-HEIGHT REVERSE-VIDEO REQUIRED AUTO.
98
99  01  CONFIRM-SCREEN.
100     05  LINE 23 COLUMN  13 UNDERLINE
101         FOREGROUND-COLOR BLUE
102         BACKGROUND-COLOR CYAN
103         VALUE 'Is the above information correct? '.
104     05  LINE 24 COLUMN 21
105         FOREGROUND-COLOR BLUE
106         BACKGROUND-COLOR CYAN
107         VALUE ' (Y - Yes, N - No) '.
108     05  SCR-CONFIRM      LINE 23 COLUMN 49  PIC X
109         FOREGROUND-COLOR BLUE
110         BACKGROUND-COLOR CYAN
111         TO CONFIRM-SWITCH.
112
113 PROCEDURE DIVISION USING INPUT-INFORMATION.
114 000-INPUT-PERSONAL-DATA.
115     INITIALIZE PROGRAM-SWITCHES.              — INITIALIZE statement resets all program switches
116     PERFORM UNTIL ALL-DATA-VALID
117         DISPLAY INPUT-SCREEN
118         CALL 'TIMESUB'
119         PERFORM 200-VALIDATE-DATA
120         PERFORM 300-CONFIRM-INPUT-SCREEN
121     END-PERFORM.
122     EXIT PROGRAM.                            — EXIT PROGRAM returns control to calling program
123
124 200-VALIDATE-DATA.
125     PERFORM 210-VALIDATE-NAME.
126     PERFORM 220-VALIDATE-AGE.
127     PERFORM 230-VALIDATE-SEX.
128     PERFORM 240-VALIDATE-WEIGHT.
129     PERFORM 250-VALIDATE-HEIGHT.
130     PERFORM 260-VALIDATE-FITNESS-LEVEL.
131
```

Figure 16.9 *(continued)*

```
132        210-VALIDATE-NAME.
133            PERFORM WITH TEST AFTER UNTIL VALID-FIELD
134            ACCEPT SCR-FULL-NAME
135                IF MISSING-NAME
136                    SET ERROR-INDEX TO 1
137                    PERFORM 299-DISPLAY-ERROR-MESSAGE
138                ELSE
139                    PERFORM 288-CLEAR-ERRORS
140                END-IF
141            END-PERFORM.
142
143        220-VALIDATE-AGE.
144            PERFORM WITH TEST AFTER UNTIL VALID-FIELD
145                ACCEPT SCR-AGE
146                IF INVALID-AGES
147                    SET ERROR-INDEX TO 2
148                    PERFORM 299-DISPLAY-ERROR-MESSAGE
149                ELSE
150                    PERFORM 288-CLEAR-ERRORS
151                END-IF
152            END-PERFORM.
153
154        230-VALIDATE-SEX.
155            PERFORM WITH TEST AFTER UNTIL VALID-FIELD
156                ACCEPT SCR-SEX
157                IF VALID-SEX
158                    PERFORM 288-CLEAR-ERRORS
159                ELSE
160                    SET ERROR-INDEX TO 3
161                    PERFORM 299-DISPLAY-ERROR-MESSAGE
162                END-IF
163            END-PERFORM.
164
165        240-VALIDATE-WEIGHT.
166            PERFORM WITH TEST AFTER UNTIL VALID-FIELD
167                ACCEPT SCR-WEIGHT
168                IF INVALID-WEIGHTS
169                    SET ERROR-INDEX TO 4
170                    PERFORM 299-DISPLAY-ERROR-MESSAGE
171                ELSE
172                    PERFORM 288-CLEAR-ERRORS
173                END-IF
174            END-PERFORM.
175
176        250-VALIDATE-HEIGHT.
177            PERFORM WITH TEST AFTER UNTIL VALID-FIELD
178                ACCEPT SCR-HEIGHT
179                EVALUATE TRUE ALSO INP-HEIGHT
180                    WHEN MALE ALSO NOT 60 THRU 76
181                        SET ERROR-INDEX TO 5
```

In-line PERFORM with TEST AFTER clause validates data as they are entered

Figure 16.9   *(continued)*

```
182                        PERFORM 299-DISPLAY-ERROR-MESSAGE
183                WHEN FEMALE ALSO NOT 54 THRU 74
184                    SET ERROR-INDEX TO 6
185                        PERFORM 299-DISPLAY-ERROR-MESSAGE
186                WHEN OTHER
187                    PERFORM 288-CLEAR-ERRORS
188            END-EVALUATE
189        END-PERFORM.
190
191    260-VALIDATE-FITNESS-LEVEL.
192        PERFORM WITH TEST AFTER UNTIL VALID-FIELD
193            ACCEPT SCR-FITNESS-LEVEL
194            IF VALID-FITNESS-LEVELS
195                PERFORM 288-CLEAR-ERRORS
196            ELSE
197                SET ERROR-INDEX TO 7
198                PERFORM 299-DISPLAY-ERROR-MESSAGE
199            END-IF
200        END-PERFORM.
201
202    288-CLEAR-ERRORS.
203        INITIALIZE VALID-FIELD-SWITCH.
204        DISPLAY ' ' LINE 24 WITH BLANK LINE.
205
206    299-DISPLAY-ERROR-MESSAGE.
207        CALL 'TIMESUB'.
208        MOVE 'NO' TO VALID-FIELD-SWITCH.
209        DISPLAY ERROR-MESSAGE (ERROR-INDEX)
210            LINE 24 COLUMN 25 WITH HIGHLIGHT BLINK BELL
211            FOREGROUND-COLOR WHITE
212            BACKGROUND-COLOR RED.
213
214    300-CONFIRM-INPUT-SCREEN.
215        DISPLAY CONFIRM-SCREEN.
216        ACCEPT SCR-CONFIRM.
```

Weight-range Program (WGTSUB) _____

The weight-range program in Figure 16.10 reviews material on multilevel programs as presented in Chapter 13. The Working-Storage Section defines two tables, for men and women's weights, in accordance with the user's view as presented in Figure 16.5. Subsequent statements in the Procedure Division determine the suggested range for an individual's weight, based on sex, height, and age.

The sex, height, and age are contained within the 01 entry WEIGHT-ARGUMENTS that is passed as an argument to the subprogram by the CALL statement in lines 88–90 of the fitness (main) program in Figure 16.8, and which coincides with the Procedure Division header in line 101 of this program. The parameter list consists of a single 01 entry, which is copied into both the calling and called program. Note the COPY statement in the Linkage Section of this program (lines 89–99,) and the corresponding COPY statement in the fitness program (lines 40–50 in Figure 16.8). Note, too, the use of COPY statements to initialize and define the tables for male and female weights, in lines 10 and 38, respectively.

Figure 16.10 Weight Subprogram

```
    1          IDENTIFICATION DIVISION.
    2          PROGRAM-ID.        WGTSUB.          Entry in PROGRAM-ID paragraph matches CALL
    3          AUTHOR.            CVV.             statement in calling program
    4
    5          DATA DIVISION.
    6          WORKING-STORAGE SECTION.
    7          01    FILLER                        PIC X(36)
    8                VALUE 'WS BEGINS HERE FOR SUBPROGRAM WGTSUB'.
    9
   10                COPY MALEWGT.
STCPY>       01    MALE-WEIGHT-VALUES.
   12             05    PIC X(30)    VALUE    '109122110133112135114137115138'.
   13             05    PIC X(30)    VALUE    '112126113136115138117140118141'.
   14             05    PIC X(30)    VALUE    '115130116139118140120142121144'.
   15             05    PIC X(30)    VALUE    '118135119143121145123147124148'.
   16             05    PIC X(30)    VALUE    '120145122147124149126151127152'.
   17             05    PIC X(30)    VALUE    '124149125151127153129155130156'.
   18             05    PIC X(30)    VALUE    '128154129156131158133160134161'.
   19             05    PIC X(30)    VALUE    '132159133161134158136165138166'.
   20             05    PIC X(30)    VALUE    '135163136165138167140169142170'.
   21             05    PIC X(30)    VALUE    '140163141169142171144173146174'.
   22             05    PIC X(30)    VALUE    '143170144173146175148178150179'.
   23             05    PIC X(30)    VALUE    '147177148179150181152183154184'.
   24             05    PIC X(30)    VALUE    '151180152184154186156188158189'.
   25             05    PIC X(30)    VALUE    '155187156189158190160193162194'.
   26             05    PIC X(30)    VALUE    '160192161194163196165198167199'.
   27             05    PIC X(30)    VALUE    '165198166199168201170203172204'.
   28             05    PIC X(30)    VALUE    '170202171204173206175208177209'.
   29
   30       01    MALE-WEIGHT-TABLE REDEFINES MALE-WEIGHT-VALUES.
   31             05    MALE-HEIGHTS OCCURS 17 TIMES
   32                   INDEXED BY MALE-HGT-INDEX.               Weight tables are
   33                   10    MALE-AGES OCCURS 5 TIMES           copied into program
   34                         INDEXED BY MALE-AGE-INDEX.
   35                         15    MALE-WGT-FROM    PIC 9(3).
EDCPY>                        15    MALE-WGT-TO      PIC 9(3).
```

Figure 16.10   *(continued)*

```
37
38              COPY FEMWGT.
STCPY>   01   FEMALE-WEIGHT-VALUES.
40           05      PIC X(30)   VALUE  '083099084101085103086104088106'.
41           05      PIC X(30)   VALUE  '084100085102086104088105090107'.
42           05      PIC X(30)   VALUE  '086101087103088105090106092108'.
43           05      PIC X(30)   VALUE  '089102090104091106092108094110'.
44           05      PIC X(30)   VALUE  '091105092106093109094111096113'.
45           05      PIC X(30)   VALUE  '093109094111095113096114099116'.
46           05      PIC X(30)   VALUE  '096112097113098115100117102119'.
47           05      PIC X(30)   VALUE  '100116101117102119103121105122'.
48           05      PIC X(30)   VALUE  '104119105121106123107125108126'.
49           05      PIC X(30)   VALUE  '106125107126108127109129111130'.
50           05      PIC X(30)   VALUE  '109130110131111132112134114135'.
51           05      PIC X(30)   VALUE  '112133113134114136116138118139'.
52           05      PIC X(30)   VALUE  '116137117138118140120142122143'.
53           05      PIC X(30)   VALUE  '121140122142123144124146126147'.
54           05      PIC X(30)   VALUE  '123144124146126148128150130150'.
55           05      PIC X(30)   VALUE  '130148131150132152133154134155'.
56           05      PIC X(30)   VALUE  '134151135154136156137158138159'.
57           05      PIC X(30)   VALUE  '138155139158140160141162142163'.
58           05      PIC X(30)   VALUE  '142160143162144164145166146167'.
59           05      PIC X(30)   VALUE  '146164147166148168149170150171'.
60           05      PIC X(30)   VALUE  '150168151170152172153174154175'.
61
62      01   FEMALE-WEIGHT-TABLE REDEFINES FEMALE-WEIGHT-VALUES.
63           05   FEMALE-HEIGHTS OCCURS 21 TIMES
64                INDEXED BY FEMALE-HGT-INDEX.
65                10   FEMALE-AGES OCCURS 5 TIMES
66                     INDEXED BY FEMALE-AGE-INDEX.
67                     15   FEMALE-WGT-FROM  PIC 9(3).
EDCPY>               15   FEMALE-WGT-TO    PIC 9(3).
69
70      01   AGE-LIMIT-VALUES.
71           05                        PIC 99    VALUE 18.
72           05                        PIC 99    VALUE 20.
73           05                        PIC 99    VALUE 22.
74           05                        PIC 99    VALUE 24.
75           05                        PIC 99    VALUE 99.
76      01   AGE-TABLE REDEFINES AGE-LIMIT-VALUES.
77           05   AGE-LIMIT OCCURS 5 TIMES
78                INDEXED BY AGE-INDEX    PIC 99.
79
80      01   CONSTANTS-AND-VARIABLES.
81           05   MALE-HGT-ADJUST-CONSTANT   PIC 99   VALUE 59.
82           05   FEMALE-HGT-ADJUST-CONSTANT PIC 99   VALUE 53.
83           05   ADJUSTED-HEIGHT           PIC 99.
84
85      01   FILLER                        PIC X(34)
86                VALUE 'WS ENDS HERE FOR SUBPROGRAM WGTSUB'.
```

Weight tables are copied into program

Figure 16.10 *(continued)*

```
87
88          LINKAGE SECTION.                    ─── Linkage Section contains arguments of called program
89              COPY WGTCOPY.
STCPY>      01  WEIGHT-ARGUMENTS.
91              05  WEIGHT-TABLE-INPUTS.
92                  10  WGT-HEIGHT            PIC 99.
93                  10  WGT-AGE              PIC 99.
94                  10  WGT-SEX             PIC X.
95                      88  MALE                        VALUE 'M' 'm'.
96                      88  FEMALE                      VALUE 'F' 'f'.
97              05  WEIGHT-GOALS.
98                  10  GOAL-WGT-FROM       PIC 999.
EDCPY>              10  GOAL-WGT-TO         PIC 999.
100
101         PROCEDURE DIVISION USING WEIGHT-ARGUMENTS.
102         FIND-GOAL-WEIGHT.
103             EVALUATE TRUE
104                 WHEN MALE
105                     PERFORM FIND-MALE-WEIGHT-RANGE
106                 WHEN FEMALE
107                     PERFORM FIND-FEMALE-WEIGHT-RANGE
108                 WHEN OTHER
109                     DISPLAY 'INVALID SEX ENTERED'
110                     INITIALIZE WEIGHT-GOALS
111             END-EVALUATE.
112             EXIT PROGRAM.                  ─── EXIT PROGRAM returns control to calling program
113
114         FIND-MALE-WEIGHT-RANGE.
115             COMPUTE ADJUSTED-HEIGHT =
116                 WGT-HEIGHT - MALE-HGT-ADJUST-CONSTANT
117                 SIZE ERROR DISPLAY 'SIZE ERROR ADJUSTED HEIGHT'
118             END-COMPUTE.
119             SET MALE-AGE-INDEX AGE-INDEX TO 1.
120             SET MALE-HGT-INDEX TO ADJUSTED-HEIGHT.
121             SEARCH AGE-LIMIT VARYING MALE-AGE-INDEX
122                 AT END DISPLAY 'MALE AGE NOT FOUND'
123                     INITIALIZE WEIGHT-GOALS
124                 WHEN
125                     WGT-AGE <= AGE-LIMIT (AGE-INDEX)
126                     SET MALE-AGE-INDEX TO AGE-INDEX
127                     MOVE MALE-WGT-FROM (MALE-HGT-INDEX, MALE-AGE-INDEX)
128                         TO GOAL-WGT-FROM
129                     MOVE MALE-WGT-TO (MALE-HGT-INDEX, MALE-AGE-INDEX)
130                         TO GOAL-WGT-TO
131             END-SEARCH.
132
133         FIND-FEMALE-WEIGHT-RANGE.
134             COMPUTE ADJUSTED-HEIGHT =
135                 WGT-HEIGHT - FEMALE-HGT-ADJUST-CONSTANT
136                 SIZE ERROR DISPLAY 'SIZE ERROR ADJUSTED HEIGHT'
```

Figure 16.10   *(continued)*

```
137          END-COMPUTE.
138          SET FEMALE-AGE-INDEX AGE-INDEX TO 1.
139          SET FEMALE-HGT-INDEX TO ADJUSTED-HEIGHT.
140      SEARCH AGE-LIMIT VARYING FEMALE-AGE-INDEX
141          AT END DISPLAY 'FEMALE AGE NOT FOUND'
142              INITIALIZE WEIGHT-GOALS
143          WHEN
144              WGT-AGE <= AGE-LIMIT (AGE-INDEX)
145              SET FEMALE-AGE-INDEX TO AGE-INDEX
146              MOVE FEMALE-WGT-FROM
147                  (FEMALE-HGT-INDEX, FEMALE-AGE-INDEX)
148                  TO GOAL-WGT-FROM
149              MOVE FEMALE-WGT-TO
150                  (FEMALE-HGT-INDEX, FEMALE-AGE-INDEX)
151                  TO GOAL-WGT-TO
152      END-SEARCH.
```

SEARCH VARYING used with two-level table

Training Program (TRAINSUB)

The training program in Figure 16.11 calculates an individual's target heart rate (after exercise) according to the formulas given in the programming specifications. The program uses the SIZE ERROR phrase and associated END-COMPUTE scope terminator in several places in the Procedure Division. It also uses the EVALUATE statement to determine the specific training range according to the user's fitness level.

The means for passing parameters between this program and the fitness program, which calls it, parallels the procedure for the other subprograms. Thus, the Linkage Section contains a COPY statement (line 29) to define the 01 parameters that constitute the parameter list; note, too, the correspondence between the Procedure Division header in this program and the CALL statement in the fitness program.

Display Program (DSPLYSUB)

The display program in Figure 16.12 uses DISPLAY statements rather than a Screen Section to control the displayed output in accordance with earlier material from Chapter 10. The means for passing parameters between this program and the fitness program does not parallel the procedure for the other subprograms. The Linkage Section contains a single line called LINKAGE-DATA (line 54). The actual parameters are defined by a COPY statement and stored in the Working-Storage Section (lines 37–48). COBOL97 does not allow 88 levels to be defined in the Linkage Section. To accommodate this restriction, the first executable line of the Procedure Division (line 59) moves the contents of the Linkage Section to DISPLAY-ARGUMENTS and the last executable line of the program (line 63) moves them back.

Observe also the presence of the identical COPY statement in the input program (line 7) to obtain the definition of foreground and background colors.

Figure 16.11   Training Subprogram

```
  1        IDENTIFICATION DIVISION.
  2        PROGRAM-ID.        TRAINSUB.
  3        AUTHOR.            CVV.
  4
  5        DATA DIVISION.
  6        WORKING-STORAGE SECTION.
  7
  8        01   FILLER                    PIC X(38)
  9                 VALUE 'WS BEGINS HERE FOR SUBPROGRAM TRAINSUB'.
 10
 11        01   RATES-AND-CONSTANTS.
 12             05   TRAIN-CONSTANT       PIC 999   VALUE 220.
 13             05   LOW-RATE             PIC V9    VALUE .6.
 14             05   HIGH-RATE            PIC V9    VALUE .9.
 15
 16        01   RANGE-CALCULATIONS.
 17             05   OVERALL-RANGES.
 18                  10   OVERALL-HIGH    PIC 99.
 19                  10   OVERALL-LOW     PIC 99.
 20             05   FITNESS-RANGES.
 21                  10   FITNESS-HIGH    PIC 99.
 22                  10   FITNESS-LOW     PIC 99.
 23             05   RANGE-INTERVAL       PIC 9.
 24
 25        01   FILLER                    PIC X(36)
 26                 VALUE 'WS ENDS HERE FOR SUBPROGRAM TRAINSUB'.
 27
 28        LINKAGE SECTION.
 29            COPY TRAINCPY.
STCPY>    01   TRAINING-ARGUMENTS.
 31            05   TRAINING-INPUTS.
 32                 10   TRAIN-AGE        PIC 99.
 33                 10   TRAIN-FITNESS-LEVEL  PIC X.
 34                      88  BEGINNER             VALUE 'B' 'b'.
 35                      88  INTERMEDIATE         VALUE 'I' 'i'.
 36                      88  ADVANCED             VALUE 'A' 'a'.
 37            05   TRAINING-RANGES.
 38                 10   TRAIN-OVERALL-RANGE  PIC X(5).
EDCPY>               10   TRAIN-FITNESS-RANGE  PIC X(5).
 40
 41        PROCEDURE DIVISION
 42            USING TRAINING-ARGUMENTS.
 43        FIND-TRAIN-RANGE.
 44            PERFORM COMPUTE-OVERALL-RANGES.
 45            PERFORM COMPUTE-FITNESS-RANGES.
 46            EXIT PROGRAM.
```

Literals used for debugging

Program parameters are copied into Linkage section

EXIT PROGRAM returns control to calling program

Figure 16.11   *(continued)*

```
47
48         COMPUTE-OVERALL-RANGES.
49            COMPUTE OVERALL-LOW ROUNDED =
50                 (TRAIN-CONSTANT - TRAIN-AGE) * LOW-RATE / 6
51                 SIZE ERROR DISPLAY 'SIZE ERROR ON LOW RANGE'
52            END-COMPUTE.
53            COMPUTE OVERALL-HIGH ROUNDED =
54                 (TRAIN-CONSTANT - TRAIN-AGE) * HIGH-RATE / 6
55                 SIZE ERROR DISPLAY 'SIZE ERROR ON HIGH RANGE'
56            END-COMPUTE.
57            STRING OVERALL-LOW '-' OVERALL-HIGH DELIMITED BY SIZE
58                 INTO TRAIN-OVERALL-RANGE
59            END-STRING.
60
61         COMPUTE-FITNESS-RANGES.
62            COMPUTE RANGE-INTERVAL =
63                 (OVERALL-HIGH - OVERALL-LOW) / 3
64                 SIZE ERROR DISPLAY 'SIZE ERROR ON RANGE INTERVAL'
65            END-COMPUTE.
66            EVALUATE TRUE
67                WHEN BEGINNER
68                    MOVE OVERALL-LOW TO FITNESS-LOW
69                    COMPUTE FITNESS-HIGH ROUNDED =
70                        OVERALL-LOW + RANGE-INTERVAL
71                        SIZE ERROR DISPLAY 'SIZE ERROR HIGH FITNESS'
72                    END-COMPUTE
73                WHEN INTERMEDIATE
74                    COMPUTE FITNESS-LOW ROUNDED =
75                        OVERALL-LOW + RANGE-INTERVAL
76                        SIZE ERROR DISPLAY 'SIZE ERROR LOW FITNESS'
77                    END-COMPUTE
78                    COMPUTE FITNESS-HIGH ROUNDED =
79                        OVERALL-HIGH - RANGE-INTERVAL
80                        SIZE ERROR
81                            DISPLAY 'SIZE ERROR HIGH FITNESS'
82                    END-COMPUTE
83                WHEN ADVANCED
84                    COMPUTE FITNESS-LOW ROUNDED =
85                        OVERALL-HIGH - RANGE-INTERVAL
86                        SIZE ERROR DISPLAY 'SIZE ERROR LOW FITNESS'
87                    END-COMPUTE
88                    MOVE OVERALL-HIGH TO FITNESS-HIGH
89                WHEN OTHER
90                    DISPLAY 'INVALID FITNESS LEVEL SEE VALIDATION'
91            END-EVALUATE.
92            STRING FITNESS-LOW '-' FITNESS-HIGH DELIMITED BY SIZE
93                 INTO TRAIN-FITNESS-RANGE
94            END-STRING.
```

Figure 16.12 Display Subprogram

```
 1        IDENTIFICATION DIVISION.
 2        PROGRAM-ID.      DSPLYSUB.
 3        AUTHOR.          CVV.
 4
 5        ENVIRONMENT DIVISION.
 6        CONFIGURATION SECTION.
 7        COPY COLORCPY.
STCPY>    SPECIAL-NAMES.
 9            SYMBOLIC CONSTANT
10                BLACK       IS 0
11                BLUE        IS 1
12                GREEN       IS 2
13                CYAN        IS 3
14                RED         IS 4
15                MAGENTA     IS 5
16                BROWN       IS 6
EDCPY>            WHITE       IS 7.
18
19        DATA DIVISION.
20        WORKING-STORAGE SECTION.
21        01   FILLER                     PIC X(38)
22                 VALUE 'WS BEGINS HERE FOR SUBPROGRAM DSPLYSUB'.
23
24        01   DISPLAY-MESSAGES.
25            05   OVER-WEIGHT-COMMENT     PIC X(41)
26                 VALUE '  OH! NO! Your weight exceeds the range'.
27            05   UNDER-WEIGHT-COMMENT    PIC X(41)
28                 VALUE ' EAT UP! Your weight is below the range'.
29            05   IN-WEIGHT-COMMENT       PIC X(41)
30                 VALUE 'CONGRATULATIONS! You are within the range'.
31            05   WEIGHT-COMMENT          PIC X(41).
32            05   ANOTHER-MESSAGE         PIC X(14)
33                 VALUE 'Must be Y or N'.
34
35        01   GOAL-WEIGHT-RANGE           PIC X(7).
36
37            COPY DISPCPY.
38        01   DISPLAY-ARGUMENTS.
39            05   DISP-TRAINING-RANGES.
40                10   DISP-TRAIN-OVERALL-RANGE  PIC X(5).
41                10   DISP-TRAIN-FITNESS-RANGE  PIC X(5).
42            05   DISP-WEIGHT-GOALS.
43                10   DISP-GOAL-WGT-FROM    PIC ZZ9.
44                10   DISP-GOAL-WGT-TO      PIC ZZ9.
45            05   DISP-INPUT-WEIGHT         PIC 9(3).
46            05   ANOTHER-PERSON-SWITCH     PIC X.
47                88   NO-MORE-PERSONS            VALUE 'N' 'n'.
48                88   VALID-ANOTHER             VALUE 'N' 'n' 'Y' 'y'.
49
```

Screen colors are copied into program

Parameters stored in Working-Storage Section

Figure 16.12   *(continued)*

```
50        01  FILLER                 PIC X(36).
51             VALUE 'WS ENDS HERE FOR SUBPROGRAM DSPLYSUB'.
52
53        LINKAGE SECTION.                              Receives parameters
54        01  LINKAGE-DATA           PIC X(20).
55
56        PROCEDURE DIVISION
57             USING LINKAGE-DATA.
58        000-UPDATE-PERSONAL-DATA.                     Moves parameters to
59             MOVE LINKAGE-DATA TO DISPLAY-ARGUMENTS.   Working-Storage Section
60             PERFORM 100-UPDATE-SCREEN.
61             CALL 'TIMESUB'.
62             PERFORM 300-INPUT-ANOTHER-PERSON.         Restores parameters
63             MOVE DISPLAY-ARGUMENTS TO LINKAGE-DATA.
64             EXIT PROGRAM.
65
66        100-UPDATE-SCREEN.
67             STRING DISP-GOAL-WGT-FROM '-' DISP-GOAL-WGT-TO
68                 DELIMITED BY SIZE
69                 INTO GOAL-WEIGHT-RANGE
70             END-STRING.
71             DISPLAY
72                 'Your Goal Weight Range: ' LINE 11 COLUMN 4
73                 GOAL-WEIGHT-RANGE LINE 11 COLUMN 28 WITH HIGHLIGHT.
74             PERFORM 150-DISPLAY-WEIGHT-COMMENT
75             DISPLAY
76                 'Training Heart Rate Range Information (10 Second)'
77                     LINE 14 COLUMN 4.
78             DISPLAY
79                 'Overall Heart Rate Range: '
80                     LINE 15 COLUMN  6
81             DISPLAY
82                 DISP-TRAIN-OVERALL-RANGE LINE 15 COLUMN 32 WITH HIGHLIGHT
83                 'Adjusted for Fitness Level: ' LINE 16 COLUMN 6
84             DISPLAY
85                 DISP-TRAIN-FITNESS-RANGE LINE 16 COLUMN 34 WITH HIGHLIGHT.
86             DISPLAY ' '  LINE 23 COLUMN 1 WITH BLANK LINE.
87             DISPLAY ' '  LINE 24 COLUMN 1 WITH BLANK LINE.
88
89        150-DISPLAY-WEIGHT-COMMENT.
90             EVALUATE TRUE
91                 WHEN DISP-INPUT-WEIGHT < DISP-GOAL-WGT-FROM
92                     MOVE UNDER-WEIGHT-COMMENT TO WEIGHT-COMMENT
93                     DISPLAY WEIGHT-COMMENT LINE 12 COLUMN 6 WITH BLINK
94                         BACKGROUND-COLOR MAGENTA
95                         FOREGROUND-COLOR BLACK
96                 WHEN DISP-INPUT-WEIGHT < DISP-GOAL-WGT-TO
97                     MOVE OVER-WEIGHT-COMMENT TO WEIGTH-COMMENT
98                     DISPLAY WEIGHT-COMMENT LINE 12 COLUMN 6 WITH BLINK
99                         BACKGROUND-COLOR RED
100                        FOREGROUND-COLOR BLACK
```

Figure 16.12   Display Subprogram

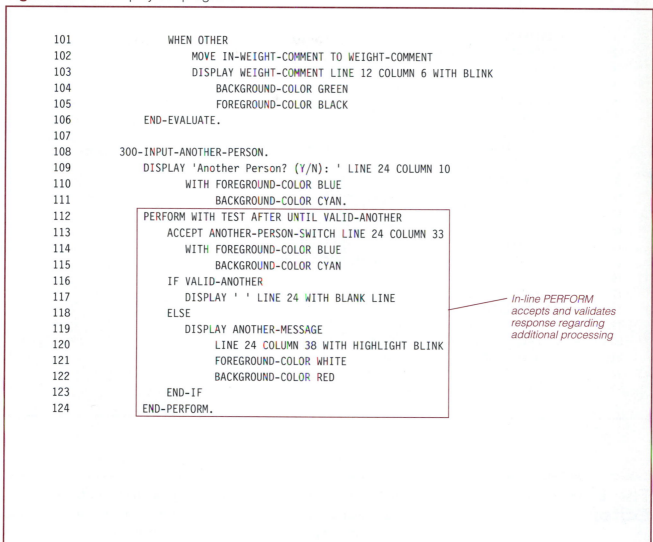

```
101                 WHEN OTHER
102                    MOVE IN-WEIGHT-COMMENT TO WEIGHT-COMMENT
103                    DISPLAY WEIGHT-COMMENT LINE 12 COLUMN 6 WITH BLINK
104                       BACKGROUND-COLOR GREEN
105                       FOREGROUND-COLOR BLACK
106              END-EVALUATE.
107
108          300-INPUT-ANOTHER-PERSON.
109              DISPLAY 'Another Person? (Y/N): ' LINE 24 COLUMN 10
110                     WITH FOREGROUND-COLOR BLUE
111                        BACKGROUND-COLOR CYAN.
112              PERFORM WITH TEST AFTER UNTIL VALID-ANOTHER
113                  ACCEPT ANOTHER-PERSON-SWITCH LINE 24 COLUMN 33
114                     WITH FOREGROUND-COLOR BLUE
115                        BACKGROUND-COLOR CYAN
116                  IF VALID-ANOTHER
117                     DISPLAY ' ' LINE 24 WITH BLANK LINE
118                  ELSE
119                     DISPLAY ANOTHER-MESSAGE
120                        LINE 24 COLUMN 38 WITH HIGHLIGHT BLINK
121                        FOREGROUND-COLOR WHITE
122                        BACKGROUND-COLOR RED
123                  END-IF
124              END-PERFORM.
```

In-line PERFORM accepts and validates response regarding additional processing

Time Program (TIMESUB)

The program to update the displayed time (Figure 16.13) uses the ACCEPT statement to obtain the current time containing hours, minutes, seconds, and hundredths of a second as per the discussion in Chapter 8. Reference modification is used in conjunction with an INSPECT statement to truncate hundredths of a second in the displayed time.

The program is called from two other programs as per the system hierarchy chart in Figure 16.6. This program is different from the other subprograms in that it does not contain any parameters; the program is completely self-contained as it obtains the current time from the system, and then displays the results directly on the monitor.

Figure 16.13 Time Subprogram

```
1        IDENTIFICATION DIVISION.
2        PROGRAM-ID.        TIMESUB.
3        AUTHOR.            CVV.
4
5        DATA DIVISION.
6        WORKING-STORAGE SECTION.
7        01   FILLER                   PIC X(37)
8                 VALUE 'WS BEGINS HERE FOR SUBPROGRAM TIMESUB'.
9
10       01   TIME-VARIABLES.
11            05   THE-TIME             PIC 9(8).
12            05   HH-MM-SS             PIC 99B99B99.
13
14       01   FILLER                   PIC X(35)
15                 VALUE 'WS ENDS HERE FOR SUBPROGRAM TIMESUB'.
16
17       PROCEDURE DIVISION.
18       000-UPDATE-TIME.
19            ACCEPT THE-TIME FROM TIME.
20            MOVE THE-TIME (1:6) TO HH-MM-SS.        ← Reference modification truncates time
21            INSPECT HH-MM-SS REPLACING ALL ' ' BY ':'.
22            DISPLAY HH-MM-SS LINE 1 COLUMN 60.
23            EXIT PROGRAM.
```

The Linkage Editor

Beginning COBOL programmers often take the *link program* (or *linkage editor* as it is called on IBM mainframes) for granted, because it functions transparently as the middle step in the compile, link, and execute sequence. Knowledge of the link program assumes greater importance, however, in systems of multiple programs as in the fitness example just presented. Accordingly, we review the compile, link, and execute sequence that was first presented in Chapter 2.

Three distinct programs are associated with the execution of a single COBOL program, a relationship that was shown earlier in Figure 2.3. The COBOL compiler translates a source program into an object (machine language) program; the link program combines the object program with object modules from other COBOL programs and/or vendor-supplied I/O routines to create an executable load module; and finally, the load module accepts the input data and produces the desired results.

Consider now a slightly different scenario in which a system of three COBOL programs (a main program and two subprograms) is to be developed. This time, a total of five steps is required in order to execute the main program:

1. Compile the main program
2. Compile the first subprogram
3. Compile the second subprogram
4. Link the three object programs to produce a load module
5. Execute the load module

It is not necessary, however, to repeat the entire five-step sequence every time the system undergoes additional testing. What if, for example, the subprograms have been successfully debugged, and only the main program is being changed? Can you see that it is inherently wasteful to continually recompile the subprograms if they remain the same? In other words, if only the main program changes, couldn't we just compile the main program (step 1), then link the object program to the existing object programs for the subprograms (step 4), and then execute the resulting load module (step 5)?

Other variations are also possible; for example, if the first subprogram changes but the other two remain the same, the run stream would consist of steps two, four, and five as only the first subprogram would have to be recompiled. Another variation would consist solely of step five, to execute the load module (without recompilation or linking) when all testing has been completed.

Figure 16.14 illustrates the compile, link, and execute sequence for the fitness system developed earlier in the chapter. Figure 16.14a displays the file names of the six programs in the system (as they might appear on a PC); the CBL extension indicates a COBOL source program.

Figure 16.14b depicts a conceptual view of the run stream. In practice, process is handled by the Project Manager in the Build process. Each of the programs is compiled individually, and then they are linked together into a load module. Step 8 executes the load module. Figure 16.14c indicates the presence of the six object modules (extension OBJ) that are produced from the individual compilations.

Figure 16.14d indicates three additional files produced by the link process. FITNESS.MAK contains the descriptive information produced by the link program . FITNESS.EXE is the executable load module, and FITNESS.LIB is a library file to handle the interaction of the various programs.

Problems with the Linkage Editor

Students are often frustrated in their attempt to produce a load module with multiple subprograms. Consider, for example, Figure 16.15, which contains—in outline form—a COBOL main (calling) program and two sub (called) programs. Observe, however, that there is an *inconsistency* between the CALL statement of the main program and the PROGRAM-ID paragraph of the first subprogram; that is, the main program is calling **SUB1,** whereas the PROGRAM-ID paragraph refers to **SUBRTN1.** This in turn produces the error message in Figure 16.15d.

The exact wording of the error message will vary from system to system; for example, the linkage editor on an IBM mainframe will cite an ***unresolved external reference,*** whereas the link program on a PC may reference an ***undefined symbol.*** Regardless of the system, however, the link program will not execute cleanly, despite the fact that all three programs compiled without error.

The reason for the problem becomes apparent when we again consider the functions of the COBOL compiler and the link program. The compiler translates COBOL source statements to machine language, and thus, must accept statements that call other (external) programs—for example, CALL SUB1. The compiler cannot access SUB1 directly, and trusts in the link program to locate the appropriate object module and produce an executable load module. The unresolved external reference detected by the link program means there was a call for a program named SUB1, but that the object module for SUB1 could not be found.

Return to the original COBOL listing of Figure 16.15a and observe once again the inconsistency between the CALL statement in the main program (CALL SUB1) and the PROGRAM-ID paragraph in the subprogram (SUBRTN1). Make the entries consistent (i.e., change SUB1 to SUBRTN1) and the problem is solved.

Figure 16.14   The Compile, Link, and Execute Sequence

```
                    DSPLYSUB.CBL
                    FITNESS .CBL
                    INPUTSUB.CBL
                    TIMESUB .CBL
                    TRAINSUB.CBL
                    WGTSUB  .CBL
```

(a) Directory before Compilation

```
Step 1: Compile fitness program (FITNESS.CBL)
Step 2: Compile input program (INPUTSUB.CBL)
Step 3: Compile weight goals program (WGTSUB.CBL)
Step 4: Compile training program (TRAINSUB.CBL)
Step 5: Compile format time program (TIMESUB.CBL)
Step 6: Compile final display program (DSPLYSUB.CBL)

Step 7: Link the object programs

Step 8: Execute the load module
```

(b) The Run Stream (Conceptual View)

```
        DSPLYSUB.CBL      DSPLYSUB.OBJ
        FITNESS .CBL      FITNESS .OBJ
        INPUTSUB .CBL     INPUTSUB.OBJ
        TIMESUB  .CBL     TIMESUB .OBJ
        TRAINSUB .CBL     TRAINSUB.OBJ
        WGTSUB   .CBL     WGTSUB  .OBJ
```

(c) Directory after Compilation

```
        FITNESS.EXE      FITNESS.LIB
        FITNESS.MAK
```

(d) Directory after Linking

LIMITATIONS OF COBOL-74

The optional BY REFERENCE and BY CONTENT phrases were not present in COBOL-74. The omission of both phrases defaults to CALLING BY REFERENCE and is the equivalent of the CALL statement in COBOL-74. The INITIAL phrase in the PROGRAM-ID paragraph is also new to COBOL-85. The optional scope terminator, END-CALL, is also new.

Two other minor changes do not add any additional capability per se, but simplify the use of subprograms. These are:

1. EXIT PROGRAM (to return control to the calling program) need not be the only statement in a paragraph, as was required in COBOL-74.

2. An elementary item may appear in the parameter list as opposed to the COBOL-74 restriction to 01- or 77-level entries.

Figure 16.15 Problems with the Linkage Editor

```
IDENTIFICATION DIVISION.
PROGRAM-ID.     MAINPROG.
       .
       .
PROCEDURE DIVISION.
       .
       .
    CALL 'SUB1' USING PARAMETER-1.
    CALL 'SUBRTN2' USING PARAMETER-2.
```
CALL statement inconsistent with PROGRAM-ID paragraph of first subroutine

(a) Main Program

```
IDENTIFICATION DIVISION.
PROGRAM-ID.     SUBRTN1.
       .
       .
PROCEDURE DIVISION
    USING PARAMETER-1.
       .
       .
    EXIT PROGRAM.
```

(b) First Subroutine

```
IDENTIFICATION DIVISION.
PROGRAM-ID.     SUBRTN2.
       .
       .
PROCEDURE DIVISION
    USING PARAMETER-2.
       .
       .
    EXIT PROGRAM.
```

(c) Second Subroutine

```
ERROR - SUB1 IS AN UNRESOLVED EXTERNAL REFERENCE
```

(d) Error Message

S U M M A R Y

Points to Remember

■ A sub (called) program is a program that is written and compiled independently of other programs but which is executed under the control of a main (calling) program.

■ A hierarchy chart shows the relationship of paragraphs within a COBOL program or programs within a system. The subprograms that comprise a system are developed in stages and tested in top-down fashion just as the paragraphs within a program.

■ The CALL statement in a calling program transfers control to the first executable statement in the called program. The EXIT PROGRAM statement returns control from the called program to the calling program.

■ The argument list is specified in the CALL USING statement of the calling program and in the Procedure Division header of the called program. The data names in the parameter lists can be, but do not have to be, the same.

■ The COPY statement inserts statements into a COBOL program (from a copy library) during compilation, as though the statements had been coded directly in the program itself. A COPY statement may appear anywhere within a program except within another COPY statement.

■ CALLING BY CONTENT prevents the value of a passed parameter modified in the calling program from being changed in the called program; CALLING BY REFERENCE, however, will change the variable in the calling program.

■ The INITIAL phrase in the PROGRAM-ID paragraph restores a program to its initial state each time it is called; that is, all data names are reset to their original values via any VALUE clauses that are present.

■ The linkage editor (link program) combines the object modules produced by compilation of one or more programs with vendor-supplied I/O routines to produce a load module.

Key Words and Concepts

Argument list	Main program
Called program	Parameter list
Calling program	Subprogram
Linkage editor (link program)	Undefined symbol
Load module	Unresolved external reference

COBOL Elements

BY CONTENT	EXIT PROGRAM
BY REFERENCE	INITIAL
CALL USING	LINKAGE SECTION
COPY	PROCEDURE DIVISION USING
END-CALL	

F i l l - i n

1. A called program returns control to its calling program via an _____ _____ statement.

2. The LINKAGE SECTION appears in the (<u>calling/called</u>) program, and indicates that space for these data names has already been allocated in the (<u>calling/called</u>) program.

3. The order of arguments in the USING clauses of the called and calling programs (<u>is/is not</u>) important.

4. If program A calls program B, then program A is the main or _____ program and program B is the sub or _____ program.

5. If program A calls program B and program B calls program C, then program B is (<u>both/neither</u>) a called and a calling program.

6. A COBOL program (<u>may/may not</u>) call multiple subprograms.

7. A _____ statement is used to bring in text from a file on disk into a COBOL program.

8. Specification of the (<u>BY CONTENT/BY REFERENCE</u>) phrase ensures that the original values will be restored when control is returned to the calling program.

9. Specification of the (<u>BY CONTENT/BY REFERENCE</u>) phrase does not restore the values and thus functions identically to the COBOL-74 implementation.

10. The _____ phrase in the PROGRAM-ID paragraph restores the data names in a called program to their initial values.

11. The PERFORM statement is to a paragraph as the _____ statement is to a subprogram.

T r u e / F a l s e

1. The COPY clause is permitted only in the Data Division.

2. The Linkage Section appears in the calling program.

3. Data names in CALL . . . USING and PROCEDURE DIVISION USING . . . must be the same.

4. A called program contains only the Data and Procedure Divisions.

5. The COPY statement can be used on an FD only.

6. A COPY statement takes effect during the linking phase of the compile, link, and execution sequence.

7. A program can contain only one CALL statement.

8. The same program can function as both a called and a calling program.

9. The parameter list may contain group items at other than a 01 level.

10. A hierarchy chart can be used to show the relationship of paragraphs in a program or programs in a system.

11. A CALL statement must include either the BY REFERENCE or BY CONTENT phrase.

12. A CALL statement must contain at least one parameter.

Problems

1. Answer the following questions with respect to the hierarchy chart in Figure 16.16:
   a. Which programs are calling programs?
   b. Which programs are called programs?
   c. Which programs are both called and calling programs?
   d. Which programs contain a CALL statement?
   e. Which programs contain a Linkage Section?
   f. Which programs might contain a COPY statement?
   g. Which programs might contain an INITIAL clause?

Figure 16.16   Hierarchy Chart for Problem 1

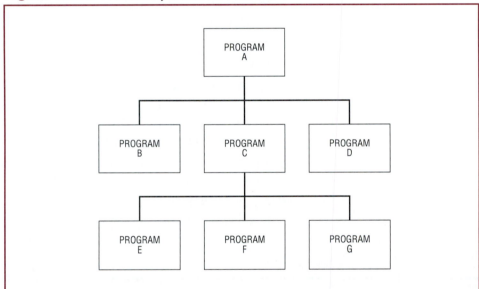

2. Figure 16.17 shows a partial listing of a called and calling program in which the first three Procedure Division statements of the subprogram initialize various counters and switches.
   a. Are these statements redundant with the existing VALUE clauses; that is, what would be the effect (if any) of removing the MOVE statements from the subprogram?
   b. What would be the effect (if any) of removing the MOVE ZERO statements, replacing them with VALUE ZERO clauses in the Data Division, and including the INITIAL phrase in the PROGRAM-ID header of the called program?
   c. Which Procedure Division statement could be substituted for the MOVE ZERO statements with no other changes to the program?

Figure 16.17   Skeleton Programs for Problem 2

```
IDENTIFICATION DIVISION.
PROGRAM-ID.    MAINPROG.
      .
      .

PROCEDURE DIVISION.
      .

      .
      CALL 'SUB1' USING PARAMETER-LIST.
```

(a) Main Program

```
IDENTIFICATION DIVISION.
PROGRAM-ID.    SUB1.
      .

      .
WORKING-STORAGE SECTION.
01  SUB-COUNTERS-AND-SWITCHES.
    05  FIRST-COUNTER        PIC 9(3)   VALUE ZERO.
    05  SECOND-COUNTER       PIC 9(3)   VALUE ZERO.
    05  TABLE-LOOKUP-SWITCH  PIC X(3)   VALUE SPACES.

PROCEDURE DIVISION
    USING PARAMTER-LIST.
      .

      .
RESET-DATA-ITEMS.
    MOVE ZEROS TO FIRST-COUNTER.
    MOVE ZEROS TO SECOND-COUNTER.
    MOVE SPACES TO TABLE-LOOKUP-SWITCH.
      .

      .
```

(b) Subprogram

3. Answer the following with respect to the COBOL fragment of Figure 16.18.
   a. What are the ending values for each of the six data names (that is, for A, B, C, D, E, and F)?
   b. What is the effect, if any, of removing the BY CONTENT phrase in the CALL statement?
   c. What is the effect, if any, of removing the BY REFERENCE phrase in the CALL statement?

Figure 16.18   COBOL Skeleton for Problem 3

```
        MOVE ZEROS TO A, B, C.
        CALL SUBRTN
            USING A
                  BY CONTENT B
                  BY REFERENCE C
        END-CALL.
```

(a) Calling Program

```
    PROGRAM-ID.    SUBRTN.

    PROCEDURE DIVISION
        USING D, E, F.
              .
              .
        MOVE 10 TO D, E, F
        EXIT PROGRAM.
```

(b) Called Program

4. Answer the following with respect to the COBOL skeleton in Figure 16.19.

   a. Indicate the necessary steps in a conceptual run stream to compile, link, and execute all three programs.

   b. Which steps would have to be repeated in the run stream of part (a), given that the subprograms were working perfectly, but that the main program needs modification?

   c. Which steps would have to be repeated in the run stream of part (a), given that the only change was in the copy member INPUTREC?

   d. What problems, if any, would arise in connection with the CALL statement for PROGA? In which step (compilation, linking, or execution) would the problem arise (be detected)?

   e. What problems, if any, would arise in connection with the CALL statement for PROGB? In which step (compilation, linking, or execution) would the problem arise (be detected)?

5. Explain how the concept of top-down testing can be applied to the fitness system as depicted by the hierarchy chart of Figure 16.6.

Figure 16.19 COBOL Programs for Problem 4

```
IDENTIFICATION DIVISION.
PROGRAM-ID.    MAINPROG.

WORKING-STORAGE SECTION.
    COPY INPUTREC
01  INPUT-DATA.
    05   INPUT-NAME      PIC X(15).
    .
       .

01  PASSED-PARAMETERS.
    05   PARM-A           PIC 9(4).
    05   PARM-B           PIC XX.

PROCEDURE DIVISION.

    CALL 'PROGA' USING PARM-A, PARM-B, INPUT-DATA.
    CALL 'PROGB' USING PARM-A.
```

(a) Main Program

```
IDENTIFICATION DIVISION.
PROGRAM-ID.    PROGA.

LINKAGE SECTION.
    COPY INPUTREC
01  INPUT-DATA.
    05   INPUT-NAME      PIC X(15).
    .
       .

01  NEW-DATA-NAMES.
    05   NEW-NAME-A      PIC XX.
    05   NEW-NAME-B      PIC 9(4).

PROCEDURE DIVISION
    USING NEW-NAME-A, NEW-NAME-B, INPUT-DATA.
```

(b) First Subroutine

```
IDENTIFICATION DIVISION.
PROGRAM-ID.    PROG-B.

LINKAGE SECTION.
01 PASSED-PARAMETERS.
   05   PARM-A           PIC 9(4).

PROCEDURE DIVISION
    USING PARM-A.
```

(b) Second Subroutine

Sequential File Maintenance

CHAPTER OUTLINE

Overview

System Concepts

Sequential versus Nonsequential Processing

Periodic Maintenance

Data Validation

Programming Specifications

Designing the Program

The Completed Program

Sequential File Maintenance

Programming Specifications

The Balance Line Algorithm

Designing the Hierarchy Chart

Top-Down Testing

The Stubs Program

The Completed Program

Summary

Fill-in

True/False

Problems

OBJECTIVES

After reading this chapter you will be able to:

■ Describe the file maintenance operation; distinguish between the old master, transaction, and new master files.

■ Describe the three transaction types associated with file maintenance.

■ Differentiate between sequential and nonsequential file maintenance.

■ Describe at least three types of errors that can be detected in a stand-alone edit program; list two errors that cannot be detected in such a program.

■ Discuss the balance line algorithm.

■ Define top-down testing; explain how a program may be tested before it is completely coded.

OVERVIEW

A large proportion of data-processing activity is devoted to file maintenance. Although printed reports are the more visible result of data processing, all files must be maintained to reflect the changing nature of the physical environment. In every system new records can be added, while existing records can be changed or deleted.

The chapter begins with a discussion of system concepts, emphasizing the importance of data validation in the maintenance process. It continues with coverage of the balance line algorithm, a completely general procedure for sequential file maintenance. The resulting program is implemented in stages through top-down testing. The initial version of the program contains several program stubs and validates the interaction among the higher-level paragraphs in the hierarchy chart. The second, and completed, version fulfills the requirements of the case study.

System Concepts

In its simplest form, file maintenance implies the existence of three files, an *old master file*, a *transaction file*, and a *new master file*, which is produced as a consequence of processing the first two files with one another. The situation is depicted in Figure 17.1, which contains a system flowchart for the traditional *sequential update*.

Figure 17.2 is an expanded version of Figure 17.1 with hypothetical data included. The old master and transaction files are both in sequence according to the same field (key), in this example, by social security number. The transaction file contains information on how the old master file is to be changed—that is, whether new records are to be *added*, or existing records *changed* or *deleted*. During the update process, every record in the old master file will be copied intact to the new master file, unless the update program detects a transaction for that record. The output produced by the program consists of the new master file and various error messages if problems are encountered.

Figure 17.1 Sequential Update

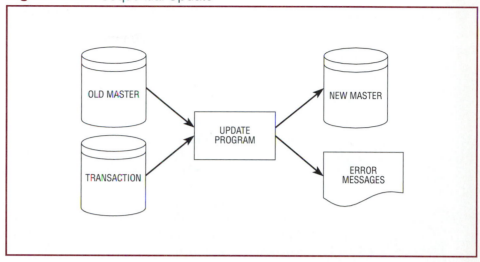

Figure 17.2 Sequential Update with Data Files

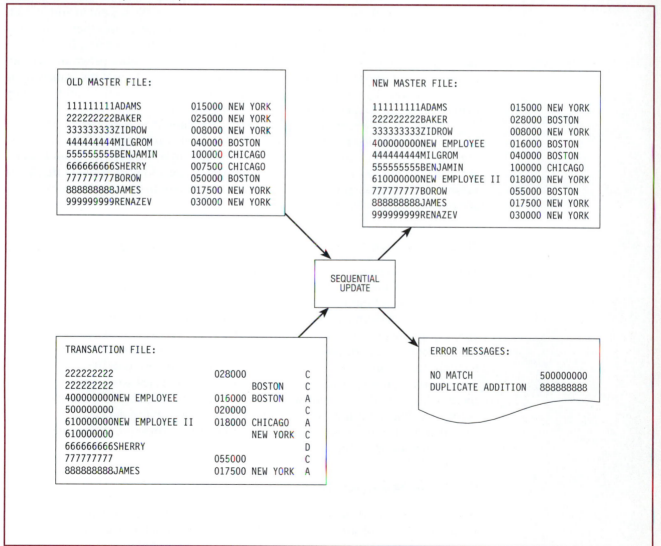

```
OLD MASTER FILE:

111111111ADAMS          015000 NEW YORK
222222222BAKER          025000 NEW YORK
333333333ZIDROW         008000 NEW YORK
444444444MILGROM        040000 BOSTON
555555555BENJAMIN       100000 CHICAGO
666666666SHERRY         007500 CHICAGO
777777777BOROW          050000 BOSTON
888888888JAMES          017500 NEW YORK
999999999RENAZEV        030000 NEW YORK
```

```
NEW MASTER FILE:

111111111ADAMS          015000 NEW YORK
222222222BAKER          028000 BOSTON
333333333ZIDROW         008000 NEW YORK
400000000NEW EMPLOYEE   016000 BOSTON
444444444MILGROM        040000 BOSTON
555555555BENJAMIN       100000 CHICAGO
610000000NEW EMPLOYEE II 018000 NEW YORK
777777777BOROW          055000 BOSTON
888888888JAMES          017500 NEW YORK
999999999RENAZEV        030000 NEW YORK
```

SEQUENTIAL UPDATE

```
TRANSACTION FILE:

222222222              028000           C
222222222                      BOSTON  C
400000000NEW EMPLOYEE  016000 BOSTON   A
500000000              020000          C
610000000NEW EMPLOYEE II 018000 CHICAGO A
610000000                      NEW YORK C
666666666SHERRY                        D
777777777              055000          C
888888888JAMES         017500 NEW YORK A
```

```
ERROR MESSAGES:

NO MATCH            500000000
DUPLICATE ADDITION  888888888
```

Every record in the old master file contains four fields: social security number, name, salary, and location. The records in the old master are in sequence by social security number, the value of which must be *unique* for every record in the file. Records in the transaction file are also in sequence by social security number, and three types of transactions (additions, changes, and deletions) are present. The update procedure must be general enough to accommodate multiple transactions for the same record; for example, employee 222222222 has two records in the transaction file, both of which are corrections.

Records with a transaction type of **A** are to be added to the new master file in their entirety. (Thus, New Employee, with social security number 400000000, does not appear on the old master but has been added to the new master.) Records with a transaction type of **D** are to be deleted. (Hence, Sherry, with social security number 666666666, appears in the old master but not the new master.) Records with a transaction code of **C** indicate a change in the value of a specific field(s) and contain only the social security number and field(s) to be changed. (Accordingly, Baker, with social security number 222222222, has had his salary and location changed to $28,000 and Boston, respectively.)

Note, too, that in addition to the records for which there is activity, the old master contains several records for which there is no corresponding transaction; for example, there are no transactions for records with social security numbers of 333333333 and 999999999. Such records are simply copied intact to the new master.

All of these illustrations assume that the transaction file is valid in and of itself by virtue of a previously executed *stand-alone edit* program. In other words, the validation of the incoming transaction file has already been accomplished in an earlier program. This enables simplified logic in the maintenance program, as it can assume that all transactions contain a valid code (A, C, or D), that the transactions are in sequence by social security number, that additions contain all necessary fields, and so on. (Data validation was first introduced in Chapter 8.)

There are, however, two types of errors that cannot be detected in the stand-alone edit, and which must be checked in the update program itself. These are the attempted correction or deletion of a nonexistent old master record (a *no match*), and the addition of a new record that is already in the old master file (a *duplicate addition*). The transaction file in Figure 17.2 illustrates both errors (with transactions 500000000 and 888888888, respectively).

Sequential versus Nonsequential Processing

This chapter is concerned entirely with a *sequential update* whereby every record in the old master is copied to the new master regardless of whether or not it changes. This technique is perfectly adequate when there is substantial activity in the old master file (that is, when many records change), but inefficient if only a few changes are made to the existing master file.

By contrast, a *nonsequential update* uses a single master file, which functions as both the old and new master. The records in the transaction file are processed one at a time, in no particular sequence, and matched against the existing master file. Nonsequential processing works best with low-activity files because unchanged records are left alone; that is, only those master records with a matching transaction record are written (rewritten) in the master file. Nonsequential processing is discussed in Chapter 18.

Periodic Maintenance

All file maintenance is done *periodically*, with the frequency depending on the application. A file of student transcripts is updated only a few times a year; a bank's checking transactions are updated daily, with other types of systems being updated

Figure 17.3 Two-period Sequential Update

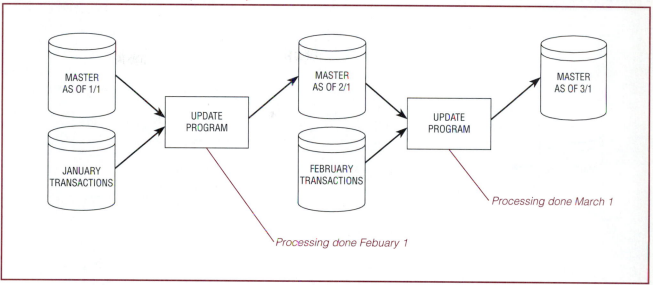

weekly or monthly. (Real-time applications, which process transactions as they occur, are covered in conjunction with nonsequential processing in the next chapter.)

A monthly cycle is depicted in Figure 17.3, beginning with a master file on January 1. Transactions are collected (batched) during the month of January. Then, on February 1, the master file of January 1 (now the old master) is processed with the transactions accrued during January, to produce a new master as of February 1. The process continues from month to month. Transactions are collected during February. On March 1, we use the file created February 1 as the old master, run it against the February transactions, and produce a new master as of March 1. The process continues indefinitely.

Figure 17.3 also serves as a basis for discussion of how ***backup procedures*** are implemented. Consider, for example, the situation on March 1 after the update has been run. The installation now has three ***generations*** of the master file; the file just produced (current master), the file produced on February 1st (previous master), and the original master file of January 1st (second previous master).

The availability of previous generations of the master file enables re-creation of the update process, should the need arise. Thus, an installation could rerun the update of March 1st, provided it retained the February master and associated transaction file. It could also go back a generation and recreate the February master, given that it retained the original January master and its associated transaction file. The number of generations that are retained depends on the individual installation, but will seldom be fewer than three. This type of backup is referred to as a ***grandfather-father-son*** strategy (with apologies to women).

Data Validation

The need for ***data validation*** is paramount, regardless of whether processing is done sequentially or nonsequentially, or how many generations of backup are retained. The example in Figure 17.2 simply assumed a valid transaction file, an assumption that is far too unrealistic in practice. Accordingly we introduce concepts of data validation within the basis of a COBOL case study.

Figure 17.4 expands the sequential update of Figure 17.1 to include a separate step for data validation, in which the transaction file is first input to a stand-alone

Figure 17.4   Sequential Update with Data Validation

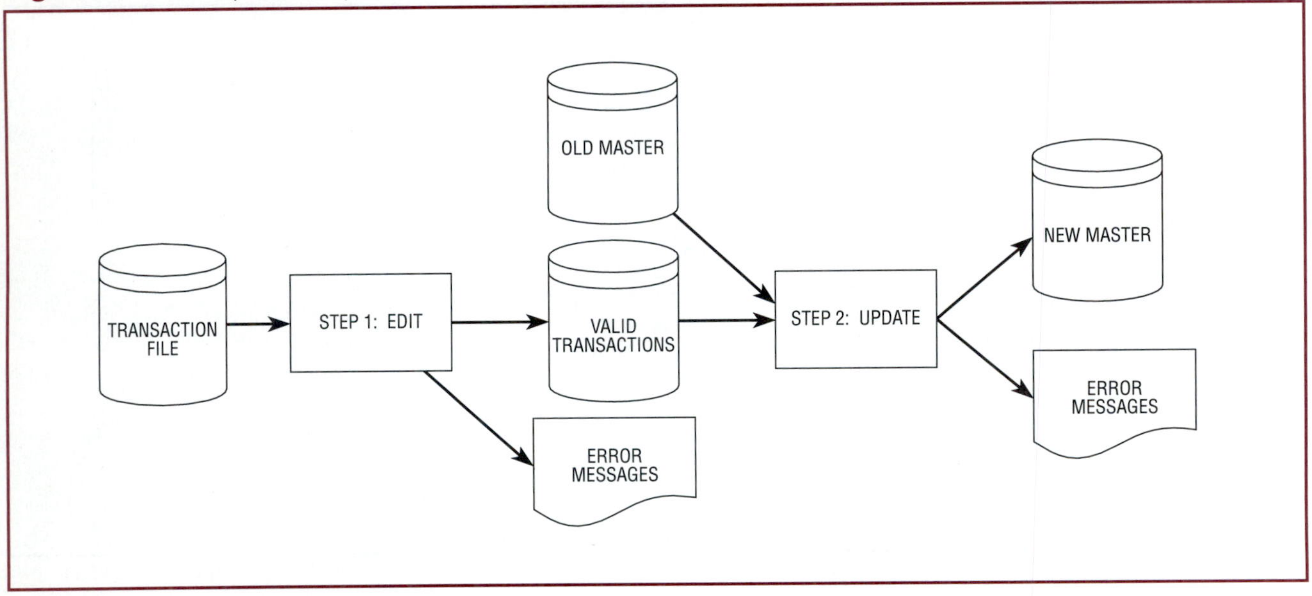

edit program. This program checks transactions for several errors (invalid transaction codes, incomplete additions, and so on), and only those transactions that pass all validity checks will be written to the output (valid) transaction file. The latter is then input to the sequential update.

In effect, Figure 17.4 is a blueprint for the remainder of the chapter. We begin with specifications for the edit program, develop the program completely, present a second set of specifications for the file maintenance (update) program, and develop that program in the second half of the chapter.

Programming Specifications

Program Name: Data Validation

Narrative: This program illustrates typical types of data validation, which are implemented in a stand-alone edit program.

Input File(s):   TRANSACTION-FILE

Input Record Layout:

```
01 TRANSACTION-RECORD.
    05  TR-SOC-SEC-NUMBER           PIC X(9).
    05  TR-NAME.
        10  TR-LAST-NAME            PIC X(15).
        10  TR-INITIALS             PIC XX.
    05  TR-LOCATION-CODE            PIC X(3).
    05  TR-COMMISSION-RATE          PIC 99.
    05  TR-SALES-AMOUNT             PIC 9(5).
    05  TR-TRANSACTION-CODE         PIC X.
        88  ADDITION        VALUE 'A'.
        88  CORRECTION      VALUE 'C'.
        88  DELETION        VALUE 'D'.
```

Test Data: See Figure 17.5a.

Output Files: VALID-TRANSACTION-FILE

ERROR-FILE

Output Record Layout: Identical to the input record layout.

Processing Requirements:

1. Process a file of incoming transactions, rejecting any (and all) invalid transactions with an appropriate error message. Each transaction is to be checked for the following:

   a. Sequence—The transactions are supposed to be in ascending sequence according to social security number by virtue of a previous program. (Multiple transactions with the same social security number are allowed). Accordingly, this program is not to sort the transaction file but to implement logic to ensure that the transactions are in fact in order. (Sorting is time consuming and should not be repeated if the transactions are already in order.)

   b. Valid transaction code—Only three types of transaction codes are permitted: A, C, or D, denoting additions, corrections, and deletions, respectively. Any other transaction code (including a blank) is to be rejected.

   c. Completeness—Additions are to contain the employee's name and initials, location, and commission rate. All fields are to be checked with individual messages written for any missing field(s). Corrections must contain a value for the sales amount.

   d. Data types—TR-COMMISSION-RATE (required for an addition) and TR-SALES-AMOUNT (required for a correction) must be numeric fields. A violation of either condition requires a specific error message.

   e. Valid location code—Additions are to contain a valid location code—that is, a location code of ATL, BOS, NYC, PHI, or SF (corresponding to the entries in a location codes table to be embedded within the program).

2. All valid transactions are to be written to a VALID-TRANSACTION-FILE, which will be created as an output file by the program. Invalid transactions may be discarded after the appropriate error message has been printed.

The function of the edit program is best understood by examining Figure 17.5, which contains the input transaction file, associated error messages, and the output (valid) transaction file. Fourteen transactions were input to the edit program (Figure 17.5a), but only eight of these passed all validity checks and thus made it to the output file (Figure 17.5c). You may find it useful to review each of the rejected transactions in conjunction with the associated error message in Figure 17.5b.

Figure 17.5 Valid Transaction File

```
000000000BOROW        JSATL07     A
000000000BOROW        JS    10000C
000000000BOROW        JS    20000C
100000000GRABER       P     30000
222222222NEW GUY      RT          A
333333333ESMAN        TNNY 09     A
400000000MOLDOF       BLATL15     A
444444444RICHARDS     IM    05000C
555555555JORDAN        BOS07      A
700000000MILGROM      A           D
666666666JOHNSON      M NYC12     A
800000000VAZQUEZ      C     55000C
```

Figure 17.5 (continued)

```
800000000VILLAR         C          C
999999999GILLENSON      MANYC10     A
```

(a) Transaction File

```
INVALID TRANSACTION CODE                100000000GRABER      P        30000
MISSING LOCATION CODE                   222222222NEW GUY     RT            A
MISSING OR NON-NUMERIC COMMISSION RATE  222222222NEW GUY     RT            A
INVALID LOCATION CODE                   333333333ESMAN       TNNY 09       A
MISSING NAME OR INITIALS                555555555JORDAN          BOS07     A
SOCIAL SECURITY NUMBER OUT OF SEQUENCE  666666666JOHNSON     M NYC12       A
MISSING OR NON-NUMERIC SALES AMOUNT     800000000VILLAR      C          C
```

(b) Error Messages

```
000000000BOROW          JSATL07     A
000000000BOROW          JS   10000C
000000000BOROW          JS   20000C
400000000MOLDOF         BLATL15     A
444444444RICHARDS       IM   05000C
700000000MILGROM        A           D
800000000VAZQUEZ        C    55000C
999999999GILLENSON      MANYC10     A
```

(c) Valid Transaction File

Figure 17.6 Hierarchy Chart for Data Validation Program

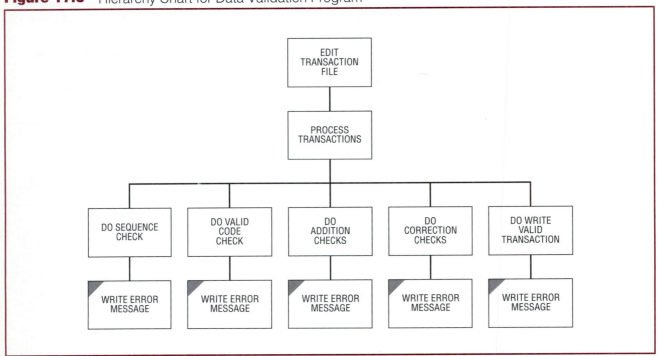

Designing the Program

The edit program is developed along the same lines as any other program, first by designing a hierarchy chart to include the functions required by the program, and then by developing pseudocode to embrace sequence and decision-making logic.

The hierarchy chart in Figure 17.6 is straightforward and should not present any difficulty. Note, however, that the module WRITE-ERROR-MESSAGE is called from several places in the program because the function is subservient to each of the error-checking modules. We have decided, therefore, to place these statements in a separate routine, rather than repeat the identical code in multiple places throughout the program.

The pseudocode for the data validation program is shown in Figure 17.7. Each incoming transaction is assumed to be valid initially, so that 'YES' is moved to

Figure 17.7 Pseudocode for Data Validation Program

```
Open files
DO while data remains
    READ transaction file
        AT END
            Indicate no more data
        NOT AT END
            Move 'YES' to valid-record-switch
            IF trans-social-security < previous-social-security
                Move 'NO' to valid-record-switch
                Write error message
            ENDIF
            Move trans-social-security to previous-social-security
            IF transaction-code is not valid
                Move 'NO' to valid-record-switch
                Write error message
            ENDIF
            IF addition
                IF transaction fails addition-check(s)
                    Move 'NO' to valid-record-switch
                    Write error message(s)
                ENDIF
            ELSE
                IF correction
                    IF sales-amount not numeric
                        Move 'NO' to valid-record-switch
                        Write error message
                    ENDIF
                ENDIF
            ENDIF
            IF valid-record-switch = 'YES'
                Write valid-transaction-record
            ENDIF
    ENDREAD
ENDDO
Close files
Stop run
```

VALID-RECORD-SWITCH. The transaction is then subjected to the various editing requirements, any one of which could cause VALID-RECORD-SWITCH to be set to 'NO'. Only if the transaction passes all of the individual checks (that is, if VALID-RECORD-SWITCH is still set to 'YES') is it written to the valid record file at the end of the loop.

The Completed Program

The completed program is shown in Figure 17.8. One technique worthy of special mention is the establishment of a table for the error messages (lines 47 through 64) and the subsequent printing of an error message in the paragraph 400-WRITE-ERROR-MESSAGE (lines 167–172).

Figure 17.8   The Edit Program

```
1       IDENTIFICATION DIVISION.
2       PROGRAM-ID.   EDIT.
3       AUTHOR.        ROBERT GRAUER.
4
5       ENVIRONMENT DIVISION.
6       INPUT-OUTPUT SECTION.
7       FILE-CONTROL.
8          SELECT TRANSACTION-FILE         ASSIGN TO TRANS
9              ORGANIZATION IS LINE SEQUENTIAL.
10         SELECT VALID-TRANSACTION-FILE   ASSIGN TO VALTRANS
11             ORGANIZATION IS LINE SEQUENTIAL.
12         SELECT ERROR-FILE               ASSIGN TO ERRORS
13             ORGANIZATION IS LINE SEQUENTIAL.
14
15      DATA DIVISION.
16      FILE SECTION.
17      FD  TRANSACTION-FILE
18          DATA RECORD IS TRANSACTION-RECORD.
19      01  TRANSACTION-RECORD              PIC X(37).
20
21      FD  VALID-TRANSACTION-FILE
22          DATA RECORD IS VALID-TRANSACTION-RECORD.
23      01  VALID-TRANSACTION-RECORD        PIC X(37).
24
25      FD  ERROR-FILE
26          DATA RECORD IS ERROR-RECORD.
27      01  ERROR-RECORD                    PIC X(132).
28
29      WORKING-STORAGE SECTION.
30      01  FILLER                          PIC X(14)
31              VALUE 'WS BEGINS HERE'.
32
33      01  WS-TRANSACTION-RECORD.
34          05  TR-SOC-SEC-NUMBER           PIC X(9).
35          05  TR-NAME.
```

Valid transactions are written to separate file (annotation pointing to lines 10–11)

Figure 17.8 *(continued)*

```
36                    10   TR-LAST-NAME              PIC X(15).
37                    10   TR-INITIALS               PIC XX.
38              05   TR-LOCATION-CODE                PIC X(3).
39              05   TR-COMMISSION-RATE              PIC 99.
40              05   TR-SALES-AMOUNT                 PIC 9(5).
41              05   TR-TRANSACTION-CODE             PIC X.
42                    88   ADDITION       VALUE 'A'.
43                    88   CORRECTION     VALUE 'C'.
44                    88   DELETION       VALUE 'D'.
45                    88   VALID-CODES    VALUES 'A', 'C', 'D'.
46
47        01   ERROR-VALUES-TABLE.
48              05   ERROR-VALUES.
49                    10   FILLER                    PIC X(40)
50                        VALUE 'SOCIAL SECURITY NUMBER OUT OF SEQUENCE'.
51                    10   FILLER                    PIC X(40)
52                        VALUE 'INVALID TRANSACTION CODE'.
53                    10   FILLER                    PIC X(40)
54                        VALUE 'MISSING NAME OR INITIALS'.
55                    10   FILLER                    PIC X(40)
56                        VALUE 'MISSING LOCATION CODE'.
57                    10   FILLER                    PIC X(40)
58                        VALUE 'INVALID LOCATION CODE'.
59                    10   FILLER                    PIC X(40)
60                        VALUE 'MISSING OR NON-NUMERIC COMMISSION RATE'.
61                    10   FILLER                    PIC X(40)
62                        VALUE 'MISSING OR NON-NUMERIC SALES AMOUNT'.
63              05   ERROR-TABLE REDEFINES ERROR-VALUES.
64                    10   ERROR-MESSAGE OCCURS 7 TIMES PIC X(40).
65
66        01   LOCATION-VALUES-TABLE.
67              05   LOCATION-VALUES.
68                    10   FILLER              PIC X(3)   VALUE 'ATL'.
69                    10   FILLER              PIC X(3)   VALUE 'BOS'.
70                    10   FILLER              PIC X(3)   VALUE 'NYC'.
71                    10   FILLER              PIC X(3)   VALUE 'PHI'.
72                    10   FILLER              PIC X(3)   VALUE 'SF '.
73              05   LOCATION-TABLE REDEFINES LOCATION-VALUES.
74                    10   LOCATION OCCURS 5 TIMES
75                        INDEXED BY LOCATION-INDEX    PIC X(3).
76
77        01   WS-ERROR-LINE.
78              05   FILLER                     PIC X(2).
79              05   EL-REASON                  PIC X(40).
80              05   EL-TRANSACTION             PIC X(37).
81              05   FILLER                     PIC X(54).
82
83        01   WS-SWITCHES-AND-DATANAMES.
84              05   WS-EOF-SWITCH              PIC X(3)   VALUE 'NO '.
85              05   WS-VALID-RECORD-SWITCH     PIC X(3)   VALUE SPACES.
```

Error messages are grouped in a common table

Figure 17.8   *(continued)*

```
86              05  WS-PREVIOUS-SOC-SEC-NUMBER      PIC X(9)  VALUE SPACES.
87              05  WS-ERROR-CODE                   PIC 99.
88
89      PROCEDURE DIVISION.
90      100-EDIT-TRANSACTION-FILE.
91          OPEN INPUT TRANSACTION-FILE
92               OUTPUT VALID-TRANSACTION-FILE
93                      ERROR-FILE.
94          PERFORM UNTIL WS-EOF-SWITCH = 'YES'
95              READ TRANSACTION-FILE INTO WS-TRANSACTION-RECORD
96                  AT END
97                      MOVE 'YES' TO WS-EOF-SWITCH
98                  NOT AT END
99                      PERFORM 210-PROCESS-TRANSACTIONS
100             END-READ
101         END-PERFORM.
102         CLOSE TRANSACTION-FILE
103               VALID-TRANSACTION-FILE
104               ERROR-FILE.
105         STOP RUN.
106
107     210-PROCESS-TRANSACTIONS.
108         MOVE 'YES' TO WS-VALID-RECORD-SWITCH.
109         PERFORM 300-DO-SEQUENCE-CHECK.
110         PERFORM 310-DO-VALID-CODE-CHECK.
111         IF ADDITION
112             PERFORM 320-DO-ADDITION-CHECKS
113         ELSE
114             IF CORRECTION
115                 PERFORM 330-DO-CORRECTION-CHECKS
116             END-IF
117         END-IF.
118         IF WS-VALID-RECORD-SWITCH = 'YES'
119             PERFORM 340-WRITE-VALID-TRANSACTION
120         END-IF.
121
122     300-DO-SEQUENCE-CHECK.
123         IF TR-SOC-SEC-NUMBER < WS-PREVIOUS-SOC-SEC-NUMBER
124             MOVE 1 TO WS-ERROR-CODE
125             PERFORM 400-WRITE-ERROR-MESSAGE
126         END-IF.
127         MOVE TR-SOC-SEC-NUMBER TO WS-PREVIOUS-SOC-SEC-NUMBER.
128
129     310-DO-VALID-CODE-CHECK.
130         IF NOT VALID-CODES
131             MOVE 2 TO WS-ERROR-CODE
132             PERFORM 400-WRITE-ERROR-MESSAGE
133         END-IF.
134
135     320-DO-ADDITION-CHECKS.
```

In-line perform and false-condition branch drives the program

Transaction is assumed valid initially

Only valid transactions are written to output file

Appropriate subscript is moved to WS-ERROR-CODE

Figure 17.8   *(continued)*

```
136          IF TR-LAST-NAME = SPACES OR TR-INITIALS = SPACES
137              MOVE 3 TO WS-ERROR-CODE
138              PERFORM 400-WRITE-ERROR-MESSAGE
139          END-IF.
140          IF TR-LOCATION-CODE = SPACES
141              MOVE 4 TO WS-ERROR-CODE
142              PERFORM 400-WRITE-ERROR-MESSAGE
143          ELSE
144              SET LOCATION-INDEX TO 1
145              SEARCH LOCATION
146                 AT END
147                    MOVE 5 TO WS-ERROR-CODE
148                    PERFORM 400-WRITE-ERROR-MESSAGE
149                 WHEN TR-LOCATION-CODE = LOCATION (LOCATION-INDEX)
150                    NEXT SENTENCE
151              END-SEARCH
152          END-IF.
153          IF TR-COMMISSION-RATE NOT NUMERIC
154              MOVE 6 TO WS-ERROR-CODE
155              PERFORM 400-WRITE-ERROR-MESSAGE
156          END-IF.
157
158      330-DO-CORRECTION-CHECKS.
159          IF TR-SALES-AMOUNT NOT NUMERIC
160              MOVE 7 TO WS-ERROR-CODE
161              PERFORM 400-WRITE-ERROR-MESSAGE
162          END-IF.
163
164      340-WRITE-VALID-TRANSACTION.
165          WRITE VALID-TRANSACTION-RECORD FROM WS-TRANSACTION-RECORD.
166
167      400-WRITE-ERROR-MESSAGE.
168          MOVE 'NO ' TO WS-VALID-RECORD-SWITCH.
169          MOVE SPACES TO WS-ERROR-LINE.
170          MOVE ERROR-MESSAGE (WS-ERROR-CODE) TO EL-REASON.
171          MOVE WS-TRANSACTION-RECORD TO EL-TRANSACTION.
172          WRITE ERROR-RECORD FROM WS-ERROR-LINE.
```

SEARCH statement nested in IF statement

All error messages are produced by a common routine

The use of an ***error message table*** enables the programmer to see at a glance all of the errors checked by the program, and further to format those messages in identical fashion. It also facilitates the use of a common routine to display the individual messages, rather than having to duplicate code throughout the program. Observe, therefore, that each error routine moves an appropriate subscript value to WS-ERROR-CODE upon detection of an error, which is then used by 400-WRITE-ERROR-MESSAGE to display the appropriate error.

Is data validation worth the extra time and trouble? Any programmer who has ever been called at two in the morning will answer strongly in the affirmative. Put another way, diligent application of data validation (sometimes known as ***defensive programming***) minimizes the need for subsequent debugging. All debugging techniques, no matter how sophisticated, suffer from the fact that they are applied *after* a problem has occurred. The inclusion of data validation within a system attempts to detect the (inevitable) errors that will occur *before* they produce a problem.

Sequential File Maintenance

We are now ready to proceed with the main objective of the chapter, the development of a program for sequential file maintenance. Specifications follow in the usual format.

Programming Specifications

Program Name: Sequential Update

Narrative: This program implements the traditional sequential update via the balance line algorithm.

Input Files: TRANSACTION-FILE

OLD-MASTER-FILE

Input Record Layout:
```
01  TRANSACTION-RECORD.
    05  TR-SOC-SEC-NUMBER          PIC X(9).
    05  TR-NAME.
        10  TR-LAST-NAME           PIC X(15).
        10  TR-INITIALS            PIC XX.
    05  TR-LOCATION-CODE           PIC X(3).
    05  TR-COMMISSION-RATE         PIC 99.
    05  TR-SALES-AMOUNT            PIC 9(5).
    05  TR-TRANSACTION-CODE        PIC X.
        88  ADDITION       VALUE 'A'.
        88  CORRECTION     VALUE 'C'.
        88  DELETION       VALUE 'D'.

01  OLD-MASTER-RECORD.
    05  OM-SOC-SEC-NUMBER          PIC X(9).
    05  OM-NAME.
        10  OM-LAST-NAME           PIC X(15).
        10  OM-INITIALS            PIC XX.
    05  OM-LOCATION-CODE           PIC X(3).
    05  OM-COMMISSION-RATE         PIC 99.
    05  OM-YEAR-TO-DATE-SALES      PIC 9(8).
```

Output File: NEW-MASTER-FILE

Output Record Layout: Identical to old master record.

Test Data: See Figure 17.9a (Old Master File) and Figure 17.9b (Valid Transaction File).

Processing Requirements:
1. Develop a sequential update program to process an incoming transaction file and the associated old master file to produce a new master file.

2. The transaction file is assumed to be valid in and of itself by virtue of a stand-alone edit program. Hence, each transaction has a valid transaction code (A, C, or D), numeric

Figure 17.9 Test Data

```
100000000GRABER          P ATL1500000000
200000000RUBIN           MABOS0800020000
300000000ANDERSON        IRBOS1000113000
400000000MOLDOF          BLATL1500000000
500000000GLASSMAN        JSNYC1000045000
600000000GRAUER          RTNYC0800087500
700000000MILGROM         A SF 0900120000
800000000VAZQUEZ         C ATL1200060000
900000000CLARK           E NYC0700002500
```

(a) Old Master

```
000000000BOROW           JSATL07      A
000000000BOROW           JS    10000C
000000000BOROW           JS    20000C
400000000MOLDOF          BLATL15      A
444444444RICHARDS        IM    05000C
700000000MILGROM         A            D
800000000VAZQUEZ         C     55000C
999999999GILLENSON       MANYC10      A
```

(b) Valid Transaction File (Output of Edit Program)

fields are numeric, and so on. Nevertheless, the update program must check (and flag) two kinds of errors that could not be detected in the stand-alone edit, as they require interaction with the old master file. These are:

a. Duplicate additions, in which the social security number of a transaction coded as an addition already exists in the old master,

b. No matches, in which the social security number of a transaction coded as either a deletion or a correction, does not exist in the old master.

3. Transactions coded as additions are to be added to the new master file in their entirety, and will contain a value for every field in the transaction record (except for TR-SALES-AMOUNT). The value of YEAR-TO-DATE-SALES in the new master record is to be initialized to zero.

4. Transactions coded as deletions are to be removed from the master file. These transactions contain only the social security number and transaction code.

5. Transactions coded as corrections contain only the social security number, name, and the transaction sales amount (TR-SALES-AMOUNT). The value of TR-SALES-AMOUNT on the incoming transaction is to be *added* to the value in the YEAR-TO-DATE-SALES field in the master record.

6. Any old master record for which there is no corresponding transaction is to be copied intact to the new master.

The Balance Line Algorithm

Every COBOL book has confronted the problem of a sequential update. Barry Dwyer[1] details a general and elegant solution to the problem known as the ***balance line***

1. B. Dwyer, "One More Time—How to Update a Master File," **Communications of the ACM,** vol. 24, no.1 (January 1981).

algorithm. To understand this solution, realize that the logic in a sequential update is more difficult than what has been encountered in previous chapters because there are multiple input files. The essence of the problem, then, is to determine whether to read from the old master file, the transaction file, or both. The solution is handled neatly in the balance line algorithm by the concept of an active key.

The *active key* is the smaller of the old master key and transaction key currently being processed. Thus, if the transaction key is less than the old master key, the active key is equal to the transaction key; if the transaction and old master keys are equal, the active key is equal to either; finally, if the old master key is less than the transaction key, the active key is the old master. (Note how easily the technique can be extended to multiple transaction files; the active key is always defined as the smallest value of all keys currently processed.)

The active key determines which records are admitted to the update process, and is illustrated with respect to the data in Figure 17.9. At the start of execution, the initial social security numbers for the old master and transaction records are 100000000 and 000000000, respectively, yielding an active key of 000000000. Thus, only the transaction record is considered for processing, while the old master record is held in abeyance. The algorithm processes this transaction, then reads another record from the transaction file, again with social security number 000000000. The keys are compared and again the transaction key is less than the master key, leaving the active key unchanged. After this transaction is processed, a third transaction is read, also with social security number 000000000, with the same results.

The fourth transaction with social security number 400000000 is read and produces a new active key of 100000000, which is the lesser of the old master (100000000) and transaction (400000000) social security numbers. The old master record is admitted to the update process, while the transaction record is held. The process continues in this fashion until eventually both files are out of data.

The balance line algorithm is expressed in pseudocode in Figure 17.10. The initial records are read from each file, and the first active key is determined. Next the major loop is executed until both the old master and transaction files are out of data. (**HIGH-VALUES** is a COBOL figurative literal and denotes the largest possible value. It is a convenient way of forcing *end-of-file* conditions, as will be seen when test data are examined later in the chapter.)

Within the outer loop, the key of the old master record is compared to the active key. If these values are equal, the old master record is moved (but **not** written) to the new master file, and another record is read from the old master file. We are not, however, finished with the original master record as it must be determined if any transactions exist for that record. Accordingly an inner loop is executed, which processes all transactions whose key is equal to the active key. (The transaction file is read repeatedly in the inner loop after each transaction is processed.) When the transaction key no longer equals the active key, a check is made to see if a deletion was processed, and if not, the new master record is written. The next active key is chosen, and the outer loop continues.

Figure 17.10 does not include the logic to accommodate error processing; that is, although the transaction file is assumed to be valid in and of itself, there are additional errors that come to light only in the actual updating process. Specifically, the update program must reject transactions that attempt to add records that already exist in the old master (duplicate additions), and must also reject transactions that attempt to change or delete records that do not exist (a no match).

The easiest way to accomplish this error processing is through the assignment of an *allocation status* to every value of the active key; that is, the value of the key is either allocated or it is not. If the allocation status is on, the record belongs in the file; if the allocation status is off, the record does not belong. Deletion of an existing record changes the status from on to off, whereas addition of a new record alters the

Figure 17.10 Balance Line Algorithm

```
Open files
Read transaction-file, at end move high-values to transaction-key
Read old-master-file, at end move high-values to old-master-key
Choose first active-key
DO WHILE active-key not equal high-values
    IF old-master-key = active-key
        Move old-master-record to new-master-record
        Read old-master-file, at end move high-values to old-master-key
    ENDIF
    DO WHILE transaction-key equal active-key
        Apply transaction to new-master-record
        Read transaction-file, at end move high-values to transaction-key
    ENDDO
    IF no deletion was processed
        Write new-master-record
    ENDIF
    Choose next active-key
ENDDO
Close files
Stop run
```

status from off to on. Any attempt to add a record whose status is already on signifies a duplicate addition. In similar fashion, attempting to change or delete a record whose allocation status is off also signifies an error, as the transaction key is not present in the old master.

Figure 17.11 expands the pseudocode of Figure 17.10 to include RECORD-KEY-ALLOCATED-SWITCH to accommodate this discussion. A record is written to the new master file only when RECORD-KEY-ALLOCATED-SWITCH is set to YES. In other words, deletions are accomplished simply by setting the switch to NO and not writing the record.

You should be convinced of the total generality of Figure 17.11 and, further, that multiple transactions for the same key may be presented in any order. For example, if an addition and correction are input in that order, the record will be added and corrected in the same run. However, if the correction precedes the addition, then the correction will be flagged as a no match, and only the addition will take effect. Two additions for the same key will result in adding the first and flagging the second as a duplicate add. An addition, correction, and deletion may be processed in that order for the same transaction. A deletion followed by an addition may also be processed but will produce an error message, indicating an attempt to delete a record that is not in the old master.

Designing the Hierarchy Chart

Recall that pseudocode and a hierarchy chart depict different things. Pseudocode indicates sequence and decision-making logic, whereas a hierarchy chart depicts function, indicating what has to be done, but not necessarily when. Accordingly, we

Figure 17.11   Expanded Balance Line Algorithm

```
Open files
Read transaction-file, at end move high-values to transaction-key
Read old-master-file, at end move high-values to old-master-key
Choose first active-key
DO WHILE active-key not equal high-values
    IF old-master-key = active-key
        Move 'yes' to record-key-allocated-switch
        Move old-master-record to new-master-record
        Read old-master-file, at end move high-values to old-master-key
    ELSE (active-key is not in old-master-file)
        Move 'no' to record-key-allocated switch
    ENDIF
    DO WHILE transaction-key equal active-key
        DO CASE transaction-code
            CASE addition
                IF record-key-allocated-switch = 'yes'
                    Write 'error - duplicate addition'
                ELSE (active-key is not in old-master-file)
                    Move transaction-record to new-master-record
                    Move 'yes' to record-key-allocated-switch
                ENDIF
            CASE correction
                IF record-key-allocated-switch = 'yes'
                    Process correction
                ELSE (active-key is not in old-master-file)
                    Write 'error - no matching record'
                ENDIF
            CASE deletion
                IF record-key-allocated-switch = 'yes'
                    Move 'no' to record-key-allocated-switch
                ELSE (active-key is not in old-master-file)
                    Write 'error - no matching record'
                ENDIF
        END CASE
        Read transaction-file, at end move high-values to transaction-key
    END DO
    IF record-key-allocated-switch = 'yes'
        write new-master-record
    ENDIF
    Choose next active-key
END DO
Close files
Stop run
```

begin by listing the functional modules necessary to accomplish a sequential update using the balance line algorithm:

Overall Program Function   UPDATE-MASTER-FILE

Functional Modules   READ-TRANSACTION-FILE

                                       READ-OLD-MASTER-FILE

                                       CHOOSE-ACTIVE-KEY

                                       PROCESS-ACTIVE-KEY

                                       BUILD-NEW-MASTER

                                       WRITE-NEW-MASTER

                                       APPLY-TRANSACTIONS-TO-MASTER

                                       ADD-NEW-RECORD

                                       CORRECT-OLD-RECORD

                                       DELETE-OLD-RECORD

The hierarchy chart in Figure 17.12 is developed in top-down fashion, beginning with the overall program function, UPDATE-MASTER-FILE. Development of a hierarchy chart requires explicit specification of the function of each module, which should be apparent from the module name, consisting of a verb, one or two adjectives, and an object. Nevertheless, the module functions are described in depth:

UPDATE-MASTER-FILE   The mainline routine that drives the entire program. It opens the program files, invokes

Figure 17.12   Hierarchy Chart for Sequential Update

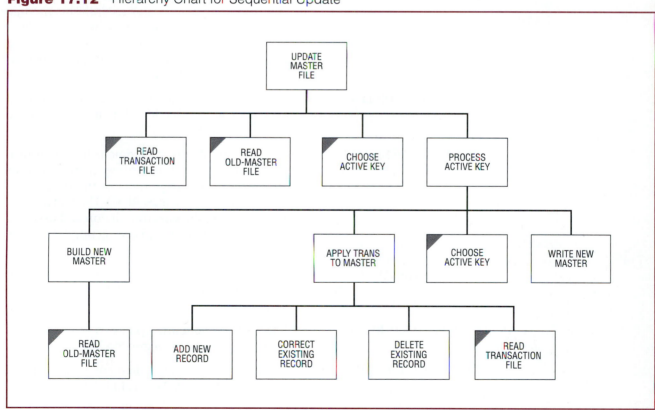

subordinate routines to do an initial read from each input file, and determines the first active key. It invokes PROCESS-ACTIVE-KEY until all files are out of data, closes the files, and terminates the run.

READ-TRANSACTION-FILE	Reads a record from the transaction file and moves HIGH-VALUES to the transaction key when the file is empty. This module is performed from more than one place in the program as indicated by the shading in the upper left-hand corner.
READ-OLD-MASTER-FILE	Reads a record from the old master file and moves HIGH-VALUES to the old master key when the file is empty. This module is performed from more than one place in the program as indicated by the shading in the upper left-hand corner.
CHOOSE-ACTIVE-KEY	Determines the active key for the balance line algorithm from the current values of the old master and transaction records. This module is also performed from more than one place.
PROCESS-ACTIVE-KEY	Performs up to four subordinates according to the value of active key. All four subordinates are invoked when the keys on the old master and transaction files equal the active key, and no deletions were processed.
BUILD-NEW-MASTER	Moves the current old master record to a corresponding new master record. This module is mandated by the nature of a sequential update, which requires that every record in the old master file be copied to the new master file, regardless of whether the record changes.
WRITE-NEW-MASTER	Writes a new master record, and is performed only after all transactions for that record have been processed.
APPLY-TRANS-TO-MASTER	Performs one of three subordinates to add, correct, or delete a record according to the current transaction code. Regardless of the transaction type, the module invokes READ-TRANSACTION-FILE to obtain the next transaction and executes repeatedly as long as the transaction key equals the active key.
ADD-NEW-RECORD	Lowest-level module to add a new record, which will set RECORD-KEY-ALLOCATED-SWITCH to YES.
CORRECT-OLD-RECORD	Lowest-level module to update (correct) the year-to-date sales total in an existing master record.
DELETE-OLD-RECORD	Lowest-level module to delete a record, which will set RECORD-KEY-ALLOCATED-SWITCH to NO.

Top-Down Testing

Top-down testing implies that the highest (most difficult) modules in a hierarchy chart be tested earlier, and more often, than the lower-level (and often trivial) routines. It requires that testing begin as soon as possible, and well before the program is finished. Testing a program before it is completed is accomplished by coding lower-level modules as program stubs, that is, abbreviated versions of completed modules.

The major advantage in this approach is that testing begins sooner in the development cycle. Errors that do exist are found earlier and consequently are easier to correct. Later versions can still contain bugs, but the more difficult problems will already have been resolved in the initial tests.

Figure 17.9 (shown previously) contains sufficient data to adequately test the update program. All transaction types are present with multiple transactions present for the same transaction record (000000000). There is a duplicate addition (400000000) that should be flagged as an error, as well as an attempted correction on a nonexisting social security number (444444444).

It is highly desirable that a person other than the programmer, preferably the user, supply the test data. The latter individual does not know how the program actually works, and thus is in a better position to make up objective data. In addition, the user knows the original specification and is not subject to distortions from the analysis phase. The programmer, on the other hand, is biased, either consciously or subconsciously, and will generate data to accommodate his or her program or interpretation of the specifications. We should also mention that anticipated results are best computed *before* testing begins. Otherwise, it is too easy to assume the program works, because the output "looks right." Indeed, trainees are often so overjoyed merely to get output that they conclude the testing phase upon receiving their first printout.

The Stubs Program

Figure 17.13 contains the stubs program for a sequential update implemented according to the balance line algorithm. It is *complete* in that it contains a paragraph for every module in the hierarchy chart of Figure 17.12, yet *incomplete* because several of the lower-level modules exist only as **program stubs**, that is, abbreviated paragraphs.

Figure 17.13 uses only two files, the old master and transaction, with record descriptions corresponding to the programming specifications. The new master file is not referenced explicitly in the program; instead, the paragraphs 0060-BUILD-NEW-MASTER and 0080-WRITE-NEW-MASTER contain DISPLAY statements to indicate that they have been executed. Indeed, the program contains many such DISPLAY statements to facilitate testing by indicating program flow.

Consider the test data in Figure 17.9, in conjunction with the program in Figure 17.13 and its associated output (Figure 17.14). The program begins by reading the first record from each file, social security numbers 000000000 and 100000000 for the transaction and old master, respectively. The active key is the smaller of the two, social security number 000000000, and corresponds to the transaction value. The paragraph 0070-APPLY-TRANS-TO-MASTER is entered for the first transaction, after which the lower-level paragraph 0090-ADD-NEW-RECORD is invoked. The second and third transactions also have a social security number of 000000000, so that 0070-APPLY-TRANS-TO-MASTER is executed twice more, each time followed by 0100-CORRECT-EXISTING-RECORD. Finally, when the transaction key no longer

Figure 17.13 Stubs Program

```
1        IDENTIFICATION DIVISION.
2        PROGRAM-ID.    SEQSTUB.
3        AUTHOR.         ROBERT GRAUER.
4
5        ENVIRONMENT DIVISION.
6        INPUT-OUTPUT SECTION.
7        FILE-CONTROL.
8            SELECT TRANSACTION-FILE      ASSIGN TO VALTRANS
9                ORGANIZATION IS LINE SEQUENTIAL.
10           SELECT OLD-MASTER-FILE       ASSIGN TO OLDMAST
11               ORGANIZATION IS LINE SEQUENTIAL.
12                                                          Two input files are required
13       DATA DIVISION.
14       FILE SECTION.
15       FD  TRANSACTION-FILE
16           DATA RECORD IS TRANSACTION-RECORD.
17       01  TRANSACTION-RECORD                 PIC X(37).
18
19       FD  OLD-MASTER-FILE
20           DATA RECORD IS OLD-MAST-RECORD.
21       01  OLD-MAST-RECORD                    PIC X(39).
22
23       WORKING-STORAGE SECTION.
24       01  FILLER                             PIC X(14)
25               VALUE 'WS BEGINS HERE'.
26
27       01  WS-TRANS-RECORD.
28           05   TR-SOC-SEC-NUMBER             PIC X(9).
29           05   TR-NAME.
30               10  TR-LAST-NAME               PIC X(15).
31               10  TR-INITIALS                PIC XX.
32           05   TR-LOCATION-CODE              PIC X(3).
33           05   TR-COMMISSION-RATE            PIC 99.
34           05   TR-SALES-AMOUNT               PIC 9(5).
35           05   TR-TRANSACTION-CODE           PIC X.
36               88  ADDITION        VALUE 'A'.
37               88  CORRECTION      VALUE 'C'.
38               88  DELETION        VALUE 'D'.          Three transaction types are permitted
39
40       01  WS-OLD-MAST-RECORD.
41           05   OM-SOC-SEC-NUMBER             PIC X(9).
42           05   OM-NAME.
43               10  OM-LAST-NAME               PIC X(15).
44               10  OM-INITIALS                PIC XX.
45           05   OM-LOCATION-CODE              PIC X(3).
46           05   OM-COMMISSION-RATE            PIC 99.
47           05   OM-YEAR-TO-DATE-SALES         PIC 9(8).
48
49       01  WS-BALANCE-LINE-SWITCHES.
50           05   WS-ACTIVE-KEY                 PIC X(9).
51           05   WS-RECORD-KEY-ALLOCATED-SWITCH PIC X(3).
```

Figure 17.13 *(continued)*

```
52
53        PROCEDURE DIVISION.
54        0010-UPDATE-MASTER-FILE.
55            OPEN INPUT TRANSACTION-FILE
56                      OLD-MASTER-FILE.
57            PERFORM 0020-READ-TRANSACTION-FILE.
58            PERFORM 0030-READ-OLD-MASTER-FILE.          Initial reads
59            PERFORM 0040-CHOOSE-ACTIVE-KEY.
60            PERFORM 0050-PROCESS-ACTIVE-KEY
61                UNTIL WS-ACTIVE-KEY = HIGH-VALUES.
62            CLOSE TRANSACTION-FILE
63                      OLD-MASTER-FILE.
64            STOP RUN.
65
66        0020-READ-TRANSACTION-FILE.
67            READ TRANSACTION-FILE INTO WS-TRANS-RECORD
68                AT END MOVE HIGH-VALUES TO TR-SOC-SEC-NUMBER
69            END-READ.
70
71        0030-READ-OLD-MASTER-FILE.
72            READ OLD-MASTER-FILE INTO WS-OLD-MAST-RECORD
73                AT END MOVE HIGH-VALUE TO OM-SOC-SEC-NUMBER
74            END-READ.
75
76        0040-CHOOSE-ACTIVE-KEY.
77            IF TR-SOC-SEC-NUMBER LESS THAN OM-SOC-SEC-NUMBER
78                MOVE TR-SOC-SEC-NUMBER TO WS-ACTIVE-KEY
79            ELSE
80                MOVE OM-SOC-SEC-NUMBER TO WS-ACTIVE-KEY    Determines active key
81            END-IF.
82
83        0050-PROCESS-ACTIVE-KEY.
84            DISPLAY '     '.
85            DISPLAY '     '.
86            DISPLAY 'RECORDS BEING PROCESSED'.
87            DISPLAY '   TRANSACTION SOC SEC #: ' TR-SOC-SEC-NUMBER.    DISPLAY statements
88            DISPLAY '   OLD MASTER SOC SEC #:  ' OM-SOC-SEC-NUMBER.    facilitate testing
89            DISPLAY '   ACTIVE KEY:           ' WS-ACTIVE-KEY.
90            DISPLAY '     '.
91
92            IF OM-SOC-SEC-NUMBER = WS-ACTIVE-KEY
93                MOVE 'YES' TO WS-RECORD-KEY-ALLOCATED-SWITCH
94                PERFORM 0060-BUILD-NEW-MASTER
95            ELSE
96                MOVE 'NO' TO WS-RECORD-KEY-ALLOCATED-SWITCH
97            END-IF.
98
99            PERFORM 0070-APPLY-TRANS-TO-MASTER
100               UNTIL WS-ACTIVE-KEY NOT EQUAL TR-SOC-SEC-NUMBER.
101
102           IF WS-RECORD-KEY-ALLOCATED-SWITCH = 'YES'
```

Figure 17.13   *(continued)*

```
103                 PERFORM 0080-WRITE-NEW-MASTER
104            END-IF.
105
106        PERFORM 0040-CHOOSE-ACTIVE-KEY.
107
108    0060-BUILD-NEW-MASTER.
109        DISPLAY '0060-BUILD-NEW-MASTER ENTERED'.
110        PERFORM 0030-READ-OLD-MASTER-FILE.
111
112    0070-APPLY-TRANS-TO-MASTER.
113        DISPLAY '0070-APPLY-TRANS-TO-MASTER ENTERED'
114            '   TRANSACTION CODE: '  TR-TRANSACTION-CODE.
115
116        EVALUATE TRUE
117            WHEN ADDITION
118                PERFORM 0090-ADD-NEW-RECORD
119            WHEN CORRECTION
120                PERFORM 0100-CORRECT-EXISTING-RECORD
121            WHEN DELETION
122                PERFORM 0110-DELETE-EXISTING-RECORD
123            WHEN OTHER
124                DISPLAY 'INVALID TRANSACTION CODE'
125        END-EVALUATE.
126
127        PERFORM 0020-READ-TRANSACTION-FILE.
128
129    0080-WRITE-NEW-MASTER.
130        DISPLAY '0080-WRITE-NEW-MASTER ENTERED'.
131
132    0090-ADD-NEW-RECORD.
133        DISPLAY '0090-ADD-NEW-RECORD ENTERED'.
134        IF WS-RECORD-KEY-ALLOCATED-SWITCH = 'YES'
135            DISPLAY '  ERROR-DUPLICATE ADDITION: ' TR-SOC-SEC-NUMBER
136        ELSE
137            MOVE 'YES' TO WS-RECORD-KEY-ALLOCATED-SWITCH
138        END-IF.
139
140    0100-CORRECT-EXISTING-RECORD.
141        DISPLAY '0100-CORRECT-EXISTING-RECORD ENTERED.'
142        IF WS-RECORD-KEY-ALLOCATED-SWITCH = 'YES'
143            CONTINUE
144        ELSE
145            DISPLAY '  ERROR-NO MATCHING RECORD: ' TR-SOC-SEC-NUMBER
146        END-IF.
147
148    0110-DELETE-EXISTING-RECORD.
149        DISPLAY '0110-DELETE-EXISTING-RECORD ENTERED'.
150        IF WS-RECORD-KEY-ALLOCATED-SWITCH = 'YES'
151            MOVE 'NO' TO WS-RECORD-KEY-ALLOCATED-SWITCH
152        ELSE
153            DISPLAY '  ERROR-NO MATCHING RECORD: ' TR-SOC-SEC-NUMBER
154        END-IF.
```

DISPLAY statement indicates paragraph has been called

Determines which lower-level module to execute

Partially coded paragraphs

RECORD-KEY-ALLOCATED-SWITCH controls deletion

Figure 17.14 Truncated Output of Stubs Program

```
RECORDS BEING PROCESSED
  TRANSACTION SOC SEC #: 000000000
  OLD MASTER SOC SEC #:  100000000
  ACTIVE KEY:            000000000

0070-APPLY-TRANS-TO-MASTER ENTERED    TRANSACTION CODE: A
0090-ADD-NEW-RECORD ENTERED
0070-APPLY-TRANS-TO-MASTER ENTERED    TRANSACTION CODE: C
0100-CORRECT-EXISTING-RECORD ENTERED.
0070-APPLY-TRANS-TO-MASTER ENTERED    TRANSACTION CODE: C
0100-CORRECT-EXISTING-RECORD ENTERED.
0080-WRITE-NEW-MASTER ENTERED

RECORDS BEING PROCESSED
  TRANSACTION SOC SEC #: 400000000
  OLD MASTER SOC SEC #:  100000000
  ACTIVE KEY:            100000000

0060-BUILD-NEW-MASTER ENTERED
0080-WRITE-NEW-MASTER ENTERED

RECORDS BEING PROCESSED
  TRANSACTION SOC SEC #: 400000000
  OLD MASTER SOC SEC #:  200000000
  ACTIVE KEY:            200000000

0060-BUILD-NEW-MASTER ENTERED
0080-WRITE-NEW-MASTER ENTERED

RECORDS BEING PROCESSED
  TRANSACTION SOC SEC #: 400000000
  OLD MASTER SOC SEC #:  300000000
  ACTIVE KEY:            300000000

0060-BUILD-NEW-MASTER ENTERED
0080-WRITE-NEW-MASTER ENTERED

RECORDS BEING PROCESSED
  TRANSACTION SOC SEC #: 400000000
  OLD MASTER SOC SEC #:  400000000
  ACTIVE KEY:            400000000

0060-BUILD-NEW-MASTER ENTERED
0070-APPLY-TRANS-TO-MASTER ENTERED    TRANSACTION CODE: A
0090-ADD-NEW-RECORD ENTERED
  ERROR-DUPLICATE ADDITION: 400000000
0080-WRITE-NEW-MASTER ENTERED
    .
        .
          .
RECORDS BEING PROCESSED
  TRANSACTION SOC SEC #: 999999999
  OLD MASTER SOC SEC #:
  ACTIVE KEY:            999999999

0070-APPLY-TRANS-TO-MASTER ENTERED    TRANSACTION CODE: A
0090-ADD-NEW-RECORD ENTERED
0080-WRITE-NEW-MASTER ENTERED
```

equals the active key, that is, when the fourth transaction (Moldof, with social security number 400000000) is read, the paragraph 0080-WRITE-NEW-MASTER is executed to write the new (and corrected) record to the new master file.

The next determination of the active key compares the transaction just read (social security number 400000000) to the current old master social record (social security number 100000000), producing an active key of 100000000. The program decides there are no transactions for this old master record and copies it immediately to the new master file, as implied by the paragraphs 0060-BUILD-NEW-MASTER and 0080-WRITE-NEW-MASTER. The next two determinations of the active key (for old master records 200000000 and 300000000) produce a similar result. The fifth determination of the active key finds the same social security number in both files in conjunction with an attempted addition in the transaction file, producing an error message for a duplicate addition.

By now you should be gaining confidence that the program is working correctly, because the paragraphs are executing in proper sequence for the test data. We can say therefore that the initial testing has concluded successfully and move on to developing the completed program.

The Completed Program

Once the stubs program has been tested and debugged, it is relatively easy to complete the program because the most difficult portion has already been written. We know that the interaction between modules works correctly; that the program will correctly read from the old master, transaction file, or both; that it will apply multiple transactions to the same master record; and that it will properly perform the appropriate lower-level module to add, correct, or delete a record.

Figure 17.15 contains the expanded update program, which defines an additional FD for the NEW-MASTER-FILE as well as completed paragraphs for the addition and correction routines. The DISPLAY statements associated with the testing procedure have also been deleted.

The files associated with the completed program are shown in Figure 17.16. Figures 17.16a and 17.16b repeat the original test data (for convenience), whereas Figures 17.16c and 17.16d contain the actual output. You should take a moment to verify the results to satisfy yourself that the program is working correctly. Observe in particular how multiple transactions were applied to a single old record (Borow), how Borow and Gillenson were successfully added to the new master, and how Milgrom was deleted. The two error messages correctly reflect both errors, an attempted duplicate addition and a nonmatching social security number.

Figure 17.15 Completed Sequential Update

```
  1        IDENTIFICATION DIVISION.
  2        PROGRAM-ID.    SEQUPDT.
  3        AUTHOR.        ROBERT GRAUER.
  4
  5        ENVIRONMENT DIVISION.
  6        INPUT-OUTPUT SECTION.
  7        FILE-CONTROL.
  8            SELECT TRANSACTION-FILE       ASSIGN TO VALTRANS
  9                ORGANIZATION IS LINE SEQUENTIAL.
 10            SELECT OLD-MASTER-FILE        ASSIGN TO OLDMAST
 11                ORGANIZATION IS LINE SEQUENTIAL.
```

Figure 17.15 *(continued)*

```
12          SELECT NEW-MASTER-FILE        ASSIGN TO NEWMAST.
13              ORGANIZATION IS LINE SEQUENTIAL.
14
15      DATA DIVISION.
16      FILE SECTION.
17      FD  TRANSACTION-FILE
18          DATA RECORD IS TRANSACTION-RECORD.
19      01  TRANSACTION-RECORD              PIC X(37).
20
21      FD  OLD-MASTER-FILE
22          DATA RECORD IS OLD-MAST-RECORD.
23      01  OLD-MAST-RECORD                 PIC X(39).
24
25      FD  NEW-MASTER-FILE
26          DATA RECORD IS NEW-MAST-RECORD.
27      01  NEW-MAST-RECORD                 PIC X(39).
28
29      WORKING-STORAGE SECTION.
30      01  FILLER                          PIC X(14)
31              VALUE 'WS BEGINS HERE'.
32
33      01  WS-TRANS-RECORD.
34          05  TR-SOC-SEC-NUMBER           PIC X(9).
35          05  TR-NAME.
36              10  TR-LAST-NAME            PIC X(15).
37              10  TR-INITIALS             PIC XX.
38          05  TR-LOCATION-CODE            PIC X(3).
39          05  TR-COMMISSION-RATE          PIC 99.
40          05  TR-SALES-AMOUNT             PIC 9(5).
41          05  TR-TRANSACTION-CODE         PIC X.
42              88  ADDITION      VALUE 'A'.
43              88  CORRECTION    VALUE 'C'.
44              88  DELETION      VALUE 'D'.
45
46      01  WS-OLD-MAST-RECORD.
47          05  OM-SOC-SEC-NUMBER           PIC X(9).
48          05  OM-NAME.
49              10  OM-LAST-NAME            PIC X(15).
50              10  OM-INITIALS             PIC XX.
51          05  OM-LOCATION-CODE            PIC X(3).
52          05  OM-COMMISSION-RATE          PIC 99.
53          05  OM-YEAR-TO-DATE-SALES       PIC 9(8).
54
55      01  WS-NEW-MAST-RECORD.
56          05  NM-SOC-SEC-NUMBER           PIC X(9).
57          05  NM-NAME.
58              10  NM-LAST-NAME            PIC X(15).
59              10  NM-INITIALS             PIC XX.
60          05  NM-LOCATION-CODE            PIC X(3).
61          05  NM-COMMISSION-RATE          PIC 99.
```

Output file has been added

Three transaction types

Record layouts are identical

Figure 17.15 *(continued)*

```
62              05  NM-YEAR-TO-DATE-SALES          PIC 9(8).
63
64          01  WS-BALANCE-LINE-SWITCHES.
65              05  WS-ACTIVE-KEY                  PIC X(9).
66              05  WS-RECORD-KEY-ALLOCATED-SWITCH PIC X(3).
67
68          PROCEDURE DIVISION.
69          0010-UPDATE-MASTER-FILE.
70              OPEN INPUT TRANSACTION-FILE
71                        OLD-MASTER-FILE
72                   OUTPUT NEW-MASTER-FILE.
73              PERFORM 0020-READ-TRANSACTION-FILE.
74              PERFORM 0030-READ-OLD-MASTER-FILE.
75              PERFORM 0040-CHOOSE-ACTIVE-KEY.
76              PERFORM 0050-PROCESS-ACTIVE-KEY
77                  UNTIL WS-ACTIVE-KEY = HIGH-VALUES.
78              CLOSE TRANSACTION-FILE
79                    OLD-MASTER-FILE
80                    NEW-MASTER-FILE.
81              STOP RUN.
82
83          0020-READ-TRANSACTION-FILE.
84              READ TRANSACTION-FILE INTO WS-TRANS-RECORD
85                  AT END MOVE HIGH-VALUES TO TR-SOC-SEC-NUMBER
86              END-READ.
87
88          0030-READ-OLD-MASTER-FILE.
89              READ OLD-MASTER-FILE INTO WS-OLD-MAST-RECORD
90                  AT END MOVE HIGH-VALUE TO OM-SOC-SEC-NUMBER
91              END-READ.
92
93          0040-CHOOSE-ACTIVE-KEY.
94              IF TR-SOC-SEC-NUMBER LESS THAN OM-SOC-SEC-NUMBER
95                  MOVE TR-SOC-SEC-NUMBER TO WS-ACTIVE-KEY
96              ELSE
97                  MOVE OM-SOC-SEC-NUMBER TO WS-ACTIVE-KEY
98              END-IF.
99
100         0050-PROCESS-ACTIVE-KEY.
101             IF OM-SOC-SEC-NUMBER = WS-ACTIVE-KEY
102                 MOVE 'YES' TO WS-RECORD-KEY-ALLOCATED-SWITCH
103                 PERFORM 0060-BUILD-NEW-MASTER
104             ELSE
105                 MOVE 'NO' TO WS-RECORD-KEY-ALLOCATED-SWITCH
106             END-IF.
107
108             PERFORM 0070-APPLY-TRANS-TO-MASTER
109                 UNTIL WS-ACTIVE-KEY NOT EQUAL TR-SOC-SEC-NUMBER.
110
111             IF WS-RECORD-KEY-ALLOCATED-SWITCH = 'YES'
112                 PERFORM 0080-WRITE-NEW-MASTER
```

Processing terminates when the active key is HIGH-VALUES: i.e., when both files are empty (annotation for lines 76–77)

Applies multiple transactions to a single master record (annotation for lines 108–109)

Figure 17.15   *(continued)*

```
113              END-IF.
114
115              PERFORM 0040-CHOOSE-ACTIVE-KEY.
116
117          0060-BUILD-NEW-MASTER.
118              MOVE WS-OLD-MAST-RECORD TO WS-NEW-MAST-RECORD.
119              PERFORM 0030-READ-OLD-MASTER-FILE.
120
121          0070-APPLY-TRANS-TO-MASTER.
122              EVALUATE TRUE
123                  WHEN ADDITION
124                      PERFORM 0090-ADD-NEW-RECORD
125                  WHEN CORRECTION
126                      PERFORM 0100-CORRECT-EXISTING-RECORD
127                  WHEN DELETION
128                      PERFORM 0110-DELETE-EXISTING-RECORD
129                  WHEN OTHER
130                      DISPLAY 'INVALID TRANSACTION CODE'
131              END-EVALUATE.
132
133              PERFORM 0020-READ-TRANSACTION-FILE.
134
135          0080-WRITE-NEW-MASTER.
136              WRITE NEW-MAST-RECORD FROM WS-NEW-MAST-RECORD.
137
138          0090-ADD-NEW-RECORD.
139              IF WS-RECORD-KEY-ALLOCATED-SWITCH = 'YES'
140                  DISPLAY '  ERROR-DUPLICATE ADDITION: ' TR-SOC-SEC-NUMBER
141              ELSE
142                  MOVE 'YES' TO WS-RECORD-KEY-ALLOCATED-SWITCH
143                  MOVE SPACES TO WS-NEW-MAST-RECORD
144                  MOVE TR-SOC-SEC-NUMBER TO NM-SOC-SEC-NUMBER
145                  MOVE TR-NAME TO NM-NAME
146                  MOVE TR-LOCATION-CODE TO NM-LOCATION-CODE
147                  MOVE TR-COMMISSION-RATE TO NM-COMMISSION-RATE
148                  MOVE ZEROS TO NM-YEAR-TO-DATE-SALES
149              END-IF.
150
151          0100-CORRECT-EXISTING-RECORD.
152              IF WS-RECORD-KEY-ALLOCATED-SWITCH = 'YES'
153                  ADD TR-SALES-AMOUNT TO NM-YEAR-TO-DATE-SALES
154              ELSE
155                  DISPLAY '  ERROR-NO MATCHING RECORD: ' TR-SOC-SEC-NUMBER
156              END-IF.
157
158          0110-DELETE-EXISTING-RECORD.
159              IF WS-RECORD-KEY-ALLOCATED-SWITCH = 'YES'
160                  MOVE 'NO' TO WS-RECORD-KEY-ALLOCATED-SWITCH
161              ELSE
162                  DISPLAY '  ERROR-NO MATCHING RECORD: ' TR-SOC-SEC-NUMBER
163              END-IF.
```

Expanded from program stub

Precludes writing a new master record

Figure 17.16   Output of the Sequential Update

```
100000000GRABER        P ATL1500000000
200000000RUBIN         MABOS0800020000
300000000ANDERSON      IRBOS1000113000
400000000MOLDOF        BLATL1500000000
500000000GLASSMAN      JSNYC1000045000
600000000GRAUER        RTNYC0800087500
700000000MILGROM       A SF 0900120000
800000000VAZQUEZ       C ATL1200060000
900000000CLARK         E NYC0700002500
```

(a) Old Master

```
000000000BOROW         JSATL07     A
000000000BOROW         JS    10000C
000000000BOROW         JS    20000C
400000000MOLDOF        BLATL15     A
444444444RICHARDS      IM    05000C
700000000MILGROM       A           D
800000000VAZQUEZ       C     55000C
999999999GILLENSON     MANYC10     A
```

(b) Valid Transaction File

```
000000000BOROW         JSATL0700030000
100000000GRABER        P ATL1500000000
200000000RUBIN         MABOS0800020000
300000000ANDERSON      IRBOS1000113000
400000000MOLDOF        BLATL1500000000
500000000GLASSMAN      JSNYC1000045000
600000000GRAUER        RTNYC0800087500
800000000VAZQUEZ       C ATL1200115000
900000000CLARK         E NYC0700002500
999999999GILLENSON     MANYC1000000000
```

(c) New Master File

```
ERROR-DUPLICATE ADDITION: 400000000
ERROR-NO MATCHING RECORD: 444444444
```

(d) Error Messages

S U M M A R Y

Points to Remember

- File maintenance is a necessity of every system and enables three types of transactions. New records may be added, while existing records may be changed or deleted.

- A sequential update copies every record from the old master file to the new master, regardless of whether it changes. By contrast, a nonsequential update uses a single file as both the old and new master. Sequential processing is best when the master file is active and has substantial activity; nonsequential processing is more efficient for inactive files with less activity.

- Data validation is an essential component of file maintenance. The transaction file is typically run through a stand-alone edit prior to the maintenance program to check for valid codes, complete records, and so on. The update program must still check for duplicate additions and/or no matches (that is, transactions entered as corrections or deletions for records that are not present in the master file).

- The balance line algorithm is a general approach to sequential file maintenance. The algorithm allows multiple transactions from one or more transaction files, to reference a single master record.

- Top-down testing was demonstrated through use of a stub program. Early testing ensures that modules are performed in proper sequence and facilitates the correction of any errors detected.

Key Words and Concepts

Active key	New master file
Addition	No match
Allocation status	Nonsequential update
Backup	Old master file
Balance line algorithm	Periodic file maintenance
Correction	Program stub
Data validation	Record-key allocated switch
Defensive programming	Sequential update
Deletion	Stand-alone edit program
Duplicate addition	Stub program
End-of-file condition	Test data
Error message table	Top-down testing and implementation
Grandfather-father-son	Transaction file
Hierarchy chart	

COBOL Element

HIGH-VALUES

F i l l - i n

1. In a sequential update, _____ record in the old master (except those slated for deletion) is copied (rewritten) to the new master, regardless of whether it changes.

2. Incoming transactions to a sequential update have generally been validated in a _____ _____ program.

3. The balance line algorithm (<u>does/does not</u>) require every record in the old master file to have a unique key.

4. The balance line algorithm (<u>does/does not</u>) require every record in the transaction file to have a unique key.

5. In general, the three transaction types that are input to a sequential update are _____, _____ and _____.

6. The RECORD-KEY-ALLOCATED-SWITCH is used in checking for two types of errors: _____ additions, and/or _____.

7. An incomplete addition (<u>can/can not</u>) be detected in a stand-alone edit program.

8. An invalid transaction code (<u>can/can not</u>) be detected in a stand-alone edit program.

9. An incorrectly entered social security number on an otherwise valid transaction (<u>can/can not</u>) be detected in a stand-alone edit program.

10. Top-down testing requires that the _____ levels in a hierarchy chart be tested _____ and more often than the lower-level routines.

11. In order to implement top-down testing, a _____ program is developed, which contains several one-line paragraphs consisting of _____ statements.

12. The grandfather-father-son backup scheme implies that at least _____ generations of files are kept.

13. _____ _____ is a figurative literal used to force the end-of-file condition.

T r u e / F a l s e

1. The balance line algorithm requires a unique key for every record in the old master file.

2. Transactions to the balance line algorithm must be presented in the following order: additions, changes, deletions.

3. The balance line algorithm permits multiple transactions for the same master record and can be generalized to any number of transaction files.

4. A program must be completely coded before any testing can begin.

5. The high-level modules in a hierarchy chart should be tested first.

6. One can logically assume that input to a maintenance program will be valid.

7. One need nct check for duplicate additions if the transaction file has been run through a stand-alone edit program.

8. A module in a hierarchy chart can be performed from more than one place.

9. Pseudocode and hierarchy charts depict the same thing.

10. A program stub may consist of a one-line DISPLAY paragraph.

11. Test data are best designed by the programmer writing the program.

12. Top-down testing can begin before a program is completely finished.

13. The balance line algorithm is restricted to a single transaction file.

14. A hierarchy chart contains decision-making logic.

P r o b l e m s

1. The transaction file in Figure 17.9b has both name and initials entered on correction transactions in addition to the social security number. Is this necessary according to the specifications and subsequent COBOL implementation (Figure 17.15)? Describe both an advantage and a disadvantage of entering the name and initials.

2. The specifications of the update program do not discuss how to change (i.e., correct) the social security number of an existing record. With respect to Figure 17.9a, for example, how could the social security number of Sugrue, who already exists in the old master file, be changed to 100000001? Discuss two different approaches, with an advantage and a disadvantage for each.

3. What problems, if any, do you see with each of the following? (Assume no data validation has been done.)

   a.
   ```
   IF SEX = 'M'
          ADD 1 TO NUMBER-OF-MEN
      ELSE
          ADD 1 TO NUMBER-OF-WOMEN
      END-IF.
   ```

   b.
   ```
   SEARCH LOCATION-TABLE
          WHEN INCOMING-LOCATION-CODE = LOCATION (LOC-INDEX)
              MOVE EXPANDED-LOCATION (LOC-INDEX) TO PRINT-LOCATION
      END-SEARCH.
   ```

18

Indexed Files

CHAPTER OUTLINE

Overview

System Concepts
COBOL Implementation
Creating an Indexed File
    Programming Specifications
    Pseudocode
    The Completed Program
Additional COBOL Elements
    OPEN
    READ
    WRITE
    REWRITE
    DELETE
Maintaining an Indexed File
    Programming Specifications
    Hierarchy Chart
    Pseudocode
    The Completed Program
Alternate Record Key
    Programming Specifications
Concatenated Key
    The START Statement
Limitations of COBOL-74
Summary
Fill-in
True/False
Problems

OBJECTIVES

After reading this chapter you will be able to:

■ Describe how an index file enables both sequential and/or nonsequential retrieval of individual records.

■ Define the specific terms associated with IBM's VSAM implementation of indexed files.

■ Discuss the clauses in the SELECT statement for an indexed file; indicate which clauses are optional and which are required.

■ Define file status bytes; state how they may be used to verify the success of an I/O operation.

■ Differentiate between the READ statements for sequential and nonsequential access of an indexed file.

■ Differentiate between the WRITE, REWRITE, and DELETE statements as they apply to file maintenance of an indexed file.

■ Describe the syntax of the START statement and give a reason for its use.

■ Distinguish between the primary and alternate keys of an indexed file, and the requirements for each.

OVERVIEW

This chapter covers all major aspects of indexed files, a type of file organization that permits both sequential and nonsequential access to individual records. It begins with a general discussion of how indexed files work, with particular reference to IBM's VSAM implementation. Different vendors use different terminology, but the underlying concepts are the same, namely, a series of indexes that access individual records on a sequential or random basis. More importantly, the COBOL syntax is identical for all vendors who adhere to the ANS 85 standard.

The chapter includes three programs that illustrate all of the COBOL elements associated with this type of file organization. The first shows how to create an indexed file, the second continues with the file maintenance example of the previous chapter, and the last illustrates how individual records may be accessed by multiple keys—for example, name and social security number.

System Concepts

Although different vendors have different physical implementations of indexed files, and consequently different terminology, the principles are the same; namely, a series of *indexes* that allow individual records to be accessed either sequentially or nonsequentially. This section provides an intuitive discussion of how an indexed file actually works.

In reality, the physical implementation of an indexed file is of little or no concern to the programmer. The operating system establishes and maintains the indexes, and the programmer is concerned primarily with accessing the file through the appropriate COBOL elements. Nevertheless, a conceptual understanding is of benefit in developing a more competent and better-rounded individual. Accordingly, we consider IBM's VSAM implementation.

A VSAM file or data set is divided into ***control areas*** and ***control intervals***. A control interval is a continuous area of auxiliary storage. A control area contains one or more control intervals. A control interval is independent of the physical device on which it resides; that is, a control interval that takes exactly one track of a given direct access device might require more or less than one track if the file were moved to another type of device.

A VSAM file is defined with an index so that individual records may be located on a random basis, with entries in the index known as index records. The lowest-level index is called the ***sequence set***. Records in all higher levels are collectively called the ***index set***.

An entry in a sequence set contains the highest key in a control interval and a vertical pointer to that interval. An entry in an index set contains the highest key in the index record at the next lower level and a vertical pointer to the sequence set. These concepts are made clearer by examination of Figure 18.1.

Figure 18.1 shows 28 records hypothetically distributed in a VSAM data set. The entire file consists of three control areas; each area in turn contains three control intervals. The shaded areas shown at the end of each control interval contain information required by VSAM. The index set has only one level of indexing. There are three entries in the index set, one for each control area. Each entry in the index

Figure 18.1   Initial VSAM Data Set

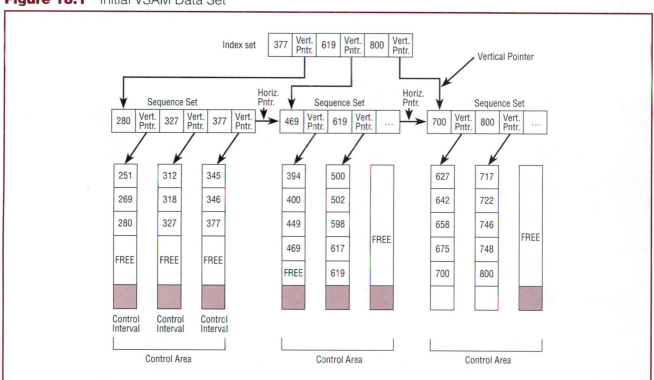

set contains the highest key in the corresponding control area; thus 377, 619, and 800 are the highest keys in the first, second, and third control areas, respectively. Each control area has its own sequence set. The entries in the first sequence set show the highest keys of the control intervals in the first control area to be 280, 327, and 377, respectively. Note that the highest entry in the third control interval, 377, corresponds to the highest entry in the first control area of the index set.

Figure 18.1 illustrates two kinds of pointers, vertical and horizontal. Vertical pointers are used for direct access to an individual record. For example, assume that the record with a key of 449 is to be retrieved. VSAM begins at the highest level of index (that is, at the index set). It concludes that record key 449, *if* it is present, is in the second control area (377 is the highest key in the first area, whereas 619 is the highest key in the second control area). VSAM follows the vertical pointer to the sequence set for the second control area and draws its final conclusion: record key 449, *if* it exists, will be in the first control interval of the second control area.

Horizontal pointers are used for sequential access only. In this instance, VSAM begins at the first sequence set and uses the horizontal pointer to get from that sequence set record to the one containing the next highest key. Put another way, the vertical pointer in a sequence set points to data; the horizontal pointer indicates the sequence set containing the next highest record.

Figure 18.1 contains several allocations of *free space*, which are distributed in one of two ways: as free space within a control interval or as a free control interval within a control area. In other words, as VSAM loads a file, empty space is deliberately left throughout the file. This is done to facilitate subsequent insertion of new records.

Figure 18.2 shows the changes brought about by the addition of two new records, with keys of 410 and 730, to the file of Figure 18.1. Addition of the first record, key 410, poses no problem, as free space is available in the control interval

Figure 18.2 Control Interval Split

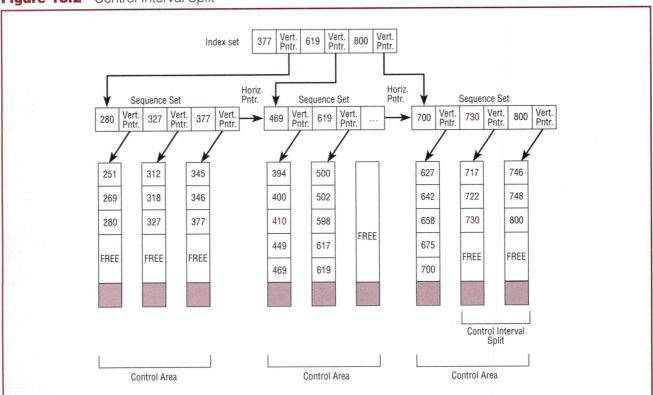

where the record belongs. Record 410 is inserted into its proper place and the other records in that control interval are moved down.

The addition of record key 730 requires different action. The control interval that should contain this record is full in Figure 18.1. Consequently VSAM causes a *control interval split*, in which some of the records in the previously filled control interval are moved to an empty control interval in the same control area. Entries in the sequence set for the third control area will change, as shown in Figure 18.2. This makes considerable sense when we realize that each record in a sequence set contains the key of the highest record in the corresponding control interval. Thus the records in the sequence set must reflect the control interval split. Note that after a control interval split, subsequent additions are facilitated, as free space is again readily available.

Figure 18.3 shows the results of including three additional records, with keys of 316, 618, and 680. Record 316 is inserted into free space in the second control interval of the first control area, with the other records initially in this interval shifted down. Record 618 causes a control interval split in the second control area.

Record 680 also requires a control interval split except that there are no longer any free control intervals in the third control area. Accordingly, a *control area split* is initiated, in which some of the records in the old control area are moved into a new control area at the end of the data set. Both the old and the new control areas will have free control intervals as a result of the split. In addition, the index set has a fourth entry, indicating the presence of a new control area. The sequence set is also expanded to accommodate the fourth control area.

Figure 18.3   Control Area Split

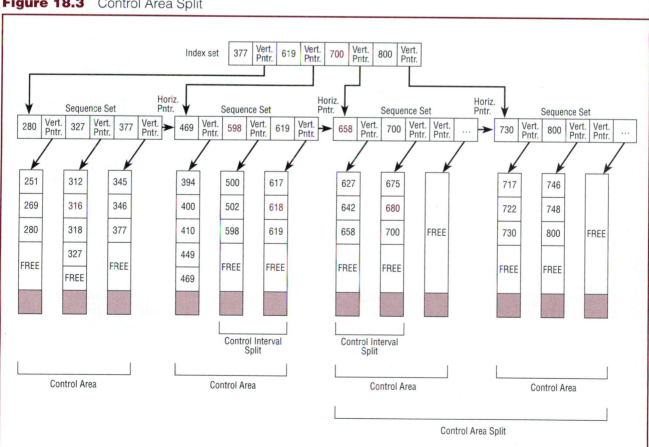

Cobol Implementation

The COBOL implementation of an indexed file centers on the SELECT statement in the Environment Division. Consider:

```
SELECT file-name

    ASSIGN TO {implementor-name-1}  . . .
              {literal-1         }

    [RESERVE integer-1 [AREA ]]
                       [AREAS]

    [ORGANIZATION IS] INDEXED

    [                  {SEQUENTIAL}]
    [ACCESS MODE IS    {RANDOM    }]
    [                  {DYNAMIC   }]

    RECORD KEY IS data-name-1

    [ALTERNATE RECORD KEY IS data-name-2 [WITH DUPLICATES]]  . . .

    [FILE STATUS IS data-name-3]
```

Three clauses are required: ASSIGN, ORGANIZATION IS INDEXED, and RECORD KEY. The function of the **ASSIGN** clause is the same as with a sequential file—to tie a programmer-chosen file name to a system name. The **ORGANIZATION IS INDEXED** clause indicates an indexed file and needs no further explanation.

The **RECORD KEY** clause references a field defined in the FD for the indexed record whose value must be unique for each record in the file. The value of the record key is used by the operating system to establish the necessary indexes for the file, which in turn enables the random retrieval of individual records.

The remaining entries—RESERVE integer AREAS, ACCESS MODE, ALTERNATE RECORD KEY, and FILE STATUS—are optional. The **RESERVE integer AREAS** clause functions identically as with a sequential file, to increase processing efficiency by allocating alternate I/O areas (or buffers) for the file. If the clause is omitted, the number of alternate areas defaults to the vendor's implementation, which is adequate in most instances. Specification of RESERVE ZERO AREAS will slow processing but will save an amount of storage equal to the buffer size. This is generally done only on smaller systems when the amount of main memory is limited.

The meaning of **ACCESS MODE** is apparent when either sequential or random (nonsequential) access is specified. ACCESS IS DYNAMIC allows a file to be read both sequentially and nonsequentially in the same program and is illustrated in Figure 18.12 later in the chapter.

ALTERNATE RECORD KEY provides a second path for random access. Unlike the record key, which must be unique for every record, the alternate key may contain duplicate values. This capability is extremely powerful and gives COBOL some limited facility for data base management. You could, for example, specify an account number as the record key and a person's name as the alternate key. Realize, however, that while the alternate key is powerful, it is expensive in terms of overhead, in that a second set of indexes must be maintained by the operating system and thus, the feature should not be used indiscriminately. The ALTERNATE RECORD KEY clause is illustrated in Figure 18.12 at the end of the chapter.

The **FILE STATUS** clause is available for any type of file organization and allows the programmer to distinguish between the many different types of I/O error conditions. The concept was first introduced in Chapter 6 in connection with debugging (see page 158). The operating system automatically returns a two-position field known as the *I/O status* (or file status bytes) to the data name designated in the FILE STATUS clause. The value of the file status bytes may be interrogated by the programmer, who is thus able to more closely monitor the results of any I/O operation.

Table 18.1 lists the various file status codes and their meaning. The use of file status codes is illustrated in the ensuing program to create an indexed file.

Table 18.1 File Status Codes

00 A successful input/output operation is performed with no further information available.

02 A successful creation of a record with duplicate alternate key value.

04 A READ is successful, but the length of the record being processed does not conform to the fixed file attributes for that file.

05 An OPEN is successful, but the referenced optional file is not present at open time.

07 An input/output statement is successful; however, for a CLOSE with NO REWIND, REEL/UNIT, or FOR REMOVAL or for an OPEN with NO REWIND the referenced file is on a nonreel/unit medium.

10 A sequential READ is attempted and no next logical record exists because (1) the end of file has been reached; or (2) an optional input file is not present.

14 A sequential READ is attempted and the number of significant digits in the record number is larger than the size of the key data item described for the file.

15 A sequential READ statement is attempted for the first time on an optional file that is not present.

21 A sequence error exists for a sequentially accessed indexed file.

22 An attempt is made to write or rewrite a record that would create a duplicate prime record key or duplicate alternate record key without the DUPLICATES phrase.

23 An attempt is made to randomly access a record that does not exist in the file, or a START or random READ is attempted on an optional input file that is not present.

24 An attempt is made to write beyond the externally defined boundaries.

25 A START statement or a random READ statement has been attempted on an optional file that is not present.

30 A permanent error exists and no further information is available concerning the input/output operation.

34 A permanent error exists because of a boundary violation; an attempt is made to write beyond the externally defined boundaries.

35 A permanent error exists because an OPEN with the INPUT, I/O, or EXTEND phrase is attempted on a nonoptional file that is not present.

37 A permanent error exists because an OPEN is attempted on a file and that file will not support the open mode specified: (1) EXTEND or OUTPUT phrase specified but not supported by the file; (2) I/O phrase is specified, but input and output operations are not supported by the file; or (3) INPUT phrase is specified, but the file will not support READ operations.

38 A permanent error exists because an OPEN is attempted on a file previously closed with a lock.

39 The OPEN is unsuccessful because a conflict has been detected between the fixed file attributes and the ones specified for that file in the program.

41 An OPEN statement is attempted for a file in the open mode.

42 A CLOSE statement is attempted for a file not in the open mode.

43 In the sequential access mode, the last input/output statement executed for the file prior to the execution of a DELETE or REWRITE statement was not a successfully executed READ statement.

44 A boundary violation exists because of an attempt to: (1) write or rewrite a record that is larger than the largest or smaller than the smallest record allowed by the RECORD IS VARYING clause of the associated file-name, or (2) rewrite a record and the record is not the same size as the record being replaced.

46 A sequential READ is attempted on a file open in the input or I/O mode and no valid next record has been established because the preceding: (1) START was unsuccessful, (2) READ was unsuccessful but did not cause an at-end condition, or (3) READ caused an at-end condition.

47 The execution of a READ or START is attempted on a file not open in the input or I/O mode.

48 The execution of a WRITE is attempted on a file not open in the I/O, output, or extend mode.

49 The execution of a DELETE or REWRITE statement is attempted on a file not open in the I/O mode.

Creating an Indexed File

Our first program creates an indexed file from sequential data, and in so doing, illustrates both the SELECT statement in the Environment Division and the use of the FILE STATUS bytes in the Procedure Division. It is important to realize that unlike sequential files, which can be created (or displayed) with an ordinary text editor or word processor, indexed files require a special procedure to create the associated indexes, and hence the need for this program. The COBOL program is not difficult and serves as a good introduction to indexed files. Specifications follow in the usual format.

Programming Specifications

Program Name: Creating an Indexed File

Narrative: This program copies the data from an incoming sequential file to an output indexed file. The logic is trivial in nature as the program is intended primarily to illustrate the SELECT statement for indexed files and the use of FILE STATUS bytes.

Input File(s): SEQUENTIAL-FILE

Input Record Layout:
```
01   SEQUENTIAL-RECORD.
     05   SEQ-SOC-SEC-NUMBER              PIC X(9).
     05   SEQ-REST-OF-RECORD              PIC X(30).
```

Output File: INDEXED-FILE

Output Record Layout:
```
01   INDEXED-RECORD.
     05   IND-SOC-SEC-NUMBER              PIC X(9).
     05   IND-REST-OF-RECORD              PIC X(30).
```

Test Data:
```
100000000GRABER       P ATL1500000000
200000000RUBIN        MABOS0800020000
300000000ANDERSON     IRBOS1000113000
222222222PANZER       S NYC0600000000
400000000MOLDOF       BLATL1500000000
500000000GLASSMAN     JSNYC1000045000
600000000GRAUER       RTNYC0800087500
700000000MILGROM      A SF 0900120000
800000000VAZQUEZ      C ATL1200060000
900000000CLARK        E NYC0700002500
```

Processing Requirements:

1. Copy the records in an incoming sequential file to an equivalent indexed file. The record layouts in both files are the same, with the first nine positions serving as the record key.

2. Display the FILE STATUS bytes after every I/O operation associated with the indexed file (OPEN, CLOSE, and WRITE).

3. Verify that the newly created indexed file has its records in sequence, and further, that every record contains a unique value for the record key. Note, for example, that the record for Panzer in the test data is out of sequence and should be flagged accordingly.

Pseudocode

The logic for this program is simple indeed as indicated in the programming specifications. In essence all we do is read a record from the sequential file, write it to the indexed file, and repeat the loop until the sequential file is out of data. We do not have to concern ourselves with building the indexes per se, as this is done automatically through the appropriate COBOL statements. The logic for the program is depicted in the pseudocode of Figure 18.4.

Figure 18.4   Pseudocode for Creating Indexed File

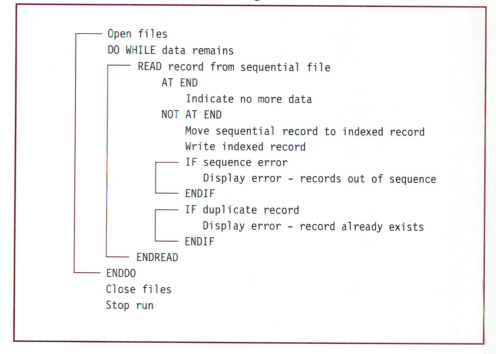

```
Open files
DO WHILE data remains
    READ record from sequential file
        AT END
            Indicate no more data
        NOT AT END
            Move sequential record to indexed record
            Write indexed record
            IF sequence error
                Display error - records out of sequence
            ENDIF
            IF duplicate record
                Display error - record already exists
            ENDIF
    ENDREAD
ENDDO
Close files
Stop run
```

The Completed Program

Figure 18.5 displays the completed program and contains little that is new in the way of COBOL other than the SELECT statement of lines 10 through 15. As indicated in the previous discussion, the ASSIGN, ORGANIZATION IS INDEXED, and RECORD KEY clauses are required, while the ACCESS IS SEQUENTIAL and FILE STATUS clauses are optional (and included here for purposes of illustration).

The RECORD KEY clause designates a field within the indexed record (IND-SOC-SEC-NUM) that will be used by the operating system to build the necessary indexes. Observe, therefore, that IND-SOC-SEC-NUM is referenced in two places, in the RECORD KEY clause of line 14 and in the FD for the indexed file in line 30.

The optional FILE STATUS clause of line 15 designates a two-position data name, INDEXED-STATUS-BYTES, which in turn is defined in Working-Storage (line 35). The operating system automatically updates the file status bytes after every I/O operation, making the result available to the program via the data name INDEXED-STATUS-BYTES. This, in turn, makes it possible to closely monitor the success (or failure) of various statements within the program.

To illustrate the utility of the file status bytes, return to the test data in the programming specifications, *noting that the record for Panzer is out of sequence.* The logic in the Procedure Division reads a record from the sequential file and

Figure 18.5   Program to Create an Indexed File

```
1        IDENTIFICATION DIVISION.
2        PROGRAM-ID.   CREATE.
3        AUTHOR.        ROBERT GRAUER.
4
5        ENVIRONMENT DIVISION.
6        INPUT-OUTPUT SECTION.
7        FILE-CONTROL.
8            SELECT SEQUENTIAL-FILE        ASSIGN TO SEQFILE
9                ORGANIZATION IS LINE SEQUENTIAL.
10           SELECT INDEXED-FILE
11               ASSIGN TO INDMAST
12               ORGANIZATION IS INDEXED
13               ACCESS IS SEQUENTIAL                        SELECT statement includes
14               RECORD KEY IS IND-SOC-SEC-NUM               ORGANIZATION, ACCESS,
15               FILE STATUS IS INDEXED-STATUS-BYTES.        RECORD KEY and FILE
16                                                            STATUS clauses
17       DATA DIVISION.
18       FILE SECTION.
19       FD  SEQUENTIAL-FILE
20           RECORD CONTAINS 39 CHARACTERS
21           DATA RECORD IS SEQUENTIAL-RECORD.
22       01  SEQUENTIAL-RECORD.
23           05  SEQ-SOC-SEC-NUM          PIC X(9).
24           05  SEQ-REST-OF-RECORD       PIC X(30).
25
26       FD  INDEXED-FILE
27           RECORD CONTAINS 39 CHARACTERS
28           DATA RECORD IS INDEXED-RECORD.
29       01  INDEXED-RECORD.
30           05  IND-SOC-SEC-NUM          PIC X(9).          RECORD KEY is defined
31           05  IND-REST-OF-RECORD       PIC X(30).         within INDEXED-RECORD
32
33       WORKING-STORAGE SECTION.
34       01  END-OF-FILE-SWITCH           PIC X(3)     VALUE 'NO'.
35       01  INDEXED-STATUS-BYTES         PIC XX.
36                                                            File status bytes defined in
37       PROCEDURE DIVISION.                                  Working-Storage
38       0010-UPDATE-MASTER-FILE.
39           OPEN INPUT SEQUENTIAL-FILE
40                OUTPUT INDEXED-FILE.
41           DISPLAY 'OPEN STATEMENT EXECUTED'.
42           DISPLAY '    FILE STATUS BYTES = ', INDEXED-STATUS-BYTES.
43           DISPLAY ' '.
44           PERFORM UNTIL END-OF-FILE-SWITCH = 'YES'
45               READ SEQUENTIAL-FILE
46                   AT END
47                       MOVE 'YES' TO END-OF-FILE-SWITCH
48                   NOT AT END
49                       MOVE SEQ-SOC-SEC-NUM TO IND-SOC-SEC-NUM       In-line perform and
50                       MOVE SEQ-REST-OF-RECORD TO IND-REST-OF-RECORD false-condition branch
51                       WRITE INDEXED-RECORD                           drive program
52                           INVALID KEY PERFORM 0020-EXPLAIN-WRITE-ERROR
53                       END-WRITE
54                       DISPLAY 'WRITE STATEMENT EXECUTED FOR  '
55                           SEQUENTIAL-RECORD
```

Figure 18.5   Program to Create an Indexed File

```
56                         DISPLAY '    FILE STATUS BYTES = '
57                             INDEXED-STATUS-BYTES
58                         DISPLAY ' '
59                 END-READ
60             END-PERFORM.
61             CLOSE SEQUENTIAL-FILE
62                   INDEXED-FILE.
63             DISPLAY 'CLOSE STATEMENT EXECUTED'.
64             DISPLAY '    FILE STATUS BYTES = ', INDEXED-STATUS-BYTES.
65             DISPLAY ' '.
66             STOP RUN.
67
68         0020-EXPLAIN-WRITE-ERROR.
69             IF INDEXED-STATUS-BYTES = '21'
70                 DISPLAY 'ERROR (SEQUENCE) FOR      ' SEQUENTIAL-RECORD
71             END-IF.
72             IF INDEXED-STATUS-BYTES = '22'
73                 DISPLAY 'ERROR (DUPLICATE KEY) FOR ' SEQUENTIAL-RECORD
74             END-IF.
```

File status bytes may be interrogated and displayed

copies it to the indexed file, repeating the loop until the sequential file is empty. A problem will result, however, because the indexed file requires its records to be in sequence, which is not true in this example. Accordingly it is good technique to include an **INVALID KEY** clause in the WRITE statement of lines 51 through 53, which is executed if, and only if, an error is detected. The paragraph performed as a consequence of the error, 0020-EXPLAIN-WRITE-ERROR (lines 68–74), interrogates the file status bytes to reveal the exact cause of the problem.

Output of the program is shown in Figure 18.6 and consists entirely of display output produced at various points in the program. The first and last lines show the results of the OPEN and CLOSE statements, respectively; both operations executed successfully as evidenced by file status bytes of 00. Note, too, how file status bytes of 00 are displayed for every *successful* write operation, but that a value of 21, corresponding to an out-of-sequence record, is displayed for Panzer.

Additional Cobol Elements

Several statements in the Procedure Division are uniquely associated with indexed files or have extended formats for indexed files. These include OPEN, READ, WRITE, REWRITE, and DELETE. We will discuss each of these statements in isolation, then include them in the illustrative programs that follow.

OPEN

The **I-O** clause of the OPEN statement, OPEN I-O, is required when updating indexed files. Consider:

```
         ┌ INPUT  ┐
OPEN    ⟨ OUTPUT ⟩  file-name
         └ I-O    ┘
```

Figure 18.6   Display Output of Create Program

```
OPEN STATEMENT EXECUTED                              ——OPEN statement executed without error
    FILE STATUS BYTES = 00

WRITE STATEMENT EXECUTED FOR   100000000GRABER        P ATL1500000000
    FILE STATUS BYTES = 00

WRITE STATEMENT EXECUTED FOR   200000000RUBIN         MABOS0800020000
    FILE STATUS BYTES = 00

WRITE STATEMENT EXECUTED FOR   300000000ANDERSON      IRBOS1000113000
    FILE STATUS BYTES = 00

ERROR (SEQUENCE) FOR        222222222PANZER        S NYC0600000000    ——Sequence error for Panzer
WRITE STATEMENT EXECUTED FOR   222222222PANZER        S NYC0600000000
    FILE STATUS BYTES = 21

WRITE STATEMENT EXECUTED FOR   400000000MOLDOF        BLATL1500000000
    FILE STATUS BYTES = 00

WRITE STATEMENT EXECUTED FOR   500000000GLASSMAN      JSNYC1000045000
    FILE STATUS BYTES = 00

WRITE STATEMENT EXECUTED FOR   600000000GRAUER        RTNYC0800087500
    FILE STATUS BYTES = 00

WRITE STATEMENT EXECUTED FOR   700000000MILGROM       A SF 0900120000
    FILE STATUS BYTES = 00

WRITE STATEMENT EXECUTED FOR   800000000VAZQUEZ       C ATL1200060000
    FILE STATUS BYTES = 00

WRITE STATEMENT EXECUTED FOR   900000000CLARK         E NYC0700002500
    FILE STATUS BYTES = 00

CLOSE STATEMENT EXECUTED                              ——CLOSE statement executed without error
    FILE STATUS BYTES = 00
```

INPUT and OUTPUT are used when an indexed file is accessed or created. In nonsequential maintenance, however, the *same* indexed file functions as both the old and new master files, and hence is both an input and an output file. The file is opened as an I-O file—for example, OPEN I-O INDEXED-FILE—to enable it to serve both functions in the same program; that is, you may read records from the file (input), as well as write records to the file (output).

READ

The **READ** statement has two distinct formats, for sequential and nonsequential access, respectively. These are:

Format 1 (Sequential Access)

```
READ file-name [NEXT] RECORD [INTO identifier-1]
    [AT END imperative-statement-1]
    [NOT AT END imperative-statement-2]
[END-READ]
```

Format 2 (Nonsequential Access)

```
READ file-name RECORD [INTO identifier-1]
    [KEY IS data-name-1]
    [INVALID KEY imperative-statement-1]
    [NOT INVALID KEY imperative-statement-2]
[END-READ]
```

The first format, for sequential access, has been used throughout the text and should present no difficulty. (The NEXT phrase is discussed in conjunction with the ACCESS IS DYNAMIC clause of the SELECT statement, and is illustrated in Figure 18.12 toward the end of the chapter.)

The second format, for nonsequential access, *must be preceded by a MOVE statement, in which the key of the desired record is moved to the data name designated as the RECORD KEY in the SELECT statement.* Consider:

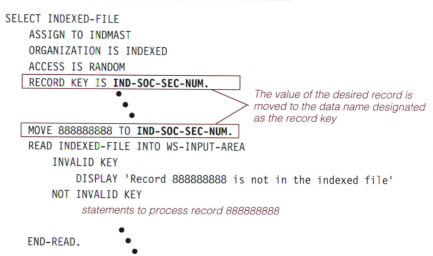

```
SELECT INDEXED-FILE
    ASSIGN TO INDMAST
    ORGANIZATION IS INDEXED
    ACCESS IS RANDOM
    RECORD KEY IS IND-SOC-SEC-NUM.
        •
          •
           •
    MOVE 888888888 TO IND-SOC-SEC-NUM.
    READ INDEXED-FILE INTO WS-INPUT-AREA
        INVALID KEY
            DISPLAY 'Record 888888888 is not in the indexed file'
        NOT INVALID KEY
            statements to process record 888888888
                •
                  •
    END-READ.          •
                         •
```

The value of the desired record is moved to the data name designated as the record key

The READ statement accesses the indexed file nonsequentially in an attempt to retrieve the record whose key is 888888888. If the record is in the file, it will be read and made available in WS-INPUT-AREA (as well as in the record area within the FD for INDEXED-FILE). If, however, the record does not exist, the INVALID KEY condition is raised and the indicated error message is displayed.

The **KEY IS** clause is necessary if multiple keys are specified in the SELECT statement (that is, if ALTERNATE RECORD KEY is included). Consider:

```
SELECT INDEXED-FILE
    ASSIGN TO INDMAST
    ORGANIZATION IS INDEXED
    RECORD KEY IS IND-SOC-SEC-NUM
    ACCESS IS RANDOM
    ALTERNATE RECORD KEY IS IND-NAME WITH DUPLICATES.
            •
              •
               •
```

```
MOVE 'Smith' TO IND-NAME.
READ INDEXED-FILE INTO WS-WORK-AREA
    KEY IS IND-NAME
    INVALID KEY
        DISPLAY 'Smith is not in the file'
    NOT INVALID KEY
        .
        .
        .
END-READ.
```

The value of the desired record is moved to the specified key

As in the case of a single key, the READ statement is preceded by a MOVE statement in which the desired value is moved to the appropriate key field. The file is then searched nonsequentially for the value specified (Smith in the example). The INVALID KEY condition is activated if the record cannot be found.

WRITE

The **WRITE** statement also has an optional INVALID KEY clause, as you already know from the COBOL program to create an indexed file (Figure 18.5). Consider:

```
WRITE record-name [FROM identifier-1]
    [INVALID KEY imperative statement-1]
    [NOT INVALID KEY imperative-statement-2]
[END-WRITE]
```

Specification of ACCESS IS SEQUENTIAL (in the SELECT statement) to create the indexed file requires that incoming records be in sequential order, and further, each record is required to have a unique key. The INVALID KEY condition is raised if either of these requirements is violated.

REWRITE

The **REWRITE** statement replaces existing records when a file has been opened as an I/O file, as in the case of nonsequential maintenance. Its syntax is similar to that of the WRITE statement:

```
REWRITE record-name [FROM identifier-1]
    [INVALID KEY imperative statement-1]
    [NOT INVALID KEY imperative-statement-2]
[END-REWRITE]
```

The INVALID KEY condition is raised if the record key of the last record read does not match the key of the record to be replaced.

DELETE

The DELETE statement removes a record from an indexed file. Consider:

```
DELETE file-name RECORD
    [INVALID KEY imperative statement-1]
    [NOT INVALID KEY imperative-statement-2]
[END-DELETE]
```

The DELETE statement is appropriate only for files opened in the I/O mode.

Maintaining an Indexed File

The distinction between *sequential* and *nonsequential* file maintenance was presented in the previous chapter, but is repeated here for emphasis. A sequential update uses two distinct master files, an old and a new master, with every record in the old master rewritten to the new master regardless of whether it changes. A nonsequential update uses a single master file that functions as both the old and new master, and only the records that change are rewritten. A sequential update is driven by the relationship between the old master and transaction files, whereas a nonsequential update is driven solely by the transaction file; that is, transactions are processed until the transaction file is empty. Finally, a sequential update requires the transaction file to be in sequence, whereas the transactions for a nonsequential update can be in any order.

The sequential update was developed in Chapter 17 through implementation of the balance line algorithm. We continue now with a parallel problem for nonsequential processing.

Programming Specifications

Program Name: Nonsequential Update

Narrative: This program parallels the update program of Chapter 17 except that the master file is accessed nonsequentially, and thus the transaction file need not be in sequence. In addition, the balance line algorithm does not apply.

Input File: TRANSACTION-FILE

Input Record Layout:
```
01 TRANSACTION-RECORD.
    05  TR-SOC-SEC-NUMBER                PIC X(9).
    05  TR-NAME.
        10  TR-LAST-NAME                 PIC X(15).
        10  TR-INITIALS                  PIC XX.
    05  TR-LOCATION-CODE                 PIC X(3).
    05  TR-COMMISSION-RATE               PIC 99.
    05  TR-SALES-AMOUNT                  PIC 9(5).
    05  TR-TRANSACTION-CODE              PIC X.
        88  ADDITION        VALUE 'A'.
        88  CORRECTION      VALUE 'C'.
        88  DELETION        VALUE 'D'.
```

Input/Output File: INDEXED-FILE

Input Record Layout:
```
01  IND-MASTER-RECORD.
    05  IND-SOC-SEC-NUMBER               PIC X(9).
    05  IND-NAME.
        10  IND-LAST-NAME                PIC X(15).
        10  IND-INITIALS                 PIC XX.
    05  IND-LOCATION-CODE                PIC X(3).
    05  IND-COMMISSION-RATE              PIC 99.
    05  IND-YEAR-TO-DATE-SALES           PIC 9(8).
```

Test Data: See Figure 18.7a and 18.7b.

Figure 18.7 Test Data for Nonsequential Update

```
100000000GRABER         P ATL1500000000
200000000RUBIN          MABOS0800020000
300000000ANDERSON       IRBOS1000113000
400000000MOLDOF         BLATL1500000000
500000000GLASSMAN       JSNYC1000045000
600000000GRAUER         RTNYC0800087500
700000000MILGROM        A SF 0900120000
800000000VAZQUEZ        C ATL1200060000
900000000CLARK          E NYC0700002500
```

(a) Indexed File (before Update)

```
444444444RICHARDS       IM      05000C
700000000MILGROM        A           D
000000000BOROW          JSATL07     A
000000000BOROW          JS      10000C
000000000BOROW          JS      20000C
400000000MOLDOF         BLATL15     A
800000000VAZQUEZ        C       55000C
999999999GILLENSON      MANYC10     A
```

Transactions are not in sequential order

(b) Transaction File

```
000000000BOROW          JSATL0700030000
100000000GRABER         P ATL1500000000
200000000RUBIN          MABOS0800020000
300000000ANDERSON       IRBOS1000113000
400000000MOLDOF         BLATL1500000000
500000000GLASSMAN       JSNYC1000045000
600000000GRAUER         RTNYC0800087500
800000000VAZQUEZ        C ATL1200115000
900000000CLARK          E NYC0700002500
999999999GILLENSON      MANYC1000000000
```

(c) Indexed File (after Update)

```
ERROR-NO MATCHING RECORD: 444444444
ERROR-DUPLICATE ADDITION: 400000000
```

(d) Error Messages

Processing Requirements:

1. Develop a nonsequential update program to process an incoming transaction file and update the associated indexed file. The processing requirements parallel those of the sequential update program of Chapter 17 with the following changes:

   a. There is only a single master file (the indexed file), which functions as both the old and new master files.

   b. The transaction file need not be in sequential order.

   c. The balance line algorithm does not apply.

2. The transaction file is assumed to be valid in and of itself by virtue of a stand-alone edit program. Hence, each transaction has a valid transaction code (A, C, or D), numeric fields are numeric, and so on. Nevertheless, the update program must check (and flag) two kinds of errors that could not be detected in the stand-alone edit, as they require interaction with the old master file. These are:

   a. Duplicate additions, in which the social security number of a transaction coded as an addition already exists in the old master,

   b. No matches, in which the social security number of a transaction coded as either a deletion or a correction does not exist in the old master.

3. Transactions coded as additions are to be added to the new master file in their entirety, and will contain a value for every field in the transaction record (except for TR-SALES-AMOUNT). The value of IND-YEAR-TO-DATE-SALES in the new master record is to be initialized to zero.

4. Transactions coded as deletions are to be removed from the master file. These transactions contain only the social security number and transaction code.

5. Transactions coded as corrections contain only the social security number, name, and the transaction sales amount (TR-SALES-AMOUNT). The value of TR-SALES-AMOUNT on the incoming transaction is to be *added* to the value in the IND-YEAR-TO-DATE-SALES field in the master record.

Figure 18.7 contains the indexed and transaction files before the update, the indexed file after the update has been run, and the associated error messages (for duplicate additions and no matches). The data parallel the example in Chapter 17 except that the transaction file is no longer in sequence. Nevertheless, the updated indexed file is the same in both examples; that is, Borow and Gillenson have been added, Milgrom has been deleted, and Vazquez has had her record changed. Note, however, that the error messages in Figure 18.7d are reversed (from those in Chapter 17) to match the order in which the transactions were processed.

Hierarchy Chart

The hierarchy chart of Figure 18.8 is simpler than its counterpart for sequential processing; it also contains four modules that were present in the hierarchy chart of Chapter 17. In other words, regardless of whether the master file is accessed sequentially or nonsequentially, it is still necessary to apply transactions to the master file, to add records to the indexed file, and to correct and/or delete existing records.

Conspicuous by its absence, however, is the module to CHOOSE-ACTIVE-KEY, because the nonsequential update is driven entirely by the transaction file. The program processes the transaction file until there are no more transactions; that is, there is no need for an active key to determine whether the record from the transaction file or the old master file will be admitted to the update process because the balance line algorithm does not apply. (See problem 7.)

Figure 18.8   Hierarchy Chart for Nonsequential Update Program

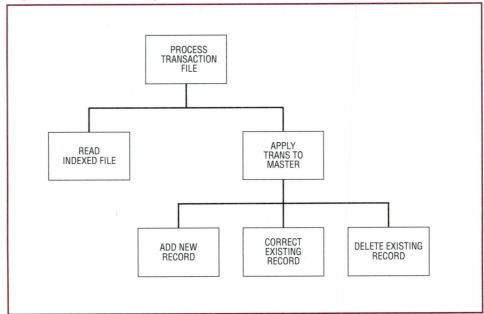

Pseudocode

The pseudocode for the nonseudential update is driven entirely by the transaction file, which reads a transaction, determines whether or not the corresponding social security number is in the indexed file, then processes the transaction as appropriate. The logic is simpler than that of the balance line algorithm, which had to determine whether the next record was to be read from the transaction file, the old master file, or both.

The pseudocode reads a record from the transaction file and immediately does a random read on the indexed file. The social security number from the transaction file is, or is not, present in the indexed file, which determines the value of the record-key-allocated-switch. The transaction is then processed according to the transaction code (addition, deletion, or correction) and the value of the record-key-allocated-switch. The process continues until the transaction file is exhausted.

The Completed Program

The completed program is shown in Figure 18.10. The SELECT statement for the INDEXED-FILE (lines 10–14) contains the required ORGANIZATION IS INDEXED and RECORD KEY clauses, and specifies ACCESS IS RANDOM. INDEXED-FILE is opened as an I/O file in line 63 because it serves as both the old and new master file; that is, it is read from and written to.

The READ statement for the indexed file (lines 79–84) is preceded by a MOVE statement, in which the key of the transaction record is moved to IND-SOC-SEC-NUM, the field defined as the RECORD KEY. The indexed file is read in an attempt to find this record, and the INVALID KEY condition is triggered if the value is not in the file.

The contents of the lowest-level modules, ADD-NEW-RECORD, CORRECT-EXISTING-RECORD and DELETE-EXISTING-RECORD, have been modified slightly (from their counterparts in the sequential update) to include the appropriate I/O statements and contain WRITE, REWRITE, and DELETE statements, respectively.

Figure 18.9   Pseudocode for Nonsequential Update Program

```
Open files
DO WHILE data remains
    READ transaction file
        AT END
            Indicate no more data
        NOT AT END
            Move transaction social security number to record key
            READ INDEXED-FILE
                INVALID KEY
                    Move 'NO' TO record-key-allocated-switch
                NOT INVALID KEY
                    Move 'YES' TO record-key-allocated-switch
            END-READ
            EVALUATE transaction-code
                WHEN addition
                    IF record-key-allocated-switch = 'yes'
                        Write 'error - duplicate addition'
                    ELSE (transaction is not in indexed file)
                        Move transaction-record to new-master-record
                        Write indexed record
                    ENDIF
                WHEN correction
                    IF record-key-allocated-switch = 'yes'
                        Process correction
                        Rewrite indexed record
                    ELSE (transaction is not in indexed file)
                        Write 'error - no matching record'
                    ENDIF
                WHEN deletion
                    IF record-key-allocated-switch = 'yes'
                        Delete indexed record
                    ELSE (transaction is not in indexed file)
                        Write 'error - no matching record'
                    ENDIF
                WHEN other
                    Write 'error - invalid transaction code
            END EVALUATE
    END READ
END DO
Close files
Stop run
```

Figure 18.10   Nonsequential Update Program

```
1        IDENTIFICATION DIVISION.
2        PROGRAM-ID.    NONSEQUP.
3        AUTHOR.         ROBERT GRAUER.
4
5        ENVIRONMENT DIVISION.
6        INPUT-OUTPUT SECTION.
7        FILE-CONTROL.
8            SELECT TRANSACTION-FILE     ASSIGN TO VALTRANS
9                ORGANIZATION IS LINE SEQUENTIAL.
10           SELECT INDEXED-FILE
11               ASSIGN TO INDMAST
12               ORGANIZATION IS INDEXED
13               ACCESS IS RANDOM
14               RECORD KEY IS IND-SOC-SEC-NUM.
15
16       DATA DIVISION.
17       FILE SECTION.
18       FD  TRANSACTION-FILE
19           RECORD CONTAINS 37 CHARACTERS
20           DATA RECORD IS TRANSACTION-RECORD.
21       01  TRANSACTION-RECORD            PIC X(37).
22
23       FD  INDEXED-FILE
24           RECORD CONTAINS 39 CHARACTERS
25           DATA RECORD IS INDEXED-RECORD.
26       01  INDEXED-RECORD.
27           05  IND-SOC-SEC-NUM           PIC X(9).
28           05  IND-REST-OF-RECORD        PIC X(30).
29
30       WORKING-STORAGE SECTION.
31       01  FILLER                        PIC X(14)
32               VALUE 'WS BEGINS HERE'.
33
34       01  WS-TRANS-RECORD.
35           05  TR-SOC-SEC-NUMBER         PIC X(9).
36           05  TR-NAME.
37               10  TR-LAST-NAME          PIC X(15).
38               10  TR-INITIALS           PIC XX.
39           05  TR-LOCATION-CODE          PIC X(3).
40           05  TR-COMMISSION-RATE        PIC 99.
41           05  TR-SALES-AMOUNT           PIC 9(5).
42           05  TR-TRANSACTION-CODE       PIC X.
43               88  ADDITION       VALUE 'A'.
44               88  CORRECTION     VALUE 'C'.
45               88  DELETION       VALUE 'D'.
46
47       01  WS-MASTER-RECORD.
48           05  MA-SOC-SEC-NUMBER         PIC X(9).
49           05  MA-NAME.
50               10  MA-LAST-NAME          PIC X(15).
```

——— *SELECT statement for INDEXED-FILE*

Figure 18.10   *(continued)*

```
51                  10  MA-INITIALS             PIC XX.
52             05  MA-LOCATION-CODE             PIC X(3).
53             05  MA-COMMISSION-RATE           PIC 99.
54             05  MA-YEAR-TO-DATE-SALES        PIC 9(8).
55
56        01  PROGRAM-SWITCHES.
57             05  END-OF-FILE-SWITCH           PIC X(3)     VALUE 'NO '.
58             05  RECORD-KEY-ALLOCATED-SWITCH  PIC X(3)     VALUE 'NO '.
59
60        PROCEDURE DIVISION.
61        0010-PROCESS-TRANSACTION-FILE.
62            OPEN INPUT TRANSACTION-FILE
63                 I-O INDEXED-FILE.
64            PERFORM UNTIL END-OF-FILE-SWITCH = 'YES'
65                READ TRANSACTION-FILE INTO WS-TRANS-RECORD
66                    AT END
67                        MOVE 'YES' TO END-OF-FILE-SWITCH
68                    NOT AT END
69                        PERFORM 0020-READ-INDEXED-FILE
70                        PERFORM 0030-APPLY-TRANS-TO-MASTER
71                END-READ
72            END-PERFORM.
73            CLOSE TRANSACTION-FILE
74                  INDEXED-FILE.
75            STOP RUN.
76
77        0020-READ-INDEXED-FILE.
78            MOVE TR-SOC-SEC-NUMBER TO IND-SOC-SEC-NUM.
79            READ INDEXED-FILE INTO WS-MASTER-RECORD
80                INVALID KEY
81                    MOVE 'NO ' TO RECORD-KEY-ALLOCATED-SWITCH
82                NOT INVALID KEY
83                    MOVE 'YES' TO RECORD-KEY-ALLOCATED-SWITCH
84            END-READ.
85
86        0030-APPLY-TRANS-TO-MASTER.
87            EVALUATE TRUE
88                WHEN ADDITION
89                    PERFORM 0090-ADD-NEW-RECORD
90                WHEN CORRECTION
91                    PERFORM 0100-CORRECT-EXISTING-RECORD
92                WHEN DELETION
93                    PERFORM 0110-DELETE-EXISTING-RECORD
94                WHEN OTHER
95                    DISPLAY 'INVALID TRANSACTION CODE'
96            END-EVALUATE.
97
98        0090-ADD-NEW-RECORD.
99            IF RECORD-KEY-ALLOCATED-SWITCH = 'YES'
100               DISPLAY ' ERROR-DUPLICATE ADDITION: ' TR-SOC-SEC-NUMBER
```

In-line perform and false-condition branch drive the program

Nonsequential READ statement

EVALUATE statement determines transaction processing

Figure 18.10   *(continued)*

```
101          ELSE
102              MOVE SPACES TO WS-MASTER-RECORD
103              MOVE TR-SOC-SEC-NUMBER TO MA-SOC-SEC-NUMBER
104              MOVE TR-NAME TO MA-NAME
105              MOVE TR-LOCATION-CODE TO MA-LOCATION-CODE
106              MOVE TR-COMMISSION-RATE TO MA-COMMISSION-RATE
107              MOVE ZEROS TO MA-YEAR-TO-DATE-SALES
108              WRITE INDEXED-RECORD FROM WS-MASTER-RECORD
109          END-IF.
110
111      0100-CORRECT-EXISTING-RECORD.
112          IF RECORD-KEY-ALLOCATED-SWITCH = 'YES'
113              ADD TR-SALES-AMOUNT TO MA-YEAR-TO-DATE-SALES
114              REWRITE INDEXED-RECORD FROM WS-MASTER-RECORD
115          ELSE
116              DISPLAY ' ERROR-NO MATCHING RECORD: ' TR-SOC-SEC-NUMBER
117          END-IF.
118
119      0110-DELETE-EXISTING-RECORD.
120          IF RECORD-KEY-ALLOCATED-SWITCH = 'YES'
121              DELETE INDEXED-FILE
122          ELSE
123              DISPLAY ' ERROR-NO MATCHING RECORD: ' TR-SOC-SEC-NUMBER
124          END-IF.
```

Modified to use appropriate I/O statements

Alternate Record Key

Our earlier discussion of the SELECT statement included the **ALTERNATE RECORD KEY** phrase to enable a second path for retrieving records from an indexed file. Unlike the record key, which must be unique, the alternate key may contain duplicate values. This capability is illustrated in the third and final program of the chapter, the specifications of which follow in the usual format.

Programming Specifications

Program Name: Alternate Indexes

Narrative: This program illustrates primary and alternate indexes, as well as nonsequential retrieval on either type of key. It does no useful processing per se, other than to illustrate COBOL syntax

Input File: INDEXED-FILE

Input Record Layout:
```
01 INDEXED-RECORD.
   05  IND-SOC-SEC-NUMBER        PIC X(9).
   05  IND-NAME                  PIC X(15).
   05  IND-REST-OF-RECORD        PIC X(16).
```

Figure 18.11 Alternate Keys

```
        100000000GRAUER
        100000001GRAUER
        100000002GRAUER
        300000000MILGROM
        300000001MILGROM
        300000002MILGROM
        400000000GRAUER
        500000000JONES
        600000000SMITH
        700000000MILGROM
```

(a) The Indexed File

```
PRIMARY KEY OK - 300000001

ALTERNATE KEY - MILGROM        300000000
ALTERNATE KEY - MILGROM        300000001
ALTERNATE KEY - MILGROM        300000002
ALTERNATE KEY - MILGROM        700000000
```

(b) Displayed Output

Test Data: See Figure 18.11a.

Report Layout: There is no formal report produced by this program; instead DISPLAY statements are used to indicate the results as in Figure 18.11b.

Processing Requirements:

1. The social security and name fields are designated as the primary and secondary keys, respectively. The value of the social security number is unique, whereas the value of name is not.

2. Execute a random read for the record whose social security number is 300000001, displaying an appropriate message to indicate whether or not the record was found.

3. Execute a random read to find the first record whose name is Milgrom, then read sequentially to display all other records with this value in the secondary key.

Figure 18.12 contains the completed program corresponding to these specifications. The SELECT statement in lines 8–13 designates IND-SOC-SEC-NUM and IND-NAME as the primary (record) and alternate key, respectively. The record key is (and must always be) unique, but the alternate key need not be; hence the **WITH DUPLICATES** phrase is included in the SELECT statement. Both fields are defined within the FD for INDEXED-FILE in lines 21 and 22, respectively. The **ACCESS IS DYNAMIC** phrase (line 11) indicates both random and sequential retrieval within the same program.

Figure 18.12 Alternate Index Program

```
1        IDENTIFICATION DIVISION.
2        PROGRAM-ID.    ALTINDEX.
3        AUTHOR.         ROBERT GRAUER.
4
5        ENVIRONMENT DIVISION.
6        INPUT-OUTPUT SECTION.
7        FILE-CONTROL.
8            SELECT INDEXED-FILE
9                ASSIGN TO ALTINDEX                         ── Indicates both random and
10               ORGANIZATION IS INDEXED                       sequential retrieval
11               ACCESS IS DYNAMIC
12               RECORD KEY IS IND-SOC-SEC-NUM
13               ALTERNATE RECORD KEY IS IND-NAME WITH DUPLICATES.   ── Nonunique alternate key
14
15       DATA DIVISION.
16       FILE SECTION.
17       FD  INDEXED-FILE
18           RECORD CONTAINS 40 CHARACTERS
19           DATA RECORD IS INDEXED-RECORD.
20       01  INDEXED-RECORD.                               ── Keys defined within index record
21           05  IND-SOC-SEC-NUM           PIC X(9).
22           05  IND-NAME                  PIC X(15).
23           05  IND-REST-OF-RECORD        PIC X(16).
24
25       WORKING-STORAGE SECTION.
26       01  END-OF-FILE-SWITCH            PIC X(3)   VALUE SPACES.
27
28       PROCEDURE DIVISION.
29       0010-DISPLAY-INDEXED-RECORDS.
30           OPEN INPUT INDEXED-FILE.
31           PERFORM 0020-RETRIEVE-BY-PRIMARY-KEY.
32           PERFORM 0030-RETRIEVE-BY-SECONDARY-KEY.
33           CLOSE INDEXED-FILE.
34           STOP RUN.                                     ── Primary key retrieval
35
36       0020-RETRIEVE-BY-PRIMARY-KEY.
37           MOVE '300000001' TO IND-SOC-SEC-NUM.
38           READ INDEXED-FILE
39               INVALID KEY
40                   DISPLAY 'RECORD NOT FOUND - 300000001'
41               NOT INVALID KEY
42                   DISPLAY 'PRIMARY KEY OK - ', IND-SOC-SEC-NUM
43           END-READ.
44           DISPLAY ' '.
45
46       0030-RETRIEVE-BY-SECONDARY-KEY.
47           MOVE 'MILGROM' TO IND-NAME.
48           READ INDEXED-FILE KEY IS IND-NAME             ── Secondary key retrieval
49               INVALID KEY
50                   DISPLAY 'RECORD NOT FOUND - MILGROM'
```

Figure 18.12 *(continued)*

```
51                      NOT INVALID KEY
52                          PERFORM 0040-RETRIEVE-DUPLICATES
53                              UNTIL IND-NAME NOT EQUAL 'MILGROM'
54                              OR END-OF-FILE-SWITCH = 'YES'
55                  END-READ.
56
57          0040-RETRIEVE-DUPLICATES.
58              DISPLAY 'ALTERNATE KEY - ' IND-NAME, IND-SOC-SEC-NUM.
59              READ INDEXED-FILE NEXT RECORD
60                  AT END
61                      MOVE 'YES' TO END-OF-FILE-SWITCH
62              END-READ.
```

Successful retrieval

The Procedure Division illustrates the retrieval of records on either field. Lines 36–44 contain the logic for the primary key and have already been covered in the program for a nonsequential update. The READ statement of lines 38–43 is preceded by a MOVE statement in which the key of the desired record (300000001 in the example) is moved to the data name designated as the RECORD KEY in the SELECT statement. If the record is in the file, it will be read into the data name INDEXED-RECORD; and the false-condition branch, NOT INVALID KEY, will indicate the primary key was found. If the record is not in the file, the INVALID KEY condition will be activated to display an appropriate error message.

Lines 46–55 contain a parallel procedure based on the alternate key, but with three important differences:

1. The key value (MILGROM) is moved to the ALTERNATE RECORD KEY (IND-NAME rather than IND-SOC-SEC-NUM).

2. The KEY IS phrase is used to indicate the retrieval is on the alternate rather than the primary key.

3. Successful retrieval causes the execution of 0040-RETRIEVE-DUPLICATES, which retrieves all records for MILGROM. The NEXT RECORD phrase (line 59) in the READ statement indicates sequential retrieval.

The DISPLAY output produced by the program is shown in Figure 18.11b. The first message indicates the successful retrieval based on the primary key (produced by the paragraph 0020-RETRIEVE-BY-PRIMARY-KEY). The second set of messages reflects all records for Milgrom.

Concatenated Key

The record key in an indexed file may be specified as a group item rather than an elementary item, producing what is known as a *concatenated key*, that is, a key consisting of two (or more) keys strung together to form a single value. Consider, for example, a system for bank loans with a concatenated key defined as follows:

```
05  CUSTOMER-LOAN-NUMBER.
    10  CUSTOMER-NUMBER        PIC 9(6).
    10  LOAN-NUMBER            PIC 9(3).
```

In this example CUSTOMER-LOAN-NUMBER is a group item and consists of the elementary items, CUSTOMER-NUMBER and LOAN-NUMBER. Every value of the record key (CUSTOMER-LOAN-NUMBER) must be unique, but there can be several loans for the same customer, with each loan assigned a new loan number. Customer 111111, for example, may have two outstanding loans, with record keys of 111111001 and 111111004, respectively. (Loans 002 and 003 may have been previously paid off.) The problem is to retrieve all loans for a given customer, which leads to a discussion of the START statement.

The START Statement

The **START** statement moves nonsequentially (randomly) into an indexed file to the first record whose value is equal to, greater than, or not less than the value contained in the identifier. The INVALID KEY condition is raised if the file does not contain a record meeting the specified criterion. Syntactically, the START statement has the form:

```
                     ⎡    ⎧IS EQUAL TO             ⎫           ⎤
                     ⎢    ⎪IS =                    ⎪           ⎥
                     ⎢    ⎪IS GREATER THAN         ⎪           ⎥
                     ⎢    ⎪IS >                    ⎪           ⎥
  START file-name KEY ⎨IS NOT LESS THAN        ⎬ identifier
                     ⎢    ⎪IS NOT <                ⎪           ⎥
                     ⎢    ⎪IS GREATER THAN OR EQUAL TO⎪        ⎥
                     ⎣    ⎩IS >=                   ⎭           ⎦

  [INVALID KEY imperative-statement-1]

  [NOT INVALID KEY imperative-statement-2]

  [END-START]
```

The START statement can be used in conjunction with a concatenated key as shown in Figure 18.13. *Note, however, that START only moves to the designated record, but does **not** read the record.* In other words, a READ statement is required immediately following START. The subsequent PERFORM statement will then retrieve all loans for the customer in question.

Limitations of COBOL-74

The READ, DELETE, WRITE, REWRITE, and START statements contain both an optional scope terminator and a false-condition branch. As indicated throughout the text, these elements are new to COBOL-85 and were not available in COBOL-74.

Sixteen I/O status codes (i.e., the majority of the entries in Table 18.1) are new to COBOL-85. The new codes (02, 04, 05, 07, 15, 24, 25, 34, 35, 37, 38, 39, 41, 42, 43, 46, and 49) were added to eliminate the need for vendor-specific file status codes that treated the same error condition in different ways.

Figure 18.13   The START Statement

```
        SELECT LOAN-FILE
            ASSIGN TO LOAN
            ORGANIZATION IS INDEXED
            ACCESS MODE IS DYNAMIC
            RECORD KEY IS CUSTOMER-LOAN-NUMBER.
        .
          .
            .
        FD  LOAN-FILE
            RECORD CONTAINS 120 CHARACTERS
            DATA RECORD IS LOAN-RECORD.
        01  LOAN-RECORD.
            05   CUSTOMER-LOAN-NUMBER.
                10   CUSTOMER-NUMBER      PIC 9(6).
                10   LOAN-NUMBER          PIC 9(3).
        .
          .
            .
        PROCEDURE DIVISION.
          .
            .
              .
            MOVE 333333000 TO CUSTOMER-LOAN-NUMBER.
            START LOAN-FILE
                KEY IS GREATER THAN CUSTOMER-LOAN-NUMBER
                INVALID KEY DISPLAY 'CUSTOMER 333333 NOT IN FILE'
            END-START.

            READ LOAN-FILE NEXT RECORD
                AT END
                    MOVE 'YES' TO END-OF-FILE-SWITCH
            END-READ.

            PERFORM UNTIL CUSTOMER-NUMBER NOT EQUAL 333333
                OR END-OF-FILE-SWITCH = 'YES'
                    DISPLAY LOAN-RECORD
                    READ LOAN-FILE NEXT RECORD
                        AT END
                            MOVE 'YES' TO END-OF-FILE-SWITCH
                    END-READ
            END-PERFORM.
```

Record key is concatenated, consisting of customer number and loan number

START statement finds the first loan for customer 333333

PERFORM statement finds all subsequent loans

S U M M A R Y

Points to Remember

■ Indexed files permit sequential and/or nonsequential access to records within a file. Different vendors have different physical implementations, but the COBOL syntax to access an indexed file is the same for all compilers adhering to the ANS 85 standard. VSAM (Virtual Storage Access Method) is IBM's implementation for indexed files.

■ The SELECT statement for an indexed file has seven clauses: three clauses (ASSIGN, ORGANIZATION IS INDEXED, and RECORD KEY) are required, and the other four (RESERVE AREAS, ACCESS MODE, ALTERNATE RECORD KEY, and FILE STATUS) are optional.

■ The RECORD KEY clause in the SELECT statement specifies a field (defined within the FD of the indexed record) whose value must be unique; the value of the optional alternate record key can contain duplicate values.

■ The Procedure Division has several statements uniquely associated with indexed files, and/or extends the formats of other statements to accommodate indexed files. These include OPEN I-O, READ . . . INVALID KEY, WRITE . . . INVALID KEY, and DELETE.

■ The transaction file does not have to be in sequence when updating an indexed file as the latter can be accessed nonsequentially. The INVALID KEY clause will be activated if the transaction record is not found.

■ The updated indexed file cannot be used as the old master to retest the update program with the same input as previously; you must retain (create) a copy of the original indexed file for repeated testing.

■ A concatenated key consists of two or more fields strung together. Concatenated keys are frequently used in conjunction with the START statement, which moves nonsequentially to the first record satisfying a specified condition.

Key Words and Concepts

Concatenated key	Indexed file
Control area	I/O status
Control area split	Multiple keys
Control interval	Nonsequential access
Control interval split	Scope terminator
False-condition branch	Sequence set
Free space	Sequential access
Index set	VSAM organization

COBOL Elements

ACCESS IS DYNAMIC
ACCESS IS RANDOM
ACCESS IS SEQUENTIAL
ACCESS MODE
ALTERNATE RECORD KEY
DELETE
END-DELETE
END-READ
END-START
END-REWRITE
END-WRITE

FILE STATUS
INVALID KEY
NOT INVALID KEY
OPEN I-O
ORGANIZATION IS INDEXED
RECORD KEY
RESERVE AREAS
REWRITE
START
WITH DUPLICATES
WRITE . . . INVALID KEY

F i l l - i n

1. _____ files make it possible to retrieve records sequentially and/or nonsequentially.

2. An active file is best updated sequentially, whereas _____ processing should be used for inactive files.

3. _____ is the IBM specific implementation of COBOL's _____ file organization.

4. In IBM's VSAM implementation, a _____ _____ contains one or more _____ _____.

5. In IBM's VSAM implementation, each entry in a sequence set contains the _____ key for the associated control interval.

6. The SELECT statement for indexed files requires three clauses: _____, _____, and _____.

7. An indexed file requires the primary key to be _____, but allows _____ values for its _____ key.

8. Records are added to an indexed file through the _____ statement; existing records are changed through _____ and removed by the _____ statement.

9. The FILE STATUS clause is (<u>optional/required</u>) and requires that a _____ byte area be defined in _____ _____.

10. FILE STATUS bytes of _____ indicate a successful I/O operation, whereas _____ indicates an end-of-file condition.

11. The _____ statement allows one to enter an indexed file randomly and read sequentially from that point on.

12. A random (nonsequential) READ statement is preceded by a MOVE statement in which the desired key is moved to the field defined as the _____ _____.

13. Specification of ACCESS IS _____ permits both sequential and nonsequential access of an indexed file in the same program.

14. When a file is open in the _____ mode, it may be read from and written to.

True/False

1. ALTERNATE RECORD KEY should always be specified for indexed files to allow for future expansion.

2. The FILE STATUS clause is permitted only for indexed files.

3. A READ statement must contain either the AT END or INVALID KEY clause.

4. Inclusion of the INTO clause in a READ statement is not recommended, as it requires additional storage space.

5. RESERVE 0 AREAS is recommended to speed up processing of an indexed file that is processed sequentially.

6. The value of RECORD KEY must be unique for every record in an indexed file.

7. The value of ALTERNATE RECORD KEY must be unique for every record in an indexed file.

8. The FILE STATUS clause is a mandatory entry in the SELECT statement for an indexed file.

9. An indexed file can be accessed sequentially and nonsequentially in the same program.

10. The first byte of an indexed record should contain either LOW- or HIGH-VALUES.

11. WRITE and REWRITE can be used interchangeably.

12. Records in an indexed file are deleted by moving HIGH-VALUES to the first byte.

13. The COBOL syntax for IBM VSAM files conforms to the ANS 85 standard.

14. Active files are best updated nonsequentially.

Problems

1. Describe the changes to Figure 18.3 if record keys 401, 723, 724, and 725 were added. What would happen if record keys 502 and 619 were deleted?

2. Assume that record key 289 is to be inserted in the first control area of the VSAM data set in Figure 18.3. Logically, it could be added as the last record in the first control interval or the first record in the second control interval. Is there a preference?

   In similar fashion, should record 620 be inserted as the last record in the third interval of the second area or as the first record in the first interval of the third area?

   Finally, will record 900 be inserted as the last record in the fourth control area, or will it require creation of a fifth control area? Can you describe in general terms how VSAM adds records at the end of control areas and/or control intervals?

3. Indicate whether each of the following SELECT statements is valid syntactically and logically. (Some of the statements have more than one error.)
   a. SELECT INDEXED-FILE
          ASSIGN INDMAST
          ORGANIZATION INDEXED
          RECORD IND-SOC-SEC-NUM.

```
b. SELECT INDEXED-FILE
       ASSIGN TO INDMAST
       RECORD KEY IS IND-SOC-SEC-NUM WITH NO DUPLICATES
       ALTERNATE KEY IS IND-NAME WITH DUPLICATES.

c. SELECT INDEXED-FILE
       ASSIGN INDMAST
       RESERVE 5 AREAS
       ORGANIZATION IS INDEXED
       ACCESS IS SEQUENTIAL
       RECORD KEY IS IND-SOC-SEC-NUM WITH DUPLICATES
       ALTERNATE RECORD KEY IS IND-NAME
       FILE STATUS IS FILE-STATUS-BYTES.

d. SELECT INDEXED-FILE
       ASSIGN TO INDMAST
       ORGANIZATION IS INDEXED
       ACCESS MODE RANDOM
       RECORD KEY IS IND-SOC-SEC-NUM, IND-NAME.
```

4. Given the COBOL definition:

```
    05    FILE-STATUS-BYTES              PIC 99.
```

What is wrong with the following entries?

```
a.  IF FILE-STATUS-BYTES EQUAL '10'
        DISPLAY 'END OF FILE HAS BEEN REACHED'
    END-IF

b.  IF FILE STATUS-BYTES EQUAL 10
        DISPLAY 'ERROR - DUPLICATE KEY'
    END-IF

c.  IF FILE-STATUS-BYTE EQUAL 1
        DISPLAY 'END OF FILE HAS BEEN REACHED'
    END-IF

d.  IF FILE STATUS BYTES EQUAL 10
        DISPLAY 'END OF FILE HAS BEEN REACHED'
    END-IF
```

5. Indicate whether each of the following entries is valid syntactically and logically. (Assume INDEXED-FILE and INDEXED-RECORD are valid as a file name and a record name, respectively.)

```
a.  OPEN INPUT INDEXED-FILE
         OUTPUT INDEXED-FILE.

b.  READ INDEXED-FILE.

c.  READ INDEXED-FILE
        AT END MOVE 'YES' TO END-OF-FILE-SWITCH.
    END-READ.
```

```
d.  READ INDEXED-FILE
        AT END
            MOVE 'YES' TO END-OF-FILE-SWITCH
        NOT AT END
            PERFORM PROCESS-RECORD
    END-READ.

e.  READ INDEXED-FILE
        AT END MOVE 21 TO FILE-STATUS-BYTES.

f.  READ INDEXED-FILE
        INVALID KEY
            DISPLAY 'RECORD IS IN FILE'
        NOT INVALID KEY
            DISPLAY 'RECORD IS NOT IN FILE'
    END-READ.

g.  WRITE INDEXED-RECORD.

h.  WRITE INDEXED-RECORD
        INVALID KEY
            DISPLAY 'INVALID KEY'
        NOT INVALID KEY
            PERFORM CONTINUE-PROCESSING
    END-WRITE.

i.  REWRITE INDEXED-RECORD
        INVALID KEY
            DISPLAY 'INVALID KEY'
            PERFORM ERROR-PROCESSING
    END-REWRITE.

j.  REWRITE INDEXED-FILE.

k.  DELETE INDEXED-RECORD.

l.  DELETE INDEXED-FILE.
```

6. Figure 18.14a contains a slightly modified paragraph from the nonsequential update program of Figure 18.10, which produces the compiler diagnostics in Figure 18.14b. Why do the errors occur?

7. The balance line algorithm was not used for the nonsequential update program (Figure 18.10) developed in the chapter. The resulting program worked correctly, but it can be made more efficient by changing its logic to include the concept of the active key.

   a. What are the advantages of including the additional logic and using the balance line algorithm?

   b. What are the disadvantages to this approach?

   c. Modify the hierarchy chart and pseudocode of Figures 18.8 and 18.9 to accommodate the algorithm.

Figure 18.14   Debugging Exercise

```
60        PROCEDURE DIVISION.
61        0010-UPDATE-MASTER-FILE.
62            OPEN INPUT TRANSACTION-FILE
63                 I-O INDEXED-FILE.
64            PERFORM UNTIL END-OF-FILE-SWITCH = 'YES'
65                READ TRANSACTION-FILE INTO WS-TRANS-RECORD
66                    AT END
67                         MOVE 'YES' TO END-OF-FILE-SWITCH
68                    NOT AT END
69                         PERFORM 0020-READ-INDEXED-FILE
70                         PERFORM 0030-APPLY-TRANS-TO-MASTER.
71                END-READ
72            END-PERFORM
```

(a) Modified Procedure Division

```
64 W Explicit scope terminator END- 'PERFORM' assumed present
71 E No corresponding active scope for 'END-READ'
72 E No corresponding active scope for 'END-PERFORM'
```

(b) Error Messages

The Year 2000 Problem

CHAPTER OUTLINE

Overview
The Year 2000 Problem
Date Arithmetic
    COBOL Intrinsic Calendar Functions
    Leap-Year Problem
Retirement Program Revisited
Summary
Fill-in
True/False
Problems
For Further Study

OBJECTIVES

After reading this chapter, you will be able to:

■ Describe the implications of the Year 2000 problem.

■ State the causes of the problem.

■ Identify the types of routines that may cause the problem.

■ Discuss several types of date arithmetic.

■ Use COBOL intrinsic calendar function to do date conversions.

OVERVIEW

This chapter discusses a major information system issue at the end of the twentieth century. This problem is known by several titles such as "the Year 2000 problem," "Millennium 2K," or simply "Y2K." Whatever the name, the problem is one the industry has brought upon itself—threatening the well-being of many companies and governmental organizations. The purpose of this chapter is to define what the problem is, show how it came about, and suggest some ways to deal with it.

The first section of the chapter discusses the nature of the problem by examining a program typical of those written in the 1960s, 1970s, and 1980s. The next section deals with the issues of date arithmetic. The discussion involves the two date formats introduced in Chapter 8: DATE format (YYMMDD) and DAY (YYDDD). The discussion shows how the DAY format can be used in calculating the number of days between two dates. This section of the chapter then looks at the COBOL intrinsic calendar functions to see how they can further simplify date arithmetic.

Leap year processing compounds the Year 2000 problem. The last portion of the chapter looks at this aspect of the problem and presents a Year 2000 compliant version of the original program. For further research on the Year 2000 problem, the section contains a listing of World Wide Web sites dedicated to the problem and its solution.

The Year 2000 Problem

Look at the retirement program listed in Figure 19.1. This program reads an employee file and computes the employee's age, years of service to the company, and the date of retirement. The program then prints a report showing the results of its calculations.

Do you see any problems with this program? First, notice the output format for the retirement date. In line 86, just before DET-RET-YR, the programmer has coded in a value of "/19." As a result, the output report will print the retirement year as "19*YY*" no matter when the employee is due to retire. Obviously, in the late 1990s, most employees will retire after 1999 and the report format needs to reflect a retirement year where the first two digits can be 19, 20, or even 21. The report should not state that the retirement date is 1904 when the year actually should be 2004.

This program is a simple example of the Year 2000 problem. When programs like this one were written, programmers assumed that all dates used would be in the twentieth century[1] and that "19" was the valid prefix for all years.

This type of thinking meant that many computer systems incorporated only two digits for representing a year instead of the four digits normally used. As a result, when these systems encounter the year 2000, they act as if the year is 1900. This apparently simple oversight means that when January 1, 2000 comes, many systems will fail entirely or will produce massive amounts of erroneous information. The remedy will not be cheap. Some authorities estimate the cost to fix the problem at $300 billion to $600 billion worldwide.[2] The Year 2000 problem is one that will not go away, and the deadline cannot be delayed.

Figure 19.1 Retirement Program, a Year 2000 Problem Example

```
1          IDENTIFICATION DIVISION.
2          PROGRAM-ID.   Y2K01.
3          AUTHOR.       ARTHUR R. BUSS
4
5          ENVIRONMENT DIVISION.
6          INPUT-OUTPUT SECTION.
7          FILE-CONTROL.
8              SELECT EMPLOYEE-FILE ASSIGN TO SYSIN
9                  ORGANIZATION IS LINE SEQUENTIAL.
10             SELECT PRINT-FILE ASSIGN TO SYSOUT
11                 ORGANIZATION IS LINE SEQUENTIAL.
12
13         DATA DIVISION.
14         FILE SECTION.
15         FD EMPLOYEE-FILE
16             RECORD CONTAINS 34 CHARACTERS.
17         01 EMPLOYEE-RECORD          PIC X(34).
18
19         FD PRINT-FILE
20             RECORD CONTAINS 80 CHARACTERS.
21         01 PRINT-LINE               PIC X(80).
22
23         WORKING-STORAGE SECTION.
24         01  EMPLOYEE-DATA.
25             05  EMP-NUM             PIC X(05).
26             05  EMP-NAME.
27                 10  EMP-LAST        PIC X(15).
28                 10  EMP-INIT        PIC X(02).
29             05  EMP-BIRTHDATE.
30                 10  EMP-BIRTH-YR    PIC 9(02).
31                 10  EMP-BIRTH-MO    PIC 9(02).
32                 10  EMP-BIRTH-DA    PIC 9(02).
33             05  EMP-SERVICE-DATE.
34                 10  EMP-SERVICE-YR  PIC 9(02).
35                 10  EMP-SERVICE-MO  PIC 9(02).
```

Figure 19.1 *(continued)*

```
36              10   EMP-SERVICE-DA      PIC 9(02).
37
38        01  DATA-REMAINS-SW           PIC X(02).
39              88  NO-DATA-REMAINS                   VALUE 'NO'.
40
41        01  INDIVIDUAL-FIELDS.
42              05  IND-AGE             PIC 9(02).
43              05  IND-SERV-YEARS      PIC 9(02).
44              05  IND-RET-DATE.
45                  10   IND-RET-YR     PIC 9(02).
46                  10   IND-RET-MO     PIC 9(02).
47                  10   IND-RET-DA     PIC 9(02).
48
49        01  TODAYS-DATE.
50              05  TODAYS-YR           PIC 9(02).
51              05  TODAYS-MO           PIC 9(02).
52              05  TODAYS-DA           PIC 9(02).
53
54        01  CONSTANTS.
55              05  RETIRE-AGE          PIC 9(02)    VALUE 65.
56
57        01  HEADING-LINE-1.
58              05                      PIC X(05)    VALUE SPACES.
59              05                      PIC X(10)    VALUE 'EMPLOYEE'.
60              05                      PIC X(17)    VALUE SPACES.
61              05                      PIC X(09)    VALUE 'SERVICE'.
62              05                      PIC X(10)    VALUE 'RETIREMENT'.
63
64        01  HEADING-LINE-2.
65              05                      PIC X(07)    VALUE SPACES.
66              05                      PIC X(14)    VALUE 'NAME'.
67              05                      PIC X(07)    VALUE 'INIT'.
68              05                      PIC X(06)    VALUE 'AGE'.
69              05                      PIC X(08)    VALUE 'YEARS'.
70              05                      PIC X(10)    VALUE 'DATE'.
71
72        01  DETAIL-LINE.
73              05                      PIC X(05)    VALUE SPACES.
74              05  DET-LAST            PIC X(15).
75              05                      PIC X(02)    VALUE SPACES.
76              05  DET-INIT            PIC X(02).
77              05                      PIC X(05)    VALUE SPACES.
78              05  DET-AGE             PIC 9(02).
79              05                      PIC X(05)    VALUE SPACES.
80              05  DET-SERV-YEARS      PIC 9(02).
81              05                      PIC X(02)    VALUE SPACES.
82              05  DET-RET-DATE.
83                  10   DET-RET-MO     PIC Z9.
84                  10                  PIC X        VALUE '/'.
85                  10   DET-RET-DA     PIC Z9.
86                  10                  PIC X(03)    VALUE '/19'.        ── Assumed year
87                  10   DET-RET-YR     PIC 9(02).
```

Figure 19.1 *(continued)*

```
88
89          PROCEDURE DIVISION.
90          100-PREPARE-RETIREMENT-REPORT.
91              OPEN INPUT EMPLOYEE-FILE
92                   OUTPUT PRINT-FILE
93              PERFORM 210-GET-TODAYS-DATE
94              PERFORM 230-WRITE-HEADERS
95              PERFORM UNTIL NO-DATA-REMAINS
96                  READ EMPLOYEE-FILE INTO EMPLOYEE-DATA
97                      AT END
98                          SET NO-DATA-REMAINS TO TRUE
99                      NOT AT END
100                         PERFORM 260-PROCESS-DETAIL
101                 END-READ
102             END-PERFORM
103             CLOSE EMPLOYEE-FILE
104                   PRINT-FILE
105             STOP RUN
106             .                              ─── Paragraph ending
107                                                period
108         210-GET-TODAYS-DATE.
109             ACCEPT TODAYS-DATE FROM DATE
110         *   MOVE '000101' TO TODAYS-DATE
111             .                              ─── Test for year 2000
112
113         230-WRITE-HEADERS.
114             WRITE PRINT-LINE FROM HEADING-LINE-1
115         AFTER ADVANCING PAGE
116             WRITE PRINT-LINE FROM HEADING-LINE-2
117             INITIALIZE PRINT-LINE
118             WRITE PRINT-LINE
119             .
120
121         260-PROCESS-DETAIL.
122             PERFORM 310-CALCULATE-EMP-AGE
123             PERFORM 330-CALCULATE-EMP-SERVICE
124             PERFORM 360-CALCULATE-IND-RET-DATE
125             PERFORM 390-WRITE-DETAIL-LINE
126             .
127
128         310-CALCULATE-EMP-AGE.
129             COMPUTE IND-AGE = TODAYS-YR - EMP-BIRTH-YR
130                       + (TODAYS-MO - EMP-BIRTH-MO) / 12   ─── Age calculation
131             .
132
133         330-CALCULATE-EMP-SERVICE.
134             COMPUTE IND-SERV-YEARS = TODAYS-YR - EMP-SERVICE-YR
135                       + (TODAYS-MO - EMP-SERVICE-MO) / 12  ─── Service calculation
136             .
137
138         360-CALCULATE-IND-RET-DATE.
139             ADD RETIRE-AGE      TO EMP-BIRTH-YR GIVING IND-RET-YR
```

Figure 19.1 *(continued)*

```
140              MOVE EMP-BIRTH-MO   TO IND-RET-MO
141              MOVE EMP-BIRTH-DA   TO IND-RET-DA
142                  .
143
144          390-WRITE-DETAIL-LINE.
145              MOVE EMP-LAST       TO DET-LAST
146              MOVE EMP-INIT       TO DET-INIT
147              MOVE IND-AGE        TO DET-AGE
148              MOVE IND-SERV-YEARS TO DET-SERV-YEARS
149              MOVE IND-RET-MO     TO DET-RET-MO
150              MOVE IND-RET-DA     TO DET-RET-DA
151              MOVE IND-RET-YR     TO DET-RET-YR
152              WRITE PRINT-LINE    FROM DETAIL-LINE
153                  .
```

At this point, you may think that the case is overstated. Certainly a simple remedy exists for the problem described above. By expanding the DET-RET-YR field size to four positions and eliminating the "19" from the preceding filler field, the program can print either 19YY or 20YY. However, having made the change, the question becomes, "How do I know which lead digits to use, 19 or 20?" It would be just as wrong to assume that all retirement dates will fall after the year 2000 as it was to assume that the dates should come before 2000. A way must be found to determine the appropriate digits.

You can now begin to see the essence of the Year 2000 problem. When there are only two digits to work with, how would the program determine the right century? Should it treat "88" as 1888, 1988, or 2088? Before answering the question, you may want to know how this problem came about in the first place.

From the 1960s through the 1980s, many organizations developed systems containing programs, and, more importantly, files that used only the last two digits of the year whenever a date was required. This practice worked well for a long time and did not seem to cause any particular problems. One exception was when a program had to look far into the future, as in calculating retirement dates. You may still wonder why the system developers did not anticipate the problem and just use four-digit years as a standard practice.

One answer is in the hardware used at the time. Mainframes were the primary computer of the era, and they ran most systems. On these machines, disk storage and primary memory were extremely expensive. Thus, programmers had to use storage economically, and eliminating two "unnecessary" digits was one way to do it. The decision was a conscious one made to save money.[3]

A second answer is in the COBOL compilers. Using the same type of logic in the previous answer, the "ACCEPT...FROM DATE" command returned the system date in YYMMDD format. This date format is the default even in the newer COBOL standards.[4] In order to maintain four-digit years, a programmer would have to deliberately add the extra digits to the year field wherever it was created. From a programming perspective, the course of least resistance was to use just two digits.

A third answer is that most system developers could not envision these programs being around long enough for the problem to matter. They expected that the programs would be replaced long before 2000, and that the new systems would deal with the problem. However, some 20 and even 30 years later, these "legacy" systems are still running, and the problem faces industry now.

Look at the program in Figure 19.1 again.[5] In paragraph 210-GET-TODAYS-DATE (line 108), the ACCEPT statement brings in the current system date and stores it in the TODAYS-DATE group item. Paragraph 310-CALCULATE-EMPLOYEE-AGE, in line 128, uses the system date information to compute the employee's age by using the age calculation introduced in Chapter 8. The code segment below shows the date items and the calculations.

```
01  EMPLOYEE-DATA.
    05  EMP-NUM                   PIC X(05).
    05  EMP-NAME.
        10  EMP-LAST              PIC X(15).
        10  EMP-INIT              PIC X(02).
    05  EMP-BIRTHDATE.
        10  EMP-BIRTH-YR          PIC 9(02).
        10  EMP-BIRTH-MO          PIC 9(02).
        10  EMP-BIRTH-DA          PIC 9(02).
    05  EMP-SERVICE-DATE.
        10  EMP-SERVICE-YR        PIC 9(02).
        10  EMP-SERVICE-MO        PIC 9(02).
        10  EMP-SERVICE-DA        PIC 9(02).

01  DATA-REMAINS-SW              PIC X(02).
    88  NO-DATA-REMAINS                        VALUE 'NO'.

01  INDIVIDUAL-FIELDS.
    05  IND-AGE                  PIC 9(02).
    05  IND-SERV-YEARS           PIC 9(02).
    05  IND-RET-DATE.
        10  IND-RET-YR           PIC 9(02).
        10  IND-RET-MO           PIC 9(02).
        10  IND-RET-DA           PIC 9(02).


01  TODAYS-DATE.
    05  TODAYS-YR                PIC 9(02).
    05  TODAYS-MO                PIC 9(02).
    05  TODAYS-DA                PIC 9(02).

310-CALCULATE-EMP-AGE.
    COMPUTE IND-AGE = TODAYS-YR - EMP-BIRTH-YR
                    + (TODAYS-MO - EMP-BIRTH-MO) / 12
    .
```

As an example, suppose that an employee was born on January 1, 1970. On January 1, 2000, this employee will be 30 years old. Following the logic of the program, you should find that it will calculate that the employee is 70 years old and overdue for retirement. (Note: If the IND-AGE field were defined as signed, the employee would be –70.) To test this for yourself, remove the asterisk in line 110 and put an asterisk in column 7 of line 109. This change overrides setting TODAYS-DATE from the system date and forces it to be January 1, 2000. Compile the program and check the results.

In the same way, the program has a problem determining how long an employee has worked. Notice paragraph 330-CALCULATE-EMP-SERVICE (line 133). This paragraph uses the same type of logic to compute the employee's time in service. However, if our employee started work on January 1, 1990, the algorithm will compute the service years as 90. This result is particularly interesting, since the program claims that the employee is only 70 years old.

The question then becomes, "How does one fix the problem?" The answer, in one sense, is quite simple. The programmer must change all of the date fields in the program to incorporate four digits for the year portion of the date. Each task is very simple if there are not too many date fields and they have clearly identified names. However, even in this simple program, you can get a feel for the problem. The programmer must find and change five fields representing years and also correct the print format line. In a larger program, the programmer may easily miss some necessary changes.

The problem becomes more complex because there is more to change than just the program. The input records also contain two-digit year fields. Thus, the file definition must be modified to make sure that all date group items contain four-digit years. In addition to changing the file definition, the data in the files must be changed as well. Thus, some program has to convert the data to the new format. While this process is going on, someone must convert all other associated programs to accept the data in its new format, even if those programs do not use the date fields directly. Coordination of all this effort is critical to ensure that nothing "drops through the cracks." While each change is simple by itself, the implications and volume can be overwhelming.

Some companies have thousands of programs affected by the Year 2000 problem. Many organizations may have 50 million lines of code to inspect and change along with all of the associated files, screens, and reports. Such changes are going to be expensive.[6]

Date Arithmetic

Another aspect of the problem occurs when a program has to calculate days and not years. Many applications need to determine how many days have occurred between two dates. To accomplish this task, COBOL provides a different type of date structure. The DAY format (YYDDD) describes the sequential number of a date within a given year. In this structure, the YY refers to the years and the DDD refers to the day of the year. December 31 would be 365 in normal years and 366 in leap years. The use of the DAY format makes date arithmetic quite simple as long as the *dates* involved are within the same calendar year.

```
01  TWO-DATES.
    05  FIRST-DATE.
        10  FIRST-YEAR                    PIC 99.
        10  FIRST-DAY                     PIC 999.
    05  SECOND-DATE.
        10  SEC-YEAR                      PIC 99.
        10  SEC-DAY                       PIC 999.
01  DAYS-DIFFERENCE                       PIC 999.

    MOVE 97234 TO FIRST-DATE.
    MOVE 97100 TO SECOND-DATE.
    SUBTRACT SEC-DAY FROM FIRST-DAY GIVING DAYS-DIFFERENCE.
```

In the code fragment above, you can see how the DAY format easily provides the number of days between two events as long as both dates are in the same year. The trick is to determine what to do if the two dates span the year boundary. The YY portion of the DAY format does not help much.

Since there are not 1,000 days in a year, simple subtraction would leave a gap of 636 days between December 31, 1997 (97365) and January 1, 1998 (98001), for example. Date calculations crossing the year boundary must take the gap into account. The following code shows one way of handling the problem.

```
MOVE 98030 TO FIRST-DATE.
MOVE 97300 TO SECOND-DATE.
IF FIRST-YEAR > SEC-YEAR
    ADD 365 TO FIRST-DAY
END-IF.
SUBTRACT SEC-DAY FROM FIRST-DAY GIVING DAYS-DIFFERENCE.
```

This code treats the date in the new year as a continuation of the old year and acts as if 98030 were actually 97395. This technique allows the program to compute the difference of 95 days.

You can see what may happen when the millennium changes. If FIRST-YEAR is 00 and SEC-YEAR is 99, the IF condition is false and DAYS-DIFFERENCE would be 270 rather than 95.

Fortunately, the 1989 extensions to COBOL provide a better way to do date arithmetic. These extensions include a number of intrinsic functions that do the kinds of standard operations available in many other languages and in spreadsheet programs. Appendix E, on COBOL 2002, covers the 1989 intrinsic functions as well as the additional functions proposed for the new standard. In the next section, you will see how to use the calendar functions to perform date arithmetic and correct the Year 2000 problem.

COBOL Intrinsic Calendar Functions

If you have worked with an electronic spreadsheet, you may know that the spreadsheet does not maintain dates YYYYMMDD format. Rather, the spreadsheet maintains a count of the number of days from some arbitrary starting point. In EXCEL, for example, the starting point is January 1, 1900. In other words, EXCEL treats January 1, 1900, as "Day 1." Each day since January 1, 1900 is a consecutively numbered integer. Date arithmetic is simply a matter of adding to or subtracting from these integers. Any date before the defined starting date is invalid.

The intrinsic functions of COBOL allow programmers to use the same type of integer date functions as in a spreadsheet. With COBOL, however, the arbitrary starting point is January 1, 1601. This early date allows consideration of more dates than EXCEL can handle and should be sufficient for most date applications. On the other hand, the early starting date means that the integer values of current dates are quite large. As an example, January 1, 2000 has an integer value of 145732. This means that programs must allow at least six digits for integer date fields.

While integer format dates ease the problem of date calculations, humans have trouble reading dates in this format. Therefore, COBOL has provided functions that convert dates from standard formats to integer and back. The 1989 extension to COBOL provides six intrinsic calendar functions for programmer use.

- CURRENT-DATE—Returns the current system date in YYYYMMDD format.

- WHEN-COMPILED—Returns the compile date in YYYYMMDD format.

- DATE-OF-INTEGER—Converts an integer date to YYYYMMDD format.

- DAY-OF-INTEGER—Converts an integer date to YYYYDDD format.

- INTEGER-OF-DATE—Converts YYYYMMDD to an integer.

- INTEGER-OF-DAY—Converts YYYYDDD to an integer.

The syntax for these functions is:

FUNCTION function-name [(argument-1 [, argument-2] . . .)]

The first two functions do not require an argument since they return specific values. The last four functions are the routines that allow COBOL to convert dates to integers and vice versa. These functions work similarly. By reviewing how the DATE-TO-INTEGER function works, you can easily see how to use the remaining functions.

The program shown in Figure 19.2 uses INTEGER-OF-DATE. You may want to compile and test the program (Y2K02.CBL) for yourself. The program interactively takes the year, month, and day from the user and returns the integer value of the date. Test the program with your birthdate, February 29, 1900, February 29, 2000, and any other date you wish. The program will return zeros for invalid dates.

Looking at the program, you should note several points. In line 8, the integer field has a length of 6. As stated above, six digits are necessary to hold the integer value of current dates. In line 13, DATE-RDF redefines DATE-INPUT because the function INTEGER-OF-DATE requires an elementary item as the input parameter. In line 23 notice that the keyword "FUNCTION" tells COBOL that "INTEGER-OF-DATE" is an intrinsic function and not an identifier.

The syntax is:

```
FUNCTION  INTEGER-OF-DATE  (argument-1)
```

The argument is an elementary item in the format YYYYMMDD, and the function returns a six-digit number.

You may want to rewrite this program to accept DAY values from the user and use the INTEGER-OF-DAY function to convert the value to an integer. You can also write programs to convert an integer to its corresponding DATE or DAY by using the DATE-OF INTEGER or DAY-OF-INTEGER functions. These problems are included in the exercises at the end of the chapter.

Date arithmetic using the intrinsic functions can be quite straightforward. For example:

```
COMPUTE NO-OF-DAYS = FUNCTION INTEGER-OF-DATE (DATE-1)
                   - FUNCTION INTEGER-OF-DATE (DATE-2).
```

This statement converts DATE-1 and DATE-2 to integers and subtracts DATE-2 from DATE-1 storing the result in NO-OF-DAYS.

As another exercise, try modifying the program to accept two days and to calculate the difference between them. You may also want to write another program that accepts a date and a number of days from the user. The program then would calculate and return a new date by adding the number of days to the integer of the original date.

One advantage to using the intrinsic calendar functions is that leap-year problems may be avoided or at least minimized.

Figure 19.2 Example of the Integer-of-Date Function

```
 1        IDENTIFICATION DIVISION.
 2        PROGRAM-ID.    Y2K02.
 3        AUTHOR.        ARTHUR R. BUSS.
 4
 5        DATA DIVISION.
 6        WORKING-STORAGE SECTION.
 7        01  DATE-DATA.
 8            05  DATE-INTEGER        PIC 9(06).          ──── Six positions for date integer
 9            05  DATE-INPUT.
10                10  DATE-YEAR       PIC 9(04).
11                10  DATE-MONTH      PIC 9(02).
12                10  DATE-DAY        PIC 9(02).
13            05  DATE-RDF  REDEFINES DATE-INPUT
14                                    PIC 9(08).
15            05  LAST-DATE-SW        PIC X.
16                88  LAST-DATE              VALUE 'N' 'n'.
17
18        PROCEDURE DIVISION.
19        CONVERT-DATE.
20            MOVE 'Y' TO LAST-DATE-SW
21            PERFORM GET-DATE
22            PERFORM UNTIL LAST-DATE
23                COMPUTE DATE-INTEGER = FUNCTION
24                                 INTEGER-OF-DATE (DATE-RDF)    ──── Intrinsic function
25                DISPLAY DATE-INTEGER
26                DISPLAY 'DO YOU WISH TO CONTINUE (Y OR N)? '
27                    WITH NO ADVANCING
28                ACCEPT LAST-DATE-SW
29                IF NOT LAST-DATE
30                    PERFORM GET-DATE
31                END-IF
32            END-PERFORM
33            STOP RUN
34            .
35
36        GET-DATE.
37            DISPLAY 'ENTER YEAR IN "YYYY" FORMAT '
38                WITH NO ADVANCING
39            ACCEPT DATE-YEAR
40            DISPLAY 'ENTER MONTH IN "MM" FORMAT '
41                WITH NO ADVANCING
42            ACCEPT DATE-MONTH
43            DISPLAY 'ENTER DAY IN "DD" FORMAT '
44                WITH NO ADVANCING
45            ACCEPT DATE-DAY
46            .
```

Leap-Year Problem

A programmer working on the Year 2000 problem and looking at date handling in COBOL programs would encounter special routines written to deal with leap years. Leap years pose special problems, and programs must account for them properly. For example, look again at the program in Figure 19.1 and examine the logic to compute the employee's retirement date (360-CALCULATE-IND-RET-DATE). Notice that the logic assumes that the retirement month and day will be the same as the birth month and day.

```
MOVE EMP-BIRTH-MO TO IND-RET-MO.
MOVE EMP-BIRTH-DA TO IND-RET-DA.
```

In most cases this assumption is valid. However, if an employee was born on February 29, by definition he or she was born in a leap year. A problem occurs because February 29 is invalid for the retirement date 65 years later. For example, a person born on February 29, 1940 would expect to retire in the year 2005. However, 2005 is not a leap year, and February 29 is invalid. In this case, the employee should retire on March 1, 2005. Code must be added to the program to detect the situation and make the adjustment.

Unfortunately, the rules for determining leap years are confusing. Most people know that leap years occur when the year value is equally divisible by four. Many people do not know that years ending in 00 are *not* leap years. There was no February 29 in 1900; yet, some versions of Microsoft's EXCEL will accept February 29 as a valid date for 1900.

Just to make things more difficult, every 400 years February 29 *does* occur in the year ending in 00. So, 1600, 2000, and 2400 are leap years. Consequently, a simple leap year routine that simply divides by 4 often works out better for the year 2000 than a more sophisticated routine that makes adjustments for the century years.

COBOL's intrinsic function INTEGER-OF-DATE manages leap years properly and will return a value of zero when it detects an invalid date. Therefore, the function also provides a way to validate dates. By testing for a zero value, the program can detect when it has encountered an invalid date. Appropriate routines can then be written to deal with the problem. Unfortunately COBOL97 also returns an error message to the user. This lessens the usefulness of the technique.

How can these techniques improve the original program?

Retirement Program Revisited

Figure 19.3 presents a revision[7] of the original retirement program. This revision eliminates the Year 2000 problems and properly deals with leap years. This new program takes advantage of the 1989 COBOL intrinsic functions and also utilizes a date conversion utility program YEAR-TO-YYYY[8] shown in Figure 19.4. This utility program simulates the COBOL 2002 intrinsic function of the same name. (Note: In order to keep things simple, this version of the program uses the same input file as the original.)

As introduced in the previous section, the CURRENT-DATE intrinsic function returns the system date in YYYYMMDD format and can replace the ACCEPT...FROM DATE statement. Line 119 uses CURRENT-DATE to get the system date. More about CURRENT-DATE can be found in the appendix on COBOL 2002.

Line 120 has been "commented out." This line sets the system date to January 1, 2000. You may test the program to see how it would work in the year 2000, by deleting the "*" and recompiling. Be sure to change line 26 of the utility program and recompile that program as well.

In line 140, the program CALLs the utility program YEAR-TO-YYYY[9] using the data group item DATE-CONVERSION-DATA shown beginning in line 44. The utility program takes the value of the first argument "CNV-YY," a two-digit year, and returns "CNV-YEAR," a four-digit year. (Similar CALLs occur in lines 147 and 154.) Because the program needs to determine the proper century, a "window" is necessary. The window is a range of 100 years. The CNV-WINDOW field serves to specify the highest year of the range. YEAR-TO-YYYY adds CNV-WINDOW to the current year determining the latest year the program can return. Thus, if the current year is 2000 and CNV-WINDOW is 15, YEAR-TO-YYYY can return 4 four-digit years from 1916 to 2015. With a current year of 2000 and a WINDOW-MAX set to –15, the utility returns four-digit years from 1886 to 1985.

If years are likely to be equally from the past or the future, the window value should be set at 50. If all of the years to be converted are expected to be less than the current year, the window value should be zero. If all dates will reflect the current and future years only, the window value should be +99.

In the revised program, lines 159 and following manage the retirement-date problem for the employees born on February 29. As explained above, an employee born on this date could not retire on February 29, 65 years later. The program takes advantage of intrinsic function INTEGER-OF-DATES's ability to validate dates. If the function returns a zero, the date proposed is invalid and the program changes the date to March 1. This technique is appropriate only if the source data (i.e., the birthdate) has been previously validated.

Figure 19.3 Revised Retirement Program

```
1          IDENTIFICATION DIVISION.
2          PROGRAM-ID.    Y2K03.
3          AUTHOR.        ARTHUR R. BUSS
4
5          ENVIRONMENT DIVISION.
6          INPUT-OUTPUT SECTION.
7          FILE-CONTROL.
8             SELECT EMPLOYEE-FILE ASSIGN SYSIN
9                ORGANIZATION IS LINE SEQUENTIAL.
10            SELECT PRINT-FILE ASSIGN TO SYSOUT
11         ORGANIZATION IS LINE SEQUENTIAL.
12
13         DATA DIVISION.
14         FILE SECTION.
15         FD EMPLOYEE-FILE
16            RECORD CONTAINS 34 CHARACTERS.
17         01 EMPLOYEE-RECORD           PIC X(34).
18
19         FD PRINT-FILE
20            RECORD CONTAINS 80 CHARACTERS.
21         01 PRINT-LINE                PIC X(80).
22
23         WORKING-STORAGE SECTION.
24         01  EMPLOYEE-DATA.
25             05  EMP-NUM              PIC X(05).
```

Figure 19.3 *(continued)*

```
26              05   EMP-NAME.
27                   10   EMP-LAST         PIC X(15).
28                   10   EMP-INIT         PIC X(02).
29              05   EMP-BIRTHDATE.
30                   10   EMP-BIRTH-YR     PIC 9(02).
31                   10   EMP-BIRTH-MO     PIC 9(02).
32                   10   EMP-BIRTH-DA     PIC 9(02).
33              05   EMP-SERVICE-DATE.
34                   10   EMP-SERVICE-YR   PIC 9(02).
35                   10   EMP-SERVICE-MO   PIC 9(02).
36                   10   EMP-SERVICE-DA   PIC 9(02).
37
38         01   DATA-REMAINS-SW           PIC X(02).
39              88   NO-DATA-REMAINS                    VALUE 'NO'.
40
41         01   CONSTANTS.
42              05   RETIRE-AGE            PIC 9(02)   VALUE 65.
43
44         01   DATE-CONVERSION-DATA.
45              05   CNV-YY               PIC 9(02).
46              05   CNV-WINDOW           PIC S9(02)  VALUE ZERO.        —— Window Specification
47              05   CNV-YEAR             PIC 9(04).                        for Conversion
48                                                                         Subprogram
49         01   INDIVIDUAL-FIELDS.
50              05   IND-AGE              PIC 9(02).
51              05   IND-SERV-YEARS       PIC 9(02).
52              05   IND-RET-DATE.
53                   10   IND-RET-YR      PIC 9(04).
54                   10   IND-RET-MO      PIC 9(02).
55                   10   IND-RET-DA      PIC 9(02).
56              05   IND-RET-DATE-RDF REDEFINES
57                        IND-RET-DATE    PIC 9(08).
58              05   IND-RET-INT-DATE     PIC 9(06).
59
60         01   TODAYS-DATE.
61              05   TODAYS-YR            PIC 9(04).
62              05   TODAYS-MO            PIC 9(02).
63              05   TODAYS-DA            PIC 9(02).
64
65         01   HEADING-LINE-1.
66              05                        PIC X(05)   VALUE SPACES.
67              05                        PIC X(10)   VALUE
68                        'EMPLOYEE'.
69              05                        PIC X(07)   VALUE SPACES.
70              05                        PIC X(10)   VALUE SPACES.
71              05                        PIC X(09)   VALUE 'SERVICE'.
72              05                        PIC X(10)   VALUE 'RETIREMENT'.
73
74         01   HEADING-LINE-2.
75              05                        PIC X(07)   VALUE SPACES.
76              05                        PIC X(14)   VALUE 'NAME'.
```

Figure 19.3 *(continued)*

```
77          05                      PIC X(07)   VALUE 'INIT'.
78          05                      PIC X(06)   VALUE 'AGE'.
79          05                      PIC X(08)   VALUE 'YEARS'.
80          05                      PIC X(10)   VALUE 'DATE'.
81
82       01  DETAIL-LINE.
83          05                      PIC X(05)   VALUE SPACES.
84          05  DET-LAST            PIC X(15).
85          05                      PIC X(02)   VALUE SPACES.
86          05  DET-INIT            PIC X(02).
87          05                      PIC X(05)   VALUE SPACES.
88          05  DET-AGE             PIC 9(02).
89          05                      PIC X(05)   VALUE SPACES.
90          05  DET-SERV-YEARS      PIC 9(02).
91          05                      PIC X(02)   VALUE SPACES.
92          05  DET-RET-DATE.
93             10  DET-RET-MO       PIC Z9.
94             10                   PIC X       VALUE '/'.
95             10  DET-RET-DA       PIC Z9.
96             10                   PIC X       VALUE '/'.
97             10  DET-RET-YR       PIC 9(04).                 ──── YYYY Format
98
99       PROCEDURE DIVISION.
100      100-PREPARE-RETIREMENT-REPORT.
101          OPEN INPUT EMPLOYEE-FILE
102               OUTPUT PRINT-FILE
103          PERFORM 210-GET-TODAYS-DATE
104          PERFORM 230-WRITE-HEADERS
105          PERFORM UNTIL NO-DATA-REMAINS
106              READ EMPLOYEE-FILE INTO EMPLOYEE-DATA
107                  AT END
108                      SET NO-DATA-REMAINS TO TRUE
109                  NOT AT END
110                      PERFORM 260-PROCESS-DETAIL
111              END-READ
112          END-PERFORM
113          CLOSE EMPLOYEE-FILE
114                PRINT-FILE
115          STOP RUN
116          .
117
118      210-GET-TODAYS-DATE.
119          MOVE FUNCTION CURRENT-DATE TO TODAYS-DATE
120      *    MOVE '20000101' TO TODAYS-DATE                    ──── Test for Year 2000
121          .
122
123      230-WRITE-HEADERS.
124          WRITE PRINT-LINE FROM HEADING-LINE-1
125              AFTER ADVANCING PAGE
126          WRITE PRINT-LINE FROM HEADING-LINE-2
127          INITIALIZE PRINT-LINE
```

Figure 19.3 *(continued)*

```
128          WRITE PRINT-LINE
129          .
130
131     260-PROCESS-DETAIL.
132          PERFORM 310-CALCULATE-EMP-AGE
133          PERFORM 330-CALCULATE-EMP-SERVICE
134          PERFORM 360-CALCULATE-IND-RET-DATE
135          PERFORM 390-WRITE-DETAIL-LINE
136          .
137
138     310-CALCULATE-EMP-AGE.
139          MOVE EMP-BIRTH-YR TO CNV-YY
140          CALL 'YEAR-TO-YYYY' USING DATE-CONVERSION-DATA
141          COMPUTE IND-AGE = TODAYS-YR - CNV-YEAR
142                       + (TODAYS-MO - EMP-BIRTH-MO) / 12
143          .
144
145     330-CALCULATE-EMP-SERVICE.
146          MOVE EMP-SERVICE-YR TO CNV-YY
147          CALL 'YEAR-TO-YYYY' USING DATE-CONVERSION-DATA
148          COMPUTE IND-SERV-YEARS = TODAYS-YR - CNV-YEAR
149                       + (TODAYS-MO - EMP-SERVICE-MO) / 12
150          .
151
152     360-CALCULATE-IND-RET-DATE.
153          MOVE EMP-BIRTH-YR TO CNV-YY
154          CALL 'YEAR-TO-YYYY' USING DATE-CONVERSION-DATA
155          ADD  RETIRE-AGE      TO CNV-YEAR GIVING IND-RET-YR
156          MOVE EMP-BIRTH-MO    TO IND-RET-MO
157          MOVE EMP-BIRTH-DA    TO IND-RET-DA
158     *    TEST FOR INVALID FEBRUARY 29 RETIREMENT DATE
159          COMPUTE IND-RET-INT-DATE = FUNCTION INTEGER-OF-DATE
160                              (IND-RET-DATE-RDF)
161          IF IND-RET-INT-DATE = 0
162     *    WHEN FOUND, SET DATE TO MARCH 1.
163              ADD  1 TO IND-RET-MO
164              MOVE 1 TO IND-RET-DA
165          END-IF
166          .
167
168     390-WRITE-DETAIL-LINE.
169          MOVE EMP-LAST       TO   DET-LAST
170          MOVE EMP-INIT       TO   DET-INIT
171          MOVE IND-AGE        TO   DET-AGE
172          MOVE IND-SERV-YEARS TO   DET-SERV-YEARS
173          MOVE IND-RET-MO     TO   DET-RET-MO
174          MOVE IND-RET-DA     TO   DET-RET-DA
175          MOVE IND-RET-YR     TO   DET-RET-YR
176          WRITE PRINT-LINE    FROM DETAIL-LINE
177     .
```

Test for Feb 29 Retirement

*Correction of
Retirement Date*

Figure 19.4 Year Conversion Utility Program

```
1        IDENTIFICATION DIVISION.
2        PROGRAM-ID.  YEAR-TO-YYYY.
3        AUTHOR.      ARTHUR R. BUSS
4
5        ENVIRONMENT DIVISION.
6
7        DATA DIVISION.
8        WORKING-STORAGE SECTION.
9        01  TEMPORARY-DATA.
10           05  WORK-YEAR.
11               10 WORK-HIGH-YY         PIC  9(02).
12               10 WORK-LOW-YY          PIC  9(02).
13           05  WORK-YYYY REDEFINES WORK-YEAR
14                                       PIC  9(04).
15       LINKAGE SECTION.
16       01  LS-CONVERSION-DATA.
17           05  LS-YY                   PIC  9(02).
18           05  LS-WIND                 PIC S9(02).
19           05  LS-YYYY.
20               10  LS-HIGH-YY          PIC  9(02).
21               10  LS-LOW-YY           PIC  9(02).
22
23       PROCEDURE DIVISION USING LS-CONVERSION-DATA.
24
25           MOVE FUNCTION CURRENT-DATE TO WORK-YEAR.
26       *   MOVE 2000 TO WORK-YYYY
27           ADD LS-WIND TO WORK-YYYY.
28           MOVE WORK-HIGH-YY TO LS-HIGH-YY
29           MOVE LS-YY TO LS-LOW-YY
30           IF LS-YY > WORK-LOW-YY
31               SUBTRACT 1 FROM LS-HIGH-YY
32           END-IF
33           EXIT PROGRAM
34               .
```

Window Specification — (line 18)

Test for Year 2000 — (line 26)

S U M M A R Y

Points to Remember

- The Year 2000 problem has been known for many years, but has drawn attention only recently. As January 1, 2000 gets nearer, interest and alarm are also growing. This problem will not go away, and the deadline cannot be postponed.

- Making the program corrections is not difficult in itself. The difficulty comes because so many programs and files must be changed and tested. Information Technology departments must find every occurrence of a date and convert each date to YYYY format.

■ Two kinds of date formats are involved: the DATE format (YYYYMMDD) and the DAY format (YYYYDDD). Both types of dates must be corrected.

■ The 1989 COBOL extensions to COBOL 85 provide several intrinsic functions that can help in the conversion process. These include CURRENT-DATE, INTEGER-OF-DATE, INTEGER-OF-DAY, DATE-OF-INTEGER, and DAY-OF-INTEGER. COBOL 2000 includes other intrinsic functions, but they may not be available in time.

■ The Year 2000 is a leap year. All date routines that accommodate leap years must be checked to assure that 2000 is handled properly.

Key Words and Concepts

Y2K
Millennium Problem
Date Arithmetic
Intrinsic Function

COBOL Elements

FUNCTION	INTEGER-OF-DAY
CURRENT-DATE	DATE-OF-INTEGER
INTEGER-OF-DATE	DAY-OF-INTEGER

F I L L - I N

1. The year 2000 problem resulted from a desire to save on _____ and _____.

2. The correction of the problem (<u>can/cannot</u>) be delayed beyond January 1, 2000.

3. Businesses have (<u>been/not been</u>) quick to recognize and to solve the problem.

4. The 1989 extensions to COBOL 85 have provided new capabilities called _____.

5. INTEGER-TO-DATE converts a(n) _____ to a _____ in _____ format.

6. DAY-TO-INTEGER converts a(n) _____ in _____ format to a(n) _____.

7. The year 2000 (<u>is/is not</u>) a leap year.

T R U E / F A L S E

1. The Year 2000 problem has been known for a number of years.

2. With the Year 2000 problem, finding the changes to make is more difficult than the actual correction.

3. Intrinsic functions were a part of the original COBOL 85 standards.

4. The decision to eliminate the first two positions of the year in dates was a conscious one.

5. INTEGER-TO-DATE and INTEGER-TO-DAY return the same date format.

6. The COBOL statement ACCEPT FROM DATE works the same under the 1985 standards as it will in the 2000 standards.

7. Business, in general, has been slow to recognize the Year 2000 problem and has to scramble to catch up.

8. Even if companies cannot make all date routine changes by December 31, 1999, they should have at least a year before problems show up.

P R O B L E M S

1. Write a program that accepts the year and day of the year and displays the integer value of that year and day. Test the program with year 1600 day 365, year 1601 day 1, year 1999 day 365, year 2000 day 1, year 2000 day 366, and any other year and day number. Invalid dates should return a 0 integer value.

2. Write a program that accepts a date and a number of days. The program should add the days to the input date and return the new date. The program should work with negative numbers for the input number of days. Test the program to make sure that it works for dates after January 1, 2000.

3. Accounts Receivable systems need to be able to detect when an invoice is overdue. Write a procedure or a subprogram that calculates the date 90 days prior to the current date and compares an invoice date to see whether or not it is overdue. Use the commenting technique demonstrated in Y2K01 and Y2K02 to test to see how the program would work in the year 2000.

4. Life insurance rates are partially based on the age of the policyholder. Write a procedure that will compute a person's age in years based on their birthdate and the current date. Test the program to see whether it will work in the year 2000.

F O R   F U R T H E R   S T U D Y

This chapter has included Year 2000 problem topics primarily involving COBOL, but the Year 2000 problem has ramifications in other contexts, as well. For example, many personal computers will fail when the system clock changes to January 1, 2000. DOS systems do not recognize dates before January 1, 1980, and when 2000 occurs, many of these systems will assume that 00 must mean that the current year is 1980.

The Year 2000 problem is getting increasing press recognition; interest is likely to grow as 2000 gets nearer. A number of World Wide Web sites address the topic and offer some places to use as starting points for further research.

```
http://www.yahoo.com/text/Computers_and_Internet/Year_2000_Problem/
http://www.wa.gov/dis/2000/y2000.htm
http://www.year2000.com/y2klinks.html
http://www.ttuhsc.edu/pages/year2000/y2k_bib.htm
```

[1] The authors recognize that the year 2000 is technically part of the twentieth century, but the problem nonetheless is one that begins on January 1, 2000.

[2] According to the Gartner Group, quoted in Leon A. Kappelman and James J. Cappel, "A Problem of Rational Origin That Requires a Rational Solution," *Journal of Systems Management* 47, 4 (July-August 1996): 6, 8.

[3] Kappelman and Cappel contend that the saving in disk space and memory space over the years actually compensates for the conversion costs that are now necessary.

[4] COBOL 2002 can return the year in either YY or YYYY form. The format "ACCEPT identifier FROM DATE YYYYMMDD" must be used to get four digits. For compatibility's sake, YYMMDD is the default format.

[5] You may have noticed the period standing alone at the end of each paragraph. Some programmers use this technique to avoid logic errors resulting from misplaced punctuation. The authors have chosen to use introduce this practice here. Scope terminators can replace most uses of the period, as explained in the Programming Tip *Use Scope Terminators* in Chapter 7. The ANS standard requires only a period at the end of a paragraph.

[6] The Gartner Group has estimated that fixing the problem will cost about $1 for *each* line of code in the organization. Many companies have 50 million or more lines of code. Quoted in Kappelman and Cappel.

[7] Y2K03.CBL.

[8] Y2K04.CBL.

[9] Y2K04.CBL.

Object-Oriented COBOL Programming

Chapter Outline

Overview

The Next Generation of COBOL

The Development of Structured Programming

Terminology

The Object-Oriented versus Structured Paradigm

The Student-Look-Up System

Student-Look-Up Program

The Registrar Class

Classes and Inheritance

ProcessRequests Method

The StudentDM Class

StudentDM Instance Definition

The Student Class

The Person Class

The StudentUI Class

The StudentPRT Class

Conclusion

Summary

Fill-in

True/False

Problems

Objectives

After reading this chapter you will be able to:

■ Discuss the concept of Object-Oriented programming as compared to structured programming.

■ Describe the structure of classes including the class definition as well as the Factory and instance definition.

■ Be able to define some major OO concepts including: encapsulation, inheritance, persistence, and polymorphism.

■ Describe the similarities and differences between the use of Objects and the use of subroutines.

■ Describe the advantages OO programming has over Structured Programming.

■ State why OO programming does not invalidate all of the principles of Structured Programming.

Overview

Object-Orientation (OO) has become an important new way to develop information systems. This technique allows for faster development of systems, reuse of program code, and better management of data. OO is now available for use with COBOL and promises to give additional life to this well-established programming language. The COBOL 2002 standards define Object-Oriented COBOL, but this standard has not been completed and accepted as yet. However, several vendors including Micro Focus have developed their own version of OO COBOL and have tried to make their versions as close as possible to the proposed standards. We use Micro Focus Personal COBOL for Windows in developing the example system in this chapter. Differences in the code presented here and code that matches the official standard should be minimal.

The chapter begins with an introduction to the concepts and reasons for OO COBOL. Next, we review the strengths and weaknesses of structured programming and then make comparisons between the two programming approaches.

The remaining portion of the chapter shows an OO system implementation of the Engineering Senior program developed in Figure 1.6. What was in one program becomes several classes. Each class serves to demonstrate one or more OO concepts. As we present each portion of the system, we attempt to demonstrate the structure of OO classes and methods to show how OO can make system development and maintenance simple.

This chapter by itself is not enough to train you in OO COBOL. You will need further study to become proficient. We have included the names of several new texts of OO COBOL at the end of the chapter. The intent of this chapter is to whet your appetite to learn more about this exciting and challenging new programming technique.

The Next Generation of COBOL

One of the most exciting new features of the COBOL 2002 Standard is its incorporation of ***Object-Orientation*** (OO) into the language. Even though the standard will not become official for several years, OO COBOL is available now and offered by several vendors including Fujitsu, IBM, Hitachi, and Micro Focus. OO COBOL provides the advantages of object-orientation to the business community without having to train programmers in new languages. In addition, there is no need to worry about making these languages work with critical legacy systems. COBOL, the dominant business language, now has object-orientated capabilities while retaining COBOL's traditional strengths: readability, easy maintenance, powerful file handling, and good reporting.

Previously, OO was limited to such languages as Smalltalk and C++. These languages were designed for highly technical applications and for small, rapidly developed systems. While there is much to commend in these OO languages, they do not have the business orientation that is the trademark of COBOL. For example, these languages do not have the powerful file-handling capabilities of COBOL, nor do their data structures work well with the files created by COBOL legacy systems. The syntax of those languages also tends to be rather abstract and hard to read, making systems developed in these languages difficult to maintain. OO COBOL, on the other hand, maintains and even improves COBOL's traditional readability and maintainability.

Other languages, such as Visual BASIC and Delphi, provide a form of OO and are relatively easy to use. They also provide a way for end users to develop their own business systems. Yet these languages are not necessarily efficient; nor are systems developed in these languages always effective for large applications. In addition, systems developed in Visual BASIC or Delphi are not easily maintained by users other than the developers.

Systems developed in OO COBOL are maintainable and able to interface with the programs and files of traditional COBOL systems. On the other hand, the COBOL 2002 standard provides for the Boolean, integer, and floating-point data types used by other common languages. Thus, the new COBOL can work with systems developed in all computer languages.

The concept of object-orientation may be somewhat threatening to someone who has devoted much time and effort to learning structured COBOL. Students, for example, may be concerned that they have spent much effort learning how to write structured programs only to have this skill made obsolete by object-orientation. These students may wonder, "Why not just learn OO and forget ***structured programming*** entirely?"

In answer to these concerns, we believe that structured COBOL will not go away soon. Yet OO is coming, and the individual who can "speak" both dialects of COBOL will become a valuable asset to employers. As businesses begin to adopt OO COBOL, they will be seeking out people who can help them make the transition. In the meantime, structured COBOL is the predominant dialect and will continue to be so for many years. The change may be inevitable, but it will be slow. As evidence, even today some legacy systems are still in *pre-structured programming* code.

A second answer is that object-orientation does not eliminate what is good about structured programming. OO promotes and even improves upon the best features of structured programming. Therefore, even though there is much new about OO COBOL, a programmer will not be starting from scratch when learning it.

At this point, many texts attempt to define object-orientation with a series of new terms and potentially confusing terms such as ***encapsulation, inheritance,*** and ***polymorphism.*** This discussion delays the introduction and definition of these and other terms until they can be demonstrated and defined within the context of a functioning system. It is difficult to define object-orientation in a few sentences or by simply introducing and explaining the new terms. This entire chapter is, in a sense, a definition. OO represents a new *paradigm* or way of thinking about programming, just as the structured programming was a new way of thinking about programming in its time.

The Development of Structured Programming

When computers were new and people were still learning how to program them, there were few guidelines as to what constituted a "good" program. Programming was more an art form than a disciplined craft. As a result, the quality of programs varied widely. Programming projects were difficult to estimate and manage because no one could be sure how long a program would take to build. Information systems were difficult to build and, when completed, were usually late and over budget. In many cases, the systems were not completed at all.

Structured programming was developed as a response to this systems development crisis. The structured approach introduced a philosophy of program development and specified "rules" for writing programs. Some of these rules were as follows:

- Break programs into short sections of code called modules. Modules were usually implemented as COBOL paragraphs.

- Build cohesive modules, where each module performs a single task.

- Build loosely coupled modules, where each module is as independent as possible from the other modules.

- Ensure that each module has a single entry and a single exit point.

- Avoid the use of GOTO statements.

The structured techniques brought a new degree of order and discipline into the programming process. As a result, the quality of programs improved and programming projects became more manageable. Structured programming was a great step forward in the evolution of programming.

Unfortunately, the structured paradigm also introduced new problems. Structured programs tend to be cumbersome because the structuring process requires an elaborate hierarchy of operations and control structures. These hierarchies and structures define the operation of a program, but they also mean that there is duplication of effort in developing programs. The higher levels of structured programs tend to follow the same patterns, but must be coded into every program. Elaborate structures also tend to make programs rigid and difficult to change quickly enough to meet new processing requirements. For example, review the Tuition Billing program developed in Chapters 4-7 and shown in Figure 7.4.

Paragraph 100-PREPARE-TUITION-REPORT in line 124 maintains overall control of the program's process. This paragraph opens and closes files, and performs four other paragraphs. One of those paragraphs, 260-PROCESS-STUDENT-RECORD, does the main processing loop in the program (lines 129 and 130). This paragraph, in lines 148–152, performs four additional paragraphs. Of these paragraphs, 310-COMPUTE-INDIVIDUAL-BILL in lines 166–172, performs four more paragraphs and makes a computation. Thus, out of the twelve paragraphs in the program, three paragraphs are primarily dedicated to controlling the process and do little actual work. For a simple program, a large part of the code is devoted just to control. Figure 3.3 shows the entire hierarchy chart for the program.

Most structured programs spend a similar proportion of code just controlling the process. Unfortunately, these control paragraphs cannot be simply copied from one program to another; each program must have its own set of control paragraphs.

The problems inherent in structured programming are not limited to the Procedure Division. Of the 80 lines in the Data Division, 63 lines specify parts of the report. Only three of the twelve paragraphs actually use those lines. Nevertheless, any paragraph in the program can access those items and every other data item. Structured COBOL provides no way to isolate data items so that only the authorized paragraphs can use them or change their values. Thus, if the structured rules are not followed, code can be inserted in any paragraph to modify data items. Under these circumstances, errors may be introduced to the program, and these errors may be difficult to find.

The Tuition program is a very good structured program. It just reflects the conditions inherent in any structured program. Object-orientation can avoid many of these problems.

Structured programming was a new way of thinking about programming. This new paradigm was far superior to the way people thought about programs before. The superiority of this approach led virtually every company to adopt structured programming as the standard. In the process of change, programmers who had learned to program under the old rules (or lack thereof) had a difficult time making the transition to structured programming. They had to learn a new way to think about programming. In the same way, the transition to object-orientation will be difficult but worthwhile.

The object-orientation approach is not a complete negation of the structured principles. In fact the most important contributions of structured programming are maintained and enhanced. For example, OO programs still incorporate the three basic control structures—sequence, selection, and iteration—discussed in Chapter 3. The principles of cohesiveness and loose coupling mentioned above are actually strengthened in OO programming. OO represents a "paradigm shift" in its approach to the overall design issues, but does not contradict the principles of good programming that have been proved in structured programming.

Terminology

In order to compare the object-oriented and structured paradigms, some terminology needs to be defined. In learning from a book like this, you should have developed a good idea of what a program is. As defined in Chapter 1, a program is a translation of an algorithm into a form the computer can understand. Usually that algorithm requires the program to input data, process it, and output information.

In working through problems and assignments, you have had to focus on writing individual programs and may have formed the impression that programs are self-sufficient units. You may not have thought about where the input files came from or where the output goes. In "real-world" applications, a program is usually just one part of a system. Systems are collections of software and data units designed to work together to perform an application.

In structured systems, the software units are programs and the data units are files. Generally, one program runs at a time, processing input files and data to create output files and reports. Each program runs to completion before the next program begins. Files provide the link from one program to another and allow the system to function as a whole.

Object-oriented systems consist not of files and programs, but rather of objects. The proposed COBOL 2002 standard defines an object as "an entity that has a unique identity, specific data values, and specific behaviors or program code." In other words, objects combine the features of files and programs. Objects not only store data, but process it as well. Within an OO system, objects pass data directly and interactively to each other without the use of files. Unlike programs that run one at a time, many objects may be active at the same time. Objects are linked by sending **messages** to each other.

The messages are requests for the receiving object to perform some action and often to return the results of that action. The messages request the objects to perform a **method**. The COBOL 2002 standard defines a method as "procedural code that defines a specific function... A method may be thought of as a module or subroutine." Objects can contain many methods, with each method designed to accomplish a particular function. When one object requests (sends a message to) another object to perform a function, the process is called **invoking** a method.

In summary, systems are made up of numerous units that carry out the purposes of the system. In structured systems, these units are programs and files. In OO systems, these units are objects. Objects contain both data and methods. Many objects may be active at one time, and they communicate with each other through messages. Messages are requests for other objects to perform a method.

The Object-Oriented versus Structured Paradigm

When developing an OO system, the designer tries to identify and represent the *nouns* of the system. The nouns come from the names of entities necessary to accomplish the system's purpose such as Student, Employee, or Invoice. These entities become candidates for **classes** in the system. In OO terminology, a class is the generic definition of an object. The term **instance** is used to refer to a specific occurrence of an object. Most authors use "instance" and "object" interchangeably. From this point on we use the term "class" to refer to the generic model and "instance" or "object" to refer to a specific example.

As OO designers begin to identify and refine the classes, they specify the types of data belonging to and the behaviors associated with the class. As additional requirements become apparent, additional data items and methods may be added. By looking at the nouns, the OO designer can determine how a class should behave in general without regard to any specific system. Thus, these general class behaviors or methods can be used by many systems. When system-specific requirements dictate the need for additional methods or data items, they can be added to the class without affecting the previously defined data items and methods in the class.

By contrast, the structured approach focuses on the *verbs* of the system. Verbs identify the things a system must do. As each activity of the system is identified, the designer specifies a program or programs to carry it out. These programs are custom designed for their specific system.

OO systems are more flexible than structured systems. By placing procedures in methods contained in classes rather than programs, OO allows common routines to be written just once. Any system that uses the class can use any of its methods. Methods are developed just once, but used in a variety of situations. The need for duplicate coding is reduced and additional functionality can be added to systems with minimum effort.

Methods, once developed and tested, can be reused with confidence and a minimum of testing. In addition, if some change is necessary in the method, the change only has to be made only once in the class. Every system using that class then automatically uses the revised method.

After a class is developed, it becomes a building block available for use in future systems. When the developers of a new system determine the need for a class, they can investigate to see if it is already available. If the new system requires new functionality from a class, new methods can be added to the class without affecting any of the old methods. As a result, classes become more useful and powerful as new functions are defined and implemented as methods. The same cannot be said for structured systems and programs.

Structured systems consist of custom-designed programs. Even when common routines occur, they cannot easily be copied into other programs, nor can other systems just use part of a structured program. As a result, each new program is built from scratch with little use of previously developed routines. Even if the routines can be copied into new programs, it is almost impossible to update all of the copies should some change need to be made.

As an example, suppose that there is a need for a Student Enrollment system. A structured analysis would look at the verbs and might determine that the system needs to:

- Generate a course schedule.

- Enroll students.

- Prepare course rosters.

- Prepare student schedules.

The structured approach would then design one or more programs to perform each of these activities. Files would be developed to link the processes together so that the system could perform as a whole. Even though preparing course rosters and preparing student schedules are very similar processes, it is unlikely that any of the programs would be reused or that routines would be copied from one program to another.

The OO approach to a Student Enrollment system would focus on the entities who participate in the system. The analysis then might come up with classes such as:

- Student

- Advisor

- Registrar

- Course

From this analysis, the OO designer would determine the functions and the data that each of these should handle. In producing the actual Course Rosters and the Student Schedules, the system would use methods from both the Student class and the Course class. Some of the same methods could be used in performing each function. In addition, most of these classes developed for Student Enrollment might be used in other systems such as Tuition Billing, Advising, or Grade Reporting. Therefore, these classes are not useful just for the Student Enrollment system, but could be building blocks for other systems as well.

Another difference between OO and structured systems is in how they actually operate. Programs run in a standalone mode with one program operating at a time. Linkages between programs are maintained by passing files. By contrast, many objects may be functioning interactively and linkages are maintained through messages. Objects, unlike programs, are aware of other objects. Since messages, rather than files, provide the linkage between objects, files per se are not necessary in an OO system except to store data while the system is not running.

Objects exist in the memory of the computer only while the system is operating. If there were no way to store the objects, data would be lost when the system shut down. Therefore, OO systems store object data in files until the system starts again. These files provide *persistence* between system runs. An OO system requires special classes called data managers to ensure that the data "persists" from one run of the system to another.

The Student-Look-Up System

To illustrate the concepts of Object-Oriented COBOL and the differences from structured programming, this chapter uses a OO version of the Engineering Senior program presented in Chapter 2.[1] The design of the system is shown in Figure 20.1. While the original program worked only for Engineering Students with more than 100 credit hours, this version has added functionality, allowing the user to specify a minimum number of credit hours required (rather than 100) and any major, not just engineering. For the purpose of this chapter the OO version is called the Student-Look-Up system.

PROGRAMMING SPECIFICATIONS

System Name: Student-Look-Up system (Object Version of Engineering Senior program)

Narrative: This system is an Object-Oriented Enhancement of the Engineering Senior program presented in Chapter 1. The system allows the user to interactively enter a major course of study and a minimum number of credits earned. The system then produces a report listing all students meeting both the major and minimum credit-hours qualifications.

Input File(s):   STUDENT-FILE

Input Record Layout: See Figure 1.3a.

Test Data: See Figure 1.3b.

Report Layout: See Figure 1.3c.

Screen Layout: See Figure 20.8.

Processing Requirements: 1. Print a heading line.

2. Prompt the user for a major.

3. Prompt the user for the minimum number of credit hours.

4. Read a file of student records.

5. For every record, determine whether that student has the major specified in step 2 and has completed more than the number of hours specified in step 3.

6. Print the name of every student who satisfies the requirements in item 5. Single-space the output.

7. At the end of the Report, print a line that says "* * * End of Report * * *."

Look at the design of the Student Look-Up system in Figure 20.1. A system of six classes replaces the original program. The figure does not show a driver program used to initiate the system. Viewing the diagram, you may feel that creating six classes and a driver program has to be more complex than developing just one program. To perform this very simple application, you may be right. However, if you look at the classes as potential building blocks for other systems, you can see that some extra effort here could mean less effort over the long run. The Engineering Senior program can do one function and one function only.

The trick to developing OO systems is not in implementing the classes, but in knowing how to partition out the data and procedures to the various classes. One accomplishes this task through Object-Oriented Analysis and Design. A full discussion of that topic is beyond the scope of this chapter, but it does need to be mentioned briefly.

Figure 20.1 Student-Look-Up System Design

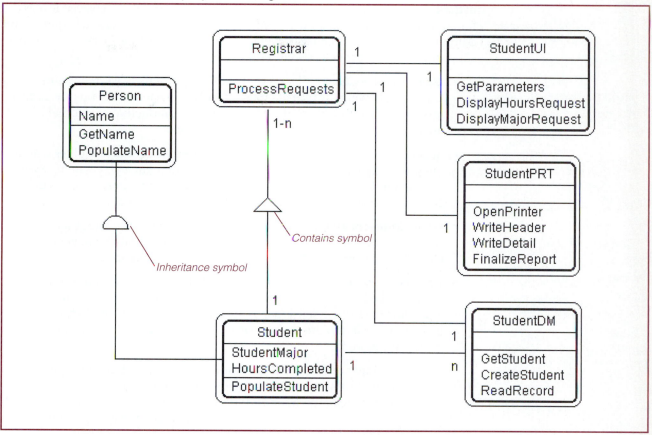

As stated before, OO analysis and design focuses on the nouns used to describe the systems. These nouns often can identify the system classes. For example, in the Student Look-Up system, Registrar and Student are obvious classes.

After identifying the class, the analyst asks three questions about each class:[2]

- What does it know? What data does it own?

- Whom does it know? What other classes are necessary for it to accomplish its work?

- What does it do? What functions does it need to perform?

After answering these questions, the analyst can develop a model of the system such as seen in Figure 20.1. The double boxes with rounded corners represent classes. Each class symbol is divided into three sections. The top section contains the class name. The middle section contains the names for data items owned by the class and the bottom section contains the names of the methods the class can perform. The lines represent the routes messages can take within the system and show the answer to the question, "Whom does it know?" The indicators at either end of the line show how many instances of another class an instance can know at one time. For example, a Student can know only one Registrar object, while the Registrar object can know from 1 to *n* instances of Student.

Special relationships between classes are shown by symbols on the connecting lines. The half-circle between Person and Student means that Student *inherits* from Person. We will discuss the concept of inheritance later. The triangle between Registrar and Student means that Student is contained in Registrar. That is, the Registrar is responsible for managing the Student class. This concept is not important to understanding how this system works.

Some of the classes represent the ***problem domain*** of the system—the purpose of the system. These classes do the primary work of the system. However, just as the functional workers in an office cannot operate efficiently without support and administrative workers such as secretaries, mailroom staff, file clerks, and the like, support classes are needed as well. Some of the support classes include:

- ***User Interface Classes.*** Classes that handle the interactive screens and windows allowing the users to interact with the system. User interfaces also involve the printing of reports for the user and production of external documents such as invoices and purchase orders.

- ***System Interaction Classes.*** These classes manage the interfaces to other systems. These other systems may be object-oriented or traditional legacy systems. System Interaction classes would handle files passed between the systems, access to centralized data bases or telecommunications between systems.

- ***Data Management Classes.*** These classes administer the storage and retrieval of data used by Problem Domain instances. Data Management classes are necessary to maintain the persistence of objects.

- ***Drivers.*** These programs are not classes at all. They are programs developed to initiate and test objects. Driver programs often are temporary in nature and allow the system developer to see how a class will behave before incorporating it into the system. Most OO systems include a driver program to start the system.

Table 20.1 shows the classes of the Student-Look-Up system, the types of class they are and comments about the functions performed.

The starting point for the system is the Student-Look-Up program. Even though Student-Look-Up is the driver program for the system and not a class, it introduces some of the elements of object-orientation.

Student-Look-Up Program

Student-Look-Up is the program shown in Figure 20.2 and may be one of the shortest COBOL programs you have ever seen. The program cannot really be called structured because it has only three statements in lines 19–21 of the Procedure Division. There are several other features in this program that may seem strange. The most obvious difference is the use of uppercase and lowercase in the source code. COBOL 85 has always allowed this practice, but acceptance of this practice has been slow. We have used mixed-cases code to symbolize a new age of COBOL.[3] The Programming Tip shows all of the coding conventions we use in this chapter.

TABLE 20.1 Student-Look-Up System Driver and Classes

Class	Category	Functions
Student-Look-Up	Driver	Initiates the system and creates the Registrar object.
Registrar	Problem Domain	Maintains overall control of the system, creates the utility objects: StudentUI, StudentDM, and StudentPRT. Interacts with Student to get the student name.
Student	Problem Domain	Maintains the Student data. Can produce the student's name, credit hours taken and major.
Person	Problem Domain	Parent Class to Student. Maintains the student name information.
StudentDM	Data Management	Controls the processing of the Student File and creates Student Instances based on requested parameters.
StudentPRT	User Interface	Controls the production of the report.
StudentUI	User Interface	Controls the interactive dialog with the user of the system.

PROGRAMMING SPECIFICATIONS

Program Name: Student-Look-Up

Narrative: This program is the primary driver program for the system. The program creates the Registrar object and initiates the system to process a request for a listing of students based on user input specifications.

Objects Created: Registrar

Objects Referenced: Registrar

Processing Requirements: 1. Create Registrar object.

2. Invoke Registrar method ProcessRequest.

Figure 20.2 Student-Look-Up Program

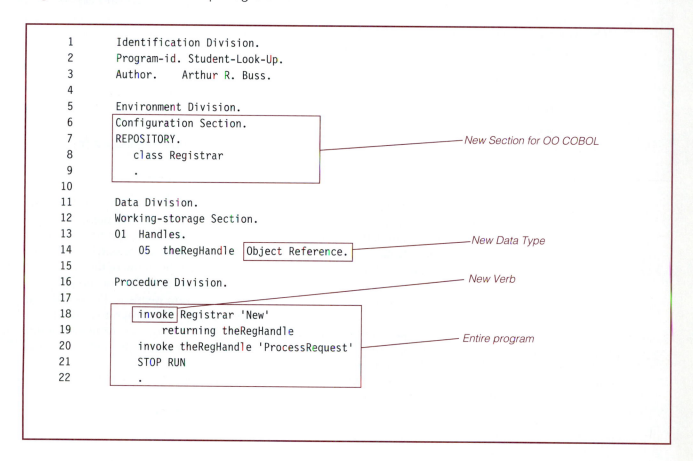

```
 1          Identification Division.
 2          Program-id. Student-Look-Up.
 3          Author.    Arthur R. Buss.
 4
 5          Environment Division.
 6          Configuration Section.
 7          REPOSITORY.                                  New Section for OO COBOL
 8             class Registrar
 9             .
10
11          Data Division.
12          Working-storage Section.
13          01  Handles.
14             05  theRegHandle  Object Reference.       New Data Type
15
16          Procedure Division.                          New Verb
17
18             invoke Registrar 'New'
19                 returning theRegHandle
20             invoke theRegHandle 'ProcessRequest'      Entire program
21             STOP RUN
22             .
```

PROGRAMMING TIP
Object-Oriented Coding Conventions

OO COBOL is so new that there are not well-established ways for coding classes. The following are the conventions for this book.

- Division and section names are capitalized. For example, Procedure Division and Working-storage Section.
- Data item name words are capitalized and separated by hyphens. For example, Student-Name.
- Linkage-storage data names are prefixed by ls-.
- Method name words are capitalized, but *not* separated by hyphens. For example, ProcessRequests.
- Handle names do not have an initial capital letter, but each succeeding word is capitalized. The words are not separated. For example: theRegHandle.
- COBOL reserved words other than division and section titles are lowercase.
- For visibility purposes, `REPOSITORY, FACTORY, OBJECT, STOP RUN, NOT, NULL, and TRUE` are uppercase.
- End statements for methods, objects, and classes are capitalized. For example, `End Method, End Object`, and `End Class`.
- Within classes, all methods are separated by a blank line.
- To ensure that method names are seen as being part of the method, Method-id statements are *not* separated from the next line.
- When a method Procedure Division has `using` or `returning` clauses, each clause is separated onto a separate line and indented. For example:

```
Procedure Division
    using  ls-Stu-Parameters
    returning ls-theStuHandle.
```

- Procedure Division code is separated from the division title by one line.
- In Procedure Division code, only one period is allowed. The period must be after the last line of code and alone on a line. End scope terminators are always used.

The Configuration Section contains a new entry—*REPOSITORY*. The Repository paragraph is similar to traditional COBOL's File-Control paragraph. The Repository paragraph defines the interface to classes used in the system. Each class needed by the program must be specified here. Notice the three entries in lines 8 through 10. Each begins with the word "class" and then the name of the class.

The Repository paragraph allows OO COBOL to answer the question "Whom do I know?" In this case, the Student-Look-Up program needs to know only the Registrar class. There are other classes in the system, but this program does not use them directly and therefore does not have to specify them. You may want to examine OO-Senior project in Chaptr-20 of the data files to see how the Fujitsu Project Manager makes these linkages.

Student-Look-Up does not contain an Input-Output Section. Since the classes do all file processing, the section can be safely omitted.

The Working-Storage Section contains a new type of data called *object reference*.

OO COBOL uses object reference data as ***pointers*** to system objects. In OO COBOL, object pointers are generally called ***handles***. The 05 level item "theRegHandle," in line 16, is the handle to the Registrar object.

The Procedure Division of the Student-Look-Up Driver program has only two statements other than `STOP RUN`. Both statements use a new COBOL verb `invoke`. Invoke is similar to a CALL in that it addresses programs outside of the current program and turns control over to that procedure. The `invoke` verb also can pass parameters or arguments to and from the invoked procedure. However, a CALL turns over control to an entire COBOL program while `invoke` only references a method within an object.

Figure 20.3 Syntax of Invoke

```
INVOKE object-name { literal-1 | data-name-1 }
               [USING {data-name-2}... ]
               [RETURNING data-name-3 ]
[END INVOKE]
```

Figure 20.3 shows the syntax of the `invoke` verb. The object name specifies the object containing the desired method. Literal-1 or data-name-1 is the message (name of the method) to be passed to the object. Any data items to be passed to the object are preceded by `using`. The data item to be returned must be preceded by `returning`. Note that multiple data items can be passed to the method but `returning` allows only one data item. The invoke verb requires that the named data items be at the 01 level, but entire data groups can be passed by using a 01 level group item. If more than one parameter must be returned, all of the parameters should be elementary items under a single 01 level group item. Arrays can be passed in either direction as long as they are contained within a 01 level group item.

The first `invoke` addresses the Registrar class and passes the message "New." New is a generic message required to create a new instance or occurrence of a class. This process is called ***instantiation***. Hence, to instantiate a class means to create a new instance of the class. For example, in the Student Look-Up system, only one Registrar instance is required. Universities only have one Registrar office, and this instance needs to emulate the functions of that office. However, many students attend the university and one would expect the system to instantiate numerous instances of the Student class.

When instantiating a class, the object name in the `invoke` statement is the name of the class. The New method instantiates the instance returns its handle. In this case, the handle is called "theRegHandle."

Look again at Figure 20.2 and line 20. The second `invoke` uses theRegHandle to request the instance method, "ProcessRequest." The statement invokes theRegHandle instead of Registrar because it points to the instance of the class and its methods are now available. ProcessRequest requires no parameters to be passed. Upon completion, ProcessRequest returns control to the driver program. The driver then stops the run.

After `STOP RUN` there is a period on a line by itself. A new standard is emerging in COBOL programming to minimize use of the period. Many programmers will use only one period at the end of each paragraph and place the period on a separate line for the sake of clarity. End statements replace periods whenever possible. Since COBOL requires that each paragraph end with a period, it is placed on a separate line for visibility.

In examining the driver program, you have encountered several important OO topics without even looking at a class. These topics include Repository and the Object Reference data type, handles, instantiation, methods, messages, and the

Invoke verb. Now, we will look at the classes to see how these and other concepts are used in a class.

Along with the discussion of each class, you will find the programming specifications of that class. Since classes are different from programs, you will notice several new entries. First, we use Class Name rather than Program Name and have a new entry to show what type of class this is. Next, we describe the purpose of the class in the Narrative. The Narrative is followed by the objects created and referenced. We specify objects rather than classes because these are actual instances of classes that are created or referenced. Finally, we specify the methods included in the class. These methods include both *factory* methods and instance methods.

The Registrar Class

PROGRAMMING SPECIFICATIONS

Class Name: Registrar

Class Type: Problem Domain

Narrative: This object represents the role of a university registrar.

Objects Created: StudentDM

Classes Referenced: FJBase
StudentDM
StudentPRT
StudentUI

Objects Referenced: StudentDM
Student

Factory Methods: None

Instance Method: Process Request

Narrative: This method controls the main processing of the system.

Processing:
1. Create the StudentDM instance.
2. Request StudentPRT to prepare for processing.
3. Get request parameters from StudentUI.
4. Get all instances of Student from StudentDM that meets the requested parameters.
5. Get the student name from each Student instance.
6. Send each Student name to StudentPRT to be printed.
7. When all names have been processed, request StudentPRT to finish the report.

The object portion of the Registrar class contains the attributes and behaviors that are needed to represent the university registrar's role in the Student-Look-Up Billing System. The registrar knows about student data and provides this data on request. The Registrar object, therefore, manages students and can provide data about them.

Figure 20.4 Class Definition of Registrar

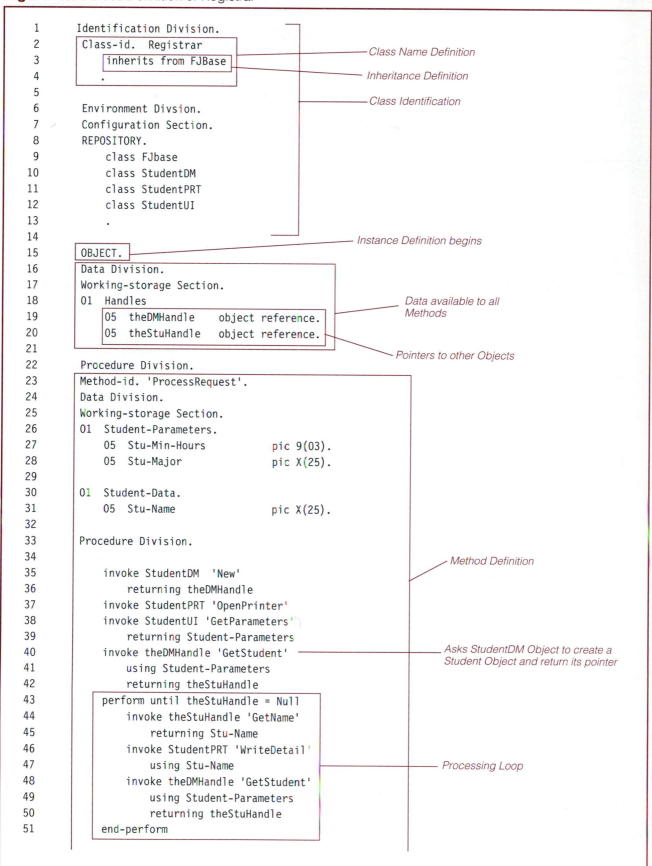

```
 1      Identification Division.
 2      Class-id.  Registrar
 3          inherits from FJBase
 4          .
 5
 6      Environment Divsion.
 7      Configuration Section.
 8      REPOSITORY.
 9          class FJbase
10          class StudentDM
11          class StudentPRT
12          class StudentUI
13          .
14
15      OBJECT.
16      Data Division.
17      Working-storage Section.
18      01  Handles
19          05  theDMHandle    object reference.
20          05  theStuHandle   object reference.
21
22      Procedure Division.
23      Method-id. 'ProcessRequest'.
24      Data Division.
25      Working-storage Section.
26      01  Student-Parameters.
27          05  Stu-Min-Hours        pic 9(03).
28          05  Stu-Major            pic X(25).
29
30      01  Student-Data.
31          05  Stu-Name             pic X(25).
32
33      Procedure Division.
34
35          invoke StudentDM  'New'
36              returning theDMHandle
37          invoke StudentPRT 'OpenPrinter'
38          invoke StudentUI 'GetParameters'
39              returning Student-Parameters
40          invoke theDMHandle 'GetStudent'
41              using Student-Parameters
42              returning theStuHandle
43          perform until theStuHandle = Null
44              invoke theStuHandle 'GetName'
45                  returning Stu-Name
46              invoke StudentPRT 'WriteDetail'
47                  using Stu-Name
48              invoke theDMHandle 'GetStudent'
49                  using Student-Parameters
50                  returning theStuHandle
51          end-perform
```

Annotations:
- Class Name Definition
- Inheritance Definition
- Class Identification
- Instance Definition begins
- Data available to all Methods
- Pointers to other Objects
- Method Definition
- Asks StudentDM Object to create a Student Object and return its pointer
- Processing Loop

Figure 20.4 *(continued)*

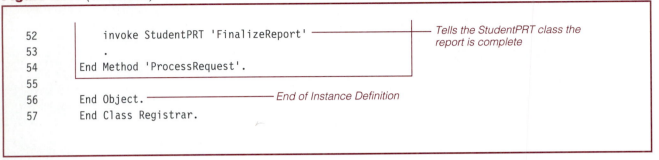

```
52            invoke StudentPRT 'FinalizeReport' ————————— Tells the StudentPRT class the
53            .                                              report is complete
54       End Method 'ProcessRequest'.
55
56       End Object. ———————————— End of Instance Definition
57       End Class Registrar.
```

The class definition can be made up of three parts:

- Class identification area that defines the class name and the linkages of the class definition files for the other classes associated with this one.

- The Factory area. The Factory is a special instance of the class that contains methods and data used for managing all other instances of the class.

- The Object or Instance area. This part of the class definition describes the data formats and methods available to each instance.

You should see a difference between the class identification area and the start of a traditional program. The Program-Id statement is replaced by a Class-Id statement. The Class-Id also includes an Inherits clause. This clause defines the *inheritance* of the class. In most cases, a class inherits from FJBase. In other words, Registrar is a "child" of FJBase. FJBase, a special class provided in COBOL97, serves as the basis for all other classes. However, as you will see later, not all classes directly inherit from FJBase. In some cases, FJBase becomes the grandparent rather than the parent of a class.

As in the Student-Look-Up program, the class identification area contains a Repository paragraph. Notice that the Repository contains four classes: FJBase, StudentDM, StudentPRT, and StudentUI. The Repository contains FJBase because it is the parent class. StudentDM is included because Registrar instantiates a StudentDM object. Finally, the Repository includes StudentPRT and StudentUI because Registrar requests these classes to perform some factory methods. The class Student is not included in the Repository because, although Registrar uses some instance methods, Registrar does not instantiate Student.

In some class definitions, a Factory definition follows the Repository. The Factory is a special instance used by the class itself for its own processing and data. The Factory instance is entirely separate from the Object instances. Registrar does not require Factory methods or data, so a Factory is not defined here. Several of the other classes do include Factories.

The definition of the instance in Figure 20.4 begins with the keyword OBJECT in line 15. As mentioned before, in defining a class the designer needs to ask:

- What does it know?

- Whom does it know?

- What does it do?

To answer the first question, in the Student-Look-Up system the Registrar does not have to have any special knowledge. If the class were to be used with some other system it is likely that some data items would have to be defined and stored in the Working-storage Section in lines 17–20.

The Working-storage Section of the Object works much as it does in a traditional program. However, one class description can have many Working-storage Sections. The Factory can have one, the Object can have one, and each Factory or instance method can have its own Working-storage Section. In the case of the Object's Working-storage Section, all instance methods can access the data. However, no other class, object, or program can access the data except by invoking an instance method.

The Working-storage Section also contains a partial answer to the question, "Whom does it know?" The group item Handles in lines 18–20 contains the pointers to the objects the Registrar needs to know.

The answer to "What does it do?" is defined by the methods. For Registrar, there is only one method, ProcessRequests. This method is discussed below.

Classes and Inheritance

Look again at the Class-id paragraph in lines 2-3. Inheritance is an important OO concept. By stating that Registrar inherits from FJBase, the clause is saying that FJBase is the parent class and all of the methods in FJBase are available to Registrar. FJBase is a special class provided by COBOL97 as part of the OO COBOL system. The FJBase class serves as a template for all other classes and has specialized methods for the management of all classes.

For an example of how inheritance works, consider the method New. New is invoked before an instance exists. New also addresses the Class-id rather than an instance handle. The Factory contains specialized methods that allow management of the instances. The method New creates the instance, and therefore it cannot be contained in an instance. New is therefore a *factory method*.

You should notice that the Registrar Class definition in Figure 20.4 does not specify a Factory or its methods. Then where is the method New? New is a factory method in FJBase. Whenever a class is instantiated, the parent class is also instantiated and is available to the child class. Because Registrar inherits from FJBase, Registrar can perform New as if it were its own method. Thus, when Student-Look-Up invokes New, Registrar receives the message and passes it on to FJBase. FJBase then creates the instance of Registrar. The invoking program did not need to know anything about FJBase, but just asks the Registrar class to create an instance of Registrar. By taking advantage of inheritance, the object programmer does not have to write a method to create an instance for every class. This example is just one way inheritance works to reuse code; other ways are discussed below.

There is one more point to make about factory methods and instance methods. Even though the Factory and instances are parts of the same class, methods belong to either the Factory or the instances. If the Factory needs to invoke an instance method, the invoke must specify the instance handle. Instance methods must use the class name (for example, Registrar) to invoke a Factory method. OO COBOL maintains a strict separation between the two types of methods.

ProcessRequests Method

The ProcessRequests method begins with the Method-id paragraph in line 24. Every method must begin with Method-id and end with End Method. These statements provide the method's boundaries. Each method may have its own Data Division and Procedure Division. The Data Division is optional and contains entries that are available only by the method itself. A method Data Division may have a Working-Storage Section and a Linkage Section.

The Working-Storage Section contains method data. The entries are reinitialized on each invocation of the method. If a Value clause is specified for an entry, the entry's contents are reset to that of the Value clause. If a data value needs to be maintained from one method invocation to another, the data should be stored in the Object's Data Division.

The Linkage Section works in conjunction with the Procedure Division to pass data to and from the method. The Linkage Section of a method is similar to that of a sub-program.

ProcessRequests needs only a few Working-storage Section entries to do its work. They may be seen in lines 27–32. In this case, the system invokes ProcessRequests just once. Therefore, it does not matter whether these data items were stored in the method or the Object. If the data were stored in the Object, there would be no need for a method Data Division. Whether or not a method has a Data Division, all methods must have Procedure Divsions.

The Procedure Division, starting in line 34, begins by creating an instance of the StudentDM class. Again the New method is invoked,. Since the system does not need more than one instance of StudentDM, whether or not an instance actually has to be created is a design decision. For example, everything could be done in the Factory using factory methods. In this case, we have elected to create an instance in order to demonstrate a feature of Object-Oriented programming—*polymorphism.* This feature is duscussed in the section about the StudentDM class.

The next step is to have the StudentPRT class open its printer file. For purposes of contrast and showing different options, we have elected to use just Factory methods in StudentPRT. Since classes are loaded as part of the system, they do not have to be created like an object. Therefore, the Factory portion of StudentPRT is available immediately. However, the Registrar needs to inform StudentPRT that the printer file should be opened. StudentPRT does not automatically know when to open the file. The OpenPrinter message requests StudentPRT to perform that action. No data is sent or returned with this message.

After requesting that the Printer be opened, ProcessRequests then gets the Student Parameters from StudentUI. Again, we have chosen to operate at the Class level rather than an instance level. However, this message expects StudentUI to return the minimum hours and the major for the students we are requesting. This request represents an improvement over the Senior program in Chapter 1. The Senior program could only process Engineering students with more than 110 hours. Once StudentUI returns the parameters, Registrar can request the StudentDM instance to get an instance of Student meeting the parameters. Registrar does this by invoking the message "GetStudent." This message passes the parameters received from StudentUI and requests the handle of a Student instance meeting these requirements. Notice that the invoke does not request the student name directly.

For StudentDM to provide the name directly would violate the OO principle of encapsulation. This principle requires that only the Student object can manipulate Student data. The StudentDM does not have the authorization to deal with Student data directly. StudentDM can only process files and use the control fields to generate a Student instance. That instance can then manipulate the data.

The concept of **encapsulation** or **data hiding,** as it is sometimes known, means that data are kept in a "capsule" called an instance. The data is the property of the instance and can be accessed only through one of the instance methods. Other objects must send messages to the instance in order to use any of its data. Encapsulation allows the instance to maintain the data's integrity since there can be no unauthorized changes by other programs or objects.

Compare encapsulation to the way data is treated in programs. In a program, all data are available to every paragraph in the program. Any paragraph could potentially alter any data item in the Data Division. In poorly designed programs or ones that have been hastily modified, logic errors can cause data to be improperly changed and as a result cause unexpected effects. The source of these errors may not be easy to detect since any paragraph could have caused the problem. By restricting all manipulation to an object and its methods, logic errors in methods are much easier to detect and fix.

Returning to ProcessRequests, in line 44 the method begins the main processing loop of the system. The control variable for the loop is theStudentHandle. When the variable becomes "null" the loop stops. Null is a predefined address used by COBOL to indicate that an object does not exist. If for some reason StudentDM cannot create an instance of Student, getStudent returns null in theStudentHandle.

Using a valid Student handle, the first statement requests the Student name from the Student object and then passes that data to StudentPRT for printing.

PROGRAMMING TIP

Memory Leakage

One problem in object-oriented systems is called ***memory leakage***. Memory leakage occurs when the system generates a new instance of a class and uses the same handle name as the previous instance. OO COBOL will place the new address into the handle overwriting the previous address. The original instance remains in the computer's memory, but since the pointer is gone there is no way to access it. The old instance has become an orphan and the memory assigned to it cannot be used for any other purpose.

As orphans accumulate, the memory available is reduced and the performance of the system degrades.

Some OO systems provide a service called "garbage collection" where the system looks for and removes orphaned instances. COBOL97 provides this service..

The Registrar object and its method ProcessRequests has served as an introduction to the concept of inheritance and demonstrated how an object interacts with other objects to accomplish a task. This discussion has also included the concept of encapsulation and the need to remove objects from memory when they are no longer necessary.

The StudentDM Class

Objects exist only in the memory of a computer while a system is running. However, a system that cannot maintain data from one run to another has little practical use. OO systems therefore must provide a way to store and recall data whenever necessary. The OO term for this requirement is ***persistence***. One method of handling persistence in a system is to have a data management class for each problem domain class. StudentDM is the data manager for the Student class.

The three questions apply here as well.

- StudentDM needs to know the file specifications for the Student persistence file.

- The object needs to know the Student object.

- StudentDM must be able to do all of the file handling to create Student instances.

Class Name: StudentDM

Class Type: Data Management

Narrative: This object performs all file processing for the Student file. The object opens, closes, and reads records from the file. StudentDM also creates Student instances from the data in the file.

Objects Created: Student

Objects Referenced: Student

Factory Methods: New

Narrative: Overrides the FJBase New in order to open the file when the object is created.

Processing:
1. Invoke New from FJBase.
2. Open the Student File.

Instance Method: GetStudent

Narrative: This method controls the process of finding a student record that meets the user's specification.

Processing:
1. Set the Student handle to null in case a record cannot be found.
2. Read the Student data file.
3. For every record, determine whether it meets the minimum credit hours required and is in the required major.
4. When a matching record is found, create and populate a Student object. Return the handle for the Student object.

Instance Method: ReadRecord

Narrative: This is a private method to read Student Records.

Processing:
1. Read records from the Student file.
2. At end of file, set an end of file switch and close the file.

Instance Method: CreateStudent

Narrative: This private method creates an instance of Student and populates it with the values from the current Student Record.

Processing:
1. Invoke a new instance of Student.
2. Populate the instance.

Figure 20.5 Class Definition of StudentDM

```
 1        Identification Division.
 2        Class-id.    StudentDM
 3           inherits FJBase
 4              .
 5
 6        Environment Division.
 7        Configuration section.
 8        REPOSITORY.
 9           class FJBase
10           class Student
11              .
12
13    FACTORY.
14    Procedure Division.
15
16    Method-Id. New override.
17    Data Division.
18    Linkage Section.
19    01  ls-theDMHandle object reference self.
20
21    Procedure Division
22        returning ls-theDMHandle.
23
24        invoke super 'New' returning ls-theDMHandle
25        invoke ls-theDMHandle 'OpenFile'
26           .
27    End Method New.
28    End Factory.
29
30    OBJECT.
31    Environment Division.
32    Input-Output Section.
33    File-Control.
34        select Student-File assign to SYSIN
35            organization is line sequential.
36
37    Data Division.
38    File Section.
39    fd  Student-File.
40    01  Student-In.
41        05  Stu-Name          pic X(25).
42        05  Stu-Credits       pic 9(03).
43        05  Stu-Major         pic X(20).
44
45    Procedure Division.
46
47    Method-id. OpenFile.
48    Procedure Division.
49
50        open input Student-file
51           .
52    End Method OpenFile.
```

Factory definition

'New' overrides FJBase method

Invoke FJBase method

File Control specification

File description

Figure 20.5 *(continued)*

```
53
54      Method-id. ReadRecord.
55      Data Division.
56      Linkage Section.
57      01  ls-Data-Remains-Switch        pic X(03).
58
59      Procedure Division
60          returning ls-Data-Remains-Switch.
61
62          move 'YES' to ls-Data-Remains-Switch
63          read Student-File
64              at end
65                  move 'NO' to ls-Data-Remains-Switch
66                  close Student-File
67          end-read
68          .
69      End Method ReadRecord.
70
71      Method-id. GetStudent.
72      Data Division.
73      Working-storage Section.
74      01  Data-Remains-Switch           pic X(03).
75
76      Linkage Section.
77      01  ls-Stu-Parameters.
78          05  ls-Stu-Credits            pic 9(03).
79          05  ls-Stu-Major              pic X(25).
80
81      01  ls-theStuHandle               object reference.
82
83      Procedure Division
84          using  ls-Stu-Parameters
85          returning ls-theStuHandle.
86
87          set ls-theStuHandle to NULL
88          invoke self 'ReadRecord'
89              returning Data-Remains-Switch
90          perform until Data-Remains-Switch = 'NO' or
91                          ls-theStuHandle NOT = NULL
92              evaluate TRUE        also Stu-Major
93                  when Stu-Credits  >= ls-Stu-Credits also ls-Stu-Major
94                      invoke self 'CreateStudent'
95                          returning ls-theStuHandle
96                  when other
97                      invoke self 'ReadRecord'
98                          returning Data-Remains-Switch
99              end-evaluate
100         end-perform
101         .
102     End Method GetStudent.
103
104     Method-id. CreateStudent.
```

New clause for Procedure Division

Close file when last record read

Uses and returns data

Invoke method in same instance

Two-condition Evaluate statement .

Figure 20.5 *(continued)*

```
105        Data Division.
106        Linkage Section.
107        01 ls-theStudentHandle        object reference.
108
109        Procedure Division
110            returning ls-theStudentHandle.
111
112            invoke Student 'New'
113                returning ls-theStudentHandle
114            invoke ls-theStudentHandle 'PopulateStudent'
115                using Student-In
116                .
117        End Method CreateStudent.
118
119        End Object.
120        End Class StudentDM.
```

The class definition for StudentDM in Figure 20.5 introduces the use of a Factory. Within the Factory is a method called "New." You may have wondered why Registrar had to tell StudentPRT to open its file, but did not tell StudentDM to open its file. Examination of New should explain what is going on. First, look at the Method-Id statement. The clause "Override" follows the method name. This clause means that this local method should be used instead of the inherited method "New." Normally FJBase performs the "New" method, but we have chosen to "override" that method with our own. By doing so, we can open the file as part of the process of creating the instance. This method shows a simple example of polymorphism.

Polymorphism is a Greek term meaning many shapes. In OO programming, polymorphism means that a message may produce different results based on the object or class it is sent to. Polymorphism is usually achieved by having one method override another, inherited method. This technique is a powerful OO tool, but we are showing just a simple example. A full discussion of polymorphism is beyond the scope of the chapter.

By defining a method called New within the Factory, StudentDM can override the New method in FJBase. When an object or class receives a message, it first checks to see if it has a method by that name. If so, the object executes the local method instead of the inherited method.

The overriding of inheritance must be done with caution, because the local method must be able to handle all of the processing expected of the inherited method. For example, New must be able to create an instance of StudentDM. The local method accomplishes this easily by calling on the inherited method. In line 24, the statement invoke super 'New' returning ls-the DMHandle requests FJBase to build the instance. "Super" refers to the parent class—FJBase. FJBase then instantiates StudentDM and returns a handle for this new instance. The handle can be returned to the invoking object, class, or program. In this case the handle serves another purpose as well.

The point of overriding was to allow StudentDM to open its own file. However, the file description is part of the Object definition and not the Factory. New has to request the instance to open its file. Even though the Factory and the Object are part of the same class definition, they are different entities. The Factory has to use a handle to reference the instance.

StudentDM Instance Definition

The instance definition of StudentDM begins with the word OBJECT in line 30. This definition looks much like a traditional COBOL program in that it has an Environment Division and a Data Division. In those divisions are the Input-Output Sections and File Sections. Although this is an object, StudentDM uses traditional file processing.

Beyond those considerations, the instance definition of Student is straightforward. To answer the three questions:

- The instance does not have to have special knowledge other than the file information.

- The only object that it knows is Student.

- What it does is read records from the file, test for records that meet the required parameters, and create Student instances to hold the data.

Of the three methods defined in the instance, only one is invoked from outside. GetStudent is a public method and can be invoked by other objects. The remaining two objects are "private" methods to be used by other methods in StudentDM.

Beginning at line 73, GetStudent maintains its own Working-storage Section to hold an end-of-file switch and a Linkage Section to receive the invoking parameters and to pass back the handle of the Student instance.

The Procedure Division has both `using` and `returning` clauses to allow use of the items in the Linkage Section. The algorithm of the method is to initialize the Student handle to `null` and then `invoke` the ReadRecord method. The `invoke` statement uses the keyword `self`. Self refers to the pointer of the current instance. An instance always knows its own memory location and can reference that location by using `self`.

Once the record is read, GetStudent evaluates the credit hours against the minimum and the major against the required major. If the test is successful, the routine invokes the CreateStudent method, and uses the result to return the Student Handle and to stop the loop. If the test was not successful, the routine invokes ReadRecord method to get the next record. When ReadRecord runs out of records, it returns "NO" to the Data-Remains-Switch. The loop stops, and because no instance of Student has been created the method returns a `null` handle to the invoking procedure.

The remaining two methods are easily understood. ReadRecord is a simple read routine that might be found in any traditional COBOL program. The only notable feature is that the routine closes the file when AT END is reached. CreateStudent is also simple. It invokes the New method to create an instance of Student and then invokes the PopulateStudent method to move data from the input file into the instance just created.

In a real system, StudentDM would have more instance methods, such as ones which could add, modify, or delete student records. Students acquainted with indexed files, direct files, or databases are well aware that the use of a sequential file as has been done here, would not be efficient for handling many student records. You should be able to see that if StudentDM were rewritten to use another file organization, Registrar and Student would never know the difference. By encapsulating the file processing in StudentDM, major file changes are invisible to the rest of the system. Polymorphism and encapsulation make system modifications simple.

The StudentDM class serves as an example of how an object can process files and interact with other objects. You have also seen an example of polymorphism and how inherited methods can be overridden.

The Student Class

PROGRAMMING SPECIFICATIONS

Class Name:	Student
Class Type:	Problem Domain
Narrative:	This class represents the data and behaviors of students in the system. An instance of the class may return the student's major and the number of credit-hours earned.
Objects Created:	None
Objects Referenced:	Person (Parent)
Factory Methods:	None
Instance Method:	PopulateStudent
Narrative:	This method moves the data from the linkage section of the method into the Object-storage Section, where the data are available to every method of the instance.
Processing:	1. Format and store the Student name.
	2. Store the rest of the Student data.
Instance Method:	GetCreditHours
Narrative:	Returns the Student credit hours.
Processing:	1. Move Credit Hours to linkage section.
Instance Method:	GetMajor
Narrative:	Returns the Student major.
Processing:	1. Move Major to linkage section.

Figure 20.6 Student Class Definition

```
1        Identification Division.
2        Class-id.   Student
3           inherits Person
4           .
5
6        Environment Division.
7        Configuration Section.
8        REPOSITORY.
9           class Person
10          .
11
12       OBJECT.
13       Data Division.
14       Working-storage Section.
15       01  Student-In.
16           05  Stu-Data.
17               10  Stu-Credits       pic 9(03).
18               10  Stu-Major         pic X(20).
19
20       Procedure Division.
21
22       Method-id. PopulateStudent.
23       Data Division.
24       Working-storage Section.
25       01  Stu-Name               PIC X(60).
26
27       Linkage Section.
28       01  ls-Student-In.
29           05  ls-Stu-Name        pic X(25).
30           05  ls-Stu-Data.
31               10  ls-Stu-Credits pic 9(03).
32               10  ls-Stu-Major   pic X(20).
33
34       Procedure Division
35           using ls-Student-In.
36
37           Move ls-Stu-Name TO Stu-Name
38           invoke self 'PopulateName'
39               using Stu-Name
40           move ls-Stu-Data to Stu-Data
41           .
42       End Method PopulateStudent.
43
44       Method-id. GetCreditHours.
45       Data Division.
46       Linkage Section.
47       01  ls-Credit-Hours         pic  9(03).
48
49       Procedure Division
50           returning ls-Credit-Hours.
51
52           move Stu-Credits to ls-Credit-Hours
```

Inherits from Person, not FJBase

Uses inherited method

Figure 20.6 *(continued)*

```
53          .
54       End Method GetCreditHours.
55
56       Method-id. GetMajor.
57       Data Division.
58       Linkage Section.
59       01  ls-Stu-Major              pic X(20).
60
61       Procedure Division
62           returning ls-Stu-Major.
63
64           move Stu-Major to ls-Stu-Major
65          .
66       End Method GetMajor.
67
68       End Object.
69       End Class Student.
```

The Student class manages the data for students. Figure 20.6 contains the definition of Student. Notice that that this object does not inherit from FJBase (line 3). Student inherits from another class, Person. We explain the reason for using inheritance under the discussion for the class Person.

The Student object represents a simple application of how inheritance can work. Student contains three instance methods. Only one, PopulateStudent, is actually used by this system. PopulateStudent stores the data in the Object-storage section after an instance has been created. GetMajor and GetCreditHours are simple methods to show how other applications might retrieve those data items.

PopulateStudent, in line 22, invokes a method called PopulateName. The `invoke` statement references `self`. However, Student does not have a method called PopulateName. That method is actually in Person.

By referencing `self`, Student looks for a method by the name PopulateName within itself. The Student cannot find the method; it will pass the message to its parent—Person. In a case like this, the programmer may want to reference `super` rather than `self`. Yet there may be some instances where `self` is actually safer. Should PopulateName be added to Student to accommodate some need for polymorphism, using `super` would bypass the local method. Using `self` assures that the proper method is invoked.

Because Student inherits from Person, an instantiation of Student means that Person is instantiated as well. Both Person and Student exist at the same time, but Student does not have to maintain a pointer to Person. The inheritance mechanism handles these relationships.

One other example of inheritance should also be noted. In Figure 20.4, line 45, the ProcessRequest method invokes theStudentHandle with the method GetName. GetName is not defined in the Student object. Student will receive the message and send it on to Person to be performed. Registrar neither knows nor cares that the work is actually done by Person instead of Student.

The Student class is an example of inheritance and of how OO programmers can take advantage of this technique to reuse code in a variety of ways. The Person class gives an example of what a parent class could look like.

The Person Class _____

Class Name: Person

Class Type: Problem Domain

Narrative: This class represents the data and behaviors of persons of any type in the system.

Objects Created: None

Objects Referenced: None

Factory Methods: None

Instance Method: PopulateName

Narrative: This method moves the formatted name data from the linkage section of the method into the Object-storage Section where the data are available to every method of the instance. The Object-storage Section holds name data in a generalized format and the input name is broken up into its parts.

Processing: 1. Find and store the first-name portion of the name and store it in the Object–storage Section.
2. Find the last-name portion of the name and store it in the Object-storage Section.

Instance Method: GetName

Narrative: Produces the Name in a formatted form.

Processing: 1. Concatenate the first name and last name and move to linkage section.

Many types of people are involved in the operation of a university. Besides students, there are faculty, administration, clerical staff, and facilities staff, to name a few. Each of these roles has its own specialized functions and data. Yet, if one were to ask either a faculty member or a facilities person what their name was, the questioner would expect that either one could respond. Therefore, if the system required a Faculty class or a Staff class in addition to a Student class, each of these classes should be able to respond to a message "GetName."

One way to accomplish this goal would be to code a "GetName" method into each of these classes. However, any change to the method would have to be made in every class using that method. Structured programs often face this problem.

A better approach to meeting the requirement is to take advantage of inheritance. Students, faculty, administration, clerical staff, and facilities staff are all persons. By defining a generic class called Person, all of the common data attributes and associated methods could be placed in Person and every class inheriting from Person could use the methods and access the data.

Some common attributes might be:

- Name

- Address

- Telephone

- Age

By coding these and other attributes into Person, they have to be coded only once, but they are available to any class inheriting from Person. Any changes to the data or the methods is automatically available to the subclasses by making changes only in Person.

Figure 20.7 Person Class Definition

```
1          Identification Division.
2      Class-id. Person
3              inherits FJBase
4              .
5      Environment Division.
6      Configuration Section.
7      REPOSITORY.
8          class FJbase
9          .
10
11     OBJECT.
12     Data Division.
13     Working-storage Section.
14     01   Person-Name.
15          05   Per-Last-Name          pic X(20).
16          05   Per-First-Name         pic X(20).
17          05   Per-Middle-Name        pic X(20).
18
19     01   Counters.
20          05   First-Name-Len         pic 9(02).
21          05   Last-Name-Len          pic 9(02).
22
23     Procedure Division.
24
25     Method-id. PopulateName.
26     Data Division.
27     Linkage Section.
28     01  ls-Person-Name            pic X(60).
29
30     Procedure Division
31         using ls-Person-Name.
32
33         initialize Counters
34         inspect ls-Person-Name
35             tallying First-Name-Len
36             for characters before initial space
37         inspect ls-Person-Name (First-Name-Len + 2:)
38             tallying Last-Name-Len
39             for characters before initial space
40         move ls-Person-Name (1:First-Name-Len)
```

Breaks Full Name to First and Last Name

Figure 20.7 *(continued)*

```
41               to Per-First-Name
42          move ls-Person-Name (First-Name-Len + 2 : Last-Name-Len)
43               to Per-Last-Name
44          .
45      End Method PopulateName.
46
47      Method-id. GetName.
48      Data Division.
49      Working-storage Section.
50      01  Blank-Char                 pic X    value space.
51
52      Linkage Section.
53      01  ls-Name                    pic X(25).
54
55      Procedure Division
56          returning ls-Name.
57
58          initialize ls-name
59          string Per-First-Name delimited by space          ── Reconstructs Full Name
60                 Blank-Char     delimited by size
61                 Per-Last-Name  delimited by space
62              into ls-Name
63          .
64      End Method GetName.
65
66      End Object.
67      End Class Person.
```

The Person class, shown in Figure 20.7, looks much like any other class. For example, Person inherits from FJBase. Note that because Student inherits from Person it also inherits from FJBase, though indirectly. There may be multiple levels of inheritance defined with lower-level classes inheriting methods and data from grandparent as well as parent classes. You should also note that Person does not have to know what classes inherit from it.

Because Student inherits from Person, any instantiation of Student creates an instantiation of Person as well. OO COBOL then allows Student to access the methods in Person without creating a special handle. Person and Student are attached to each other. However, even though Student knows about Person, Person does not need to know about Student.

The Working-storage Section in lines 14–17 defines how the Name is stored. The format specified here is quite different from that actually stored in the Student file and printed on the output report. The designers of the class wanted to be able to output the name in a variety of formats. Therefore, a more general name format has been specified in the Object-storage Section.

Therefore, PopulateName has to be able to convert a single name field into the three attribute fields. The routine uses the `inspect` statement to break down the name and to store the results in the proper fields.

GetName reformats the Name into the full-name format and returns the name as a single data item.

The Person class shows how a super class and its methods might be used in an OO system. The class definition shows how objects can input and output data in formats different from the way the class stores them.

The StudentUI Class

Class Name: StudentUI

Class Type: User Interface

Screen Layout: See Figure 20.8a.

Narrative: This class controls the interface to the user. The class gathers the requested minimum number of credit hours and the name of the desired major.

Objects Created: None

Objects Referenced: None

Factory Method: GetParameters

Narrative: This method controls the display of requests to the system user and accepts the responses.

Processing:
1. Invoke DisplayHoursRequest and store the result in the linkage section.
2. Invoke DisplayMajorRequest and store the result in the linkage section.

Factory Method: DisplayHoursRequest

Narrative: This is a private method that displays a user prompt for the minimum number of credit hours desired and accepts the response.

Processing:
1. Display Prompt.
2. Accept response into the linkage section.

Factory Method: DisplayMajorRequest

Narrative: This is a private method that displays a user prompt for the desired major and accepts the response.

Processing:
1. Display Prompt.
2. Accept response into the linkage section.

Instance Methods: None

Figure 20.8 Screen Sample

```
                    Enter Minimum Hours: 100
                    Enter Student Major: Engineering
                    (a) Display Parameter Prompts


                    STUDENT NAME

                    ORVILLE WRIGHT
                    JOHN ROEBLING


                    * * *  End of Report * * *
                    (b)  Report Sample
```

Figure 20.9 StudentUI Class Definition

```
1        Identification Division.
2        Class-id.   StudentUI
3           inherits FJBase
4              .
5
6        Environment Division.
7        Configuration Section.
8        REPOSITORY.
9           class FJbase
10             .
11
12       FACTORY.
13       Procedure Division.
14
15       Method-id. GetParameters.
16       Data Division.
17       Linkage Section.
18       01  ls-Student-Parameters.
19           05  ls-Stu-Hours          pic 9(03).
20           05  ls-Stu-Major          pic X(25).
21
22       Procedure Division
23           returning ls-Student-Parameters.
24
25           invoke self 'DisplayHoursRequest'
26               returning ls-Stu-Hours                     Private methods
27           invoke self 'DisplayMajorRequest'
28               returning ls-Stu-Major
29               .
30       End Method GetParameters.
31
32       Method-id. DisplayHoursRequest.
33       Data Division.
34       Linkage Section.
35       01  ls-Stu-Hours              pic 9(03).
36
```

Figure 20.9 *(continued)*

```
37      Procedure Division
38          returning ls-Stu-Hours.
39
40          display 'Enter Minmum Hours: ' with no advancing
41          accept ls-Stu-Hours from console
42          .
43      End Method DisplayHoursRequest.
44
45      Method-id. DisplayMajorRequest.
46      Data Division.
47      Linkage Section.
48      01  ls-Stu-Major              pic X(25).
49
50      Procedure Division
51          returning ls-Stu-Major.
52
53          display 'Enter Student Major: ' with no advancing
54          accept ls-Stu-Major from console
55          move function Upper-Case (ls-Stu-Major) to ls-Stu-Major
56          .
57      End Method DisplayMajorRequest.
58
59      End Factory.
60      End Class StudentUI.
```

Figure 20.9 shows the class definition for the StudentUI object. This object controls the user interface to the system. There are no OO techniques that have not been addressed elsewhere.

StudentUI has been kept very simple for instructional purposes, but more elaborate user interfaces could be developed even to the point of using Windows screens without affecting the rest of the system. These more elaborate objects would simply replace StudentUI. OO allows "plug compatibility." When an object needs enhancement, the changes can be made and tested outside of the production system. When ready, the old version of the object can simply be replaced by the new version.

The instance method GetParameters controls the process and uses the private methods DisplayHoursRequest and DisplayMajorRequest to get the user's input.

In lines 41 and 54, the `accept` statements use the clause `from console`. This clause allows the user to enter a response shorter than the full length of the receiving field.

The StudentPRT Class

The final class in the system is a print manager, a form of user interface class. This class manages the printing of the report and has been slightly enhanced from the Engineering Senior program in Figure 1.6.

PROGRAMMING SPECIFICATIONS

Class Name: StudentPRT

Class Type: User Interface

Narrative: This class controls the printing of the selected student report.

Report Format: Figure 20.8b

Objects Created: None

Objects Referenced: None

Factory Method: OpenPrinter

Narrative: Opens the printer and causes the report headers to be printed.

Processing:
1. Open Print File.
2. Invoke WriteHeader.

Factory Method: WriteHeader

Narrative: This is a private method that Writes the Report Header.

Processing:
1. Write Header Line.
2. Write Blank Line.

Factory Method: WriteDetail

Narrative: This is a private method that prints the Detail Line containing a student name.

Processing:
1. Move name to Print Line.
2. Write Print Line.

Factory Method: FinalizeReport

Narrative: Prints the final report line and closes the print file.

Processing:
1. Move End of Report Line to Print Line.
2. Write the Print Line.
3. Close the Print File.

Figure 20.10 StudentPRT Class Definition

```
1        Identification Division.
2        Class-id.    StudentPRT
3            inherits FJBase
4            .
5
6        Environment Division.
7        Configuration Section.
8        REPOSITORY.
9            class FJbase
10           .
11
12       FACTORY.
13
14       Environment Division.
15       Input-Output Section.
16       File-Control.
17           select PrintFile assign to SYSOUT
19               organization is line sequential
20               .
21
22       Data Division.
23       File Section.
24       fd  PrintFile.
25       01  Print-Line           pic X(45).
26
27       Procedure Division.
28
29       Method-id. OpenPrinter.
30       Procedure Division.
31
32           open output PrintFile.
33           invoke self 'WriteHeader'
34               .
35       End Method OpenPrinter.
36
37       Method-id. WriteHeader.
38       Data Division.
39       Working-storage Section.
40       01  Heading-Line.
41           05              pic X(10)      value Spaces.
42           05  Head-1      pic X(12)      value 'STUDENT NAME'.
43           05              pic X(58)      value Spaces.
44
45       Procedure Division.
46
47           move Heading-Line to Print-Line
48           write Print-Line after advancing page
49           move spaces to Print-Line
50           write Print-Line after advancing 1
51               .
52       End Method WriteHeader.
53
```

Figure 20.10 *(continued)*

```
54      Method-id. WriteDetail.
55      Data Division.
56      Working-storage Section.
57      01  Detail-Line.
58          05                  pic X(10)           value spaces.
59          05   Print-Name     pic X(25).
60          05                  pic X(45)           value spaces.
61
62      Linkage Section.
63      01  ls-Stu-Name         pic X(25).
64
65      Procedure Division
66          using ls-Stu-Name.
67
68          move ls-Stu-Name to Print-Name
69          move Detail-Line to Print-Line
70          write Print-Line after advancing 1
71          .
72      End Method WriteDetail.
73
74      Method-id.  FinalizeReport.
75      Procedure Division.
76
77          invoke self 'WriteDetail' using ' '
78          invoke self 'WriteDetail' using
79          '* * * End of Report * * *'
80          close PrintFile
81          .
82      End Method FinalizeReport.
83
84      End Factory.
85      End Class StudentPRT.
```

Like StudentDM, Student PRT, shown in Figure 20.10, has to manage a file, in this case a print file. However, StudentPRT works entirely in the Factory rather than using an instance. Therefore, the File-Control and File Sections are defined in the Factory. The methods are all Factory Methods.

Since the Factory is loaded at tun-time, Student PRT does not know when to open the file. Therefore, Registrar has to run the method OpenPrinter as shown in Figure 20.4, line 38. OpenPrinter opens the file and invokes the private method WriteHeader.

WriteHeader advances the page and prints out the report header.

WriteDetail is the "workhorse" of the class and prints out the Student Name. This method is used both as a public method from Registrar in line 47 of Figure 20.4 and privately by FinalizeReport in lines 77–78 of Figure 20.10.

StudentPRT, unlike StudentDM, cannot tell when the file should be closed. Only Registrar can determine when all of the records have been processed. Thus, Registrar has to invoke FinalizeReport. FinalizeReport prints an End of Report line and then closes the print file.

There are no new OO concepts in StudentPRT, but this class does show how a report can be produced by an object-oriented system.

Conclusion

In summary, why use object-orientation for COBOL programs instead of structured programming? Object-Orientation allows systems to use:

- Shorter code elements

- Reusable code

- Simpler control structures

- Ways to have better control over data

Object-Orientation does not invalidate the concept of structured programming. OO simply is the next step in providing the capabilities that structured programming claimed to supply.

One might observe that OO COBOL may have advantages for new development, but might question how it would work with the massive amount of COBOL code developed with the traditional methods. The answer is that OO does not have to be "either-or." Traditional programs can invoke objects. We saw that the driver program for the Student-Look-Up system is a traditional program. On the other hand, objects can call traditional programs as well.

An organization can examine its legacy systems and develop a plan to evolve their systems to OO by determining the objects present in the system. Each object can then evolve as common procedures in the traditional programs are converted to methods. The traditional programs can then initially invoke the methods from objects. As the organization develops its OO skills and understanding, the legacy programs can be slowly eliminated. This process can become part of the regular maintenance process and does not have to be overly expensive if good OO analysis and design has been done.

S u m m a r y

Points to Remember

■ Even though the COBOL 2002 standard has not been adopted yet, OO COBOL compilers are available and can be used to learn this new "dialect."

■ The emphasis in OO programming is on the development of systems, not just programs. Objects are developed to serve as building blocks for many systems.

■ The structure of methods is similar to that of programs, but methods are simpler and do not need elaborate control structures.

■ Programmers who know both structured and OO COBOL will have an advantage as companies begin to migrate their legacy systems toward object-orientation.

■ Structured systems will not disappear soon, and the migration to OO will be evolutionary rather than revolutionary.

Key Words and Concepts

Class	System
Instance	Persistence
Factory	User Interface Class
Method	System Interface Class
Message	Data Manager Class
Encapsulation	Problem Domain Class
Polymorphism	Driver
Inheritance	Pointer
Paradigm	Handle
Structured Programming	Data Hiding
Object-oriented Programming	Static

COBOL Elements

```
Invoke
Class-id
REPOSITORY
OBJECT
FACTORY
Method-id
Object Reference
```

F I L L - I N

1. Object-oriented COBOL (<u>is/is not</u>) part of the COBOL 2002 standard.

2. _____ is the COBOL verb for running methods in classes.

3. A(n) _____ is the definition of an object; a(n) _____ is a specific occurrence of an object.

4. The special instance that allows manipulation of all other instances is called the _____.

5. _____ is the feature of OO that allows one class to act as if it contained the data and methods of another class.

6. The OO feature that protects the data contained in an object from access by other objects except through methods is called _____.

7. _____ is a special class and contains methods that are inherited by all other classes.

8. The change to OO represents a _____ shift because it represents a new way of thinking about programming.

9. Sometimes, one class overrides a method in a parent class to provide some new capability. This OO feature is called _____.

10. A new data type designed for specifying instance handles is called _____ _____.

T R U E / F A L S E

1. Object-Orientation reverses all of the principles of structured programming.

2. The Identification Division does not have to be specified in class definitions.

3. The Procedure Division does not have to be specified in a method.

4. COBOL is the first language to have OO capability.

5. It is not likely that OO COBOL will completely replace structured COBOL in the near future.

6. When developing the specifications for a class, the designer should ask:
   What does it know?
   Whom does it know?
   What does it do?

7. Classes that specifically deal with processing of the application are said to belong to the Problem Domain.

8. OO systems have no need of files.

9. Files provide the links between programs in structured systems.

10. OO systems use files to provide persistence between runs of the system.

PROBLEMS

1. Why is the class name used to invoke a Factory method and a handle to invoke an instance method?

2. How does object-orientation promote the reuse of program code?

3. Write a method for the Person class that would format a name starting with the last name followed by ", " and followed by the first name.

4. Which class should contain a campus phone number if it should be needed by the system?

5. Differentiate between system, program, and class.

For Further Study

Several texts are now available for learning OO COBOL. These include:

Arranga, E., and Coyle, F. *Object-Oriented COBOL.* SIGS Publications, 1996.

Chapin, N. *Standard Object-Oriented COBOL.* John Wiley & Sons, 1997.

Doke, E. R., and Hardgrave, B. C. *An Introduction to Object COBOL.* John Wiley & Sons, 1998.

Obin, R. *Object-Orientation: An Introduction for COBOL Programmers.* 2nd ed., Micro Focus Publishing, 1995.

Price, W. *Elements of Object-Oriented COBOL.* Object-Z Publishing, 1997.

---

[1] This system can downloaded from `http://www.prenhall.com/grauer_cobol`.

[2] This discussion is an oversimplification of the analysis and design process. For students interested in the OO Analysis and Design process, many books are available. This discussion is based on Peter Coad's book *Object Models: Strategies, Patterns, and Applications,* 2nd ed., Yourdan Press.

[3] COBOL 2002 goes a step beyond and allows free formatting of COBOL programs. This chapter does not show this technique because of the awkward way that the Animator handles free format. Future versions of the compiler should improve in that respect. Students interested in trying free format should place `$set sourceformat "free"` starting in column 7 before the first line of the source code. In free format the comment indicator becomes "*" and can be placed anywhere in a line. All entries to the right of the comment indicator are ignored.

Getting Started

Overview: This appendix consists of hands-on exercises that provide instruction in the use of Fujitsu COBOL 4.0—COBOL97 and its associated tools. The exercises are straightforward and offer systematic instructions to make you proficient in the use of the Project Manager for COBOL97. COBOL 4.0 is a complete COBOL development suite. These exercises do not explore the full range of options but are limited to the tools that you will need with the book— primarily the Project Manager.

Exercise 1: Installing Fujitsu COBOL97.
Exercise 2: Downloading Data Files from the World Wide Web.
Exercise 3: Compiling, Linking and Executing a COBOL Program.
Exercise 4: The Fujitsu Editor and Correcting Errors.
Exercise 5: Debugging Programs Using the Project Manager.
Exercise 6: Using Enviornmental Variables to Specify Files.
Exercise 7: Building Projects with Multiple Programs.
Exercise 8: COBOL97 File Utility.

COBOL97 provides you with all the functionality you will need for the projects in the book. We are pleased to offer it as a feature of *COBOL: From Micro to Mainframe*.

EXERCISE A1:

Installing Fujitsu COBOL97

Discussion: This exercise leads through the installation of Fujitsu COBOL97. Begin by taking note of the system requirements on the CD jacket. Be sure your computer can handle the specifications. As you go through the installation, the process will give you a Serial Number; record that number for future reference.

This exercise covers the Windows95 installation; the processing is similar in Windows 3.1, Windows98, and Windows NT. It is like most Windows installations, and experienced Windows users should have little difficulty.

Step A.1.1: Start-Up Procedures

Before beginning to install the program, you should shut down all other Windows tasks such as a Web browser, your e-mail, or any other application you may be using. Installing new software can be tricky and it is best to avoid system conflicts if possible.

There are several methods for determining what applications are running. One method, common to all versions of Windows, is to press <Alt-Tab> and hold the Alt key. This action brings up a list of all active appalications. By holding the Alt key and clicking the Tab key, you can move from one active application to the other. Once the system has highlighted the desired application, release the Alt key. At this point, the system brings that application to the front and you can close it.

To begin the process, place the *Fujitsu COBOL* CD into your CD-ROM drive. If you have the AutoRun feature installed, the process should begin automatically. If not, open the Start menu and select Run. You will need to run a program called "Autorun.Exe".

Figure A1.1 Fujitsu COBOL Master Setup Screen

Step A.1.2: Installing Fujitsu COBOL

The installation displays a Welcome screen that warns you about trying to install the suite when you have other Windows programs running. If you haven't already shut down any other programs, you should do so now. Read the copyright warning (Figure A1.2) and then click on Next to proceed.

Figure A1.5 Welcome Screen and Warnings

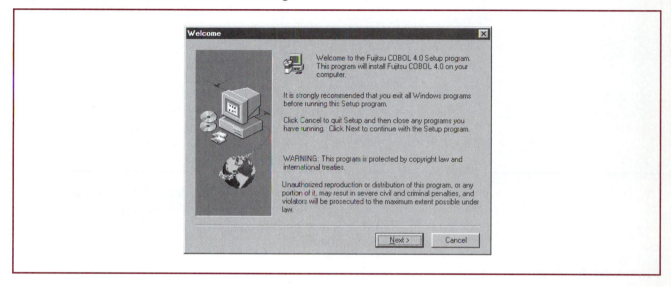

In the screen shown in Figure A1.3 the system asks for the Serial Number supplied with the CD. This number should already be entered for you. If not, enter the number you were given on the CD. Enter the dashes as well as the numbers. Click on Next.

Figure A1.3 Serial Number Entry Screen

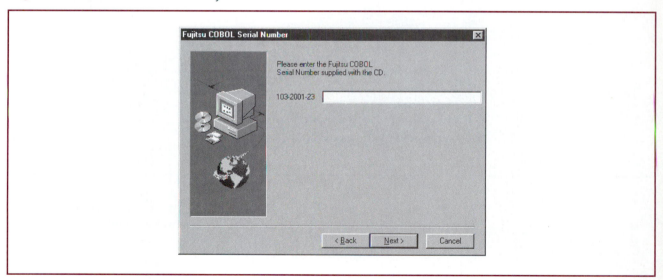

After the system has accepted the serial number, it displays the software license agreement as in Figure A1.4. Read the agreement and then press Yes to continue.

Figure A1.4 Fujitsu Software License Agreement

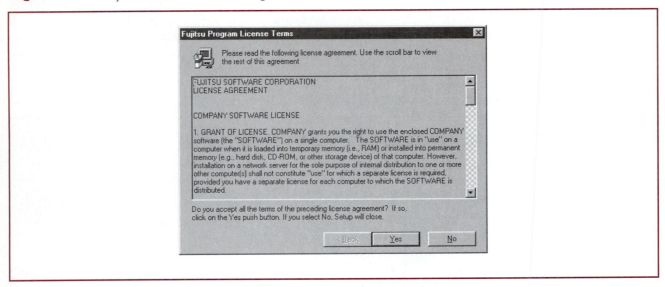

Now the system suggests a location for the files to be stored, as shown in Figure A1.5. You should accept this location, unless there is a good reason to store the data in another folder. If you do change the default folder, make sure that you write it down so you can find it.

Figure A1.5 Choose Destination for Files

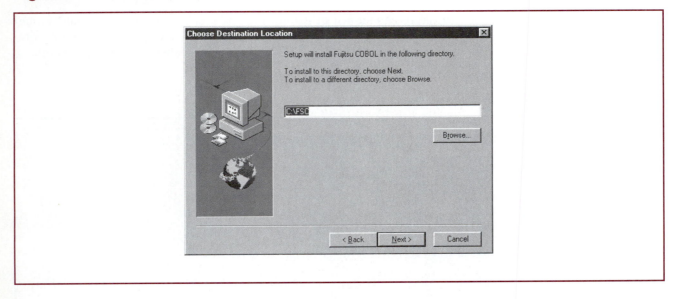

The system then suggests a Program Folder to use for starting COBOL97. Figure A1.6 shows the options. Click on Next to accept the default.

Figure A1.6 Program Folder Selection

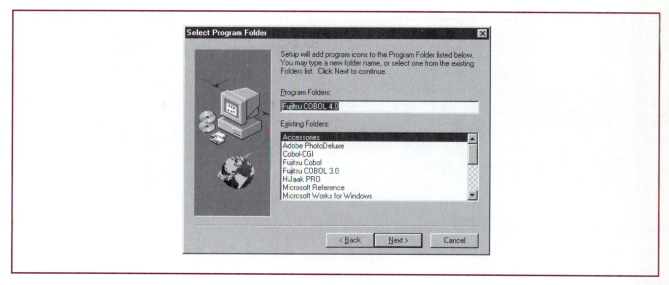

The next window (Figure A1.7) allows you to decide what portions of the product to install. We recommend that you install both options. Be sure that you have enough disk space. Notice also that some of the more advanced tools have a 90-day time limit.

Once you have determined your options, select Next to continue.

Figure A1.7 Installation Options Screen

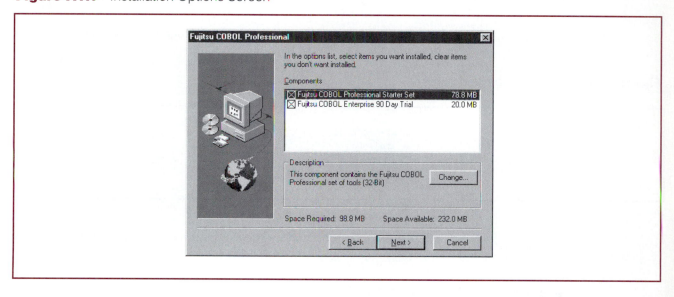

Figure A1.8 Start Copying Files Screen

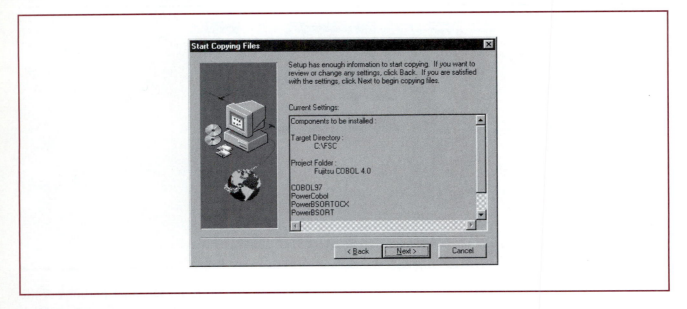

The next window gives you a list of what will be installed. Review the list, as shown in Figure A1.9, for any changes you might want to make. Clicking Back allows you to return to previous screens. Clicking Next starts the actual installation.

Step A.1.4: System Copies Files and Installs Programs

While the system is copying files and installing programs, you will see several screens similar to that in Figure A1.9.

Figure A1.9 Typical Installation Screen

There is nothing for you to do while the system copies files, so it might be a good time to get a cup of coffee or a soft drink.

Step A.1.5: Register with Fujitsu

After installing the programs, the system requests information for registration (Figure A1.10). This material is optional for students. Registration can be done on-line or printed out, depending on your choice.

Figure A1.10 Fujitsu Registration Form

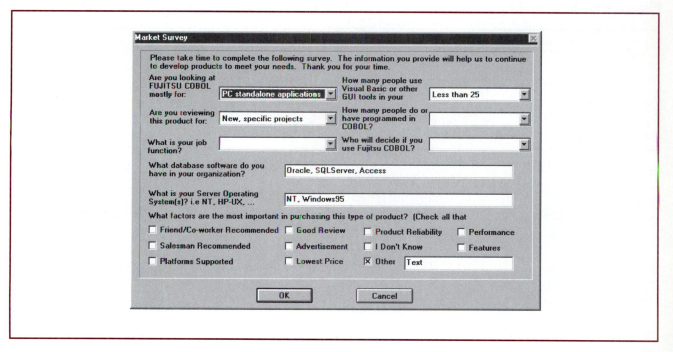

If you choose to register, fill out all of the appropriate fields. The serial number field is automatically filled. Click on OK to register or Cancel to ignore registration.

If you choose to continue with registration, Fujitsu requests some marketing information from you (Figure A1.11). Again, this information is optional. Click *OK* to proceed.

Figure A1.11 Fujitsu Marketing Form

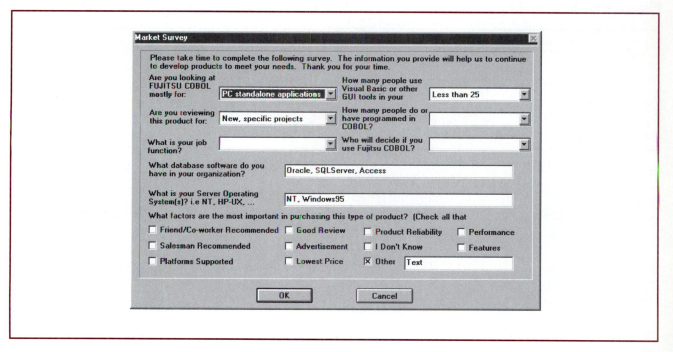

If you continue with registration, the system attempts to connect you first by modem and then by Internet. To save space, we are showing only the first of these screens (Figure A1.12). You can cancel at any point.

Figure A1.12 Select Country for Modem

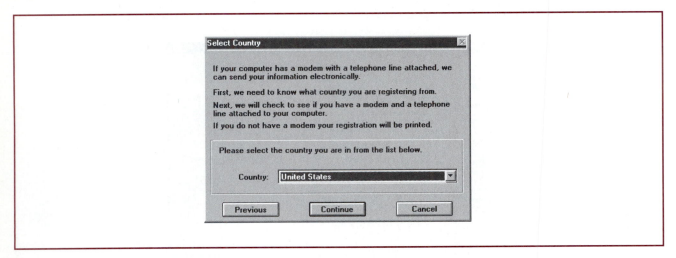

Step A.1.6: Restart the Computer

At this point the installation is complete, but there are two more screens. The first is a warning similar to the one shown in Figure A1.13. The system notifies you that the "AUTOEXEC.BAT" has been changed and that the old file is still available but renamed. You may want to record this information, should you need to go back to the previous configuration.

Figure A1.13 AUTOEXE.BAT Information

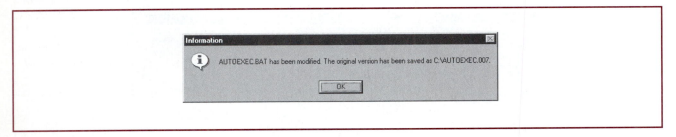

Finally, the system gives you the option to restart the computer (Figure A1.14). Normally you should do so. Click Finish to complete the installation and restart your computer.

Figure A1.14 Restart Computer Dialog Box

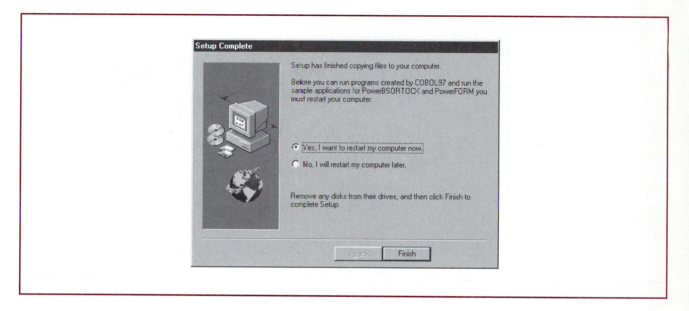

EXERCISE A2:

Downloading Data Files from the World Wide Web

Discussion: In this exercise you will download data files from the Web and have a chance to explore our Web site. You will open a self-extracting Zip file and store the data files on a diskette or in a hard-drive folder of your choice.

We assume that you know how to use a Web browser and are somewhat comfortable in navigating the Web. If not, have someone who is proficient help you with this exercise.

The sample figures were done with Microsoft Explorer. Your browser may give you some slightly different windows and perhaps different messages.

Step A2.1: Find the COBOL Web Site

The first step is to find the COBOL Web site. This site is `http://www.prenhall.com/grauer_cobol/`. (*Note:* There is an (_) between the words "grauer" and "cobol".) If your computer shows the previous URL as a hyperlink and you are connected to the Internet, you can click on the hyperlink and be directly connected to the Web site. Otherwise, log on to the Web and enter the URL, you should arrive at the screen shown in Figure A2.1. At times we may need to change certain aspects of the web site and the data files. Do not be disturbed if the screens do not look exactly the same as shown in this exercise.

Figure A2.1 Welcome Screen for *COBOL: From Micro to Mainframe*

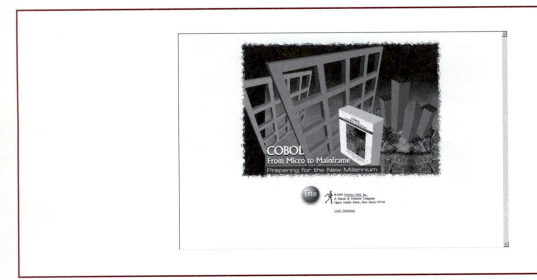

Step A2.2: Explore the Main Content Page

Once you have located the Web site, click on the Enter circle; you will then find the main content page (Figure A2.2). You should explore these options and may want to mark this page as a "Favorite."

Figure A2.2 Main Content Screen of Web Site

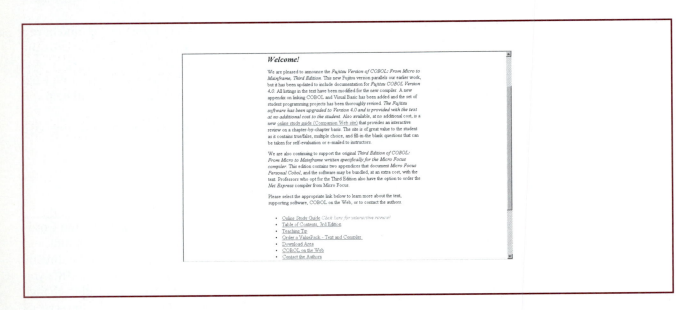

Click on the bulleted item "Download Area" to proceed.

Step A2.3: Download the Data Files

The page shown in Figure A2.3 provides several options.

Figure A2.3 File Download Options

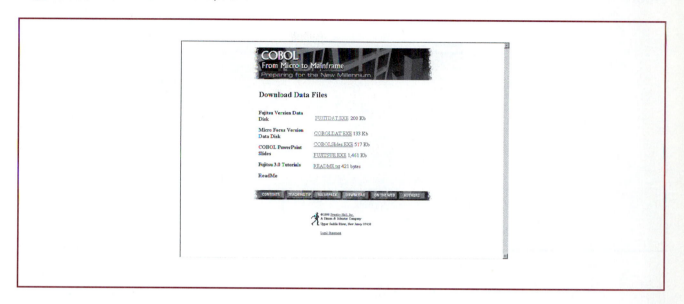

The "Fujitsu Version Data Disk" entry allows you to download the Fujitsu programs and data files to store them on a diskette or hard disk. You will also see an entry for a ReadMe file and Micro Focus programs and files. The ReadMe file gives you our greeting. The Micro Focus programs are used with the Micro Version of the text. Be sure you click on the "'Fujitsu Tutorial' files".

Step A2.4: Process Warning Messages

Depending on the browser you use, you may receive a message similar to that in Figure A2.4. Since the file to be downloaded is self-extracting, you can extract it from our site or just save it on your hard disk and run it later. If your browser does not provide the option, just go ahead and save the file and proceed to Step A2.5. Be sure you know where the file has been stored.

Click on the Open it radio button to have the files directly installed on your disk device. Save it to disk saves the file on to your hard disk, and you can run it later outside of the browser.

Figure A2.4 Download Option Window

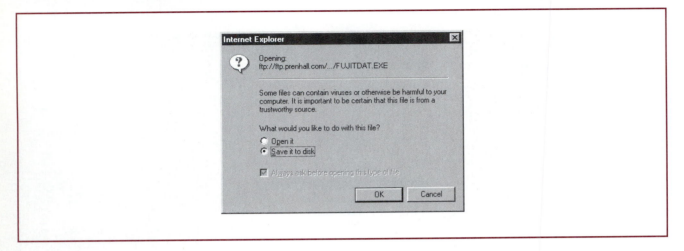

Click on OK to start the process. However, you may also receive the message in Figure A2.5. In this case, you can select Yes to continue the process.

Figure A2.5 Security Warning Message

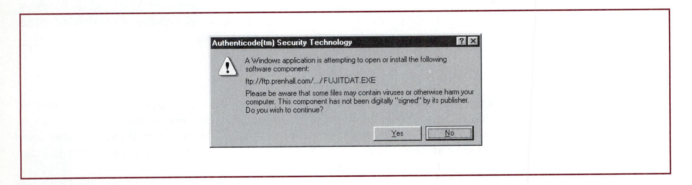

Step A2.5: Run the Self-Extracting File

If you have saved the self-extracting file, you need to open the folder where it was saved. Click on the icon to start the process.

The next window is our thank you message. (Figure A2.6) The default location for the restored files is "A:\"—the diskette drive. Click *OK* to proceed. To save time and space we have compressed all of the files into a Zip format. This file contains the compressed data files and programs along with a program to uncompress them.

Figure A2.6 Thank You Message Window

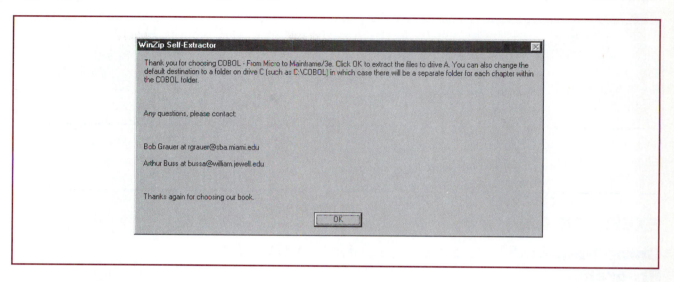

In the next window, click on Unzip to store the restored files on your machine (Figure A2.7). If you chose to store the data files on a diskette, be sure that you have an empty, formatted diskette in your diskette drive.

Figure A2.7 Unzip to Folder

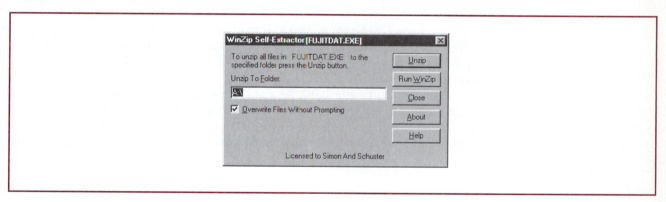

When the self-extracting program has completed its work, you should see the window in Figure A2.8.

Figure A2.8 Completion

EXERCISE A3:
Compiling, Linking, and Executing a COBOL Program

Discussion: This exercise shows the compilation, linking, and execution process using Fujitsu COBOL97 tools. The process is quite similar to the one employed on mainframe computers but allows the use of a Windows environment on a personal computer.

COBOL97 uses a program project approach like that of several other programming languages. The approach makes it possible to compile an entire system all at once. Most of your work with this text will not fully utilize this capability. However, as you gain experience, you will find that COBOL97's project management is a powerful tool and makes COBOL97 a valuable resource. Exercise A7 gives an example of how to build a small system.

COBOL97 makes the compile-and-link process easy for the programmer but also maintains a great deal of flexibility. It also allows the creation of fully executable files. In addition, the Fujitsu approach allows the user to define the input and output files at execution time rather than having to hard-code them in the program.

Figure A3.1 Starting Fujitsu COBOL 4.0

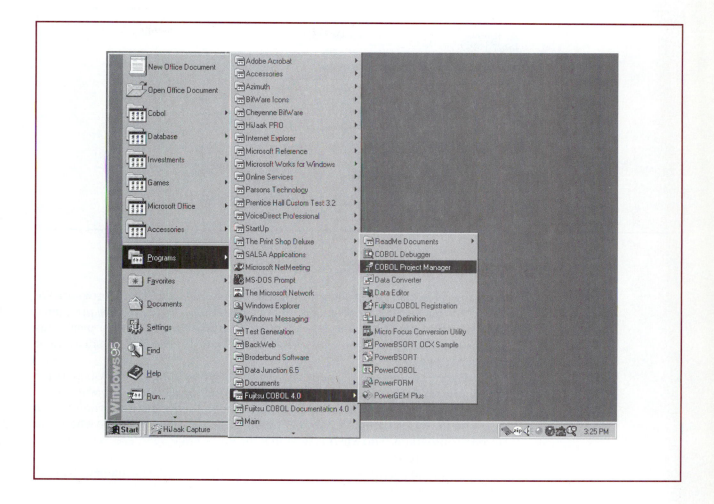

Step A3.1: Start Project Manager

All of the work in the COBOL97 is done in the Project Manager. Open COBOL Project Manager by using the Start Menu. You can begin the program from the Start Menu in the section called Fujitsu COBOL 4.0. Figure A3.1 shows how the Start Menu might look.

Once the Project Manager is opened, it presents a blank window with menus and a tool bar. The File menu (Figure A3.2), allows the user to open a previously developed project or to create a new one. For this exercise we will use an already created project.

Figure A3.2 Project Manager Main Window with File Menu

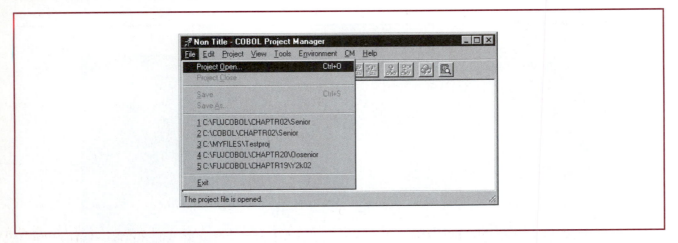

Step A3.2: Create or Retrieve a Source File

Normally you would have to create the project containing the COBOL program. We have made life easier by including all of the illustrative COBOL projects, programs, and associated data files in a self-extracting file available on our Web page. This discussion assumes that you have already downloaded those files to a diskette or your hard drive.

Clicking on the Project Open entry in the File menu brings up the Open dialog box (Figure A3.3). This dialog box resembles the Windows Explorer. You will have to specify to the dialog box the exact folder containing the project you want. In this case, find the folder named "Chaptr02" on the diskette or the hard drive where you stored the programs. You will find later that the Project Manager retains memory of the last-used directory.

You should see a listing of projects in Chaptr02. Select the file named "Senior" and click the *Open* button.

Figure A3.3 Open Dialog Box

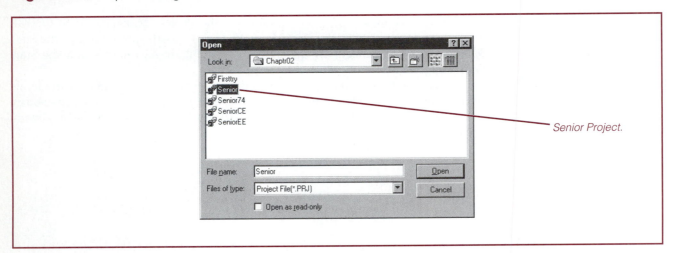

Senior Project.

Step A3.3: Expand the Project Definition

Figure A3.4 Reduced Project Configuration

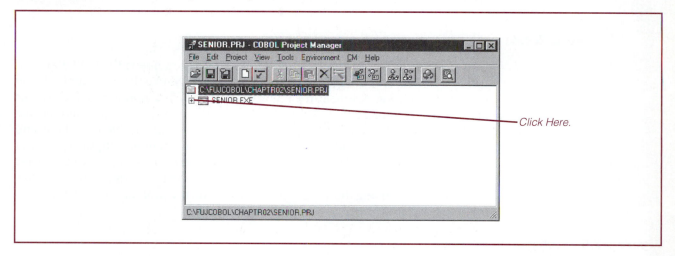

Click Here.

Selecting a project brings it into the Project Manager window. Figure A3.4 shows how SENIOR includes the name of the project and the name of the executable file. Here, the filename is SENIOR.EXE. The executable file does not actually exist at this point, but you will soon create it. To the left of the file name is a "plus" sign. This sign means that there are items hidden from view. Click on the plus sign and continue doing so until you see the configuration in Figure A3.5.

Figure A3.5 Expanded Project Configuration

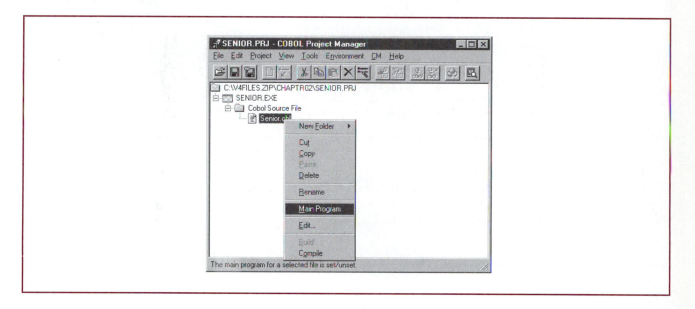

Highlight the item called SENIOR.CBL by clicking on it. This item is the source program for your project. When you first start the project, the icon will be white. Right-click on the program name and select Main Program from the menu, as shown in Figure A3.5. (You can accomplish the same thing by using <Ctrl-M> on the keyboard or selecting the Project menu, the Option entry and then Main.) What you are doing is telling Project Manager that this is the starting program of your project. When many programs are in a project, this step is particularly important. Even in a one-program project, however, the step is required. Once you have established the main program, the icon turns red.

Step A3.4: View the Program Source Listing

Double-click on the filename SENIOR.CBL. This action opens the COBOL Editor window and shows the source file as in Figure A3.6. Notice the line numbering at the left of the listing. Normally the Editor maintains the line numbers in increments of 10. However, for consistency with the text presentation, we have altered the numbering to increments of 1. Therefore, the first line is line 1, the second is 2, and so forth. Notice lines 8 and 10. These lines identify the program's input and output devices. SYSIN and SYSOUT are symbolic names for the devices and more specifically the files that are used when the program runs. These symbolic device names allow you to delay specifying the actual files until you run the program. You will see how this works later.

Figure A3.6 Source Listing in Editor

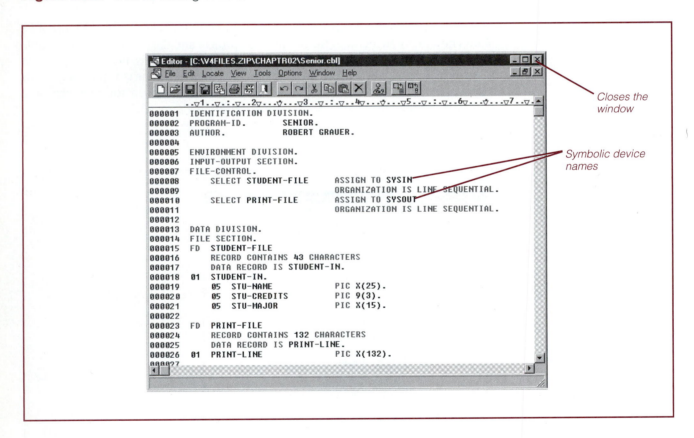

You may want to look through the program, but you should not make any changes at this point. Once you are through, return to the Project Manager window by clicking the Close Window (X) on the Editor title bar.

Step A3.5: Build the Project

The next part is easy and there are several ways to do it. In the Project Manager window, click on the SENIOR.PRJ filename to highlight it. Then, click on the Rebuild Project button shown in Figure A3.7. The project manager proceeds to compile and link the program and create SENIOR.EXE.

Figure A3.7 Building a Project

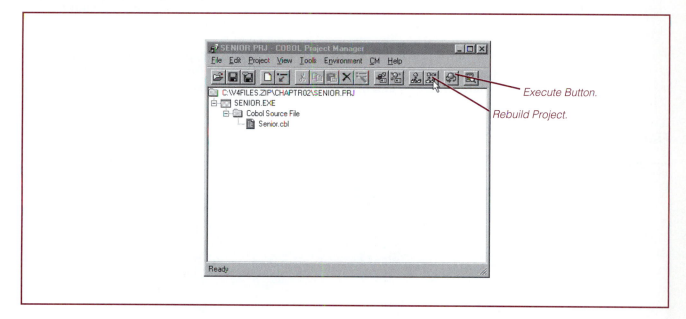

The Project Manager reports on its progress in a make-file window. The make file contains information about project. Figure A3.8 shows the results of a successful build.

Figure A3.8 A Successful Project Build

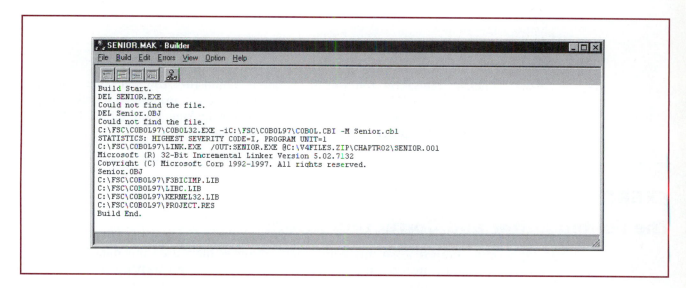

Step A3.6:   Run the Project

All that is left at this point is to run the project. You accomplish this by highlighting either the Project File or the EXE file and clicking on the Execute button. You can find that button in Figure A3.7.

Before the Program Manager can actually run the program, it needs to know where the input file is and where the output should go. To do this, the Project Manager brings up the Run-time Environment Setup window shown in Figure A3.9.

Normally, you would have to create the input file, but we have already created it for you in a file called Senior.Dat. Do you remember the items SYSIN and SYSOUT in Figure A3.6? Now you have the chance to specify the actual files used by the program. Look at the List text box. We have already specified the input and output files for you. SYSIN is replaced by Senior.Txt as the input file, and all output will go to Print.Txt. You can override these files by typing in new assignments. Refer to Exercise A6 to see how this can be done.

Figure A3.9   Run-time Environment Setup Window

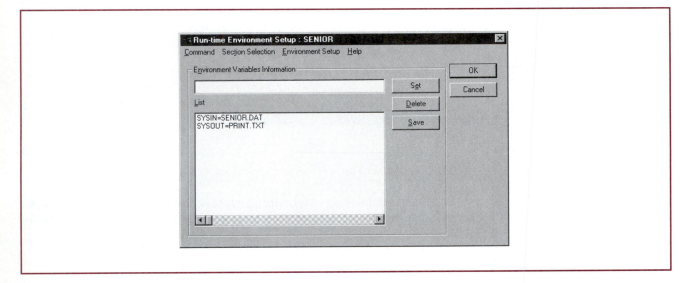

Step A3.7:   Click on OK

Click on the OK button and the program should run. You will not receive any notification that the program has completed. You can use the Windows NotePad program to check the results of the program by looking at the PRINT.TXT file in Chaptr02. The program will have created this file for you.

EXERCISE A4:

The Fujitsu Editor and Correcting Errors

Discussion: To this point, these exercises have used our data-file COBOL programs, but eventually you will have to create your own programs. COBOL programs can be developed in a variety of ways. You can use Notepad or any other editor with which you are familiar. You can also use a word processor (e.g., Microsoft Word or Word Perfect), provided you save the file as an ASCII or text file. Alternatively, you can use the Editor in the Project Manager.

Editor is very powerful, but there is no need to learn all of its features to use it effectively. Indeed, you can probably use it immediately, applying the experience you have had with other editors—for example, you probably know how to use insertion and replacement. The on-line help facility can help you to master the more sophisticated commands and gain proficiency.

The steps that follow show how to initiate the editor, how to find and correct compilation errors, how to make changes easily, and how to save the edited program. Finally, the exercise suggests a change you might wish to make in the standard configuration.

Step A4.1:   Build a Project Containing Errors

Following the procedure in Exercise 3, build the project called SENIORCE in the Chaptr02 data files directory. Be sure to set SENIORCE.CBL as the Main program. Refer to Exercise 3, Step 3, if you are unsure about doing this.

SENIORCE.CBL contains intentionally inserted syntax errors.

Step A4.2:   Interpreting the Build Process

After the Project Manager has attempted to build the project, you should see the Make File window (Figure A4.1). The error messages are highlighted in red. You can use these messages to identify syntax errors and to move directly to the error in the source code. You may want to expand the window to see the entire message.

Figure A4.1 Make File Window with Errors

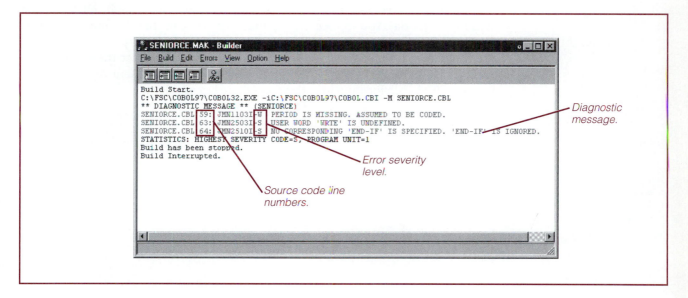

Since there are errors in the source code, the Project Manager is unable to complete the Build process. The last two messages indicate that the Build was unsuccessful.

Step A4.3: Correcting Errors by Moving between the Messages and Source Code

The Project Manager provides an easy way to make source-code corrections by moving between the listing and the source code. While there are several ways to make the move, the simplest is to double-click on an error message. This action opens the source-code Editor and positions the cursor on the line where the problem occurs. (You may get a warning message about renumbering. If so, reply Yes.)

Figure A4.2 Windows Task Bar Menu

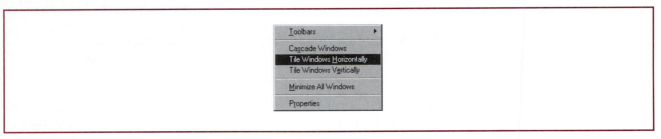

When the Project Manager opens the Editor window, the Builder window is not closed. Therefore, both windows are available for access. You can use a Windows trick to make movement between these two windows easy. "Right click" on the Windows Task Bar. You will see a menu that allows you to "tile" the open windows. Figure A4.2 shows the Windows Task Bar Menu.

Figure A4.3 shows the two windows tiled horizontally. Once the windows are tiled, you can simply click on either window to move between them. At that point, it is easy to find each location in code where there is a problem.

Figure A4.3 Windows Tiled for Error Correction

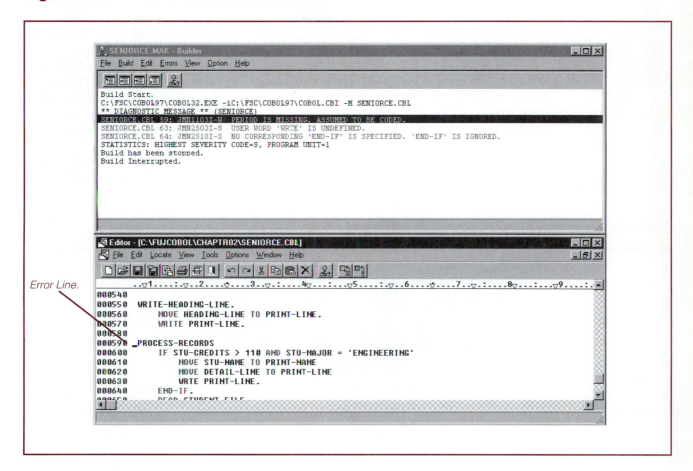

Error Line.

At the top of the Builder window are four icons. These icons are useful when the program has a long list of syntax errors. Clicking one or another of the icons allows you to move to the first, last, previous, or next error in the list.

Step A4.4: Correct the Errors

Using the technique described in Step 4.3 make the following corrections:

- Place a period after PROCESS-RECORDS
- Change WRTE to WRITE
- Delete the period at the end of line 63.

The last error message given is somewhat misleading. The message should probably read: "NO CORRESPONDING 'IF' IS SPECIFIED. 'END-IF' IS IGNORED".

Rebuild the project. There should be no further errors associated with the program. Do not attempt to run the program at this point. This program is included to show how to correct errors.

Step A4.5: Adjusting the Editor Defaults

You may have noted tab-setting differences between the examples and the results on your computer. These differences reflect some changes we have made in the configuration of the compiler. You may want to consider the same changes.

In English-speaking countries, most COBOL programs are coded between columns 8 and 72 with tabbing occurring at intervals of 4 columns. One would expect the tab settings for a COBOL editor to be at 8, 12, 16, etc. The Fujitsu Editor was evidently developed for use with the Japanese language. Japanese characters each take the equivalent of two columns of data. Thus, the default tab settings start at 9 and are incremented in units of 8 columns.

Unfortunately, in this version of the Editor, the first tab mark cannot be changed from column 9, but it is possible to adjust the number of spaces between tabs.

Figure A4.4 Select Editor Setup Environment

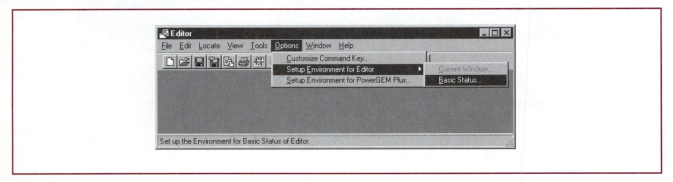

Open the Editor from the Project Manager by clicking Editor in the Tools menu. From the Editor Options menu, select *Environment for Editor* and then *Basic Status.* Figure A4.4 shows the menus needed.

You should now see the Setup Environment for Editor dialog box as in Figure A4.5. Leave most of the parameters alone. However, you can change the Tab Interval to 4.

Click on *OK* to make the change.

Figure A4.5 Setup Basic Status Window

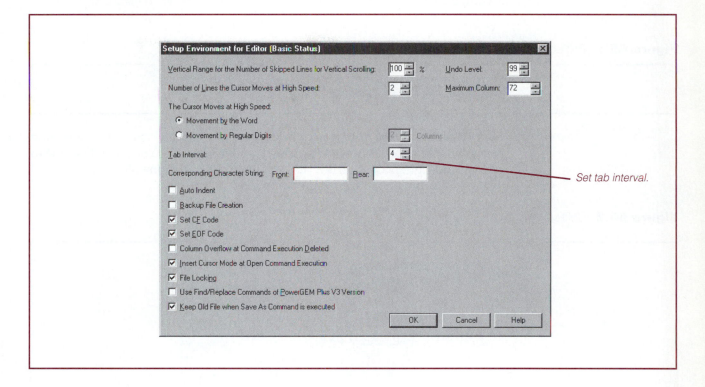

EXERCISE A5:

Debugging Programs using the Project Manager

Discussion: In this exercise we introduce you to the Fujitsu interactive debugging feature of the Project Manager. You will go through the steps to compile and link a project but this time will prepare the load module for debugging. You will see several features of the debugger, including animation, stepping, watch windows, and breakpoints.

The debugger is a powerful tool, and mastering its commands and features will take you a while. This brief introduction should get you started

Step A5.1: Load the Project

In order to use the debugger you must prepare the project for debugging. Follow the process in Exercise 3 to build a project, but this time use TUITION5.PRJ in folder Chaptr05.

When you have loaded the project, make sure the TUITION5.CBL is set as the MAIN program.

Step A5.2: Add the TEST Compiler Option

Now you need to add a compiler option that allows the debugger to work. There are several steps to this process, and they are all important. Be sure that you follow carefully.

The first step is to open the Compiler Options dialog box. This step is accomplished by clicking the Compile Option button shown in Figure A5.1.

Figure A5.1 Project Manager Buttons

—Debug.

—Compile Options.

When the dialog box opens, click on the Add button. This opens a second dialog box called Add Compiler Options. Type the letter "T". You should be able to see the TEST option. Click on the TEST option to select it. Figure A5.2 shows the two dialog windows with the TEST option selected.

Figure A5.2 Selecting the TEST Compiler Option

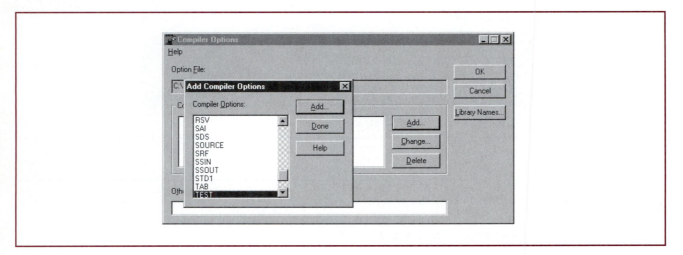

Once TEST has been selected, click on Add. Before actually adding the Compiler Option, some additional information is required, so you will see another dialog box. This box verifies that you want to add the TEST option and allows you to specify where the debugging data should be stored. Click on the radio button called "Generate WINSVD DEBUG information." Click on the Browse button before clicking on OK or pressing the Enter key. A Folder window opens. This window should point to the Chaptr05 folder. Click OK to accept this folder for storing the debugging information. Chaptr05 is probably the best option, but the data can be stored anywhere. For example, if you are compiling from a diskette, you might want to consider storing the debugging information on the hard disk. Figure A5.3 shows the completed Test Compiler Option dialog box.

Figure A5.3 Completed Test Compiler Option Dialog

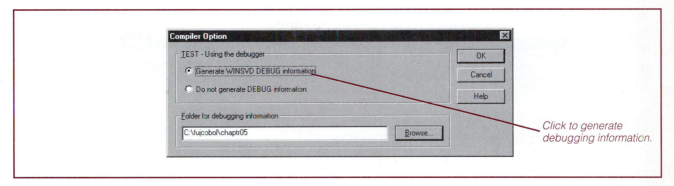

Click to generate debugging information.

Click on OK and then Done to return to the Compiler Option dialog box, which should now look like Figure A5.4. Click on OK to return to the Project Manager.

Figure A5.4 Compiler Options Ready for Debugging

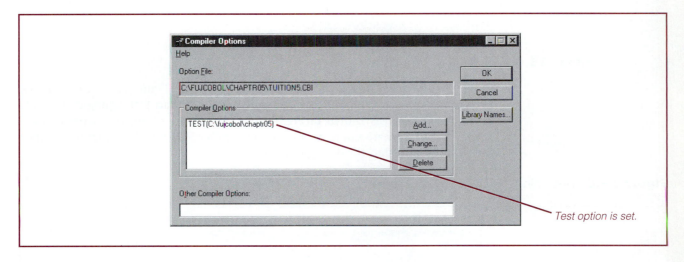

Test option is set.

Step A5.3: Build the Project

After setting the compiler options, you are ready to build the project. You can click the build or rebuild button. The Builder window appears as in Figure A5.5. You might note that the Link step has some additional statements including "/DEBUG / DEBUGTYPE:COFF". The builder is telling you that additional subprograms are being added to your program. These subprograms manage the debugging process. Because you have specified the TEST option for the compiler, the builder also changes the Link options.

Figure A5.5 Building a Project for Debugging

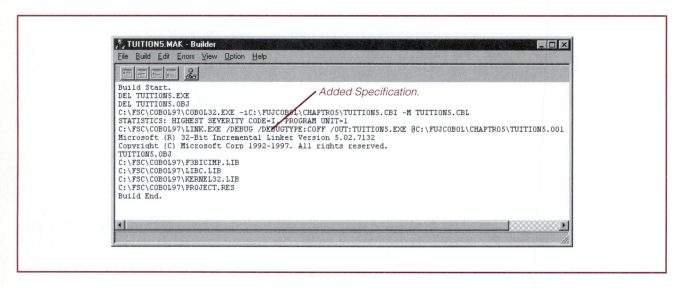

Step A5.4: Start the Debugger

From the Project Manager, select the Debug button (Figure A5.1) to open the debugger. The Debugger window opens along with a Start Debugging dialog box. This configuration is shown in Figure A5.6. A number of advanced options are available, but they are not necessary to perform basic debugging operations. Click the OK button to start the debugging process.

Figure A5.6 Beginning the Debugging Process

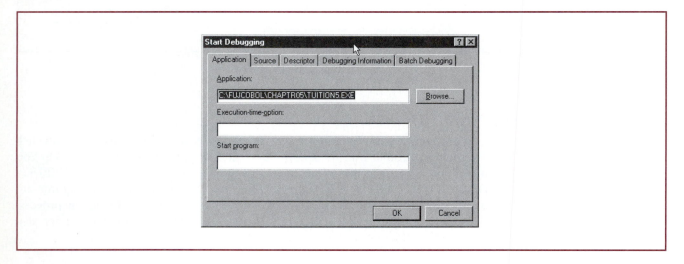

Step A5.5:   Begin Debugging

After going through the Environment Setup window, the Debugger window now displays the source listing with the first executable statement highlighted. The program is ready to run, as shown in Figure A5.7.

Figure A5.7   Program in Debug Mode

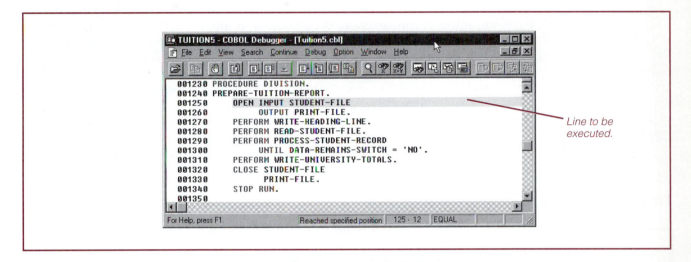

Line to be executed.

Before running the program, take some time to explore the icons across the tool bar. Simply move the mouse across the icons without clicking and allow the icon to tell you what it does. Be patient; the icon names may take a few seconds to appear. Figure A5.8 shows the tool bar.

Figure A5.8   Debugger Toolbar

Note particularly the following buttons:
- Set/Delete Breakpoint
- Re-debug
- Go
- Animate
- Break
- Step into
- Data
- Watch-data

Step A5.6:   Test the Buttons

Click on the Animate Button of the Tool Bar to watch the program step through the process slowly. This allows you to view the operation of program in "slow motion." Often logic errors can be spotted this way. You may want to click on Break to stop the program from running.

When the execution has been stopped, you can click on Animate again or on GO. GO runs the program at full speed until it stops.

Another option is to use Step into. This button executes the program one step at a time. You have to click on the button each time to execute a step.

You may find that you want to start the program all over again without running to the conclusion. The Re-debug button does this for you.

In some cases, there is a problem in a certain area of code and you do not want to wait for Animate to reach that point. You would rather have the program run directly to the problem area of code and stop. You could then use Animate or Step into to see what is wrong. The Set/Delete Breakpoint button is what you need. Find a line of code just before the problem area and click this button.

The line is highlighted to show that it is a breakpoint. You can then start the program and use Go to run the program; it will stop at the breakpoint.

So far, all you have seen is how to move around in the program. Often it is not enough just to see the flow of the logic. You also may want to see what is happening to the data.

The Data button allows you to place the cursor on a data item and see what is in that field. Figure A5.9 shows the value of IND-BILL.

Figure A5.9 Using the Data Button

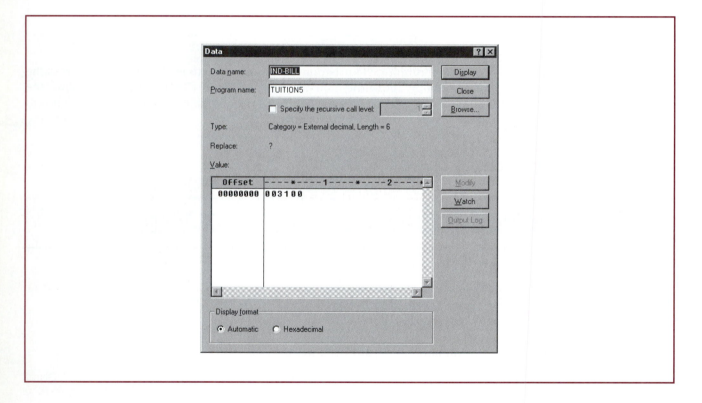

At times, you may want to see how the data is changing as the program progresses. The Watch Data button allows you monitor the data. You have to choose the particular items that you want to watch. The debugger then creates a window that shows the current value of the data as the program runs.

As before, place the cursor on the data item you want to watch. Click on Watch Data. This opens the Watch Data dialog box (Figure A5.10).

Figure A5.10 Watch Data Window

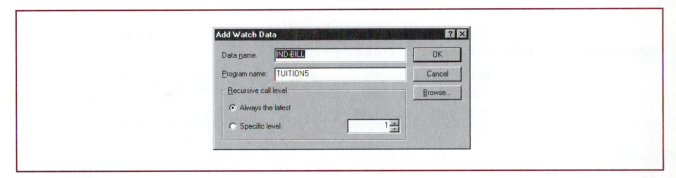

Click on OK to add the data name to the list of watched data.

Click on Cancel to exit the box. The Debugger creates a new window with the value of the data item. From the Windows menu, you can have the Debugger tile the windows horizontally or vertically. You can rearrange the windows any way you wish. Figure A5.11 shows the source window and the watch window tiled horizontally.

Figure A5.11 Windows Tiled Horizontally

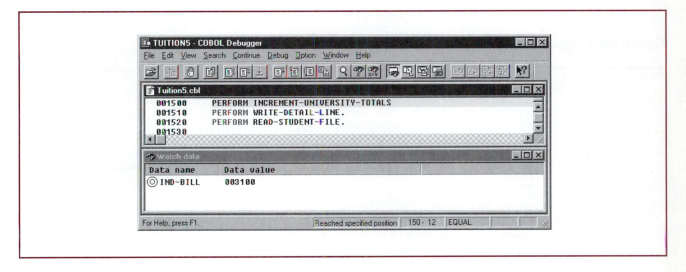

Step A5.7: Conclusion

This exercise has introduced the capabilities of the interactive debugger. You should read the Help messages supplied on-line and the Fujitsu COBOL Debugging Guide on the CD for more information on debugging techniques.

EXERCISE A6:

Using Environmental Variables to Specify Files

Discussion: In this exercise you will see how you can customize the input and output files used by a program at Execution time. This capability means that you do not have to specify a particular file name in a program as you are writing it; you can use a file identifier as an alias. Only when you run the program do you have to give the actual file name.

IBM mainframe programs use a similar process. One purpose of the Job Control Language (JCL) is to specify the run-time file names. The Program Manager does not use JCL but can accomplish the same result using environmental variables.

In previous exercises an Environmental Variables window appeared, but you simply clicked on OK and continued. In this exercise you will learn how to use that window.

Step A6.1: Enter File Identifiers into the Program

In order to use environmental variables, the program needs to make use of file descriptors. File descriptors are special variable names used only with the ASSIGN clause. Use the Project Manager to open Senior.Cbl in Chaptr02. Review the ASSIGN statements used in the program, as shown in Figure A6.1.

Figure A6.1 Senior Program Showing File Descriptors

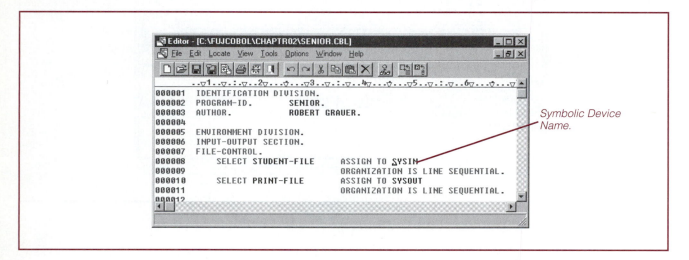

Notice the names SYSIN and SYSOUT. These names are called Symbolic Devices. In other words, they are names that stand for an actual device. If we were to follow the IBM mainframe convention used with JCL, we would have used UT-S-SYSIN and UT-S-SYSOUT. The "UT-S-" portion is not needed by the Fujitsu compiler; therefore, we have omitted it. SYSIN is the file descriptor for the input file, and SYSOUT is for the print file.

When you direct print files to the file descriptor as in the program, the output goes to a file, and you will have to print the information using some other program such as Notepad. If you want the COBOL program to print the file directly, you should specify PRINTER instead of SYSOUT or some other file descriptor. Printer is a COBOL reserved word for directing output to the system printer. The Environmental Variables window will allow you to specify a particular printer if you have access to network printers.

Step A6.2: Compile and Link the Program

Following the steps in Exercise 3, compile and link the program as usual. Make sure that the program is set as MAIN. The program does not have to be compiled and linked in test mode.

Now you are ready to execute the program.

Step A6.3: Set Environmental Variables

The window shown in Figure A6.2 is the Runtime Environment Setup window. This window allows you to specify the actual files used by the program just before it runs. You can also set other environmental variables. For example, you can specify the printer used by the program. A number of other environmental variables can be set, but they are beyond the scope of this exercise.

Figure A6.2 Run-time Environment Setup Window

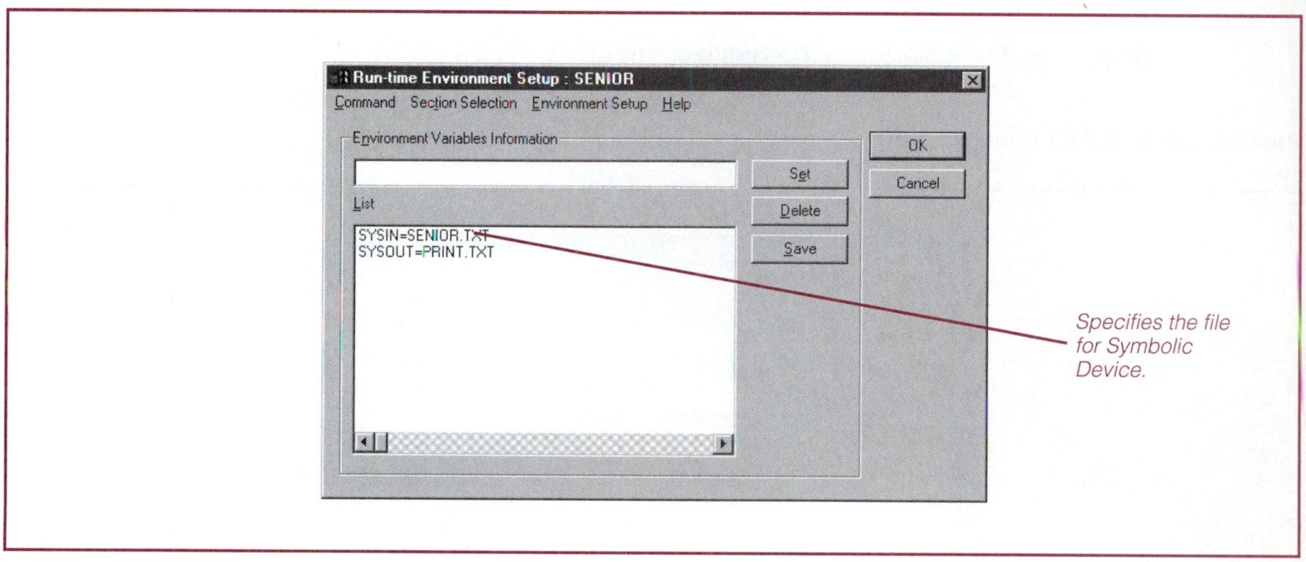

We have already given you some default files. If you wanted to use other files with the program, you could easily override these file names. Just remember that the data in the input files must be in the correct format.

To change the file names or to enter a new file name for a program you have written, simply type the program file descriptor and the file name in the Environmental Variables Information box.

As a test, change the output file name. In the Environmental Variables Information box, type SYSOUT=MYPRINT.TXT. Click on the Set button; the variable in the List box is changed as in Figure A6.3.

Figure A6.3 SYSOUT Directed to New File

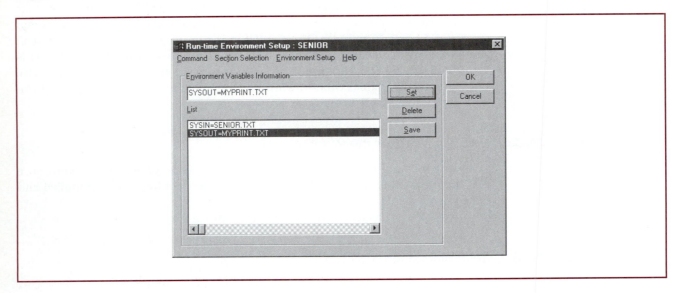

You can save the variable if you choose. If you do not, you will have to reenter it each time you execute the program. If the file name should change, you can change its name at any time.

Click *OK* to run the program as before. This time it will create a file called MYPRINT.TXT. Everything else should be the same. If you receive any error messages, make sure you have spelled environmental variable correctly.

Step A6.4: Changing the System Printer

Figure A6.4 Select Printer Dialog Box

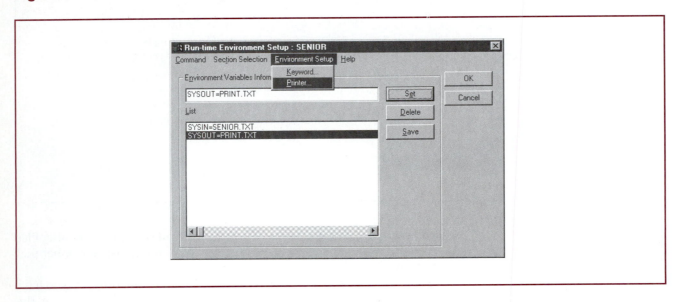

If you have used the PRINTER option in the ASSIGN portion of the program, you can specify the specific printer you want to use. From the Environment Setup menu select the Printer option, then choose the appropriate printer from the available list in the Select Printer dialog box shown in Figure A6.4. If you do not select a specific printer, the Project Manager will assume the Default Printer.

When you do select a printer, Project Manager gives you the option of using a dialog box with a drop-down list as shown in Figure A6.5.

Figure A6.5 Drop-Down Listing of Printers

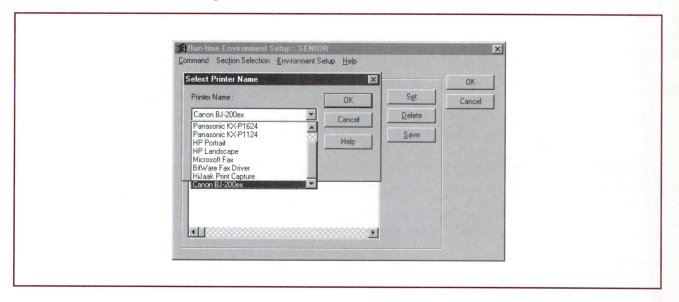

EXERCISE A7:

Building Projects with Multiple Programs

Discussion: This exercise shows you some of the real power of the Project Manager. The Project Manager is designed not just to compile and run one program at a time but to manage a number of integrated programs that constitute a system. This concept may seem a little strange, but you can pursue the topic in Chapter 16, where a number of programs are working together to provide an interactive check on your fitness.

In this exercise you will build a much smaller project, one that just uses two programs working together to accomplish a task. You will see most of the concepts that can be applied to projects that are more extensive.

Step A7.1: Create a New Project

In this exercise you will create a new project. Follow the process in Exercise 3 to start up Project Manager and open a project. This time select the folder AppndxA as shown in Figure A7.1. You should not see any project files. Therefore, you will need to create one. Type "TwoProg" into the File Name text box and click on *Open*.

Figure A7.1 Open Project File Dialog Box

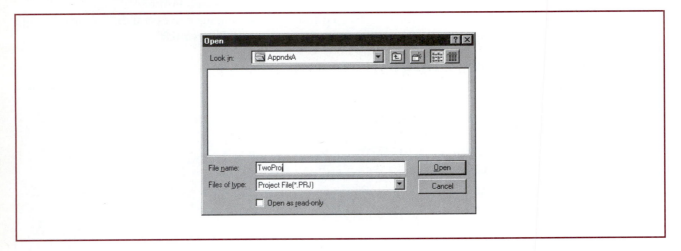

Since TwoProg.Prj does not exist, the Project Manager checks to make sure that this is what you want to do. Figure A7.2 shows the confirmation message box. When this box appears, click on *Yes.*

Figure A7.2 Confirmation Message Box

Step A7.2: Add an EXE File to the Project

Figure A7.3 Project Manager Window with Project File

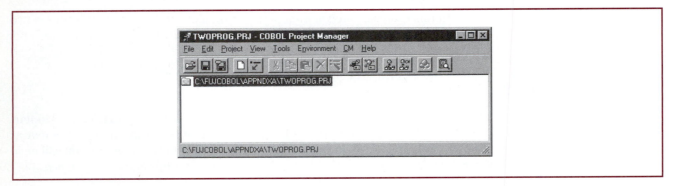

Figure A7.3 shows the Project File loaded into the Project Manager window. This is the only file that is loaded. Now you need to add the other components to the project. The first step is to create an EXE file to hold the compiled and linked project.

Figure A7.4 Add New EXE File

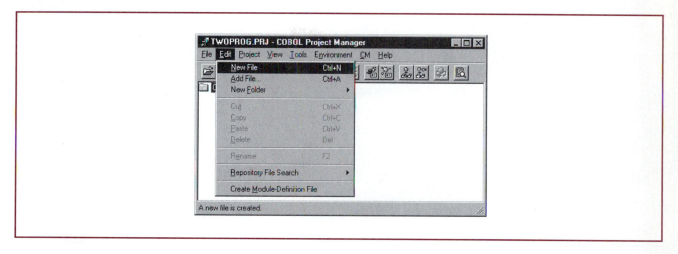

Open the Edit menu and select New File as shown in Figure A7.4. The Project Manager then creates an EXE file and enters it into the project. Figure A7.5 shows the new EXE file. Rename the file TwoProg.EXE.

Figure A7.5 Project Manager Window with EXE file.

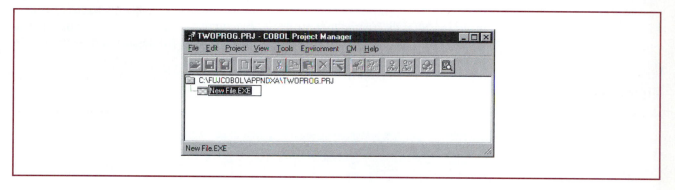

Step A7.3: Add COBOL Source File Folder

The next step is to create the COBOL Source File folder. The folder needs to be associated with the EXE file. Make sure that the TwoProg.EXE file is highlighted. From the Edit menu select New Folder and then COBOL Source File. Figure A7.6 shows this process.

Figure A7.6 Create COBOL Source File Folder

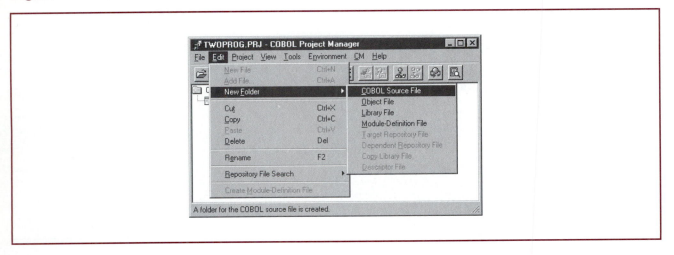

Step A7.4: Add the Source Files and Select Main Program

Now the project needs some COBOL programs. In most cases you would have to code the programs yourself, and you would want to select New File from the Edit menu or click on the New File button. For this exercise you will only have to bring in programs already created for you. Thus, instead of the New File button, you can use the Add File button. Figure A7.7 displays the Project Manager window with both buttons shown.

Figure A7.7 New File and Add File Buttons in Project Manager

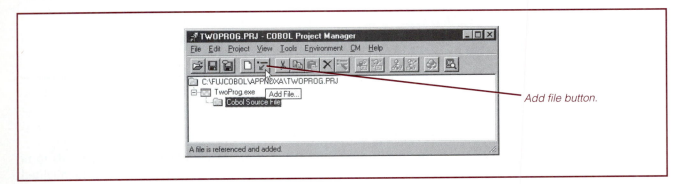

Add file button.

The Add File button or the Add File option in the Edit menu brings up a Browse window. Use the Browse window to look in the Folder ApndixB. There should be two files available-Senior.cbl and Stureq.cbl. Figure A7.8 shows the files. Select and open each file into the COBOL Source File folder.

Figure A7.8 Browse Window with COBOL Source Files

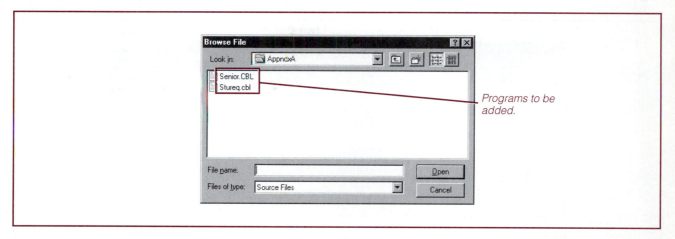

Programs to be added.

Right-click on Senior.cbl and then select Main Program to designate this program as the starting point. The Project Manager always needs to know the starting point for a project. The reason becomes more obvious when there are several programs in a project. Figure A7.9 shows how Senior.cbl is selected as the Main Program.

Figure A7.9 Selecting the Main Program

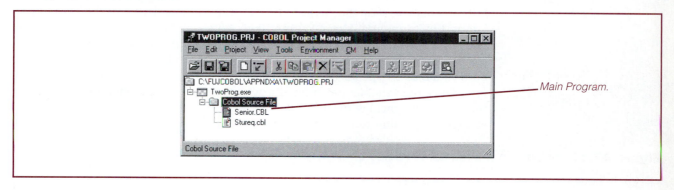

Main Program.

Step A7.5: Build the Project

Following the procedures in Exercise 3, build the project. Figure A7.10 shows the Builder window. You may want to compare the entries to those of single-program projects.

Figure A7.10 Building the Project

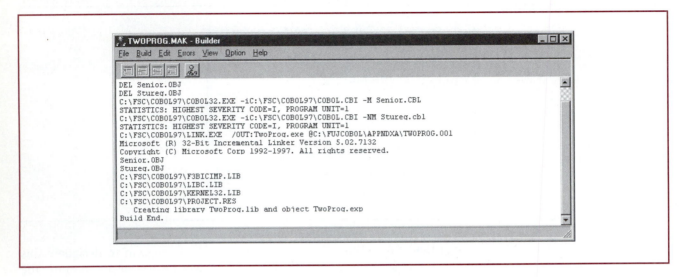

Step A7.6: Run the Project and Set the Environmental Variables

You are now ready to run the project. Start the process by clicking on the *Run* button. This brings up the Environmental Setup window. This time, however, there are no Environmental Variables specified. Figure A7.11 shows the variables that need to be entered. Carefully type each variable into the top text box and click on the *Set* button to enter them into the List box. Do not click on *OK* or hit *Enter* until both variables are specified.

Once the variables are entered, you may want to save them for future runs of the system by clicking on the *Save* button. Then you do not have to type in the variables each time you run the program.

Figure A7.11 Setting Environmental Variables

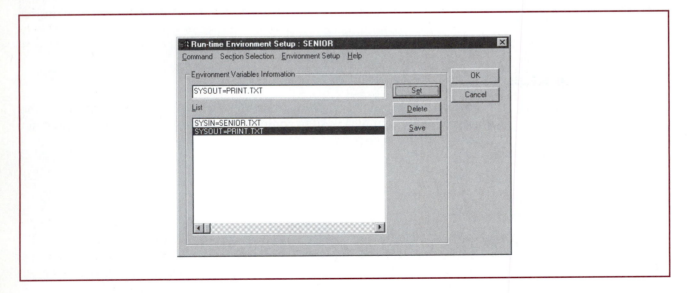

If you make a mistake in typing the variables, you can just retype them and reset them. If you have somehow added too many variables, you can always delete the extra ones by highlighting them and clicking the *Delete* button.

When the variables are correct, click on *OK* to start the program. The program brings up a screen as shown in Figure A7.12. Enter the values shown in the screen. The program executes and places the results in a file called Print.Txt. You can find this file in the AppndxA folder.

Figure A7.12 Entering Values

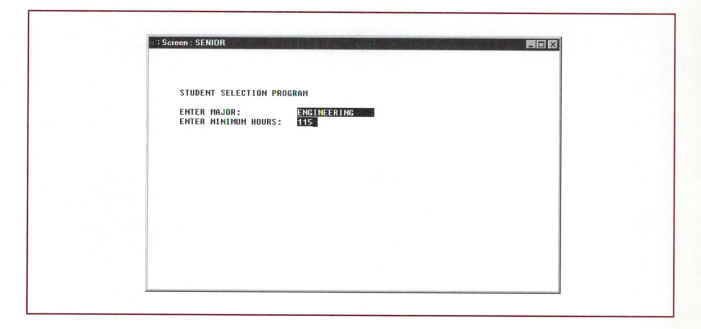

Step A7.7: Conclusion

This exercise shows how you can build your own project and how more than one program can be used in a project. In order to understand how these programs actually work together, you will need to look at Chapters 10 and 16 for further information.

EXERCISE A8:

COBOL97 File Utility

Discussion: The Fujitsu COBOL97 system provides a way to convert and edit data files without having to write COBOL programs just for that purpose. The File Utility program allows the conversion of text files to sequential, relative, or indexed data files. In addition, any one of these data file types may be converted to another. Once a data file is created, it can be edited, added to, or just browsed.

You need to understand something about file types to be able to use the File Utility effectively. For example, it is possible to create data files in an editor like Notepad. These files are often called text files or ASCII files. In COBOL terminology, such files are called *line-sequential* files. Most of the data files included with the data disk download are line sequential. COBOL can read these files but the programmer must tell COBOL to expect them by using the ORGANIZATION IS LINE SEQUENTIAL clause in the SELECT ... ASSIGN statements.

Mainframe programs generally use a different type of sequential file—record-sequential. COBOL uses this file as its default file organization. PC COBOL programs can also process record-sequential files. The problem is that it is difficult to create record-sequential files without writing special programs. This is where the File Utility comes in. This utility can convert line-sequential files to record-sequential files. Perhaps of even more importance, you can also convert record-sequential files into relative or indexed files. A full discussion of these advanced file types is beyond the scope of this exercise, but you can read about indexed files in Chapter 18 of the text.

In this exercise you will learn how to convert a line-sequential file to a record-sequential file and then to create an indexed file from that file. You will also create an indexed file with an alternate index.

Before you start, you need to know about one other file concept—fixed-length records vs. variable-length records. In a file with fixed-length records, all records have exactly the same length. In a variable-length file, each record can be of a different length, but no record should exceed a maximum size. Line-sequential files are usually considered variable-length records. Record-sequential files generally are fixed-length records, although they can be variable as well. The important point is that you need to know the maximum record length of files, regardless of type, in order to use the File Utility.

Step A8.1: Start the File Utility Program

Begin the Project Manager and from the Tools menu select File Utility. This action brings up the File Utility Screen (Figure A8.1). There are only three options:

- Exit—Quit the Program
- Commands—List of operations that can be performed.
- Help—Help for the Utility. This help file is well done and can be of great use as you learn to use the utility.
  Click on Commands to start the process.

Figure A8.1 File Utility Window with Commands Menu

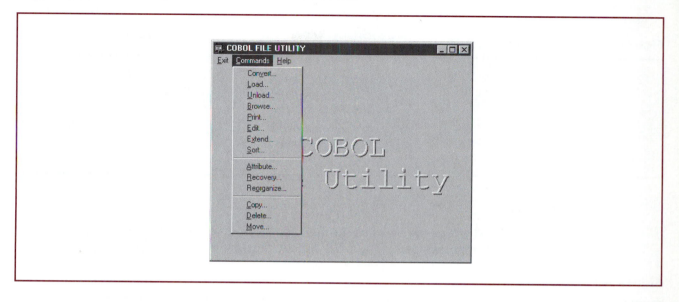

Step A8.2: Convert a Line-Sequential File

The Convert option converts line-sequential files to record-sequential files. Click on the Convert option to bring up the dialog box (Figure A8.2).

Figure A8.2 Convert Window

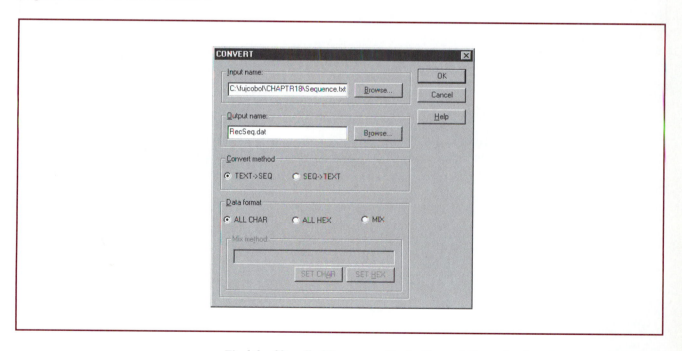

Find the file called Sequence.Txt in Chaptr18 by using Browse. Enter RecSeq.dat into the Output name box. Click OK to begin the process. The Convert process creates a new record-sequential file called RecSeq.dat. Convert assumes that the lines in the text (line-sequential) file may vary in length. Therefore, it creates a variable-length record-sequential file.

After the process has been run, you should see the completion message shown in Figure A8.3.

Figure A8.3   Completion Message

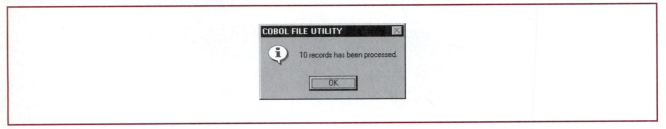

Step A8.3:   Browse the File

When you have created the file, you may want to look at it. Select Browse from the Commands menu. Figure A8.4 shows the Browse dialog window.

Figure A8.4   Browse Dialog Window

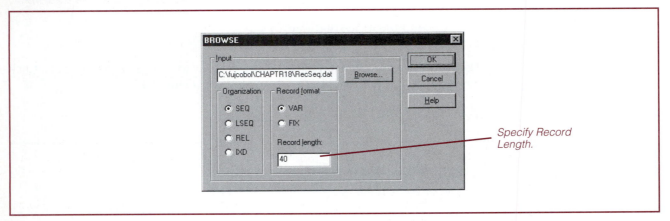

Open the RecSeq.dat file into the Input box. Enter the record length (40, in this example). Clicking OK brings up a view of the record in both hexadecimal and character mode. Figure A8.5 shows a record in Browse mode.

Figure A8.5 Record Contents in Hexadecimal and Character Format

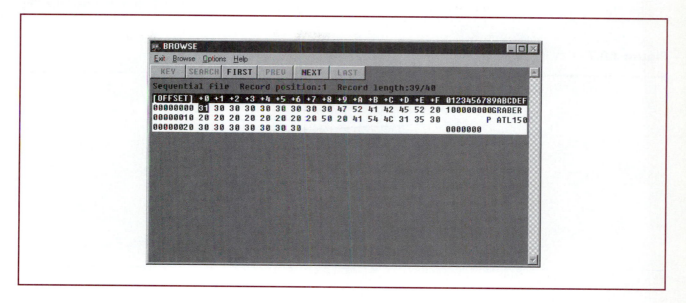

The Browse function allows you to look all of the records in the file, but you cannot change them. The hexadecimal format represents the ASCII codes for the characters using the hexadecimal numbering system. To close the Browse function, click on *Exit* in the Menu bar and then *Cancel* in the Browse Dialog Box.

Step A8.4: Load a Sequential File into an Indexed File

The Load command creates copies of data files in new formats. Load can be used only with record-sequential, indexed, and relative files. We do not deal with relative files, but in this step you will create an indexed file from RecSeq.dat.

Click on Load in the Commands menu to bring up the Load dialog box (Figure A8.6).

Figure A8.6 Load Dialog Box

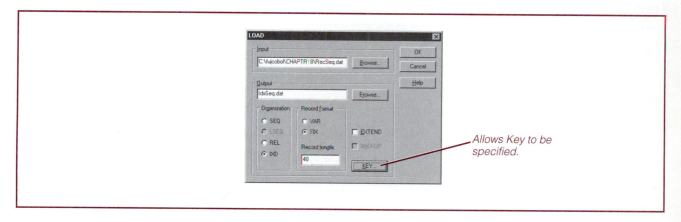

Allows Key to be specified.

Place the path for RecSeq.dat in the Input box and type IdxSeq.dat in the Output box. Make sure that the Organization is IDX and the record format is FIX. The record length is 40.

Before creating the file, you will need to establish the KEY. A key is used by indexed files to find individual records. Click on the KEY button to open the Key dialog box (Figure A8.7).

Figure A8.7 Key Information Dialog Box

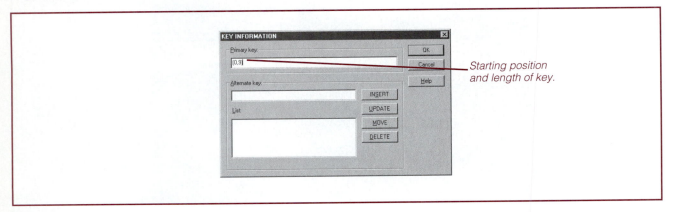

In this case, the key field for the file is a Social Security Number that starts the record. This field is 9 characters long. Enter "(0,9)" into the Primary key box. Do not type the quote marks. The first number is the offset from the start of the record; the second number is the length of the field. Since the key starts in the first position of the record, it has an offset of 0.

Click on OK twice, and the new file is created. Click OK a final time after you see a message similar to Figure A8.3, indicating that all records have been processed.

Step A8.5: Browse the Indexed File

Now that you have created an index file, you can look at it in the BROWSE function. Following the procedure in Step 7.3, you should open the dialog box, find the proper file, and check IXD for the Organization. Figure A8.8 shows the completed Browse dialog box.

Figure A8.8 Browse Dialog Box with Indexed File

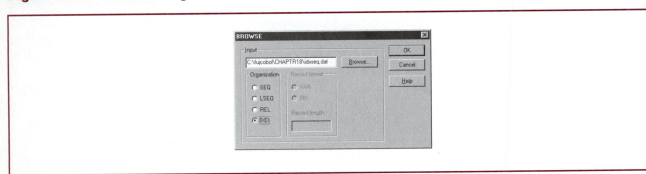

Click on *OK* to view the file.

Figure A8.9 shows the indexed file in Browse mode. Click on the Options menu and choose Character mode to make things easier. In Character mode, you can simply type into the hexadecimal area of the window. The File Utility does not allow direct entry into the character area.

Figure A8.9 Indexed File in Browse Mode

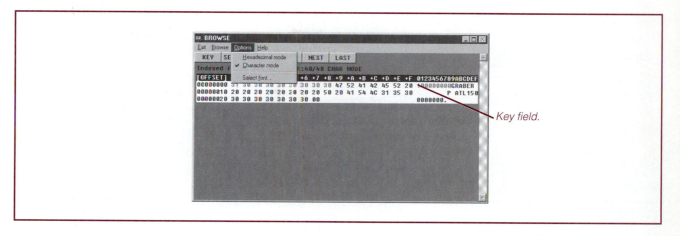

Key field.

Notice that you have more buttons available to use than with a sequential file. Experiment with moving around in the file. You may want to perform a search. Enter "222222222" into the key field (shown in red). If you get strange results, double-check to make sure that you are in Character mode and not Hexadecimal. Hexadecimal mode requires the entry of Hexadecimal values. In Browse mode you cannot change any of the records, so don't be afraid to try things.

Step A8.6: Create an Alternate Index

At times you may need to look at data in sequences different from that of the primary key. Indexed files allow you to create other ways of looking at data, called alternate indexes. The File Utility does not allow you to add an alternate index to an already created index file, but it does allow you to define alternate indexes when it is being created. Follow the procedure in Step 7.4 to build a file called IdxSeqA.dat.

This time, however, you will be building an alternate key.

Click on KEY. Enter the data from Figure A8.10 into the KEY INFORMATION dialog box. The primary key is the same as before. Now, we also want to be able to look up people by their location. This information has an offset of 26 and a length of 3. Since there can be more than one person at a location, you need to show duplicates are allowed. Without typing the quote marks, enter "D(26,3)" into the Alternate key box and click INSERT. The "D" at the beginning stands for duplicates. You can then click OK twice to create the file.

Figure A8.10   Key Information Dialog Box with Alternate Key

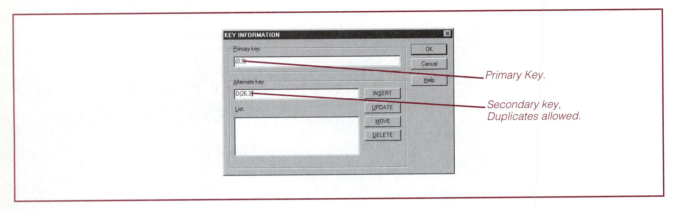

Step A8.7:   Browse the File Using the Alternate Index

Use the browse option to open IndSeqA.dat. The window will look the same as in Figure A8.9.

Click on Key and highlight the alternate key in the Record Key dialog box (Figure A8.11).

Figure A8.11   Record Key Dialog with Alternate Key Highlighted

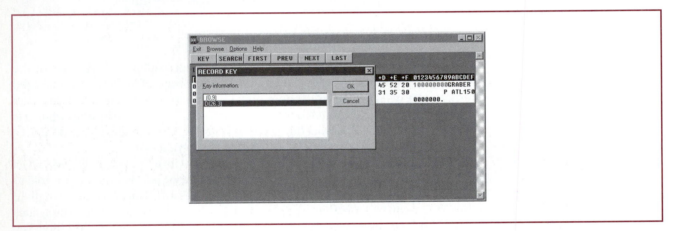

Click on OK to reshow the Browse window.

Notice that now "ATL" is highlighted in red. This is the alternate key field. Use the various buttons to move around in the file. Notice how the sequence of records seems be different from when you used the primary key.

Figure A8.12 Browse Screen with Alternate Key

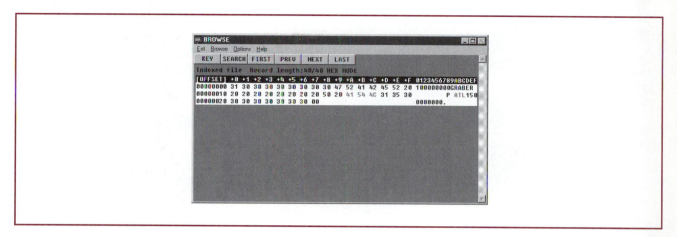

The use of alternate keys increases the flexibility and usefulness of indexed files, since they allow the file to be processed in a variety of sequences.

Connecting COBOL97 and Visual Basic

Overview: In Chapter 10 we presented the interactive capabilities of COBOL. These capabilities are character based with limited graphic possibilities. The new visual languages, such as Visual Basic, Delphi, Visual C++, and others, allow programmers to quickly implement graphical user interfaces (GUI) with their programs. COBOL compiler vendors have responded by producing COBOL tools and products that provide similar GUI capabilities for COBOL. Products such as Fujitsu's Power COBOL and Micro Focus' Net Express are good examples of these tools.

Unfortunately, as of this writing, no COBOL standard has been adopted for incorporating GUIs with COBOL. Consequently each vendor has developed its own proprietary product to answer the need. These products are extensions to and not actually part of COBOL. We have elected not to include instruction in any proprietary extension to the language but rather to use a more generic approach to show how COBOL can be used with a GUI.

Visual Basic is a widely used and taught programming language. This language can be used to quickly develop Windows-based interactive applications. Since Visual Basic supports calls to programs developed in other languages and modern COBOL compilers can create Windows-based subprograms called DLLs, we have chosen to show you how to link a COBOL program to a GUI written in Visual Basic.

This appendix contains four sections
Creating the COBOL Subprogram
Creating the Visual Basic Program
Connecting the Two Programs
Final Comments

Caveats: We are not attempting to teach Visual Basic in this appendix. Students who already know Visual Basic will find the discussion quite elementary except for the discussion of combining the programs. Those who have not written Visual Basic programs will have a more difficult time but should be able to follow the discussion. Finally, this discussion and the Visual Basic program files presume Visual Basic 5.0 as a minimum.

Creating the COBOL Subprogram

Review of Subprograms

In Chapter 16 we discussed the concept of calling subprograms. We considered the CALL verb and the concepts of BY REFERENCE and BY CONTENT. We also introduced the LINKAGE SECTION and showed how it passes parameters or arguments from one program to another. You may remember that the Procedure Division of a subprogram must include a USING clause to specify parameters. Finally, we pointed out that subprograms used EXIT PROGRAM instead of STOP RUN. You may want to review Chapter 16 if these concepts are a little vague.

Building a DLL Project

In Appendix A we showed you how to build COBOL projects resulting in an EXE file. In this section we will show you how to use the Project Manager to build a DLL file.

DLLs are files that contain one or more subprograms. In a Windows environment, these subprograms may be called by any other program as long as the proper interfaces are established. The calling program and the subprogram do not have to be written in the same source language. Therefore, a COBOL program should be able to use a C++ DLL and vice versa. For this project, we build a DLL that can be used by a Visual Basic program.

The first step is to create a new project following the procedures in Exercise 8 of Appendix A. Figure B.1a shows the standard result of opening a project and adding a file to the project. This time, however, change the name of the file to "Scrntuit.dll". The results appear in Figure B.1b. Notice the cogged-wheel icon denoting a DLL.

Figure B.1 Creating a DLL Project

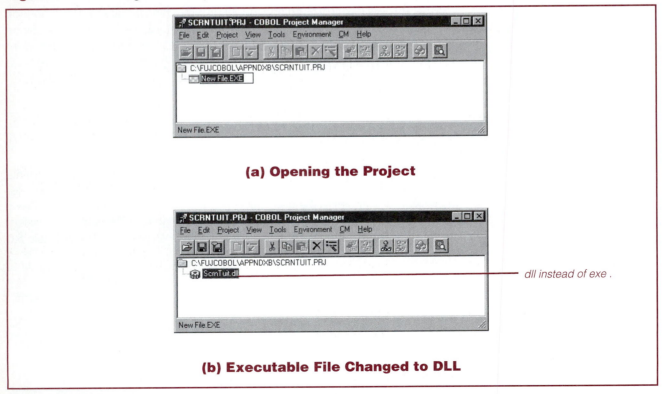

(a) Opening the Project

dll instead of exe .

(b) Executable File Changed to DLL

Figure B.2   Creating a Module Definition File

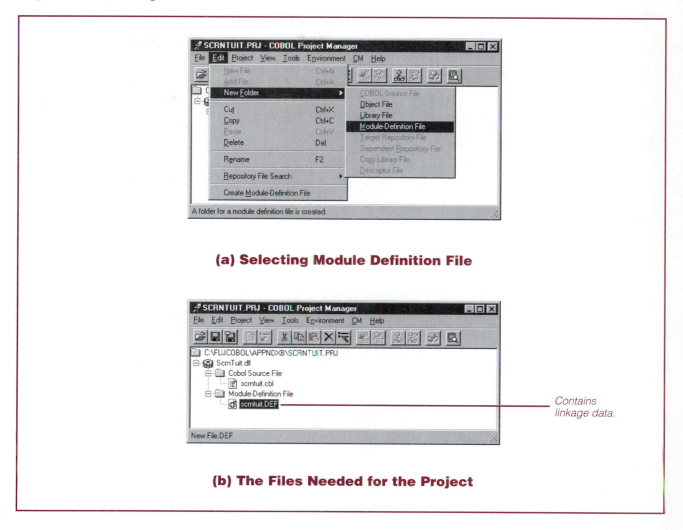

(a) Selecting Module Definition File

Contains
linkage data.

(b) The Files Needed for the Project

Next you need to add file folders to your program. The first is the standard COBOL Source File, and you should add Scrntuit.cbl from the AppndixB folder. However, for Visual Basic we need to create a Module Definition File. Select Edit, New Folder, and Module-Definition File as shown in Figure B.2a. Add a new file to the new folder and rename it "scrntuit.def". Figure B.2b shows all of the files needed for the project.

Do **not** make Scrntuit.cbl the main program. The purpose of the project is to create a subprogram. The Visual Basic program will become the main program.

Redesign of Tuition Program

We have rewritten the Scrntuit program from Chapter 10 to work as a subprogram. Figure B.3 shows the new version of the program.

Figure B.3 Revised Scrntuit Program

```
1     IDENTIFICATION DIVISION.
2     PROGRAM-ID.     SCRNTUIT.
3     AUTHOR.         CVV AND ARB.
4
5     DATA DIVISION.
6     WORKING-STORAGE SECTION.
7     01  STUDENT-DATA.
8         05  STU-CREDITS          PIC 9(2).
9         05  STU-UNION-MEMBER     PIC X.
10        05  STU-SCHOLARSHIP      PIC 9(4).
11        05  STU-GPA              PIC 9V99.
12
13    01  INDIVIDUAL-CALCULATIONS.
14        05  IND-TUITION          PIC 9(4)  VALUE ZEROS.
15        05  IND-ACTIVITY-FEE     PIC 9(2)  VALUE ZEROS.
16        05  IND-UNION-FEE        PIC 9(2)  VALUE ZEROS.
17        05  IND-SCHOLARSHIP      PIC S9(4) VALUE ZEROS.
18        05  IND-BILL             PIC S9(6) VALUE ZEROS.
19
20    01  CONSTANTS-AND-RATES.
21        05  PRICE-PER-CREDIT     PIC 9(3)  VALUE 200.
22        05  UNION-FEE            PIC 9(2)  VALUE 25.
23        05  ACTIVITY-FEES.
24            10  1ST-ACTIVITY-FEE PIC 99    VALUE 25.
25            10  1ST-CREDIT-LIMIT PIC 99    VALUE 6.
26            10  2ND-ACTIVITY-FEE PIC 99    VALUE 50.
27            10  2ND-CREDIT-LIMIT PIC 99    VALUE 12.
28            10  3RD-ACTIVITY-FEE PIC 99    VALUE 75.
29        05  MINIMUM-SCHOLAR-GPA  PIC 9V9   VALUE 2.5.
30
31    LINKAGE SECTION.
32    01 LS-CREDITS               PIC S9(4) COMP-5.
33    01 LS-UNION-MEMBER          PIC X.
34    01 LS-SCHOLARSHIP           PIC S9(10)V9(4) COMP-5.
35    01 LS-GPA                   COMP-1.
36    01 LS-TUITION-FEE           PIC S9(10)V9(4) COMP-5.
37    01 LS-ACTIVITY-FEE          PIC S9(10)V9(4) COMP-5.
38    01 LS-UNION-FEE             PIC S9(10)V9(4) COMP-5.
39    01 LS-SCHOLARSHIP-FEE       PIC S9(10)V9(4) COMP-5.
40    01 LS-BILL                  PIC S9(10)V9(4) COMP-5.
41
42     PROCEDURE DIVISION WITH STDCALL LINKAGE
43        USING                   LS-CREDITS
44                                LS-UNION-MEMBER
45                                LS-SCHOLARSHIP
46                                LS-GPA
47                                LS-TUITION-FEE
48                                LS-ACTIVITY-FEE
49                                LS-UNION-FEE
50                                LS-SCHOLARSHIP-FEE
51                                LS-BILL.
```

Figure B.3 Revised Scrntuit Program *(continued)*

```
52    000-PROCESS-STUDENT-DATA.
53        PERFORM 200-INPUT-STUDENT-INFO
54        PERFORM 310-COMPUTE-INDIVIDUAL-BILL
55        PERFORM 500-DISPLAY-STUDENT-BILL
56        EXIT PROGRAM.
57
58    200-INPUT-STUDENT-INFO.
59        MOVE LS-CREDITS TO STU-CREDITS
60        MOVE LS-UNION-MEMBER TO STU-UNION-MEMBER
61        MOVE LS-SCHOLARSHIP TO STU-SCHOLARSHIP
62        MOVE LS-GPA TO STU-GPA.
63
64    310-COMPUTE-INDIVIDUAL-BILL.
65        PERFORM 410-COMPUTE-TUITION.
66        PERFORM 430-COMPUTE-UNION-FEE.
67        PERFORM 460-COMPUTE-ACTIVITY-FEE.
68        PERFORM 490-COMPUTE-SCHOLARSHIP.
69        COMPUTE IND-BILL = IND-TUITION + IND-UNION-FEE +
70            IND-ACTIVITY-FEE - IND-SCHOLARSHIP
71            SIZE ERROR DISPLAY 'SIZE ERROR FOR INDIVIDUAL BILL'
72        END-COMPUTE.
73
74    410-COMPUTE-TUITION.
75        COMPUTE IND-TUITION = PRICE-PER-CREDIT * STU-CREDITS
76            SIZE ERROR DISPLAY 'SIZE ERROR FOR INDIVIDUAL TUITION'
77        END-COMPUTE.
78
79    430-COMPUTE-UNION-FEE.
80        IF STU-UNION-MEMBER = 'Y' or 'y'
81            MOVE UNION-FEE TO IND-UNION-FEE
82        ELSE
83            MOVE ZERO TO IND-UNION-FEE
84        END-IF.
85
86    460-COMPUTE-ACTIVITY-FEE.
87        EVALUATE TRUE
88            WHEN STU-CREDITS <= 1ST-CREDIT-LIMIT
89                MOVE 1ST-ACTIVITY-FEE TO IND-ACTIVITY-FEE
90            WHEN STU-CREDITS > 1ST-CREDIT-LIMIT
91                AND STU-CREDITS <= 2ND-CREDIT-LIMIT
92                    MOVE 2ND-ACTIVITY-FEE TO IND-ACTIVITY-FEE
93            WHEN STU-CREDITS > 2ND-CREDIT-LIMIT
94                MOVE 3RD-ACTIVITY-FEE TO IND-ACTIVITY-FEE
95        END-EVALUATE.
96
97    490-COMPUTE-SCHOLARSHIP.
98        IF STU-GPA > MINIMUM-SCHOLAR-GPA
99            MOVE STU-SCHOLARSHIP TO IND-SCHOLARSHIP
100       ELSE
101           MOVE ZERO TO IND-SCHOLARSHIP
102       END-IF.
```

Figure B.3   Revised Scrntuit Program *(continued)*

```
103
104    500-DISPLAY-STUDENT-BILL.
105        MOVE IND-TUITION TO LS-TUITION-FEE
106        MOVE IND-ACTIVITY-FEE TO LS-ACTIVITY-FEE
107        MOVE IND-UNION-FEE TO LS-UNION-FEE
108        MOVE IND-SCHOLARSHIP TO LS-SCHOLARSHIP-FEE
109        MOVE IND-BILL TO LS-BILL.
```

This program is somewhat shorter than the original program in Chapter 10. We have taken out all code that is no longer necessary. For example, there is no Screen Section in the Data Division, since the Visual Basic program will make screen. On the other hand, a Linkage Section has been added for parameter passing. As you examine the Linkage Section, the PIC clauses and the associated USAGE may seem to be strange. These PIC and USAGEs are necessary to coordination with Visual Basic data types. You will see further discussion in the Coordinating Data Types section.

The Procedure Division header lists all parameters of the Linkage Section. Consider that some of these parameters are input parameters (e.g., LS-CREDITS to LS-GPA) and are needed to make the calculations. The remaining parameters (LS-TUITION-FEE to LS-BILL) are output parameters to be returned to the Visual Basic program.

Within the Procedure Division, we have taken out the paragraphs that were needed for the user interface. The remaining paragraphs get the input parameters from the Linkage Section, calculate the fees, and move the fees to the Linkage Section output parameters. We have kept the same paragraph names and numbers so that you can compare the new version to the old.

The new program does not have a main processing loop because it only has to deal with one calculation at a time. The Visual Basic program controls handling multiple transactions.

Compiling and Linking the Program

We are now ready to compile and link the project to become a functioning DLL. You may have noticed that we have not done anything with the Scrntuit.def file. As the Project Manager builds the project, it will automatically fill in the values for this file.

Proceed to build the project using the Build Button. Figure B.4 shows the Builder Results. You can now close the Project Manager, saving all of your files.

Figure B.4   Build of Scrntuit.dll

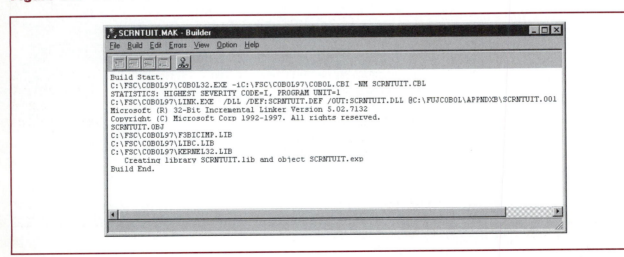

Creating the Visual Basic Program

A Brief Introduction to Visual Basic

Visual Basic is a widely used programming language that can create Windows applications quickly and easily. Visual Basic differs from traditional languages such as COBOL or even the original BASIC language in that much of the programming is "built in" already. For example, the Visual Basic programmer does not have to know the intricacies of graphical programming. The programmer simply *drags and drops* predefined controls onto a form.

Visual Basic develops *event-driven* programs. Events are generally actions taken by the user of the program such as clicking on a button or selecting a particular option from a list. These events may occur in any order, and Visual Basic is designed to handle their random nature. Once the interface is developed and the program is running, Visual Basic is in the background monitoring the events that occur.

By contrast, traditional languages produce *sequence-oriented* programs. COBOL programs, for example, generally are designed to handle transactions in a predictable order. The possible combinations of events are much more limited than in a truly interactive situation. Both types of languages have their strengths and weaknesses. Visual Basic allows the program to deal with unpredictable series of events but requires a great deal of overhead. Traditional programming languages can be more efficient but are not as flexible.

Controls, Properties, and Events

Understanding some of the Visual Basic concepts and terms is important. The Visual Basic interface is created by using a number of templates called *controls*. You have used controls any time you have used a Windows program. Some common controls include:

- Command Buttons
- Option Buttons
- Text Boxes
- Labels
- Frames

Each control has a series of *properties*. A property is some feature of the control and is generally changeable by the Visual Basic program and sometimes by the user. Common properties include:

- Name
- Caption
- Color
- Size
- Fonts
- Visible

When a Visual Basic program is running, the programming is detecting events as they occur. Events are things that happen to controls. A number of differing events are associated with each control type. Visual Basic has the responsibility to detect events and determine if the program should act when the event occurs. Common events include:

- Click
- DoubleClick
- GotFocus
- LoadForm

A Visual Basic programmer's primary job is to determine what actions should be taken when an event occurs and write the appropriate code.

Designing the Form

First, start up Visual Basic and create a new project. Figure B.5 shows the dialog box used in one version of Visual Basic.

As Visual Basic opens it presents a complex set of windows that may appear something like Figure B.6.

Figure B.5   Creating a New Visual Basic Project

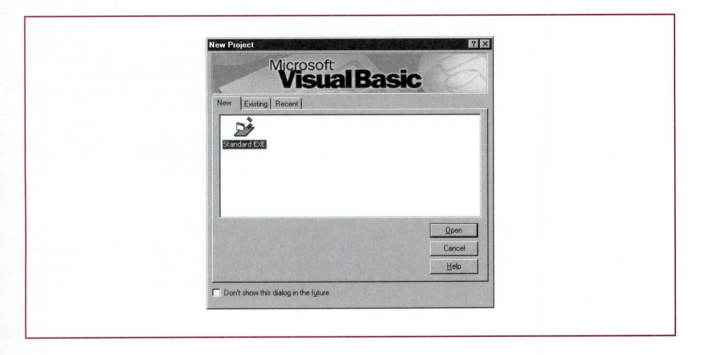

Figure B.6 Visual Basic Design Work Space

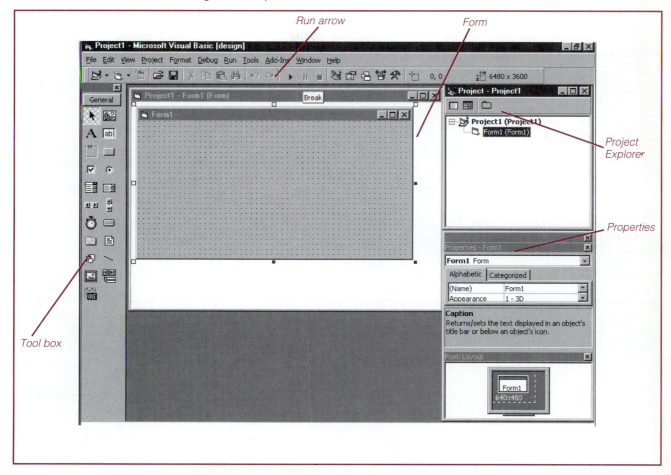

For this project, the most important features to note are:

- The Toolbox, which contains the controls.
- The Project Explorer, which is used to move from the form image to the procedure code.
- The Properties Window, which maintains the properties of each control.
- The Form itself.
- The Run Arrow to start processing the program.

In order to build the Visual Basic portion of the system, we need to build a form. In Figure B.7 we have started a form, showing an example of all the controls used in this project. To recreate this form, click first on the Frame control and move the cursor over the form. A "plus" or "cross-hair" pattern appears, allowing us to draw the frame by clicking and dragging. Frames are containers for other controls. It is easier to create the frame first and add other controls to it, rather than to try to put a frame around already created controls.

Figure B.7 Sample Visual Basic Form Using Frame, Label, Text Box, and Command Button

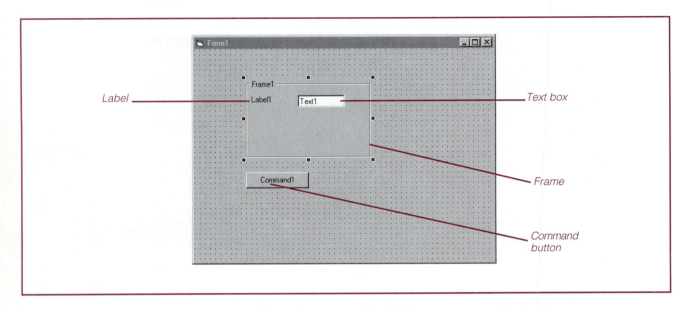

Next click on the Label tool and move the cursor into the frame before clicking and drawing the label. Do the same thing for the text box, again within the frame. Now, create a command button outside of the frame. This exercise shows how quickly a form can be built.

As each control was created, Visual Basic filled in a default value identifying the control. Visual Basic will automatically name each control and will use that name in the Caption property for most controls, or in the Text property for text boxes. Visual Basic programmers change the names and captions of controls as they create them. This practice assures that meaningful names can be used for each control.

Building the Interface

Figure B.8 shows the final form interface that we designed for the project. We have included this Visual Basic project in the AppndxB Folder under the name "Tuition.vbp". You can use our project or build one of your own if you wish. There are two frames; one is for the input and the second is for the calculated totals. Notice the use of labels and text boxes within the frames. In addition to the frames and their contents, we have specified three command buttons.

Figure B.8 Interface Design

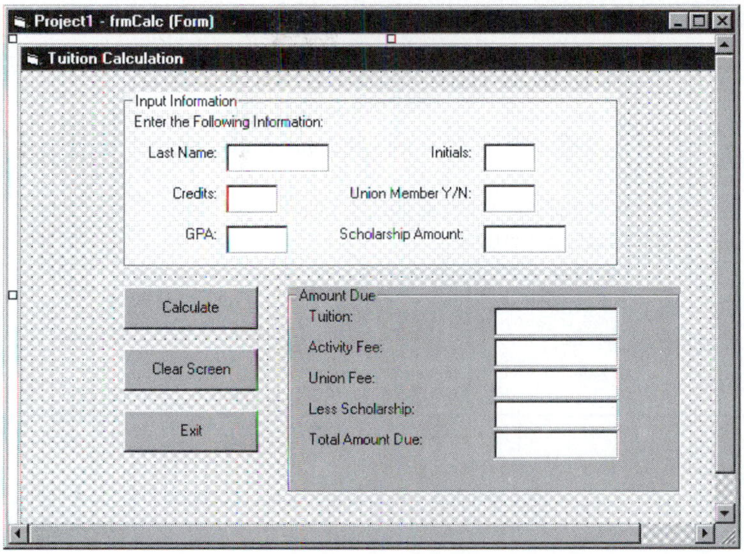

Control Property Specifications

Figure B.9 shows the name and essential property specifications for the active controls in the program. For space reasons, we have not included the label controls. The Command Buttons and Frames are associated with the Form. Text boxes (and Labels) are associated with the appropriate Frame. The Visible property of fraAmount is set to False. As a result, this frame will be hidden when the program starts.

Figure B.9 Control Names and Properties

```
Form frmCalc
    Caption        =   "Tuition Calculation"

CommandButton cmdExit
    Caption        =   "Exit"
CommandButton cmdClear
    Caption        =   "Clear Screen"
CommandButton cmdCalculate
    Caption        =   "Calculate"
Frame fraAmount
    BackColor      =   &H00FF0000&
    Caption        =   "Amount Due"
    ForeColor      =   &H00FFFFFF&
    Visible        =   0   'False

    TextBox txtTotalAmt
    TextBox txtScholarshipAmt
```

Figure B.9 Control Names and Properties *(continued)*

```
                          TextBox txtUnionFee
                          TextBox txtActivityFee
                          TextBox txtTuitionFee

                      Frame fraInput
                          BackColor      =   &H00FFFF00&
                          Caption        =   "Input Information"

                          TextBox txtScholarship
                          TextBox txtGPA
                          TextBox txtUnion
                          TextBox txtCredits
                          TextBox txtInit
                          TextBox txtLastName
```

The BackColor and ForeColor properties can be selected from a palette of colors, and the user does not have to enter the hexadecimal values shown in the figure.

Programming Specifications

Figure B.10 shows the programming code for each of the three command buttons and for the FormLoad event. You can double-click on the control to bring up the code window.

Figure B.10 Visual Basic Programming Code

```
                      Private Sub cmdCalculate_Click()
                          Dim StuCredits As Integer
                          Dim UnionMember As String
                          Dim GPA As Single
                          Dim Scholarship As Currency
                          Dim Tuition As Currency
                          Dim ActivityFee As Currency
                          Dim UnionFee As Currency
                          Dim ScholarshipAmt As Currency
                          Dim Total As Currency

                          StuCredits = Val(txtCredits.Text)
                          UnionMember = txtUnion.Text
                          GPA = Val(txtGPA.Text)
                          Scholarship = Val(txtScholarship.Text)

                          Call SCRNTUIT(StuCredits, UnionMember, Scholarship, GPA, Tuition, _
                                      ActivityFee, UnionFee, ScholarshipAmt, Total)

                          txtTuitionFee.Text = Format$(Tuition, "Currency")
                          txtActivityFee.Text = Format$(ActivityFee, "Currency")
```

Figure B.10 Visual Basic Programming Code *(continued)*

```
                        txtUnionFee.Text = Format$(UnionFee, "Currency")
                        txtScholarshipAmt.Text = Format$(ScholarshipAmt, "Currency")
                        txtTotalAmt.Text = Format$(Total, "Currency")

                        fraAmount.Visible = True
                    End Sub

                    Private Sub cmdClear_Click()
                        fraAmount.Visible = False
                        txtLastName.Text = ""
                        txtInit.Text = ""
                        txtCredits.Text = ""
                        txtUnion.Text = ""
                        txtGPA.Text = ""
                        txtScholarship.Text = ""
                    End Sub

                    Private Sub cmdExit_Click()
                        Call JMPCINT3
                        End
                    End Sub

                    Private Sub Form_Load()
                        Call JMPCINT2
                    End Sub
```

For the three command buttons, this code is executed when the user clicks on the button. The button named cmdCalculate does the most work. First, you see a number of "Dim" statements. Dim statements perform the function of the COBOL Working-storage Section, in that they define variables or fields used by the program. Visual Basic uses data types instead of PIC to define the format of variables. We provide a conversion table in the next section, so you can see how they relate.

The next four statements store values from the various text boxes into the input variables. The Call statement sends the input data to the COBOL DLL and receives the calculations back. The next five statements format the calculations and place them into the Output text boxes, and last statement makes the Amount Due frame visible.

The cmdClear button makes the Amount Due frame invisible again and clears out all of the text boxes.

The cmdExit button releases the COBOL DLL from memory and ends the program.

There is one more event procedure—Form_Load. This event occurs when the program starts and the form is loaded onto the screen. In this project the event occurs only once. When it does occur, the call statement loads the COBOL DLL into memory for execution.

Connecting the Two Programs

At this point we have developed the two parts of the puzzle. Each piece was not difficult in itself. However, now we have to connect the two together. COBOL and Visual Basic are substantially different programming languages having differing data types. Fortunately, the Windows environment has become a de facto standard. Both the COBOL vendors and Microsoft have provided means to meet the interconnection standard. In this section you will see how to connect the two programs. There are three aspects involved:

- Declaring subprograms in Visual Basic so it can find the COBOL subprogram.
- Formatting the passed parameters to be recognizable by both languages.
- Formatting the call statement.

Declaring Subprograms in Visual Basic

Figure B.11   Subprogram Declare Statements

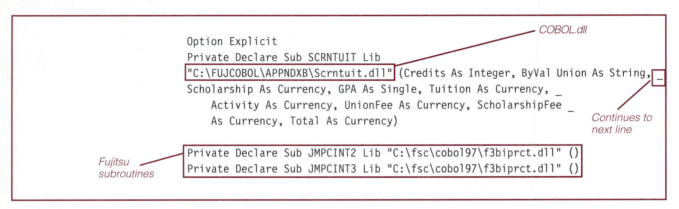

For our Visual Basic program to know that the COBOL DLL exists, the DLL must be declared as part of the Visual Basic General Procedures. Figure B.11 shows the Declare statements linking the two programs. There are three Declare statements. The first is quite long, taking five lines. (In Visual Basic, a blank space and an underscore mean that a single statement is continued on the next line.) "SCRNTUIT" is the name of the subroutine being declared. This name is case sensitive and needs to be all uppercase. "Lib" states that this subroutine is contained in the DLL which follows. The name and full path of the DLL must be specified within double quotes. Following the DLL name and enclosed in parentheses are the parameter names and their data types. Thus, Credit is an Integer, Union is a String, and so forth until all parameters are defined. String data types must be passed using the ByVal keyword. ByVal is the Visual Basic equivalent of COBOL BY REFERENCE.

Two more Declare statements are required. "JMPCINT2" and "JMPCINT3" are special subprograms provided by Fujitsu. These subprograms connect Visual Basic with our COBOL subroutine. JMPCINT2 initializes the connection and JMPCINT3 removes the connection. The Visual Basic program must call JMPCINT2 before executing SCRNTUIT (or any other COBOL DLL), and JMPCINT3 when SCRNTUIT is no longer needed. These two subprograms do not have any parameters, but the full path must be specified. Be sure to refer to the folder where COBOL97 is loaded.

Coordinating Data Types

In declaring subprograms, it is very important to assure the correct specification and sequence of variables and their associated data types. COBOL and Visual Basic do not use the same method of specifying data, but there are equivalent representations.

Table B.1 shows the standard Visual Basic data types and the corresponding COBOL PICTURE clauses. If you should write your own Windows programs, this table will become invaluable.

Table B.1 Data Type Equivalencies

Visual Basic		COBOL
Type Name	**Storage Size**	**PICTURE Clause**
Boolean (16 bit)	2 Bytes	S9(4) COMP-5
Boolean (32 bit)	4 Bytes	S9(9) COMP-5
Byte	1 Byte	X
Currency	8 Bytes	S9(10)V9(4) COMP-5
Double	8 Bytes	COMP-2
Integer	2 Bytes	S9(4) COMP-5
Long	4 Bytes	S9(9) COMP-5
Single	4 Bytes	COMP-1
String	1 Byte per character	X(n)

Review the Linkage Section of in Figure B.3 and the Variable definitions in Figure B.10 to see how these data types work together.

Calling Subprograms in Visual Basic

In Visual Basic, the Call statement transfers control to the subprogram. The Call statement below comes from Figure B.10.

```
Call SCRNTUIT(StuCredits, UnionMember, Scholarship, GPA, Tuition, _
              ActivityFee, UnionFee, ScholarshipAmt, Total)
```

In the call statement, you call the name of the subprogram as defined in a Declare statement and list the parameters in order. The parameters must be of the correct data type and in the proper sequence.

Processing the Project

Once the Visual Basic project has been completed, you can run the program by clicking on the Run Arrow shown in Figure B.6. As the program starts, the interface shown in Figure B.12 appears. The frame containing the computed values is hidden.

Figure B.12 Program Interface

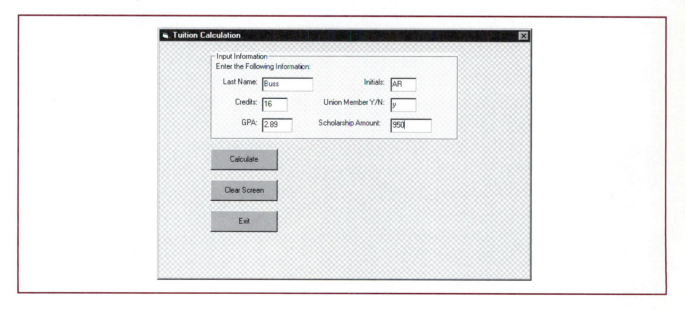

When you click on the Calculate button, the Environmental Variables dialog box, shown in Figure B.13, appears. This dialog box should appear only on the first calculation. Once you are satisfied that everything is working, you may want to suppress the dialog box entirely. The variable setting below causes COBOL97 to bypass the Environmental Variables dialog box. Set and Save the variable setting.

```
@EnvSetWindow=UNUSE
```

Be sure to enter the data exactly as above. The setting is case sensitive.

Figure B.13 Environmental Variables Dialog Box

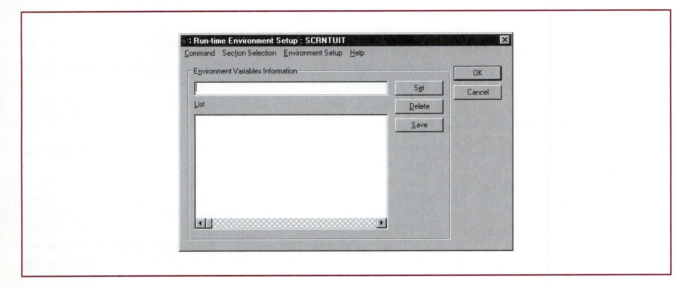

When you click on OK, the program will run, and the Amount frame appears with the calculated amounts as shown in Figure B.14. Click on the Clear button to restore the screen and enter a new transaction. When you are done, click on the Exit button to close the subprogram and exit the Visual Basic project.

Figure B.14 Program Interface Showing Calculated Results

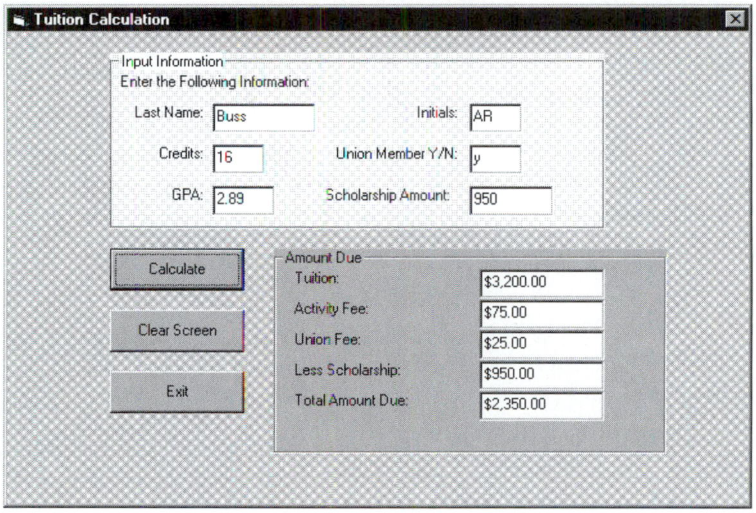

Final Comments

This appendix has attempted to show how a COBOL program can have a Windows-based user interface by linking with Visual Basic. The task may initially seem daunting, but as you gain experience with COBOL and Visual Basic, such interfaces can be developed very quickly.

The marriage between the two languages means that a project can have the processing efficiencies of COBOL and the user-friendly interface of Visual Basic. We hope that you can see that COBOL is a powerful language that still has a place in the Windows-oriented world. We would also remind you that there are vendor-developed extensions to COBOL that allow programmers to develop COBOL-based Windows programs without resorting to the use of Visual Basic or some other visual language. Whatever route is chosen, COBOL continues to be a viable language even in a Windows environment.

Reserved Words

ACCEPT	CLASS	DEBUG-SUB-1	END-RETURN
ACCESS	CLOCK-UNITS	DEBUG-SUB-2	END-REWRITE
ADD	CLOSE	DEBUG-SUB-3	END-SEARCH
ADVANCING	COBOL	DEBUGGING	END-START
AFTER	CODE	DECIMAL-POINT	END-STRING
ALL	CODE-SET	DECLARATIVES	END-SUBTRACT
ALPHABET	COLLATING	DELETE	END-UNSTRING
ALPHABETIC	COLUMN	DELIMITED	END-WRITE
ALPHABETIC-LOWER	COMMA	DELIMITER	ENTER
ALPHABETIC-UPPER	COMMON	DEPENDING	ENVIRONMENT
ALPHANUMERIC	COMMUNICATION	DESCENDING	EOP
ALPHANUMERIC-EDITED	COMP	DESTINATION	EQUAL
ALSO	COMPUTATIONAL	DETAIL	ERROR
ALTER	COMPUTE	DISABLE	ESI
ALTERNATE	CONFIGURATION	DISPLAY	EVALUATE
AND	CONTAINS	DIVIDE	EVERY
ANY	CONTENT	DIVISION	EXCEPTION
ARE	CONTINUE	DOWN	EXIT
AREA	CONTROL	DUPLICATES	EXTEND
AREAS	CONTROLS	DYNAMIC	EXTERNAL
ASCENDING	CONVERTING		
ASSIGN	COPY	EGI	FALSE
AT	CORR	ELSE	FD
AUTHOR	CORRESPONDING	EMI	FILE
	COUNT	ENABLE	FILE-CONTROL
BEFORE	CURRENCY	END	FILLER
BINARY		END-ADD	FINAL
BLANK	DATA	END-CALL	FIRST
BLOCK	DATE	END-COMPUTE	FOOTING
BOTTOM	DATE-COMPILED	END-DELETE	FOR
BY	DATE-WRITTEN	END-DIVIDE	FROM
	DAY	END-EVALUATE	
CALL	DAY-OF-WEEK	END-IF	GENERATE
CANCEL	DE	END-MULTIPLY	GIVING
CD	DEBUG-CONTENTS	END-OF-PAGE	GLOBAL
CF	DEBUG-ITEM	END-PERFORM	GO
CH	DEBUG-LINE	END-READ	GREATER
CHARACTER	DEBUG-NAME	END-RECEIVE	GROUP
CHARACTERS			

HEADING	NO	REMAINDER	SYNC
HIGH-VALUE	NOT	REMOVAL	SYNCHRONIZED
HIGH-VALUES	NUMBER	RENAMES	
	NUMERIC	REPLACE	TABLE
I-O	NUMERIC-EDITED	REPLACING	TALLYING
I-O-CONTROL		REPORT	TAPE
IDENTIFICATION	OBJECT-COMPUTER	REPORTING	TERMINAL
IF	OCCURS	REPORTS	TERMINATE
IN	OF	RERUN	TEST
INDEX	OFF	RESERVE	TEXT
INDEXED	OMITTED	RESET	THAN
INDICATE	ON	RETURN	THEN
INITIAL	OPEN	REVERSED	THROUGH
INITIALIZE	OPTIONAL	REWIND	THRU
INITIATE	OR	REWRITE	TIME
INPUT	ORDER	RF	TIMES
INPUT-OUTPUT	ORGANIZATION	RH	TO
INSPECT	OTHER	RIGHT	TOP
INSTALLATION	OUTPUT	ROUNDED	TRAILING
INTO	OVERFLOW	RUN	TRUE
INVALID			TYPE
IS	PACKED-DECIMAL	SAME	
	PADDING	SD	UNIT
JUST	PAGE	SEARCH	UNSTRING
JUSTIFIED	PAGE-COUNTER	SECTION	UNTIL
	PERFORM	SECURITY	UP
KEY	PF	SEGMENT	UPON
	PH	SEGMENT-LIMIT	USAGE
LABEL	PIC	SELECT	USE
LAST	PICTURE	SEND	USING
LEADING	PLUS	SENTENCE	
LEFT	POINTER	SEPARATE	VALUE
LENGTH	POSITION	SEQUENCE	VALUES
LESS	POSITIVE	SEQUENTIAL	VARYING
LIMIT	PRINTING	SET	
LIMITS	PROCEDURE	SIGN	WHEN
LINAGE	PROCEDURES	SIZE	WITH
LINAGE-COUNTER	PROCEED	SORT	WORDS
LINE	PROGRAM	SORT-MERGE	WORKING-STORAGE
LINE-COUNTER	PROGRAM-ID	SOURCE	WRITE
LINES	PURGE	SOURCE-COMPUTER	
LINKAGE		SPACE	ZERO
LOCK	QUEUE	SPACES	ZEROES
LOW-VALUE	QUOTE	SPECIAL-NAMES	ZEROS
LOW-VALUES	QUOTES	STANDARD	
		STANDARD-1	+
MEMORY	RANDOM	STANDARD-2	–
MERGE	RD	START	*
MESSAGE	READ	STATUS	/
MODE	RECEIVE	STOP	**
MODULES	RECORD	STRING	>
MOVE	RECORDS	SUB-QUEUE-1	<
MULTIPLE	REDEFINES	SUB-QUEUE-2	=
MULTIPLY	REEL	SUB-QUEUE-3	>=
	REFERENCE	SUBTRACT	<=
NATIVE	REFERENCES	SUM	
NEGATIVE	RELATIVE	SUPPRESS	
NEXT	RELEASE	SYMBOLIC	

COBOL-85
Reference Summary

This appendix contains the composite language skeleton of the revised version of the American National Standard COBOL. It is intended to display complete and syntactically correct formats.

The leftmost margin on pages 712 through 720 is equivalent to margin A in a COBOL source program. The first indentation after the leftmost margin is equivalent to margin B in a COBOL source program.

On pages 721 through 731 the leftmost margin indicates the beginning of the format for a new COBOL verb. The first indentation after the leftmost margin indicates continuation of the format of the COBOL verb. The appearance of the italic letter *S*, *R*, *I*, or *W* to the left of the format for the verbs CLOSE, OPEN, READ, and WRITE indicates the **Sequential** I-O module, **Relative** I-O module, **Indexed** I-O module, or Report **Writer** module in which that general format is used. The following formats are presented:

Identification Division 714

Environment Division 714

File Control Entry 715

Data Division 716

File Description Entry 717

Data Description Entry 719

Communication Description Entry 720

Report Description Entry 721

Report Group Description Entry 721

Procedure Division 722

COBOL Verbs 723

COPY and REPLACE Statements 733

Conditions 734

Qualification 735

Miscellaneous Formats 736

Nested Source Programs 736

A Series of Source Programs 737

Identification Division

```
IDENTIFICATION DIVISION.

PROGRAM-ID.  program-name  [ IS  {|COMMON |}  PROGRAM ]
                                 {|INITIAL|}

[AUTHOR.  [comment-entry] . . . ]

[INSTALLATION.  [comment-entry] . . . ]

[DATE-WRITTEN.  [comment-entry] . . . ]

[DATE-COMPILED.  [comment-entry] . . . ]

[SECURITY.  [comment-entry] . . . ]
```

Environment Division

```
[ENVIRONMENT DIVISION.

[CONFIGURATION SECTION.

[SOURCE-COMPUTER.  [computer-name  [WITH DEBUGGING MODE] . ] ]

[OBJECT-COMPUTER.  [computer-name

     [PROGRAM COLLATING  SEQUENCE  IS alphabet-name-1]

     [SEGMENT-LIMIT  IS  segment-number] . ] ]

[SPECIAL-NAMES.  [ [implementor-name-1

         ⎧ IS mnemonic-name-1  [ON STATUS IS  condition-name-1  [OFF STATUS IS  condition-name-2] ] ⎫
         ⎪ IS mnemonic-name-2  [OFF STATUS IS  condition-name-2  [ON STATUS IS  condition-name-1] ] ⎪  ] . . .
         ⎨ [ON STATUS IS  condition-name-1  [OFF STATUS IS  condition-name-2] ]                       ⎬
         ⎩ [OFF STATUS IS  condition-name-2  [ON STATUS IS  condition-name-1] ]                       ⎭

     [ALPHABET  alphabet-name-1  IS

         ⎧ STANDARD-1                                         ⎫
         ⎪ STANDARD-2                                         ⎪
         ⎪ NATIVE                                             ⎪
         ⎨ implementor-name-2                                 ⎬  ] . . .
         ⎪ ⎧              ⎡ ⎧THROUGH⎫  literal-2 ⎤     ⎫       ⎪
         ⎪ ⎨ literal-1    ⎢ ⎨THRU   ⎬           ⎢ . . ⎬       ⎪
         ⎩ ⎩              ⎣ {ALSO  literal-3} . . . ⎦   ⎭       ⎭

     ⎡ SYMBOLIC  CHARACTERS  ⎧ {symbolic-character-1} . . . ⎧IS ⎫ {integer-1} . . . ⎫ . . . [IN alphabet-name-2] ⎫ ⎤ . . .
     ⎣                        ⎩                             ⎩ARE⎭                     ⎭                             ⎭ ⎦

     ⎡ CLASS  class-name  IS  ⎧ literal-4 ⎡ ⎧THROUGH⎫  literal-5 ⎤ ⎫ . . . ⎤ . . .
     ⎣                        ⎩           ⎣ ⎨THRU   ⎬            ⎦ ⎭       ⎦

     [CURRENCY  SIGN  IS  literal-6]

     [DECIMAL-POINT  IS  COMMA]. ] ] ]

[INPUT-OUTPUT SECTION.

FILE-CONTROL.

     {file-control-entry} . . .
```

Environment Division *(continued)*

[I-O-CONTROL.

```
    ⎡                                      ⎧⎧          ⎧REEL⎫           ⎫ ⎤
    ⎢        ⎡   ⎧file-name-1       ⎫⎤      ⎪⎢[END OF] ⎨    ⎬ OF file-name-2⎬ ⎥
    ⎢ RERUN  ⎢ON ⎨                  ⎬⎥ EVERY⎨⎣          ⎩UNIT⎭              ⎭⎥...⎥
    ⎢        ⎣   ⎩implementor-name-1⎭⎦      ⎪ integer-1 RECORDS            ⎥ ⎥
    ⎢                                      ⎪ integer-2 CLOCK-UNITS         ⎥ ⎥
    ⎢                                      ⎩ condition-name-1              ⎭ ⎥
    ⎣                                                                       ⎦

    ⎡      ⎡RECORD   ⎤                                      ⎤
    ⎢ SAME ⎢SORT     ⎥ AREA FOR file-name-1 {file-name-2} ...⎥...
    ⎢      ⎣SORT-MERGE⎦                                      ⎦
                                                                ]]
    ⎡ MULTIPLE FILE  TAPE CONTAINS                   ⎤
    ⎢       {file-name-3 [POSITION IS integer-1] }...⎥...   .
    ⎣                                                ⎦
```

File Control Entry

SEQUENTIAL FILE

SELECT [OPTIONAL] file-name-1

    ASSIGN TO ⎧implementor-name-1⎫ ...
                ⎩literal-1   ⎭

    ⎡RESERVE integer-1 ⎡AREA ⎤⎤
    ⎣   ⎣AREAS⎦⎦

    [[ORGANIZATION IS] [LINE]SEQUENTIAL]

    ⎡PADDING CHARACTER IS ⎧data-name-1⎫⎤
    ⎣   ⎩literal-2 ⎭⎦

    ⎡RECORD DELIMITER IS ⎧STANDARD-1   ⎫⎤
    ⎣   ⎩implementor-name-2⎭⎦

    [ACCESS MODE IS SEQUENTIAL]

    [FILE STATUS IS data-name-2] .

RELATIVE FILE

SELECT [OPTIONAL] file-name-1

    ASSIGN TO ⎧implementor-name-1⎫ ...
                ⎩literal-1   ⎭

    ⎡RESERVE integer-1 ⎡AREA ⎤⎤
    ⎣   ⎣AREAS⎦⎦

    [ORGANIZATION IS] RELATIVE

    ⎡   ⎧SEQUENTIAL [RELATIVE KEY IS data-name-1]⎫⎤
    ⎢ACCESS MODE IS ⎨⎧RANDOM ⎫   ⎬⎥
    ⎢   ⎨⎨DYNAMIC⎬ RELATIVE KEY IS data-name-1   ⎬⎥
    ⎣   ⎩⎩   ⎭   ⎭⎦

    [FILE STATUS IS data-name-2] .

File Control Entry *(continued)*

INDEXED FILE

SELECT [OPTIONAL] file-name-1

    ASSIGN TO $\begin{Bmatrix} \text{implementor-name-1} \\ \text{literal-1} \end{Bmatrix}$ . . .

    $\left[\text{RESERVE integer-1} \begin{bmatrix} \text{AREA} \\ \text{AREAS} \end{bmatrix} \right]$

    [ORGANIZATION IS] INDEXED

    $\left[\text{ACCESS MODE IS} \begin{Bmatrix} \text{SEQUENTIAL} \\ \text{RANDOM} \\ \text{DYNAMIC} \end{Bmatrix} \right]$

    RECORD KEY IS data-name-1

    [ALTERNATE RECORD KEY IS data-name-2 [WITH DUPLICATES]] . . .

    [FILE STATUS IS data-name-3] .

SORT OR MERGE FILE

SELECT file-name-1 ASSIGN TO $\begin{Bmatrix} \text{implementor-name-1} \\ \text{literal-1} \end{Bmatrix}$ . . .

Data Division

[DATA DIVISION.

[FILE SECTION.

[file-description-entry

{record-description-entry} . . .] . . .

[sort-merge-file-description-entry

{record-description-entry} . . .] . . .

[report-file-description-entry] . . .]

[WORKING-STORAGE SECTION.

$\begin{bmatrix} \text{77-level-description-entry} \\ \text{record-description-entry} \end{bmatrix}$ . . .]

[LINKAGE SECTION.

$\begin{bmatrix} \text{77-level-description-entry} \\ \text{record-description-entry} \end{bmatrix}$ . . .]

[COMMUNICATION SECTION.

[communication-description-entry

[record-description-entry] . . .] . . .]

[REPORT SECTION.

[report-description-entry

{record-group-description-entry} . . .] . . .]]

File Description Entry

SEQUENTIAL FILE

FD file-name-1

    [IS EXTERNAL]

    [IS GLOBAL]

$$\left[\text{BLOCK CONTAINS [integer-1 TO] integer-2} \begin{Bmatrix} \text{RECORDS} \\ \text{CHARACTERS} \end{Bmatrix} \right]$$

$$\left[\text{RECORD} \begin{Bmatrix} \text{CONTAINS integer-3 CHARACTERS} \\ \text{IS VARYING IN SIZE [[FROM integer-4] [TO integer-5] CHARACTERS]} \\ \text{[DEPENDING ON data-name-1]} \\ \text{CONTAINS integer-6 TO integer-7 CHARACTERS} \end{Bmatrix} \right]$$

$$\left[\text{LABEL} \begin{Bmatrix} \text{RECORD IS} \\ \text{RECORDS ARE} \end{Bmatrix} \begin{Bmatrix} \text{STANDARD} \\ \text{OMITTED} \end{Bmatrix} \right]$$

$$\left[\text{VALUE OF} \left\{ \text{implementor-name-1 IS} \begin{Bmatrix} \text{data-name-2} \\ \text{literal-1} \end{Bmatrix} \right\} \ldots \right]$$

$$\left[\text{DATA} \begin{Bmatrix} \text{RECORD IS} \\ \text{RECORDS ARE} \end{Bmatrix} \{\text{data-name-3}\} \ldots \right]$$

$$\left[\text{LINAGE IS} \begin{Bmatrix} \text{data-name-4} \\ \text{integer-8} \end{Bmatrix} \text{LINES} \left[\text{WITH FOOTING AT} \begin{Bmatrix} \text{data-name-5} \\ \text{integer-9} \end{Bmatrix} \right] \right.$$
$$\left. \left[\text{LINES AT TOP} \begin{Bmatrix} \text{data-name-6} \\ \text{integer-10} \end{Bmatrix} \right] \left[\text{LINES AT BOTTOM} \begin{Bmatrix} \text{data-name-7} \\ \text{integer-11} \end{Bmatrix} \right] \right]$$

    [CODE-SET IS alphabet-name-1] .

RELATIVE FILE

FD file-name-1

    [IS EXTERNAL]

    [IS GLOBAL]

$$\left[\text{BLOCK CONTAINS [integer-1 TO] integer-2} \begin{Bmatrix} \text{RECORDS} \\ \text{CHARACTERS} \end{Bmatrix} \right]$$

$$\left[\text{RECORD} \begin{Bmatrix} \text{CONTAINS integer-3 CHARACTERS} \\ \text{IS VARYING IN SIZE [[FROM integer-4] [TO integer-5] CHARACTERS]} \\ \text{[DEPENDING ON data-name-1]} \\ \text{CONTAINS integer-6 TO integer-7 CHARACTERS} \end{Bmatrix} \right]$$

$$\left[\text{LABEL} \begin{Bmatrix} \text{RECORD IS} \\ \text{RECORDS ARE} \end{Bmatrix} \begin{Bmatrix} \text{STANDARD} \\ \text{OMITTED} \end{Bmatrix} \right]$$

$$\left[\text{VALUE OF} \left\{ \text{implementor-name-1 IS} \begin{Bmatrix} \text{data-name-2} \\ \text{literal-1} \end{Bmatrix} \right\} \ldots \right]$$

$$\left[\text{DATA} \begin{Bmatrix} \text{RECORD IS} \\ \text{RECORDS ARE} \end{Bmatrix} \{\text{data-name-3}\} \ldots \right] \quad .$$

File Description Entry *(continued)*

SORT - MERGE FILE

```
SD  file-name-1

    ⌈      ⌈CONTAINS  integer-1  CHARACTERS                                          ⌉⌉
    │      │IS  VARYING  IN SIZE  [ [FROM  integer-2] [TO  integer-3]  CHARACTERS] ││
    │RECORD│      [DEPENDING  ON  data-name-1]                                       ││
    │      │CONTAINS  integer-4  TO  integer-5  CHARACTERS                           ││
    ⌊      ⌊                                                                          ⌋⌋

    ⌈     ⌈RECORD  IS ⌉                      ⌉
    │DATA │RECORDS ARE│ {data-name-2} . . . │
    ⌊     ⌊           ⌋                      ⌋
```

REPORT FILE

```
FD  file-name-1

    [IS  EXTERNAL]

    [IS  GLOBAL]

    ⌈                                      ⌈RECORDS   ⌉ ⌉
    │BLOCK  CONTAINS  [integer-1  TO]  integer-2 │CHARACTERS│ │
    ⌊                                      ⌊          ⌋ ⌋

    ⌈      ⌈CONTAINS  integer-3  CHARACTERS                                          ⌉⌉
    │      │IS  VARYING  IN SIZE  [ [FROM  integer-4] [TO  integer-5]  CHARACTERS] ││
    │RECORD│      [DEPENDING  ON  data-name-1]                                       ││
    │      │CONTAINS  integer-6  TO  integer-7  CHARACTERS                           ││
    ⌊      ⌊                                                                          ⌋⌋

    ⌈      ⌈RECORD  IS ⌉ ⌈STANDARD⌉ ⌉
    │LABEL │RECORDS ARE│ │OMITTED │ │
    ⌊      ⌊           ⌋ ⌊        ⌋ ⌋

    ⌈                                  ⌈data-name-2⌉    ⌉
    │VALUE OF │implementor-name-1  IS │literal-1  │ │ . . . │
    ⌊                                  ⌊           ⌋    ⌋

    [CODE-SET  IS  alphabet-name-1]

    ⌈REPORT  IS ⌉
    │REPORTS ARE│ {report-name-1} . . .
    ⌊           ⌋
```

INDEXED FILE

```
FD  file-name-1

    [IS  EXTERNAL]

    [IS  GLOBAL]

    ⌈                                      ⌈RECORDS   ⌉ ⌉
    │BLOCK  CONTAINS  [integer-1  TO]  integer-2 │CHARACTERS│ │
    ⌊                                      ⌊          ⌋ ⌋

    ⌈      ⌈CONTAINS  integer-3  CHARACTERS                                          ⌉⌉
    │      │IS  VARYING  IN SIZE  [ [FROM  integer-4] [TO  integer-5]  CHARACTERS] ││
    │RECORD│      [DEPENDING  ON  data-name-1]                                       ││
    │      │CONTAINS  integer-6  TO  integer-7  CHARACTERS                           ││
    ⌊      ⌊                                                                          ⌋⌋

    ⌈      ⌈RECORD  IS ⌉ ⌈STANDARD⌉ ⌉
    │LABEL │RECORDS ARE│ │OMITTED │ │
    ⌊      ⌊           ⌋ ⌊        ⌋ ⌋

    ⌈                                  ⌈data-name-2⌉    ⌉
    │VALUE OF │implementor-name-1  IS │literal-1  │ │ . . . │
    ⌊                                  ⌊           ⌋    ⌋

    ⌈     ⌈RECORD  IS ⌉                      ⌉
    │DATA │RECORDS ARE│ {data-name-3} . . . │ .
    ⌊     ⌊           ⌋                      ⌋
```

Data Description Entry

FORMAT 1

```
level-number  ⎡data-name-1⎤
              ⎣FILLER    ⎦

     [REDEFINES  data-name-2]

     [IS  EXTERNAL]

     [IS  GLOBAL]

     ⎡⎧PICTURE⎫                        ⎤
     ⎢⎨PIC    ⎬  IS  character-string  ⎥
     ⎣⎩       ⎭                        ⎦

     ⎡             ⎧BINARY         ⎫⎤
     ⎢             ⎪COMPUTATIONAL  ⎪⎥
     ⎢             ⎪COMP           ⎪⎥
     ⎢[USAGE IS]   ⎨DISPLAY        ⎬⎥
     ⎢             ⎪INDEX          ⎪⎥
     ⎢             ⎩PACKED-DECIMAL ⎭⎥
     ⎣                             ⎦

     ⎡           ⎧LEADING ⎫                    ⎤
     ⎢[SIGN  IS] ⎨TRAILING⎬ [SEPARATE CHARACTER]⎥
     ⎣           ⎩        ⎭                    ⎦

     ⎡OCCURS  integer-2  TIMES                              ⎤
     ⎢                                                      ⎥
     ⎢   ⎡⎧ASCENDING ⎫                        ⎤             ⎥
     ⎢   ⎢⎨DESCENDING⎬ KEY IS  {data-name-3} ...⎥ ...       ⎥
     ⎢   ⎣⎩          ⎭                        ⎦             ⎥
     ⎢   [INDEXED  BY  {index-name-1} . . . ]               ⎥
     ⎢OCCURS  integer-1  TO  integer-2  TIMES DEPENDING ON data-name-4⎥
     ⎢   ⎡⎧ASCENDING ⎫                        ⎤             ⎥
     ⎢   ⎢⎨DESCENDING⎬ KEY IS  {data-name-3} ...⎥ ...       ⎥
     ⎢   ⎣⎩          ⎭                        ⎦             ⎥
     ⎣   [INDEXED  BY  {index-name-1} . . . ]               ⎦

     ⎡⎧SYNCHRONIZED⎫ ⎡LEFT ⎤⎤
     ⎢⎨SYNC        ⎬ ⎣RIGHT⎦⎥
     ⎣⎩            ⎭        ⎦

     ⎡⎧JUSTIFIED⎫        ⎤
     ⎢⎨JUST     ⎬  RIGHT ⎥
     ⎣⎩         ⎭        ⎦

     [BLANK  WHEN  ZERO]

     [VALUE  IS  literal-1] .
```

FORMAT 2

```
66  data-name-1  RENAMES  data-name-2  ⎡⎧THROUGH⎫            ⎤
                                       ⎢⎨THRU   ⎬ data-name-3⎥ .
                                       ⎣⎩       ⎭            ⎦
```

FORMAT 3

```
88  condition-name-1  ⎧VALUE IS  ⎫ ⎧literal-1 ⎡⎧THROUGH⎫          ⎤⎫ ...  .
                      ⎨VALUES ARE⎬ ⎨          ⎢⎨THRU   ⎬ literal-2⎥⎬
                      ⎩          ⎭ ⎩          ⎣⎩       ⎭          ⎦⎭
```

Communication Description Entry

FORMAT 1

CD cd-name-1

```
              ┌                                                    ┐
              │ [ [SYMBOLIC QUEUE IS data-name-1]                  │
              │                                                    │
              │   [SYMBOLIC SUB-QUEUE-1 IS data-name-2]            │
              │                                                    │
              │   [SYMBOLIC SUB-QUEUE-2 IS data-name-3]            │
              │                                                    │
              │   [SYMBOLIC SUB-QUEUE-3 IS data-name-4]            │
              │                                                    │
              │   [MESSAGE DATE IS data-name-5]                    │
              │                                                    │
              │   [MESSAGE TIME IS data-name-6]                    │
              │                                                    │
              │   [SYMBOLIC SOURCE IS data-name-7]                 │
FOR [INITIAL] INPUT                                               │
              │   [TEXT LENGTH IS data-name-8]                     │
              │                                                    │
              │   [END KEY IS data-name-9]                         │
              │                                                    │
              │   [STATUS KEY IS data-name-10]                     │
              │                                                    │
              │   [MESSAGE COUNT IS data-name-11] ]                │
              │   [data-name-1, data-name-2, data-name-3,          │
              │    data-name-4, data-name-5, data-name-6,          │
              │    data-name-7, data-name-8, data-name-9,          │
              │    data-name-10, data-name-11]                     │
              └                                                    ┘
```

FORMAT 2

CD cd-name-1 FOR OUTPUT

[DESTINATION COUNT IS data-name-1]

[TEXT LENGTH IS data-name-2]

[STATUS KEY IS data-name-3]

[DESTINATION TABLE OCCURS integer-1 TIMES

    [INDEXED BY {index-name-1} . . .]]

[ERROR KEY IS data-name-4]

[SYMBOLIC DESTINATION IS data-name-5] .

FORMAT 3

CD cd-name-1

```
              ┌                                                ┐
              │ [ [MESSAGE DATE IS data-name-1]                │
              │                                                │
              │   [MESSAGE TIME IS data-name-2]                │
              │                                                │
              │   [SYMBOLIC TERMINAL IS data-name-3]           │
FOR [INITIAL] I-O                                              │
              │   [TEXT LENGTH IS data-name-4]                 │
              │                                                │
              │   [END KEY IS data-name-5]                     │
              │                                                │
              │   [STATUS KEY IS data-name-6] ]                │
              │   [data-name-1, data-name-2, data-name-3,      │
              │    data-name-4, data-name-5, data-name-6]      │
              └                                                ┘
```

Report Description Entry

```
RD  report-name-1

    [IS GLOBAL]

    [CODE literal-1]

    ⎡⎧CONTROL IS ⎫  ⎧{data-name-1} . . .      ⎫⎤
    ⎢⎩CONTROLS ARE⎭  ⎨FINAL  [data-name-1] . . .⎬⎥
    ⎣               ⎩                          ⎭⎦

    ⎡      ⎡LIMIT IS ⎤           ⎡LINE ⎤                     ⎤
    ⎢[PAGE ⎣LIMITS ARE⎦ integer-1 ⎣LINES⎦ [HEADING integer-2]⎥
    ⎣                                                        ⎦

        [FIRST DETAIL integer-3]  [LAST DETAIL integer-4]

        [FOOTING integer-5] ] .
```

Report Group Description Entry

FORMAT 1

```
01  [data-name-1]

    ⎡                  ⎧integer-1 [ON NEXT PAGE]⎫⎤
    ⎢LINE  NUMBER  IS  ⎨PLUS integer-2          ⎬⎥
    ⎣                  ⎩                        ⎭⎦

    ⎡                  ⎧integer-3           ⎫⎤
    ⎢NEXT GROUP  IS    ⎨PLUS  integer-4     ⎬⎥
    ⎢                  ⎪NEXT PAGE           ⎪⎥
    ⎣                  ⎩                    ⎭⎦

                      ⎧⎧REPORT HEADING⎫                 ⎫
                      ⎪⎩RH            ⎭                 ⎪
                      ⎪⎧PAGE HEADING⎫                   ⎪
                      ⎪⎩PH          ⎭                   ⎪
                      ⎪⎧CONTROL HEADING⎫ ⎧data-name-2⎫  ⎪
                      ⎪⎩CH             ⎭ ⎩FINAL      ⎭  ⎪
        TYPE  IS      ⎨⎧DETAIL⎫                         ⎬
                      ⎪⎩DE    ⎭                         ⎪
                      ⎪⎧CONTROL FOOTING⎫ ⎧data-name-3⎫  ⎪
                      ⎪⎩CF             ⎭ ⎩FINAL      ⎭  ⎪
                      ⎪⎧PAGE FOOTING⎫                   ⎪
                      ⎪⎩PF          ⎭                   ⎪
                      ⎪⎧REPORT FOOTING⎫                 ⎪
                      ⎩⎩RF            ⎭                 ⎭

    [ [USAGE IS] DISPLAY] .
```

FORMAT 2

```
level-number  [data-name-1]

    ⎡                  ⎧integer-1 [ON NEXT PAGE]⎫⎤
    ⎢LINE  NUMBER  IS  ⎨PLUS integer-2          ⎬⎥
    ⎣                  ⎩                        ⎭⎦

    [ [USAGE IS] DISPLAY] .
```

Report Group Description Entry *(continued)*

FORMAT 3

```
level-number  [data-name-1]

    ⎰PICTURE⎱  IS  character-string
    ⎱PIC    ⎰

    [ [USAGE  IS]  DISPLAY]

    ⎡           ⎰LEADING ⎱                      ⎤
    ⎢[SIGN  IS] ⎱TRAILING⎰ SEPARATE  CHARACTER  ⎥

    ⎡ ⎰JUSTIFIED⎱          ⎤
    ⎢ ⎱JUST     ⎰ RIGHT    ⎥

    [BLANK  WHEN  ZERO]

    ⎡                  ⎰integer-1  [ON  NEXT PAGE]⎱ ⎤
    ⎢LINE  NUMBER  IS  ⎱PLUS  integer-2           ⎰ ⎥

    [COLUMN  NUMBER  IS  integer-3]

    ⎰SOURCE  IS  identifier-1                                          ⎱
    ⎪VALUE  IS  literal-1                                              ⎪
    ⎨{SUM  {identifier-2} . . .  [UPON  {data-name-2} . . . ] } . . .  ⎬
    ⎪    ⎡          ⎰data-name-3⎱ ⎤                                    ⎪
    ⎩    ⎢RESET  ON ⎱FINAL      ⎰ ⎥                                    ⎭

    [GROUP  INDICATE] .
```

Procedure Division

FORMAT 1

```
[PROCEDURE DIVISION   [USING  {data-name-1} . . . ] .

[DECLARATIVES.

{section-name  SECTION  [segment-number] .

    USE statement.

[paragraph-name.

    [sentence] . . . ] . . . } . . .

END DECLARATIVES.]

{section-name  SECTION  [segment-number] .

[paragraph-name.

    [sentence] . . . ] . . . } . . . ]
```

FORMAT 2

```
[PROCEDURE DIVISION   [USING  {data-name-1} . . . ] .

[paragraph-name.

    [sentence] . . . } . . . ]
```

COBOL Verbs

```
ACCEPT  identifier-1   [FROM  mnemonic-name-1]
```

```
                              ⎧DATE       ⎫
                              ⎪DAY        ⎪
ACCEPT  identifier-2  FROM    ⎨DAY-OF-WEEK⎬
                              ⎪TIME       ⎪
                              ⎩           ⎭
```

```
ACCEPT  cd-name-1  MESSAGE COUNT
```

```
ADD  ⎧identifier-1⎫ . . .  TO  {identifier-2  [ROUNDED] } . . .
     ⎩literal-1   ⎭

     [ON  SIZE ERROR  imperative-statement-1]

     [NOT ON  SIZE ERROR  imperative-statement-2]

     [END-ADD]
```

```
ADD  ⎧identifier-1⎫ . . .  TO  ⎧identifier-2⎫
     ⎩literal-1   ⎭             ⎩literal-2   ⎭

     GIVING  {identifier-3}  [ROUNDED] } . . .

     [ON  SIZE ERROR  imperative-statement-1]

     [NOT ON  SIZE ERROR  imperative-statement-2]

     [END-ADD]
```

```
ADD  ⎧CORRESPONDING⎫  identifier-1  TO  identifier-2  [ROUNDED]
     ⎩CORR         ⎭

     [ON  SIZE ERROR  imperative-statement-1]

     [NOT ON  SIZE ERROR  imperative-statement-2]

     [END-ADD]
```

```
ALTER {procedure-name-1  TO  [PROCEED TO]  procedure-name-2} . . .
```

```
CALL  ⎧identifier-1⎫ ⎡USING ⎧[BY REFERENCE]  {identifier-2} . . . ⎫ . . .⎤
      ⎩literal-1   ⎭ ⎣      ⎩BY CONTENT   {identifier-2} . . .    ⎭     ⎦

     [ON  OVERFLOW  imperative-statement-1]  [END-CALL]
```

```
CALL  ⎧identifier-1⎫ ⎡USING ⎧[BY REFERENCE]  {identifier-2} . . . ⎫ . . .⎤
      ⎩literal-1   ⎭ ⎣      ⎩BY CONTENT   {identifier-2} . . .    ⎭     ⎦

     [ON  EXCEPTION  imperative-statement-1]

     [NOT ON  EXCEPTION  imperative-statement-2]

     [END-CALL]
```

COBOL Verbs *(continued)*

<u>CANCEL</u> {identifier-1 / literal-1} . . .

<u>CLOSE</u> {file-name-1 [[{<u>REEL</u> / <u>UNIT</u>} [FOR <u>REMOVAL</u>]] / [WITH {<u>NO REWIND</u> / <u>LOCK</u>}]] } . . .

<u>CLOSE</u> {file-name-1}   [WITH <u>LOCK</u>] } . . .

<u>COMPUTE</u> {identifier-1 [<u>ROUNDED</u>] } . . . = arithmetic-expression-1

    [ON <u>SIZE ERROR</u> imperative-statement-1]

    [<u>NOT</u> ON <u>SIZE ERROR</u> imperative-statement-2]

    [<u>END-COMPUTE</u>]

<u>CONTINUE</u>

<u>DELETE</u>   file-name-1   RECORD

    [<u>INVALID</u> KEY imperative-statement-1]

    [<u>NOT INVALID</u> KEY imperative-statement-2]

    [<u>END-DELETE</u>]

<u>DISABLE</u> {<u>INPUT</u> [<u>TERMINAL</u>] / <u>I-O TERMINAL</u> / <u>OUTPUT</u>} cd-name-1 [WITH <u>KEY</u> {identifier-1 / literal-1}]

<u>DISPLAY</u> {identifier-1 / literal-1} . . . [<u>UPON</u> mnemonic-name-1] [WITH <u>NO ADVANCING</u>]

<u>DIVIDE</u> {identifier-1 / literal-1} <u>INTO</u> {identifier-2 [<u>ROUNDED</u>] } . . .

    [ON <u>SIZE ERROR</u> imperative-statement-1]

    [<u>NOT</u> ON <u>SIZE ERROR</u> imperative-statement-2]

    [<u>END-DIVIDE</u>]

<u>DIVIDE</u> {identifier-1 / literal-1} <u>INTO</u> {identifier-2 / literal-2}

    <u>GIVING</u> {identifier-3 [<u>ROUNDED</u>] } . . .

    [ON <u>SIZE ERROR</u> imperative-statement-1]

    [<u>NOT</u> ON <u>SIZE ERROR</u> imperative-statement-2]

    [<u>END-DIVIDE</u>]

COBOL Verbs *(continued)*

```
DIVIDE   {identifier-1}  BY  {identifier-2}
         {literal-1   }      {literal-2   }

   GIVING {identifier-3 [ROUNDED] } . . .

   [ON SIZE ERROR imperative-statement-1]

   [NOT ON SIZE ERROR imperative-statement-2]

   [END-DIVIDE]
```

```
DIVIDE   {identifier-1}  INTO  {identifier-2}  GIVING  identifier-3  [ROUNDED]
         {literal-1   }        {literal-2   }

   REMAINDER identifier-4

   [ON SIZE ERROR imperative-statement-1]

   [NOT ON SIZE ERROR imperative-statement-2]

   [END-DIVIDE]
```

```
DIVIDE   {identifier-1}  BY  {identifier-2}  GIVING  identifier-3  [ROUNDED]
         {literal-1   }      {literal-2   }

   REMAINDER identifier-4

   [ON SIZE ERROR imperative-statement-1]

   [NOT ON SIZE ERROR imperative-statement-2]

   [END-DIVIDE]
```

```
ENABLE   {INPUT [TERMINAL]}                    {identifier-1}
         {I-O TERMINAL    }  cd-name-1 [WITH KEY {literal-1   }]
         {OUTPUT          }
```

```
EVALUATE {identifier-1}        {identifier-2}
         {literal-1   }        {literal-2   }
         {expression-1}  ALSO  {expression-2}  . . .
         {TRUE        }        {TRUE        }
         {FALSE       }        {FALSE       }

   { {WHEN

         {ANY                                                                        }
         {condition-1                                                                }
         {TRUE                                                                       }
         {FALSE                                                                      }
         {      {identifier-3           }  {THROUGH} {identifier-4           }        }
         {[NOT] {literal-3             }  {THRU   } {literal-4             }          }
         {      {arithmetic-expression-1}            {arithmetic-expression-2}       }
```

COBOL Verbs *(continued)*

```
 ┌ALSO                                                          ┐
 │  ┌ANY                                                     ┐  │
 │  │condition-2                                             │  │
 │  │TRUE                                                    │  │ ... } ...
 │  │FALSE                                                   │  │
 │  │      ┌identifier-5          ┐ ┌THROUGH┐ ┌identifier-6          ┐ │  │
 │  │[NOT] │literal-5             │ │THRU   │ │literal-6             │ │  │
 │  └      └arithmetic-expression-3┘ └       ┘ └arithmetic-expression-4┘ ┘  │
 └                                                              ┘

    imperative-statement-1} . . .

[WHEN OTHER  imperative-statement-2]

[END-EVALUATE]


EXIT


EXIT PROGRAM


GENERATE   ┌data-name-1  ┐
           └report-name-1┘


GO  TO  [procedure-name-1]


GO  TO  {procedure-name-1} . . .  DEPENDING  ON  identifier-1


IF  condition-1  THEN  ┌{statement-1} . . .┐ ┌ELSE {statement-2} . . . [END-IF]┐
                       └NEXT SENTENCE      ┘ │ELSE NEXT SENTENCE              │
                                             └END-IF                          ┘


INITIALIZE  {identifer-1} . . .

   ┌                ┌ALPHABETIC          ┐              ┌identifier-2┐    ┐
   │                │ALPHANUMERIC        │              │literal-1   │    │
   │REPLACING       │NUMERIC             │ DATA BY      └            ┘... │
   │                │ALPHANUMERIC-EDITED │                                │
   └                └NUMERIC-EDITED      ┘                                ┘


INITIATE  {report-name-1} . . .


INSPECT  identifier-1  TALLYING

 ┌                     ┌CHARACTERS ┌┌BEFORE┐ INITIAL ┌identifier-4┐┐ . . .       ┐    ┐
 │                     │           └└AFTER ┘         └literal-2   ┘┘             │    │
 │identifier-2  FOR    │                                                         │... │ ...
 │                     │┌ALL    ┐┌identifier-3┐┌┌BEFORE┐ INITIAL┌identifier-4┐┐...│... │
 └                     └└LEADING┘└literal-1   ┘└└AFTER ┘        └literal-2   ┘┘   ┘    ┘
```

COBOL Verbs *(continued)*

```
INSPECT  identifier-1  REPLACING

   ⎧                 ⎧identifier-5⎫ ⎡⎧BEFORE⎫         ⎧identifier-4⎫⎤      ⎫
   ⎪ CHARACTERS BY   ⎨           ⎬ ⎢⎨     ⎬ INITIAL ⎨           ⎬⎥ ...  ⎪
   ⎪                 ⎩literal-3  ⎭ ⎣⎩AFTER ⎭         ⎩literal-2  ⎭⎦      ⎪
   ⎨                                                                      ⎬ ...
   ⎪ ⎧ALL    ⎫ ⎧identifier-3⎫    ⎧identifier-5⎫ ⎡⎧BEFORE⎫         ⎧identifier-4⎫⎤       ⎪
   ⎪ ⎨LEADING⎬ ⎨           ⎬ BY ⎨           ⎬ ⎢⎨     ⎬ INITIAL ⎨           ⎬⎥ ... ... ⎪
   ⎩ ⎩FIRST  ⎭ ⎩literal-1  ⎭    ⎩literal-3  ⎭ ⎣⎩AFTER ⎭         ⎩literal-2  ⎭⎦         ⎭
```

```
INSPECT  identifier-1  TALLYING

   ⎧            ⎧ CHARACTERS ⎡⎧BEFORE⎫         ⎧identifier-4⎫⎤                        ⎫
   ⎪            ⎪            ⎢⎨     ⎬ INITIAL ⎨           ⎬⎥ ...                     ⎪
   ⎪            ⎪            ⎣⎩AFTER ⎭         ⎩literal-2  ⎭⎦                         ⎪
   ⎨identifier-2 FOR ⎨                                                                ⎬ ...
   ⎪            ⎪ ⎧ALL    ⎫ ⎧identifier-3⎫ ⎡⎧BEFORE⎫         ⎧identifier-4⎫⎤           ⎪
   ⎪            ⎪ ⎨LEADING⎬ ⎨           ⎬ ⎢⎨     ⎬ INITIAL ⎨           ⎬⎥ ... ...   ⎪
   ⎩            ⎩ ⎩       ⎭ ⎩literal-1  ⎭ ⎣⎩AFTER ⎭         ⎩literal-2  ⎭⎦            ⎭

   REPLACING

   ⎧                 ⎧identifier-5⎫ ⎡⎧BEFORE⎫         ⎧identifier-4⎫⎤      ⎫
   ⎪ CHARACTERS BY   ⎨           ⎬ ⎢⎨     ⎬ INITIAL ⎨           ⎬⎥ ...  ⎪
   ⎪                 ⎩literal-3  ⎭ ⎣⎩AFTER ⎭         ⎩literal-2  ⎭⎦      ⎪
   ⎨                                                                      ⎬ ...
   ⎪ ⎧ALL    ⎫ ⎧identifier-3⎫    ⎧identifier-5⎫ ⎡⎧BEFORE⎫         ⎧identifier-4⎫⎤       ⎪
   ⎪ ⎨LEADING⎬ ⎨           ⎬ BY ⎨           ⎬ ⎢⎨     ⎬ INITIAL ⎨           ⎬⎥ ... ... ⎪
   ⎩ ⎩FIRST  ⎭ ⎩literal-1  ⎭    ⎩literal-3  ⎭ ⎣⎩AFTER ⎭         ⎩literal-2  ⎭⎦         ⎭
```

```
INSPECT  identifier-1  CONVERTING  ⎧identifier-6⎫  TO  ⎧identifier-7⎫
                                   ⎨           ⎬      ⎨           ⎬
                                   ⎩literal-4  ⎭      ⎩literal-5  ⎭

   ⎡⎧BEFORE⎫         ⎧identifier-4⎫⎤
   ⎢⎨     ⎬ INITIAL ⎨           ⎬⎥ ...
   ⎣⎩AFTER ⎭         ⎩literal-2  ⎭⎦
```

```
MERGE  file-name-1  ⎧ON ⎧ASCENDING ⎫ KEY {data-name-1} ... ⎫ ...
                    ⎨   ⎨          ⎬                        ⎬
                    ⎩   ⎩DESCENDING⎭                        ⎭

   [COLLATING  SEQUENCE  IS  alphabet-name-1]

   USING  file-name-2  {file-name-3} ...

   ⎧ OUTPUT PROCEDURE  IS  procedure-name-1  ⎡⎧THROUGH⎫ procedure-name-2⎤ ⎫
   ⎨                                         ⎢⎨      ⎬                 ⎥ ⎬
   ⎩ GIVING {file-name-4} ...                ⎣⎩THRU  ⎭                 ⎦ ⎭
```

```
MOVE  ⎧identifier-1⎫  TO  {identifier-2} ...
      ⎨           ⎬
      ⎩literal-1  ⎭
```

```
MOVE  ⎧CORRESPONDING⎫  identifier-1  TO  identifier-2
      ⎨             ⎬
      ⎩CORR         ⎭
```

```
MULTIPLY  ⎧identifier-1⎫  BY  {identifier-2  [ROUNDED] } ...
          ⎨           ⎬
          ⎩literal-1  ⎭

   [ON  SIZE ERROR  imperative-statement-1]

   [NOT ON  SIZE ERROR  imperative-statement-2]

   [END-MULTIPLY]
```

COBOL Verbs *(continued)*

MULTIPLY $\begin{Bmatrix} \text{identifier-1} \\ \text{literal-1} \end{Bmatrix}$ <u>BY</u> {identifier-2 [<u>ROUNDED</u>] } . . .

    [ON <u>SIZE ERROR</u> imperative-statement-1]

    [<u>NOT</u> ON <u>SIZE ERROR</u> imperative-statement-2]

    [<u>END-MULTIPLY</u>]

MULTIPLY $\begin{Bmatrix} \text{identifier-1} \\ \text{literal-1} \end{Bmatrix}$ <u>BY</u> $\begin{Bmatrix} \text{identifier-2} \\ \text{literal-2} \end{Bmatrix}$

    <u>GIVING</u> {identifier-3 [<u>ROUNDED</u>] } . . .

    [ON <u>SIZE ERROR</u> imperative-statement-1]

    [<u>NOT</u> ON <u>SIZE ERROR</u> imperative-statement-2]

    [<u>END-MULTIPLY</u>]

<u>OPEN</u> $\begin{Bmatrix} \underline{\text{INPUT}}\ \{\text{file-name-1}\ \ [\text{WITH}\ \underline{\text{NO REWIND}}]\ \}\ .\ .\ . \\ \underline{\text{OUTPUT}}\ \{\text{file-name-2}\ \ [\text{WITH}\ \underline{\text{NO REWIND}}]\ \}\ .\ .\ . \\ \underline{\text{I-O}}\ \ \{\text{file-name-3}\}\ .\ .\ . \\ \underline{\text{EXTEND}}\ \ \{\text{file-name-4}\}\ .\ .\ . \end{Bmatrix}$ . . .

<u>OPEN</u> $\begin{Bmatrix} \underline{\text{INPUT}}\ \{\text{file-name-1}\}\ .\ .\ . \\ \underline{\text{OUTPUT}}\ \{\text{file-name-2}\}\ .\ .\ . \\ \underline{\text{I-O}}\ \ \{\text{file-name-3}\}\ .\ .\ . \\ \underline{\text{EXTEND}}\ \ \{\text{file-name-4}\}\ .\ .\ . \end{Bmatrix}$ . . .

<u>OPEN</u> $\begin{Bmatrix} \underline{\text{OUTPUT}}\ \{\text{file-name-1}\ \ [\text{WITH}\ \underline{\text{NO REWIND}}]\ \}\ .\ .\ . \\ \underline{\text{EXTEND}}\ \ \{\text{file-name-2}\}\ .\ .\ . \end{Bmatrix}$ . . .

<u>PERFORM</u> $\left[\text{procedure-name-1}\ \left[\begin{Bmatrix} \underline{\text{THROUGH}} \\ \underline{\text{THRU}} \end{Bmatrix}\ \text{procedure-name-2} \right] \right]$

    [imperative-statement-1 <u>END-PERFORM</u>]

<u>PERFORM</u> $\left[\text{procedure-name-1}\ \left[\begin{Bmatrix} \underline{\text{THROUGH}} \\ \underline{\text{THRU}} \end{Bmatrix}\ \text{procedure-name-2} \right] \right]$

    $\begin{Bmatrix} \text{identifier-1} \\ \text{integer-1} \end{Bmatrix}$ <u>TIMES</u> [imperative-statement-1 <u>END-PERFORM</u>]

<u>PERFORM</u> $\left[\text{procedure-name-1}\ \left[\begin{Bmatrix} \underline{\text{THROUGH}} \\ \underline{\text{THRU}} \end{Bmatrix}\ \text{procedure-name-2} \right] \right]$

    $\left[\text{WITH}\ \underline{\text{TEST}}\ \begin{Bmatrix} \underline{\text{BEFORE}} \\ \underline{\text{AFTER}} \end{Bmatrix} \right]$ <u>UNTIL</u> condition-1

    [imperative-statement-1 <u>END-PERFORM</u>]

COBOL Verbs *(continued)*

```
PERFORM [procedure-name-1 [{THROUGH} procedure-name-2]]
                           {THRU   }

        [WITH TEST {BEFORE}]
                   {AFTER }

        VARYING {identifier-2 } FROM {identifier-3 }
                {index-name-1}      {index-name-2}
                                    {literal-1    }

            BY {identifier-4} UNTIL condition-1
               {literal-2   }

        [AFTER {identifier-5} FROM {identifier-6 }
               {literal-3   }      {index-name-4}
                                   {literal-3    }  . . .

            BY {identifier-7} UNTIL condition-2]
               {literal-4   }

        [imperative-statement-1 END-PERFORM]


PURGE cd-name-1


READ file-name-1 [NEXT] RECORD [INTO identifier-1]

     [AT END imperative-statement-1]

     [NOT AT END imperative-statement-2]

     [END-READ]


READ file-name-1 RECORD [INTO identifier-1]

     [INVALID KEY imperative-statement-3]

     [NOT INVALID KEY imperative-statement-4]

     [END-READ]


READ file-name-1 RECORD [INTO identifier-1]

     [KEY IS data-name-1]

     [INVALID KEY imperative-statement-3]

     [NOT INVALID KEY imperative-statement-4]

     [END-READ]


RECEIVE cd-name-1 {MESSAGE} INTO identifier-1
                  {SEGMENT}

     [NO DATA imperative-statement-1]

     [WITH DATA imperative-statement-2]

     [END-RECEIVE]


RELEASE record-name-1 [FROM identifier-1]
```

COBOL Verbs *(continued)*

```
RETURN file-name-1 RECORD [INTO identifier-1]

    AT END imperative-statement-1

    [NOT AT END imperative-statement-2]

    [END-RETURN]


REWRITE record-name-1 [FROM identifier-1]


REWRITE record-name-1 [FROM identifier-1]

    [INVALID KEY imperative-statement-1]

    [NOT INVALID KEY imperative-statement-2]

    [END-REWRITE]
```

```
SEARCH identifier-1 [ VARYING { identifier-2  } ]
                                { index-name-2 }

    [AT END imperative-statement-1]

    { WHEN condition-1 { imperative-statement-2 } }  . . .
                        { NEXT-SENTENCE          }

    [END-SEARCH]
```

```
SEARCH ALL identifier-1 [AT END imperative-statement-1]

    WHEN { data-name-1 { IS EQUAL TO }  { identifier-3            } }
         {             { IS =         }  { literal-1              } }
         {                               { arithmetic-expression-1 } }
         { condition-name-2                                          }

    [ AND { data-name-2 { IS EQUAL TO }  { identifier-4            } } ]  . . .
          {             { IS =         }  { literal-2              } }
          {                               { arithmetic-expression-2 } }
          { condition-name-2                                          }

    { imperative-statement-2 }
    { NEXT SENTENCE          }

    [END-SEARCH]
```

```
SEND cd-name-1 FROM identifier-1


SEND cd-name-1 [FROM identifier-1]  { WITH identifier-2 }
                                     { WITH ESI         }
                                     { WITH EMI         }
                                     { WITH EGI         }

    [ { BEFORE } ADVANCING { identifier-3 } [ LINE  ] ]
      { AFTER  }           { integer-1    } [ LINES ]
                           { mnemonic-name-1 }
                           { PAGE         }

    [REPLACING LINE]
```

COBOL Verbs *(continued)*

```
SET {index-name-1 }  . . .  TO  {index-name-2 }
    {identifier-1 }             {identifier-2 }
                               {integer-1   }


SET {index-name-3} . . . {UP BY  } {identifier-3}
                         {DOWN BY} {integer-2  }


SET {{mnemonic-name-1} . . . TO {ON }} . . .
                                {OFF}


SET {condition-name-1} . . . TO TRUE


SORT file-name-1 {ON {ASCENDING }  KEY {data-name-1} . . . } . . .
                     {DESCENDING}

    [WITH DUPLICATES IN ORDER]

    [COLLATING SEQUENCE IS alphabet-name-1]

    {INPUT PROCEDURE IS procedure-name-1 [{THROUGH} procedure-name-2]}
    {                                     {THRU   }                  }
    {USING [file-name-2] . . .                                       }

    {OUTPUT PROCEDURE IS procedure-name-3 [{THROUGH} procedure-name-4]}
    {                                      {THRU   }                  }
    {GIVING [file-name-3] . . .                                       }


START file-name-1 [KEY {IS EQUAL TO             }               ]
                       {IS =                    }               
                       {IS GREATER THAN         }               
                       {IS >                    } data-name-1   
                       {IS NOT LESS THAN        }               
                       {IS NOT <                }               
                       {IS GREATER THAN OR EQUAL TO}            
                       {IS >=                   }               

    [INVALID KEY imperative-statement-1]

    [NOT INVALID KEY imperative-statement-2]

    [END-START]


STOP {RUN      }
     {literal-1}
```

COBOL Verbs *(continued)*

STRING {identifier-1 / literal-1} . . . DELIMITED BY {identifier-2 / literal-2 / SIZE} . . .

    INTO   identifier-3

    [WITH POINTER   identifier-4]

    [ON   OVERFLOW   imperative-statement-1]

    [NOT ON   OVERFLOW   imperative-statement-2]

    [END-STRING]

SUBTRACT {identifier-1 / literal-1} . . . FROM {identifier-3 [ROUNDED] } . . .

    [ON   SIZE ERROR   imperative-statement-1]

    [NOT ON   SIZE ERROR   imperative-statement-2]

    [END-SUBTRACT]

SUBTRACT {identifier-1 / literal-1} . . . FROM {identifier-2 / literal-2}

    GIVING   {identifier-3}   [ROUNDED] } . . .

    [ON   SIZE ERROR   imperative-statement-1]

    [NOT ON   SIZE ERROR   imperative-statement-2]

    [END-SUBTRACT]

SUBTRACT {CORRESPONDING / CORR} identifier-1 FROM identifier-2 [ROUNDED]

    [ON   SIZE ERROR   imperative-statement-1]

    [NOT ON   SIZE ERROR   imperative-statement-2]

    [END-SUBTRACT]

SUPPRESS   PRINTING

TERMINATE   {report-name-1} . . .

UNSTRING   identifier-1

    [DELIMITED   BY   [ALL]   {identifier-2 / literal-1}   [OR   [ALL]   {identifier-3 / literal-2}]] . . .

    INTO   {identifier-4   [DELIMITER   IN   identifier-5]   [COUNT   IN   identifier-6] } . . .

    [WITH   POINTER   identifier-7]

    [TALLYING   IN   identifier-8]

    [ON   OVERFLOW imperative-statement-1]

    [NOT   ON   OVERFLOW imperative-statement-2]

    [END-UNSTRING]

COBOL Verbs *(continued)*

```
USE [GLOBAL] AFTER STANDARD {EXCEPTION} PROCEDURE ON {{file-name-1} ...
                            {ERROR    }                {INPUT
                                                       {OUTPUT
                                                       {I-O
                                                       {EXTEND
```

```
USE [GLOBAL] BEFORE REPORTING identifier-1
```

```
USE FOR DEBUGGING ON {cd-name-1                      } ...
                     {[ALL REFERENCES OF] identifier-1}
                     {file-name-1                    }
                     {procedure-name-1               }
                     {ALL PROCEDURES                 }
```

```
WRITE record-name-1 [FROM identifier-1]

  [{BEFORE}  ADVANCING {{identifier-2} [LINE ]}]
  [{AFTER }            {{integer-1   } [LINES]}]
                       {{mnemonic-name-1}      }
                       {{PAGE          }       }

  [AT {END-OF-PAGE} imperative-statement-1]
  [   {EOP        }                       ]

  [NOT AT {END-OF-PAGE} imperative-statement-2]
  [       {EOP        }                       ]

  [END-WRITE]
```

```
WRITE record-name-1 [FROM identifier-1]

  [INVALID KEY imperative-statement-1]

  [NOT INVALID KEY imperative-statement-2]

  [END-WRITE]
```

COPY and REPLACE Statements

```
COPY text-name-1 [{OF} library-name-1]
                 [{IN}               ]

  [REPLACING {{== pseudo-text-1 ==}  BY  {== pseudo-text-2 ==}} ...]
  [          {identifier-1        }      {identifier-2        }    ]
  [          {literal-1           }      {literal-2           }    ]
  [          {word-1              }      {word-2              }    ]
```

```
REPLACE {== pseudo-text-1 ==  BY  == pseudo-text-2 ==} ...
```

```
REPLACE OFF
```

Conditions

RELATION CONDITION

$$
\begin{Bmatrix} \text{identifier-1} \\ \text{literal-1} \\ \text{arithmetic-expression-1} \\ \text{index-name-1} \end{Bmatrix}
\begin{Bmatrix} \text{IS [NOT] } \underline{\text{GREATER}} \text{ THAN} \\ \text{IS [NOT] } > \\ \text{IS [NOT] } \underline{\text{LESS}} \text{ THAN} \\ \text{IS [NOT] } < \\ \text{IS [NOT] } \underline{\text{EQUAL}} \text{ TO} \\ \text{IS [NOT] } = \\ \text{IS } \underline{\text{GREATER}} \text{ THAN } \underline{\text{OR}} \underline{\text{EQUAL}} \text{ TO} \\ \text{IS } >= \\ \text{IS } \underline{\text{LESS}} \text{ THAN } \underline{\text{OR}} \underline{\text{EQUAL}} \text{ TO} \\ \text{IS } <= \end{Bmatrix}
\begin{Bmatrix} \text{identifier-2} \\ \text{literal-2} \\ \text{arithmetic-expression-2} \\ \text{index-name-2} \end{Bmatrix}
$$

CLASS CONDITION

$$
\text{identifier-1 IS [NOT] }
\begin{Bmatrix} \underline{\text{NUMERIC}} \\ \underline{\text{ALPHABETIC}} \\ \underline{\text{ALPHABETIC-LOWER}} \\ \underline{\text{ALPHABETIC-UPPER}} \\ \text{class-name} \end{Bmatrix}
$$

CONDITION-NAME CONDITION

condition-name-1

SWITCH-STATUS CONDITION

condition-name-1

SIGN CONDITION

$$
\text{arithmetic-expression-1 IS [NOT] }
\begin{Bmatrix} \underline{\text{POSITIVE}} \\ \underline{\text{NEGATIVE}} \\ \underline{\text{ZERO}} \end{Bmatrix}
$$

NEGATED CONDITION

<u>NOT</u> condition-1

COMBINED CONDITION

$$
\text{condition-1 } \left\{ \begin{Bmatrix} \underline{\text{AND}} \\ \underline{\text{OR}} \end{Bmatrix} \text{condition-2} \right\} \ldots
$$

ABBREVIATED COMBINED RELATION CONDITION

$$
\text{relation-condition } \left\{ \begin{Bmatrix} \underline{\text{AND}} \\ \underline{\text{OR}} \end{Bmatrix} \text{[NOT] [relational-operator] object} \right\} \ldots
$$

Qualification

FORMAT 1

$$\left\{ \begin{matrix} \text{data-name-1} \\ \text{condition-name} \end{matrix} \right\} \left\{ \begin{matrix} \left\{ \begin{matrix} \text{IN} \\ \text{OF} \end{matrix} \right\} \text{data-name-2} \end{matrix} \right\} \cdots \left[\begin{matrix} \text{IN} \\ \text{OF} \end{matrix} \right] \left\{ \begin{matrix} \text{file-name} \\ \text{cd-name} \end{matrix} \right\} \right] \left\{ \begin{matrix} \text{IN} \\ \text{OF} \end{matrix} \right\} \left\{ \begin{matrix} \text{file-name} \\ \text{cd-name} \end{matrix} \right\}$$

FORMAT 2

$$\text{paragraph-name} \left\{ \begin{matrix} \text{IN} \\ \text{OF} \end{matrix} \right\} \text{section-name}$$

FORMAT 3

$$\text{text-name} \left\{ \begin{matrix} \text{IN} \\ \text{OF} \end{matrix} \right\} \text{library-name}$$

FORMAT 4

$$\underline{\text{LINAGE-COUNTER}} \left\{ \begin{matrix} \text{IN} \\ \text{OF} \end{matrix} \right\} \text{report-name}$$

FORMAT 5

$$\left\{ \begin{matrix} \underline{\text{PAGE-COUNTER}} \\ \underline{\text{LINE-COUNTER}} \end{matrix} \right\} \left\{ \begin{matrix} \text{IN} \\ \text{OF} \end{matrix} \right\} \text{report-name}$$

FORMAT 6

$$\text{data-name-3} \left\{ \begin{matrix} \left\{ \begin{matrix} \text{IN} \\ \text{OF} \end{matrix} \right\} \text{data-name-4} \left[\begin{matrix} \text{IN} \\ \text{OF} \end{matrix} \right] \text{report-name} \\ \left\{ \begin{matrix} \text{IN} \\ \text{OF} \end{matrix} \right\} \text{report-name} \end{matrix} \right\}$$

Miscellaneous Formats

SUBSCRIPTING

$$
\begin{Bmatrix} \text{condition-name-1} \\ \text{data-name-1} \end{Bmatrix}
\left(
\begin{Bmatrix} \text{integer-1} \\ \text{data-name-2} \quad [\ \{\pm\}\ \text{integer-2}] \\ \text{index-name-1} \quad [\ \{\pm\}\ \text{integer-3}] \end{Bmatrix} \ldots
\right)
$$

REFERENCE MODIFICATION

data-name-1 $\left(\text{leftmost-character-position:}\quad [\text{length}]\right)$

IDENTIFIER

data-name-1 $\left[\begin{Bmatrix} \underline{\text{IN}} \\ \underline{\text{OF}} \end{Bmatrix} \text{data-name-2}\right]$ . . . $\left[\begin{Bmatrix} \underline{\text{IN}} \\ \underline{\text{OF}} \end{Bmatrix} \begin{Bmatrix} \text{cd-name} \\ \text{file-name} \\ \text{report-name} \end{Bmatrix}\right]$

[({subscript} . . .)]　　[(leftmost-character-position:　[length])]

Nested Source Programs

IDENTIFICATION DIVISION.

PROGRAM-ID. program-name-1 [IS INITIAL PROGRAM] .

[ENVIRONMENT DIVISION. environment-division-content]

[DATA DIVISION. data-division-content]

[PROCEDURE DIVISION. procedure-division-content]

[[nested-source-program] . . .

END PROGRAM program-name-1.]

NESTED-SOURCE-PROGRAM

IDENTIFICATION DIVISION.

PROGRAM-ID.　program-name-2 $\left[\text{IS} \begin{Bmatrix} \underline{\text{COMMON}} \\ \underline{\text{INITIAL}} \end{Bmatrix} \text{PROGRAM}\right]$.

[ENVIRONMENT DIVISION. environment-division-content]

[DATA DIVISION. data-division-content]

[PROCEDURE DIVISION. procedure-division-content]

[nested-source-program] . . .

END PROGRAM　program-name-2.

A Series of Source Programs

```
{IDENTIFICATION DIVISION.

PROGRAM-ID.  program-name-3  [IS  INITIAL  PROGRAM ] .

[ENVIRONMENT DIVISION. environment-division-content]

[DATA DIVISION. data-division-content]

[PROCEDURE DIVISION. procedure-division-content]

[nested-source-program] . . .

END PROGRAM program-name-3.} . . .

IDENTIFICATION DIVISION.

PROGRAM-ID.  program-name-4  [IS  INITIAL  PROGRAM ] .

[ENVIRONMENT DIVISION. environment-division-content]

[DATA DIVISION. data-division-content]

[PROCEDURE DIVISION. procedure-division-content]

[ [nested-source-program] . . .

END PROGRAM  program-name-4.]
```

E

COBOL in the New Millennium

Overview: The COBOL language is overdue for its next major revision. Since its origination in 1958, COBOL has had several major revisions reflecting the changing needs of business information systems. Each revision has added to the power and capability of the language. and now perhaps the most sweeping revision is waiting in the wings.

COBOL was originally designed to be as English-like as possible. Even mathematical expressions were to be stated in English. Thus, COBOL has verbs like ADD, SUBTRACT, MULTIPLY, and DIVIDE. Every effort was made to make the language readable, so that even a non-programmer could read it. Eventually, it became apparent that this idealistic approach was too limiting. Programmers found that specifying complex expressions only through the use of ADD, SUBTRACT, MULTIPLY, and DIVIDE verbs was too restrictive. COBOL needed a way to make writing mathematical expressions easy in a way similar to FORTRAN and other languages. The 1964 revision made COBOL more flexible with the addition of the COMPUTE verb and other changes.

By 1974 a new revision was needed. Business applications needed to manipulate character data as well as numbers. Thus, new string operations were added and the INSPECT verb was improved. However, by the 1980s, structured programming had become the standard way to write programs, and COBOL needed to change in order to take advantage of this new technique.

After much discussion in the COBOL community and after the delay of several years, COBOL 1985 was finally released. COBOL 1985 had many new and important features. For the first time, in-line PERFORM statements meant that loops were available directly in the code without having to set up separate paragraphs. Statement terminators such as END-IF and END-READ meant that logic errors caused by the careless placement of the period could be reduced. COBOL 1985 provided a powerful new Case statement, EVALUATE, reducing the programmer's reliance on nested IFs. Another major development in COBOL 1985 was the use of subprograms and new ways of structuring programs. COBOL 1985 was a major step forward in the development of the language. The new COBOL was less English-like, but still maintained its readability, business orientation, and compatibility with previous versions.

In 1989, an enhanced version of the 1985 standard was released. The major change in this version was the introduction of intrinsic functions that were common in other programs but had been neglected in COBOL. Now COBOL programs could use statistical functions such as Average and Standard Deviation as well as business functions such as Present Value and Annuity.

Now, a new COBOL standard is being prepared. Just as the paradigm shift to Structured programming meant a revision to the COBOL standards, the new paradigm shift to object-oriented programming means that COBOL must again be revised. The major addition to the new COBOL is object-orientation, and Chapter 20 deals extensively with those changes. However, there are a number of less dramatic changes in the next version of COBOL that programmers should know about even if they do not use OO COBOL.

That is the good news; the bad news is that the wheels of standardization grind very slowly. The new standards were scheduled to be approved and become official in 1997. However, for a variety of reasons the final approval appears to be delayed until the year 2002. This delay is extremely unfortunate and does not help the cause of the COBOL language.

In spite of this setback, some compiler vendors have made good faith efforts to begin implementing some of the new language features. The COBOL community should push for a quick adoption of the new standards and ask their language vendors how they are supporting the new standards.

The purpose of this appendix is to describe the enhancements to COBOL that were included in the 1989 revisions and the projected enhancements for COBOL 2002. The appendix does not describe these changes in detail; our aim is intended to provide a summary of the major improvements and their impact.

The major change in the 1989 revision was the addition of intrinsic functions. This appendix includes a section on intrinsic functions that presents:

- The concept of functions.
- The format of the FUNCTION statement.
- Classification of the functions by type.
- Brief descriptions of key functions.
- An introduction to the proposed additions to the functions.
- A discussion of user-defined functions.

The second section of the appendix discusses new data types including Boolean and the operators allowed by the new standards.

Finally, we discuss some of the changes that improve the language, but are difficult to classify.

Intrinsic Functions

Most computer languages provide a set of predefined functions that save programming effort. These functions do standard and well-understood mathematical, business, and statistical operations. COBOL has been slow to adopt this capability, but at last, there was a general recognition that the language had moved beyond being just a specialized business language. Therefore, in 1989 an enhancement to the 1985 standards defined 42 "intrinsic" functions. Intrinsic means "inherent" or "part of." Thus, these functions are now part of the language.

A function performs an operation and returns a result. Generally functions are used within assignment statements and can be used instead of a variable or literal. Within COBOL the assignment verbs are MOVE and COMPUTE. An example would be:

```
MOVE FUNCTION UPPER CASE ("abcdef") TO DATA-STRING
```

The function-identifier specifies the function as UPPER CASE, and the single argument shown in the parentheses is "abcdef." The UPPER CASE function converts alphanumeric data to upper case, and as a result DATA-STRING contains the value "ABCDEF" after the MOVE statement has been performed.

An example of a numeric function-identifier would be:

```
COMPUTE NUMERIC-ITEM = FUNCTION SIN(10)
```

The COMPUTE statement calculates the sine of 10 and return the value to NUMERIC-ITEM so that the final value of NUMERIC-ITEM is 0.544. SIN is the function identifier and 10 is the argument.

The format of a function-identifier is as follows:

```
FUNCTION function-name-1 [({argument-1}. . .)]
```

Numeric functions must be used with COMPUTE cannot be used with ADD, SUBTRACT, MULTIPLY, or DIVIDE.

Function Types

The various types of intrinsic functions are shown in the following tables. We have categorized them according to their purpose.

Two business functions are now provided to make the computation of annuities and the value of investments easier.

Table E.1 Business Functions

Function Name	Argument-1	Argument-2	Result
ANNUITY	Interest rate for period	Number of Periods	The ratio of an annuity paid for an initial investment of $1.00
PRESENT-VALUE	Discount Rate	A series of Future Payments	The present value of the Future Payments based on the Discount Rate

Date functions are based primarily on a starting date of January 1, 1601. This arbitrary date is established to assure accuracy for date arithmetic under virtually all circumstances. All dates are based on the Gregorian calendar. Dates supplied to a date function must be valid calendar dates after December 31, 1600.

Table E.2 Date Functions

Function Name	Argument-1	Argument-2	Result
CURRENT-DATE	None	None	Returns the current system date and time in YYYYMMDDHHMMSShh format
DATE-OF-INTEGER	Number of Days succeeding December 31, 1600		Returns the date in YYYYMMDD format
DAY-OF-INTEGER	Number of Days succeeding December 31, 1600		Returns the date in YYYYDDD format
INTEGER-OF DATE	Date in YYYYMMDD format		Returns an integer for the number of days succeeding December 31, 1600
INTEGER OF DAY	Date in YYYYDDD format		Returns an integer for the number of days succeeding December 31, 1600

There are a number of mathematical functions available as intrinsic functions. All except the Sum function have a single argument. The Sum function can have as many arguments as required, since it adds up a series of numbers.

Table E.3 Mathematical Functions

Function Name	Argument-1	Argument-2	Results
ACOS	Number	None	Returns the Arcosine of the number
ASIN	Number	None	Returns the Arcsine of the number
ATAN	Number	None	Returns the Arctangent of the number
COS	Number	None	Returns the Cosine of the number
FACTORIAL	Number	None	Returns the Factorial of the number
LOG	Number	None	Returns the natural Logarithm of the number
LOG10	Number	None	Returns the Logarithm to base 10 of the number
SIN	Number	None	Returns the Sine of the number
SUM	Number	Number (as many as needed)	Returns the total of all values specified
SQRT	Number	None	Returns the Square Root of the number
TAN	Number	None	Returns the Tangent of the number

The intrinsic functions also include a number of statistical functions. Statistical functions work on a series of numbers. The number series can be specified by using one argument for each value. When tables are involved, there is an easier method. Statistical functions can specify ALL for the subscript in the argument, as in the following example:

```
01   TEST-ARRAY.
     05   TEST-RESULT      PIC  9(03).
     05   TEST-ITEMS       OCCURS 5 TIMES PIC  9(02).


COMPUTE TEST-RESULT = FUNCTION SUM (TEST-ITEMS (ALL)).
```

This statement adds all of the values in the table TEST-ITEMS and stores the results in TEST-RESULT. The SUM function can be considered as a mathematical or statistical function.

Table E.4 Statistical Functions

Function Name	Argument-1	Argument-2	Results
MAX	Number series	As needed	Returns the value of the highest number in the series
MEAN	Number series	As needed	Returns the arithmetic average of the series
MEDIAN	Number series	As needed	Returns the middle value of the series where there are as many values above as below
MIDRANGE	Number series	As needed	Returns the average of the maximum argument and the minimum argument
RANDOM	Number (not required)	None	Returns a random number between 0 and 1. If argument-1 is specified, it must be zero or a positive integer and is used as a seed value
RANGE	Number series	As needed	Returns a value that is equal to the value of the maximum argument minus the value of the minimum argument
STANDARD-DEVIATION	Number series	As needed	Returns the standard deviation of the series
SUM	Number series	As needed	Returns the sum of the number series
VARIANCE	Number series	As needed	Returns the variance of the number series

Another set of functions deals with the use of alphanumeric data and conversion between alphanumeric and numeric data.

Table E.5 Alphanumeric and Conversion Functions

Function Name	Argument-1	Argument-2	Results
CHAR	Integer	None	The alphanumeric character corresponding to ordinal position in the collating sequence
LENGTH	Alphanumeric string	None	Returns the number of characters in the string
LOWER-CASE	Alphanumeric string	None	Converts all alphabetic characters to lower case
NUMVAL	Edited numeric string	None	Returns the numeric value of the edited string. Cannot be used with currency symbol
NUMVAL-C	Edited numeric string with currency symbol	Symbol used as currency symbol	Returns the numeric value of the edited string. Uses argument-2 to determine the currency symbol
ORD	Alphanumeric character	None	Returns the ordinal position number of the alphanumeric character
ORD-MAX	Alphanumeric or numeric series	None	Returns the ordinal position number within the series of the element having the highest collating value
ORD-MIN	Alphanumeric or numeric series	None	Returns the ordinal position number within the series of the element having the lowest collating value
REVERSE	Alphanumeric string	None	Returns an alphanumeric string the same length as argument-1 with the characters in reverse order
UPPER-CASE	Alphanumeric string	None	Converts all alphabetic characters to upper case

Finally, a set of miscellaneous functions that are not easily categorized into one of the above tables is provided.

Table E.6 Miscellaneous Functions

Function Name	Argument-1	Argument-2	Results
INTEGER	Numeric value		Largest Integer not greater than Argument-1. If Argument-1 is +2.3, +2 is returned. If Argument-1 is -2.3, the value returned is -3
INTEGER-PART	Numeric value		Integer portion of Argument-1. If Argument-1 is +2.3, +2 is returned. If Argument-1 is -2.3, -2 is returned
MOD	Integer	Integer	Returns the value of the remainder when Argument-1 is divided by Argument-2. The result is an integer value
REM	Numeric value	Numeric value	Same as MOD but can use and return non-integer values.
WHEN-COMPILED	None	None	Returns the compile date and time in YYYYMMDDHHMMDD format

Intrinsic Functions Added in COBOL 2002

COBOL 2002 adds a number of functions to the 1989 extensions. Several of these functions deal with manipulation of national characters—symbols that are not part of the English language, but are used in other languages. There are also functions that handle special collating sequences in other languages. The following table includes only the new functions that are of more general interest. Other functions may be added or changed before the new standards are adopted.

Table E.7 COBOL 2002 Functions

Function Name	Argument-1	Argument-2	Results
ABS	Numeric value		Returns the absolute value of Argument-1
ALLOCATED-OCCURRENCES	Dynamic Table		Returns an integer value for the number of occurrences allocated in the table
BOOLEAN-OF	Positive Integer	Positive Integer	Returns the binary value of Argument-1 in a binary field with Argument-2 number of bits
DATE-TO-YYYYMMDD	Positive Integer	Integer	Converts YYMMDD date format to YYYYMMDD format. Argument-2 allows adjustment to the century range Argument-2 defines the ending year as a displacement from the current system year. If Argument-2 is omitted, the default is 50
DAY-TO-YYYYDDD	Positive Integer	Integer	Converts YYDDD date to format to YYYYDDD format. Argument-2 allows adjustment to century range
E	None	None	Returns the value of *e*, the natural logarithm base
EXP	Numeric Item		Returns the value of *e* raised to the Argument-1 power
EXP10	Numeric Item		Returns the value of 10 raised to the Argument-1 power
FRACTION-PART	Numeric Item		Returns the fractional part of Argument-1 eliminating the integer portion
NUMVAL-B	Boolean Value		Returns the decimal equivalent of the Binary value of Argument-1. Function may use the SIGNED keyword following Argument-1 to indicate that Argument-1 is a signed value
NUMVAL-F	Numeric value specified as floating point		Returns the decimal equivalent of Argument-1
PI	None		Returns the value of PI up to 31 decimal places
YEAR-TO-YYYY	Positive Integer	Integer	Converts YY to YYYY. Argument-2 specifies a window for candidate dates.

In addition to the new intrinsic functions defined above, COBOL 2002 also allows the creation and use of user defined functions.

New Data Types

The COBOL 2002 standards allow for several new data types that have been available to other languages. These data types include new fixed length BINARY data fields, Floating-Point data types, and new pointer types. These data types can be specified by the USAGE clause of data items within the DATA DIVISION.

COBOL 1985 allowed the BINARY data type. This data type has a variable length dependent upon places specified in the picture clause. The binary options have been expanded to a Boolean data type and several fixed length BINARY data types.

- BIT—this data type is a Boolean Data type used for Boolean Operations. The size of the field is specified by the Picture clause.

- BINARY-CHAR—a binary field using 1 byte for representation.

- BINARY-SHORT—a binary file 2 bytes in length.

- BINARY-LONG —a binary field 4 bytes in length.

- BINARY-DOUBLE—a binary field 8 bytes in length.

COMP(UTATIONAL) usage is left up to the compiler implementers, but is generally the equivalent of BINARY.

Floating point numbers are specified as FLOAT-SHORT or FLOAT-LONG. The size of the fields is dependent on the implementor. Generally, the FLOAT-SHORT will use 2 bytes of storage and FLOAT-LONG uses 4 bytes. In other languages, these data types may be called "Single" or "Double."

These new data types will make the linking of COBOL programs with programs developed in other languages much easier. COBOL will be able to receive and pass data directly to programs written in other languages. This new compatibility is also enhanced by an new INTEGER data type. This data type accepts Integer data in the format of other languages. The use of INTEGER is limited to use in the LINKAGE SECTION of programs and must be associated with a BY VALUE reference.

In connection with object-oriented COBOL, the 2002 standard provides a new pointer type to specify the pointers for Objects. This USAGE is OBJECT REFERENCE. The pointer type follows the conventions of other pointer and index data types. The SET verb must be used to update these fields.

Miscellaneous New Features

Free Form Source Code: In the new COBOL standards, the COBOL programmer is freed from the confines of the 80-column card. The new standards allow source code lines to be from 0 to 255 characters in length, and the code can be placed anywhere in the line. In order to achieve this new freedom, the standards committee has decided to change the comment indicator from a "*" in column 7 to the characters "*>" placed anywhere in the source code line. Any characters to the right of the comment indicator are treated as comments. The comment stops at the end of a line. Therefore, if a comment needs to go onto two or more lines, each comment line or area must begin with "*>". There is no symbol to stop the comment.

The free format also provides new capability in continuing literals from one line to another. The partial literal on the first line should be ended by a "- or '-. The second line of the can start anywhere on the second line, but must begin with a " or '. The literal must conclude with a " or '.

The new free format provides new flexibility in writing code and in program documentation.

Fewer Required Entries: Another change in the coding of programs is a loosening of the rules for required entries in a program. For example, the Division headers do not have to be specified at all. Section headers are still needed, but only for the sections actually used. One exception to the new rule about Division headers is when the Procedure Division needs a Linkage Section. The Procedure Division header has to specify the use of the Linkage Section. Therefore, the Procedure Division header to define Linkage Section entries.

Conclusion

COBOL 2002 is part of the language's gradual evolution. While the introduction of object-orientation is the primary new language feature, the addition of new intrinsic functions, the new data types, and the new freedom for coding programs will all make the COBOL programmer's life easier.

Answers to Odd-Numbered Exercises

Chapter 1

Fill-in

1. Input, processing, output
3. Flowchart
5. Decision
7. Programmer-supplied-name
9. Relational
11. Fields

True/False

1. False. Nonnumeric literals may contain numbers, letters, or special characters.
3. False. A dataname may contain hyphens.
5. True.
7. True.
9. False. They must appear in order: IDENTIFICATION, ENVIRONMENT, DATA, and PROCEDURE.
11. True.
13. False. They must be told exactly what to do, and the instructions take the form of a computer program.
15. False. A diamond indicates a decision; a rectangle implies straightforward processing.
17. False. Reserved words are restricted to a preassigned use.
19. False. The rules for pseudocode are at the discretion of the programmer.

Chapter 2

Fill-in

1. Compiler, source, object (machine)
3. A margin
5. 12, 72
7. Editor (word processor)
9. Debugging
11. Linker
13. Different
15. Execution

True/False

1. False. A compiler translates a problem-oriented language into a machine-oriented language.
3. True.
5. True.
7. False. Division headers may begin anywhere in the A margin (columns 8 to 11), although many people begin them in column 8.
9. False. Paragraph names begin in the A margin.

11. False. A clean compile means only that the program has been translated into machine language; it says nothing about whether the logic of the program is correct.

13. True.

15. False. Each text editor has its own unique commands.

17. False. The compiler produces an object module which is input to the linker, which in turn produces the load module.

Chapter 3

Fill-in

1. Sequence, selection, and iteration
3. One, one
5. Hierarchy chart
7. Completeness, functionality, and span of control
9. Pseudocode
11. Span of control
13. Bohm, Jacopini
15. Top down

True/False

1. False. It may still contain logic errors, but presumably fewer than nonstructured code.
3. False. Initialization and termination are too vague and do not follow the verb, adjective, object convention for naming paragraphs.
5. True.
7. False. It is an extension to sequence, selection, and iteration.
9. False. The rules of pseudocode are at the discretion of the programmer, although individual shops may impose standards.

11. False. Testing should begin as soon as possible with the aid of program stubs.
13. False. The name implies that the paragraph is doing three distinct things, as opposed to having a single function.
15. False. Program testing should be ongoing throughout the life of the project.
17. False. The optimal number of modules is a function of the program's design.

Chapter 4

Fill-in

1. Identification
3. Braces
5. Programmer supplied
7. SELECT
9. PICTURE
11. FILE, WORKING-STORAGE
13. may not
15. BLOCK CONTAINS, logical, physical

True/False

1. True.
3. False. Square brackets indicate the entry is optional.
5. False. Some modification, generally in the Environment Division is required.
7. False. It will have a picture clause if it is an elementary item.
9. False. A group item never has a picture clause.

11. False. The determination of whether a data item is a group or elementary item depends on the definition of subordinate data items.
13. True.
15. False. Technically, a program may be written without a File Section, although this is unusual.
17. False. It is optional as indicated by the brackets in the COBOL notation.

Chapter 5

Fill-in

1. COMPUTE
3. ROUNDED
5. Before
7. Does not
9. STOP RUN
11. N + 1

13. AFTER ADVANCING PAGE
15. One, left, right
17. Decimal alignment
19. May not
21. SIZE ERROR

True/False

1. True.
3. False. An ADD statement must contain one word or the other.
5. True.
7. False. The use of BY or INTO determines which operand is the dividend, and which one is the divisor.
9. True.
11. False. If multiplication and division are both present, the order of operations is from left to right.
13. True.
15. True.

17. False. STOP RUN is the last statement executed, but it need not be (and usually isn't) the last physical statement in the program.
19. False. The READ statement specifies a file name.
21. False. They are required whenever a file is present. (Strictly speaking, if a program did not reference any files, then the statements would not be used).
23. True.
25. False. ROUNDED is an optional clause in all the arithmetic statements.
27. False. It is an optional clause.

Chapter 6

Fill-in

1. Compilation
3. Execution
5. Compiles

7. Structured walkthrough
9. Detection, correction
11. Run Time Errors

True/False

1. False. A clean compile means only that the program has been successfully translated into machine language.
3. False. The compiler checks for syntax only and has no way of determining the validity of a program's logic.
5. True.
7. True.

9. False. Spaces are generally required after punctuation symbols, but not before.
11. False. A data name may contain hyphens, letters, or digits only.
13. False. One reads a file and writes a record.
15. False. Walkthroughs should be held for everyone.
17. False. A walkthrough should take a maximum of two hours.

Chapter 7

Fill-in

1. Coding standards
3. Floating, fixed
5. V, S

7. Verb, adjective, object
9. Indentation
11. Negative

True/False

1. False. Indentation is used to improve the readability of a program.
3. False. Coding standards are a function of the individual shop.
5. False. Data names should be meaningful to simplify program maintenance, an activity which takes far more time than initial coding and data entry.
7. False. Comments should be used with caution, and always for a specific purpose; a common fault of beginners is to overcomment.
9. False. The name implies that the paragraph is performing two functions.

11. False. A VALUE clause is used only to assign an initial value; for example for heading lines in Working-Storage. (VALUE clauses are not permitted in the FILE SECTION.)
13. False. The assignment of CR and/or DB depends on the accounting system in use.
15. False. One or the other should be selected, depending on the accounting system.
17. True.
19. True.

Chapter 8

Fill-in

1. Validated (checked)
3. Numeric
5. Completeness

7. 88
9. END-IF

True/False

1. False. The output of the edit program is input to the reporting program.
3. True.
5. False. The alphabetic class test can be applied to only alphabetic or alphanumeric data.

7. True.
9. True.
11. False. DAY and DATE imply the Julian and calendar dates, respectively.

Chapter 9

Fill-in

1. Two
3. Section
5. Qualified, OF, IN

7. STRING, UNSTRING, and INSPECT
9. BEFORE, AFTER
11. In-line

True/False

1. True.
3. False. An in-line perform does not specify a procedure.
5. False. CORRESPONDING is always optional.
7. False. The CORRESPONDING option has several fine points, but level number is not one of them.

9. False. It is an optional statement which is not favored by the authors.
11. True.

Chapter 10

Fill-in

1. Is not
3. SECURE
5. Last

7. Should not
9. TEST BEFORE
11. Interactive

True/False

1. False. Both sections may appear in the same program.
3. False. The clauses are optional.
5. True.

7. False. The text would be illegible; i.e., it would blend into the background.
9. True.

Chapter 11

Fill-in

1. OCCURS
3. Variable, OCCURS DEPENDING ON
5. May

7. Is
9. Does not change

True/False

1. False. Tables are established through an OCCURS clause.
3. True.
5. True. However if a subscript does assume a zero value, it would indicate a logic error in the program.

7. False. An index can be used only with the table for which it was defined.
9. False. Variable length records means that records in a file are of different lengths.
11. False. An index is modified by a SET or PERFORM statement.

Chapter 12

Fill-in

1. 100, 676, 1296
3. Hard-coded
5. Positional
7. REDEFINES

9. KEY
11. INDEXED BY
13. Compilation
15. Range step

True/False

1. True.
3. True.
5. True.
7. True.
9. True.

11. False. Examination of the COBOL syntax shows an additional WHEN clause enclosed in brackets.
13. True.
15. True. Good practice however, dictates that a separate subscript be used for every table.

17. True.
19. True.
21. True.
23. False. All codes should be unique.

25. True.
27. False. A range step table occurs when a one-to-one correspondence no longer exists.

Chapter 13

Fill-in

1. OCCURS
3. Seven
5. May not, OCCURS, REDEFINES

7. 1, 6, 2, 1, 6
9. 1, 2, 3.

True/False

1. True.
3. True in COBOL-85, but not in COBOL-74.
5. True.

7. False. The program would compile cleanly, but produce problems during execution.
9. False. The clauses are all optional

Chapter 14

Fill-in

1. Key
3. EBCDIC, ASCII
5. Primary (major), secondary (intermediate), tertiary (minor)

7. GIVING, OUTPUT PROCEDURE
9. SELECT, SD
11. Trailing, embedded
13. Identical

True/False

1. False. It can be used on a calculated field if INPUT PROCEDURE is specified.
3. False. INPUT PROCEDURE may also be specified with GIVING.
5. True.
7. False. They are associated with INPUT PROCEDURE and OUTPUT PROCEDURE, respectively.
9. True.
11. True.

13. False. The INPUT PROCEDURE is used if you want to selectively pass records to the sort work file; for example, to increase efficiency by sorting on fewer records.
15. True.
17. False. INPUT PROCEDURE is not used with the MERGE statement.
19. False. The MERGE statement requires that all input files have identical record layouts and appear in the same sequence.

Chapter 15

Fill-in

1. Change, control break
3. Is
5. Before

7. Pseudocode
9. Less
11. Rolling

True/False

1. False. Control breaks can theoretically extend to any number of levels, although they lose meaning after three or four.
3. True.

5. True.
7. True.
9. True.

Chapter 16

Fill-in

1. EXIT PROGRAM
3. Is
5. Both

7. COPY
9. BY REFERENCE
11. CALL

True/False

1. False. The COPY statement is permitted anywhere except within another COPY.
3. False. They can be the same, but there is no COBOL requirement stating they must be the same.
5. False. The COPY statement is permitted anywhere except within another COPY.

7. False. A program may call several subprograms.
9. False. All parameters must be elementary items except for those passed at the 01 level.
11. False. Both are optional; omission of both phrases defaults to calling BY REFERENCE which is equivalent to a CALL statement in COBOL-74.

Chapter 17

Fill-in

1. Every
3. Does
5. Additions, changes (corrections), deletions
7. Can

9. Can not
11. Stubs, DISPLAY
13. HIGH-VALUES

True/False

1. True.
3. True.
5. True.
7. False. Duplicate additions can only be checked against the master file; i.e., during the actual update.
9. False. Pseudocode is procedural in nature and indicates sequence and decision making. Hierarchy charts are functional and indicate what has to be done, not necessarily when or if.

11. False. The programmer is biased (either consciously or unconsciously), as he or she wrote the program and knows what it does or doesn't do. Ideally test data should be designed by the user, but this is often difficult to achieve.
13. False. The balance line algorithm may be used with multiple transaction files (as was done in the chapter).

Chapter 18

Fill-in

1. Indexed
3. VSAM, indexed
5. Highest
7. Unique, duplicate, alternate (secondary)

9. Optional, two, WORKING-STORAGE
11. START
13. DYNAMIC

True/False

1. False. Specification of ALTERNATE RECORD KEY will require substantial amounts of overhead in retrieving records from an indexed file; it should not be used indiscriminately.
3. False. The COBOL notation places both clauses in brackets to indicate optional entries. Logically, however, one of the two conditions must pertain, and consequently either clause should be specified. (The authors find these clauses easier to follow than testing the equivalent FILE STATUS entries.)

5. False. Specification of zero alternate areas will slow processing.
7. False. The ALTERNATE RECORD KEY need not be unique, as per the WITH DUPLICATES clause.
9. True.
11. False. They have different functions; to enter a new record and to change an existing record.
13. True.

Chapter 19

Fill-in

1. storage, memory
3. not been

5. integer, date, YYYYMMDD
7. is

True/False

1. True
3. False, they were added in 1989
5. False, INTEGER-TO-DATE returns YYYYMMDD and INTEGER-TO-DAY returns YYYYDDD

7. True

Chapter 20

Fill-in

1. is
3. class, instance
5. Inheritance

7. Base
9. polymorphism

True/False

1. False, many of the basic concepts remain.
3. False, the Procedure Division is necessary to specify the use of the Linkage Section.
5. True

7. True
9. True

Projects

Project 2-1

Program Name: Price Break Report

Narrative: Write a program to determine whether a customer receives a price break based on quantity ordered.

Input File: ORDER-TRANSACTION-FILE

Input Record Layout:

Order Record			
Customer Number		Quantity Ordered	Item Number
1 ... 8	9	10 ... 12	13 ... 17

Test Data:

```
          1         2         3         4         5         6
1234567890123456789012345678901234567890123456789012345678901234 5
51347935 00511111
42309847 10021222
38901974 12532333
21564823 50043444
10024567 90054555
```

Report Layout:

```
          1         2         3         4         5         6         7
1234567890123456789012345678901234567890123456789012345678901234567890 12
1 XXXXXXXX   XXXXX   999      99
2    |         |       |       |
3 Customer   Item    Qty    Discount
4 Number   Number  Ordered  Percent
5
```

Processing Requirements:

1. Read a file of order records.

2. For every record read, determine the discount the customer will receive. The discounting of an item is based on the Item Series and Quantity Ordered. Item Series is indicated by the first byte of the Item Number. For example, Item Number 12345 is Item Series 1 because it starts with a 1. The eligibility of discounting is determined as follows.

	Quantity Ordered	Discount Percent
Item Series 1 & 2	0–100	0%
	101–500	10%
	501–999	20%
Item Series 3, 4, & 5	0–50	0%
	51–100	15%
	101–500	20%
	501–999	25%

3. Print the Customer Number, Item Number, Quantity Ordered, and Discount Percent allowed for each customer record. Single-space the output.

Project 2-2

Program Name: Inter-City Piano Program

Narrative: Write a program for the Inter-City Piano Company. The program is to process a file of customer records and produce a list of people eligible for a discount in buying a piano.

Input File: CUSTOMER-LESSON-FILE

Input Record Layout:

Customer Lesson Record				
Last Name	First Name	# of Lesson		Purchase Indicator
1 ... 15	16 ... 25	26 ... 28	29	30

Test Data:

```
         1         2         3         4         5         6
1234567890123456789012345678901234567890123456789012345678901234567890

CRAWFORD       SHERRY    011 N
KARVAZY        KAREN     017 Y
MORSE          KENNETH   014 N
PLUMETREE      MICHELE   027 N
SLY            MATTHEW   019 N
POWERS         NANCY     024 Y
BLAKELY        KRISTEN   008 Y
```

Report Layout:

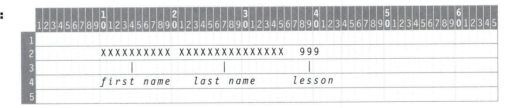

```
         1         2         3         4         5         6
1234567890123456789012345678901234567890123456789012345678901234567890

XXXXXXXXXX XXXXXXXXXXXXXXX  999
     |             |          |
 first name    last name    lesson
```

Processing Requirements:

1. Read a file of customer records.

2. For every record read, determine whether that person is eligible for a discount to buy a piano. Individuals who have taken 15 or more lessons and have not yet purchased a piano qualify. Do not consider as eligible anyone with a "Y" in position 30 of the input record which indicates that a piano has already been purchased.

3. Print the names of all qualified individuals according to item 2 above. Single-space the output. (Do not print the names of individuals who are not eligible.)

Project 2-3

Program Name: Delinquent Accounts

Narrative: Write a program to process a corporation's account file to select a list of problem accounts. The generated list will then be brought to the attention of the comptroller.

Input File: CUSTOMER-ACCOUNT-FILE

Input Record Layout:

Customer Account Record							
Name		Account No.		Account Owed		Days Overdue	
1 ... 15	16	17 ... 22	23	24 ... 28	29	30 ... 32	

Test Data:

```
         1         2         3         4         5         6
1234567890123456789012345678901234567890123456789012345678901 2345
ACME ENTERPRISE 111111 01000 010
BAKER BROTHERS   222222 20000 030
BENJAMIN CO      333333 00500 015
FRANKEL CORP     444444 27500 045
CLARK PROGRESS   555555 32000 005
MARSHAK BOOKS    666666 03500 060
KARLSTROM INC    777777 00100 045
MILGROM THEATRE  888888 15000 014
SPRINGS WATER    999999 20000 007
```

Report Layout: Design your own report layout.

Processing Requirements:

1. Read a file of customer account records.

2. Determine if the record is a problem account. An account is considered a problem if the amount owed is over 20,000 or the account is more than 30 days overdue.

3. Print the name and associated information (account number, amount owed, and days overdue) of all problem accounts. Space this information reasonably over a print line. Double-space the report.

Project 2-4

Program Name: Shoe Inventory Program

Narrative: Write a program to process a file of shoe inventory records and produce a list of shoes that need reordering.

Input File: SHOE-INVENTORY-FILE

Input Record Layout:

Shoe Inventory Record			
Vendor Name	Style No.	Quantity on Hand	Reorder Quantity
1 … 12	13 … 18	19 … 22	23 … 26

Test Data:

```
         1         2         3         4         5         6
1234567890123456789012345678901234567890123456789012345
BASS        12121204500300
BRUNO MAGLI 23232305000500
KEDS        34343407000750
JOAN & DAVID45454500500025
LA GEAR     56565605000550
FLORSHEIM   67676701000075
NIKE        78787803000200
REEBOK      89898907000800
```

Report Layout:

```
         1         2         3         4         5         6
1234567890123456789012345678901234567890123456789012345

    XXXXXXXXXXXX   XXXXXX    9999    9999

    vendor name   style #   QOH     Reorder
```

Processing Requirements:

1. Read a file of shoe inventory records.

2. For each record read, determine whether a particular shoe style should be reordered. Shoes should be reordered when the quantity on hand falls below the reorder quantity.

3. Print the vendor name, style number, quantity on hand, and reorder quantity for only the shoes that should be reordered.

Project 2-5

Program Name: Mailing List Program

Narrative: Write a program to process a file of mailing list records and produce a mailing list.

Input File: MAILING-LIST-FILE

Input Record Layout:

Mailing List Record			
Name	Street Address	City and State	Zip
1 … 20	21 … 45	46 … 63	64 … 68

Test Data:

```
          1         2         3         4         5         6
1234567890123456789012345678901234567890123456789012345678
ROBERT T. GRAUER     60 PACIFIC COAST HWY     SANTA BARBARA, CA 93101
JANE DOE             123 SOUTH STREET         CHARLOTTE, NC     28203
JOHN SMITH           21 JUMP STREET           AUSTIN, TX        78701
DEBRA L. FEIT        59 BROADWAY              NEW YORK, NY      10006
MEGAN J. ALVORD      9 SOUTH SHORE DRIVE      BEVERLY HILLS, CA 90210
GEORGE BERENS        73 WEST FLAGLER          MIAMI, FL         33130
GARY FEIN            45 MAIN STREET W         CHICAGO, IL       60648
CAROL VAZQUEZ VILAR  9 ROAD TO HANA           MAUI, HI          96713
```

Report Layout:

```
            1         2         3         4         5         6
  1234567890123456789012345678901234567890123456789012345678901234 5
1
2       XXXXXXXXXXXXXXXXXXXX – name
3       XXXXXXXXXXXXXXXXXXXXXXXXXX – street address
4       XXXXXXXXXXXXXXXXXX XXXXX
5               |             |
6          city & state     zip
```

Processing Requirements:

1. Read a file of mailing list records.

2. For each record read, create a mailing label. Double-space between each record.

Project 2-6

Program Name: Church Building Fund Report

Narrative: Write a program to print a Church Building Fund Report containing all church members who are behind on their contributions.

Input File: CHURCH-BLD-FUND-MSTR-FILE

Input Record Layout:

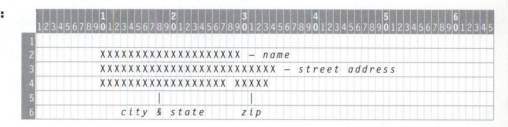

Church Building Fund Master Record					
Member Name		Pledged Amount		Member Number	Amount Given
1 ... 15	16 ... 20	21 ... 25	26 ... 30	31 ... 34	35 ... 39

Test Data:

```
          1         2         3         4         5         6
1234567890123456789012345678901234567890123456789012345
JOHN SMITH          00100     000100050
ANN LOVING          00200     000200025
MARY BROWN          00500     000300500
TOM SAWYER          00075     000400000
JACK CAPPS          03400     000503400
JILL JACOBS         40000     000603500
SUSAN CLUB          02000     000702000
MIKE CLOUD          00300     000800150
```

Report Layout:

```
         1         2         3         4         5         6         7
1234567890123456789012345678901234567890123456789012345678901234567890 12
1  XXXXXXXXXXXXXX   99999      99999       99999
2       |           |          |           |
3    MEMBER        AMOUNT     GIVEN       AMOUNT
4    NAME          PLEDGED    AMOUNT      OWED
5                             TO DATE
```

Processing Requirements:

1. Read a file of church member building fund master records.

2. For every record read:

   a. Calculate the AMOUNT OWED = AMOUNT PLEDGED - AMOUNT GIVEN

   b. Print the church member name, the amount pledged, the amount paid to date, and the amount owed for each church member who owes money to the church. Single–space each line.

Project 2-7

Program Name: Telephone Long Distance Carrier Program

Narrative: Write a program to process a file of telephone records to produce a report list of customers who are *not* using ET&T as a long distance carrier.

Input File: TELEPHONE-FILE

Input Record Layout:

Telephone Record			
Name	Area Code	Phone No.	Long Distance Carrier
1 ... 18	19 ... 21	22 ... 28	29 ... 35

Test Data:

```
         1         2         3         4         5         6
123456789012345678901234567890123456789012345678901234567890 12345
MARYANN BARBER    3055557634AT&T
JOEL STUTZ        4076341234ET&T
ROBERT PLANT      3124374962SPRINT
GREGG ELOFSON     2032469368MCI
SARA RUSHINEK     2126662916ET&T
MARK GILLENSON    3163969476TELTEC
DAVID HERTZ       6132463618MCI
JOHN STEWART      8133246846TELTEC
```

Report Layout:

```
         1         2         3         4         5         6
123456789012345678901234567890123456789012345678901234567890 12345
1
2     XXXXXXXXXXXXXXXXXX   (XXX) XXX-XXXX    XXXXXX
3          |                 |       |         |
4         name              area  phone #   long distance
5                           code             carrier
```

Processing Requirements:

1. Read a file of telephone records.

2. For each record read, determine whether the long distance carrier is ET&T or not.

3. Print the name, complete phone number, and the current long distance carrier of the records that are *not* using ET&T.

Programming Specifications

Project 3-1

Program Name: Insurance Policy Holder Report

Narrative: Develop a hierarchy chart and either flowchart, pseudocode, or Warnier-Orr diagram for a program to determine which customers have group life insurance policies.

Input File: CUSTOMER -INSURANCE-FILE

Input Record Layout:

Customer Insurance Record				
Customer Number		First Insurance Policy Held	Effective Date	Expiration Date
1 ... 8	9	10 ... 11	12 ... 19	20 ... 27
		Second Insurance Policy Held	Effective Date	Expiration Date
		28 ... 29	30 ... 37	38 ... 45
		Third Insurance Policy Held	Effective Date	Expiration Date
		46 ... 47	48 ... 55	56 ... 63
		First Policy Premium	First Insurance Policy Method of Payment	
		64 ... 68	69	
		Second Policy Premium	Second Insurance Policy Method of Payment	
		70 ... 74	75	
		Third Policy Premium	Third Insurance Policy Method of Payment	
		76 ... 80	81	

Test Data:

```
         1         2         3         4         5         6         7         8
123456789012345678901234567890123456789012345678901234567890123456789012345678901234567890123456789012345
51347935 GL09101999091020000UL0801199808012000HE0515199905152001015000A00400Q00025M
42309847 SA04281998042820000HE1108199811082001                    00010M00300Q
38901974 UL06131999061320000GL0101200001012002                    00400A00500M
21564823 AS05031998050320000XL1210199912102002GL01041999010420010000300M00150Q05000A
10024567 HE04041998040420000                                      00500M
```

Report Layout:

```
         1         2         3         4         5         6         7
1234567890123456789012345678901234567890123456789012345678901234567890123456789012
1              USA INSURANCE COMPANY
2              GROUP LIFE POLICY REPORT
3
4  CUSTOMER      EFFECTIVE      EXPIRATION      POLICY
5  NUMBER        DATE           DATE            PREMIUM
   XXXXXXX       XX/XX/XXXX     XX/XX/XXXX      9999999


   TOTAL GROUP POLICY PREMIUMS   99999999
```

Processing Requirements:

1. Read a file of customer records.

2. For every record read:

   a. Determine whether the customer has a group life insurance policy. Each customer can have as many as three different insurance policies. Check all three policies to determine whether they are group life. A group life insurance policy is indicated with the code 'GL'.

   b. Calculate the POLICY PREMIUM for each group life insurance policy by checking the METHOD OF PAYMENT field. If the METHOD OF PAYMENT field contains an "M," multiply the rate times 12 (months). If the METHOD OF PAYMENT field contains a "Q," multiply the rate times 4 (quarterly). If the METHOD OF PAYMENT field contains an "A," the rate is the POLICY PREMIUM (annual).

   c. Accumulate the POLICY PREMIUMS, giving the TOTAL GROUP POLICY PREMIUMS.

   d. Print the customer number, effective date, expiration date, rate, and policy premium for each customer who has a group life insurance policy. Single-space the output.

3. After all records have been read, print the total group life policy premiums.

Project 3-2

Program Name: Price Break Report

Narrative: This project builds on Project 2-1. Develop the hierarchy chart and either flowchart, pseudocode, or Warnier-Orr diagram to determine whether a customer receives a price break based on quantity ordered, and calculate the unit price and extended price.

Input file: ORDER-TRANSACTION-FILE

Input Record Layout:

Order Record					
Customer Number		Quantity Ordered	Item Number		Unit Price
1 ... 8	9	10 ... 12	13 ... 17	18	19 ... 21

Test Data:

```
         1         2         3         4         5         6
1234567890123456789012345678901234567890123456789012345
513479350005111119105
423098470100212228020
389019740125323337300
215648230500434446340
100245670900545555065
```

Report Layout:

```
          1         2         3         4         5         6         7
 123456789012345678901234567890123456789012345678901234567890123456789012
1                    AUSTIN    RETAIL    COMPANY
2
3 CUSTOMER   ITEM       QTY      UNIT     EXTENDED    TOTAL       TOTAL
4 NUMBER     NUMBER   ORDERED   PRICE      PRICE    QUANTITY      SALES
5 XXXXXXXX   XXXXX      999      999      999999    ORDERED
                                                     999999    999999999
```

Processing Requirements:

1. Read a file of order records.

2. For every record read:

    a. Determine whether the customer will receive a discount based on the specifications in Project 2-1.

    b. Calculate the Unit Price by applying the appropriate discount as determined in 2a.

    c. Calculate the Extended Price by multiplying the Quantity Ordered by the Unit Price.

    d. Accumulate the Total Quantity Ordered by adding the Quantity Ordered. Accumulate the Total Sales by adding the Extended Price.

    e. Print the customer number, item number, quantity ordered, unit price (calculated), and extended price for each customer record. Single-space the output.

3. After all records have been read, print the total quantity ordered and the total sales.

Project 3-3

Program Name: Barcoded Price List

Narrative: Develop the hierarchy chart and either flowchart, pseudocode, or Warnier-Orr diagram for a program to create and print a barcoded price list.

Input File: ITEM-PRICE-FILE

Input Record Layout:

Item Price Record		
Item Number	Quantity on Hand	Unit Price
1 ... 5	6 ... 9	10 ... 14

Test Data:

```
                    1         2         3         4         5         6
           1234567890123456789012345678901234567890123456789012345678901234 5
           11080105000100
           12400120001400
           13050001000200
           14450020001350
           23010010000200
           31054100000050
           05100006000213
           02187090600045
           95678002000300
           10234001000024
```

Report Layout:

```
                 1         2         3         4         5         6         7
        123456789012345678901234567890123456789012345678901234567890123456789012
     1                    COMPANY ABC BARCODED PRICE LIST
     2
     3   BARCODED           BARCODED            ITEM          UNIT
     4  ITEM NUMBER         UNIT PRICE          NUMBER        PRICE
     5   <9999999>          <9999999>           99999         99999

        TOTAL ITEMS:        9999999
```

Processing Requirements:

1. Read a file of price records.

2. For every record read:

   a. Determine the check digits for the barcoded item number and unit price as follows:

   Add each number in the field together and divide by the number of digits being added, then multiply the result by 3.

   Place the check digits to the right of the field for 2 positions and place a < to the left of the first digit and > to the right of the last digit.

   When the price list prints, a barcode font should be used to cause the appropriate fields to be barcoded (this cannot be done in the lab environment, the fields will just print normal).

   For example: ITEM NUMBER = 12345

   check digit = 1 + 2 + 3 + 4 + 5 = 15

   15/5 = 3

   3 * 3 = 9

   check digit = 09

   BARCODED ITEM NUMBER = <1234509>

   < indicates the beginning of a barcode field and > indicates the end of a barcode field.

   Check digits are used to ensure that proper transmission has occurred. The program that uses the data after transmission uses the above algorithm to determine whether the proper data has been sent. If the answer derived does not match the check digits, something was not transmitted properly.

   b. Increment an accumulator for number of items.

   c. Print the barcoded item number, barcoded unit price, item number, and unit price.

3. After all records have been read, print the total items.

Project 3-4

Program Name: Savings Dividends

Narrative: Develop the hierarchy chart and either flowchart, pseudocode, or Warnier-Orr diagram for a program to process a file of savings account records and compute and print a dividend report for each account and a total. The Identification, Environment, and Data Divisions for this project can be developed after Chapter 4. Completion of the project requires you to finish Chapter 5 in order to do the Procedure Division.

Input File: SAVINGS-FILE

Input Record Layout:

Savings Record			
Account Number	Name	Amount	Term
1 ... 8	9 ... 25	26 ... 32	33 34

Test Data:

```
          1         2         3         4         5         6
1234567890123456789012345678901234567890123456789012345678901234 5

11000-01MILGROM          004556018
23000-05PETERS           003067016
31001-02SMITH            002589012
43045-03JONES            006988024
51005-01VILLAR           000455006
35010-02HANSEN           010936036
```

Report Layout:

```
          1         2         3         4         5         6
1234567890123456789012345678901234567890123456789012345678901234567
  ACCOUNT                         SAVINGS   DIVIDEND       TOTAL
  NUMBER        NAME              AMOUNT      PAID       SAVINGS

  XXXXXXXX    XXXXXXXXXXXXXXXXX   9999999   9999999     99999999



                        TOTALS  ---------  ---------  ----------
                                99999999   99999999   999999999
```

Processing Requirements:

1. Print a heading at the beginning of the report.

2. Read a file of savings account records.

3. Process each record read by:

   a. Determining the interest rate as follows:

     (1) 6% interest on terms of 6 months or less.

     (2) 7% interest on terms of more than 6 months but less than 12.

     (3) 8% interest on terms of more than 12 months but less than 18.

     (4) 9% interest on terms of more than 18 months but less than 24.

       (5)   10% interest on terms of more than 24 months but less than 30.

       (6)   12% interest on terms of more than 30 months.

    b. Calculating the dividend to be paid by multiplying the amount by the interest rate.

    c. Calculating the total savings by adding the interest to be paid to the account amount.

    d. Incrementing savings totals for savings amount, dividend paid, and total savings.

    e. Printing a detail line for each record read.

  4. Print a total line at the end of the report.

Project 3-5

Program Name: Evaluation of Student Curriculum Records

Narrative: Develop the hierarchy chart and either flowchart, pseudocode, or Warnier-Orr diagram for a program to evaluate a student's curriculum record and determine the percentage of courses a student has left in order to to graduate, the percentage of courses a student has transferred, the percentage of courses for which a student has been awarded proficiency credit, and the percentage of courses a student has completed.

Input File: STUDENT-CURRICULUM-FILE

Input Record Layout:

Student Curriculum Record			
Student Id Number	Course Number 1	Grade 1	
1 ... 5	6 ... 12	13	
Course Number 2	Grade 2	Course Number 3	Grade 3
14 ... 20	21	22 ... 28	29
Course Number 4	Grade 4	Course Number 5	Grade 5
30 ... 36	37	38 ... 44	45
Course Number 6	Course Grade 6	Number 7	Grade 7
46 ... 52	53	54 ... 60	61
Course Number 8	Course Grade 8	Number 9	Grade 9
62 ... 68	69	70 ... 76	77
Course Number 10	Grade 10		
78 ... 84	85		

Test Data:

```
         1         2         3         4         5         6         7         8
1234567890123456789012345678901234567890123456789012345678901234567890123456789012345
11345COMP110AENGL110AMATH148KMATH168PCIS150 FCIS230  PSYC105BBUSN110AHUMN410PHUMN4285
34567ENGL110CENGL120CMATH048CMATH210DCIS150 PCIS230 ACIS330
78921BUSN110 BUSN120 ENGL110AENGL120PMATH048KMATH168BMATH220
34678PSYC105APSYC305AENGL110AENGL120 ECON210AHUMN410KHUMN420PHUMN430AACCT213AACCT347
47830SPCH275AENGL110AACCT205AACCT210PACCT347K
```

Report Layout:

```
          1         2         3         4         5         6         7
 1234567890123456789012345678901234567890123456789012345678901234567890123456789012
 1                          UNIVERSITY OF NOWHERE
 2                     STUDENT CURRICULUM EVALUATION
 3
 4 STUDENT ID                        PERCENTAGE OF COURSES
 5  NUMBER      COMPLETED    REMAINING    TRANSFERRED PROFICIENCY

     XXXXX         999          999          999         999
```

Processing Requirements:

1. Read a file of student curriculum records.

2. For every record read:

   a. Add the total number of courses (course name, not spaces) for each student (a maximum of 10).

   b. Add the total number of courses where the student was awarded a grade (A, B, C, or D), proficiency (P), or transfer credit (K).

   c. Add the total number of courses where the student was awarded transfer credit (K).

   d. Add the total number of courses where the student was awarded proficiency credit (P).

   e. Determine the percentages of courses left in order to graduate, courses completed, courses transferred, and courses awarded proficiency credit.

   f. Print student id number and the percentages of courses left in order to graduate, courses completed, courses transferred, and courses awarded proficiency credit.

Project 3-6

Program Name: Inventory Parts List

Narrative: Develop the hierarchy chart and either flowchart, pseudocode, or Warnier-Orr diagram for a program to produce an inventory report. The Identification, Environment, and Data Divisions for this project can be developed after Chapter 4. Completion of the project requires you to finish Chapter 5 in order to do the Procedure Division.

Input File: INVENTORY-FILE

Input Record Layout:

Inventory Record				
Part Name	Quantity on Hand	Amount Received	Amount Shipped	Unit Price
1 20	21 ... 23	24 ... 26	27 ... 29	30 ... 33

Test Data:

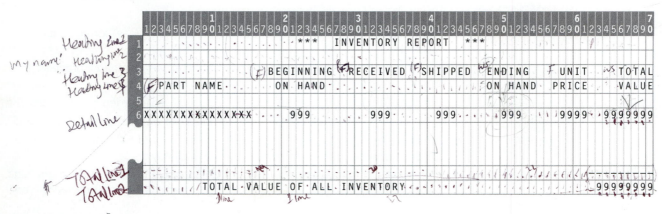

```
                     1         2         3         4         5         6
            1234567890123456789012345678901234567890123456789012345
WIDGETS, SIZE S      1500500960070
WIDGETS, SIZE M      2000750760080
WIDGETS, SIZE L      0005004000090
WHOSIWHATSIS         3501100460100
GIZMOS, TYPE A       2500800360200
GIZMOS, TYPE B       0000500250300
GADGETS, SIZE S      0250180260015
GADGETS, SIZE L      0900280350025
```

Report Layout:

```
                 1         2         3         4         5         6         7
        1234567890123456789012345678901234567890123456789012345678901234567890
1                         *** INVENTORY REPORT ***
2
3                  BEGINNING  RECEIVED  SHIPPED   ENDING    UNIT    TOTAL
4        PART NAME. . .ON HAND. . . . . . . . . .ON HAND   PRICE    VALUE
5
6        XXXXXXXXXXXXXX    999       999       999       999      9999   9999999


         TOTAL VALUE OF ALL INVENTORY                                  99999999
```

(Handwritten annotations: Heading Line 1, my name Heading line 2, Heading line 3, Heading line 4, Detail Line, Total line 1, Total line 2)

Processing Requirements:

1. Read a file of inventory records, and for every record read:

   a. Determine the quantity on hand at the end of the period. This is equal to the quantity on hand at the start of the period (contained in the input record), plus the amount received, minus the amount shipped.

   b. Determine the value of the inventory on hand at the end of the period. This is equal to the unit price (contained in the input record) multiplied by the quantity on hand at the end of the period [computed in part a.].

   c. Print a detail line for every part containing the part name, quantity on hand at the beginning of the period, the amount received, the amount shipped, the quantity on hand at the end of the period, the unit price, and the value of the inventory at the end of the period. Double-space detail lines.

2. When all records have been read, print the total value of all inventory on hand at the end of the period.

Project 3-7

Program Name: Money Changer

Narrative: The ACME Widget Corporation has decided to pay its employees in cash rather than by check. Develop the hierarchy chart and either flowchart, pseudocode, or Warnier-Orr diagram for a program to read a file of payroll amounts and determine the required number of bills in each denomination. The Identification, Environment, and Data Divisions for this project can be developed after Chapter 4. Completion of the project requires you to finish Chapter 5 in order to do the Procedure Division.

Input File: PAYROLL-FILE

Input Record Layout:

Payroll Record		
Employee Name	Soc Sec No.	Gross Pay
1 ... 18	19 ... 27	28 ... 30

Test Data:

```
                   1         2         3         4         5         6
          1234567890123456789012345678901234567890123456789012345
          JOHN SMITH        123456789350
          JESSICA GRAUER    333444555475
          CHANDLER LAVOR    987654321178
          JEFFRY BOROW      777668888219
          MARION MILGROM    999887777341
          LYNN FRANKEL      492336789492
          KARL KARLSTROM    333228888314
          KATHY MARSHAK     245347878368
          RHODA HAAS        111111111305
          JIM FEGEN         222222222522
          MARIO VILLAR      333333333378
```

Report Layout:

```
          1         2         3         4         5         6         7
1234567890123456789012345678901234567890123456789012345678901234567890123456789012
1  EMPLOYEE NAME                    $100   $50   $20   $10    $5    $1  PAY
2
3  XXXXXXXXXXXXXXXXXX   XXX-XX-XXXX    9     9     9     9     9     9  999
4
5  XXXXXXXXXXXXXXXXXX   XXX-XX-XXXX    9     9     9     9     9     9  999

                                    ---   ---   ---   ---   ---   ---  ----
          TOTALS                     99    99    99    99    99    99  9999
```

Processing Requirements:

1. Read a file of employee pay records.

2. For each record read:

    a. Determine the number of bills of each denomination required to pay the employee in cash, rather than by check. (Do not include cents in your computation.)

    b. Use denominations of $100, $50, $20, $10, $5, and $1. Pay employees in the highest denominations possible; e.g., an employee with a gross pay of $300 should be paid with three $100 bills rather than six $50 bills.

    c. Maintain a running total of the total payroll as well as the number of bills in each denomination for the company as a whole.

    d. Print a detail line for each employee according to the report format. Double-space detail lines.

3. When all records have been read, print a total line for the company according to specification 2c. above.

Project 3-8

Program Name: Real Estate Sales

Narrative: Develop the hierarchy chart and either flowchart, pseudocode, or Warnier-Orr diagram for a program to process a file of real estate records and produce a monthly report based on transaction types, commissions paid, and summary. The Identification, Environment, and Data Divisions for this project can be developed after Chapter 4. Completion of the project requires you to finish Chapter 5 in order to do the Procedure Division.

The sales commission on any real estate sale is 6 percent of the total sale and is divided equally between the listing and selling agencies. This produces three possible sales types, which in turn determine the commissions paid to the company and its agents.

1. *The company both sells and lists the property (CO-CO).* The agent who listed the property receives 25 percent of the total (6 percent) commission, and the remaining 75 percent of the commission is divided equally (50 percent each) between the agent who sold the property and the company.

2. *The company sells the property listed by an outside agency (CO-OUT).* The agent who sells the property listed by an outside agency receives 70 percent of the commission due to the company (the commission due to the company is 3 percent of the total sales price, or one half of the total 6 percent commission). The company retains the remaining 30 percent of the 3 percent commission to the selling agency.

3. *An outside agency sells the property that was listed by the company (OUT-CO).* The company receives 50 percent of the sales commission (3 percent of the total price), which is split equally between the company and the listing agent.

Input File: REAL-ESTATE-FILE

Input Record Layout:

Real Estate Record									
Salesperson	Date			CO-CO		CO-OUT		OUT-CO	
	Month	Day	Year	Amount	Status	Amount	Status	Amount	Status
1 ... 12	12 14	15 16	17 20	21...26	27	28...33	34	35...40	41

Test Data:

```
         1         2         3         4         5         6
1234567890123456789012345678901234567890123456789012345678901234 5
ALVORD      08032000138500C0000000123900K
VILLAR      08052000215500C130300C234000C
VAZQUEZ     08052000345500C123000C273400C
GARCIA      08082000134500K145000C295600C
GRAUER      08102000234000C395000C124400K
ALVORD      08122000000000230000C234000K
VAZQUEZ     08152000138500K234000K0000000
GARCIA      08172000245000C123000C398400K
VILLAR      08182000345000C0000000278400C
GRAUER      08212000234500C145500K225000C
GARCIA      08222000245500V178000C298600K
GRAUER      08302000263500C0000000169600C
ALVORD      08312000423000C130000K247000C
```

Report Layout:

```
         1111111111222222222233333333334444444444555555555566666666667777777777
1234567890123456789012345678901234567890123456789012345678901234567890123456789
```

		PROPERTY SOLD	PROPERTY SOLD	OUTSIDE SALE
DATE	SALESPERSON	CO LISTING	OUTSIDE LISTING	CO LISTING
------	-----------	------------	---------------	-----------
MM/DD	XXXXXXXXXXX	999999	999999	999999
------	-----------	------------	---------------	-----------
	TOTAL SALES:	9999999	9999999	9999999
	GROSS TO LOTSA:	9999999	9999999	9999999
	COMMISSIONS PAID:	9999999	9999999	9999999
	NET TO LOTSA:	9999999	9999999	9999999
	MONTHLY SUMMARY			
	TOTAL SALES:	9999999		
	COMMISSIONS PAID:	9999999		
	NET TO LOTSA:	9999999		

Heading line 1: LOTSA HOUSES REALTY COMPANY

Processing Requirements:

1. Print the appropriate report headings as shown in the report layout.

2. Read a file of real estate records and process each record read by:
   a. Incrementing each of the three sales type totals with closed sales only. A closed sale is denoted by a "C" in the appropriate STATUS field.
   b. Printing a detail line of the closed sales for each sales type.

3. For all three sales types:
   a. Process the total sales by:
      (1) Printing the total sales for each of the three types of sale.
   b. Process the gross commission to the company by:
      (1) Calculating the gross commissions to the company for each of the three sales types as described in the program narrative.
      (2) Printing the calculated gross commissions for each sales type.
   c. Process the commissions paid by:
      (1) Calculating the commissions paid for each of the three sales types as described in the program narrative.
      (2) Printing the calculated commissions paid for each sales type.
   d. Process the net commissions to the company by:
      (1) Calculating the net commissions to the company for each of the three sales types as described in the program narrative.
      (2) Printing the calculated net commissions for each sales type.

4. Process the monthly summary by:
   a. Printing the total sales for the month.
   b. Printing the total commission paid for the month.
   c. Printing the total net commission to the company for the month.

Programming Specifications

Projects 4-1 through 4-8

Program Name: Insurance Policy Holder Report, Price Break Report, Barcoded Price List, Savings Dividends, Evaluation of Student Curriculum Records, Inventory Parts List, Money Changer, and Real Estate Sales

Narrative: The specifications for these projects were introduced in Chapter 3, at which time you were to attempt the hierarchy charts, pseudocode, flowcharts, and/or Warnier-Orr diagrams. Now we ask you to develop the Identification, Environment, and Data Divisions, but completion of the projects requires you to finish Chapter 5 in order to do the Procedure Division.

Programming Specifications

Projects 5-1 through 5-8

Program Name: Insurance Policy Holder Report, Price Break Report, Barcoded Price List, Savings Dividends, Evaluation of Student Curriculum Records, Inventory Parts Lists, Money Changer, and Real Estate Sales

Narrative: The specifications for these projects were introduced in Chapter 3, at which time you were to attempt the hierarchy charts, pseudocode, flowcharts, and/or Warnier-Orr diagrams. Completion of Chapter 4 enabled you to code the first three COBOL divisions. Now you are expected to develop the Procedure Division and complete the projects.

Programming Specifications

Project 7-1

Program Name: Payroll Report

Narrative: This project will produce a payroll report of employees, which will include their compensation..

Input File: EMPLOYEE-FILE

Input Record Layout:

Employee Record			
Soc Sec No.	Name & Initial	Compensation Rate	Compensation Code
1 ... 9	10 ... 24	25 *(2 decimals)* 31	32

Test Data:

```
          1         2         3         4         5         6
 1234567890123456789012345678901234567890123456789012345678901234 5
 111111111GRAUER       RT012002 5M
 222222222JONES        JJ000065 0H
 333333333MILGROM      EA000057 5H
 444444444RICHARDS     IM021000 0M
 555555555JEFFRIES     JB000055 5H
 666666666STEVEN       SS037004 5M
 777777777BROWN        BB000089 5H
 888888888BAKER        ED025001 0M
 999999999SUGRUE       PK015009 0M
 000000000VAZQUEZ      C 023503 3M
```

Report Layout:

```
                  1         2         3         4         5         6         7
       1234567890123456789012345678901234567890123456789012345678901234567890123456789012
    1                       IVAN PAYROLL
    2
    3   SSN              NAME            COMP    COMP     PAY
    4                                    RATE    CODE    AMOUNT
    5  999 99 9999  XXXXXXXXXXXXXX  $$$99 99     9    $$$9 99


                     TOTAL PAYROLL                    $$$$9 99
```

Develop your own report layout in compliance with the processing requirements. Be sure to give enough detail on the error report for the user to make the appropriate corrections.

Additional Requirements:

1. If compensation code is hourly, multiply hourly rate by 160 hours to obtain pay amount.

Project 7-2

Program Name: Price Break Report

Narrative: The specifications for this project were introduced in Chapter 3. The input record and data file have been updated to include two decimal places in the unit price, which requires that the extended price be extended to two decimal places as well. Use COBOL's editing facility to dress up the reports produced by these changes. Redo the report layout, using any editing features you deem appropriate.

Input File: ORDER-TRANSACTION-FILE

Input Record Layout:

Order Record					
Customer Number		Quantity Ordered	Item Number		Unit Price
1 ... 8	9	10 ... 12	13 ... 17	18	19 (2 decimals) 23

Test Data:

```
          1         2         3         4         5         6
 123456789012345678901234567890123456789012345678901234567890123456
 1000000010005111119105340
 2000000201002122280205056
 3000000301253233373300450
 4000000405004344463402100
 5000000509005455555657800
 1000000100151345691353400
 2000000200102123480105600
 3000000301003432173304500
 4000000404004432463702100
 5000000507004245655657800
 1000000100604111191553400
 2000000200255662280405600
 3000000303153113373330450
 4000000404002421463202100
 5000000507801645555157800
```

Report Layout: Use the Report Layout from Project 3-2 and modify it to look good, using the editing facility ($, commas, decimal points, etc.).

Project 7-3

Program Name: Payroll Calculation

Narrative: This program produces a payroll report from an employee-input file. The program calculates weekly gross pay, income tax owed, and the resulting net pay. By defining constants as part of Working-Storage, you can change the tax calculation algorithm with minimal changes to the rest of the program. Make use of the editing facilities to give the report a professional appearance.

Input File: EMPLOYEE-FILE

Input Record Layout:

	Employee Record				
Soc Sec No.	Name		Hourly Rate	Hours Worked
	Last	Initials		
1 ... 9	10 ... 22	23 24	25 *(2 decimals)* 29	30 *(2 decimals)* 33

Test Data:

```
         1         2         3         4         5         6
1234567890123456789012345678901234567890123456789012345678901234 5
111111111GRAUER      RT010253550
222222222JONES       JJ015004075
333333333MILGROM     EA005754550
444444444RICHARDS    IM011005000
555S55555JEFFRIES    JB055503025
666666666STEVENS     SS007803500
777777777BROWN       BB080252550
888888888BAKER       ED025453075
999999999SUGRUE      PK015352500
000000000VAZQUEZ     C 040505025
```

Report Layout:

```
          1         2         3         4         5         6         7
1234567890123456789012345678901234567890123456789012345678901234567890 12
                IVAN PAYROLL

 SSN          NAME         PAY     HRS    GROSS   INCOME    NET
                           RATE    WRKD   PAY     TAX       PAY

 999 99 9999  XXXXXXXXXXXXXXX  $$9 99  Z9 99  $$$9 99  $$$9 99  $$$$9 99
```

Additional Requirements:

1. As an aid in maintainability, define the overtime rates, overtime thresholds, tax rates, and tax thresholds as constants in Working-Storage. Use the corresponding data names in your calculations and comparisons instead of the actual values. For example:

   Change: `IF HOURS-WORKED <= 40`

   To: `IF HOURS-WORKED <= STRAIGHT-TIME`

2. Update your program and verify your results, then make the following changes. (Hint: You should need to change the values in only one place in your program.)

   a. Calculate the gross pay as follows:

      Straight time for the first 35 hours

      Time and a half for the next 7 hours (more than 35 and up to 42 hours)

      Double time for anything over 42 hours

b. Calculate federal withholding tax as follows:

10% on first $100 of gross

15% on amounts between $100 and less than $150

20% on amounts between $150 and less than $200

25% on amounts over $200

After the above changes are made, rerun the program to get new results and verify them with your projected answers.

3. Note that the hourly rate and hours worked have been extended to two decimal places. You should also extend all the other calculated amounts to two decimal places.

Project 7-4

Program Name: Extended Savings Dividends

Narrative: The specifications for this project were introduced in Chapter 3. The input record and data file have been updated to include two decimal places in the amount field, mandating a similar change in the fields for the dividend and total savings. Use COBOL's editing facility to appropriately dress up the reports produced by these changes. Redo the report layout, using any editing features you deem appropriate.

Input File: SAVINGS-FILE

Input Record Layout:

Savings Record			
Account No.	Name	Amount	Term
1 ... 8	9 ... 25	26 *(2 decimals)* 34	35 36

Test Data:

```
         1         2         3         4         5         6
1234567890123456789012345678901234567890123456789012345678901234 5
11000-01MILGROM        00455600518
23000-05PETERS         00306700016
31001-02SMITH          00258905712
43045-03JONES          00698809024
51005-01VILLAR         00045503906
35010-02HANSEN         01093602936
```

Report Layout: Use the Report Layout from Project 3-4 and modify it to look good, using the editing facility ($, commas, decimal points, etc.). Don't forget to show the calculated average from additional processing requirement two.

Additional Requirements: 1. As an aid in maintainability, define the six interest rates in Working-Storage and use these data names in your calculations instead of the raw percentage rates. For example, for a six month or less account term, change the computation

Change: `COMPUTE IND-DIVIDEND-PAID = SAV-AMOUNT * .06`

To: `COMPUTE IND-DIVIDEND-PAID = SAV-AMOUNT * UPTO-6MO-RATE`

where UPTO-6MO-RATE is defined in Working-Storage with a value of .06.

2. Calculate and print the average savings amount for all savings accounts processed.

3. The savings amount has been extended to two decimal places; extend all other calculated amounts to two decimal places as well.

Update the program and verify your results, then make the following changes. (Hint: You should need to change each rate in only one place in the program.)

(1) 7% interest on 6 months or less.

(2) 8% interest on more than 6 months but up to 12.

(3) 9% interest on more than 12 months but up to 18.

(4) 10% interest on more than 18 months but up to 24.

(5) 11% interest on more than 24 months but up to 30.

(6) 14% interest on more than 30 months.

Project 7-5

Program Name: Church Building Fund Report

Narrative: The specifications for this project were introduced in Project 2-6. The input record and data file have been updated to include two decimal places in the pledged amount field, mandating a similar extension in the amount given. Use COBOL's editing facility to dress up the report. Redo the report layout, using any editing features you deem appropriate. Add total amount pledged, given, and owed. Print all church members, not just those owing money.

Input File: CHURCH-BLD-FUND-MSTR-FILE

Input Record Layout:

Church Building Fund Master Record					
Master Name		Pledged Amount		Member Number	Amount Given
1 ... 15	16 ... 20	21 ... 27	28 ... 30	31 ... 34	35 ... 41

Test Data:

```
         1         2         3         4         5         6
1234567890123456789012345678901234567890123456789012345678901234 5
JOHN  SMITH         0010055   00010005000
ANN  LOVING         0020050   00020002550
MARY  BROWN         0050000   00030050000
TOM  SAWYER         0007500   00040000000
JACK  CAPPS         0340034   00050340034
JILL  JACOBS        4000012   00060350000
SUSAN  CLUB         0200025   00070200025
MIKE  CLOUD         0030030   00080015000
```

Project 7-6

Program Name: Inventory Parts List

Narrative: The specifications for this project were introduced in Chapter 3. The input record and data file have been updated to include two decimal places in the unit price field, mandating a similar extension in the total value. Use COBOL's editing facility to dress up the reports produced by these changes. Redo the report layout, using any editing features you deem appropriate.

Input File: INVENTORY-FILE

Input Record Layout:

Inventory Record				
Part Name	Quantity on Hand	Amount Received	Amount Shipped	Unit Price
1 ... 20	21 ... 23	24 ... 26	27 ... 29	30 *(2 decimals)* 35

Test Data:

```
         1         2         3         4         5         6
1234567890123456789012345678901234567890123456789012345678901234 5
WIDGETS, SIZE S    150050096007050
WIDGETS, SIZE M    200075076008075
WIDGETS, SIZE L    000500400009034
WHOSIWHATSIS       350110046010000
GIZMOS,  TYPE A    250080036020055
GIZMOS,  TYPE B    000050025030087
GADGETS, SIZE S    025018026001599
GADGETS, SIZE L    090028035002565
```

Project 7-7

Program Name: Money Changer

Narrative: The specifications for this project were introduced in Chapter 3. The input record and data file have been updated to include 2 decimal places in the gross pay field; accordingly extend the pay to 2 decimal places. Use COBOL's editing facility to appropriately dress up the reports produced by these changes. Accordingly redo the report layout, using any editing features you deem appropriate.

Input File: PAYROLL-FILE

Input Record Layout:

Payroll Record		
Employee Name	Soc Sec No.	Gross Pay
1 ... 18	19 ... 27	28 *(2 decimals)* 32

Test Data:

```
         1         2         3         4         5         6
1234567890123456789012345678901234567890123456789012345678901234 5
JOHN SMITH          1234567893505 0
JESSICA GRAUER      3334445554757 7
CHANDLER LAVOR      9876543211785 5
JEFFRY BOROW        7776688882198 3
MARION MILGROM      9998877773412 2
LYNN FRANKEL        4923367894923 7
KARL KARLSTROM      3332288883144 4
KATHY MARSHAK       2453478783682 8
RHODA HAAS          1111111113059 8
JIM FEGEN           2222222225224 4
MARIO VILLAR        3333333333786 9
```

Processing Requirements: Extend the calculations to determine the proper number of coins with which to pay the individual. Use quarters, dimes, nickels, and pennies in your computations.

Project 7-8

Program Name: Extended Real Estate Sales

Narrative: The specifications for this project were introduced in Chapter 3. Use COBOL's editing facility to dress up the reports produced by these changes. Redo the report layout, using any editing features you deem appropriate.

Input File: REAL-ESTATE-FILE

Input Record Layout: Same as project 3-8

Report Layout: Use the Report Layout from Project 3-8 and modify it to look good, using the editing facility ($, commas, decimal points, etc.).

Processing Requirements:
1. As an aid in maintainability, define the gross and commission rate for all three sales types in Working-Storage and use these data names in your calculations. For example, change the gross to company

Change: `COMPUTE TOT-GROSS-CO-CO = TOT-SALES-CO-CO * .06`

To: `COMPUTE TOT-GROSS-CO-CO = TOT-SALES-CO-CO * GROSS-CO-CO-RATE`

where GROSS-CO-CO-RATE is defined in Working-Storage with a value of .06.

2. Print the gross percent to the company for each of the three sales types as shown on the report layout.

3. Print the commission percent paid out for each of the three sales types as shown on the report layout.

Update the program and verify your results, then make the following changes. (Hint: You should need to change each rate in only one place in the program.)

The sales commission on any real estate sale is 8 percent of the total sale and is divided equally between the listing and selling agencies. This produces three possible sales types, which in return determine the commissions paid to the company and its agents.

1. *The company both sells and lists the property (CO-CO).* The agent who listed the property receives 35 percent of the total (8 percent) commission, and the remaining 65 percent of the commission is divided equally (50 percent each) between the agent who sold the property and the company.

2. *The company sells the property listed by an outside agency (CO-OUT).* The agent who sells the property listed by an outside agency receives 60 percent of the commission due to the company (the commission due to the company is 4 percent of the total sales price, or one half of the total 8 percent commission). The company retains the remaining 40 percent of the 4 percent commission to the selling agency.

3. *An outside agency sells the property that was listed by the company (OUT-CO).* The company receives 50 percent of the sales commission (4 percent of the total price), which is split equally between the company and the listing agent.

Project 7-9

Program Name: Car Sales Program

Narrative: Develop the hierarchy chart and either flowchart or pseudocode for a program to process a file of car sales records to produce a commission report.

Input File: CAR-SALES-FILE

Input Record Layout:

	Car Sales Record					
Invoice No.	Type Information			Sales Information		
	Year	Make	Model	Asking Price	Sold Price	Salesperson
1 ... 5	6 ... 9	10 ... 20	21 ... 33	34 ... 39	40 ... 45	46 ... 52

Test Data:

```
         1         2         3         4         5         6
1234567890123456789012345678901234567890123456789012345678901234 5
781751997NISSAN     PATHFINDER   018999017899WILLCOX
148511994ACURA      LEGEND COUPE 018988016987SCHULZ
574761998CHEVROLET  CORVETTE ZRI 039450039000MORIN
586811997BMW        5251         034900032789TORRES
856441993LOTUS      ESPRIT       073500073250WENDEL
874651996FERRARI    TESTAROSSA   105000097500FIXLER
254891999SATURN     SL           011995011995JONES
255441997RANGEOVER  4 DOOR       034900032568MORIN
724621999MERCEDES   ML430        049700045900CULVER
568431998CADILLAC   DEVILLE      026977025362TORRES
157461987ROLLS ROYCESILVER SPUR  045888045000WILCOX
148421994FERRARI    308GTB       048500046299FIXLER
255851997JAGUAR     XJS CONV     040000038565CULVER
479141988ALFA ROMEO SPYDER       012000011298WENDEL
285321998LEXUS      GS400        041995039750SCHULZ
165411995PORSCHE    911 CABRIOLET054500052988JONES
```

Report Layout:

```
                                                    VERY VERY NICE CARS INC.
                                                      COMMISSION REPORT

                              CAR          CAR          CAR        ASKING      PRICE     % OF       COMM       NET TO
       INVOICE #  SALESPERSON YEAR        MAKER        MODEL       PRICE       SOLD     ASKING      PAID       DEALER

       ZZZZ9      XXXXXXX     9999  XXXXXXXXXXX  XXXXXXXXXXX ZZZ,ZZ9     ZZZ,ZZ9      99       ZZ,ZZ9     ZZZ,ZZ9

                                                                    ----------              --------   ----------
                                                                    $Z,ZZZ,ZZ9              $ZZZ,ZZ9   $Z,ZZZ,ZZ9
```

Processing Requirements:

1. Print a heading at the beginning of the report.

2. Read a file of Car Sales records.

3. For each record read:

   a. Calculate the percent of the asking price at which the car was sold. For example, a $10,000 car which sold for $9,500, sold for 95% of the asking price. Note: Allow for decimal places in your calculations, but do not print them in your report as shown in the report layout.

   b. Calculate the commission paid to the salesperson as follows:

      (1) For any car sold above 95 percent of the asking price the salesperson receives a 5% commission rate. In addition, the salesperson is paid a bonus equal to 40% of the amount in excess of 95%. For example, a $10,000 car selling at $9,800 yields a commission of $610.00 ($490.00 + $120.00).

      (2) For any car sold between 90 and 95 percent of the asking price the salesperson's 5% commission is reduced by 10% for every percentage point below 95%. For example, a $10,000 car selling at $9,400 results in 94% of the asking price and a 4.5% commission rate; therefore the commission paid is $423.00.

      (3) For any car sold below 90 percent of the asking price the amount below 90% comes straight out of the salesperson's remaining commission at the 90% level as calculated in paragraph (2)—that is, 2.5% of the asking price is all that's left to play with. For example, a $10,000 car selling at $8,900 yields a commission of only $122.50 ($222.50 - $100.00).

   c. Calculate the Net to the Dealer, assuming the dealer's markup is 25%—that is, the asking price is the dealer's cost plus 25%. For example, a $10,000 car selling at $9,400 yields a net of $977.00 since the cost to the dealer was $8000.00.

   d. Print a detail line for each record. Double-space all detail lines.

   e. Increment appropriate totals as shown on the report layout.

4. As an aid in maintainability, define the 5% commission rate, the 40% bonus rate, 95% upper level, 90% lower level, the 10% reduction per percentage point below the lower level, and the 25% markup as constants in Working-Storage. Use the corresponding data names in your calculations instead of the actual values. For example:

   To: COMPUTE IND-BONUS ROUNDED = **BONUS-RATE** * CAR-ASKING=
            PRICE * (IND-PERCENT-ASKING - **UPPER-LEVEL**)

            COMPUTE IND-COMM-PAID ROUNDED = CAR-PRICE-SOLD
              * **COMM-RATE** + IND-BONUS

5. **The Final Challenge!** Once you have verified that your program works with the original rates, determine what effect a *6%* commission rate, a *50%* bonus, a *15%* reduction for every percentage point below the upper level, and a *30%* markup would have on the net to the dealer as well as commissions paid by making the appropriate

changes in Working-Storage and rerunning the program. Make sure you hand in both reports (.RPT). If this was *your* dealership, which rates would you choose?

6. Print the totals when all records have been processed.

Programming Specifications

Project 8-1

Program Name: Order Transaction File Validation

Narrative: Write a data validation program that will validate an order transaction file. Note to instructors: We have found this project particularly difficult for students. You may want to delay assignment of this task until they have had experience with at least one data validation program and other more advanced programming techniques.

Input File: ORDER-TRANSACTION-FILE

Input Record Layout:

```
01    ORDER-ENTRY-TYPE-1-REC.
      05          REC-TYPE-1                          PIC X.
      05          CUSTOMER-NO-1.
                  10          REGION-1                PIC X.
                  10          REST-CUST-NO-1          PIC X(5).
      05          PURCH-ORDER-NO-1                    PIC X(5).
      05          PURCHASE-DATE.
                  10          PURCHASE-MM             PIC 99.
                  10          PURCHASE-DD             PIC 99.
                  10          PURCHASE-YYYY           PIC 9999.
      05          PARTIAL-SHIP-IND                    PIC X.
      05          TAXABLE-IND                         PIC X.
      05          HOLD-DELIVERY-DATE.
                  10          HOLD-DEL-MM             PIC 99.
                  10          HOLD-DEL-DD             PIC 99.
                  10          HOLD-DEL-YYYY           PIC 9999.
01    ORDER-ENTRY-TYPE-2-REC.
      05          REC-TYPE-2                          PIC X.
      05          CUSTOMER-NO-2.
                  10          REGION-2                PIC X.
                  10          REST-CUST-NO-2          PIC X(5).
      05          PURCH-ORDER-NO-2                    PIC X(5).
      05          CUSTOMER-NAME                       PIC X(15).
      05          CUSTOMER-ADDRESS                    PIC X(25).
      05          CUSTOMER-ZIP                        PIC 9(5).
      05          CREDIT-LIMIT                        PIC 9.
      05          BALANCE-DUE                         PIC 9(5)V99.
      05          PHONE-NUMBER                        PIC X(12).
01    ORDER-ENTRY-TYPE-3-REC.
      05          REC-TYPE-3                          PIC X.
      05          CUSTOMER-NO-3.
                  10          REGION-3                PIC X.
                  10          REST-CUST-NO-3          PIC X(5).
      05          PURCH-ORDER-NO-3                    PIC X(5).
```

```
      05    ORDER-ITEM-NO1.
                              10                        ITEM-NUM1              PIC 9(5).
                              10                        ITEM1-QUANTITY        PIC X.
                              10                        ITEM1-UNIT-PRICE      PIC 9(4)V99
            05              ORDER-ITEM-NO2.
                              10                        ITEM-NUM2             PIC 9(5).
                              10                        ITEM2-QUANTITY        PIC X.
                              10                        ITEM2-UNIT-PRICE      PIC 9(4)V99.
            05              ORDER-ITEM-NO3.
                              10                        ITEM-NUM3             PIC 9(5).
                              10                        ITEM3-QUANTITY        PIC X.
                              10                        ITEM3-UNIT-PRICE      PIC 9(4)V99.
            05              ORDER-ITEM-NO4.
                              10                        ITEM-NUM4             PIC 9(5).
                              10                        ITEM4-QUANTITY        PIC X.
                              10                        ITEM4-UNIT-PRICE      PIC 9(4)V99.
            05              ORDER-ITEM-NO5.
                              10                        ITEM-NUM5             PIC 9(5).
                              10                        ITEM5-QUANTITY        PIC X.
                              10                        ITEM5-UNIT-PRICE      PIC 9(4)V99.
```

Test Data:

```
         1         2         3         4         5         6         7         8
1234567890123456789012345678901234567890123456789012345678901234567890123456789012345
1004100AA10208051999NY10201999
3004100AA102C1245L001000
3004100AA10244011A025000
3108000AM11172950P015000
1773100A100309021999YN01151999
2773100A1003BIZ SMART       210 FIRST ST.   IRVING      7503850002000817-949-8275
3773100A100390600I002000
3143000A3B3333333C008000
1016040BR54902281999NN12161999
3016040BR549586G3C040050
1998100B4D22090192YY013093
2998100B4D22RYX CORP        55512 NOEL DR   DALLAS      7552292222222214-741-9999
3998100B4D2272600J09000
3998100B4D2233333K000500
1360500CD88808281999YN11021999
2360500CD888ABC CORP        9559 KNOB HILL SAN DIEGO 8650050010000805-744-9889
3360500CD88816789A099900
3360500CD88832600E008800
1999990CL99902291999NY11011999
3999990CL99966666G022000
3999990CL99912345H002200
3999990CL99955555I001050
3999990CL99972600D015050
2350200DB895THE MONEY PIT  10 DOWNTOWN AVEDALLAS      7505220100000214-845-9676
1105105D5M0010101999NN11021999
2105105D5M00CANDY INC.      666 WYLIE LANE HUMBUG      9998830010000717-666-6656
3105105D5M0026666A005000
1025000KM66610101999YN11021999
2025000KM666WIDGET CORP     9995 ABC STREETCARROLLTON7520179000000818-666-9000
3025000KM66637777F025000
1200100KT95509281999NN12121999
3200100KT95533333B001000
3200100KT95555555C000150
2000100NB456ABC COMPANY    N. 123 STREET              7250QQ005000215-626-4153
1631600NN20007301999NN11191999
```

```
3631600NN20072600A030000
1143000RT33303311999YY12051999
3143000RT333595XXR040000
3143000RT333X2X005005000
1312000XXX3J04271999BN06011999
3312000XXX3J5555Z1090000
1771600XX20007301999NN11021999
2771600XX200SMITH INDUSTRY N. 333 HAVEN    COPPELL    7501630010000214-123-6613
3771600XX20032600A030000
3771600XX20012345E003000
1881600ZZ20007301999NN11021999
3881600ZZ20032600B03000092
3881600ZZ20012345E002000
3881600ZZ20034567K003000
3881600ZZ20045678F001500
3881600ZZ20016789A000100
1101000330410928I999XN11011999
```

Report Layout: Develop your own report layout in compliance with the processing requirements. Be sure to give enough detail on the error report for the user to make the appropriate corrections.

Processing Requirements:

1. Read a file of order transaction records.

2. The current run date is typically accepted from a file, but for this lab set up a literal in working storage with the run date as November 2, 1999.

3. Validate each input record field for all of the following:

   All numeric fields should be validated for numeric values and should be greater than zero.

   On the type 1 record, the PARTIAL SHIP and TAXABLE fields should contain either a "Y" or an "N."

   The HOLD DELIVERY DATE should be a future date.

   The PURCHASE DATE should be the current date or prior to the current date.

   On the type 2 record, all fields should contain data.

   The quantity field on the type 3 record is a 1-byte alphanumeric field. This is a code that translates as follows:

A = 1	E = 300	I = 700
B = 10	F = 400	J = 800
C = 100	G = 500	K = 900
D = 200	H = 600	

   The quantity field should be validated for a valid code.

4. Any record that fails any validity test is to be written to an error file, and an appropriate error message should appear on the error report. It is possible that a record may contain more than one error, and all errors are to be flagged.

5. Valid records are to be written to a valid transaction file. The valid transaction file should be the same format as the input Order Transaction file with the exception that the quantity code on the Type 3 record should be converted to the quantity amount, causing the unit price to be moved to the right two bytes. See code below:

```
        05      ORDER-ITEM.
                10            ITEM-NUM              PIC 9(5).
                10            ITEM-QUANTITY         PIC 9(3).
                10            ITEM-UNIT-PRICE       PIC 9(4)V99.
```

6. Each valid transaction is to be written to a file to be used in Project 9-1..

Project 8-2

Program Name: Stock Transactions Validation Program

Narrative: This project will validate a stock transaction file and produce both a valid stock file and an error report.

Input File: STOCK-TRANSACTION-FILE

Input Record Layout:

```
01  STOCK-RECORD.
    05  ST-TRANSACTION-INFORMATION.
        10 ST-TRANSACTION-SHARES      PIC 9(3).
        10 ST-TRANSACTION-STOCK       PIC X(14).
    05  ST-PURCHASE-INFORMATION.
        10  ST-PURCHASE-PRICE         PIC 9(5)V99.
        10  ST-PURCHASE-DATE.
            15  ST-PURCHASE-YEAR       PIC 9999.
            15  ST-PURCHASE-MONTH      PIC 99.
            15  ST-PURCHASE-DAY        PIC 99.
    05  ST-SALE-INFORMATION.
        10  ST-SALE-PRICE             PIC 9(5)V99.
        10  ST-SALE-DATE.
            15  ST-SALE-YEAR           PIC 9999.
            15  ST-SALE-MONTH          PIC 99.
            15  ST-SALE-DAY            PIC 99.
```

Test Data:

```
         1         2         3         4         5         6
123456789012345678901234567890123456789012345678901234567890123456789012345
100XYZ CORP      2000000199901153000000020000103
200ABC CORP      1200000199903052200000019980305
100ACME WIDGETS  1150000199911095000000020000331
100BOROW ASSOC   005000019990229000048
300LEE ENTERPRISE45000001999132290000000019990422
200NATL GADGET   0100A001999051511000000019990631
100NATL GISMO    1000000199906181200000019990606
400AMER WIDGETS  0900000199907070800000019990906
350MIGROM POWER  1000000199804052500000020000431
200PARKER INC    00300001999073101000A20000428
100SHELLY CO     003000019990431000200
200STEVENS INC   2000000199908312200000019990922
```

Report Layout: Design your own report layout. Be sure to comply with all the processing requirements.

Processing Requirements: 1. Read a file of stock records.

2. Validate each input record for all of the following:

    a. The month, day, and year of both the purchase and sale date must be numeric.

    b. The month must be a valid value, that is, between 1 and 12, inclusive.

    c. The day cannot exceed the maximum days in the corresponding month.

    d. The date of sale cannot be earlier than the date of purchase.

    e. The dollar amount of both purchase and sale must be numeric.

3. Design an appropriate report layout. Invalid transactions are to be displayed with an appropriate error message. If a given transaction contains more than one invalid field, multiple error messages are required. No further processing is required for invalid transactions.

4. Each valid transaction is to be written to a file to be used in Project 9-2.

Project 8-3

Program Name:	Payroll Validation Program
Narrative:	Develop a program to validate a payroll file and produce both a valid payroll file and an error report.
Input File:	PAYROLL-FILE

Input Record Layout:

```
01  PAYROLL-RECORD.
    05  PAY-SOC-SEC-NUM             PIC 9(9).
    05  PAY-NAME.
        10  PAY-LAST                PIC X(14).
        10  PAY-FIRST               PIC X(12).
        10  PAY-INITIAL             PIC X.
    05  PAY-INFO.
        10  PAY-HOURLY-RATE         PIC 9(3)V99.
        10  PAY-HOURS-WORKED        PIC 9(3)V99.
        10  PAY-SALARY-TYPE         PIC X.
        10  PAY-DEPENDENTS          PIC 99.
        10  PAY-TAX-STATUS          PIC 9.
        10  PAY-INSURANCE           PIC X.
    05  PAY-YTD-INFO.
        10  PAY-YTD-EARNINGS        PIC 9(6)V99.
        10  PAY-YTD-TAXES           PIC 9(5)V99.
        10  PAY-YTD-FICA            PIC 9(4)V99.
        10  PAY-YTD-INSURANCE       PIC 9(4)V99.
```

Test Data:

```
         1         2         3         4         5         6         7
1234567890123456789012345678901234567890123456789012345678901234567890123456789012345678
100000000                           01000 4000H  3D02315022011434013451205000
111111111BOYER         WARD         E0150004000S013B027000000548524202770045000
200000000MERA          SASHA        X01400045005045B
222222222DAVERSA       NICK         A00550040005014A009900000148500074349063000
300000000MENENDEZ      LOURDES      Y02350040005X152C045298220891300025053057500
333333333FRENCH        MICHELLE     P0650003500H082B11700000267113987867010800 0
400000000BARBER        MARYANN       A18000400LH06  AA85927400719262143290900000
444444444GEHLE         SHELLY       T0157504350H002Z028350000444055212909000000
500000000GRAUER        ROBERT       T1500 46000  052Z029104050513950214890000000
555555555RICO          CHERYL       S00745052005H013C01341000020115010070904 5000
600000000                           04000S10AB00990000013765007343606000 0
```

```
666666666ROWE            CANDACE        M0300004200S031A05400000123243804055409 0000
700000000HEMMERDE CLARKRICHARD           06500        H008Z116000002571143854320000000
777777777SHIM            ANNA           M0080004800H044C01440000022910610814409 0000
800000000STUTZ           JOEL            005500500H0L11 0991500           075607
888888888VASQUEZ         DONNA          A0237504000M022C0427500008488133210530585 00
900000000PLANT           ROBERT          0075005300S013001441000021005010009004500 0
999999999VAZQUEZ VILLARCAROL             0180004000M053B032400000699724243324108 000
```

Report Layout: Design your report layout based on the requirements below.

Processing Requirements:

1. Read a file of sales payroll records.

2. Validate each input record for all of the following:

   a. The incoming record must contain data for the following fields: social security number, name, hourly rate, hours worked, salary type, number of dependents, tax status, and insurance. If any field is missing, display the message "INCOMING RECORD MISSING DATA" and the input record.

   b. The incoming fields of hourly rate, hours worked, number of dependents, tax status, ytd earnings, taxes, fica, and insurance must be numeric. If not, display an appropriate error message that contains the entire input record.

   c. The salary type must be either hourly or salaried (H or S). If it is not, display an appropriate error message, such as "INVALID SALARY TYPE FOR", the social security number, name, and salary type. (Hint: Use a condition name test.)

   d. *Salaried* employees are not paid overtime; therefore hours worked for salaried employees cannot be over 40 hours. Use the message "NO OVERTIME FOR SALARIED EMPLOYEES", the social security number, name, and hours worked.

   e. The tax status must be valid (1 through 4). Use the message "INVALID TAX STATUS FOR", the social security number, name, and tax status. (Hint: Use a condition name test.)

   f. The insurance type must be valid (A, B, C, or Z). Use the message "INVALID INSURANCE FOR", the social security number, name, and insurance type. (Hint: Use a condition name test.)

   g. A reasonable number of dependents; flag any record where the number of dependents is over 10. (Hint: Use a condition name test.)

3. Any record that fails any validity test is to be rejected with no further processing, other than displaying the appropriate error message(s). It is possible that a record may contain more than one error (flag all errors). Valid records are to be written to a new file to be used in Projects 9-3 and 16-3.

Project 8-4

Program Name: Car Sales Commissions Validation Program

Narrative: This project will validate a file of car sales records and produce both a valid car file and an error report.

Input File: CAR-SALES-FILE

Input Record Layout:

FIELD NAME	POSITIONS	FIELD TYPE
Location	1 - 11	Alphanumeric
Branch	12 - 15	Numeric
Salesperson	16 - 25	Alphanumeric
Customer Name	26 - 35	Alphanumeric
Sale Date	36 - 43	Numeric
Sale Amount	44 - 49	Numeric
Commission Rate	50 - 52	Numeric
Car Model	53 - 65	Alphanumeric
Car Year	66 - 69	Numeric

Test Data:

```
         1         2         3         4         5         6
1234567890123456789012345678901234567890123456789012345678901234567789
BROWARD    1234SHIM    REIMAN    13121999 24900002SAAB 900  CSE  1998
MONROE     4528VASQUEZ HAFEZ     10131998 35275003JAGUAR XJS   1995
DADE       4679DAVERSA           11141999048974005INFINITI Q45 1999
BROWARD    1234SHIM    PORTO     10321998025575004MB 300E      1916
MONROE     4528BOYER             06331998 14125004MAZDA 929    1994
BROWARD    1234GEHLE   LARSH     11121998005995003PEUGOT 405GLS1993
DADE       9879FRENCH            09281999029750003BMW 850iX    1991
BROWARD    1234GEHLE   HOLME      9311997014700002PRELUDE SI   1992
DADE       9879FRENCH  DEGGS     01311999017925004NISS MAXIMA  1996
BROWARD    1234GEHLE   MORENO    10121998 08500  5TOY SUPRA    1991
DADE       0124RICO    GORMAN    10311998048500184LEXUS LS450  1997
MONROE     4528VASQUEZ HWANG     12311997 25000  4LEGEND C LS  1990
BROWARD    4567ROWE    TOCKMAN   01041998074980006BMW 750iL    1997
DADE       0124RICO    CHUA       8151999024700004TOY CAMRY XLE1998
DADE       9879FRENCH  SPEARS    10161999014975001NISS ALTIMA  1998
MONROE     4528BOYER   AUGUSMA   04101999079000002MB 500 SL    1998
DADE       4679DAVERSA RENESCA   10421999009550002HYUN ELANTRA 1999
BROWARD    4567ROWE    VIERA     11 51999012300002STUDEBAKER   1962
MONROE     4528BOYER   LOUIS     10291998 12175104MAZ MILLENIA 1995
BROWARD    4567ROWE    PINEDA    12241999069395  3AUDI QUATTRO 1999
DADE       0124RICO    DILEGO    11261998012800004MAZDA MIATA  1994
```

Report Layout: Design your own report layout, subject to the processing requirements.

Processing Requirements:
1. Read a file of car sales records.

2. Validate each input record for all of the following:

a. The incoming record must contain data for the following fields: location, branch, salesperson, customer, sale amount, commission rate, and model year. If any field is missing, display a single message "INCOMING RECORD MISSING DATA", followed by the input record.

b. The incoming fields of branch, sale date, sale amount, and commission rate must be numeric. If not, display an appropriate error message that contains the entire input record.

c. Valid dates (sale date): month must be between 1 and 12, inclusive; day should be in conjunction with the month; and year must be the current year or the year before. Display a suitable message "INVALID MONTH", "INVALID DAY", and/or "INVALID YEAR", followed by the input record.

d. A reasonable commission rate: flag any record where the rate is not between 0% and 100%. Use the message "INVALID COMMISSION RATE", followed by the input record.

e. A reasonable car year: flag any record where the car year is not between 1930 and the current year +1, inclusive. Use the message "INVALID CAR YEAR", followed by the input record.

3. Any record that fails any validity test is to be rejected with no further processing, other than displaying the appropriate error message(s). It is possible that a record may contain more than one error (all errors are to be flagged).

4. Valid records are to be written to a file to be used in Project 9-4.

Project 8-5

Program Name: Invoice Validation Program

Narrative: Write a data validation program that will validate an invoice file and produce both a valid invoice file and an error report.

Input File: INVOICE-FILE

Input Record Layout:
```
01  INVOICE-RECORD-IN.
    05  INV-INVOICE-NO        PIC X(4).
    05  INV-DATE.
        10  INV-MONTH         PIC 9(2).
        10  INV-DAY           PIC 9(2).
        10  INV-YEAR          PIC 9(4).
    05  INV-CUSTOMER-INFO.
        10  INV-CUST-NAME     PIC X(10).
        10  INV-CUST-ADDRESS  PIC X(10).
        10  INV-CUST-CITY     PIC X(10).
        10  INV-CUST-STATE    PIC XX.
        10  INV-CUST-ZIP      PIC X(5).
```

Test Data:

```
         1         2         3         4         5         6
1234567890123456789012345678901234567890123456789012345678901234 5
246710041999Scully    20 Main StChicago   IL60666
38451312      Minnie            Disney    TZ
157808122000Schultz   45 5th St Los AngeleCA90024
344612312000Goofy     Main St   Orlando   FX39575
034209101999Culver    1 Sunny LnSeattle   WA98008
479011121999Perez     4 Long Dr New OrleanLA79345
      09    2000       NoName St Somewhere   49576
683607041999Fixler    3 42nd St New York  NY10020
234G    322000Pluto    2 Dog Dr  Dogville  PR67453
480703182000Morin     9 7th Ave Newark    NJ07632
049806301999Munroe    10 Long StTulsa     OK59345
6234          Mickey   Disney St           FL33480
```

Report Layout: Develop your own report layout in compliance with the processing requirements.

Processing Requirements: 1. Read a file of invoice records.

2. Validate each input record field for all of the following:

   a. **Invoice No:**

      (1) If the invoice number is missing, print an appropriate error message:

         Record missing data in INVOICE NO field for: Smith

> (2) *If the invoice number is not missing*, verify that the value is numeric; if not, display an error message:
>
> ```
> Nonnumeric INVOICE NO for: Smith      Invoice No: ABC4
> ```

  b. **Date:**

> (1) If the invoice date (i.e., Month, Day, or Year) is missing, print an appropriate error message:
>
> ```
> Record missing data in INVOICE DATE field for: Smith
> ```
>
> (2) *If the invoice date is not missing*, verify that the month is valid (i.e., 1 thru 12); error message:
>
> ```
> Invalid MONTH for: Smith        Invoice No: 1234 Month: 20
> ```
>
> (Hint: Use a condition name test for valid months.)
>
> (3) Verify that the day is valid (i.e., cannot exceed the maximum days in the corresponding month); error message:
>
> ```
> Invalid DAY for: Smith         Invoice No: 1234 Month: 12 Day: 35
> ```
>
> (Hint: Yes, use another condition name test for valid days.)
>
> (4) Verify that the year is valid; the year must be either the current or previous year; error message:
>
> ```
> Invalid YEAR for: Smith    Invoice No: 1234  Year: 1995
> ```
>
> (5) If the date is valid, then verify the complete date against today's date; error message:
>
> ```
> Invalid DATE for: Smith  Invoice No: 1234 Month: 12 Day: 31 Year: 2005
> ```

  c. **Name:** If the name is missing, print an appropriate error message:

> ```
> Record missing data in NAME field for Invoice No: 1234
> ```

  d. **Address:** If the city is missing, print an appropriate error message:

> ```
> Record missing data in ADDRESS field for: Smith Invoice No: 1234
> ```

  e. **City:** If the address is missing, print an appropriate error message:

> ```
> Record missing data in CITY field for: Smith   Invoice No: 1234
> ```

  f. **State:**

> (1) If the state is missing, print an appropriate error message:
>
> ```
> Record missing data in STATE field for: Smith   Invoice No: 1234
> ```
>
> (2) If the state is not missing, then verify that it is a valid state. Valid States are AK, AL, AR, AZ, CA, CO, CT, DC, DE, FL, GA, HI, IA, ID, IL, IN, KS, KY, LA, MA, MD, ME, MI, MN, MO, MS, MT, NC, ND, NE, NH, NJ, NM, NV, NY, OH, OK, OR, PA, RI, SC, SD, TN, TX, UT, VA, VT, WA, WI, WV, and WY; error message:
>
> ```
> Invalid STATE for: Smith      Invoice No: 1234 State: AT
> ```
>
> (Hint: Another condition name test for valid states.)

  g. **Zip:**

> (1) If the zip is missing, print an appropriate error message:
>
> ```
> Record missing data in ZIP field for: Smith        Invoice No: 1234
> ```
>
> (2) *If the zip is not missing*, verify that the value is numeric; if not, display an error message:
>
> ```
> Nonnumeric ZIP for: Smith        Invoice No: 1234 Zip: 08307
> ```

3. Any record that fails any validity test is to be rejected with no further processing, other than displaying or printing the error message(s). It is possible that a record may contain more than one error (flag all errors except where noted).

4. Valid records are to be written to a new file to be used in Project 9-5.

Project 8-6

Program Name: Student Record Validation Program

Narrative: Write a data validation program that will validate a student file and produce both a valid student file and an error report.

Input File: STUDENT-FILE

Input Record Layout:

```
01   STUDENT-RECORD.
     05   STU-ID                    PIC X(9).
     05   STU-NAME                  PIC X(16).
     05   STU-SCHOOL-INFORMATION.
          10   STU-SCHOOL-CODE      PIC X(3).
          10   STU-MAJOR-CODE       PIC X(3).
          10   STU-AID-TYPE         PIC X.
          10   STU-GPA              PIC 9V999.
          10   STU-CREDIT-HOURS     PIC 99.
```

Test Data:

```
          1         2         3         4         5         6
 1234567890123456789012345678901234567890123456789012345678901234 5

235980890Kostner, Kevin  BUSMKTS349908
293765635Roberts, Julia  COMMKTG365710
328576407Murphy, Eddie   COMPHYS249912
         Smith, John     MDDECOZ000003
378575600Baldwin, Alec   MUSEEGS   0G
397575906Hawn, Goldie    MEDBIOG345015
427496794Russell, Kurt   ARTCISG369018
434562734Tweety Bird     BUSFINS387103
459797G01Stallone, Sly   COMPHYL210500
470876493Gable, Clark    EMGBIOL250L
475673723Bird, Big       LAWSTAS300509
492729475Freeman, Morgan MUSCISG379012
524956063Newman, Paul    MEDSTAS332101
540394065Redford, Robert ARTACCL267510
S84784755                ENGSTTL310520
586432980Runner, Road    COMACCL250006
593639456Davis, Geena    BUSFINS299911
635968690Sarandon, Susan ENGSTAG349909
658294585Douglas, MichealBUSMKTS300004
693764956Hitchcock, Al   MISACCL355500
732947566Mouse, Mickey   MUSCISS400016
740685676Bunny, Bugs     MEDPHYS350002
753546833Duck, Donald    LAYMKTL2499
769048304Streep, Merril  ARTFINS397002
779309498Goldberg, Woopi LAWMKTG289918
794784830Grant, Cary     MESEEGL2399 G
816274855Crystal, Billy  COMBIOL300105
826495896Letterman, DavidCOMCISS300116
834858653Clark, Dick     BUSFINS379817
843020375Williams, Robin ENGENGS276910
924649576ET              EEGENGZ400112
967707888Hall, Arsenio   COMMKTG398017
```

Report Layout: Develop your own report layout in compliance with the processing requirements.

Processing Requirements: 1. Read a file of student records.

2. Validate each input record field for all of the following:
   a. **Name:** If the name is missing, print an appropriate error message:

   `Record missing data in NAME field for Student ID: 123456789`

   b. **Student ID:**
      (1) If the student ID is missing, print an appropriate error message:

      `Record missing data in STUDENT ID field for: Smith, AB`

      (2) Verify that the value is numeric; if not, display an error message:

      `Nonnumeric STUDENT ID for: Smith, AB Student ID: 123456789`

   c. **GPA:**
      (1) If the GPA is missing, print an appropriate error message:

      `Record missing data in GPA field for: Smith, AB Student ID: 123456789`

      (2) *If the GPA is not missing*, verify that the value is numeric; if not, display an error message:

      `Nonnumeric GPA for: Smith, AB Student ID: 123456789  GPA: ABCD`

      (3) *If the GPA is numeric*, then verify that the GPA is between 2.5 and 4.0, inclusively (students with a GPA below 2.5 are ineligible for any kind of aid); if not, display an error message:

      `GPA out of limits for: Smith, AB  Student ID: 123456789 GPA: 5000`

   d. **Credit Hours:**
      (1) If the credit hours are missing, print an appropriate error message:

      `Record missing data in CREDIT HOURS field for: Smith, AB Student ID: 123456789`

      (2) *If the credit hours are not missing*, verify that the value is numeric; if not, display an error message:

      `Nonnumeric CREDIT HOURS for: Smith, AB Student ID: 123456789  Credit Hours: AB`

      (3) *If the credit hours are numeric*, then verify that the hours are between 1 and 18, inclusively; if not, display an error message:

      `CREDIT HOURS out of limits for: Smith, AB  Student ID: 123456789 Credit Hours: 22`

   e. **Codes:**
      (1) Valid school codes are ART, BUS, COM, ENG, LAW, MED, and MUS; error message:

      `Invalid SCHOOL for: Smith, AB  Student ID: 123456789 School: ABC`

      (2) Valid major codes are ACC, BIO, ECO, ENG, FIN, CIS, MKT, PHY, and STA; error message:

      `Invalid MAJOR for: Smith, AB  Student ID: 123456789 MAJOR: ABC`

      (3) Valid aid types are S, G, and L; error message:

      `Invalid AID TYPE for: Smith, AB    Student ID: 123456789 Aid Type: Z`

3. Any record that fails any validity test is to be rejected with no further processing, other than displaying or printing the appropriate error message(s). It is possible that a record may contain more than one error (all errors are to be flagged except where noted).

4. Valid records are to be written to a new file, which will be used in Projects 9-6 and 16-2.

Project 8-7

Program Name: Salary Report Validation Program

Narrative: Write a data validation program that will validate a salary file and produce a valid salary file.

Input File: SALARY-FILE

Input Record Layout:

```
01   SALARY-RECORD.
     05   SAL-SOC-SEC-NO              PIC X(9).
     05   SAL-NAME-AND-INITIALS       PIC X(15).
     05   SAL-BIRTH-DATE.
          10   SAL-BIRTH-MONTH        PIC 9(2).
          10   SAL-BIRTH-YEAR         PIC 9(4).
     05   SAL-LOCATION-CODE           PIC X(3).
     05   SAL-EDUCATION-CODE          PIC 9.
     05   SAL-TITLE-DATA.
          10   SAL-TITLE-CODE         PIC 9(3).
          10   SAL-TITLE-DATE.
               15   SAL-TITLE-MONTH   PIC 9(2).
               15   SAL-TITLE-YEAR    PIC 9(4).
     05   SAL-RATING                  PIC 9.
     05   SAL-SALARY                  PIC 9(6).
```

Test Data:

```
         1         2         3         4         5         6
1234567890123456789012345678901234567890123456789012345678901234 5
125896790Beckelse, GG    031957MIA404003199020 54000
235980890Bennett, JA     161967LA 406003194440 46700
293765635Blaney, WC      041974CHI504004199550 78027
312458697Chatani, DH     061967NY 605006199741 23000
328576407Chen, EI        091966MIA204002199810 45999
         Crumity, TR     161971AT 407106199850 83078
378575600Dailey, TP      051981ATL508007199920 67200
397575906Feuer, D        051981CHI309006199440 90680
427496794Garcia, A       061974LA 607002199320 18050
459797808Gonzalez, L     021974NY 309008198550 30480
470876493Gutierrez, CM   031972ATL210001199540 27090
492729475Jackson, NL     041974MIA304003199840 14 0980
524956063Largesse, CL    021959CHI405011198730 30856
540394065Levy, MS        051960LA 203012199110 37452
S84784755                021965SATL015014199233 5001
593639456Moscatelli, EJ  031979ATL207012199750 50120
635968690Muarata, Y      061973MIA502002199240 38546
658294585Nilsson, P      011980CHI206003199650 36456
693764956Pauncefort, C   051996LA 507002199920 63740
732947566Raffle, AG      061968LA 205007197950 46589
740685G7GRobinson, PJ    121980NYC507007199 80
769048304Rodriquez, AM   111980MIA503003199210 28345
779309498Sanchez, MC     071965NY 208007199640 47242
794784830Schand, MI      041972LAX709006199170 6490
816274855Shinawatra, R   031966CHI410007199930 36478
826495896Tozzi, GA       031961ATL408007199251 92375
834858653Villar, CV      081938MIA501002195553 50000
843020375Wilcoxon, B     041967ATL507004199740 47566
924649576Yadav, S        041971MIA209012200010 37856
967707888Yau, SC         031977CHI310003199922 38745
```

Report Layout: Develop your own report layout in compliance with the processing requirements.

Processing Requirements: 1. Read a file of salary records.

2. Validate each input record field for all of the following:

    a. **Name:** If the name is missing, print an appropriate error message:

```
Record missing data in NAME field for Soc Sec No: 123456789
```

    b. **Soc Sec No:**

      (1) If the social security number is missing, print an appropriate error message:

```
Record missing data in SOC SEC NO field for: Smith, AB
```

      (2) *If the social security number is not missing*, verify that the value is numeric; if not, display an error message:

```
Nonnumeric SOC SEC NO for: Smith, AB    Soc Sec No: ABCD6789
```

    c. **Salary:**

      (1) If the salary is missing, print an appropriate error message:

```
Record missing data in SALARY field for: Smith, AB    Soc Sec No: 123456789
```

      (2) *If the salary is not missing*, verify that the value is numeric; if not, display an error message:

```
Nonnumeric SALARY for: Smith, AB      Soc Sec No: 123456789 Salary: 083078
```

      (3) If the salary is numeric, then verify that salary is over $10,000 and under $350,000; if not, display an error message:

```
SALARY out of limits (under $010000 or over $350000) for: Smith, AB
Soc Sec No: 123456789 Salary: 350001
```

    d. **Codes:**

      (1) Valid location codes are MIA, CHI, LA, NY, and ATL; error message:

```
Invalid LOCATION for: Smith, AB     Soc Sec No: 123456789 Location: AT
```

      (2) Valid education codes are 1 through 6; error message:

```
Invalid EDUCATION for: Smith, AB    Soc Sec No: 123456789 Education: 0
```

      (3) Valid title codes are 010, 020, 030, 040, 050, 060, 070, 080, 090, and 100; error message:

```
Invalid TITLE for: Smith, AB        Soc Sec No: 123456789 Title: 150
```

      (4) Valid ratings are 1 through 5; error message:

```
Invalid RATING for: Smith, AB       Soc Sec No: 123456789 Rating: 0
```

    e. **Birth Date and Age:**

      (1) Verify that the values in the birth date are valid; error message:

```
Invalid BIRTH MONTH for: Smith, AB Soc Sec No:  123456789
Birth Month: 16
```

    (2) Verify the employee is not under 16 years of age; error message:

        AGE under 16 for: Smith, AB   Soc Sec No: 123456789 Age: 13

  f. **Title Date:**

    (1) Verify that the title month is valid; error message:

        Invalid TITLE MONTH for: Smith, AB Soc Sec No: 123456789
        Title Month: 20

    (2) Verify that the title year is valid; the company was established in 1955; therefore no employee should have had a title before that year; error message:

        TITLE YEAR beyond 1999 for: Smith, AB   Soc Sec No: 123456789
        Title Year: 2001

    (3) Verify that the title year is valid; therefore no employee should have had a title year beyond the current year; error message:

        TITLE YEAR beyond 1993 for: Smith, AB   Soc Sec No: 123456789 Title
        Year: 95

    (4) If the title year is valid, be sure the month is not greater than the current month; error message:

        Invalid TITLE DATE for: Smith, AB Soc Sec No: 123456789 Month: 12 Year:
        1999

3. Any record that fails any validity test is to be rejected with no further processing, other than displaying or printing the appropriate error message(s). It is possible that a record may contain more than one error (all errors are to be flagged except where noted).

4. Valid records are to be written to a new file to be used in Projects 9-7 and 16-3.

Project 8-8

Program Name: Stock Validation Program

Narrative: Write a data validation program that will validate a stock file and produce both a valid stock file and an error report.

Input File: STOCK-FILE

Input Record Layout:

```
01  STOCK-RECORD-IN.
    05  STOCK-INFO.
        10  STOCK-NAME              PIC X(8).
        10  STOCK-EXCHANGE-CODE     PIC 9.
        10  STOCK-INDUSTRY-CODE     PIC X(3).
    05  STOCK-CURRENT-INFO.
        10  STOCK-PRICE             PIC 9(3)V9(3).
        10  STOCK-PE                PIC 9(3).
        10  STOCK-DIVIDEND          PIC 9V99.
    05  STOCK-PROJECTION-INFO.
        10  STOCK-RISK-CODE         PIC 9.
        10  STOCK-GROWTH-RATE       PIC 9V9(4).
        10  STOCK-SHARES-TO-BUY     PIC 9(4).
```

Test Data:

```
          1         2         3         4         5         6
 1234567890123456789012345678901234567890123456789012345678901234 5
Hhhhhhh  0BEE0010009995556001 00
Aaaaaaa  1BAN01234001222200543200 00
Anheus   1BEE 52750016112300500 0015
AT&T     1TEL0421250881324025500 100
BellSo   1TEL0477500152764029750 065
Chevron  10IL0727500243304009500 050
Chryslr  1AUT0200000150602003000 025
Compq    1CMP0287500382303015500 025
Eeeeeee  1ELL1500000118900000000 168
Exxon    10IL0627500142883007000 035
Fffffff  1F&L     0102500100010 000
Kellogg  1F0005837502211230245500 10
Kmart    1RET0460000111763005000 005
GenEl    1ELE0775000152203009500 050
GnMotr   1AUT0441250153312006750 010
IBM      1CMP0903750134843011000 050
Marriot  1F&L0180000230283005000 020
McDonld  1F&L0465000190404013500 010
Norwst   1AIR0377500121002004500 015
Reebok   1RET0235000090302007750 075
Sears    1RET0425000152003011500 050
SwBell   1TEL0603750122923007000 030
Upjohn   1DRU0326250111364008000 025
USWst    1AIR0356250122121004500 025
Wendys   1F&L0120000220244029500 050
Bankrs   2BAN0022750080581003200 030
Iomega   2ELE0065000090503006750 040
Maxwel   2F0001300001304040070000 10
Oracle   2CMP0155000552253012000 010
PolkAu   2ELE0062500350752005500 025
Seagate  2ELE0171253431303008900 045
         3TEL1250000345500045450 200
Ccccccc  3BEN0125500120153012340 250
CmceBk   3BAN0155000050152004000 019
LdmkB    3BAN0000630070101003250 500
Ddddddd  4dru0000000204551023000 750
Excel    4CMP0117500280244035000 075
Ggggggg  4air0100000227500000250 100
LilVern  4RET0140000140052006500 050
Luria    4RET0071250290952007500 025
Metrbk   4BAN0112500090603004000 050
Skywst   4AIR0077500200053005000 035
Sonesta  4F&L0055000021003008900 050
Trustco  4BAN0270000120602004000 010
Tyson    4F0001862501700430055000 25
Bbbbbbb  5SD 00134501207511250 01500
```

Report Layout: Develop your own report layout in compliance with the processing requirements.

Processing Requirements:

1. Read a file of stock records.

2. Validate each input record field for all of the following:

   a. **Stock Name:** If the name is missing, print an appropriate error message:

   ```
   Record missing data in NAME field Industry Code: XXX
   ```

   b. **Exchange Code:**

(1) Verify that the value is numeric; if not, display an error message:

`Nonnumeric EXCHANGE CODE for Stock: XXXXXXXX`

(2) *If the* **exchange code** *is numeric*, verify that the code is valid. Valid exchanges are 1 through 4.

Error message: `Invalid EXCHANGE for Stock: XXXXXXXX  Exchange: X`

(Hint: Use condition name test for valid exchanges.)

c. **Industry Code:** Verify that the industry code is valid. Valid industry codes are: AIR, AUT, BAN, BEE, CMP, DRU, ELE, F&L, FOO, OIL, RET, S&L, and TEL.

Error message: `Invalid INDUSTRY CODE for Stock: XXXXXXXX Industry: XXX`

(Hint: Use condition name test for valid types.)

d. **PE and Dividend:** Verify that these values are numeric; if not, display the appropriate error message:

`Nonnumeric PE for Stock: XXXXXXXX  PE: 999`

`Nonnumeric DIVIDEND for Stock: XXXXXXXX  Dividend: 9.99`

e. **Price and Shares to Buy**

(1) Verify that these values are numeric; if not, display the appropriate error message:

`Nonnumeric PRICE for Stock: XXXXXXXX  Price: 999.999`

`Nonnumeric SHARES TO BUY for Stock: XXXXXXXX  Shares to Buy: 9999`

(2) Verify that both are not zero; if either is zero, display an error message:

`Zero Price and/or Shares to Buy for Stock: XXXXXXXX Price: 999.999 Shares: 9999`

(3) *Finally, when both the* **price** *and* **shares to buy** *are numeric and not zero*, verify that the potential stock purchase is not over the limit of $25,000. That is, if the product of the stock price and the shares to buy exceeds $25,000, the record should be rejected. Display the following error message:

`Total Purchase exceeds limit for Stock: XXXXXXXX Limit: 9999999`

f. **Risk Code and Growth Rate:**

(1) Verify that the value is numeric; if not, display the appropriate error message:

`Nonnumeric RISK CODE for Stock: XXXXXXXX  Risk Code: X`

`Nonnumeric GROWTH RATE for Stock: XXXXXXXX  Growth Rate: XXXXX`

(2) *If the* **risk code** *or* **growth rate** *is numeric*, verify that the codes are valid. Valid risk codes are 1 through 5. Valid growth rates are .01% through 100%. Appropriate error messages are:

`Invalid RISK CODE for Stock: XXXXXXXX  Risk Code: X`

`Invalid GROWTH RATE for Stock: XXXXXXXX  Growth Rate: 9.9999`

(Hint: Use a condition name test for valid risks and growth rates.)

3. Any record that fails any validity test is to be rejected with no further processing, other than displaying or printing the appropriate error message(s). It is possible that a record may contain more than one error (all errors are to be flagged except where noted).

4. Valid records are to be written to a file to be used in Projects 9-8, 16-4, and 17-6.

Project 8-9

Program Name: Electricity Bill Validation Program

Narrative: Write a data validation program that will validate an electric file and produce a valid electric file.

Input File: ELECTRIC-FILE

Input Record Layout:

```
01  ELECTRIC-RECORD-IN.
    05  EL-ACCOUNT-NO                  PIC X(6).
    05  EL-ACCOUNT-TYPE.
        10  EL-TYPE-CODE               PIC X.
        10  EL-CATEGORY-CODE           PIC XX.
        10  EL-DEMAND-CODE             PIC X.
        10  EL-TIME-OF-USE-CODE        PIC X.
    05  EL-METER-INFO.
        10  EL-KW-DEMAND-LEVEL         PIC 9(4).
        10  EL-SERVICE-USED-FROM-DATE.
            15  EL-FROM-YEAR           PIC 9(4).
            15  EL-FROM-MONTH          PIC 99.
            15  EL-FROM-DAY            PIC 99.
        10  EL-SERVICE-USED-TO-DATE.
            15  EL-TO-YEAR             PIC 9(4).
            15  EL-TO-MONTH            PIC 99.
            15  EL-TO-DAY              PIC 99.
        10  EL-METER-READ-INFO.
            15  EL-CURRENT-READING     PIC 9(5).
            15  EL-PREVIOUS-READING    PIC 9(5).
```

Test Data:

```
         1         2         3         4         5         6
1234567890123456789012345678901234567890123456789012345678901234 5
342545RRSN10000200001232000022235748349 53
238945CCSX13467200002212000032239081345 76
689353RRSN20000200001272000022900234010 02
466567CGSS10045200002252000032640242329 34
000000CCSL12199200003152000011002357034 65
465758CCSL23456199911131999121400456023 45
763645CGSN10000200001242000021583493724 52
111111RRSN10123200002272000022606678056 78
457686CGSM10512200002012000030336133356 88
487653CGSN20000200002232000032800387378 46
222222CCSM22195200214332000053056754024 66
333333CGSS10550199906391999111112344575 75
349766CGSS20499200001222000021600346627 45
456977CGSL25553200003072000031500643032 45
444444CCSS20025200001182000141237742756 38
945766CCSL12145200002212000032255455445 44
457897CGSM20937200002252000032200425021 45
555555CCSX11590199908322000061512425474 26
460674CGSM10750200001202000021934234212 12
906654RRSN20000200001152000021400335008 56
548645CCSL22100200003092000032900364047 42
666666CGSS10000200005301999063212424242 44
486467RRSN10000199912312000013145867237 45
```

```
859734CGSM20500200002182000003200136409736
146557CGSL12345200001182000002229721995984
387643CCSM11999200001172000002106453342345
777777XXXX12345200013282005121205325 06643
984545CGSN1      1999090319991004903 0289734
895098CGSL12000200001162000002199427483423
567455CGSX14243200001062000002084932845834
387464CCSM10500200002022000003035845333845
345456CGSS10030199912082000001087348773464
463454CGSL22382200003012000032709347 10374
888888CCSM20311199909352000008110864636431
436355CCSM21821200001142000030108863818346
234557RRSN10000200002272000032517274 17234
       CGSL25678200005302000052912342 02345
489753CGSX12000200001132000021053947 39843
487635CCSL12001199911122000001119475384653
784567CGSX25689199903142000033102384 09549
845543CGSN20000200002132000032500895 03453
387454CCSL22003200001172000021501893 10763
999999CGSS11130200002131999123135215 35218
223456CCSM11456200002232000032378446 73523
348756CCSX12150199911111999121178642 65987
345464RRSN20000200001302000032200458 04975
646757CCSM21234200003012000032700030 02985
758346CGSX22123200002022000031510384 00384
457466CCSX23123199912122000012302788 18236
ZZZZZZCGSN20000201002152010 02163642686637
545465CGSS20050199905191999062000023 00384
346768CCSL14356200002172000031745985 45643
859567CCSX25574199907201999082004534 00454
```

Report Layout: Develop your own report layout in compliance with the processing requirements.

Processing Requirements: 1. Read a file of electric records.

2. Validate each input record field for all of the following:
   a. **Account No:**
      (1) If the account number is missing, print an appropriate error message:
      `Record missing data in ACCOUNT NO field Account Type: RRSN1`
      (2) *If the **account number** is not missing*, then verify that the value is numeric; if not, display an error message:
      `Nonnumeric ACCOUNT NO for Account No: 123456`
   b. **Account Type:** Verify that the account type is a valid account type. Valid account types are RRSN1, RRSN2, CGSN1, CGSN2, CGSS1, CGSS2, CGSM1, CGSM2, CGSL1, CGSL2, CGSX1, CGSX2, CCSM1, CCSM2, CCSL1, CGCL2, CGCX1, CCSX2;
      Error message: `Invalid ACCOUNT TYPE for Account: 123456 Type: XXXXX`
      (Hint: Use a condition name test for valid types.)
   c. **KW Demand Level:**
      (1) Verify that the value is numeric; if not, display an error message:
      `Nonnumeric KW DEMAND LEVEL for Account No: 123456`
      (2) *If the **kw demand level** is numeric*, then verify that the value is consistent with the demand code in the account type as shown below:

Demand Code	KW Demand Level Range
N	n/a (0)
S	21-499
M	500-1999
L	2000-9999
X	2000-9999

Error Message:

```
Inconsistent DEMAND CODE & DEMAND LEVEL for Account No: 123456
Demand Code: S  Demand Level: 545
```

d. **Service Used From and To Dates:**

(1) Verify that the from or to month is valid (i.e., 1 thru 12); error message:

```
Invalid FROM MONTH for Account No: 123456 Month: 20
```
or `Invalid TO MONTH for Account No: 123456 Month: 20`

(2) Verify that the from or to day is valid (i.e., cannot exceed the maximum days in the corresponding month); error message:

```
Invalid FROM DAY for Account No: 123456 Month: 12 Day: 35
```
or `Invalid TO DAY for Account No: 123456 Month: 12 Day: 35`

(Hint: Use a condition name test for valid months and days.)

(3) Verify that the from or to year is valid; the year must be either the current or previous year; error message:

```
Invalid FROM YEAR for Account No: 123456  Year: 1995
```
or `Invalid TO YEAR for Account No: 123456  Year: 1995`

(4) If the from or to date is valid, then verify the complete date (year, month, and day) is less than today's date; error message:

```
Invalid FROM DATE for Account No: 123456 Mon: 05 Day: 31 Yr: 2005
```
or `Invalid TO DATE for Account No: 123456 Mon: 05 Day: 31 Yr: 2005`

(5) Verify that the from date is prior to the to date; error message:

```
FROM DATE is not prior to TO DATE for Account No: 123456
Current Date: 920325 Previous Date: 920220
```

e. **Current and Previous Readings:** Verify that the value is numeric; if not, display an error message:

```
Nonnumeric CURRENT READING for Account No: 123456 Current Reading:
346C4
```

or `Nonnumeric PREVIOUS READING for Account No: 123456 Previous Reading:`
`346C4`

3. Any record that fails any validity test is to be rejected with no further processing, other than displaying or printing the appropriate error message(s). It is possible that a record may contain more than one error (all errors are to be flagged except where noted).

4. Valid records are to be written to a file to be used in Projects 9-9, 16-5.

Project 9-1

Program Name: Order Transactions Report Program.

Narrative: This program accepts the valid output file produced by Project 8-1 as input and produces a report as output.

Input File: ORDER-TRANSACTION-FILE

Input Record Layout: Identical to the output record of Project 8-1.

Test Data: Use the output file of valid records created in Project 8-1 as input.

Report Layout: Design your own report layout, subject to the processing requirements.

Processing Requirements: 1. Read a file of valid order records.

2. Write an appropriate heading at the top of each page showing the date the report was run and page number.

3. Write an order report line for each type-1 record listing all of the order information including the purchase order number and date.

4. On the next line write the customer information from the associated type-2 record including customer name and address, credit limit, balance due, and phone number.

5. Write one line for *each* type-3 record showing the item number, quantity, unit price, and the extended price (quantity * unit price). Use any editing facilities you deem appropriate.

6. At the end, provide a total line for the total balance due. The balance due is contained in the type-2 record.

Project 9-2

Program Name: Stock Transactions Report Program

Narrative: This program accepts the valid output file produced by Project 8-2 as input and produces a report as output.

Input File: STOCK-TRANSACTION-FILE

Input Record Layout: Identical to the output record of Project 8-2.

Test Data: Use the output file of valid records created in Project 8-2 as input.

Report Layout:

```
                           We Make U Money, Inc.                          Page Z9
                     Stock Activity Report as of MM/DD/YYYY

                    Purchase Info                         Sell Info            Profit
              ------------------------------------   ----------------------------   / Loss
Stock        Shares  Date    Price/Share    Total    Date    Price/Share   Total
XXXXXXXXXXXXX  ZZ9  MM/DD/YYYY  ZZ,ZZ9.99  ZZZ,ZZ9.99 MM/DD/YYYY ZZ,ZZ9.99 ZZZ,ZZZ9.99  ---,--9.99
                .     .    .          .         .        .          .          .            .
                .     .    .          .         .        .          .          .            .
                .     .    .          .         .        .          .          .            .
              -----                        ------------              ------------ ------------
Totals        Z,ZZ9                        Z,ZZZ,ZZ9.99              Z,ZZZ,ZZ9.99 -,---,--9.99
```

Processing Requirements:

1. Read a file of valid stock records.

2. Write the appropriate headings showing the date and page number.

3. For each record read:
   a. Calculate the
      (1) total purchase by multiplying the number of shares by the purchase price per share.
      (2) total sale by multiplying the shares by the selling price per share.
      (3) profit/loss by subtracting the total purchase from the total sale.
   b. String the record's purchase and sale date into a month, day, and year format.
   c. Write a detail line for every transaction; print 4 transactions per page.

4. Write totals as shown in the report layout after all records are processed.

Project 9-3

Program Name: Payroll Report Program

Narrative: This program accepts the valid output file produced by Project 8-3 as input and produces a report as output.

Input File: PAYROLL-FILE

Input Record Layout: Identical to the output record of Project 8-3.

Test Data: Use the output file of valid records created in Project 8-3 as input.

Report Layout:

```
                        HardWorkers of America as of mm/dd/yyyy        Page Z9

        Name                          Gross Pay      Taxes  Insurance     Net Pay

        last name, first name         $$$,$$9.99    $$$9.99   $$$9.99   $$$,$$9.99
                    .                      .            .         .           .
                    .                      .            .         .           .
                    .                      .            .         .           .
                                      $$$$,$$9.99  $$,$$9.99 $$,$$9.99 $$$$,$$9.99
```

Processing Requirements:

1. Read a file of valid payroll records.

2. Write the appropriate headings showing the date and page number.

3. For each input record read:
   a. Calculate the gross pay as:
      (1) Straight time for the first 40 hours worked
      (2) Time and a half for hours worked over 40

      Note: Salaried workers DO NOT get overtime.
   b. Calculate the deductions:
      (1) Federal withholding tax is based on the gross pay.
         (a) 18% on the first $400
         (b) 23% on amounts over $400 and up to $600, inclusive
         (c) 25% on amounts over $600
      (2) FICA is 6.2% of the gross pay.
      (3) Insurance as indicated below depending on the Plan Type.

Plan	Amount Deducted
A	$5
B	$8
C	$10
Z	$0 (no insurance)

   c. Calculate net pay by subtracting all of the deductions (tax, FICA, and insurance) from the gross pay.
   d. Write a detail line for each employee. String the name as shown in the report layout. Print only 5 employees per page.

4. Write totals as shown on the report layout after ten records have been processed.

Project 9-4

Program Name: Car Sales Commissions Report Program

Narrative: This program accepts the valid output file produced by Project 8-4 as input and produces a report as output.

Input File: CAR-SALES-FILE

Input Record Layout: Identical to the output record of Project 8-4.

Test Data: Use the output file of valid records created in Project 8-4 as input.

Report Layout:

```
                        Very Very Nice Cars, Inc.            Page Z9
                        Commission Report MM/DD/YYYY

        Salesperson  Date         Car           Sale   Commission    Net

        XXXXXXXXXX MM/DD/YYYY 'YY XXXXXXXXXXXX  ZZZ,ZZ9   ZZZ,ZZ9    ZZZ,ZZ9
            .         .      .      .              .         .          .
            .         .      .      .              .         .          .
            .         .      .      .              .         .          .
                                             ---------- ---------- ----------
                                             Z,ZZZ,ZZ9  Z,ZZZ,ZZ9  Z,ZZZ,ZZ9
```

Processing Requirements:

1. Read a file of valid car sales records.

2. Write the appropriate headings showing the current date and page.

3. For each record read:
   a. Calculate the commission paid to the salesperson by multiplying the commission rate by the sale amount.
   b. Calculate the net to the company by subtracting the commission paid from the sale amount.
   c. Write a detail line, printing 8 sales per page. Use reference modification to show only the last two digits in the car year on the report line.

4. Write totals as shown on the report layout after all the records have been processed.

Project 9-5

Program Name: Invoice Mailing Labels Program

Narrative: This program accepts the valid output file produced by Project 8-5 as input and produces a mailing label as output.

Input File:	INVOICE-FILE
Input Record Layout:	Identical to the output record of Project 8-5.
Test Data:	Use the output file of valid records created in Project 8-5 as input.
Report Layout:	

```
Scully                    Schultz
20 Main St                45 5th St
Chicago, IL 60666         Los Angeles, CA 90024
```

Processing Requirements:

1. Read a file of valid invoice records.

2. For each input record read create a mailing label.
   a. String the city, state, and zip as shown in the report layout.
   b. Print the labels in two columns as shown in the report layout.

Project 9-6

Program Name:	Student Record Report Program
Narrative:	This program accepts the valid output file produced by Project 8-6 as input and produces a report as output.
Input File:	STUDENT-FILE
Input Record Layout:	Identical to the output record of Project 8-6.
Test Data:	Use the output file of valid records created in Project 8-6 as input.
Report Layout:	

```
                              Smart U                              Page Z9
                      Student Aid Report 99/99/9999

                                      Credit   Total      Total    Tuition
    StudentID  Name          School  Aid Hours Tuition      Aid       Due

    999999999  XXXXXXXXXXXXXX   XXX   X    Z9   ZZZ,ZZ9   ZZZ,ZZ9   ZZZ,ZZ9

        .          .            .    .    .      .          .         .

        .          .            .    .    .      .          .         .

        .          .            .    .    .      .          .         .

                                          ---  --------- --------- ---------

                                          ZZ9 Z,ZZZ,ZZ9 Z,ZZZ,ZZ9 Z,ZZZ,ZZ9
```

Processing Requirements:
1. Read a file of valid student records.

2. Write appropriate headings showing the current date and page number.

3. For each input record read:
   a. Calculate total tuition based on $300 per credit.
   b. Calculate total aid based on the GPA as follows:

GPA	% Aid
2.5 to 3.0	60%
3.1 to 3.5	70%
3.6 to 4.0	80%

   c. Calculate the tuition due by subtracting the total aid from the total tuition.
   d. Write a detail line with the information shown on the report layout, printing 10 students per page.

4. Write the totals shown on the report layout after all the records have been processed.

Project 9-7

Program Name: Salary Report Program

Narrative: This program accepts the valid output file produced by Project 8-7 as input and produces a report as output.

Input File: SALARY-FILE

Input Record Layout: Identical to the output record of Project 8-7.

Test Data: Use the output file of valid records created in Project 8-7 as input.

Report Layout: Develop your own report layout in compliance with the processing requirements.

Processing Requirements:
1. Read a file of valid salary records.

2. Write an appropriate heading showing the current date and page number.

3. For each input record read write a detail line showing all of the information in the record. Print 10 employees per page.

4. Write a total for the salary amounts after all records have been processed.

Project 9-8

Program Name: Stock Purchases Report Program

Narrative: This program accepts the valid output file produced by Project 8-8 as input and produces a report as output.

Input File: STOCK-FILE

Input Record Layout: Identical to the output record of Project 8-8.

Test Data: Use the output file of valid records created in Project 8-8 as input.

Report Layout:

```
                        Stock Purchases              Page Z9
                      day of Week MM/DD/YYYY


          Name     Exchange    Shares     Price        Total
          XXXXXXXX   XXX       Z,ZZ9    $ZZ9.999    $ZZ,ZZ9.99
            .         .          .          .            .
            .         .          .          .            .
            .         .          .          .            .
                                ------                -----------
                                ZZ,ZZ9                $ZZZ,ZZ9.99
```

Processing Requirements:
1. Read a file of valid stock records.

2. Write an appropriate heading, showing the page, day of week, and current date.

3. For each input record read:
   a. Calculate the total by multiplying the shares to buy by the stock price.
   b. Write a detail line showing all of the information on the report layout, printing 10 stocks per page.

4. When all the records are processed, print totals as shown on the report layout.

Project 9-9

Program Name: Electricity Bill Report Program

Narrative: This program accepts the valid output file produced by Project 8-9 as input and produces a report as output.

Input File: ELECTRIC-FILE

Input Record Layout: Identical to the output record of Project 8-9.

Test Data: Use the output file of valid records created in Project 8-9 as input.

Report Layout:

```
                              Bright Power & Light                    Page Z9
                              Residential Kilowatt Usage


          Account Info      Service Used     Meter Readings      Total    Estimated
        ----------------    ------------    ------------------  Kilowatt     Bill
                                                                ----------   ----------
        Number    Type      From   To      Previous  Current   Hrs Used
        999999    XXXXX     MM/DD  MM/DD    ZZ,ZZ9    ZZ,ZZ9    ZZ,ZZ9    Z,ZZ9.99
          .         .         .     .         .         .         .          .
          .         .         .     .         .         .         .          .
          .         .         .     .         .         .         .          .
                                                                -------    --------
                                                                ZZZ,ZZ9   ZZ,ZZ9.99
```

Processing Requirements:

1. Read a file of valid electric records.

2. Write an appropriate heading showing the page number.

3. For each input record read:

   a. If the account category is residential:

      (1) Calculate the total kilowatt hours used by subtracting the previous reading from the current reading.

      (2) Calculate an estimated bill:

          The first 750 kw hours used will be charged at 3.922¢ per kw hour.

          Additional kw hours used will be charged at 4.922¢.

   b. Print a detail line showing the information in the report layout.

4. Write the totals shown on the report layout after all records have been processed.

Programming Specifications

Projects 10-1 through 10-9

Program Name: Order Transactions, Stock Transactions, Payroll, Car Sales Commissions, Invoice Mailing Labels, Student Record, Salary, Stock Purchases, and Electricity Bill

Narrative: These projects combine the requirements of projects 8-1 through 8-9 and 9-1 through 9-9 as presented earlier in Chapters 8 and 9. The fields in each incoming record transaction are accepted and validated one at a time, after which the necessary computations are done and the report is displayed on the screen.

Test Data: Use one or more records from the original data in Chapter 8.

Screen Layout: Design your own input and output screen layout (based on the record layout in projects 8-1 through 8-9 and report layout in projects 9-1 through 9-9).

Processing Requirements:

1. Display a screen to input and validate a record, repeating the appropriate validations in the corresponding projects in Chapter 8.

2. Display the calculated information from the corresponding projects in Chapter 9 on the screen.

3. Optional: write the validated input records to a file after displaying it on the screen.

Programming Specifications

Project 11-1

Program Name: Employee Profiles

Narrative: The requirements of this project are typical of compensation reports done in large organizations, which compare individuals with similar skills to one another. (The project is expanded to include material on table lookups in Project 12-1 at the end of the next chapter.)

Input File: EMPLOYEE-FILE

Input Record Layout:

```
01  EMPLOYEE-RECORD.
    05  EMP-SOC-SEC-NUMBER                  PIC X(9).
    05  EMP-NAME-AND-INITIALS               PIC X(16).
    05  EMP-DATE-OF-BIRTH.
        10  EMP-BIRTH-MONTH                 PIC 99.
        10  EMP-BIRTH-YEAR                  PIC 9(4).
    05  EMP-DATE-OF-HIRE.
        10  EMP-HIRE-MONTH                  PIC 99.
        10  EMP-HIRE-YEAR                   PIC 9(4).
    05  EMP-SEX                             PIC X.
    05  EMP-SALARY-DATA OCCURS 3 TIMES.
        10  EMP-SALARY                      PIC 9(5).
        10  EMP-SALARY-TYPE                 PIC X.
        10  EMP-SALARY-DATE.
            15  EMP-SALARY-MONTH            PIC 99.
            15  EMP-SALARY-YEAR             PIC 9(4).
        10  EMP-SALARY-GRADE                PIC 9.
    05  EMP-TITLE-DATA.
        10  EMP-TITLE-CODE                  PIC XX.
        10  EMP-TITLE-DATE.
            15  EMP-TITLE-MONTH             PIC 99.
            15  EMP-TITLE-YEAR              PIC 9(4).
    05  EMP-LOCATION-CODE                   PIC 99.
    05  EMP-EDUCATION-CODE                  PIC 9.
```

Test Data:

```
         1         2         3         4         5         6         7         8
1234567890123456789012345678901234567890123456789012345678901234567890123456789012345
100000000DOE             J 121979091998M33000M092000331500H0919993              35091999104
200000000WILCOX          PA101969111991M29000M112000227500H1119992              35111999104
400000000LEVINE          S 011950081990F31000M082000229000M081999228000M021999232081990104
500000000SMITHERS        M 031950011972M48000M081999745500M081998740000M081995428051994204
600000000SUPERPROG       S 041957101991F59000H1019986                          50101998106
700000000LEE             B 101953021985F40000P052000837500M021999835000M021998740051997405
800000000PERSNICKETYP 081975031999M25600H0320003                               50031999306
900000000MILGROM         MB111965091996F32000M111999329000M051998227500M051996132111996103
```

Report Layout: The report below shows required information and illustrative calculations for A. B. Jones. Print your report according to these general specifications, but do not be concerned about exact line and column positions on a page. (See item 2b in the processing requirements for additional guidelines.)

```
                            PERSONNEL PROFILE
              NAME:   JONES A.B.      SOC-SEC-NO.:  123-45-6789
              AGE:    31.4 YEARS      HIRE DATE:    1/1991
--------------------------------------------------------------------------
SALARY    DATE  TYPE  % INC.   MBI    RSI     GRADE   MIDPOINT   % MIDPOINT
$24,200   7/94  P      10.0     6    20.0%      4     $28,000       86.4
$22,000   1/94  M      10.0    12    10.0%      3     $21,000      104.7
$20,000   1/93  H                               3     $21,000       95.2
```

Processing Requirements: 1. Read a file of employee records.

2. For every record read:

   a. Compute and print the employee's age, using the date of birth and date of execution. (The age calculation will be approximate, as the input birth date contains only the month and year.)

   b. Print all indicated fields with appropriate editing. Print three employees per page; leave six blank lines between employees.

   c. Print all associated salary information as described in items 3–6.

3. Each employee has a salary history with 1, 2, or 3 levels of salary data, denoting present, previous, and second previous salary, respectively. Not every employee will have all three salaries indicated, but every employee must have a present salary.

4. Associated with every salary is a salary grade, indicative of the level of responsibility in the company (for example, the janitor and president might have grade levels of 1 and 9, respectively). Each grade has an associated average salary, or midpoint. The salary midpoint is computed by multiplying the grade by $7,000. The percent of grade midpoint is found by dividing the salary by the grade midpoint and multiplying by 100.

5. Associated with every pair of salaries are three fields: percent salary increase, months between increase (MBI), and annual rate of salary increase (RSI).

   a. Percent salary increase is found by subtracting the old salary from the new salary, dividing by the old salary, and multiplying by 100. For example, new and old salaries of $22,000 and $20,000 yield a percent increase of 10%.

   b. Months between increase (MBI) is simply the number of months between the two salary dates.

   c. Annual rate of salary increase (RSI) is computed by converting the percent salary increase to a 12-month basis; for example, 10% after 6 months is equivalent to an annual rate of 20%; 10% after 2 years is an annual rate of 5%.

6. Calculate percent salary increase, MBI, and RSI for each pair of salaries as appropriate. Realize, however, that not every employee will have all three salary levels, and hence the calculations cannot be made in every instance. Use an OCCURS clause, subscripts, and a PERFORM VARYING statement to do the calculations. Be sure to include a suitable test to avoid the computation if historical data are not present.

Project 11-2

Program Name: Benefit Statement

Narrative: Most employees do not realize the value of their fringe benefits, which often run to 30% of their annual salaries. Accordingly, benefit statements are often prepared to remind employees how well (their employer thinks) they are being treated. Develop a program to read a file of confidential employee data and to compute and print the fringe benefits for each employee.

Input File: EMPLOYEE-FILE

Input Record Layout: Use the same record layout as for Project 11-1.

Test Data: Use the same test data as for Project 11-1.

Report Layout:

```
                       Employee Benefit Statement
  NAME: XXXXXXXXXXXXXXX                          BIRTH DATE: 99/9999
   ANNUAL SALARY: $$$,$$9                        HIRE DATE: 99/9999
  ------------------------ Sick Pay Benefit --------------------------------
  WEEKS AT FULL PAY: Z9        WEEKS AT HALF PAY: Z9
  ------------------------ Retirement Benefit ------------------------
  COMPANY CONTRIBUTES: $$$,$$9  INTEREST RATE: .99  AMT AT AGE 65: $$,$$$,$$9
  ------------------------ Life Insurance = $$$$,$$9 ----------------------
```

Processing Requirements:

1. Read a file of employee records, preparing an individual benefit statement for every record. Each individual statement is to appear on a separate page.

2. For every record read:

   a. Calculate the retirement benefit based on an annual company contribution for each employee. The contribution is equal to 5% of the first $15,000 of salary plus 3% on any salary in excess of $15,000. Hence the company would contribute $840 annually for an employee earning $18,000 (5% of 15,000 = 750, plus 3% of 3,000 = 90). The money is invested for the employees and assumed to earn 8% annually. Use the following formula:

   $$\text{Amount at age 65} = \frac{\left(\left(1+i\right)^{n} - 1\right)}{i} * \text{Company Contribution}$$

   where i = interest rate (for example, .08) and n = years until age 65 (specify the ROUNDED option of any arithmetic statement used in computing n).

   b. Calculate the life insurance benefit as twice an employee's annual salary if the employee earns $23,000 or less; it is three times the annual salary for those earning more than $23,000.

   c. Calculate the amount of sick pay, which is dependent on the individual's length of service. An employee is entitled to one week of full pay and an additional two weeks of half pay, for every year (or fraction thereof) of employment. The maximum benefit, however, is 10 weeks of full salary and 20 of half salary, which is reached after 10 years. (An employee with two years' service, for example, is entitled to two weeks full pay and an additional four weeks of half pay.)

   d. Use the individual's present salary, EMP-SALARY (1), in all benefit calculations.

Project 11-3

Program Name: Evaluation of Student Curriculum Records

Narrative: This project builds on Project 3-5. Write a program using table handling to evaluate a student's curriculum record and determine the percentage of courses a student has left in order to graduate, the percentage of courses a student has transferred, the percentage of courses for which a student has been awarded proficiency credit, and the percentage of courses a student has completed. Print the names of students who are close to graduation and the courses they have left to complete.

Input File: STUDENT-CURRICULUM-FILE

Student Curriculum Record		
Student Id Number	Course Number	Grade
1 ... 5	6 ... 12	13

Input Record Layout:

```
         1         2         3         4         5         6         7         8
1234567890123456789012345678901234567890123456789012345678901234567890123456789012345
11345COMP110AENGL110AMATH148KMATH168PCIS150 FCIS230  PSYC105BBUSN110AHUMN410PHUMN4285
34567ENGL110CENGL120CMATH048CMATH210DCIS150 PCIS230 ACIS330
78921BUSN110 BUSN120 ENGL110AENGL120PMATH048KMATH168BMATH220
34678PSYC105APSYC305AENGL110AENGL120 ECON210AHUMN410KHUMN420PHUMN430AACCT213AACCT347
47830SPCH275AENGL110AACCT205AACCT210PACCT347K
```

Test Data:

Report Layout: Use the same report layout as in Project 3-5. Add editing where appropriate. Add the remaining courses to complete for a student who is near graduation (see specifications) using an appropriate format.

Processing Requirements: 1. Read a file of student curriculum records.

2. Dynamically load a table containing all the student curriculum records for one student.

3. Once all records for one student are loaded into the table:
   a. Add the total number of courses (course name, not spaces) for each student.
   b. Add the total number of courses where the student was awarded a grade (A, B, C, or D), proficiency credit (P), or transfer credit (K).
   c. Add the total number of courses where the student was awarded transfer credit (K).
   d. Add the total number of courses where the student was awarded proficiency credit (P).
   e. Determine the percentages of courses left in order to graduate, courses completed, courses transferred, and courses awarded proficiency credit.

f. Print student id number and the percentages of courses left to graduate, courses completed, courses transferred, and courses awarded proficiency credit.

g. If the student has less than 20% of courses left in order to graduate, print the courses the student has not completed.

Project 11-4

Program Name: Computer Status Report

Narrative: This program will create an individual status report for each record in the file. When all the records have been processed, print a summary report showing totals for each status. (The project is expanded to include material on table lookups in Project 12-4 in the next chapter.)

Input File: COMPUTER-FILE

Input Record Layout:

```
01  COMPUTER-RECORD.
    05  COM-INVOICE-NO              PIC 9(5).
    05  COM-CUSTOMER-NAME           PIC X(18).
    05  COM-PAYMENT-METHOD          PIC XX.
    05  COM-SHIP-INFO.
        10  COM-SHIP-STATUS         PIC X.
        10  COM-SHIP-CHARGE         PIC 99V99.
    05  COM-COMPONENT-INFO.
        10  COM-NO-COMPONENTS       PIC 9.
        10  COM-COMPONENTS   OCCURS 1 TO 4 TIMES
                    DEPENDING ON COM-NO-COMPONENTS.
            15  COM-COMPONENT       PIC X(12).
            15  COM-COST            PIC 9(4).
```

Test Data:

```
         1         2         3         4         5         6         7         8         9
1234567890123456789012345678901234567890123456789012345678901234567890123456789012345678901234 5

12834Blanco, Erick       AM145502II  450MHz  15891.5MB Modem  0099
79845Casali, Joseph      AM375002III 500MHz  2499Laser Printr1399Supertape    0199
59789Davis, Kevin        VII65502II  400MHz  1995Laser Pritnr1399
85778Demler, Linda       CO380254III 450MHz  2199InkJet Ptr   0250Scanner     0150Modem/FAX 0080
47597EChavarria, Felipe  CK265002II  333MHz  1195TapeStore    0324
58684Flemming, Sharon    MC145002540 Laptop  1899InkJet Ptr   0250
48577Gonzalez, Maria     VI135003II  350MHz  1575Modem/FAX    0080Video Card  0139
56749Katan, Maharan      CK245001810 Laptop  2799
95877Parmenter, Donita   CO335002II  450MHz  1995CD/ROM       0120
38476Pinkwasser, Randi   VI389004III 500MHz  159556K Modem    0143InkJet Ptr 0250Scanner    0150
37586Stewart, Roberto    CK250002II  333MHz  0800FAX          1279
```

Report Layout:

```
                      FLY BY NITE COMPUTERS, INC.
                           STATUS REPORT

     INVOICE #:  XXXXX                STATUS: X
     CUSTOMER NAME: XXXXXXXXXXXXXXX   PAYMENT METHOD: XX


           COMPONENT                      COST
           XXXXXXXXXXXX                $$,$$9.99

                 .
                   .
                     .

                                      ----------
           SUBTOTAL                    $$$,$$9.99
           SHIPPING CHARGES              $$$9.99
           TOTAL                       $$$,$$9.99
```

```
                      FLY BY NITE COMPUTERS, INC.
                           SUMMARY BY STATUS

        STATUS    ITEMS    SHIP CHARGES        COST
          1        Z9       $$,$$9.99      $$,$$9.99
          2        Z9       $$,$$9.99      $$,$$9.99
          3        Z9       $$,$$9.99      $$,$$9.99
                  ----     ----------     ----------
        TOTAL     ZZ9       $$,$$9.99     $$$,$$9.99
```

Processing Requirements:

1. Read a file of customer records.

2. For each record read:

   a. Print the report for each customer on a separate page; print headings as shown on the report layout.

   b. Process each component ordered by

      (1) Printing a detail line as shown on the report layout.

      (2) Incrementing the cost totals for that customer.

   c. When all items for one customer have been processed:

      (1) Calculate the customer total by adding the shipping charges to the cost totals.

      (2) Print the customer total lines as shown in the report layout.

   d. Increment the appropriate status in the summary table with the above information.

3. After all records have been read, print the summary table showing totals for each status (as shown on the report layout).

Project 11-5

Program Name: Credit Report

Narrative: This program produces a credit report for store accounts. The store offers three types of accounts: 20, 40, or 60; a customer may have one of each. The report will show detail lines for each type of account for each customer. The last page is a summary of payments, purchases, interest charged, and current balance by account type.

Input File: CREDIT-FILE

Input Record Layout:

```
01  CREDIT-RECORD.
    05  CR-ACCOUNT-NO              PIC 9(7).
    05  CR-NAME-AND-INITIALS       PIC X(18).
    05  CR-NO-OF-ACCOUNTS          PIC 9.
    05  CR-TRANSACTIONS OCCURS 1 TO 3 TIMES
            DEPENDING ON CR-NO-OF-ACCOUNTS.
        10  CR-TYPE                PIC 99.
        10  CR-BALANCE             PIC 9(4)V99.
        10  CR-PAYMENT             PIC 9(4)V99.
        10  CR-PURCHASES           PIC 9(4)V99.
```

Test Data:

```
          1         2         3         4         5         6         7         8
 1234567890123456789012345678901234567890123456789012345678901234567890123456789012345 6
1234520STUTZ, JD          12005860003430004 5444
1957620FROST, RD          14004534505000000 5055
2947660BARBER, MM         320023390010000009545400047534031500034212602334122334120433 32
3856740GOLDSMITH, KN      24002343401233403432360342330362330005443
4209540GRAUER, RG         320034222023422185344400634440300000343326055641203421206452 3
4908560PLANT, RK          22003430003430002232360043400050000000000
5748920ELOFSON, GS        24008640005640003422360675400375400045334
6847660STEWART, JB        16005560000560016 4543
7457620GILLENSON, ML      14006551300551303 5434
8466740RUSHINEK, SF       22004533400500012343460074554084554045334
9436560VAZQUEZ VILLAR, C  3200453450500000034454006566606500000455060054656044656043534
```

Report Layout:

```
┌──────────────────────────────────────────────────────────────────────────────┐
│                  NEEDLESS MARKUP STORES ACCOUNT CREDIT REPORT        PAGE Z9    │
│                                                                                │
│     ACCOUNT # 9999999    NAME: XXXXXXXXXXXXXXXXXX                               │
│                                                                                │
│        TYPE   PREVIOUS                    INTEREST   CURRENT    CREDIT  AVAILABLE│
│               BALANCE   PAYMENT PURCHASES  CHARGE    BALANCE    LIMIT    CREDIT  │
│                                                                                │
│        99     Z,ZZ9.99  Z,ZZ9.99 Z,ZZ9.99  ZZ9.99   Z,ZZ9.99CR Z,ZZ9.99 Z,ZZ9.99│
│        99     Z,ZZ9.99  Z,ZZ9.99 Z,ZZ9.99  ZZ9.99   Z,ZZ9.99CR Z,ZZ9.99 Z,ZZ9.99│
│        99     Z,ZZ9.99  Z,ZZ9.99 Z,ZZ9.99  ZZ9.99   Z,ZZ9.99CR Z,ZZ9.99 Z,ZZ9.99│
│                        --------- ---------- -------- ----------                 │
│        TOTALS          ZZ,ZZ9.99 ZZ,ZZ9.99 Z,ZZ9.99 ZZ,ZZ9.99CR                 │
│          .                                                                     │
│            .                                                                   │
│              .                                                                 │
└──────────────────────────────────────────────────────────────────────────────┘
```

```
                    NEEDLESS MARKUP STORES ACCOUNT TYPE SUMMARY

        TYPE                              INTEREST      CURRENT
                    PAYMENT    PURCHASES    CHARGE       BALANCE

         20        Z,ZZ9.99    Z,ZZ9.99    ZZ9.99     Z,ZZ9.99CR
         40        Z,ZZ9.99    Z,ZZ9.99    ZZ9.99     Z,ZZ9.99CR
         60        Z,ZZ9.99    Z,ZZ9.99    ZZ9.99     Z,ZZ9.99CR
                   ---------   ---------   --------   ---------
        TOTALS     ZZ,ZZ9.99  ZZ,ZZ9.99  Z,ZZ9.99    ZZ,ZZ9.99CR
```

Processing Requirements:

1. Read a file of credit records.

2. Develop a page heading routine which prints 5 accounts on every page.

3. For each record read:
   a. Print the appropriate account headings.
   b. Process each account type by
      (1) Calculating the monthly interest charge on the account based on the account balance after the payment has been applied. (To make life a lot easier, use simple interest and a rate of 18.5%.)
      (2) Calculating the current balance by adding the interest charge and purchases and subtracting the payment. (Note: a customer could overpay the account, therefore you should remember to make the field signed and display it as such on the report as shown in the report layout or as desired.)
      (3) Determining the credit limit for each account as follows:

Type	Credit Limit
20	$1,500
40	$3,500
60	$5,000

      (4) Calculating the available credit on the account by subtracting the current balance from the credit limit determined in (3).
      (5) Printing a detail line as shown on the report layout.
      (6) Incrementing the appropriate totals.
   c. When all accounts for one customer have been processed, print the total lines as shown in the report layout.
   d. Increment the appropriate account type in the summary table with the above information.

4. After all records have been read, print a summary table showing totals for each account type (as shown on the report layout).

Project 11-6

Program Name: Software Cost Analysis

Narrative: The program will determine the following:

1. The break-even units and revenue for each software product.

2. The break-even units and revenue for each software product if a $50,000 profit is desired.

3. The break-even units and revenue for each software product if the selling price is reduced by 25%.

Input File: SOFTWARE-FILE

Input Record Layout:

```
01  SOFTWARE-RECORD.
    05  SOFT-PROGRAM-INFO.
        10  SOFT-PRODUCT-LINE            PIC X.
        10  SOFT-PRODUCT-NO              PIC 9(4).
        10  SOFT-PROGRAM-NAME            PIC X(18).
    05  SOFT-VARIABLE-COSTS.
        10  SOFT-PREP-COSTS.
            15  SOFT-LOADING-PER-DISK    PIC 9V99.
            15  SOFT-NO-DISKS-USED       PIC 99.
        10  SOFT-MANUAL-PRINTING         PIC 99V99.
        10  SOFT-SHIPPING-N-HANDLING     PIC 99V99.
    05  SOFT-SELL-PRICE                  PIC 999V99.
    05  SOFT-FIXED-COST                  PIC 9(5).
```

Test Data:

```
         1         2         3         4         5         6
1234567890123456789012345678901234567890123456789012345678901234 5
G4695Flight Simulator   1500110000325042 9525000
B3764WordPerfect 8.0    2251135501025346 9523000
G1634Leisure Suit Larry 10002108502000399520000
U3476Fastback Plus      1750115000350119 5021000
G6424ChessMaster 6000   0500107500550033 0018000
B4676Word 98            2500855500850366 7530000
M9775Streetfinder       0750108250250043 0018000
G2555Police Quest       0750204550445045 5505000
D4954PowerPoint 4.0     2251035000950303 0008000
U7558PROCOMM Plus 4.6   0750110500525098 0007500
B2154Excel 5.0          2650725751025302 9528750
E5775Carmen San Diego   0800103500225029 0003000
B75841-2-3 5.0          2450845500555303 9035800
D2585Harvard Graphics   2150525250725206 0034500
E6555Kid Pix Studios    0250105400250024 0003650
B4954Quicken 99         1950645001250059 9515950
U7588Corel Print Office 10002185007500640017000
```

Report Layout:

```
                        Nexus Software Inc.
                Product Cost Analysis as of 99/99/9999
                based on Total Fixed Costs:  $ZZ,ZZ9


    Product Line: X
    Product Name: XXXXXXXXXXXXXXXXX
    Sell Price: ZZ9.99     Total Variable Cost: ZZ9.99
                                  Units      Revenue
           Breakeven              Z,ZZ9  ZZZ,ZZ9.99
           Profit: $$$,$$9.99     Z,ZZ9  ZZZ,ZZ9.99
           Price Decline: Z9%     Z,ZZ9  ZZZ,ZZ9.99
                    .
                 .
              .
```

```
                     Nexus Software Inc.
                    Product Cost Analysis
           Summary Report by Product Line as of 99/99/9999


        Product   Breakeven      Profit:         Price
         Line                    $ZZ,ZZ9       Decline: Z9%


          X        $$$$,$$9      $$$$,$$9       $$$$,$$9
          .           .             .              .
          .           .             .              .
          .           .             .              .
        Totals $$,$$$,$$9     $$,$$$,$$9     $$,$$$,$$9
```

Processing Requirements:

1. Read a file of software records.

2. For each record read:

   a. Calculate the total variable costs for each product using the data in each record; include an additional cost of $1.00 for the disk itself. The software preparation costs will be the loading cost per disk multiplied by the number of disks used; don't forget to add the cost of the blank disk(s) by multiplying the cost of a blank disk by the number of disks used.

   b. Create a three-item table containing units and revenues. This table should hold break-even units and revenue calculated as described below:

      (1) Calculate the break-even point and revenue for each product.

      (2) Calculate the required number of units and associated revenue to yield a $50,000 profit for each product.

      (3) Calculate the price decline break-even units and revenue if the selling price is reduced by 25%.

   c. Print a detail line for each record as shown on the report layout. Design your detail line with a table that mimics the information calculated in item b. above.

   d. Increment the appropriate revenue totals in your summary table.

3. After all records have been read, print the summary report and totals on a separate page as shown on the report layout. This will require you to create a table to hold all the product lines and revenue information.

Programming Specifications

Project 12-1

Program Name: Employee Profiles

Narrative: This project continues the employee profile program of Project 11-1 by introducing additional material on table lookups.

Input File: EMPLOYEE-FILE and TITLE-FILE (see processing requirement 3)

Input Record Layout: Use the same record layout as Project 11-1.

Test Data: Use the same test data as Project 11-1.

Report Layout: Expand the report layout of the earlier project to include space for the various table lookups. You may display the information anywhere you deem appropriate.

Processing Requirements: 1. The education table is to be initialized through hard-coding and expanded through a direct lookup according to the following table:

Code	Description	Code	Description
1	Some High School	5	Some Grad School
2	High School Diploma	6	Master's Degree
3	Two Year Degree	7	Ph. D.
4	Four Year Degree	8	Other Graduate Degree

2. The location table is to be initialized through hard-coding and expanded with a sequential search according to the following table:

Code	Description	Code	Description
05	Atlanta	30	Los Angeles
10	Boston	35	Minneapolis
15	Chicago	40	New York
20	Detroit	45	Philadelphia
25	Kansas City		

3. The title table is to be input loaded and expanded with a binary search according to the following table:

Code	Title
15	Accountant
18	Senior Accountant
30	Jr. Programmer
32	Senior Programmer
40	Analyst
45	Senior Analyst
50	Programming Manager

Project 12-2

Program Name: Student Profile Program

Narrative: Develop a program to print a set of student profiles, showing detailed information on each student. Among other functions, the program is to convert an incoming set of codes for each student to an expanded, and more readable, format.

Input File: STUDENT-FILE and COURSE-FILE (see processing requirement 12)

Input Record Layout:

```
01  STUDENT-RECORD-IN.
    05  STU-SOC-SEC-NUMBER                      PIC 9(9).
    05  STU-NAME-AND-INITIALS.
        10  STU-LAST-NAME                       PIC X(18).
        10  STU-INITIALS                        PIC XX.
    05  STU-DATE-OF-BIRTH.
        10  STU-BIRTH-MONTH                     PIC 99.
        10  STU-BIRTH-YEAR                      PIC 9(4).
    05  STU-SEX                                 PIC X.
    05  STU-MAJOR-CODE                          PIC X(3).
    05  STU-SCHOOL-CODE                         PIC 9.
    05  STU-CUMULATIVE-CREDITS                  PIC 999.
    05  STU-CUMULATIVE-POINTS                   PIC 999.
    05  STU-UNION-MEMBER-CODE                   PIC X.
    05  STU-SCHOLARSHIP                         PIC 999.
    05  STU-DATE-OF-ENROLLMENT                  PIC 9(6).
    05  STU-COURSES-THIS-SEMESTER OCCURS 7 TIMES.
        10  STU-COURSE-NUMBER      PIC XXX.
        10  STU-COURSE-CREDITS     PIC 9.
```

Test Data:

```
                1                 2                 3                 4                 5                 6                 7                 8
1234567890123456789012345678901234567890123456789012345678901234567890123456789012345678901234
100000000ALBERT            A 011980MSTA1059118Y0150919981002200330044004501360026011
200000000BROWN             B 021981FSTA1089275N0250919981002200330044004
300000000CHARLES           GG061981MHIS2109286Y100091999501350335043505350653
400000000SMITH             D 071982FXXX2090269N0100919981002200330044194
500000000BAKER             EF101980MGEN3032049Y00009200022233334443
600000000GULFMAN           SF111979FELE4029059N00009199920033333444355536663675270001
700000000BOROW             JS121981MIEN3030090Y0000919982223
800000000MILGROM           MB031982F    5015045Y00009199911313138315031603
900000000MILLER            K 011980MFRL2015054Y0000919991113140315031503
999919999WAYNE             N 041979FHIS2090270Y00009200050135033504350653
```

Report Layout:

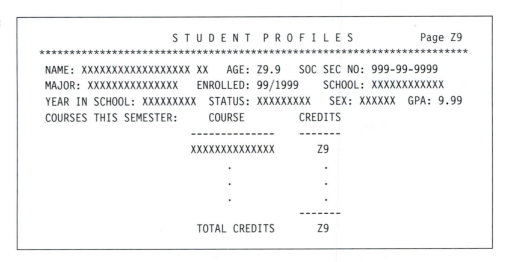

```
                    S T U D E N T   P R O F I L E S           Page Z9
    ***************************************************************************
    NAME: XXXXXXXXXXXXXXXXXX XX    AGE: Z9.9    SOC SEC NO: 999-99-9999
    MAJOR: XXXXXXXXXXXXXXX    ENROLLED: 99/1999    SCHOOL: XXXXXXXXXXXX
    YEAR IN SCHOOL: XXXXXXXXX   STATUS: XXXXXXXXX   SEX: XXXXX   GPA: 9.99
    COURSES THIS SEMESTER:       COURSE          CREDITS
                                -------------    -------
                                XXXXXXXXXXXXXX    Z9
                                      .            .
                                      .            .
                                      .            .
                                                 -------
                                TOTAL CREDITS    Z9
```

Processing Requirements:

1. Process a file of student records, printing a complete student profile for each record.

2. Two students are to appear on each page, with eight blank lines after the last line of the first profile on each page. The page number and literal heading S T U D E N T P R O F I L E S are to appear only before the first profile on each page.

3. The detailed layout for each profile can be seen from the report layout. Additional specifications are given in items 4–11.

4. Student age is to be calculated from date of birth and date of program execution.

5. The social security number requires the insertion of hyphens; accomplish this by defining an output picture containing blanks in appropriate positions and then replace the blanks through the INSPECT verb.

6. The status of the student is either part-time or full-time. Part-time students take fewer than 12 credits per semester.

7. GPA is defined as the cumulative points divided by the cumulative credits and does not include credits taken this semester. Calculate this field to two decimal places.

8. Year in school is a function of cumulative credits and again does not include credits taken this semester. Freshmen have completed fewer than 30; sophomores between 30 and 59, inclusive; juniors between 60 and 89, inclusive; and seniors 90 or more.

9. The incoming STU-SCHOOL-CODE is to be expanded via a direct lookup. Hard-code the following table in your program:

CODE	SCHOOL	CODE	SCHOOL
1	BUSINESS	3	ENGINEERING
2	LIBERAL ARTS	4	EDUCATION

10. The incoming STU-MAJOR-CODE is to be expanded via a sequential search. Hard-code the following major table:

CODE	MAJOR	CODE	MAJOR
STA	STATISTICS	ECO	ECONOMICS
FIN	FINANCE	FRL	FOREIGN LANG
MKT	MARKETING	EEN	ELECTRICAL ENG
MAN	MANAGEMENT	MEN	MECHANICAL ENG
EDP	DATA PROCESSING	CEN	CHEMICAL ENG
PHY	PHYSICS	IEN	INDUSTRIAL ENG
ENG	ENGLISH	ELE	ELEMENTARY EDUC
BIO	BIOLOGY	SEE	SECONDARY EDUC
HIS	HISTORY	SPE	SPECIAL EDUC

11. Expand each value of STU-COURSE-NUMBER to an expanded course name using a binary search. An incoming record contains up to seven courses; blanks (that is, spaces) appear in an incoming record with fewer than seven courses.

12. The table of course codes is to be established by reading values from a separate COURSE-FILE, with the following format: course code in positions 1–3 and course name in positions 4–18. The maximum table length is 100 courses, and the table of course codes appears below:

CODE	COURSE	CODE	COURSE
100	ENGLISH I	503	EUR HISTORY
111	COMPUTER SCI	504	ECONOMICS
140	SPANISH I	505	POL SCIENCE
150	MUSIC	506	CREATIVE WRIT
160	ART APPREC	555	EDUC THEORY
200	BIOLOGY	601	COBOL
222	CHEMISTRY	666	PSYCHOLOGY
300	CALCULUS	675	SPECIAL EDUC
333	ELECT ENG 1	700	THESIS
501	AM HISTORY		

Project 12-3

Program Name: Furniture Shipments

Narrative: Develop a program to print invoices for each furniture record. Display customer information and the individual items ordered, including the item number. When all the records are processed, print a summary report showing totals for each warehouse. Use table lookups for the item numbers and warehouses.

Input File: FURNITURE-FILE and ITEM-FILE (see processing requirement 1a)

Input Record Layout:

```
01  FURNITURE-RECORD.
    05  FURN-INVOICE-NO                 PIC 9(5).
    05  FURN-CUSTOMER-NAME-N-INITIALS   PIC X(18).
    05  FURN-DELIVERY-INFO.
        10  FURN-DELIVERY-WAREHOUSE     PIC X.
        10  FURN-DELIVERY-DATE          PIC 9(8).
    05  FURN-ORDER-INFO.
        10  FURN-DEPOSIT-PERCENT        PIC 9V99.
        10  FURN-NO-ITEMS-ORDERED       PIC 9.
        10  FURN-ITEMS-ORDERED   OCCURS 1 TO 3 TIMES
                DEPENDING ON FURN-NO-ITEMS-ORDERED.
            15  FURN-ITEM-NO            PIC 9(4).
```

Test Data:

```
         1         2         3         4         5         6
1234567890123456789012345678901234567890123456789012345678901234567890
23485ELELSTEIN, M        A0610199900521345 1386
12834ALIAS, Y            B0724199900421787 1798
79845RAHIM, S            A0927199900732300235023 75
59789KELLY, C            B0824199900323609 3650
85778WILSON, D           C0712199901234575459045 98
47597GUDAT, G            A0628199900821345 1397
58684HYMOWITZ, A         C1028199900912350
48577BOOZ, B             C1212199902834599360936 50
46749HENNESSY, L         A0909199900415500
95877MOHD-RAZALLI        B0112199907811345
38476THOMPSON, J         A0923199900911397 1399
48565JACOMINO, R         A0923199901021397 1345
67566DESCHPELLES, M      B0704199900921787 1798
09777SANCHEZ-CARRION,V   C0812199900222350 4599
48576WENNEMAN, M         B0816199900412300
45337AL-DAKHIL, A        A0722199900515500
47567HARDING, J          C0822199900221345 1397
```

Report Layout

```
                    MANSIONS FURNITURE, INC.
                       CUSTOMER INVOICE
            INVOICE #:   XXXX              WAREHOUSE:   X
     CUSTOMER NAME:  XXXXXXXXXXXX, X.   SHIP DATE: MM/DD/YYYY
        ITEM #   ITEM              WEIGHT          COST
        XXXX     XXXXXXXXXX          ZZ9      $$,$$9.99
           .
            .
             .
                                    ------    ----------
        SUBTOTAL                   Z,ZZ9     $$$,$$9.99
        SHIPPING CHARGES                       $$$9.99
        TOTAL                                $$$,$$9.99
        LESS DEPOSIT                         $$$,$$9.99
        BALANCE DUE                          $$$,$$9.99

                    MANSIONS FURNITURE, INC.
                       WAREHOUSE SUMMARY
           WAREHOUSE           WIEGHT               COST
               A                ZZ9          $$,$$9.99
               B                ZZ9          $$,$$9.99
               C                ZZ9          $$,$$9.99
                               ----         ----------
           TOTAL              Z,ZZ9         $$$,$$9.99
```

Processing Requirements:

1. Read a file of furniture shipment records.

2. Fore each record read:

   a. Print headings as shown on the report layout. Use the STRING statement to add a period after the first-name initial in the name.

   b. Process each item ordered by

      (1) Printing a detai line as shown on the report layout.

      (2) Incrementing the weight and cost totals for the customer.

   c. Determine the description, cost, and weight via a binary lookup. Initialize the following table by reading values from a separate ITEM-FILE and input-load it:

Item #	Description	Cost	Weight	Item #	Description	Cost
1345	72" Sofa	$2,300.00	100	2375	Nightstand	$300.00
1386	Love Seat	$1,300.00	80	3609	Desk	$450.00
1397	Chair	$545.00	50	3650	Desk Chair	$395.00
1399	Ottoman	$350.00	40	4575	Dining Table	$3,575.00
1787	Sofa Table	$600.00	50	4590	6 Dining Chairs	$1,278.00
1798	End Table	$545.50	35	4598	Console	$2,225.50
2300	Dresser	$4,300.00	95	4599	Credenza	$1,235.00
2350	Armoire	$5,500.00	100	5500	Pool Table	$2,300.00

d. The warehouse code is to be expanded via a sequential lookup. Hard-code the following table in your program:

Warehouse Code	Description
A	Miami
B	N. Carolina
C	New York

e. When the items for one customer have been processed:
   (1) Calculate the shipping charges as follows: the first 500 pounds are charged at $2.00 per pound; additional pounds over 500 are charged at $1.75 per pound.
   (2) Calculate an intermediate total by adding the shipping charges to the cost totals.
   (3) Calculate the deposit by multiplying the total [calculated in (2) above] by the deposit percent.
   (4) Calculate the balance due by subtracting the deposit from the total.
   (5) Print the balance due as shown in the report layout.
   f. Increment the totals for the appropriate warehouse in the summary table with the above information.

3. After all records have been read, print the summary table showing totals for each warehouse (as shown on the report layout).

Project 12-4

Program Name: Computer Status Report

Narrative: This program takes Project 11-4 and adds table lookups for payment method, status, and component information.

Input File: COMPUTER-FILE and COMPONENT-FILE (see processing requirement 1a)

Input Record Layout:

```
01  COMPUTER-RECORD.
    05  COM-INVOICE-NO              PIC 9(5).
    05  COM-CUSTOMER-NAME           PIC X(18).
    05  COM-PAYMENT-METHOD          PIC XX.
    05  COM-SHIP-INFO.
        10  COM-SHIP-STATUS         PIC X.
        10  COM-SHIP-CHARGE         PIC 99V99.
    05  COM-COMPONENT-INFO.
        10  COM-NO-COMPONENTS       PIC 9.
        10  COM-COMPONENTS   OCCURS 1 TO 4 TIMES
                DEPENDING ON COM-NO-COMPONENTS.
            15  COM-COMPONENT-NO       PIC 9(4).
```

Test Data:

```
          1         2         3         4         5         6
1234567890123456789012345678901234567890123456789012345678901234 5
12834Blanco, Erick       AM14550243306250
79845Casali, Joseph      AM37500233050008120
59789Davis, Kevin        VI16550243305000
85778Demler, Linda       CO380254330055009201 6750
47597Echavarria, FelipeCK26500243308250
58684Flemming, Sharon    MC14500245005500
48577Gonzalez, Maria     VI135003450067509300
56749Katan, Maharan      CK2450013250
95877Parmenter, Donita   CO33500242509001
38476Pinkwasser, Randi   VI38900446606500550 09300
37586Stewart, Roberto    CK25000232507000
```

Report Layout: Use the same report layout as Project 11-4, but expand the status and payment method from the table lookups in both the detail and summary reports. Include the component number in the detail line.

Processing Requirements: 1. Follow the same processing requirements as Project 11-4 with the following changes.

    a. Note that the component description and cost have been replaced in the input record layout by a single component number. Determine the description and cost via a binary lookup for the detail report. Hardcode the following table:

Component	Description	Cost	Component	Description	Cost
3250	Pent II 333MHz	$800.00	6250	1.5 Modem	$99.00
3330	Pent II 400MHz	$1,995.00	6500	56K Modem	$143.00
3400	Pent II 450MHz	$1,589.00	6750	Modem/FAX Card	$80.00
4250	540MB Laptop	$1,899.00	7000	FAX	$1,279.00
4330	Pent III 450MHz	$2,199.00	8120	Supertape	$324.00
4500	Pent III 500MHz	$2,499.00	8250	Tape Stor	$199.00
4660	810MB Laptop	$2,799.00	90001	CD/ROM	$120.00
5000	Laser Printer	$1,399.00	9201	Scanner	$150.00
5500	Ink Jet Printer	$250.00	9300	Video Card	$139.00

    b. The status code (printed in both the detail and summary reports) is to be expanded via a binary lookup. Hard-code the following table in your program:

Status	Description
1	Assembly
2	Packing
3	Testing

c. The payment method code is to be expanded via a sequential lookup. Hard-code the following table in your program:

Payment Code	Method of Payment
AM	American Express
MC	MasterCard
VI	Visa
CO	COD
CK	Check

Project 12-5

Program Name: Credit Report

Narrative: This program takes Project 11-5 and adds table lookups for the interest rate, credit limit, and account type.

Input File: CREDIT-FILE

Input Record Layout: Use the same record layout as Project 11-5.

Test Data: Use the same test data as Project 11-5.

Report Layout: Use the same report layout as Project 11-5, but expand the account type with the appropriate description.

Processing Requirements: 1. Follow the same processing requirement as Project 11-5 with the following changes.

a. Determine the description, credit limit, and interest rate via a sequential lookup. Hard-code the following table:

Type	Description	Credit Limit	Interest Rate
20	Regular	$1,500	18.5%
40	3Pay	$3,500	0%
60	Household	$5,500	17.5%

Project 12-6

Program Name: Software Cost Analysis

Narrative: This program takes Project 11-6 and adds table lookups for product line description.

Input File: SOFTWARE-FILE

Input Record Layout: Use the same record layout as Project 11-6.

Test Data: Use the same test data as Project 11-6.

Report Layout: Use the same report layout as Project 11-6, but expand the product line with the appropriate description.

Processing Requirements: 1. Use the processing requirements from Project 11-6 and add the following:

a. The product line code should be expanded in the summary report using the following code definitions:

Code	Product Line	Code	Product Line
G	Games	D	Drawing/Graphics
B	Business Applications	E	Educational
U	Utility Applications	M	Miscellaneous

b. Today's date is to be printed as shown on the report layout. The current month is to be expanded via a direct lookup. Hard-code the following table in your program:

Month	Expanded Month	Month	Expanded Month
1	January	7	July
2	February	8	August
3	March	9	September
4	April	10	October
5	May	11	November
6	June	12	December

Project 12-7

Program Name: Catalog Orders Program

Narrative: Develop a program to calculate the total orders and the total handling charges for the Regal Catalog Company's monthly orders. The order file has been sorted by date.

Input File: CATALOG-ORDER-FILE and HANDLING-CLASS-FILE (see processing requirement 7)

Input Record Layout:
```
01  CATALOG-ORDER-RECORD.
    05  CAT-ITEM-NO                  PIC 9(4).
    05  CAT-DATE.
        10  CAT-MONTH               PIC 99.
        10  CAT-DAY                 PIC 99.
        10  CAT-YEAR                PIC 9(4).
    05  CAT-QUANTITY                PIC 9(3).
    05  CAT-PRICE                   PIC 9(3)V99.
    05  CAT-HANDLING-CLASS          PIC X.
```

Test Data:

```
                    1         2         3         4         5         6
          1234567890123456789012345678901234567890123456789012345678901234 5
          44140104199901011545A
          17780120199901047995G
          31310129199904004995E
          11830131199901008995D
          47650205199902008925F
          59920214199901007945C
          51860218199901043500F
          34750222199902008995E
          83440228199901005495B
```

Report Layout: Design your own report layout in accordance with the processing specifications.

Processing Requirements:

1. Process a file of catalog orders to determine the monthly total for orders and handling charges.

2. Print the month's orders with five blank lines between each month. Print an appropriate heading at the beginning of each new month.

3. The detailed layout can be determined from the report layout. Additional specifications are given in items 4–7.

4. The incoming CAT-MONTH is to be expanded via a direct lookup. Hard-code the following table in your program:

Month	Expanded Month	Month	Expanded Month
1	January	7	July
2	February	8	August
3	March	9	September
4	April	10	October
5	May	11	November
6	June	12	December

5. The incoming CAT-ITEM-NO is to be expanded via a binary search. Input-load the following item table:

Item No.	Item Description	Item No.	Item Description
1183	Portable Phone	4414	Chess Set
1778	20" Television	4765	Table Lamp
2686	Coffee Maker	5186	35mm Camera
3131	Ceiling Fan	5992	Tennis Racquet
3475	Bedspread	8344	Vase

6. Total price is calculated by multiplying the quantity by the price per item.

7. The incoming CAT-HANDLING-CLASS is to be expanded via a sequential search. The table for handling classes is to be established by reading values from a separate HANDLING-CLASS-FILE, with the following format: handling class code in position 1 and handling charges in positions 2–5. The maximum table length is 26. The table of class codes is shown:

Code	Handling Charges
A	6.25
B	12.00
C	14.25
D	16.50
E	18.50
F	21.25
G	25.50

Project 12-8

Program Name: Check Register

Narrative: The dollar amount of any check is written out in words, in addition to appearing as a number. This project is intended to accomplish that conversion.

Input File: CHECKING-ACCOUNT-FILE

Input Record Layout:
```
01  CHECKING-RECORD.
    05  CHECK-NUMBER          PIC 9(4).
    05  CHECK-AMOUNT          PIC 9(5).
```

Test Data:
```
         1         2         3         4         5         6
1234567890123456789012345678901234567890123456789012345678901234 5
111101234
222245000
333345200
444445986
666645906
777700689
888800089
999900008
100001000
200000100
300023000
```

Report Layout: The resulting report need not be elaborate. All that is required is a single detail line for each input record, containing the dollar amount and associated conversion.

Processing Requirements: 1. Read a file of checking account records.

2. For each record read:

a. Convert the dollar amount to a written amount, with the word "dollars" appended at the end; for example, 234 should be converted to TWO HUNDRED THIRTY-FOUR DOLLARS.

b. Cents are not included; that is, all incoming amounts are integer amounts. The maximum dollar amount to be converted is 99,999.

c. The report is to contain one line for each record, with the amount expressed in both numbers and words.

Programming Specifications

Project 13-1

Program Name: Price Break Report

Narrative: This project builds on Projects 2-1 and 7-2. Write a program to determine whether a customer receives a price break based on quantity ordered, and calculate the unit price and extended price. Create a report that prints each customer's order, as well as the Total Quantity Ordered and Total Sales for the company.

Input File: ORDER-TRANSACTION-FILE

Input Record Layout:

Order Record					
Customer Number		Quantity Ordered	Item Number		Unit Price
1 ... 8	9	10 ... 12	13 ... 17	18	19 (2 decimals) 23

Test Data: Use same test data as in Project 7-2.

Report Layout: Use the same layout designed in Project 7-2.

Processing Requirements: 1. Read a file of order records.

2. For every record read:

a. Determine whether the customer will receive a discount. The discounting of an item is based on specifications presented in Project 2-1; only 5-item series are included in this exercise, but the program should support up to 100-item series. Because of this additional criterion, utilize a two-dimensional table to determine the discount percent based on the item series and quantity ordered.

b. Calculate the unit price by applying the appropriate discount as determined in 2a.

c. Calculate the extended price by multiplying the quantity ordered by the unit price.

d. Accumulate the customer's and the company's order totals.

3. Print the customer number, item number, quantity ordered, unit price (calculated), and extended price for each customer record. Single-space the output.

4. Print the total quantity ordered and the total sales. Double-space the totals.

Project 13-2

Program Name: Movies

Narrative: Develop a program to compute the amount due the hundreds of movie extras who participated in the latest Hollywood extravaganza.

Input File: MOVIE-EXTRA-FILE

Input Record Layout:

POSITIONS	FIELD	PICTURE
1–9	SOC-SEC-NUMBER	9(9)
10–27	NAME	X(18)
28–29	MOVIE-EXPERIENCE	99
30	TYPE-ROLE	X
31–34	HOURS-WORKED	999V9
35–36	EXPANDED-ROLE	XX

Test Data:

```
         1         2         3         4         5         6
123456789012345678901234567890123456789012345678901234567890123456
000000001JONES, J.         00G0800GN
000000002JONES, ROY        02F0450FA
000000003WILLIAMS, JOHN    01E0450EA
000000004FOSTER, RAYMOND   11B0425BN
000000005HIGH, LUCY        08A0450AR
000000006HARDING, HOWARD   04A0450AV
000000007ZHE, KEVIN        05D0450DN
000000008JENNINGS, VIVIAN  D0200DA
000000009ROOSEVELT, TIMOTHY07E0230XX
000000010TRUELOVE, BILL    09G0450EN
```

Report Layout:

```
            HOLLYWOOD EXTRAVAGANZA, INC.                        PAGE Z9

SOC SEC NO   MOVIE EXTRA          EXP  ROLE  HOURLY-RATE  REG-HOURS  EXTRA-HOURS    PAY
999-99-9999  XXXXXXXXXXXXXXXXXX   99    X      $Z9.99       ZZ9.9        Z9       $$,$$9.99
     .            .                .    .         .            .          .           .
     .            .                .    .         .            .          .           .
     .            .                .    .         .            .          .           .
```

Processing Requirements:

1. Process a file of pay records for movie extras, to determine the pay owed to each individual.

2. An hourly pay scale is used, with the individual's hourly rate a function of the type of role and his or her experience in previous movies. The following table contains the pay scale and is to be hard-coded in your program:

Type of Role	Previous experience (number of movies)						
	0	1	2	3	4	5-7	8 and Up
A	20.00	25.00	30.00	32.00	34.00	38.00	40.00
B	14.00	17.00	18.00	19.00	21.00	23.00	24.00
C	7.00	7.00	7.50	8.00	8.50	8.50	9.00
D	4.00	4.00	5.00	5.50	5.50	6.00	6.00
E	3.75	4.50	5.00	5.25	5.25	5.50	5.50
F	3.50	3.50	3.50	3.75	3.75	3.75	4.00

The number of previous movies for an individual must be converted into a number from 1 to 7, so that it can be used as a subscript for access into the table.

3. Incoming pay records are to be checked for valid data; specifically:
   a. Verify that the value in MOVIE-EXPERIENCE is numeric; if not, display an error message and do no further processing for that record.
   b. Verify that the value in TYPE-ROLE is valid (i.e., A, B, C, D, E, or F); if not, display an error message and do no further processing for that record.

4. Each employee is to receive, as a bonus, a number of extra hours (not appearing on the employee's pay record), for which the employee will be paid at his or her regular hourly rate. The number of extra hours is a function of the EXPANDED-ROLE field in the incoming record as shown in the following table:

Expanded Role	Extra Hours	Expanded Role	Extra Hours
AA	01	DN	08
AV	01	DR	09
BA	03	EA	14
BN	05	EN	03
CA	05	ER	03
CN	04	FA	01
DA	08	FN	06

5. The bonus table for extra hours is in ascending sequence by the expanded role field. Use a binary search to determine the number of extra hours an individual will receive; that is, if a match is found, take the hours shown in the table and add it to the hours in the incoming record to determine pay. If no match is found, do not add any extra hours. An individual with no extra hours will be paid just for the number of hours on his or her incoming record.

6. The printed report should print no more than four valid records per page. (The employees with invalid data should be displayed in a separate error report.) Double-space between detail lines.

Project 13-3

Program Name: Two-level Tables

Narrative: This program illustrates two-level tables and PERFORM VARYING in two dimensions. Incoming employee records are checked for one of three locations and one of two performance levels, producing six location-performance combinations. The average salary for each of these six combinations is computed.

Input File: EMPLOYEE-FILE

Input Record Layout:

```
01  EMPLOYEE-RECORD-IN.
    05  EMP-PERSONAL-INFO.
        10  EMP-SOC-SEC-NUM        PIC X(9).
        10  EMP-NAME-AND-INITIALS  PIC X(16).
        10  EMP-DATE-OF-BIRTH.
            15  EMP-BIRTH-MONTH     PIC 9(2).
            15  EMP-BIRTH-YEAR      PIC 9(4).
    05  EMP-COMPANY-INFO.
        10  EMP-DATE-OF-HIRE.
            15  EMP-HIRE-MONTH      PIC 9(2).
            15  EMP-HIRE-YEAR       PIC 9(4).
        10  EMP-LOCATION-CODE      PIC 9(2).
        10  EMP-EDUCATION-CODE     PIC 9.
        10  EMP-TITLE-DATA.
            15  EMP-TITLE-CODE      PIC 9(3).
            15  EMP-TITLE-DATE      PIC 9(6).
        10  EMP-PERFORMANCE        PIC 9.
        10  EMP-SALARY             PIC 9(5).
```

Test Data:

```
         1         2         3         4         5         6
1234567890123456789012345678901234567890123456789012345678901234 5
254679876KERBEL,  NX         071966011997802564061990115500
264480529CLARK,   JS         111967071998303999011991125300
223340090HUMMER,  MR         071959021999806734061990143980
556667856BENWAY,  CX         091966111999605999011991132554
667893343FITZPATRICK, DT     041964062000803878011991221550
433556767NORIEGA, LA         111967041998602453061990218500
455399829VOGEL,   VD         031967062000803233061990124825
688773423BEINHORN, CB        091987081999304455061990129850
100334234GARCIA,  PJ         071966011997602564061990212000
899843328TOWER,   DR         051967071997303999011991119000
776338380MCDONALD, J         071960111997806734061990154380
```

Report Layout:

```
              LOCATION/PERFORMANCE AVERAGE SALARY REPORT


    LOCATION        HIGH PERFORMANCE        LOW PERFORMANCE
    MIAMI               ZZ,ZZ9.99               ZZ,ZZ9.99
    LOS ANGELES         ZZ,ZZ9.99               ZZ,ZZ9.99
    NEW YORK            ZZ,ZZ9.99               ZZ,ZZ9.99
```

Processing Requirements: 1. Read a file of employee records.

2. For each record read, determine if the employee is in Miami (code 30), Los Angeles (code 60), or New York (code 80) and has a performance rating of 1 (high performance) or 2 (low performance). Any employee meeting both requirements—that is, an employee with a valid location and performance rating—is a qualified employee. No further processing is necessary for nonqualified employees.

3. Establish a 3-by-2 table to compute salary statistics for the 6 location-performance combinations. Rows 1, 2, and 3 are for Miami, Los Angeles, and New York. Columns 1 and 2 designate high and low performance, respectively.

4. For each qualified employee:

   a. Determine the appropriate row-column (i.e., location-performance) combination.

   b. Increment the total of all employee salaries for that row-column combination by this employee's salary.

   c. Increment the number of employees in that row-column combination by 1.

5. When all employees have been processed, divide the total salaries for each combination by the number of employees in that combination, producing the average salary for that combination. Produce the required report shown in the report layout, showing the six values of average salary.

Project 13-4

Program Name: Three-level Tables

Narrative: This program extends the previous project to illustrate three-level tables and PERFORM VARYING in three dimensions. Incoming employee records are checked for one of three locations, one of six education codes, and one of two performance levels, producing 36 location-education-performance combinations. The average salary for each of these 36 combinations is computed.

Input File: EMPLOYEE-FILE

Input Record Layout: Same as Project 13-3.

Test Data: Same as Project 13-3.

Report Layout:

```
                    AVERAGE SALARY REPORT FOR LOCATION: MIAMI

        EDUCATION LEVEL    HIGH PERFORMANCE        LOW PERFORMANCE
           GRADE SCHOOL         ZZ,ZZ9.99              ZZ,ZZ9.99
           HIGH SCHOOL          ZZ,ZZ9.99              ZZ,ZZ9.99
           ASSOCIATE            ZZ,ZZ9.99              ZZ,ZZ9.99
           BACHELOR             ZZ,ZZ9.99              ZZ,ZZ9.99
           MASTER               ZZ,ZZ9.99              ZZ,ZZ9.99
           DOCTORATE            ZZ,ZZ9.99              ZZ,ZZ9.99
```

```
┌─────────────────────────────────────────────────────────────┐
│                                                               │
│          AVERAGE SALARY REPORT FOR LOCATION: LOS ANGELES      │
│                                                               │
│       EDUCATION LEVEL     HIGH PERFORMANCE      LOW PERFORMANCE│
│          GRADE SCHOOL         ZZ,ZZ9.99            ZZ,ZZ9.99   │
│          HIGH SCHOOL          ZZ,ZZ9.99            ZZ,ZZ9.99   │
│          ASSOCIATE            ZZ,ZZ9.99            ZZ,ZZ9.99   │
│          BACHELOR             ZZ,ZZ9.99            ZZ,ZZ9.99   │
│          MASTER               ZZ,ZZ9.99            ZZ,ZZ9.99   │
│          DOCTORATE            ZZ,ZZ9.99            ZZ,ZZ9.99   │
│                                                               │
└─────────────────────────────────────────────────────────────┘
```

```
┌─────────────────────────────────────────────────────────────┐
│                                                               │
│          AVERAGE SALARY REPORT FOR LOCATION: NEW YORK         │
│                                                               │
│       EDUCATION LEVEL     HIGH PERFORMANCE      LOW PERFORMANCE│
│          GRADE SCHOOL         ZZ,ZZ9.99            ZZ,ZZ9.99   │
│          HIGH SCHOOL          ZZ,ZZ9.99            ZZ,ZZ9.99   │
│          ASSOCIATE            ZZ,ZZ9.99            ZZ,ZZ9.99   │
│          BACHELOR             ZZ,ZZ9.99            ZZ,ZZ9.99   │
│          MASTER               ZZ,ZZ9.99            ZZ,ZZ9.99   │
│          DOCTORATE            ZZ,ZZ9.99            ZZ,ZZ9.99   │
│                                                               │
└─────────────────────────────────────────────────────────────┘
```

Processing Requirements:

1. Read a file of employee records.

2. For each record read, determine if the employee is in Miami, Los Angeles, or New York; has an education code of 1 through 6 for Grade School, High School, Associate, Bachelor, Master, and Doctorate; and has a performance rating of 1 (high performance) or 2 (low performance). Any employee meeting all three requirements—that is, an employee with a valid location, education, and performance rating—is a qualified employee. No further processing is necessary for nonqualified employees.

3. Establish a 3-by-6-by-2 table to compute salary statistics for the 36 location-education-performance combinations. Each location contains rows 1 through 6 for Grade School, High School, Associate, Bachelor, Master, and Doctorate; and columns 1 and 2 designate high and low performance, respectively.

4. For each qualified employee:

   a. Determine the appropriate row-column (i.e., education-performance) combination for each location.

   b. Increment the total of all employee salaries for that row-column combination for each location by this employee's salary.

   c. Increment the number of employees in that row-column combination for that location by 1.

5. When all employees have been processed, divide the total salaries for each combination by the number of employees in that combination, producing the average salary for that combination. Produce the required report shown in the report layout, showing the 36 values of average salary, printing every location on a separate page.

Project 13-5

Program Name: Payroll Program

Narrative: Develop a program to print complete paycheck (including a check stub) and a payroll journal reflecting all checks printed.

Input File: PAYROLL-FILE

Input Record Layout:

```
01  PAYROLL-RECORD-IN.
    05  PAY-SOC-SEC-NUM        PIC 9(9).
    05  PAY-NAME.
        10  PAY-LAST           PIC X(14).
        10  PAY-FIRST          PIC X(12).
        10  PAY-INITIAL        PIC X.
    05  PAY-INFO.
        10  PAY-HOURLY-RATE    PIC 9(3)V99.
        10  PAY-HOURS-WORKED   PIC 9(3)V99.
        10  PAY-SALARY-TYPE    PIC X.
        10  PAY-DEPENDENTS     PIC 99.
        10  PAY-TAX-STATUS     PIC 9.
        10  PAY-INSURANCE      PIC X.
    05  PAY-YTD-INFO.
        10  PAY-YTD-EARNINGS   PIC 9(6)V99.
        10  PAY-YTD-TAXES      PIC 9(5)V99.
        10  PAY-YTD-FICA       PIC 9(4)V99.
        10  PAY-YTD-INSURANCE  PIC 9(4)V99.
```

Test Data: Use the validated payroll file from Project 8-3.

Report Layout:

```
                          ANDREW INC.                                    PAGE Z9
                 PAYROLL JOURNAL AS OF 99/99/9999
                                                    DEDUCTIONS
                                        GROSS    -----------------------------------
                                        EARNINGS    TAXES     FICA    INSURANCE   NET PAY
 SOC SEC NO    NAME
 999-99-9999  XXXXXXXXXXXXXX, XXXXXXXXXXXX X.  ZZ,ZZ9.99  Z,ZZ9.99  Z,ZZ9.99   Z9.99   ZZ,ZZ9.99
     .                .                          .          .         .          .         .
     .                .                          .          .         .          .         .
     .                .                          .          .         .          .         .
                                              ----------  ---------  --------- -------  ----------
                                              ZZZ,ZZ9.99 ZZ,ZZ9.99 ZZ,ZZ9.99  ZZ9.99  ZZZ,ZZ9.99
```

Processing Requirements:

1. Read a file of payroll records.

2. For each record read calculate:

    a. Gross earnings, which is dependent on salary type (salaried or hourly) and can be calculated in one of two ways:

        (1) Salaried employees are not paid overtime. Gross pay for salaried employees is rate of pay multiplied by the standard 40 hours. If hours exceed 40, place an asterisk (*) next to the hours worked in the detail line of the payroll journal and calculate the gross earnings using 40 hours.

(2) Hourly employees are paid overtime at a rate of time and a half for hours beyond 40 through 48 and double time for hours beyond 48.

b. The yearly taxes, which are dependent on two factors: tax status and yearly salary. This amount is divided by 52 to obtain the weekly tax deduction.

Tax Status Code	Tax Status
1	Head of Household
2	Married Filing Jointly
3	Single
4	Married Filing Separately

(1) The tax status is used to determine the proper tax table. Establish a two-level table with the following information to determine the taxes deducted (you may pick the type of initialization and lookup technique):

Head of Household

Yearly salary over -	but not over	The tax is:		of the amount over -
0	24,850	$0	+ 15%	$0
24,850	64,200	$3,727.50	+ 28%	24,850
64,200	128,810	14,745.50	+ 33%	64,200

Married Filing Jointly

Yearly salary over -	but not over	The tax is:		of the amount over -
0	30,950	$0	+ 15%	$0
30,950	74,800	$4,642.50	+ 28%	30,950
74,800	140,000	16,934.50	+ 33%	74,800

Single

Yearly salary over -	but not over	The tax is:		of the amount over -
0	18,500	$0	+ 15%	$0
18,500	44,900	$2,782.50	+ 28%	18,500
44,900	93,130	10,160.50	+ 33%	44,900

Married Filing Separately

Yearly salary over -	but not over	The tax is:		of the amount over -
0	15,475	$0	+ 15%	$0
15,475	37,425	$2,321.50	+ 28%	15,475
37,425	117,895	8,467.50	+ 33%	37,425

    (2) Yearly salary for both salaried and hourly employees is estimated based on a 40-hour week and a 52-week year.

  c. FICA deduction, which is calculated as 7.51% of gross pay for the first $56,000. After year-to-date earnings reach $56,000, no FICA will be deducted.

  d. Insurance deducted, which is also determined by the type of insurance plan and number of dependents. Determine the insurance deducted via a table lookup in the following two-level table:

Number of Dependents	Health Plan		
	Blue Cross	AvMed	Humana
1	14.00	10.00	10.00
2	15.00	12.00	12.00
3	20.00	15.00	15.00
4	23.00	18.00	18.00
5	25.00	24.00	24.00

Note: Beyond 5 dependents the cost of the plan remains the same. Therefore, an employee with 8 dependents pays the 5-dependent rate. No insurance is deducted for those with a Z (NO-INSURANCE).

  e. Net earnings, which is calculated as gross earnings minus deductions (taxes, FICA [if any], and insurance [if any]).

3. Print a payroll journal detail line as shown in the report layout. Use the STRING statement to print the employee name in the following format:

    lastname, firstname initial

4. Print a heading on top of each new page. Each page is to contain 10 employees. The date of execution should appear on the heading as indicated.

5. When all records have been read, print totals for hours worked, gross pay, all deductions (taxes deducted, FICA deducted, insurance deducted), and net pay.

Project 13-6

Program Name: Extended Student Profile Program

Narrative: This program continues the student profile program of Project 12-2 by adding a summary report. The summary report will utilize a three-dimensional table to accumulate totals for each school, major within school, and year in school within major.

Input File: STUDENT-FILE and COURSE-FILE from Project 12-2

Input Record Layout: Use the same record layout as Project 12-2.

Test Data: Use the same test data as Project 12-2.

Report Layout:

```
                    S T U D E N T   P R O F I L E S         Page Z9
                 Summary Report for School of XXXXXXXXXX as of 99/99/9999
       **************************************************************************
                             Major: XXXXXXXXXXXXXXX
                              Number of       Total      Average
              Year in School   Students      Credits     Credits
                Freshman         ZZ9         ZZ,ZZ9       Z,ZZ9
                Sophomore          .            .            .
                Junior             .            .            .
                Senior             .            .            .
                               ----------   ----------   --------
              Totals             Z,ZZ9       ZZZ,ZZ9     ZZ,ZZ9


       **************************************************************************
                             Major: XXXXXXXXXXXXXXX
                              Number of       Total      Average
              Year in School   Students      Credits     Credits
                   .               .            .            .

              School of XXXXXXXXXX  ZZ,ZZ9    Z,ZZZ,ZZ9   ZZZ,ZZ9
```

Processing Requirements:

1. The following are additional processing requirements to Project 12-2 for the summary report:

   a. Create a 4 x 18 x 4 (3-dimensional) table to accumulate number of students and total credits for the appropriate school-major-year (in school) combination.

   b. When all records have been processed, print the summary as shown in the report layout. Each school should begin on a new page.

Programming Specifications

Project 14-1

Program Name: Price Break Report

Narrative: This project builds on Project 13-1. Write a program to determine whether a customer receives a price break based on quantity ordered and calculate the unit price and extended price. Create a report that prints each customer's order, as well as the total ordered for each customer and a grand total for the company.

Input File: ORDER-TRANSACTION-FILE

Input Record Layout:

Customer Order Record						
Customer Number		Quantity Ordered	Item Number		Unit Price	Salesrep Number
1 ... 8	9	10 ... 12	13 ... 17	18	19 (2 decimals) 23	24 ... 27

Test Data:

```
             1         2         3         4         5         6
   123456789012345678901234567890123456789012345678901234567890123456789012345
   1000000100051111191105 34A100
   2000000201002122280205 6B200
   3000000301253233373004 5A100
   4000000405004344463402 1B202
   5000000509005455555657 8C300
   1000000100151345691353 4A101
   2000000200102123480105 6B202
   3000000301003432173304 5C300
   4000000404004432463702 1A100
   5000000507004245655657 8B202
   1000000100604111191553 4A100
   2000000200255662280405 6B200
   3000000303153113373304 5C300
   4000000404002421463202 1B200
   5000000507801645555157 8B200
```

Report Layout: Modify the report designed in Project 7-2, adding salesrep number and region area name.

Processing Requirements: 1. Sort the incoming order file by customer number and within customer number by salesrep number.

2. Read the sorted file of order records.

3. For every record read:
   a. Determine whether the customer will receive a discount. The discounting is determined based on the specifications of Project 13-1.
   b. Calculate the unit price by applying the appropriate discount as determined in 3a.
   c. Calculate the extended price by multiplying the quantity ordered by the unit price.
   d. Determine the region a salesrep is assigned to based on the first byte of the salesrep number and utilizing the following table.

Region Code	Region Area Name
A	Arlington
B	Bridgeport
C	Coppell
D	Dallas
E	Euless

4. Print the customer number, item number, quantity ordered, unit price (calculated), and extended price for each customer record. Single-space the output.

5. Print the total quantity ordered and the total sales. Double-space the totals.

Project 14-2

Program Name: Order Transaction File Validation

Narrative: This project builds on Project 8-1, utilizing more advanced programming techniques such as table handling, redefines, internal sort, and control break logic. Write a data validation program that will validate an order transaction file.

Input File: ORDER-TRANSACTION-FILE, same as Project 8-1.

Test Data: Same as Project 8-1.

Report Layout: Same as Project 8-1.

Processing Requirements:
1. Read a file of order transaction records.

2. Sort the order transaction records so that all records for one order can be processed together and so that the record types 1, 2, and 3 are in the appropriate order.

3. The current run date is typically accepted from a file, but for this lab set up a literal in working storage with the run date as November 2, 1999.

4. Validate each input record field for all of the following:

   All validations from Project 8-1.

   Change the Quantity Code conversion to Quantity Amount logic in Project 8-1 to utilize a hard coded table containing the Quantity Code and the appropriate Quantity Amount.

5. Any record that fails any validity test is to be written to an error file, and an appropriate error message should appear on the error report. It is possible that a record may contain more than one error, and all errors are to be flagged.

6. Valid records are to be written to a valid transaction file. The valid transaction file should be the same format as the input Order Transaction file, with the exception that the quantity code on the Type 3 record should be converted to the quantity amount, causing the unit price to be moved to the right two bytes.

Project 14-3

Program Name: Sorted Car Sales Program

Narrative: Develop a program to process a sales file in order to determine the amount earned by each salesperson.

Input File: SALES-FILE

Input Record Layout:
```
01  SALES-RECORD-IN.
    05  SA-DEALER            PIC X(8).
    05  SA-BRANCH            PIC 9(3).
    05  SA-SALESPERSON       PIC X(10).
    05  SA-SALES-INFO.
        05  SA-CUSTOMER      PIC X(10).
        05  SA-SALE-PRICE    PIC 9(6).
        05  SA-COMMISSION-RATE PIC 9V99.
    05  SA-CAR-INFO.
        10  SA-CAR-MAKE      PIC X(8).
        10  SA-CAR-MODEL     PIC X(8).
```

```
        10  SA-CAR-YEAR          PIC 9(4).
```

Test Data:

```
    1         2         3         4         5         6
12345678901234567890123456789012345678901234567890123456789012345
BROWARD 010GEHLE     MORENO   016125005TOYOTA  SUPRA    1991
DADE    110DAVERSA   RENESCA  008950002HYNDAI  ELANTRA  1999
BROWARD 020ROWE      VIERA    014300002STERLING825SL    1987
DADE    100RICO      GORMAN   048500004LEXUS   450 LS   1997
BROWARD 010SHIM      PORTO    025575004M BENZ  300E     1996
DADE    110FRENCH    DEGGS    017025004NISSAN  MAXIMA   1996
MONROE  210BOYER     PIRES    014125004MAZDA   929      1994
DADE    100RICO      CHUA     024700004TOYOTA  CAMRY    1998
BROWARD 020ROWE      PINEDA   009200003AUDI    5000     1996
DADE    110DAVERSA   MCDONALD 048900005INFINITIQ45      1999
BROWARD 010GEHLE     LARSH    009475003PUEGOT  405GLS   1993
DADE    110FRENCH    SPEARS   014975001NISSAN  ALTIMA   1998
BROWARD 020ROWE      TOCKMAN  027150006BMW     635 CSI  1986
MONROE  210BOYER     AUGUSMA  079799002M BENZ  560 SL   1998
BROWARD 010GEHLE     HOLME    901370002HONDA   PRELUDE  1992
MONROE  210BOYER     LOUIS    012175004MAZDA   MILLENIA1995
BROWARD 010SHIM      REINMAN  024725002SAAB    900 CSE  1998
DADE    100RICO      DILEGO   012800004MAZDA   MIATA    1994
MONROE  210VASQUEZ   HAFEZ    032875003JAGUAR  XJJ6     1995
DADE    110FRENCH    GRAHE    014750003BMW     325 ES   1986
MONROE  210VASQUEZ   HWANG    023000004LEGEND  COUPE LS1990
```

Report Layout:

```
                    VERY VERY NICE CARS INC.                    PAGE Z9

                CAR INFORMATION                   COMMISSION    NET TO
 DEALER   SALESPERSON  YEAR   MAKE    MODEL  CUSTOMER    PRICE      PAID      DEALER

XXXXXXXX XXXXXXXXXX   9999 XXXXXXXX XXXXXXXX XXXXXXXXXX ZZZ,ZZ9  ZZ,ZZ9.99  ZZZ,ZZ9.99
   .        .          .       .       .        .         .         .          .
   .        .          .       .       .        .         .         .          .
   .        .          .       .       .        .         .         .          .
                                                       ----------  -----------  -------------
 VERY VERY NICE CARS TOTALS                            $Z,ZZZ,ZZ9  $ZZZ,ZZ9.99  $Z,ZZZ,ZZ9.99
```

Processing Requirements:

1. Sort the incoming sales file by dealer, within dealer by salesperson, and within year by car make.

2. Read the file of sorted sales records, and for each record read:

   a. Calculate the commission paid to the salesperson by multiplying the sale amount by the commission rate.

   b. Calculate the net to the dealer by subtracting the commission from the sale amount.

   c. Print a detail line for each sale.

   d. Increment the totals as shown on the report layout.

3. After all records have been read, print Very Very Nice Cars totals. Skip three lines prior to printing the company total.

Project 14-4

Program Name: Sorted Bonus Program

Narrative: Write a program to process a bonus file to determine which employees are eligible for a bonus and the bonus amount.

Input File: BONUS-FILE

Input Record Layout:

```
01  BONUS-RECORD-IN.
    05  BO-MANU-PLANT    PIC XX.
    05  BO-DEPARTMENT    PIC X(8).
    05  BO-EMPLOYEE      PIC X(15).
    05  BO-MANAGER       PIC X(10).
    05  BO-SALARY        PIC 99999.
    05  BO-PERCENTAGE    PIC 9V99.
    05  BO-ELIGIBILTY    PIC X.
```

Test Data:

```
         1         2         3         4         5         6
1234567890123456789012345678901234567890123456789012345678901234 5
TNInteriorKnowles, CD    GARCIA    30100008Y
KYFenders Price, MD      VILLAR    24000000N
OHTrim    Inniss, ML     SPENCER   32000012Y
KYFenders Kanning, DS    VILLAR    28000008Y
OHPaint   Prates, LS     ALVORD    29000015Y
KYInteriorSangastiano, LAFEIN      32000011Y
TNTrim    Gibbs, GJ      JONES     26000006Y
KYFenders Barnabas, SJ   GRAUER    30000010Y
TNInteriorDavis, JL      GARCIA    31000007Y
OHPaint   Montes, J      ALVORD    27000012Y
KYFenders Lamania, NC    GRAUER    32000005Y
TNTrim    Romero, CM     WILLIAMS  32000018Y
OHPaint   Simonton, DM   ALVORD    25000000N
TNTrim    Wilson, RJ     JONES     24000000N
OHPaint   Keiler, M      SMITH     28000006Y
TNInteriorTwinn, SA      JAMES     22000004Y
OHPaint   Chua, CE       SMITH     31000007Y
KYInteriorAl-Askar, EK   BARBER    30100009Y
OHTrim    Cardone, J     FRANK     32000008Y
KYInteriorWinter, EK     FEIN      22000000N
TNTrim    Hess, AM       WILLIAMS  36000014Y
OHTrim    Boberg, DM     FRANK     36000012Y
KYInteriorBehrend, TR    BARBER    31000005Y
OHTrim    Smith, GM      FRANK     26000000N
KYFenders Giberson, CJ   GRAUER    34000015Y
TNTrim    Clasen, CC     JONES     32000010Y
OHTrim    Al-Khuwiter, A SPENCER   24000011Y
TNInteriorAlberni, WJ    JAMES     32000010Y
KYInteriorChilders, RL   BARBER    35000012Y
TNInteriorWarren, AE     JAMES     35000011Y
```

Report Layout:

```
                    FASSSTCARS MANUFACTURERS                    PAGE Z9

      PLANT  DEPT     MANAGER      SOC SEC NO   SALARY  BONUS    TOTAL
       XX   XXXXXXXX  XXXXXXXXXX  999-99-9999   ZZ,ZZ9  Z,ZZ9   ZZZ,ZZ9
        .      .          .            .           .      .        .

        .      .          .            .           .      .        .

        .      .          .            .           .      .        .
                                                ---------  -------  ---------
      FASSSTCARS TOTALS                         Z,ZZZ,ZZ9  ZZ,ZZ9  Z,ZZZ,ZZ9
```

Processing Requirements:

1. Sort the incoming bonus file by plant, within plant by department, and within department by manager. Sort only the employees that are eligible for a bonus, that is, those that contain a "Y" in the eligibility field.

2. Read the file of sorted bonus records, and for each record read:
   a. Calculate the bonus amount by multiplying the salary by the bonus percentage.
   b. Calculate the total compensation by adding the salary and the bonus.
   c. Print a detail line as shown on the report layout.
   d. Increment the appropriate totals as shown on the report layout.

3. After all records have been read, print totals for Fassstcars.

Project 14-5

Program Name: Sorted Store Sales Commissions Program

Narrative: Develop a program to process sales records for the Needless Markup company. The report is to show sales, commissions paid, and net sales for each transaction.

Input File: SALES-FILE

Input Record Layout:

```
01 SALES-RECORD.
    05  SAL-PERSON-NAME          PIC X(10).
    05  SAL-DATE.
        10  SAL-MONTH            PIC 9(2).
        10  SAL-DAY              PIC 9(2).
        10  SAL-YEAR             PIC 9(2).
    05  SAL-AMOUNT               PIC 9(5)V99.
    05  SAL-COMMISSION-RATE      PIC V99.
    05  SAL-STORE-NUMBER         PIC 9(2).
    05  SAL-DEPARTMENT-NAME      PIC X(12).
```

Test Data:

```
          1         2         3         4         5         6
 1234567890123456789012345678901234567890123456789012345678901 2345
ADAMS      042220000214000 0603DESIGNER
HILL       043120000009800 0501SPORTSWEAR
SMITH      042820000008000 0502LINGERIE
HARRISON   042320000002600 0504SPORTSWEAR
HILL       040920000036900 0401SHOES & BAGS
HARRISON   041820000012550 0504SPORTSWEAR
HILL       041520000026300 0401SHOES & BAGS
CLARK      042420000000455 0504LINGERIE
TURNER     041820000007500 0302ACCESSORIES
JONES      042520000025600 0501SPORTSWEAR
ADAMS      041620000839600 0603DESIGNER
CLARK      041520000047800 0504SPORTSWEAR
SMITH      042520000015500 0502LINGERIE
JONES      043020000015799 0501SPORTSWEAR
JONES      043020000023099 0401SHOES & BAGS
ADAMS      040820000031500 0503SPORTSWEAR
LUDLUM     042620000612099 0603DESIGNER
ADAMS      040520000083600 0503SPORTSWEAR
SMITH      041220000004525 0302ACCESSORIES
VANBERGER  042920000005500 0502LINGERIE
CLARK      040920000023799 0504SPORTSWEAR
HARRISON   042920000022500 0504LINGERIE
HARRISON   043020000249825 0604DESIGNER
```

Report Layout:

```
                NEEDLESS MARKUP        99/99/9999                    PAGE Z9


    STORE        DEPARTMENT    SALESPERSON    DATE       SALES   COMMISSION  NET SALES
XXXXXXXXXXX  XXXXXXXXXXX   XXXXXXXXXX   99/99/9999  ZZ,ZZ9.99   Z,ZZ9.99  ZZ,ZZ9.99
    .            .             .           .            .          .          .
    .            .             .           .            .          .          .
    .            .             .           .            .          .          .
                                                     ----------  --------- ----------
NEEDLESS MARKUP TOTALS                                ZZZ,ZZ9.99 ZZ,ZZ9.99 ZZZ,ZZ9.99
```

Processing Requirements:

1. Sort the incoming sales file by store, within store by department, and within department by salesperson.

2. Read the file of sorted sales records, and for each record read:

   a. Calculate the commission by multiplying the sales amount by the commission rate.

   b. Calculate the net sales by subtracting the commission from the sale amount.

   c. Expand the store code via a direct lookup:

LOCATION CODE	LOCATION NAME
1	Bal Harbor
2	Dadeland
3	The Galleria
4	Worth Avenue

d. Print a detail line for each record.

e. Increment the totals for sale amount, commission paid, and net sales.

3. Print the totals at the end of the report.

Project 14-6

Program Name: Sorted Zoo Program

Narrative: Write a program to process a zoo's inventory file.

Input File: ZOO-FILE

Input Record Layout:

```
01  ZOO-RECORD.
    05  ZOO-SPECIES            PIC X(8).
    05  ZOO-TYPE               PIC X(11).
    05  ZOO-GROUP              PIC X(7).
    05  ZOO-SEX                PIC X.
    05  ZOO-QUANTITY           PIC 99.
    05  ZOO-SPECIES-VALUE      PIC 9(6)V99.
    05  ZOO-ACQUISITION-LEVEL  PIC 99.
```

Test Data:

```
         1         2         3         4         5         6
1234567890123456789012345678901234567890123456789012345678901234 5
Whale    Humpback   Mammal F010012509001
Tiger    White      Mammal F050166008508
Parrot   Macaw      Bird   M050006600005
Tiger    White      Mammal M070156008505
Parrot   Macaw      Bird   F120007509915
Bear     Black Bear Mammal M000102330502
Ray      Manta      Fish   F040004004002
Whale    Killer     Mammal F020045005002
Ray      Manta      Fish   M020004500504
Whale    Killer     Mammal M010042005001
Shark    Great WhiteFish   F010120120004
Tiger    Bengal     Mammal M020040209002
Shark    Mako       Fish   F020008990002
Whale    Humpback   Mammal M000017509001
Bear     Grizzly    Mammal F030090000002
Shark    Mako       Fish   M060009500508
Bear     Black Bear Mammal F030102330503
Parrot   Cockatoo   Bird   F450003050430
Bear     Grizzly    Mammal M040091010003
Shark    Great WhiteFish   M040113000004
Tiger    Bengal     Mammal F100020508008
```

Report Layout:

```
            Wild Kingdom Zoo Inventory Report   99/99/9999        Page Z9
                                                                  No. to
    Group   Species     Type    Sex   Value  Quantity    Total    Acquire
    XXXXXXX XXXXXXXX XXXXXXXXXXX  X   ZZZ,ZZ9.99   Z9   ZZZ,ZZ9.99    Z9
      .        .          .       .      .          .        .        .
      .        .          .       .      .          .        .        .
      .        .          .       .      .          .        .        .
                                                  ----  ------------  ----
    Total for Wild Kingdom                        ZZ9  Z,ZZZ,ZZ9.99   ZZ9
```

Processing Requirements:

1. Sort the incoming animal file by group, within group by species, and within species by type.

2. Read the file of sorted animal records, and for each record read:
   a. Calculate the value of each animal (quantity times value).
   b. Determine whether acquisition of addition animals is justified; the zoo should acquire more animals if the acquisition level is below the quantity level.
   c. Print animal information in that record and calculated values on a detail line.
   d. Accumulate the animal quantity totals, total values, and acquisition totals.

3. After all records have been read, print totals for Wild Kingdom.

Project 14-7

Program Name: Sorted PC Software Program

Narrative: Write a program to process a PC software file to determine totals for PC software totals.

Input File: PC-SOFTWARE-FILE

Input Record Layout:
```
01  PC-SOFTWARE-RECORD-IN.
    05  PC-ORDER-INFO.
        10  PC-ORDER-NO            PIC 9(5).
        10  PC-ORDER-TYPE          PIC X.
        10  PC-CUSTOMER-NAME       PIC X(16).
    05  PC-PURCHASE-INFO.
        10  PC-QUANTITY            PIC 999.
        10  PC-PRICE               PIC 9(3)V99.
        10  PC-DATE                PIC 9(8).
    05  PC-PROGRAM-INFO.
        10  PC-PROGRAM-ID.
            15  PC-PROGRAM-NO       PIC 9(4).
            15  PC-PLATFORM-CODE    PIC X.
        10  PC-PROGRAM-NAME        PIC X(16).
        10  PC-VENDOR              PIC X(16).
```

Test Data:

```
         1         2         3         4         5         6         7
1234567890123456789012345678901234567890123456789012345678901234567890123
02634PZeuqzav-Ralliv  01502899020320005514WEntertainmnt PacMicrosoft
79456PRacal Datacomm  00333495020120005653D1-2-3 5.0       Lotus
74523PAmerican Express00801900122219993338WMoney 99        Microsoft
13473PRacal Datacomm  03508495092519993146DNorton Anti-ViruSymantec
34342RNeiman Marcus    02532895092519998000WIllustrator 8   Adobe
63452PAmerican Express01009900011620003424W1-2-3 Upgrade    Lotus
53623PRacal Datacomm  03524900013020005799WApproach 97      Lotus
43646PNeiman Marcus    01832500010320009695DBorland C++ 4.0 Borland Int'l
43623PRacal Datacomm  03009900022220003424W1-2-3 Upgrade    Lotus
27345RNeiman Marcus    00313900101519996223WFont Control     Adobe
58424RAmerican Express00533495011620005653D1-2-3 5.0        Lotus
64564PNeiman Marcus    01549895092519991332WPageMaker 6.5    Adobe
47635PZeuqzav-Ralliv  01503895020320002858DFlight SimulatorMicrosoft
46353PRacal Datacomm  07509999122119992359WNorton UtilitiesSymantec
63454PZeuqzav-Ralliv  01529900020320002856WExcel 97        Microsoft
84563PRacal Datacomm  08509999122119993784WNorton 2000     Symantec
45364PZeuqzav-Reilly  01529900020320007387WPowerPoint 97   Microsoft
44535PRacal Datacomm  05534895122319993523WFreelance       Lotus
34593PZeuqzav-Ralliv  01529900020320006195WWord 98         Microsoft
74387PNeiman Marcus    01831850100719996242DMidas           Borland Int'l
24256PRacal Datacomm  00539900020120005417D1-2-3 4.0 Plus  Lotus
75357RNeiman Marcus    01552995112519991514DJBuilder 4000   Borland Int'l
24246RAmerican Express01039900012020005417D1-2-3 4.0 Plus  Lotus
34534RRacal Datacomm  02033500101419992755W1-2-3           Lotus
23333PAmerican Express05033500011620002755W1-2-3           Lotus
32453PRacal Datacomm  02508900021520007010WWindows 98      Microsoft
74387PNeiman Marcus    00519900121719997540WAcrobat 4       Adobe
85634RAmerican Express01534895022620003523WFreelance       Lotus
43244PAmerican Express020129000112019992735WWorks 4.5       Microsoft
49785PZeuqzav-Ralliv  05502300011320001162DMickey&Friends  Walt Disney Comp
43352PRacal Datacomm  02544595111419997388WProject 98      Microsoft
47633PZeuqzav-Rallliv 01502900011320002629DMickey's 123's  Walt Disney Comp
56352PNeiman Marcus    02508900101619991624WVisual Basic 6.0Microsoft
46523PZeuqzav-Ralliv  01503200020320008731WAtlas Map       3rd Planet
43274PRacal Datacomm  09047900121419996188DOffice 97       Microsoft
26342PZeuqzav-Ralliv  01502900011320002624DMickey's ABC's  Walt Disney Comp
26437PNeiman Marcus    09505900122619991620DOffice 2000     Microsoft
37466PAmerican Express02505900101619991620DOffice 2000     Microsoft
47324RNeiman Marcus    04509500111419992904DWorks 4.5       Microsoft
26437PRacal Datacomm  04505900101619991620DOffice 2000     Microsoft
24364PZeuqzav-Ralliv  01510900020320008101WLand Form C3    Rapid Imaging
63454PNeiman Marcus    03529900021720002856WExcel 97        Microsoft
94534PZeuqzav-Ralliv  01503400020320006649WStar Trek:ScreenBerkeley Systems
48536PNeiman Marcus    05529900021700007387WPower Point 97  Microsoft
73623PRacal Datacomm  01026900122219993804DWordPerfect 7.0 WordPerfect Corp
```

Report Layout:

```
                        Software R Us, Inc. 99/99/9999                    PAGE Z9

    Customer          Vendor              Platform   Program            Quantity   Price    Total
    XXXXXXXXXXXXXX    XXXXXXXXXXXXXXX     XXXXXXX    XXXXXXXXXXXXXXX       ZZ9      ZZ9.99   ZZ9.99
         .                 .                 .            .                .         .        .
         .                 .                 .            .                .         .        .
         .                 .                 .            .                .         .        .
                                                                        -------            --------
    Total for Software R Us                                              Z,ZZ9             Z,ZZ9.99
```

Processing Requirements:

1. Sort the incoming PC software file by customer, within customer by vendor, and within vendor by platform.

2. Read the file of sorted PC software records, and for each record read:

   a. Calculate the total for each program by multiplying the quantity by the price.

   b. Determine whether the order is either a purchase (P) or a return (R) by examining the order type field. If the order is a return, then the quantity and total calculated should be negated. Make sure your report will show this (use CR, DB, +, or – editing symbols).

   c. Print information in that record and total on a detail line. Expand the platform code as follows: "D" for "DOS", and "W" for "Windows". Print the platform name only for the first detail line.

   d. Accumulate totals for quantity and total.

3. After all the records have been read, print company totals for Software R Us.

Project 14-8

Program Name: Video Program

Narrative: Write a program to process a video file to determine totals for video rental and sales revenue.

Input File: VIDEO-FILE

Input Record Layout:

```
01  VIDEO-RECORD-IN.
    05  VID-TITLE-INFO.
        10  VID-TITLE          PIC X(19).
        10  VID-CATEGORY       PIC X(11).
        10  VID-RATING         PIC X(5).
    05  VID-RENTAL-INFO.
        10  VID-RENTAL-FEE     PIC 99V99.
        10  VID-RENTED         PIC 9(3).
    05  VID-SELL-INFO.
        10  VID-SELL-PRICE     PIC 9(3)V99.
        10  VID-SOLD           PIC 9(3).
        10  VID-RETURNED       PIC 9(3).
    05  VID-STORE              PIC X(10).
```

Test Data:

```
          1         2         3         4         5         6
1234567890123456789012345678901234567890123456789012345678901234 5
Rocky Horror          Drama       PG-13020040005995101050Coco Grove
Dirty Harry           Action      R    017501002000025002Miami
Basic Instinct        New ReleaseR    030020003995099002Hialeah
My Girl               Drama       PG   020007002000060005Miami Bch
Cutting Edge          Drama       PG-13025010002000035008Coco Grove
Lethal Weapon III     Action      R    030015002995103000Miami
Candy Man             New ReleaseR    030020005995105040Hialeah
Cape Fear             Drama       R    020008001995020002Miami Bch
Nighmare on Elm St    Horror      R    025006001995006006Ft. Laud
ET                    Childrens   G    015006001995045012Hialeah
Caddy Shack           Comedy      PG   010004501095023005Miami
Caddy Shack           Comedy      PG   010004501095023005Coco Grove
Final Analysis        Suspense    R    030012002995076003Miami Bch
Dr. Giggles           New ReleaseR    030030007795092030Hialeah
Star Wars II          Action      G    017505001995050020Miami
Wayne's World         Comedy      PG   030005001595045055Miami
Care Bears            Childrens   G    010007500995035003Hialeah
Halloween             Horror      PG-13025004001995090095Ft. Laud
Dances with Wolves    Drama       R    030010004995010000Coco Grove
The Blues Brothers    Comedy      PG   020001001095015005Coco Grove
One Flew Over...      Drama       R    017502501095009000Coco Grove
The Birds             Horror      PG-13015001001495010000Ft. Laud
The Fly               Suspense    R    020007502995065005Miami Bch
Pinnochio             Childrens   G    010003501495080003Hialeah
The Little Mermaid    Childrens   G    025020001995098003Hialeah
To Kill a Mocking..   Drama       PG   010001000995002001Miami Bch
Sneakers              New ReleaseR    030040007500125000Hialeah
The Shining           Suspense    R    015001501500010004Ft. Laud
T2 - Judgement Day    New ReleaseR    030035003995135001Hialeah
Hell Raiser II        Horror      R    015007701095075080Ft. Laud
Wayne's World         Comedy      PG   030005001595045055Coco Grove
Star Wars             Action      G    017505001495030010Miami
Beauty & the Beast    Childrens   G    030020001995200000Hialeah
```

Report Layout:

```
        BlokBuzter Monthly Video Rentals & Sales 99/99/9999                    PAGE Z9

                                    Rental Information          Sell Information
                                 ------------------------------  ------------------------------
Category     Rating  Movie Title      Fee  # Rented    Revenue   Price     Net     Revenue
XXXXXXXXXX   XXXXX   XXXXXXXXXXXXXXXXXXXX  Z9.99   ZZ9    ZZ9.99   ZZ9.99   ZZ9    ZZ9.99
    .          .          .           .      .         .          .       .         .
    .          .          .           .      .         .          .       .         .
    .          .          .           .      .         .          .       .         .
                                            -------  -----------  -------  -----------
Total for BlokBuzter                         Z,ZZ9   Z,ZZ9.99     Z,ZZ9    Z,ZZ9.99
```

Processing Requirements:

1. Sort the incoming video file by store, within each store by rating, and within each rating by movie title.

2. Read the file of sorted video records, and for each record read:

   a. Calculate the rental revenue by multiplying the rental fee by the number of times rented.

b. Calculate the net sales by subtracting the videos returned from the videos sold. Returns are accepted from other stores so your net could be negative! Make sure your report will show this (use CR, DB, +, or – editing symbols).

c. Calculate the sales revenue for each movie by multiplying the selling price by the net sales.

d. Print a detail line.

e. Accumulate totals as indicated on the report layout.

3. After all the records have been read, print totals for BlokBuzter.

Programming Specifications

Project 15-1

Program Name: Price Break Report (Continuation of Project 14-1)

Narrative: Write a control break program to determine whether a customer receives a price break based on quantity ordered, and calculate the unit price and extended price. Create a report which prints each customer's order as well as the total ordered for each customer and a grand total for the company.

Input File: Order Transaction File

Input Record Layout:

Order Record						
Customer Number		Quantity Ordered	Item Number		Unit Price	Salesrep Number
1 ... 8	9	10 ... 12	13 ... 17	18	19 (2 decimals) 23	24 ... 27

Test Data: Use the same test data as Project 14-1.

Report Layout: You may continue to use the report layout you designed in Project 7-2, or utilize the following specifications.

Two-Level Report Layout:

```
                              AUSTIN RETAIL COMPANY

         SALESREP:            XXXX     REGION AREA: XXXXXXXXXXXXXX
         CUSTOMER NUMBER:     XXXXXXXX
         ITEM                 QUANTITY      UNIT           EXTENDED
         NUMBER               ORDERED       PRICE          PRICE
         XXXXX                ZZ9           $$$$.99        $$,$$$,$$$.99
         XXXXX                ZZ9           $$$$.99        $$,$$$,$$$.99
         CUSTOMER TOTAL SALES:          $$,$$$,$$$,$$$.99
```

```
CUSTOMER NUMBER:            XXXXXXXX
ITEM              QUANTITY       UNIT          EXTENDED
NUMBER            ORDERED        PRICE         PRICE
XXXXX             ZZ9            $$$$.99       $$,$$$,$$$.99
XXXXX             ZZ9            $$$$.99       $$,$$$,$$$.99

CUSTOMER TOTAL SALES:       $$,$$$,$$$,$$$.99
SALESREP TOTAL SALES:       $$,$$$,$$$,$$$.99
SALESREP:          XXXX    REGION AREA: XXXXXXXXXXXXXX
CUSTOMER NUMBER:   XXXXXXXX
ITEM              QUANTITY       UNIT          EXTENDED
NUMBER            ORDERED        PRICE         PRICE
XXXXX             ZZ9            $$$$.99       $$,$$$,$$$.99
XXXXX             ZZ9            $$$$.99       $$,$$$,$$$.99
CUSTOMER TOTAL SALES:       $$,$$$,$$$,$$$.99
CUSTOMER NUMBER:            XXXXXXXX
ITEM              QUANTITY       UNIT          EXTENDED
NUMBER            ORDERED        PRICE         PRICE
XXXXX             ZZ9            $$$$.99       $$,$$$,$$$.99
XXXXX             ZZ9            $$$$.99       $$,$$$,$$$.99
CUSTOMER TOTAL SALES:       $$,$$$,$$$,$$$.99
SALESREP TOTAL SALES:       $$,$$$,$$$,$$$.99
TOTAL SALES FOR COMPANY:    $$,$$$,$$$,$$$.99
```

Three-level Report Layout:

```
                   AUSTIN RETAIL COMPANY
REGION AREA:       XXXXXXXXXXXXXX
SALESREP:          XXXX
CUSTOMER NUMBER:   XXXXXXXX
ITEM              QUANTITY       UNIT          EXTENDED
NUMBER            ORDERED        PRICE         PRICE
XXXXX             ZZ9            $$$$.99       $$,$$$,$$$.99
XXXXX             ZZ9            $$$$.99       $$,$$$,$$$.99
CUSTOMER TOTAL SALES:       $$,$$$,$$$,$$$.99
CUSTOMER NUMBER:            XXXXXXXX
ITEM              QUANTITY       UNIT          EXTENDED
NUMBER            ORDERED        PRICE         PRICE
XXXXX             ZZ9            $$$$.99       $$,$$$,$$$.99
XXXXX             ZZ9            $$$$.99       $$,$$$,$$$.99
CUSTOMER TOTAL SALES:       $$,$$$,$$$,$$$.99
SALESREP TOTAL SALES:       $$,$$$,$$$,$$$.99
REGION TOTAL SALES:         $$,$$$,$$$,$$$.99
TOTAL NUMBER OF SALESREP IN REGION:  ZZZ9
REGION AREA:                XXXXXXXXXXXXXX
SALESREP:                   XXXX
CUSTOMER NUMBER:            XXXXXXXX
ITEM              QUANTITY       UNIT          EXTENDED
NUMBER            ORDERED        PRICE         PRICE
XXXXX             ZZ9            $$$$.99       $$,$$$,$$$.99
XXXXX             ZZ9            $$$$.99       $$,$$$,$$$.99
CUSTOMER TOTAL SALES:         $$,$$$,$$$,$$$.99
SALESREP TOTAL SALES:         $$,$$$,$$$,$$$.99
REGION TOTAL SALES:           $$,$$$,$$$,$$$.99
TOTAL NUMBER OF SALESREP IN REGION:  ZZZ9
TOTAL SALES FOR COMPANY:      $$,$$$,$$$,$$$.99
```

**Two-level
Processing Requirements:** 1. Perform an internal sort on the file of customer records so that the report will break on customer number within salesrep number.

2. Read the sorted file of order records.

3. For every record read:

    a. Determine whether the customer will receive a discount. The discounting of an item is based on specifications in Project 13-1.

    b. Calculate the unit price by applying the appropriate discount as determined in 2a.

    c. Calculate the extended price by multiplying the quantity ordered by the unit price.

    d. Accumulate the customer's and the company's order total.

4. Print the customer number, item number, quantity ordered, unit price (calculated), and extended price for each customer record. Single-space the output. Use group indication when printing the salesrep number and customer number, only print the salesrep number and customer number when the customer number changes. Print the totals when appropriate. Double-space between headings and totals.

Three-level Extension: Extend the report to include a third (higher-level) control break on region as shown in the report format. Begin each region on a new page (expand the region area in the heading) and include multiple salesreps in a region on the same page. Be sure to modify the format of the heading and detail lines, to change the SORT statement to include the extra level control break, and to modify the program to increment totals as necessary.

Project 15-2

Program Name: Order Transaction File Validation

Narrative: This project builds on Project 14-2, utilizing more advanced programming techniques such as table handling, redefines, and control break logic. Write a data validation program that will validate an order transaction file.

Input File: ORDER-TRANSACTION-FILE, same as Project 14-2.

Test Data: Same as Project 14-2.

Report Layout: Same as Project 14-2.

Processing Requirements: 1. Read a file of order transaction records.

2. Sort the order transaction records so that all records for one order can be processed together, and so that the record types 1, 2, and 3 are in the appropriate order.

3. The current run date is typically accepted from a file, but for this lab set up a literal in working storage with the run date as November 2, 1999.

4. Validate each input record field for all of the following:

    All validations from Project 8-1, Project 15-2.

    Each order must have a type 1 record and cannot have more than 1 type 1 record.

    Each order must have a type 2 record and cannot have more than 1 type 2 record.

    Each order must have at least 1 type 3 record and can have up to 5 type 3 records.

(Hint: in order to process the order in its entirety, you will need to process the order using control break logic, and you will need to hold onto all the records for the order in a table until ready to process.)

5. If an error occurs in any part of the order, write the entire order, including all type 1, 2, and 3 records, to an error file. An order may contain more than one error, and all errors are to be flagged.

6. Valid records are to be written to either a Valid Transaction File or a Future/Back–order File. Both files should be the same format as the input Order Transaction file, with the exception that the quantity code on the Type 3 record should be converted to the Quantity Amount, as in Project 14-2.

7. If the hold delivery date is greater than the current run date of November 2, 1999, then write the entire order, including the type 1, 2, and 3 records, to the Future/Back-order Transaction File; otherwise write the order to the new Order Transaction File, assuming that the order passed the validation.

Project 15-3

Program Name: Car Sales Control Break (Continuation of Project 14-3)

Narrative: Develop a control break program to process a sales file in order to determine totals by year, salesperson, and dealer. The choice between a two- or three-level report is between you and your instructor.

Input File: SALES-FILE

Input Record Layout: Use the same record layout as Project 14-3.

Test Data: Use the same test data as Project 14-3.

Two-level Report Layout:

```
                            VERY VERY NICE CARS INC.              PAGE Z9
                  salesperson name COMMISSION REPORT AS OF 99/99/9999

     YEAR: 9999
        CAR INFORMATION                         COMMISSION       NET TO
        MAKE     MODEL      CUSTOMER    PRICE       PAID          DEALER
     XXXXXXXX XXXXXXXX    XXXXXXXXXX   ZZZ,ZZ9    ZZ,ZZ9.99     ZZZ,ZZ9.99
           .        .            .        .           .             .
           .        .            .        .           .             .
           .        .            .        .           .             .
        **  TOTAL FOR year             $Z,ZZZ,ZZ9  $ZZZ,ZZ9.99 $Z,ZZZ,ZZ9.99

        *   TOTAL FOR salesperson name $Z,ZZZ,ZZ9  $ZZZ,ZZ9.99 $Z,ZZZ,ZZ9.99
                                       ----------  ----------- -------------
        VERY VERY NICE CARS TOTALS     $Z,ZZZ,ZZ9  $ZZZ,ZZ9.99 $Z,ZZZ,ZZ9.99
```

Three-level Report Layout:

```
                         VERY VERY NICE CARS INC.                PAGE Z9
               dealer name COMMISSION REPORT AS OF 99/99/9999

SALESPERSON: XXXXXXXXX
   CAR INFORMATION           CUSTOMER              COMMISSION      NET TO
YEAR MAKE       MODEL                   PRICE        PAID          DEALER

9999 XXXXXXXX XXXXXXXX   XXXXXXXXXX   ZZZ,ZZ9     ZZ,ZZ9.99     ZZZ,ZZ9.99
          .          .           .         .            .             .
          .          .           .         .            .             .
          .          .           .         .            .             .
***   TOTAL FOR year                 $Z,ZZZ,ZZ9  $ZZZ,ZZ9.99  $Z,ZZZ,ZZ9.99

 **   TOTAL FOR salesperson name     $Z,ZZZ,ZZ9  $ZZZ,ZZ9.99  $Z,ZZZ,ZZ9.99

 *    TOTAL FOR dealer name          $Z,ZZZ,ZZ9  $ZZZ,ZZ9.99  $Z,ZZZ,ZZ9.99
                                     ----------  -----------  -------------
VERY VERY NICE CARS TOTALS           $Z,ZZZ,ZZ9  $ZZZ,ZZ9.99  $Z,ZZZ,ZZ9.99
```

Two-level Processing Requirements:

1. Sort the incoming sales file by salesperson, and within salesperson by year.

2. Read the file of sorted sales records and for each record read:
   a. Print a detail line as shown in the report layout using the processing requirements for Project 14-3.
   b. Increment the year, salesperson, and company totals as appropriate.
   c. Begin every salesperson on a new page with an appropriate heading containing the salesperson name, current date, and page number of the report.
   d. Print year and salesperson headings whenever the fields change.
   e. Print year and salesperson totals whenever the fields change.

3. Print the Very Very Nice Cars totals on a separate page at the conclusion of the report.

Three-level Extension: Extend the report to include a third (higher-level) control break on dealer as shown in the report format. Begin each dealer on a new page and include multiple salespersons in the same dealer on the same page. Be sure to modify the format of the heading and detail lines, to change the SORT statement to include the extra level control break, and to modify the program to increment all totals as necessary.

Project 15-4

Program Name: Bonus Control Break Program (Continuation of Project 14-4)

Narrative: Write a control break program to process a bonus file to determine bonus totals by manager, department, and plant. The choice between a two- or three-level report is between you and your instructor.

Input File: BONUS-FILE

Input Record Layout: Use the same record layout as Project 14-4.

Test Data: Use the same test data as Project 14-4.

Two-level Report Layout:

```
                        FASSSTCARS MANUFACTURERS                PAGE Z9
                     BONUS REPORT FOR DEPARTMENT: XXXXXXXX


   MANAGER: XXXXXXXXXX
   SOC SEC NO        EMPLOYEE                SALARY   BONUS    TOTAL
   999-99-9999       XXXXXXXXXXXXXXX         ZZ,ZZ9   Z,ZZ9   ZZZ,ZZ9
              .                  .                .       .        .
              .                  .                .       .        .
              .                  .                .       .        .
                                              --------- ------- ---------
   ** TOTAL FOR manager name                 Z,ZZZ,ZZ9 ZZ,ZZ9 Z,ZZZ,ZZ9
                                              --------- ------- ---------
   *** TOTAL FOR department name             Z,ZZZ,ZZ9 ZZ,ZZ9 Z,ZZZ,ZZ9
                                              --------- ------- ---------
   TOTAL FOR FASSSTCARS                       Z,ZZZ,ZZ9 ZZ,ZZ9 Z,ZZZ,ZZ9
```

Three-level Report Layout:

```
                        FASSSTCARS MANUFACTURERS                PAGE Z9
                        BONUS REPORT FOR PLANT: XX


   DEPARTMENT: XXXXXXXX
   MANAGER      SOC SEC NO    EMPLOYEE          SALARY  BONUS    TOTAL
   XXXXXXXXXX   999-99-9999   XXXXXXXXXXXXXXX   ZZ,ZZ9  Z,ZZ9   ZZZ,ZZ9
                        .             .             .       .        .
                        .             .             .       .        .
                        .             .             .       .        .
                                              --------- ------- ---------
   * TOTAL FOR manager name                   Z,ZZZ,ZZ9 ZZ,ZZ9 Z,ZZZ,ZZ9
                                              --------- ------- ---------
   ** TOTAL FOR department name               Z,ZZZ,ZZ9 ZZ,ZZ9 Z,ZZZ,ZZ9
                                              --------- ------- ---------
   *** TOTAL FOR plant name                   Z,ZZZ,ZZ9 ZZ,ZZ9 Z,ZZZ,ZZ9
                                              --------- ------- ---------
   TOTAL FOR FASSSTCARS                        Z,ZZZ,ZZ9 ZZ,ZZ9 Z,ZZZ,ZZ9
```

Two-level Processing Requirements:

1. Sort the incoming bonus file, sorting only the employees that are eligible for a bonus (i.e., those that contain a "Y" in the eligibility field) by department, and within department by manager.

2. Read the file of sorted bonus records and for each record read:

   a. Print a detail line as shown in the report layout using the processing requirements for Project 14-4.

   b. Increment the manager, department, and company totals as appropriate.

   c. Begin every department on a new page with an appropriate heading containing the department name and page number of the report.

    d. Print manager and department headings whenever the fields change.

    e. Print manager and department totals whenever the fields change.

3. Print the FassstCars Manufacturers totals at the conclusion of the report.

Three-level Extension: Extend the report to include a third (higher-level) control break on plant as shown in the report format. Begin each plant on a new page and include multiple departments in the same plant on the same page. Be sure to modify the format of the heading and detail lines, to change the SORT statement to include the extra level control break, and to modify the program to increment all totals as necessary.

Project 15-5

Program Name: Store Sales Commissions Program (Continuation of Project 14-5)

Narrative: Write a control break program to process sales records for Needless Markup to produce totals by salesperson, department, and store. The choice between a two- or three-level report is between you and your instructor.

Input File: SALES-FILE

Input Record Layout: Use the same record layout as Project 14-5.

Test Data: Use the same test data as Project 14-5.

Two-level Report Layout:

```
                         NEEDLESS MARKUP INC    99/99/9999        PAGE Z9
                    COMMISSION REPORT FOR DEPARTMENT: XXXXXXXXXXXX


        SALESPERSON: XXXXXXXXXX
                    DATE            SALES      COMMISSION     NET SALES
                 99/99/9999       ZZ,ZZ9.99     Z,ZZ9.99      ZZ,ZZ9.99
                     .               .             .              .
                     .               .             .              .
                     .               .             .              .
                                  ----------    ---------     ----------
        TOTAL FOR salesperson     ZZZ,ZZ9.99    ZZ,ZZ9.99     ZZZ,ZZ9.99
                                  ----------    ---------     ----------
        TOTAL FOR department      ZZZ,ZZ9.99    ZZ,ZZ9.99     ZZZ,ZZ9.99
                                  ----------    ---------     ----------
        TOTAL FOR NEEDLESS MARKUP ZZZ,ZZ9.99    ZZ,ZZ9.99     ZZZ,ZZ9.99
```

Three-level Report Layout:

```
                          NEEDLESS MARKUP INC   99/99/9999          PAGE Z9
                     COMMISSION REPORT FOR STORE: XXXXXXXXXXXX


           DEPARTMENT: XXXXXXXXXXXX
           SALESPERSON      DATE        SALES      COMMISSION      NET SALES
           XXXXXXXXXX    99/99/9999    ZZ,ZZ9.99    Z,ZZ9.99       ZZ,ZZ9.99
                              .            .            .              .
                              .            .            .              .
                              .            .            .              .
                                       ----------   ---------     ----------
           TOTAL FOR salesperson       ZZZ,ZZ9.99  ZZ,ZZ9.99     ZZZ,ZZ9.99
                                       ----------   ---------     ----------
           TOTAL FOR department name   ZZZ,ZZ9.99  ZZ,ZZ9.99     ZZZ,ZZ9.99
                                       ----------   ---------     ----------
           TOTAL FOR store name        ZZZ,ZZ9.99  ZZ,ZZ9.99     ZZZ,ZZ9.99
                                       ----------   ---------     ----------
           TOTAL FOR NEEDLESS MARKUP   ZZZ,ZZ9.99  ZZ,ZZ9.99     ZZZ,ZZ9.99
```

Two-level Processing Requirements:

1. Sort the incoming sales file by department, and within department by salesperson.

2. Read the file of sorted bonus records, and for each record read:
   a. Print a detail line as shown in the report layout using the processing requirements for Project 14-5.
   b. Increment the salesperson, department, and company totals as appropriate.
   c. Begin every department on a new page with an appropriate heading containing the department name, current date, and page number of the report.
   d. Print salesperson and department headings whenever the fields change.
   e. Print salesperson and department totals whenever the fields change.

3. Print the Needless Markup total at the conclusion of the report.

Three-level Extension:

Extend the report to include a third (higher-level) control break on store as shown in the report format. Begin each store on a new page (expand the store code in the store heading) and include multiple departments in the same store on the same page. Be sure to modify the format of the heading and detail lines, to change the SORT statement to include the extra level control break, and to modify the program to increment all totals as necessary.

Project 15-6

Program Name: Zoo Control Break Program (Continuation of Project 14-6)

Narrative: Write a control break program to process a zoo's inventory animal file to determine totals by group, species, and type of animal. The choice between a two- or three-level report is between you and your instructor.

Input File: ZOO-FILE

Input Record Layout: Use the same record layout as Project 14-6.

Test Data: Use the same test data as Project 14-6.

Two-level Report Layout:

```
                         WILD KINGDOM ZOO     99/99/9999           PAGE Z9
                         INVENTORY REPORT - species name


TYPE: XXXXXXXXXX

                                                                NO. TO
         SEX                 VALUE    QUANTITY      TOTAL        ACQUIRE
          F              ZZZ,ZZ9.99      Z9       ZZZ,ZZ9.99       Z9
          M              ZZZ,ZZ9.99      Z9       ZZZ,ZZ9.99       Z9
                                       ----     ------------     ----
   ** TOTAL FOR type name               ZZ9    Z,ZZZ,ZZ9.99      ZZ9
                                       ----     ------------     ----
    * TOTAL FOR species name            ZZ9    Z,ZZZ,ZZ9.99      ZZ9
                                       ----     ------------     ----
 TOTAL FOR WILD KINGDOM                 ZZ9    Z,ZZZ,ZZ9.99      ZZ9
```

Three-level Report Layout:

```
                         WILD KINGDOM ZOO     99/99/9999           PAGE Z9
                         INVENTORY REPORT - group name


SPECIE: XXXXXXX

                                                                NO. TO
 TYPE              SEX     VALUE    QUANTITY      TOTAL          ACQUIRE
 xxxxxxxxxxxx       F   ZZZ,ZZ9.99     Z9      ZZZ,ZZ9.99         Z9
                    M   ZZZ,ZZ9.99     Z9      ZZZ,ZZ9.99         Z9
                                     ----     ------------       ----
 *** TOTAL FOR type                   ZZ9    Z,ZZZ,ZZ9.99        ZZ9
                                     ----     ------------       ----
  ** TOTAL FOR species name           ZZ9    Z,ZZZ,ZZ9.99        ZZ9
                                     ----     ------------       ----
   * TOTAL FOR group name             ZZ9    Z,ZZZ,ZZ9.99        ZZ9
                                     ----     ------------       ----
 TOTAL FOR WILD KINGDOM               ZZ9    Z,ZZZ,ZZ9.99        ZZ9
```

Two-level Processing Requirements:

1. Sort the incoming zoo file by species, and within species by type.

2. Read a file of sorted zoo records and for each record read:

   a. Print a detail line as shown in the report layout using the processing requirements for Project 14-6.

   b. Increment the type, species, and Wild Kingdom totals as appropriate.

   c. Begin every species on a new page with an appropriate heading containing the species name, current date, and page number of the report.

    d. Print type and species headings whenever the fields change.

    e. Print type and species totals whenever the fields change.

3. Print the Wild Kingdom totals at the conclusion of the report.

Three-level Extension: Extend the report to include a third (higher-level) control break on group as shown in the report format. Begin each group on a new page and include multiple species in the same group on the same page. Be sure to modify the format of the heading and detail lines, to change the SORT statement to include the extra level control break, and to modify the program to increment all totals as necessary.

Project 15-7

Program Name: PC Software Control Break Program (Continuation of Project 14-7)

Narrative: Write a control break program to process a PC software file to determine totals by customer, vendor, and platform. The choice between a two- or three-level report is between you and your instructor.

Input File: PC-SOFTWARE-FILE

Input Record Layout: Use the same record layout as Project 14-7.

Test Data: Use the same test data as Project 14-7.

Two-level Report Layout:

```
                          SOFTWARE R US, INC      99/99/9999        PAGE Z9
                          SALES REPORT FOR vendor name


PLATFORM: XXXXXXX
CUSTOMER          PROGRAM NAME        DATE    QUANTITY   PRICE      TOTAL
XXXXXXXXXXXXXXX XXXXXXXXXXXXXXX 99/99/9999        ZZ9    ZZ9.99     ZZ9.99
      .               .              .            .        .          .
      .               .              .            .        .          .
      .               .              .            .        .          .
                                              -------            ----------
TOTAL FOR platform                             Z,ZZ9            ZZZ,ZZ9.99
                                              -------            ----------
TOTAL FOR vendor name                          Z,ZZ9            ZZZ,ZZ9.99
                                              -------            ----------
SOFTWARE R US TOTAL                            Z,ZZ9            ZZZ,ZZ9.99
```

Three-level Report Layout:

```
            SOFTWARE R US, INC      99/99/9999         PAGE Z9
              SALES REPORT FOR customer name


VENDOR: XXXXXXXXXXXXXXX
PLATFORM    PROGRAM NAME        DATE      QUANTITY    PRICE     TOTAL
XXXXXXX     XXXXXXXXXXXXXXX   99/99/9999     ZZ9      ZZ9.99    ZZ9.99
      .           .               .          .        .          .
      .           .               .          .        .          .
      .           .               .          .        .          .
                                           -------             ----------
TOTAL FOR platform                          Z,ZZ9              ZZZ,ZZ9.99
                                           -------             ----------
TOTAL FOR vendor name                       Z,ZZ9              ZZZ,ZZ9.99
                                           -------             ----------
TOTAL FOR customr name                      Z,ZZ9              ZZZ,ZZ9.99
                                           -------             ----------
SOFTWARE R US TOTAL                         Z,ZZ9              ZZZ,ZZ9.99
```

Two-level Processing Requirements:

1. Sort the incoming PC software file by vendor, and within vendor by platform.

2. Read the file of sorted PC software records and for each record read:
   a. Print a detail line as shown in the report layout using the processing requirements for Project 14-7.
   b. Increment the platform, vendor, and company totals as appropriate.
   c. Begin every vendor on a new page with an appropriate heading containing the vendor name, current date, and page number of the report.
   d. Print platform and vendor headings whenever the fields change.
   e. Print platform and vendor totals whenever the fields change.

3. Print the Software R Us totals at the conclusion of the report.

Three-level Extension:

Extend the report to include a third (higher-level) control break on customer as shown in the report format. Begin each customer on a new page and include multiple vendors for the same customer on the same page. Be sure to modify the format of the heading and detail lines, to change the SORT statement to include the extra level control break, and to modify the program to increment all totals as necessary.

Project 15-8

Program Name: Video Control Break Program (Continuation of Project 14-8)

Narrative: Write a control break program to process a video file to determine totals by each store, category, and rating. The choice between a two- or three-level report is between you and your instructor.

Input File: VIDEO-FILE

Input Record Layout: Use the same record layout as Project 14-8.

Test Data: Use the same test data as Project 14-8.

**Two-level
Report Layout:**

```
                        Blokbuzter Video    99/99/9999        Page Z9
             MONTHLY VIDEO RENTALS & SALES FOR category name


RATING: XXXXXXX

                      Rental Information        Sell Information
                    ----------------------  ----------------------
MOVIE TITLE           FEE  #RENTED  REVENUE  PRICE    NET   REVENUE
XXXXXXXXXXXXXXXXXXX  Z9.99     ZZ9   ZZ9.99  ZZ9.99   ZZ9   ZZ9.99
       .              .       .       .       .       .       .
       .              .       .       .       .       .       .
       .              .       .       .       .       .       .
                            ------ ---------        ------- -----------
** TOTAL FOR rating           Z,ZZ9 Z,ZZ9.99        Z,ZZ9   Z,ZZ9.99
                            ------ ---------        ------- -----------
 * TOTAL FOR category name    Z,ZZ9 Z,ZZ9.99        Z,ZZ9   Z,ZZ9.99
                            ------ ---------        ------- -----------
TOTAL FOR BLOKBUZTER          Z,ZZ9 Z,ZZ9.99        Z,ZZ9   Z,ZZ9.99
```

**Three-level
Report Layout:**

```
                        Blokbuzter Video    99/99/9999        PageZ9
             MONTHLY VIDEO RENTALS & SALES FOR store name

CATEGORY: XXXXXXXXXXX

RATING: XXXXXXX      Rental Information        Sell Information
                    ----------------------  ----------------------
MOVIE TITLE           FEE  #RENTED  REVENUE  PRICE    NET   REVENUE
XXXXXXXXXXXXXXXXXXX  Z9.99     ZZ9   ZZ9.99  ZZ9.99   ZZ9   ZZ9.99
       .              .       .       .       .       .       .
       .              .       .       .       .       .       .
       .              .       .       .       .       .       .
                            ------ ---------        ------- -----------
*** TOTAL FOR rating          Z,ZZ9 Z,ZZ9.99        Z,ZZ9   Z,ZZ9.99
                            ------ ---------        ------- -----------
** TOTAL FOR category name    Z,ZZ9 Z,ZZ9.99        Z,ZZ9   Z,ZZ9.99
                            ------ ---------        ------- -----------
 * TOTAL FOR store name       Z,ZZ9 Z,ZZ9.99        Z,ZZ9   Z,ZZ9.99
                            ------ ---------        ------- -----------
TOTAL FOR BLOKBUZTER          Z,ZZ9 Z,ZZ9.99        Z,ZZ9   Z,ZZ9.99
```

**Two-level
Processing Requirements:**

1. Sort the incoming video file by category, and within category by rating.

2. Read the file of sorted video records and for each record read:
    a. Print a detail line as shown in the report layout using the processing requirements for Project 14-8.
    b. Increment the rating, category, and Blokbuzter totals as appropriate.

c. Begin every category on a new page with an appropriate heading containing the category name, current date, and page number of the report.

d. Print rating and category headings whenever the fields change.

e. Print rating and category totals whenever the fields change.

3. Print the BlokBuzter totals on a separate page at the conclusion of the report.

Three-level Extension: Extend the report to include a third (higher-level) control break on store as shown in the report format. Begin each store on a new page and include multiple categories in the same store on the same page. Be sure to modify the format of the heading and detail lines, to change the SORT statement to include the extra level control break, and to modify the program to increment all totals as necessary.

Programming Specifications

Project 16-1

Program Name: Invoice Program with Subprogram

Narrative: Write a program to produce an invoice for each record in a validated invoice file.

Input File: INVOICE-FILE
STATE-FILE

Input Record Layout:

```
01   INVOICE-RECORD-IN.
     05   INV-INVOICE-NO        PIC X(4).
     05   INV-DATE.
          10   INV-MONTH        PIC 9(2).
          10   INV-DAY          PIC 9(2).
          10   INV-YEAR         PIC 9(4).
     05   INV-CUSTOMER-INFO.
          10   INV-CUST-NAME    PIC X(10).
          10   INV-CUST-ADDRESS PIC X(10).
          10   INV-CUST-CITY    PIC X(10).
          10   INV-CUST-STATE   PIC XX.
          10   INV-CUST-ZIP     PIC X(5).
     05   INV-NO-OF-ITEMS       PIC 9.
     05   INV-ITEMS-ORDERED OCCURS 1 TO 4 TIMES
               DEPENDING ON INV-NO-OF-ITEMS.
          10   INV-ITEM-NO      PIC 9(4).
          10   INV-QUANTITY     PIC 9.

01   STATE-RECORD.
     05   ST-STATE              PIC XX.
     05   ST-ZONE               PIC 9.
```

Test Data:

```
         1         2         3         4         5         6         7
1234567890123456789012345678901234567890123456789012345678901234567890123
246710042000Scully    20 Main StChicago   IL435353125021100115501
157808122000Schultz   45 5th St Los Angele CA5678624500232001
034209102000Culver    1 Sunny LnSeattle   WA55986190003
479011121999Perez     4 Long Dr New Orlean LA7934526800245001
683607042000Fixler    3 42nd St New York  NY2000121250115503
480703182000Morin     9 7th Ave Newark    NJ30697432001900031100230002
049806302000Munroe    10 Long StTulsa     OK59345190005
```

Report Layout:

```
┌─────────────────────────────────────────────────────────────────────────────┐
│   Date 99/99/9999          Dominoe Catalog Orders      Invoice Number    9999 │
│   Ship To:          Name                          Invoice Order Date 99/99/9999│
│                     XXXXXXXXXX                                                 │
│                     Address                                                   │
│                     XXXXXXXXXX                                                 │
│                     City          State   Zip                                 │
│                     XXXXXXXXXX    XX      XXXXX                                │
├───────────────────────────────────────────────────────────────────────────────┤
│   Item No.      Description   Qty    Price Each   Total Price   Tot Ship Wt    │
│   XXXX          XXXXXXXXXXXXXXX  9    Z,ZZ9.99     ZZ,ZZ9.99       ZZ9.99       │
│     .               .         .          .            .             .         │
│     .               .         .          .            .             .         │
│     .               .         .          .            .             .         │
│   XXXX          XXXXXXXXXXXXXXX  9    Z,ZZ9.99     ZZ,ZZ9.99       ZZ9.99       │
│                                       Totals    $ZZZ,ZZ9.99    Z,ZZ9.99        │
│                         Total delivery charge       ZZ9.99                     │
│                             Handling charge           1.50                     │
│                             Total amount        $ZZZ,ZZ9.99                    │
├───────────────────────────────────────────────────────────────────────────────┤
│              Questions? Call Toll Free 1-800-DOMINOE                           │
└───────────────────────────────────────────────────────────────────────────────┘
```

Processing Requirements:

1. Create an invoice, one per page, for each record read.

    a. Write appropriate invoice headings.

    b. For each item ordered:

    (1) The incoming item number is to be used to find the description, price, and shipping weight via a sequential lookup. Hard-code the following table in the program:

Item Information			
Item #	**Item Description**	**Price (each)**	**Ship Wt (each)**
1100	Handwoven Rug	129.00	9.50
1550	Crystal Frame	39.40	3.00
1250	Floor Lamp	99.00	20.30
3000	Ceiling Fan	299.00	50.01
4500	Wicker Basket	25.00	2.00
6800	Wall Clock	169.00	19.30
3200	Ceramic Figure	39.90	10.00
9000	Wood Wall Shelf	14.90	1.00

    (2) Compute the total price and total shipping weight.

    (3) Write a detail line for the item.

(4) Increment appropriate invoice totals.

c. After all the items ordered in the record have been processed, calculate the total delivery charge and the total invoice amount as follows:

(1) The total delivery charge should be calculated in a subprogram. There are two steps in obtaining the total delivery charge:

(a) You must first determine the appropriate zone. The incoming state is to be used via a binary lookup to determine the appropriate zone (there are three zones in total). Input-load this state/zone table (only once per execution of the program). The state file (16-1STAT.DAT) can be found on the data disk.

(b) The total delivery charge is based on the zone and total shipping weight. Once the correct zone has been found, it is to be used in combination with the sum of the total shipping weight as follows:

Delivery Rates				
Total Ship Wgt Range (in lbs)		Zone Number		
From	To (inclusive)	Zone 1	Zone 2	Zone 3
0	2	$4.00	$4.25	$4.50
2	4	$5.75	$6.25	$6.75
4	9	$7.75	$8.50	$9.25
9	20	$10.75	$12.00	$14.75
20	30	$14.00	$15.50	$18.25
30	50	$18.25	$20.75	$25.25
50	70	$21.25	$25.00	$30.50
70	999	$25.50	$29.00	$35.00

Develop a two-dimensional table to hold the above information and perform a table-lookup to determine the correct charge. Establish this table via a COPY statement. Use a direct lookup for zone dimension.

(2) The final total amount is calculated by adding the total price, the total delivery charge, and the handling charge. The current handling charge is $1.50; code this in your program so in the event this charge changes, it can be easily updated.

d. Print appropriate totals (total price, total delivery charge, handling charge, and total amount) as shown on the layout.

e. Increment the totals for price, shipping weight, total delivery charge, handling charge, and amount for the Summary Report (see #3).

2. When all records have been processed, write the Summary Report, on a separate page, of all the totals accumulated in e. (Design your summary report.)

Project 16-2

Program Name: Student Aid Report Program with Subprogram

Narrative: Write the program to print a detailed student aid report for all validated students and a summary page depicting totals for each school.

Input File: STUDENT-FILE
SCHOOL-FILE (See requirement 1b.)

Input Record Layout: Use the same record layout as Project 8-6.

Test Data: Use the validated student file from Project 8-6.

Report Layout:

Detailed Student Aid Report:

```
                                    Smart U                                    Page 1
                               Student Aid Report                            99/99/9999


                                                   Credit      Total      Total    Tuition
  Student ID       Name          School        Type of Aid  Hours     Tuition      Aid        Due

  999999999    XXXXXXXXXXXXXX   XXXXXXXXXX     XXXXXXXXXXX      99    $ZZZ,ZZ9  $ZZZ,ZZ9  $ZZZ,ZZ9
      .             .              .               .           .         .         .          .
      .             .              .               .           .         .         .          .
      .             .              .               .           .         .         .          .
```

Summary Report of Total Aid per School:

```
                                    Smart U                                    Page n
                       Summary Report of Total Aid per School                99/99/9999

                                  Total                  Total                 Tuition
  School                        Tuition                   Aid                    Due

  Art                       $ZZ,ZZZ,ZZ9            $ZZ,ZZZ,ZZ9            $ZZ,ZZZ,ZZ9
    .                             .                      .                      .
    .                             .                      .                      .
    .                             .                      .                      .
                              =======                =======                =======
  University Totals         $ZZZ,ZZZ,ZZ9           $ZZZ,ZZZ,ZZ9           $ZZZ,ZZZ,ZZ9
```

Processing Requirements: 1. For each valid record read:

a. The incoming aid type is to be expanded via a sequential lookup. The table-lookup procedure should be coded in a separate subprogram. Hard-code the following table:

Aid Type & Expanded Aid Types	
Aid Type	**Expanded Aid Type**
S	Scholarship
G	Grant
L	Loan

b. The incoming school code is to be expanded via a binary lookup. The lookup procedure should be coded in a separate subprogram. Use the following table and input-load it in the subprogram (only once per execution of the program).

| School Codes & Expanded Schools ||||
School Code	Expanded School	School Code	Expanded School
ART	Arts & Sciences	LAW	Law
BUS	Business	MED	Medicine
COM	Communications	MUS	Music
ENG	Engineering		

c. Calculate total tuition based on $300 per credit hour.

d. Calculate total aid based on the percent of total tuition. This percent is determined by a combination of credit hours and GPA as follows:

| Credit Hours || GPA ||||||
| | | from 2.5 | to 3 | from > 3 | to 3.5 | from > 3.5 | to 4.0 |
from	to						
1	3	30%		40%		50%	
> 3	6	44%		52%		63%	
> 6	9	53%		64%		72%	
> 9	12	62%		75%		84%	
>12	15	70%		80%		92%	
>15	18	75%		88%		100%	

Develop a two-dimensional table to hold the above information and perform a table-lookup to determine the percent to be used. Establish this table via a COPY statement.

e. Calculate tuition due by subtracting the total aid from the total tuition.

f. Write a detail line with the information shown on the Detailed Student Aid Report, printing ten students per page.

g. Increment the school's totals for total tuition, total aid, and total due. (Establish a table to compute the aid statistics for each school that will print at the conclusion of processing, remembering that the number of schools is variable.)

3. When all records have been processed, write the Summary Report of Total Aid per School from the table established in (g).

Project 16-3

Program Name: Salary Report Program

Narrative: Write a program to print a detailed salary report and average salary summary per location for all employees in a validated salary file.

Input File: SALARY-FILE

LOCATION-FILE (See requirement 2b.)

Input Record Layout: Use the same record layout as Project 8-7.

Test Data: Use the validated salary file from Project 8-7.

Report Layout:

Detailed Salary Report:

```
                              Big Bucks, Inc.                          Page 1
                     Detailed Salary Report for 99/99/9999
Soc Sec No.    Name              Title       Location      Education      Rating    Salary
XXXXXXXXX      XXXXXXXXXXXXXXX   XXXXXXXX    XXXXXXXXXXXX  XXXXXXXXXXXX      9     $ZZZ,ZZ9
     .            .                            .             .             .
     .            .                            .             .             .
     .            .                            .             .             .
```

Summary Report of Average Salaries per Location:

```
                              Big Bucks, Inc.                          Page n
               Average Salary Summary - XXXXXXXXXXXX Location for 99/99/9999
Education          ------------------------------- Rating -------------------------------
Level                  1              2              3              4              5

Grade School      $ZZZ,ZZZ,ZZ9   $ZZZ,ZZZ,ZZ9   $ZZZ,ZZZ,ZZ9   $ZZZ,ZZZ,ZZ9   $ZZZ,ZZZ,ZZ9
     .                  .              .              .              .              .
     .                  .              .              .              .              .
     .                  .              .              .              .              .
Doctorate         $ZZZ,ZZZ,ZZ9   $ZZZ,ZZZ,ZZ9   $ZZZ,ZZZ,ZZ9   $ZZZ,ZZZ,ZZ9   $ZZZ,ZZZ,ZZ9
```

Processing Requirements:

1. Read a file of salary records.

2. For each record read:

   a. The incoming title code is to be expanded via a sequential lookup. The table-lookup procedure should be coded in a separate subprogram. Establish the following table via the COPY statement:

Title Codes & Expanded Titles			
Title Code	Expanded Title	Title Code	Expanded Title
010	President	060	DP VP
020	Vice Pres	070	DP Mgr
030	Mkt VP	080	DP Prog
040	Mkt Mgr	090	Clerk
050	Mkt Rep	100	Adm Asst

   b. The incoming location code is to be expanded via a binary lookup from the following table which is to be input-loaded. Code the lookup and initialization in a subprogram (only once per execution of the program).

Location Code	Expanded Location	Location Code	Expanded Location
MIA	Miami	NY	New York
CHI	Chicago	ATL	Atlanta
LA	Los Angeles		

c. The incoming education code is to be expanded via a direct lookup from the following table, which is to be hard-coded in your program.

Education Code	Expanded Education	Education Code	Expanded Education
1	Grade School	4	Bachelors
2	High School	5	Masters
3	Associates	6	Doctorate

d. Write a detail line with the information shown on the Detailed Salary Report, printing ten employees per page.

e. Establish a three-dimensional (5 by 6 by 5) table to compute the salary statistics for the 150 location-education-rating combinations.

(1) Determine the appropriate row-column (i.e., education-rating) combination for each location.

(2) Increment the employee salary total for that row-column combination for each location by the employee's salary.

(3) Increment the number of employees in that row-column combination for that location by 1.

3. When all employees have been processed, write the Summary Report of Average Salaries per Location. Obtain the average salary by dividing the salary total for each combination by the number of employees in that combination. Print all 150 values of average salaries with every location on a separate page (i.e., 30 education-rating combinations per page).

Project 16-4

Program Name: Stock Program

Narrative: Write a program to produce a stock report for each record in a validated stock file.

Input File: STOCK-FILE
INDUSTRY-FILE (See requirement 1b.)

Input Record Layout: Use the same record layout as Project 8-8.

Test Data: Use the validated stock file from Project 8-8.

Report Layout:

```
                    Stock Evaluation Report as of 99/99/9999                          Page Z9


                                     Market            Dividend              Est.  Est.  Ind
Exchange  Stock    Industry           Price    EPS      Yield      PE     Growth   PE    PE   Comments

XXXXXX    XXXXXXXX  XXXXXXXXXXXXXXX ZZ9.999   Z9.9     ZZ9.99     ZZ9   ZZ9.99%  ZZ9    Z9   XXXXXXXXXXXX
  .          .          .              .        .         .        .       .      .      .        .
  .          .          .              .        .         .        .       .      .      .        .
  .          .          .              .        .         .        .       .      .      .        .
```

```
       Summary of Stocks to Buy as of 99/99/9999


                        Market     No. of
Exchange    Stock        Price     Shares          Total

XXXXXX      XXXXXXXX     ZZ9.99     Z,ZZ9       ZZZ,ZZ9.99
  .            .            .         .             .
  .            .            .         .             .
  .            .            .         .             .
Total                               ZZ,ZZ9     $Z,ZZZ,ZZ9.99
```

Processing Requirements:

1. Read a file of stock records, and for each record read:

   a. Expand the exchange code, from the incoming record, to the appropriate exchange name as shown below. To determine the exchange name, hard-code the table in your program and implement a direct (positional) table lookup.

Exchange Code	Exchange Name
1	NYSE
2	NASDAQ
3	OTC
4	AMEX

   b. Determine the industry description and industry PE. The industry code is to be used to find the description and PE via a binary lookup. Input-load this table (only once per execution of the program).

Industry Code	Industry Description	Industry PE Range
AIR	Airline	12
AUT	Automobile	7
BAN	Bank	7
BEE	Beer	9
CMP	Computers	30
DRU	Drugs	15
ELE	Electronics	25
F&L	Food & Lodging	10
FOO	Food Products	8
OIL	Oil	12
RET	Retail	9
S&L	Savings & Loan	7
TEL	Telephone	8

c. Calculate earnings per share (EPS) by dividing the PE into the stock price.

d. Calculate the dividend yield by dividing the stock price into the dividend.

e. Determine the estimated annual rate of growth in EPS (Est. Growth) over the next 3–5 years by multiplying the annual growth rate by the risk factor. To determine the risk factor, hard-code the table in your program and implement a direct (positional) table lookup.

Risk Code	Risk Factor
1	.7
2	.8
3	.95
4	1.1
5	1.3

f. Calculate the estimated price-to-earnings ratio (Est. PE) based on the estimated annual rate of growth in EPS and the current interest rate.

(1) The current interest rate should be obtained at execution. Use appropriate DISPLAY/ACCEPT statements to prompt for the interest rate and to enter it. The current interest rate limits are from .5% to 15%. (Remember data validation.)

(2) Develop a subprogram to determine the estimated PE. Create a two-dimensional table to hold the information below and perform a table lookup to determine the appropriate PE. Establish this table via a COPY statement in your subprogram.

Estimated Annual Rate of Growth in EPS		Current Interest Rate		
from	to	.5% - 7.9%	8% - 10.9%	11 - 15%
.01%	5%	18	9	6
5.01%	10%	20	15	8
10.01%	15%	25	20	11
15.01%	20%	30	21	14
20.01%	25%	40	30	18
25.01%	30%	45	35	21
30.01%	35%	50	40	24
35.01%	130%	65	55	31

   g. Determine the comments by comparing the PE in the record, estimated PE, and the industry PE.

   (1) Print "BUY NOW" in the comments column when the PE is less than both the estimated PE and the industry PE.

   (2) Print "Consider" in the comments column when the PE is less than estimated PE.

   (3) Print "Potential" in the comments column when the PE is less than the industry PE.

   h. Print a detail line for the record in the file, as shown on the layout. Detail lines are to be double spaced with 10 records per page. Print appropriate headings (and page numbers) on the top of every page in the report.

   i. Create a summary table to hold the stocks deemed to be bought. This table should contain the exchange, stock name, market price, and shares to purchase.

2. When all records have been processed, create the Summary Report showing all the "BUY NOW" stocks and appropriate investment totals in the headings.

Project 16-5

Program Name: Electric Program

Narrative: Write a program to produce an electric report for each record in a validated electric file.

Input File: ELECTRIC-FILE
TYPE-FILE (See requirement 1a.)

Input Record Layout: Use the same record layout as Project 8-9.

Test Data: Use the validated electric file from project 8-9.

Report Layout:

```
                                   Bright Power & Light                          Page Z9
                              Billing Report as of   XXX Z9, 9999

                             Service Used      Meter Readings        Kilowatt Hours
                             --------------   ------------------   --------------------------   Amount
Account
Number   Rate Schedule/Class of Service  From    To    Previous  Current   On-Peak   Off-Peak   Total      Billed


999999   XXXXXXXXXXXXXXXXXXXXXXXXXXXXXX   XXX Z9  XXX Z9   ZZ,ZZ9   ZZ,ZZ9    ZZ,ZZ9   ZZ,ZZ9   ZZ,ZZ9    ZZZ,ZZ9.99
           .              .              .       .        .        .          .         .        .           .
           .              .              .       .        .        .          .         .        .           .
           .              .              .       .        .        .          .         .        .           .

                                                                            -------  -------  -------  ------------
TOTALS                                                                       ZZZ,ZZ9  ZZZ,ZZ9  ZZZ,ZZ9 $Z,ZZZ,ZZ9.99
```

Processing Requirements:

1. Read a file of electric records; for each record read:

   a. In a subprogram, determine the corresponding description, customer charge, and minimum charge. The incoming account type is to be used to find the description, customer, and minimum charges via a binary lookup. Input-load this table (only once per execution of the program).

Account Type	Description Type, Category, Demand, Time of Use	Customer Charge	Minimum Charge
CCSL1	Comm, Curt Svc, 2000+	170.00	12,670.00
CCSL2	Comm, Curt Svc, 2000+, ToU	175.00	12,699.00
CCSM1	Comm, Curt Svc, 500-1999	110.00	3,235.00
CCSM2	Comm, Curt Svc, 500-1999, ToU	120.00	3,150.99
CCSX1	Comm, Curt Svc, 2000+(TV)	400.00	13,000.00
CCSX2	Comm, Curt Svc, 2000+(TV), ToU	410.00	12,900.00
CGSL1	Comm, Gen Svc, 2000+	170.00	12,670.00
CGSL2	Comm, Gen Svc, 2000+, ToU	180.00	12,550.00
CGSM1	Comm, Gen Svc, 500-1999	41.00	3,166.00
CGSM2	Comm, Gen Svc, 500-1999, ToU	55.00	3,100.00
CGSN1	Comm, Gen Svc, non-demand	9.00	9.00
CGSN2	Comm, Gen Svc, non-demand, ToU	12.30	12.30
CGSS1	Comm, Gen Svc, 21-499	35.00	166.25
CGSS2	Comm, Gen Svc, 21-499, ToU	41.50	1,365.00
CGSX1	Comm, Gen Svc, 2000+(TV)	400.00	12,500.00
CGSX2	Comm, Gen Svc, 2000+(TV), ToU	425.00	12,900.00
RRSN1	Res, Residential Svc	5.65	5.65
RRSN2	Res, Residential Svc, ToU	8.95	8.95

b. The energy charge is determined differently for residential and commercial accounts and whether the account is or is not Time of Use:

   (1) Residential Accounts

Non Time of Use

The first 750 kw hours used will be charged at 3.922¢ per kw hour.

Additional kw hours used will be charged at 4.922¢ per kw hour.

(Remember total kw hours used is the current reading minus the previous reading.)

Time of Use

The On-Peak kw hours used will be charged at 7.962¢ per kw hour.

The Off-Peak kw hours used will be charged at 2.729¢ per kw hour.

(Remember total kw hours used is the on-peak kw hours plus the off-peak kw hours.)

   (2) Commercial Accounts

Non Time of Use

Develop a subprogram to determine the appropriate energy charge. Create a two-dimensional table to hold the information below and perform a table-lookup to determine the appropriate energy rates. Establish this table via a COPY statement in your subprogram. The energy charge is energy rate multiplied by the kw hours used. (Remember the kw hours used is the current reading minus the previous reading.)

Demand Type	Commercial Account Category	
	General Service (GS)	**Curtailable Services (CS)**
	Energy Rate	**Energy Rate**
N	4.564¢	
S	1.884¢	
M	1.576¢	1.473¢
L	1.573¢	1.373¢
X	1.014¢	0.945¢

Time of Use

Develop another subprogram to determine the appropriate energy and fuel rates. Create a two-dimensional table to hold the information below and perform a table-lookup to determine the appropriate energy and fuel rates. Establish this table via a COPY statement in your subprogram. The energy charge is the on-peak rate multiplied by the on-peak kw hours used plus the off-peak rate multiplied by the off-peak kw hours used. (Remember total kw hours used is the on-peak kw hours plus the off-peak kw hours.) This subprogram is almost identical to the other; debug the first before going on to this one.

Demand Type	Commercial Account Category			
	General Service (GS)		Curtailable Services (CS)	
	On-Peak	Off-Peak	On-Peak	Off-Peak
N	8.525¢	2.752¢		
S	3.846¢	1.355¢		
M	2.715¢	1.111¢	2.615¢	1.102¢
L	1.573¢.	1.066¢	2.733¢	1.046¢
X	1.082¢	0.949¢	1.062¢	0.939¢

c. The fuel charge is based on the demand code in the following table. Hard-code this table into the program and reference it via a sequential lookup.

Demand Code	Fuel Rate
N	1.824¢
S	1.824¢
M	1.823¢
L	1.816¢
X	1.769¢

d. The demand charge is calculated by multiplying the kw demand level by the demand charge. The current demand charge is $6.25. Note: Residential accounts do not have a demand charge.

e. Calculate the amount billed, which is the customer charge plus the energy charge plus the fuel charge plus the demand charge (if any). Verify the amount against the minimum charge; if amount calculated is less than the minimum charge, then use the minimum charge as the amount billed.

f. Use a hard-coded table and a direct lookup to translate the numerical From- and To- month in the record to a 3-character abbreviation (using the first 3 letters of the month) to be printed on the detail line.

g. Print a detail line for the record in the file, as shown on the layout. Detail lines are to be double spaced with 10 records per page. Print appropriate headings (and page numbers) on the top of every page in the report. Use the table in 1f. to create the format of the date as shown on the layout.

h. Increment all totals shown in the report layout.

2. When all records have been processed, write the totals accumulated in 1h.

Basic Definitions for Account Codes and Types:

Type Code: C   for Commercial Accounts

                 R   for Residential Accounts

Category Code: RS   for Residential Service

                   GS   for General Service (Commercial)

                   CS   for Curtailable Service (Commercial)

Demand Code: Demand is the kw to the nearest whole kw, as determined from the metering equipment for the 30-minute period of the customer's greatest use.

N   for non demand

S   for 21–499 kw demand

M   for 500–1999 kw demand

L   for 2000+ kw demand

X   for 2000+ Transmission Voltage kw demand

Time of Use: The energy rate is determined by the time in which the electricity is used, either On-Peak or Off-Peak. Usually the Off-Peak rate is less than the On-Peak rate.

On-Peak Hours are:

from Nov 1–Mar 31, Monday–Friday, 6am–10am & 6pm–10pm
excluding Thanksgiving, Christmas, and New Year Days
from Apr 1–Oct 31, Monday–Friday, 12noon–9pm
excluding Memorial, Independence, and Labor Days

1   for non Time of Use

2   for Time of Use

(EL-CURRENT-READING contains On-Peak kw hours used and EL-PREVIOUS-READING contains Off-Peak kw hours used.)

Project 16-6

Program Name: Extended Movies Program with Subprograms

Narrative: This program extends Project 13-2 to contain two subprograms.

Input File: MOVIE-EXTRA-FILE

Input Record Layout: Use the same record layout as Project 13-2.

Test Data: Use the same test data as Project 13-2.

Report Layout: Use the same report layout as Project 13-2.

Processing Requirements: Make the following changes to Project 13-2: the table-lookups for pay scale (processing requirement #2) and bonus (processing requirement #4) are to be implemented in a subprogram.

Project 16-7

Program Name: Extended Payroll Program with Subprogram

Narrative: This program extends Project 13-5 to contain subprograms.

Input File: PAYROLL-FILE

Input Record Layout: Use the same record layout as Project 13-5.

Test Data: Use the same test data as Project 13-5.

Report Layout: Use the same report layout as Project 13-5.

Processing Requirements: Make the following changes to Project 13-5: the table-lookups for taxes (processing requirement #2b) and insurance deduction (processing requirement #2d) are to be implemented in a subprogram.

P r o g r a m m i n g   S p e c i f i c a t i o n s

Project 17-1

Program Name: Extended Program Maintenance

Narrative: This project deals with program maintenance, in that some of the specifications for the data validation and sequential update programs presented in the chapter, have been changed as indicated below. Implement the changes in whatever program you deem appropriate.

Input File: As indicated in the chapter.

Input Record Layout: As indicated in the chapter.

Output File: NEW-MASTER-FILE

Output Record Layout: As indicated in the chapter.

Test Data: Use the existing files of Figure 17.5a and 17.9a for the unedited transaction and old master files, respectively.

Report Layout: There is no new report other than the indicated error messages.

Processing Requirements: 1. Change the stand-alone edit and/or sequential update program (as you deem appropriate) to implement all of the following:
   a. SORT the valid transaction file (at the end of the edit program or the beginning of the update program). This change also implies that out-of-sequence transactions (which are input to the edit program) are no longer invalid (assuming that is the only error).
   b. Replace lines 33–45 in the edit program, which describe the transaction file, with a COPY statement; use the same COPY statement in the sequential update program.

    c. Deleted records are to be written to a new file, DELETED-RECORD-FILE, for possible recall at a future date.

    d. Enable the OM-LASTNAME, OM-INITIALS, OM-LOCATION-CODE, and/or OM-COMMISSION-RATE fields in the old master to be changed if necessary. The change is accomplished by coding any (all) of these fields as a correction in the transaction file; that is, the update program is to check if a value is present in the transaction file, and if so, it will replace the value in the master file with the value in the transaction file.

    e. The change involved in item d. above implies it is permissible for a correction not to contain a value in the TR-SALES-AMOUNT field. For example, the transaction,

        `800000000VILLAR        C          C`

    is now valid and implies a name change for the record in question. (The transaction was previously rejected for not containing a sales amount.)

    f. The value in the commission field (on both additions and corrections) is to be between 5 and 10 inclusive; any other value is to be rejected with an appropriate error message.

2. Create additional test data (if necessary) so that all of the program modifications can be tested. Rerun both programs with the modified test data.

Project 17-2

Program Name: Customer Master Sequential File Update

Narrative: This project processes output from Project 15-2. Write a program that takes the Valid Order Transaction File created in Project 15-2 and update the Customer Master Sequential File.

Input File: VALID-ORDER-TRANSACTION-FILE, created in Project 15-2.

SEQ-CUSTOMER-MSTR.

Input Record Layout:

		Sequential Customer Master Record	
01		SEQ-CUSTOMER-MSTR-REC.	
	05	CUSTOMER-NUMBER	PIC X(6).
	05	CUSTOMER-NAME	PIC X(15).
	05	CUSTOMER-ADDRESS	PIC X(15).
	05	CUSTOMER-CITY	PIC X(10).
	05	CUSTOMER-ZIP	PIC 9(5).
	05	CUSTOMER-CREDIT-LIMIT	PIC 9.
	05	DATE-OF-LAST-REV	PIC 9(8).
	05	BALANCE-DUE	PIC 9(5)V99.
	05	CUSTOMER-PHONE-NUM	PIC X(12).
	05	FILLER	PIC X.

Test Data: VALID-ORDER-TRANSACTION-FILE: Created in Project 15-2

```
         1         2         3         4         5         6         7         8
1234567890123456789012345678901234567890123456789012345678901234567890123456789012345
                                                  SEQ-CUSTOMER-MSTR:

105105 TARGETWORLD    123 THIS IS IT IRVING      77123305101992000123421214-123-4567
661400 MILLERS OUTLAW 999 W. BELTLINE IRVING     77430305241992007642121214-847-0000
771600 COMPANY 123    S. 440 CIRCLE  DALLAS      75016302071992001003838 5-999-4444
795300 SOUND STUDIO   26 AIRPORT FRWYIRVING      75032411271992023500081 7-295-4327
852300 PET WORLD      210 N. LION DR.FT. WORTH   73284212031992002995977 7-398-3843
881600 GRAND CHICKEN  5600 LUNCH AVE.ANYTOWN     79305110261992007800091 5-350-4088
900000 CHRISTMAS, INC.100 SNOW DR.    NORTH POLE00001612251992000000080 0-010-7252
902900 PARTY'S UNLIMTD500 NEW YR'S AVEVERYWHERE99999401011992050000091 5-295-6859
998000 E-Z CATERING   250 N. MACARTHURIRVING     73027109201992001527021 4-695-5432
```

Report Layout: Create a Customer Master Audit Report showing the data before and after the change, as well as the appropriate message indicating the action taken. Create a Customer Master report showing all data on the Customer Master.

Processing Requirements:
1. Sort the order transaction records by record type, keeping only the type 2 records, and by customer number.
2. Process a file of sorted transactions to accomplish both of the following:
   a. Add a new customer (if the customer does not exist on the current customer master file)—enter all information from the transaction record to the new master record.
   b. Change (correct) information on a customer (customer master number equals valid order transaction customer number)—transactions to correct will contain all of the information, even if it does not change.
3. All error messages are to appear in one report.
4. The FD's and record descriptions for both the master and transaction files are to be copied into the program. This requires that you establish the necessary COPY members as separate files, and bring them in at compile time.

Project 17-3

Program Name: Inventory Master Sequential File Update

Narrative: This project processes output from Project 15-2. Write a program that takes the Valid Order Transaction File created in Project 15-2, and update the Inventory Master Sequential File.

Input File: VALID-ORDER-TRANSACTION-FILE, created in Project 15-2.

SEQ-INVENTORY-MSTR.

Output File: SHIP-BACKORDER-TRANS-FILE

Input Record Layout: Sequential Inventory Master Record

```
01   SEQ-INVENTORY-MSTR-REC.
05   INV-ITEM-NUMBER            PIC 9(5).
05   INV-DESCRIPTION            PIC X(20).
05   INV-QTY-ON-HAND            PIC 9(4).
05   INV-LOCATION               PIC X(5).
```

Test Data: VALID-ORDER-TRANSACTION-FILE: Created in Project 15-2.

```
              SEQ-INVENTORY-MSTR:
              12345ITEM 0              0000LOC09
              15555ITEM 5              0000LOC12
              16789ITEM 6              0049LOC32
              18633ITEM 1              0700LOC10
              26666ITEM 7              0099LOC14
              32600ITEM 8              0189LOC14
              32950ITEM 9              0100LOC14
              32966ITEM 10             0500LOC13
              33333ITEM 2             1499LOC11
              34567ITEM 3              0100LOC12
              37777ITEM 11             0000LOC13
              45678ITEM 4             1600LOC12
              49880ITEM 12             0010LOC14
```

Output Record Layout: Same as VALID-ORDER-TRANSACTION-FILE, with a ship/back-order indicator alphanumeric field added to the last byte of the record.

Report Layout: Create an Inventory Master Audit Report showing the data before and after the change, as well as the appropriate message indicating the action taken. Create an Inventory Master report showing all data on the Inventory Master.

Processing Requirements: 1. Sort the order transaction records by order number and record type, keeping only the type 1 and 3 records.

2. Process a file of sorted transactions to accomplish the following:

   a. If a type 1 record, hold onto the partial ship indicator and write the entire record to the SHIP-BACKORDER-TRANS-FILE.

   b. If the item ordered is found on the inventory master file (inventory item number equals valid order transaction item number on type 3 record), determine whether there is enough quantity on hand to ship.

   If there is enough quantity on hand to ship:

   * Update the appropriate inventory master record quantity on hand.
   * Create a ship transaction indicating the quantity shipped, placing an 's' in the ship/back-order indicator.

   If there is not enough quantity on hand to ship, and a partial ship is okay (check the partial ship indicator on the type 1 record):

   * Update the appropriate inventory master record quantity on hand to zero.
   * Create a ship transaction indicating the quantity shipped, placing an 's' in the ship/back-order indicator.
   * Create a back-order transaction indicating the quantity not shipped, placing a 'b' in the ship/back-order indicator.

If there is not enough quantity on hand to ship, and a partial ship is not okay (check the partial ship indicator on the type 1 record):

   * Create a back-order transaction indicating the entire quantity ordered not shipped, placing a 'b' in the ship/back-order indicator.

c. If an item is not on the inventory master file, create a back-order transaction for the entire quantity and indicate that an error has occurred with an appropriate error message on the report.

3. All error messages are to appear in one report.

4. The FD's and record descriptions for both the master and the transaction files are to be copied into the program. This requires that you establish the necessary COPY members as separate files, and bring them in at compile time.

Project 17-4

Program Name: Employee Sequential File Update

Narrative: This project and the next are more complex applications of the balance line algorithm.

Input Files: OLD-MASTER-FILE
TRANSACTION-FILE

Input Record Layouts:

```
01  OLD-MASTER-RECORD.
    05  OLD-SOC-SEC-NUMBER        PIC X(9).
    05  OLD-NAME.
        10  OLD-LAST-NAME         PIC X(12).
        10  OLD-INITIALS          PIC XX.
    05  OLD-DATE-OF-BIRTH.
        10  OLD-BIRTH-MONTH       PIC 99.
        10  OLD-BIRTH-YEAR        PIC 9(4).
    05  OLD-DATE-OF-HIRE.
        10  OLD-HIRE-MONTH        PIC 99.
        10  OLD-HIRE-YEAR         PIC 9(4).
    05  OLD-LOCATION-CODE         PIC X(3).
    05  OLD-PERFORMANCE-CODE      PIC X.
    05  OLD-EDUCATION-CODE        PIC X.
    05  OLD-TITLE-DATA OCCURS 2 TIMES.
        10  OLD-TITLE-CODE        PIC 9(3).
        10  OLD-TITLE-DATE        PIC 9(6).
    05  OLD-SALARY-DATA OCCURS 3 TIMES.
        10  OLD-SALARY            PIC 9(6).
        10  OLD-SALARY-DATE       PIC 9(6).

01  TRANSACTION-RECORD.
    05  TR-SOC-SEC-NUMBER         PIC X(9).
    05  TR-NAME.
        10  TR-LAST-NAME          PIC X(12).
        10  TR-INITIALS           PIC XX.
    05  TR-DATE-OF-BIRTH.
        10  TR-BIRTH-MONTH        PIC 99.
        10  TR-BIRTH-YEAR         PIC 9(4).
```

```
                    05  TR-DATE-OF-HIRE.
                        10  TR-HIRE-MONTH        PIC 99.
                        10  TR-HIRE-YEAR         PIC 9(4).
                    05  TR-LOCATION-CODE         PIC X(3).
                    05  TR-PERFORMANCE-CODE      PIC X.
                    05  TR-EDUCATION-CODE        PIC X.
                    05  TR-TITLE-DATA.
                        10  TR-TITLE-CODE        PIC 9(3).
                        10  TR-TITLE-DATE        PIC 9(6).
                    05  TR-SALARY-DATA.
                        10  TR-SALARY            PIC 9(6).
                        10  TR-SALARY-DATE       PIC 9(6).
                    05  TR-TRANSACTION-CODE      PIC X.
                        88  ADDITION                        VALUE    'A'.
                        88  CORRECTION                      VALUE    'C'.
                        88  DELETION                        VALUE    'D'.
```

Output File: NEW-MASTER-FILE

Output Record Layout: Identical to the old master record.

Test Data: **Old Master File:**

```
          1         2         3         4         5         6         7         8         9
1234567890123456789012345678901234567890123456789012345678901234567890123456789012345678901234567890123456789012

100000000SUGRUE    PK12195508199580SE8100081995                 08000009199907000008199 8
200000000CRAWFORD  MA08194309197380SE8100081995                 08000009199907000008199 8
200000000CRAWFORD  MA08194309197380SE8100081995                 08000009199907000008199 8
300000000MILGROM   MB
400000000LEE        101974111989NYCG4441011993         034000111999
500000000TATER     CR12195005198280SE8100081995 2210111998029000010199902800001019980270001019980
600000000GRAUER    JE11196803198880SE8100081995  069000111998
700000000JONES     JJ11196906198680SE8100081995  110111996032000010199803000001019970280001019960
800000000SMITH      11194804198680SE8100081995  410111996029000010199802600001019970240001019960
900000000BAKER     ED11195206197880SE8100081995  1230111996068000010199806400001019970600001019960
```

Transaction File:

```
          1         2         3         4         5         6
1234567890123456789012345678901234567890123456789012345

000000000RUBIN        J  10197012198 9MIA 5010121992025000121989A
000000000RUBIN        J            X                              C
200000000CRAWFORD     MA0819430919 73WASE22000519920750001019 89A
400000000LEE          BL                                        C
400000000LEE             101973                                 C
400000000LEE                   121989                           C
400000001LEE                          MIA                        C
500000000TATER        CR                                        D
555555555NEW EMPLOYEEXX                                         C
555555555NEW EMPLOYEENE091954121989WASE22001219920750001219 89A
555555555NEW EMPLOYEENE             NYC                          C
700000000JONES        A                      034000121989C
800000000SMITH        SS              300                        C
```

Report Layout: There is no report produced by this program, other than the error messages indicated in the processing requirements. The latter may be produced using DISPLAY statements with programmer discretion as to the precise layout.

Processing Requirements:

1. Develop a sequential update program to process an incoming transaction file and the associated old master file to produce a new master file.

2. Three transaction codes are permitted: A, C, and D, denoting additions, corrections, and deletions, respectively.

3. The transaction file is assumed to be valid in itself because it has been processed by a stand-alone edit program. Hence each transaction has a valid transaction code (A, C, or D), numeric fields are numeric, and so on. Nevertheless, the update program must check (and flag) two kinds of errors that could not be detected in the stand-alone edit, as they require interaction with the old master file. These are:
   a. Duplicate additions, in which the social security number of a transaction coded as an addition already exists in the old master.
   b. No matches, in which the social security number of a transaction coded as either a deletion or a correction, does not exist in the old master.

4. Transactions coded as additions are added to the new master file in their entirety. These transactions require all fields in the transaction record to be present.

5. Transactions coded as deletions are removed from the master file. These transactions need contain only the social security number and transaction code.

6. Transactions coded as corrections contain only the social security number and the corrected value of any field(s) to be changed and are handled on a parameter-by-parameter basis. For example, if birth date and location are to be corrected, the incoming transaction will contain only the social security number and corrected values of birth date and location code in the designated positions on the transaction record.

7. Any old master record for which there is no corresponding transaction is to be copied intact to the new master.

Project 17-5

Program Name: Extended Employee Sequential File Update

Narrative: This program shows the generality of the balance line algorithm by expanding the specifications in the previous project to include a second transaction file. You will find that even though a new input file has been added, there are no additional modules required for the algorithm per se. It will, however, be necessary to change the logic of CHOOSE-ACTIVE-KEY in that the active key is now the smallest of three values.

Input File: PROMOTION-FILE

Input Record Layout:

```
01  PROMOTION-RECORD.
    05  PR-SOC-SEC-NUMBER       PIC X(9).
    05  PR-NAME.
        10  PR-LAST-NAME        PIC X(12).
        10  PR-INITIALS         PIC XX.
    05  PR-SALARY-DATA.
        10  PR-SALARY           PIC 9(6).
```

```
          10  PR-SALARY-DATE        PIC 9(6).
      05  PR-TITLE-DATA.
          10  PR-TITLE-CODE         PIC 9(3).
          10  PR-TITLE-DATE         PIC 9(6).
      05  PR-PROMOTION-CODE         PIC X.
          88  SALARY-RAISE                        VALUE 'R'
          88  PROMOTION                           VALUE 'P'.
```

Test Data:

```
          1         2         3         4         5         6
 1234567890123456789012345678901234567890123456789012345678901234 5
 100000000SUGRUE     PK090000091999            R
 100000000SUGRUE     PK              9990199 90P
 400000000LEE        BL050000111999            R
 666666666GLASSMAN   C 045000101999            R
 800000000SMITH      SS075000101999            R
```

Report Layout: Identical to the previous project.

Processing Requirements: Modify the specifications of Project 17-4 to accommodate all of the following:

1. Inclusion of a second transaction (i.e., a promotion) file to accommodate promotions and/or salary increases.

2. Salary increases are to be handled in the following manner: the transaction salary becomes the present salary in the new master, causing the present salary in the old master to become the previous salary in the new master. In similar fashion, the previous salary in the old master becomes the second previous salary in the new master. (The record layout of the master file in the programming specifications allowed three salary levels.)

   Each occurrence of salary is accompanied by a salary date in both the old master and promotion record layouts. Accordingly, the salary dates and the salaries are to be adjusted simultaneously.

3. Promotions (i.e., title changes in the new file) are to be handled in a manner analogous to salary increases. Hence the transaction title, PR-TITLE-CODE, becomes the present title in the new master, causing the present title in the old master to become the previous title in the new master. The associated dates are to be adjusted simultaneously.

4. Deletions (in the original transaction file) are to be written in their entirety to a new file, DELETED-RECORD-FILE, for possible recall at a future date.

5. All error messages are to be expanded to print the entire transaction that is in error.

Project 17-6

Program Name: Stock Sequential File Update

Narrative: Develop a sequential update program to process an incoming transaction file and the associated master stock file to produce a new master stock file.

Input File: MASTER-STOCK-FILE

   TRANSACTION-FILE

Input Record Layout: Use the record layout in Project 8-8 for the MASTER-STOCK-FILE.

```
01  TRANSACTION-FILE.
    05  TR-INFO.
        10  TR-NAME          PIC X(8).
        10  TR-EXCHANGE-CODE  PIC 9.
        10  TR-INDUSTRY-CODE  PIC X(3).
    05  TR-CURRENT-INFO.
        10  TR-PRICE          PIC 9(3)V9(3).
        10  TR-PE             PIC 9(3).
        10  TR-DIVIDEND       PIC 9V99.
    05  TR-PROJECTION-INFO.
        10  TR-RISK-CODE      PIC 9.
        10  TR-GROWTH-RATE    PIC 9V9(4).
        10  TR-SHARES-TO-BUY  PIC 9(4).
    05  TRANS-CODE            PIC X.
        88  ADDITION                      VALUE 'A'.
        88  CORRECTION                    VALUE 'C'.
        88  DELETION                      VALUE 'D'.
```

Output File: NEW-MASTER-STOCK-FILE

Output Record Layout: Same as master stock file.

Test Data: Use the validated stock file from Project 8-8 as the MASTER-STOCK-FILE.

Transaction File:

```
         1         2         3         4         5         6
1234567890123456789012345678901234567890123456789012345678901234 5
Anheus                   200550         C
Citicorp1BAN02625001900020255 00123A
Chevron 10IL0727500243304009500050A
Compq            030550032285          C
GenEl                              0100C
GnMotr                                 D
HBO     2RET0230000290302065000075A
Hilton  1F&L0497750221223055000025A
IBM              383 01000         C
Kmart                                  D
Marrion    0155000130143          C
PolkAu     005250020   4          C
Reebok         007   3      0055C
OBrien  4RET0048750150000403300110A
Seagate 2ELE01712534313030089000045A
Skywst                                 D
Trustco          0653             C
Wendys  1F&L0120000220244029500050A
```

Report Layout: There is no output report other than the error messages; use whatever form you deem appropriate.

Processing Requirements:
1. Sort the master file by stock name.

2. Three transaction codes are permitted: A, C, and D, denoting additions, corrections, and deletions, respectively:

3. The transaction file is assumed to be valid in itself because it has been processed by a stand-alone edit program. Hence each transaction has a valid transaction code (A,

C, or D), numeric fields are numeric, and so on. Nevertheless, the update program must check (and flag) two kinds of errors that could not be detected in the stand-alone edit, as they require interaction with the master file. These are:

a. Duplicate additions, in which the stock name of a transaction coded as an addition already exists in the master.

b. No matches, in which the stock name of a transaction coded as either a deletion or a correction, does not exist in the master.

4. Transactions coded as additions are added to the new master file in their entirety. These transactions require all fields in the transaction record to be present.

5. Transactions coded as deletions are removed from the master file. These transactions need contain only the stock name and transaction code.

6. Transactions coded as corrections contain only the stock name and the corrected value of any field(s) to be changed and are handled on a parameter-by-parameter basis. For example, if price and PE are to be corrected, the incoming transaction will contain only the stock name and corrected values of price and PE in the designated positions on the transaction record.

7. Any master stock record for which there is no corresponding transaction is to be copied intact to the new master.

Project 17-7

Program Name: Church Building Fund Sequential File Maintenance

Narrative: Write a program to update the church members' balance based on their contributions to the church building fund.

Input File: CHURCH-BLD-FUND-MSTR-FILE

CHURCH-BLD-FUND-TRAN-FILE

Church Building Fund Master Record					
Member Name		Pledge Amount	Member Number	Amount Given	
1 ... 15	16 ... 18	19 (2 decimals) 27	28–32	33 (2 decimals) 41	42 ... 43

Church Building Fund Transaction Record			
Member Number		Amount Given	Date Given
1 ... 5	6 ... 15	16 (2 decimals) 24	25 ... 32

Output File: NEW-CHURCH-BLD-FUND-MSTR

ERROR-TRANS-FILE

Output Record Layout: NEW-CHURCH-BLD-FUND-MSTR: same as Church Member Master Record.

ERROR-TRANS-FILE: same as Church Member Transaction File.

Test Data:

```
                  1         2         3         4         5         6
         1234567890123456789012345678901234567890123456789012345678901234 5
         Master File:

         JOHN  SMITH             0010000000000001000010000
         ANN  LOVING             0020000000000002000015200
         MARY  BROWN             0000500000000003000003000
         TOM  SAWYER             0007500000000004000025000
         JACK  CAPPS             0340000000000005000005000


         Transaction File:

         00002               0010000000010021999
         00003               0000030000008051999
         00001               0000020000006111999
         00001               0001300000003021999
         00005               0100000000007031999
         00002               0009000000002101999
         00004               0000040000001101999
         00001               0000500000002021999
         00005               0100000000001011999
         00004               0000040000003031999
         00003               0000030000004041999
         00003               0000030000005051999
         00002               0000980000006061999
```

Report Layout:

```
          1         2         3         4         5         6         7
1234567890123456789012345678901234567890123456789012345678901234567890123 4  5 6789012
1 DATE:          XX/XX/XXXX                                    PAGE:  ZZZ
2
3 ABC  CHURCH  MEMBER  BUILDING  FUND  REPORT
4
5
  MEMBER               AMOUNT              AMOUNT  GIVEN        AMOUNT
  NAME                 PLEDGED             TO  DATE             OWED

  XXXXXXXXXXXXXXX      $$,$$$,$$$.99        $$,$$$,$$$.99        $$,$$$,$$$.99




  TOTAL               $$$,$$$,$$$,$$$.99   $$$.$$$,$$$,$$$.99   $$$,$$$,$$$.99
```

Error Report: Design any report you deem appropriate in conjunction with the processing specifications.

Processing Requirements: 1. Read a file of church member building fund transaction records.

2. Perform an internal sort, sorting the transaction records by church member number.

3. For every record read, accumulate the total amount a church member has given. After all transaction records have been read for a church member:

   a. Read the sequential church member building fund master record until the church member numbers on the transaction file match the church member numbers on the master file.

   Make sure that the master records are coming in sorted by church member number by doing a data validation check.

   b. Calculate the AMOUNT OWED = AMOUNT PLEDGED - AMOUNT GIVEN.

   c. Update the master record with the new amount given.

   d. If transaction records exist for a church member who does not have a master record, put this on the error report and keep the transactions on an error file. The Error File should have the same layout of the Transaction File. The error report should contain all the information on the transaction file with an appropriate error message.

   e. Accumulate the total amount given, the total amount pledged, and the total amount owed by all church members.

   f. Print the CHURCH MEMBER NAME, the AMOUNT PLEDGED, the AMOUNT PAID TO DATE, and the AMOUNT OWED for each church member. Single-space each line.

4. Print the TOTAL AMOUNT PLEDGED, AMOUNT PAID, and AMOUNT OWED at the end of the report.

Project 17-8

Program Name: Two-file Merge

Narrative: This project merges two sequential files to produce a third file; all three files have different record layouts.

Input Files: EMPLOYEE-MASTER-FILE

SALARY-FILE

Input Record Layout:

```
01   EMPLOYEE-MASTER-RECORD.
     05   EMP-SOC-SEC-NUMBER          PIC X(9).
     05   EMP-NAME.
          10   EMP-LAST-NAME          PIC X(15).
          10   EMP-INITIALS           PIC XX.
     05   EMP-BIRTH-DATE              PIC 9(6).
     05   EMP-HIRE-DATE               PIC 9(6).
     05   EMP-LOC-CODE                PIC X(3).
     05   EMP-TITLE-CODE              PIC 9(3).

01   SALARY-RECORD.
     05   SAL-SOC-SEC-NUMBER          PIC X(9).
     05   SAL-ANNUAL-SALARY           PIC 9(6).
```

Test Data: **Employee Master File:**

```
              1         2         3         4         5         6
    1234567890123456789012345678901234567890123456789012345678901234 5
    111111111ADAMS          J0101972101995ATL111
    222222222MOLDOF         ML101979041998FLA222
    333333333FRANKEL        LY061956051989NJ 111
    555555555BOROW          JE011983062000NY 222
    666666666MILGROM        IR031948011987NY 222
    888888888JONES          JJ091980062000NY 222
```

Salary File:

```
              1         2         3         4         5         6
    1234567890123456789012345678901234567890123456789012345678901234 5
    111111111050000
    222222222100000
    444444444075000
    555555555040000
    777777777043500
    888888888035000
    999999999042000
```

Input Files: MERGED-FILE

Output Record Layout:
```
01  MERGED-DATA-RECORD.
    05  MGD-SOC-SEC-NUMBER          PIC X(9).
    05  MGD-NAME.
        10  MGD-LAST-NAME           PIC X(15).
        10  MGD-INITIALS            PIC XX.
    05  MGD-BIRTH-DATE              PIC 9(6).
    05  MGD-HIRE-DATE               PIC 9(6).
    05  MGD-LOC-CODE                PIC X(3).
    05  MGD-TITLE-CODE              PIC 9(3).
    05  MGD-ANNUAL-SALARY           PIC 9(6).
```

Report Layout: There is no report produced by this program, other than the error messages indicated in the processing requirements. The latter may be produced using DISPLAY statements with programmer discretion as to the precise layout.

Processing Requirements:

1. Write a program to merge two input files, each in sequence by social security number, to produce a third file as output.

2. In order to produce an output record with a given key, that key must be present on both input files. With respect to the test data, for example, records 111111111 and 222222222 should both appear on the merged file. A record is written to the MERGED-FILE by combining fields on the two input records as per the record layouts.

3. If a key appears on only one input file, that record key is not to appear in the MERGED-FILE. With respect to the test data, for example, record 333333333 should not appear in the MERGED-FILE, as it is not present in the SALARY-FILE. Nor should record key 444444444, as it is not present in the EMPLOYEE-MASTER-FILE.

4. Any key appearing in only one file should be flagged with an appropriate error message, for example:

   ```
   ERROR - RECORD 333333333 NOT IN SALARY-FILE

   ERROR - RECORD 444444444 NOT IN EMPLOYEE-MASTER-FILE
   ```

Project 18-1

Program Name: Extended Program Maintenance

Narrative: Change the nonsequential update program of Figure 18.10 to accommodate the various changes in specifications listed below.

Input File: As indicated in the chapter.

Input Record Layout: As indicated in the chapter.

Test Data: Use the existing files of Figure 18.7a and 18.7b for the transaction and indexed files, respectively.

Report Layout: There is no new report other than the indicated error messages.

Processing Requirements:
1. Change the existing program to accommodate all of the following:
    a. Replace the record descriptions in Working-Storage, (lines 34–45 and 47–54 for the transaction and master files, respectively) with a COPY statement. This in turn requires you to create the necessary copy members.
    b. Deleted records are to be written to a new file, DELETED-RECORD-FILE, for possible recall at a future date.
    c. Enable the MA-LAST-NAME, MA-INITIALS, MA-LOCATION-CODE, and/or MA-COMMISSION-RATE fields in the indexed file to be changed if necessary. The change is accomplished by coding any (all) of these fields as a correction in the transaction file; that is, the update program is to check if a value is present in the transaction file, and if so, it will replace the value in the master file with the value in the transaction file.
    d. The change involved in item c. above implies it is permissible for a correction not to contain a value in the TR-SALES-AMOUNT field. For example, the transaction,

        ```
        800000000VILLAR          C          C
        ```

        is now valid and implies a name change for the record in question. (The transaction was previously rejected for not containing a sales amount.)

2. Create additional test data so that all of the program modifications can be tested. Rerun the program with the modified test data.

Projects 18-2 through 18-7

Program Name: Nonsequential File Update

Narrative: Implement the programming specifications for Projects 17-2 through 17-7 as a nonsequential (rather than a sequential) update. The file descriptions, test data, and programming specifications given with the sequential program apply here as well, except that the indexed file in this example functions as both the old and new master files in the sequential version.

Project 18-8

Program Name: Catalog Orders

Narrative: Develop an interactive program that will process additions, changes, deletions, and inquiries to an indexed file of catalog orders.

Input File: ORDER-FILE

Input Record Layout:

```
01  ORDER-RECORD-IN.
    05  ORD-NUMBER              PIC 9(6).
    05  ORD-INFO.
        10  ORD-NAME            PIC X(10).
        10  ORD-TELEPHONE       PIC 9(10).
    05  ORD-ITEMS-ORDERED  OCCURS 3 TIMES.
        10  ORD-ITEM-NUMBER     PIC 9(4).
        10  ORD-QUANTITY-ORDERED PIC 9.
```

Test Data:

```
         1         2         3         4         5         6
1234567890123456789012345678901234567890123456789012345678901234 5
212467Scully    305233123412502110011550 1
561578Schultz   2013471535450023200 1
036442Culver    4013452347900 03
479350Perez     305976745668002450 01
683736Fixler    20136218231250115503
488907Morin     41374353433200190003110 02
043498Munroe    305331485490005
```

Screen Layouts: **Screen A**

```
┌─────────────────────────────────────────────┐
│              Catalog Orders                   │
│                                               │
│          Order #: ▓▓▓▓▓▓                       │
│                                               │
│          Transaction Types:                   │
│              Add                              │
│              Change                           │
│              Delete                           │
│              Inquiry                          │
│                                               │
│          Enter transaction type: ▓            │
│                                               │
└─────────────────────────────────────────────┘
```

Screen B

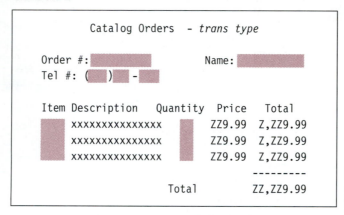

```
                    Catalog Orders   - trans type

      Order #:▮▮▮▮▮▮          Name:▮▮▮▮▮▮▮▮▮

      Tel #: (▮▮) ▮▮ -▮▮


      Item Description   Quantity  Price    Total
      ▮                  xxxxxxxxxxxxxxx ▮   ZZ9.99  Z,ZZ9.99
                         xxxxxxxxxxxxxxx     ZZ9.99  Z,ZZ9.99
                         xxxxxxxxxxxxxxx     ZZ9.99  Z,ZZ9.99
                                                    ---------
                                    Total           ZZ,ZZ9.99
```

Processing Requirements:

1. Display Screen A to accept an order # and transaction type (valid transaction types are A, C, D, or I).

2. Depending on the transaction type, display an appropriate screen using Screen B as a model, and processing the transaction as follows:

   a. Additions:

      (1) Accept and validate the order # (don't forget to check for duplicate additions), name, telephone number (numeric), item number (valid item numbers are found in the item table, see requirement #3), and quantity (numeric).

      (2) For each valid item, look up the price and description from the item table, calculate the total (quantity multiplied by price), and display the item detail line.

      (3) When all items are entered, display a total for all ordered items.

      (4) Prompt the user for confirmation and write the record to the indexed file.

   b. Changes:

      (1) Display Screen B showing the information found in the order file.

      (2) For each item, look up and display the price and description from the item table along with the calculated total.

      (3) Allow modification to the name, telephone, item number, and quantity fields.

      (4) Validate each item changed against the item table, and for each valid item display the description and price and calculate the total.

      (5) Prompt the user for confirmation and replace the modified record in the indexed file.

   c. Deletions:

      (1) Display Screen B showing the information found in the order file, the corresponding information from the item table for each item, and all totals.

      (2) Prompt the user for confirmation to delete, and delete the record.

   d. Inquiries: Display Screen B showing the information found in the order file, the corresponding information from the item table for each item, and all totals.

3. Hard-code the following item table in the program and use a sequential lookup:

Item Information		
Item #	**Item Description**	**Price (each)**
1100	Handwoven Rug	129.00
1550	Crystal Frame	39.40
1250	Floor Lamp	99.00
3000	Ceiling Fan	299.00
4500	Wicker Basket	25.00
6800	Wall Clock	169.00
3200	Ceramic Figure	39.90
9000	Wood Wall Shelf	14.90

4. All error messages are to be displayed on the bottom of the screen and will allow the user to reenter the desired information.

Project 18-9

Program Name: Create Customer Bills

Narrative: This project processes output from Projects 17-2 and 17-3. Write a program that takes the Ship/Back-order Transaction File and the VSAM Customer Master file updated in Project 18-2, and create a bill for each customer.

Input File: SHIP-BACK-ORDER-TRANS-FILE, created in Project 17-3/Project 18-3.

VSAM-CUSTOMER-MASTER, updated in Project 18-2.

Input Record Layout: Ship/back-order transaction record: same as Project 17-3.

VSAM customer master record: same as Project 18-2.

Test Data: Ship/back-order transaction record: created in Project 17-3.

VSAM customer master record: updated in Project 18-2.

Report Layout: Create a Customer Bill

```
BILL DATE: XX/XX/XXXX

CUSTOMER NAME: XXXXXXXXXXXXXX      CUSTOMER NUMBER:      XXXXXX
CUSTOMER ADDRESS: XXXXXXXXXXXXXX   XXXXXXXXXXXXXX        XXXXX

ORDER NUMBER: XXXXX                PURCHASE DATE: XX/XX/XXXX

_____

ITEM NUMBER              QUANTITY       UNIT PRICE      EXTENDED PRICE
99999                    ZZZ            $ZZ,ZZZ.99      $ZZ,ZZZ,ZZZ.99
99999                    ZZZ            $ZZ,ZZZ.99      $ZZ,ZZZ,ZZZ.99

SUBTOTAL:                                               $ZZZ,ZZZ,ZZZ.99
TAX:                                                        $ZZZ,ZZZ.99
TOTAL AMT DUE:                                        $Z,ZZZ,ZZZ,ZZZ.99
_____

ITEMS BACKORDERED:

ITEM NUMBER              QUANTITY

XXXXX                    ZZZ
XXXXX                    ZZZ


_____

TOTAL ITEMS BACKORDERED  ZZZ,ZZZ,ZZZ
TOTAL ITEMS SHIPPED      ZZZ,ZZZ,ZZZ
```

Processing Requirements: 1. Sort the order transaction records by order number, record type, and ship/back-order indicator

2. Process a file of sorted transactions to create a customer bill.

   a. The customer number comes from the transaction file and is used to access the customer name and address from the VSAM CUSTOMER MASTER file.

   b. The order number and purchase date come from the type 1 record on the new transaction file.

   c. Item number and quantity come from the transaction file.

   d. Unit price and extended price are calculated based on the item number and quantity as follows:

   Check the first byte of the item number and then check the quantity to determine the percent of markup on the item. Take the unit cost from the transaction file and use the percent markup to determine the unit price.

```
UNIT-PRICE = UNIT-COST * 1.PERCENT MARKUP
EXTENDED PRICE = UNIT-PRICE * QUANTITY
PERCENT MARKUP

FIRST BYTE       QTY      QTY      QTY      QTY      QTY
of ITEM NUMBER   <50      50-99    100-199  200-300  >300

1                30%      25%      20%      15%      10%
2                25%      20%      15%      10%      5%
3                35%      30%      25%      20%      15%
4                40%      35%      30%      25%      20%
```

e. The subtotal is the extended price for each item accumulated per order.

f. The amount of tax is zero if the taxable item indicator on the type 1 transaction record contains an "N." If the taxable item indicator on the type 1 transaction is a "Y," compute the amount of tax = subtotal * 8.25%. The total amount due is calculated by adding the subtotal plus tax.

g. If an item is backordered, a B will exist in the ship/back-order indicator field on the type 3 record of the new Transaction file.

h. The total items back-ordered is an accumulation of the quantity for each item back-ordered, and the total items shipped is an accumulation of the quantity for each item shipped.

Index

A

ACCEPT statement, 206-7, 242-43, 266, 267-69
AUTO clause, 268
   BACKGROUND-COLOR clause, 267
   BELL clause, 268
   BLINK clause, 268
   COLUMN clause, 267
   FOREGROUND-COLOR clause, 267
   HIGHLIGHT clause, 268
   LEFT-JUSTIFY clause, 269
   LINE clause, 267
   REVERSE-VIDEO clause, 268
   RIGHT-JUSTIFY clause, 268
   SECURE clause, 269
   SPACE-FILL clause, 268
   UNDERLINE clause, 268
   UPDATE clause, 269
   ZERO-FILL clause, 268
ACCESS IS DYNAMIC phrase, SELECT statement, 561, 571
ACCESS IS RANDOM phrase, SELECT statement, 566
ACCESS IS SEQUENTIAL phrase, SELECT statement, 562
ACCESS MODE clause, 554
Action list, 162
Active key, 530
Actual decimal point, 172
ADD statement, 112-13
ALL literal, 84
Allocation status, 530

Alphabetic codes, 333
Alphabetic data items, 103
Alphabetic pictures, 17
Alphabetic test, 197
Alphanumeric codes, 333
Alphanumeric data items, 79, 103
Alternate indexes program, 570-74
   programming specifications, 570-73
ALTERNATE RECORD KEY clause, 554, 570
A margin, 29
Arithmetic statements, 109-18
   ADD statement, 112-13
   COMPUTE statement, 110-11
   DIVIDE statement, 115-17
   MULTIPLY statement, 114-15
   ROUNDED clause, 109-10
   SIZE ERROR clause, 110
   SUBTRACT statement, 113-14
Arithmetic symbols, 16
Ascending order, sorts, 405
ASCII collating sequence, 405, 407
ASSIGN clause, 554
Assumed decimal point, 81-82, 117-18
Asterisks, and check protection, 175
AT END clause, READ statement, 183
AUTO clause, ACCEPT statement, 268

B

BACKGROUND-COLOR clause, ACCEPT statement, 267
Backup procedures, 519
Bad command or file name, 33
Balance line algorithm, 529-31
Barcoded Price List (project), 763-64, 772
Basic structures, sufficiency of, 56
Batch processing, 30
BELL clause, ACCEPT statement, 268
Benefit Statement (project), 809-10
Binary table lookups, 335-36
BLANK WHEN ZERO clause, 177
BLINK clause, ACCEPT statement, 268
BLOCK CONTAINS clause, 78
Blocked vs. unblocked records, 78
Blocking factor, 78
B margin, 29
Bonus Control Break Program (project), 855-57
Braces, 74-75
Brackets, 74

C

Calculated field, 410
Called and calling programs, 477-79

Calorie counter's delight, 392-97
   completed program, 394-97
   hierarchy chart, 394
   programming specifications, 392
   pseudocode, 395
   range-step tables, 392-94
Car billing program, 246-58
   completed program, 249-57
   hierarchy chart, 248
   program design, 248-49
   programming specifications, 246-47
   pseudocode, 249
Car rental validation program, 208-21
   completed program, 213-21
   error messages, 211
   hierarchy chart, 212-13
   programming specifications, 208-9
   pseudocode, 211-12
   transaction files/error reports, 209-11
Car Sales Commissions Report Program (project), 802-3
Car Sales Commissions Validation Program (project), 786-87
Car Sales Control Break (project), 854-55
Car Sales Program (project), 779-81
Car validation and billing program, 278-97

completed program, 287-96

hierarchy, 284

programming specifications, 279-80

pseudocode, 284-86

Screen Section, 280-84

Catalog Orders (project), 827-29, 891-93

Check protection, and asterisks, 175

Check Register (project), 829-30

Church Building Fund Report (project), 559-60, 776

Church Building Fund Sequential File Maintenance (project), 886-88

Classes, 608, 619

Class test, 199

CLOSE statement, 99

COBOL, 9-13

    coding form, 28

    Data Division, 11-12, 77-84

    data names, 14

    elements of, 13-17

    Environment Division, 11, 76-77

    evolution of, 38-40

    file names, 14

    first program, 9-13

    Identification Division, 11, 75-76

    intrinsic calendar functions, 591-92

    intrinsic functions, 740-44

      alphanumerical and conversions functions, 743

      business functions, 741

    COBOL 2000 functions, 743-44

      data functions, 741

      function types, 741-43

      mathematical functions, 742

      miscellaneous functions, 743

statistical functions, 742

    level numbers, 16

    literals, 15-16

    miscellaneous new features, 745

    new data types, 744-45

    next generation of, 605-9

    notation, 74-75

    paragraph name, 14

    pictures, 17

    Procedure Division, 12-13, 97-137

    program:

      development, 86

      skeleton outline of, 129

      structure of, 234

    programmer-supplied names, 14-15

    reserved words, 13-14

    revisions, 739-45

    symbols, 16

    See also Subprograms

COBOL-74, 17, 38-40, 90, 128, 221-22, 258, 297, 325, 357, 471, 506, 574

COBOL-75, 38-40

COBOL-84, 38-40

COBOL-85, 18, 38, 90, 221

COBOL-85 reference summary, 713-37

    COBOL verbs, 723-33

    ommunication description entry, 720

    conditions, 734

    COPY and REPLACE statements, 733

    data description entry, 719

    Data Division, 716

    Environment Division, 714-15

    file control entry, 715-16

    file description entry, 717-18

    Identification Division, 714

    miscellaneous formats, 736

    nested source programs, 736

    Procedure Division, 722

    qualification, 735

    report description entry, 721

    report group description entry, 721-22

    series of source programs, 737

COBOL97:

    connecting COBOL97 and, 693-709

    connecting Visual Basic and, 693, 705-8

      calling subprograms in Visual Basic, 707

      coordinating data types, 706-7

      declaring subprograms in Visual Basic, 706

      program interface, 707-9

    data types, coordinating, 706-7

COBOL 2000:

    data types, 744-45

    intrinsic functions, 743-44

    miscellaneous new features, 745

COBOL: From Micro to Mainframe Web site:

    Download Option Window, 654

    main content page, 652

    security warning message, 654

    Thank You Message Window, 655

    Welcome screen, 652

Coding, 26-32

    defined, 26-27

Coding conventions, object-oriented, 614

Coding form, 28-30

    editor, 28-30

    rules for, 28-29

Coding standards, 179-84

    constants, avoiding, 183-84

    Data Division, 179-81

      data-name prefixes, 179

      data names, 179

      indenting successive level numbers, 181

      PICTURE clauses, 179

      77-level entries, 181

    overcommenting, 184

    Procedure Division, 181-83

      avoiding commas, 181

      functional paragraph development, 181

      indenting successive level numbers, 183

      scope terminators, 181-83

      sequencing paragraph names, 181

    spacing, 183

Collating sequence, 405-8

    ASCII, 405, 407

    defined, 405

    EBCDIC, 405, 407

    embedded sign, 406-8

COLLATING SEQUENCE clause, SORT statement, 409

COLUMN clause, ACCEPT statement, 267

Comma, 174-75

Compilation, 27

Compilation errors:

    conflicting picture/value clause, 150

    conflicting RECORD CONTAINS clause and FD record description, 150

    going past column 72, 151

    inadvertent use of COBOL reserved words, 150

    invalid picture clause for numeric entry, 150

    misspelled data names/reserved words, 151

    nonunique data names, 149-51

    omitted/extra hyphens in data name, 151

    omitted/extra periods, 150

    omitted space before/after arithmetic operator, 150

receiving field too small to accommodate sending field, 150
Compiler, 30-31
Compiler diagnostics, 36, 141
Completeness check, 197
Compound conditions, 202, 454
Compound test, 200-201
Computer, from coding form to, 26-32
Computer program, 6
Computer Status Report (project), 812-13, 824-26
COMPUTE statement, 110-11
using for multiple arithmetic operations, 116
Concatenated key, 573-74
Condition-name test, 200
Configuration Section, 76
Environment Division, 76
SPECIAL-NAMES paragraph, 267
SYMBOLIC CONSTANT clause, 267
Consistency check, 197
Continuation of nonnumeric literals, 29
Control areas, 551, 553
Control area split, 553
Control breaks, 435-74
control field, 437
control totals, 437
defined, 437
one-level, 438, 443-51
algorithm, 445
completed program, 446-50
hierarchy chart, 444-46
programming specifications, 443
pseudocode, 446
rolling company total, 441
running company total, 440-41

system concepts, 436-42
three-level, 439-42
algorithm, 461-62
completed program, 463-70
hierarchy chart, 460-61
pseudocode, 462-63
two-level, 439-40
algorithm, 453
completed program, 454-60
hierarchy chart, 451-52
pseudocode, 452-54
writing a control break program, 471
Control field, 437
Control intervals, 551-52
Control interval split, 552-53
Control statements, 27
Control totals, 437
COPY statement, 479-80
CR character, 176-77
Create Customer Bills (project), 893-95
Creating an Indexed File program, 556-59
completed program, 557-59
programming specifications, 556
pseudocode, 557
Credit Report (project), 814-15, 826
Customer Master Sequential File Update (project), 878-79

D

Data Division, 11-12, 77-84
coding standards, 179-81
File Section, 12, 77-82
assumed decimal point, 81-82
BLOCK CONTAINS clause, 78
blocking factor, 78
DATA RECORD clause, 79

file description (FD), 77-79
LABEL RECORDS clause, 79
level numbers, 79-81
PICTURE clause, 17, 79
RECORD CONTAINS clause, 79
record description, 79
order of, 11
Working-Storage Section, 12, 151
figurative constant, 84-85
FILLER entry, 82-83
VALUE clause, 83-84
Data hiding, 620-21
Data input errors, 37
Data management classes, 612
Data names, 14
DATA RECORD clause, 79
Data validation, 195-228, 278
ACCEPT statements, 206-7
calculations involving dates, 206-7
alphabetic test, 197
car rental validation program, 208-21
completed program, 213-21
error messages, 211
hierarchy chart, 212-13
programming specifications, 208-9
pseudocode, 211-12
transaction files/error reports, 209-11
car validation and billing program, 278-97
completeness check, 197
consistency check, 197
date check, 197
existing code check, 197
IF statement, 197-206
class test, 199
compound test, 200-201

condition-name test, 200
hierarchy of operations, 201-2
implied conditions, 203
nested IFs, 203-5
NEXT SENTENCE clause, 205-6
relational condition, 198
sign test, 200
numeric test, 197
reasonableness check, 197
sequence check, 197
stand-alone edit program, 207-22
completed program, 220-21
error messages, 211
hierarchy chart, 212-13
pseudocode, 211-12
subscript check, 197
Data validation program, 519-28
completed program, 524-28
defensive programming, 527
designing, 523-24
error message table, 527
hierarchy chart, 522
programming specifications, 520-22
pseudocode, 523
sequential update with, 520
Date arithmetic, 590-93
COBOL intrinsic calendar functions, 591-92
Date check, 197
DB character, 176-77
Debugging, 139-67
compilation errors, 33-35, 140-51
execution errors, 35-37, 151-56
file status errors, 157
logic errors, 158-59
proficiency in, 141-42

run-time errors, 156-58

structured walkthrough, 162-63

tips for, 159-60

Decimal point, 172

Defensive programming, 527

DELETE statement, and indexed files, 562

Delinquent Accounts (project), 757

DEPENDING ON clause, 310-11

Descending order, sorts, 405

Direct lookups, 344-45

and positional tables, 336

DISPLAY statement, 266

BLANK LINE clause, 269

BLANK SCREEN clause, 269

DIVIDE statement, 115-17

Doctor Visits Report Program (project), 799-800

Doctor Visits Validation Program (project), 781-83

Dollar signs, 174

Drivers, 612

Duplicate addition, 518

Duplicate data names, 243-45

MOVE CORRESPONDING statement, 245

qualification, 243, 244-45

E

EBCDIC collating sequence, 405, 407

Editing, 170-79

asterisks, and check protection, 175

BLANK WHEN ZERO clause, 177

comma, 174-75

decimal point, 172

dollar signs, 174

editing characters, 170-71

insertion characters, 175

numeric-edited fields, 170

review of, 175-76

signed numbers, 176-77

zero suppression, 172-74

Editor, use of, 28-30

88-level entry, 200-201

Electricity Bill Report Program (project), 806

Electricity Bill Validation Program (project), 796-98

Electric Program (project), 872-76

Elementary item, 79

Ellipsis, 74

ELSE clause, IF statement, 106, 108

Embedded sign, 406-8

Employee Profiles (project), 807-9, 818-19

Employee Sequential File Update (project), 881-83

Encapsulation, 605, 620

END-IF scope terminator, 106, 181-83

End-of-file conditions, 6, 99, 530

END-READ scope terminator, 100, 183

Engineering senior program:

COBOL-74 implementation, 38

with compilation errors, 33-35

data input errors, 37

with execution errors, 35-37

flowchart, 7

programming specifications, 5

Entering the program, errors in, 33

Environment Division, 11, 76-77

Configuration Section, 76

SPECIAL-NAMES paragraph, 267

SYMBOLIC CONSTANT clause, 267

Input-Output Section, 76-77

order of, 11

Error diagnostics, 141

Error message table, 527

Errors, 32-37

in compilation, 33-35, 140-51

in data input, 37

in entering the program, 33

in execution, 35-37, 151-56

file status, 157

logic, 158-59

in operating system commands, 33

run-time, 156-58

EVALUATE statement, 109

advanced use of, 274

Evaluation of Student Curriculum Records (project), 766-67, 772, 810-11

Execution errors, 35-37, 151-56

Existing code check, 197

Expandable table codes, 333-34

Extended Employee Sequential File Update (project), 883-84

Extended Movies Program with Subprograms (project), 876

Extended Payroll Program with Subprogram (project), 877

Extended Program Maintenance (project), 877-78, 890

Extended Real Estate Sales (project), 778-79

Extended Savings Dividends (project), 775-76

Extended Student Profile Program (project), 838-39

Extra periods, as compilation error, 150

F

Factory method, 619

False-condition branch, READ statement, 235

Field, 2-3

Figurative constant, 84-85

File, 2-3

processed, 3

File names, 14

File Section:

Data Division, 12, 77-82

assumed decimal point, 81-82

BLOCK CONTAINS clause, 78

blocking factor, 78

DATA RECORD clause, 79

file description (FD), 77-79

LABEL RECORDS clause, 79

level numbers, 79-81

PICTURE clause, 17, 79

RECORD CONTAINS clause, 79

record description, 79

FILE STATUS clause, 555

File status codes, 555

File status errors, 157

FILLER entry, 82-83

Fitness program, 482-504

Fixed position, dollar sign, 174

Fixed sign, 177

Floating position, dollar sign, 174

Floating sign, 177

Flowcharts, 6-8, 57

and test data, 8

FOREGROUND-COLOR clause, ACCEPT statement, 267

Free space, 552

Fujitsu COBOL 4.0— COBOL97:

building projects, 661

building projects with multiple programs, 677-83

adding an EXE file to the project, 678-79

adding COBOL source file folder, 679-80

adding the source files and selecting the main program, 680-81

Builder window, 681-82

creating a new program, 677-79

running the project, 682-83

setting environmental variables, 682-83

COBOL2002 file utility, 683-90

Browse dialog window, 686-87

browsing an indexed file, 688-89

browsing a file, 686-87

browsing a file using the alternate index, 690

Commands Menu, 685

converting a line-sequential file, 685-86

Convert option, 685

creating an alternate index, 689-90

Key Information dialog box, 688, 690

Load dialog box, 687-88

loading a sequential file into an indexed file, 687-88

Record Key dialog box, 690

starting, 684-85

COBOL: From Micro to Mainframe Web site:

Download Option Window, 654

main content page, 652

security warning message, 654

Thank You Message Window, 655

Welcome screen, 652

COBOL program, compiling/linking/ executing, 656-62

debugging programs, 667-73

adding the TEST compiler option, 667-69

Animate button, 671-72

building the project, 669-70

Compiler Option dialog box, 669

Completed Test Compiler Option dialog box, 669

Data button, 672

Debugger toolbar, 671-72

Debugger window, 671

loading the project, 667

Re-debug button, 672

Set/Delete Breakpoint button, 672

Start Debugging dialog box, 670

Step Into button, 672

testing the Debugging toolbar buttons, 671-73

Watch Data button, 672

Watch Data dialog box, 672-73

downloading data files from the Web, 651-56

file download options, 652-53

finding the COBOL Web site, 651-52

self-extracting file, 654-55

unzipping files to a folder, 655-56

warning messages, 653

See also COBOL: From Micro to Mainframe Web site

environmental variables, 674-77

directing SYSOUT to a new file, 675-76

error correction, 662-67

adjusting Project Manager Editor defaults, 666

building a project containing errors, 663

by moving between messages and source code, 664-65

interpreting the build process, 663-64

techniques for, 665

windows tiled for, 665

file descriptors, 674-75

installation of, 644-51

AUTOEXE.BAT information, 650

Choose Destination for Files screen, 646

Fujitsu Software License Agreement, 646

Installation Options screen, 647

program folder selection screen, 647

Restart Computer dialog box, 651

restarting the computer, 650

Serial Number Entry screen, 645

Start Copying Files screen, 648

start-up procedures, 644

typical installation screen, 648

Welcome screen and warnings, 645

master start-up screen, 644

Open dialog box, 658

program source listing, viewing, 660

project definition, expanding, 659-60

Project Manager:

debugging programs using, 667-73

starting, 656-57

Project Manager Editor, 662-67

adjusting defaults, 666

Setup Environment for Editor window, 667

reduced/expanded project configuration, 659

registration, 648-49

Fujitsu Marketing Form, 649

Fujitsu Registration Form, 649

Select Country for Modem screen, 650

running a project, 662

Runtime Environment Setup window, 662, 675

source file, creating/ retrieving, 658

system printer, changing, 676-77

Fujitsu COBOL 97 compiler, 31fn

Furniture Shipments (project), 822-24

G

Garbage in, garbage out (GIGO), 37, 196

Grandfather-father-son strategy, 519

Group item, 79

Group moves, 105

H

Handles, 615

Hard-coded tables, 336-38

Hierarchy chart, 50-52

completeness of, 53

development of, 51

evaluating, 52-54

functionality of, 54

levels of, 51-52

span of control, 54

HIGHLIGHT clause,
ACCEPT statement,
268

Hopper, Grace Murray, 38

I

Identification Division,
11, 75-76

division header/
paragraphs, 75-76

order of, 11

IF statement, 106-8,
197-206

class test, 199

compound test, 200-201

condition-name
test, 200

ELSE clause, 106

hierarchy of operations,
201-2

implied conditions, 203

indentation in, 106-8

nested IFs, 203-5

NEXT SENTENCE clause,
205-6

relational condition, 198

sign test, 200

Implementor-name, 77

Implied conditions, 203

Implied decimal point,
81-82

Incompatibilities, 38

INDEXED BY clause, 311

Indexed files, 549-81

alternate indexes
program, 570-74

programming
specifications,
570-73

COBOL implementation,
554-55

ACCESS MODE
clause, 554

ALTERNATE RECORD
KEY clause, 554

ASSIGN clause, 554

FILE STATUS
clause, 555

RECORD KEY
clause, 554

RESERVE integer
AREAS clause, 554

concatenated key,
573-74

control areas, 551, 553

control area split, 553

control intervals, 551-52

control interval split,
552-53

Creating an Indexed File
program, 556-59

completed program,
557-59

programming
specifications, 556

pseudocode, 557

DELETE statement, 562

free space, 552

indexes, 550-51

index set, 551

I/O status, 555

maintaining, 563-70

nonsequential update
program, 563-70

completed program,
566-70

hierarchy chart,
565-66

programming
specifications,
563-65

pseudocode, 566-67

test data, 564

OPEN statement, 559-60

READ statement, 561-62

REWRITE statement, 562

sequence set, 551

START statement,
574-75

system concepts, 550-53

WRITE statement, 562

Indexes, 550-51

defined, 321

as a displacement, 321

SET statement, 322

subscripts vs., 321-24

Index set, 551

Informational
diagnostics, 141

Inheritance, 605, 619, 625

INITIAL clause, 482

Initialization, 8

INITIALIZE statement,
236-37

In-line perform, 232

Input, 2-3, 26

Input-loaded tables,
338-39

Input-Output Section,
Environment Division,
76-77

Insertion characters, 175

INSPECT statement,
237-38

Instances, 608

Instantiation, 615

Insurance Policy Holder
Report (project),
761-62, 772

INTEGER-OF-DATE
function, 594

example of, 593

Interactive program, 270

Inter-City Piano Program
(project), 756

INVALID KEY clause, 559

Inventory Master
Sequential File Update
(project), 879-81

Inventory Parts List
(project), 767-68,
772, 777

Invoice Mailing Labels
Program (project), 803

Invoice Program with
Subprogram (project),
863-65

Invoice Validation Program
(project), 788-89

Invoking a method, 608

I-O clause, OPEN
statement, 559-60

I/O status, 555

Iteration, 9

J-K

Job not run due to JCL
error, 33

KEY IS clause, 561-62

L

LABEL RECORDS
clause, 79

Leap-year problem, 594

Learning by doing, 32-37

LEFT-JUSTIFY clause,
ACCEPT statement,
269

Level numbers, 12, 16,
79-81

and PICTURE clause, 81

LINE clause, ACCEPT
statement, 267

Linkage editor, 504-7

problems with, 505, 507

Linkage Section, 477, 694

Linker, 30-31

Literals, 15-16

avoiding, 180

Load module, 30-31

Logical expressions, 57-61

flowchart, 57

pseudocode, 57-59

Warnier-Orr diagrams,
59-61

Logical records, 78

Logic errors, 158-59

Lookups, 331-62

binary, 335-36

complete example,
347-56

completed program,
350-56

program design,
349-50

programming
specifications,
347-49

direct, 344-45

PERFORM VARYING
statement, 340

procedure, 339-47

SEARCH ALL
statement, 344

SEARCH statement,
340-44

sequential, 334-35

Lowercase letters, in
COBOL, 74

M

Mailing List Program (project), 558-59
Major key, 405
Memory leakage, 621
MERGE statement, 426-27
Messages, 608
Methods, 608
Minor key, 405
Minus sign, 177
Mnemonic table codes, 333-34
Moderator, 162
Money Changer (project), 768-69, 772, 777-78
MOVE CORRESPONDING statement, 245
MOVE statement, 102-5
  group moves, 105
  moving data:
    from alphanumeric field to alphanumeric field, 103-4
    from numeric field to numeric field, 104
  restrictions on, 103
  rules of, 103
Movies (project), 831-32
Multilevel tables, 363-402
  COBOL implementation, 366
  one-level tables, 366-67
    PERFORM VARYING statement, 366-67
  sample program, 373-75
    completed program, 375-79
    hierarchy chart, 375
    program design, 375
    pseudocode, 376
  system concepts, 364-66
  three-level tables, 380-90
    PERFORM VARYING statement, 382
    sample program, 384-90
  two-level tables, 368-73
    compilation errors, 369-70
    PERFORM VARYING statement, 370-73
  See also Tables
MULTIPLY statement, 114-15

N

Nested IF statements, 203-5
Nested SEARCH statement, 394
New master file, 516
NEXT SENTENCE clause, 205-6
No match, 518
Nonnumeric literals, 15-16
Nonsequential File Update (project), 890
Nonsequential update, 518
Nonsequential update program, 563-70
  completed program, 566-70
  hierarchy chart, 565-66
  programming specifications, 563-65
  pseudocode, 566-67
  test data, 564
Nonunique data names, 149-51
NOT AT END clause, READ statement, 18, 235
Notation, COBOL, 74-75
Numeric codes, 333
Numeric data items, 79, 103
Numeric-edited data items, 103
Numeric-edited fields, 170
Numeric literals, 15-16
Numeric test, 197

O

Object-oriented (OO) programming, 603-42
  classes, 608
  COBOL, next generation of, 605-9
  coding conventions, 614
  data hiding, 620-21
  encapsulation, 605, 620-21
  handles, 615
  inheritance, 605, 619, 625
  instances, 608
  instantiation, 615
  invoking a method, 608
  memory leakage, 621
  messages, 608
  methods, 608
    object-oriented vs. structured paradigm, 608-9
  persistence, 609, 621
  pointers, 615
  polymorphism, 605, 625
  structured programming, development of, 606-7
  student-look-up program, 612-16
    programming specifications, 613
    system driver and classes, 612
  student-look-up system, 610-12
    classes and inheritance, 619
    Person class, 630-32
    ProcessRequests method, 619-21
    programming specifications, 610
    Registrar class, 616-19
    Student class, 627-29
    StudentDM class, 621-27
    StudentPRT class, 635-39
    StudentUI class, 633-35
    terminology, 607-8
  See also Student-look-up program; Student-look-up system
OCCURS clause, 303, 306-8
  and hard-coded tables, 336-38
  problems with, 308
OCCURS DEPENDING ON clause, 310-11
Old master file, 516
Omitted periods, as compilation error, 150
One-level control breaks, 438
  algorithm, 445
  completed program, 446-50
  hierarchy chart, 444-46
  programming specifications, 443
  pseudocode, 446
One-level tables, 366-67
  PERFORM VARYING statement, 366-67
OPEN statement, 98-99
  and indexed files, 559-60
  I-O clause, 559-60
Operating system, 31
Operating system commands, errors in, 33
Optional sequence numbers, 29
Order Transaction File Validation (project), 840-41, 853-54
Organization:
  tables:
    by frequency of occurrence, 334-35
    positional, 336
Orr, Kenneth, 59
Output, 3-4, 26

P

Paradigm, 606
Paragraph name, 14
Paragraphs, 12
Password protection, 269
Payroll Calculation (project), 774-75
Payroll Program (project), 836-38
Payroll Report Program (project), 801-2
Payroll Report (project), 772-73
Payroll Validation Program (project), 785-86
PC Software Control Break Program (project), 860-61

PERFORM statement, 12, 18, 105-6, 231-34
  in-line perform, 232
  paragraph, 232-33
  performing sections, 232-33
  section, 232
  TEST BEFORE/TEST AFTER clause, 231-32
  THROUGH (THRU) clause, 233-34
PERFORM VARYING statement, 304-6
  and one-level tables, 366-67
  and table lookups, 340-41
  and three-level tables, 382-84
  and two-level tables, 370-73
Periodic maintenance, 518-19
Persistence, 609, 621
Person class, 630-32
  definition, 631-32
  programming specifications, 630
Physical fitness system, 482-504
  display program (DSPLYSUB), 498, 501-3
  fitness screen, 483
  hierarchy chart, 485
  input program (INPUTSUB), 490-94
  main program (FITNESS), 486-89
  programming specifications, 482-84
  pseudocode, 485-86
  table of goal weights, 484
  time program (TIMESUB), 503-4
  training program (TRAINSUB), 498-500
  weight-range program (WGTSUB), 494-98
Physical record, 58
PICTURE clause, 17, 79, 177
  and level numbers, 81

Pictures, 17, 79
Plus sign, 177
Pointers, 615
Polymorphism, 605, 625
Positional tables, and direct lookup, 336
Precise table codes, 333-34
Price Break Report (project), 755-56, 762-63, 772, 773, 830, 839-40, 851-53
Primary key, 405
Print layout chart, 3-4
Problem domain, 612
Procedure Division, 12-13, 97-137
  ACCEPT statement, 242-43
  arithmetic statements, 109-18
    ADD statement, 112-13
    assumed decimal point, 117-18
    COMPUTE statement, 110-11, 116
    DIVIDE statement, 115-17
    MULTIPLY statement, 114-15
    ROUNDED clause, 109-10
    SIZE ERROR clause, 110
    SUBTRACT statement, 113-14
  car billing program, 246-58
    completed program, 249-57
    hierarchy chart, 248
    program design, 248-49
    programming specifications, 246-47
    pseudocode, 249
  CLOSE statement, 99
  Coding standards, 181-83
  duplicate data names, 243-45

MOVE CORRESPONDING statement, 245
  qualification, 243, 244-45
EVALUATE statement, 109
IF statement, 106-8
INITIALIZE statement, 236-37
logic, 13
MOVE statement, 102-5
OPEN statement, 98-99
order of, 11
PERFORM statement, 105-6, 231-34
  in-line perform, 232
  paragraph, 232-33
  performing sections, 232-33
  section, 232
  TEST BEFORE/TEST AFTER, 231-32
  THROUGH (THRU) clause, 233-34
READ statement, 99-100, 234-36
  false-condition branch, 235
  NOT AT END clause, 235
  READ INTO statement, 235-36
STOP RUN statement, 102, 694
string processing, 237-42
  INSPECT statement, 237-38
  reference modification, 240-42
  STRING statement, 237-38
  UNSTRING statement, 240
tuition billing program, 118-27
WRITE FROM statement, 236
WRITE statement, 100-102
Processing, 3-4, 8, 26
  tables, 304

PROCESS-RECORDS block, 6, 106
ProcessRequests method, 619-21
Program development, 47-72
  constants/rates, 85
  File Section, 85
  hierarchy chart, 50-52
    development of, 51
    evaluating, 52-54
    levels of, 51-52
  logical expressions, 57-61
  print lines, 86
  structured design, 50-52
  structured programming, 54-56
    case structure, 56
    iteration, 54, 56
    logic structures, 54-55
    selection, 54, 56
    sequence, 54-55
    sufficiency of basic structures, 56
  top-down testing, 61-66
  tuition building program, 48-50
Program identification, 29
Programmer-supplied names, 14-15
Programming process (flowchart), 27
Programming specifications, 3-5
Projects, 755-98
Pseudocode, 6, 8-9, 57-59
  block structure, 57
  for building blocks, 59
  car validation and billing program, 284-86
  development of, 57-59
  stand-alone edit program, 211-12
Punched card, 30
Punctuation symbols, 16

Q

Qualification, duplicate data names, 243, 244-45

R

Range-step tables, 345-47, 392-94

READ INTO statement, 235-36

READ statement, 6, 99-100, 234-36
  false-condition branch, 235
  and indexed files, 561-62
  NOT AT END clause, 235
  placement of, 100
  READ INTO statement, 235-36

Real Estate Sales (project), 770-71, 772

Reasonableness check, 197

Record, 2-3

RECORD CONTAINS clause, 79, 150

Record description, 12, 79

RECORD KEY clause, 554

REDEFINES clause, and hard-coded tables, 336-38

Reference modification, 240-42

Registrar class, 616-19
  class definition of registrar, 617-18
  programming specifications, 616

Relational condition, 198

Relational symbols, 16

Relative subscripting, 308-9

RELEASE statement, 410-11

Required logic, 5-9

Reserved words, 13-14, 711-12

RESERVE integer AREAS clause, 554

RETURN statement, 410-11

REVERSE-VIDEO clause, ACCEPT statement, 268

REWRITE statement, and indexed files, 562

RIGHT-JUSTIFY clause, ACCEPT statement, 268

Rolling company total, 441

ROUNDED clause, 109-10

Running company total, 440-41

Run-time errors, 156-58

S

Salary Report Program (project), 804-5, 867-70

Salary Report Validation Program (project), 792-94

Savings Dividends (project), 765-66, 772

Scope terminators, 12, 182

Screen I-O, 265-300
  ACCEPT statement, 266, 267-69
  car validation and billing program, 278-97
  DISPLAY statement, 266
  tuition billing program, 270-78
  See also ACCEPT statement; DISPLAY statement

Scrntuit.dll, build of, 698

Scrntuit program, 695-98

SD statement, 410

SEARCH ALL statement, 344

SEARCH statement:
  SEARCH ALL statement vs., 344
  and table lookups, 340-44

Secondary key, 405

Secretary, 162

SECURE clause, ACCEPT statement, 269

Selection, 9

SELECT statement, 76
  ACCESS IS DYNAMIC phrase, 561, 571
  ACCESS IS RANDOM phrase, 566
  ACCESS IS SEQUENTIAL phrase, 562

implementor-name in, 77
  WITH DUPLICATES phrase, 571

Sequence check, 197

Sequence set, 551

Sequential file maintenance, 515-47
  backup procedures, 519
  data validation program, 519-28
    completed program, 524-28
    defensive programming, 527
    designing, 523-24
    error message table, 527
    hierarchy chart, 522
    programming specifications, 520-22
    pseudocode, 523
    sequential update with, 520
  duplicate addition, 518
  grandfather-father-son strategy, 519
  multiple generations of the master file, 519
  new master file, 516
  no match, 518
  nonsequential update, 518
  old master file, 516
  periodic maintenance, 518-19
    sequential update, 517-19
    two-period, 519
  sequential update program, 528-34
    active key, 530
    allocation status, 530
    balance line algorithm, 529-31
    completed program, 540-43
    end-of-file conditions, 530
    expanded balance line algorithm, 532

hierarchy chart, 531-34
    output, 544
    programming specifications, 528-29
    stand-alone edit program, 518
    stubs program, 535-44
      completed program, 540-43
      truncated output of, 539
    system concepts, 516-18
    top-down testing, 535-44
    transaction file, 516

Sequential table lookups, 334-35

Sequential update, 517, 518

Sequential update program, 528-34
  active key, 530
  allocation status, 530
  balance line algorithm, 529-31
  end-of-file conditions, 530
  expanded balance line algorithm, 532
  hierarchy chart, designing, 531-34
  programming specifications, 528-29

Serious diagnostics, 141

SET statement, 322

Shoe Inventory Program (project), 757-58

Signed field, 176

Signed numbers, 176-77
  CR, 176-77
  DB, 176-77
  minus sign, 177
  plus sign, 177

Sign test, 200

SIZE ERROR clause, 110

Size of field, 12, 79

Software Cost Analysis (project), 816-17, 826-27

Sorted Bonus Program (project), 843-44

Sorted Car Sales Program (project), 841-42

Sorted PC Software Program (project), 847-49

Sorted Store Sales Commissions Program (project), 844-46

Sorted Zoo Program, 846-47

Sorting, 403-34
  ascending order, 405
  COBOL implementation, 408-13
  collating sequence, 405-8
    embedded sign, 406-8
  comparing options, 426
  descending order, 405
  INPUT PROCEDURE/ OUTPUT PROCEDURE, 410, 419-26
    implicit transfers of control, 420-21
    sort program, 422-26
  major key, 405
  MERGE statement, 426-27
  minor key, 405
  primary key, 405
  RELEASE statement, 410-11
  RETURN statement, 410-11
  sample program, 411-13
    programming specifications, 411
    sorted reports, 412
    test data, 412
  SD statement, 410
  secondary key, 405
  sort key, 405
  SORT statement, 409-10
  system concepts, 405
  USING/GIVING option, 414-19
  vocabulary, 406

Sort key, 405

SORT statement, 409-10
  COLLATING SEQUENCE clause, 409

  WITH DUPLICATES IN ORDER phrase, 409
  See also Sorting

Sort work file, 410

SPACE-FILL clause, ACCEPT statement, 268

Stand-alone edit program, 207-22, 518
  error messages, 211
  hierarchy chart, 212-13
  programming specifications, 208-9
  pseudocode, 211-12

START statement, and indexed files, 574-75

Stock Program (project), 869-72

Stock Purchases Report Program (project), 805

Stock Sequential File Update (project), 884-86

Stock Transactions Report Program (project), 800-801

Stock Transactions Validation Program (project), 784-85

Stock Validation Program (project), 794-95

STOP RUN statement, 12, 102, 694

Store Sales Commissions Program (project), 857-58

String processing, 237-42
  INSPECT statement, 237-38
  reference modification, 240-42
  STRING statement, 237-38
  UNSTRING statement, 240

STRING statement, 237-38

Structured design, 50-52

Structured programming, 9, 54-56, 605
  building blocks, 55-56
    pseudocode for, 59
    sufficiency of, 56
    Warnier-Orr diagrams for, 61

  case structure, 56
  development of, 606-7
  iteration, 54, 56
  logic structures, 54-55
  selection, 54, 56
  sequence, 54-55

Structured walkthrough, 162-63
  desk check, 162

Stubs, 61, 535

Stubs program, 535-44

Student Aid Report Program with Subprogram (project), 865-67

Student-look-up program, 612-16
  programming specifications, 613
  system driver and classes, 612

Student-look-up system, 610-12
  classes and inheritance, 619
  Person class, 630-32
    definition, 631-32
    programming specifications, 630
  ProcessRequests method, 619-21
  programming specifications, 610
  Registrar class, 616-19
    class definition of registrar, 617-18
    programming specifications, 616
  Student class, 627-29
    definition, 628-29
    programming specifications, 627
  StudentDM class, 621-27
    class definition of, 623-25
    instance definition, 626-27
    programming specifications, 622
  StudentPRT class, 635-39
    definition, 637-38

  programming specifications, 636
  StudentUI class, 633-35
    definition, 634
    programming specifications, 633
    screen sample, 634

Student Profile Program (project), 819-21

StudentPRT class, 635-39
  definition, 637-38
  programming specifications, 636

Student Record Report Program (project), 803-4

Student Record Validation Program (project), 790-91

Student transcript program, 311-21
  completed program, 314-21
  program design, 313-14
  programming specifications, 311-13

StudentUI class, 633-35
  definition, 634
  programming specifications, 633
  screen sample, 634

Subprograms, 475-513
  argument list, 477
  called and calling programs, 477-79
  calling in Visual Basic, 707
  COPY statement, 479-80
  declaring in Visual Basic, 706
  defined, 477
  DLL file, building, 694-95
  Exit Program, 694
  INITIAL clause, 482
  linkage editor, 504-7
    problems with, 505, 507
  Linkage Section, 477, 694
  main (calling) program, 477
  parameter list, 477

physical fitness system, 482-504
  display program (DSPLYSUB), 498, 501-3
  fitness screen, 483
  hierarchy chart, 485
  input program (INPUTSUB), 490-94
  main program (FITNESS), 486-89
  programming specifications, 482-84
  pseudocode, 485-86
  table of goal weights, 484
  time program (TIMESUB), 503-4
  training program (TRAINSUB), 498-500
  weight-range program (WGTSUB), 494-98
Scrntuit.dll, build of, 698
Scrntuit program, 695-98
USING BY CONTENT phrase, 480, 694
USING BY REFERENCE phrase, 481, 694
Subscript check, 197, 308
Subscripts:
  indexes vs., 321-24
  restricting to a single use, 342
  rules for, 308
SUBTRACT statement, 113-14
Sufficiency of basic structures, 56
Symbols, 16
System interaction classes, 612

T

Table codes, 332
  characteristics of, 333-34
  expandable codes, 333-34
  mnemonic codes, 333-34
  precise codes, 333-34
  types of, 333
Table lookups:
  defined, 332
  See also Lookups
Tables:
  concept, 303
  hard coding, 336-38
  hierarchical levels of, 369-70
  indexes:
    defined, 321
    as a displacement, 321
    SET statement, 322
    subscripts vs., 321-24
  initializing, 336-39
  input-loaded, 338-39
  introduction to, 302-5
  lookups, 331-62
    binary, 335-36
    complete example, 347-56
    direct, 344-45
    procedure, 339-47
    SEARCH ALL statement, 344
    sequential, 334-35
    two-level, 390-91
  multilevel, 363-402
  OCCURS clause, 303
    problems with, 308
  OCCURS DEPENDING ON clause, 310-11
  organization:
    by frequency of occurrence, 334-35
    positional, 336
  PERFORM VARYING statement, 304-6
  positional, and direct lookup, 336
  processing, 304
  range-step, 345-47
  relative subscripting, 308-9
  student transcript program, 311-21
    completed program, 314-21
  program design, 313-14
  programming specifications, 311-13
  subscript check, 308
  subscripts:
    indexes vs., 321-24
    restricting to a single use, 342
    rules for, 308
  USAGE clause, 309-10
  See also Multilevel tables
Telephone Long Distance Carrier Program (project), 760-61
Termination, 8
TEST BEFORE/TEST AFTER clause, 231-32
Test data, 13
Three-level control breaks, 439, 441-42
  algorithm, 461-62
  completed program, 463-70
  hierarchy chart, 460-61
  pseudocode, 462-63
Three-level tables, 380-90
  PERFORM VARYING statement, 382-84
  sample program, 384-90
    completed program, 386-90
    programming specifications, 384-86
Three-level Tables (project), 834-35
THROUGH (THRU) clause, 233-34
Top-down testing, 61-66
  advantages of, 66
  stubs, 61
Transaction file, 516
Tuition billing program, 48-50, 84-90, 118-27, 270-78
  COBOL entries, 87
  COBOL program skeleton, 128-29
  with compilation errors, 142-46
  Data Division, 87-90
  edited vs. unedited PICTURE clauses, 178-79
  Environment Division, 87-90
  with execution errors, 151-56
  flowchart, 58
  hierarchy chart for, 51-53
    development of, 51
    evaluating, 52-53
    levels of, 51-52
  Identification Division, 87-90
  Procedure Division, 118-27
    developing, 119-20
    hierarchy chart, 127
    test data, 127
  programming specifications, 49, 84-86
  pseudocode, 60, 271-72
  record layouts, 50
  screen version, 270-71
    completed program, 273-78
    hierarchy chart for, 52, 271-72
    programming specifications, 270-71
  with stubs, 63-64
  testing, 65
Two-file Merge (project), 888-89
Two-level control breaks, 439-40
  algorithm, 453
  completed program, 454-60
  hierarchy chart, 451-52
  pseudocode, 452-54
Two-level tables, 368-73
  PERFORM VARYING statement, 370-73
Two-level tables lookups, 390-91
Two-level Tables (project), 833-34
Type of field, 12, 79

U

Undefined symbol, 505
UNDERLINE clause, ACCEPT statement, 268
Unrecoverable diagnostics, 141
Unresolved external reference, 505
UNSTRING statement, 240
UNTIL clause, 105
UPDATE clause, ACCEPT statement, 269
Uppercase letters, in COBOL, 74
USAGE clause, 309-10
User interface classes, 612
USING BY CONTENT phrase, 480, 694
USING BY REFERENCE phrase, 481, 694

V

VALUE clause, 83-84, 183
  and hard-coded tables, 336-38
Video Control Break Program (project), 861-63
Video Program (project), 849-51
Visual Basic, 699
  calling subprograms in, 707
  connecting to COBOL97, 705-8
  control property specifications, 703-4
  controls, 699
  data types, coordinating, 706-7
  declaring subprograms in, 706
  design work space, 701
  events, 699
  form interface, 702-3
  New Project dialog box, 700
  programming specifications, 704-5
  project features, 701

properties, 699
  sample form, 701-2
VSAM file, 551-52

W

Warnier, Jean-Dominique, 59
Warnier-Orr diagrams, 59-61
  for building blocks, 61
  for tuition billing program, 62
Warning diagnostics, 141
Well-written program, 184-89, 196
WITH DUPLICATES IN ORDER phrase, SORT statement, 409
WITH DUPLICATES phrase, SELECT statement, 571
Working-Storage Section:
  Data Division, 12, 151
    figurative constant, 84-85
    FILLER entry, 82-83
    VALUE clause, 83-84
WRITE FROM statement, 236
WRITE statement, 100-102
  general format of, 236
  and indexed files, 562

X

Year 2000 problem, 583-602
  date arithmetic, 590-93
    COBOL intrinsic calendar functions, 591-92
  leap-year problem, 594
  retirement program:
    example, 584-90
    revised, 594-99

Z

ZERO-FILL clause, ACCEPT statement, 268

Zero suppression, 172-74
Zoo Control Break Program (project), 858-60